Master
Visual C++ 2

Second Edition

Ori Gurewich and

Nathan Gurewich

201 West 103rd Street
Indianapolis, Indiana 46290

SAMS
PUBLISHING

Trademarks

Publisher
Richard K. Swadley

Acquisitions Manager
Greg Wiegand

Managing Editor
Greg Wiegand

Acquisitions Editor
Gregory Croy

Development Editor
Phillip W. Paxton

Software Development Specialist
Keith Davenport

Production Editor
Kitty Wilson

Editor
Matthew Usher

Editorial Coordinator
Bill Whitmer

Editorial Assistants
Carol Ackerman
Sharon Cox
Lynette Quinn

Technical Reviewer
Robert Bogue

Marketing Manager
Gregg Bushyeager

Assistant Marketing Manager
Michelle Milner

Cover Designer
Alyssa Yesh

Book Designer
Alyssa Yesh

Director of Production and Manufacturing
Jeff Valler

Imprint Manager
Juli Cook

Manufacturing Coordinator
Paul Gilchrist

Production Analysts
Angela D. Bannan
Dennis Clay Hager
Mary Beth Wakefield

Graphics Image Specialists
Clint Lahnen
Tim Montgomery
Dennis Sheehan
Greg Simsic
Susan VandeWalle
Jeff Yesh

Page Layout
Mary Ann Cosby
Judy Everly
Aleata Howard
Louisa Klucznik
Ayanna Lacey
Shawn MacDonald
Chad Poore
Susan Shepard
Jill Tompkins
Dennis Wesner

Proofreading
Carol Bowers
Michael Brumitt
DiMonique Ford
Donna Haigerty
Erika Millen
Brian-Kent Proffitt
SA Springer
Holly Wittenburg

Indexer
Jeanne Clark

Overview

1   What Do You Need to Know?   1

2   Your First C++ DOS Program   21

3   Hierarchy   67

4   Writing Your First True Windows Application   87

5   Designing a Menu   117

6   Edit Boxes   145

7   Check Boxes   169

8   Scroll Bars   189

9   List and Combo Boxes   229

10   Radio Buttons   267

11   Displaying Dialog Boxes   289

12   Writing a Single-Document Interface Application   325

13   Writing and Reading Data (with Serialization) to and from Files   349

14   Writing and Reading Lists (with Serialization) to and from Files   385

15   Customizing Serialization   431

16   Writing and Reading Data (Without Serialization) to and from Files   447

17   The Mouse   487

18   The Keyboard   545

19   Writing a Multiple-Document Interface Application   567

20   Menus   611

21   The Toolbar and Status Bar   665

22   Multimedia: Playing and Recording WAV Files   695

23   Multimedia: Playing MIDI Files   735

24   Multimedia: Video for Windows   757

25   Multimedia: CD Audio   795

26   The Timer   823

27   Animation   841

28   The `OnIdle()` Function   875

29   Animation and Sound with and Without Synchronization   899

30   Creating C++ Classes for Distribution and Profit   955

31   Creating Your Own DLLs   983

32   Drawing Geometric Shapes and Text with Different Fonts   1007

33   Creating OCX Controls   1061

34   Customizing OCX Controls   1077

35   Adding Events and Messages to OCX Controls   1119

     Index   1145

Contents

1   What Do You Need to Know?   1

The Book's CD 2
What's Next? 3
   C++ Topics 3
   Creating Your First Visual C++ Windows Program 3
   Creating Menus 3
   Dialog Boxes and Single-Document Interface (SDI) Applications 5
   Serialization 6
   The Mouse and the Keyboard 7
   Multiple-Document Interface (MDI) Applications 9
   More About Menus, Toolbars, and Status Bars 11
   Multimedia 12
   Timers 14
   Animation 14
   The `OnIdle()` Function 15
   Animation and Sound 15
   Writing and Distributing Your Own Classes 16
   Creating Your Own DLLs 17
   Drawing Geometric Shapes and Displaying Text with Different
      Fonts 17
   OCX Technology—How to Create Your Own OCX Controls 19
Many Topics, Many Applications… 20

2   Your First C++ DOS Program   21

What Is a Console Application? 22
Why Learn How to Write Console Applications? 22
Writing a Simple DOS C++ Program 22
   Writing the Code of the Hello.CPP Program 24
   Compiling and Linking the Hello.CPP Program 25
   Executing the Hello.EXE Program 27
   Examining the Hello.CPP Program's Code 27
Target: Debug and Release 30
C++ Versus C 32
Classes in C++ 32
   Declaring a Class 33
   The Destructor Function 35
   The `Public` and `Private` Keywords 36

The Circle Program 36
    Writing the Code of the Circle.CPP Program 36
    Examining the Circle.CPP Program's Code 39
    Compiling and Linking the Circle.CPP Program 43
The Circle2 Program 44
    Writing the Code of the Circle2.CPP Program 44
    Examining the Code of the Circle2.CPP Program 46
    Compiling, Linking, and Executing the Circle2.CPP Program 48
The Circle3.CPP Program 49
    Writing the Code of the Circle3.CPP Program 50
    Examining the Code of the Circle3.CPP Program 52
Overloaded Functions 54
    Writing the Code of the Circle4.CPP Program 54
    Examining the Code of the Circle4.CPP Program 57
Declaring Variables in C++ Versus C 62
Default Parameters 62
Final Words 65

3   Hierarchy   67

The RECT Program 68
    The RECT.CPP Program's Code 70
What if You Need Additional Member Functions? 72
Class Hierarchy 72
    The Rect2.CPP Program's Code 75
Class Hierarchy Pictorial Representation 78
Overriding a Member Function 79
Using Pointers to Objects 82
The New and Delete Operators 83
What's It All About? 85

4   Writing Your First True Windows Application   87

The SAY Application 88
    Creating the Project of the SAY Application 90
    Running the SAY Application Before Customizing It 98
    The Visual Implementation of the SAY Application 100
What You've Accomplished So Far 107
    Attaching Code to the Say Hello Push Button 108

Attaching Code to the Exit Push Button 114
Final Words… 116

5   **Designing a Menu**   **117**

The Beep Application 118
 Creating the Project of the Beep Application 119
 The Visual Implementation of the Dialog Box That Serves as
  the Main Window of the Beep Application 122
 The Visual Implementation of the Menu Bar 124
 Associating the IDR_MENU1 Menu with a Class 131
 Attaching the IDR_MENU1 Menu to the Main Window of the
  Application 133
 Attaching Code to the Exit Menu Item of the File Menu 135
 Attaching Code to the Beep 1 Time Menu Item 137
 Attaching Code to the Beep 2 Times and Beep 3 Times Menu
  Items 138
 Attaching Code to the Push Buttons of the Beep Application 140

6   **Edit Boxes**   **145**

The MyEdit Application 146
 Creating the Project of the MyEdit Application 147
 The Visual Implementation of the MyEdit Application 150
 Attaching Variables to the Dialog Box of the MyEdit Program 152
 Attaching Code to the BN_CLICKED Events of the Test 1 and
  Clear 1 Buttons 153
 Adding More Controls to the MyEdit Program 156
 Attaching a Control Variable to the Lower Edit Box 157
 Modifying the Properties of the IDC_EDIT2 Edit Box 158
 Attaching Code to the Test 2 Button 159
 Attaching Code to the Clear 2 Button 161
 Attaching Code to the Copy Button 163
 Implementing the Paste Feature 165

7   **Check Boxes**   **169**

The ChkBox Application 170
 Creating the Project of the ChkBox Application 171
 The Visual Implementation of the ChkBox Application 174
 Attaching Variables to the Dialog Box of the ChkBox Program 175
 Initializing the Controls of the Dialog Box 176
 Attaching Code to the BN_CLICKED Event of the Exit Button 178
 Attaching Code to the Click Event of the Check Box 179
 Attaching Code to the Hide and Show Buttons 181
 Attaching Code to the Disable and Enable Buttons 186

8   Scroll Bars   **189**

The ScrollMe Application 190

    Creating the Project of the ScrollMe Application 191

    The Visual Implementation of the ScrollMe Application 194

    Attaching Variables to the Controls Inside the Dialog Box of the
        ScrollMe Program 196

    Initializing the Controls of the Dialog Box 197

    Attaching Code to the `BN_CLICKED` Event of the Exit Button 200

    Attaching Code to the `WM_HSCROLL` Event of the Dialog
        Box 201

    Determining Which Scroll Bar Is Associated with the Event 204

    Attaching Code to the Other Scroll Bar Messages 206

    Displaying the Scroll Bar's Thumb Tab Position While the
        Thumb Tab Is Being Dragged 211

    Attaching Code to the Hide and Show Buttons 213

    Attaching Code to the Disable and Enable Buttons 216

    Attaching Code to the Min. Button 218

    Attaching Code to the Max. Button 219

    Attaching Code to the Reset Button 220

    Debugging and Fixing the ScrollMe Program 222

    The Last Touch… 224

Making the Edit Box Read-Only 227

9   List and Combo Boxes   **229**

The MyList Application 230

    Creating the Project of the MyList Application 231

    The Visual Implementation of the MyList Application 234

    Attaching Variables to the Controls Inside the Dialog Box of
        the MyList Program 236

    Initializing the List Box 237

    Attaching Code to the `BN_CLICKED` Event of the Exit
        Button 238

    Reading an Item from the List Box 239

    Adding an Item to the List Box from Within Your Code 243

    Experimenting with Other Member Functions of the `CListBox`
        Class 246

The MyCombo Program 250

    Creating the Project of the MyCombo Application 251

    The Visual Implementation of the MyCombo Application 255

    Attaching Variables to the Dialog Box of the MyCombo
        Program 256

    Initializing the Combo Box 258

Attaching Code to the `BN_CLICKED` Event of the Exit
Button 260
Reading an Item from the List Box 261
Why Not Use Copy and Paste? 265

10   Radio Buttons   267
The MyRadio Application 268
Creating the Project of the MyRadio Application 269
The Visual Implementation of the MyRadio Application 272
Declaring the Radio Buttons Groups 276
Attaching Variables to the Controls Inside the Dialog Box of
the MyRadio Program 278
Initializing the Radio Buttons 280
Attaching Code to the `BN_CLICKED` Event of the Exit
Button 283
Determining the Status of the Radio Buttons 284

11   Displaying Dialog Boxes   289
The MyDialog Application 290
Creating the Project of the MyDialog Application 291
The Visual Implementation of MyDialog's
Main Window 295
Attaching Code to the `BN_CLICKED` Event of the Exit
Button 296
Creating a Dialog Box for Taking Users' Data 297
Declaring a Class for the IDD_DIALOG1 Dialog Box 299
Attaching a Variable to the Edit Box of the IDD_DIALOG1
Dialog Box 300
Creating an Object of Class `CMyDlg` 301
Displaying the m_Dlg1 Dialog Box 303
Attaching Code to the Display Data Button 304
Going Over the Whole Process One More Time... 305
Displaying Another Dialog Box 306
The Visual Implementation of the IDD_DIALOG2 Dialog
Box 307
Associating the IDD_DIALOG2 Scroll Bar with a Class 309
Attaching Variables to the Controls of the IDD_DIALOG2
Dialog Box 309
Creating an Object m_Dlg2 of Class `CSpeedDlg` 309
Attaching Code to the Enter Speed Button 312
Attaching Code to the Display Speed Button 313
Initializing the m_Dlg2 Dialog Box 314
Attaching Code to the `WM_HSCROLL` Event of the
m_Dlg2 Dialog Box 317

12   Writing a Single-Document Interface Application   323

Single-Document Interface Versus Multiple-Document Interface 324

The Test Application 326

Creating the Project of the Test Application 328

Running the Test Application Before Customizing It 336

The Visual Implementation of the Test Application's Form 339

Attaching a Variable to the IDC_EDIT1 Edit Box 341

The Visual Implementation of the Menu Bar 341

Attaching Code to the Test and Clear Buttons 345

Final Words... 347

13   Writing and Reading Data (with Serialization) to and from Files   349

The MEMO Application 350

Creating the Project of the MEMO Application 353

The Visual Implementation of the Application's Form 357

Attaching Variables to the Controls Inside the
IDD_MEMO_FORM Dialog Box 359

Changing the Properties of the Memo Edit Box 361

The Visual Implementation of the Menu Bar 362

The Document Class of the MEMO Application 363

Initializing the Data Members of the Document Class 364

Initializing the Data Members of the View Class 366

Updating the Data Members of the Document Class 369

Writing and Reading Data to and from Files 373

Executing the MEMO Application 377

Enhancing the MEMO application 378

Executing the Final Version of the MEMO Application 381

Serializing Different Types of Data Members 382

Final Words... 382

**14   Writing and Reading Lists (with Serialization) to and
from Files   385**

The PHN Application 386

Creating the Project of the PHN Application 389

Designing the Form of the Application 393

Attaching Variables to the Controls of the IDD_PHN_FORM
Dialog Box 395

The Visual Implementation of the Menu 395

Executing the PHN Application 396

Declaring the Phone Class 396

Adding the PHONE.CPP File to the PHN Project 398

The Document Class of the PHN Application 400

The MFC CObList Class 400

Initializing the Data Member of the Document Class 401

Deleting the Objects of the m_PhoneList List 404
The View Class of the PHN Application 408
Declaring the Data Members of the View Class 408
Initializing the Data Members of the View Class 409
Updating the Data Members of the Document Class 413
Attaching Code to the Previous Button 416
Attaching Code to the Next Button 419
Attaching Code to the Add Button 420
Attaching Code to the Delete Button 422
Executing the PHN Application 424
Serializing the List 425
Adding Overhead Code to PHONE.H and PHONE.CPP 425
Calling the List's Serialize() Function 428
Executing the PHN Application 430
The Final Touch 430

15   Customizing Serialization   431
The CArchive Class 432
The ARCH Application 432
Creating the Project of the ARCH Application 434
The Visual Implementation of the ARCH Application's Form 439
Attaching Variables to the Edit Boxes of the Form 440
The Visual Implementation of the Menu Bar 441
Attaching Code to the Save Button 441
Attaching Code to the Load Button 444
Executing the Finished ARCH Application 446

**16   Writing and Reading Data (Without Serialization) to and
        from Files   447**
The FileIt Application 448
Creating the Project of the FileIt Application 450
The Visual Implementation of the FileIt Application 454
The Visual Implementation of the Menu of the FileIt
    Application 454
The Visual Implementation of the Main Window of the FileIt
    Application 456
The Visual Implementation of the Try It Dialog Box 457
Attaching a Class to the Try It Dialog Box 458
Attaching Variables to the Controls Inside the IDD_DIALOG1
    Dialog Box 459
Declaring the Try It Dialog Box Object as a Data Member of
    the View Class 460
Attaching Code to the FileIt Menu Item 461
Providing Your User with a Save Button 463

The CFile MFC Class 465
Reading the MyFile.TXT File 466
The SeekIt Application 469
The Sampling Rate of a WAV File 469
Executing the SeekIt Application 471
Creating the Project of the SeekIt Application 473
The Visual Implementation of the SeekIt Application Main
Window 477
The Visual Implementation of the Menu of the SeekIt
Application 477
Modifying the About Dialog Box 478
Attaching Code to the Sampling Rate Menu Item of the SeekIt
Application 482

17   The Mouse   487

The MyMouse Application 488
Creating the Project of the MyMouse Application 490
The Visual Implementation of the Application's Form 494
Attaching Variables to the Controls Inside the
IDD_MYMOUSE_FORM Dialog Box 495
Changing the Properties of the Edit Box 496
The Visual Implementation of the Menu Bar 497
Attaching Code to the OnLButtonDown() Function 499
Attaching Code to the Left Button Up Event 502
Who Receives the Messages? 504
The Parameters of the OnLButtonDown() Function 506
The point Parameter of the OnLButtonUp() and
OnLButtonDown() Functions 513
The WhereAmI Application 513
Creating the Project of the WhereAmI Application 515
The Visual Implementation of the Application's Form 519
Attaching Variables to the Controls Inside the
IDD_WHEREAMI_FORM Dialog Box 520
Changing the Properties of the Edit Box 521
The Visual Implementation of the Menu Bar 522
Responding to Mouse Events 523
The DragIt Application 525
Determining Mouse Movement 525
Creating the Project of the DrawIt Application 527
The Visual Implementation of the Application's Form 532
Attaching Variables to the Controls Inside the
IDD_DRAWIT_FORM Dialog Box 533
The Visual Implementation of the Menu Bar 534
Responding to Mouse Events 535

18   The Keyboard   545

The MyKey Application 546

   Creating the Project of the MyKey Application 548

   The Visual Implementation of the Menu Bar 552

   Processing Keyboard Messages 553

   Attaching Code to the OnKeyDown() Function 553

   Determining Which Key Is Pressed 555

   Other Virtual Keys 556

   Checking for the Pressing of the Ctrl Key 559

   Checking for Other Combinations of Keys 561

   The WM_CHAR Message 564

19   Writing a Multiple-Document Interface Application   567

What Is a Multiple-Document Interface Application? 568

The PAD Application 568

   Creating the Project of the PAD Application 579

   Creating the Form of the Application 583

   Attaching Variables to the Controls of the IDD_PAD_FORM

      Dialog Box 585

   The Visual Implementation of the Menus 585

   Executing the PAD Application 588

   The Document Class of the PAD Application 589

   Initializing the Data Members of the Document Class 591

   Initializing the Data Members of the View Class 592

   Updating the Data Members of the Document Class 594

   Writing and Reading Data to and from Files 597

   Using the String Editor to Enhance the PAD Application 598

   Multiple Views of the Same Document 602

   The UpdateAllViews() and OnUpdate() Functions 603

   Calling the UpdateAllViews() Function 603

   The OnUpdate() Member Function of the View Class 605

   Splitter Windows 607

   Adding the Split Option to the Window Menu 609

   Executing the Final Version of the PAD Application 610

20   Menus   611

The MyMenu Application 612

   Creating the Project of the MyMenu Application 615

   The Visual Design of the Menu 619

   The Visual Implementation of the Main Window of MyMenu 620

   Attaching Code to a Menu Item 620

   Adding Accelerator Keys to the Menu 621

   Implementing Submenus 626

   Placing a Checkmark in a Menu Item 632

Disabling a Menu Item 636
Using the UPDATE_COMMAND_UI Message 639
The GROW Application 644
Creating the Project of the GROW Application 647
The Visual Design of the Menu 651
The Visual Implementation of the Application's Main Window ... 652
Attaching Code to the Menu Items 652
Removing the Items from the Growing Menu 654
Attaching Code to the Add Item Menu Item 657
Adding Five Items at Runtime 659
Deleting and Inserting Items 663
Attaching Code to the Added Menu Items 663

21   The Toolbar and Status Bar   665

The MyTool Application 666
Creating the Project of the MyTool Application 669
The Visual Design of the Menu 673
The Visual Implementation of the MyTool Application's Main
Window 675
Attaching Code to the Menu Items 678
What About the Toolbar? 683
Replacing the Icons on the Toolbar 685
Customizing the Status Bar for Menu Prompts 688
Further Helping the User… 691

22   Multimedia: Playing and Recording WAV Files   695

What Is the CTegMM.LIB Advanced Multimedia Library? 696
The WAVE.EXE Application 697
Creating the Project of the WAVE.EXE Application 700
Creating the Form of the Application 704
Attaching Variables to the Controls of the IDD_WAVE_FORM
Dialog Box 706
The Visual Implementation of the Menu 707
Adding the CTegMM.LIB Library to the Wave.MAK Project 707
Declaring an Object of Class CTegMM 708
Opening the WAV File 710
Attaching Code to the Play Button 715
Attaching Code to the MM_MCINOTIFY Event 718
Attaching Code to the Prev Button 721
Attaching Code to the Next Button 723
Rewinding the Playback Position Automatically 724
Attaching Code to the Stop Button 727
Attaching Code to the Pause Button 728
Attaching Code to the Record Button 729

Saving the User's Recording in the WAV File 732
Using the CTegMM.LIB Multimedia Library for Playing
Through the PC Speaker 732

23 Multimedia: Playing MIDI Files   **735**

The MIX Application 736
Creating the Project of the MIX.EXE Application 738
Creating the Form of the Application 743
The Visual Implementation of the Menu 744
Adding the CTegMM.LIB Library to the MIX.MAK Project 745
Declaring Two Objects of Class CTegMM 745
Attaching Code to the Play Bourbon6.MID Button 747
Attaching Code to the Stop Bourbon6.MID Button 751
Attaching Code to the Play 8Kenned3.WAV Button 753
Attaching Code to the Stop 8Kenned3.WAV Button 754

24 Multimedia: Video for Windows   **757**

Playing Video Files 758
Before You Can Play Video Files on Your PC… 758
Installing the Video for Windows Software Drivers 759
Playing a Video File with Media Player 760
Creating Your Own Video Files 762
The AVI Application 762
Creating the Project of the AVI Application 765
Creating the Form of the Application 769
Attaching Variables to the Controls of the IDD_AVI_FORM
Dialog Box 771
The Visual Implementation of the Menu 772
Adding the CTegMM.LIB Library to the AVI.MAK Project 773
Declaring an Object of Class CTegMM 773
Opening the AVI File 775
Attaching Code to the Play Button 780
Attaching Code to the MM_MCINOTIFY Event 782
Attaching Code to the Stop Button 786
Attaching Code to the Step Button 788
Attaching Code to the Back Button 789
Attaching Code to the Silent Check Box 790
Attaching Code to the WM_PAINT Event 791
Experimenting with Other Video Files 793

25 Multimedia: CD Audio   **795**

Playing an Audio CD with Media Player 796
The CD Application 798
Creating the Project of the CD Application 800
Creating the Form of the Application 805

Attaching Variables to the Controls of the IDD_CD_FORM
  Dialog Box 806
The Visual Implementation of the Menu 807
Adding the CTegMM.LIB Library to the CD.MAK Project 808
Declaring an Object of Class CTegMM 808
Loading an Audio CD 810
Attaching Code to the Load Button 812
Attaching Code to the Play Button 814
Attaching Code to the Stop Button 814
Attaching Code to the Prev Button 816
Attaching Code to the Next Button 817
Attaching Code to the Eject Button 818
Updating the Track Edit Box Continuously 820

26   The Timer   823

The MyTimer Application 824
Creating the Project of the MyTimer Application 825
The Visual Implementation of the MyTimer Application's
  Menu 829
The Visual Implementation of the MyTimer Application's
  Main Window 830
Installing a Timer in the MyTimer Application 831
Attaching Code to the WM_TIMER Event 832
Executing the MyTimer Application 834
Displaying the Current Time in the MyTimer Application's
  Window 834
Changing the Default Characteristics of the MyTimer
  Application's Main Window 836
Executing the Final Version of the MyTimer Application 838
Killing the Timer 838

27   Animation   841

The BALL Application 842
Creating the Project of the BALL Application 845
The Visual Implementation of the BALL Application's Main
  Window 849
Attaching Variables to the Controls of the IDD_BALL_FORM
  Dialog Box 850
The Visual Implementation of the Menu 851
Adding Bitmap Files to the BALL Application 851
Executing the BALL Application 857

Declaring Variables for the Animation Show 858

Loading the Bitmaps 859

Displaying the First Frame of the Show 862

Deleting the Bitmaps 865

Starting the Animation Show 867

The Animation Show 868

Setting the Default Size of the Application's Window 871

28   The `OnIdle()` Function   875

What Is the `OnIdle()` Function? 876

The ANNOUNCE Application 876

Creating the Project of the ANNOUNCE Application 878

The Visual Implementation of the ANNOUNCE Application's
Main Window 882

The Visual Implementation of the Menu 883

Writing Code in the ANNOUNCE Application's `OnIdle()`
Function 884

Executing the ANNOUNCE Application 886

Declaring the `CTegMM` Advanced Multimedia Class 887

Creating a Multimedia Object of Class `CTegMM` 888

Adding the CTegMM.LIB Library to the Announce.MAK
Project 890

Monitoring the Windows Session 891

Displaying Text in the Main Window of the ANNOUNCE
Application 894

Changing the Default Size of the ANNOUNCE Application's
Main Window 896

29   Animation and Sound with and Without Synchronization   899

Animation with Asynchronous Sound—The DANCE
Application 900

Creating the Project of the DANCE Application 901

Creating the Form of the DANCE Application 906

The Visual Implementation of the Menu 907

Adding Bitmap Files to the DANCE Application 908

Executing the DANCE Application 911

Declaring Variables for the Animation Show 912

Loading the Bitmaps and Creating a Multimedia Object 913

Displaying the First Frame of the Show 918

Deleting the Bitmaps 919

Starting the Animation Show 921

The Animation Show 923

Stopping the Animation Show 925

Attaching Code to the Stop Button 928

Setting the Default Size of the Application Window 929

Animation with Synchronized Sound—The KENNEDY
    Application 930
    Creating the Project of the KENNEDY Application 932
    The Visual Implementation of the Dialog Box 936
    The Visual Implementation of the Menu 937
    Adding Bitmap Files to the KENNEDY Application 938
    Executing the KENNEDY Application 939
    Declaring Variables for the Animation Show 940
    Loading the Bitmaps and Initializing the Multimedia Object 942
    Displaying the First Frame of the Show 944
    Deleting the Bitmaps 946
    Starting the Animation Show 946
    The Synchronized Animation Show 948
    Stopping the Animation Show 950
    Setting the Default Size of the Application's Window 953

30   Creating C++ Classes for Distribution and Profit   955
    Why Create Professional Software Modules? 956
    Different Formats for Software Modules 957
    Creating the Circle.CPP and Circle.H Files 957
    Creating the Circle.MAK Project 958
    Declaring the CCircle Class 963
    Writing Code Inside the Circle.CPP File 964
    Making the Circle.LIB Library 967
    Testing the Library—The TestLib.EXE Program 968
    The Visual Implementation of the TestLib Main Window 972
    Attaching Code to the My Circle Button of the
        IDD_TESTLIB_FORM Dialog Box 973
    Attaching Code to the His Circle Button of the
        IDD_TESTLIB_FORM Dialog Box 975
    Attaching Code to the Her Circle Button of the
        IDD_TESTLIB_FORM Dialog Box 976
    Attaching Code to the Our Circle Button of the
        IDD_TESTLIB_FORM Dialog Box 977
    Plugging In the TestLib.LIB Library 978
    Compiling, Linking, and Executing the TestLib Program 980
    Distributing Your Software Modules 981

31   Creating Your Own DLLs   983
    What Is a DLL? 984
    Creating a DLL 984
    Using Generic Files to Start Your DLL Project 985
    Creating the Project of MyDLL.DLL 985

Customizing the MyDLL.CPP File 988
Customizing the MyDLL.DEF File 992
Writing a Visual C++ Program That Uses MyDLL.DLL 993
Creating the Project of the TestDLL Application 994
Creating the Form of the Application 998
The Visual Implementation of the Menu 999
Declaring Global Variables 1000
Loading MyDLL.DLL 1001
Attaching Code to the Test MyDLL.DLL Button 1004

32   Drawing Geometric Shapes and Text with Different Fonts   1007

Drawing from Within Visual C++ Versus Drawing from Within
Paintbrush 1008
The DRAW Application 1008
Creating the Project of the DRAW Application 1011
The Visual Design of the Menu 1016
The OnDraw() Function 1018
Attaching Code to the OnDraw() Function 1019
Drawing Inside the Window 1021
Attaching Code to the Menu Items 1022
Drawing a Line from within the OnDraw() Function 1026
Changing the Characteristics of the Line 1027
Drawing a Circle 1030
Drawing a Rectangle 1033
The CircleIt Application 1036
Creating the Project of the CircleIt Application 1039
The Visual Design of the Menu of the CircleIt Application 1044
Adding Code to the OnDraw() Function 1044
Drawing Outside the OnDraw() Function 1046
The MyText Application 1050
Creating the Project of the MyText Application 1051
The Visual Design of the Menu of the MyText Application 1056
Displaying Text with Different Fonts 1056

33   Creating OCX Controls   1061

What Is an OCX Control? 1062
The MYCLOCK OCX Control 1063
Creating the Project of the MyClock.OCX Control 1063
Testing the MYCLOCK Control Before Customizing It 1068
Registering the MYCLOCK Control 1070
Testing the MYCLOCK Control 1070
Customizing the Picture of the MYCLOCK Control Tool 1074
What You Have Accomplished So Far 1075

34 Customizing OCX Controls   **1077**

Drawing Inside the MYCLOCK Control 1078

Displaying the Current Time Inside the MYCLOCK Control 1082

Displaying the Current Time Continuously 1085

Adding Stock (Standard) Properties to the MYCLOCK

    Control 1088

Making the BackColor and ForeColor Properties Functional 1094

Setting the Initial Size of the MYCLOCK Control 1097

Adding a Custom Property to the MYCLOCK Control 1099

Initializing the UpdateInterval Property 1102

Making the UpdateInterval Property Functional 1104

Validating the Value of the UpdateInterval Property 1107

Adding a Properties Page to the MYCLOCK Control 1109

Customizing the General Properties Page 1113

What You Have Accomplished So Far 1117

35 Adding Events and Methods to OCX Controls   **1119**

Adding Stock Events to the MYCLOCK Control 1120

Adding a Custom Event to the MYCLOCK Control 1126

Firing the NewMinute Event 1130

Adding Methods to the MYCLOCK Control 1133

The AboutBox() Method—A Gift from ControlWizard 1133

Adding a Stock Method to the MYCLOCK Control 1135

Adding a Custom Method to the MYCLOCK Control 1139

Final Words 1143

Index   **1145**

Acknowledgments

We would like to thank Greg Croy, acquisitions editor at Sams Publishing, for asking us to write this book, and especially for the various suggestions and recommendations that he made during the development and production of the book.

We would also like to thank Phil Paxton, the development editor of this book; Robert Bogue, the technical editor; Kitty Wilson, the production editor; and Wayne Blankenbeckler and Keith Davenport, who helped in the production of the book's CD-ROM.

We would also like to thank all the other people at Sams who contributed to this book.

Thanks also to Microsoft Corporation, which supplied us with technical information and various betas and upgrades of the software product.

About the Author

Ori Gurewich and Nathan Gurewich are the authors of several best-selling books in the areas of Visual Basic for Windows, C/C++ programming, multimedia programming, database design and programming, and other topics.

Ori Gurewich holds a bachelor's degree in electrical engineering from Stony Brook University, Stony Brook, New York. His background includes working as a senior software engineer and as a software consultant engineer for companies, developing professional multimedia and Windows applications. He is an expert in the field of PC programming and network communications, and has developed various multimedia algorithms for the PC. Ori Gurewich can be contacted via CompuServe (CompuServe ID 72072,312).

Nathan Gurewich holds a master's degree in electrical engineering from Columbia University, New York, and a bachelor's degree in electrical engineering from Hofstra University, Long Island, New York. Since the introduction of the PC, the author has been involved in the design and implementation of commercial software packages for the PC. He is an expert in the field of PC programming and in providing consulting services in the area of local area networks, wide area networks, database management and design, and software marketing. Nathan Gurewich can be contacted via CompuServe (CompuServe ID 75277,2254).

Introduction

Why Visual C++?

Welcome to the fascinating world of programming powerful, professional Windows applications with the Microsoft Visual C++ 2.0 package.

Currently, Windows is the most popular operating system for the PC, and consequently, almost all vendors ship their PCs with a mouse and the Windows operating system already installed.

16-bit and 32-bit Windows Operating Systems

Currently, there are two types of Windows operating systems: the 16-bit operating system and the 32-bit operating system.

For example, Windows 3.1 is a 16-bit operating system. Windows for Workgroups 3.11 is also a 16-bit operating system.

Windows 95 (commonly known by its code name *Chicago*) is a 32-bit operating system. Windows NT 3.5 (commonly known by its code name *Daytona*) is also a 32-bit operating system.

Visual C++ 1.5x and Visual C++ 2.0

Currently, Microsoft ships the product Visual C++ 2.0 with two versions of Visual C++ in it: Visual C++ 1.5x and Visual C++ 2.0.

You use Visual C++ 1.5x to develop 16-bit Windows applications. A 16-bit Windows application can be executed on a 16-bit Windows operating system and on a 32-bit Windows operating system.

You use Visual C++ 2.0 to develop 32-bit Windows applications. A 32-bit Windows application can be executed only on a 32-bit Windows operating system. You cannot execute a 32-bit Windows application on a 16-bit Windows operating system.

In this book you'll develop 32-bit Windows applications by using Visual C++ 2.0.

NOTE

In this book you'll develop 32-bit Windows applications by using Visual C++ 2.0.

For developing 16-bit Windows applications with Visual C++ 1.5x, use the Sams Publishing book *Master Visual C++ 1.5* by Gurewich & Gurewich.

Why Use Windows? Why Use Visual C++?

There are several reasons why Windows became so popular in a relatively short time:

- Windows lets you write device-independent programs.

  This means that while you write the application, you don't have to concern yourself with issues such as what type of printer, mouse, monitor, keyboard, sound card, CD-ROM drive, or other devices your users own. Your application should work fine no matter what hardware is used by your users. So does this mean, for example, that your user can use *any* sound card? Not at all! It is your user's responsibility to install the sound card into his/her PC. During the installation, Windows asks the user to install the appropriate drivers, and Windows either accepts or rejects the sound card. Windows will accept the sound card provided that the hardware and the software (drivers) that your user receives from the vendor of the sound card were implemented in accordance with Windows requirements. Once Windows accepts the sound card, the Windows applications you write should work with that sound card. The same applies for other devices such as the printer, the monitor, and the CD-ROM drive.

- A lot of code is already installed in your user's PC.

  Once Windows is installed, the PC contains much Windows-related software. This code exists on your PC (the developer's PC) and on your users' PCs. This means that before you even start writing the first line of code yourself, your user already has more than half of your program in his or her PC! Not only do you not have to write this code, you don't even have to distribute that code to your users.

- Standard user interface.

  The user-interface mechanism is the same for all Windows applications. For example, without reading the documentation of your application, your users know how to execute your application, they can use the icon that appears on the corner of the window of your application to minimize the window, they know the meaning of the OK and Cancel buttons, they know what the About dialog box is, and they understand many other features of your program before you even start writing your programs!

These reasons for using Windows are applicable no matter what programming language you use for developing the application. The question is Why should you use Visual C++ for writing Windows applications, and not a "regular" C with the SDK for Windows?

Visual C++: What Is That?

The *C++* in *Visual C++* means that you have to use C++ for writing the code. However, this book assumes no previous C++ experience. That is, during the course of this book, you will learn all the C++ stuff that you'll need for writing professional, powerful Windows applications by using the C++ programming language. It is assumed, however, that you do have some previous programming experience with the "regular" C programming language. This book does not assume that you have any Windows programming experience. That is, if you have some minimal C DOS programming experience, you will do fine.

Now that you know the meaning of the *C++* in *Visual C++,* what is the meaning of *Visual?* It means that you'll accomplish many of your programming tasks by using the keyboard and the mouse device to visually design and write your applications. You'll select controls such as push buttons and scroll bars with the mouse, drag them to your application, and size them—and you'll be able to see your application as you build it (this is called *design time*). In other words, you'll be able to see how your application will look before you execute it. This is a great advantage because it saves you considerable time (you can see your application without compiling/linking it), and you can change your mind regarding placement and sizes of edit boxes, push buttons, and other objects, by simply using the mouse device.

ClassWizard: What Is That?

The most powerful feature of Visual C++ is a program called *ClassWizard.* ClassWizard writes code for you! In the industry, this type of program is often referred to as a CASE (computer-aided software engineering) program. Of course, ClassWizard is not a magic program—you have to tell it what you want it to write for you. For example, suppose that you visually (with the mouse) placed a push button inside the window of your application. Once you have placed the button, you want to write code that is executed whenever the user clicks that button. This is the time to use ClassWizard. By clicking various buttons in the window of ClassWizard, you tell ClassWizard to prepare all the overhead code. ClassWizard responds by preparing all the overhead code and then showing you where you should insert your own code. Therefore, your job is to type your code in the area that ClassWizard prepared.

Visual C++ is an interesting and fun package to use because it lets you develop very sophisticated Windows applications in a very short time. So relax, and prepare yourself for a very pleasant journey!

> **NOTE**
>
> Make sure to install the book's CD according to the instructions on the Install Page and in Chapter 1.

Windows NT and SCSI CD-ROM Drive

As stated at the beginning of this chapter, with Visual C++ you can generate 32-bit EXE programs, 32-bit OCX controls, and 32-bit DLLs. These 32-bit files can be executed on a 32-bit Windows operating system such as Windows NT and Windows '95 (also known as *Chicago*). Therefore, you must install a 32-bit Windows operating system on your PC. You should know that you can purchase Windows NT 3.5 on diskettes and on a CD. However, if you intend to install Windows NT from a CD, your PC must be equipped with a special CD-ROM drive (called an SCSI CD-ROM drive). A non-SCSI CD-ROM drive is not recognized by Windows NT. So if you plan to install Windows NT from a CD, you must have an SCSI CD-ROM drive that is compatible with Windows NT.

NOTE

Before purchasing an SCSI CD-ROM drive, make sure that the particular SCSI CD-ROM drive that you are purchasing is compatible with Windows NT.

1

What Do You Need to Know?

This book teaches you how to write Windows applications by using the Microsoft Visual C++ 2.0 package. As implied by its name, Microsoft Visual C++ 2.0 enables you to write Windows programs by using the C++ programming language. But wait a minute! Do you know how to use the C++ programming language? Well, if you don't know C++, you can read Chapters 2 and 3 of this book to learn the essentials of C++. In these chapters you'll learn C++ topics and concepts that are prerequisites for the rest of the chapters of this book. The book assumes that you have some "regular" C programming experience.

The Book's CD

This book comes with a CD, on which you'll find all the book's programs, BMP files, WAV files, MIDI files, movie files, and other files that you'll need during the course of this book.

To install the book's CD on your hard drive, follow these steps:

☐ Start Windows.

☐ Insert the CD into your CD-ROM drive.

☐ Execute the INSTALL.EXE program that resides in the root directory of the CD.

☐ Follow the directions of the INSTALL.EXE program.

NOTE

The INSTALL program creates the directory C:\MVCPROG and subdirectories below C:\MVCPROG.

Throughout this book you'll be instructed to execute various EXE programs. These EXE programs are located in the subdirectory \MVCPROG\EXE of the CD. For example, in Chapter 20 you'll learn to write two applications: MyMenu.EXE and Grow.EXE. These applications reside inside the \MVCPROG\EXE directory of the CD. The source code files of these applications reside in the \MVCPROG\CH20\MYMENU directory of the CD and the \MVCPROG\CH20\GROW directory of the CD.

The \MVCPROG\EXE directory of the CD is supplied so that you'll be able to execute the applications prior to writing them yourself.

Note that the EXE programs are 32-bit programs generated with the Visual C++ 2.0 32-bit compiler. This means that to execute these programs, you need to run them on a 32-bit Windows operating systems such as Windows NT or Windows '95 (Chicago).

Also, the EXE directory of the book's CD does not include the various DLL files that are needed for the execution of these programs. This means that to execute the EXE programs, you must have Visual C++ 2.0 already installed on your PC because during the installation of Visual C++ 2.0, the SETUP program of Visual C++ 2.0 copies various DLL files to the \System directory of your 32-bit Windows operating system.

The \MVCPROG\CH?? directories of the CD are supplied so that you'll be able to compare the supplied source code files with the source code files you'll generate yourself.

Throughout this book, you'll be instructed to write the code of the book's program in the C:\MVCPROG\CH?? directories. For example, in Chapter 20, you'll be instructed to write the MyMenu application in the C:\MVCPROG\CH20\MYMENU directory, and you'll be instructed to write the Grow application in the C:\MVCPROG\CH20\GROW directory.

What's Next?

The objective of this book is to teach you how to write powerful professional Windows applications with the Visual C++ 2.0 package. The following sections describe how the book is organized. Due to the large amount of information and large number of applications that are presented in this book, you may wish to refer to the following sections and their corresponding figures for locating a particular topic or application in the future.

C++ Topics

In Chapters 2 and 3, you'll learn C++ topics. These chapters assume that you know how to write simple C DOS programs. The material that is covered in these chapters is a prerequisite for the rest of the chapters in this book.

Creating Your First Visual C++ Windows Program

In Chapter 4 you'll learn how to write your first Visual C++ Windows application and how to use the visual tools of Visual C++. (See Figure 1.1.)

Figure 1.1. Your first Visual C++ Windows program.

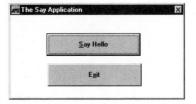

Creating Menus

In Chapter 5 you'll learn how to implement menus in your applications. (See Figure 1.2.) (More sophisticated menu topics will also be discussed in Chapter 20.)

Figure 1.2. Creating menus.

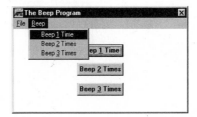

In Chapters 6 through 10 you'll learn how to implement Visual C++ programs that include standard Windows user-interface mechanisms such as edit boxes, check boxes, scroll bars, list boxes, combo boxes, and radio buttons. (See Figures 1.3 through 1.8.)

Figure 1.3. Implementing
edit boxes.

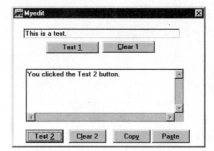

Figure 1.4. Implementing
check boxes.

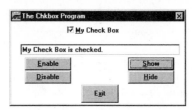

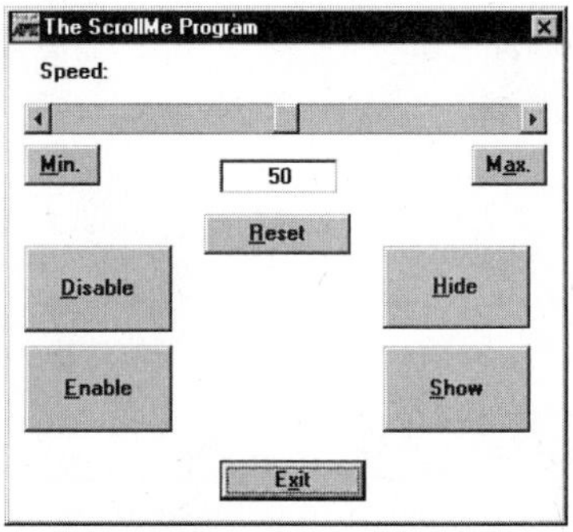

Figure 1.5. Implementing
scroll bars.

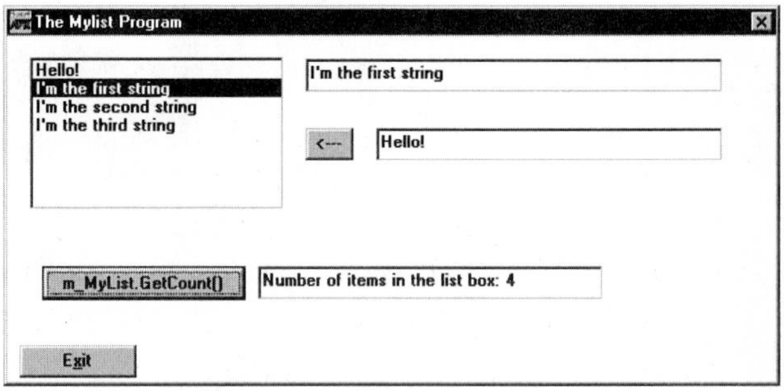

Figure 1.6. Implementing
list boxes.

Figure 1.7. Implementing combo boxes.

Figure 1.8. Implementing option buttons.

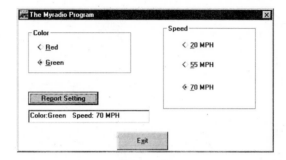

Dialog Boxes and Single-Document Interface (SDI) Applications

In Chapter 11 you'll learn how to design and display dialog boxes, and in Chapter 12 you'll learn how to design single-document interface applications. (See Figures 1.9 through 1.12.)

Figure 1.9. Implementing a main window that activates other dialog boxes.

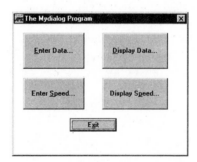

Figure 1.10. Implementing dialog boxes that contain edit boxes.

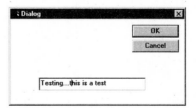

*Figure 1.11. Implementing
dialog boxes that contain
scroll bars.*

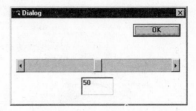

*Figure 1.12. Implementing
SDI applications.*

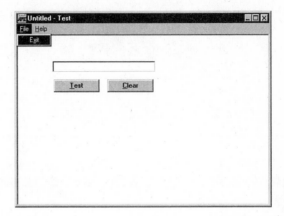

Serialization

Chapters 13 through 15 cover the important and powerful serialization feature of Visual C++. In Chapter 13 you'll learn how to write and read data to and from files with serialization. (See Figure 1.13.) In Chapter 14 you'll learn how to use serialization to write and read lists to and from files. (See Figure 1.14.) In Chapter 15 you'll learn how to customize serialization. (See Figure 1.15.) In Chapter 16 you'll learn how to write and read data without serialization. (See Figure 1.16.)

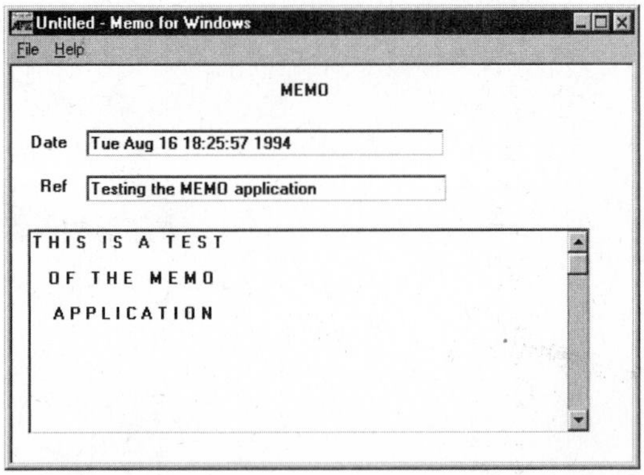

*Figure 1.13. Writing and
reading data to and from
files with serialization.*

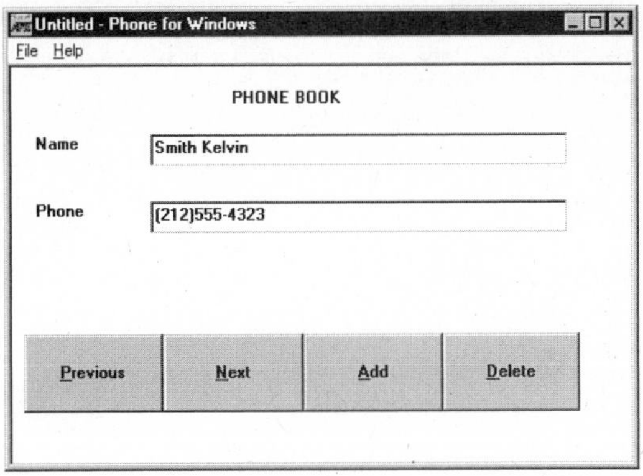

Figure 1.14. Writing and reading lists to and from files with serialization.

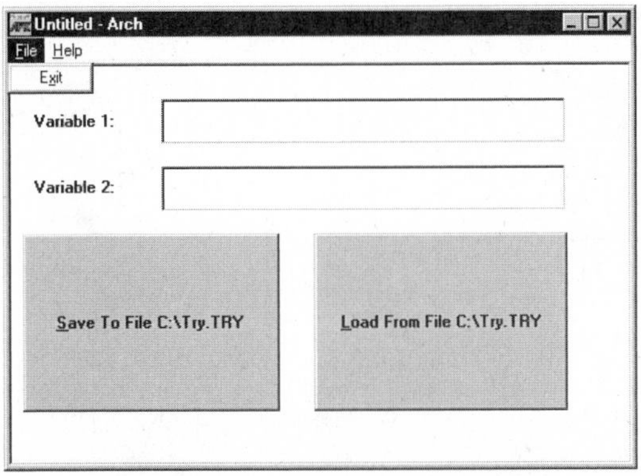

Figure 1.15. A program that uses customized serialization.

Figure 1.16. Reading and writing data without serialization.

The Mouse and the Keyboard

In Chapter 17 you'll learn how to take advantage of the mouse from within your Visual C++ programs (See Figures 1.17 through 1.20.), and in Chapter 18 you'll learn how to take advantage of the keyboard.

Figure 1.17. Detecting mouse-keyboard clicking.

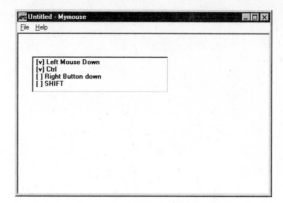

Figure 1.18. Detecting mouse position.

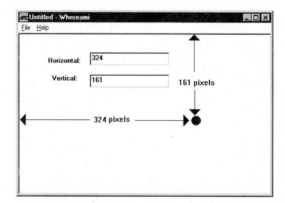

Figure 1.19. Drawing with the mouse.

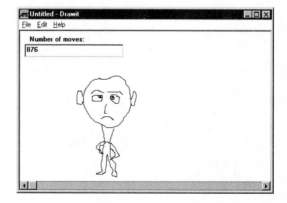

Figure 1.20. Writing with the mouse.

Multiple-Document Interface (MDI) Applications

Chapter 19 discusses multiple-document interface applications. For example, Figure 1.21 shows the MDI window (which you'll design in Chapter 21) with two child windows in it. You'll learn how to tile the child windows and manipulate the child windows in other ways. (See Figure 1.22.)

One of the interesting and powerful features of Visual C++ is its capability to let you design Windows applications with the Split feature. Figure 1.23 shows an unsplit window, Figure 1.24 shows the window of Figure 1.23 split into two, and Figure 1.25 shows the same window split into four parts. Figure 1.26 shows an MDI window with five minimized child windows.

Figure 1.21. An MDI window with two child windows in it.

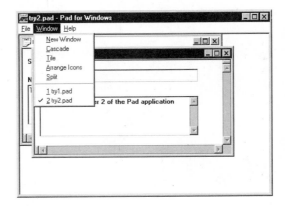

Figure 1.22. Tiling the child windows of the MDI application.

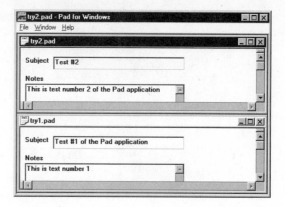

Figure 1.23. An unsplit window.

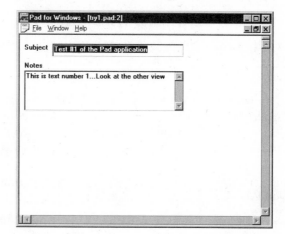

Figure 1.24. Splitting the window into two parts.

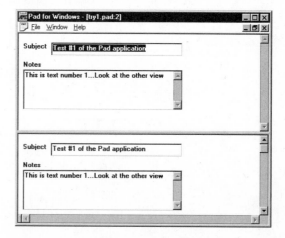

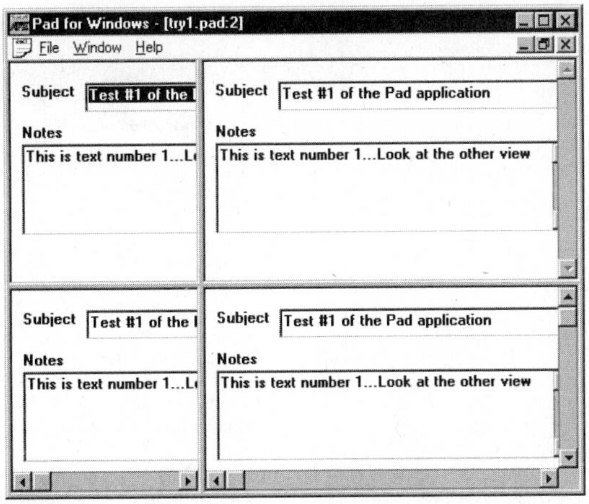

Figure 1.25. Splitting the window into four parts.

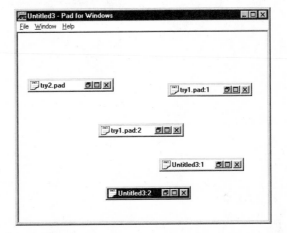

Figure 1.26. Minimizing the child windows.

More About Menus, Toolbars, and Status Bars

In Chapter 20 you'll learn how to incorporate sophisticated menus into your Visual C++ programs. For example, you'll learn how to generate "next level" menus, and you'll learn to place checkmarks next to menu items. (See Figure 1.27.) In Chapter 21 you'll also learn how to incorporate toolbars and status bars. (See Figure 1.28.)

*Figure 1.27. Placing
checkmarks next to menu
items.*

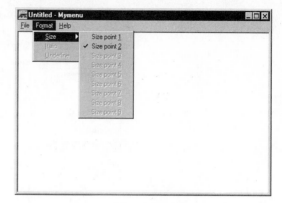

*Figure 1.28. Incorporating
toolbars and status bars in
an application.*

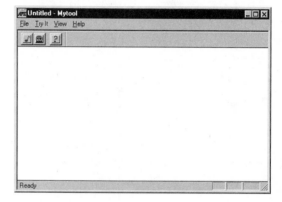

Multimedia

In Chapters 22 through 25 you'll implement multimedia Visual C++ applications. In Chapter 22 you'll learn how to play and record WAV files. (See Figure 1.29.) In Chapter 23 you'll learn how to play MIDI files simultaneously with the playback of WAV files. (See Figure 1.30.) In Chapter 24 you'll learn how to play movie files (AVI files). (See Figures 1.31 and 1.32.) In Chapter 25 you'll learn how to load and play CD audio. (See Figure 1.33.)

*Figure 1.29. Playing and
recording WAV files.*

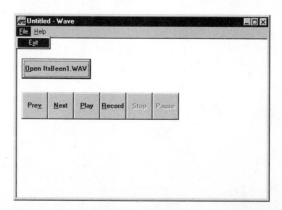

Figure 1.30. Playing MIDI and WAV files simultaneously.

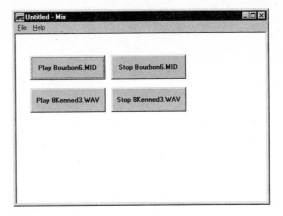

Figure 1.31. Generating movie AVI files.

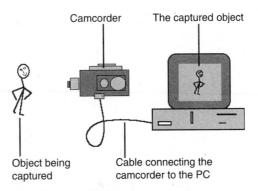

Figure 1.32. Playing movie AVI files.

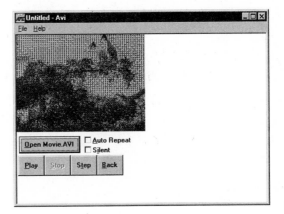

Figure 1.33. Loading and
playing CD audio.

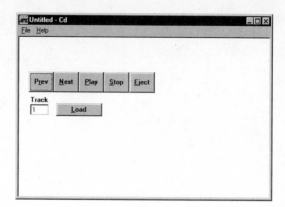

Timers

In Chapter 26 you'll learn how to implement programs that use timers. You'll implement a clock
program similar to the Clock program that comes with Windows. (See Figure 1.34.)

Figure 1.34. Implementing
a clock program with an
always-on-top window.

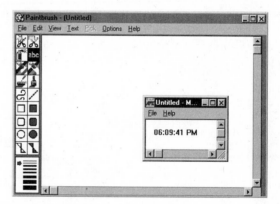

Animation

In Chapter 27 you'll learn how to implement Animation programs. For example, you'll implement
a program that throws a basketball into the basket (and never misses). (See Figure 1.35.)

Figure 1.35. Implementing the basketball animation program.

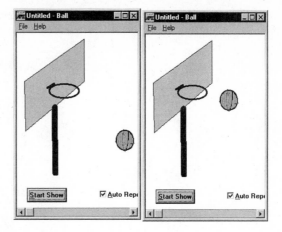

The *OnIdle()* Function

Chapter 28 shows you how to take advantage of the powerful `OnIdle()` function for performing background operations. For example, you'll learn to implement a program that runs in the background and automatically monitors and detects the presence of other Windows applications. (See Figure 1.36.)

Figure 1.36. Writing programs that work in the background.

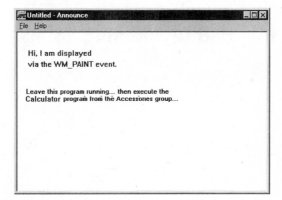

Animation and Sound

In Chapter 29 you'll implement programs that include both animation and sound. You'll learn how to design programs that include nonsynchronized as well as synchronized sound. For example, you'll implement the Dance program, a program that displays a couple dancing to music. (See Figure 1.37.) You'll also write the Kennedy program, which plays a famous speech by former President John F. Kennedy and displays the spoken words in synchronization with the played speech. (See Figure 1.38.)

Figure 1.37. The Dance program.

Figure 1.38. The Kennedy program.

Writing and Distributing Your Own Classes

Throughout this book you will extensively utilize the Microsoft Foundation Class (MFC) library. In Chapter 30 you'll learn how to design and distribute your own classes. (See Figures 1.39 and 1.40.)

Figure 1.39. Distributing your classes.

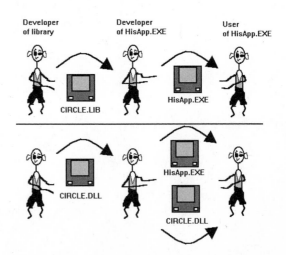

Figure 1.40. Testing your classes.

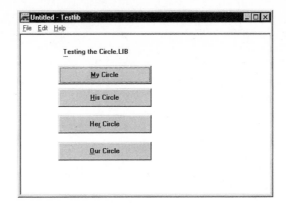

Creating Your Own DLLs

In Chapter 31 you'll learn how to create your own DLLs and you'll learn how to test the DLL that you write. (See Figure 1.41.)

Figure 1.41. Testing the DLL that you implement.

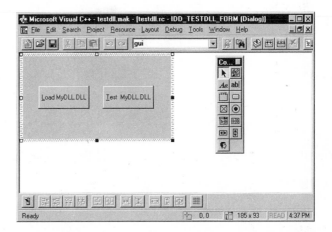

Drawing Geometric Shapes and Displaying Text with Different Fonts

Chapter 32 shows you how to create programs that draw geometric shapes and text with different fonts. (See Figures 1.42 through 1.46.)

Figure 1.42. Drawing lines with different thicknesses.

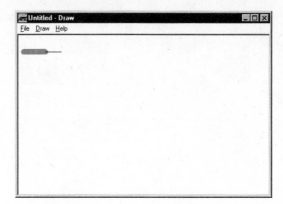

Figure 1.43. Drawing circles with different thicknesses.

Figure 1.44. Drawing geometric shapes with different fillings.

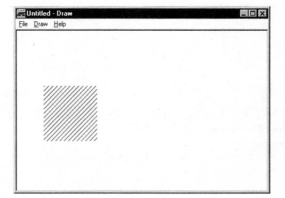

Figure 1.45. Drawing circles with the mouse.

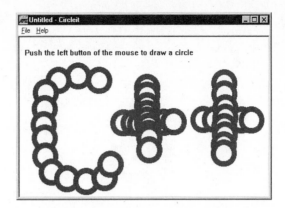

Figure 1.46. Displaying text with different fonts.

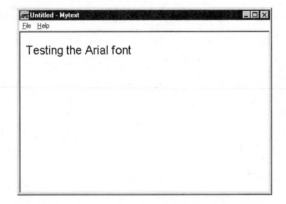

OCX Technology—How to Create Your Own OCX Controls

Chapters 33 through 35 are a very detailed tutorial that teaches you OCX technology. You'll learn what OCX controls are, how to create your own OCX controls, and how to test the OCX control that you create in these chapters.

Figure 1.47 shows the icon tool of the OCX control that you'll write, and Figure 1.48 shows the window that tests the OCX control that you'll write.

Figure 1.47. The new icon tool of the OCX that you'll design.

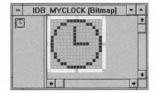

Figure 1.48. Testing the OCX that you designed and implemented.

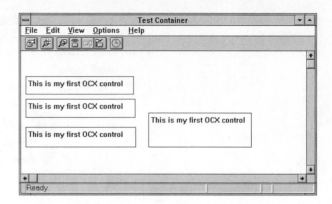

Many Topics, Many Applications...

You'll study many topics in this book, and you'll design and write many applications. In fact, there are more than 50 applications in this book. As you'll soon see, the Visual C++ knowledge that you'll get in this book is supplied on a need-to-know basis. That is, you'll write an application, and as you develop your application, you'll learn how to implement and apply new Visual C++ features and topics as they are related to the particular application that you are developing. The best way to grasp the material is to follow the tutorials by actually implementing the applications.

Remember, the only way to learn programming (any programming language) is by actually doing programming! So, once you finish studying an application, try to modify the application in some ways and experiment with it.

2

Your First C++ DOS Program

In this chapter and Chapter 3,
"Hierarchy," you'll learn some basic
C++ concepts and topics that are
prerequisites for the subsequent
chapters of this book.

What Is a Console Application?

Visual C++ comes with a capability to create console applications. Basically, *console applications* are DOS programs that are executed in a Windows shell. This means that the console programs that you write can use C statements such as `printf()`, but you execute these programs from within Windows.

> **NOTE**
>
> Visual C++ enables you to write C and C++ DOS programs that are executed in a Windows shell.

Why Learn How to Write Console Applications?

Visual C++ enables you to write DOS programs that are executed in a Windows shell. The objective of this book is to teach you how to write C++ Windows applications with the Visual C++ package. Why, then, does this chapter teach about console programs? To use Visual C++ to write Windows applications you need to know some C++ topics. As you know, even the simplest Windows program is long and contains several overhead files. Therefore, it is much simpler to learn the basics of C++ by writing simple DOS programs than by writing Windows programs.

Who needs the console programs that Visual C++ can generate? Well, this feature has several uses. For example, you need this feature to demonstrate C++ topics without using all the overhead code that true Windows applications require.

Writing a Simple DOS C++ Program

In this section, you'll write a simple C++ DOS program with Visual C++.

> **NOTE**
>
> The purpose of this chapter and the next chapter is to teach you C++ concepts and topics. These topics are prerequisites to the subsequent chapters of the book. This book assumes that you have no previous C++ programming experience, so if you've never done C++ programming or if you need to refresh your C++ knowledge, read this chapter and the next chapter.
>
> If you already know C++ and feel that you can jump directly into the Visual C++ ocean, feel free to just browse through this chapter and the next chapter.
>
> In Chapter 4, "Writing Your First True Windows Application," you'll write your first true Windows application with Visual C++.

☐ Start Visual C++ by double-clicking the Visual C++ icon. (See Figure 2.1.)

Windows responds by running the Visual C++ program. (See Figure 2.2.)

Figure 2.1. The Visual C++ program group.

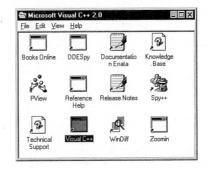

Figure 2.2. The Microsoft Visual C++ window.

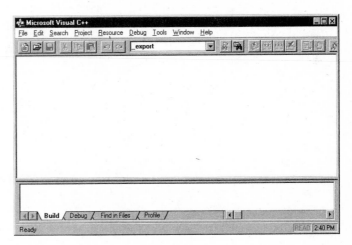

☐ Select New from the File menu. (See Figure 2.3.)

Visual C++ responds by displaying the New dialog box. (See Figure 2.4.)

As Figure 2.4 shows, the New dialog box enables you to select an item from a list. Your objective now is to create a text file that contains the code of your program. Therefore, you have to select the Code/Text item from the list of items in the New dialog box.

☐ Select the Code/Text item from the list of items in the New dialog box, and then click the OK button.

Visual C++ responds by opening a new window called Text1. (See Figure 2.5.)

Figure 2.3. Selecting New from the File menu of Visual C++.

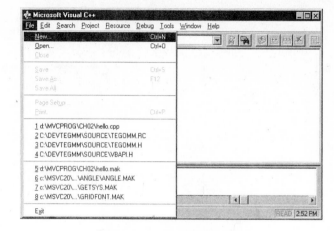

Figure 2.4. The New dialog box that Visual C++ displays after you select New from the File menu.

Figure 2.5. The new window (the Text1 window) that Visual C++ opens.

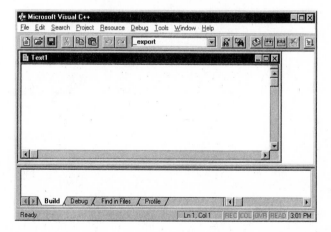

Writing the Code of the Hello.CPP Program

Now you are ready to write the C++ code of the program, which you will call Hello.CPP.

☐ Type the code of the Hello.CPP program in the Text1 window. Listing 2.1 shows the code of the program.

Listing 2.1. The code of the Hello.CPP program.

```
/////////////////////////////
// Program Name: Hello.CPP
/////////////////////////////

/////////////////////////////////////////////////////////
// Program Description:
//
// This program illustrates the use of the cout operator.
/////////////////////////////////////////////////////////

///////////////
// #include
///////////////
#include <iostream.h>

///////////////////////////
// Function Name: main()
///////////////////////////
void main()
{

cout << "Hello, this is my first C++ program";

}
```

Now save your program:

☐ Select Save As from the File menu.

    Visual C++ responds by displaying the Save As dialog box.

☐ Save your program in the directory \MVCPROG\CH02 as Hello.CPP.

    Your Save As dialog box should now look like the one shown in Figure 2.6.

Figure 2.6. The Save As dialog box.

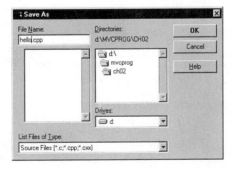

Compiling and Linking the Hello.CPP Program

Now it's time to compile and link your Hello.CPP program.

☐ Select Build Hello.EXE from the Project menu.

Visual C++ responds by displaying the dialog box shown in Figure 2.7.

Figure 2.7. The dialog box that Visual C++ displays after you select Build Hello.EXE from the Project menu.

☐ Click the Yes button in the dialog box shown in Figure 2.7.

Visual C++ responds by compiling and linking the Hello.CPP program.

If you followed the instructions outlined in the previous sections and typed the code exactly as you were instructed, you will get the window shown in Figure 2.8. This window, which is called the output window, contains the results of the compiling and linking process. (When the output window contains the message `0 error(s)`, `0 warning(s)`, this window is referred to as the happy window.)

Figure 2.8. The output window of Visual C++.

The results of the compiling and linking are shown here.

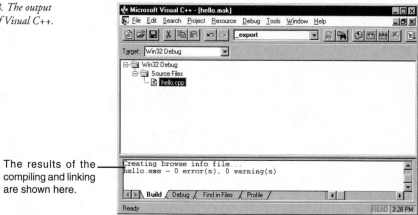

If the output window is not shown on your screen, select Output from the Window menu of Visual C++.

You can enlarge the area of the output window by placing the mouse cursor on the upper edge of the window and dragging the mouse upward.

Notice that the output window has several tabs: Build, Debug, Find in Files, and Profile. To view the results of the compiling and linking, make sure that the Build tab is selected, as shown in Figure 2.8.

If you did not get the `0 error(s)` message, display the Hello.CPP file, and make sure that you typed everything without any syntax errors.

To display the Hello.CPP window do the following:

☐ Select Hello.CPP from the Window menu.

Executing the Hello.EXE Program

Now you are in a position to execute the Hello.EXE program.

☐ Use Windows to execute the MS-DOS program (MS-DOS prompt).

> *Windows responds by executing the MS-DOS program.*

☐ Log in to the \MVCPROG\CH02 directory.

☐ At the DOS prompt type the following:

```
Hello.EXE  {Enter}
```

> *DOS responds by executing the Hello.EXE program.*

As you can see, the Hello.EXE program displays this text:

```
Hello, this is my first C++ program.
```

To terminate the DOS program do the following:

☐ At the DOS prompt, type **Exit**, and then press the Enter key.

NOTE

You should be aware that console EXE files generated by Visual C++ are not true DOS programs. In fact, if you can run MS-DOS as the true operating system of your PC, exit to the DOS prompt, log in to the \MVCPROG\CH02 directory, and type the following text at the DOS prompt:

```
HELLO  {Enter}
```

You'll get this message:

```
This program cannot be run in DOS mode.
```

Examining the Hello.CPP Program's Code

Go over the code of the Hello.CPP program.

Notice that the code contains many // characters. Comments in C++ start with the // characters. For example, the following is a valid C++ comment:

```
// This is my comment.
```

Unlike comments in C, comments in C++ do not have to terminate with the comment characters.

In C, you would write the following comment:

```
/*
   This is my comment.
   I can write here whatever I want.
*/
```

In C++, however, you can write the preceding comment like this:

```
//
//   This is my comment.
//   I can write here whatever I want.
//
```

NOTE

Generally, C is a subset of C++. Therefore, you can apply everything that you know in C to your C++ programs. For example, the following code is valid in a C++ program:

```
// This is my comment.
/* I can mix C and C++ syntax, */
// because C is a subset of C++.
```

The Hello.CPP program starts by using `#include` on the iostream.h file:

```
#include <iostream.h>
```

This `#include` statement is needed because the iostream.h file includes all the prototypes of the functions that enable you to stream characters to and from the input/output (I/O) device.

The following statements of the Hello.CPP program contain the `main()` function:

```
void main()
{

cout << "Hello, this is my first C++ program";

}
```

Just like DOS C programs, DOS C++ programs require a `main()` function. `main()` contains a single statement:

```
cout << "Hello, this is my first C++ program";
```

As you have probably guessed, `cout` serves the same role as the `printf()` function of C. The `<<` characters indicate the direction of the stream. Because the `<<` characters point from the string `Hello,...` to the `cout`, the characters of the string flow to the `cout` device (the screen).

As stated earlier, C is a subset of C++. This means that you can use the `printf()` function of C.

☐ Display the Hello.CPP file—that is, select `Hello.CPP` from the Window menu.

> *If the Window menu does not contain the Hello.CPP item, select Open from the File menu to open the Hello.CPP file from the \MVCPROG\CH02 directory.*

☐ Modify the Hello.CPP file so that it looks like this:

```
/////////////////////////////
// Program Name: Hello.CPP
/////////////////////////////

/////////////////////////////////////////////////////////////
// Program Description:
//
// This program illustrates the use of the cout operator.
/////////////////////////////////////////////////////////////

//////////////
// #include
//////////////
#include <iostream.h>

/////////////////////////////
// Function Name: main()
/////////////////////////////
void main()
{

// cout << "Hello, this is my first C++ program";
printf ("Hello, this is my first C program");

}
```

☐ Save the Hello.CPP file by selecting Save from the File menu.

Now compile and link the Hello.CPP program:

☐ Select Rebuild All from the Project menu.

Visual C++ responds by displaying the error messages shown in Figure 2.9.

Figure 2.9. The error messages Visual C++ displays.

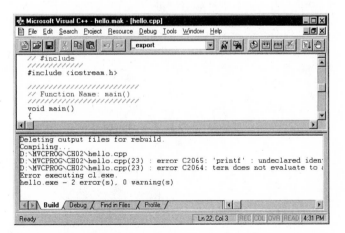

Errors? Why? From the errors that you received, you may conclude that the compiler does not know the meaning of printf(). This conclusion makes sense, of course, because you did not use #include on the stdio.h file.

NOTE

During the compiling process, the compiler and linker display error messages (if any) in the output window. To go directly to the line that causes the error, you can double-click the error message in the output window.

☐ Add the following statement at the beginning of the Hello.CPP file:

```
#include <stdio.h>
```

☐ Select Rebuild All from the Project menu.

Visual C++ responds by compiling and linking the Hello.CPP program.

☐ Exit to an MS-DOS shell—that is, execute the MS-DOS program from Windows.

☐ Log in to the \MVCPROG\CH02 directory and execute the Hello.EXE program.

DOS responds by executing the Hello.EXE program.

As expected, the program displays this message:

```
"Hello, this is my first C program".
```

To terminate the DOS program do the following:

☐ At the DOS prompt, type Exit, and then press the Enter key.

Target: Debug and Release

When compiling and linking, you can specify debug or release as the target. When you specify debug as the target, the compiler and linker generate an EXE file that contains various code lines. This code is used by other debug utilities that come with Visual C++. You typically specify a debug target when you plan to debug your program. On the other hand, when you specify a release target, no debugging code is embedded inside the EXE file. This is how you tell Visual C++ to generate a release EXE file:

☐ Select Hello.MAK from the Window menu.

Visual C++ responds by making the Hello.MAK window the active window. (See Figure 2.10.)

As you can see from Figure 2.10, the target is debug. Notice that the Hello.MAK file consists of a source file called Hello.CPP.

To change the target to release do the following:

☐ Click the down-arrow icon of the Target list box and select Release. (See Figure 2.11.)

Figure 2.10. The Hello.MAK window as the active window.

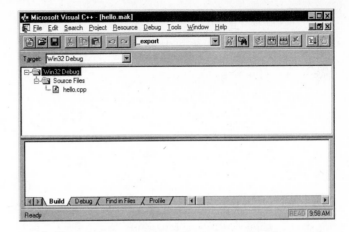

Figure 2.11. Changing the target to release.

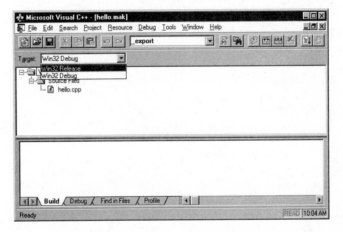

Figure 2.12 shows the Hello.MAK window in release mode.

Figure 2.12. The Hello.MAK window in release mode.

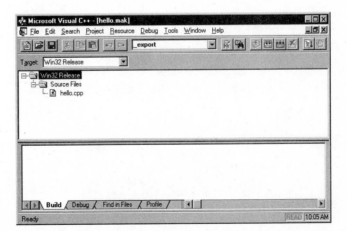

C++ Versus C

You learned in the preceding sections that C++ uses a different comment syntax from C, and that C++ uses the cout statement instead of the printf() function. These are not the only differences between C and C++, of course.

C++ was invented after several years of extensive C use—that is, people had used C for a long time, and this programming language proved to be very reliable and convenient. The EXE files that are generated with the C programming language are short and are executed quickly.

So why bother with a new programming language? People started to demand more from C. In essence, C++ is the second version of the C programming language. This version contains all the enhancements that C programmers desired when they wrote their C programs.

Briefly, the C++ programming language incorporates improvements on the C programming language, based on huge amounts of experience. The resulting C++ language is an excellent language that is very easy and convenient to use, and like the C language, it produces small, fast EXE files.

You can take advantage of C++ for writing DOS programs, but the main advantage of using C++ probably is for writing Windows applications. This book assumes that you have no previous experience programming Windows applications. If you know how to write Windows applications with the C language, however, you know that the process of writing such applications involves typing a great deal of code—code that simply serves as the overhead for the application! There is nothing ingenious about that code, and it must appear in each and every C Windows application that you write. Does this requirement make sense to you?

By using C++, you can use something called classes. You'll get into the business of C++ classes soon enough, but for now, you can think of C++ classes as being program modules that you can plug in to your programs easily. You can write the classes yourself or purchase them from software vendors. The Microsoft Visual C++ package, for example, comes with the MFC library, which stands for *Microsoft Foundation Class* library. The MFC library contains many useful code modules that are available for your C++ Windows applications. Throughout the book, you'll have an opportunity to use many of the classes that come with the MFC library.

Classes in C++

The most important concept in C++ is the concept of *classes*.

C++ classes are similar to C structures. A C structure, however, defines only the data that is associated with the structure. The following example is a C structure:

```
struct MYSTRUCT
{
int radius;
int color;
};
```

After you declare the structure, you can use it from within your main() statement, as follows:

```
void main()
{
```

```
MYSTRUCT MyCircle;
...
...
...

MyCircle.radius = 10;
MyCircle.color = 255; /* 255 represents a color */
...
...
...
}
```

As stated earlier, the `MyCircle` structure has data associated with it (`radius` and `color`).

A class in C++, on the other hand, has both data and functions associated with it. The data of the class are called *data members*, and the functions of the class are called *member functions*. In a program that uses classes, therefore, the following code is allowed:

```
MyCircle.radius = 20;
MyCircle.Color = 255;
MyCircle.DisplayCircle();
```

The first two statements update the `radius` and the `color` data members of `MyCircle`; the third statement uses the member function `DisplayCircle()` to display the `MyCircle` circle.

Declaring a Class

Before you can do anything with the class, your program must declare the class. In this section, you learn about the syntax used to declare a class.

For practice, you'll declare a class called `Circle`. Following is the declaration of the `Circle` class:

```
class Circle
{
public:
  Circle();
  void SetRadius(void);
  void GetRadius(void);
  ~Circle();
private:
  void CalculateArea(void);
  int radius;
  int color;
};
```

The class declaration has the following skeleton:

```
class Circle
{
........
........
........
Here you type the declaration of the class
........
........
........
};
```

The `class` keyword is an indication to the compiler that whatever is typed between the curly brackets ({}) belongs to the class declaration. Don't forget to include the semicolon (;) character at the end of the declaration.

The declaration of the class contains the declarations of data members (for example, `int radius`), as well as the declarations of the prototypes of the member functions of the class. In the `Circle` class declaration, the declaration contains two data members:

```
int radius;
int color;
```

The declaration also contains five prototypes of member functions:

```
Circle();
void SetRadius(void);
void GetRadius(void);
~Circle();
void CalculateArea(void);
```

The first and fourth prototypes look strange. The first prototype is `Circle();`, which is the prototype of the *constructor* function. You'll learn about the role of the constructor function later in this chapter; for now, examine the syntax that C++ uses for the prototype of the constructor function.

When you write the prototype of the constructor function, you must follow these rules:

- Every class declaration must include the prototype of the constructor function.
- The name of the constructor function must be the same as the class name, followed by `()`.

  If you declare a class called `Rectangle`, for example, the declaration of this class must include the declaration of its constructor function, and the name of the constructor function must be `Rectangle()`. The declaration of the `Rectangle` class, therefore, looks like the following example:

  ```
  class Rectangle
  {
  public:
    Rectangle(); // The constructor
  ...
  ...
  ...
  private:
  ...
  ...
  ...
  };
  ```

- Don't mention any returned value for the constructor function. (The constructor function must be of type `void`, but do not mention it.)
- The constructor function must be under the `public` keyword.

NOTE

At this point, you are probably asking What are the `public` and `private` keywords that are mentioned in the class declaration? These keywords indicate the visibility of the data members and member functions of the class. You'll learn about these keywords later in this chapter. For now, just remember that the constructor function must be under the `public` keyword.

As stated earlier, the constructor function always has a return value of type `void` (even though you should not mention it in the prototype). As you'll soon see, the constructor function usually has one or more parameters.

The Destructor Function

The destructor function is mentioned in the class declaration as follows:

```
class Circle
{
public:
     ......
     ......
     ......
     ~Circle(); // The destructor
private:
     ......
     ......
     ......
};
```

Notice the ~ character that precedes the prototype of the destructor function. (On most keyboards you type the ~ character by pressing the Shift key together with the key to the left of the 1 key.)

When you write the prototype of the destructor function, observe the following rules:

- The name of the destructor function must be the same as the class name, preceded by the ~ character.

    If you declare a class called `Rectangle`, for example, the name of the destructor function must be `~Rectangle`. The declaration of the `Rectangle` class, therefore, looks like the following example:

    ```
    class Rectangle
    {
    public:
        Rectangle();  // The constructor
        .......
        .......
        .......
        ~Rectangle(); // The destructor
    ```

```
private:
   .......
   .......
   .......
};
```

- Don't mention any returned value for the destructor function. (The constructor function must be of type `void`, but do not mention it.)
- The destructor function does not have any parameters.

The *Public* and *Private* Keywords

As you saw in the preceding section, you include the prototype of the functions and the declaration of the data members under the `public` or the `private` section of the class declaration.

The `public` and `private` keywords tell the compiler the accessibility of the functions and the accessibility of the data members. For example, the `SetRadius()` function is defined under the `public` section, which means that any function in the program can call the `SetRadius()` function. Because the `CalculateArea()` function is declared under the `private` section, however, only member functions of the `Circle` class can call the `CalculateArea()` function.

Similarly, because the `radius` data member is declared under the `private` section, only member functions of the `Circle` class program can update or read the value of this data member directly. Had you declared the `radius` data member under the `public` section, however, any function in the program could access (read and update) the `radius` data member.

To summarize, the class declaration defines the accessibility of its member functions and data members with the `public` and `private` keywords.

> **NOTE**
>
> The class declaration defines the accessibility of its member functions and data members with the `public` and `private` keywords.

The Circle Program

So far, you've learned about some important syntax topics in C++ (for example, the syntax of class declaration). Now you are ready to write a program that makes use of a class. The program that you'll write is called Circle.CPP.

Writing the Code of the Circle.CPP Program

Follow these steps to write the Circle.CPP program:

☐ Select Hello.CPP from the Window menu, and then select Close from the File menu to close the Hello.CPP window.

☐ Select Hello.MAK from the Window menu, and then select Close from the File menu to close the Hello.MAK project.

☐ Select New from the File menu.

> *Visual C++ responds by displaying the New dialog box.*

☐ Select the Code/Text item in the list of the New dialog box, and then click the OK button.

> *Visual C++ responds by displaying a new window that will contain the code of your program.*

☐ Save the new (empty) file as Circle.CPP in the \MVCPROG\CH02 directory.

☐ In the Circle.CPP window, type the code shown in Listing 2.2.

☐ Select Save from the File menu of Visual C++.

Listing 2.2. The code of the Circle.CPP program.

```
/////////////////////////////
// Program Name: Circle.CPP
/////////////////////////////

///////////////////////
// #include files
///////////////////////
#include <iostream.h>

// Declare the CCircle class
class CCircle
{
public:
  CCircle( int r);    // Constructor
  void    SetRadius(int r);
  int     GetRadius(void);
```

continues

Listing 2.2. continued

```
  void    DisplayArea(void);
  ~CCircle();          // Destructor
private:
  float CalculateArea(void);
  int m_Radius;
  int m_Color;
};

//////////////////////////
// The constructor function
//////////////////////////
CCircle::CCircle ( int r )
{

// Set the radius
m_Radius = r;

}


//////////////////////////
// The destructor function
//////////////////////////
CCircle::~CCircle ()
{


}


////////////////////////////////
// Function Name: DisplayArea()
////////////////////////////////
void CCircle::DisplayArea ( void )
{

float fArea;

fArea = CalculateArea ( );

// Print the area
cout << "The area of the circle is: " << fArea;


}


////////////////////////////////////
// Function Name: CalculateArea()
////////////////////////////////////
float CCircle::CalculateArea ( void )
{

float f;

f = (float) (3.14 * m_Radius * m_Radius);
```

```
return f;

}


void main(void)
{
// Create an object of class Circle with
// radius equals to 10.
CCircle MyCircle ( 10 );

// Display the area of the circle
MyCircle.DisplayArea();

}
```

Examining the Circle.CPP Program's Code

In this section, you go over the code of the Circle.CPP program.

The program uses #include on the iostream.h file:

```
#include <iostream.h>
```

You must use #include on this file because the cout statement is used in this program.

The Circle.CPP program declares the CCircle class:

```
class CCircle
{
public:
  CCircle( int r);        // Constructor
  void   SetRadius(int r);
  int    GetRadius(void);
  void   DisplayArea(void);
  ~CCircle();             // Destructor
private:
  float CalculateArea(void);
  int m_Radius;
  int m_Color;
};
```

The `public` section contains five prototypes. The first is the prototype of the constructor function:

```
CCircle( int r);       // Constructor
```

As always, the prototype of the constructor function does not mention the fact that the function is of type `void`. Notice that the constructor function has the parameter `int r`.

Next are three more prototypes:

```
void    SetRadius(int r);
int     GetRadius(void);
void    DisplayArea(void);
```

Remember that you'll be able to access these functions from any function in the program because these functions are `public` member functions.

The fifth prototype under the `public` section is the prototype of the destructor function:

```
~CCircle();
```

Again, the prototype of the destructor function does not mention the fact that this function is of type `void`. Notice that the ~ character precedes the name of the destructor function.

The `private` section of the `CCircle` class declaration contains the prototype of one function and the declaration of two data members:

```
private:
  float CalculateArea(void);
  int m_Radius;
  int m_Color;
```

Because `CalculateArea()` is declared under the `private` section of the `CCircle` class declaration, you will be able to call the `CalculateArea()` function only from within member functions of the `CCircle` class.

Now look at the `main()` function:

```
void main(void)
{

// Create an object of class CCircle with radius
// equals to 10.
CCircle MyCircle ( 10 );

// Display the area of the circle
MyCircle.DisplayArea();

}
```

The first statement in `main()` creates an object called `MyCircle`, of class `CCircle`:

```
CCircle MyCircle ( 10 );
```

This statement causes the execution of the constructor function. At first glance, the notation for executing the constructor function may look strange. As you'll see later in this chapter, however, this notation makes sense; for now, just accept the fact that this is the correct way to execute the constructor function. As stated earlier, the statement creates an object called `MyCircle` of class `CCircle`.

Before continuing to examine the main() function, look at the constructor function:

```
/////////////////////////////
// The constructor function
/////////////////////////////
CCircle::CCircle ( int r )
{

// Set the radius
m_Radius = r;

}
```

As committed in its prototype, the constructor function has one parameter: int r. Notice the first line of the function:

```
CCircle::CCircle ( int r )
{
 . . .
 . . .
 . . .
}
```

The name of the function is preceded by the text CCircle::, which means that the CCircle() function is a member function of the CCircle class.

The code inside the constructor function consists of a single statement:

```
m_Radius = r;
```

r is the parameter that was passed to the constructor function. Because you created the MyCircle (in main()):

```
CCircle MyCircle ( 10 );
```

10 is passed to the constructor function.

The statement inside the constructor function sets the value of m_Radius to r:

```
m_Radius = r;
```

After the MyCircle object is created in main(), the constructor function is executed, and the code of the constructor function sets the value of m_Radius to 10. Recall that m_Radius was declared as a data member of the CCircle class, so any member function (public or private) of the CCircle class can read or update m_Radius.

At this point, an object MyCircle of class CCircle was created, and its data member m_Radius was set to 10 with the constructor function.

The next statement in main() executes the DisplayArea() member function:

```
MyCircle.DisplayArea();
```

Recall that you declared the DisplayArea() function in the public section of the CCircle class declaration. Therefore, main() can access the DisplayArea() function. Notice the dot (.) operator that separates the name of the object MyCircle and the DisplayArea() function, giving the following instruction to the compiler:

```
Execute the DisplayArea() function on the MyCircle object.
```

The DisplayArea() function displays the area of the MyCircle object. Look at the code of this function:

```
void Circle::DisplayArea ( void )
{

float fArea;

fArea = CalculateArea ( );

// Print the area
cout << "The area of the circle is: " << fArea;

}
```

Again, the compiler knows that this function is a member function of the CCircle class, because the first line uses the CCircle:: notation. The function declares a local float variable called fArea:

```
float fArea;
```

Then the CalculateArea() function is executed:

```
fArea = CalculateArea ( );
```

Recall that CalculateArea() is a member function of the CCircle class; therefore, DisplayArea() can call the CalculateArea() function.

The CalculateArea() function returns the area of the circle as a float number. The next statement in DisplayArea() uses cout to display the value of fArea:

```
cout << "The area of the circle is: " << fArea;
```

This statement streams the value of fArea and the string The area of the circle is: onto the screen.

Now examine the CalculateArea() function. Again, the first line of the CalculateArea() function uses the CCircle:: text to indicate that this function is a member function of the CCircle class.

```
float CCircle::CalculateArea ( void )
{

float f;

f = (float) (3.14 * m_Radius * m_Radius);

return f;

}
```

The CalculateArea() function declares a local variable, f:

```
float f;
```

Then the area of the circle is calculated and assigned to the f variable:

```
f = (float) (3.14 * m_Radius * m_Radius);
```

Notice that CalculateArea() does not have any parameters. How, then, does this function know to substitute 10 for m_Radius? During the execution of the Circle program, the history of executing functions is traced. First, main() creates the MyCircle object:

```
Circle MyCircle ( 10 );
```

This code causes the execution of the constructor function, which causes the m_Radius of the MyCircle object to be equal to 10. Then main() executes the DisplayArea() function on the MyCircle object:

```
MyCircle.DisplayArea();
DisplayArea() executes the CalculateArea() function:
```

```
fArea = CalculateArea ( );
```

CalculateArea() knows to use 10 for the value of m_Radius because CalculateArea() is executed due to the fact that DisplayArea() was executed on the MyCircle object. CalculateArea() can access m_Radius because CalculateArea() is a member function of the CCircle class and m_Radius also is a member of the CCircle class.

The last statement in CalculateArea() returns the calculated area:

```
return f;
```

The destructor function looks like this:

```
CCircle::~CCircle ()
{
}
```

The first line of the destructor function starts with the CCircle:: text, an indication that this function is a member function of the CCircle class.

No code is used inside the destructor function. You should know, however, that the destructor function is executed automatically whenever the MyCircle object is destroyed. In the case of the Circle.CPP program, the MyCircle object is destroyed when the program terminates.

Notice that the SetRadius() and GetRadius() functions were not used in the program. You'll have an opportunity to use these functions later in this chapter.

Compiling and Linking the Circle.CPP Program

☐ Select Build Circle.EXE from the Project menu.

Visual C++ responds by displaying a dialog box that asks whether you want to create a project.

☐ Click the Yes button.

Visual C++ responds by compiling and linking the Circle.CPP program.

Now execute the Circle.EXE program:

☐ Use the Program Manager to execute the MS-DOS program, log in to the \MVCPROG\CH02 directory, and execute the Circle.EXE program.

> *The Circle.EXE program displays the message* `The area of the circle is: 314.`

☐ At the DOS prompt, type **Exit**, and then press the Enter key.

The Circle2 Program

So far you have declared a class called `CCircle`, created an object (`MyCircle`) of class `CCircle`, and calculated and displayed the area of the `MyCircle` object.

Notice that although `main()` looks very elegant and short, it does not demonstrate the object-oriented nature of C++. The Circle2 program demonstrates how you can create more than one object of class `CCircle`.

NOTE

C++ is known as an *OOP* (object-oriented programming) language. As you'll see in this chapter and the following chapter, in C++ your program deals with objects.

Writing the Code of the Circle2.CPP Program

The code of the Circle2.CPP program appears in Listing 2.3.

Listing 2.3. The code of the Circle2.CPP program.

```
/////////////////////////////
// Program Name: Circle2.CPP
/////////////////////////////

///////////////////////
// #include files
///////////////////////
#include <iostream.h>

// Declare the Circle class
class CCircle
{
public:
  CCircle( int r);    // Constructor
  void   SetRadius(int r);
  int    GetRadius(void);
  void   DisplayArea(void);
  ~CCircle();         // Destructor
private:
```

```
  float CalculateArea(void);
  int m_Radius;
  int m_Color;
};

//////////////////////////
// The constructor function
//////////////////////////
CCircle::CCircle ( int r )
{

// Set the radius
m_Radius = r;

}

//////////////////////////
// The destructor function
//////////////////////////
CCircle::~CCircle ()
{

}

//////////////////////////////
// Function Name: DisplayArea()
//////////////////////////////
void CCircle::DisplayArea ( void )
{

float fArea;

fArea = CalculateArea ( );

// Print the area
cout << "The area of the circle is: " << fArea;

}

//////////////////////////////////
// Function Name: CalculateArea()
//////////////////////////////////
float CCircle::CalculateArea ( void )
{

float f;

f = (float) (3.14 * m_Radius * m_Radius);

return f;

}

void main(void)
{
// Create an object of class CCircle with
// radius equal to 10.
CCircle MyCircle ( 10 );
```

continues

Listing 2.3. continued

```
// Create an object of class CCircle with
// radius equal to 20.
CCircle HerCircle ( 20 );

// Create an object of class CCircle with
// radius equal to 30.
CCircle HisCircle ( 30 );

// Display the area of the circles
MyCircle.DisplayArea();
cout << "\n";
HerCircle.DisplayArea();
cout << "\n";
HisCircle.DisplayArea();

}
```

Examining the Code of the Circle2.CPP Program

In this section, you go over the code of the Circle2.CPP program.

Because the Circle2 program uses cout, you need to use #include on the iostream.h file:

```
#include <iostream.h>
```

Then the class declaration of the CCircle class appears:

```
class CCircle
{
public:
  CCircle( int r);      // Constructor
  void    SetRadius(int r);
  int     GetRadius(void);
  void    DisplayArea(void);
  ~CCircle();           // Destructor
private:
  float CalculateArea(void);
  int m_Radius;
  int m_Color;
};
```

Notice that this class declaration is identical to the one that appears in the Circle.CPP program discussed earlier in this chapter.

The constructor function of the CCircle class also is identical to the constructor function that appears in the Circle.CPP program, as are the destructor function, the DisplayArea() function, and the CalculateArea() function. In fact, the only thing different in the Circle2.CPP program is the code in the main() function. The following is the code of the main() function:

```
void main(void)
{
```

```
// Create an object of class Circle with
// radius equal to 10.
CCircle MyCircle ( 10 );

// Create an object of class Circle with
// radius equal to 20.
CCircle HerCircle ( 20 );

// Create an object of class Circle with
// radius equal to 30.
CCircle HisCircle ( 30 );

// Display the area of the circles
MyCircle.DisplayArea();
cout << "\n";
HerCircle.DisplayArea();
cout << "\n";
HisCircle.DisplayArea();

}
```

The first statement in main() creates an object called MyCircle of class CCircle:

```
CCircle MyCircle ( 10 );
```

Notice that the MyCircle object is created with its m_Radius data member equal to 10.

The next two statements create two more objects:

```
CCircle HerCircle ( 20 );
CCircle HisCircle ( 30 );
```

The HerCircle object is created with its m_Radius data member equal to 20, and the HisCircle object is created with its m_Radius data member equal to 30.

Now that these three objects are created, main() displays the areas of these circles by using the DisplayArea() member function on the corresponding circle objects:

```
MyCircle.DisplayArea();
cout << "\n";
HerCircle.DisplayArea();
cout << "\n";
HisCircle.DisplayArea();
```

Between the execution of the DisplayArea() functions, cout is used to print a carriage-return/line-feed character (\n) so that the areas will be displayed on different lines.

Look at the execution of the first DisplayArea() function:

```
MyCircle.DisplayArea();
```

When DisplayArea() is executed, it calls the CalculateArea() function. Recall that CalculateArea() makes use of the m_Radius data member. Which m_Radius will be used? The m_Radius of the MyCircle object is used because DisplayArea() works on the MyCircle object.

Similarly, the following statement works on the HerCircle object:

```
HerCircle.DisplayArea();
```

This means that when the `CalculateArea()` function is executed from `DisplayArea()`, the `m_Radius` of the `HerCircle` object is used. Likewise, when the area of the `HisCircle` object is displayed, the `m_Radius` of `HisCircle` is used to calculate the area.

Compiling, Linking, and Executing the Circle2.CPP Program

To see your code in action, follow these steps:

☐ Close the Circle.CPP window and close the Circle.MAK project. (That is, select Circle.CPP from the Window menu and then select Close from the File menu; select Circle.MAK from the Window menu and then select Close from the File menu.)

☐ Select Open from the File menu and load the \MVCPROG\CH02\Circle.CPP file, which you created earlier in this chapter.

☐ Select Save As from the File menu, and save the file as Circle2.CPP in the \MVCPROG\CH02 directory.

You now have to type the code of the Circle2.CPP program, which appears in Listing 2.3 earlier in this chapter. Notice that most of the code of the Circle2.CPP program is typed already, because you created the Circle2.CPP file from the Circle.CPP file. As you are probably starting to realize, that's the idea of object-oriented programming. You created the class during the development of the Circle.CPP program. From now on, you can develop other programs (such as the Circle2.CPP program) with minimum typing, because you did most of the work during the development of the Circle.CPP program. In fact, the only thing that you have to do to the Circle2.CPP program is modify its `main()` function. (When you create Windows programs, your job is even easier, because Microsoft provides the classes for you.)

☐ Modify the `main()` function of Circle2.CPP so that it matches the one shown in Listing 2.3.

☐ Save the Circle2.CPP file (by selecting Save from the File menu).

☐ Select Rebuild All from the Project menu, and then click the Yes button in the dialog box that Visual C++ displays.

    Visual C++ responds by compiling and linking the Circle2.CPP program.

☐ Execute the MS-DOS program, log in to the \MVCPROG\CH02 directory, and execute the Circle2.EXE program.

    DOS responds by executing the Circle2.EXE program.

As expected, the Circle2 program displays the areas of the three circle objects.

☐ At the DOS prompt, type **Exit**, and then press the Enter key.

The Circle3.CPP Program

Notice how short and elegant the `main()` function of the Circle2 program is. This function is easy to read and, more important, very easy to maintain. If you decide that you need more accuracy in the calculation of the circle areas, you can simply change the code of the `CalculateArea()` function. (You can change 3.14 to 3.1415, for example.)

If you type the class declaration in a file called CCircle.H, you can remove the `CCircle` class declaration from the Circle.CPP and Circle2.CPP files, and then add the following statement:

```
#include "CCIRCLE.H"
```

Notice that in both Circle.CPP and Circle2.CPP, `m_Radius` was set by the constructor function. You cannot change the value of `m_Radius` from within `main()`, however, because `m_Radius` was declared inside the `private` section of the class declaration.

If you want to be able to change the value of `m_Radius` from within `main()`, you have to move the `m_Radius` declaration from the `private` section to the `public` section:

```
class Circle
{
public:
        Circle( int r);     // Constructor
  void    SetRadius(int r);
  int     GetRadius(void);
  void    DisplayArea(void);
        ~Circle();          // Destructor
  int m_Radius; // *** Here m_Radius is public  ***
private:
  float CalculateArea(void);
  // int m_Radius;
  int m_Color;
};
```

Then `main()` can read and write the value of `m_Radius`:

```
void main ( void)
{

// Create the MyCircle object with m_Radius equal to 10
CCircle MyCircle (10);

// Display the area of the circle
MyCircle.DisplayArea();
cout << "\n";

//Set the Radius of MyCircle to 20.
MyCircle.m_Radius = 20;

// Display the area of the circle
MyCircle.DisplayArea();

}
```

Similarly, you can read the value of m_Radius from main():

```
void main ( void)
{

// Create the MyCircle object with m_Radius equal to 10
CCircle MyCircle (10);

// Display the area of the circle
MyCircle.DisplayArea();
cout << "\n";

//Set the Radius of MyCircle to 20.
MyCircle.m_Radius = 20;

// Display the radius of the circle
cout << "The radius is: " << MyCircle.m_Radius;

}
```

There is nothing wrong with the preceding implementation of reading and updating the value of m_Radius directly from within main(). The recommended way to read and write important data members of a class, however, is to use *access functions*. The access functions serve as a focal point for reading and writing data into the data members. The advantage of using access functions is that the code of the access function can perform additional tasks. For example, the code can check to see whether the value that is assigned to m_Radius is a positive number.

> **NOTE**
>
> By using access functions, you can add code that checks the validity of the data members.

The next program that you'll write in this chapter is called Circle3.CPP. This program demonstrates how you can set and read the value of m_Radius with access functions.

Writing the Code of the Circle3.CPP Program

The code of the Circle3.CPP program, shown in Listing 2.4, is very similar to that of the Circle.CPP and Circle2.CPP programs.

Listing 2.4. The code of the Circle3.CPP program.

```
/////////////////////////////
// Program Name: Circle3.CPP
/////////////////////////////

////////////////////
// #include files
////////////////////
#include <iostream.h>

// Declare the CCircle class
class CCircle
{
```

```
public:
  CCircle( int r);      // Constructor
  void   SetRadius(int r);
  int    GetRadius(void);
  void   DisplayArea(void);
  ~CCircle();           // Destructor
private:
  float CalculateArea(void);
  int m_Radius;
  int m_Color;
};

/////////////////////////////
// The constructor function
/////////////////////////////
CCircle::CCircle ( int r )
{

// Set the radius
m_Radius = r;

}

/////////////////////////////
// The destructor function
/////////////////////////////
CCircle::~CCircle ()
{

}

/////////////////////////////
// Function Name: SetRadius()
/////////////////////////////
void CCircle::SetRadius ( int r)
{

m_Radius = r;

}

/////////////////////////////
// Function Name: GetRadius()
/////////////////////////////
int CCircle::GetRadius ( void)
{

return m_Radius;

}

/////////////////////////////
// Function Name: DisplayArea()
/////////////////////////////
void CCircle::DisplayArea ( void )
{
```

continues

Listing 2.4. continued

```
float fArea;

fArea = CalculateArea ( );

// Print the area
cout << "The area of the circle is: " << fArea;

}

////////////////////////////////
// Function Name: CalculateArea()
////////////////////////////////
float CCircle::CalculateArea ( void )
{

float f;

f = (float) (3.14 * m_Radius * m_Radius);

return f;

}

void main ( void)
{

// Create the MyCircle object with
// m_Radius equal to 10
CCircle MyCircle (10);

// Display the area of the circle
MyCircle.DisplayArea();
cout << "\n";

//Set the m_Radius of MyCircle to 20.
MyCircle.SetRadius (20);

// Display the radius of the circle
cout << "The Radius is: " << MyCircle.GetRadius();

}
```

Examining the Code of the Circle3.CPP Program

The code of the Circle3.CPP program is similar to that of the Circle.CPP and Circle2.CPP programs. As shown in Listing 2.4, the m_Radius data member in Circle3.CPP is in the private section, so main() cannot access this data member directly. For example, you cannot have the following statement in main():

```
//Not allowed when m_Radius is private
MyCircle.m_Radius = 20; // *** ERROR ***
```

Instead, two access functions are used. The `SetRadius()` member function is used to set the `m_Radius` data member, and the `GetRadius()` member function is used to read it. Recall that `SetRadius()` and `GetRadius()` are defined as `public` in the `CCircle` class declaration. This means that `main()` can use these functions:

```
void main ( void)
{

// Create the MyCircle object with
// m_Radius equal to 10
CCircle MyCircle (10);

// Display the area of the circle
MyCircle.DisplayArea();
cout << "\n";

//Set the Radius of MyCircle to 20.
MyCircle.SetRadius (20);

// Display the radius of the circle
cout << "The Radius is: " << MyCircle.GetRadius();

}
```

The `SetRadius()` function simply sets the value of `m_Radius`:

```
void CCircle::SetRadius ( int r)
{

m_Radius = r;

}
```

The `GetRadius()` function simply returns the value of `m_Radius`:

```
int CCircle::GetRadius ( void)
{

return m_Radius;

}
```

As stated earlier, the `SetRadius()` and `GetRadius()` functions are called access functions. Typically, these functions contain additional code. For example, the `SetRadius()` function may include code that checks whether `m_Radius` is set within a certain range.

To see the Circle3.CPP program in action, follow these steps:

☐ Close the Circle2.MAK project (select Circle2.MAK from the Window menu, and then select Close from the File menu).

☐ Select Open from the File menu, and then load the Circle2.CPP file.

☐ Select Save As from the File menu, and save the Circle2.CPP file as Circle3.CPP in the directory C:\MVCPROG\CH02.

☐ Add to the Circle3.CPP file the code of the `SetRadius()` and `GetRadius()` functions. (Refer to Listing 2.4 for the code of these functions.)

☐ Modify the `main()` function of Circle3.CPP according to Listing 2.4.

☐ Select Save from the File menu to save the Circle3.CPP file.

☐ Select Rebuild All from the Project menu to compile and link the Circle3.CPP program.

☐ Use the Program Manager to execute the MS-DOS program, log in to the \MVCPROG\CH02 directory, and execute the Circle3.EXE program from the Project menu.

☐ Verify that the Circle3.EXE program operates as expected.

☐ At the DOS prompt, type **Exit**, and then press the Enter key.

Overloaded Functions

In C++, you can use the same function name for more than one function. For example, you can declare two `SetRadius()` functions in the class declaration of the `CCircle` class.

The Circle4.CPP program demonstrates how a program can have two different functions with the same name. Such functions are called *overloaded* functions.

Writing the Code of the Circle4.CPP Program

Listing 2.5 shows the code of the Circle4.CPP program.

Listing 2.5. The code of the Circle4.CPP program.

```
/////////////////////////////
// Program Name: Circle4.CPP
/////////////////////////////

///////////////////////
// #include files
///////////////////////
#include <iostream.h>

// Declare the CCircle class
class CCircle
{
public:
  CCircle( int r);    // Constructor

  void    SetRadius(int r);          // Overloaded
  void    SetRadius(int r, int c );  // Overloaded

  int     GetRadius(void);
  void    DisplayArea(void);
  ~CCircle();               // Destructor

  int m_Color;
```

```
private:
  float CalculateArea(void);
  int m_Radius;
  // int Color;
};

/////////////////////////
// The constructor function
/////////////////////////
CCircle::CCircle ( int r )
{

// Set the radius
m_Radius = r;
m_Color = 0;

}

/////////////////////////
// The destructor function
/////////////////////////
CCircle::~CCircle ()
{

}

/////////////////////////////
// Function Name: SetRadius()
/////////////////////////////
void CCircle::SetRadius ( int r)
{

m_Radius = r;
m_Color = 255;

}

/////////////////////////////
// Function Name: SetRadius()
/////////////////////////////
void CCircle::SetRadius ( int r, int c)
{

m_Radius = r;
m_Color = c;

}

/////////////////////////////
// Function Name: GetRadius()
/////////////////////////////
int CCircle::GetRadius ( void)
{

return m_Radius;

}
```

continues

Listing 2.5. continued

```
///////////////////////////////
// Function Name: DisplayArea()
///////////////////////////////
void CCircle::DisplayArea ( void )
{

float fArea;

fArea = CalculateArea ( );

// Print the area
cout << "The area of the circle is: " << fArea;


}


///////////////////////////////
// Function Name: CalculateArea()
///////////////////////////////
float CCircle::CalculateArea ( void )
{

float f;

f = (float) (3.14 * m_Radius * m_Radius);

return f;

}

void main ( void)
{
// Create the MyCircle object with Radius equal to 10
CCircle MyCircle (10);

// Display the radius of the circle
cout << "The Radius is: " << MyCircle.GetRadius();
cout << "\n";

// Display the color of the circle
cout << "The Color of the circle is: " << MyCircle.m_Color;
cout << "\n";

//Set the Radius of MyCircle to 20.
MyCircle.SetRadius (20);

// Display the radius of the circle
cout << "The Radius is: " << MyCircle.GetRadius();
cout << "\n";

// Display the color of the circle
cout << "The Color of the circle is: " << MyCircle.m_Color;
cout << "\n";

// Use the other SetRadius() function
MyCircle.SetRadius (40, 100);
```

```
// Display the radius of the circle
cout << "The Radius is: " << MyCircle.GetRadius();
cout << "\n";

// Display the color of the circle
cout << "The Color of the circle is: " << MyCircle.m_Color;


}
```

Examining the Code of the Circle4.CPP Program

The Circle4.CPP program uses #include on the iostream.h file (because it uses the cout statement):

```
#include <iostream.h>
```

Then the CCircle class is declared:

```
class CCircle
{
public:
  Circle( int r);     // Constructor

  void    SetRadius(int r);        // Overloaded
  void    SetRadius(int r, int c );  // Overloaded

  int     GetRadius(void);
  void    DisplayArea(void);
  ~Circle();            // Destructor

  int m_Color;

private:
  float CalculateArea(void);
  int m_Radius;
  // int m_Color;
};
```

This CCircle class is similar to the CCircle class that was used in the previous programs, except that the int m_Color data member has been moved from the private section to the public section. (This was done for the sake of simplicity, because you want to access m_Color from main(), and you don't want to write an access function such as GetColor().)

Also, the CCircle class declaration now has the following set of overloaded functions:

```
void    SetRadius(int r);        // Overloaded
void    SetRadius(int r, int c );  // Overloaded
```

In other words, the CCircle class has two SetRadius() functions: one with a single parameter (int r), and the other with two parameters (int r, int c).

The constructor function of this CCircle class is similar to the constructor functions that were introduced previously in this chapter, except that this constructor function also sets the value of m_Color to 0:

```
CCircle::CCircle ( int r )
{

// Set the radius
m_Radius = r;
m_Color = 0;

}
```

The destructor function is identical to the destructor function of the previous programs (it contains no code).

One of the SetRadius() functions in Circle4.CPP sets m_Radius to the value that was passed to it, and it also sets m_Color to 255:

```
void CCircle::SetRadius ( int r)
{

m_Radius = r;
m_Color = 255;

}
```

The other SetRadius() function in Circle4.CPP sets m_Radius to the value that was passed to it. The function also sets m_Color to the value that was passed to it:

```
void CCircle::SetRadius ( int r, int c)
{

m_Radius = r;
m_Color = c;

}
```

The GetRadius() function is identical to the GetRadius() functions of the previous programs:

```
int CCircle::GetRadius ( void)
{

return m_Radius;

}
```

Following is the main() function of Circle4.CPP:

```
void main ( void)
{

// Create the MyCircle object with
// Radius equal to 10
Circle MyCircle (10);

// Display the radius of the circle
cout << "The Radius is: " << MyCircle.GetRadius();
cout << "\n";

// Display the color of the circle
cout << "The Color of the circle is: " << MyCircle.m_Color;
cout << "\n";
```

```
//Set the Radius of MyCircle to 20.
MyCircle.SetRadius (20);

// Display the radius of the circle
cout << "The Radius is: " << MyCircle.GetRadius();
cout << "\n";

// Display the color of the circle
cout << "The Color of the circle is: " << MyCircle.m_Color;
cout << "\n";

// Use the other SetRadius() function
MyCircle.SetRadius (40, 100);

// Display the radius of the circle
cout << "The Radius is: " << MyCircle.GetRadius();
cout << "\n";

// Display the color of the circle
cout << "The Color of the circle is: " << MyCircle.m_Color;

}
```

The main() function starts by creating the MyCircle() object:

```
Circle MyCircle (10);
```

Recall that the constructor function is executed whenever an object is created. Because 10 is passed in the preceding statement, the constructor function sets m_Radius of the MyCircle object to 10. The constructor function also sets m_Color to 0. So after the MyCircle object is created, the MyCircle object has m_Radius equal to 10 and m_Color equal to 0.

This fact is verified by the next statements in main():

```
cout << "The Radius is: " << MyCircle.GetRadius();
cout << "\n";

cout << "The Color of the circle is: " << MyCircle.m_Color;
cout << "\n";
```

Notice that m_Color can be accessed with MyCircle.m_Color because m_Color was moved to the public section in the CCircle class declaration.

When the Circle4.CPP program is executed, it outputs the messages The Radius is: 10 and The Color of the circle is: 0.

The next statement in main() sets the m_Radius data member of MyCircle to 20:

```
MyCircle.SetRadius (20);
```

Which SetRadius() function will be executed? Remember that there are two SetRadius() functions! The C++ compiler is smart, however; it knows that there are two SetRadius() functions, and because you specified only one parameter in the MyCircle.SetRadius (20) statement, it knows that you want to execute the SetRadius() function with the single parameter.

To verify that the compiler uses the `SetRadius()` function that has one parameter, the next statements in `main()` display `m_Radius` and `m_Color`:

```
cout << "The Radius is: " << MyCircle.GetRadius();
cout << "\n";

cout << "The Color of the circle is: " << MyCircle.m_Color;
cout << "\n";
```

These statements display the messages `The Radius is: 20` and `The Color of the circle is: 255`.

Indeed, `m_Radius` should be equal to 20 (because you passed 20 as the parameter of `SetRadius()`), and `m_Color` should be equal to 255, because the `SetRadius()` function that was executed sets `m_Color` to 255.

The next statement in `main()` uses the other `SetRadius()` function:

```
MyCircle.SetRadius (40, 100);
```

The compiler knows that you mean to use the other `SetRadius()` function because you supplied two parameters to this function. The next statements in `main()` display `m_Radius` and `m_Color`:

```
cout << "The Radius is: " << MyCircle.GetRadius();
cout << "\n";

cout << "The Color of the circle is: " << MyCircle.m_Color;
```

When you execute the Circle4 program, the program displays the messages `The Radius is: 40` and `The Color of the Circle is: 100`.

Indeed, you supplied 40 as the first parameter of `SetRadius()`, and you supplied 100 as the second parameter of `SetRadius()`.

☐ Close the Circle3.MAK project.

☐ Select New from the File menu.

>   *Visual C++ responds by displaying the New dialog box.*

☐ Select Code/Text from the New dialog box, and then click the OK button in the New dialog box.

☐ Save the empty new text file as Circle4.CPP in the \MVCPROG\CH02 directory.

☐ Type the code shown in Listing 2.5 in the Circle4.CPP window.

☐ Save the Circle4.CPP file.

☐ Compile and link the Circle4 program (select Rebuild All from the Project menu).

>   *Visual C++ responds by compiling and linking the Circle4.CPP program.*

☐ Use the Program Manager to execute the MS-DOS program, log in to the \MVCPROG\CH02 directory, and execute the Circle4.EXE program.

☐ Verify that the Circle4.EXE program operates as expected.

☐ At the DOS prompt, type **Exit**, and then press the Enter key.

NOTE

The Circle4.CPP program illustrates how to implement and use overloaded functions, but it does not demonstrate how overloaded functions are used in practice. To understand the practical use of overloaded functions, consider a program that calculates the area of a circle and the area of a rectangle. As you know, the area of a circle is calculated in the following way:

```
Circle Area = Radius * Radius * 3.14
```

You also know that the area of a rectangle is calculated like this:

```
Rectangle Area = SideA * SideB
```

One way to implement a program that calculates both the circle's and the rectangle's area is to write this function:

```
CalculateCircleArea(Radius)
```

as well as this function:

```
CalculateRectangleArea(SideA, SideB)
```

With overloaded functions, however, you can use a single function from within your program: the CalculateArea() function. The CalculateArea() function is an overloaded function. When only one parameter is supplied to the CalculateArea() function, the program knows that the circle's area is to be calculated, and when two parameters are supplied to the CalculateArea() function, the program knows that the rectangle's area is to be calculated.

At first glance, this business of overloaded functions seems not to help at all. After all, you have to write two separate functions; one function calculates the circle's area, and the other function calculates the rectangle's area. So what's the big deal about overloaded functions?

Consider what your main program looks like. Instead of remembering that the program has one function for calculating the circle's area and another function for calculating the rectangle's area, all you have to remember is that the program has one function—CalculateArea()—and that this function takes care of both the circle and the rectangle. (You have to know how to use the function, of course, which means that you have to know what parameters, and how many parameters, you should supply to the function.)

Still, you may not agree that overloaded functions really help when it comes to calculating the areas of circles and rectangles. You'll learn to appreciate overloaded functions, however, when you create Windows applications. As you'll see in this book, Visual C++ comes with hundreds of useful Windows functions, many of which are overloaded functions. When you use these functions, your programs are easy to write, easy to read, and easy to maintain.

Declaring Variables in C++ Versus C

In C, you have to declare your variables at the beginning of the function. The following `main()` function declares the variable i at its beginning; then, 1000 lines forward, it uses the variable i:

```
void main(void)
{
i = 3;
.....
.....
.....
/* 1,000 lines of code */
.....
.....
.....

while (i<0)
    {
    ...
    ...
    ...
    }

}
```

In C++, however, you don't have to declare your variables at the beginning of the function. The preceding C `main()` function can be written in C++:

```
void main(void)
{
.....
.....
.....
// 1,000 lines of code
.....
.....
.....
int i =3;
while (i<0)
    {
    ...
    ...
    ...
    }

}
```

Don't try to use the i variable before it is declared, of course.

Default Parameters

Another convenient feature of C++ that doesn't exist in C is default parameters.

In C, you can declare the following function prototype:

```
int MyFunction (int a,
                int b,
```

```
            int c,
            int d);
```

The actual function may look like the following example:

```
int MyFunction (int a,
                int b,
                int c,
                int d)
{
...
...
...
}
```

If you execute `MyFunction()` from within `main()`, you must supply four parameters, because that's what you specified in the prototype of the function.

C++ is more liberal than C. The designers of C++ knew that although you specified four parameters for the `MyFunction()` function, in most cases, you'll use the same values for some of the parameters of the function. Therefore, C++ enables you to specify default parameters in the prototype of `MyFunction()`:

```
int MyFunction ( int a = 10,
                 int b = 20,
                 int c = 30,
                 int d = 40 );
```

From `main()`, you can execute `MyFunction()`:

```
main()
{
...
...
...
int iResult;
iResult = MyFunction();
...
...
...
}
```

Because you did not supply any parameters for `MyFunction()`, the compiler automatically interprets your statement this way:

```
main()
{
...
...
...
int iResult;
iResult = MyFunction(10,
                     20
                     30
                     40);
...
...
...
```

```
}
```

In addition, you can override the default parameters:

```
main()
{
...
...
...
int iResult;
iResult = MyFunction(100,
                     200);
...
...
...
}
```

Because you did not supply any third and fourth parameters to `MyFunction()`, the compiler automatically interprets your statement in the following way:

```
main()
{
...
...
...
int iResult;
iResult = MyFunction(100,
                     200,
                     30,
                     40);
...
...
...
}
```

In other words, you overrode the first and second parameters, and the compiler automatically substituted the third and fourth parameters (as indicated in the prototype of the function).

NOTE

When using a default parameter, you must use all the default parameters that appear after that parameter. For example, the following is not allowed:

```
void main(void)
{
...
...

...
int iResult;
iResult = MyFunction(100,
                     ,    // Not allowed
                 300
                 400);
```

```
      ...
      ...
      ...
      }
```

Because you overrode the third parameter, you must specify a value for the second parameter as well.

Final Words...

In this chapter you learned about the major differences between C and C++. As you see, the C++ concepts are not difficult; they represent the natural evolution of the C programming language. C++ enables you to write complex programs that are easy to read and understand.

Consider the following declaration of the `CPersonGoToWork` class:

```
class CPersonGoToWork
{
public:
        CPersonGoToWork(); // The constructor
        void WakeUp(void);
        void Wash(void);
        void Dress(void);
        void Eat(void);
        void TakeBus(void);
        void TakeCar(void);
        void TakeSubway(void);
        void TurnPCon(void);
        void TurnIrrigationOn(void);
        void CalibrateRadar(void);
       ~CPersonGoToWork(); // The destructor

private:
        .....
        .....
        .....
}
```

This class contains member functions that display cartoon characters doing something during the course of going to work. The `TakeCar()` function displays a person getting into a car, for example, and the `TakeSubway()` function displays a person taking a subway to work.

Consider the following `main()` program:

```
void main(void)
{
// Create an object called Jim
// for Mr. Jim Smart the programmer.
CPersonGoToWork Jim;

// Show Jim going to work.
Jim.WakeUp(void);
Jim.Wash(void);
```

```
Jim.Dress(void);
Jim.Eat(void);
Jim.TakeCar(void);
Jim.TurnPCon(void);

// Create an object called Jill
// for Ms. Jill Officer, the policewoman.
CPersonGoToWork Jill;

// Show Jill going to work.
Jill.WakeUp(void);
Jill.Wash(void);
Jill.Dress(void);
Jill.Eat(void);
Jill.TakeCar(void);
Jill.CalibrateRadar();

// Create an object called Don
// for Mr. Don Farmer the farmer.
CPersonGoToWork Don;

// Show Don going to work.
Don.WakeUp(void);
Don.Wash(void);
Don.Dress(void);
Don.Eat(void);
Don.TurnIrrigationOn(void);

}
```

As you can see, `main()` can be written in a matter of minutes, and `main()` can be easily understood and maintained. The real work of writing such a program, of course, is writing the member functions of the `CPersonGoToWork` class.

When the class is ready, however, writing `main()` is very easy—this is the main advantage of using Visual C++ for writing Windows applications. The MFC is supplied with the Visual C++ package, so in fact most of your program is written already. All you have to do is understand the powerful member functions that exist in the MFC and apply them to your Windows applications.

Chapter 3 discusses other important C++ concepts. Starting with Chapter 4, you'll write Windows applications.

3

Hierarchy

In this chapter you'll learn about
additional C++ topics that are
prerequisites for the rest of the book.

As stated in Chapter 2, "Your First C++ DOS Program," you'll start writing a true Windows application in Chapter 4, "Writing Your First True Windows Application." In this chapter, however, you'll learn the material by writing DOS console programs.

The RECT Program

You begin by writing the RECT.CPP program.

☐ Close all the open windows that appear inside the desktop of Visual C++ (if there are any).

☐ Select New from the File menu.

   Visual C++ responds by displaying the New dialog box.

☐ Select Code/Text from the list of items in the New dialog box, and then click the OK button.

☐ Select Save As from the File menu, and save the new (empty) file as RECT.CPP in the directory \MVCPROG\CH03.

☐ In the RECT.CPP window, type the code shown in Listing 3.1.

☐ Select Rebuild All from the Project menu.

☐ Click the Yes button in the dialog box that Visual C++ displays. (You are telling Visual C++ Yes, create the RECT.MAK project.)

   Visual C++ responds by compiling and linking the RECT program.

☐ Execute the MS-DOS program (MS-DOS prompt), log in to the \MVCPROG\CH03 directory, and execute the RECT.EXE program.

   DOS responds by executing the RECT.EXE program.

As you can see, the RECT.EXE program displays a message that tells you the area of a rectangle.

☐ At the DOS prompt type **Exit**, and then press the Enter key.

Listing 3.1. The RECT.CPP program.

```
/////////////////////////
// Program Name: Rect.CPP
/////////////////////////

////////////
// #include
////////////
#include <iostream.h>

//////////////////////////////////////
// The CRectangle class declaration
//////////////////////////////////////
class CRectangle
{
```

```
public:
      CRectangle(int w, int h);   // Constructor

      void DisplayArea (void);    // Member function

      ~CRectangle();              // Destructor

      int m_Width;    // Data member
      int m_Height;   // Data member

};

/////////////////////////////
// The constructor function
/////////////////////////////
CRectangle::CRectangle( int w, int h )
{

m_Width = w;
m_Height = h;

}

/////////////////////////////
// The destructor function
/////////////////////////////
CRectangle::~CRectangle()
{

}

///////////////////////////////////
// Function Name: DisplayArea()
///////////////////////////////////
void CRectangle::DisplayArea(void)
{

int iArea;

iArea = m_Width * m_Height;

cout << "The area is: " << iArea << "\n";

}

void main(void)
{

CRectangle MyRectangle ( 10, 5 );

MyRectangle.DisplayArea();

}
```

The RECT.CPP Program's Code

In this section you'll go over the code of the RECT.CPP program.

The program starts by using #include on the iostream.h file (because the cout statement is used):

```
#include <iostream.h>
```

Then the program declares the CRectangle class:

```
class CRectangle
{
public:
      CRectangle(int w, int h);  // Constructor

      void DisplayArea (void);   // Member function

      ~CRectangle();             // Destructor

      int m_Width;    // Data member
      int m_Height;   // Data member

};
```

The CRectangle class declaration contains its constructor function, the destructor function, the DisplayArea() function, and two data members.

The constructor function simply initializes the data members:

```
CRectangle::CRectangle( int w, int h)
{

m_Width = w;
m_Height = h;

}
```

No code appears inside the destructor function, and the DisplayArea() function calculates the area of the rectangle and then displays it:

```
void CRectangle::DisplayArea(void)
{

int iArea;

iArea = m_Width * m_Height;

cout << "The area is: " << iArea << "\n";

}
```

main() creates an object called MyRectangle of class CRectangle:

```
CRectangle MyRectangle ( 10, 5 );
```

Because (10, 5) is passed to the constructor function, the MyRectangle object has width equal to 10 and height equal to 5.

main() then displays the area of MyRectangle:

```
MyRectangle.DisplayArea();
```

As you see, the CRectangle class enables you to calculate the area of the rectangle.

Suppose that you want to calculate the area of a rectangle with width equal to 20 and height equal to 5. What would you do? You could add SetWidth() and SetHeight() member functions that set the values of m_Width and m_Height. Therefore, the CRectangle class declaration would look like this:

```
/////////////////////////////////
// The CRectangle class declaration
/////////////////////////////////
class CRectangle
{
public:
      CRectangle(int w, int h);  // Constructor

      void DisplayArea (void);

      void SetWidth ( int w );
      void SetHeight ( int h );

      ~CRectangle();            // Destructor

      int m_Width;
      int m_Height;
};
```

The SetWidth() and SetHeight() member functions may look like this:

```
/////////////////////////////
// Function Name: SetWidth()
/////////////////////////////
void CRectangle::SetWidth(int w)
{

m_Width = w;

}


/////////////////////////////
// Function Name: SetHeight()
/////////////////////////////
void CRectangle::SetHeight(int h)
{

m_Height = h;

}
```

Your main() function then looks like this:

```
void main(void)
{

// Create the MyRectangle with width equals to 10
// and height equals to 5
CRectangle MyRectangle (10,5);
```

```
// Display the area
MyRectangle.DisplayArea();

// Change the width and height
MyRectangle.SetWidth(20);
MyRectangle.SetHeight(5);

// Display the area
MyRectangle.DisplayArea();

}
```

What if You Need Additional Member Functions?

There is nothing wrong with the preceding implementation, but it assumes that you own the source code of the CRectangle class and therefore can modify it at any time. In many cases, the software vendors do not give you the source code of the class. For one thing, the vendors don't want you to have the source code. Also, they don't want you to mess with the source code of the class, because you could accidentally damage the class.

Nevertheless, in many cases you need to add some of your own member functions, just as you need to add the SetWidth() and SetHeight() functions to the CRectangle class.

Class Hierarchy

To solve the problem discussed in the preceding section, you use the class hierarchy concept of C++, which enables you to create a new class from the original class. The original class is called the *base* class, and the class that you create from the original class is called the *derived* class. The derived class inherits data members and member functions from its base class. When you create the derived class, you can add to it member functions and data members.

In this section, you create a class called CNewRectangle from the CRectangle class. The base class is CRectangle, and the derived class is CNewRectangle.

Listing 3.2 shows the code of the RECT2.CPP program.

Listing 3.2. The RECT2.CPP program.

```
/////////////////////////////
// Program Name: Rect2.CPP
/////////////////////////////

////////////
// #include
////////////
#include <iostream.h>

///////////////////////////////////////////////////
// The CRectangle class declaration (base class)
```

```
//////////////////////////////////////////////
class CRectangle
{
public:
      CRectangle(int w, int h);   // Constructor

      void DisplayArea (void);

      ~CRectangle();               // Destructor

     int m_Width;
     int m_Height;

};

//////////////////////////////////////////////////
// The declaration of the derived class CNewRectangle
//////////////////////////////////////////////////
class CNewRectangle : public CRectangle
{

public:
    CNewRectangle(int w, int h);   // Constructor

    void SetWidth (int w);
    void SetHeight (int h);

    ~CNewRectangle();              // Destructor

};

//////////////////////////////////////////////////
// The constructor function of CRectangle (base)
//////////////////////////////////////////////////
CRectangle::CRectangle( int w, int h)
{

cout << "In the constructor of the base class" << "\n";

m_Width = w;
m_Height = h;

}

//////////////////////////////////////////////////
// The destructor function of CRectangle (base)
//////////////////////////////////////////////////

CRectangle::~CRectangle()
{

cout << "In the destructor of the base class" << "\n";

}

//////////////////////////////////////////
// Function Name: DisplayArea() (base)
//////////////////////////////////////////
```

continues

Listing 3.2. continued

```
void CRectangle::DisplayArea(void)
{

int iArea;

iArea = m_Width * m_Height;

cout << "The area is: " << iArea << "\n";

}

//////////////////////////////////////////////////////
// The constructor function of CNewRectangle (derived)
//////////////////////////////////////////////////////
CNewRectangle::CNewRectangle( int w,
                             int h):CRectangle( w, h)
{

cout << "In the constructor of the derived class" << "\n";

}

//////////////////////////////////////////////////////
// The destructor function of CNewRectangle (derived)
//////////////////////////////////////////////////////
CNewRectangle::~CNewRectangle()

{

cout << "In the destructor of the derived class" << "\n";

}

////////////////////////////////////////////
// Function Name: SetWidth() (derived)
////////////////////////////////////////////
void CNewRectangle::SetWidth(int w)
{

m_Width = w;

}

////////////////////////////////////////////
// Function Name: SetHeight() (derived)
////////////////////////////////////////////
void CNewRectangle::SetHeight(int h)
{

m_Height = h;

}

void main(void)
{

CNewRectangle MyRectangle (10, 5);
```

```
MyRectangle.DisplayArea();

MyRectangle.SetWidth (100);
MyRectangle.SetHeight (20);

MyRectangle.DisplayArea();

}
```

The RECT2.CPP Program's Code

The RECT2.CPP program declares the CRectangle class exactly as it was declared in the RECT.CPP program:

```
class CRectangle
{
public:
      CRectangle(int w, int h);  // Constructor

      void DisplayArea (void);

      ~CRectangle();             // Destructor

      int m_Width;
      int m_Height;

};
```

The RECT2.CPP program then declares a class called CNewRectangle, which is derived from the CRectangle class:

```
/////////////////////////////////////////////////////
// The declaration of the derived class CNewRectangle
/////////////////////////////////////////////////////
class CNewRectangle : public CRectangle
{

public:
    CNewRectangle(int w, int h);  // Constructor

    void SetWidth (int w);
    void SetHeight (int h);

    ~CNewRectangle();             // Destructor

};
```

Notice the first line of the declaration of the derived class:

```
class CNewRectangle : public CRectangle
{
....
....
....
};
```

The text : `public CRectangle` is an indication that `CNewRectangle` is derived from `CRectangle`.

The derived class has a constructor function, a destructor function, the `SetWidth()` function, and the `SetHeight()` function. As you'll see, the `CNewRectangle` class has all the features of the `CRectangle` class. For example, even though the data members `m_Width` and `m_Height` do not appear as data members of `CNewRectangle`, `CNewRectangle` inherited these data members from `CRectangle`. Also, even though `CNewRectangle` does not have the `DisplayArea()` function as one of its member functions, for all practical purposes, you can think as if `CNewRectangle` has a member function called `DisplayArea()`, because `CNewRectangle` inherited the `DisplayArea()` function from its base class.

The constructor function of the base class simply sets the values of the data members of the class:

```
CRectangle::CRectangle( int w, int h)
{

cout << "In the constructor of the base class" << "\n";

m_Width = w;
m_Height = h;

}
```

The `cout` statement is used in the preceding constructor function so that you can tell during the execution of the program that this constructor function was executed.

Following is the destructor function of the base class:

```
CRectangle::~CRectangle()
{

cout << "In the destructor of the base class" << "\n";

}
```

Again, the `cout` statement is used so that you'll be able to tell that this function was executed.

The `DisplayArea()` function of the base class calculates and displays the area:

```
void CRectangle::DisplayArea(void)
{

int iArea;

iArea = m_Width * m_Height;

cout << "The area is: " << iArea << "\n";

}
```

Now look at the constructor function of the derived class.

```
CNewRectangle::CNewRectangle(int w,
                            int h):CRectangle(w,h)
{

cout << "In the constructor of the derived class" << "\n";

}
```

The first line of the preceding function includes this text:

```
:CRectangle(w,h)
```

This code means that when an object of class CNewRectangle is created the constructor function of the base class is executed and the parameters (w and h) are passed to the constructor function of the base class.

The code inside the constructor function of the derived class uses the cout statement so that during the execution of the program you'll be able to tell that this function was executed.

Following is the destructor function of the derived class:

```
CNewRectangle::~CNewRectangle()
{

cout << "In the destructor of the derived class" << "\n";

}
```

Again, the cout statement is used so that you'll be able to tell when this function is executed.

Following are the SetWidth() and SetHeight() functions of the derived class:

```
void CNewRectangle::SetWidth(int w)
{

m_Width = w;

}

void CNewRectangle::SetHeight(int h)
{

m_Height = h;

}
```

main() starts by creating an object of class CNewRectangle:

```
CNewRectangle MyRectangle (10, 5);
```

The preceding statement creates the MyRectangle object of class CNewRectangle. Because CNewRectangle is derived from CRectangle, however, you can use member functions from the base class:

```
MyRectangle.DisplayArea();
```

The preceding statement executes the DisplayArea() member function on the MyRectangle object. Note that even though the CNewRectangle class does not have the DisplayArea() member function in its class declaration, CNewRectangle inherited the DisplayArea() member function of the base class CRectangle.

main() then uses the SetWidth() and SetHeight() member functions to set new values of m_Width and m_Height:

```
MyRectangle.SetWidth (100);
MyRectangle.SetHeight (20);
```

Finally, `main()` uses the `DisplayArea()` function to display the area of the rectangle:

```
MyRectangle.DisplayArea();
```

Now that you understand the code of the RECT2.CPP program, you're ready to see it in action.

☐ Close all the windows inside the desktop of Visual C++ (select RECT.MAK from the Window menu, and then select Close from the File menu).

☐ Select New from the File menu, select Code/Text in the New dialog box that Visual C++ displays, and then click the OK button.

☐ Save the new, empty text file as RECT2.CPP in the \MVCPROG\CH03 directory.

☐ In the RECT2.CPP window, type the code shown in Listing 3.2 earlier in this chapter.

You now can compile, link, and execute the RECT2.CPP program, as follows:

☐ Select Rebuild All from the Project menu.

     Visual C++ displays a dialog box that asks whether you want to create a default project.

☐ In the dialog box, click the Yes button.

☐ Execute the MS-DOS program, log in to the \MVCPROG\CH03 directory, and execute the RECT2.EXE program.

As you see, the RECT2.CPP program first executes the constructor function of the base class and then executes the constructor function of the derived class, because of the following statement in `main()`:

```
CNewRectangle MyRectangle(10, 5);
```

The RECT2.CPP program then displays the area of a rectangle with width equal to 10 and height equal to 5.

Next, the program displays the area of a rectangle with width equal to 100 and height equal to 20.

Finally, upon completion of the `main()` function, the `MyRectangle` object is destroyed. As you see, the destructor function of the derived class was executed, and then the destructor function of the base class was executed.

Notice that when the object was created the constructor function of the base class was executed, and then the constructor function of the derived class was executed. Also notice that when the object was destroyed the destructor function of the derived class was executed, and then the destructor function of the base class was executed.

Class Hierarchy Pictorial Representation

Figure 3.1 shows the class-hierarchy relationship between `CRectangle` and `CNewRectangle`.

Figure 3.1. The class hierarchy of `CRectangle` *and* `CNewRectangle`.

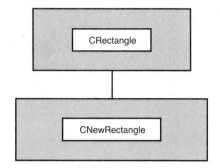

The relationship shown in Figure 3.1 is simple, and you probably don't even need a diagram to show this relationship. The class hierarchy can be as complex as you want it to be. For example, you may want to construct another derived class, called `CNewNewRectangle`, that is derived from the `CNewRectangle` class. In this case, the class declaration of `CNewNewRectangle` would look like this:

```
class CNewNewRectangle: public CNewRectangle
{
....
....
....
};
```

In the preceding declaration, `CNewNewRectangle` serves as the derived class and `CNewRectangle` serves as the base class. You now can declare another derived class for which `CNewNewRectangle` serves as the base class.

Figure 3.2 shows a complex class hierarchy. You should be aware that the complex class hierarchy shown in Figure 3.2 was not created for academic reasons. In fact, as you'll see later in this book, the class hierarchy of the MFC is far more complex than the one shown in the figure.

How can you use this representation of a class hierarchy? By looking at the class hierarchy you can tell which member functions you can execute. By looking at Figure 3.2, you can tell that you can execute a member function that exists in class A on objects of class B, C, D, E, F, G, and H. You also can execute a member function that appears in class F on an object of class G, E, and H. But you cannot execute a member function that appears in class F on objects of class A, B, C, D, and E.

Overriding a Member Function

Sometimes, you may find it necessary to override a particular member function. Suppose that you purchase the `CRectangle` class; you like this class, and you want to use it in your applications. The only problem is that you don't like the way the author of the `CRectangle` class wrote the `DisplayArea()` function. Can you override that function? Sure. The RECT3.CPP program demonstrates how to accomplish this task.

Figure 3.2. A complex class hierarchy.

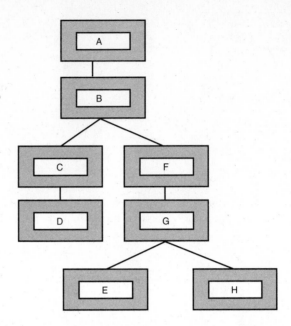

Because the RECT3.CPP program is very similar to the RECT2.CPP program, follow these steps to create the RECT3.CPP program:

☐ Save the RECT2.CPP program as RECT3.CPP in the \MVCPROG\CH03 directory, and then close the RECT2.MAK project (select RECT3.MAK from the Window menu, and then select Close from the File menu).

☐ Add another prototype function to the declaration of the CNewRectangle class in the RECT3.CPP file.

After you add the prototype, the declaration of the CNewRectangle class should look like this:

```
/////////////////////////////////////////////////////
// The declaration of the derived class CNewRectangle
/////////////////////////////////////////////////////
class CNewRectangle : public CRectangle
{

public:
    CNewRectangle(int w, int h);  // Constructor

    void SetWidth (int w);
    void SetHeight (int h);

    void DisplayArea();

    ~CNewRectangle(); // Destructor

};
```

In the preceding example, the prototype of the DisplayArea() function was added.

☐ Add to the RECT3.CPP file the code of the DisplayArea() function. Here is the code of the DisplayArea() function of the derived class:

```
/////////////////////////////////////////
// Function Name: DisplayArea() (derived)
/////////////////////////////////////////
void CNewRectangle::DisplayArea(void)
{

int iArea;

iArea = m_Width * m_Height;

cout << "================= \n";
cout << "The area is: " << iArea << "\n";
cout << "================= \n";

}
```

As you see, the RECT3.CPP program now has two DisplayArea() functions. One function is a member function of the CRectangle class (the base class), and the other DisplayArea() function is a member function of the CNewRectangle class (the derived class).

main() remains exactly as it was in the RECT2.CPP program:

```
void main(void)
{

CNewRectangle MyRectangle (10, 5);

MyRectangle.DisplayArea();

MyRectangle.SetWidth (100);
MyRectangle.SetHeight (20);

MyRectangle.DisplayArea();

}
```

☐ Save your work (select Save from the File menu).

☐ Select Rebuild All from the Project menu, and then click the Yes button in the dialog box that appears.

> *Visual C++ responds by compiling and linking the RECT3.CPP program.*

☐ Execute the MS-DOS program, log in to the \MVCPROG\CH03 directory, and then execute RECT3.EXE from the Project menu.

As you see, the output of RECT3.CPP is the same as the output of RECT2.CPP, except that the areas are displayed with the DisplayArea() function of the derived class. This means that when the MyRectangle.DisplayArea(); statement is executed, the DisplayArea() of the derived class is executed (not the DisplayArea() function of the base class).

Using Pointers to Objects

In many cases, it is convenient to use pointers to objects. The RECT4.CPP program demonstrates this concept.

☐ Save the RECT3.CPP file as RECT4.CPP in the directory C:\VCPROG\PRACTICE\CH03 (select Save As from the File menu).

☐ Close the RECT3.MAK project.

☐ Modify the `main()` function of RECT4.CPP.

After you modify `main()`, it should look like this:

```
void main(void)
{

CNewRectangle MyRectangle (10, 5);

CNewRectangle * pMyRectangle = &MyRectangle;

pMyRectangle->DisplayArea();


pMyRectangle->SetWidth (100);
pMyRectangle->SetHeight (20);


pMyRectangle->DisplayArea();

}
```

As you see, `main()` creates an object `MyRectangle` of class `CNewRectangle`:

```
CNewRectangle MyRectangle (10, 5);
```

Then `main()` declares a pointer `pMyRectangle` of type `CNewRectangle`:

```
CNewRectangle * pMyRectangle = &MyRectangle;
```

In the preceding statement, the address of the `MyRectangle` object is assigned to `pMyRectangle`.

The rest of the statements in `main()` are similar to the statements in the `main()` function of the RECT3.CPP program. Unlike the `main()` function in RECT3.CPP, however, the `main()` function in RECT4.CPP uses the pointer of the `MyRectangle` object to execute the member function.

The `DisplayArea()` function is executed as follows:

```
pMyRectangle->DisplayArea();
```

You execute the `SetWidth()` and `SetHeight()` functions this way:

```
pMyRectangle->SetWidth (100);
pMyRectangle->SetHeight (20);
```

☐ Compile and link the RECT4.CPP program (select Rebuild All from the Project menu, and then click the Yes button when Visual C++ displays the dialog box that asks whether you want to create the default project, which is the RECT4.MAK file).

☐ Execute the MS-DOS program, log in to the \MVCPROG\CH03 directory, and execute the RECT4.EXE program.

☐ Verify that the results of the RECT4.EXE program are identical to those of the RECT3.CPP program.

The New and Delete Operators

In the RECT4.CPP program, you created the MyRectangle object in main():

```
void main(void)
{

CNewRectangle MyRectangle (10, 5);

CNewRectangle * pMyRectangle = &MyRectangle;

pMyRectangle->DisplayArea();

...
...
...

}
```

In the preceding main() function, the object is destroyed when main() terminates. If you create the object from within a function, however, as shown in the following example, the memory that was used for storing the MyRectangle object is freed automatically when MyFunction() terminates.

```
void MyFunction(void)
{

CNewRectangle MyRectangle (10, 5);

CNewRectangle * pMyRectangle = &MyRectangle;

pMyRectangle->DisplayArea();

...
...
...

}
```

The object is created with the following statement:

```
CNewRectangle MyRectangle (10, 5);
```

Then the pointer to the object is created:

```
CNewRectangle * pMyRectangle = &MyRectangle;
```

Alternatively, you can use the new operator, which is equivalent to the malloc() function of C.

The RECT5.CPP program demonstrates how you can use the new operator.

☐ Close the RECT4.MAK project, open the RECT4.CPP file, and then save the RECT4.CPP file as RECT5.CPP in the \MVCPROG\CH03 directory.

☐ Modify the `main()` function of RECT5.CPP so that it looks like this:

```
void main(void)
{

CNewRectangle* pMyRectangle;
pMyRectangle = new CNewRectangle(10,5);

pMyRectangle->DisplayArea();


pMyRectangle->SetWidth (100);
pMyRectangle->SetHeight (20);


pMyRectangle->DisplayArea();

delete pMyRectangle;
}
```

☐ To save your work, select Save from the File menu.

☐ Select Rebuild from the Project menu, and when Visual C++ displays the dialog box asking whether you want to create a default project (the RECT5.MAK file), click the Yes button.

   Visual C++ responds by compiling and linking the RECT5.CPP program.

☐ Execute the MS-DOS program, log in to the \MVCPROG\CH03 directory, and execute the RECT5.EXE program.

As you see, the output of RECT5.EXE is identical to the output of the RECT4.EXE program.

Now look at the code of the `main()` function of the RECT5.CPP program.

A pointer `pMyRectangle` is declared. This pointer is declared as a pointer to an object of class `CNewRectangle`:

```
CNewRectangle* pMyRectangle;
```

Then the `new` operator is used to create a new object of class `CNewRectangle`. The address of this new object is stored in the pointer `pMyRectangle`:

```
pMyRectangle = new CNewRectangle(10,5);
```

The rest of the code in `main()` remains the same as it was in the RECT4.CPP program. To execute the `DisplayArea()` member function on the object, for example, you use this statement:

```
pMyRectangle->DisplayArea();
```

The last thing that `main()` does is free the memory occupied by the object:

```
delete pMyRectangle;
```

Note that the delete operator must be used to free objects that were created with the new operator.

> **NOTE**
>
> If you use the new operator from within a function, when the function terminates the memory occupied by the pointer is freed automatically (because the pointer is just a local variable to the function). The pointer holds a memory address where the actual object is stored, however, and that memory is *not* freed when the function terminates. You must use the delete operator to free the memory occupied by the object.

> **NOTE**
>
> In the RECT5.CPP program, you created the object by using two statements in main():
>
> ```
> CNewRectangle* pMyRectangle;
> pMyRectangle = new CNewRectangle(10,5);
> ```
>
> In Visual C++ you typically see these statements combined in one statement:
>
> ```
> CNewRectangle* pMyRectangle = new CNewRectangle(10,5);
> ```
>
> This statement is identical to the preceding two statements.

What's It All About?

Congratulations! You've completed the quick C++ tutorial.

Starting in the next chapter, you'll write true C++ Windows applications. Visual C++ enables you to write powerful, sophisticated, professional applications in a very short time. This is possible because Microsoft ships the Visual C++ package with a set of very powerful classes called the MFC library. As it turns out, learning Visual C++ amounts to knowing how to use the powerful member functions of the MFC.

In addition, Visual C++ enables you to design your windows, dialog boxes, menus, bitmaps, and icons visually—that is, you use the mouse and the visual tools of Visual C++ to design these objects.

Visual C++ also includes a program called AppWizard, which writes the overhead code for you. A Windows application usually requires several overhead files; these overhead files appear in every Windows application that you'll write. Instead of typing these repetitive, boring overhead files yourself, you can use the AppWizard program to generate and write these overhead files for you.

Finally, Visual C++ is equipped with a program called ClassWizard. As you learned in this chapter, when you know that a certain class is available (for example, the CRectangle class), you can derive other classes that inherit the data members and member functions of the base class.

Unlike the CRectangle and CNewRectangle classes that were discussed in this chapter, the classes of the MFC are very powerful, and deriving classes from the MFC requires a great deal of typing. Don't worry, though; ClassWizard takes care of this task. ClassWizard inserts the prototypes of the member functions into the declaration of the derived classes and even starts writing the function for you. All you have to do is type your own specific code inside the functions ClassWizard prepares for you.

These wizard programs are what Visual C++ is all about. Throughout this book you'll use these wizards extensively.

4

Writing Your First True Windows Application

In this chapter you will write your
first true Windows application with
Visual C++. As you will soon see,
writing a true Windows application
with Visual C++ is easy because a lot
of the code is generated for you
automatically by Visual C++.

Writing a Visual C++ Windows application involves the following two steps:

1. The visual programming step
2. The code programming step

During the visual programming step, you design your application by using software tools that come with the Visual C++ package. With these tools, you design your application by using the mouse and the keyboard. You don't have to write any code in this step! You just have to know how to use the visual tools of the package to place objects (for example, menus, push buttons, scroll bars) inside the windows of your application.

In the code programming step, you write code using the text editor that comes with the Visual C++ package. The code statements are written in the C++ programming language.

The SAY Application

In the following sections you will find step-by-step instructions to create a simple Windows application called SAY.

Before you start writing the SAY application, execute it. This way, you will have a better understanding of what the SAY application is supposed to do. The SAY.EXE application resides in the \MVCPROG\EXE directory of the book's CD.

To execute the SAY application do the following:

☐ Insert the book's CD into your CD-ROM drive and execute the X:\mvcProg\EXE\SAY.EXE program (where *X* is the letter of your CD-ROM drive).

Windows responds by executing the SAY application. The main window of the SAY application appears, as shown in Figure 4.1.

Figure 4.1. The main window of the SAY application.

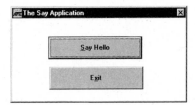

As you can see from Figure 4.1, the main window of the SAY application has two buttons: Say Hello and Exit.

☐ Click the Say Hello button.

The SAY application responds by displaying a Hello message box. (See Figure 4.2.)

☐ Close the Hello message box by clicking its OK button.

Figure 4.2. The Hello message box of the SAY application.

The System menu of the SAY application has an About menu item. To see this menu item in action do the following:

☐ Open the System menu of the SAY application by clicking the small icon at the top-left corner of the application window.

 The SAY application responds by displaying the System menu. (See Figure 4.3.)

Figure 4.3. The System menu of the SAY application.

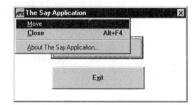

Display the About dialog box of the SAY application:

☐ Select About The Say Application from the System menu.

 The SAY application responds by displaying an About dialog box. (See Figure 4.4.)

Figure 4.4. The About dialog box of the SAY application.

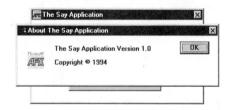

☐ Close the About dialog box by clicking its OK button.

Terminate the SAY application:

☐ Click the Exit button.

 The SAY application responds by terminating.

You now know what the SAY application is supposed to do. Now it's time to write the SAY application from scratch. In the following sections you will follow a set of step-by-step instructions to implement the SAY application yourself.

Creating the Project of the SAY Application

The first thing to do when you design a new application is to create the project of the application.

☐ Use the Start menu of Windows to start the Visual C++ program.

> *Windows responds by running the Visual C++ program. The main window of Visual C++ appears, as shown in Figure 4.5.*

Figure 4.5. The main window of Visual C++.

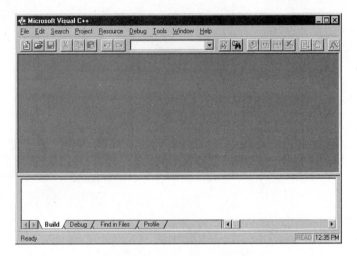

NOTE

In Figure 4.5 the desktop of Visual C++ has no open files. If you have an open file, close it by selecting Close from the File menu of Visual C++.

☐ Select New from the File menu of Visual C++.

> *Visual C++ responds by displaying the New dialog box. (See Figure 4.6.)*

Figure 4.6. The New dialog box.

☐ Select Project inside the New dialog box (because you are now creating a new project) and then click the OK button.

> *Visual C++ responds by displaying the New Project dialog box. (See Figure 4.7.)*

*Figure 4.7. The New
Project dialog box.*

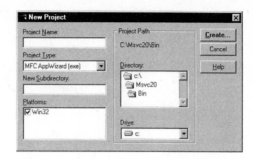

Tell Visual C++ the name of the new project:

☐ Type **SAY** inside the Project Name edit box.

Tell Visual C++ the directory where you want to create the new application:

☐ Use the Directory list box to select the directory C:\MVCPROG\CH04. That is, inside
the directory list box double-click c:\, then double-click mvcprog, and finally, double-click
ch04.

The project path should now be C:\MVCPROG\CH04\SAY\SAY.MAK.

☐ Make sure Project Type is set to MFC AppWizard (exe).

By setting the project type to MFC AppWizard (exe) you are telling Visual C++ that you want to
create the new project by using AppWizard.

What is AppWizard? It is a very powerful "wizard" that writes for you the skeleton code of your
application. Instead of you writing overhead code every time you start writing a new application,
AppWizard will write this overhead code for you.

At this point your New Project dialog box should look like the one shown in Figure 4.8.

*Figure 4.8. The New
Project dialog box (after
you finish specifying the
project name, project path,
and project type).*

Now that you have finished specifying the name, type, and path of the new project, you can start
creating the project:

☐ Click the Create button of the New Project dialog box.

Visual C++ responds by displaying the MFC AppWizard—Step 1 dialog box. (See Figure 4.9.)

Figure 4.9. The MFC AppWizard—Step 1 dialog box.

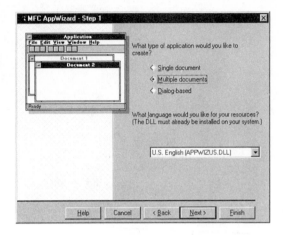

Because in the New Project dialog box you specified that you want the new project to be of type MFC AppWizard (exe), AppWizard will now take you through several steps. In these steps you'll tell AppWizard what type of application you want to create. When you complete all the AppWizard steps, AppWizard will create for you the project file of the application (say.mak) as well as the skeleton files of the application.

As you can see in Figure 4.9, AppWizard is currently asking you what type of application you want to create. Select the type of application:

☐ Click the Dialog-based radio button.

By selecting the Dialog-based radio button you are telling AppWizard that you want to create a dialog-based application. A dialog-based application is an application whose main window is a dialog box. As you saw earlier in Figure 4.1, the main window of the SAY application should be a dialog box that has two push buttons in it. You'll design this dialog box later in this chapter.

The other two types of applications (single-document and multiple-document) are covered in later chapters of the book.

As shown in Figure 4.9, the AppWizard—Step 1 dialog box also asks you what language you would like to use for your resources. You select the desired language from the Language drop-down list box of the dialog box.

☐ Leave the Language drop-down list box at the default setting: U.S. English (APPWIZUS.DLL).

Your AppWizard—Step 1 dialog box should now look like the one shown in Figure 4.10.

*Figure 4.10. The MFC
AppWizard—Step 1 dialog
box for the SAY application.*

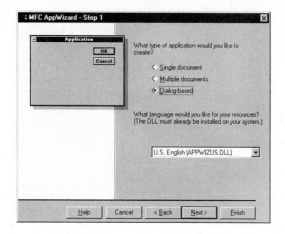

To advance to the next AppWizard step do the following:

☐ Click the Next button.

> *Visual C++ responds by displaying the MFC AppWizard—Step 2 dialog box. (See Figure 4.11.)*

*Figure 4.11. The
AppWizard—Step 2 of 4
dialog box.*

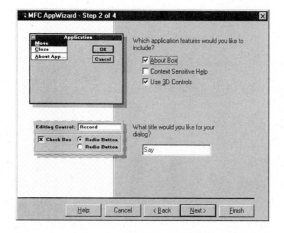

As you can see, the AppWizard—Step 2 of 4 dialog box lets you specify which features you want to include (or exclude) in the application as well as the title of the application's dialog box (that is, the title of the application's main window).

☐ Set the options of the AppWizard—Step 2 of 4 dialog box as shown in Figure 4.12. That is, leave the application features check boxes at their default values, and set the title of the dialog box to The Say Application.

Figure 4.12. The
AppWizard—Step 2 of 4
dialog box for the SAY
application.

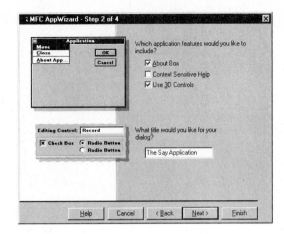

By setting the AppWizard—Step 2 of 4 dialog box as shown in Figure 4.12, you are telling AppWizard that you want to create an application with the following features:

Has an About dialog box

Does not include context-sensitive help

Uses three-dimensional controls

Has a main window with the title The Say Application

To advance to the next AppWizard step do the following:

☐ Click the Next button.

Visual C++ responds by displaying the MFC AppWizard—Step 3 of 4 dialog box. (See Figure 4.13.)

Figure 4.13. The
AppWizard—Step 3 of 4
dialog box.

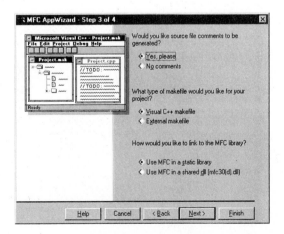

As you can see, the AppWizard—Step 3 of 4 dialog box asks you three questions. Answer the three questions as shown in Figure 4.14.

Figure 4.14. The AppWizard—Step 3 of 4 dialog box for the SAY application.

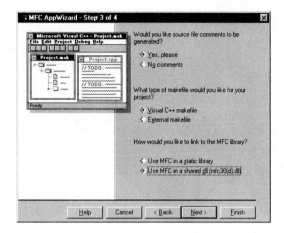

By setting the AppWizard—Step 3 of 4 dialog box as shown in Figure 4.14, you are specifying the following:

- When AppWizard creates for you the skeleton code of application it should include comments. Including comments in the skeleton files will help you understand the code that AppWizard will write for you (in case you want to go over this code).

- The MAK file (project file) of the application should be a Visual C++ MAK file.

- The application will use the MFC dynamic linked library (DLL) MFC30D.DLL and not a static library. Using a DLL instead of a static library has the advantage that the resultant EXE file is shorter. The disadvantage of using the DLL file is that when you distribute your application to others, in addition to the EXE file of your application you also have to distribute the DLL file and copy the DLL file to your user's \WINDOWS\SYSTEM directory.

NOTE

In Figure 4.14 the name of the MFC DLL is specified as mfc30(d).dll. This means that depending on how you create the application's EXE file, your EXE program will use either the mfc30.dll file or the mfc30d.dll file.

If you'll create the application's EXE file for debugging, then your EXE program will use the mfc30d.dll file. If, however, you'll create the application's EXE file for release, then your EXE program will use the mfc30.dll file.

Soon you'll learn how to set the application's EXE file for debugging or for release.

To advance to the last AppWizard step do the following:

☐ Click the Next button.

Visual C++ responds by displaying the AppWizard—Step 4 of 4 dialog box. (See Figure 4.15.)

Figure 4.15. The
AppWizard—Step 4 of 4
dialog box.

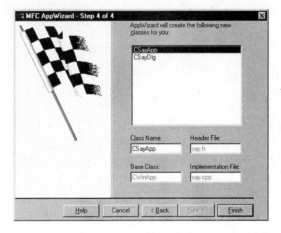

As you can see, the AppWizard—Step 4 of 4 dialog box tells the names of the classes and files that AppWizard will create for you. You don't have to change anything in this dialog box.

You can now tell AppWizard to create the project and skeleton files of the SAY application:

☐ Click the Finish button.

AppWizard responds by displaying the New Project Information dialog box. (See Figure 4.16.) This dialog box summarizes all the information you specified in the previous steps.

Figure 4.16. The New
Project Information
dialog box.

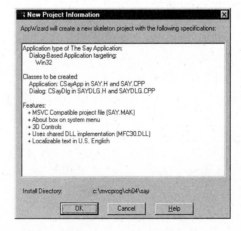

☐ Click the OK button of the New Project Information dialog box.

AppWizard responds by creating the project file (say.mak) and all the skeleton files of the SAY application in the directory C:\MVCPROG\CH04\SAY, and then it displays the window of Visual C++, as shown in Figure 4.17.

Figure 4.17. The window of Visual C++ after the project of the SAY application has been created.

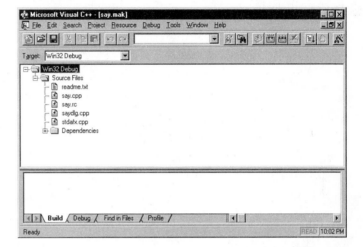

As you can see in Figure 4.17, Visual C++ displays the SAY.MAK window. SAY.MAK is the project file of the SAY application. The SAY.MAK window displays a visual presentation of the SAY.MAK project—it lists all the files that make up the SAY application.

What exactly did AppWizard do for you? If you examine your hard drive, you'll see that AppWizard created several files inside your C:\MVCPROG\CH04\SAY directory. These files are the "bones" (that is, the skeleton) of your application. Your job, with the aid of Visual C++, is to customize these files so that the SAY application will do what it's supposed to do.

> **NOTE**
>
> As you can see in Figure 4.17, the top of the say.mak window has a Target drop-down list box. The Target drop-down list box is currently set to Win32Debug. When the Target list box is set to Win32Debug, Visual C++ generates an EXE file that contains various code lines that are needed for debugging.
>
> You can set the Target drop-down list box to Win32Release. If you do that, no debugging code will be embedded inside the EXE file. To set the Target drop-down list box to Win32Release, simply click the down-arrow icon of the Target list box and select Win32Release.

Running the SAY Application Before Customizing It

Before you start customizing the files of the SAY application, first compile, link, and execute the SAY application in its current state. As you'll see, the skeleton files that AppWizard created for you have code in them that actually does something.

To compile and link the SAY application do the following:

☐ Select Rebuild All from the Project menu of Visual C++.

> *Visual C++ responds by compiling and linking the SAY application.*

> **NOTE**
>
> If during the compiling and linking process you get a memory error (an out-of-memory error or an out-of-heap-space error), close any open applications and then try to build the application again. If you still get a memory error, terminate Visual C++ and then run Visual C++ again and try to build the application again. If you still get a memory error, restart Windows and build the application again.

When Visual C++ finishes compiling and linking the application, you can run the application:

☐ Select Execute say.exe from the Project menu.

> *Visual C++ responds by executing the SAY application. The main window of the SAY application looks like the one shown in Figure 4.18.*

Figure 4.18. The main window of the SAY application (before you customize it).

As you can see, the main window of the SAY application has two push buttons—OK and Cancel—and it displays the text TODO: Place dialog controls here.

The SAY application also has an About dialog box. It has an About dialog box because when you specified the features of the application in the AppWizard—Step 2 of 4 dialog box you specified that you want an About dialog box. (See Figure 4.12.)

☐ Open the System menu of the SAY application by clicking the small icon at the top-left corner of the application window.

> *The SAY application responds by displaying the System menu. (See Figure 4.19.)*

Figure 4.19. The System menu of the SAY application.

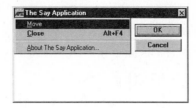

To display the About dialog box of the SAY application do the following:

☐ Select About The Say Application… from the System menu.

    The SAY application responds by displaying an About dialog box. (See Figure 4.20.)

☐ Close the About dialog box by clicking its OK button.

Figure 4.20. The About dialog box of the SAY application.

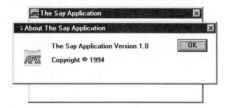

Terminate the SAY application:

☐ Click the OK button.

    The SAY application responds by terminating.

As you can see, even though you have not yet written a single line of code, you already have a true working Windows application in your hands—a gift from AppWizard. Of course, this application is not exactly what you wanted it to be. So in the following sections you will design the files of the SAY application, until finally, the SAY application does what it is supposed to do.

As stated at the beginning of the chapter, the design process involves two steps:

    1. The visual implementation step
    2. The code-writing step

You'll perform these steps in the remaining sections of this chapter.

NOTE

In the preceding steps you executed the SAY.EXE application by selecting Execute say.exe from the Project menu of Visual C++.

Alternatively you can execute the SAY.EXE file directly from Windows.

Visual C++ created the SAY.EXE file in one of the following two directories:

- \MVCPROG\CH04\SAY\WINDEBUG

- \MVCPROG\CH04\SAY\WINREL

If you set the Release drop-down list box at the top of the SAY.MAK window to Win32Debug (See Figure 4.17.), then Visual C++ created the SAY.EXE file in the \MVCPROG\CH04\SAY\WINDEBUG directory.

If, however, you set the Release drop-down list box to Win32Release, then Visual C++ created the SAY.EXE file in your \MVCPROG\CH04\SAY\WINREL directory.

The Visual Implementation of the SAY Application

Currently, the main window of the SAY application has an OK button, a Cancel button, and the text TODO: Place dialog controls here. Your objective is to customize the dialog box that serves as the application's main window so that the application's main window looks like the one shown in Figure 4.1.

To modify the dialog box that serves as the main window of the SAY application you have to work on the resource file (RC file) of the SAY application. The resource file of the application is where all the resources of the application (for example, dialog boxes and menus) are defined. The resource file of the SAY application is SAY.RC. Visual C++ includes powerful visual tools that enable you to work on the RC file visually. In the following steps you'll use the visual tools of Visual C++ to customize the dialog box that serves as the main window of the application.

☐ Double-click say.rc in the say.mak window. (say.rc is the third item under the Source Files item inside the say.mak window.)

Visual C++ responds by displaying the say.rc window. (See Figure 4.21.)

Figure 4.21. The say.rc window.

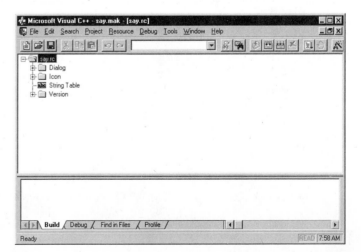

The say.rc window is a visual presentation of the RC file (resource file) of the SAY application. Notice the title of the Visual C++ window:

```
Microsoft Visual C++ — say.mak — [say.rc]
```

That's because you are currently viewing the say.rc file that is part of the say.mak project.

As you can see from Figure 4.21, the say.rc window lists several types of resources: Dialog, Icon, String Table, and Version. Currently your objective is to modify a dialog box. Therefore, you have to double-click the Dialog item:

☐ Double-click Dialog in the say.rc window.

> *Visual C++ responds by displaying the names of the dialog boxes of the SAY application under the Dialog item. (See Figure 4.22.)*

Figure 4.22. Listing the names of the dialog boxes of the SAY application.

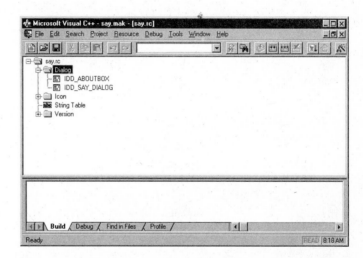

As shown in Figure 4.22, currently the SAY application has two dialog boxes: IDD_ABOUTBOX and IDD_SAY_DIALOG. Both of these dialog boxes were created for you by AppWizard.

As you might have guessed, IDD_ABOUTBOX is the About dialog box of the SAY application, and IDD_SAY_DIALOG is the dialog box that serves as the main window of the SAY application. Currently your objective is to customize the dialog box that serves as the main window of the application. Therefore, you have to double-click the IDD_SAY_DIALOG item:

☐ Double-click IDD_SAY_DIALOG in the say.rc window.

> *Visual C++ responds by displaying the IDD_SAY_DIALOG dialog box in design mode. (See Figure 4.23.)*

Figure 4.23. The
IDD_SAY_DIALOG
dialog box in design mode.

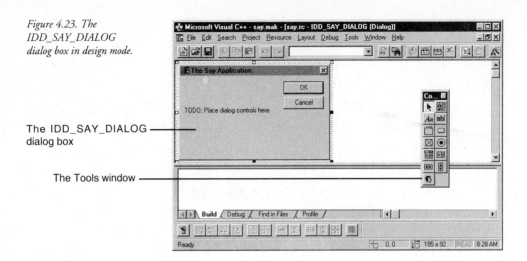

The IDD_SAY_DIALOG ————
dialog box

The Tools window ————

NOTE

As shown in Figure 4.23, besides displaying the IDD_SAY_DIALOG dialog box, Visual C++ also displays the Tools window. As you'll soon see, the Tools window is used for placing controls inside the dialog box.

As shown in Figure 4.23, currently the IDD_SAY_DIALOG dialog box has three objects: an OK button, a Cancel button, and the text TODO: Place dialog controls here. Your objective is to remove these three objects and to replace them with two new controls: a Say Hello button and an Exit button. (See Figure 4.1.)

Follow these steps to remove the three controls that are currently inside the IDD_SAY_DIALOG dialog box:

☐ Click the OK button inside the IDD_SAY_DIALOG dialog box and then press the Delete key on your keyboard.

   Visual C++ responds by removing the OK button from the IDD_SAY_DIALOG dialog box.

☐ Click the Cancel button inside the IDD_SAY_DIALOG dialog box and then press the Delete key on your keyboard.

   Visual C++ responds by removing the Cancel button from the IDD_SAY_DIALOG dialog box.

☐ Click the text TODO: Place dialog controls here. inside the IDD_SAY_DIALOG dialog box and then press the Delete key on your keyboard.

Visual C++ responds by removing the text that you selected from the IDD_SAY_DIALOG dialog box.

Your IDD_SAY_DIALOG dialog box is now empty. (See Figure 4.24.)

Figure 4.24. The IDD_SAY_DIALOG dialog box after you have deleted all the controls inside it.

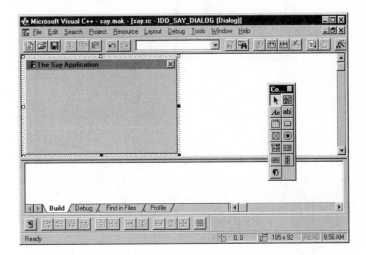

You'll now place two push button controls (Say Hello and Exit) inside the IDD_SAY_DIALOG dialog box.

To place a push button control inside the dialog box you have to use the push button tool of the Tools window. The push button tool inside the Tools window is shown in Figure 4.25.

Figure 4.25. The push button tool.

The push button tool

NOTE

If your Tools window is currently not displayed, follow these steps to display it:

☐ Select Toolbars from the Tools menu

Visual C++ responds by displaying the Toolbars dialog box.

☐ Place a checkmark inside the Controls check box and then click the Close button of the Toolbars dialog box.

Visual C++ responds by displaying the Tools window.

As stated, you have to place two push buttons inside the dialog box: Say Hello and Exit. Start with the Say Hello button:

☐ Click the push button tool inside the Tools window and then click the mouse anywhere inside the IDD_SAY_DIALOG dialog box.

Visual C++ responds by placing a push button control at the point where you clicked the mouse. (See Figure 4.26.)

Figure 4.26. The IDD_SAY_DIALOG dialog box after you place a push button inside it.

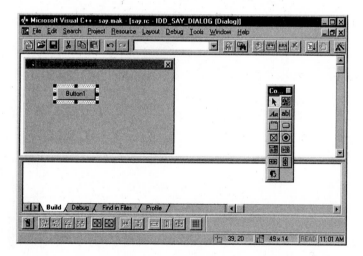

Currently, the caption of the push button is Button1. As shown back in Figure 4.1, the caption of this button should be Say Hello. Here is how you change the caption of the button from Button1 to Say Hello:

☐ Double-click the Button1 button.

Visual C++ responds by displaying the Push Button Properties dialog box. (See Figure 4.27.)

*Figure 4.27. The Push
Button Properties
dialog box.*

As you can see from Figure 4.27, the Caption box contains the text Button1. You want to change the caption to Say Hello:

☐ Click inside the Caption box, and type `&Say Hello`.

NOTE

The `&` character that prefixes the `S` in `&Say Hello` causes the character `S` to appear underlined. This means that during the execution of the program when the dialog box is displayed, pressing Alt+S produces the same results as clicking the Say Hello button. (You make the character `&` by pressing Shift+7.)

Your dialog box should now look like the one shown in Figure 4.28.

*Figure 4.28. Changing the
caption of Button1 to Say
Hello.*

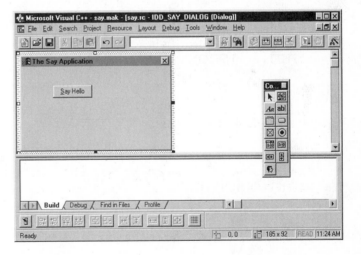

As shown back in Figure 4.1, the Say Hello button should be larger than the Say Hello button of Figure 4.28. To enlarge the Say Hello button do the following:

☐ Select the Say Hello button (that is, click inside the Say Hello button), and then drag the handles of the button until the button is at the desired size. (The handles are the solid squares on the rectangle that encloses the button.)

The enlarged Say Hello button is shown in Figure 4.29.

Figure 4.29. The Say Hello button after it has been enlarged.

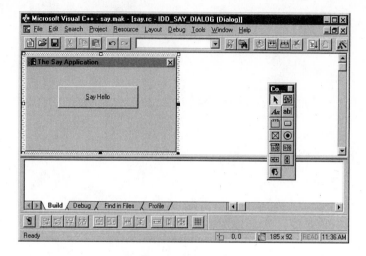

Note that you can move the Say Hello button to any desired location by dragging it with the mouse. That is, click the mouse on the button, and then drag the button to any desired location in the dialog box.

When you placed the button inside the dialog box, Visual C++ assigned the ID IDC_BUTTON1 to the button. It would be better if the ID of the Say Hello button had a more friendly name, one that would identify it as the ID of the Say Hello button (for example, IDC_SAYHELLO_BUTTON).

Change the ID name of the Say Hello button from IDC_BUTTON1 to IDC_SAYHELLO_BUTTON:

☐ Double-click the Say Hello button.

Visual C++ responds by displaying the Push Button Properties dialog box.

As you can see, currently the ID box contains the text IDC_BUTTON1. You want to change it to IDC_SAYHELLO_BUTTON:

☐ Click inside the ID box and type **IDC_SAYHELLO_BUTTON**.

From now on, Visual C++ will refer to the Say Hello button as IDC_SAYHELLO_BUTTON.

As shown back in Figure 4.1, the dialog box should also contain an Exit button:

☐ Place a new button inside the dialog box. That is, click the push button tool inside the Tools window and then click anywhere inside the dialog box.

☐ Move the new button so that it is below the Say Hello button. (That is, click on the new button and then drag it to the desired location.)

☐ Size the new button so that it is the same size as the Say Hello button. (That is, drag the handles of the new button until the button is at the desired size.)

Change the properties of the new button as follows:

☐ Double-click the new button.

☐ Set the Caption property to E&xit.

☐ Set the ID property to IDC_EXIT_BUTTON.

Your dialog box should now look like the one shown in Figure 4.30.

Figure 4.30. The dialog box with the Say Hello and Exit buttons.

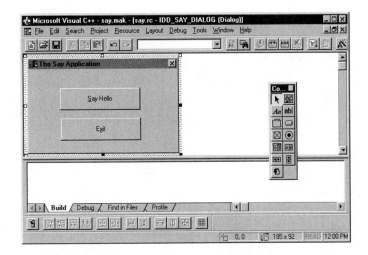

Congratulations! You have completed the visual design of the SAY application.

Now save your work:

☐ Select Save from the File menu.

What You've Accomplished So Far

Although you have not yet written a single line of code, you have finished the visual design of the SAY application. To see your visual design in action do the following:

☐ Select Build say.exe from the Project menu of Visual C++.

> *Visual C++ responds by compiling and linking the SAY application.*

When Visual C++ finishes compiling and linking the application, you can run the application:

☐ Select Execute say.exe from the Project menu.

> *Visual C++ responds by executing the SAY application. The main window of the SAY application appears as shown in Figure 4.31.*

Figure 4.31. The main
window of the SAY
application.

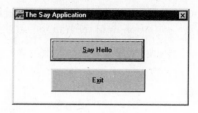

As you can see, the main window of the SAY application displays the IDD_SAY_DIALOG dialog box just as you designed it—with a Say Hello button and an Exit button.

☐ Try to click the Say Hello and Exit buttons.

As you can see, when you click the Say Hello button or Exit button, nothing happens. That's because you have not yet attached code to these buttons. You'll attach code to these buttons in the next section.

Terminate the SAY application:

☐ Open the System menu of the SAY application by clicking the small icon at the top-left corner of the application window and select Close from the System menu. (Alternatively, you can press Alt+F4 on your keyboard.)

   The SAY application responds by terminating.

Attaching Code to the Say Hello Push Button

As you have seen, at this point when you click the Say Hello and Exit buttons nothing happens. In this section you'll attach code to the Say Hello button so that when the user clicks this button the application will do what it's supposed to do. In the next section you'll attach code to the Exit button.

Recall that when the user clicks the Say Hello button, the SAY application should display a Hello message box. (See Figure 4.2.) You'll now attach code to the Say Hello button.

☐ Select ClassWizard from the Project menu of Visual C++.

   Visual C++ responds by displaying the ClassWizard dialog box. (See Figure 4.32.)

What is ClassWizard? ClassWizard is a powerful "wizard" that lets you write and maintain the code of the application very easily. In the following steps you'll use ClassWizard to attach code to the Say Hello push button.

As shown in Figure 4.32 the top of ClassWizard's dialog box has four tabs: Message Maps, Member Variables, OLE Automation, and OLE Events.

☐ Make sure that the Message Maps tab is currently selected.

☐ Make sure that the Class Name drop-down list box at the top of the dialog box is set to CSayDlg.

*Figure 4.32. The
ClassWizard dialog box.*

What is the `CSayDlg` class? It is the class that is associated with the IDD_SAY_DIALOG dialog box (the dialog box that serves as the main window of the SAY application). This class was created for you by AppWizard when you created the application.

In the preceding step you were asked to select the `CSayDlg` class because you are now going to attach code to the Say Hello button, and the Say Hello button is inside the IDD_SAY_DIALOG dialog box. Therefore, the code that you will attach to the Say Hello button will be written in the `CSayDlg` class.

You will now use ClassWizard to write the code that is automatically executed whenever the user clicks the Say Hello button.

As you can see from Figure 4.32, the middle section of the ClassWizard dialog box has two list boxes: the Object IDs list box (on the left side of the window) and the Messages list box (on the right side of the window).

The Object IDs list box is used to select the object to which you want to attach code. As you can see from Figure 4.32, currently IDC_EXIT_BUTTON (the ID of the Exit button) is selected in the Object IDs list box. However, now you want to attach code to the Say Hello button. Therefore, you have to select IDC_SAYHELLO_BUTTON:

☐ Select IDC_SAYHELLO_BUTTON in the Object IDs list of ClassWizard.

Your ClassWizard dialog box should now look like the one shown in Figure 4.33.

The Messages list box (to the right of the Object IDs list) lists messages that represent events that relate to the selected object. As you can see from Figure 4.33 there are two possible events that relate to the IDC_SAYHELLO_BUTTON button: BN_CLICKED and BN_DOUBLECLICKED. BN_CLICKED represents the event "the user clicked the button," and BN_DOUBLECLICKED represents the event "the user double-clicked the button."

*Figure 4.33. The
ClassWizard dialog box
after you select the
IDC_SAYHELLO_BUTTON
object.*

So in order to tell ClassWizard that you want to write code for the event "the user clicked the Say Hello button," you need to select IDC_SAYHELLO_BUTTON in the Object IDs list box and then you need to select BN_CLICKED in the Messages list box.

☐ Select BN_CLICKED inside the Messages list box (that is, click the BN_CLICKED item inside the Messages list box).

Your ClassWizard window should now look like the one shown in Figure 4.34—IDC_SAYHELLO_BUTTON is selected inside the Object IDs list box, and BN_CLICKED is selected inside the Messages list box.

*Figure 4.34. Selecting
BN_CLICKED inside the
Messages list box.*

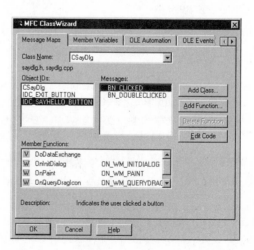

Next you have to tell ClassWizard to add the function that corresponds to the event that you just selected. That is, you have to tell ClassWizard to add the function that is executed automatically whenever the user clicks the Say Hello button.

Tell ClassWizard to add this function:

☐ Click the Add Function button of ClassWizard.

> *ClassWizard responds by displaying the Add Member Function dialog box. (See Figure 4.35.)*

*Figure 4.35. The Add
Member Function
dialog box.*

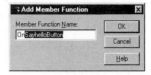

As you can see from Figure 4.35, ClassWizard suggests naming the new function `OnSayhelloButton()`.

☐ Click the OK button to accept the default name that ClassWizard suggests.

> *ClassWizard responds by adding the function `OnSayhelloButton()` to the SAY application. This function will be automatically executed whenever the user clicks the Say Hello button.*

Your ClassWizard dialog box should now look like the one shown in Figure 4.36. As shown in Figure 4.36, now the function `OnSayhelloButton()` is listed inside the Member Functions list box of ClassWizard's dialog box (at the bottom of the dialog box). Notice that now the `BN_CLICKED` item in the Messages list box has a small icon of a hand next to it. This icon serves as an indication that the `BN_CLICKED` event of the IDC_SAYHELLO_BUTTON object has a function attached to it.

*Figure 4.36. ClassWizard
after you add the function
`OnSayhelloButton()`.*

Note that ClassWizard made the `OnSayhelloButton()` function a member function of the `CSayDlg` class. That's because earlier you set the Class Name drop-down list box (at the top of the ClassWizard dialog box) to `CSayDlg`.

ClassWizard wrote only the code that declares the OnSayhelloButton() function and the skeleton of the function. It's your job to write the code inside the OnSayhelloButton() function.

To write the code inside the OnSayhelloButton() function do the following:

☐ Click the Edit Code button of ClassWizard.

> *ClassWizard responds by opening the file SAYDLG.CPP, with the function* OnSayhelloButton() *ready to be edited by you. (See Figure 4.37.)*

Figure 4.37. The OnSayhelloButton() *function, ready to be edited by you.*

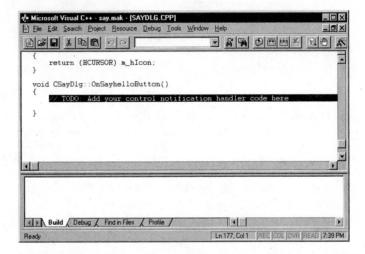

It is important to see the correlation between Figure 4.34 and Figure 4.37. As you can see in Figure 4.34 you told ClassWizard the following: The class name is CSayDlg, the object ID is ID_SAYHELLO_BUTTON, and the message is BN_CLICKED.

After you clicked the Add Function button of ClassWizard, ClassWizard generated the code shown in Figure 4.37.

As you can see from Figure 4.37, ClassWizard generated a member function called OnSayhelloButton() of the class CSayDlg. In addition, ClassWizard also added all the other code that has to be written when adding a member function to a class. For example, ClassWizard added to the declaration of the CSayDlg class the prototype of the OnSayhelloButton() function.

☐ Write code inside the OnSayhellobutton() function so that it looks like this:

```
void CSayDlg::OnSayhelloButton()
{
// TODO: Add your control notification handler code here

//////////////////////////
// MY CODE STARTS HERE
//////////////////////////

MessageBox("Hello! This is my first Visual C++ program.");
```

```
//////////////////////
// MY CODE ENDS HERE
//////////////////////
```

}

☐ Save your work by selecting Save from the File menu of Visual C++.

NOTE

As you have just seen, when you use AppWizard to attach code to a control, you have to type your code inside an existing function. To make it easy for you to distinguish between code that Visual C++ wrote for you and code that you have to type, the following convention is used in this book:

Code that you have to write is presented in the following manner:

```
//////////////////////
// MY CODE STARTS HERE
//////////////////////


............................
... Your code appears here ...
............................


//////////////////////
// MY CODE ENDS HERE
//////////////////////
```

The MY CODE STARTS HERE and MY CODE ENDS HERE comments will help you to distinguish between code that Visual C++ wrote for you and code that you have to type or modify. Any code that is not enclosed within the MY CODE STARTS HERE and MY CODE ENDS HERE comments is code that was written by Visual C++.

The code you just typed is quite simple (one line):

```
MessageBox("Hello! This is my first Visual C++ program.");
```

It uses the MessageBox() function to display this message:

```
Hello! This is my first Visual C++ program.
```

You have finished attaching code to the Say Hello button. To see your code in action do the following:

☐ Select Build say.exe from the Project menu of Visual C++.

Visual C++ responds by compiling and linking the SAY application.

When Visual C++ finishes compiling and linking the application, you can run the application:

☐ Select Execute say.exe from the Project menu.

> *Visual C++ responds by executing the SAY application. The main window of the SAY application appears.*

☐ Click the Say Hello button.

> *The SAY application responds by displaying a Hello message box. The code you attached to the* Click *event of the Say Hello button is working!*

☐ Close the Hello message box by clicking its OK button.

Terminate the SAY application:

☐ Open the System menu of the SAY application by clicking the small icon at the top-left corner of the application window and select Close from the System menu. (Alternatively, you can press Alt+F4 on your keyboard.)

> *The SAY application responds by terminating.*

Attaching Code to the Exit Push Button

Recall that when the user clicks the Exit button, the SAY application should terminate. You'll now attach code to the Click event of the Exit button.

☐ Display the ClassWizard dialog box by selecting ClassWizard from the Project menu of Visual C++.

> *Visual C++ responds by displaying the ClassWizard dialog box.*

☐ Select the Message Maps tab at the top of the ClassWizard dialog box.

☐ Use ClassWizard to select the event:

CSayDlg -> IDC_EXIT_BUTTON -> BN_CLICKED

Then click the Add Function button.

☐ Name the new function OnExitButton().

NOTE

In the preceding steps you were instructed to use ClassWizard to select the event:

CSayDlg -> IDC_EXIT_BUTTON -> BN_CLICKED

What does this instruction mean? It is a shorthand instruction for the following series of steps:

☐ Select the CSayDlg class in the Class Name drop-down list of ClassWizard.

☐ Select IDC_EXIT_BUTTON inside the Object IDs list of ClassWizard.

☐ Select BN_CLICKED inside the Messages list of ClassWizard.

From now on, this shorthand notation will be used whenever you are instructed to make selections in ClassWizard.

Write the code of the OnExitButton() function:

☐ Click the Edit Code button of ClassWizard.

> *ClassWizard responds by opening the file SAYDLG.CPP, with the function* OnExitButton() *ready to be edited by you.*

☐ Write code inside the OnExitButton() function so that it looks like this:

```
void CSayDlg::OnExitButton()
{
// TODO: Add your control notification handler code here

/////////////////////////
// MY CODE STARTS HERE
/////////////////////////

// Close the dialog box (i.e. terminate the application).
OnOK();

////////////////////////
// MY CODE ENDS HERE
////////////////////////

}
```

☐ Save your work by selecting Save from the File menu of Visual C++.

The code you just typed is quite simple (one line):

```
OnOK();
```

This statement closes the dialog box of the SAY application (IDD_SAY_DIALOG) by calling the OnOK() member function of the CSayDlg class. You can call the OnOK() member function of the CSayDlg class from the OnExitButton() function, because the OnExitButton() function is also a member function of the CSayDlg class.

But wait a minute! Who wrote the code of the OnOK() function? The OnOK() function is a gift from Visual C++!

When AppWizard created for you the skeleton of the SAY application, it created for you the class CSayDlg and it associated this class with the IDD_SAY_DIALOG dialog box (the dialog box that serves as the main window of the application).

The `CSayDlg` class that AppWizard created for you is derived from the MFC class `CDialog`. Therefore, `CSayDlg` inherited the data members and member functions of the MFC class `CDialog`.

As implied by its name, the `CDialog` MFC class was specifically designed to let you manipulate dialog boxes. That is, the member functions of the `CDialog` class let you manipulate dialog boxes in almost any conceivable way. For example, one of the member functions of the `CDialog` class is the `OnOK()` function. The `OnOK()` function closes the dialog box.

Because the dialog box that is associated with the `CSayDlg` class is the IDD_SAY_DIALOG dialog box, and the IDD_SAY_DIALOG dialog box serves as the main window of the SAY application, calling the `OnOK()` function (that is, closing the IDD_SAY_DIALOG dialog box) causes the termination of the application.

You may ask how did we know that the `OnOK()` function is a member function of the `CDialog` class, and how did we know that the `OnOK()` member function closes the dialog box? In this book, you'll learn about the major member functions of various MFC classes. As you can imagine, closing a dialog box is an important function of the `CDialog` class, and you have to remember that this function is available.

To get information about all the member functions of the `CDialog` class, you can select Foundation Classes from the Help menu of Visual C++ and then use the Search dialog box to search for the keyword `CDialog`.

You have finished attaching code to the Exit button. The SAY application is now complete!

To see the code you attached to the Exit button in action do the following:

☐ Select Build say.exe from the Project menu of Visual C++.

☐ Select Execute say.exe from the Project menu.

The main window of the SAY application appears.

☐ Click the Exit button.

As expected, the SAY application terminates!

Final Words...

In this chapter you have learned the following:

- How to use AppWizard to create the project file and skeleton files of a dialog-based application (an application whose main window is a dialog box).
- How to use the visual tools of Visual C++ to visually design the dialog box of the application (for example, how to place controls inside the dialog box).
- How to use ClassWizard to attach code to the controls of the dialog box.

In Chapter 5, "Designing a Menu," you'll learn how to design a menu bar, how to attach a menu bar to the main window of the application, and how to attach code to the menu items of the menu bar.

5

Designing a Menu

In this chapter you'll learn how
to design a menu bar, how to
attach the menu bar to a dialog
box, and how to attach code to
the menu items of the menu bar.
The application that you'll write
in this chapter is a dialog-based
type—an application whose
main window is a dialog box.

The Beep Application

You'll now write the Beep application. The Beep application is an example of a dialog-based application that has a menu bar.

Before you start writing the Beep application yourself, execute the copy of it that resides in the \MVCPROG\EXE directory of the book's CD.

To execute the Beep application do the following:

☐ Select Run from the Start menu of Windows.

> *Windows responds by displaying the Run Application dialog box.*

☐ Type **X:\mvcProg\EXE\SAY.EXE** inside the Command Line box (where *X* represents the drive letter of your CD-ROM drive) and then click the OK button.

> *Windows responds by executing the Beep.EXE application. The window of Beep.EXE appears, as shown in Figure 5.1.*

Figure 5.1. The main window of the Beep application.

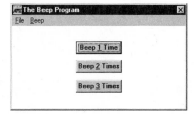

As you can see, the main window of the Beep application has three push buttons (Beep 1 Time, Beep 2 Times, and Beep 3 Times), and a menu bar with two pop-up menus (File and Beep).

The File and Beep pop-up menus of the Beep application are shown in Figures 5.2 and 5.3.

Figure 5.2. The File menu of the Beep application.

Figure 5.3. The Beep menu of the Beep application.

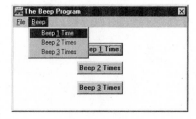

☐ Experiment with the three Beep buttons.

As you can hear, when you click one of the Beep buttons, the Beep application beeps the number of times stated on the button you clicked. For example, when you click the Beep 2 Times button, the Beep application beeps twice.

☐ Experiment with the three menu items of the Beep menu.

As you can hear, the three menu items of the Beep menu have the same functionality as the three Beep push buttons.

Terminate the Beep application:

☐ Select Exit from the File menu.

Now that you know what the Beep application should do, you can begin learning how to write it.

Creating the Project of the Beep Application

To create the project of the Beep application do the following:

☐ Start Visual C++ and close all the open windows that appear on the desktop of Visual C++ (if there are any).

☐ Select New from the File menu.

  Visual C++ responds by displaying the New dialog box.

☐ Select Project inside the New dialog box and then click the OK button of the New dialog box.

  Visual C++ responds by displaying the New Project dialog box.

☐ Set the project name to Beep.

☐ Set the project path to \MVCPROG\CH05\Beep\Beep.MAK.

Your New Project dialog box should now look like the one shown in Figure 5.4.

Figure 5.4. The New Project dialog box of the Beep.MAK project.

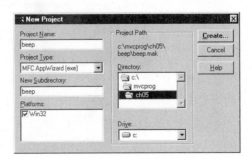

☐ Click the Create button of the New Project dialog box.

Visual C++ responds by displaying the AppWizard—Step 1 window.

☐ Set the Step 1 window as shown in Figure 5.5. As shown in Figure 5.5, the Beep.MAK project is set as a dialog-based application (an application whose main window is a dialog box), and U.S. English (APPWIZUS.DLL) is used as the language for the application's resources.

Figure 5.5. The AppWizard—Step 1 window for the Beep application.

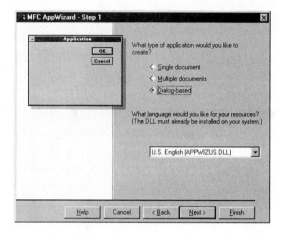

☐ Click the Next button of the Step 1 window.

Visual C++ responds by displaying the AppWizard—Step 2 of 4 window.

☐ Set the Step 2 of 4 window as shown in Figure 5.6. That is, place a checkmark inside the About Box check box (to incorporate an About dialog box into the application), and place a checkmark inside the Use 3D Controls check box (so that the application will use 3D controls). Also, set the title of the application to The Beep Program.

Figure 5.6. The AppWizard—Step 2 of 4 window for the Beep application.

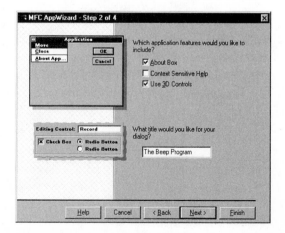

☐ Click the Next button of the Step 2 of 4 window.

    Visual C++ responds by displaying the AppWizard—Step 3 of 4 window.

☐ Set the Step 3 of 4 window as shown in Figure 5.7.

As shown in Figure 5.7, the project will be generated with comments, a Visual C++ makefile will be generated, and the application will use the MFC library from a DLL.

Figure 5.7. The
AppWizard—Step 3 of 4
window for the Beep
application.

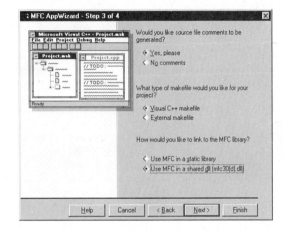

☐ Click the Next button of the Step 3 of 4 window.

    Visual C++ responds by displaying the AppWizard—Step 4 of 4 window, as shown in
    Figure 5.8.

Figure 5.8. The
AppWizard—Step 4 of 4
window for the Beep
application.

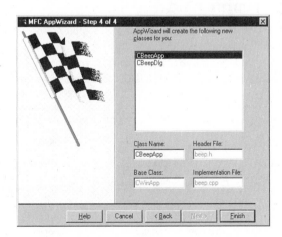

☐ Click the Finish button of the Step 4 of 4 window.

Visual C++ responds by displaying the New Project Information window, as shown in Figure 5.9.

Figure 5.9. The New Project Information window of the Beep.MAK project.

☐ Click the OK button of the New Project Information window.

Visual C++ responds by creating the project file and all the skeleton files of the application.

The Visual Implementation of the Dialog Box That Serves as the Main Window of the Beep Application

Because the Beep application is a dialog-based application, when you created the project and the skeleton files of the Beep application with AppWizard, AppWizard created for you a dialog box that serves as the main window of the application. AppWizard named this dialog box IDD_BEEP_DIALOG. You'll now customize the IDD_BEEP_DIALOG dialog box so that it looks like the one shown back in Figure 5.1.

☐ Double-click beep.rc inside the beep.mak window.

Visual C++ responds by displaying the beep.rc window.

☐ Double-click Dialog inside the beep.rc window and then double-click IDD_BEEP_DIALOG.

Visual C++ responds by displaying the IDD_BEEP_DIALOG dialog box in design mode.

☐ Delete the default controls that Visual C++ placed inside the dialog box (the OK button, the Cancel button, and the TODO: Place dialog controls here. text).

☐ Implement the dialog box according to the specifications in Table 5.1. When you finish implementing the dialog box, it should look like the one shown in Figure 5.10.

NOTE

In the preceding steps you were instructed to implement the IDD_BEEP_DIALOG dialog box by following a Properties table.

Following a Properties table to implement a dialog box is easy. Simply place the controls that are listed in the Properties table inside the dialog box and set the Properties of the controls as specified in the table. For example, Table 5.1 lists the properties of the first push button as follows:

Object	Property	Setting
Push button	ID	IDC_BEEP1_BUTTON
	Caption	Beep &1 Time

This means that you have to use the Tools window to place a push button control inside the dialog box, then double-click the push button control inside the dialog box to display the Properties window, and finally use the Properties window to set the ID property to IDC_BEEP1_BUTTON and the Caption property to Beep &1 Time.

The push button tool inside the Tools window is shown in Figure 5.11.

Table 5.1. The Properties table of the IDD_BEEP_DIALOG dialog box.

Object	Property	Setting
Dialog box	ID	IDD_BEEP_DIALOG
Push button	ID	IDC_BEEP1_BUTTON
	Caption	Beep &1 Time
Push button	ID	IDC_BEEP2_BUTTON
	Caption	Beep &2 Times
Push button	ID	IDC_BEEP3_BUTTON
	Caption	Beep &3 Times

☐ Save your work by selecting Save from the File menu.

You have completed the visual implementation of the IDD_BEEP_DIALOG dialog box. To see your visual design in action do the following:

☐ Select Build Beep.EXE from the Project menu.

Visual C++ responds by compiling and linking the Beep application.

Figure 5.10. The dialog box that serves as the main window of the Beep application (in design mode).

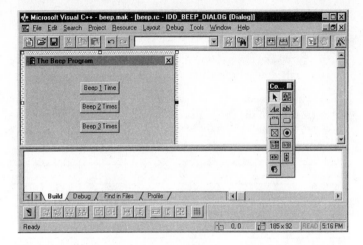

Figure 5.11. The push button tool inside the Tools window of Visual C++.

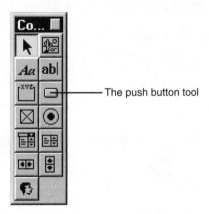

The push button tool

☐ Select Execute Beep.EXE from the Project menu.

Visual C++ responds by executing the Beep.EXE application. As expected, the IDD_BEEP_DIALOG dialog box that you designed appears as the main window of the application.

Terminate the Beep application:

☐ Click the × icon at the top-right corner of the Beep application window.

The Visual Implementation of the Menu Bar

Recall from Figure 5.1 that the menu bar of the Beep application should have two pop-up menus: File and Beep. You'll now design the menu bar of the Beep application.

To design a menu you have to use the visual tools of Visual C++ to work on the resource file of the application (BEEP.RC).

☐ Select beep.rc from the Window menu of Visual C++.

Visual C++ responds by displaying the beep.rc window. (See Figure 5.12.)

NOTE

If the beep.rc window is currently not open, then you have to do the following:

☐ Display the beep.mak window by selecting beep.mak from the Window menu of Visual C++.

☐ Double-click beep.rc inside the beep.mak window.

Visual C++ responds by displaying the beep.rc window.

Figure 5.12. The
beep.rc window.

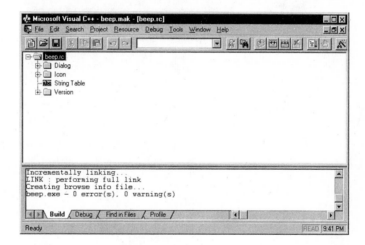

You'll now add a new resource (a menu) to the beep.rc file:

☐ Select New from the Resource menu of Visual C++.

Visual C++ responds by displaying the New Resource dialog box. (See Figure 5.13.)

Figure 5.13. The New
Resource dialog box.

☐ Select Menu from the list of resources and then click the OK button.

Visual C++ responds by creating a new blank menu and displaying this menu in design mode, ready to be edited by you. (See Figure 5.14.)

Figure 5.14. The new blank menu.

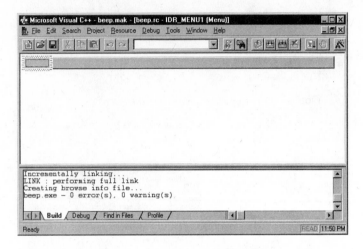

As you can see in Figure 5.14, the title of the Visual C++ window is currently

```
Microsoft Visual C++—beep.mak—[beep.rc-IDR_MENU1(Menu)]
```

Just by looking at this title you can tell that you are currently working on a menu whose ID is IDR_MENU1, and this menu is part of the resource file beep.rc, which is part of the project file beep.mak.

As you can see from Figure 5.14, the menu that Visual C++ created for you, IDR_MENU1, is currently blank. That is, the menu bar has no titles. Your objective is to customize this menu bar until it looks like the one shown back in Figures 5.2 and 5.3. Here is how you do that:

As you can see from Figure 5.14, the extreme-left side of the menu bar has a small blank rectangle that is surrounded by black dots. This rectangle represents the title of the extreme-left pop-up menu of the menu bar. You'll now set the title of the extreme-left pop-up menu to File:

☐ Double-click the rectangle at extreme-left side of the menu bar (that is, double-click the title of the extreme-left pop-up menu).

Visual C++ responds by displaying the Menu Item Properties dialog box. (See Figure 5.15.)

☐ Set the Caption field inside the Menu Item Properties dialog box to &File.

Notice that as you type inside the Caption field the title of the extreme-left pop-up menu of the menu bar changes accordingly. Your menu bar should now look like the one shown in Figure 5.16. That is, the title of the extreme-left pop-up menu is no longer blank; it is now set to File.

*Figure 5.15. The Menu
Item Properties dialog box.*

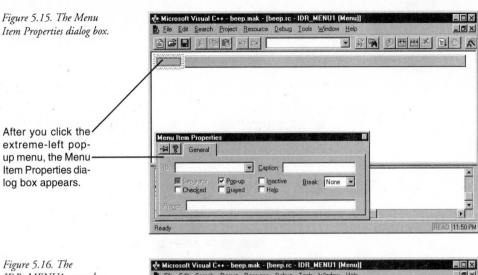

After you click the
extreme-left pop-
up menu, the Menu
Item Properties dia-
log box appears.

*Figure 5.16. The
IDR_MENU1 menu bar
after you've set the title of
the extreme-left pop-up
menu to File.*

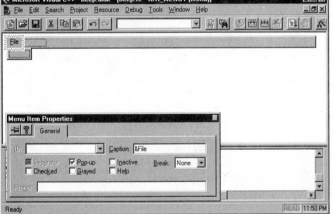

Note that the F in File is underlined. That's because you prefixed the F of File with the & character. The fact that the F is underlined in File means that during runtime when the user presses Alt+F on the keyboard, the File pop-up menu will open.

As shown in Figure 5.16, there is now a small rectangle under the File menu title. This rectangle represents the caption of the first menu item of the File menu. (If you don't see this rectangle on your screen, click the File title.)

Set the caption of the first item in the File pop-up menu:

☐ Double-click the blank rectangle under the File title.

> *Visual C++ responds by again displaying the Menu Item Properties dialog box, this time so that you can set the caption of the first menu item of the File pop-up menu.*

☐ Set the Caption field inside the Item Properties dialog box to E&xit.

Notice that as you type inside the Caption field, the caption of the first menu item of the File pop-up menu changes accordingly. Your IDR_MENU1 menu bar should now look like the one shown in Figure 5.17. That is, the caption of the first menu item in the File pop-up menu is no longer blank, but is now set to Exit.

Figure 5.17. The IDR_MENU1 menu bar after you've set the caption of the first menu item in the File pop-up menu to Exit.

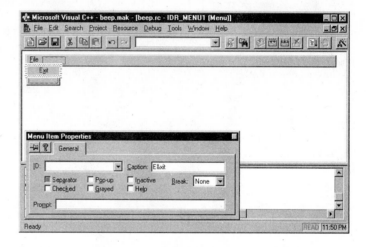

Note that the x in Exit is underlined. That's because you prefixed the x of Exit with the & character. The fact that the x is underlined in Exit means that during runtime whenever the File menu is open, pressing X on the keyboard will have the same effect as selecting the Exit menu item

As shown in Figure 5.17, besides the Caption field, the Menu Item Properties dialog box also has an ID field (for the ID of the menu item). However, you do not have to set the ID of the menu item. Visual C++ will automatically assign an ID to each menu item that you add to the pop-up menu.

To verify that Visual C++ automatically set the ID of the Exit menu item do the following:

☐ Double-click the Exit item of the File pop-up menu.

> *Visual C++ responds by again displaying the Menu Item Properties dialog box. (See Figure 5.18.) As shown in Figure 5.18, the ID field for the Exit menu item is ID_FILE_EXIT.*

The File pop-up menu is now complete! As shown back in Figure 5.2, the File pop-up menu in the Beep application should have only one item (Exit).

You'll now implement the Beep pop-up menu:

☐ Double-click the small rectangle on the menu bar that is located to the right of the File pop-up menu title.

> *Visual C++ responds by displaying the Menu Item Properties dialog box.*

*Figure 5.18. The ID of
the Exit menu item was
automatically set to
ID_FILE_EXIT by
Visual C++.*

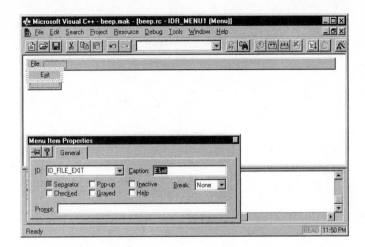

☐ Set the Caption field inside the Item Properties dialog box to &Beep.

Your IDR_MENU1 menu bar should now look like the one shown in Figure 5.19.

*Figure 5.19. The
IDR_MENU1 menu bar
after you've set the title of
the second pop-up menu to
Beep.*

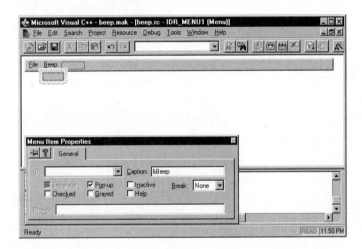

Note that the B in Beep is underlined. That's because you prefixed the B of Beep with the & character. The fact that the B in Beep is underlined means that during runtime when the user presses Alt+B
on the keyboard, the Beep pop-up menu will open.

As shown in Figure 5.19, there is now a small rectangle under the Beep menu title. This rectangle
represents the caption of the first menu item of the Beep menu. (If you don't see this rectangle on
your screen, click the Beep title.)

Set the caption of the first item in the Beep pop-up menu:

☐ Double-click the blank rectangle under the Beep title.

Visual C++ responds by again displaying the Menu Item Properties dialog box, this time so that you can set the caption of the first menu item of the Beep pop-up menu.

☐ Set the Caption field inside the Item Properties dialog box to Beep &1 Time.

Your IDR_MENU1 bar menu should now look like the one shown in Figure 5.20. That is, the caption of the first menu item in the Beep pop-up menu is no longer blank, it is now set to Beep 1 Time.

Figure 5.20. The IDR_MENU1 menu bar after you've set the caption of the first item in the Beep pop-up menu to Beep 1 Time.

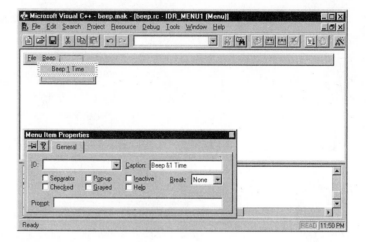

☐ Repeat the preceding steps to add another menu item to the Beep menu. Set the caption of this menu item to Beep 2 Times.

☐ Repeat the preceding steps to add another menu item to the Beep menu. Set the caption of this menu item to Beep 3 Times.

The Beep pop-up menu should now look like the one shown in Figure 5.21.

Figure 5.21. The Beep pop-up menu after you've added to it three menu items.

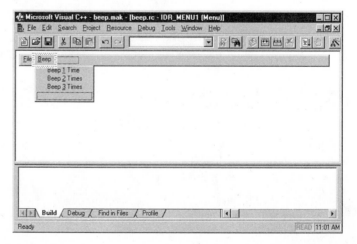

The IDR_MENU1 menu bar is now complete! As stated earlier, you do not have to set the IDs of the menu items. Visual C++ automatically sets the IDs of the menu items according to the caption of each menu item. For example, to see the ID that Visual C++ assigned to the Beep 2 Times menu item of the Beep pop-up menu do the following:

☐ If the Beep pop-up menu is not open, open it by clicking the Beep menu title.

☐ Double-click the Beep 2 Times menu item.

> *Visual C++ responds by displaying the Menu Item Properties dialog box for the Beep 2 Times menu item. (See Figure 5.22.) As you can see, the ID that Visual C++ assigned to the Beep 2 Times menu item is ID_BEEP_BEEP2TIMES.*

Figure 5.22. The ID of the Beep 2 Times menu item was automatically set to ID_BEEP_BEEP2TIMES by Visual C++.

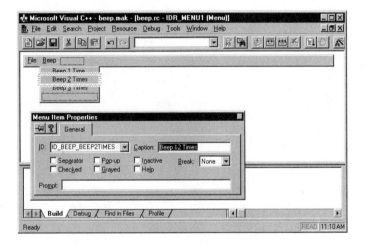

Note that if you wish you can change the ID of the menu item by typing your own ID inside the ID field. However, in most cases, the ID that Visual C++ assigns makes sense. For example, the ID_BEEP_BEEP2TIMES ID implies that this ID belongs to the Beep 2 Times menu item that is part of the Beep pop-up menu.

☐ Save your work by selecting Save from the File menu of Visual C++.

Associating the IDR_MENU1 Menu with a Class

In the previous section you created and designed the IDR_MENU1 menu. You'll now associate the IDR_MENU1 menu with a class.

You'll associate the IDR_MENU1 menu with the CBeepDlg class. The CBeepDlg class is the class that is associated with the IDD_BEEP_DIALOG dialog box. Therefore, the code that you will later attach to the menu items of the IDR_MENU1 menu bar will be able to access member functions and data members that are associated with the dialog box.

To associate the IDR_MENU1 menu with the CBeepDlg class do the following:

☐ Make sure that the IDR_MENU1 menu is currently displayed. That is, if the IDR_MENU1 menu is currently not displayed, display it by selecting beep.rc—IDR_MENU1 [Menu] from the Window menu of Visual C++.

☐ Select ClassWizard from the Project menu of Visual C++.

Visual C++ responds by displaying the Add Class dialog box. (See Figure 5.23.)

Figure 5.23. The Add Class dialog box.

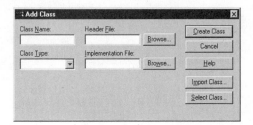

The reason that Visual C++ displays the Add Class dialog box is that the IDR_MENU1 menu is currently not associated with any class.

☐ Click the Select Class button inside the Add Class dialog box.

Visual C++ responds by displaying the Select Class dialog box. (See Figure 5.24.)

Figure 5.24. The Select Class dialog box.

☐ Select the CBeepDlg class from the class list and then click the OK button.

Visual C++ responds by displaying the ClassWizard dialog box. (See Figure 5.25.)

☐ Close the ClassWizard dialog box by clicking its OK button.

The IDR_MENU1 menu is now associated with the CBeepDlg class.

Figure 5.25. The
ClassWizard dialog box.

Attaching the IDR_MENU1 Menu to the Main Window of the Application

In the previous sections you designed the IDR_MENU1 menu and you associated it with the `CBeepDlg` class. In this section you'll attach the IDR_MENU1 menu to the dialog box that serves as the main window of the Beep application (that is, to the IDD_BEEP_DIALOG dialog box). Here is how you do that:

☐ Display the IDD_BEEP_DIALOG dialog box by selecting
beep.rc—IDD_BEEP_DIALOG [Dialog] from the Window menu of Visual C++.

> *Visual C++ responds by displaying the IDD_BEEP_DIALOG dialog box in design mode.*
> *(See Figure 5.26.)*

Figure 5.26. The
IDD_BEEP_DIALOG
dialog box (in design
mode).

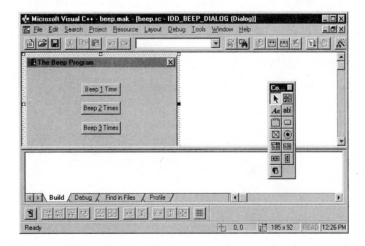

☐ Double-click inside a free area inside the IDD_BEEP_DIALOG dialog box. (That is, double-click inside the IDD_BEEP_DIALOG dialog box in any area that is not occupied by a control.)

Visual C++ responds by displaying the Dialog Properties dialog box. (See Figure 5.27.)

Figure 5.27. The Dialog Properties dialog box for the IDD_BEEP_DIALOG dialog box.

As you can see, the Dialog Properties dialog box includes a Menu drop-down list (under the Caption field). You have to use this drop-down list to select the menu that you want to attach to the dialog box:

☐ Click the arrow of the Menu drop-down list and select the IDR_MENU1 menu.

The Dialog Properties dialog box should now look like the one shown in Figure 5.28.

Figure 5.28. The Dialog Properties dialog box after you've set the Menu drop-down list to IDR_MENU1.

☐ Save your work by selecting Save from the File menu of Visual C++.

That's it! The IDR_MENU1 menu that you designed is now attached to the IDD_BEEP_DIALOG box. To see the IDR_MENU1 menu in action do the following:

☐ Select Build Beep.EXE from the Project menu.

Visual C++ responds by compiling and linking the Beep application.

☐ Select Execute Beep.EXE from the Project menu.

Visual C++ responds by executing the Beep.EXE application. As you can see, the main window of the Beep application now has a menu bar—the menu bar that you designed. (Refer to Figures 5.2 and 5.3.)

☐ Experiment with the menu items in the File menu and Beep menu.

Of course, when you select any of the menu items, nothing happens. That's because you have not yet attached any code to the menu items. You'll do that in the following sections.

☐ Terminate the Beep application by clicking the × icon on the top-right corner of the application's main window.

Attaching Code to the Exit Menu Item of the File Menu

When the user selects Exit from the File menu, the Beep application should terminate. You'll now attach code to the COMMAND event of the Exit menu item. The COMMAND event of a menu item occurs when the user selects the menu item.

☐ Display the IDR_MENU1 menu by selecting beep.rc—IDR_MENU1 [Menu] from the Window menu of Visual C++.

☐ Display the ClassWizard dialog box by selecting ClassWizard from the Project menu of Visual C++.

NOTE

If after you select ClassWizard from the Project Menu the Add Class dialog box appears instead of the ClassWizard window, you have to do the following:

☐ Click the Select Class button inside the Add Class dialog box.

Visual C++ responds by displaying the Select Class dialog box. (See Figure 5.24.)

☐ Select the CBeepDlg class from the class list and then click the OK button.

Visual C++ responds by displaying the ClassWizard dialog box. (See Figure 5.25.)

☐ Make sure the Message Maps tab at the top of ClassWizard's dialog box is selected.

☐ Use ClassWizard to select the event:

CBeepDlg -> ID_FILE_EXIT -> COMMAND

Then click the Add Function button.

☐ Name the new function OnFileExit().

NOTE

In the preceding steps, before you used ClassWizard you were instructed to display the IDR_MENU1 menu. That was because in the preceding steps you were attaching a function to the ID_FILE_EXIT menu item of the IDR_MENU1 menu. If you do not display the IDR_MENU1 menu prior to using ClassWizard, ClassWizard will not list the IDs of the IDR_MENU1 menu items inside the ClassWizard window.

To write the code of the OnFileExit() function do the following:

☐ Click the Edit Code button of ClassWizard.

> *ClassWizard responds by opening the file BeepDlg.CPP, with the function* OnFileExit() *ready to be edited by you.*

☐ Write code inside the OnFileExit() function so that it looks like this:

```
void CBeepDlg::OnFileExit()
{
// TODO: Add your command handler code here

//////////////////////////
// MY CODE STARTS HERE //
//////////////////////////

// Close the dialog box (terminate the program).
OnOK();

//////////////////////////
// MY CODE ENDS HERE    //
//////////////////////////

}
```

☐ Save your work by selecting Save from the File menu of Visual C++.

The code you typed inside the OnFileExit() function closes the dialog box by calling the OnOK() member function of the CBeepDlg class:

```
// Close the dialog box (terminate the program).
OnOK();
```

Note that the reason you can call the OnOK() member function of the CBeepDlg class from the OnFileExit() function is that the OnFileExit() function is also a member function of the CBeepDlg class. That is, because earlier you associated the IDR_MENU1 menu with the CBeepDlg class, the functions that you are attaching to the menu items of the IDR_MENU1 menu are member functions of the CBeepDlg class.

To see the code you attached to the Exit menu item in action do the following:

☐ Select Build Beep.EXE from the Project menu.

> *Visual C++ responds by compiling and linking the Beep application.*

☐ Select Execute Beep.EXE from the Project menu.

> *Visual C++ responds by executing the Beep.EXE application.*

☐ Select Exit from the File menu of the Beep application.

> *As expected, the Beep application terminates itself.*

Attaching Code to the Beep 1 Time Menu Item

Recall that when the user selects Beep 1 Time from the Beep menu, the Beep application should beep one time. You'll now attach code to the COMMAND event of the Beep 1 Time menu item.

☐ Display the IDR_MENU1 menu by selecting beep.rc—IDR_MENU1 [Menu] from the Window menu of Visual C++.

☐ Display the ClassWizard dialog box by selecting ClassWizard from the Project menu of Visual C++.

☐ Make sure that the Message Maps tab at the top of ClassWizard's dialog box is selected.

☐ Use ClassWizard to select the event:

```
CBeepDlg -> ID_BEEP_BEEP1TIME -> COMMAND
```

Then click the Add Function button.

☐ Name the new function OnBeepBeep1time().

To write the code of the OnBeepBeep1time() function do the following:

☐ Click the Edit Code button of ClassWizard.

> *ClassWizard responds by opening the file BeepDlg.CPP, with the function OnBeepBeep1time() ready to be edited by you.*

☐ Write code inside the OnBeepBeep1time() function so that it looks like this:

```
void CBeepDlg::OnBeepBeep1time()
{
// TODO: Add your command handler code here

/////////////////////////
// MY CODE STARTS HERE //
/////////////////////////

// Beep.
MessageBeep((WORD)-1);

/////////////////////////
// MY CODE ENDS HERE   //
/////////////////////////

}
```

☐ Save your work by selecting Save from the File menu of Visual C++.

The code that you typed inside the OnBeepBeep1time() function is made of a single statement:

```
MessageBeep((WORD)-1);
```

This statement calls the MessageBeep() function. Therefore, whenever the user selects Beep 1 Time from the Beep menu, the application will beep.

To hear the code that you attached to the Beep 1 Time menu item in action do the following:

☐ Select Build Beep.EXE from the Project menu.

   Visual C++ responds by compiling and linking the Beep application.

☐ Select Execute Beep.EXE from the Project menu.

   Visual C++ responds by executing the Beep.EXE application.

☐ Select Beep 1 Time from the File menu of the Beep application.

   As expected, the Beep application beeps.

☐ Terminate the Beep application by selecting Exit from the File menu.

Attaching Code to the Beep 2 Times and Beep 3 Times Menu Items

Recall that when the user selects Beep 2 Times from the Beep menu, the Beep application should beep twice, and when the user selects Beep 3 Times from the Beep menu, the Beep application should beep three times. You'll now attach code to the COMMAND events of the Beep 2 Times and Beep 3 Times menu items.

To attach code to the COMMAND event of the Beep 2 Times menu item do the following:

☐ Display the IDR_MENU1 menu by selecting beep.rc—IDR_MENU1 [Menu] from the Window menu of Visual C++.

☐ Display the ClassWizard dialog box by selecting ClassWizard from the Project menu of Visual C++.

☐ Make sure that the Message Maps tab at the top of ClassWizard's dialog box is selected.

☐ Use ClassWizard to select the event:

```
CBeepDlg -> ID_BEEP_BEEP2TIMES -> COMMAND
```

Then click the Add Function button.

☐ Name the new function OnBeepBeep2times().

To write the code of the OnBeepBeep2times() function do the following:

☐ Click the Edit Code button of ClassWizard.

   ClassWizard responds by opening the file BeepDlg.CPP, with the function
   OnBeepBeep2times() ready to be edited by you.

☐ Write code inside the OnBeepBeep2times() function so that it looks like this:

```
void CBeepDlg::OnBeepBeep2times()
{
// TODO: Add your command handler code here
```

```
/////////////////////////
// MY CODE STARTS HERE //
/////////////////////////

// Beep.
MessageBeep((WORD)-1);

// 500 milliseconds delay.
DWORD start = GetCurrentTime();
while ( GetCurrentTime() < start + 500 );

// Beep.
MessageBeep((WORD)-1);

/////////////////////////
// MY CODE ENDS HERE    //
/////////////////////////

}
```

☐ Save your work by selecting Save from the File menu of Visual C++.

> *As you can see, the code of the* OnBeepBeep2times() *function causes the PC to beep two times, with a 500-millisecond delay between the beeps.*

To attach code to the COMMAND event of the Beep 3 Times menu item do the following:

☐ Display the IDR_MENU1 menu by selecting beep.rc—IDR_MENU1 [Menu] from the Window menu of Visual C++.

☐ Display the ClassWizard dialog box by selecting ClassWizard from the Project menu of Visual C++.

☐ Make sure that the Message Maps tab at the top of ClassWizard's dialog box is selected.

☐ Use ClassWizard to select the event:

```
CBeepDlg -> ID_BEEP_BEEP3TIMES -> COMMAND
```

Then click the Add Function button.

☐ Name the new function OnBeepBeep3times().

To write the code of the OnBeepBeep3times() function do the following:

☐ Click the Edit Code button of ClassWizard.

> *ClassWizard responds by opening the file BeepDlg.CPP, with the function* OnBeepBeep3times() *ready to be edited by you.*

☐ Write code inside the OnBeepBeep3times() function so that it looks like this:

```
void CBeepDlg::OnBeepBeep3times()
{
// TODO: Add your command handler code here

/////////////////////////
// MY CODE STARTS HERE //
/////////////////////////
```

```
// Beep.
MessageBeep((WORD)-1);

// 500 milliseconds delay.
DWORD start = GetCurrentTime();
while ( GetCurrentTime() < start + 500 );

// Beep.
MessageBeep((WORD)-1);

// 500 milliseconds delay.
start = GetCurrentTime();
while ( GetCurrentTime() < start + 500 );
// Beep.
MessageBeep((WORD)-1);

/////////////////////////
// MY CODE ENDS HERE    //
/////////////////////////

}
```

☐ Save your work by selecting Save from the File menu of Visual C++.

> *As you can see, the code of the* OnBeepBeep3times() *function causes the PC to beep three times, with a 500-millisecond delay between the beeps.*

To hear in action the code that you attached to the Beep 2 Times and Beep 3 Times menu items do the following:

☐ Select Build Beep.EXE from the Project menu.

> *Visual C++ responds by compiling and linking the Beep application.*

☐ Select Execute Beep.EXE from the Project menu.

> *Visual C++ responds by executing the Beep.EXE application.*

☐ Experiment with the menu items of the Beep menu and verify that they work properly.

☐ Terminate the Beep application by selecting Exit from the File menu.

Attaching Code to the Push Buttons of the Beep Application

The last thing you have to do to complete the Beep application is attach code to the three Beep push buttons. Recall that the three Beep push buttons should have the same functionality as their corresponding Beep menu items.

To attach code to the Click event of the Beep 1 Time push button do the following:

☐ Display the ClassWizard dialog box by selecting ClassWizard from the Project menu of Visual C++.

☐ Select the Message Maps tab at the top of ClassWizard's dialog box.

☐ Use ClassWizard to select the event:

```
CBeepDlg -> IDC_BEEP1_BUTTON -> BN_CLICKED
```

Then click the Add Function button.

☐ Name the new function `OnBeep1Button()`.

To write the code of the `OnBeep1Button()` function do the following:

☐ Click the Edit Code button of ClassWizard.

> *ClassWizard responds by opening the file BeepDlg.CPP, with the function `OnBeep1Button()` ready to be edited by you.*

☐ Write code inside the `OnBeep1Button()` function so that it looks like this:

```
void CBeepDlg::OnBeep1Button()
{
// TODO: Add your control notification handler code here

/////////////////////////
// MY CODE STARTS HERE //
/////////////////////////

// Beep one time.
OnBeepBeep1time();

/////////////////////////
// MY CODE ENDS HERE    //
/////////////////////////

}
```

☐ Save your work by selecting Save from the File menu of Visual C++.

The code that you typed inside the `OnBeep1Button()` function calls the `OnBeepBeep1time()` function that you wrote earlier:

```
OnBeepBeep1time();
```

Therefore, clicking the Beep 1 Time push button produces the same result as selecting Beep 1 Time from the Beep menu. Note that the reason you can call the `OnBeepBeep1time()` function from the `OnBeep1Button()` function is that both `OnBeepBeep1time()` and `OnBeep1Button()` are member functions of the `CBeepDlg` class.

To attach code to the Click event of the Beep 2 Times push button do the following:

☐ Display the ClassWizard dialog box by selecting ClassWizard from the Project menu of Visual C++.

☐ Select the Message Maps tab at the top of ClassWizard's dialog box.

☐ Use ClassWizard to select the event:

```
CBeepDlg -> IDC_BEEP2_BUTTON -> BN_CLICKED
```

Then click the Add Function button.

☐ Name the new function `OnBeep2Button()`.

To write the code of the `OnBeep2Button()` function do the following:

☐ Click the Edit Code button of ClassWizard.

> *ClassWizard responds by opening the file BeepDlg.CPP, with the function `OnBeep2Button()` ready to be edited by you.*

☐ Write code inside the `OnBeep2Button()` function so that it looks like this:

```
void CBeepDlg::OnBeep2Button()
{
// TODO: Add your control notification handler code here

//////////////////////////
// MY CODE STARTS HERE //
//////////////////////////

// Beep two times.
OnBeepBeep2times();

//////////////////////////
// MY CODE ENDS HERE    //
//////////////////////////

}
```

☐ Save your work by selecting Save from the File menu of Visual C++.

The code you typed inside the `OnBeep2Button()` function calls the `OnBeepBeep2times()` function that you wrote earlier:

```
OnBeepBeep2times();
```

Therefore, clicking the Beep 2 Times push button produces the same result as selecting Beep 2 Times from the Beep menu. Note that the reason you can call the `OnBeepBeep2times()` function from the `OnBeep2Button()` function is that both `OnBeepBeep2times()` and `OnBeep2Button()` are member functions of the `CBeepDlg` class.

To attach code to the Click event of the Beep 3 Times push button do the following:

☐ Display the ClassWizard dialog box by selecting ClassWizard from the Project menu of Visual C++.

☐ Select the Message Maps tab at the top of ClassWizard's dialog box.

☐ Use ClassWizard to select the event:

```
CBeepDlg -> IDC_BEEP3_BUTTON -> BN_CLICKED
```

Then click the Add Function button.

☐ Name the new function `OnBeep3Button()`.

To write the code of the OnBeep3Button() function do the following:

☐ Click the Edit Code button of ClassWizard.

ClassWizard responds by opening the file BeepDlg.CPP, with the function OnBeep3Button() ready to be edited by you.

☐ Write code inside the OnBeep3Button() function so that it looks like this:

```
void CBeepDlg::OnBeep3Button()
{
// TODO: Add your control notification handler code here
/////////////////////////////
// MY CODE STARTS HERE //
/////////////////////////////

// Beep three times.
OnBeepBeep3times();

/////////////////////////////
// MY CODE ENDS HERE    //
/////////////////////////////

}
```

☐ Save your work by selecting Save from the File menu of Visual C++.

The code you typed inside the OnBeep3Button() function calls the OnBeepBeep3times() function that you wrote earlier:

```
OnBeepBeep3times();
```

Therefore, clicking the Beep 3 Times push button produces the same result as selecting Beep 3 Times from the Beep menu. Note that the reason you can call the OnBeepBeep3times() function from the OnBeep3Button() function is that both OnBeepBeep3times() and OnBeep3Button() are member functions of the CBeepDlg class.

The Beep application is now complete! To hear in action the code that you attached to the three Beep push buttons do the following:

☐ Select Build Beep.EXE from the Project menu.

Visual C++ responds by compiling and linking the Beep application.

☐ Select Execute Beep.EXE from the Project menu.

Visual C++ responds by executing the Beep.EXE application.

☐ Experiment with the three Beep push buttons.

As expected, clicking the three Beep push buttons has the same effect as selecting the corresponding Beep menu items from the Beep menu.

☐ Terminate the Beep application by selecting Exit from the File menu.

6

Edit Boxes

In this chapter you'll learn how to incorporate edit boxes in a dialog box. As you know, edit boxes serve an important role in the Windows user-interface mechanism. The application that you'll write in this chapter is a dialog-based type—an application in which a dialog box serves as the main window of the application.

The MyEdit Application

Before you start writing the MyEdit application yourself, execute the copy of it that resides in the \MVCPROG\EXE directory of the book's CD.

To execute the MyEdit application do the following:

☐ Execute the X:\MVCPROG\EXE\MyEdit.EXE program (where *X* represents the drive letter of your CD-ROM drive).

> *Windows responds by executing the MyEdit.EXE application. The window of MyEdit.EXE appears, as shown in Figure 6.1.*

Figure 6.1. The window of the MyEdit application.

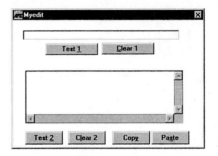

☐ Click the Test 1 button.

> *MyEdit responds by placing the text* This is a test. *inside the upper edit box. (See Figure 6.2.)*

Figure 6.2. The window of the MyEdit application after you click the Test 1 button.

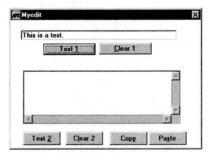

☐ Click the Clear 1 button.

> *MyEdit responds by clearing the contents of the upper edit box.*

☐ Click inside the upper edit box, and then type something in it.

As you can see, the edit box behaves as you expect an edit box to behave in a Windows program.

☐ Click the Test 2 button.

> *MyEdit responds by placing the text* You clicked the Test 2 button. *inside the lower edit box. (See Figure 6.3.)*

Figure 6.3. The window of
the MyEdit application
after you click the Test 2
button.

☐ Click the Clear 2 button.

MyEdit responds by clearing the contents of the lower edit box.

The MyEdit program also implements the Copy and Paste features. You'll learn how to use (and implement) these features later in this chapter.

Now that you know what the MyEdit application should do, you can begin to write it.

Creating the Project of the MyEdit Application

To create the project of the MyEdit application do the following:

☐ Start Visual C++ and close all the open windows that appear inside the desktop of Visual C++ (if there are any).

☐ Select New from the File menu.

Visual C++ responds by displaying the New dialog box.

☐ Select Project inside the New dialog box and then click the OK button of the New dialog box.

Visual C++ responds by displaying the New Project dialog box.

☐ Set the project name to MyEdit.

☐ Set the project path to \MVCPROG\CH06\MyEdit\MyEdit.MAK.

Your New Project dialog box should now look like the one shown in Figure 6.4.

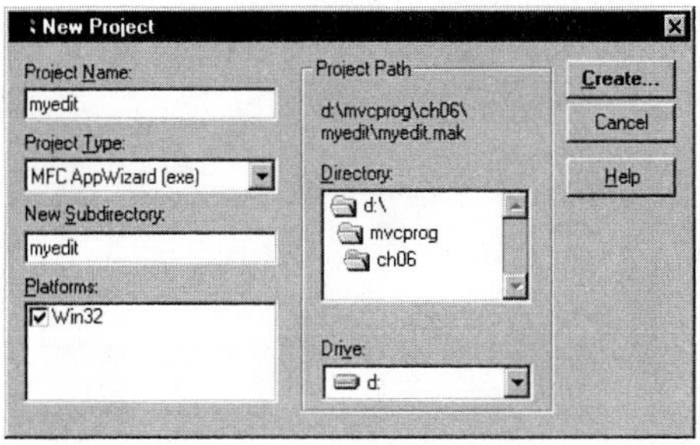

Figure 6.4. The New
Project dialog box of the
MyEdit.MAK project.

☐ Click the Create button of the New Project dialog box.

Visual C++ responds by displaying the AppWizard—Step 1 window.

☐ Set the Step 1 window as shown in Figure 6.5. As shown in Figure 6.5, the MyEdit.MAK project is set as a dialog-based application, and U.S. English (APPWIZUS.DLL) is used as the language for the MyEdit.MAK project's resources.

Figure 6.5. The AppWizard—Step 1 window of the MyEdit.MAK project.

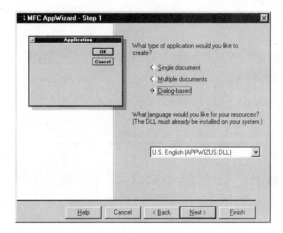

☐ Click the Next button of the Step 1 window.

Visual C++ responds by displaying the AppWizard—Step 2 of 4 window.

☐ Set the Step 2 of 4 window as shown in Figure 6.6. That is, place a checkmark inside the About Box check box (to incorporate an About dialog box into the application), and place a checkmark inside the Use 3D Controls check box (so that the application will use 3D controls).

Figure 6.6. The AppWizard—Step 2 of 4 window of the MyEdit.MAK project.

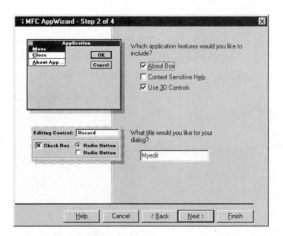

☐ Click the Next button of the Step 2 of 4 window.

> *Visual C++ responds by displaying the AppWizard—Step 3 of 4 window.*

☐ Set the Step 3 of 4 window as shown in Figure 6.7.

As shown in Figure 6.7, the project will be generated with comments, a Visual C++ makefile will be generated, and the application will use the MFC library from a DLL.

Figure 6.7. The AppWizard—Step 3 of 4 window of the MyEdit.MAK project.

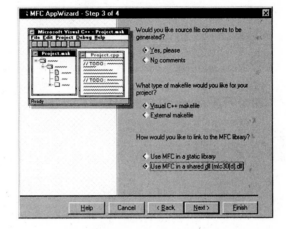

☐ Click the Next button of the Step 3 of 4 window.

> *Visual C++ responds by displaying the AppWizard—Step 4 of 4 window, as shown in Figure 6.8.*

Figure 6.8. The AppWizard—Step 4 of 4 window of the MyEdit.MAK project.

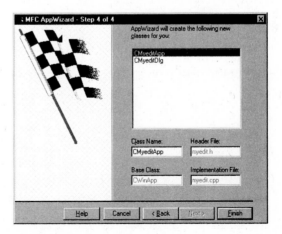

☐ Click the Finish button of the Step 4 of 4 window.

> *Visual C++ responds by displaying the New Project Information window, as shown in Figure 6.9.*

Figure 6.9. The New Project Information window of the MyEdit.MAK project.

☐ Click the OK button of the New Project Information window.

Visual C++ responds by creating the project file and all the skeleton files of the application.

The Visual Implementation of the MyEdit Application

Because the MyEdit application is a dialog-based application, when you created the project and the skeleton files of the MyEdit application with AppWizard, AppWizard created for you a dialog box that serves as the main window of the application. AppWizard named this dialog box IDD_MYEDIT_DIALOG. You'll now customize the IDD_MYEDIT_DIALOG dialog box.

☐ Select MyEdit.MAK from the Window menu to display the MyEdit.MAK window.

Visual C++ responds by displaying the MyEdit.MAK window.

☐ Double-click MyEdit.rc inside the MyEdit.MAK window.

Visual C++ responds by displaying the MyEdit.rc window.

☐ Double-click Dialog inside the MyEdit.rc window and then double-click IDD_MYEDIT_DIALOG.

Visual C++ responds by displaying the IDD_MYEDIT_DIALOG dialog box in design mode.

☐ Implement the dialog box according to the specifications in Table 6.1. When you finish implementing the dialog box, it should look like the one shown in Figure 6.10.

Table 6.1. The Properties table of the IDD_MYEDIT_DIALOG dialog box.

Object	Property	Setting
Dialog box	ID	IDD_MYEDIT_DIALOG
Edit box	ID	IDC_EDIT1

Object	Property	Setting
Push button	ID	IDC_TEST1_BUTTON
	Caption	Test &1
Push button	ID	IDC_CLEAR1_BUTTON
	Caption	&Clear 1

Figure 6.10. The dialog box that serves as the main window of the MyEdit program (in design mode).

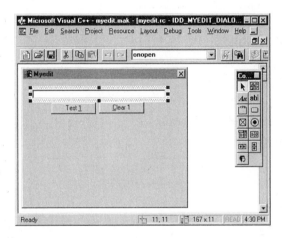

NOTE

Table 6.1 instructs you to place an edit box control inside the dialog box. The edit box tool inside the Tools window is shown in Figure 6.11.

Figure 6.11. The edit box and push button tools inside the Tools window of Visual C++.

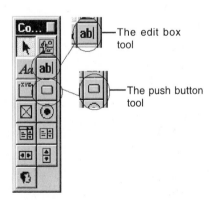

Attaching Variables to the Dialog Box of the MyEdit Program

You'll now attach a variable called m_Edit1 to the edit box IDC_EDIT1.

☐ Select ClassWizard from the Project menu.

> *Visual C++ responds by displaying the ClassWizard dialog box.*

☐ Select the Member Variables tab.

☐ Make sure the Class Name is set to CMyeditDlg.

☐ Click the IDC_EDIT1 item.

☐ Click the Add Variable button.

> *Visual C++ responds by displaying the Add Member Variable dialog box.*

☐ Set the member variable name to m_Edit1, set the category to Value, set the variable type to CString, and finally, click the OK button. (See Figure 6.12.)

> *Visual C++ responds by adding the m_Edit1 variable to the CMyediDlg class. Your ClassWizard dialog box should now look like the one shown in Figure 6.13.*

Figure 6.12. Attaching a variable (m_Edit1) to the IDC_EDIT1 edit box.

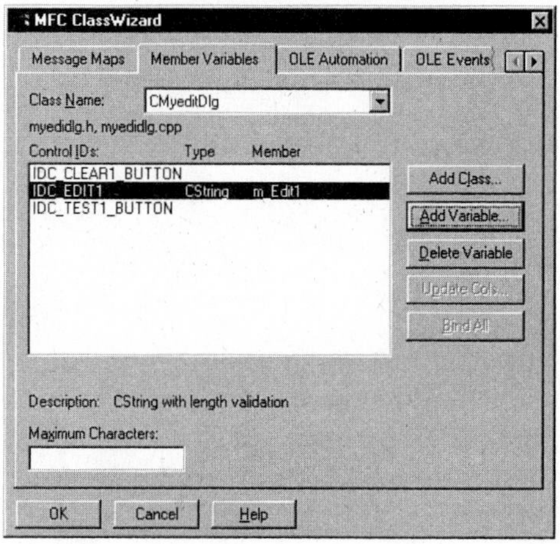

Figure 6.13. The ClassWizard dialog box after you attach the variable m_Edit1 to the IDC_EDIT1 edit box.

☐ To save your work, select Save from the File menu.

In the preceding steps, you attached the variable m_Edit1 to the IDC_EDIT1 edit box. This is necessary because, as you'll see when you'll write the code of the application, you'll use this variable to set the contents of the IDC_EDIT1 edit box.

To see your visual design in action do the following:

☐ Select Build MyEdit.EXE from the Project menu.

> *Visual C++ responds by compiling and linking the MyEdit application.*

☐ Select Execute MyEdit.EXE from the Project menu.

> *Visual C++ responds by executing the MyEdit.EXE application.*

As expected, the IDD_MYEDIT_DIALOG dialog box that you designed appears as the main window of the application.

☐ Click the icon that appears on the upper-left corner of the MyEdit application window, and select About from the System menu that pops up.

> *MyEdit responds by displaying the About dialog box.*

☐ Click the OK button of the About dialog box to close the About dialog box.

☐ Click the Test 1 and Clear 1 buttons, and notice that nothing happens. This of course makes sense because you have not yet attached any code to these buttons.

☐ Click the icon that appears on the upper-left corner of the MyEdit application, and select Close from the System menu that pops up.

> *MyEdit responds by terminating itself.*

Attaching Code to the *BN_CLICKED* Events of the Test 1 and Clear 1 Buttons

Recall that when the user clicks the Test 1 button, the MyEdit program should place text inside the edit box. You'll now attach code to the Click event (BN_CLICKED) of the Test 1 button.

☐ Display the ClassWizard dialog box by selecting ClassWizard from the Project menu of Visual C++.

☐ Select the Message Maps tab at the top of ClassWizard's dialog box.

☐ Use ClassWizard to select the event:

```
CMyEditDlg -> IDC_TEST1_BUTTON -> BN_CLICKED
```

Then click the Add Function button.

☐ Accept the name OnTest1Button() that Visual C++ suggests.

To write the code of the OnTest1Button() function do the following:

☐ Click the Edit Code button of ClassWizard.

ClassWizard responds by opening the file MyEdiDlg.CPP, with the function OnTest1Button() *ready to be edited by you.*

☐ Write code inside the OnTest1Button() function so that it looks like this:

```
void CMyeditDlg::OnTest1Button()
{
// TODO: Add your control notification
// handler code here

/////////////////////////
// MY CODE STARTS HERE
/////////////////////////

// Set the variable of the IDC_EDIT1 edit box.
m_Edit1 = "This is a test.";

// Update the screen.
UpdateData (FALSE);

/////////////////////////
// MY CODE ENDS HERE
/////////////////////////

}
```

☐ Save your work by selecting Save from the File menu of Visual C++.

The code you typed updates the m_Edit1 variable (the variable you attached to the IDC_EDIT dialog box):

```
m_Edit1 = "This is a test.";
```

However, updating the variable m_Edit1 will *not* cause the program to display the contents of the m_Edit1 variable inside the edit box. That is, to actually transfer the contents of the m_Edit1 variable to the IDC_EDIT1 control, you need to use the UpdateData() function with FALSE as its parameter:

```
UpdateData (FALSE);
```

You'll now attach code to the BN_CLICKED event of the Clear 1 button:

☐ Use ClassWizard (from the Project menu) to select the event:

```
CMyEditDlg -> IDC_CLEAR1_BUTTON -> BN_CLICKED
```

Then click the Add Function button.

☐ Accept the name OnClear1Button() that Visual C++ suggests.

To write the code of the OnClear1Button() function do the following:

☐ Click the Edit Code button of ClassWizard.

ClassWizard responds by opening the file MyEdiDlg.CPP, with the function OnClear1Button() *ready to be edited by you.*

☐ Write code inside the `OnClear1Button()` function so that it looks like this:

```
void CMyeditDlg::OnClear1Button()
{
// TODO: Add your control notification
// handler code here

///////////////////////
// MY CODE STARTS HERE
///////////////////////

// Set the variable of the IDC_EDIT1 edit box to null.
m_Edit1 = "";

// Update the screen.
UpdateData (FALSE);

///////////////////////
// MY CODE ENDS HERE
///////////////////////

}
```

To save your work do the following:

☐ Select Save from the File menu.

The code you typed inside the `OnTest1Button()` function is similar to the code you typed inside the `OnClear1Button()` function. The only difference is that now you are updating the `m_Edit1` variable with a null string:

```
// Set the variable of the IDC_EDIT1 edit box to null.
m_Edit1 = "";

// Update the screen.
UpdateData (FALSE);
```

To see the code that you attached to the Exit button in action do the following:

☐ Select Build MyEdit.EXE from the Project menu.

Visual C++ responds by compiling and linking the MyEdit program.

☐ Select Execute MyEdit.EXE from the Project menu.

Visual C++ responds by executing the MyEdit.EXE program.

☐ Click the Test 1 button.

MyEdit responds by filling the edit box with the text `This is a test`.

☐ Click the Clear 1 button,

MyEdit responds by clearing the edit box.

☐ Experiment with the MyEdit program and then terminate the program.

Adding More Controls to the MyEdit Program

So far you have implemented an edit box and two push buttons inside the IDD_MYEDIT_DIALOG dialog box. You'll now add a second edit box and four more push buttons to the dialog box.

☐ Using the specifications in Table 6.2, add a second edit box and four additional push buttons to the IDD_MYEDIT_DIALOG so that the dialog box looks like the one shown in Figure 6.14. That is, select myedit.rc from the Window menu to display the MyEdit.RC window, double-click Dialog, and finally, double-click IDD_MYEDIT_DIALOG to display the dialog box in design mode.

Table 6.2. Adding a second edit box and four push buttons to the IDD_MYEDIT_DIALOG dialog box.

Object	Property	Setting
Edit box	ID	IDC_EDIT2
Push button	ID	IDC_TEST2_BUTTON
	Caption	Test &2
Push button	ID	IDC_CLEAR2_BUTTON
	Caption	Clear 2
Push button	ID	IDC_COPY_BUTTON
	Caption	Cop&y
Push button	ID	IDC_PASTE_BUTTON
	Caption	Pa&ste

Figure 6.14. The IDC_MYEDIT_DIALOG dialog box (in design mode).

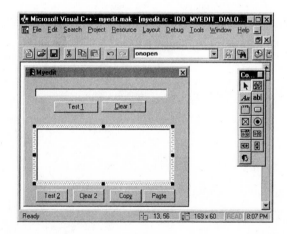

Attaching a Control Variable to the Lower Edit Box

Earlier in this chapter you attached a variable (m_Edit1) to the upper edit box (IDC_EDIT1). Recall from Figure 6.12 that you set the Category of the m_Edit1 variable to Value, and you set the Variable Type of m_Edit1 to CString. As you'll soon see, the variable m_Edit2 that you'll attach to the IDC_EDIT2 edit box is a variable of a different type and category.

Here is how you attach the variable m_Edit2 to the IDC_EDIT2 edit box:

☐ Select ClassWizard from the Project menu.

Visual C++ responds by displaying the ClassWizard dialog box.

☐ Select the Member Variables tab.

☐ Make sure the class name is set to CMyeditDlg.

☐ Click the IDC_EDIT2 item.

☐ Click the Add Variable button.

Visual C++ responds by displaying the Add Member Variable dialog box.

☐ Set the Member Variable Name to m_Edit2, set the Category to Control, set the Variable Type to CEdit, and finally, click the OK button. (See Figure 6.15.)

Visual C++ responds by adding the m_Edit2 variable to the CMyediDlg class. Your ClassWizard dialog box should now look like the one shown in Figure 6.16.

Figure 6.15. Attaching a variable (m_Edit2) to the IDC_EDIT2 edit box.

☐ To save your work, select Save from the File menu.

Just to make sure that you performed all the steps correctly, compile, link, and execute the MyEdit program:

☐ Compile and link the MyEdit program.

☐ Execute the MyEdit program.

☐ Experiment with the MyEdit program and note the following points about the lower edit box (IDC_EDIT2):

- You can click inside the edit box and type characters in it, but you can't advance to the next line.
- The IDC_EDIT2 edit box does not have a horizontal scroll bar.
- The IDC_EDIT2 edit box does not have a vertical scroll bar.

☐ Terminate the MyEdit program.

Figure 6.16. The ClassWizard dialog box after you attach the variable m_Edit2 to the IDC_EDIT2 edit box.

Modifying the Properties of the IDC_EDIT2 Edit Box

Now modify the properties of the IDC_EDIT2 edit box so that it will let you type multiple lines.

☐ Display the IDD_MYEDIT_DIALOG dialog box. That is, select myedit.rc from the Window menu, double-click Dialog, and then double-click IDD_MYEDIT_DIALOG.

Visual C++ responds by displaying the IDD_MYEDIT_DIALOG dialog box in design mode.

☐ Double-click the IDC_EDIT2 edit box.

Visual C++ responds by displaying the Edit Properties dialog box of the IDC_EDIT2 edit box.

☐ Click the Style tab of the Edit Properties dialog box.

☐ Place a checkmark inside the Multiline check box.

☐ Place checkmarks inside the Horiz. Scroll, Auto HScroll, Vert. Scroll, Auto VScroll, Want Return, and Border check boxes.

The Edit Properties dialog box should now look like the one shown in Figure 6.17.

Figure 6.17. Setting the IDC_EDIT2 edit box as a multiple-line edit box with scroll bars.

One of the most important check boxes of the edit box is the Want Return check box. This property enables the user to press the return key on the keyboard, and the program will interpret this key by inserting a carriage return/line feed characters as the contents of the edit box.

In effect, currently the MyEdit program has a little bug in it. If you execute the MyEdit program, click inside the upper edit box, and press the Return key on your keyboard, the program will terminate. You can correct this by setting the Want Return check box of the IDC_EDIT1 edit box as follows:

☐ Double-click inside the IDC_EDIT1 edit box (the upper edit box) of the IDD_MYEDIT_DIALOG dialog box to display the edit properties of IDC_EDIT1 edit box.

☐ Click the Style tab.

☐ Place a checkmark inside the Multiline, Auto HScroll, Want Return, and Border check boxes.

The Edit Properties dialog box of IDC_EDIT1 should now look like the one shown in Figure 6.18.

Figure 6.18. Setting the edit properties of the IDC_EDIT1 edit box.

☐ Compile, link, and execute the MyEdit program.

☐ Experiment with the MyEdit program. In particular, note that the IDC_EDIT2 edit box has the capability of receiving multiple lines from the user.

☐ Terminate the MyEdit program.

Attaching Code to the Test 2 Button

You'll now attach code to the Test 2 button.

☐ Select ClassWizard from the Project menu, and select the event (See Figure 6.19.):

```
CMyeditDlg -> IDC_TEST2_BUTTON -> BN_CLICKED
```

Then click the Add Function button.

*Figure 6.19. Attaching
code to the* BN_CLICKED
event of the Test 2 button.

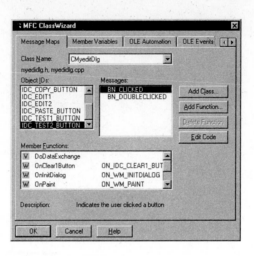

☐ Accept the name *OnTest2Button()* that Visual C++ suggests.

☐ Click the Edit Code button.

>   *Visual C++ responds by displaying the* OnTest2Button() *function, ready to be edited by you.*

☐ Add code to the OnTest2Button() function. After you add the code, the OnTest2Button() function should look like this:

```
void CMyeditDlg::OnTest2Button()
{
// TODO: Add your control notification
// handler code here



///////////////////////
// MY CODE STARTS HERE
///////////////////////

// Select the entire text
m_Edit2.SetSel (0,-1);

// Replace the select text
m_Edit2.ReplaceSel ("You clicked the Test 2 button.");

///////////////////////
// MY CODE ENDS HERE
///////////////////////

}
```

The first statement you typed selects the entire text inside the edit box (if there is any):

```
m_Edit2.SetSel (0,-1);
```

The second statement you typed replaces the selected text with new text:

```
m_Edit2.ReplaceSel ("You clicked the Test 2 button.");
```

To save your work do the following:

☐ Select Save from the File menu.

NOTE

In the preceding steps you wrote code that executes the functions `SetSel()` and `ReplaceSel()` on the `m_Edit2` variable:

```
m_Edit2.SetSel (0,-1);
m_Edit2.ReplaceSel ("You clicked the Test 2 button.");
```

Recall that when you attached the variable `m_Edit2` to the IDC_EDIT2 edit box (See Figure 6.15.), you defined `m_Edit2` as a variable of type `CEdit`. This means that `m_Edit2` is an object of class `CEdit`. `CEdit` is an MFC class that was specifically designed for edit boxes. Therefore, it includes powerful member functions (such as `SetSel()` and `ReplaceSel()`) that enable you to manipulate edit boxes easily.

Attaching Code to the Clear 2 Button

You'll now attach code to the Clear 2 button.

☐ Select ClassWizard from the Project menu, and select the event (See Figure 6.20.):

```
CMyeditDlg -> IDC_CLEAR2_BUTTON -> BN_CLICKED
```

Then click the Add Function button.

Figure 6.20. Attaching code to the BN_CLICKED event of the Clear 2 button.

☐ Accept the name `OnClear2Button()` that Visual C++ suggests.

☐ Click the Edit Code button.

Visual C++ responds by displaying the OnClear2Button() *function, ready to be edited by you.*

☐ Add code to the OnClear2Button() function. After you add the code, the OnClear2Button() function should look like this:

```
void CMyeditDlg::OnClear2Button()
{
// TODO: Add your control notification
// handler code here

/////////////////////////
// MY CODE STARTS HERE
/////////////////////////

// Select the entire text
m_Edit2.SetSel (0,-1);

// Replace the select text
m_Edit2.ReplaceSel ("");


/////////////////////////
// MY CODE ENDS HERE
/////////////////////////

}
```

The first statement you typed selects the entire text inside the edit box (if there is any):

```
m_Edit2.SetSel (0,-1);
```

The second statement you typed replaces the selected text with NULL:

```
m_Edit2.ReplaceSel ("");
```

To save your work do the following:

☐ Select Save from the File menu.

To test your work do the following:

☐ Compile, link, and then execute the MyEdit program.

☐ Click the Test 2 button.

> *MyEdit responds by placing the text* You clicked the Test 2 button. *inside the IDC_EDIT2 edit box. (See Figure 6.21.)*

☐ Click the Clear 2 button.

> *MyEdit responds by clearing the contents of the IDC_EDIT2 edit box.*

☐ Experiment with the MyEdit program and then terminate the program.

Figure 6.21. The
IDC_EDIT2 edit box after
you click the Test 2 button.

NOTE

Note the difference between the m_Edit1 variable and the m_Edit2 variable.

During the visual design, you set m_Edit1 as CString. You fill the IDC_EDIT1 edit box as follows:

```
// Set the variable of the IDC_EDIT1 edit box to ABC.
m_Edit1 = "ABC";

// Update the screen.
UpdateData (FALSE);
```

During the visual design you set m_Edit2 as Control. You fill the IDC_EDIT2 edit box as follows:

```
m_Edit2.SetSel (0,-1);

m_Edit2.ReplaceSel ("ABC");
```

At first glance, you might think that setting the variable of the edit box to CString is less trouble than setting it as an object of class CEdit. However, as you'll soon see, setting the variable of the edit box as an object of class CEdit has its advantages. You'll realize it when you implement the Copy and Paste buttons in the following sections.

Attaching Code to the Copy Button

You'll now attach code to the Copy button.

☐ Use ClassWizard from the Project menu to select the event (See Figure 6.22.):

```
CMyeditDlg -> IDC_COPY_BUTTON -> BN_CLICKED
```

Then click the Add Function button.

Figure 6.22. Adding the
`OnCopyButton()`
function.

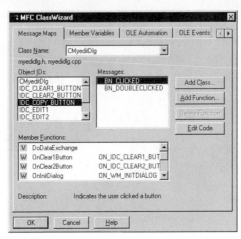

☐ Accept the name `OnCopyButton()` that Visual C++ suggests.

☐ Click the Edit Code function.

> *Visual C++ responds by displaying the* `OnCopyButton()` *function, ready to be edited by you.*

☐ Add code to the `OnCopyButton()` function. After you add the code, the `OnCopyButton()` function should look like this:

```
void CMyeditDlg::OnCopyButton()
{
// TODO: Add your control notification
// handler code here

/////////////////////////
// MY CODE STARTS HERE
/////////////////////////

// Select the entire text
m_Edit2.SetSel (0,-1);

// Copy to the Clipboard
m_Edit2.Copy();

/////////////////////////
// MY CODE ENDS HERE
/////////////////////////


}
```

The code you typed selects the text of the IDC_EDIT2 edit box:

```
m_Edit2.SetSel (0,-1);
```

Then the `Copy()` member function of the `CEdit` class is executed:

```
m_Edit2.Copy();
```

After the preceding statement is executed, the Clipboard is filled with the contents of the IDC_EDIT2 edit box.

To save your work do the following:

☐ Select Save from the File menu.

To see your work in action do the following:

☐ Compile, link, and execute the MyEdit program.

☐ Execute the MyEdit program.

☐ Type something inside the lower edit box, and then click the Copy button.

   MyEdit responds by copying the contents of the lower edit box to the Clipboard of Windows.

☐ Switch to your word processor program.

☐ Paste the contents of the Clipboard to your word processor.

As you can see, indeed the Copy button of the MyEdit program copied the contents of the IDC_EDIT2 edit box to the Clipboard.

☐ Experiment with the MyEdit program and then terminate the program.

Implementing the Paste Feature

You'll now implement the Paste feature.

☐ Use ClassWizard from the Project menu to select the event (See Figure 6.23.):

```
CMyeditDlg -> IDC_PASTE_BUTTON -> BN_CLICKED
```

Then click the Add Function button.

Figure 6.23. Adding the
`OnPasteButton()`
function.

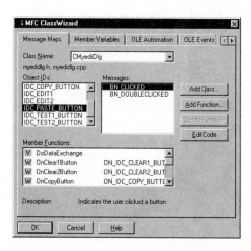

☐ Accept the name `OnPasteButton()` that Visual C++ suggests.

☐ Click the Edit Code button.

>   *Visual C++ responds by displaying the* `OnPasteButton()` *function, ready to be edited by you.*

☐ Add code to the *OnPasteButton()* function. After you add the code, the `OnPasteButton()` function should look like this:

```
void CMyeditDlg::OnPasteButton()
{
// TODO: Add your control notification
// handler code here

////////////////////////
// MY CODE STARTS HERE
////////////////////////

// Select the entire text
m_Edit2.SetSel (0,-1);

// Paste from the Clipboard
m_Edit2.Paste();

////////////////////////
// MY CODE ENDS HERE
////////////////////////

}
```

The code you typed pastes the contents of the Clipboard to the IDC_EDIT2 edit box:

```
m_Edit2.Paste();
```

After the preceding statement is executed, the Clipboard's contents are copied to the IDC_EDIT2 edit box.

To save your work do the following:

☐ Select Save from the File menu.

To see your work in action do the following:

☐ Compile and link the MyEdit program.

☐ Execute the MyEdit program.

☐ Type `Will it work?` inside the lower edit box, and then click the Copy button.

>   *MyEdit responds by copying the contents of the lower edit box to the Clipboard of Windows.*

☐ Click the Test 2 button.

>   *MyEdit responds by filling the lower edit box with the text* `You clicked the Test 2 button.`

☐ Click the Paste button.

MyEdit responds by pasting the contents of the Clipboard (which is currently filled with the text Will it work?*) to the IDC_EDIT2 edit box.*

☐ Experiment with the MyEdit program and then terminate the program.

NOTE

Note how easy it is to implement powerful standard Windows features such as Copy and Paste. This is possible because you set the m_Edit2 variable as an object of class CEdit.

Copy() and Paste() are member functions of the CEdit class, and because m_Edit2 is an object (Control) of class CEdit, you have the "right" to execute the member functions of the CEdit class on the m_Edit2 object.

7

Check Boxes

In this chapter you'll learn how to incorporate check boxes in a dialog box. As you know, check boxes serve an important role in the Windows user-interface mechanism. The application that you'll write in this chapter is a dialog-based type—an application in which a dialog box serves as the main window of the application.

The ChkBox Application

Before you start writing the ChkBox application yourself, execute the copy of it that resides in the \MVCPROG\EXE directory of the book's CD.

To execute the ChkBox application do the following:

☐ Use the Program Manager of Windows to execute the X:\MVCPROG\EXE\ChkBox.EXE program (where *X* represents the drive letter of your CD-ROM drive).

> *Windows responds by executing the ChkBox.EXE application. The window of ChkBox.EXE appears, as shown in Figure 7.1.*

Figure 7.1. The window of the ChkBox application.

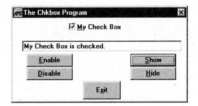

☐ Click the My Check Box check box.

> *ChkBox responds by removing the checkmark inside the check box and by displaying the text* My Check Box is NOT checked *inside the edit box.*

☐ Click the My Check Box check box again.

> *ChkBox responds by placing the checkmark inside the check box and by displaying the text* My Check Box is checked *inside the edit box.*

☐ Try the other buttons of the dialog box.

As you can see, the Disable button makes the check box unavailable (dimmed) and the Enable button makes the check box available. Similarly, the Hide button makes the check box invisible (See Figure 7.2.), and the Show button makes the check box visible.

☐ Click the Exit button to terminate the ChkBox application.

Figure 7.2. Making the check box invisible.

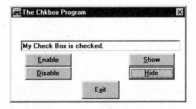

Now that you know what the ChkBox application should do, you can begin to write it.

Creating the Project of the ChkBox Application

To create the project of the ChkBox application do the following:

☐ Start Visual C++ and close all the open windows that appear inside the desktop of Visual C++ (if there are any).

☐ Select New from the File menu.

> *Visual C++ responds by displaying the New dialog box.*

☐ Select Project inside the New dialog box and then click the OK button of the New dialog box.

> *Visual C++ responds by displaying the New Project dialog box.*

☐ Set the project name to ChkBox.

☐ Set the project path to \MVCPROG\CH07\ChkBox\ChkBox.MAK.

Your New Project dialog box should now look like the one shown in Figure 7.3.

*Figure 7.3. The New
Project dialog box of the
ChkBox.MAK project.*

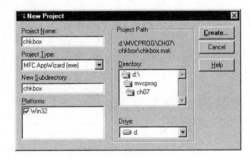

☐ Click the Create button of the New Project dialog box.

> *Visual C++ responds by displaying the AppWizard—Step 1 window.*

☐ Set the Step 1 window as shown in Figure 7.4. As shown in Figure 7.4, the ChkBox.MAK project is set as a dialog-based application, and U.S. English (APPWIZUS.DLL) is used as the language for the ChkBox.MAK project's resources.

☐ Click the Next button of the Step 1 window.

> *Visual C++ responds by displaying the AppWizard—Step 2 of 4 window.*

☐ Set the Step 2 of 4 window as shown in Figure 7.5. That is, place a checkmark inside the About Box check box (to incorporate an About dialog box into the application) and place a checkmark inside the Use 3D Controls check box (so that the application will use 3D controls). Also, set the title of the application to The Chkbox Program.

Figure 7.4. The AppWizard—Step 1 window of the ChkBox.MAK project.

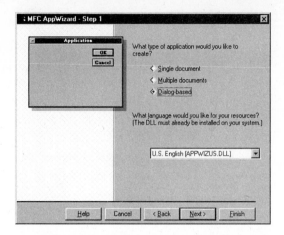

Figure 7.5. The AppWizard—Step 2 of 4 window of the ChkBox.MAK project.

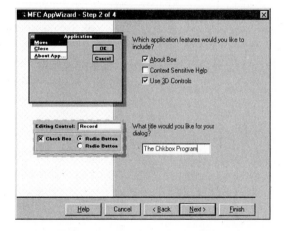

☐ Click the Next button of the Step 2 of 4 window.

Visual C++ responds by displaying the AppWizard—Step 3 of 4 window.

☐ Set the Step 3 of 4 window as shown in Figure 7.6.

As shown in Figure 7.6, the project will be generated with comments, a Visual C++ makefile will be generated, and the application will use the MFC library from a DLL.

☐ Click the Next button of the Step 3 of 4 window.

Visual C++ responds by displaying the AppWizard—Step 4 of 4 window, as shown in Figure 7.7.

☐ Click the Finish button of the Step 4 of 4 window.

Visual C++ responds by displaying the New Project Information window, as shown in Figure 7.8.

Figure 7.6. The AppWizard—Step 3 of 4 window of the ChkBox.MAK project.

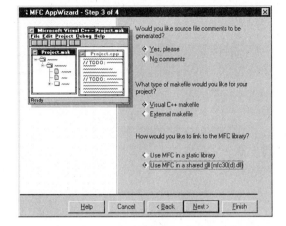

Figure 7.7. The AppWizard—Step 4 of 4 window of the ChkBox.MAK project.

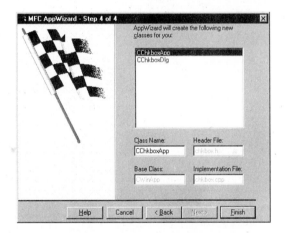

Figure 7.8. The New Project Information window of the ChkBox.MAK project.

☐ Click the OK button of the New Project Information window.

Visual C++ responds by creating the project file and all the skeleton files of the application.

The Visual Implementation of the ChkBox Application

Because the ChkBox application is a dialog-based application, when you created the project and the skeleton files of the ChkBox application with AppWizard, AppWizard created for you a dialog box that serves as the main window of the application. AppWizard named this dialog box IDD_CHKBOX_DIALOG. You'll now customize the IDD_CHKBOX_DIALOG dialog box until it looks like the one shown back in Figure 7.1.

☐ Double-click chkbox.rc inside the chkbox.mak window.

Visual C++ responds by displaying the chkbox.rc window.

☐ Double-click Dialog inside the chkbox.rc window and then double-click IDD_CHKBOX_DIALOG.

Visual C++ responds by displaying the IDD_CHKBOX_DIALOG dialog box in design mode.

☐ Implement the dialog box according to the specifications in Table 7.1. When you finish implementing the dialog box, it should look like the one shown in Figure 7.9.

Table 7.1. The Properties table of the IDD_CHKBOX_DIALOG dialog box.

Object	Property	Setting
Dialog box	ID	IDD_CHKBOX_DIALOG
Check box	ID	IDC_MY_CHECKBOX
	Caption	&My Check Box
Push button	ID	IDC_EXIT_BUTTON
	Caption	E&xit
Edit box	ID	IDC_MY_EDITBOX
Push button	ID	IDC_ENABLE_BUTTON
	Caption	&Enable
Push button	ID	IDC_DISABLE_BUTTON
	Caption	&Disable
Push button	ID	IDC_SHOW_BUTTON
	Caption	&Show
Push button	ID	IDC_HIDE_BUTTON
	Caption	&Hide

Figure 7.9. The dialog box
that serves as the main
window of the ChkBox
program (in design mode).

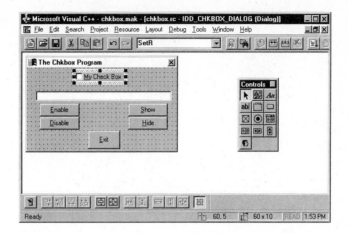

NOTE

Table 7.1 instructs you to place a check box control inside the dialog box. The check box
tool in the Tools window is shown in Figure 7.10.

Figure 7.10. The check box
tool inside the Tools
window of Visual C++.

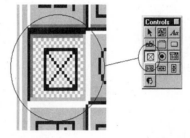

Attaching Variables to the Dialog Box of the ChkBox Program

You'll now attach variables to the controls of the ChkBox application's dialog box.

☐ Use ClassWizard (from the Project menu) to attach variables to the controls of the
IDD_CHKBOX_DIALOG dialog box according to the specifications in Table 7.2.

Table 7.2. The Variables table of the ChkBox application's dialog box.

Control ID	Variable Name	Category	Variable Type
IDC_MY_CHECKBOX	m_MyCheckBox	Value	BOOL
IDC_MY_EDITBOX	m_MyEditBox	Value	CString

☐ To save your work, select Save from the File menu.

To see your visual design in action do the following:

☐ Select Build ChkBox.EXE from the Project menu.

> *Visual C++ responds by compiling and linking the ChkBox application.*

☐ Select Execute ChkBox.EXE from the Project menu.

> *Visual C++ responds by executing the ChkBox.EXE application. As expected, the IDD_CHKBOX_DIALOG dialog box that you designed appears as the main window of the application.*

☐ Click the icon that appears on the upper-left corner of the ChkBox application window, and select About from the System menu that pops up.

> *ChkBox responds by displaying the About dialog box.*

☐ Click the OK button of the About dialog box to close the About dialog box.

☐ Click the My Check Box control several times and note that each click causes a checkmark to be placed or to be removed from the My Check Box control.

☐ Click the icon that appears on the upper-left corner of the ChkBox application, and select Close from the System menu that pops up.

> *ChkBox responds by terminating itself.*

The point of the preceding exercise is to show you that no code is needed to place and remove the checkmark from the check box.

Initializing the Controls of the Dialog Box

As you saw, the ChkBox application initially displays the My Check Box control without a checkmark in it. You'll now write code that causes the My Check Box check box to have a checkmark in it upon start-up of the ChkBox program.

You'll now attach code to the WM_INITDIALOG event of the IDD_CHKBOX_DIALOG dialog box. The WM_INITDIALOG event occurs just before the dialog box is displayed.

☐ Select ClassWizard from the Project menu of Visual C++.

> *Visual C++ responds by displaying the ClassWizard dialog box.*

☐ Select the Message Maps Tab at the top of ClassWizard's dialog box.

☐ Use ClassWizard to select the event:

```
CChkboxDlg -> CChkboxDlg -> WM_INITDIALOG
```

Then click the Edit Code button.

Visual C++ responds by opening the CHKBODLG.CPP file and displaying the OnInitDialog() *function, ready to be edited by you.*

☐ Write code inside the OnInitDialog() function so that it looks like this:

```
BOOL CChkboxDlg::OnInitDialog()
{
CDialog::OnInitDialog();
CenterWindow();
// Add "About..." menu item to system menu.
// IDM_ABOUTBOX must be in the system command range.
ASSERT((IDM_ABOUTBOX & 0xFFF0) == IDM_ABOUTBOX);
ASSERT(IDM_ABOUTBOX < 0xF000);
CMenu* pSysMenu = GetSystemMenu(FALSE);
CString strAboutMenu;
strAboutMenu.LoadString(IDS_ABOUTBOX);
if (!strAboutMenu.IsEmpty())
    {
    pSysMenu->AppendMenu(MF_SEPARATOR);
    pSysMenu->AppendMenu(MF_STRING, IDM_ABOUTBOX,
    strAboutMenu);
    }
// TODO: Add extra initialization here
/////////////////////////
// MY CODE STARTS HERE //
/////////////////////////

// Update the variable of the check box
m_MyCheckBox = TRUE;
// Update the variable of the edit box
m_MyEditBox = _T("My Check Box is checked.");
// Update the screen with the variables values
UpdateData(FALSE);
/////////////////////////
// MY CODE ENDS HERE //
/////////////////////////
return TRUE;
// return TRUE  unless you set the focus to a control
}
```

☐ Save your work by selecting Save from the File menu of Visual C++.

The first statement that you typed inside the OnInitDialog() function

```
m_MyCheckBox = TRUE;
```

sets the variable of the check box to TRUE.

The next statement

```
m_MyEditBox = _T("My Check Box is checked.");
```

sets the variable of the edit box to the My Check Box is checked string. Note that the m_MyEditBox variable expects a CString. This explains why you can convert the string to a CString with the _T() macro.

Finally, the contents of the m_MyTextBox and m_MyEditBox variables are transferred to the screen by using the UpdateData() function with its parameter set to FALSE:

```
UpdateData(FALSE);
```

To see your initialization code in action do the following:

☐ Select Build ChkBox.EXE from the Project menu.

>   *Visual C++ responds by compiling and linking the ChkBox program.*

☐ Select Execute ChkBox.EXE from the Project menu.

>   *Visual C++ responds by executing the ChkBox.EXE program. As you can see, the check box appears with a checkmark in it. Also, the edit box displays the text My Check Box is checked.*

☐ Click the × icon that appears on the upper-right corner of the ChkBox program's window.

>   *ChkBox responds by terminating itself.*

Attaching Code to the *BN_CLICKED* Event of the Exit Button

Recall that when the user clicks the Exit button, the ChkBox program should terminate. You'll now attach code to the Click event (BN_CLICKED) of the Exit button.

☐ Display the ClassWizard dialog box by selecting ClassWizard from the Project menu of Visual C++.

☐ Select the Message Maps tab at the top of ClassWizard's dialog box.

☐ Use ClassWizard to select the event:

```
CChkboxDlg -> IDC_EXIT_BUTTON -> BN_CLICKED
```

Then click the Add Function button.

☐ Name the new function OnExitButton().

To write the code of the OnExitButton() function do the following:

☐ Click the Edit Code button of ClassWizard.

>   *ClassWizard responds by opening the file ChkBoDlg.CPP, with the function OnExitButton() ready to be edited by you.*

☐ Write code inside the OnExitButton() function so that it looks like this:

```
void CChkboxDlg::OnExitButton()
{
// TODO: Add your control notification handler code here
```

```
/////////////////////////
// MY CODE STARTS HERE //
/////////////////////////
// Close the dialog box (terminate the program).
OnOK();
/////////////////////////
// MY CODE ENDS HERE //
/////////////////////////
}
```

☐ Save your work by selecting Save from the File menu of Visual C++.

The code you typed closes the dialog box by calling the `OnOK()` member function of the `CChkboxDlg` class.

To see the code that you attached to the Exit button in action do the following:

☐ Select Build ChkBox.EXE from the Project menu.

   Visual C++ responds by compiling and linking the ChkBox program.

☐ Select Execute ChkBox.EXE from the Project menu.

   Visual C++ responds by executing the ChkBox.EXE program.

☐ Click the Exit button.

   As expected, the ChkBox program terminates itself.

Attaching Code to the *Click* Event of the Check Box

Recall that when the user clicks the check box, the edit box should display the new status of the check box. You'll now attach code to the `Click` event of the check box.

☐ Display the ClassWizard dialog box by selecting ClassWizard from the Project menu of Visual C++.

   Visual C++ responds by displaying the ClassWizard dialog box.

☐ Select the Message Maps tab at the top of ClassWizard's dialog box.

☐ Use ClassWizard to select the event:

`CChkboxDlg -> IDC_MY_CHECKBOX -> BN_CLICKED`

Then click the Add Function button.

☐ Name the new function `OnMyCheckbox()`.

To write the code of the `OnMyCheckbox()` function do the following:

☐ Click the Edit Code button of ClassWizard.

   ClassWizard responds by opening the file ChkBoDlg.CPP, with the function
   `OnMyCheckbox()` *ready to be edited by you.*

☐ Write code inside the OnMyCheckbox() function so that it looks like this:

```
void CChkboxDlg::OnMyCheckbox()
{
// TODO: Add your control notification handler code here

/////////////////////////
// MY CODE STARTS HERE //
/////////////////////////
// Update the controls' variables
// (the screen contents are transferred
// to the controls' variables).
UpdateData(TRUE);
// Update the variable of the edit box
if (m_MyCheckBox == TRUE)
   m_MyEditBox = _T("My Check Box is checked.");
else
   m_MyEditBox = _T("My Check Box is NOT checked.");
// Update the screen.
// (the contorls' variables are transferred
// to the screen).
UpdateData(FALSE);
/////////////////////////
// MY CODE ENDS HERE //
/////////////////////////
}
```

☐ Save your work by selecting Save from the File menu of Visual C++.

The first statement you typed inside the OnMyCheckbox() function updates the variables of the controls with the current contents of the screen:

```
UpdateData(TRUE);
```

Next, an if…else statement is executed to update the variable of the edit box according to the value of the m_MyCheckBox variable:

```
if (m_MyCheckBox == TRUE)
   m_MyEditBox = _T("My Check Box is checked.");
else
   m_MyEditBox = _T("My Check Box is NOT checked.");
```

And finally, the screen is updated (so that the new value of m_MyEditBox will be displayed):

```
UpdateData(FALSE);
```

To see your code in action do the following:

☐ Select Build ChkBox.EXE from the Project menu.

   Visual C++ responds by compiling and linking the ChkBox program.

☐ Select Execute ChkBox.EXE from the Project menu.

   Visual C++ responds by executing the ChkBox.EXE program.

☐ Click the My Check Box control.

As expected, the ChkBox program changes the status of the check box, and the new status of the check box is displayed inside the edit box.

☐ Experiment with the ChkBox program and then click the Exit button to terminate the program.

Attaching Code to the Hide and Show Buttons

Recall that when the user clicks the Hide button, the My Check Box control should become invisible. You'll now attach code to the Click event of the Hide button.

☐ Display the ClassWizard dialog box by selecting ClassWizard from the Project menu of Visual C++.

☐ Select the Message Maps tab at the top of ClassWizard's dialog box.

☐ Use ClassWizard to select the event:

CChkboxDlg -> IDC_HIDE_BUTTON -> BN_CLICKED

Then click the Add Function button.

☐ Name the new function OnHideButton().

To write the code of the OnHideButton() function do the following:

☐ Click the Edit Code button of ClassWizard.

ClassWizard responds by opening the file ChkBoDlg.CPP, with the function OnHideButton() ready to be edited by you.

☐ Write code inside the OnHideButton() function so that it looks like this:

```
void CChkboxDlg::OnHideButton()
{
// TODO: Add your control notification handler code here
/////////////////////////
// MY CODE STARTS HERE //
/////////////////////////
// Hide the check box
GetDlgItem(IDC_MY_CHECKBOX)->ShowWindow(SW_HIDE);

/////////////////////////
// MY CODE ENDS HERE //
/////////////////////////
}
```

The code that you typed hides the check box:

```
GetDlgItem(IDC_MY_CHECKBOX)->ShowWindow(SW_HIDE);
```

The GetDlgItem() function extracts the pointer of a control that is located inside the dialog box. The parameter of the GetDlgItem() function is the ID of the control whose pointer you wish to extract. Therefore, you supplied IDC_MY_CHECKBOX as the parameter of the GetDlgItem() function because you want to extract the pointer of the check box control.

The ShowWindow() function hides or shows the control. If you supply SW_HIDE as the parameter of the ShowWindow() function, the control is made invisible, and if you supply SW_SHOW as the parameter of the ShowWindow() function, the control is made visible.

In the OnHideButton() function you want to make the check box invisible. Therefore, you extract the pointer of the check box and then apply the ShowWindow(SW_HIDE) function on the extracted pointer.

☐ To save your work, select Save from the File menu.

Recall that when the user clicks the Show button, the My Check Box control should become visible. You'll now attach code to the Click event of the Show button.

☐ Display the ClassWizard dialog box by selecting ClassWizard from the Project menu of Visual C++.

☐ Select the Message Maps tab at the top of ClassWizard's dialog box.

☐ Use ClassWizard to select the event:

CChkboxDlg -> IDC_SHOW_BUTTON -> BN_CLICKED

Then click the Add Function button.

☐ Name the new function *OnShowButton()*.

To write the code of the OnShowButton() function do the following:

☐ Click the Edit Code button of ClassWizard.

> *ClassWizard responds by opening the file ChkBoDlg.CPP, with the function OnShowButton() ready to be edited by you.*

☐ Write code inside the OnShowButton() function so that it looks like this:

```
void CChkboxDlg::OnShowButton()
{
// TODO: Add your control notification handler code here
////////////////////////
// MY CODE STARTS HERE
////////////////////////
// Show the check box
GetDlgItem(IDC_MY_CHECKBOX)->ShowWindow(SW_SHOW);

////////////////////////
// MY CODE ENDS HERE
////////////////////////
}
```

The code you typed extracts the pointer of the check box and applies the ShowWindow() function on the extracted pointer with SW_SHOW as a parameter. This makes the check box visible.

To see your code in action do the following:

☐ Select Build ChkBox.EXE from the Project menu.

Visual C++ responds by compiling and linking the ChkBox program.

☐ Select Execute ChkBox.EXE from the Project menu.

Visual C++ responds by executing the ChkBox.EXE program.

☐ Click the Hide button.

As expected, the ChkBox program makes the check box invisible.

☐ Click the Show button.

As expected, the ChkBox program makes the check box visible.

☐ Experiment with the ChkBox program and then click the Exit button to terminate the program.

In this book you'll learn about the existence of many important member functions such as the GetDlgItem() and ShowWindow() functions. Whenever you use a function in this book, you should always ask yourself Where did this function come from?

Now examine the GetDlgItem() function.

☐ Select Foundation Classes from the Help menu.

Visual C++ responds by displaying the Search dialog box, as shown in Figure 7.11.

Figure 7.11. The Search dialog box.

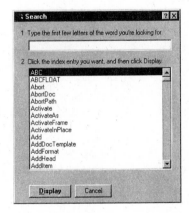

☐ Inside the top edit box of the Search dialog box type GetDlgItem.

☐ Click the Display button.

Visual C++ responds by displaying the help window of the GetDlgItem() function. (See Figure 7.12.)

*Figure 7.12. The help
window of the
GetDlgItem() function.*

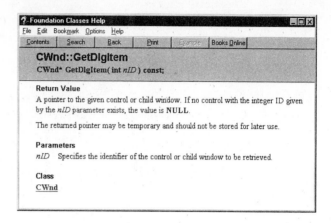

At first glance, it looks as if you did something wrong! That is, you used the GetDlgItem() function as though it is a member function of the CChkboxDlg class:

```
void CChkboxDlg::OnShowButton()
{
// TODO: Add your control notification handler code here
//////////////////////////
// MY CODE STARTS HERE //
//////////////////////////
// Show the check box
GetDlgItem(IDC_MY_CHECKBOX)->ShowWindow(SW_SHOW);

//////////////////////////
// MY CODE ENDS HERE //
//////////////////////////
}
```

In other words, you used the GetDlgItem() function from within a member function of the CChkboxDlg class, which means that you considered the GetDlgItem() function to be a member function of the CChkboxDlg class.

Yet, as shown in Figure 7.12, the GetDlgItem() function is shown to be a member function of the CWnd class. This is shown in the title of help window of Figure 7.12:

```
CWnd::GetDlgItem
```

To understand what is going on here, examine the CDialog class:

☐ Search for help about the CDialog class.

The CDialog help window is shown in Figure 7.13.

As shown in Figure 7.13, CDialog is a derived class from the CWnd class. This means that it is okay to use the GetDlgItem() function (a member function of the CWnd class) on objects of the CDialog class. That is, CDialog inherited the function GetDlgItem() from its parent CWnd.

Figure 7.13. The CDialog
help window.

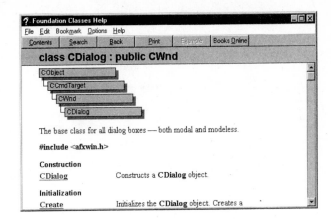

However, you treated the GetDlgItem() function as a member function of the CChkboxDlg class. This is okay because CChkboxDlg is a derived class from the CDialog class. You can verify this as follows:

☐ Select ClassWizard from the Project window, and then click the Class Info tab. (Note that you may have to scroll the tabs to the right in order to be able to click the Class Info tab.)

Visual C++ responds by displaying the Class Info dialog box. (See Figure 7.14.)

☐ Make sure that Class Name is set to CChkboxDlg.

As you can see in Figure 7.14, the Case Class indicates that CDialog is the base class of CChkboxDlg.

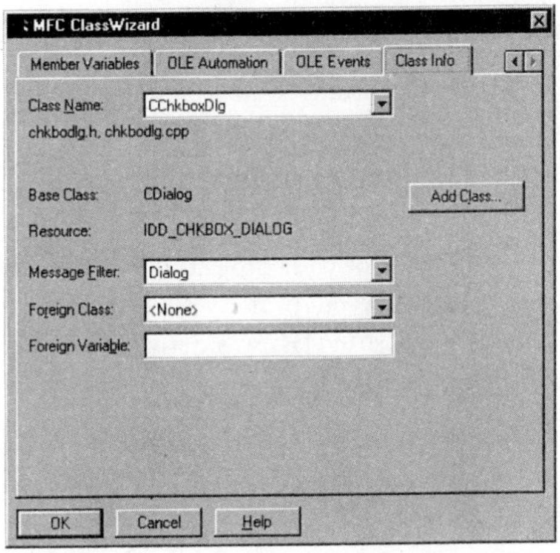

*Figure 7.14. The Class Info
window.*

As you can see in Figure 7.14, the CChkboxDlg class is derived from the CDialog class. You already verified that CDialog is a derived class from the CWnd class. So the CChkboxDlg class can use the GetDlgItem() member function of the CWnd class.

In a similar manner, you can use the Help menu to verify that the ShowWindow() function is a member function of the CWnd class (See Figure 7.15.), and hence you can apply this function to classes that are derived from the CWnd class.

Figure 7.15. The ShowWindow() help window.

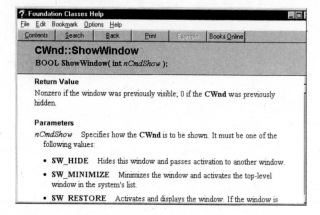

It is important to understand how to apply the member functions. For example, Figure 7.15 shows the possible values that can be supplied as the parameter of the ShowWindow() member function.

Take a look at Figure 7.12. As shown, the GetDlgItem() function returns a pointer. This pointer points to a control that is of class CWnd (or of a class derived from the CWnd class). This explains the syntax used for showing the control in the OnShowButton() function:

```
GetDlgItem(IDC_MY_CHECKBOX)->ShowWindow(SW_SHOW);
```

If this is your first experience with the MFC, you might be overwhelmed and possibly confused by this business of classes. However, it all makes sense as long as you think about the whole mechanism of classes from an "object" point of view. That is, the CWnd class is a general class, with many powerful member functions—it is a gift from Microsoft.

During the development of your project, you'll use classes such as the CChkboxDlg class to create dialog boxes. The classes of your projects (such as the CChkboxDlg class) are derived from other classes. In particular, the CChkboxDlg class was derived from the CDialog class. CDialog was itself derived from the CWnd class. Thus, the CChkboxDlg class inherited the powerful member functions of the CWnd class.

Attaching Code to the Disable and Enable Buttons

Recall that when the user clicks the Disable button, the My Check Box control should become disabled. You'll now attach code to the Click event of the Disable button.

☐ Display the ClassWizard dialog box by selecting ClassWizard from the Project menu of Visual C++.

Visual C++ responds by displaying the ClassWizard dialog box.

☐ Select the Message Maps tab at the top of ClassWizard's dialog box.

☐ Use ClassWizard to select the event:

```
CChkboxDlg -> IDC_DISABLE_BUTTON -> BN_CLICKED
```

Then click the Add Function button.

☐ Name the new function OnDisableButton().

To write the code of the `OnDisableButton()` function do the following:

☐ Click the Edit Code button of ClassWizard.

> *ClassWizard responds by opening the file ChkBoDlg.CPP, with the function* `OnDisableButton()` *ready to be edited by you.*

☐ Write code inside the OnDisableButton() function so that it looks like this:

```
void CChkboxDlg::OnDisableButton()
{
// TODO: Add your control notification handler code here
/////////////////////////
// MY CODE STARTS HERE //
/////////////////////////
// Disable the check box
GetDlgItem(IDC_MY_CHECKBOX)->EnableWindow(FALSE);

/////////////////////////
// MY CODE ENDS HERE //
/////////////////////////

}
```

The code you typed inside the `OnDisableButton()` function disables the check box control:

```
GetDlgItem(IDC_MY_CHECKBOX)->EnableWindow(FALSE);
```

That is, the pointer to the check box is extracted with the `GetDlgItem()` function, and the `EnableWindow()` function is applied on the extracted pointer. When the parameter of the `EnableWindow()` is FALSE, the `EnableWindow()` function disables the control.

Recall that when the user clicks the Enable button, the My Check Box control should become enabled. You'll now attach code to the Click event of the Enable button.

☐ Display the ClassWizard dialog box by selecting ClassWizard from the Project menu of Visual C++.

☐ Select the Message Maps tab at the top of ClassWizard's dialog box.

☐ Use ClassWizard to select the event:

```
CChkboxDlg -> IDC_ENABLE_BUTTON -> BN_CLICKED
```

Then click the Add Function button.

☐ Name the new function OnEnableButton().

To write the code of the `OnEnableButton()` function do the following:

☐ Click the Edit Code button of ClassWizard.

> *ClassWizard responds by opening the file ChkBoDlg.CPP, with the function* `OnEnableButton()` *ready to be edited by you.*

☐ Write code inside the OnEnableButton() function so that it looks like this:

```
void CChkboxDlg::OnEnableButton()
{
// TODO: Add your control notification handler code here

/////////////////////////
// MY CODE STARTS HERE //
/////////////////////////
// Enable the check box
GetDlgItem(IDC_MY_CHECKBOX)->EnableWindow(TRUE);

/////////////////////////
// MY CODE ENDS HERE //
/////////////////////////

}
```

The code you typed inside the `OnEnableButton()` function enables the check box:

```
// Enable the check box
GetDlgItem(IDC_MY_CHECKBOX)->EnableWindow(TRUE);
```

To see your code in action do the following:

☐ Select Build ChkBox.EXE from the Project menu.

> *Visual C++ responds by compiling and linking the ChkBox program.*

☐ Select Execute ChkBox.EXE from the Project menu.

> *Visual C++ responds by executing the ChkBox.EXE program.*

☐ Click the Disable button.

> *As expected, the ChkBox program makes the check box disabled.*

☐ Click the Enable button.

> *As expected, the ChkBox program makes the check box enabled.*

☐ Experiment with the ChkBox program and then click the Exit button to terminate the program.

8

Scroll Bars

In this chapter you'll learn how to incorporate scroll bars in a dialog box. As you know, scroll bars serve an important role in the Windows user-interface mechanism. The application that you'll write in this chapter is a dialog-based type—that is, it is an application in which a dialog box serves as the main window of the application.

The ScrollMe Application

You'll now write the ScrollMe application, which is an example of an application that uses a scroll bar. Before you start writing the ScrollMe application yourself, execute the copy of it that resides in the \MVCPROG\EXE directory of the book's CD.

To execute the ScrollMe application do the following:

☐ Execute the X:\VCPROG\EXE\ScrollMe.EXE program (where *X* represents the drive letter of your CD-ROM drive).

> *Windows responds by executing the ScrollMe.EXE application. The main window of ScrollMe.EXE appears, as shown in Figure 8.1.*

Figure 8.1. The main window of the ScrollMe application.

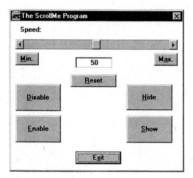

In the ScrollMe program, the scroll bar was designed so that it represents a number between 1 and 100. The current position of the scroll bar is 50.

You can change the scroll bar's position in the following way:

☐ Click the arrow icons that appear on the left or the right side of the scroll bar.

> *ScrollMe responds by increasing or decreasing by 1 the number that appears inside the edit box. That is, each click on the left-arrow icon decreases the number by 1, and each click on the right-arrow icon increases the number by 1.*

☐ Click inside an area on the scroll bar between the thumb tab of the scroll bar and the arrow icons that appear on the left or the right side of the scroll bar.

> *ScrollMe responds by increasing or decreasing the number that appears inside the edit box by 10.*

☐ Drag the thumb tab of the scroll bar to the right or to the left.

> *ScrollMe responds by increasing or decreasing the number that appears inside the edit box according to your mouse movement.*

☐ Try using the other buttons of the dialog box.

As you can see, the Disable button makes the scroll bar unavailable (dimmed), and the Enable button makes the scroll bar available. Similarly, the Hide button makes the scroll bar invisible and the Show button makes the scroll bar visible. (See Figure 8.2.)

☐ Click the Exit button to terminate the ScrollMe application.

Figure 8.2. Making the scroll bar invisible.

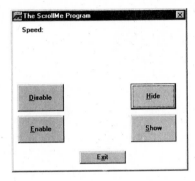

Now that you know what the ScrollMe application should do, you can begin writing it.

Creating the Project of the ScrollMe Application

To create the project of the ScrollMe application do the following:

☐ Start Visual C++ and close all the open windows that appear inside the desktop of Visual C++ (if there are any).

☐ Select New from the File menu.

Visual C++ responds by displaying the New dialog box.

☐ Select Project inside the New dialog box and then click the OK button of the New dialog box.

Visual C++ responds by displaying the New Project dialog box.

☐ Set the project name to ScrollMe.

☐ Set the project path to \MVCPROG\CH08\ScrollMe\ScrollMe.MAK.

Your New Project dialog box should now look like the one shown in Figure 8.3.

☐ Click the Create button of the New Project dialog box.

Visual C++ responds by displaying the AppWizard—Step 1 window.

☐ Set the Step 1 window as shown in Figure 8.4. As shown in Figure 8.4, the ScrollMe.MAK project is set as a dialog-based application, and U.S. English (APPWIZUS.DLL) is used as the language for the ScrolDlg.MAK project's resources.

Figure 8.3. The New Project dialog box of the ScrollMe.MAK project.

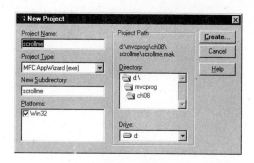

Figure 8.4. The AppWizard—Step 1 window of the ScrollMe.MAK project.

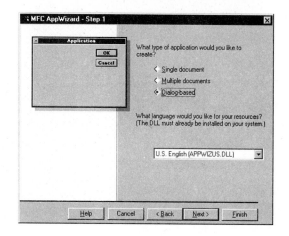

☐ Click the Next button of the Step 1 window.

> *Visual C++ responds by displaying the AppWizard—Step 2 of 4 window.*

☐ Set the Step 2 of 4 window as shown in Figure 8.5. That is, place a checkmark inside the About Box check box (to incorporate an About dialog box into the application), and place a checkmark inside the Use 3D Controls check box (so that the application will use 3D controls). Also, set the title of the application to The ScrollMe Program.

☐ Click the Next button of the Step 2 of 4 window.

> *Visual C++ responds by displaying the AppWizard—Step 3 of 4 window.*

☐ Set the Step 3 of 4 window as shown in Figure 8.6.

As shown in Figure 8.6, the project will be generated with comments, a Visual C++ makefile will be generated, and the application will use the MFC library from a DLL.

Figure 8.5. The AppWizard—Step 2 of 4 window of the ScrollMe.MAK project.

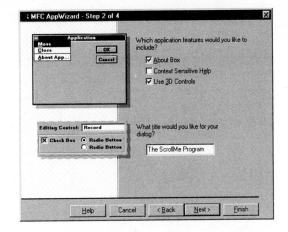

Figure 8.6. The AppWizard—Step 3 of 4 window of the ScrollMe.MAK project.

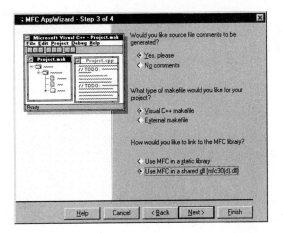

☐ Click the Next button of the Step 3 of 4 window.

> *Visual C++ responds by displaying the AppWizard—Step 4 of 4 window, as shown in Figure 8.7.*

☐ Click the Finish button of the Step 4 of 4 window.

> *Visual C++ responds by displaying the New Project Information window, as shown in Figure 8.8.*

☐ Click the OK button of the New Project Information window.

> *Visual C++ responds by creating the project file and all the skeleton files of the application.*

Figure 8.7. The
AppWizard—Step 4 of 4
window of the
ScrollMe.MAK project.

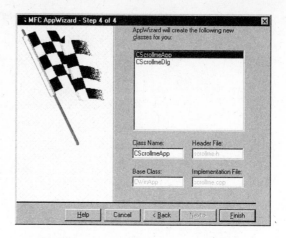

Figure 8.8. The New
Project Information
window of the
ScrollMe.MAK project.

The Visual Implementation of the ScrollMe Application

Because the ScrollMe application is a dialog-based application, when you created the project and the skeleton files of the ScrollMe application with AppWizard, AppWizard created for you a dialog box that serves as the main window of the application. AppWizard named this dialog box IDD_SCROLLME_DIALOG. You'll now customize the IDD_SCROLLME_DIALOG dialog box until it looks like the one shown back in Figure 8.1.

☐ Double-click scrollme.rc inside the scrollme.mak window.

   Visual C++ responds by displaying the scrollme.rc window.

☐ Double-click Dialog inside the scrollme.rc window and then double-click IDD_SCROLLME_DIALOG.

   Visual C++ responds by displaying the IDD_SCROLLME_DIALOG dialog box in design mode.

☐ Implement the dialog box according to the specifications in Table 8.1. When you finish implementing the dialog box, it should look like the one shown in Figure 8.9.

NOTE

Table 8.1 instructs you to place a horizontal scroll bar control inside the dialog box. The horizontal scroll bar tool inside the Tools window is shown in Figure 8.10.

Table 8.1. The Properties table of the IDD_SCROLLME_DIALOG dialog box.

Object	Property	Setting
Dialog box	ID	IDD_SCROLLME_DIALOG
Push button	ID	IDC_EXIT_BUTTON
	Caption	E&xit
Horizontal scroll bar	ID	IDC_SCROLLME
Edit box	ID	IDC_SPEED
	Multiline	Checked
	Align Text	Centered
Static	ID	IDC_STATIC
	Caption	Speed:
Push button	ID	IDC_MIN_BUTTON
	Caption	&Min.
Push button	ID	IDC_MAX_BUTTON
	Caption	M&ax.
Push button	ID	IDC_DISABLE_BUTTON
	Caption	&Disable
Push button	ID	IDC_ENABLE_BUTTON
	Caption	&Enable
Push button	ID	IDC_HIDE_BUTTON
	Caption	&Hide
Push button	ID	IDC_SHOW_BUTTON
	Caption	&Show
Push button	ID	IDC_RESET_BUTTON
	Caption	&Reset

*Figure 8.9. The dialog box
that serves as the main
window of the ScrollMe
program (in design mode).*

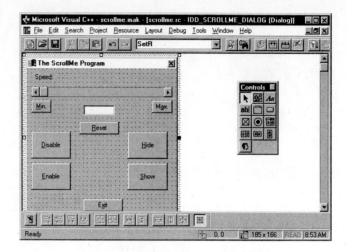

*Figure 8.10. The
horizontal scroll bar tool
inside the Tools window of
Visual C++.*

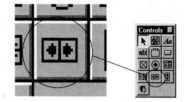

Attaching Variables to the Controls Inside the Dialog Box of the ScrollMe Program

You'll now attach variables to the controls of the ScrollMe dialog box.

☐ Use ClassWizard (from the Project menu) to attach variables to the controls of the IDD_SCROLLME_DIALOG dialog box according to the specifications in Table 8.2.

Table 8.2. The Variables table of the ScrollMe dialog box.

Control ID	Variable Name	Category	Type
IDC_MY_EDITBOX	m_Speed	Control	CEdit
IDC_SCROLLME	m_ScrollMe	Control	CScrollBar

NOTE

As specified in Table 8.2, when you add the two variables (m_Speed and m_ScrollMe), you must set the category of these variables to Control (not to Value).

☐ To save your work, select Save from the File menu.

To see your visual design in action do the following:

☐ Select Build ScrollMe.EXE from the Project menu.

> *Visual C++ responds by compiling and linking the ScrollMe application.*

☐ Select Execute ScrollMe.EXE from the Project menu.

> *Visual C++ responds by executing the ScrollMe.EXE application. As expected, the IDD_SCROLLME_DIALOG dialog box that you designed appears as the main window of the application.*

☐ Click the icon that appears on the upper-left corner of the ScrollMe application window, and select About from the System menu that pops up.

ScrollMe responds by displaying the About dialog box.

☐ Click the OK button of the About dialog box to close the About dialog box.

☐ Try to change the thumb tab position of the scroll bar and note that the scroll bar does not respond to the clicking. (This, of course, makes sense because you have not yet attached code that causes the scroll bar to respond.)

☐ Click the icon that appears in the upper-left corner of the ScrollMe application, and select Close from the System menu that pops up.

> *ScrollMe responds by terminating itself.*

The point of the above exercise is to show you that you have to write code to cause the scroll bar to act as a scroll bar.

Initializing the Controls of the Dialog Box

In this section you'll write initialization code that causes the scroll bar to place its thumb tab at a value of 50. Also, the minimum value that the scroll bar represents will be set to 0, and the maximum value that the scroll bar represents will be set to 100.

Because the edit box of the ScrollMe program always displays the value of the scroll bar, the initialization code will also cause the edit box to display the value 50.

You'll now attach code to the WM_INITDIALOG event of the IDD_SCROLLME_DIALOG dialog box. The WM_INITDIALOG event occurs just before the dialog box is displayed.

☐ Select ClassWizard from the Project menu of Visual C++.

> *Visual C++ responds by displaying the ClassWizard dialog box.*

☐ Select the Message Maps tab at the top of ClassWizard's dialog box.

☐ Use ClassWizard to select the event:

CScrollmeDlg -> CScrollmeDlg -> WM_INITDIALOG

Then click the Edit Code button.

> *Visual C++ responds by opening the SCROLDLG.CPP file and displaying the*
> OnInitDialog() *function, ready to be edited by you.*

☐ Write code inside the OnInitDialog() function so that it looks like this:

```
BOOL CScrollmeDlg::OnInitDialog()
{
CDialog::OnInitDialog();
CenterWindow();

// Add "About..." menu item to system menu.

// IDM_ABOUTBOX must be in the system command range.
ASSERT((IDM_ABOUTBOX & 0xFFF0) == IDM_ABOUTBOX);
ASSERT(IDM_ABOUTBOX < 0xF000);

CMenu* pSysMenu = GetSystemMenu(FALSE);
CString strAboutMenu;
strAboutMenu.LoadString(IDS_ABOUTBOX);
if (!strAboutMenu.IsEmpty())
    {
    pSysMenu->AppendMenu(MF_SEPARATOR);
    pSysMenu->AppendMenu(MF_STRING, IDM_ABOUTBOX,
    strAboutMenu);
    }

// TODO: Add extra initialization here

/////////////////////////
// MY CODE STARTS HERE
/////////////////////////

// Set the range of the scroll bar
m_ScrollMe.SetScrollRange (0,100);

// Set the current position of the scroll bar
m_ScrollMe.SetScrollPos (50);


// Fill sPos with the value of the scroll bar
char sPos[25];
itoa (m_ScrollMe.GetScrollPos(), sPos, 10 );

// Select the entire text inside the edit box
m_Speed.SetSel (0,-1);

 // Replace the selected text
m_Speed.ReplaceSel (sPos);

// Update the screen
UpdateData(FALSE);
```

```
////////////////////////
// MY CODE ENDS HERE
////////////////////////
```

```
return TRUE;
// return TRUE  unless you set the focus to a control
}
```

☐ Save your work by selecting Save from the File menu of Visual C++.

The first statement that you typed inside the `OnInitDialog()` function:

```
m_ScrollMe.SetScrollRange (0,100);
```

sets the range of the scroll bar by using the `SetScrollRange()` member function of the `CScrollBar` class. So from now on the minimum value that the scroll bar represents is 0, and the maximum value that the scroll bar represents is 100.

Next, the current position of the scroll bar is set to 50:

```
m_ScrollMe.SetScrollPos (50);
```

Note that in the preceding statement, the `SetScrollPos()` member function of the `CScrollBar` class is used on `m_ScrollMe`. Recall that `m_ScrollMe` is the variable that you attached to the scroll bar.

The `sPos` string variable is then filled with the value of the scroll bar's current position:

```
char sPos[25];
itoa (m_ScrollMe.GetScrollPos(), sPos, 10 );
```

Then the entire text inside the edit box is selected with the `SetSel()` member function of the `CEdit` class:

```
m_Speed.SetSel (0,-1);
```

Finally, the selected text of the edit box is replaced with the value of `sPos`:

```
m_Speed.ReplaceSel (sPos);
```

To transfer the contents of the variables to the screen, the `UpdateData()` function is used with `FALSE` as its parameter:

```
UpdateData(FALSE);
```

To see your initialization code in action do the following:

☐ Select Build ScrollMe.EXE from the Project menu.

> *Visual C++ responds by compiling and linking the ScrollMe program.*

☐ Select Execute ScrollMe.EXE from the Project menu.

> *Visual C++ responds by executing the ScrollMe.EXE program. As you can see, the scroll bar appears with its thumb tab in the middle of the scroll bar, and the edit box contains the text 50.*

☐ Try to change the scroll bar's position, and note that the scroll bar still does not behave as a scroll bar. This, of course, makes sense because you have not yet written the code that causes the scroll bar control to behave as a scroll bar.

☐ Click the × icon that appears on the upper-right corner of the ScrollMe program's window.

ScrollMe responds by terminating itself.

Attaching Code to the *BN_CLICKED* Event of the Exit Button

Recall that when the user clicks the Exit button the ScrollMe program should terminate. You'll now attach code to the Click event (BN_CLICKED) of the Exit button.

☐ Display the ClassWizard dialog box by selecting ClassWizard from the Project menu of Visual C++.

☐ Select the Message Maps tab at the top of ClassWizard's dialog box.

☐ Use ClassWizard to select the event:

CScrollmeDlg -> IDC_EXIT_BUTTON -> BN_CLICKED

Then click the Add Function button.

☐ Name the new function OnExitButton().

To write the code of the OnExitButton() function do the following:

☐ Click the Edit Code button of ClassWizard.

ClassWizard responds by opening the file SCROLDLG.CPP, with the function OnExitButton() *ready to be edited by you.*

☐ Write code inside the OnExitButton() function so that it looks like this:

```
void CScrollmeDlg::OnExitButton()
{
// TODO: Add your control notification handler code here

///////////////////////
// MY CODE STARTS HERE
///////////////////////

// Close the dialog box (terminate the program).
OnOK();

///////////////////////
// MY CODE ENDS HERE
///////////////////////

}
```

☐ Save your work by selecting Save from the File menu of Visual C++.

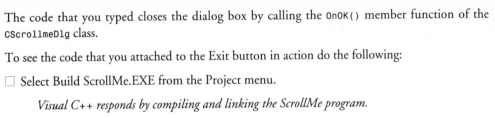

The code that you typed closes the dialog box by calling the OnOK() member function of the CScrollmeDlg class.

To see the code that you attached to the Exit button in action do the following:

☐ Select Build ScrollMe.EXE from the Project menu.

   Visual C++ responds by compiling and linking the ScrollMe program.

☐ Select Execute ScrollMe.EXE from the Project menu.

   Visual C++ responds by executing the ScrollMe.EXE program.

☐ Click the Exit button.

As expected, the ScrollMe program terminates itself.

Attaching Code to the *WM_HSCROLL* Event of the Dialog Box

You'll now write the code that causes the horizontal scroll bar to behave like a scroll bar.

☐ Display the ClassWizard dialog box by selecting ClassWizard from the Project menu of Visual C++.

   Visual C++ responds by displaying the ClassWizard dialog box.

☐ Select the Message Maps tab at the top of ClassWizard's dialog box.

☐ Use ClassWizard to select the event:

```
CScrollmeDlg -> CScrollmeDlg -> WM_HSCROLL
```

Then click the Add Function button.

> **NOTE**
>
> You might think that to add a function to the scroll bar you have to use ClassWizard and select the event:
>
> ```
> CScrollmeDlg -> IDC_SCROLLME -> WM_HSCROLL
> ```
>
> However, as you can see from the ClassWizard dialog box, there are no events associated with the scroll bar.
>
> To attach an event to a horizontal scroll bar, you have to select the event like this:
>
> ```
> CScrollmeDlg -> CScrollmeDlg -> WM_HSCROLL
> ```
>
> The WM_HSCROLL event occurs whenever the user changes a horizontal scroll bar inside the dialog box.

Note that Visual C++ does not ask you to name the function. This is because Visual C++ forces you to use the OnHScroll() function for the WM_HSCROLL event.

To write the code of the OnHScroll() function do the following:

☐ Click the Edit Code button of ClassWizard.

> *ClassWizard responds by opening the file SCROLDLG.CPP, with the function OnHScroll() ready to be edited by you.*

☐ Write code inside the OnHScroll() function so that it looks like this:

```
void CScrollmeDlg::OnHScroll(UINT nSBCode, UINT nPos,
                  CScrollBar* pScrollBar)
{
// TODO: Add your message handler code
// here and/or call default

/////////////////////////
// MY CODE STARTS HERE
/////////////////////////

char sPos[25];

switch (nSBCode)
{

case SB_THUMBPOSITION:

    // Set the thumb of the scroll bar to its new position
    m_ScrollMe.SetScrollPos ( nPos );

    // Fill sPos with the value of the scroll bar
    itoa (m_ScrollMe.GetScrollPos(), sPos, 10 );

    // Select the entire text
    m_Speed.SetSel (0,-1);

    // Replace the select text
    m_Speed.ReplaceSel (sPos);

break;

}

/////////////////////////
// MY CODE ENDS HERE
/////////////////////////

CDialog::OnHScroll(nSBCode, nPos, pScrollBar);
}
```

☐ Save your work by selecting Save from the File menu of Visual C++.

The code that you typed declares the sPos variable:

```
char sPos[25];
```

Then a `switch` is implemented:

```
switch (nSBCode)
{

case SB_THUMBPOSITION:
        .....
        .....
        .....
break;

}
```

The code inside case `SB_THUMBPOSITION` is executed provided that `nSBCode` is equal to `SB_THUMBPOSITION`.

Take a look at the `OnHScroll()` function:

```
void CScrollmeDlg::OnHScroll(UINT nSBCode, UINT nPos,
                       CScrollBar* pScrollBar)
{
.....
.....
.....
}
```

As you can see, `nSBCode` is the first parameter of the function. This parameter indicates which event occurs to the scroll bar. If `nSBCode` is equal to `SB_THUMBPOSITION`, you know that the user dragged the thumb tab of the scroll bar. You may ask Which scroll bar? because a window can contain several horizontal scroll bars. So when the `OnHScroll()` function is executed with its parameter `nSBCode` equal to `SB_THUMBPOSITION`, you know that the thumb tab of one of these horizontal scroll bars was dragged. In the case of the ScrollMe program, there is only one horizontal scroll bar, so you don't have to worry about it. However, when a window contains more than one scroll bar, you have to write code that determines which scroll bar is associated with the event. This issue is discussed again later in this chapter.

The thumb tab of the scroll bar is then set to the value specified by the `nPos` parameter:

```
m_ScrollMe.SetScrollPos ( nPos );
```

`nPos` is the second parameter of the `OnHScroll()` function. `nPos` indicates the new position of the thumb tab.

The `sPos` variable is filled with a string that indicates the current position of the scroll bar:

```
itoa (m_ScrollMe.GetScrollPos(), sPos, 10 );
```

Then the edit box is filled with a string that indicates the current position of the scroll bar:

```
m_Speed.SetSel (0,-1);
m_Speed.ReplaceSel (sPos);
```

To see your code in action do the following:

☐ Select Build ScrollMe.EXE from the Project menu.

Visual C++ responds by compiling and linking the ScrollMe program.

☐ Select Execute ScrollMe.EXE from the Project menu.

> *Visual C++ responds by executing the ScrollMe.EXE program.*

☐ Drag the thumb tab of the scroll bar.

As expected, the ScrollMe program changes the status of the scroll bar, and the new status of the scroll bar is displayed inside the edit box.

☐ Experiment with the ScrollMe program and then click the Exit button to terminate the program. In particular, note that clicking the arrow icons of the scroll bar does not cause the scroll bar to change its position. This makes sense because you have not yet attached the appropriate code. Also, clicking between the thumb tab and the arrow icon does not cause the scroll bar to change its position.

Determining Which Scroll Bar Is Associated with the Event

As previously stated, for an application that has more than one horizontal scroll bar, you need to write code that determines which scroll bar is associated with the event that caused the OnHScroll() function to execute.

☐ Edit the OnHScroll() function so that it looks like this:

```
void CScrollmeDlg::OnHScroll(UINT nSBCode, UINT nPos,
                        CScrollBar* pScrollBar)
{
// TODO: Add your message
// handler code here and/or call default

/////////////////////////
// MY CODE STARTS HERE
/////////////////////////

char sPos[25];


switch (nSBCode)
{

if (pScrollBar == &m_ScrollMe )
   {
   case SB_THUMBPOSITION:

      // Set the thumb of the scroll bar to its new position
      m_ScrollMe.SetScrollPos ( nPos );

      // Fill sPos with the value of the scroll bar
      itoa (m_ScrollMe.GetScrollPos(), sPos, 10 );

      // Select the entire text
      m_Speed.SetSel (0,-1);

      // Replace the select text
```

```
        m_Speed.ReplaceSel (sPos);

        break;

    } //end of if

} // end of switch

//////////////////////////
// MY CODE ENDS HERE
//////////////////////////

CDialog::OnHScroll(nSBCode, nPos, pScrollBar);
}
```

As you can see, an if statement was added:

```
void CScrollmeDlg::OnHScroll(UINT nSBCode, UINT nPos,
                        CScrollBar* pScrollBar)
{
....
....
....
if (pScrollBar == &m_ScrollMe )
    {
      ......
      ......
      ......
    }
}
```

The if statement compares pScrollBar, the fourth parameter of the OnHScroll() function, to &m_ScrollMe. If the if condition is satisfied, you know that the scroll bar associated with the m_ScrollMe variable caused the event.

☐ To save your work, select Save from the File menu.

To see your code in action do the following:

☐ Select Build ScrollMe.EXE from the Project menu.

   Visual C++ responds by compiling and linking the ScrollMe program.

☐ Select Execute ScrollMe.EXE from the Project menu.

   Visual C++ responds by executing the ScrollMe.EXE program.

☐ Drag the thumb tab of the scroll bar.

As expected, the ScrollMe program changes the status of the scroll bar, and the new status of the scroll bar is displayed inside the edit box.

☐ Experiment with the ScrollMe program and then click the Exit button to terminate the program.

Attaching Code to the Other Scroll Bar Messages

So far the scroll bar responds only to its thumb tab being dragged. You'll now attach additional code to the OnHScroll() function that causes the scroll bar to respond the way a standard scroll bar does.

☐ Edit the OnHScroll() function so that it looks like this:

```
void CScrollmeDlg::OnHScroll(UINT nSBCode, UINT nPos,
                   CScrollBar* pScrollBar)
{
// TODO: Add your message handler code
// here and/or call default

//////////////////////////
// MY CODE STARTS HERE
//////////////////////////

char sPos[25];
int iCurrent;


switch (nSBCode)
{

if (pScrollBar == &m_ScrollMe )
    {
    case SB_THUMBPOSITION:

        ///////// User dragged the thumb ////////

        // Set the thumb to its new position
        m_ScrollMe.SetScrollPos ( nPos );

        // Fill sPos with the value of the scroll bar
        itoa (m_ScrollMe.GetScrollPos(), sPos, 10 );

        // Select the entire text
        m_Speed.SetSel (0,-1);

        // Replace the select text
        m_Speed.ReplaceSel (sPos);


        break;

    case SB_LINEDOWN:

        ///////// User clicked the right arrow icon //////

        iCurrent = m_ScrollMe.GetScrollPos();

        iCurrent = iCurrent + 1;

        if ( iCurrent > 100 )
            iCurrent = 100;

        // Set the thumb to its new position
```

```
        m_ScrollMe.SetScrollPos(iCurrent);

        // Fill sPos with the value of the scroll bar
        itoa (m_ScrollMe.GetScrollPos(), sPos, 10 );

        // Select the entire text
        m_Speed.SetSel (0,-1);

        // Replace the select text
        m_Speed.ReplaceSel (sPos);


    break;


case SB_LINEUP:

        ///////// User clicked the left arrow icon //////

        iCurrent = m_ScrollMe.GetScrollPos();

        iCurrent = iCurrent - 1;

        if ( iCurrent < 0 )
           iCurrent = 0;

        // Set the thumb to its new position
        m_ScrollMe.SetScrollPos(iCurrent);

        // Fill sPos with the value of the scroll bar
        itoa (m_ScrollMe.GetScrollPos(), sPos, 10 );

        // Select the entire text
        m_Speed.SetSel (0,-1);

        // Replace the select text
        m_Speed.ReplaceSel (sPos);


    break;

 case SB_PAGEDOWN:

        ///////// User clicked in between the thumb
        ///////// and the right arrow icon.

        iCurrent = m_ScrollMe.GetScrollPos();

        iCurrent = iCurrent + 10;

        if ( iCurrent > 100 )
           iCurrent = 100;

        // Set the thumb to its new position
        m_ScrollMe.SetScrollPos(iCurrent);

        // Fill sPos with the value of the scroll bar
        itoa (m_ScrollMe.GetScrollPos(), sPos, 10 );
```

```
        // Select the entire text
        m_Speed.SetSel (0,-1);

        // Replace the select text
        m_Speed.ReplaceSel (sPos);


        break;

    case SB_PAGEUP:

        ///////// User clicked in between the thumb
        ///////// and the left arrow icon.

        iCurrent = m_ScrollMe.GetScrollPos();

        iCurrent = iCurrent – 10;

        if ( iCurrent < 0 )
           iCurrent = 0;


        // Set the thumb to its new position
        m_ScrollMe.SetScrollPos(iCurrent);

        // Fill sPos with the value of the scroll bar
        itoa (m_ScrollMe.GetScrollPos(), sPos, 10 );

        // Select the entire text
        m_Speed.SetSel (0,-1);

        // Replace the select text
        m_Speed.ReplaceSel (sPos);


        break;

    }// end of if

}// end of switch


//////////////////////
// MY CODE ENDS HERE
//////////////////////

CDialog::OnHScroll(nSBCode, nPos, pScrollBar);
}
```

The code that you typed takes care of other messages that are related to the user's activity on the scroll bar. As stated earlier, the SB_THUMBPOSITION message is generated whenever the user drags the thumb tab of the scroll bar.

The SB_LINEDOWN message is generated whenever the user clicks the right-arrow icon of the scroll bar. The code under the SB_LINEDOWN is the following:

```
case SB_LINEDOWN:

        ///////// User clicked the right arrow icon //////
```

```
        iCurrent = m_ScrollMe.GetScrollPos();

        iCurrent = iCurrent + 1;

        if ( iCurrent > 100 )
           iCurrent = 100;

        // Set the thumb to its new position
        m_ScrollMe.SetScrollPos(iCurrent);

        // Fill sPos with the value of the scroll bar
        itoa (m_ScrollMe.GetScrollPos(), sPos, 10 );

        // Select the entire text
        m_Speed.SetSel (0,-1);

        // Replace the select text
        m_Speed.ReplaceSel (sPos);

     break;
```

The preceding code increases the current position of the scroll bar by 1. Note that an `if` statement is used to ensure that the scroll bar position does not exceed 100. (Recall that you set the range of the scroll bar to `0,100`.)

The `SB_LINEUP` message is generated whenever the user clicks the left-arrow icon of the scroll bar. The code under `SB_LINEDOWN` is the following:

```
  case SB_LINEUP:

        ///////// User clicked the left arrow icon //////

        iCurrent = m_ScrollMe.GetScrollPos();

        iCurrent = iCurrent—1;

        if ( iCurrent < 0 )
           iCurrent = 0;

        // Set the thumb to its new position
        m_ScrollMe.SetScrollPos(iCurrent);

        // Fill sPos with the value of the scroll bar
        itoa (m_ScrollMe.GetScrollPos(), sPos, 10 );

        // Select the entire text
        m_Speed.SetSel (0,-1);

        // Replace the select text
        m_Speed.ReplaceSel (sPos);

     break;
```

The preceding code decreases the current position of the scroll bar by 1. Note that an `if` statement is used to ensure that the scroll bar position is not set below 0. (Recall that you set the range of the scroll bar to `0,100`.)

The SB_PAGEDOWN message is generated whenever the user clicks between the thumb tab of the scroll bar and the right-arrow icon of the scroll bar. The code under the SB_PAGEDOWN is the following:

```
case SB_PAGEDOWN:

    ///////// User clicked in between the thumb
    ///////// and the right arrow icon.

    iCurrent = m_ScrollMe.GetScrollPos();

    iCurrent = iCurrent + 10;

    if ( iCurrent > 100 )
       iCurrent = 100;

    // Set the thumb to its new position
    m_ScrollMe.SetScrollPos(iCurrent);

    // Fill sPos with the value of the scroll bar
    itoa (m_ScrollMe.GetScrollPos(), sPos, 10 );

    // Select the entire text
    m_Speed.SetSel (0,-1);

    // Replace the select text
    m_Speed.ReplaceSel (sPos);

    break;
```

The code of SB_PAGEDOWN is very similar to the code of SB_LINEDOWN. In fact, the only difference is that under the SB_LINEDOWN case you increase the thumb tab position by 1, whereas under the SB_PAGEDOWN case you increase the thumb tab position by 10.

The SB_PAGEUP message is generated whenever the user clicks between the thumb tab of the scroll bar and the left-arrow icon of the scroll bar. The code under the SB_PAGEUP is the following:

```
case SB_PAGEUP:

    ///////// User clicked in between the thumb
    ///////// and the left arrow icon.

    iCurrent = m_ScrollMe.GetScrollPos();

    iCurrent = iCurrent-10;

    if ( iCurrent < 0 )
       iCurrent = 0;


    // Set the thumb to its new position
    m_ScrollMe.SetScrollPos(iCurrent);

    // Fill sPos with the value of the scroll bar
    itoa (m_ScrollMe.GetScrollPos(), sPos, 10 );

    // Select the entire text
    m_Speed.SetSel (0,-1);
```

```
    // Replace the select text
    m_Speed.ReplaceSel (sPos);

    break;

}// end of if
```

The code of SB_PAGEUP is very similar to the code of SB_LINEUP. In fact, the only difference is that under the SB_LINEUP case you decrease the thumb tab position by 1, whereas under the SB_PAGEUP case you decrease the thumb tab position by 10.

☐ To save your work, select Save from the File menu.

To see your code in action do the following:

☐ Select Build ScrollMe.EXE from the Project menu.

   Visual C++ responds by compiling and linking the ScrollMe program.

☐ Select Execute ScrollMe.EXE from the Project menu.

   Visual C++ responds by executing the ScrollMe.EXE program.

☐ Drag the thumb tab of the scroll bar.

   As expected, the ScrollMe program changes the status of the scroll bar, and the new status of the scroll bar is displayed inside the edit box.

☐ Click the right- and left-arrow icons of the scroll bar.

   As expected, the ScrollMe program changes the status of the scroll bar by 1 unit, and the new status of the scroll bar is displayed inside the edit box.

☐ Click between the thumb tab of the scroll bar and the right- or left-arrow icons of the scroll bar.

   As expected, the ScrollMe program changes the status of the scroll bar by 10 units, and the new status of the scroll bar is displayed inside the edit box.

Note that while you drag the thumb tab of the scroll bar the edit box does not display the current position of the scroll bar. The edit box displays the current position of the scroll bar only after you release the dragged thumb tab. In the next section you'll modify the OnHScroll() function so that the edit box will continuously display the current position of the scroll bar while you drag the scroll bar's thumb tab.

☐ Experiment with the ScrollMe program and then click the Exit button to terminate the program.

Displaying the Scroll Bar's Thumb Tab Position While the Thumb Tab Is Being Dragged

As was demonstrated in the previous section, the edit box displays the position of the dragged thumb tab only after you release the thumb tab. In many applications it is necessary that the scroll bar position be displayed while the thumb tab is being dragged. In this section you'll learn how to accomplish that.

☐ Edit the OnHScroll() function by adding another case to the switch:

```
case SB_THUMBTRACK:

        ///////// User is dragging the thumb


        // Set the thumb to its new position
        m_ScrollMe.SetScrollPos(nPos);

        // Fill sPos with the value of the scroll bar
        itoa (nPos, sPos, 10 );

        // Select the entire text
        m_Speed.SetSel (0,-1);

        // Replace the select text
        m_Speed.ReplaceSel (sPos);

        break;
```

The code that you typed is executed whenever the thumb tab of the scroll bar is dragged. That is, while the thumb tab is dragged, Windows generates the SB_THUMBTRACK message, and the OnHScroll() function is executed with nSBCode equal to SB_THUMBTRACK.

NOTE

Should you include the SB_THUMBTRACK case in your applications? It depends on the application. For example, if you drag the thumb tab of the vertical scroll bar of a document in Microsoft Word for Windows, you'll see that the document does not scroll while you drag the thumb tab. The document scrolls only after you release the thumb tab. In other words, the SB_THUMBTRACK case was not implemented! This is because a document can contain graphics and formatted text. Therefore, scrolling the document while the thumb tab is dragged is difficult, because it requires a huge amount of calculations whenever the thumb tab is moved. In fact, if the SB_THUMBTRACK were implemented, the user would observe such great delays that it would be difficult to understand what is going on.

On the other hand, in the ScrollMe program there is not much code under the SB_THUMBTRACK case, and therefore the user does not notice any significant delays.

☐ To save your work, select Save from the File menu.

To see your code in action do the following:

☐ Select Build ScrollMe.EXE from the Project menu.

> *Visual C++ responds by compiling and linking the ScrollMe program.*

☐ Select Execute ScrollMe.EXE from the Project menu.

> *Visual C++ responds by executing the ScrollMe.EXE program.*

☐ Drag the thumb tab of the scroll bar.

As expected, the ScrollMe program changes the status of the edit box as you drag the scroll bar's thumb tab.

☐ Experiment with the ScrollMe program and then click the Exit button to terminate the program.

Attaching Code to the Hide and Show Buttons

Recall that when the user clicks the Hide button the scroll bar should become invisible. You'll now attach code to the Click event of the Hide button.

☐ Display the ClassWizard dialog box by selecting ClassWizard from the Project menu of Visual C++.

☐ Select the Message Maps tab at the top of ClassWizard's dialog box.

☐ Use ClassWizard to select the event:

```
CScrollmeDlg -> IDC_HIDE_BUTTON -> BN_CLICKED
```

Then click the Add Function button.

☐ Name the new function `OnHideButton()`.

To write the code of the `OnHideButton()` function do the following:

☐ Click the Edit Code button of ClassWizard.

> *ClassWizard responds by opening the file SCROLDLG.CPP, with the function* `OnHideButton()` *ready to be edited by you.*

☐ Write code inside the `OnHideButton()` function so that it looks like this:

```
void CScrollmeDlg::OnHideButton()
{
// TODO: Add your control notification handler code here


/////////////////////////
// MY CODE STARTS HERE
/////////////////////////

// Hide the scroll bar

// To hide the scroll bar, you  use
//
// m_ScrollMe.ShowScrollBar(FALSE);
//
//      or
//
```

```
// m_ScrollMe.ShowWindow(SW_HIDE);

m_ScrollMe.ShowWindow(SW_HIDE);

/////////////////////////
// MY CODE ENDS HERE
/////////////////////////

}
```

The code that you typed hides the scroll bar:

```
m_ScrollMe.ShowWindow(SW_HIDE);
```

The ShowWindow() function hides or shows the control. If you supply SW_HIDE as the parameter of the ShowWindow() function, the control is made invisible, and if you supply SW_SHOW as the parameter of the ShowWindow() function, the control is made visible.

> **NOTE**
>
> To hide the scroll bar, you used this statement:
>
> ```
> m_ScrollMe.ShowWindow(SW_HIDE);
> ```
>
> Alternatively, you can hide the scroll bar by using the ShowScrollBar() member function of the CScrollBar class:
>
> ```
> m_ScrollMe.ShowScrollBar(FALSE);
> ```

☐ To save your work, select Save from the File menu.

Recall that when the user clicks the Show button the scroll bar control should become visible. You'll now attach code to the Click event of the Show button.

☐ Display the ClassWizard dialog box by selecting ClassWizard from the Project menu of Visual C++.

☐ Select the Message Maps tab at the top of ClassWizard's dialog box.

☐ Use ClassWizard to select the event:

```
CScrollmeDlg -> IDC_SHOW_BUTTON -> BN_CLICKED
```

Then click the Add Function button.

☐ Name the new function OnShowButton().

To write the code of the OnShowButton() function do the following:

☐ Click the Edit Code button of ClassWizard.

> *ClassWizard responds by opening the file SCROLDLG.CPP, with the function OnShowButton() ready to be edited by you.*

☐ Write code inside the OnShowButton() function so that it looks like this:

```
void CScrollmeDlg::OnShowButton()
{
// TODO: Add your control notification handler code here


////////////////////////
// MY CODE STARTS HERE
////////////////////////

// Show the scroll bar

// To show the scroll bar, you  use
//
// m_ScrollMe.ShowScrollBar(TRUE);
//
//     or
//
// m_ScrollMe.ShowScrollBar(SW_SHOW);

m_ScrollMe.ShowWindow(SW_SHOW);

////////////////////////
// MY CODE ENDS HERE
////////////////////////

}
```

The code that you typed uses the ShowWindow() function with parameter equal to SW_SHOW. This makes the scroll bar visible.

NOTE

To make the scroll bar visible, you used this statement:

```
m_ScrollMe.ShowWindow(SW_SHOW);
```

Alternatively, you can make the scroll bar visible by using the ShowScrollBar() member function of the CScrollBar class:

```
m_ScrollMe.ShowScrollBar(TRUE);
```

To see your code in action do the following:

☐ Select Build ScrollMe.EXE from the Project menu.

   Visual C++ responds by compiling and linking the ScrollMe program.

☐ Select Execute ScrollMe.EXE from the Project menu.

   Visual C++ responds by executing the ScrollMe.EXE program.

☐ Click the Hide button.

As expected, the ScrollMe program makes the scroll bar invisible.

☐ Click the Show button.

As expected, the ScrollMe program makes the scroll bar visible.

☐ Experiment with the ScrollMe program and then click the Exit button to terminate the program.

Attaching Code to the Disable and Enable Buttons

Recall that when the user clicks the Disable button the scroll bar control should become disabled. You'll now attach code to the Click event of the Disable button.

☐ Display the ClassWizard dialog box by selecting ClassWizard from the Project menu of Visual C++.

Visual C++ responds by displaying the ClassWizard dialog box.

☐ Select the Message Maps tab at the top of ClassWizard's dialog box.

☐ Use ClassWizard to select the event:

```
CScrollmeDlg -> IDC_DISABLE_BUTTON -> BN_CLICKED
```

Then click the Add Function button.

☐ Name the new function OnDisableButton().

To write the code of the OnDisableButton() function do the following:

☐ Click the Edit Code button of ClassWizard.

ClassWizard responds by opening the file SCROLDLG.CPP, with the function OnDisableButton() ready to be edited by you.

☐ Write code inside the OnDisableButton() function so that it looks like this:

```
void CScrollmeDlg::OnDisableButton()
{
// TODO: Add your control notification handler code here


/////////////////////
// MY CODE STARTS HERE
/////////////////////


// Disable the scroll bar
m_ScrollMe.EnableWindow(FALSE);

/////////////////////
// MY CODE ENDS HERE
/////////////////////


}
```

8

The code you typed inside the OnDisableButton() function disables the scroll bar control:

```
m_ScrollMe.EnableWindow(FALSE);
```

Recall that when the user clicks the Enable button the scroll bar control should become enabled. You'll now attach code to the Click event of the Enable button.

☐ Display the ClassWizard dialog box by selecting ClassWizard from the Project menu of Visual C++.

☐ Select the Message Maps tab at the top of ClassWizard's dialog box.

☐ Use ClassWizard to select the event:

```
CScrollmeDlg -> IDC_ENABLE_BUTTON -> BN_CLICKED
```

Then click the Add Function button.

☐ Name the new function OnEnableButton().

To write the code of the OnEnableButton() function do the following:

☐ Click the Edit Code button of ClassWizard.

ClassWizard responds by opening the file SCROLDLG.CPP, with the function OnEnableButton() ready to be edited by you.

☐ Write code inside the OnEnableButton() function so that it looks like this:

```
void CScrollmeDlg::OnEnableButton()
{
// TODO: Add your control notification handler code here

//////////////////////////
// MY CODE STARTS HERE
//////////////////////////


// Enable the scroll bar
m_ScrollMe.EnableWindow(TRUE);

//////////////////////////
// MY CODE ENDS HERE
//////////////////////////


}
```

The code you typed inside the OnEnableButton() function enables the scroll bar:

```
m_ScrollMe.EnableWindow(TRUE);
```

To see your code in action do the following:

☐ Select Build ScrollMe.EXE from the Project menu.

Visual C++ responds by compiling and linking the ScrollMe program.

☐ Select Execute ScrollMe.EXE from the Project menu.

> *Visual C++ responds by executing the ScrollMe.EXE program.*

☐ Click the Disable button.

> *As expected, the ScrollMe program makes the scroll bar disabled.*

☐ Click the Enable button.

> *As expected, the ScrollMe program makes the scroll bar enabled.*

☐ Experiment with the ScrollMe program and then click the Exit button to terminate the program.

NOTE

You enabled and disabled the scroll bar by using this statement:

```
m_ScrollMe.EnableWindow(FALSE);
```

and this statement:

```
m_ScrollMe.EnableWindow(TRUE);
```

Alternatively, you may use the EnableScrollBar() member function of the CScrollBar class.

You can display the help window of the CScrollBar class and then click the EnableScrollBar() function that appears as one of the member functions of the CScrollBar class. As you can see, you can enable the scroll bar:

```
m_ScrollMe.EnableScrollBar(ESB_ENABLE_BOTH);
```

You can disable the complete scroll bar:

```
m_ScrollMe.EnableScrollBar(ESB_DISABLE_BOTH);
```

You can also disable only the left-arrow icon of the scroll bar:

```
m_ScrollMe.EnableScrollBar(ESB_DISABLE_LTUP);
```

You can also disable only the right-arrow icon of the scroll bar:

```
m_ScrollMe.EnableScrollBar(ESB_DISABLE_RTDN);
```

Attaching Code to the Min. Button

Recall that when the user clicks the Min. button the scroll bar's position should be set to 0. You'll now attach code to the Click event of the Min. button.

☐ Display the ClassWizard dialog box by selecting ClassWizard from the Project menu of Visual C++.

> *Visual C++ responds by displaying the ClassWizard dialog box.*

☐ Select the Message Maps tab at the top of ClassWizard's dialog box.

☐ Use ClassWizard to select the event:

```
CScrollmeDlg -> IDC_MIN_BUTTON -> BN_CLICKED
```

Then click the Add Function button.

☐ Name the new function `OnMinButton()`.

To write the code of the `OnMinButton()` function do the following:

☐ Click the Edit Code button of ClassWizard.

> *ClassWizard responds by opening the file SCROLDLG.CPP, with the function* `OnMinButton()` *ready to be edited by you.*

☐ Write code inside the `OnMinButton()` function so that it looks like this:

```
void CScrollmeDlg::OnMinButton()
{
// TODO: Add your control notification handler code here


/////////////////////
// MY CODE STARTS HERE
/////////////////////

       // Set the thumb to its minimum position
       m_ScrollMe.SetScrollPos(0);


       // Select the entire text inside the edit box
       m_Speed.SetSel (0,-1);

       // Replace the selected text
       m_Speed.ReplaceSel ("0");

/////////////////////
// MY CODE ENDS HERE
/////////////////////

}
```

The code you typed sets the scroll bar's position to 0 and updates the edit box accordingly.

Attaching Code to the Max. Button

Recall that when the user clicks the Max. button the scroll bar's position should be set to 100. You'll now attach code to the `Click` event of the Max. button.

☐ Display the ClassWizard dialog box by selecting ClassWizard from the Project menu of Visual C++.

> *Visual C++ responds by displaying the ClassWizard dialog box.*

☐ Select the Message Maps tab at the top of ClassWizard's dialog box.

☐ Use ClassWizard to select the event:

```
CScrollmeDlg -> IDC_MAX_BUTTON -> BN_CLICKED
```

Then click the Add Function button.

☐ Name the new function `OnMaxButton()`.

To write the code of the `OnMaxButton()` function do the following:

☐ Click the Edit Code button of ClassWizard.

> *ClassWizard responds by opening the file SCROLDLG.CPP with the function* `OnMaxButton()` *ready to be edited by you.*

☐ Write code inside the `OnMaxButton()` function so that it looks like this:

```
void CScrollmeDlg::OnMaxButton()
{
// TODO: Add your control notification handler code here


/////////////////////
// MY CODE STARTS HERE
/////////////////////

        // Set the thumb to its maximum position
        m_ScrollMe.SetScrollPos(100);


        // Select the entire text inside the edit box
        m_Speed.SetSel (0,-1);

        // Replace the selected text
        m_Speed.ReplaceSel ("100");

/////////////////////
// MY CODE ENDS HERE
/////////////////////

}
```

The code you typed sets the scroll bar's position to 100 and updates the edit box accordingly.

Attaching Code to the Reset Button

Recall that when the user clicks the Reset button the scroll bar's position should be set to 50. You'll now attach code to the `Click` event of the Reset button.

☐ Display the ClassWizard dialog box by selecting ClassWizard from the Project menu of Visual C++.

> *Visual C++ responds by displaying the ClassWizard dialog box.*

☐ Select the Message Maps tab at the top of ClassWizard's dialog box.

☐ Use ClassWizard to select the event:

```
CScrollmeDlg -> IDC_RESET_BUTTON -> BN_CLICKED
```

Then click the Add Function button.

☐ Name the new function OnResetButton().

To write the code of the OnResetButton() function do the following:

☐ Click the Edit Code button of ClassWizard.

> *ClassWizard responds by opening the file SCROLDLG.CPP, with the function OnResetButton() ready to be edited by you.*

☐ Write code inside the OnResetButton() function so that it looks like this:

```
void CScrollmeDlg::OnResetButton()
{
// TODO: Add your control notification handler code here

/////////////////////
// MY CODE STARTS HERE
/////////////////////

        // Set the thumb to its middle position
        m_ScrollMe.SetScrollPos(50);


        // Select the entire text inside the edit box
        m_Speed.SetSel (0,-1);

        // Replace the selected text
        m_Speed.ReplaceSel ("50");

/////////////////////
// MY CODE ENDS HERE
/////////////////////

}
```

The code you typed sets the scroll bar's position to 50 and updates the edit box accordingly.

To save your work do the following:

☐ Select Save from the File menu.

To see your code in action do the following:

☐ Select Build ScrollMe.EXE from the Project menu.

> *Visual C++ responds by compiling and linking the ScrollMe program.*

☐ Select Execute ScrollMe.EXE from the Project menu.

> *Visual C++ responds by executing the ScrollMe.EXE program.*

☐ Experiment with the Min., Max., and Reset buttons and then click the Exit button to terminate the program.

Debugging and Fixing the ScrollMe Program

Did you notice a small bug in the ScrollMe program? Here it is:

☐ Execute the ScrollMe program.

☐ Click the Disable button.

Now the scroll bar should be disabled! You should not be able to set the scroll bar's position.

☐ Click the Min., Max., and Reset buttons and note that the moment you click any of these buttons, the scroll bar becomes enabled.

☐ Click the Exit button to terminate the application.

You can fix this bug by adding code to the OnDisableButton() function that makes the Min., Max., and Reset buttons disabled. Also, you'll have to add code to the OnEnableButton() function that makes the Min., Max., and Reset buttons enabled.

☐ Display the ClassWizard dialog box by selecting ClassWizard from the Project menu of Visual C++.

   Visual C++ responds by displaying the ClassWizard dialog box.

☐ Select the Message Maps tab at the top of ClassWizard's dialog box.

☐ Use ClassWizard to select the event:

CScrollmeDlg -> IDC_DISABLE_BUTTON -> BN_CLICKED

Then click the Edit Function button.

   ClassWizard responds by opening the file SCROLDLG.CPP, with the function OnDisableButton() ready to be edited by you.

☐ Add code inside the OnDisableButton() function. After you add the code, your OnDisableButton() function should look like this:

```
void CScrollmeDlg::OnDisableButton()
{
// TODO: Add your control notification handler code here


//////////////////////////
// MY CODE STARTS HERE
//////////////////////////


// Disable the scroll bar
m_ScrollMe.EnableWindow(FALSE);
```

```
// Disable the Min, Max and Reset buttons
GetDlgItem(IDC_MIN_BUTTON)->EnableWindow(FALSE);
GetDlgItem(IDC_MAX_BUTTON)->EnableWindow(FALSE);
GetDlgItem(IDC_RESET_BUTTON)->EnableWindow(FALSE);

/////////////////////////
// MY CODE ENDS HERE
/////////////////////////

}
```

The code you added disables the Min., Max., and Reset buttons:

```
GetDlgItem(IDC_MIN_BUTTON)->EnableWindow(FALSE);
GetDlgItem(IDC_MAX_BUTTON)->EnableWindow(FALSE);
GetDlgItem(IDC_RESET_BUTTON)->EnableWindow(FALSE);
```

> **NOTE**
>
> The OnDisableButton() function disables the buttons by using the EnableWindow() function as follows:
>
> ```
> GetDlgItem(IDC_MIN_BUTTON)->EnableWindow(FALSE);
> ```
>
> That is, you extract the pointer of the button by using the GetDlgItem() function. The parameter of the GetDlgItem() function is the ID of the button whose pointer you extract.
>
> Alternatively, you could attach a variable to the button (for example, you could have used ClassWizard to attach the m_Min variable of type Control to the Min. button). Then you could disable the button by using the following statement:
>
> ```
> m_Min.EnableWindow(FALSE);
> ```

☐ Display the ClassWizard dialog box by selecting ClassWizard from the Project menu of Visual C++.

Visual C++ responds by displaying the ClassWizard dialog box.

☐ Select the Message Maps tab at the top of ClassWizard's dialog box.

☐ Use ClassWizard to select the event:

```
CScrollmeDlg -> IDC_ENABLE_BUTTON -> BN_CLICKED
```

Then click the Edit Function button.

ClassWizard responds by opening the file SCROLDLG.CPP, with the function OnEnableButton() ready to be edited by you.

☐ Add code inside the OnEnableButton() function. After you add the code, your OnEnableButton() function should look like this:

```
void CScrollmeDlg::OnEnableButton()
{
```

```
// TODO: Add your control notification handler code here

/////////////////////////
// MY CODE STARTS HERE
/////////////////////////

// Enable the scroll bar
m_ScrollMe.EnableWindow(TRUE);

// Enable the Min, Max and Reset buttons
GetDlgItem(IDC_MIN_BUTTON)->EnableWindow(TRUE);
GetDlgItem(IDC_MAX_BUTTON)->EnableWindow(TRUE);
GetDlgItem(IDC_RESET_BUTTON)->EnableWindow(TRUE);

/////////////////////////
// MY CODE ENDS HERE
/////////////////////////

}
```

You extracted the pointer of the button by using the GetDlgItem() function. The parameter of the GetDlgItem() function is the ID of the button whose pointer you extract. Then you applied the EnableWindow() function with TRUE as a parameter on the extracted pointer.

To save your work do the following:

☐ Select Save from the File menu.

To see your code in action do the following:

☐ Select Build ScrollMe.EXE from the Project menu.

  Visual C++ responds by compiling and linking the ScrollMe program.

☐ Select Execute ScrollMe.EXE from the Project menu.

  Visual C++ responds by executing the ScrollMe.EXE program.

☐ Click the Disable button.

  ScrollMe responds by disabling the scroll bar and the Min., Max., and Reset buttons.

☐ Click the Enable button.

  ScrollMe responds by enabling the scroll bar and the Min., Max., and Reset buttons.

☐ Experiment with the ScrollMe program and then click the Exit button to terminate the program.

The Last Touch...

You fixed the bug in the ScrollMe program. However, there is still something wrong with the ScrollMe program. When you hide the scroll bar, the Min., Max., and Reset buttons and the edit box are visible! Because the scroll bar is invisible, it makes sense to hide these other controls, as well.

You'll now add code that hides the Min., Max., and Reset buttons and the edit box whenever the user clicks the Hide button.

☐ Display the ClassWizard dialog box by selecting ClassWizard from the Project menu of Visual C++.

> *Visual C++ responds by displaying the ClassWizard dialog box.*

☐ Select the Message Maps tab at the top of ClassWizard's dialog box.

☐ Use ClassWizard to select the event:

```
CScrollmeDlg -> IDC_HIDE_BUTTON -> BN_CLICKED
```

Then click the Edit Function button.

> *ClassWizard responds by opening the file SCROLDLG.CPP, with the function* OnHideButton() *ready to be edited by you.*

☐ Add code inside the OnHideButton() function. After you add the code, your OnHideButton() function should look like this:

```
void CScrollmeDlg::OnHideButton()
{
// TODO: Add your control notification handler code here

/////////////////////////
// MY CODE STARTS HERE
/////////////////////////

// Hide the scroll bar

// To hide the scroll bar, you  use
//
// m_ScrollMe.ShowScrollBar(FALSE);
//
//      or
//
// m_ScrollMe.ShowWindow(SW_HIDE);

m_ScrollMe.ShowWindow(SW_HIDE);

// Hide the buttons and the edit box
GetDlgItem(IDC_MIN_BUTTON)->ShowWindow(SW_HIDE);
GetDlgItem(IDC_MAX_BUTTON)->ShowWindow(SW_HIDE);
GetDlgItem(IDC_RESET_BUTTON)->ShowWindow(SW_HIDE);
m_Speed.ShowWindow(SW_HIDE);

/////////////////////////
// MY CODE ENDS HERE
/////////////////////////

}
```

The code you added hides the Min., Max., and Reset buttons and the edit box:

```
GetDlgItem(IDC_MIN_BUTTON)->ShowWindow(SW_HIDE);
GetDlgItem(IDC_MAX_BUTTON)->ShowWindow(SW_HIDE);
```

```
GetDlgItem(IDC_RESET_BUTTON)->ShowWindow(SW_HIDE);
m_Speed.ShowWindow(SW_HIDE);
```

NOTE

You can hide the edit box like this:

```
m_Speed.ShowWindow(SW_HIDE);
```

Alternatively, you can hide the edit box like this:

```
GetDlgItem(IDC_SPEED)->ShowWindow(SW_HIDE);
```

☐ Add code inside the OnShowButton() function (inside the SCROLDLG.CPP file). After you add the code, your OnShowButton() function should look like this:

```
void CScrollmeDlg::OnShowButton()
{
// TODO: Add your control notification handler code here


/////////////////////////
// MY CODE STARTS HERE
/////////////////////////

// Show the scroll bar

// To show the scroll bar, you  use
//
// m_ScrollMe.ShowScrollBar(TRUE);
//
//      or
//
// m_ScrollMe.ShowScrollBar(FALSE);

m_ScrollMe.ShowWindow(SW_SHOW);

// Show the buttons and the edit box
GetDlgItem(IDC_MIN_BUTTON)->ShowWindow(SW_SHOW);
GetDlgItem(IDC_MAX_BUTTON)->ShowWindow(SW_SHOW);
GetDlgItem(IDC_RESET_BUTTON)->ShowWindow(SW_SHOW);
m_Speed.ShowWindow(SW_SHOW);

/////////////////////////
// MY CODE ENDS HERE
/////////////////////////

}
```

The code you added makes the Min., Max., and Reset buttons and the edit box visible:

```
GetDlgItem(IDC_MIN_BUTTON)->ShowWindow(SW_SHOW);
GetDlgItem(IDC_MAX_BUTTON)->ShowWindow(SW_SHOW);
GetDlgItem(IDC_RESET_BUTTON)->ShowWindow(SW_SHOW);
m_Speed.ShowWindow(SW_SHOW);
```

To save your work do the following:

☐ Select Save from the File menu.

To see your code in action do the following:

☐ Select Build ScrollMe.EXE from the Project menu.

> *Visual C++ responds by compiling and linking the ScrollMe program.*

☐ Select Execute ScrollMe.EXE from the Project menu.

> *Visual C++ responds by executing the ScrollMe.EXE program.*

☐ Click the Hide button.

> *ScrollMe responds by hiding the scroll bar, the Min., Max., and Reset buttons, and the edit box.*

☐ Click the Show button.

> *ScrollMe responds by making visible the scroll bar, the Min., Max., and Reset buttons, and the edit box.*

☐ Experiment with the ScrollMe program and then click the Exit button to terminate the program.

Making the Edit Box Read-Only

The last modification you'll make to the ScrollMe program is to make the edit box read-only (so that the user will not be able to type inside the edit box).

☐ Double-click scrollme.rc inside the scrollme.mak window.

> *Visual C++ responds by displaying the scrollme.rc window.*

☐ Double-click Dialog inside the scrollme.rc window and then double-click IDD_SCROLLME_DIALOG.

☐ Double-click the edit box.

> *Visual C++ responds by displaying the Properties dialog box of the edit box.*

☐ Click the Style tab of the Edit Box Properties dialog box, and place a checkmark inside the Read Only check box.

☐ Select Save from the File menu to save your work.

To verify that the edit box is now read-only do the following:

☐ Select Build ScrollMe.EXE from the Project menu.

> *Visual C++ responds by compiling and linking the ScrollMe program.*

☐ Select Execute ScrollMe.EXE from the Project menu.

   Visual C++ responds by executing the ScrollMe.EXE program.

☐ Try to type something inside the edit box.

   As you can see, you cannot type inside the edit box.

☐ Experiment with the ScrollMe program and then click the Exit button to terminate the program.

List and Combo Boxes

In this chapter you'll learn how to incorporate list boxes and combo boxes into a dialog box. As you know, these controls serve an important role in the Windows user-interface mechanism. The applications you'll write in this chapter are dialog-based type—that is, they are applications in which a dialog box serves as the main window of the application.

The MyList Application

You'll now write the MyList application, which is an example of an application that uses a list box control. Before you start writing the MyList application yourself, execute the copy of it that resides in the \MVCPROG\EXE directory of the book's CD.

To execute the MyList application do the following:

☐ Select Run from the Start menu of Windows and execute the X:\MVCPROG\EXE\MyList.EXE program (where *X* represents the drive letter of your CD-ROM drive).

> *Windows responds by executing the MyList.EXE application. The main window of MyList.EXE appears, as shown in Figure 9.1. As you can see, the window of Figure 9.1 contains three edit boxes (an upper edit box, a middle edit box, and a lower edit box).*

Figure 9.1. The main window of the MyList application.

☐ Double-click any of the items inside the list box.

> *MyList responds by copying the item that you double-clicked to the upper edit box.*

☐ Try to double-click any of the other items inside the list box.

> *MyList responds by copying the item that you double-clicked to the upper edit box.*

☐ Type something inside the middle edit box, and then click the button that has an arrow pointing from right to left.

> *MyList responds by copying the contents of the middle edit box and adding the contents as a new item to the list box.*

☐ Click the m_MyList.GetCount( ) button.

> *MyList responds by reporting the number of items that exist inside the list box. This number is reported inside the lower edit box.*

Figure 9.2 shows the window of the MyList program after you have experimented with it.

☐ Click the Exit button to terminate the MyList program.

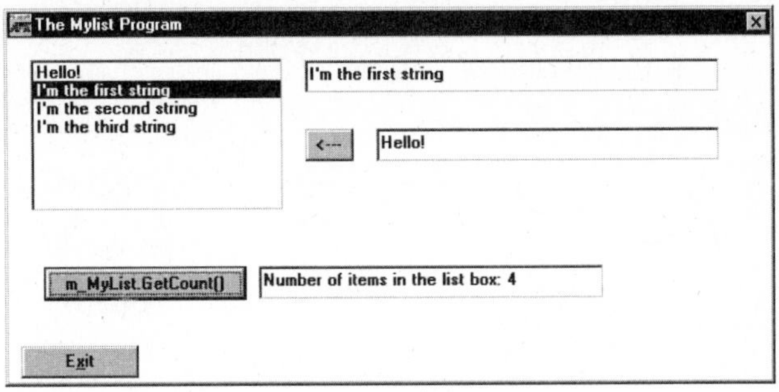

Figure 9.2. The window of
the MyList program after
you have experimented
with it.

The MyList Program

Hello!
I'm the first string
I'm the second string
I'm the third string

I'm the first string

<--- Hello!

m_MyList.GetCount()   Number of items in the list box: 4

E_xit

Now that you know what the MyList application should do, you can begin learning how to write it.

Creating the Project of the MyList Application

To create the project of the MyList application do the following:

☐ Start Visual C++ and close all the open windows that appear inside the desktop of Visual C++ (if there are any).

☐ Select New from the File menu.

   Visual C++ responds by displaying the New dialog box.

☐ Select Project inside the New dialog box and then click the OK button of the New dialog box.

   Visual C++ responds by displaying the New Project dialog box.

☐ Set the project name to MyList.

☐ Set the project path to \MVCPROG\CH09\MyList\MyList.MAK.

Your New Project dialog box should now look like the one shown in Figure 9.3.

Figure 9.3. The New
Project dialog box of the
MyList.MAK project.

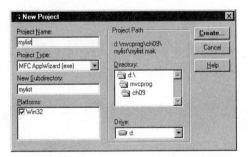

☐ Click the Create button of the New Project dialog box.

   Visual C++ responds by displaying the AppWizard—Step 1 window.

☐ Set the AppWizard—Step 1 window as shown in Figure 9.4. As shown in Figure 9.4, the MyList.MAK project is set as a dialog-based application, and U.S. English (APPWIZUS.DLL) is used as the language for the MyList.MAK project's resources.

Figure 9.4. The AppWizard—Step 1 window of the MyList.MAK project.

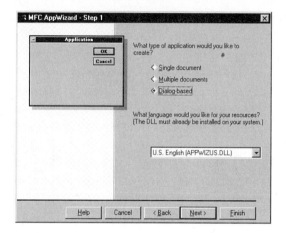

☐ Click the Next button of the AppWizard—Step 1 window.

Visual C++ responds by displaying the AppWizard—Step 2 of 4 window.

☐ Set the AppWizard—Step 2 of 4 window as shown in Figure 9.5. That is, place a checkmark inside the About Box check box (to incorporate an About dialog box into the application), and place a checkmark inside the Use 3D Controls check box (so that the application will use 3D controls). Also, set the title of the application to The MyList Program.

Figure 9.5. The AppWizard—Step 2 of 4 window of the MyList.MAK project.

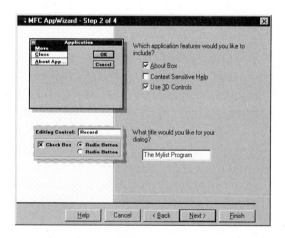

☐ Click the Next button of the AppWizard—Step 2 of 4 window.

> *Visual C++ responds by displaying the AppWizard—Step 3 of 4 window.*

☐ Set the Step 3 of 4 window as shown in Figure 9.6.

As shown in Figure 9.6, the project will be generated with comments, a Visual C++ makefile will be generated, and the application will use the MFC library from a DLL.

Figure 9.6. The AppWizard—Step 3 of 4 window of the MyList.MAK project.

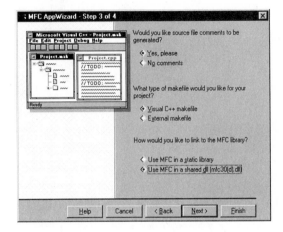

☐ Click the Next button of the AppWizard—Step 3 of 4 window.

> *Visual C++ responds by displaying the AppWizard—Step 4 of 4 window, as shown in Figure 9.7.*

Figure 9.7. The AppWizard—Step 4 of 4 window of the MyList.MAK project.

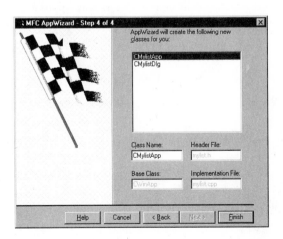

☐ Click the Finish button of the AppWizard—Step 4 of 4 window.

Visual C++ responds by displaying the New Project Information window, as shown in Figure 9.8.

Figure 9.8. The New Project Information window of the MyList.MAK project.

☐ Click the OK button of the New Project Information window.

Visual C++ responds by creating the project file and all the skeleton files of the application.

The Visual Implementation of the MyList Application

Because the MyList application is a dialog-based application, when you created the project and the skeleton files of the MyList application with AppWizard, AppWizard created for you a dialog box that serves as the main window of the application. AppWizard named this dialog box IDD_MYLIST_DIALOG. You'll now customize the IDD_MYLIST_DIALOG dialog box.

☐ Double-click mylist.rc inside the mylist.mak window.

Visual C++ responds by displaying the mylist.rc window.

☐ Double-click Dialog inside the mylist.rc window and then double-click IDD_MYLIST_DIALOG.

Visual C++ responds by displaying the IDD_MYLIST_DIALOG dialog box in design mode.

☐ Implement the dialog box using the specifications in Table 9.1. When you finish implementing the dialog box, it should look like the one shown in Figure 9.9.

Table 9.1. The Properties table of the IDD_MYLIST_DIALOG dialog box.

Object	Property	Setting
Dialog box	ID	IDD_MYLIST_DIALOG
Push button	ID	IDC_EXIT_BUTTON
	Caption	E&xit
List box	ID	IDC_MYLIST

Figure 9.9. The dialog box that serves as the main window of the MyList program (in design mode).

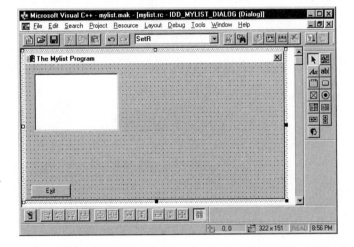

NOTE

Table 9.1 instructs you to place a list box control inside the dialog box. The list box tool inside the Tools window is shown in Figure 9.10.

Figure 9.10. The list box tool inside the Tools window of Visual C++.

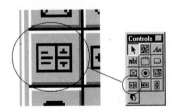

Attaching Variables to the Controls Inside the Dialog Box of the MyList Program

You'll now attach variables to the controls of the IDD_MYLIST_DIALOG dialog box.

☐ Use ClassWizard (from the Project menu) to attach variables to the controls of the IDD_MYLIST_DIALOG dialog box, using the specifications in Table 9.2.

Table 9.2. The Variables table of the MyList dialog box.

Control ID	Variable Name	Category Type
IDC_MYLIST	m_MyList	Control CListBox

> **NOTE**
>
> As specified in Table 9.2, when you add the variable m_MyList, you must set the Category of the variable to Control (not to Value). The Variable Type is set to CListBox.
>
> The variable type is CListBox. This means that the variable m_MyList that you attached to the IDC_MYLIST list box is an object of class CListBox.

☐ To save your work, select Save from the File menu.

To see your visual design in action do the following:

☐ Select Build MyList.EXE from the Project menu.

Visual C++ responds by compiling and linking the MyList application.

☐ Select Execute MyList.EXE from the Project menu.

Visual C++ responds by executing the MyList.EXE application. (See Figure 9.11.) As expected, the IDD_MYLIST_DIALOG dialog box that you designed appears as the main window of the application. Of course, the list box does not have any items in it, because you have not yet written code that accomplishes this.

☐ Click the icon that appears in the upper-left corner of the MyList application window, and select About from the System menu that pops up.

MyList responds by displaying the About dialog box.

☐ Click the OK button of the About dialog box to close the About dialog box.

☐ Click the icon that appears in the upper-left corner of the MyList application window, and select Close from the System menu that pops up.

MyList responds by terminating itself.

Figure 9.11. The MyList
window with its Exit
button and list box.

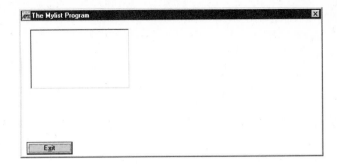

Initializing the List Box

In this section you'll write initialization code that fills the list box with three items.

You'll now attach code to the WM_INITDIALOG event of the IDD_MYLIST_DIALOG dialog box. The WM_INITDIALOG event occurs just before the dialog box is displayed.

☐ Select ClassWizard from the Project menu of Visual C++.

Visual C++ responds by displaying the ClassWizard dialog box.

☐ Select the Message Maps tab at the top of ClassWizard's dialog box.

☐ Use ClassWizard to select the event:

CMylistDlg -> CMyListDlg -> WM_INITDIALOG

Then click the Edit Code button.

Visual C++ responds by opening the MYLISDLG.CPP file and displaying the OnInitDialog() function, ready to be edited by you.

☐ Write code inside the OnInitDialog() function so that it looks like this:

```
BOOL CMylistDlg::OnInitDialog()
{
CDialog::OnInitDialog();
CenterWindow();

// Add "About..." menu item to system menu.

// IDM_ABOUTBOX must be in the system command range.
ASSERT((IDM_ABOUTBOX & 0xFFF0) == IDM_ABOUTBOX);
ASSERT(IDM_ABOUTBOX < 0xF000);

CMenu* pSysMenu = GetSystemMenu(FALSE);
CString strAboutMenu;
strAboutMenu.LoadString(IDS_ABOUTBOX);
if (!strAboutMenu.IsEmpty())
   {
   pSysMenu->AppendMenu(MF_SEPARATOR);
   pSysMenu->AppendMenu(MF_STRING, IDM_ABOUTBOX,
                     strAboutMenu);
   }
```

```
// TODO: Add extra initialization here

///////////////////////////
// MY CODE STARTS HERE
///////////////////////////

// Insert 3 strings inside the list box
m_MyList.AddString("I'm the first string");
m_MyList.AddString("I'm the second string");
m_MyList.AddString("I'm the third string");

///////////////////////////
// MY CODE ENDS HERE
///////////////////////////


return TRUE;
// return TRUE  unless you set the focus to a control
}
```

The code you typed uses the AddString() function to add three items to the list box:

```
m_MyList.AddString("I'm the first string");
m_MyList.AddString("I'm the second string");
m_MyList.AddString("I'm the third string");
```

Attaching Code to the *BN_CLICKED* Event of the Exit Button

Recall that when the user clicks the Exit button the MyList program should terminate. You'll now attach code to the Click event (BN_CLICKED) of the Exit button.

☐ Display the ClassWizard dialog box by selecting ClassWizard from the Project menu of Visual C++.

☐ Select the Message Maps tab at the top of ClassWizard's dialog box.

☐ Use ClassWizard to select the event:

```
CMylistDlg -> IDC_EXIT_BUTTON -> BN_CLICKED
```

Then click the Add Function button.

☐ Name the new function OnExitButton().

To write the code of the OnExitButton() function do the following:

☐ Click the Edit Code button of ClassWizard.

> *ClassWizard responds by opening the file MYLISDLG.CPP, with the function* OnExitButton() *ready to be edited by you.*

☐ Write code inside the OnExitButton() function so that it looks like this:

```
void CMylistDlg::OnExitButton()
{
```

```
// TODO: Add your control notification handler code here


/////////////////////////
// MY CODE STARTS HERE
/////////////////////////

// Close the dialog box (terminate the program).
OnOK();

/////////////////////////
// MY CODE ENDS HERE
/////////////////////////

}
```

☐ Save your work by selecting Save from the File menu of Visual C++.

To see your initialization code in action do the following:

☐ Select Build MyList.EXE from the Project menu.

> *Visual C++ responds by compiling and linking the MyList program.*

☐ Select Execute MyList.EXE from the Project menu.

> *Visual C++ responds by executing the MyList.EXE program. As you can see from Figure 9.12, the list box appears with three strings in it.*

Figure 9.12. The list box with three strings in it.

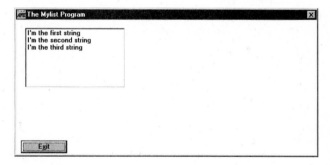

☐ Click the Exit button.

> *MyList responds by terminating itself.*

Reading an Item from the List Box

In the preceding section, you added three strings to the list box. In this section you'll write code that reads the contents of the list box.

☐ Select mylist.rc—IDD_MYLIST_DIALOG from the Window menu of Visual C++.

☐ Place an edit box inside the dialog box. After you add the edit box, your dialog box should look like the one shown in Figure 9.13.

☐ Set the ID of the edit box to IDC_FROM_LISTBOX.

Figure 9.13. Adding an
edit box to the dialog box
(in design mode).

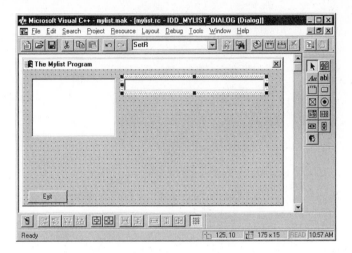

☐ Use ClassWizard to attach a variable to the IDC_FROM_LISTBOX edit box. The variable that you attach should have the following properties:

ID:	IDC_FROM_LISTBOX (edit box)
Variable Name:	m_FromListBox
Category:	Control
Class:	CEdit

Your objective now is to write code so that when the user double-clicks an item in the list box, the clicked item is copied to the edit box.

> **NOTE**
>
> You added the m_FromListBox variable to the IDC_FROM_LISTBOX edit control as a variable with category equal to Control and Class equal to CEdit. This means that you'll be able to apply the member functions of the CEdit class on the IDC_FROM_LISTBOX edit control.

You'll now attach code to the LBN_DCLICK event of the IDC_MYLIST list box. The LBN_DCLICK event occurs when the user double-clicks an item inside the list box.

☐ Select ClassWizard from the Project menu of Visual C++.

  Visual C++ responds by displaying the ClassWizard dialog box.

☐ Select the Message Maps tab at the top of ClassWizard's dialog box.

☐ Use ClassWizard to select the event:

```
CMylistDlg -> IDC_MYLIST -> LBN_DCLICK
```

Then click the Edit Code button.

> *Visual C++ responds by opening the MYLISDLG.CPP file and displaying the* OnDblclkMyList() *function, ready to be edited by you.*

☐ Write code inside the OnDblclkMyList() function so that it looks like this:

```
void CMylistDlg::OnDblclkMylist()
{
// TODO: Add your control notification handler code here


/////////////////////////
// MY CODE STARTS HERE
/////////////////////////

// A buffer that will hold the string
char sFromList[50];


// Update the contents of the sFromList string variable
m_MyList.GetText (m_MyList.GetCurSel(), sFromList);

// Select the entire text inside the edit box
m_FromListBox.SetSel (0,-1);

// Replace the selected text of the edit box
//   with the contents of the sFromList variable.
m_FromListBox.ReplaceSel (sFromList);

/////////////////////
// MY CODE ENDS HERE
/////////////////////

}
```

The OnDblclkMylist() function is automatically executed whenever the user double-clicks an item in the list box.

The code you typed declares a string variable:

```
char sFromList[50];
```

The sFromList variable will hold the double-clicked item from the list box.

The GetCurSel() function is used as the first parameter of the GetText() function:

```
m_MyList.GetText ( m_MyList.GetCurSel(), sFromList );
```

GetCurSel() returns the index of the item that is currently selected. For example, if the user double-clicked the first item in the list box, GetCurSel() returns 0. If the user double-clicked the second item in the list box, GetCurSel() returns 1, and so on.

The second parameter of the GetText() function is the variable that will hold the string mentioned as the first parameter of the GetText() function. So the sFromList variable is filled with the contents of the item that the user double-clicked.

Next, the edit box is filled with the contents of the sFromList variable:

```
// Select the entire text inside the edit box
m_FromListBox.SetSel (0,-1);

// Replace the selected text of the edit box
//  with the contents of the sFromList variable.
m_FromListBox.ReplaceSel (sFromList);
```

☐ Save your work by selecting Save from the File menu of Visual C++.

To see your code in action do the following:

☐ Select Build MyList.EXE from the Project menu.

   Visual C++ responds by compiling and linking the MyList program.

☐ Select Execute MyList.EXE from the Project menu.

   Visual C++ responds by executing the MyList.EXE program. As you can see, the list box appears with three strings in it.

☐ Double-click the second item in the list.

   Visual C++ responds by filling the edit box with the string you double-clicked. (See Figure 9.14.)

Figure 9.14. Filling the edit box with contents of the second item from the list box.

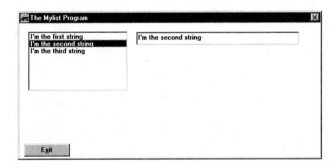

☐ Double-click the first item in the list.

   Visual C++ responds by filling the edit box with the string you double-clicked.

☐ Double-click the third item in the list.

   Visual C++ responds by filling the edit box with the string you double-clicked.

☐ Click the Exit button.

   MyList responds by terminating itself.

Adding an Item to the List Box from Within Your Code

In the preceding section, you learned how to read a list box item from within your code. You'll now add code that adds an item to the list box.

☐ Use ClassWizard (from the Project menu) to add an edit box and a button to the IDD_MYLIST_DIALOG dialog box using the specifications in Table 9.3. When you finish adding the button and the edit box to the dialog box, the dialog box should look like the one shown in Figure 9.15.

Table 9.3. Adding a button and an edit box to the IDD_MYLIST_DIALOG dialog box.

Object	Property	Setting
Push button	ID	IDC_TO_LISTBOX_BUTTON
	Caption	<—
Edit box	ID	IDC_TO_LISTBOX

Figure 9.15. Adding a button and an edit box to the dialog box.

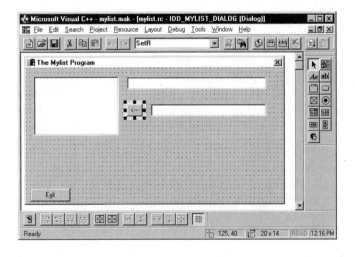

You'll now attach a variable to the edit box that you added to the MyList dialog box.

☐ Use ClassWizard (from the Project menu) to attach a variable to the IDC_TO_LISTBOX edit box of the IDD_MYLIST_DIALOG dialog box, using the following specifications:

Control ID:	IDC_TO_LISTBOX
Variable Name:	m_ToListBox
Category:	Control
Type:	CEdit

As specified, when you add the variable m_ToListBox, you must set the Category of this variable to Control (not to Value). The Variable Type is set to CEdit. This means that the variable that you attached to the IDC_TO_LISTBOX edit box is an object of class Cedit.

Recall that when the user clicks the <— button, the MyList program should copy the contents of the IDC_TO_LISTBOX edit box to a new item in the list box. You'll now attach code to the Click event (BN_CLICKED) of the <— button.

☐ Display the ClassWizard dialog box by selecting ClassWizard from the Project menu of Visual C++.

☐ Select the Message Maps tab at the top of ClassWizard's dialog box.

☐ Use ClassWizard to select the event:

CMylist -> IDC_TO_LISTBOX_BUTTON -> BN_CLICKED

Then click the Add Function button.

☐ Name the new function OnToListboxButton().

To write the code of the OnToListboxButton() function do the following:

☐ Click the Edit Code button of ClassWizard.

> *ClassWizard responds by opening the file MYLISDLG.CPP, with the function* OnToListboxButton() *ready to be edited by you.*

☐ Write code inside the OnToListboxButton() function so that it looks like this:

```
void CMylistDlg::OnToListboxButton()
{
// TODO: Add your control notification handler code here


/////////////////////////
// MY CODE STARTS HERE
/////////////////////////

// A variable that will hold the contents of the edit box
char sFromEditBox[50];

// Fill sFromEditBox with blanks
int i;
for ( i=0; i<25; i++ )
    sFromEditBox[i] = ' ';

// Fill sFromEditBox with the contents of the edit box
m_ToListBox.GetLine ( 0, sFromEditBox, 25 );

// Terminate the string
sFromEditBox[25] = 0;

// Add an item to the list box
m_MyList.AddString ( sFromEditBox );
```

```
/////////////////////
// MY CODE ENDS HERE
/////////////////////

}
```

The code you typed declares a string variable:

```
char sFromEditBox[50];
```

The sFromEditBox variable will hold the contents of the edit box.

The sFromEditBox is then filled with 25 spaces:

```
int i;
for ( i=0; i<25; i++ )
    sFromEditBox[i] = ' ';
```

The contents of the edit box are then copied to the FromEditBox variable:

```
m_ToListBox.GetLine ( 0, sFromEditBox, 25 );
```

The first parameter of the GetLine() function indicates the line number to be copied. In this case, you are copying the first and only line of the edit box, line number 0.

The second parameter of the GetLine() function indicates the name of the string variable that will hold the contents of the edit box.

The third parameter of the GetLine() function is set to 25. This means that a maximum of 25 characters will be copied to the sFromEditBox string.

The null terminator is added to the sFromEditBox string:

```
sFromEditBox[25] = 0;
```

Finally, the AddString() function is executed:

```
m_MyList.AddString ( sFromEditBox );
```

So the contents of the edit box were copied to the sFromEditBox variable, and then the contents of the sFromEditBox variable were added as a new item to the list box.

To see your code in action do the following:

☐ Select Build MyList.EXE from the Project menu.

> *Visual C++ responds by compiling and linking the MyList application.*

☐ Select Execute MyList.EXE from the Project menu.

> *Visual C++ responds by executing the MyList.EXE application. As expected, the IDD_MYLIST_DIALOG dialog box that you designed appears with two edit boxes.*

☐ Type Add to list box inside the lower edit box, and then click the button that has the <— caption on it.

> *MyList responds by adding the contents of the lower edit box to the list box. (See Figure 9.16.)*

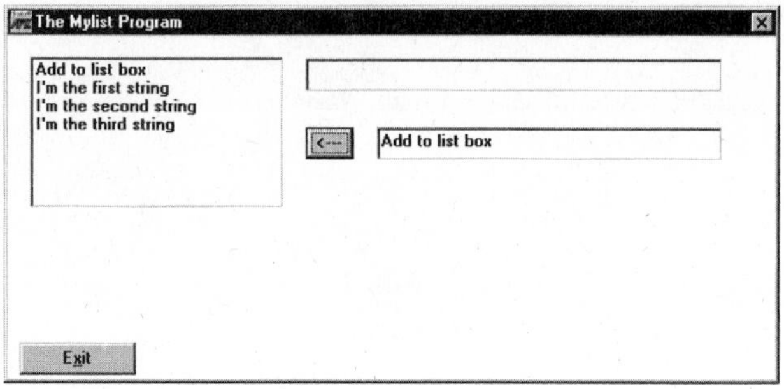

Figure 9.16. Adding the contents of the edit box to the list box.

☐ Practice with the MyList program and then click the Exit button to terminate the program.

Experimenting with Other Member Functions of the *CListBox* Class

In this chapter you have learned how to apply some of the member functions of the CListBox class. For example, you have learned how to apply the AddString(), GetText(), and GetCurSel() member functions of the CListBox class.

As you can see, applying the member functions of the CListBox class is a straightforward process. You should be aware of the fact that the CListBox class has many more powerful member functions.

☐ Select Foundation Classes from the Help menu of Visual C++.

> *Visual C++ responds by displaying the Search dialog box.*

☐ Search for the CListBox topic, and display the help window of the CListBox class.

As you can see, the CListBox class has many useful member functions. To learn about a particular member function, you have to click the member function.

☐ Click the GetCount function that appears inside the help window of the CListBox window.

> *Visual C++ responds by displaying the help window of the* GetCount() *member function of the CListBox class. (See Figure 9.17.)*

Of course, you can apply the GetCount() function to m_MyList because m_MyList is an object of class CListBox.

☐ Add a button to the dialog box of the MyList program. The button should have the following properties:

ID: IDC_GETCOUNT_BUTTON
Caption: m_MyList.GetCount()

☐ Add an edit box to the dialog box of the MyList program. The edit box should have the following property:

   ID: IDC_GETCOUNT_EDITBOX

Figure 9.17. The help window of the `GetCount()` *member function of the* `CListBox` *class.*

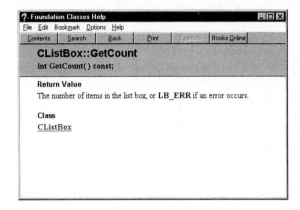

When you finish adding the new button and the new edit box to the dialog box, the dialog box should look like the one shown in Figure 9.18.

Figure 9.18. Adding a button and an edit box to the dialog box of the MyList program.

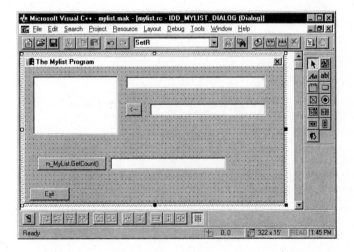

☐ Use ClassWizard to add a variable to the IDC_GETCOUNT_EDITBOX edit box. The variable should have the following properties:

Control ID:	IDC_GETCOUNT_EDITBOX
Variable Name:	m_GetCountEditBox
Category:	Control
Variable Type:	CEdit

You'll now add a function that fills IDC_GETCOUNT_EDITBOX with the number of items in the list box whenever the user clicks the GetCount button:

☐ Display the ClassWizard dialog box by selecting ClassWizard from the Project menu of Visual C++.

☐ Select the Message Maps tab at the top of ClassWizard's dialog box.

☐ Use ClassWizard to select the event:

```
CMylist -> IDC_GETCOUNT_BUTTON -> BN_CLICKED
```

Then click the Add Function button.

☐ Name the new function OnGetcountButton().

To write the code of the OnGetcountButton() function do the following:

☐ Click the Edit Code button of ClassWizard.

> *ClassWizard responds by opening the file MYLISDLG.CPP, with the function* OnGetcountButton() *ready to be edited by you.*

☐ Write code inside the OnGetcountButton() function so that it looks like this:

```
void CMylistDlg::OnGetcountButton()
{
// TODO: Add your control notification handler code here


///////////////////////////
// MY CODE STARTS HERE
///////////////////////////

// Variable that will hold the contents of the edit box
char sToEditBox[50];

// Start building the sToEditBox variable
strcpy(sToEditBox, "Number of items in the list box: ");

// Get the number of items inside the list box
int iNumberOfItems;
iNumberOfItems = m_MyList.GetCount();

// Convert the number of items to a string
char sNumberOfItems[25];
itoa (iNumberOfItems, sNumberOfItems, 10 );

// Build the sToEditBox variable
strcat(sToEditBox, sNumberOfItems);

// Select the entire text inside the edit box
m_GetCountEditBox.SetSel (0,-1);
```

```
// Replace the selected text
m_GetCountEditBox.ReplaceSel (_T(sToEditBox));
```

```
////////////////////
// MY CODE ENDS HERE
////////////////////
```

```
}
```

The code you typed declares a string variable:

```
char sToEditBox[50];
```

Then `sToEditBox` is filled with the text `Number of items in the list box`:

```
strcpy( sToEditBox, "Number of items in the list box: " );
```

The `GetCount()` function is used to fill the `iNumberOfItems` variable with the number of items that exist inside the list box:

```
int iNumberOfItems;
iNumberOfItems = m_MyList.GetCount();
```

Then the integer `iNumberOfItems` is converted to a string:

```
char sNumberOfItems[25];
itoa (iNumberOfItems, sNumberOfItems, 10 );
```

`itoa()` is a regular C/C++ function (not an MFC function) that converts integers to ASCII (hence the name `itoa()`). The first parameter of `itoa()` is the integer to be converted, the second parameter is the name of the string that will be updated by `itoa()`, and the third parameter is the radix. When you are converting base 10 numbers (that is, regular integers), the third parameter should be 10.

The `sToEditBox` string is updated by using the `strcat()` function:

```
strcat(sToEditBox, sNumberOfItems);
```

Finally, the m_GetCountEditBox edit box is updated with the value of the `sToEditBox` string:

```
// Select the entire text inside the edit box
m_GetCountEditBox.SetSel (0,-1);
```

```
// Replace the selected text
m_GetCountEditBox.ReplaceSel (_T(sToEditBox));
```

To save your work do the following:

☐ Select Save from the File menu of Visual C++.

To see your code in action do the following:

☐ Select Build MyList.EXE from the Project menu.

> *Visual C++ responds by compiling and linking the MyList application.*

☐ Select Execute MyList.EXE from the Project menu.

Visual C++ responds by executing the MyList.EXE application. As expected, the IDD_MYLIST_DIALOG dialog box that you designed appears with three edit boxes.

☐ Click the m_MyList.GetCount button.

MyList responds by filling the lower edit box with the number of items inside the list box. (See Figure 9.19.)

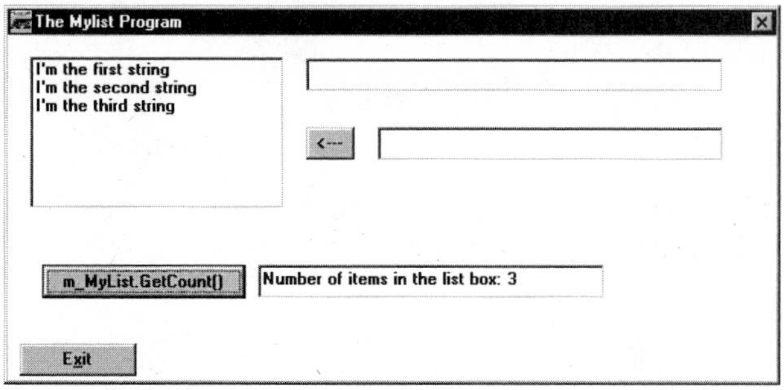

Figure 9.19.
Clicking the
m_MyList.GetCount()
button to report the
number of items in the
list box.

☐ Practice with the MyList program and then click the Exit button to terminate the program.

This exercise illustrates how you can use the Help feature of Visual C++ to find out about the available member functions of the CListBox class, and how to apply the member functions.

In a similar manner, you can practice with the other member functions of the CListBox class.

The MyCombo Program

A list box only lets you select an item from a list of items. A combo box, on the other hand, lets you select an item from a list, as well as type characters just like you type them in an edit box. Thus, the combo box is a combination of a list box and an edit box (hence the name combo box).

You'll now write the MyCombo application, which is an example of an application that uses a combo box control. Before you start writing the MyCombo application yourself, execute the copy of it that resides inside the \MVCPROG\EXE directory of the book's CD.

To execute the MyCombo application do the following:

☐ Select Run from the Start menu of Windows and execute the X:\MVCPROG\EXE\MyCombo.EXE program (where *X* represents the drive letter of your CD-ROM drive).

Windows responds by executing the MyCombo.EXE application. The main window of MyCombo.EXE appears, as shown in Figure 9.20.

Figure 9.20. The main
window of the MyCombo
application.

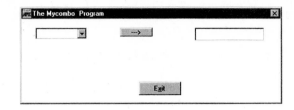

☐ Click the arrow icon of the combo box.

> *MyCombo responds by dropping down a list.*

☐ Click on any of the items in the list.

> *MyCombo responds by copying the item that you double-clicked to the edit box of the
> combo box.*

☐ Click the button that has a caption of an arrow pointing from left to right.

> *MyCombo responds by copying the contents of the edit box of the combo box to the edit box
> that is located on the right side of the window.*

☐ Type something inside the edit box of the combo box, and then click the button that has
the caption of an arrow pointing from left to right.

> *MyCombo responds by copying the contents of the combo box edit box to the right edit box.
> (See Figure 9.21.)*

☐ Click the Exit button to terminate the MyCombo program.

Figure 9.21. Copying the
combo box's edit box.

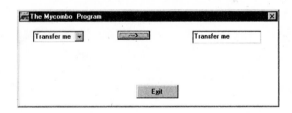

Now that you know what the MyCombo application should do, you can begin learning how to
write it.

Creating the Project of the MyCombo Application

To create the project of the MyCombo application do the following:

☐ Start Visual C++ and close all the open windows that appear inside the desktop of Visual
C++ (if there are any).

☐ Select New from the File menu.

> *Visual C++ responds by displaying the New dialog box.*

☐ Select Project inside the New dialog box and then click the OK button of the New dialog box.

Visual C++ responds by displaying the New Project dialog box.

☐ Set the project name to MyCombo.

☐ Set the project path to \MVCPROG\CH09\MyCombo\MyCombo.MAK.

Your New Project dialog box should now look like the one shown in Figure 9.22.

Figure 9.22. The New Project dialog box of the MyCombo.MAK project.

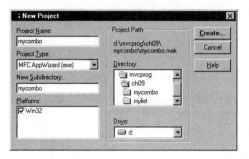

☐ Click the Create button of the New Project dialog box.

Visual C++ responds by displaying the AppWizard—Step 1 window.

☐ Set the AppWizard—Step 1 window as shown in Figure 9.23. As shown in Figure 9.23, the MyCombo.MAK project is set as a dialog-based application and U.S. English (APPWIZUS.DLL) is used as the language for the MyList.MAK project's resources.

Figure 9.23. The AppWizard—Step 1 window of the MyCombo.MAK project.

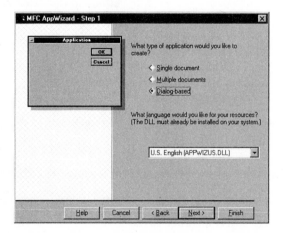

☐ Click the Next button of the AppWizard—Step 1 window.

   Visual C++ responds by displaying the AppWizard—Step 2 of 4 window.

☐ Set the AppWizard—Step 2 of 4 window as shown in Figure 9.24. That is, place a
   checkmark inside the About Box check box (to incorporate an About dialog box into the
   application), and place a checkmark inside the Use 3D Controls check box (so that the
   application will use 3D controls). Also, set the title of the application to The MyCombo
   Program.

*Figure 9.24. The
AppWizard—Step 2 of 4
window of the
MyCombo.MAK project.*

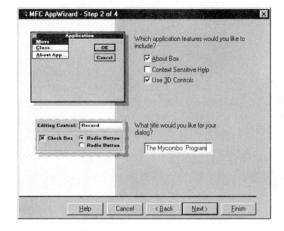

☐ Click the Next button of the AppWizard—Step 2 of 4 window.

   Visual C++ responds by displaying the AppWizard—Step 3 of 4 window.

☐ Set the Step 3 of 4 window as shown in Figure 9.25.

As shown in Figure 9.25, the project will be generated with comments, a Visual C++ makefile will
be generated, and the application will use the MFC library from a DLL.

*Figure 9.25. The
AppWizard—Step 3 of 4
window of the
MyCombo.MAK project.*

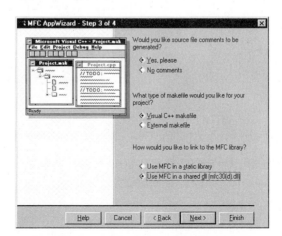

☐ Click the Next button of the AppWizard—Step 3 of 4 window.

Visual C++ responds by displaying the AppWizard—Step 4 of 4 window, as shown in Figure 9.26.

Figure 9.26. The
AppWizard—Step 4 of 4
window of the
MyCombo.MAK project.

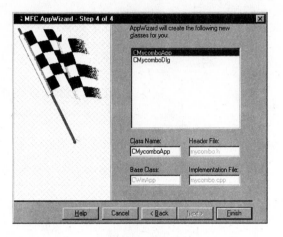

☐ Click the Finish button of the AppWizard—Step 4 of 4 window.

Visual C++ responds by displaying the New Project Information window, as shown in Figure 9.27.

Figure 9.27. The New
Project Information
window of the
MyCombo.MAK project.

☐ Click the OK button of the New Project Information window.

Visual C++ responds by creating the project file and all the skeleton files of the application.

The Visual Implementation of the MyCombo Application

Because the MyCombo application is a dialog-based application, when you created the project and the skeleton files of the MyCombo application with AppWizard, AppWizard created a dialog box that serves as the main window of the application. AppWizard named this dialog box IDD_MYCOMBO_DIALOG. You'll now customize the IDD_MYCOMBO_DIALOG dialog box.

☐ Double-click mycombo.rc inside the mycombo.mak window.

Visual C++ responds by displaying the mycombo.rc window.

☐ Double-click Dialog inside the mycombo.rc window and then double-click IDD_MYCOMBO_DIALOG.

Visual C++ responds by displaying the IDD_MYCOMBO_DIALOG dialog box in design mode.

☐ Implement the dialog box using the specifications in Table 9.4. When you finish implementing the dialog box, it should look like the one shown in Figure 9.28.

Table 9.4. The Properties table of the IDD_MYCOMBO_DIALOG dialog box.

Object	Property	Setting
Dialog box	ID	IDD_MYCOMBO_DIALOG
Combo box	ID	IDC_MY_COMBO
Push button	ID	IDC_EXIT_BUTTON
	Caption	E&xit
Push button	ID	IDC_TO_EDIT_BOX
	Caption	—>
Edit box	ID	IDC_FROM_COMBO

NOTE

Table 9.4 instructs you to place a combo box control inside the dialog box. The combo box tool inside the Tools window is shown in Figure 9.29.

Figure 9.28. The dialog box that serves as the main window of the MyCombo program (in design mode).

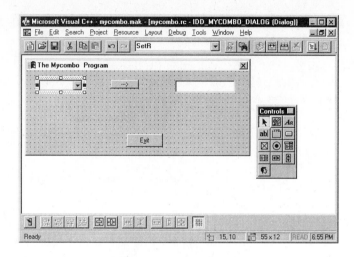

Figure 9.29. The combo box tool inside the Tools window of Visual C++.

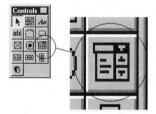

NOTE

During design time you can set the size of the list section of the combo box as follows:

☐   Click the arrow icon of the combo box.

Visual C++ responds by dropping down the list section of the combo box. (See Figure 9.30.)

☐   Use the mouse to drag the handles of the list box to any desired size.

Attaching Variables to the Dialog Box of the MyCombo Program

You'll now attach variables to the controls of the MyCombo dialog box.

☐ Use ClassWizard (from the Project menu) to attach variables to the controls of the IDD_MYCOMBO_DIALOG dialog box, using the specifications in Table 9.5.

Figure 9.30. Sizing the list section of the combo box.

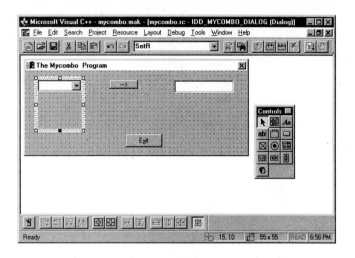

Table 9.5. The Variables table of the MyCombo dialog box.

Control ID	Variable Name	Category	Type
IDC_MY_COMBO	m_MyCombo	Control	CComboBox
IDC_FROM_COMBO	m_FromCombo	Control	CEdit

NOTE

As specified in Table 9.5, when you add the variable m_MyCombo, you must set the Category of this variable to Control (not to Value). The variable type is set to CComboBox. This means that you'll be able to apply all the member functions of the CComboBox class on your combo box.

Also, m_FromCombo (the variable of the edit box) is set to Control and the variable type is CEdit. This means that you'll be able to apply all the member functions of the CEdit class to your edit box.

☐ To save your work, select Save from the File menu.

To see your visual design in action do the following:

☐ Select Build MyCombo.EXE from the Project menu.

> *Visual C++ responds by compiling and linking the MyCombo application.*

☐ Select Execute MyCombo.EXE from the Project menu.

Visual C++ responds by executing the MyCombo.EXE application. (See Figure 9.31.) As expected, the IDD_MYCOMBO_DIALOG dialog box that you designed appears as the main window of the application.

Figure 9.31. The MyCombo window with its combo box.

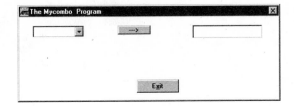

☐ Click the arrow icon of the combo box.

Visual C++ responds by dropping down the list section of the combo box. (See Figure 9.32.) Of course, the list box of the combo box does not have any items in it, because you have not yet written code that accomplishes this.

Figure 9.32. The empty list section of the combo box.

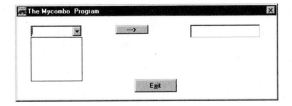

☐ Click the icon that appears in the upper-left corner of the MyCombo application window, and select About from the System menu that pops up.

MyList responds by displaying the About dialog box.

☐ Click the OK button of the About dialog box to close the About dialog box.

☐ Click the icon that appears in the upper-left corner of the MyCombo application window, and select Close from the System menu that pops up.

MyCombo responds by terminating itself.

Initializing the Combo Box

In this section you'll write initialization code that fills the combo box with four items.

You'll now attach code to the WM_INITDIALOG event of the IDD_MYCOMBO_DIALOG dialog box. The WM_INITDIALOG event occurs just before the dialog box is displayed.

☐ Select ClassWizard from the Project menu of Visual C++.

Visual C++ responds by displaying the ClassWizard dialog box.

☐ Select the Message Maps tab at the top of ClassWizard's dialog box.

☐ Use ClassWizard to select the event:

```
CMycomboDlg -> CMycomboDlg -> WM_INITDIALOG
```

Then click the Edit Code button.

> *Visual C++ responds by opening the MYCOMDLG.CPP file and displaying the* `OnInitDialog()` *function, ready to be edited by you.*

☐ Write code inside the `OnInitDialog()` function so that it looks like this:

```
BOOL CMycomboDlg::OnInitDialog()
{
CDialog::OnInitDialog();
CenterWindow();

// Add "About..." menu item to system menu.

// IDM_ABOUTBOX must be in the system command range.
ASSERT((IDM_ABOUTBOX & 0xFFF0) == IDM_ABOUTBOX);
ASSERT(IDM_ABOUTBOX < 0xF000);

CMenu* pSysMenu = GetSystemMenu(FALSE);
CString strAboutMenu;
strAboutMenu.LoadString(IDS_ABOUTBOX);
if (!strAboutMenu.IsEmpty())
   {
   pSysMenu->AppendMenu(MF_SEPARATOR);
   pSysMenu->AppendMenu(MF_STRING, IDM_ABOUTBOX,
                 strAboutMenu);
   }

// TODO: Add extra initialization here

/////////////////////////
// MY CODE STARTS HERE
/////////////////////////

// Insert 4 strings inside the list box
// section of the combo box
m_MyCombo.AddString("I'm string a");
m_MyCombo.AddString("I'm string b");
m_MyCombo.AddString("I'm string c");
m_MyCombo.AddString("I'm string d");

/////////////////////////
// MY CODE ENDS HERE
/////////////////////////


return TRUE;
// return TRUE  unless you set the focus to a control
}
```

The code you typed uses the AddString() function to add four items to the list box section of the combo box:

```
m_MyCombo.AddString("I'm string a");
m_MyCombo.AddString("I'm string b");
m_MyCombo.AddString("I'm string c");
m_MyCombo.AddString("I'm string d");
```

Attaching Code to the *BN_CLICKED* Event of the Exit Button

Recall that when the user clicks the Exit button the MyCombo program should terminate. You'll now attach code to the Click event (BN_CLICKED) of the Exit button.

☐ Display the ClassWizard dialog box by selecting ClassWizard from the Project menu of Visual C++.

☐ Select the Message Maps tab at the top of ClassWizard's dialog box.

☐ Use ClassWizard to select the event:

```
CMycomboDlg -> IDC_EXIT_BUTTON -> BN_CLICKED
```

Then click the Add Function button.

☐ Name the new function OnExitButton().

To write the code of the OnExitButton() function do the following:

☐ Click the Edit Code button of ClassWizard.

> *ClassWizard responds by opening the file MYCOMDLG.CPP, with the function* OnExitButton() *ready to be edited by you.*

☐ Write code inside the OnExitButton() function so that it looks like this:

```
void CMycomboDlg::OnExitButton()
{
// TODO: Add your control notification handler code here


/////////////////////////
// MY CODE STARTS HERE
/////////////////////////

// Close the dialog box (terminate the program).
OnOK();


/////////////////////////
// MY CODE ENDS HERE
/////////////////////////

}
```

☐ Save your work by selecting Save from the File menu of Visual C++.

To see your initialization code in action do the following:

☐ Select Build MyCombo.EXE from the Project menu.

Visual C++ responds by compiling and linking the MyCombo program.

☐ Select Execute MyCombo.EXE from the Project menu.

Visual C++ responds by executing the MyCombo.EXE program.

☐ Click the arrow icon of the combo box.

MyCombo responds by dropping down the list section of the combo box. As shown in Figure 9.33, the list contains the strings that you added to it in the OnInitDialog() *function.*

Figure 9.33. The combo box with four string in it.

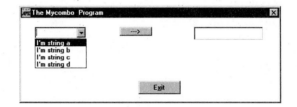

☐ Click one of the items in the list.

MyCombo responds by copying the clicked item into the edit box section of the combo box. (See Figure 9.34.)

Figure 9.34. Copying the clicked item of the list to the edit box section of the combo box.

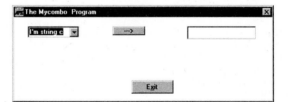

☐ Click the Exit button.

MyList responds by terminating itself.

Reading an Item from the List Box

In the preceding section, you added three strings to the combo box. In this section you'll write code that reads the contents of the list section of the combo box.

Your objective now is to write code that does the following: When the user clicks the button that has a caption of an arrow pointing from left to right, the contents of the edit box section of the combo box are copied to the right edit box.

You'll now attach code to the BN_CLICKED event of the IDC_TO_EDIT_BOX button. The BN_CLICKED event occurs when the user clicks the button.

☐ Select ClassWizard from the Project menu of Visual C++.

> *Visual C++ responds by displaying the ClassWizard dialog box.*

☐ Select the Message Maps tab at the top of ClassWizard's dialog box.

☐ Use ClassWizard to select the BN_CLICKED event of the IDC_TO_EDIT_BOX button:

```
CMycombo -> IDC_TO_EDIT_BOX -> BN_CLICKED
```

Then click the Edit Code button.

> *Visual C++ responds by opening the MYCOBDLG.CPP file and displaying the*
> OnToEditBox() *function, ready to be edited by you.*

☐ Write code inside the OnToEditBox() function so that it looks like this:

```
void CMycomboDlg::OnToEditBox()
{
// TODO: Add your control notification handler code here

/////////////////////////
// MY CODE STARTS HERE
/////////////////////////

// A buffer that will hold the string
char sFromCombo[50];


// Fill the sFromCombo variable with the contents of
// the edit box section of the combo box.
m_MyCombo.GetWindowText ( sFromCombo, 25);


// Select the entire text inside the right edit box
m_FromCombo.SetSel (0,-1);
// Replace the selected text of
// the right edit box
m_FromCombo.ReplaceSel (sFromCombo);



/////////////////////////
// MY CODE ENDS HERE
/////////////////////////

}
```

The code you typed declares a string variable sFromCombo:

```
char sFromCombo[50];
```

The sFromCombo variable is then filled with the contents of the edit box section of the combo box:

```
m_MyCombo.GetWindowText ( sFromCombo, 25);
```

The first parameter of the `GetWindowText()` function is the string variable that will be filled with the contents of the edit box section of the combo box, and the second parameter is the maximum number of characters that will be copied to the string variable mentioned in the first parameter of the `GetWindowText()` function.

It is interesting to note that the `CComboBox` class does not have a member function that fills a string variable with the contents of the edit box section of the combo box. You can verify that by displaying the help menu of the `CComboBox` class. So the question is, of course, Where did the `GetWindowText()` function come from?

Take a look at the help window of the `CComboBox`. (See Figure 9.35.)

As shown in Figure 9.35, the `CComboBox` class was derived from the `CWnd` class. So because `CComboBox` does not have a member function that reads the edit box section of the combo box, maybe you'll be lucky and the base class `CWnd` will have such a member function.

Figure 9.35. The help window of the CComboBox class.

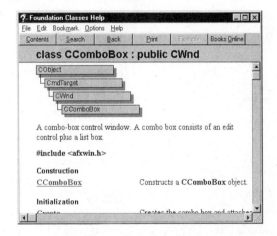

Displaying the help window of the `CWnd` class shows that the `CWnd` class has a member function called `GetWindowText()`. When the `GetWindowText()` function is applied on a combo box, this function fills a string variable with the contents of the edit box section of the combo box (which is exactly what you need).

So the `m_MyCombo` variable is an object of class `CComboBox`. And because the `CComboBox` class is derived from the `CWnd` class, you are able to use the `GetWindowText()` member function of CWnd on the `m_MyCombo` variable.

Next, the IDC_FROM_COMBO (right) edit box is filled with the contents of the `sFromCombo` variable:

```
// Select the entire text inside the right edit box
m_FromCombo.SetSel (0,-1);
// Replace the selected text of
// the right edit box
m_FromCombo.ReplaceSel (sFromCombo);
```

☐ Save your work by selecting Save from the File menu of Visual C++.

To see your code in action do the following:

☐ Select Build MyCombo.EXE from the Project menu.

  Visual C++ responds by compiling and linking the MyCombo program.

☐ Select Execute MyCombo.EXE from the Project menu.

☐ Click the arrow icon of the combo box.

  MyCombo responds by dropping down the list section of the combo box.

☐ Click any of the items in the list box.

  MyCombo responds by copying the clicked item to the edit box section of the combo box.

☐ Click the button that has a caption with an arrow pointing from left to right.

  MyCombo responds by copying the contents of the edit box section of the combo box to the IDC_FROM_COMBO (right) edit box. (See Figure 9.36.)

Figure 9.36. Copying the second item in the list section of the combo box to the IDC_FROM_COMBO (right) edit box.

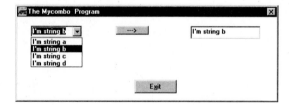

You can also type characters inside the edit box section of the combo box, and then copy the characters to the IDC_FROM_COMBO (right) edit box:

☐ Type something inside the edit box section of the combo box, and then click the button that has a caption with an arrow pointing from left to right.

  MyCombo responds by copying the contents of the edit box section of the combo box to the IDC_FROM_COMBO (right) edit box. (See Figure 9.37.)

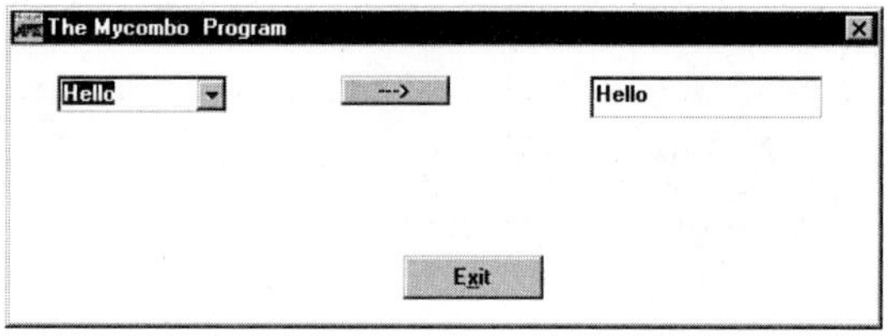

Figure 9.37. Copying the contents of the edit box section of the combo box to the IDC_FROM_COMBO (right) edit box.

Why Not Use Copy and Paste?

An alternate way of transferring the contents of the list box and combo box to an edit box is to copy the string to the Clipboard, and then copy the Clipboard to the edit box.

However, this is not the recommended way because of the following reason: Suppose that the user works with Windows and copies something to the Clipboard. Then the user needs to copy a string from a list box or from a combo box to an edit box. If you implement the transfer of the string from the list box or the combo box to the edit box via the Clipboard, the previous contents of the Clipboard are removed. When the user pastes the contents of the Clipboard, the user expects to paste the string that he or she copied to the Clipboard, not a string that your code copied to the Clipboard!

The Windows interface rule is therefore the following:

Don't change the Clipboard from within your code! Only the user is allowed to change the contents of the Clipboard.

10

Radio Buttons

In this chapter you'll learn how to incorporate radio buttons in a dialog box. As you know, radio buttons serve an important role in the Windows user-interface mechanism. The application you'll write in this chapter is a dialog-based type—that is, it's an application in which a dialog box serves as the main window of the application.

The MyRadio Application

You'll now write the MyRadio application, which is an example of an application that uses radio buttons. Before you start writing the MyRadio application yourself, execute the copy of it that resides in the \MVCPROG\EXE directory of the book's CD.

To execute the MyRadio application do the following:

☐ Select Run from the Start menu of Windows and execute the X:\MVCPROG\EXE\MyRadio.EXE program (where *X* represents the drive letter of your CD-ROM drive).

> *Windows responds by executing the MyRadio.EXE application. The main window of MyRadio.EXE appears, as shown in Figure 10.1.*

As you can see, the main window of Figure 10.1 contains two groups of radio buttons.

Figure 10.1. The main window of the MyRadio application.

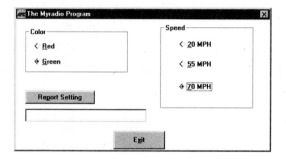

☐ Click an unselected radio button inside the Color group of radio buttons.

> *MyRadio responds by placing a dot inside the radio button that you clicked and removing the dot from the other radio button.*

☐ Click an unselected radio button inside the Speed group of radio buttons.

> *MyRadio responds by placing a dot inside the radio button that you clicked and removing the dot from the other radio button.*

☐ Click the Report Setting button.

> *MyRadio responds by placing text inside the edit box that reports the status of the radio buttons. (See Figure 10.2.)*

Now that you know what the MyRadio application should do, you can begin learning how to write it.

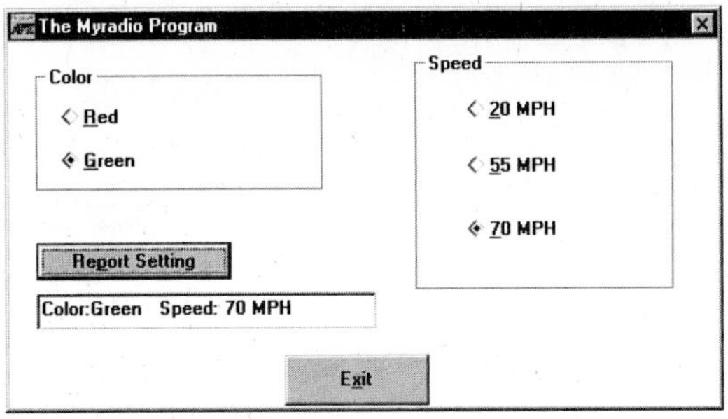

Figure 10.2. The window
of the MyRadio program
after you have experi-
mented with it.

The Myradio Program

Color
‹ Red
← Green

Speed
‹ 20 MPH
‹ 55 MPH
← 70 MPH

Report Setting

Color:Green   Speed: 70 MPH

Exit

Creating the Project of the MyRadio Application

To create the project of the MyRadio application do the following:

☐ Start Visual C++ and close all the open windows that appear inside the desktop of Visual C++ (if there are any).

☐ Select New from the File menu.

Visual C++ responds by displaying the New dialog box.

☐ Select Project inside the New dialog box and then click the OK button of the New dialog box.

Visual C++ responds by displaying the New Project dialog box.

☐ Set the project name to MyRadio.

☐ Set the project path to \MVCPROG\CH10\MyRadio\MyRadio.MAK.

Your New Project dialog box should now look like the one shown in Figure 10.3.

Figure 10.3. The New
Project dialog box of the
MyRadio.MAK project.

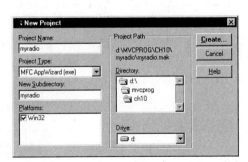

☐ Click the Create button of the New Project dialog box.

Visual C++ responds by displaying the AppWizard—Step 1 window.

☐ Set the AppWizard—Step 1 window as shown in Figure 10.4. As shown in Figure 10.4, the MyRadio.MAK project is set as a dialog-based application, and U.S. English (APPWIZUS.DLL) is used as the language for the MyRadio.MAK project's resources.

Figure 10.4. The AppWizard—Step 1 window of the MyRadio.MAK project.

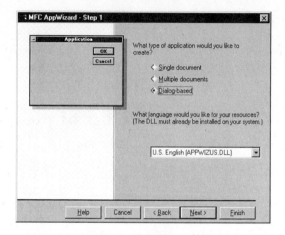

☐ Click the Next button of the AppWizard—Step 1 window.

Visual C++ responds by displaying the AppWizard—Step 2 of 4 window.

☐ Set the AppWizard—Step 2 of 4 window as shown in Figure 10.5. That is, place a checkmark inside the About Box check box (to incorporate an About dialog box into the application), and place a checkmark inside the Use 3D Controls check box (so that the application will use 3D controls). Also, set the title of the application to The MyRadio Program.

Figure 10.5. The AppWizard—Step 2 of 4 window of the MyRadio.MAK project.

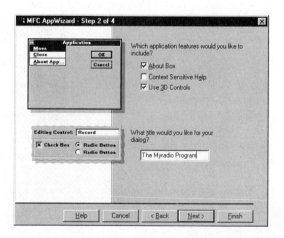

☐ Click the Next button of the AppWizard—Step 2 of 4 window.

Visual C++ responds by displaying the AppWizard—Step 3 of 4 window.

☐ Set the Step 3 of 4 window as shown in Figure 10.6.

As shown in Figure 10.6, the project will be generated with comments, a Visual C++ makefile will be generated, and the application will use the MFC library from a DLL.

Figure 10.6. The AppWizard—Step 3 of 4 window of the MyRadio.MAK project.

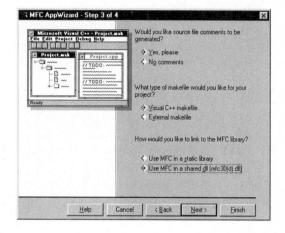

☐ Click the Next button of the AppWizard—Step 3 of 4 window.

Visual C++ responds by displaying the AppWizard—Step 4 of 4 window, as shown in Figure 10.7.

Figure 10.7. The AppWizard—Step 4 of 4 window of the MyRadio.MAK project.

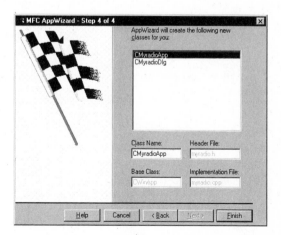

☐ Click the Finish button of the AppWizard—Step 4 of 4 window.

Visual C++ responds by displaying the New Project Information window, as shown in Figure 10.8.

Figure 10.8. The New Project Information window of the MyRadio.MAK project.

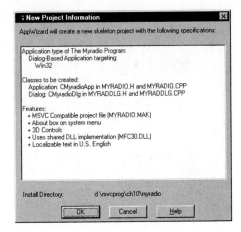

☐ Click the OK button of the New Project Information window.

Visual C++ responds by creating the project file and all the skeleton files of the application.

The Visual Implementation of the MyRadio Application

Because the MyRadio application is a dialog-based application, when you created the project and the skeleton files of the MyRadio application with AppWizard, AppWizard created for you a dialog box that serves as the main window of the application. AppWizard named this dialog box IDD_MYRADIO_DIALOG. You'll now customize the IDD_MYRADIO_DIALOG dialog box.

☐ Double-click myradio.rc inside the myradio.mak window.

Visual C++ responds by displaying the myradio.rc window.

☐ Double-click Dialog inside the myradio.rc window and then double-click IDD_MYRADIO_DIALOG.

Visual C++ responds by displaying the IDD_MYRADIO_DIALOG dialog box in design mode.

☐ Implement the dialog box using the specifications in Table 10.1. When you finish implementing the dialog box, it should look like the one shown in Figure 10.9.

Table 10.1. The Properties table of the IDD_MYRADIO_DIALOG dialog box.

Object	Property	Setting
Dialog box	ID	IDD_MYRADIO_DIALOG
Push button	ID	IDC_EXIT_BUTTON
	Caption	E&xit
Radio button	ID	IDC_RED_RADIO
	Caption	Red
Radio button	ID	IDC_GREEN_RADIO
	Caption	Green
Static frame	ID	IDC_STATIC
	Caption	Color
Radio button	ID	IDC_20_RADIO
	Caption	&20 MPH
Radio button	ID	IDC_55_RADIO
	Caption	&55 MPH
Radio button	ID	IDC_70_RADIO
	Caption	&70 MPH
Static frame	ID	IDC_STATIC
	Caption	Speed
Edit box	ID	IDC_EDIT1
Push button	ID	IDC_REPORT_BUTTON
	Caption	Re&port Setting

Figure 10.9. The dialog box that serves as the main window of the MyRadio program (in design mode).

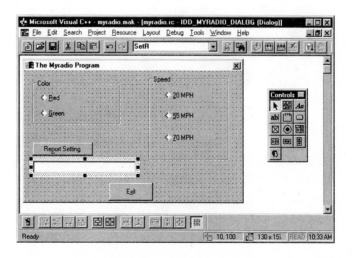

NOTE

Table 10.1 instructs you to place radio button controls inside the dialog box. The radio button tool inside the Tools window is shown in Figure 10.10.

Figure 10.10. The radio button tool inside the Tools window of Visual C++.

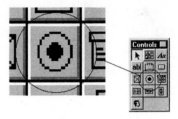

NOTE

In Windows literature, the radio button is also referred to as an option button.

In this book, *radio button* and *option button* mean the same thing.

NOTE

Note that the ID of each of the two static frames in Table 10.1 is IDC_STATIC. Two different controls with identical ID? Yes, this is okay, because the static frame is not used from within your code.

NOTE

When placing the radio buttons, use the following steps:

☐ Place the Red and Green radio buttons.

☐ Place a static frame control, and then drag the static frame so that it encloses the Red and Green radio buttons.

In a similar manner, place the 20 MPH, 55 MPH, and 70 MPH radio buttons inside the dialog box, place a second static frame control, and then drag and size the static frame control so that it encloses the 20 MPH, 55 MPH, and 70 MPH radio buttons.

Now test your work. As you'll see, currently there is something wrong with the visual implementation of the dialog box!

☐ Select Test from the Resource menu. (See Figure 10.11.)

Visual C++ responds by displaying the dialog box as it will appear during runtime. (See Figure 10.12.)

Figure 10.11. Selecting Test from the Resource menu to test the visual implementation.

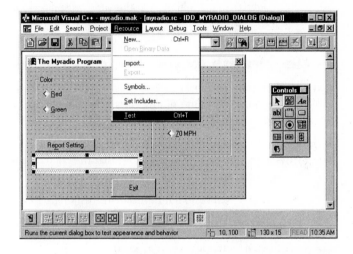

Figure 10.12. Displaying the IDC_MYRADIO_DIALOG dialog box in test mode.

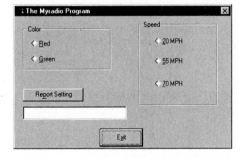

☐ Click any of the radio buttons inside the Color group, and then click any of the radio buttons inside the Speed group.

As you can see, there is something wrong with the visual implementation. That is, Visual C++ does not let you select one radio button inside the Color group and another radio button inside the Speed group. In other words, Visual C++ considers the five radio buttons to be one group of buttons.

☐ Click the × icon that appears on the upper-right corner of the test window.

Visual C++ responds by terminating the test.

NOTE

As you can see from the preceding experiment, the Test feature is a very useful feature. It lets you test your visual design without the need for compiling and linking the application.

You should use the Test feature during your visual design process, because it is best to discover (and fix) your application at this early stage of your design.

Declaring the Radio Buttons Groups

In the preceding section you discovered that Visual C++ treats the five radio buttons as belonging to one single group. You'll now inform Visual C++ that the Red and Green radio buttons belong to one group and that the 20 MPH, 55 MPH, and 70 MPH radio buttons belong to a second group.

In essence, you already gave this information to Visual C++. That is, by enclosing the radio buttons with the static frames, you told Visual C++ that the radio buttons that are enclosed by the static frame belong to one group. Nevertheless, there is one additional step that you must perform:

☐ Double-click the Red radio button inside the Color group.

   Visual C++ responds by displaying the Properties dialog box of the Red radio button.

☐ Place a checkmark inside the Group check box.

☐ Double-click the 20 MPH radio button inside the Speed group.

   Visual C++ responds by displaying the Properties dialog box of the 20 MPH radio button.

☐ Place a checkmark inside the Group check box.

NOTE

You should place a checkmark inside the Group check box of only the first radio button of the group. That is, only the Red radio button should have its Group property checked, and only the 20 MPH radio button should have its Group property checked.

NOTE

When you design a dialog box with radio buttons, it is very important that you place the radio buttons one after the other.

When you place a control inside the dialog box, Visual C++ assigns an ID number to the control. The IDs are assigned in sequential order. For example, the first radio control that you placed was assigned with a number such as 1017, the second radio control that you placed will therefore have an ID of 1018, and so on.

The idea is to place the radio buttons one after another so that they will have sequential IDs. As you'll see later in this chapter, the functions that deal with radio buttons assume that the radio buttons of any group have sequential ID numbers.

You can check the ID numbers of the radio buttons (as well as the IDs of the other controls of the dialog box) in the following way:

☐ Select Symbols from the Resource menu.

Visual C++ responds by displaying a dialog box containing all the controls listed with their corresponding ID numbers.

If your radio buttons do not have sequential numbers, delete them from the dialog box and then place new radio buttons inside the dialog box.

Remember, the radio buttons inside a group must have sequential IDs. For example, it is okay to have the following IDs:

Color group:
Red   1017
Green   1018

Speed group:
20 MPH   2001
55 MPH   2002
70 MPH   2003

Now test your visual design:

☐ Select Test from the Resources menu.

> *Visual C++ responds by displaying the Test window. (See Figure 10.12.)*

☐ Click the Red radio button, and then click the 55 MPH radio button.

Your Test window should now look like the one shown in Figure 10.13.

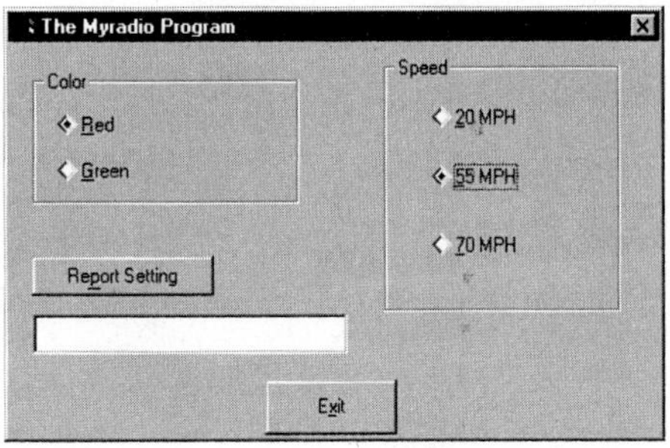

Figure 10.13. Selecting the Red radio button from the Color group and the 55 MPH radio button from the Speed group.

☐ Click the Green radio button and then click the 70 MPH radio button.

Your Test window should now look like the one shown in Figure 10.14.

Figure 10.14. Selecting the Green radio button from the Color group and the 70 MPH radio button from the Speed group.

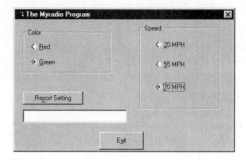

☐ Experiment with the Test window and verify that Visual C++ considers the Red and Green radio buttons to be one group, and the 20 MPH, 55 MPH, and 70 MPH radio buttons as an independent second group.

☐ Click the × icon of the Test window to terminate the test.

NOTE

Before proceeding with this chapter, make sure that Visual C++ accepted the radio buttons as two separate groups. If for some reason you can't accomplish this, delete the two static frames and the five radio buttons, and then start implementing the two groups all over again. Don't forget, only the first radio button in each group gets its Group property checked.

Attaching Variables to the Controls Inside the Dialog Box of the MyRadio Program

You'll now attach variables to the controls inside the IDD_MYRADIO_DIALOG dialog box.

☐ Display the ClassWizard dialog box by selecting ClassWizard from the Project menu of Visual C++.

☐ Select the Member Variables tab at the top of ClassWizard's dialog box.

☐ Make sure that the Class Name drop-down list is set to CMyradioDlg.

☐ Attach variables to the controls of the IDD_MYRADIO_DIALOG dialog box as specified in Table 10.2.

Table 10.2. The Variables table of the MyRadio dialog box.

Control ID	Variable Name	Category	Variable Type
IDC_RED_RADIO	m_RedRadio	Control	CButton
IDC_20_RADIO	m_SpeedRadio	Value	int
IDC_EDIT1	m_Edit1	Control	CEdit

NOTE

As specified in Table 10.2, when you add the variable m_RedRadio, you have to set the category of the variable to Control (not to Value). The variable type is set to CButton.

The variable type is CButton. This means that the variable that you attached to the IDC_RED_RADIO radio button is an object of the CButton class.

However, the variable you attached to the IDC_20_RADIO radio button is of type int.

Why do you attach a variable of type CButton to the first group of radio buttons and attach a variable of type int to the second group of radio buttons? Because you should see two different ways of manipulating radio buttons. You'll see the two different ways in the next section.

The variable that you attached to the IDC_EDIT1 edit box is of type CEdit. This means that you'll be able to use the member functions of the CEdit class on the m_Edit1 edit box.

NOTE

Note that only the first radio button in each group gets a variable. That is, you attached a variable to the Red radio button, and you should not attach a variable to the Green radio button.

Also, you attached a variable to the 20 MPH radio button, and you should not attach variables to the 55 MPH and 70 MPH radio buttons.

☐ To save your work, select Save from the File menu.

To see your visual design in action do the following:

☐ Select Build MyRadio.EXE from the Project menu.

Visual C++ responds by compiling and linking the MyRadio application.

☐ Select Execute MyRadio.EXE from the Project menu.

Visual C++ responds by executing the MyRadio.EXE application. (See Figure 10.15.) As expected, the IDD_MYRADIO_DIALOG dialog box that you designed appears as the main window of the application. Of course, none of the radio buttons is selected because you have not yet written code that accomplishes this.

Figure 10.15. The MyRadio window with its radio buttons not initialized.

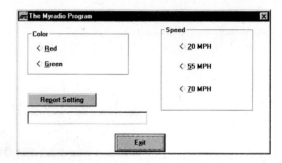

☐ Click the Green radio button and then click the 70 MPH radio button.

MyRadio responds by placing dots inside the Green and 70 MPH radio buttons. (See Figure 10.16.)

Figure 10.16. The MyRadio window with its Green and 70 MPH radio button selected.

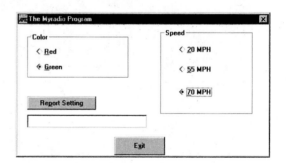

☐ Click the other radio buttons, and verify that MyRadio treats the two radio button groups as separate groups.

☐ Click the icon that appears on the upper-left corner of the MyRadio application, and select Close from the System menu that pops up.

MyRadio responds by terminating itself.

Initializing the Radio Buttons

In this section you'll write initialization code that selects a radio button from each group.

You'll now attach code to the WM_INITDIALOG event of the IDD_MYRADIO_DIALOG dialog box. The WM_INITDIALOG event occurs just before the dialog box is displayed.

☐ Select ClassWizard from the Project menu of Visual C++.

Visual C++ responds by displaying the ClassWizard dialog box.

☐ Select the Message Maps tab at the top of ClassWizard's dialog box.

☐ Use ClassWizard to select the event:

CMyradioDlg -> CMyradioDlg -> WM_INITDIALOG

Then click the Edit Code button.

Visual C++ responds by opening the MYRADDLG.CPP file and displaying the
OnInitDialog() *function, ready to be edited by you.*

The question is What code should you type to initialize the radio buttons? It depends on the type of variable that you attached to the group of radio buttons.

When you attached variables to the Color radio buttons, you set the variable type to CButton. The variable you attached to the Speed radio buttons is of type int.

☐ Write code inside the OnInitDialog() function so that it looks like this:

```
BOOL CMyradioDlg::OnInitDialog()
{
CDialog::OnInitDialog();
CenterWindow();

// Add "About..." menu item to system menu.

// IDM_ABOUTBOX must be in the system command range.
ASSERT((IDM_ABOUTBOX & 0xFFF0) == IDM_ABOUTBOX);
ASSERT(IDM_ABOUTBOX < 0xF000);

CMenu* pSysMenu = GetSystemMenu(FALSE);
CString strAboutMenu;
strAboutMenu.LoadString(IDS_ABOUTBOX);
if (!strAboutMenu.IsEmpty())
    {
    pSysMenu->AppendMenu(MF_SEPARATOR);
    pSysMenu->AppendMenu(MF_STRING, IDM_ABOUTBOX,
            strAboutMenu);
    }

// TODO: Add extra initialization here


/////////////////////////
// MY CODE STARTS HERE
/////////////////////////

// Initialize the Red and 55 MPH radio buttons
// (Two methods are shown)

// Method #1
CheckRadioButton ( IDC_RED_RADIO,
                   IDC_GREEN_RADIO,
                   IDC_GREEN_RADIO );
```

```
// Method #2
m_SpeedRadio = 2;

UpdateData(FALSE);

///////////////////////
// MY CODE ENDS HERE
///////////////////////


return TRUE;
// return TRUE unless you set the focus to a control
}
```

The code you typed selects the Green radio button:

```
CheckRadioButton ( IDC_RED_RADIO,
                   IDC_GREEN_RADIO,
                   IDC_GREEN_RADIO );
```

That is, the CheckRadioButton() function is used. The first parameter of the CheckRadioButton() is the ID of the first radio button in the group. The second parameter of the CheckRadioButton() function is the ID of the last radio button in the group. The third parameter of the CheckRadioButton() function is the ID of the radio button that you want to select. Because you want to select the Green radio button, the third parameter of the CheckRadioButton() is set to IDC_GREEN_RADIO.

NOTE

Note that the CheckRadioButton() function assumes that the IDs of the radio buttons have sequential numbers. That is, you have to specify the ID of the first radio button of the group and the ID of the last radio button in the group. The third parameter of the CheckRadioButton() function must be a number greater than or equal to the first parameter and less than or equal to the second parameter.

The 70 MPH radio button in the Speed group is selected in the following way:

```
m_SpeedRadio = 2;
UpdateData(FALSE);
```

That is, the integer variable that you attached to the Speed group of radio buttons indicates which radio button in the group is selected. Therefore, setting m_SpeedRadio to 0 causes the 20 MPH radio button to be selected; setting m_SpeedRadio to 1 causes the 55 MPH radio button to be selected; and setting m_SpeedRadio to 2 causes the 70 MPH radio button to be selected. After you set the variables of the radio buttons group, the UpdateData() function is called with its parameter set to FALSE so that the screen will be updated.

Attaching Code to the *BN_CLICKED* Event of the Exit Button

Recall that when the user clicks the Exit button the MyRadio program should terminate. You'll now attach code to the click event (BN_CLICKED) of the Exit button.

☐ Display the ClassWizard dialog box by selecting ClassWizard from the Project menu of Visual C++.

☐ Select the Message Maps tab at the top of ClassWizard's dialog box.

☐ Use ClassWizard to select the event:

CMyradioDlg -> IDC_EXIT_BUTTON -> BN_CLICKED

Then click the Add Function button.

☐ Name the new function OnExitButton().

To write the code of the OnExitButton() function do the following:

☐ Click the Edit Code button of ClassWizard.

> *ClassWizard responds by opening the file MYRADDLG.CPP, with the function* OnExitButton() *ready to be edited by you.*

☐ Write code inside the OnExitButton() function so that it looks like this:

```
void CMyradioDlg::OnExitButton()
{
// TODO: Add your control notification handler code here


/////////////////////////
// MY CODE STARTS HERE
/////////////////////////

// Close the dialog box (terminate the program).
OnOK();

/////////////////////////
// MY CODE ENDS HERE
/////////////////////////

}
```

☐ Save your work by selecting Save from the File menu of Visual C++.

To see your initialization code in action do the following:

☐ Select Build MyRadio.EXE from the Project menu.

> *Visual C++ responds by compiling and linking the MyRadio program.*

☐ Select Execute MyRadio.EXE from the Project menu.

Visual C++ responds by executing the MyRadio.EXE program. As you can see, the radio buttons appear as you set them inside the OnInitDialog() *function.*

☐ Click the Exit button.

MyRadio responds by terminating itself.

Determining the Status of the Radio Buttons

In this section you'll write code that reads the status of the radio buttons.

Recall that when the user clicks the Report Status button the MyRadio program should display the status of the radio buttons inside the m_Edit1 edit box. You'll now attach code to the Click event (BN_CLICKED) of the Report Status push button.

☐ Display the ClassWizard dialog box by selecting ClassWizard from the Project menu of Visual C++.

☐ Select the Message Maps tab at the top of ClassWizard's dialog box.

☐ Use ClassWizard to select the event:

CMyradio -> IDC_REPORT_BUTTON -> BN_CLICKED

Then click the Add Function button.

☐ Name the new function OnReportButton().

To write the code of the OnReportButton() function do the following:

☐ Click the Edit Code button of ClassWizard.

ClassWizard responds by opening the file MYRADDLG.CPP, with the function OnReportButton() *ready to be edited by you.*

☐ Write code inside the OnReportButton() function so that it looks like this:

```
void CMyradioDlg::OnReportButton()
{
// TODO: Add your control notification handler code here


/////////////////////////
// MY CODE STARTS HERE
/////////////////////////

// Read the status of the radio buttons
// (Two methods are shown)

UpdateData(TRUE);

char sRadioButtonsStatus[50];
```

```
// Method #1
int iWhichRadioButton;
iWhichRadioButton = GetCheckedRadioButton ( IDC_RED_RADIO, IDC_GREEN_RADIO );

if (iWhichRadioButton == 0 )
   strcpy ( sRadioButtonsStatus, "Color:None" );

if (iWhichRadioButton == IDC_RED_RADIO )
   strcpy ( sRadioButtonsStatus, "Color:Red" );

if (iWhichRadioButton == IDC_GREEN_RADIO )
   strcpy ( sRadioButtonsStatus, "Color:Green" );

// Method #2

if ( m_SpeedRadio == 0 )
   strcat ( sRadioButtonsStatus, "   Speed: 20 MPH");

if ( m_SpeedRadio == 1 )
   strcat ( sRadioButtonsStatus, "   Speed: 55 MPH");

if ( m_SpeedRadio == 2 )
   strcat ( sRadioButtonsStatus, "   Speed: 70 MPH");


// Select the entire text inside the edit box
m_Edit1.SetSel (0,-1);
 // Replace the selected text
m_Edit1.ReplaceSel (sRadioButtonsStatus);


/////////////////////
// MY CODE ENDS HERE
/////////////////////

}
```

The code you typed executes the UpdateData() function with TRUE as its parameter:

```
UpdateData(TRUE);
```

This means that the variables of the controls will be updated with the contents of the controls. In particular, the m_SpeedRadio variable will be updated with an integer that reflects the status of the Speed group of radio buttons. If the 20 MPH radio button is selected, m_SpeedRadio will be updated with the value 1, if the 55 MPH radio button is selected, m_SpeedRadio will be updated with the value 2, and if the 70 MPH radio button is selected, m_SpeedRadio will be updated with the value 2.

NOTE

Whenever you attach a variable to a control and the type of variable is Value, you must use UpdateData(FALSE) to transfer the contents of the variable to the control, and you must update the variable by using UpdateData(TRUE).

On the other hand, there is no need to use the UpdateData() function when you are using a Control variable.

A string variable is declared:

```
char sRadioButtonsStatus[50];
```

Then the status of the radio button from the Color group is determined:

```
int iWhichRadioButton;
iWhichRadioButton =
   GetCheckedRadioButton ( IDC_RED_RADIO,
                           IDC_GREEN_RADIO );
```

The `GetCheckedRadioButton()` function returns an integer. This integer represents the ID of the selected radio button.

The first parameter of the `GetCheckedRadioButton()` function is the ID of the first radio button in the group, and the second parameter of the `GetCheckedRadioButton()` function is the ID of the last radio button in the group.

NOTE

The `GetCheckedRadioButton()` function assumes that the IDs of the radio buttons in the group have sequential numbers.

A series of three `if` statements is then executed to analyze the returned value of the `GetCheckedRadioButton()` function:

```
if (iWhichRadioButton == 0 )
   strcpy ( sRadioButtonsStatus, "Color:None" );

if (iWhichRadioButton == IDC_RED_RADIO )
   strcpy ( sRadioButtonsStatus, "Color:Red" );

if (iWhichRadioButton == IDC_GREEN_RADIO )
   strcpy ( sRadioButtonsStatus, "Color:Green" );
```

As you can see from the preceding code, when the `GetCheckedRadioButton()` function returns 0, you know that none of the radio buttons of the group is checked; when the `GetCheckedRadioButton()` function returns `IDC_RED_RADIO`, you know that the red radio button of the group is checked; and when the `GetCheckedRadioButton()` function returns `IDC_GREEN_RADIO`, you know that the green radio button of the group is checked. (Note that instead of using a series of three `if` statements, you can use a `switch` statement with three `case` statements in it.)

Next, three `if` statements are executed to analyze the value of `m_SpeedRadio`:

```
if ( m_SpeedRadio == 0 )
   strcat ( sRadioButtonsStatus, "   Speed: 20 MPH");

if ( m_SpeedRadio == 1 )
   strcat ( sRadioButtonsStatus, "   Speed: 55 MPH");

if ( m_SpeedRadio == 2 )
   strcat ( sRadioButtonsStatus, "   Speed: 70 MPH");
```

Finally, the m_Edit1 edit box is updated:

```
// Select the entire text inside the edit box
m_Edit1.SetSel (0,-1);
 // Replace the selected text
m_Edit1.ReplaceSel (sRadioButtonsStatus);
```

☐ Save your work by selecting Save from the File menu of Visual C++.

To see your code in action do the following:

☐ Select Build MyRadio.EXE from the Project menu.

Visual C++ responds by compiling and linking the MyRadio program.

☐ Select Execute MyRadio.EXE from the Project menu.

Visual C++ responds by executing the MyRadio.EXE program. As you can see, the radio buttons appear as you set them inside the OnInitDialog() *function.*

☐ Click the Report Setting button.

MyRadio responds by displaying the status of the radio buttons inside the edit box.

☐ Change the setting of the radio buttons, and then click the Report Setting button.

MyRadio responds by displaying the status of the radio buttons inside the edit box.

☐ Click the Exit button.

MyRadio responds by terminating itself.

11

Displaying Dialog Boxes

In this chapter you'll learn how to display dialog boxes.

In the applications of the previous chapters you placed controls inside the dialog boxes that serve as application main windows. You did not create these dialog boxes— AppWizard created the dialog boxes—and then you placed controls inside the dialog boxes.

In the application you'll write in this chapter, you'll create a dialog box from scratch, you'll place controls inside the dialog box, and you'll write the code that displays the dialog box.

The MyDialog Application

The MyDialog program illustrates how to implement an application that displays a dialog box and lets the user enter data via the dialog box.

Before you start writing the MyDialog application yourself, execute the copy of it that resides in the \MVCPROG\EXE directory of the book's CD.

To execute the MyDialog application do the following:

☐ Select Run from the Start menu of Windows and execute the X:\MVCPROG\EXE\MyDialog.EXE program (where *X* represents the drive letter of your CD-ROM drive).

> *Windows responds by executing the MyDialog.EXE application. The main window of MyDialog.EXE appears, as shown in Figure 11.1.*

Figure 11.1. The main window of the MyDialog application.

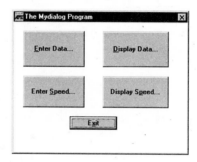

☐ Click the Enter Data button.

> *MyDialog responds by displaying a dialog box.*

☐ Type `Testing...this is a test` inside the edit box and then click the OK button of the dialog box. (See Figure 11.2.)

> *MyDialog responds by closing the dialog box and returning to the main window.*

Figure 11.2. The dialog box of the MyDialog application. This dialog box is used for accepting data from the user.

☐ Click the Display Data button.

> *MyDialog responds by displaying a message box with the string `Testing...this is a test` inside the message box.*

☐ Click the Enter Data button.

> *MyDialog responds by displaying the dialog box again. As you can see, the old data that you entered in the dialog box is maintained.*

☐ Type New test inside the edit box and then click the Cancel button.

> *MyDialog responds by closing the dialog box and returning to the main window.*

☐ Click the Display Data button.

> *MyDialog responds by displaying a message box with the string* Testing...this is a test *inside the message box. In other words, because you closed the dialog box with the Cancel button, the string* New test *is not maintained.*

☐ Click the Enter Speed button.

> *MyDialog responds by displaying the dialog box shown in Figure 11.3.*

Figure 11.3. The dialog box that lets the user enter the speed.

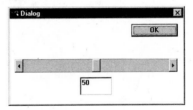

☐ Use the scroll bar to set a new speed, and then click the OK button.

☐ Click the Display Speed button of the main window.

> *MyDialog responds by displaying the speed that you set with the scroll bar.*

☐ Experiment with the MyDialog program, and then click its Exit button to terminate the program.

Now that you know what the MyDialog application should do, you can begin to write it.

Creating the Project of the MyDialog Application

To create the project of the MyDialog application do the following:

☐ Start Visual C++ and close all the open windows that appear inside the desktop of Visual C++ (if there are any).

☐ Select New from the File menu.

> *Visual C++ responds by displaying the New dialog box.*

☐ Select Project inside the New dialog box and then click the OK button of the New dialog box.

> *Visual C++ responds by displaying the New Project dialog box.*

☐ Set the project name to MyDialog.

☐ Set the project path to \MVCPROG\CH11\MyDialog\MyDialog.MAK.

Your New Project dialog box should now look like the one shown in Figure 11.4.

Figure 11.4. The New Project dialog box of the MyDialog.MAK project.

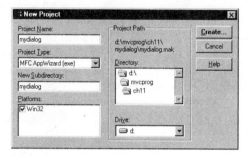

☐ Click the Create button of the New Project dialog box.

> *Visual C++ responds by displaying the AppWizard—Step 1 window.*

☐ Set the AppWizard—Step 1 window as shown in Figure 11.5. As shown in Figure 11.5, the MyDialog.MAK project is set as a dialog-based application, and U.S. English (APPWIZUS.DLL) is used as the language for the MyDialog.MAK project's resources.

Figure 11.5. The AppWizard—Step 1 window of the MyDialog.MAK project.

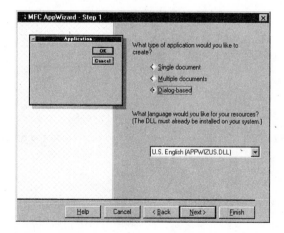

☐ Click the Next button of the AppWizard—Step 1 window.

Visual C++ responds by displaying the AppWizard—Step 2 of 4 window.

☐ Set the AppWizard—Step 2 of 4 window as shown in Figure 11.6. That is, place a checkmark inside the About Box check box (to incorporate an About dialog box into the application), and place a checkmark inside the Use 3D Controls check box (so that the application will use 3D controls). Also, set the title of the application to The MyDialog Program.

Figure 11.6. The AppWizard—Step 2 of 4 window of the MyDialog.MAK project.

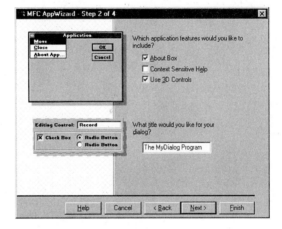

☐ Click the Next button of the AppWizard—Step 2 of 4 window.

Visual C++ responds by displaying the AppWizard—Step 3 of 4 window.

☐ Set the Step 3 of 4 window as shown in Figure 11.7.

As shown in Figure 11.7, the project will be generated with comments, a Visual C++ makefile will be generated, and the application will use the MFC library from a DLL.

Figure 11.7. The AppWizard—Step 3 of 4 window of the MyDialog.MAK project.

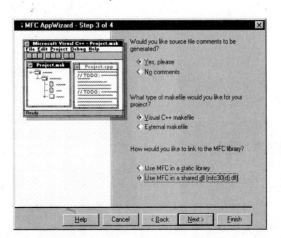

☐ Click the Next button of the AppWizard—Step 3 of 4 window.

Visual C++ responds by displaying the AppWizard—Step 4 of 4 window, as shown in Figure 11.8.

Figure 11.8. The AppWizard—Step 4 of 4 window of the MyDialog.MAK project.

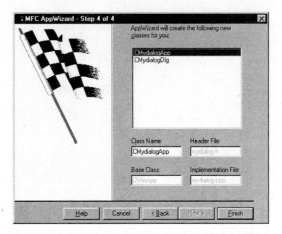

☐ Click the Finish button of the AppWizard—Step 4 of 4 window.

Visual C++ responds by displaying the New Project Information window, as shown in Figure 11.9.

Figure 11.9. The New Project Information window of the MyDialog.MAK project.

☐ Click the OK button of the New Project Information window.

Visual C++ responds by creating the project file and all the skeleton files of the application.

The Visual Implementation of MyDialog's Main Window

You'll now visually design the main window of the MyDialog application.

Because the MyDialog application is a dialog-based application, when you created the project and the skeleton files of the MyDialog application with AppWizard, AppWizard created for you a dialog box that serves as the main window of the application. AppWizard named this dialog box IDD_MYDIALOG_DIALOG. You'll now customize the IDD_MYDIALOG_DIALOG dialog box.

☐ Double-click mydialog.rc inside the mydialog.mak window.

> *Visual C++ responds by displaying the mydialog.rc window.*

☐ Double-click Dialog inside the mydialog.rc window and then double-click IDD_MYDIALOG_DIALOG.

> *Visual C++ responds by displaying the IDD_MYDIALOG_DIALOG dialog box in design mode.*

☐ Implement the dialog box according to the specifications in Table 11.1. When you finish implementing the dialog box, it should look like the one shown in Figure 11.10.

Table 11.1. The Properties table of the IDD_MYDIALOG_DIALOG dialog box.

Object	Property	Setting
Dialog box	ID	IDD_MYDIALOG_DIALOG
Push button	ID	IDC_EXIT_BUTTON
	Caption	E&xit
Push button	ID	IDC_ENTERDATA_BUTTON
	Caption	&Enter Data…
Push button	ID	IDC_DISPLAYDATA_ BUTTON
	Caption	&Display Data…

To save your work do the following:

☐ Select Save from the File menu.

To see your visual design in action do the following:

☐ Select Build MyDialog.EXE from the Project menu.

> *Visual C++ responds by compiling and linking the MyDialog application.*

Figure 11.10. The dialog box that serves as the main window of the MyDialog program (in design mode).

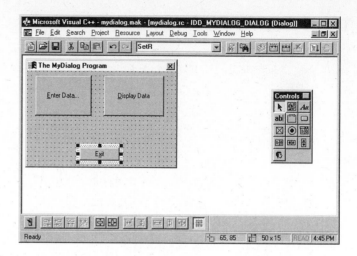

☐ Select Execute MyDialog.EXE from the Project menu.

> *Visual C++ responds by executing the MyDialog.EXE application. As expected, the IDD_MYDIALOG_DIALOG dialog box that you designed appears as the main window of the application. Of course, none of the buttons are functional because you have not yet attached code to these buttons.*

☐ Click the × icon that appears in the upper-right corner of the window to terminate the program.

Attaching Code to the *BN_CLICKED* Event of the Exit Button

Recall that when the user clicks the Exit button the MyDialog program should terminate. You'll now attach code to the Click event (BN_CLICKED) of the Exit button.

☐ Display the ClassWizard dialog box by selecting ClassWizard from the Project menu of Visual C++.

☐ Select the Message Maps tab at the top of ClassWizard's dialog box.

☐ Use ClassWizard to select the event:

CMydialogDlg -> IDC_EXIT_BUTTON -> BN_CLICKED

Then click the Add Function button.

☐ Name the new function OnExitButton().

To write the code of the OnExitButton() function do the following:

☐ Click the Edit Code button of ClassWizard.

ClassWizard responds by opening the file MyDiaDlg.CPP, with the function OnExitButton() ready to be edited by you.

☐ Write code inside the OnExitButton() function so that it looks like this:

```
void CMydialogDlg::OnExitButton()
{
// TODO: Add your control notification handler code here



/////////////////////////
// MY CODE STARTS HERE //
/////////////////////////

// Close the dialog box (terminate the program).
OnOK();

/////////////////////////
// MY CODE ENDS HERE   //
/////////////////////////


}
```

☐ Save your work by selecting Save from the File menu of Visual C++.

To see your Exit button in action do the following:

☐ Select Build MyDialog.EXE from the Project menu.

Visual C++ responds by compiling and linking the MyDialog program.

☐ Select Execute MyDialog.EXE from the Project menu.

Visual C++ responds by executing the MyDialog.EXE program.

☐ Click the Exit button.

MyDialog responds by terminating itself.

Creating a Dialog Box for Taking Users' Data

You'll now visually design a dialog box that is used for taking users' input.

☐ Select New from the Resource menu (because you are now building a new resource for the project).

Visual C++ responds by displaying the New Resource dialog box.

☐ Select Dialog from the New Resource dialog box (because you are now building a new dialog box), and then click the OK button.

Visual C++ responds by displaying the new dialog box in design mode. (See Figure 11.11.)

Figure 11.11. The new dialog box (in design mode).

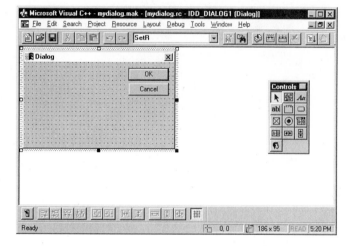

Your job now is to modify the dialog box shown in Figure 11.11 so that it looks like the one shown in Figure 11.2.

NOTE

Visual C++ displays the new dialog box with OK and Cancel buttons. Do not delete these buttons. As you know, most dialog boxes contain these buttons.

NOTE

Note that Visual C++ named the new dialog box IDD_DIALOG1.

☐ Place an edit box inside the new dialog box, as shown in Figure 11.12.

☐ Double-click the edit box that you placed inside the IDD_DIALOG1 dialog box, and name the edit box IDC_EDIT1.

Figure 11.12. Placing an edit box inside the new dialog box.

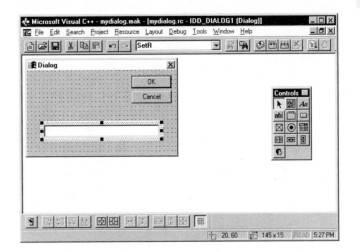

Declaring a Class for the IDD_DIALOG1 Dialog Box

Your project now has a new dialog box, IDD_DIALOG1. But what class is associated with this dialog box?

You'll now create a new class and you'll associate this class with the IDD_DIALOG1 dialog box. You'll derive the new class from the MFC class CDialog. Therefore, your new class will inherit the powerful member functions of the CDialog class—functions that were specifically designed to work with dialog boxes.

To create a new class and associate this class with the IDD_DIALOG1 dialog box do the following:

☐ Select ClassWizard from the Project menu.

Visual C++ responds by displaying the Add Class dialog box. (See Figure 11.13.)

Figure 11.13. The Add Class dialog box.

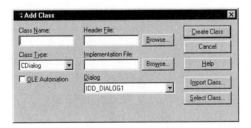

You'll now use the Add Class dialog box to create a new class, derived from the MFC CDialog.

Why did Visual C++ display the Add Class dialog box? You are currently working on the IDD_DIALOG1 dialog box (a new dialog box that you just created), and Visual C++ knows that this dialog box is not yet associated with any class.

☐ Type CMyDlg inside the Class Name edit box of the Add Class dialog box. (See Figure 11.14.)

Figure 11.14. Adding the CMyDlg class.

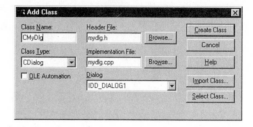

As you can see from Figure 11.14, when you type CMyDlg inside the Class Name edit box, Visual C++ automatically assumes that the header file that will be used for the new class is mydlg.h, and the implementation file that will be used for this new class is mydlg.cpp.

☐ Make sure that the Class Type edit box of the Add Class dialog box is set to CDialog (because you want the new class CMyDlg to be derived from CDialog).

☐ Click the Create Class button of the Add Class dialog box.

   Visual C++ responds by returning to the ClassWizard dialog box.

☐ Click the OK button of the ClassWizard dialog box.

The IDD_DIALOG1 dialog box is now associated with a new class called CMyDlg. The CMyDlg class is derived from the CDialog class.

Attaching a Variable to the Edit Box of the IDD_DIALOG1 Dialog Box

You'll now attach a variable to the edit box that you placed inside the IDD_DIALOG1 dialog box.

☐ Select ClassWizard from the Project menu, select the Member Variables tab, and attach a variable to the IDC_EDIT1 edit box. The variable that you attach to the IDC_EDIT1 edit box should have the following properties:

Control ID:	IDC_EDIT1
Variable Name:	m_Edit1
Category:	Value
Variable Type:	Cstring

When you attach this variable, make sure that the Class is set to CMyDlg.

To save your work do the following:

☐ Select Save from the File menu.

In the preceding steps, you added a new class, the CMyDlg class that was derived from the CDialog class. The IDD_DIALOG1 dialog box is associated with the CMyDlg class.

Just to make sure that you added the new class correctly, try to compile and link the project:

☐ Select Build MyDialog.EXE from the Project menu.

   Visual C++ responds by compiling and linking the MyDialog program.

☐ Select Execute MyDialog.EXE from the Project menu.

   Visual C++ responds by executing the MyDialog.EXE program.

☐ Click the Exit button.

   MyDialog responds by terminating itself.

Creating an Object of Class *CMyDlg*

Before displaying the IDD_DIALOG1 dialog box, you have to create an object of class CMyDlg. Here is how you create an object of class CMyDlg:

☐ Select Open from the File menu, and open the MyDiaDlg.H file.

The MyDiaDlg.H file contains the class declaration of the CMydialogDlg class. (When you created the MyDialog.MAK project, AppWizard wrote for you the CMydialogDlg class declaration.) Note that AppWizard also created a file called MyDialog.H. However, currently you are interested in the MyDiaDlg.H file (not in the MyDialog.H file).

> **NOTE**
>
> Don't get confused between the MyDiaDlg.H file and the MyDialog.H file. The MyDiaDlg.H file contains the declaration of the CMydialogDlg class—which is the class that is associated with the dialog box that serves as the main window of the application.

☐ Add code inside the CMydialogDlg class declaration (inside the MyDiaDlg.H file). After you add the code, the CMydialogDlg class declaration should look like this:

```
/////////////////////////////////////////////////////
// CMydialogDlg dialog

class CMydialogDlg : public CDialog
{
// Construction
public:
CMydialogDlg(CWnd* pParent = NULL);//standard constructor
```

```
/////////////////////////
// MY CODE STARTS HERE //
/////////////////////////

// Create an object of class CMyDlg
CMyDlg m_Dlg1;

/////////////////////////
// MY CODE ENDS HERE //
/////////////////////////


// Dialog Data
//{{AFX_DATA(CMydialogDlg)
enum { IDD = IDD_MYDIALOG_DIALOG };
   // NOTE: the ClassWizard will add data members here
   //}}AFX_DATA

  // ClassWizard generated virtual function overrides
  //{{AFX_VIRTUAL(CMydialogDlg)
protected:
virtual void DoDataExchange(CDataExchange* pDX);
// DDX/DDV support
//}}AFX_VIRTUAL

// Implementation
protected:
  HICON m_hIcon;

   // Generated message map functions
   //{{AFX_MSG(CMydialogDlg)
   virtual BOOL OnInitDialog();
   afx_msg void OnSysCommand(UINT nID, LPARAM lParam);
   afx_msg void OnPaint();
   afx_msg HCURSOR OnQueryDragIcon();
   afx_msg void OnExitButton();
   afx_msg void OnEnterdataButton();
   afx_msg void OnDisplaydataButton();
   //}}AFX_MSG
DECLARE_MESSAGE_MAP()
};
```

If you now compile and link the MyDialog.MAK project you'll get errors! This is to be expected, because the `CMydialogDlg` class declaration now contains the statement `CMyDlg m_Dlg1;`.

However, the `CMyDlg` class is unknown in the MyDiaDlg.H file. The `CMyDlg` class is declared inside the MyDlg.H file. So you have to use `#include` on the CMyDlg.H file inside the MyDiaDlg.H file.

☐ Add an `#include` statement at the beginning of the MyDiaDlg.H file. After you add the `#include` statement, the beginning of the MyDiaDlg.H file should look like this:

```
// mydiadlg.h : header file
//
```

```
/////////////////////////
// MY CODE STARTS HERE //
/////////////////////////

// The CMyDialogDlg class declaration contains
// the statement:
//
// CMyDlg m_Dlg1;
//
// This means that you must #include the file that
// contains the class declaration of the CMyDlg class.
// The file that contains the CMyDlg class declaration
// is the MyDlg.H file. Thus, you must #include the
// MyDlg.H file.


#include "MyDlg.H"

/////////////////////////
// MY CODE ENDS HERE //
/////////////////////////
```

You have created the `m_Dlg1` object, which is an object of class `CMyDlg`. The `CMyDlg` class is associated with the IDD_DIALOG1 dialog box. Therefore, from now on you can think of the `m_Dlg1` object as the IDD_DIALOG1 dialog box. In other words, the member functions that you will execute on the `m_Dlg1` object will be performed on the IDD_DIALOG1 dialog box.

Displaying the m_Dlg1 Dialog Box

In this section you'll write the code that displays the m_Dlg1 dialog box. Recall that when the user clicks the Enter Data button the MyDialog program should display the m_Dlg1 dialog box.

☐ Display the ClassWizard dialog box by selecting ClassWizard from the Project menu of Visual C++.

☐ Select the Message Maps tab at the top of ClassWizard's dialog box.

☐ Use ClassWizard to select the event:

CMydialogDlg -> IDC_ENTERDATA_BUTTON -> BN_CLICKED

In the preceding step, it is very important that you set the Class Name edit box to `CMydialogDlg`. At this point in your development, the project contains several classes. The default class name that ClassWizard displays is not necessarily the class name you want!

NOTE

If you are new to Visual C++, probably the most common mistakes you'll make during the implementation of the programs of this book will involve selecting the wrong class name inside the ClassWizard dialog box.

For example, in the preceding steps you were instructed to add a function to the event:

CMydialogDlg -> IDC_ENTERDATA_BUTTON -> BN_CLICKED

Again, this line means that you must set the Class Name edit box of the ClassWizard dialog box to CMydialogDlg.

☐ Click the Add Function button.

Visual C++ responds by suggesting OnEnterdataButton() *as the name of the function.*

☐ Click the OK button to accept the function's name.

☐ Click the Edit Code button to edit the OnEnterdataButton() function.

☐ Add code to the OnEnterdataButton() function. After you add the code, your OnEnterdataButton() function should look like this:

```
void CMydialogDlg::OnEnterdataButton()
{
// TODO: Add your control notification handler code here


/////////////////////////
// MY CODE STARTS HERE
/////////////////////////

// Display the m_Dlg1 dialog box
m_Dlg1.DoModal();

/////////////////////////
// MY CODE ENDS HERE
/////////////////////////


}
```

The code you typed executes the following statement:

```
m_Dlg1.DoModal();
```

That is, you already created the m_Dlg1 object of class CMyDlg. The statement that you typed displays the m_Dlg1 dialog box as a modal dialog box. (A modal dialog box is a dialog box that does not let you switch to any of the other windows of the same applications unless you close the currently open modal dialog box.)

Attaching Code to the Display Data Button

You'll now attach code to the Click event of the Display Data button.

☐ Use ClassWizard (from the Project menu) to add a function to the following event:

```
CMydialogDlg -> IDC_DISPLAYDATA_BUTTON -> BN_CLICKED
```

☐ Name the new function OnDisplaydataButton().

☐ Click the Edit Code button, and add code to the OnDisplaydataButton() function. After you add the code, your OnDisplaydataButton() function should look like this:

```
void CMydialogDlg::OnDisplaydataButton()
{
// TODO: Add your control notification handler code here


///////////////////////////
// MY CODE STARTS HERE//
///////////////////////////


// Display the contents of the edit box
// of the m_Dlg1 dialog box.
MessageBox (m_Dlg1.m_Edit1);


///////////////////////////
// MY CODE ENDS HERE//
///////////////////////////
}
```

The code that you added simply uses the MessageBox() function to display the contents of the m_Edit1 edit box of the m_Dlg1 dialog box:

```
MessageBox (m_Dlg1.m_Edit1);
```

To save your work do the following:

☐ Select Save from the File menu.

To see your code in action do the following:

☐ Select Build MyDialog.EXE from the Project menu.

    Visual C++ responds by compiling and linking the MyDialog program.

☐ Select Execute MyDialog.EXE from the Project menu.

    Visual C++ responds by executing the MyDialog.EXE program.

☐ Experiment with the MyDialog program and verify its proper operation. In particular, verify that when you close the m_Dlg1 dialog box by clicking its OK button the data of the m_Edit1 edit box is maintained.

☐ Click the Exit button.

    MyDialog responds by terminating itself.

Going Over the Whole Process One More Time...

If you are new to Visual C++, you might have gotten the impression that the process of displaying dialog boxes in Visual C++ is long and complex. In fact, after practicing for a while, you'll realize that this process is actually short and easy!

This section goes over the steps of the implementation.

When you created the MyDialog.MAK project, you told AppWizard that you want to create an application in which a dialog box serves as the main window.

Therefore, AppWizard created for you a dialog box called IDD_MYDIALOG_DIALOG that serves as the main window of the application. AppWizard also created a class called `CMydialogDlg` that is associated with the IDD_MYDIALOG_DIALOG dialog box.

Using the visual tools of Visual C++, you visually designed a new dialog box called IDD_DIALOG1 that serves as a dialog box for accepting users' data.

You then selected ClassWizard and associated a new class, (the `CMyDlg` class) with the IDD_DIALOG1 dialog box. You told ClassWizard that `CMyDlg` should be derived from the `CDialog` MFC class.

You created the `m_Dlg1` object as an object of class `CMyDlg` inside the `CMydialogDlg` class declaration. The class declaration of the `CMydialogDlg` class is inside the MyDiaDlg.H file.

Because the compiler does not know about the `CMyDlg` class, you had to use `#include` on the `MyDlg.H` statement at the beginning of the MyDiaDlg.H file.

From this point on, the `m_Dlg1` object is created and ready to work for you.

Inside the function that is executed whenever the user clicks the Enter Data button, you typed the code

```
m_Dlg1.DoModal();
```

`DoModal()` is a member function of the `CDialog` class. You can use the `DoModal()` function on the `m_Dlg1` object because `m_Dlg1` is an object of class `CMyDlg`, and `CMyDlg` was derived from the `CDialog` class.

Note that the code that you added to the function that is executed whenever the user clicks the Display Data button is this:

```
MessageBox (m_Dlg1.m_Edit1);
```

`m_Dlg1` is, of course, accessible from within the member functions of the `CMydialogDlg` class, because you created the `m_Dlg1` object as a data member of the `CMydialogDlg` class.

Displaying Another Dialog Box

You'll now add two additional buttons to the IDC_MYDIALOG_DIALOG dialog box of the MyDialog program:

☐ Select mydialog.rc- IDC_MYDIALOG_DIALOG from the Window menu of Visual C++.

Visual C++ responds by displaying the IDC_MYDIALOG_DIALOG dialog box in design mode.

☐ Drag the handles of the dialog box to make the dialog box larger, and add the following buttons to the dialog box:

Object	Property	Setting
Push button	ID	IDC_ENTERSPEED_BUTTON
	Caption	Enter &Speed...
Push button	ID	IDC_DISPLAYSPEED_BUTTON
	Caption	Display S&peed...

When you finish adding the two buttons, the IDC_DIALOG1_DIALOG dialog box should look like the one shown in Figure 11.15.

Figure 11.15. Adding two buttons to the IDC_DIALOG1_DIALOG dialog box (in design mode).

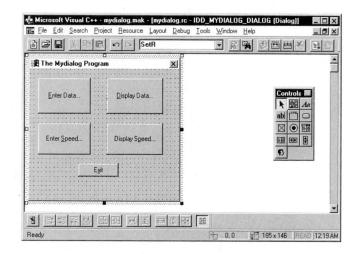

The Visual Implementation of the IDD_DIALOG2 Dialog Box

You'll now visually design the IDD_DIALOG2 dialog box (a dialog box that contains a scroll bar).

☐ Select New from the Resource menu.

Visual C++ responds by displaying the New Resource dialog box.

☐ Select the Dialog item (because you are now designing a new dialog box), and then click the OK button.

Visual C++ responds by displaying the IDD_DIALOG2 dialog box in design mode. (See Figure 11.16.)

☐ Implement the IDD_DIALOG2 dialog box according to the specifications in Table 11.2. When you finish implementing the dialog box, it should look like the one shown in Figure 11.17. Note that you are instructed to leave the OK button, but you have to delete the Cancel button (by highlighting the Cancel button and then pressing the Delete button).

Figure 11.16. The default
IDD_DIALOG2 dialog
box (in design mode).

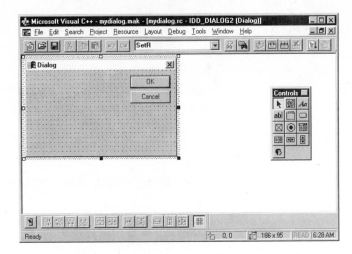

Table 11.2. The Properties table of the IDD_DIALOG2 dialog box.

Object	Property	Setting
Dialog box	ID	IDD_DIALOG2
Horizontal scroll bar	ID	IDC_SPEED_SCROLLBAR
Edit box	ID	IDC_SPEED_EDIT

Note that the IDD_DIALOG2 dialog box also contains the default OK button.

Figure 11.17. The
IDD_DIALOG2 dialog
box (in design mode).

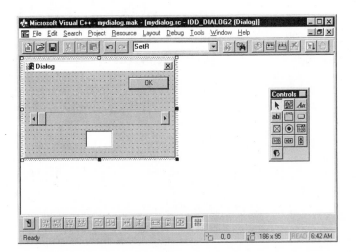

Associating the IDD_DIALOG2 Scroll Bar with a Class

You'll now associate the IDD_DIALOG2 dialog box with a class.

☐ Select ClassWizard from the Project window.

    Visual C++ responds by displaying the Add Class dialog box.

☐ Set the class name to CSpeedDlg, make sure the class type is CDialog, and then click the Create Class button. (See Figure 11.18.)

    Visual C++ responds by creating the CSpeedDlg class.

Figure 11.18. The Add Class dialog box of the IDD_DIALOG2 dialog box.

Attaching Variables to the Controls of the IDD_DIALOG2 Dialog Box

You'll now attach variables to the scroll bar and edit box of the IDD_DIALOG2 dialog box.

☐ Use ClassWizard to attach the variables listed in Table 11.3.

Table 11.3. The Variables table of the IDD_DIALOG2 dialog box.

Control ID	Variable Name	Category	Variable Type
IDC_SPEED_EDIT	m_SpeedEdit	Variable	CString
IDC_SPEED_SCROLLBAR	m_SpeedScroll	Control	CScrollBar

Note that when you are attaching the variables of Table 11.3 you need to make sure that the class name of the Add Variable dialog box is set to CSpeedDlg.

Creating an Object m_Dlg2 of Class *CSpeedDlg*

You'll now create the m_Dlg2 dialog box object of class CSpeedDlg.

☐ Open the MyDiaDlg.H file, and add code to the CMydialogDlg class declaration. After you add the code, the MyDialogDlg class declaration inside the MyDiaDlg.H file should look like this:

```
/////////////////////////////////////////////////////
// CMydialogDlg dialog

class CMydialogDlg : public CDialog
{
// Construction
public:
CMydialogDlg(CWnd* pParent = NULL);// standard constructor

/////////////////////////////
// MY CODE STARTS HERE  //
/////////////////////////////

// Create an object of class CMyDlg
CMyDlg m_Dlg1;


// Create an object of class CSpeedDlg
CSpeedDlg m_Dlg2;


///////////////////////////
// MY CODE ENDS HERE  //
///////////////////////////


// Dialog Data
   //{{AFX_DATA(CMydialogDlg)
   enum { IDD = IDD_MYDIALOG_DIALOG };
   // NOTE: the ClassWizard will add data members here
   //}}AFX_DATA

   // ClassWizard generated virtual function overrides
   //{{AFX_VIRTUAL(CMydialogDlg)
protected:
 virtual void DoDataExchange(CDataExchange* pDX);
   // DDX/DDV support
   //}}AFX_VIRTUAL

// Implementation
protected:
   HICON m_hIcon;

      // Generated message map functions
      //{{AFX_MSG(CMydialogDlg)
      virtual BOOL OnInitDialog();
      afx_msg void OnSysCommand(UINT nID, LPARAM lParam);
      afx_msg void OnPaint();
      afx_msg HCURSOR OnQueryDragIcon();
      afx_msg void OnExitButton();
      afx_msg void OnEnterdataButton();
      afx_msg void OnDisplaydataButton();
      //}}AFX_MSG
      DECLARE_MESSAGE_MAP()
};
```

The code you typed declares the m_Dlg2 dialog box object of class CSpeedDlg. So now the MydialogDlg class declaration contains two object-creation statements:

```
CMyDlg m_Dlg1;
CSpeedDlg m_Dlg2;
```

Of course, if you now compile and link the MyDialog.MAK project you'll get errors, because the CSpeedDlg class is unknown in the MyDiaDlg.H file. So you need to use #include on SpeedDlg.H in the MyDiaDlg.H file:

☐ Add an #include statement to the beginning of the MyDiaDlg.H file. After you use #include on the statement, the beginning of the MyDiaDlg.H file should look like this:

```
// mydiadlg.h : header file
//

/////////////////////////
// MY CODE STARTS HERE //
/////////////////////////

// The CMyDiaDlg class declaration contains
// the statement:
//
// CMyDlg m_Dlg1;
//
// This means that you must #include the file that
// contains the class declaration of the CMyDlg class.
// The file that contains the CMyDlg class declaration
// is the MyDlg.H file.
// Thus, you must #include the MyDlg.H file.
//
// Because the CMydialogDlg class also creates an object of
// class CSpeedDlg, you also have to #include the
// SpeedDlg.H file.

#include "MyDlg.H"

#include "SpeedDlg.H"

/////////////////////////
// MY CODE ENDS HERE //
/////////////////////////
```

To ensure that you implemented everything properly, try to compile and link the MyDialog.MAK project:

☐ Select Save from the File menu.

To see your code in action do the following:

☐ Select Build MyDialog.EXE from the Project menu.

   Visual C++ responds by compiling and linking the MyDialog program.

☐ Select Execute MyDialog.EXE from the Project menu.

   Visual C++ responds by executing the MyDialog.EXE program.

□ Experiment with the MyDialog program and verify its proper operation. (Of course, at this point the Enter Speed and Display Speed buttons are not functional because you have not yet implemented the code that makes them functional.)

□ Click the Exit button.

MyDialog responds by terminating itself.

Attaching Code to the Enter Speed Button

Recall that when the user clicks the Enter Speed button the MyDialog program should display the IDD_DIALOG2 dialog box. You'll now attach code to the click event (BN_CLICKED) of the Enter Speed button.

□ Display the ClassWizard dialog box by selecting ClassWizard from the Project menu of Visual C++.

□ Select the Message Maps tab at the top of ClassWizard's dialog box.

□ Use ClassWizard to select the event:

CMydialogDlg -> IDC_ENTERSPEED_BUTTON -> BN_CLICKED

Then click the Add Function button.

□ Name the new function OnEnterspeedButton().

To write the code of the OnEnterspeedButton() function do the following:

□ Click the Edit Code button of ClassWizard.

ClassWizard responds by opening the file MyDiaDlg.CPP, with the function OnEnterspeedButton() ready to be edited by you.

□ Write code inside the OnEnterspeedButton() function so that it looks like this:

```
void CMydialogDlg::OnEnterspeedButton()
{
// TODO: Add your control notification handler code here


/////////////////////////
// MY CODE STARTS HERE //
/////////////////////////

// Display the m_Dlg2 dialog box as a modal dialog box
m_Dlg2.DoModal();


/////////////////////////
// MY CODE ENDS HERE //
/////////////////////////


}
```

The code you typed displays the m_Dlg2 dialog box as a modal dialog box:

```
m_Dlg2.DoModal();
```

Attaching Code to the Display Speed Button

Recall that when the user clicks the Display Speed button the MyDialog program should display the value of the speed (as it was set by the scroll bar of the IDD_DIALOG2 dialog box). You'll now attach code to the Click event (BN_CLICKED) of the Display Speed button.

☐ Display the ClassWizard dialog box by selecting ClassWizard from the Project menu of Visual C++.

☐ Select the Message Maps tab at the top of ClassWizard's dialog box.

☐ Use ClassWizard to select the event:

```
CMydialogDlg -> IDC_DISPLAYSPEED_BUTTON -> BN_CLICKED
```

Then click the Add Function button.

☐ Name the new function OnDisplayspeedButton().

To write the code of the OnDisplayspeedButton() function do the following:

☐ Click the Edit Code button of ClassWizard.

ClassWizard responds by opening the file MyDiaDlg.CPP, with the function OnDisplayspeedButton() *ready to be edited by you.*

☐ Write code inside the OnDisplayspeedButton() function so that it looks like this:

```
void CMydialogDlg::OnDisplayspeedButton()
{
// TODO: Add your control notification handler code here


/////////////////////////
// MY CODE STARTS HERE //
/////////////////////////

char sSpeed[50];

strcpy(sSpeed, "Speed: ");

strcat (sSpeed, m_Dlg2.m_SpeedEdit);

MessageBox (sSpeed);

/////////////////////////
// MY CODE ENDS HERE //
/////////////////////////

}
```

The code you typed declares the sSpeed variable:

```
char sSpeed[50];
```

Then the sSpeed string variable is updated:

```
strcpy(sSpeed, "Speed: ");
strcat (sSpeed, m_Dlg2.m_SpeedEdit);
```

Finally, the MessageBox() function is executed to display the speed:

```
MessageBox (sSpeed);
```

Initializing the m_Dlg2 Dialog Box

The m_Dlg2 dialog box contains a scroll bar. Recall from Chapter 8, "Scroll Bars," that certain initialization must be performed to make the scroll bar an operational scroll bar.

You'll now type code that initializes the scroll bar.

☐ Display the ClassWizard dialog box by selecting ClassWizard from the Project menu of Visual C++.

☐ Select the Message Maps tab at the top of ClassWizard dialog box.

☐ Use ClassWizard to select the event:

```
CSpeedDlg -> CSpeedDlg—> WM_INITDIALOG
```

Recall that the WM_INITDIALOG event is executed when the m_Dlg2 dialog box is initialized (which is when the m_Dlg2 object is created).

☐ Click the Add Function button.

> *Visual C++ responds by adding the function* OnInitDialog().

☐ Click the Add Code button.

> *Visual C++ responds by opening the* OnInitDialog() *function (inside the SpeedDlg.CPP file), ready to be edited by you.*

☐ Add code to the OnInitDialog() function. After you add the code, your OnInitDialog() function should look like this:

```
BOOL CSpeedDlg::OnInitDialog()
{
CDialog::OnInitDialog();

// TODO: Add extra initialization here


/////////////////////////////
// MY CODE STARTS HERE //
/////////////////////////////

static BOOL iFirstTime = TRUE;
```

```
CScrollBar* pSB =
(CScrollBar*) GetDlgItem (IDC_SPEED_SCROLLBAR);

if ( iFirstTime == TRUE )
   {

   iFirstTime = FALSE;

   // Set the range of the scroll bar
   pSB->SetScrollRange (0,100);

   // Set the current position of the scroll bar
   pSB->SetScrollPos (50);
   }
else
   {

   // Set the range of the scroll bar
   pSB->SetScrollRange (0,100);

   // Set the current position of the scroll bar
   pSB->SetScrollPos ( atoi(m_SpeedEdit) );

   }



// Fill sPos with the value of the scroll bar
char sPos[25];
itoa (pSB->GetScrollPos(), sPos, 10 );

// Update the contents of the edit box
m_SpeedEdit = sPos;
UpdateData(FALSE);

////////////////////////
// MY CODE ENDS HERE //
////////////////////////


return TRUE;
// return TRUE unless you set the focus to a control
// EXCEPTION: OCX Property Pages should return FALSE
}
```

The code you typed initializes the scroll bar.

A static variable is declared and initialized to TRUE:

```
static BOOL iFirstTime = TRUE;
```

The GetDlgItem() function is then executed to extract the pointer of the IDC_SPEED_SCROLLBAR scroll bar:

```
CScrollBar* pSB =
 (CScrollBar*) GetDlgItem (IDC_SPEED_SCROLLBAR);
```

In the preceding statement the pSB variable is updated with the pointer of the scroll bar. Note that a cast is used to convert the returned value from the GetDlgItem() function to a pointer of type CScrollBar*.

Also note that in the preceding statement you declared the pSB variable and updated it on a single line.

An if…else statement is then executed to determine whether the OnInitDialog() function is executed for the very first time:

```
if ( iFirstTime == TRUE )
   {
   .....
   .....
   .....
   }
else
   {
   .....
   .....
   .....
   }
```

If iFirstTime is equal to TRUE, you know that the OnInitDialog() function is executed for the very first time. The code under the if statement sets the iFirstTime variable to FALSE, the range of the scroll bar is set to (0,100), and the current position is set to 50:

```
if ( iFirstTime == TRUE )
   {

   iFirstTime = FALSE;

   // Set the range of the scroll bar
   pSB->SetScrollRange (0,100);

   // Set the current position of the scroll bar
   pSB->SetScrollPos (50);
   }
else
   {
   .....
   .....
   .....
   }
```

If the user closes the dialog box and then clicks the Enter Speed button again, the OnInitDialog() function is executed again. However, because iFirstTime is declared as a static variable, its value is maintained from the last execution of the OnInitDialog() function. This means that on the second execution of the OnInitDialog() function, iFirstTime is equal to FALSE, and the statements under the else statement are executed:

```
if ( iFirstTime == TRUE )
   {
   ....
   ....
   ....
```

```
else
   {

   // Set the range of the scroll bar
   pSB->SetScrollRange (0,100);

   // Set the current position of the scroll bar
   pSB->SetScrollPos ( atoi(m_SpeedEdit) );

   }
```

The statements under the `else` statement set the range of the scroll bar to (`0,100`):

```
pSB->SetScrollRange (0,100);
```

Then the current position of the scroll bar is set to the value that is being displayed inside the edit box:

```
pSB->SetScrollPos ( atoi(m_SpeedEdit) );
```

So when the `OnInitDialog()` function is executed for the first time, the position of the scroll bar is set to 50, and on subsequent execution of the `OnInitDialog()` function, the position of the scroll bar is set according to the value of the edit box.

The variable `sPos` is then declared and updated with a string that represents the current position of the scroll bar:

```
// Fill sPos with the value of the scroll bar
char sPos[25];
itoa (pSB->GetScrollPos(), sPos, 10 );
```

Finally, the edit box is updated with a string that represents the current position of the scroll bar:

```
// Update the contents of the edit box
m_SpeedEdit = sPos;
UpdateData(FALSE);
```

Attaching Code to the *WM_HSCROLL* Event of the m_Dlg2 Dialog Box

You'll now attach code to the `WM_HSCROLL` event. Recall that the `WM_HSCROLL` event occurs whenever the user changes the scroll bar position.

☐ Display the ClassWizard dialog box by selecting ClassWizard from the Project menu of Visual C++.

☐ Select the Message Maps tab at the top of ClassWizard's dialog box.

☐ Use ClassWizard to select the event:

```
CSpeedDlg -> CSpeedDlg -> WM_HSCROLL
```

> **NOTE**
>
> You are adding code to the WM_HSCROLL event of the CSpeedDlg class because this event occurs when the user changes the horizontal scroll bar of the m_Dlg2 dialog box, which is an object of class CSpeedDlg.

☐ Click the Add Function button.

Visual C++ responds by adding the function OnHScrollUpdate() *member function inside the SpeedDlg.CPP file.*

☐ Click the Edit Code button of ClassWizard.

ClassWizard responds by opening the file SpeedDlg.CPP, with the function OnHScrollUpdate() *ready to be edited by you.*

☐ Write code inside the OnHScrollUpdate() function so that it looks like this:

```
void CSpeedDlg::OnHScroll(UINT nSBCode, UINT nPos,
        CScrollBar* pScrollBar)
{
// TODO: Add your message handler code
// here and/or call default


////////////////////////////
// MY CODE STARTS HERE //
////////////////////////////

char sPos[25];
int iCurrent;



if ( pScrollBar == &m_SpeedScroll )
    {
    switch (nSBCode)
    {
    case SB_THUMBPOSITION:

        ////////// User dragged the thumb ////////

        // Set the thumb of the scroll bar to its new position
        pScrollBar->SetScrollPos ( nPos );

        // Fill sPos with the value of the scroll bar
        itoa (pScrollBar->GetScrollPos(), sPos, 10 );

        // Update the contents of the edit box
        m_SpeedEdit = sPos;
        UpdateData(FALSE);
```

```
   break;

case SB_LINEDOWN:

   ///////// User clicked the right arrow icon ////////


   iCurrent = pScrollBar->GetScrollPos();

   iCurrent = iCurrent + 1;

   if ( iCurrent > 100 )
      iCurrent = 100;

   // Set the thumb to its new position
   pScrollBar->SetScrollPos(iCurrent);

   // Fill sPos with the value of the scroll bar
   itoa (pScrollBar->GetScrollPos(), sPos, 10 );

   // Update the contents of the edit box
   m_SpeedEdit = sPos;
   UpdateData(FALSE);

   break;


 case SB_LINEUP:

///////// User clicked the left arrow icon ////////


   iCurrent = pScrollBar->GetScrollPos();

   iCurrent = iCurrent - 1;

   if ( iCurrent < 0 )
       iCurrent = 0;

   // Set the thumb to its new position
   pScrollBar->SetScrollPos(iCurrent);


   // Fill sPos with the value of the scroll bar
   itoa (pScrollBar->GetScrollPos(), sPos, 10 );

   // Update the contents of the edit box
   m_SpeedEdit = sPos;
   UpdateData(FALSE);

   break;

 case SB_PAGEDOWN:

   ///////// User clicked in between the thumb
   ///////// and the right arrow icon.
```

```
   iCurrent = pScrollBar->GetScrollPos();

   iCurrent = iCurrent + 10;

 if ( iCurrent > 100 )
    iCurrent = 100;

 // Set the thumb to its new position
 pScrollBar->SetScrollPos(iCurrent);


 // Fill sPos with the value of the scroll bar
 itoa (pScrollBar->GetScrollPos(), sPos, 10 );

 // Update the contents of the edit box
 m_SpeedEdit = sPos;
 UpdateData(FALSE);

 break;

case SB_PAGEUP:

 ///////// User clicked in between the thumb
 ///////// and the left arrow icon.

 iCurrent = pScrollBar->GetScrollPos();

 iCurrent = iCurrent - 10;

 if ( iCurrent < 0 )
     iCurrent = 0;


 pScrollBar->SetScrollPos(iCurrent);

 // Fill sPos with the value of the scroll bar
 itoa (pScrollBar->GetScrollPos(), sPos, 10 );

 // Update the contents of the edit box
 m_SpeedEdit = sPos;
 UpdateData(FALSE);


 break;



case SB_THUMBTRACK:

    ///////// User is dragging the thumb


    // Set the thumb to its new position
    pScrollBar->SetScrollPos(nPos);
```

```
        // Fill sPos with the value of the scroll bar
        itoa (nPos, sPos, 10 );

        // Update the contents of the edit box
        m_SpeedEdit = sPos;
        UpdateData(FALSE);

        break;


    }// end of switch


}// end of if


/////////////////////////
// MY CODE ENDS HERE //
/////////////////////////


CDialog::OnHScroll(nSBCode, nPos, pScrollBar);
}
```

The code you typed is very similar to the code you typed for the ScrollMe program in Chapter 8. As you can see, this code makes the scroll bar operational, and it updates the edit box with a value that represents the scroll bar's position.

Note, however, that unlike the code that is attached to the OnHScroll() function in Chapter 8, here you access the scroll bar in the following manner:

```
pScrollBar->SetScrollPos ( nPos );
```

That is, pScrollBar is the third parameter of the OnHScroll() function:

```
void CSpeedDlg::OnHScroll(UINT nSBCode, UINT nPos,
        CScrollBar* pScrollBar)
{
....
....
....
}
```

pScrollBar is the pointer of the scroll bar that was changed.

In Chapter 8 you access the scroll bar this way:

```
m_ScrollMe.SetScrollPos(nPos);
```

The only reason for using the pScrollBar pointer instead of the m_SpeedScroll variable is just to show you that you can access the scroll bar in different ways.

☐ Select Save from the File menu.

To see your code in action do the following:

☐ Select Build MyDialog.EXE from the Project menu.

> *Visual C++ responds by compiling and linking the MyDialog program.*

☐ Select Execute MyDialog.EXE from the Project menu.

> *Visual C++ responds by executing the MyDialog.EXE program.*

☐ Experiment with the MyDialog program and verify its proper operation.

☐ Click the Exit button.

> *MyDialog responds by terminating itself.*

12

Writing a Single-Document Interface Application

So far in the book you have written dialog-based applications. In this chapter you'll write a single-document interface (SDI) application.

Single-Document Interface Versus Multiple-Document Interface

As implied by its name, an SDI application lets the user work with a document. The document is where the data of the application is stored. For example, in a text editor program the document that the user works on is text. Similarly, in a sound editor program the document that the user works on is sound.

In an SDI application the user can work on only one document at a time. That is, the user cannot open several documents simultaneously. That's the reason for the word "single" in single-document interface. That is, at any given time the user can work on only a single document.

An example of an SDI application is the Notepad program that is shipped with Windows. The Notepad program lets the user view and edit various types of files (for example, text files). However, at any given time the user can view and edit only one file. The user cannot open several files simultaneously. Figure 12.1 shows the Notepad program with an open file.

Figure 12.1. The Notepad program of Windows. An example of an SDI application. (At any given time, the user can work on only a single document.)

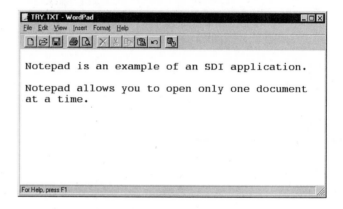

A typical SDI application includes a File menu that lets the user open a file, close a file, save a file, and print the currently open file. Figure 12.2 shows the File menu of a typical SDI application (the File menu of Notepad).

A multiple-document interface (MDI) application also works with documents. However, an MDI application lets the user work on several documents simultaneously. For example, an MDI text editor application lets the user open several text files simultaneously. Similarly, an MDI sound editor application lets the user open several sound files simultaneously.

An example of an MDI application is the Word for Windows word processor program. The Word for Windows program lets the user work on several documents simultaneously. Figure 12.3 shows Word for Windows with several documents open.

Figure 12.2. A typical File menu of an SDI application. (The File menu of the Notepad program of Windows.)

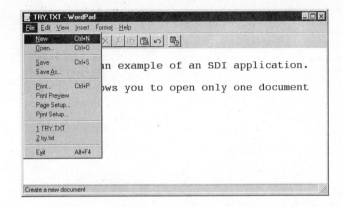

Figure 12.3. The Word for Windows program, which is an example of an MDI application. (At any given time, the user can work on several documents.)

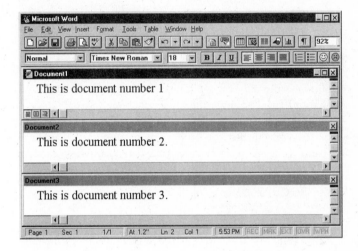

Like an SDI application, an MDI application includes a File menu that lets the user open files, close files, save files, and print files. Besides a File menu, an MDI application also includes a Window menu. The Window menu lets the user switch between the windows of the currently open documents and arrange the windows of the documents in various ways. Figure 12.4 shows the Window menu of a typical MDI application (the Window menu of Word for Windows).

In this chapter you will learn how to write an SDI application. In Chapter 19, "Writing a Multiple-Document Interface Application," you'll learn how to write an MDI application.

*Figure 12.4. A typical
Window menu of an MDI
application. (The Window
menu of the Word for
Windows program.)*

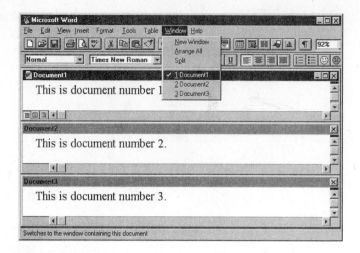

The Test Application

You'll now write the Test application. The Test application is an example of a very simple SDI application. The Test application is simple because it only lets the user view and edit data on the screen. It does not include standard SDI features such as saving data to a file or loading data from a file. In the next chapter you'll write a more complex SDI application—one that lets the user view and edit data as well as save and load the data to and from files.

Before you start writing the Test application yourself, execute the copy of it that resides in the \MVCPROG\EXE directory of the book's CD.

To execute the Test application do the following:

☐ Select Run from the Start menu of Windows and execute the
X:\mvcProg\EXE\TEST.EXE program (where *X* represents the drive letter of your
CD-ROM drive).

   The window of Test.EXE appears, as shown in Figure 12.5.

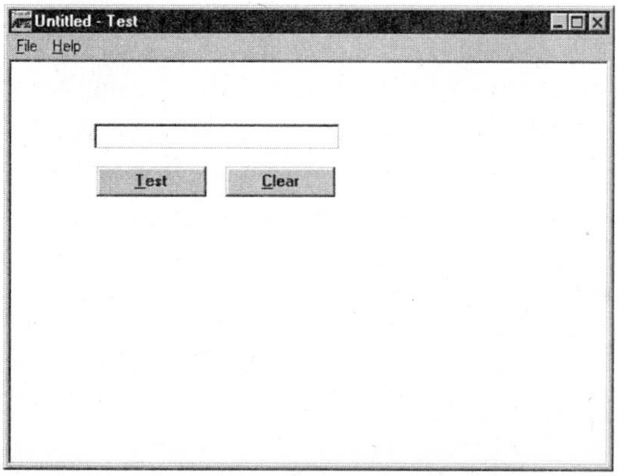

*Figure 12.5. The main
window of the Test
application.*

As you can see, the main window of the Test application has an edit box, two push buttons (Test and Clear), and a menu bar with two pop-up menus: File and Help.

The File and Help pop-up menus of the Test application are shown in Figures 12.6 and 12.7.

Figure 12.6. The File menu of the Test application.

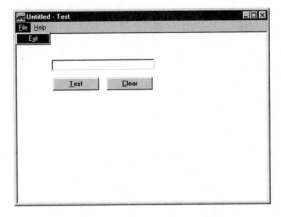

Figure 12.7. The Help menu of the Test application.

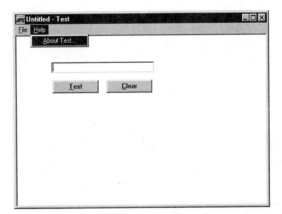

As you can see, the File menu of the Test application falls short of a typical SDI-application File menu. That is, it has the Exit menu item, but it does not include other standard important File menu options such as Open, Save, and Save As. As discussed earlier, in the next chapter you'll write a more complex SDI application—one whose File menu looks more like a standard SDI File menu.

☐ Click the Test button.

The Test application responds by placing the text This is a test! *inside the edit box. (See Figure 12.8.)*

*Figure 12.8. The window
of the Test application after
you click the Test button.*

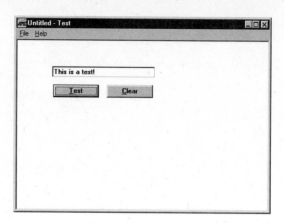

☐ Click the Clear button.

   The Test application responds by clearing the edit box.

☐ Type something inside the edit box, and then click the Clear button.

   The Test application responds by clearing the edit box.

The Test application has an About dialog box. To see this dialog box do the following:

☐ Select About from the Help menu.

   The Test application responds by displaying an About dialog box. (See Figure 12.9.)

*Figure 12.9. The About
dialog box of the Test
application.*

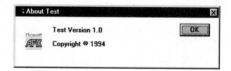

To terminate the Test application do the following:

☐ Select Exit from the File menu.

Now that you know what the Test application should do, you can begin learning how to write it.

Creating the Project of the Test Application

To create the project of the Test application do the following:

☐ Start Visual C++ and close all the windows that appear inside the desktop of Visual C++ (if there are any).

☐ Select New from the File menu.

   Visual C++ responds by displaying the New dialog box.

☐ Select Project inside the New dialog box and then click the OK button of the New dialog box.

Visual C++ responds by displaying the New Project dialog box.

☐ Set the project name to Test.

☐ Set the project path to \MVCPROG\CH12\Test\Test.MAK.

Your New Project dialog box should now look like the one shown in Figure 12.10.

Figure 12.10. The New Project dialog box of the Test.MAK project.

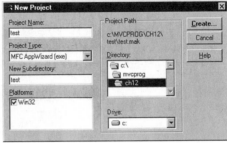

☐ Click the Create button of the New Project dialog box.

Visual C++ responds by displaying the AppWizard—Step 1 window.

☐ Set the Step 1 window as shown in Figure 12.11. As shown in Figure 12.11, the Test.MAK project is set as a single-document application, and U.S. English (APPWIZUS.DLL) is used as the language for the application's resources.

NOTE

In the applications of the previous chapters you set the application type to Dialog-based (because all these applications were dialog-based applications).

The Test application that you are now implementing is an SDI application. Therefore, as shown in Figure 12.11, make sure to select the Single document radio button.

☐ Click the Next button of the Step 1 window.

Visual C++ responds by displaying the AppWizard—Step 2 of 6 window.

☐ Set the Step 2 of 6 window as shown in Figure 12.12. That is, in the Test application you don't want any database support.

*Figure 12.11. The
AppWizard—Step 1
window for the Test
application.*

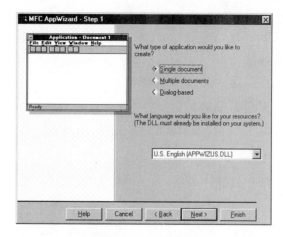

*Figure 12.12. The
AppWizard—Step 2 of 6
window for the Test
application.*

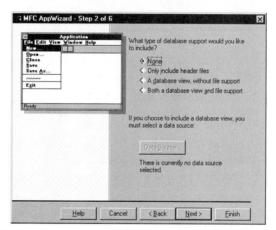

☐ Click the Next button of the Step 2 of 6 window.

  Visual C++ responds by displaying the AppWizard—Step 3 of 6 window.

☐ Set the Step 3 of 6 window as shown in Figure 12.13. That is, in the Test application you
  don't want any OLE support.

☐ Click the Next button of the Step 3 of 6 window.

  Visual C++ responds by displaying the AppWizard—Step 4 of 6 window.

☐ Set the Step 4 of 6 window as shown in Figure 12.14.

Figure 12.13. The AppWizard—Step 3 of 6 window for the Test application.

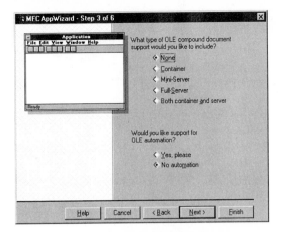

Figure 12.13. The AppWizard—Step 3 of 6 window for the Test application.

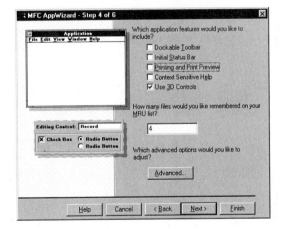

Figure 12.14. The AppWizard—Step 4 of 6 window for the Test application.

As shown in Figure 12.14, the features Dockable Toolbar, Initial Status Bar, Printing and Print Preview, and Context Sensitive Help will not be included in the Test application.

As shown in Figure 12.14, the How many files would you like remembered on your MRU list? edit box is set to 4. The MRU list feature is covered in the next chapter. In the Test application you don't use the MRU list feature.

☐ Click the Next button of the Step 4 of 6 window.

Visual C++ responds by displaying the AppWizard—Step 5 of 6 window.

☐ Set the Step 5 of 6 window as shown in Figure 12.15.

As shown in Figure 12.15, the project will be generated with comments, a Visual C++ makefile will be generated, and the application will use the MFC library from a DLL.

Figure 12.15. The AppWizard—Step 5 of 6 window for the Test application.

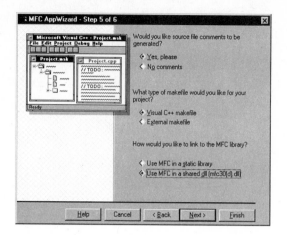

☐ Click the Next button of the Step 5 of 6 window.

Visual C++ responds by displaying the AppWizard—Step 6 of 6 window, as shown in Figure 12.16.

Figure 12.16. The AppWizard—Step 6 of 6 window for the Test application.

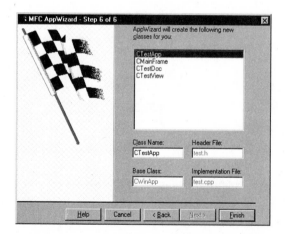

NOTE

In all the applications that you wrote in the previous chapters you did not have to change anything in the last AppWizard step (that is, you just clicked the Finish button). However, for the Test application you have to change one of the default settings of AppWizard. So do not click the Finish button yet!

Take a close look at Figure 12.16. As you can see, AppWizard is telling you that it will create for you the following four classes: CTestApp, CMainFrame, CTestDoc, and CTestView.

The CTestApp class is the application class. AppWizard will derive this class from the MFC class CWinApp. The member functions of the CTestApp class (functions that were inherited from the CWinApp class) are used for initializing a Windows application and running it. In most cases, you will not have to change or write any code in the application class. That is, you'll be able to use the code that AppWizard will write for you in this class as is.

The CMainFrame class is the main frame window class. AppWizard will derive this class from the MFC class CFrameWnd. The member functions of the CMainFrame class (functions that were inherited from the CFrameWnd class) are used for creating a frame window for the application and for managing the frame window. In most cases, you will not have to change or write any code in the main frame window class. That is, you'll be able to use the code that AppWizard will write for you in this class as is.

The CTestDoc class is the document class of the Test application. AppWizard will derive this class from the MFC class CDocument. What is the document class? You can think of the document class as the place where you will define and initialize the data (variables) of the application. It is your job to add data members to the document class of the applications. These data members will be the document (data) of your application.

The CTestView class is the view class of the Test application. What is the view class? The view class is where all the action takes place. The code that you'll write in the view class is the code that is responsible for what the user sees (views) on the screen.

The purposes of the view class and the document class can be summarized as follows:

- The code that you'll write in the document class is responsible for storing and maintaining the data of your application.
- The code that you'll write in the view class is responsible for displaying the data that is stored in the document class.

As discussed previously, AppWizard will derive the document class of the Test application (CTestDoc) from the MFC class CDocument. What about the view class of the Test application? From which MFC class will AppWizard derive the view class (CTestview) of the Test application? It happens that AppWizard lets you specify from which class you want to derive the view class of the application. Here is how you do that:

☐ Select the CTestView class inside the AppWizard—Step 6 of 6 window.

Your AppWizard—Step 6 of 6 window should now look like the one shown in Figure 12.17.

As you can see from Figure 12.17, one of the fields inside the AppWizard—Step 6 of 6 window is a drop-down list box that displays the base class from which AppWizard will derive the CTestView class. Currently the base class drop-down list box is set to CView. To see the other view classes from which you can derive the view class of the application do the following:

Figure 12.17. The AppWizard—Step 6 of 6 window after you have selected the CTestView *class.*

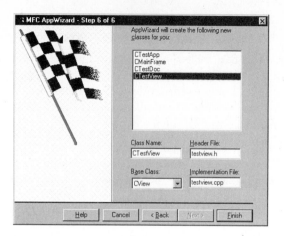

☐ Click the arrow icon of the Base Class drop-down list box.

>   *The Base Class drop-down list opens, as shown in Figure 12.18.*

Figure 12.18. The Base Class drop-down list box for the application's view class.

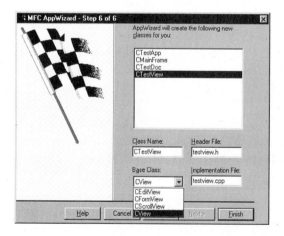

As you can see from Figure 12.18, the Base Class drop-down list box lists four MFC classes from which you can derive the view class of the application: CEditView, CFormView, CScrollView, and CView.

The Test application should have a view class that is derived from the MFC class CFormView. Therefore, you have to set the Base Class drop-down list to CFormView:

☐ Set the Base Class drop-down list box to CFormView.

Your AppWizard—Step 6 of 6 window should now look like the one shown in Figure 12.19.

Figure 12.19. The AppWizard—Step 6 of 6 window after you have set the base class of the application view class to `CFormView`.

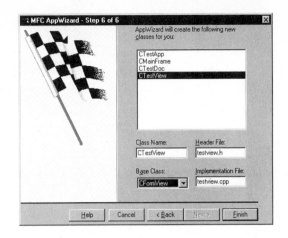

A view class that is derived from the `CFormView` class can be connected to a dialog box. This dialog box then becomes the view of the application. That is, you display information to the user by placing controls inside the dialog box. This dialog box serves as the main window of the application.

So by setting the Base Class drop-down list for the view class of the Test application to `CFormView`, you are specifying the following:

- AppWizard should derive the view class of the Test application (`CTestView`) from the MFC class `CFormView`.

- AppWizard should create a dialog box and attach this dialog box to the view class of the Test application. This dialog box will serve as the main window of the Test application.

Now that the AppWizard—Step 6 of 6 window is set properly for the Test application you can click the Finish button:

☐ Click the Finish button of the Step 6 of 6 window.

  Visual C++ responds by displaying the New Project Information window, as shown in Figure 12.20.

☐ Click the OK button of the New Project Information window.

  Visual C++ responds by creating the project file and all the skeleton files of the application.

Figure 12.20. The New Project Information window of the Test.MAK project.

Running the Test Application Before Customizing It

Before you start customizing the files of the Test application, first compile, link, and execute the Test application in its current status. As you'll see, the skeleton files that AppWizard created for you yield an SDI application that has some functionality.

To compile and link the Test application do the following:

☐ Select Build Test.exe from the Project menu of Visual C++.

Visual C++ responds by compiling and linking the Test application.

NOTE

If during the compiling and linking process you get a memory error (an out-of-memory error or an out-of-heap-space error) close any open applications and then try to rebuild the application. If you still get a memory error, terminate Visual C++ and then run Visual C++ again and try to build the application again. If you still get a memory error, restart Windows and build the application again.

When Visual C++ finishes compiling and linking the application, you can run the application:

☐ Select Execute Test.exe from the Project menu.

Visual C++ responds by executing the Test application. The main window of the Test application appears, as shown in Figure 12.21.

Figure 12.21. The main window of the Test application (before customization).

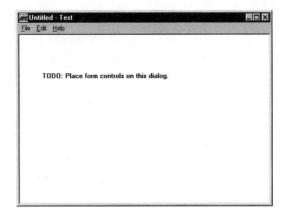

The main window of the Test application displays the text TODO: Place form controls on this dialog. AppWizard placed this text inside the dialog box that serves as the main window of the application. Later you will customize this dialog box so that the main window of the Test application will look like the one shown back in Figure 12.1.

As you can see, the Test application has three pop-up menus: File, Edit, and Help. These pop-up menus are shown in Figures 12.22, 12.23, and 12.24.

Figure 12.22. The File menu of the Test application (before customization).

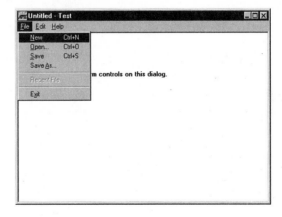

Figure 12.23. The Edit menu of the Test application (before customization).

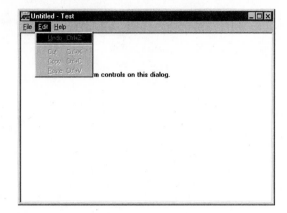

Figure 12.24. The Help menu of the Test application (before customization).

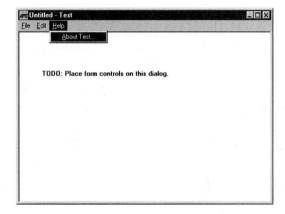

The code that AppWizard wrote for you includes an About dialog box. To see the About dialog box do the following:

☐ Select About from the Help menu of the Test application.

> *The Test application responds by displaying an About dialog box. (Refer back to Figure 12.9.)*

☐ Close the About dialog box by clicking its OK button.

WARNING

Although you haven't attached any code to the menu items of the File menu, these menu items have some functionality. For example, if you select Open from the File menu, a File Open dialog box appears. Of course, once you select a file nothing will be displayed on the screen because you have not written code to accomplish that.

However, be careful with the Save and Save As menu items. Even though you haven't written code for the Save and Save As menu items, they write data to the disk. For example, if you have a file TRY.TXT that has some data in it and you select Save As from the File menu and then select the TRY.TXT file, the original TRY.TXT is overwritten by a new, blank TRY.TXT. Similarly, if you select Open from the File menu to open the file TRY.TXT, and then you select Save from the File menu, the original TRY.TXT will be overwritten by a new, blank TRY.TXT.

To terminate the Test application do the following:

☐ Select Exit from the File menu.

As you have just seen, even though you haven't written a single line of code yet, you have the skeleton of a true working SDI Windows application in your hands—a gift from AppWizard. Of course, this application is not exactly what you want it to be. In the following sections, you will customize the Test application so that it does what it's supposed to do.

The Visual Implementation of the Test Application's Form

Because in AppWizard you specified that the base class of the application's view class is CFormView, AppWizard created for you a form (a dialog box) that is attached to the view class of the application. This dialog box serves as the main window of the application. AppWizard named this dialog box IDD_TEST_FORM. You'll now customize the IDD_TEST_FORM dialog box until it looks like the one shown back in Figure 12.5.

☐ Double-click test.rc inside the test.mak window.

   Visual C++ responds by displaying the test.rc window.

☐ Double-click Dialog inside the test.rc window and then double-click IDD_TEST_FORM.

   Visual C++ responds by displaying the IDD_TEST_FORM dialog box in design mode. (See Figure 12.25.)

☐ Delete the text TODO: Place form controls on this dialog. that Visual C++ placed inside the dialog box.

☐ Implement the dialog box according to the specifications in Table 12.1. When you finish implementing the dialog box, it should look like the one shown in Figure 12.26.

Figure 12.25. The IDD_TEST_FORM dialog box (before customization).

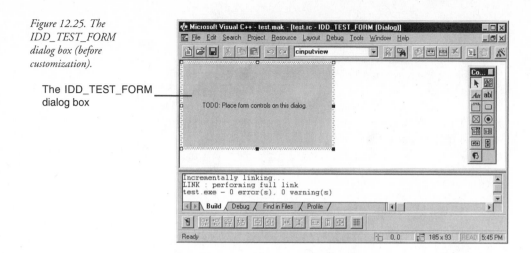

The IDD_TEST_FORM dialog box

Table 12.1. The Properties table of the IDD_TEST_FORM dialog box.

Object	Property	Setting
Dialog box	ID	IDD_TEST_DIALOG
Edit box	ID	IDC_EDIT1
Push button	ID	IDC_TEST_BUTTON
	Caption	&Test
Push button	ID	IDC_CLEAR_BUTTON
	Caption	&Clear

Figure 12.26. The dialog box that serves as the main window of the Test application (in design mode).

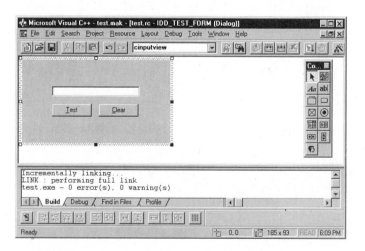

☐ Save your work by selecting Save from the File menu.

Attaching a Variable to the IDC_EDIT1 Edit Box

You'll now attach a variable to the IDC_EDIT1 edit box.

☐ Use ClassWizard (from the Project menu) to attach a variable to the IDC_EDIT1 edit box of the IDD_TEST_FORM dialog box according to the specifications in Table 12.2. (Make sure that Class Name in the ClassWizard dialog box is set to CTestView.)

Table 12.2. The Variables table of the IDD_TEST_FORM dialog box.

Control ID	Variable Name	Category	Variable Type
IDC_EDIT1	m_MyEditBox	Value	Cstring

☐ To save your work, select Save from the File menu.

To see your visual design in action do the following:

☐ Select Build Test.EXE from the Project menu.

  Visual C++ responds by compiling and linking the Test application.

☐ Select Execute Test.EXE from the Project menu.

  Visual C++ responds by executing the Test.EXE application.

As expected, the IDD_TEST_FORM dialog box that you designed appears as the main window of the application.

☐ Select Exit from the File menu of the Test application.

  The Test application responds by terminating itself.

The Visual Implementation of the Menu Bar

AppWizard created for you a standard SDI menu bar. (Refer back to Figures 12.22, 12.23, and 12.24.) However, the Test application should have a simpler menu bar. (Refer back to Figures 12.6 and 12.7.)

You'll now customize the menu bar of the Test application until it finally looks like the one shown back in Figures 12.6 and 12.7.

The menu bar that AppWizard created for you is called IDR_MAINFRAME. Follow these steps to customize the IDR_MAINFRAME menu:

☐ Select test.rc from the Window menu of Visual C++.

  Visual C++ responds by displaying the test.rc window.

☐ Double-click Menu inside the test.rc window and then double-click IDR_MAINFRAME.

Visual C++ responds by displaying the IDR_MAINFRAME menu bar in design mode. (See Figure 12.27.)

Figure 12.27. The IDR_MAINFRAME menu bar (before customization).

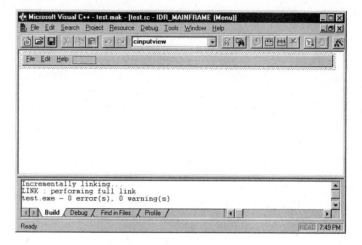

As you can see from Figure 12.27, the IDR_MAINFRAME menu currently has three pop-up menus: File, Edit, and Help.

Because the Test application should not have an Edit menu (Refer back to Figure 12.5), you have to remove the Edit pop-up menu:

☐ Click the Edit item on the menu bar.

Visual C++ responds by opening the Edit pop-up menu. (See Figure 12.28.)

Figure 12.28. The Edit pop-up menu.

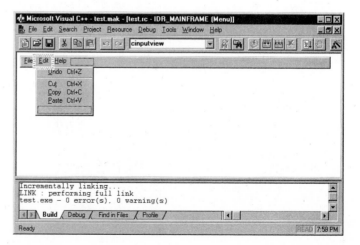

☐ Now press the Delete key on your keyboard.

Visual C++ responds by displaying a dialog box warning you that you're about to delete an entire pop-up menu. (See Figure 12.29.)

Figure 12.29. The warning
that Visual C++ displays
when you try to delete an
entire pop-up menu.

☐ Click the OK button of the dialog box.

Visual C++ responds by deleting the Edit pop-up menu. Now the IDR_MAINFRAME menu looks like the one shown in Figure 12.30.

Figure 12.30. The
IDR_MAINFRAME menu
after you delete the Edit
pop-up menu.

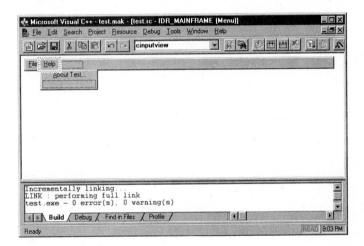

Now modify the File pop-up menu so that it looks like the one shown in Figure 12.7:

☐ Click the File item on the menu bar.

Visual C++ responds by opening the File pop-up menu. (See Figure 12.31.)

Currently the File pop-up menu has the following items:

New
Open...
Save
Save As...
Recent File
Exit

*Figure 12.31. The File
pop-up menu.*

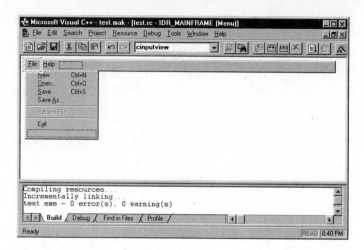

As you can see from Figure 12.7, the only item you need from this list is the Exit item. Therefore, you have to delete all the items from the File pop-up menu except the Exit item:

☐ To delete the New menu item, click it and then press the Delete key on your keyboard.

☐ Repeat the preceding step to delete all the other items in the File pop-up except the Exit item.

Your File pop-up menu should now look like the one shown in Figure 12.32.

*Figure 12.32. The File
pop-up menu after you
remove all the items except
the Exit item.*

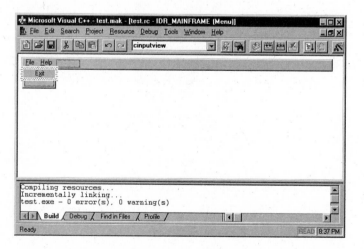

The IDR_MAINFRAME menu bar is now complete!

☐ Save your work by selecting Save from the File menu of Visual C++.

To see your visual design in action do the following:

☐ Select Build Test.EXE from the Project menu.

> *Visual C++ responds by compiling and linking the Test application.*

☐ Select Execute Test.EXE from the Project menu.

> *Visual C++ responds by executing the Test.EXE application.*

As expected, the menu bar of the application appears as you have customized it—it now has only two pop-up menus: File and Help.

☐ Verify that the File and Help menus look like the ones shown in Figures 12.6 and 12.7.

☐ Terminate the Test application by selecting Exit from the File menu.

Attaching Code to the Test and Clear Buttons

You have completed the visual implementation of the Test application menu and dialog box. The last thing that you have to do to complete the Test application is attach code to the Test and Clear buttons.

The Test and Clear buttons are inside the IDD_TEST_FORM dialog box. Recall that the IDD_TEST_FORM dialog box is associated with the view class of the Test application (CTestView). Therefore, the code that you'll now attach to the Test and Clear buttons will be written inside the CTestView class.

To attach code to the Click event of the Test button do the following:

☐ Display the ClassWizard dialog box by selecting ClassWizard from the Project menu of Visual C++.

☐ Select the Message Maps tab at the top of ClassWizard's dialog box.

☐ Use ClassWizard to select the event:

```
CTestView -> IDC_TEST_BUTTON -> BN_CLICKED
```

Then click the Add Function button.

☐ Name the new function OnTestButton().

To write the code of the OnTestButton() function do the following:

☐ Click the Edit Code button of ClassWizard.

> *ClassWizard responds by opening the file TestView.CPP, with the function OnTestButton() ready to be edited by you.*

☐ Write code inside the `OnTestButton()` function so that it looks like this:

```
void CTestView::OnTestButton()
{
// TODO: Add your control notification handler code here

//////////////////////////
// MY CODE STARTS HERE //
//////////////////////////

// Fill the variable of the edit box with text.
m_MyEditBox = _T("This is a test!");

// Update the screen.
UpdateData(FALSE);

//////////////////////////
// MY CODE ENDS HERE    //
//////////////////////////

}
```

☐ Save your work by selecting Save from the File menu of Visual C++.

The code that you typed inside the `OnTestButton()` function is made of two statements. The first statement

```
m_MyEditBox = _T("This is a test!");
```

updates the variable of the edit box with the string `This is a test!`.

The second statement

```
UpdateData(FALSE);
```

updates the screen by calling the `UpdateData()` function with its parameter set to `FALSE`.

To attach code to the `Click` event of the Clear button do the following:

☐ Display the ClassWizard dialog box by selecting ClassWizard from the Project menu of Visual C++.

☐ Select the Message Maps tab at the top of ClassWizard's dialog box.

☐ Use ClassWizard to select the event:

```
CTestView -> IDC_CLEAR_BUTTON -> BN_CLICKED
```

Then click the Add Function button.

☐ Name the new function `OnClearButton()`.

To write the code of the `OnClearButton()` function do the following:

☐ Click the Edit Code button of ClassWizard.

> *ClassWizard responds by opening the file TestView.CPP, with the function `OnClearButton()` ready to be edited by you.*

☐ Write code inside the `OnClearButton()` function so that it looks like this:

```
void CTestView::OnClearButton()
{
// TODO: Add your control notification handler code here

////////////////////////////
// MY CODE STARTS HERE //
////////////////////////////

// Fill the variable of the edit box with null.
m_MyEditBox = _T("");

// Update the screen.
UpdateData(FALSE);

////////////////////////////
// MY CODE ENDS HERE    //
////////////////////////////

}
```

☐ Save your work by selecting Save from the File menu of Visual C++.

The code you typed inside the `OnClearButton()` function is similar to the code you wrote inside the `OnTestButton()` function. The only difference is that now the variable of the edit box is filled with a null string:

```
m_MyEditBox = _T("");
```

The Test application is now complete! To see the code that you attached to the Test and Clear push buttons in action do the following:

☐ Select Build Test.EXE from the Project menu.

   Visual C++ responds by compiling and linking the Test application.

☐ Select Execute Test.EXE from the Project menu.

   Visual C++ responds by executing the Test.EXE application.

☐ Experiment with the Test and Clear push buttons and verify that they work properly.

☐ Terminate the Test application by selecting Exit from the File menu.

Final Words...

In this chapter you have learned how to create the skeleton of an SDI application with AppWizard.

As you've seen, when you create an SDI application with AppWizard, AppWizard creates for you a view class and a document class. The code that you write inside the view class is responsible for what the user sees (views) on the screen, and the code that you write inside the document class is responsible for storing and maintaining the data of the application.

In the application that you wrote in this chapter, you wrote code only in the view class of the application. You did not have to write any code inside the document class because the application in this chapter is a very simple one—it displays three controls (an edit box and two push button controls), but it does not maintain any data. For example, when the user terminates the application, whatever the user typed inside the edit box is gone forever. The application does not save what the user typed in the edit box.

In the next chapter you'll write a more involved SDI application. In that application you'll write code in the document class of the application as well as in the view class of the application. The code that you'll write in the document class will store and maintain the data of the application, and the code that you'll write in the view class will enable the user to view and edit the data.

In the application you wrote in this chapter (the Test application), writing code inside the view class was very easy. That's because when you created the skeleton of the application with AppWizard, you asked AppWizard to derive the view class of the application from the MFC class `CFormView`. Therefore, AppWizard created for you a dialog box (IDD_TEST_FORM) and associated it with the view class of the application (`CTestView`). Your job was very easy. All you had to do was customize the IDD_TEST_FORM dialog box. You placed controls inside the dialog box and you attached code to these controls. The code you attached to these controls was written inside the view class. For example, the `OnClearButton()` function that you attached to the Clear push button is a member function of the view class. Similarly, the variable that you attached to the edit box control (`m_MyEditBox`) is a data member of the view class.

13

Writing and Reading Data (with Serialization) to and from Files

In Chapter 12, "Writing a Single-Document Interface Application," you wrote a very simple single-document interface (SDI) application that lets the user view and edit data on the screen but does not let the user save the data. For example, you can type data into the edit box, but all the data that you enter is gone forever once you terminate the application.

In this chapter you'll write a more practical SDI application—one that lets the user edit data and save it in a file. Then the user can terminate the application and load the saved data the next time the application is executed. As you will soon see, Visual C++ supports a mechanism called *serialization* that enables you to write code that writes and reads data to and from files with great ease.

In the application you wrote in Chapter 12 (the Test.EXE application), you wrote code only in the view class of the application. You did not have to write any code inside the document class because the Test.EXE application displays data, but it does not maintain any data. In the application that you'll write in this chapter, you'll write code in the view class of the application as well as in the document class of the application. The code that you'll write in the document class will store and maintain the data of the application and the code that you'll write in the view class will enable the user to view and edit the data.

At the end of this chapter you'll learn how to modify the string table of the application to change default characteristics of the application, such as the title of the application's main window.

The MEMO Application

You'll now write the MEMO application, an example of an SDI application that reads and writes data to the disk.

Before you start writing the MEMO application yourself, execute the copy of it that resides in the \MVCPROG\EXE directory of the book's CD.

To execute the MEMO application do the following:

☐ Select Run from the Start menu of Windows and execute the X:\mvcProg\EXE\Memo.EXE program (where *X* represents the drive letter of your CD-ROM drive).

The window of Memo.EXE appears, as shown in Figure 13.1.

Figure 13.1. The main window of the MEMO application.

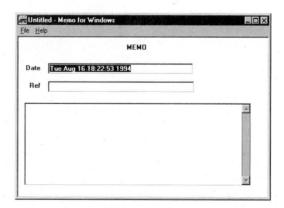

As you can see from Figure 13.1, the main window of the application displays a memo form ready to be filled in. The title of the window is Untitled—Memo for Windows.

The MEMO application has two pop-up menus: File and Help. These pop-up menus are shown in Figures 13.2 and 13.3.

Figure 13.2. The File pop-up menu of the MEMO application.

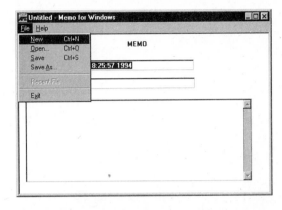

Figure 13.3. The Help pop-up menu of the MEMO application.

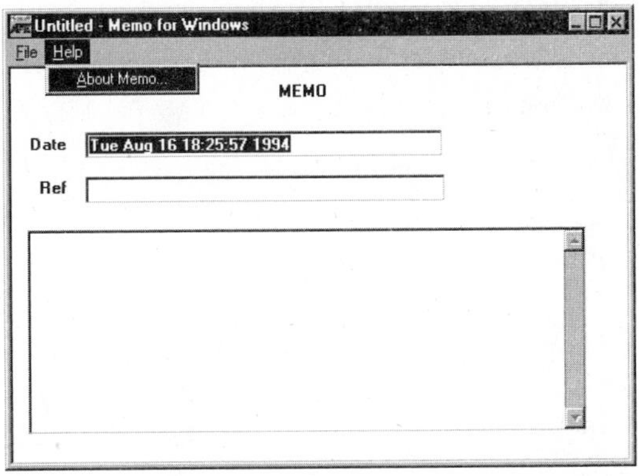

☐ Fill the memo's fields with data. Figure 13.4 shows the memo form after it's completed.

Figure 13.4. A completed memo form.

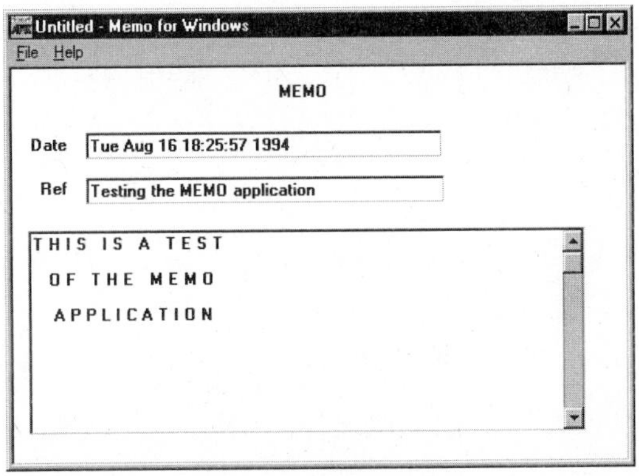

☐ Select Save from the File menu of the MEMO application.

The MEMO application responds by displaying the Save As dialog box. (See Figure 13.5.)

Figure 13.5. The Save As
dialog box of the MEMO
application.

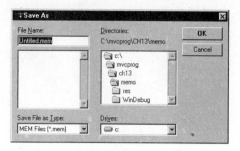

☐ Save the file as TRY.MEM. (The default filename is untitled.mem, so change it to
TRY.MEM and then click the OK button.)

*The MEMO application responds by saving your memo in the file TRY.MEM and
changing the window's title to Memo for Windows—TRY.MEM.*

To verify that indeed your memo is saved in the file TRY.MEM do the following:

☐ Exit the MEMO application by selecting Exit from the File menu.

☐ Execute the MEMO application again.

☐ Select Open from the File menu of the MEMO application.

The MEMO application responds by displaying the Open dialog box. (See Figure 13.6.)

Figure 13.6. The Open
dialog box of the MEMO
application.

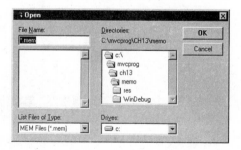

☐ Select the file TRY.MEM.

The MEMO application responds by displaying the TRY.MEM memo file on the screen.

Experiment with the other menu items of the File menu (New and Save As). As you can see, all
the File menu items behave as you would expect them to behave in a standard SDI Windows
application.

To exit the MEMO application do the following:

☐ Select Exit from the File menu.

> **NOTE**
>
> If you make changes to the memo and then you try to exit the application without first saving your changes, the MEMO application will display a Yes/No/Cancel message box asking you if you want to save your changes.

Now that you know what the MEMO application should do, you can start writing it.

Creating the Project of the MEMO Application

To create the project of the MEMO application do the following:

☐ Start Visual C++ and close all the open windows that appear inside the desktop of Visual C++ (if there are any).

☐ Select New from the File menu.

Visual C++ responds by displaying the New dialog box.

☐ Select Project inside the New dialog box and then click the OK button of the New dialog box.

Visual C++ responds by displaying the New Project dialog box.

☐ Set the project name to Memo.

☐ Set the project path to \MVCPROG\CH13\Memo\Memo.MAK.

Your New Project dialog box should now look like the one shown in Figure 13.7.

Figure 13.7. The New Project dialog box of the Memo.MAK project.

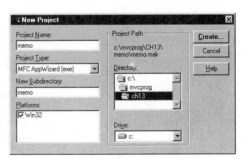

☐ Click the Create button of the New Project dialog box.

Visual C++ responds by displaying the AppWizard—Step 1 window.

☐ Set the Step 1 window as shown in Figure 13.8. As shown in Figure 13.8, the Memo.MAK project is set as an SDI application, and U.S. English (APPWIZUS.DLL) is used as the language for the application's resources.

Figure 13.8. The AppWizard—Step 1 window for the MEMO application.

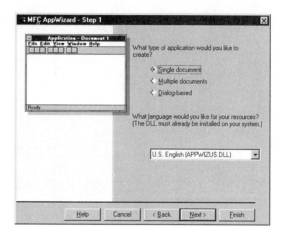

☐ Click the Next button of the Step 1 window.

Visual C++ responds by displaying the AppWizard—Step 2 of 6 window.

☐ Set the Step 2 of 6 window as shown in Figure 13.9. That is, in the MEMO application you don't want any database support.

Figure 13.9. The AppWizard—Step 2 of 6 window for the MEMO application.

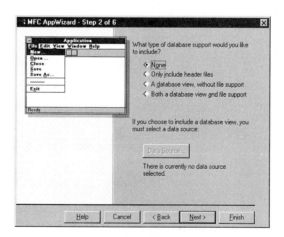

☐ Click the Next button of the Step 2 of 6 window.

Visual C++ responds by displaying the AppWizard—Step 3 of 6 window.

☐ Set the Step 3 of 6 window as shown in Figure 13.10. That is, in the MEMO application you don't want any OLE support.

Figure 13.10. The
AppWizard—Step 3 of 6
window for the MEMO
application.

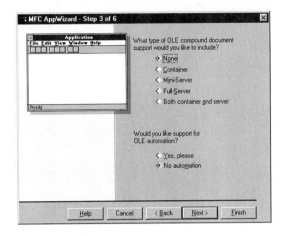

☐ Click the Next button of the Step 3 of 6 window.

Visual C++ responds by displaying the AppWizard—Step 4 of 6 window.

☐ Set the Step 4 of 6 window as shown in Figure 13.11.

Figure 13.11. The
AppWizard—Step 4 of 6
window for the MEMO
application.

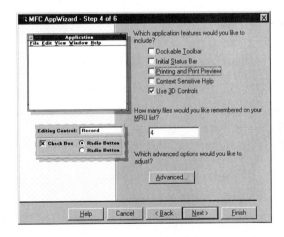

As shown in Figure 13.11, the features Dockable Toolbar, Initial Status Bar, Printing and Print Preview, and Context Sensitive Help will not be included in the MEMO application.

NOTE

As shown in Figure 13.11, you should leave the How many files would you like remembered on your MRU list? edit box at the default setting, which is 4.

The MRU list feature is covered later in this chapter.

☐ Click the Next button of the Step 4 of 6 window.

   Visual C++ responds by displaying the AppWizard—Step 5 of 6 window.

☐ Set the Step 5 of 6 window as shown in Figure 13.12.

As shown in Figure 13.12, the project will be generated with comments, a Visual C++ makefile will be generated, and the application will use the MFC library from a DLL.

Figure 13.12. The AppWizard—Step 5 of 6 window for the MEMO application.

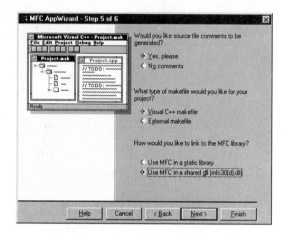

☐ Click the Next button of the Step 5 of 6 window.

   Visual C++ responds by displaying the AppWizard—Step 6 of 6 window.

Just as you did in Chapter 12, you'll now use the AppWizard—Step 6 of 6 window to tell AppWizard to derive the view class of the application from the MFC class CFormView:

☐ Select the CMemoView class inside the AppWizard—Step 6 of 6 window.

☐ Set the Base Class drop-down list box to CFormView.

Your AppWizard—Step 6 of 6 window should now look like the one shown in Figure 13.13.

☐ Click the Finish button of the Step 6 of 6 window.

   Visual C++ responds by displaying the New Project Information window, as shown in Figure 13.14.

☐ Click the OK button of the New Project Information window.

   Visual C++ responds by creating the project file and all the skeleton files of the application.

Figure 13.13. The AppWizard—Step 6 of 6 window after you set the base class of the application view class to CFormView.

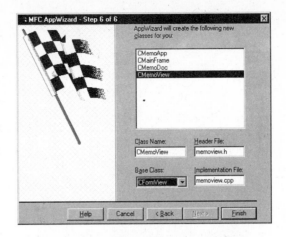

Figure 13.14. The New Project Information window of the Memo.MAK project.

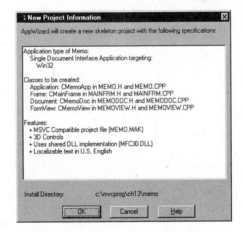

The Visual Implementation of the Application's Form

Because in AppWizard you specified that the base class of the application's view class is CFormView, AppWizard created for you a form (a dialog box) that is attached to the view class of the application. This dialog box serves as the main window of the application. AppWizard named this dialog box IDD_MEMO_FORM. You'll now customize the IDD_MEMO_FORM dialog box until it looks like the one shown back in Figure 13.1.

☐ Double-click memo.rc inside the memo.mak window.

Visual C++ responds by displaying the memo.rc window.

☐ Double-click Dialog inside the memo.rc window and then double-click IDD_MEMO_FORM.

Visual C++ responds by displaying the IDD_MEMO_FORM dialog box in design mode.

☐ Delete the text TODO: Place form controls on this dialog. that Visual C++ placed inside the dialog box.

☐ Implement the dialog box according to the specifications in Table 13.1. When you finish implementing the dialog box, it should look like the one shown in Figure 13.15.

Table 13.1. The Properties table of the IDD_MEMO_FORM dialog box.

Object	Property	Setting
Dialog box	ID	IDD_MEMO_FORM
Static text	ID	IDC_STATIC
	Caption	MEMO
Static text	ID	IDC_STATIC
	Caption	Date
Edit box	ID	IDC_DATE
Static text	ID	IDC_STATIC
	Caption	Ref
Edit box	ID	IDC_REF
Edit box	ID	IDC_MEMO

Figure 13.15. The dialog box that serves as the main window of the MEMO application (in design mode).

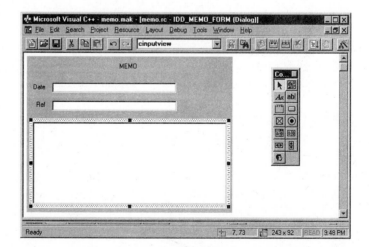

NOTE

The static text tool and edit box tool inside the Tools window are shown in Figure 13.16.

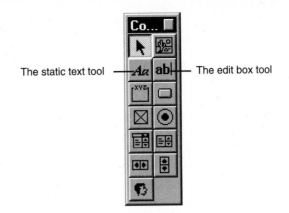

Figure 13.16. The static text tool and edit box tool inside the Tools window of Visual C++.

The static text tool ——— The edit box tool

☐ Save your work by selecting Save from the File menu.

Attaching Variables to the Controls Inside the IDD_MEMO_FORM Dialog Box

You'll now attach variables to the controls inside the IDD_MEMO_FORM dialog box.

☐ Display the ClassWizard dialog box by selecting ClassWizard from the Project menu of Visual C++.

☐ Select the Member Variables tab at the top of ClassWizard's dialog box.

☐ Make sure that the Class Name drop-down list is set to CMemoView.

☐ Attach variables to the controls of the IDD_MEMO_FORM dialog box as specified in Table 13.2.

Table 13.2. The Variables table of the IDD_MEMO_FORM dialog box.

Control ID	Variable Name	Category	Variable Type
IDC_DATE	m_Date	Value	CString
IDC_REF	m_Ref	Value	CString
IDC_MEMO	m_Memo	Value	CString

☐ To save your work, select Save from the File menu.

To see your visual design in action do the following:

☐ Select Build Memo.EXE from the Project menu.

Visual C++ responds by compiling and linking the MEMO application.

☐ Select Execute Memo.EXE from the Project menu.

Visual C++ responds by executing the Memo.EXE application.

As expected, the IDD_MEMO_FORM dialog box that you designed appears as the main window of the application. (See Figure 13.17.)

Figure 13.17. The main window of the MEMO application.

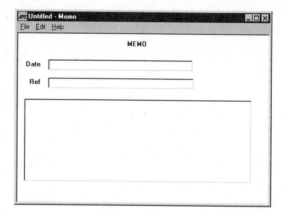

As you can see in Figure 13.17, the menu bar of the MEMO application (the menu bar that AppWizard created for you) has an Edit pop-up menu. However, the menu bar of the MEMO application should not have an Edit pop-up menu. (Refer back to Figure 13.1.) Later you'll customize the menu bar of the MEMO application so that it will not have an Edit pop-up menu.

WARNING

Although you haven't yet written any code for opening and saving memo files, the menu items of the File menu have some functionality. For example, if you select Open from the File menu, a File Open dialog box appears. Of course, once you select a file nothing will be loaded because you have not yet written code to accomplish that.

Be careful with the Save and Save As menu items. Even though you haven't written code for the Save and Save As menu items, they write data to the disk. For example, if you have a file TRY.TXT that has some data in it and you select Save As from the File menu and then select the TRY.TXT file, the original TRY.TXT is overwritten by a new, blank TRY.TXT. Similarly, if you select Open from the File menu to open the file TRY.TXT, and then you select Save from the File menu, the original TRY.TXT will be overwritten by a new, blank TRY.TXT.

Experiment with the memo form:

☐ Type something inside the Date and Ref fields.

Note that you can move from one field to another by pressing the Tab key.

☐ Type something inside the memo edit box (the large edit box at the bottom of the form) and then try to press the Enter key.

As you can see, there is a small problem when the cursor is inside the memo edit box. When you press the Enter key, nothing happens. That is, the keyboard cursor does not move to the next line in the edit box as it should. In the next section you'll fix this problem.

☐ Terminate the MEMO application by selecting Exit from the File menu.

Changing the Properties of the Memo Edit Box

As you've just seen, when you press the Enter key while the cursor is in the memo edit box, nothing happens. You have to change the properties of the memo edit box so that when you press the Enter key a carriage return is inserted in the edit box. Here is how you do that:

☐ Display the IDD_MEMO_FORM dialog box in design mode by selecting memo.rc-IDD_MEMO_FORM [Dialog] from the Window menu of Visual C++.

☐ Double-click the IDC_MEMO edit box.

Visual C++ responds by displaying the Edit Properties dialog box for the IDC_MEMO edit box.

☐ Select the Styles tab of the Edit Properties dialog box.

☐ Set the Styles properties of the IDC_MEMO edit box as follows:

Place a checkmark inside the Multiline check box.

Place a checkmark inside the Want Return check box.

Place a check mark inside the Vert. Scroll check box (this will provide the edit box with a vertical scroll bar).

The Style Properties window of your IDC_MEMO edit box should now look like the one shown in Figure 13.18.

Figure 13.18. Setting the Style properties of the IDC_MEMO edit box.

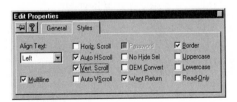

☐ Save your work by selecting Save from the File menu of Visual C++.

To see the effects of these settings on the program do the following:

☐ Select Build Memo.EXE from the Project menu.

Visual C++ responds by compiling and linking the MEMO application.

☐ Select Execute Memo.EXE from the Project menu and experiment with the memo form.

As you can see, when you press the Enter key when the cursor is inside the memo edit box, the program responds by inserting a carriage return in the edit box, which moves the keyboard cursor to the next line.

☐ Terminate the MEMO application by selecting Exit from the File menu.

The Visual Implementation of the Menu Bar

The MEMO application should have a menu, as shown in Figures 13.2 and 13.3.

Implementing this menu is very easy because the menu bar that AppWizard created for you (IDR_MAINFRAME) is almost what you need. All you have to do is delete the Edit pop-up menu. The File pop-up menu and Help pop-up menu that App Wizard generated for you are exactly what you need for the MEMO application.

Follow these steps to customize the IDR_MAINFRAME menu:

☐ Select memo.rc from the Window menu of Visual C++.

Visual C++ responds by displaying the memo.rc window.

☐ Double-click Menu inside the memo.rc window and then double-click IDR_MAINFRAME.

Visual C++ responds by displaying the IDR_MAINFRAME menu bar in design mode.

As you can see, the IDR_MAINFRAME menu currently has three pop-up menus: File, Edit, and Help.

Because the MEMO application should not have an Edit menu, you have to remove the Edit pop-up menu:

☐ Click the Edit item on the menu bar.

Visual C++ responds by opening the Edit pop-up menu.

☐ Now press the Delete key on your keyboard.

Visual C++ responds by displaying a dialog box warning you that you're about to delete an entire pop-up menu.

☐ Click the OK button of the warning dialog box.

Visual C++ responds by deleting the Edit pop-up menu.

☐ Save your work by selecting Save from the File menu of Visual C++.

The visual implementation of the menu of the MEMO application is complete. To see your visual design in action do the following:

☐ Select Build Memo.EXE from the Project menu.

Visual C++ responds by compiling and linking the MEMO application.

☐ Select Execute Memo.EXE from the Project menu.

Visual C++ responds by executing the Memo.EXE application.

As expected, the menu bar of the application appears as you customized it—it now has only two pop-up menus: File and Help.

☐ Verify that the File and Help menus look like those shown in Figures 13.2 and 13.3.

☐ Terminate the MEMO application by selecting Exit from the File menu.

The Document Class of the MEMO Application

As you know, the document class is used to hold the data of the application, and the view class is used to display the data and to enable the user to edit the data.

As you will see later in this chapter, storing the data of the application in the document class is very useful because it enables you to read and write data into files easily.

Recall that during the visual implementation of the IDD_MEMO_FORM dialog box you created three variables: m_Date (the variable for the IDC_DATE edit box), m_Ref (the variable for the IDC_REF edit box), and m_Memo (the variable for the IDC_MEMO edit box).

Because the IDD_MEMO_FORM is connected to the view class of the application (CMemoView), these variables are data members of the view class.

Now you'll add three data members to the document class. You'll give these variables the same names as the three data members of the view class.

The document class of the MEMO application is CMemoDoc, and the declaration of this class is inside the header file MEMODOC.H.

☐ Select Open from the File menu of Visual C++ and open the file MEMODOC.H.

☐ Add code to the MEMODOC.H file that defines the three variables (m_Date, m_Ref, and m_Memo) as public data members of the CMemoDoc class. Declare each of these variables as type CString. After you write this code, the CMemoDoc class declaration should look like this:

```
class CMemoDoc : public CDocument
{
protected: // create from serialization only
    CMemoDoc();
    DECLARE_DYNCREATE(CMemoDoc)

// Attributes
public:

    /////////////////////////
    // MY CODE STARTS HERE
    /////////////////////////

    CString m_Date;
    CString m_Ref;
    CString m_Memo;
```

```
////////////////////
// MY CODE ENDS HERE
////////////////////


// Operations
public:

// Overrides
    // ClassWizard generated virtual function overrides
    //{{AFX_VIRTUAL(CMemoDoc)
    public:
    virtual BOOL OnNewDocument();
    //}}AFX_VIRTUAL

// Implementation
public:
virtual ~ CMemoDoc();
virtual void Serialize(CArchive& ar); // overridden for
                                      // document i/o
#ifdef _DEBUG
    virtual void AssertValid() const;
    virtual void Dump(CDumpContext& dc) const;
#endif

protected:

// Generated message map functions
protected:
//{{AFX_MSG(CMemoDoc)
// NOTE—the ClassWizard will add and remove member
//       functions here.
// DO NOT EDIT what you see in these blocks of generated
// code !
//}}AFX_MSG
DECLARE_MESSAGE_MAP()
};
```

☐ Save your work by selecting Save from the File menu of Visual C++ and then close the MEMODOC.H file by selecting Close from the File menu.

You've finished declaring the data members of the document class. Next you will initialize these variables.

Initializing the Data Members of the Document Class

When the user starts the application or selects New from the File menu, the data members of the document class should be initialized. Why? Whenever a new memo is created you want the data of this new memo to have values as shown back in Figure 13.1. That is, you want the Date field to hold the current date and time and you want the Ref and Memo fields to be blank.

The document class has a member function called OnNewDocument(). Whenever a new document is created (either when the application begins or when the user selects New from the File menu), this member function is executed automatically. Therefore, the code that initializes the data members of the document class should be written inside this function.

☐ Display the ClassWizard dialog box by selecting ClassWizard from the Project menu of Visual C++.

☐ Select the Message Maps tab at the top of ClassWizard's dialog box.

☐ Use ClassWizard to select the event:

```
CMemoDoc -> CMemoDoc -> OnNewDocument
```

> **NOTE**
>
> In the preceding step you were asked to use ClassWizard to select the event `CMemoDoc -> CMemoDoc -> OnNewDocument`. This means that you have to set the Class Name drop-down list of ClassWizard to `CMemoDoc`, then select `CMemoDoc` inside the Object IDs list, and finally select `OnNewDocument` inside the Messages list.

☐ Click the Edit Code button of ClassWizard.

> *ClassWizard responds by opening the file MemoDoc.CPP, with the function* `OnNewDocument()` *ready to be edited by you.*

☐ Write code inside the `OnNewDocument()` function so that it looks like this:

```
BOOL CMemoDoc::OnNewDocument()
{
if (!CDocument::OnNewDocument())
   return FALSE;

// TODO: add reinitialization code here
// (SDI documents will reuse this document)

///////////////////////////
// MY CODE STARTS HERE
///////////////////////////

// Get the current time.
long lTime;
time(&lTime);
struct tm *newtime = localtime(&lTime);

// Convert the time into a string.
char CurrentTime[30];
strcpy(CurrentTime, asctime(newtime));
CurrentTime[24] = '\0';

// Initialize the data of the new memo.
m_Date = CurrentTime;
m_Ref  = "";
m_Memo = "";
```

```
/////////////////////
// MY CODE ENDS HERE
/////////////////////

return TRUE;
}
```

☐ Save your work by selecting Save from the File menu.

The first three statements that you typed inside the OnNewDocument() function

```
long lTime;
time(&lTime);
struct tm *newtime = localtime(&lTime);
```

store the current time and date in newtime (a structure of type tm). So at this point the fields of the structure newtime store the current time and date.

The next three statements

```
char CurrentTime[30];
strcpy(CurrentTime, asctime(newtime));
CurrentTime[24] = '\0';
```

use the asctime() function to convert the current time stored in newtime into a string. The resultant string is assigned to the CurrentTime string. So at this point CurrentTime contains a string with 24 characters that represents the current time. This string includes the day and date, month, time, and year. Note that the statement

```
CurrentTime[24] = '\0';
```

terminates the CurrentTime string.

The last three statements that you typed inside the OnNewDocument() function

```
m_Date = CurrentTime;
m_Ref  = "";
m_Memo = "";
```

assign the CurrentTime string to the m_Date data member of the document class and assign null strings to the m_Ref and m_Memo data members of the document class.

So when the user starts the application or selects New from the File menu, the OnNewDocument() member function of the document class is automatically executed, and the code that you wrote in this function initializes the data members of the document class. m_Date is initialized to the current date and time, and m_Ref and m_Memo are initialized to null.

Initializing the Data Members of the View Class

The code you wrote inside the OnNewDocument() member function of the document class initializes the data members of the document class. But what about the data members of the view class? After all, the data members of the view class are very important—they represent what the user sees (views) on the screen. You need to initialize the data members of the view class inside the OnInitialUpdate() member function of the view class.

The OnInitialUpdate() member function of the view class is executed automatically under the following circumstances:

> When the user starts the application
>
> When the user selects New from the File menu
>
> When the user selects Open from the File menu

The code that you write inside the OnInitialUpdate() function should update the data members of the view class with the current values of the data members of the document class. Therefore, whenever the user starts the application, creates a new memo file, or opens an existing memo file, the data members of the view class will be updated with data members of the document class.

Follow these steps to write the code of the OnInitialUpdate() member function of the view class:

☐ Display the ClassWizard dialog box by selecting ClassWizard from the Project menu of Visual C++.

☐ Select the Message Maps tab at the top of ClassWizard's dialog box.

☐ Use ClassWizard to select the event:

```
CMemoView -> CMemoView -> OnInitialUpdate
```

> **NOTE**
>
> In the preceding step you are asked to use ClassWizard to select the event CMemoView -> CMemoView -> OnInitialUpdate. This means that you have to set the Class Name drop-down list of ClassWizard to CMemoView, then select CMemoView inside the Object IDs list, and finally select OnInitialUpdate inside the Messages list.

☐ Click the Add Function button.

> *Visual C++ responds by adding the* OnInitialUpdate() *member function to the* CMemoView *class.*

☐ Click the Edit Code button of ClassWizard.

> *ClassWizard responds by opening the file MemoView.CPP, with the function* OnInitialUpdate() *ready to be edited by you.*

☐ Write code inside the OnInitialUpdate() function so that it looks like this:

```
void CMemoView::OnInitialUpdate()
{
// TODO: Add your specialized code here and/or call the base
//       class

/////////////////////////
// MY CODE STARTS HERE
/////////////////////////
```

```
// Get a pointer to the document.
CMemoDoc* pDoc = GetDocument();

// Update the data members of the view class with the
// current values of the data members of the document class.
m_Date = pDoc->m_Date;
m_Ref  = pDoc->m_Ref;
m_Memo = pDoc->m_Memo;

// Update the screen with the new values of the variables.
UpdateData(FALSE);

////////////////////
// MY CODE ENDS HERE
////////////////////

CFormView::OnInitialUpdate();

}
```

☐ Save your work by selecting Save from the File menu.

Now go over the code you wrote inside the `OnInitialUpdate()` function.

The first statement

```
CMemoDoc* pDoc = GetDocument();
```

uses the `GetDocument()` function to extract `pDoc` (the pointer for the document).

Then, using the `pDoc` pointer, the data members of the view class are updated with the current values of the document:

```
m_Date = pDoc->m_Date;
m_Ref  = pDoc->m_Ref;
m_Memo = pDoc->m_Memo;
```

Finally, the `UpdateData()` function is used to transfer the new values of the view class data members to the screen:

```
UpdateData(FALSE);
```

That is, the data members of the view class, `m_Date`, `m_Ref`, and `m_Memo`, are the variables that you attached to the `IDC_DATE`, `IDC_REF`, and `IDC_MEMO` edit boxes. Therefore, calling `UpdateData()` with its parameter set to `FALSE` updates the contents of the edit boxes on the screen with the new values of the `m_Date`, `m_Ref`, and `m_Memo` data members of the view class.

NOTE

As you have seen in the preceding code, the `GetDocument()` function (a member function of the view class) is a very useful function. It enables you to access the data members of the document class from the view class.

So what have you accomplished so far? You have written the code that initializes the data members of the document class, and you have written the code that initializes the data members of the view class.

Updating the Data Members of the Document Class

Whenever the user edits the memo form of the application, the data members of the document class should be updated with the new values that the user types. For example, if the IDC_DATE edit box is empty, and the user types inside it the character A, the data member m_Date of the document class should be updated with A.

Who is responsible for updating the data members of the document class? You! Whenever the user changes a data member of the view class, you have to update the corresponding data member in the document class with the new value.

In the MEMO application, the view class has three data members: m_Date (this variable is attached to the IDC_DATE edit box), m_Ref (this variable is attached to the IDC_REF edit box), and m_Memo (this variable is attached to the IDC_MEMO edit box).

Whenever the user changes any of these variables (that is, when the user types something inside an edit box), the code of the application should update the corresponding data member in the document class. Here is how you do that:

☐ Display the ClassWizard dialog box by selecting ClassWizard from the Project menu of Visual C++.

☐ Select the Message Maps tab at the top of ClassWizard's dialog box.

☐ Use ClassWizard to select the event:

```
CMemoView -> IDC_DATE -> EN_CHANGE
```

Then click the Add Function button.

☐ Name the new function OnChangeDate().

NOTE

The EN_CHANGE event corresponds to the message "The user changed the contents of the edit box."

Therefore, whenever the user changes the IDC_DATE edit box, the OnChangeDate() function is executed automatically.

To write the code of the OnChangeDate() function do the following:

☐ Click the Edit Code button of ClassWizard.

ClassWizard responds by opening the file MemoView.CPP, with the function OnChangeDate() ready to be edited by you.

☐ Write code inside the OnChangeDate() function so that it looks like this:

```
void CMemoView::OnChangeDate()
{
// TODO: Add your control notification handler code here


/////////////////////////
// MY CODE STARTS HERE
/////////////////////////

// Update the variables of the controls.
UpdateData(TRUE);

// Get a pointer to the document.
CMemoDoc* pDoc = GetDocument();

// Update the m_Date data member of the document class.
pDoc->m_Date = m_Date;

// Set the Modified flag of the document class to TRUE.
pDoc->SetModifiedFlag();

/////////////////////////
// MY CODE ENDS HERE
/////////////////////////

}
```

☐ Save your work by selecting Save from the File menu.

The first statement that you typed inside the OnChangeDate() function

```
UpdateData(TRUE);
```

updates the variables of the controls with the current values inside the controls. So at this point the data members of the view class (m_Date, m_Ref, and m_Memo) are filled with whatever text their corresponding edit boxes contain.

The next statement

```
CMemoDoc* pDoc = GetDocument();
```

extracts pDoc (the pointer for the document class).

The next statement

```
pDoc->m_Date = m_Date;
```

updates the m_Date data member of the document class with the new contents of the IDC_DATE edit box. That is, the m_Date data member of the document class is set to the current value of the m_Date data member of the view class.

The last statement in the OnChangeDate() function is

```
pDoc->SetModifiedFlag();
```

This statement executes a member function of the document class called `SetModifiedFlag()`. The `SetModifiedFlag()` function sets the Modified flag in the document class to `TRUE`. This flag serves as an indication that data has been changed by the user.

When the user saves the document (by selecting either Save or Save As from the File menu), the Modified flag is automatically set to `FALSE`. You don't have to write the code that sets the Modified flag to `FALSE`! This code is a gift from Visual C++.

If the Modified flag is set to `TRUE` and the user tries to quit the application or load a new file, the application will display a warning message, informing the user that the file has not been saved. Again, you don't have to write the code that displays this warning message—this code is also a gift from Visual C++.

So whenever the user changes the IDC_DATE edit box the `OnChangeDate()` function is automatically executed. The code you wrote inside the `OnChangeDate()` function transfers the new contents of the edit box to the `m_Date` data member of the document class. In addition, the `OnChangeDate()` function sets a Modified flag in the document class to indicate that data has been changed by the user.

In a similar manner, you'll now attach code to the EN_CHANGE events of the other two edit boxes in the memo form.

To attach code to the EN_CHANGE event of the IDC_MEMO edit box do the following:

☐ Display the ClassWizard dialog box by selecting ClassWizard from the Project menu of Visual C++.

☐ Select the Message Maps tab at the top of ClassWizard's dialog box.

☐ Use ClassWizard to select the event:

```
CMemoView -> IDC_MEMO -> EN_CHANGE
```

☐ Then click the Add Function button.

☐ Name the new function `OnChangeMemo()`.

☐ Click the Edit Code button of ClassWizard.

> *ClassWizard responds by opening the file MemoView.CPP, with the function* `OnChangeMemo()` *ready to be edited by you.*

☐ Write code inside the `OnChangeMemo()` function so that it looks like this:

```
void CMemoView::OnChangeMemo()
{
// TODO: Add your control notification handler code here

/////////////////////////
// MY CODE STARTS HERE
/////////////////////////
```

```
// Update the variables of the controls.
UpdateData(TRUE);

// Get a pointer to the document.
CMemoDoc* pDoc = GetDocument();

// Update the m_Memo data member of the document class.
pDoc->m_Memo = m_Memo;

// Set the Modified flag of the document class to TRUE.
pDoc->SetModifiedFlag();

//////////////////////
// MY CODE ENDS HERE
//////////////////////

}
```

Now attach code to the EN_CHANGE event of the IDC_REF edit box:

☐ Display the ClassWizard dialog box by selecting ClassWizard from the Project menu of Visual C++.

☐ Select the Message Maps tab at the top of ClassWizard's dialog box.

☐ Use ClassWizard to select the event:

```
CMemoView -> IDC_REF -> EN_CHANGE
```

Then click the Add Function button.

☐ Name the new function OnChangeRef().

☐ Click the Edit Code button of ClassWizard.

> *ClassWizard responds by opening the file MemoView.CPP, with the function* OnChangeRef() *ready to be edited by you.*

☐ Write code inside the OnChangeRef() function so that it looks like this:

```
void CMemoView::OnChangeRef()
{
// TODO: Add your control notification handler code here


//////////////////////
// MY CODE STARTS HERE
//////////////////////

// Update the variables of the controls.
UpdateData(TRUE);

// Get a pointer to the document.
CMemoDoc* pDoc = GetDocument();

// Update the m_Ref data member of the document class.
pDoc->m_Ref = m_Ref;
```

```
// Set the Modified flag of the document class to TRUE.
pDoc->SetModifiedFlag();

/////////////////////
// MY CODE ENDS HERE
/////////////////////

}
```

☐ Save your work by selecting Save from the File menu.

You have finished attaching code to all the edit boxes of the memo form!

Here's a review of what you have accomplished so far:

- You wrote the code that initializes the data members of the document class.
- You wrote the code that initializes the data members of the view class.
- You wrote the code that updates the data members of the document class whenever the user changes the data members of the view class (that is, whenever the user changes the contents of the edit boxes of the memo form).

Next you will write the code that enables the user to write data to the disk and to read data from the disk.

NOTE

Okay, you have written enough code! To make sure that you typed the correct code, compile and link the application:

☐ Select Build Memo.EXE from the Project menu, and make sure that there are no compiling or linking errors.

Do not execute the application. The only reason that you are instructed to compile and link the program is to verify that you entered the code correctly.

Writing and Reading Data to and from Files

When the user selects Save or Save As from the File menu the application should write the data members of the document class onto a file. When the user selects Open from the File menu the application should read the data from the file that the user selects and assign this data to the data members of the document class.

Accomplishing these tasks is very easy. It's easy because most of the code that accomplishes these tasks was already written by Visual C++.

The document class of the MEMO application (`CMemoDoc`) has a member function called `Serialize()`. The `Serialize()` function of the document class is automatically executed when the user selects Save, Save As, or Open from the File menu. All you have to do is customize the `Serialize()` function for the MEMO application.

The `Serialize()` member function of the `CMemoDoc` class looks like this:

```
void CMemoDoc::Serialize(CArchive& ar)
{
    if (ar.IsStoring())
    {
        // TODO: add storing code here
    }
    else
    {
        // TODO: add loading code here
    }
}
```

As you can see, the code inside the `Serialize()` function consists of a simple `if` statement that checks for the condition:

```
if (ar.IsStoring())
```

In this code, `ar` is the parameter of the `Serialize()` function and it represents the archive (that is, the file) that you are trying to read (or write). If the user selects Save or Save As from the File menu, then the condition of the `if` statement is satisfied and the code under the `if` is executed. If the user selects Open from the File menu, then the condition of the `if` statement is not satisfied, and the code under the `else` is executed.

Therefore, your job is to do the following:

- Write the code that writes data to the file under the `if`
- Write the code that reads the data from the file under the `else`

The code for writing and reading data to/from the file is very easy. Follow these steps to write this code:

☐ Select Open from the File menu of Visual C++ and open the file MEMODOC.CPP.

☐ Locate the `Serialize()` function inside the MEMODOC.CPP file.

☐ Write code inside the `Serialize()` function so that it looks like this:

```
void CMemoDoc::Serialize(CArchive& ar)
{
    if (ar.IsStoring())
    {
        // TODO: add storing code here

        //////////////////////////
        // MY CODE STARTS HERE
        //////////////////////////

        // Write to the file.
        ar << m_Date;
        ar << m_Ref;
        ar << m_Memo;
```

```
/////////////////////
// MY CODE ENDS HERE
/////////////////////

    }
    else
    {
        // TODO: add loading code here

        /////////////////////////
        // MY CODE STARTS HERE
        /////////////////////////

        // Read from the file.
        ar >> m_Date;
        ar >> m_Ref;
        ar >> m_Memo;

        /////////////////////
        // MY CODE ENDS HERE
        /////////////////////

    }
}
```

☐ Save your work by selecting Save from the File menu.

Now go over the code you just typed inside the `Serialize()` function:

The code that is responsible for saving the data into the file (the code under the `if`) is this:

```
ar << m_Date;
ar << m_Ref;
ar << m_Memo;
```

The insertion operator (`<<`) indicates that you want to save data into the file. For example, the statement

```
ar << m_Date;
```

stores the data member `m_Date` of the document class into the file. Into what file? It depends on what the user did. As mentioned earlier, the `Serialize()` member function of the document class is executed automatically whenever the user selects Open, Save, or Save As from the File menu. If, for example, the user selects Save As, and then the user selects the file TRY.MEM (from the Save As dialog box), then the statement `ar << m_Date;` will store the `m_Date` variable inside the TRY.MEM file. (So think of `ar` as the file that the user selected.)

NOTE

`ar` is the archive object (an object of class `CArchive`) that corresponds to the file that the user selected. The `CArchive` class is discussed in greater detail in Chapter 15, "Customizing Serialization."

The code that is responsible for loading the data from the file into the variables (the code under the `else`) is this:

```
ar >> m_Date;
ar >> m_Ref;
ar >> m_Memo;
```

The extractor operator (>>) indicates that you want to load data from the file into the variable. For example, the statement

```
ar >> m_Date;
```

fills the data member `m_Date` of the document class with data from the file. From what file? Again, it depends on what the user did. If, for example, the user selects Open from the File menu, and then the user selects the file TRY.MEM (from the Open File dialog box), then the statement `ar >> m_Date;` will fill the `m_Date` variable with data from the TRY.MEM file.

Note that the order in which you extract the data must be the same order used for saving the data. For example, if you save data to the file with these statements:

```
ar << Var1;
ar << Var2;
ar << Var3;
```

then when you extract the data from the file into the variables you must use the same order:

```
ar >> Var1;
ar >> Var2;
ar >> var3;
```

NOTE

In the previous code you used the insertion (<<) and extractor (>>) operators on several lines. You also can use these operators on a single line. For example, these three statements:

```
ar << Var1;
ar << Var2;
ar << Var3;
```

are equivalent to this single statement:

```
ar << Var1 << Var2 << Var3;
```

Similarly, these three statements:

```
ar >> Var1;
ar >> Var2;
ar >> Var3;
```

are equivalent to this single statement:

```
ar >> Var1 >> Var2 >> Var3;
```

Executing the MEMO Application

You have finished writing the code for the MEMO application! To see your code in action do the following:

☐ Select Build Memo.EXE from the Project menu.

☐ Select Execute Memo.EXE from the Project menu.

> *Visual C++ responds by executing the Memo.EXE application. The main window of the application appears with a new memo form—the Date field is filled with the current date and time and the Ref and Memo fields are blank. The title of the window is Untitled—Memo.*

☐ Fill the memo form with data.

☐ Select Save from the File menu and save your memo as TRY.MEM.

> *The MEMO application responds by saving your memo into the file TRY.MEM, and by changing the title of the window to this:*

```
try.mem—Memo
```

Experiment with all the other menu items of the File menu. As you can see, all the File menu items behave as you would expect them to behave in a standard SDI Windows application. For example, if you modify the memo form, and you try to exit from the application without saving the memo, the application will prompt you with a warning message. Recall that you did not have to write the code that displays this warning message. All you had to do was use the `SetModifiedFlag()` function to ensure that the Modified flag of the document class would be set to TRUE whenever the user made changes to the form.

Also note that the File menu maintains a most recently used file list. (See Figure 13.19.) The MRU list in the File menu lists the files that the user worked with most recently. When the user clicks one of the files in the MRU list, the file is opened. Again, you did not have to write any code for this very useful feature. Note that the application stores the names of the most recently used files in the INI file of the application, which resides in your Windows directory (that is, C:\WINDOWS\MEMO.INI).

The MRU list of the MEMO application lists the most recent four files that the user worked on. Why four? Recall that when you created the skeleton of the application with AppWizard, in the AppWizard—Step 4 of 6 window you accepted the default setting of 4 for the How many files would you like remembered on your MRU list? edit box. (Refer back to Figure 13.11.)

☐ Terminate the MEMO application by selecting Exit from the File menu.

Figure 13.19. The File menu with a most recently used file list.

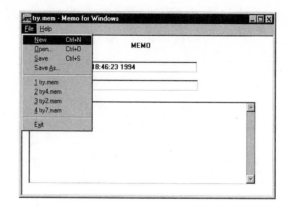

Enhancing the MEMO application

You will now enhance the MEMO application, in two ways:

- Change the caption that appears in the title of the application's window from Memo to Memo for Windows.

- Change the default file type that is displayed inside the Save As and Open dialog boxes from *.* to *.MEM. This means that whenever the user selects Open or Save As from the dialog box, the default files that will be displayed inside the File list box will have a .MEM file extension.

Complete the following steps to implement these enhancements:

☐ Select memo.rc from the Window menu of Visual C++.

Visual C++ responds by displaying the memo.rc window.

☐ Double-click String Table inside the memo.rc window.

Visual C++ responds by displaying the String Table dialog box. (See Figure 13.20.)

As implied by its name, the String Table dialog box lets you view and edit various strings that are used by the application.

As you can see from Figure 13.20, the string whose ID is IDR_MAINFRAME is currently highlighted, and the current value of this string is this:

Memo\n\nMemo\n\n\nMemo.Document.1\nMemo Document

Figure 13.20. The String Table dialog box.

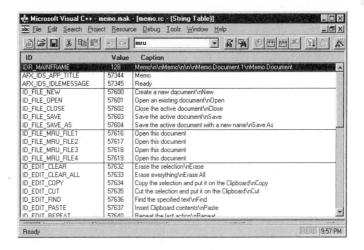

The \n in the string serves as a separator between substrings. Therefore, the preceding string is made of the following seven substrings:

```
Memo
Null
Memo
Null
Null
Memo.Document.1
Memo Document
```

The substrings that are currently of interest are the first, fourth, and fifth substrings.

The first substring specifies the title that appears in the application's main window. Recall that your objective is to make the application's main window title this:

`Memo for Windows`

Therefore, you need to change the first substring from `Memo` to `Memo for Windows`.

The fourth and fifth substrings specify the default document type that is displayed in the Save As dialog box and Open File dialog box of the application. For example, if you set the fourth substring to this:

`MEM Files (*.mem)`

and the fifth substring to this:

`.mem`

then when the user selects Save As or Open from the File menu, the files that will be listed inside the File list box will be files with this extension:

```
.mem
```

and the text that will appear inside the File Type box will be this:

```
MEM Files (*.mem)
```

Figure 13.21 shows the Save As dialog box, listing files with extension .mem. The text MEM Files (*.mem) appears inside the File Type box.

Figure 13.21. The Save As dialog box, listing files with .mem extension.

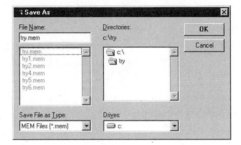

You'll now change the IDR_MAINFRAME string so that the first substring will be Memo for Windows, the fourth substring will be MEM Files (*.mem), and the fifth substring will be .mem. All the rest of the substrings will remain as they are now. Here is how you do that:

☐ Double-click on the IDR_MAINFRAME string.

> *Visual C++ responds by displaying the String Properties window for the IDR_MAINFRAME string. (See Figure 13.22.)*

Figure 13.22. The String Properties window for the IDR_MAINFRAME string.

The value of the string is displayed inside the Caption box.

☐ Change the value of the string to this:

```
Memo for Windows\n\nMemo\nMEM Files (*.mem)\n.mem\nMemo.Document.1\nMemo Document
```

> **NOTE**
>
> This text should be typed on a single line (that is, you should not press the Enter key).
> Visual C++ will wrap the line when the line is too long.

Your String Properties window for the IDR_MAINFRAME string should now look like the one shown in Figure 13.23.

Figure 13.23. The String Properties window, with a new string value.

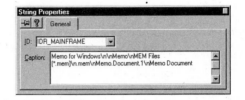

☐ Save your work by selecting Save from the File menu of Visual C++.

Executing the Final Version of the MEMO Application

The MEMO application is now complete!

To see the effects of the modification that you made to the IDR_MAINFRAME string do the following:

☐ Select Build Memo.EXE from the Project menu.

☐ Select Execute Memo.EXE from the Project menu.

Now the main window of the application appears with the title Untitled—Memo for Windows.

☐ Fill the memo form with data.

☐ Select Save from the File menu.

> *The MEMO application responds by displaying a Save As dialog box. Now the Save As dialog box lists files with .mem extension.*

☐ Save your memo form as: TRY.MEM.

> *The MEMO application responds by saving the memo form onto the file TRY.MEM and by changing the title of the application window to try.mem—Memo for Windows.*

You have enhanced the MEMO application significantly by simply customizing the IDR_MAINFRAME string.

Serializing Different Types of Data Members

In the MEMO application you serialized `CString` data members of the document class. That is, the code of the MEMO application writes and reads `CString` data members of the document class (for example, m_Memo) to and from the files by utilizing the `Serialize()` function of the document class.

Can you serialize other types of variables? Yes, you can!

However, you should know that an `int` variable cannot be serialized. So whenever you need to serialize integers, serialize a `long` type instead.

If you try to serialize an integer, as in the following:

```
ar << m_MyInteger;
```

where `m_MyInteger` is an integer, you will get a compiling error:

```
'operator <<' is ambiguous
```

Final Words...

In this chapter you wrote an SDI application called Memo.EXE that behaves like a standard Windows SDI application. It lets the user view and edit data as well as store the data in files and load the data from files.

Here is a summary of the steps you took in implementing the MEMO application:

- You used AppWizard to create the skeleton of a single-document application. You asked AppWizard to derive the view class of the application from the MFC class `CFormView`. Therefore, AppWizard created for you a form (dialog box) called IDD_MEMO_FORM and connected this dialog box to the view class of the application. The dialog box that AppWizard created for you serves as the main window of the application.

- You customized the IDD_MEMO_FORM dialog box that AppWizard created so that it would look like a memo form. You placed three edit boxes in the dialog box: IDC_DATE, IDC_REF, and IDC_MEMO.

- You attached three `CString` variables to the edit boxes of the IDD_MEMO_FORM dialog box: m_Date, m_Ref, and m_Memo. These variables are data members of the view class (because the IDD_MEMO_FORM dialog box is connected to the view class).

- You customized the menu bar IDR_MAINFRAME that AppWizard created for you. This was easy—all you had to do was remove the Edit pop-up menu. The other two pop-up menus that AppWizard created for you, the File and Help pop-up menus, did not require modification.

- You added three `CString` data members to the document class of the application. You gave these data members the same names as the names of the view class data members: m_Date, m_Ref, and m_Memo.

- You wrote the code that initializes the data members of the document class. You wrote this code inside the OnNewDocument() member function of the document class. This member function is automatically executed whenever a new document is created (when either the application begins or the user selects New from the File menu).

- You wrote the code that initializes the data members of the view class. You wrote this code inside the OnInitialUpdate() member function of the view class. The OnInitialUpdate() member function of the view class is executed automatically upon start-up of the application, when the user selects New from the File menu, and when the user selects Open from the File menu. The code you wrote inside the OnInitialUpdate() function updates the data members of the view class with the current values of the data members of the document class. Therefore, whenever the user starts the application, creates a new memo file, or opens an existing memo file, the data members of the view class are updated with data members of the document class.

- You wrote the code that updates the data members of the document class whenever the user edits the data members of the view class. That is, you attached code to the EN_CHANGE events of the three edit boxes inside the memo form so that whenever the user types something inside any of the edit boxes, the corresponding data member of the document class is updated with the new data. For example, when the user types something inside the IDC_DATE edit box, the code that you attached to the EN_CHANGE event of the IDC_DATE edit box updates the m_Date data member of the document class with the new value of the m_Date data member of the view class.

- You wrote the code that is responsible for writing and reading the data of the application (that is, the data members of the document class) to and from files. You wrote this code inside the Serialize() function of the document class.

- The last thing you did for the MEMO application is customize the IDR_MAINFRAME string of the application. You changed the title that appears inside the application's main window and you changed the type of files that are listed inside the Save As and Open File dialog boxes of the application by simply customizing the IDR_MAINFRAME string.

14

Writing and Reading Lists (with Serialization) to and from Files

In Chapter 13, "Writing and Reading Data (with Serialization) to and from Files," you learned how to serialize data members of the document class. That is, you learned how to write and read data members of the document class to and from files by utilizing the `Serialize()` function of the document class.

In this chapter you will learn how to serialize *lists*. First you will learn how to create and maintain a list of objects, and then you will learn how to serialize the list (that is, how to read and write the list to and from files).

> **NOTE**
>
> This chapter is not a typical chapter, because it requires you to type a substantial amount of code before you see any action. Therefore, you'll be instructed throughout the tutorial to compile and link (but not to execute) the application. The sole purpose of this compiling and linking is to verify that you entered the code without typographic errors.
>
> Although this chapter is more complex than other chapters in this book, it's worth your efforts, because maintaining a list of objects is a powerful and useful feature that can be incorporated into serious Windows applications.
>
> You can use the steps presented in this chapter (for maintaining a list of objects) as a framework for your future projects.

The PHN Application

You'll now write the PHN application. The PHN application is an example of an application that reads and writes a list of objects to and from files by using serialization—it enables the user to maintain a list of phone numbers of different people.

Before you start writing the PHN application, first execute the copy of it that resides in the \MVCPROG\EXE directory of the book's CD.

☐ Execute the \MVCPROG\EXE\PHN.EXE application that resides on the book's CD.

Windows responds by executing the PHN application. The main window of PHN.EXE appears, as shown in Figure 14.1.

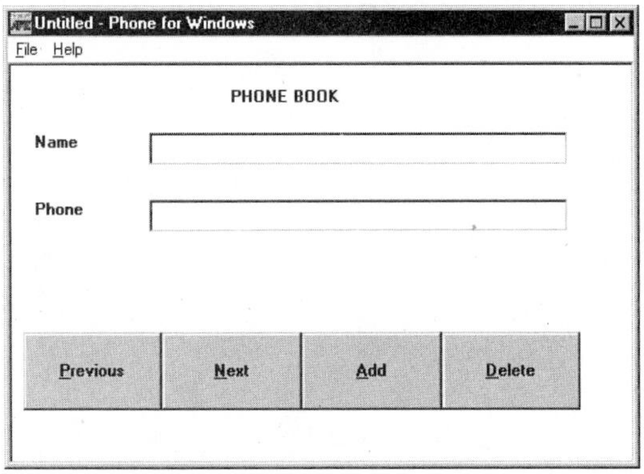

Figure 14.1. The main window of the PHN application.

As you can see from Figure 14.1, the main window of the application displays a blank record of a phone entry form, ready to be edited by you.

The PHN application has two pop-up menus: File and Help. These pop-up menus are shown in Figures 14.2 and 14.3.

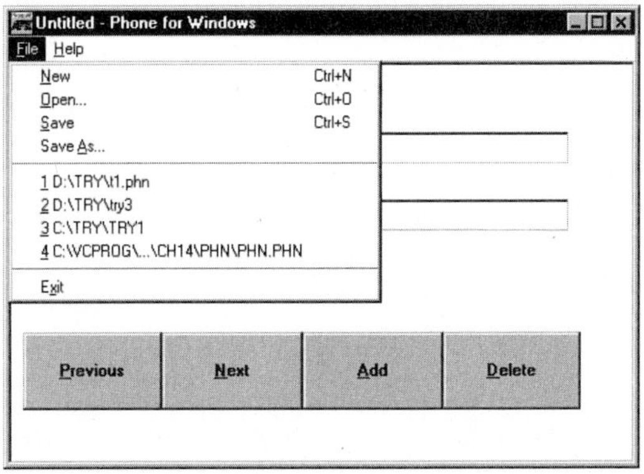

Figure 14.2. The File pop-up menu of the PHN application.

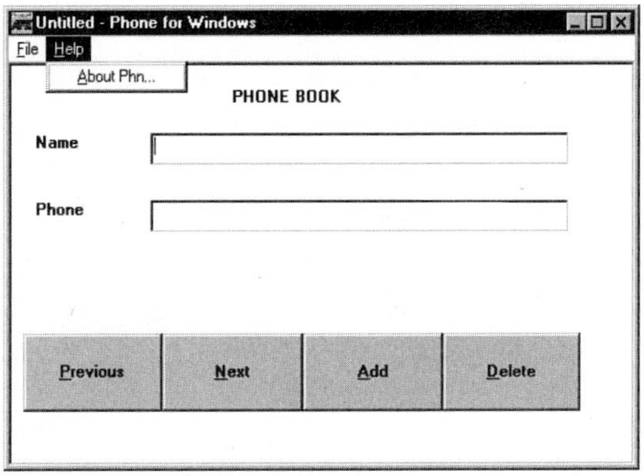

Figure 14.3. The Help pop-up menu of the PHN application.

Fill the Name and Phone fields of the blank phone entry form. Figure 14.4 shows the phone entry form after it is filled.

☐ Click the Add button of the Phone entry form.

  The PHN application responds by adding a new blank record.

☐ Fill the Name and Phone fields of the new record with new data.

☐ Repeat the previous steps to add several other records.

You can now experiment with the other buttons of the PHN application:

☐ Experiment with the Next and Previous buttons to navigate between the records that you added.

As you can see, when you click the Next button the next record is displayed, and when you click the Previous button the previous record is displayed.

☐ Experiment with the Delete button. Use the Next and Previous buttons to display any record, and then click the Delete button.

> *The PHN application responds by deleting the record that you displayed.*

To save the list of phone numbers that you entered into a file do the following:

☐ Select Save from the File menu.

> *The PHN application responds by displaying the File Save As dialog box.*

☐ Save your phone list as PHONE1.PHN on your C: or D: drive.

> *The PHN application responds by saving your phone list into the file PHONE1.PHN, and by changing the title of the application window to Phone for Windows—PHONE1.PHN.*

☐ Experiment with the other menu items in the File menu (New, Open, and Save As).

As you can see, all the File menu items behave as you would expect them to behave in a standard Windows application.

To exit the PHN application do the following:

☐ Select Exit from the File menu.

Now that you know what the PHN application should do, you can begin to write it.

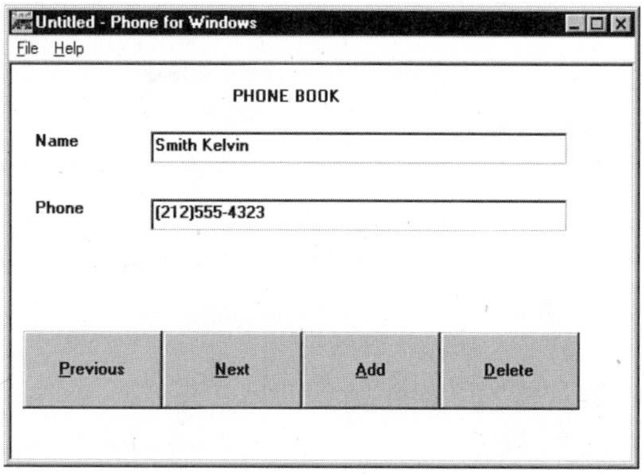

Figure 14.4. A completed phone entry form.

Creating the Project of the PHN Application

To create the project of the PHN application do the following:

☐ Start Visual C++ and close all the open windows that appear inside the desktop of Visual C++ (if there are any).

☐ Select New from the File menu.

> *Visual C++ responds by displaying the New dialog box.*

☐ Select Project inside the New dialog box and then click the OK button of the New dialog box.

> *Visual C++ responds by displaying the New Project dialog box.*

☐ Set the project name to PHN.

☐ Set the project path to \MVCPROG\CH14\PHN\PHN.MAK.

Your New Project dialog box should now look like the one shown in Figure 14.5.

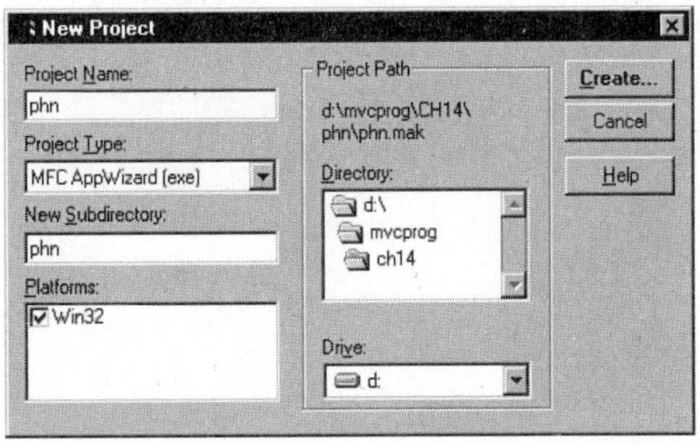

Figure 14.5. The New Project dialog box of the Phn.MAK project.

☐ Click the Create button of the New Project dialog box.

> *Visual C++ responds by displaying the AppWizard—Step 1 window.*

☐ Set the Step 1 window as shown in Figure 14.6. As shown in Figure 14.6, the Phn.MAK project is set as a single-document interface application, and U.S. English (APPWIZUS.DLL) is used as the language for the application's resources.

☐ Click the Next button of the Step 1 window.

> *Visual C++ responds by displaying the AppWizard—Step 2 of 6 window.*

☐ Set the Step 2 of 6 window as shown in Figure 14.7. That is, in the PHN application you don't want any database support.

Figure 14.6. The AppWizard—Step 1 window for the PHN application.

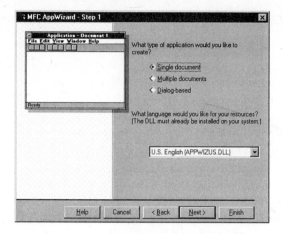

Figure 14.7. The AppWizard—Step 2 of 6 window for the PHN application.

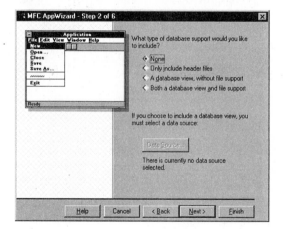

☐ Click the Next button of the Step 2 of 6 window.

 Visual C++ responds by displaying the AppWizard—Step 3 of 6 window.

☐ Set the Step 3 of 6 window as shown in Figure 14.8. That is, in the PHN application you don't want any OLE support.

☐ Click the Next button of the Step 3 of 6 window.

 Visual C++ responds by displaying the AppWizard—Step 4 of 6 window.

☐ Set the Step 4 of 6 window as shown in Figure 14.9.

*Figure 14.8. The
AppWizard—Step 3 of 6
window for the PHN
application.*

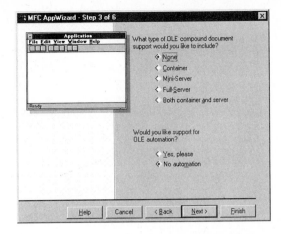

*Figure 14.9. The
AppWizard—Step 4 of 6
window for the PHN
application.*

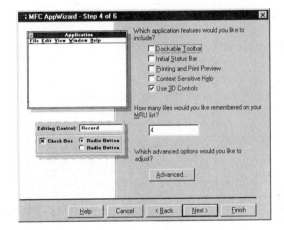

As shown in Figure 14.9, the features Dockable Toolbar, Initial Status Bar, Printing and Print Preview, and Context Sensitive Help will not be included in the PHN application.

☐ Click the Next button of the Step 4 of 6 window.

   Visual C++ responds by displaying the AppWizard—Step 5 of 6 window.

☐ Set the Step 5 of 6 window as shown in Figure 14.10.

As shown in Figure 14.10, the project will be generated with comments, a Visual C++ makefile will be generated, and the application will use the MFC library from a DLL.

☐ Click the Next button of the Step 5 of 6 window.

   Visual C++ responds by displaying the AppWizard—Step 6 of 6 window.

You'll now use the AppWizard—Step 6 of 6 window to tell AppWizard to derive the view class of the application from the MFC class CFormView:

☐ Select the CPhnView class inside the AppWizard—Step 6 of 6 window.

☐ Set the Base Class drop-down list box to CFormView.

Your AppWizard—Step 6 of 6 window should now look like the one shown in Figure 14.11.

Figure 14.10. The AppWizard—Step 5 of 6 window for the PHN application.

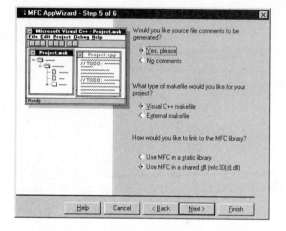

Figure 14.11. The AppWizard—Step 6 of 6 window after you set the base class of the application view class to CFormView.

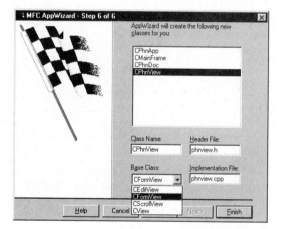

NOTE

As you can see from Figure 14.1, the main window of the PHN program does have controls inside it. Therefore, there is a need to derive the view class of the application from the CFormView class.

☐ Click the Finish button of the Step 6 of 6 window.

Visual C++ responds by displaying the New Project Information window, as shown in Figure 14.12.

Figure 14.12. The New Project Information window of the Phn.MAK project.

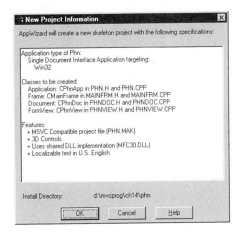

☐ Click the OK button of the New Project Information window.

Visual C++ responds by creating the project file and all the skeleton files of the application.

Designing the Form of the Application

As shown in Figure 14.1, the main window of the PHN application should contain a data entry form for entering a name and a phone number. You'll now visually implement this data entry form.

☐ Double-click the phn.mak item in the Window menu to display the phn.mak window, double-click the phn.rc item inside the phn.mak window to display the phn.rc window, double-click the Dialog item that appears inside the phn.rc window to display the list of dialog boxes, and finally, double-click the IDD_PHN_FORM item that appears under the Dialog item. Visual C++ prepared the IDD_PHN_FORM dialog box for you because in the Step 6 of 6 window you set the base class to `CFormView`. This dialog box serves as the main window of the application.

Visual C++ responds by displaying the IDD_PHN_FORM dialog box in design mode. (See Figure 14.13.) The IDD_PHN_FORM dialog box serves as the main window of the PHN application.

☐ Highlight the static text `TODO: Place form controls on this dialog.` and press the Delete button on your keyboard.

Visual C++ responds by deleting the `TODO` static text.

☐ Drag the handles of the IDD_PHN_FORM dialog box to enlarge its area horizontally and vertically.

Figure 14.13. The IDD_PHN_FORM dialog box before you customize it.

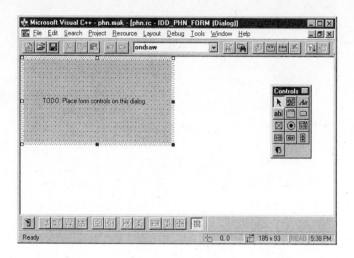

☐ Design the IDD_PHN_FORM dialog box according to the specifications in Table 14.1. When you finish implementing the dialog box, it should look like the one shown in Figure 14.14.

Table 14.1. The Properties table of the dialog box of the PHN application.

Object	Property	Setting
Dialog box	ID	IDD_PHN_FORM
Static label	ID	IDC_STATIC
	Caption	PHONE BOOK
Static label	ID	IDC_STATIC
	Caption	Name
Edit box	ID	IDC_NAME
Static label	ID	IDC_STATIC
	Caption	Phone
Edit box	ID	IDC_PHONE
Push button	ID	IDC_PREVIOUS_BUTTON
	Caption	&Previous
Push button	ID	IDC_NEXT_BUTTON
	Caption	&Next
Push button	ID	IDC_ADD_BUTTON
	Caption	&Add
Push button	ID	IDC_DELETE_BUTTON
	Caption	&Delete

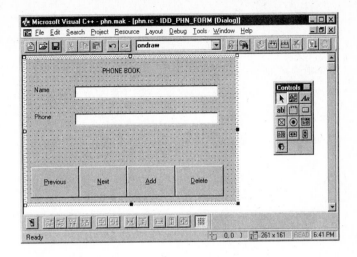

Figure 14.14. The dialog box of the PHN application.

Save your work:

☐ Select Save from the File menu.

Attaching Variables to the Controls of the IDD_PHN_FORM Dialog Box

You'll now attach variables to the edit boxes of the IDD_PHN_FORM dialog box.

☐ Use ClassWizard to attach variables to the controls of the IDD_PHN_FORM dialog box, as specified in Table 14.2.

Table 14.2. The Variables table of the IDD_PHN_FORM dialog box.

Control ID	Variable Name	Category	Variable Type
IDC_NAME	m_Name	Value	CString
IDC_PHONE	m_Phone	Value	CString

The Visual Implementation of the Menu

The PHN application should have a menu, as shown in Figures 14.1, 14.2, and 14.3.

Implementing this menu is easy, because all you have to do is delete the Edit pop-up menu. The File and Help pop-up menus that App Wizard generated for you are exactly what you need for the PHN application.

☐ Select phn.mak from the Window menu to display the phn.mak window, double-click the phn.rc item to display the phn.rc window, double-click the Menu item inside the phn.rc window, and finally, double-click the IDR_MAINFORM item that appears under the Menu item.

> *Visual C++ responds by displaying the IDR_MAINFRAME menu in design mode.*

☐ Delete the Edit menu.

To save your work do the following:

☐ Select Save from the File menu.

The visual implementation of the menu of the PHN application is complete.

Executing the PHN Application

Although you have not yet finished writing the PHN application, execute it to see what you have accomplished so far:

☐ Select Rebuild All PHN.EXE from the Project menu of Visual C++.

> *Visual C++ responds by compiling and linking the PHN application.*

☐ Select Execute PHN.EXE from the Project menu.

> *Visual C++ responds by executing the PHN application. As you can see, the dialog box that you designed appears as the main window of the application.*

Of course, none of the buttons in the dialog box are working because you haven't yet written any code. In the following sections you will write the code of the PHN application.

To exit the PHN application do the following:

☐ Select Exit from the File menu.

Declaring the Phone Class

The PHN application needs to store a list of names and phone numbers. Therefore, you need to create a class that will be used to store a person's name and a phone number. You will name this class CPhone, and you'll declare it with two data members: m_Name and m_Phone. Both of these data members will be defined as CString types.

You will define the CPhone class as a derived class from the MFC class CObject. Why is this necessary? It's necessary because later in this chapter you will write code that serializes the data members of the CPhone class—and in order to serialize a class, the class must be a derived class from the MFC CObject class.

In the following steps you'll create the CPhone class. You will create two new files: PHONE.H and PHONE.CPP. You'll declare the CPhone class inside PHONE.H, and you'll write the functions of the CPhone class (for example, the constructor function of the CPhone class) inside PHONE.CPP.

To create the PHONE.H file do the following:

☐ Select New from the File menu of Visual C++ and then select Code/Text from the New
dialog box that Visual C++ displays (because you are now creating a new text file).

> *Visual C++ responds by opening a new file.*

☐ Type the following code inside the new file:

```
/////////////////////
// MY CODE STARTS HERE
/////////////////////

// PHONE.H
//
// Header file for the CPhone class.


// CPhone class declaration.
class CPhone : public CObject
{

public:

    // Constructor
    CPhone();

    // Data members
    CString m_Name;
    CString m_Phone;
};

/////////////////////
// MY CODE ENDS HERE
/////////////////////
```

☐ Select Save As from the File menu and save the file as PHONE.H in the
C:\MVCPROG\CH14\PHN directory.

Note that the constructor function of the CPhone class is declared without any arguments. That's
because later you want to be able to serialize the CPhone class, and one of the constructor functions
of a serializeable class must be declared with no arguments. Of course, if you want you can add to
the class more constructor functions that take parameters (overload functions).

To create PHONE.CPP do the following:

☐ Select New from the File menu of Visual C++ and then select Code/Text from the New
dialog box that Visual C++ displays (because you are now creating a new text file).

> *Visual C++ responds by opening a new file.*

☐ Type the following code inside the new file:

```
/////////////////////
// MY CODE STARTS HERE
/////////////////////
```

```
// PHONE.CPP
//
// Implementation file of the CPhone class.

#include "stdafx.h"
#include "phone.h"

// Constructor.
CPhone::CPhone()
 {
    m_Name  = "";
    m_Phone = "";
 }

/////////////////////////
// MY CODE ENDS HERE
/////////////////////////
```

☐ Select Save As from the File menu and save the file as PHONE.CPP in the C:\MVCPROG\CH14\PHN directory.

Here's a summary of what you did in the preceding steps:

- You created a class CPhone with two CString data members: m_Name and m_Phone.

- You declared the CPhone class as a derived class from the MFC CObject class. This is necessary because you want to be able to serialize the CPhone class, and therefore CPhone must be derived from CObject.

- You declared the constructor function of the CPhone class with no arguments. This is necessary because you want to be able to serialize the CPhone class, and a serializeable class must have a constructor function that has no arguments. As stated earlier, if you wish you can add to the CPhone class additional constructor functions that have arguments.

Adding the PHONE.CPP File to the PHN Project

In the previous steps you created two new files, PHONE.H and PHONE.CPP. The PHONE.CPP file must be included in the project of the application (PHN.MAK) so that Visual C++ will compile PHONE.CPP without errors.

Follow these steps to add PHONE.CPP into the PHN.MAK project:

☐ Select Files from the Project menu.

Visual C++ responds by displaying the Project Files dialog box. (See Figure 14.15.)

The list at the bottom of the dialog box (the Files in Group list) contains all the files that are currently included in the PHN.MAK project.

To add the PHONE.CPP file to the list do the following:

☐ Select the \MVCPROG\CH14\PHN\PHONE.CPP file and then click the Add button.

Visual C++ responds by adding the PHONE.CPP file to the Files in Group list. Your Project Files dialog box should now look like the one shown in Figure 14.16.

Figure 14.15. The Project Files dialog box.

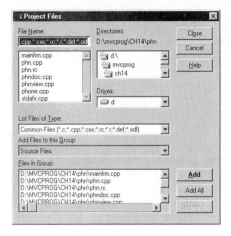

Figure 14.16. The Project Files dialog box after you add the Phone.CPP file to the project.

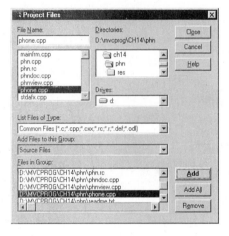

☐ Click the Close button of the dialog box.

Visual C++ responds by adding PHONE.CPP to the project.

NOTE

Okay, you have written enough code! To make sure that you typed the code correctly, compile and link the application:

☐ Select Rebuild All PHN.EXE from the Project menu, and make sure that there are no compiling and linking errors.

Do not execute the application. The only reason that you are instructed to compile and link the program is to verify that you entered the code correctly.

The Document Class of the PHN Application

As you know, the document class of the application should hold the data of the application. The question is What is the data of the PHN application? Recall that the PHN application should maintain a list of names and phone numbers. You already defined the CPhone class with two data members: m_Name and m_Phone. So now you can declare a list of objects of class CPhone. Each object in this list will store the name and phone number of a particular person. You will declare this list as a data member of the document class.

The MFC *CObList* Class

The MFC CObList class is a very useful and powerful class that enables you to maintain a list of objects with great ease. After you declare an object of class CObList, you can use member functions of the CObList class to maintain a list of objects (for example, add objects to the list, delete objects from the list, and so on).

In the PHN application you will create an object of class CObList to maintain a list of CPhone objects. You will name this list m_PhoneList and you will make m_PhoneList a data member of the document class. Therefore, the document class of the application will store a list of names and phone numbers.

Follow these steps to declare m_PhoneList as a data member of the document class:

☐ Open the file PHNDOC.H, and add to the CPhnDoc class declaration the m_PhoneList data member. Declare m_PhoneList as an object of class CObList, and make it a public data member of CPhnDoc. After you write this declaration, the CPhnDoc class declaration should look like this:

```
// phndoc.h : interface of the CPhnDoc class
//
/////////////////////////////////////////////////

class CPhnDoc : public CDocument
{
protected: // create from serialization only
CPhnDoc();
DECLARE_DYNCREATE(CPhnDoc)

// Attributes
public:


        /////////////////////////
        // MY CODE STARTS HERE
        /////////////////////////

        CObList m_PhoneList;

        /////////////////////////
        // MY CODE ENDS HERE
        /////////////////////////
```

```
// Operations
public:

// Overrides
// ClassWizard generated virtual function overrides
//{{AFX_VIRTUAL(CPhnDoc)
public:
virtual BOOL OnNewDocument();
//}}AFX_VIRTUAL

// Implementation
public:
virtual ~CPhnDoc();
virtual void Serialize(CArchive& ar);    // overridden for document i/o
#ifdef _DEBUG
virtual void AssertValid() const;
virtual void Dump(CDumpContext& dc) const;
#endif

protected:

// Generated message map functions
protected:
//{{AFX_MSG(CPhnDoc)
// NOTE—the ClassWizard will add and remove member functions here.
//    DO NOT EDIT what you see in these blocks
//    of generated code !
//}}AFX_MSG
DECLARE_MESSAGE_MAP()
};
```

///

Note that m_PhoneList is declared as a public data member (that is, it is declared below the public: keyword) because as you will see later in the chapter, the view class needs to have access to m_PhoneList. Alternatively, you can declare m_PhoneList as private, but then you will need to write a public access function (for example, GetPhoneList()) that will return the address of m_PhoneList.

Save your work:

☐ Select Save from the File menu of Visual C++.

You've finished declaring the data member of the document class. Next, you will initialize this data member.

Initializing the Data Member of the Document Class

In the previous steps you added the data member m_PhoneList to the document class. You declared m_PhoneList as an object of class CObList. Therefore, m_PhoneList can store a list of objects. At this point m_PhoneList is empty (that is, it does not have any objects inside it).

As you learned in Chapter 13, a good place to initialize the data members of the document class is inside the OnNewDocument() member function of the document class. That's because OnNewDocument()

is automatically executed whenever a new document is created (either when the application begins or whenever the user selects New from the File menu).

☐ Open the file PHNDOC.CPP and edit the `OnNewDocument()` function. After you edit this function, your `OnNewDocument()` function should look like this:

```
BOOL CPhnDoc::OnNewDocument()
{
if (!CDocument::OnNewDocument())
return FALSE;

// TODO: add reinitialization code here
// (SDI documents will reuse this document)


    /////////////////////////
    // MY CODE STARTS HERE
    /////////////////////////

    // Create an object of class CPhone.
    CPhone* pPhone  = new CPhone();
    pPhone->m_Name  = "";
    pPhone->m_Phone = "";

    // Add the new object to the m_PhoneList list.
    m_PhoneList.AddHead(pPhone);

    /////////////////////////
    // MY CODE ENDS HERE
    /////////////////////////

return TRUE;
}
```

Now go over the code that you just entered inside the `OnNewDocument()` function.

The first statement

```
CPhone* pPhone  = new CPhone();
```

creates an object of class CPhone and assigns the address of this object to the pPhone pointer. So pPhone contains the address of the new CPhone object.

The next two statements assign null values to the data members of the pPhone object:

```
pPhone->m_Name  = "";
pPhone->m_Phone = "";
```

Note that these statements are not really necessary because the constructor function of the CPhone class already assigned null values to the m_Name and m_Phone data members. However, you write these statements anyway to make the code easier to read (that is, you emphasize the fact that now m_Name and m_Phone are blank).

The last statement in the `OnNewDocument()` function is

```
m_PhoneList.AddHead(pPhone);
```

This statement uses the AddHead() member function of the CObList class to add the new CPhone object that you created to the m_PhoneList list. Therefore, whenever a new document is created (for example, upon start-up of the application), a blank CPhone object is added to the m_PhoneList list.

> **NOTE**
>
> The AddHead() member function of the CObList class adds an object to the "head" (that is, to the beginning) of the list.
>
> Pass to this function the address of the object that you want to add to the list. Here is an example:
>
> ```
> MyList.AddHead(pMyObject);
> ```

If you try to compile the PHNDOC.CPP file now, you will get a compiling error. Why? In the preceding code you referred to the CPhone class, but the CPhone class is not known in the PHNDOC.CPP file. Therefore, you must use #include on the PHONE.H file (the header file of the CPhone class) at the beginning of the PHNDOC.CPP file:

☐ Add the #include "phone.h" statement at the beginning of the PHNDOC.CPP file (immediately before the #include statement of the phndoc.h file). After you add this #include statement, the beginning of the PHNDOC.CPP file should look like this:

```
// phndoc.cpp : implementation of the CPhnDoc class
//

#include "stdafx.h"
#include "phn.h"


/////////////////////////
// MY CODE STARTS HERE
/////////////////////////

#include "phone.h"

/////////////////////////
// MY CODE ENDS HERE
/////////////////////////

#include "phndoc.h"
.......
.......
.......
```

Save your work:

☐ Select Save from the File menu of Visual C++.

NOTE

To make sure that you typed the code correctly, compile and link the application:

☐ Select Build PHN.EXE from the Project menu, and make sure that there are no compiling and linking errors.

Do not execute the application. The only reason that you are instructed to compile and link the program is to verify that you entered the code correctly.

Deleting the Objects of the *m_PhoneList* List

You need to delete (from memory) the objects that are listed in the m_PhoneList list whenever any of the following three events takes place:

- The user exits the application.
- The user starts a new document (that is, the user selects New from the File menu).
- The user opens an existing document (that is, the user selects Open from the File menu).

The DeleteContents() member function of the document class is automatically executed whenever any of these three events takes place. Therefore, a good place to write the code that deletes the objects that are listed inside the m_PhoneList list is inside the DeleteContents() function.

Visual C++ did not write for you the declaration and skeleton of the DeleteContents() function. You have to declare this function and write the skeleton of this function yourself. Here is how you do that:

☐ Open the file PHNDOC.H and add code to it that defines the function DeleteContents() as a member function of the CPhnDoc class. After you write this code, the CPhnDoc class declaration should look like this:

NOTE

In the following listing, there are two sections that look like this:

```
/////////////////////
MY CODE STARTS HERE
/////////////////////
. . . . . .
. . . . . .
. . . . . .
/////////////////////////
MY CODE ENDS HERE
/////////////////////////
```

You already typed the first section. Now just add the second section.

```
class CPhnDoc : public CDocument
{
protected: // create from serialization only
CPhnDoc();
DECLARE_DYNCREATE(CPhnDoc)

// Attributes
public:


    /////////////////////
    // MY CODE STARTS HERE
    /////////////////////

    CObList m_PhoneList;

    /////////////////////
    // MY CODE ENDS HERE
    /////////////////////


// Operations
public:

    /////////////////////
    // MY CODE STARTS HERE
    /////////////////////

    virtual void DeleteContents();

    /////////////////////
    // MY CODE ENDS HERE
    /////////////////////



// Overrides
// ClassWizard generated virtual function overrides
//{{AFX_VIRTUAL(CPhnDoc)
public:
virtual BOOL OnNewDocument();
//}}AFX_VIRTUAL

// Implementation
public:
virtual ~CPhnDoc();
virtual void Serialize(CArchive& ar);
// overridden for document i/o
#ifdef _DEBUG
virtual void AssertValid() const;
virtual void Dump(CDumpContext& dc) const;
#endif

protected:


// Generated message map functions
protected:
//{{AFX_MSG(CPhnDoc)
```

```
// NOTE—the ClassWizard will add and remove
// member functions here.
// DO NOT EDIT what you see in these blocks
// of generated code !
//}}AFX_MSG
DECLARE_MESSAGE_MAP()
};
```

Save your work:

☐ Select Save from the File menu.

Now write the code of the DeleteContents() function:

☐ Open the file PHNDOC.CPP, and add to it (at the end of the file) the DeleteContents() function. After you write this function, the PHNDOC.CPP file should look like this:

```
// phndoc.cpp : implementation of the CPhnDoc class
//

#include "stdafx.h"
#include "phn.h"


/////////////////////////
// MY CODE STARTS HERE
/////////////////////////

#include "phone.h"

/////////////////////////
// MY CODE ENDS HERE
/////////////////////////



#include "phndoc.h"

#ifdef _DEBUG
#undef THIS_FILE
static char BASED_CODE THIS_FILE□ = __FILE__;
#endif

/////////////////////////////////////////////////////
// CPhnDoc

IMPLEMENT_DYNCREATE(CPhnDoc, CDocument)

BEGIN_MESSAGE_MAP(CPhnDoc, CDocument)
//{{AFX_MSG_MAP(CPhnDoc)
// NOTE—the ClassWizard will add and
// remove mapping macros here.
// DO NOT EDIT what you see in these blocks
// of generated code!
//}}AFX_MSG_MAP
END_MESSAGE_MAP()
```

```
/////////////////////
// MY CODE STARTS HERE
/////////////////////


void CPhnDoc::DeleteContents()
{

   // Remove all the items in the list and free the
   // memory occupied by the listed objects.
   while ( !m_PhoneList.IsEmpty() )
        {
        delete m_PhoneList.RemoveHead();
        }
}
```

```
////////////////////
// MY CODE ENDS HERE
////////////////////
```

As you can see, the `DeleteContents()` function uses a `while()` loop to delete all the objects that are listed in the `m_PhoneList` list:

```
while ( !m_PhoneList.IsEmpty() )
     {
     delete m_PhoneList.RemoveHead();
     }
```

The `IsEmpty()` member function of the `CObList` class returns `TRUE` if the list is empty. Therefore, the `while()` condition

```
!m_PhoneList.IsEmpty()
```

is satisfied as long as the list is not empty.

The statement inside the `while()` loop

```
delete m_PhoneList.RemoveHead();
```

does two things:

- It removes the head item (that is, the first item) of the `m_PhoneList` list.
- It frees (deletes) the memory that was occupied by the object that the head item listed.

The `RemoveHead()` member function removes the first item from the list and it returns the address of the removed object.

Therefore, in the preceding statement the `delete` operator deletes the memory that was occupied by the removed object.

Note that the `RemoveHead()` function does more than just remove the head item. It also updates the new locations of the remaining items in the list. That is, item number 2 in the list now becomes item number 1, item number 3 becomes item number 2, and so on.

The View Class of the PHN Application

In the following sections you will write the code of the view class of the PHN application.

Declaring the Data Members of the View Class

So far the view class has two data members: m_Name (the variable of the IDC_NAME edit box) and m_Phone (the variable of the IDC_PHONE edit box). You created these data members during the visual implementation of the application when you designed the form of the application.

Now you'll declare two additional data members: m_pList and m_position.

m_pList will be used to store the address of the m_PhoneList data member of the document class.

m_position will be used to store the element number of the item that is currently displayed. That is, at any given time, the form of the application will display a particular object from the objects that are listed in m_PhoneList, and m_position will point to the item that is currently displayed.

Do the following to declare m_pList and m_position:

☐ Open the file PHNVIEW.H and add code to the class declaration of CPhnView that defines m_pList and m_position as data members. After you write this code, the CPhnView class declaration should look like this:

```
class CPhnView : public CFormView
{
protected: // create from serialization only
CPhnView();
DECLARE_DYNCREATE(CPhnView)

    /////////////////////////
    // MY CODE STARTS HERE
    /////////////////////////

    POSITION m_position; // Current position in DOC list.
    CObList* m_pList;    // Pointer to the DOC list.

    /////////////////////////
    // MY CODE ENDS HERE
    /////////////////////////
```

```
public:
//{{AFX_DATA(CPhnView)
enum { IDD = IDD_PHN_FORM };
CString    m_Name;
CString    m_Phone;
//}}AFX_DATA

// Attributes
public:
CPhnDoc* GetDocument();

// Operations
public:

// Overrides
// ClassWizard generated virtual function overrides
//{{AFX_VIRTUAL(CPhnView)
public:
protected:
virtual void DoDataExchange(CDataExchange* pDX);
// DDX/DDV support
//}}AFX_VIRTUAL

// Implementation
public:
virtual ~CPhnView();
#ifdef _DEBUG
virtual void AssertValid() const;
virtual void Dump(CDumpContext& dc) const;
#endif

protected:

// Generated message map functions
protected:
//{{AFX_MSG(CPhnView)
// NOTE—the ClassWizard will add and
// remove member functions here.
// DO NOT EDIT what you see in these blocks
// of generated code !
//}}AFX_MSG
DECLARE_MESSAGE_MAP()
};
```

Initializing the Data Members of the View Class

Recall from Chapter 13 that you write the code that initializes the data members of the view class inside the OnInitialUpdate() member function of the view class. The OnInitialUpdate() function is executed automatically in the following situations:

- Upon start-up of the application
- When the user selects New from the File menu
- When the user selects Open from the File menu

The code that you write inside the OnInitialUpdate() function should update the m_Name and m_Phone data members of the view class with the values of the object that is at the head position of the list.

☐ Select ClassWizard from the Project menu, select the OnInitialUpdate() member function of the CPhnView class, and click the Add Function button. (See Figure 14.17.)

Figure 14.17. Using ClassWizard to add the OnInitialUpdate() function to the CPhnView class.

☐ Click the Edit Code button to display the OnInitialUpdate() function (inside the PHNVIEW.CPP file), and add code to the OnInitialUpdate() function. After you write this code, the OnInitialUpdate() function should look like this:

```
void CPhnView::OnInitialUpdate()
{
// TODO: Add your specialized code here and/or
// call the base class


    ////////////////////////
    // MY CODE STARTS HERE
    ////////////////////////

    // Get a pointer to the document.
    CPhnDoc* pDoc = (CPhnDoc*) GetDocument();

    // Get the address of m_PhoneList of the document class.
    m_pList = &(pDoc->m_PhoneList);

    // Get head position.
    m_position = m_pList->GetHeadPosition();


    // Update m_Name and m_Phone with values from the list.
    CPhone* pPhone = (CPhone*)m_pList->GetAt(m_position);
    m_Name  = pPhone->m_Name;
    m_Phone = pPhone->m_Phone;

    // Update the screen with the new values of the variables.
    UpdateData(FALSE);

    // Place the cursor inside the IDC_NAME edit box.
    ((CDialog*) this)->GotoDlgCtrl(GetDlgItem(IDC_NAME));
```

```
////////////////////
// MY CODE ENDS HERE
////////////////////
```

```
CFormView::OnInitialUpdate();
}
```

Now go over the code of the `OnInitialUpdate()` function:

The first statement

```
CPhnDoc* pDoc = (CPhnDoc*) GetDocument();
```

extracts `pDoc` (the pointer for the document class).

Then the address of `m_PhoneList` of the document class is assigned to the pointer `m_pList`:

```
m_pList = &(pDoc->m_PhoneList);
```

From now on, `m_pList` will be used to access `m_PhoneList` of the document class. Recall that you declared `m_pList` as a data member of the view class. Therefore, it will be visible in all the other member functions of the view class.

Then `m_position` is initialized to the head position (the first position) of the list:

```
m_position = m_pList->GetHeadPosition();
```

Again, because you also declared `m_position` as a data member of the view class, it will be visible in all the other functions of the view class.

Then the `m_Name` and `m_Phone` data members of the view class are updated with the values in the list that correspond to the position `m_position`:

```
CPhone* pPhone = (CPhone*)m_pList->GetAt(m_position);
m_Name  = pPhone->m_Name;
m_Phone = pPhone->m_Phone;
```

Because currently `m_position` is in the head position, the preceding three statements update `m_Name` and `m_Phone` with the values of the first object in the list. In the preceding code the statement

```
CPhone* pPhone = (CPhone*)m_pList->GetAt(m_position);
```

uses the `GetAt()` member function of the `CObList` class to update `pPhone` (pointer of an object of class `CPhone`) with the address of element `m_position` of the list. That is, `GetAt()` returns the address of the object in position `m_position`.

After you update `m_Name` and `m_Phone`, the `UpdateData()` function is used to transfer the new values of these variables to the screen:

```
UpdateData(FALSE);
```

Finally, the last statement in the `OnInitialUpdate()` function places the cursor inside the `IDC_NAME` edit box:

```
((CDialog*) this)->GotoDlgCtrl(GetDlgItem(IDC_NAME));
```

Therefore, whenever the user starts the application, selects New from the File menu, or selects Open from the File menu (that is, whenever the OnInitialUpdate() function is executed), the cursor appears inside the IDC_NAME edit box.

If you try to compile the PHNVIEW.CPP file now, you will get a compiling error. Why? In the preceding code you referred to the CPhone class, but this class is not known in the PHNVIEW.CPP file. Therefore, you must use #include PHONE.H (the header file of the CPhone class) at the beginning of the PHNVIEW.CPP file:

☐ Add the statement #include "phone.h" at the beginning of the PHNVIEW.CPP file (immediately before the #include statement of the phndoc.h file). After you add the #include statement, the beginning of the PHNVIEW.CPP file should look like this:

```
// phnview.cpp : implementation of the CPhnView class
//

#include "stdafx.h"
#include "phn.h"

/////////////////////////
// MY CODE STARTS HERE
/////////////////////////

#include "phone.h"

/////////////////////////
// MY CODE ENDS HERE
/////////////////////////


#include "phndoc.h"
#include "phnview.h"

#ifdef _DEBUG
#undef THIS_FILE
static char BASED_CODE THIS_FILE[] = __FILE__;
#endif

......
......
......
```

To save your work do the following:

☐ Select Save from the File menu.

> **NOTE**
>
> To make sure that you typed the code correctly, compile and link the application:
>
> ☐ Select Build PHN.EXE from the Project menu, and make sure that there are no compiling and linking errors.
>
> Do not execute the application. The only reason that you are instructed to compile and link the program is to verify that you entered the code correctly.

Updating the Data Members of the Document Class

Whenever the user edits the IDC_NAME edit box or the IDC_PHONE edit box, the data members of the document class should be updated accordingly. For example, if currently m_position points to the fifth item in the list, and the user types something in the IDC_NAME edit box, the data member m_Name of the fifth object in the list m_PhoneList (in the document class) should be updated with the same value that the user typed.

So you need to write code that detects when the user types something inside the IDC_NAME and IDC_PHONE edit boxes and then changes the m_PhoneList data member of the document class accordingly. Here is how you do that:

☐ Select ClassWizard from the Project menu, and add a function to the following event (See Figure 14.18):

```
CPhnView -> IDC_NAME -> EN_CHANGE
```

> *Visual C++ suggests the name* OnChangeName() *as the name of the new function.*

☐ Accept the OnChangeName() as the name of the new function.

Figure 14.18. Adding a function to the CPhnView *->* IDC_NAME *->* EN_CHANGE *event.*

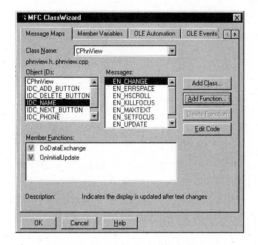

☐ Click the Edit Code button and edit the OnChangeName() function that you added to the PHNVIEW.CPP file. After you edit the function, your OnChangeName() function should look like this:

```
void CPhnView::OnChangeName()
{
// TODO: Add your control notification handler code here

    /////////////////////////
    // MY CODE STARTS HERE
    /////////////////////////

    // Update controls variables with screen contents.
```

```
    UpdateData(TRUE);

    // Get a pointer to the document.
    CPhnDoc* pDoc = (CPhnDoc*) GetDocument();

    // Update the document.
    CPhone* pPhone = (CPhone*)m_pList->GetAt(m_position);
    pPhone->m_Name = m_Name;

    // Set the Modified flag to TRUE.
    pDoc->SetModifiedFlag();

    /////////////////////
    // MY CODE ENDS HERE
    /////////////////////

}
```

Now go over the code that you just typed:

The first statement in the function

```
C1UpdateData(TRUE);
```

updates the variables of the controls with the current values inside the controls.

The next statement

```
CPhnDoc* pDoc = (CPhnDoc*) GetDocument();
```

extracts pDoc (the pointer for the document class).

The next two statements

```
CPhone* pPhone = (CPhone*)m_pList->GetAt(m_position);
pPhone->m_Name = m_Name;
```

update the m_Name data member of the object that is listed at position m_position of the list. Recall that GetAt(m_position) returns the address of the object in position m_position.

The last statement in the function is

```
pDoc->SetModifiedFlag();
```

This statement executes the SetModifiedFlag() member function of the document class to set the Modified flag to TRUE, signaling that the data of the document was modified. Recall from Chapter 13 that when the Modified flag is set to TRUE, and the user tries to quit the application or to load a new file, the application will display a warning message informing the user that the file has not been saved.

In a similar manner, you now need to attach code to the IDC_PHONE edit box:

☐ Use ClassWizard to select the event (See Figure 14.19.):

```
CPhnView -> IDC_PHONE -> EN_CHANGE
```

Then click the Add Function button.

Figure 14.19. Adding the OnChangePhone() *function.*

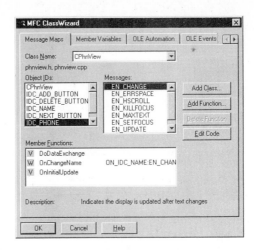

The CPhnView -> IDC_PHONE -> EN_CHANGE event occurs whenever the user changes the contents of the IDC_PHONE edit box.

☐ Accept the name OnChangePhone() that Visual C++ suggests.

☐ Click the Edit Code button to edit the OnChangePhone() function, and edit the function. After you edit the function, the OnChangePhone() function (inside the PHNVIEW.CPP file) should look like this:

```
void CPhnView::OnChangePhone()
{
// TODO: Add your control notification
// handler code here

    ////////////////////////
    // MY CODE STARTS HERE
    ////////////////////////

    // Update controls variables with screen contents.
    UpdateData(TRUE);

    // Get a pointer to the document.
    CPhnDoc* pDoc = (CPhnDoc*) GetDocument();

    // Update the document.
    CPhone* pPhone = (CPhone*)m_pList->GetAt(m_position);
    pPhone->m_Phone = m_Phone;

    // Set the Modified flag to TRUE.
    pDoc->SetModifiedFlag();

    ///////////////////////
    // MY CODE ENDS HERE
    ///////////////////////

}
```

As you can see, the OnChangePhone() function is similar to the OnChangeName() function. The only difference is that now m_Phone, not m_Name, is updated.

You have finished attaching code to the IDC_NAME and IDC_PHONE edit boxes. Whenever the user changes these edit boxes, m_PhoneList of the document class will be updated accordingly.

To save your work do the following:

☐ Select Save from the File menu.

Here's a review of what you have accomplished so far:

- You wrote the code that initializes the data members of the document class.
- You wrote the code that initializes the data members of the view class.
- You wrote the code that updates the data members of the document class whenever the user changes the data members of the view class (that is, whenever the user changes the contents of the edit boxes of the form).

In the following sections you will attach code to the Previous, Next, Add, and Delete buttons.

NOTE

To make sure that you typed the code correctly, compile and link the application:

☐ Select Build PHN.EXE from the Project menu, and make sure that there are no compiling and linking errors.

Do not execute the application. The only reason that you are instructed to compile and link the program is to verify that you entered the code correctly.

Attaching Code to the Previous Button

Whenever the user clicks the Previous button, m_position should be updated with the previous position in the list, and the IDC_NAME and IDC_PHONE edit boxes should be updated accordingly.

Follow these steps to attach code to the Previous button:

☐ Use ClassWizard to select the event:

CPhnView -> IDC_PREVIOUS_BUTTON -> BN_CLICKED

Then click the Add Function button.

The CPhnView -> IDC_PREVIOUS_BUTTON -> BN_CLICKED event occurs whenever the user clicks the Previous button.

☐ Accept the OnPreviousButton() function name that Visual C++ suggests.

☐ Click the Edit Code button and edit the OnPreviousButton() function that you added to the PHNVIEW.CPP file. After you edit the function, your OnPreviousButton() function should look like this:

```
void CPhnView::OnPreviousButton()
{
// TODO: Add your control notification
// handler code here

//////////////////////
// MY CODE STARTS HERE
//////////////////////

// Declare a Temporary POSITION variable.
POSITION temp_pos;

// Update temp_pos with the current position of the list.
temp_pos = m_position;

// Update temp_pos with the previous position.
m_pList->GetPrev(temp_pos);

if (temp_pos == NULL)
   {
   // No previous element.
   MessageBox("Bottom of file encountered!",
              "Phone for Windows");
   }
else
   {
   // Update m_position, m_Name, and m_Phone.
   m_position = temp_pos;
   CPhone* pPhone = (CPhone*)m_pList->GetAt(m_position);
   m_Name  = pPhone->m_Name;
   m_Phone = pPhone->m_Phone;
   UpdateData (FALSE);
   }

// Place the cursor inside the IDC_NAME edit box.
((CDialog*) this)->GotoDlgCtrl(GetDlgItem(IDC_NAME));

//////////////////////
// MY CODE ENDS HERE
//////////////////////

}
```

Now go over the code of the OnPreviousButton() function.

The first statement

```
POSITION temp_pos;
```

declares a temporary variable temp_pos (of type POSITION). You need this temporary temp_pos variable because you want to update the "real" POSITION variable m_position only after you are sure that there is a previous position. That is, if the current position is the head position (the first position in the list), there is no previous position.

The next statement updates temp_pos with the value of m_position:

```
C1temp_pos = m_position;
```

So now temp_pos contains the current position in the list.

The next statement uses the GetPrev() member function of the CObList class to update temp_pos with the previous position in the list (if there is one):

```
m_pList->GetPrev(temp_pos);
```

Note that the GetPrev() function changes the value of the variable that is passed to it. So now temp_pos points to the previous position. If there is no previous position (that is, the current position is the head position), then GetPrev() will update temp_pos with NULL.

The next block of statements is an if...else that checks for the value of temp_pos:

```
if (temp_pos == NULL)
    {
    // No previous element.
    MessageBox("Bottom of file encountered!",
               "Phone for Windows");
    }
else
    {
    // Update m_position, m_Name, and m_Phone.
    m_position = temp_pos;
    CPhone* pPhone = (CPhone*)m_pList->GetAt(m_position);
    m_Name  = pPhone->m_Name;
    m_Phone = pPhone->m_Phone;
    UpdateData (FALSE);
    }
```

If temp_pos is NULL, then you know that there is no previous position (that is, the current position is the head position), so the user is prompted with a "Bottom of file encountered" message:

```
MessageBox("Bottom of file encountered!",
           "Phone for Windows");
```

If, however, temp_pos is not NULL, then the code under the else is executed:

```
m_position = temp_pos;
CPhone* pPhone = (CPhone*)m_pList->GetAt(m_position);
m_Name  = pPhone->m_Name;
m_Phone = pPhone->m_Phone;
UpdateData (FALSE);
```

The first statement

```
m_position = temp_pos;
```

updates m_position with the value of temp_pos (which is the previous position in the list).

The next statement updates pPhone with the address of the object pointed to by m_position:

```
CPhone* pPhone = (CPhone*)m_pList->GetAt(m_position);
```

Then the data members of the view class are updated with the values of the data members from the document class:

```
m_Name  = pPhone->m_Name;
m_Phone = pPhone->m_Phone;
```

The next statement

```
UpdateData (FALSE);
```

transfers the new values of `m_Name` and `m_Phone` to the screen.

The last statement in the `OnPreviousButton()` function is

```
((CDialog*) this)->GotoDlgCtrl(GetDlgItem(IDC_NAME));
```

This statement places the cursor inside the `IDC_NAME` edit box. Therefore, after you click the Previous button the cursor will always appear inside the `IDC_NAME` edit box.

Don't forget to save your work:

☐ Select Save from the File menu.

Attaching Code to the Next Button

Whenever the user clicks the Next button, `m_position` should be updated with the next position in the list, and the IDC_NAME and IDC_PHONE edit boxes should be updated accordingly.

Follow these steps to attach code to the Next button:

☐ Use ClassWizard to select the event:

```
CPhnView -> IDC_NEXT_BUTTON -> BN_CLICKED
```

Then click the Add Function button.

☐ Accept `OnNextButton()` as the name of the new function.

☐ Click the Edit Code button to edit the `OnNextButton()` function that you added to the PHNVIEW.CPP file. After you edit the function, your `OnNextButton()` function should look like this:

```
void CPhnView::OnNextButton()
{
// TODO: Add your control notification
// handler code here

    //////////////////////////
    // MY CODE STARTS HERE
    //////////////////////////

    // Declare a temporary POSITION variable.
    POSITION temp_pos;

    // Update temp_pos with the current position of the list.
    temp_pos = m_position;
```

```
// Update temp_pos with the next position.
m_pList->GetNext(temp_pos);

if (temp_pos == NULL)
   {
   // No next element.
   MessageBox("End of file encountered!",
              "Phone for Windows");
   }
else
   {
   // Update m_position, m_Name, and m_Phone.
   m_position = temp_pos;
   CPhone* pPhone = (CPhone*)m_pList->GetAt(m_position);
   m_Name = pPhone->m_Name;
   m_Phone = pPhone->m_Phone;
   UpdateData (FALSE);
   }

// Place the cursor inside the IDC_NAME edit box.
((CDialog*) this)->GotoDlgCtrl(GetDlgItem(IDC_NAME));

///////////////////////
// MY CODE ENDS HERE
///////////////////////


}
```

As you can see, the `OnNextButton()` is similar to the `OnPreviousButton()` function. The only difference is that in `OnNextButton()` you use the `GetNext()` member function of the `CObList` class, not the `GetPrevious()` function.

Save your work:

☐ Select Save from the File menu.

> ### NOTE
>
> To make sure that you typed the code correctly, compile and link the application:
>
> ☐ Select Build PHN.EXE from the Project menu, and make sure that there are no compiling and linking errors.
>
> Do not execute the application. The only reason that you are instructed to compile and link the program is to verify that you entered the code correctly.

Attaching Code to the Add Button

Whenever the user clicks the Add button, a new blank object should be added to the tail of the list (that is, to the end of the list), and `m_position` should be updated accordingly.

Follow these steps to attach code to the Add button:

☐ Use ClassWizard to select the event:

```
CPhnView -> IDC_ADD_BUTTON -> BN_CLICKED
```

Then click the Add Function button.

☐ Accept the name OnAddButton() that Visual C++ suggests.

☐ Click the Edit Code button to edit the OnAddButton() function that you added to the PHNVIEW.CPP file. After you edit the function, your OnAddButton() function should look like this:

```
void CPhnView::OnAddButton()
{
// TODO: Add your control notification
// handler code here


//////////////////////////
// MY CODE STARTS HERE
//////////////////////////

// Update m_Name, m_Phone and the screen with blanks.
m_Name  = "";
m_Phone = "";
UpdateData (FALSE);

// Create a new object of class CPhone.
CPhone* pPhone  = new CPhone();
pPhone->m_Name  = m_Name;
pPhone->m_Phone = m_Phone;

// Add the new object to the tail of the list, and
// update m_position with the new position.
m_position = m_pList->AddTail(pPhone);

// Get a pointer to the document.
CPhnDoc* pDoc = (CPhnDoc*) GetDocument();

// Set the Modified flag to TRUE.
pDoc->SetModifiedFlag();

// Place the cursor inside the IDC_NAME edit box.
((CDialog*) this)->GotoDlgCtrl(GetDlgItem(IDC_NAME));

//////////////////////////
// MY CODE ENDS HERE
//////////////////////////


}
```

Now go over the code of the OnAddButton() function.

The first two statements

```
m_Name   = "";
m_Phone  = "";
```

update the data members m_Name and m_Phone of the view class with blanks.

The next statement

```
UpdateData (FALSE);
```

transfers the new values of m_Name and m_Phone to the screen.

Then a new object (pPhone) of class CPhone is created, and its data members are initialized:

```
CPhone* pPhone   = new CPhone();
pPhone->m_Name   = m_Name;
pPhone->m_Phone  = m_Phone;
```

So now the data members of pPhone are also blanks.

The next statement in the function is

```
m_position = m_pList->AddTail(pPhone);
```

This statement uses the AddTail() member function of the CObList class to add the pPhone object to the tail of the list. Note that the returned value of the AddTail() function is the new position of the added object. Therefore, after you execute the preceding statement, m_position is updated with the position of the pPhone object, which is the new tail position of the list.

The next statement

```
CPhnDoc* pDoc = (CPhnDoc*) GetDocument();
```

extracts pDoc (the pointer for the document class).

Then pDoc is used to execute the SetModifiedFlag() member function of the document class:

```
pDoc->SetModifiedFlag();
```

This is done to signal that the document data has been changed.

The last statement in the function is

```
((CDialog*) this)->GotoDlgCtrl(GetDlgItem(IDC_NAME));
```

This statement places the cursor inside the IDC_NAME edit box. Therefore, after you click the Add button, the cursor will always appear inside the IDC_NAME edit box.

Don't forget to save your work:

☐ Select Save from the File menu.

Attaching Code to the Delete Button

Whenever the user clicks the Delete button, the item in the list that is pointed to by m_position should be removed.

Follow these steps to attach code to the Delete button:

☐ Use ClassWizard (from the Project menu) to select the event:

```
CPhnView -> IDC_DELETE_BUTTON -> BN_CLICKED
```

Then click the Add Function button.

☐ Accept the name OnDeleteButton() that Visual C++ suggests.

☐ Edit the OnDeleteButton() function that you added to the PHNVIEW.CPP file. After you edit the function, your OnDeleteButton() function should look like this:

```
void CPhnView::OnDeleteButton()
{
// TODO: Add your control notification
// handler code here

    ////////////////////////
    // MY CODE STARTS HERE
    ////////////////////////

    // Save the old pointer for deletion.
    CObject* pOld;
    pOld = m_pList->GetAt( m_position );

    // Remove the element from the list.
    m_pList->RemoveAt( m_position );

    // Delete the object from memory.
    delete pOld;

    // If the list is now completely empty, add a blank item.
    if ( m_pList->IsEmpty() )
        OnAddButton();

    // Get a pointer to the document.
    CPhnDoc* pDoc = (CPhnDoc*) GetDocument();

    // Set the Modified flag to TRUE.
    pDoc->SetModifiedFlag();

    // Display the first item of the list.
    OnInitialUpdate();

    ////////////////////////
    // MY CODE ENDS HERE
    ////////////////////////


}
```

Now go over the code of the `OnDeleteButton()` function.

The first two statements are

```
CObject* pOld;
pOld = m_pList->GetAt( m_position );
```

These statements save the address of the object to be deleted in the pointer `pOld`.

Then the object to be deleted is removed from the list by using the `RemoveAt()` member function of the `CObList` class:

```
m_pList->RemoveAt( m_position );
```

Note that the `RemoveAt()` function does not delete the object from memory. It merely removes the object from the list.

The next statement actually deletes the object from memory:

```
delete pOld;
```

Then the `IsEmpty()` member function of the `CObList` class is used to check whether the list is now completely empty:

```
if ( m_pList->IsEmpty() )
   OnAddButton();
```

If the list is completely empty, the `OnAddButton()` function (which you wrote earlier) is called, so the list will have one blank object.

The next statement in the function

```
CPhnDoc* pDoc = (CPhnDoc*) GetDocument();
```

extracts `pDoc` (the pointer for the document class).

Then `pDoc` is used to execute the `SetModifiedFlag()` member function of the document class:

```
pDoc->SetModifiedFlag();
```

This is done to signal that the document data has been changed.

The last statement in the function is

```
OnInitialUpdate();
```

This statement calls the `OnInitialUpdate()` function (which you wrote earlier) so that the first object in the list will be displayed.

Don't forget to save your work:

☐ Select save from the File menu.

Executing the PHN Application

Although you have not yet written the code that writes and reads the list to and from the disk, you have finished writing most of the code. That is, you have finished writing the code that lets the user add items to the list, navigate between items in the list, and delete items in the list.

To see this code in action do the following:

☐ Select Build PHN.EXE from the Project menu of Visual C++.

Visual C++ responds by compiling and linking the PHN application.

☐ Select Execute PHN.EXE from the Project menu.

Visual C++ responds by executing the application.

Experiment with the application:

☐ Add several names and phone numbers to the list with the Add button and try the Previous, Next, and Delete buttons.

As you can see, you can add items to the list, you can delete items from the list, and you can navigate between the items in the list. In the following sections you will write the code that enables the user to write and read the list to and from files.

To terminate the PHN application do the following:

☐ Select Exit from the File menu.

Serializing the List

In the following sections you will write the code that serializes the m_PhoneList list. That is, you will utilize the Serialize() function of the CObList class to write and read the m_PhoneList list to and from files.

Adding Overhead Code to PHONE.H and PHONE.CPP

In order to support the serialization of the m_PhoneList list, you must add some overhead code in the CPhone class files (PHONE.H and PHONE.CPP). Why in the code of the CPhone class? m_PhoneList lists objects of class CPhone.

☐ Open the file PHONE.H and add code to it so that it looks like this:

```
/////////////////////////
// MY CODE STARTS HERE
/////////////////////////

// PHONE.H
//
// Header file for the CPhone class.


// CPhone class declaration.
class CPhone : public CObject
{

    // Needed for serialization.
    DECLARE_SERIAL(CPhone)

public:

    // Constructor
    CPhone();
```

```
          // Data members
          CString m_Name;
          CString m_Phone;

          // The Serialize() function.
          virtual void Serialize(CArchive& ar);

     };

     ////////////////////////
     // MY CODE ENDS HERE
     ////////////////////////
```

That is, you have to add at the beginning of the CPhone class declaration the DECLARE_SERIAL statement, and you have to add the prototype of the Serialize() member function.

Save the modifications that you made to PHONE.H:

☐ Select Save from the File menu.

Now modify the PHONE.CPP file:

☐ Open the file PHONE.CPP and add code so that it looks like this:

```
////////////////////////
// MY CODE STARTS HERE
////////////////////////

// PHONE.CPP
//
// Implementation file of the CPhone class.


#include "stdafx.h"
#include "phone.h"

// Needed for serialization.
IMPLEMENT_SERIAL(CPhone, CObject, 0)

// Constructor.
CPhone::CPhone()
{
   m_Name  = "";
   m_Phone = "";
}

// Serialize function of the CPhone class.
void CPhone::Serialize(CArchive& ar)
{
     if (ar.IsStoring())
         {
         ar << m_Name << m_Phone;
         }
     else
         {
         ar >> m_Name >> m_Phone;
         }
}
```

```
///////////////////
// MY CODE ENDS HERE
///////////////////
```

That is, you have to add the `IMPLEMENT_SERIAL` statement at the beginning of the file (immediately after the `#include phone.h` statement), and you have to add the `serialize()` function.

Save the modifications that you made to PHONE.CPP:

☐ Select Save from the File menu.

Now go over the code that you added to PHONE.H and PHONE.CPP:

Inside the declaration of `CPhone` (in PHONE.H) you wrote the statement

```
// Needed for serialization.
DECLARE_SERIAL(CPhone)
```

`DECLARE_SERIAL` is a macro that is needed for serialization. This macro takes one parameter: the name of the class.

You also added the prototype of the `Serialize()` function to the `CPhone` class declaration:

```
// The Serialize() function.
virtual void Serialize(CArchive& ar);
```

This prototype is necessary because you want to serialize a list of objects of class `CPhone`. Therefore, the `CPhone` class itself must have a `Serialize()` function.

You added this statement to the beginning of the file PHONE.CPP:

```
// Needed for serialization.
IMPLEMENT_SERIAL(CPhone, CObject, 0)
```

`IMPLEMENT_SERIAL` is another macro that is needed for serialization. Note that this macro takes three parameters. The first parameter is the name of the class (`CPhone`), the second parameter is the name of the base class (`CObject`), and the third parameter is the version number of the application. You can specify any value you wish for the version number. The version number that you specify will be written into the file when you serialize the data into the file.

Inside PHONE.CPP you wrote the code of the `Serialize()` function of the `CPhone` class:

```
// Serialize function of the CPhone class.
void CPhone::Serialize(CArchive& ar)
{
    if (ar.IsStoring())
       {
       ar << m_Name << m_Phone;
       }
    else
       {
       ar >> m_Name >> m_Phone;
       }
}
```

As you can see, the `Serialize()` function of the `CPhone` class looks very much like the `Serialize()` function of the document class, which you saw in the previous chapter. The code under the `if` is responsible for writing the data members `m_Name` and `m_Phone` into the file:

```
ar << m_Name << m_Phone;
```

The code under the `else` is responsible for reading the contents of the file into the data members `m_Name` and `m_Phone`:

```
ar >> m_Name >> m_Phone;
```

> **NOTE**
>
> To be able to utilize the `Serialize()` member function of a `CObList` class list (for example, `m_PhoneList`) there are several overheads that you have to perform:
>
> - The objects that the list lists must be objects of a class that is derived from the MFC `CObject` class. That's why when you declared the `CPhone` class you declared it as a derived class from the MFC class `CObject`.
>
> - The class of the objects that the list lists (for example, `CPhone`) must have a constructor function with no arguments. That's why when you declared the `CPhone` class, you declared its constructor function with no arguments. If you wish, you can add to the `CPhone` additional constructor functions classes that have arguments.
>
> - You must declare and write the `Serialize()` member function of the class of the objects that the list lists (for example, `CPhone::Serialize()`).
>
> - When you write the code of the class of the objects that the list lists (for example, `CPhone`), you must use the `IMPLEMENT_SERIAL` and `DECLARE_SERIAL` macros.

Calling the List's *Serialize()* Function

Okay, you have finished writing all the overhead code necessary for serializing the list. Now it's finally time to serialize the `m_PhoneList` list. That is, it's time to call the `Serialize()` member function of `m_PhoneList`.

The question is From where should you call this function? Recall that the `Serialize()` function of the document class is executed automatically whenever the user selects Save, Save As, or Open from the File menu. Therefore, you should call the `Serialize()` function of `m_PhoneList` from the `Serialize()` function of the document class.

This way, whenever the user selects Save or Save As from the File menu, `m_PhoneList` will be saved into the file that the user selected. Also, whenever the user selects Open from the File menu, `m_PhoneList` will be filled with the list that is stored inside the file that the user opened.

Follow these steps to write the code that calls the `Serialize()` function of `m_PhoneList`:

☐ Open the file PHNDOC.CPP and modify the `Serialize()` function of the document class so that it looks like this:

```
void CPhnDoc::Serialize(CArchive& ar)
```

```
{
    if (ar.IsStoring())
    {
        // TODO: add storing code here
    }
    else
    {
        // TODO: add loading code here
    }

/////////////////////
// MY CODE STARTS HERE
/////////////////////

m_PhoneList.Serialize(ar);

/////////////////////
// MY CODE ENDS HERE
/////////////////////

}
```

As you can see, you did not have to write any code under the if and else of the Serialize() function (as you did in Chapter 13). Instead you wrote the statement

```
m_PhoneList.Serialize(ar);
```

at the end of the function. You do that because you want to run the Serialize() function of m_PhoneList. The Serialize() function of m_PhoneList will do all the work for you; it will serialize all the objects listed in m_PhoneList to or from the file that the user selected.

Note that you pass the parameter ar to the Serialize() function of m_PhoneList. Recall that ar is the archive object that corresponds to the file that the user selected. You need to pass ar because the serialize function of m_PhoneList needs to know which file the user selected.

Note that you did not have to write the code of the Serialize() function of m_PhoneList. In fact, you cannot edit the code of this Serialize() function, because m_PhoneList is an object of the MFC class CObList and you cannot modify the code of an MFC class.

What does the Serialize() function of the CObList class (PhoneList.Serialize()) do?

The statement

```
m_PhoneList.Serialize()
```

will execute the Serialize() function of each of the objects that are listed in m_PhoneList. Because m_PhoneList lists objects of class CPhone, the preceding statement will cause the execution of the Serialize() function of the CPhone class for each of the objects listed in m_PhoneList.

Don't forget to save the changes that you made to PHNDOC.CPP:

☐ Select Save from the File menu.

Executing the PHN Application

You've finished writing the code that serializes the m_PhoneList list to and from files.

To see this code in action do the following:

☐ Select Build PHN.EXE from the Project menu of Visual C++.

> *Visual C++ responds by compiling and linking the PHN application.*

☐ Select Execute PHN.EXE from the Project menu.

> *Visual C++ responds by executing the application.*

Experiment with the application:

☐ Add several names and phone numbers to the list.

☐ Select Save from the File menu and save your list as TRY.PHN.

☐ Experiment with the other File menu options (Save As, Open, and New).

☐ As you can see, you can save lists of names and phone numbers into files, and you can load saved lists from files.

To terminate the PHN application do the following:

☐ Select Exit from the File menu.

The Final Touch

There are several cosmetic enhancements that you can now apply to the PHN application:

☐ Use the string table editor of Visual C++ to modify the IDR_MAINFRAME string so that it looks as follows:

```
Phone for Windows\n\nPhn\nPHN Files (*.phn)\n.phn\nPhn.Document.1\nPhn Document
```

You must type this without pressing the Enter key. Visual C++ will automatically wrap the line.

> **NOTE**
>
> If you have forgotten how to use the string table editor, refer to the end of Chapter 13, where this topic is covered via a detailed step-by-step example.

The PHN application is now complete! You can build and execute it to verify that the changes that you just made to the IDR_MAINFRAME string work.

15

Customizing Serialization

In the previous two chapters you learned about the process of serialization. In Chapter 13, "Writing and Reading Data (with Serialization) to and from Files," you wrote a program that serializes data members of the document class, and in Chapter 14, "Writing and Reading Lists (with Serialization) to and from Files," you wrote a program that serializes a list of objects. In this chapter you will learn how to customize serialization.

The *CArchive* Class

Recall from the previous two chapters that the parameter of the `Serialize()` function is an object of class `CArchive`. For example, a typical `Serialize()` function of the document class looks like this:

```
void CTryDoc::Serialize(CArchive& ar)
{
    if (ar.IsStoring())
    {

////////////////////////
// MY CODE STARTS HERE
////////////////////////

ar << m_Var1 << m_Var2 << m_Var3;

////////////////////////
// MY CODE ENDS HERE
////////////////////////

    }
    else
    {

////////////////////////
// MY CODE STARTS HERE
////////////////////////

ar >> m_Var1 >> m_Var2 >> m_Var3;

////////////////////////
// MY CODE ENDS HERE
////////////////////////

    }
```

The parameter of the `Serialize()` function (ar) is an archive object (an object of class `CArchive`) and it corresponds to a file. In the case of the document class, ar corresponds to the file that the user selects from the File menu. For example, if the user selects Open from the File menu and then selects the file MyFile.TXT, then the code for the application (code that Visual C++ wrote for you) is executed automatically. This code creates a `CArchive` object that corresponds to the MyFile.TXT file and passes this `CArchive` object to the `Serialize()` function of the document class.

Sometimes you'll find it useful to create and customize a `CArchive` object yourself, such as in cases in which you don't want the user to select the file, but rather you want to serialize data to or from a specific file.

The ARCH application illustrates how you can create and customize a `CArchive` object.

The ARCH Application

You'll now write the ARCH application. The code that you'll write creates an object of class `CArchive` and uses this object to write and read data to and from a file.

Before you start writing the ARCH application, first execute the copy of it that resides in the \MVCPROG\EXE directory of the book's CD.

To execute the ARCH application do the following:

☐ Execute the file X:\MVCPROG\EXE\ARCH.EXE from the book's CD (where *X* represents the drive letter of your CD-ROM drive).

> *Windows responds by executing the ARCH.EXE application. The main window of ARCH.EXE appears, as shown in Figure 15.1.*

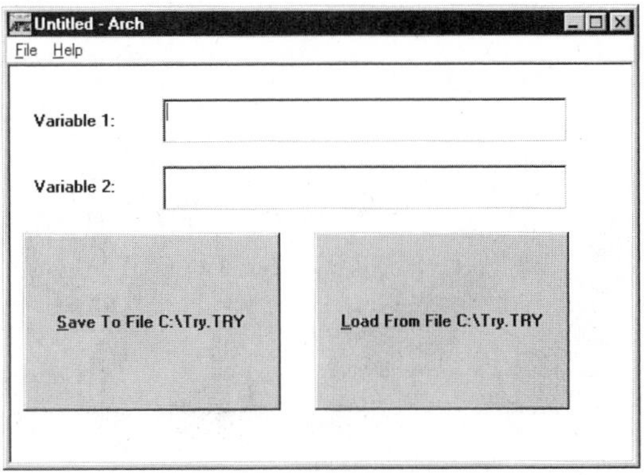

Figure 15.1. The main window of the ARCH application.

As you can see from Figure 15.1, the main window of the application displays a blank form with two fields (Variable 1 and Variable 2) and two push buttons (Save To File C:\TRY.TRY and Load From File C:\TRY.TRY).

The ARCH application has two pop-up menus: File and Help. These pop-up menus are shown in Figures 15.2 and 15.3.

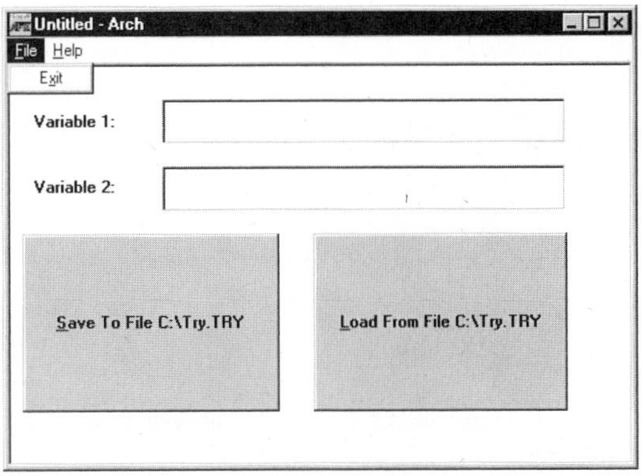

Figure 15.2. The File menu of the ARCH application.

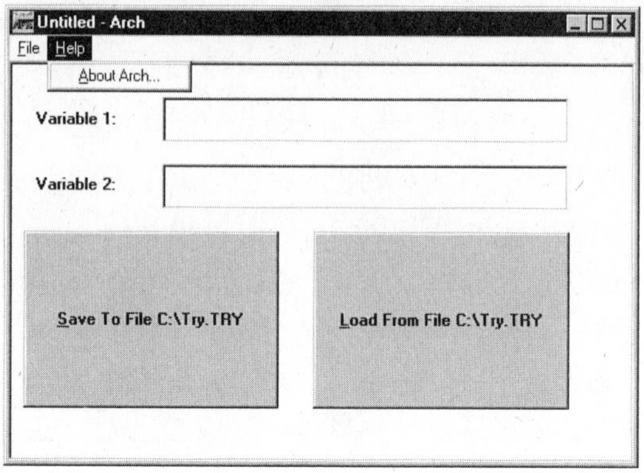

*Figure 15.3. The Help
menu of the ARCH
application.*

☐ Fill the Variable 1 and Variable 2 fields of the blank entry form with any string values you like.

☐ Click the Save To File C:\TRY.TRY button.

> *The ARCH application responds by saving the two strings you typed into the file C:\TRY.TRY.*

To verify that the strings are saved do the following:

☐ Delete the contents of the two fields and then click the Load From File C:\TRY.TRY button.

> *The ARCH application responds by loading the contents of the file C:\TRY.TRY into the Variable 1 and Variable 2 fields. As you can see, the two fields are now filled with the values that you saved.*

To terminate the ARCH application do the following:

☐ Select Exit from the File menu.

Now that you know what the ARCH application is supposed to do, you can start writing it.

Creating the Project of the ARCH Application

To create the project of the ARCH application do the following:

☐ Start Visual C++ and close all the windows that appear inside the desktop of Visual C++ (if there are any).

☐ Select New from the File menu.

> *Visual C++ responds by displaying the New dialog box.*

☐ Select Project inside the New dialog box and then click the OK button of the New dialog box.

> *Visual C++ responds by displaying the New Project dialog box.*

☐ Set the project name to ARCH.

☐ Set the project path to \MVCPROG\CH15\ARCH\ARCH.MAK.

Your New Project dialog box should now look like the one shown in Figure 15.4.

Figure 15.4. The New Project dialog box of the ARCH.MAK project.

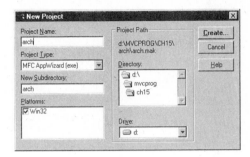

☐ Click the Create button of the New Project dialog box.

Visual C++ responds by displaying the AppWizard—Step 1 window.

☐ Set the Step 1 window as shown in Figure 15.5. As shown in Figure 15.5, the ARCH.MAK project is set as a single-document interface application, and U.S. English (APPWIZUS.DLL) is used as the language for the application's resources.

Figure 15.5. The AppWizard—Step 1 window for the ARCH application.

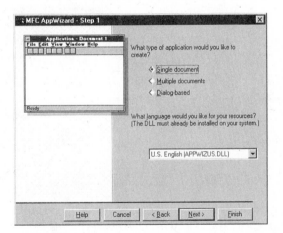

☐ Click the Next button of the Step 1 window.

Visual C++ responds by displaying the AppWizard—Step 2 of 6 window.

☐ Set the Step 2 of 6 window as shown in Figure 15.6. That is, in the ARCH application you don't want any database support.

Figure 15.6. The AppWizard—Step 2 of 6 window for the ARCH application.

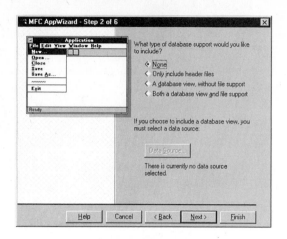

☐ Click the Next button of the Step 2 of 6 window.

Visual C++ responds by displaying the AppWizard—Step 3 of 6 window.

☐ Set the Step 3 of 6 window as shown in Figure 15.7. That is, in the ARCH application you don't want any OLE support.

Figure 15.7. The AppWizard—Step 3 of 6 window for the ARCH application.

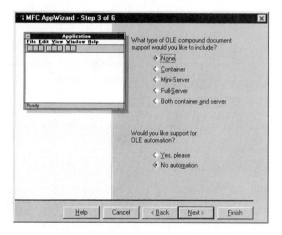

☐ Click the Next button of the Step 3 of 6 window.

Visual C++ responds by displaying the AppWizard—Step 4 of 6 window.

☐ Set the Step 4 of 6 window as shown in Figure 15.8.

As shown in Figure 15.8, the features Dockable Toolbar, Initial Status Bar, Printing and Print Preview, and Context Sensitive Help will not be included in the ARCH application.

*Figure 15.8. The
AppWizard—Step 4 of 6
window for the ARCH
application.*

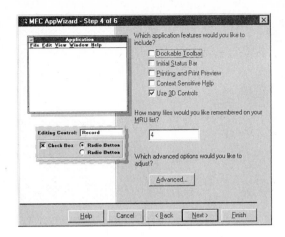

☐ Click the Next button of the Step 4 of 6 window.

   Visual C++ responds by displaying the AppWizard—Step 5 of 6 window.

☐ Set the Step 5 of 6 window as shown in Figure 15.9.

As shown in Figure 15.9, the project will be generated with comments, a Visual C++ makefile will
be generated, and the application will use the MFC library from a DLL.

*Figure 15.9. The
AppWizard—Step 5 of 6
window for the ARCH
application.*

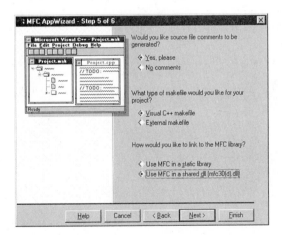

☐ Click the Next button of the Step 5 of 6 window.

   Visual C++ responds by displaying the AppWizard—Step 6 of 6 window.

You'll now use the AppWizard—Step 6 of 6 window to tell AppWizard to derive the view class of
the application from the MFC class `CFormView`:

☐ Select the `CArchView` class inside the AppWizard—Step 6 of 6 window.

☐ Set the Base Class drop-down list box to `CFormView`.

Your AppWizard—Step 6 of 6 window should now look like the one shown in Figure 15.10.

Figure 15.10. The AppWizard—Step 6 of 6 window after you the base class of the application view class to `CFormView`.

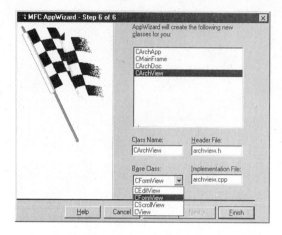

NOTE

As you can see from Figure 15.1, the main window of the ARCH program does have controls inside it. Therefore, you need to derive the view class of the application from the `CFormView` class.

☐ Click the Finish button of the Step 6 of 6 window.

Visual C++ responds by displaying the New Project Information window, as shown in Figure 15.11.

Figure 15.11. The New Project Information window of the ARCH.MAK project.

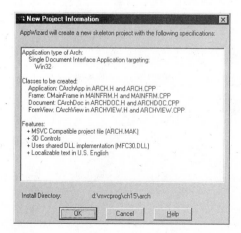

☐ Click the OK button of the New Project Information window.

Visual C++ responds by creating the project file and all the skeleton files of the application.

The Visual Implementation of the ARCH Application's Form

You'll now visually design the dialog box that serves as the main window of the ARCH application. Visual C++ created for you the IDD_ARCH_FORM dialog box because in the Step 6 of 6 window you specified CFormView as the base class.

☐ Select arch.mak from the Window menu to display the arch.mak window. Double-click arch.rc inside the arch.mak window, double-click Dialog, and finally, double-click IDD_ARCH_FORM, which appears under the Dialog item.

Visual C++ responds by displaying the IDD_ARCH_FORM dialog box in design mode. This dialog box serves as the main window of the ARCH application.

☐ Design the dialog box of the ARCH application according to the specifications in Table 15.1. When you finish designing the dialog box, it should look like the one shown in Figure 15.12.

Table 15.1. The Properties table of the dialog box of the ARCH application.

Object	Property	Setting
Dialog box	ID	IDD_ARCH_FORM
Label	ID	IDC_STATIC
	Caption	Variable 1:
Edit box	ID	IDC_VAR1
	Type	CString
Label	ID	IDC_STATIC
	Caption	Variable 2:
Edit box	ID	IDC_VAR2
	Type	CString
Push button	ID	IDC_SAVE_BUTTON
	Caption	&Save To File C:\\TRY.TRY
Push button	ID	IDC_LOAD_BUTTON
	Caption	&Load From File C:\\TRY.TRY

Figure 15.12. The dialog box of the ARCH application.

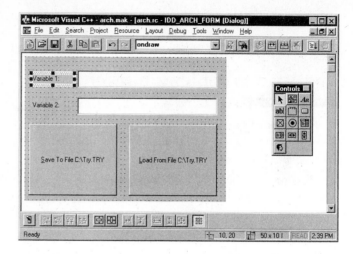

Save your work:

☐ Select Save from the File menu of Visual C++.

You've finished designing the form of the application!

> **NOTE**
>
> Note that in Table 15.1 the caption of the push button is &Save To File C:\\TRY.TRY.
>
> That is, when you want to use the \ character, you have to precede it with the \ character. This is the reason for typing \\.

Attaching Variables to the Edit Boxes of the Form

You'll now attach variables to the edit boxes of the IDD_ARCH_FORM dialog box.

☐ Use ClassWizard to attach variables to the controls of the IDD_ARCH_FORM dialog box, as specified in Table 15.2.

Table 15.2. The Variables table of the IDD_ARCH_FORM dialog box.

Control ID	Variable Name	Category	Variable Type
IDC_VAR1	m_Var1	Value	CString
IDC_VAR2	m_Var2	Value	CString

The Visual Implementation of the Menu Bar

The ARCH application should have a menu bar, as shown in Figures 15.1, 15.2, and 15.3.

☐ Select arch.mak from the Window menu to display the arch.mak window. Double-click arch.rc inside the arch.mak window, double-click Menu, and finally double-click IDR_MAINFRAME under the Menu item.

> *Visual C++ responds by displaying the IDR_MAINFRAME menu in design mode.*

☐ Design the menu of the ARCH application so that it has the following items:

&File
    E&xit
&Help
    &About Arch…

To save your work do the following:

☐ Select Save from the File menu of Visual C++.

The visual implementation of the menu of the ARCH application is complete.

Even though you haven't finished writing the ARCH application, execute it to see what you've accomplished so far:

☐ Select Rebuild All ARCH.EXE from the Project menu in Visual C++.

> *Visual C++ responds by compiling and linking the ARCH application.*

☐ Select Execute ARCH.EXE from the Project menu.

> *Visual C++ responds by executing the ARCH application. As you can see, the dialog box that you designed appears as the main window of the application. (See Figure 15.1.)*

Of course none of the buttons in the dialog box are functional because you haven't yet written any code. In the following sections you'll attach code to the two buttons in the form.

To exit the ARCH application do the following:

☐ Select Exit from the File menu.

Attaching Code to the Save Button

Whenever the user clicks the Save To File C:\TRY.TRY button, the contents of the two edit boxes (IDC_VAR1 and IDC_VAR2) should be serialized into the file C:\TRY.TRY.

Follow these steps to attach code to the Save button:

☐ Select ClassWizard from the Project menu, and select the following event (see Figure 15.13):

```
CArchView -> IDC_SAVE_BUTTON -> BN_CLICKED
```

Then click the Add Function button.

Figure 15.13. Selecting the
CArchView ->
IDC_SAVE_BUTTON ->
BN_CLICKED event.

☐ Accept OnSaveButton() as the name of the new function and then click the Edit Code button to edit the OnSaveButton() function.

Visual C++ responds by displaying the OnSaveButton() function, ready to be edited by you.

☐ Edit the OnSaveButton() function that you added to the ARCHVIEW.CPP file. After you edit the function, your OnSaveButton() function should look like this:

```
void CArchView::OnSaveButton()
{
// TODO: Add your control notification
// handler code here

/////////////////////////
// MY CODE STARTS HERE
/////////////////////////

// Update m_Var1 and m_Var2 with the screen contents.
UpdateData(TRUE);

// Create the file C:\TRY.TRY.
CFile f;
f.Open("C:\\TRY.TRY",
       CFile::modeCreate | CFile::modeWrite );

// Create an archive object.
CArchive ar( &f, CArchive::store );

// Serialize m_Var1 and m_Var2 into the archive.
ar << m_Var1 << m_Var2;

// Close the archive
ar.Close();

// Close the file.
f.Close();
```

```
///////////////////
// MY CODE ENDS HERE
///////////////////
```

}

Now go over the code for the OnSaveButton() function.

The first statement

```
UpdateData(TRUE);
```

updates the variables of the edit boxes (m_Var1 and m_Var2) with the current values displayed in the edit boxes.

The next two statements create the file C:\\TRY.TRY:

```
CFile f;
f.Open("C:\\TRY.TRY", CFile::modeCreate | CFile::modeWrite );
```

The first statement creates an object of class CFile, called f, and the second statement uses the Open() member function of the CFile class to create the C:\TRY.TRY file. The CFile class will be discussed in more detail in Chapter 16, "Writing and Reading Data (Without Serialization) to and from Files."

The next statement creates an object, called ar, of class CArchive:

```
CArchive ar( &f, CArchive::store );
```

As you can see, this statement passes two parameters to the constructor of CArchive. The first parameter is the address of the CFile object that is associated with the archive. In this statement the first parameter is &f, the address of the CFile object of the C:\TRY.TRY file. Therefore, the archive object ar will be associated with the file C:\TRY.TRY.

The second parameter in this statement specifies the mode of the archive object. An archive object can be created for storage purposes (to save variables into the archive) or for loading purposes (to load data from the archive into variables). In this statement, the second parameter is

```
CArchive::store
```

Therefore, the archive object ar will be used for storage purposes. You want to use ar for storage purposes because you want the m_Var1 and m_Var2 variables to be saved into the archive whenever the user clicks the Save button.

Now that you have an archive object that is associated with the file C:\TRY.TRY, and this archive object is in a storage mode, you can serialize variables into TRY.TRY. The next statement in the function serializes the two data members, m_Var1 and m_Var2, into TRY.TRY:

```
ar << m_Var1 << m_Var2;
```

The next statement uses the Close() member function of the CArchive class to close the ar archive:

```
ar.Close();
```

The last statement uses the Close() member function of the CFile class to close the file associated with the f object (TRY.TRY):

```
f.Close();
```

Don't forget to save your work:

☐ Select Save from the File menu.

Attaching Code to the Load Button

Whenever the user clicks the Load From File C:\TRY.TRY button, the contents of the two edit boxes (IDC_VAR1 and IDC_VAR2) should be filled with the values stored in the file TRY.TRY.

☐ Select ClassWizard from the Project menu, and select the following event:

CArchView -> IDC_LOAD_BUTTON -> BN_CLICKED

Then click the Add Function button.

☐ Accept OnLoadButton() as the name of the new function and then click the Edit Code button to edit the OnLoadButton() function.

Visual C++ responds by displaying the OnLoadButton() function, ready to be edited by you.

☐ Edit the OnLoadButton() function that you added to the ARCHVIEW.CPP file. After you edit the function, your OnLoadButton() function should look like this:

```
void CArchView::OnLoadButton()
{
// TODO: Add your control notification
// handler code here

    ///////////////////////////
    // MY CODE STARTS HERE
    ///////////////////////////

    // Open the file C:TRY.TRY.
    CFile f;
    if ( f.Open("C:\\TRY.TRY",
        CFile::modeRead)== FALSE )
      return;

    // Create an archive object.
    CArchive ar( &f, CArchive::load );

    // Serialize data from the archive into m_Var1 and m_Var2.
    ar >> m_Var1 >> m_Var2;

    // Close the archive
    ar.Close();

    // Close the file.
    f.Close();

    // Update screen with the new values of m_Var1 and m_Var2.
    UpdateData(FALSE);
```

16

Writing and Reading Data (Without Serialization) to and from Files

In this chapter you'll learn how to write and read data to and from files. Unlike the programs in the previous chapters that use serialization, the programs in this chapter do not use serialization—instead, they utilize the MFC CFile.

In this chapter you'll also learn how to attach to the application your own icon (instead of the default AFX icon that Visual C++ attaches to the application).

The FileIt Application

Before you start writing the FileIt application yourself, execute the copy of it that resides in the \MVCPROG\EXE directory of the book's CD.

To execute the FileIt application do the following:

☐   Select Run from the Start menu of Windows and execute the X:\MVCPROG\EXE\FileIt.EXE program (where *X* represents the drive letter of your CD-ROM drive).

   The main window of FileIt.EXE appears, as shown in Figure 16.1.

Figure 16.1. The main window of the FileIt application.

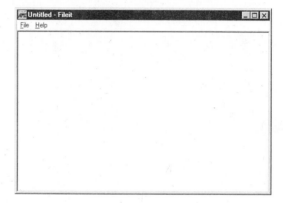

The FileIt application has two pop-up menus: File and Help. These pop-up menus are shown in Figures 16.2 and 16.3.

Figure 16.2. The File menu of the FileIt application.

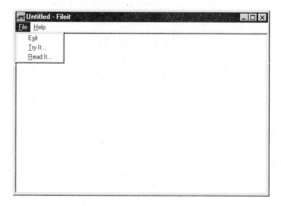

Figure 16.3. The Help
menu of the FileIt
application.

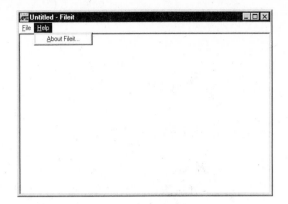

☐ Select Try It from the File menu.

FileIt responds by displaying the Try It dialog box. (See Figure 16.4.)

Figure 16.4. The Try It
Dialog Box of the FileIt
application

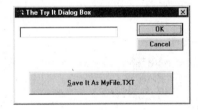

As you can see, the Try It dialog box contains an edit box and the Save It As MyFile.TXT push button.

☐ Click inside the edit box and type something.

☐ Click the Save It As MyFile.TXT button.

FileIt responds by creating the file MyFile.TXT in the root directory of the C: drive. This text file contains the text that you typed inside the edit box.

Verify that this is indeed the case:

☐ Switch to the Notepad program that comes with Windows (it's usually inside the Accessories group).

☐ Load the file C:\MyFile.TXT.

As you can see, this file contains the text that you typed inside the edit box.

☐ Click either the OK or Cancel button of the Try It dialog box to close the dialog box.

☐ Select Read It from the File menu.

FileIt responds by reading the MyFile.TXT file and displaying its contents.

☐ Experiment with the FileIt application and then select Exit from the File menu.

Note that when you select About FileIt from the Help menu, FileIt responds by displaying the standard About dialog box. The icon that appears inside the dialog box is the regular Microsoft AFX icon. Later in this chapter you'll learn how to insert a more appropriate icon into the About dialog box.

Now that you know what the FileIt program should do, you can write it.

Creating the Project of the FileIt Application

To create the project of the FileIt application do the following:

☐ Start Visual C++ and close all the open windows that appear inside the desktop of Visual C++ (if there are any).

☐ Select New from the File menu.

Visual C++ responds by displaying the New dialog box.

☐ Select Project inside the New dialog box and then click the OK button of the New dialog box.

Visual C++ responds by displaying the New Project dialog box.

☐ Set the project name to FileIt.

☐ Set the project path to \MVCPROG\CH16\FileIt\FileIt.MAK.

Your New Project dialog box should now look like the one shown in Figure 16.5.

Figure 16.5. The New Project dialog box of the FileIt.MAK project.

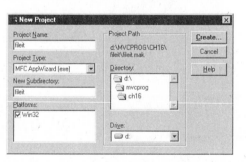

☐ Click the Create button of the New Project dialog box.

Visual C++ responds by displaying the AppWizard—Step 1 window.

☐ Set the Step 1 window as shown in Figure 16.6. As shown in Figure 16.6, the FileIt.MAK project is set as a single-document interface application, and U.S. English (APPWIZUS.DLL) is used as the language for the application's resources.

☐ Click the Next button of the Step 1 window.

Figure 16.6. The AppWizard—Step 1 window for the FileIt application.

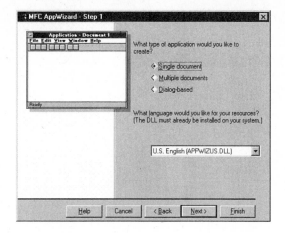

Visual C++ responds by displaying the AppWizard—Step 2 of 6 window.

☐ Set the Step 2 of 6 window as shown in Figure 16.7. That is, in the FileIt application you don't want any database support.

☐ Click the Next button of the Step 2 of 6 window.

Figure 16.7. The AppWizard—Step 2 of 6 window for the FileIt application.

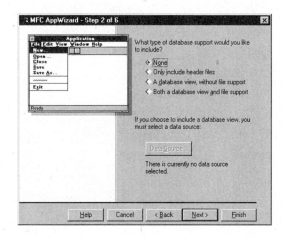

Visual C++ responds by displaying the AppWizard—Step 3 of 6 window.

☐ Set the Step 3 of 6 window as shown in Figure 16.8. That is, in the FileIt application you don't want any OLE support.

☐ Click the Next button of the Step 3 of 6 window.

*Figure 16.8. The
AppWizard—Step 3
of 6 window for the
FileIt application.*

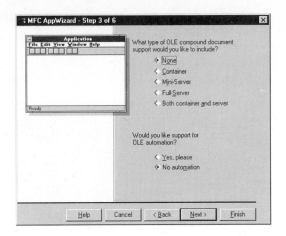

Visual C++ responds by displaying the AppWizard—Step 4 of 6 window.

☐ Set the Step 4 of 6 window as shown in Figure 16.9.

As shown in Figure 16.9, the features Dockable Toolbar, Initial Status Bar, Printing and Print

*Figure 16.9. The
AppWizard—Step 4
of 6 window for the
FileIt application.*

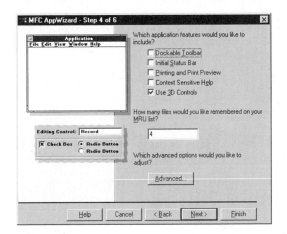

Preview, and Context Sensitive Help will not be included in the FileIt application.

☐ Click the Next button of the Step 4 of 6 window.

Visual C++ responds by displaying the AppWizard—Step 5 of 6 window.

☐ Set the Step 5 of 6 window as shown in Figure 16.10.

As shown in Figure 16.10, the project will be generated with comments, a Visual C++ makefile will
be generated, and the application will use the MFC library from a DLL.

☐ Click the Next button of the Step 5 of 6 window.

Figure 16.10. The
AppWizard—Step 5
of 6 window for the
FileIt application.

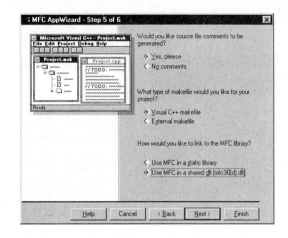

Visual C++ responds by displaying the AppWizard—Step 6 of 6 window.

You'll now use the AppWizard—Step 6 of 6 window to tell AppWizard to derive the view class of the application from the MFC class `CFormView`:

☐ Select the `CFileitView` class inside the AppWizard—Step 6 of 6 window.

☐ Set the Base Class drop-down list box to `CFormView`.

Your AppWizard—Step 6 of 6 window should now look like the one shown in Figure 16.11.

Figure 16.11. The
AppWizard—Step 6 of 6
window after you set the
base class of the application
view class to `CFormView`.

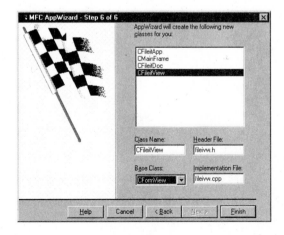

NOTE

As you can see from Figure 16.1, the main window of the FileIt program does not have any controls inside it. Therefore, there is really no need to derive the view class of the application from the `CFormView` class. That is, you could have derived the view class of the application from the default `CView` class that ClassExpert suggested.

The reason you were instructed to use the `CFormView` class as the base class is that if in the future you want to add controls to the main window of the application, you'll be able to do so easily.

☐ Click the Finish button of the Step 6 of 6 window.

> *Visual C++ responds by displaying the New Project Information window, as shown in Figure 16.12.*

Figure 16.12. The New Project Information window of the FileIt.MAK project.

☐ Click the OK button of the New Project Information window.

> *Visual C++ responds by creating the project file and all the skeleton files of the application.*

The Visual Implementation of the FileIt Application

The FileIt application has a menu, a custom dialog box, and an About dialog box. In the following sections you'll visually design the menu and the custom dialog box of the FileIt application.

The Visual Implementation of the Menu of the FileIt Application

The FileIt application should have a menu, as shown in Figures 16.2 and 16.3.

Follow these steps to customize the menu of the FileIt application (the IDR_MAINFRAME menu):

☐ Select fileit.rc from the Window menu of Visual C++.

Visual C++ responds by displaying the fileit.rc window.

☐ Double-click Menu inside the fileit.rc window and then double-click IDR_MAINFRAME item that appears under the Menu item.

Visual C++ responds by displaying the IDR_MAINFRAME menu bar in design mode.

As you can see, the IDR_MAINFRAME menu currently has three pop-up menus: File, Edit, and Help.

Because the FileIt application should not have an Edit menu, you have to remove the Edit pop-up menu:

☐ Click the Edit item on the menu bar.

Visual C++ responds by opening the Edit pop-up menu.

☐ Now press the Delete key on your keyboard.

Visual C++ responds by displaying a dialog box warning you that you're about to delete an entire pop-up menu.

☐ Click the OK button of the warning dialog box (yes, you want to delete the entire pop-up menu).

Visual C++ responds by deleting the Edit pop-up menu.

Take a look at the Help menu. As you can see, the Help menu is exactly as you want it to be, so there is no need to modify this menu. However, the File menu is not exactly as you want it to be.

You'll now modify the File menu.

☐ Delete all the items in the File menu except the Exit item.

☐ Add the Try It menu item to the File menu.

☐ Add the Read It menu item to the File menu.

Set up the menu of the FileIt program so that it has the following items:

```
&File
  E&xit
  &Try It…
  &Read It…
&Help
  &About Fileit…
```

☐ Save your work by selecting Save from the File menu of Visual C++.

The visual implementation of the menu of the FileIt application is complete. To see your visual design in action do the following:

☐ Select Build FileIt.EXE from the Project menu.

    Visual C++ responds by compiling and linking the FileIt application.

☐ Select Execute FileIt.EXE from the Project menu.

    Visual C++ responds by executing the FileIt.EXE application.

As expected, the menu bar of the application appears as you customized it.

☐ Verify that the File and Help menus look as shown in Figures 16.2 and 16.3.

☐ Terminate the FileIt application by selecting Exit from the File menu.

The Visual Implementation of the Main Window of the FileIt Application

Because in AppWizard you specified that the base class of the application's view class is CFormView, AppWizard created for you a form (a dialog box) that is attached to the view class of the application. This dialog box serves as the main window of the application. AppWizard named this dialog box IDD_FILEIT_FORM. You'll now customize the IDD_FILEIT_FORM dialog box.

☐ Select FileIt.MAK from the Window menu, double-click the Dialog item to drop down the list of dialog boxes that FileIt contains, and then double-click the IDD_FILEIT_FORM item.

    Visual C++ responds by displaying the IDD_FILEIT_FORM dialog box in design mode. (See Figure 16.13.) The IDD_FILEIT_FORM dialog box serves as the main window of the FileIt application.

Figure 16.13. The default IDD_FILEIT_FORM dialog box in design mode. (This dialog box serves as the main window of the FileIt application.)

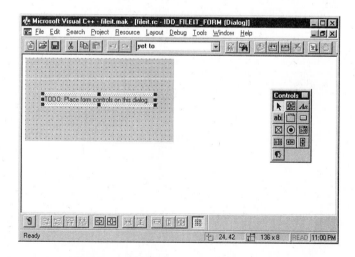

☐ Click inside the static text TODO: Place form controls on this dialog to highlight it, and then press the Delete button to delete the TODO static text.

The IDD_FILEIT_FORM dialog box should now look like the one shown in Figure 16.14.

*Figure 16.14. The
IDD_FILEIT_FORM
dialog box in design mode.*

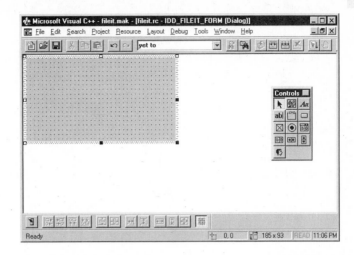

As shown back in Figure 16.1, the main window of the FileIt program should not have any controls in it. Therefore, you don't have to place any controls inside the IDD_FILEIT_FORM dialog box.

The Visual Implementation of the Try It Dialog Box

You'll now visually implement the Try It dialog box of the FileIt application. Recall that the Try It dialog box appears whenever the user selects Try It from the File menu.

☐ Select New from the Resource menu, select Dialog from the list of the New Resource dialog box, and click the OK button.

Visual C++ responds by creating and displaying the IDD_DIALOG1 dialog box in design mode. (See Figure 16.15.)

*Figure 16.15. The Try
It dialog box before you
customize it.*

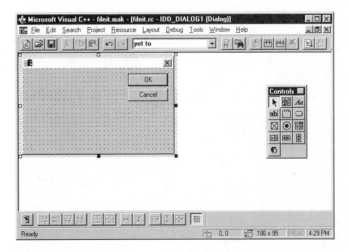

You'll now customize the IDD_DIALOG1 dialog box.

☐ Implement the Try It dialog box of the FileIt application according to the specifications in Table 16.1. When you finish implementing the dialog box it should look like the one shown in Figure 16.16.

Table 16.1. The Properties table of the IDD_DIALOG1 dialog box (the Try It dialog box).

Object	Property	Setting
Dialog box	ID	IDD_DIALOG1
	Caption	The Try It Dialog Box
Push button	ID	IDC_SAVE_IT
	Caption	&Save It As MyFile.TXT
Edit box	ID	IDC_EDIT1

Figure 16.16. The customized Try It dialog box.

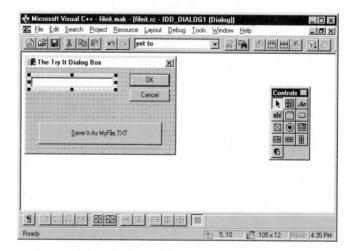

Attaching a Class to the Try It Dialog Box

You'll now attach a class to the Try It dialog box.

☐ Select Class Wizard from the Project menu.

Visual C++ notices that no class is associated with the IDD_DIALOG1 dialog box, so Visual C++ displays the Add Class dialog box.

☐ Set the Class Name of the Add Class dialog box to CTryItDlg.

☐ Make sure that the Class Type is set to `CDialog` (because you want to derive the `CTryItDlg` class from the `CDialog` class so that you'll be able to utilize the member functions of the `CDialog` class).

Your Add Class dialog box should now look like the one shown in Figure 16.17.

Figure 16.17. Associating the IDD_DIALIG1 dialog box with the `CTryItDlg` *class.*

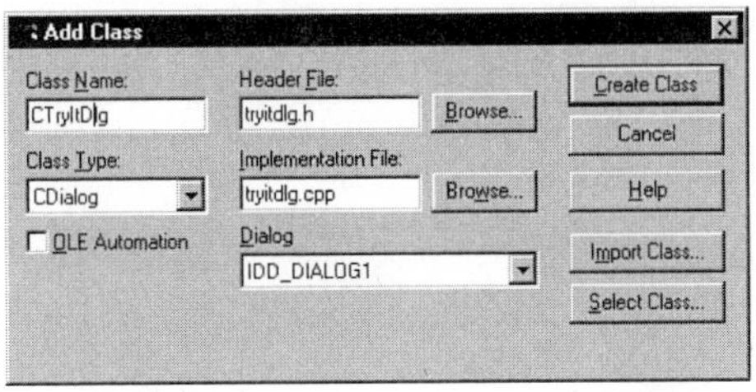

☐ Click the Create Class button of the Add Class dialog box.

☐ Click the OK Button of the ClassWizard dialog box.

Attaching Variables to the Controls Inside the IDD_DIALOG1 Dialog Box

You'll now attach variables to the controls inside the IDD_DIALOG1 dialog box.

☐ Display the ClassWizard dialog box by selecting ClassWizard from the Project menu of Visual C++.

☐ Select the Member Variables tab at the top of ClassWizard's dialog box.

☐ Make sure the Class Name drop-down list is set to `CTryItDlg`.

☐ Attach variables to the controls of the IDD_DIALOG1 dialog box as specified in Table 16.2.

Table 16.2. The Variables table of the IDD_DIALOG1 dialog box (the Try It dialog box).

Control ID	Variable Name	Category	Variable Type
IDC_EDIT1	m_EditBoxContents	Value	Cstring

☐ To save your work, select Save from the File menu.

That's it! You've completed the visual implementation of the Try It dialog box.

Declaring the Try It Dialog Box Object as a Data Member of the View Class

You'll now create an object dlg of class CTryItDlg. You'll declare this object as a data member of the view class (the CFileitView class).

☐ Open the FILEIVW.H file, and modify the declaration of the CFileitView class. After the modification, the CFileitView class declaration should look like this:

```
class CFileitView : public CFormView
{
protected: // create from serialization only
CFileitView();
DECLARE_DYNCREATE(CFileitView)

public:
//{{AFX_DATA(CFileitView)
enum{ IDD = IDD_FILEIT_FORM };
// NOTE: the ClassWizard will add data members here
//}}AFX_DATA

// Attributes
public:
CFileitDoc* GetDocument();


/////////////////////////
// MY CODE STARTS HERE
/////////////////////////

// Create an object dlg (a dialog box)
// of class CTryItDlg.
CTryItDlg dlg;

/////////////////////////
// MY CODE ENDS HERE
/////////////////////////


// Operations
public:

// Overrides
// ClassWizard generated virtual function overrides
//{{AFX_VIRTUAL(CFileitView)
public:
protected:
virtual void DoDataExchange(CDataExchange* pDX);
// DDX/DDV support
//}}AFX_VIRTUAL

// Implementation
public:
virtual ~CFileitView();
#ifdef _DEBUG
virtual void AssertValid() const;
virtual void Dump(CDumpContext& dc) const;
```

```
#endif

protected:

// Generated message map functions
protected:
//{{AFX_MSG(CFileitView)
// NOTE—the ClassWizard will add and remove
// member functions here.
//    DO NOT EDIT what you see in these blocks
// of generated code !
//}}AFX_MSG
DECLARE_MESSAGE_MAP()
};
```

Because the `CTryItDlg` class is unknown inside the file FILEIVW.H, you have to use `#include` on the file TryItDlg.h (which contains the class declaration of `CTryItDlg`) at the beginning of the FILEIVW.H file:

☐ Add the `#include "TryItDlg.h"` statement at the beginning of the FILEIVW.H file.

After you use `#include` on this file, the beginning of the FILEIVW.H file should look like this:

```
// fileivw.h : interface of the CFileitView class
//
/////////////////////////////////////////////////


/////////////////////////
// MY CODE STARTS HERE
/////////////////////////

#include "TryItDlg.h"

/////////////////////////
// MY CODE ENDS HERE
/////////////////////////

......
......
......
```

Attaching Code to the FileIt Menu Item

You'll now attach code to the Try It menu item. Recall that when you select the Try It menu item, the FileIt application should display the Try It dialog box.

☐ Select fileit.rc from the Window menu, double-click the Menu item, and then double-click the IDR_MAINFRAME item that appears under the Menu item.

Visual C++ responds by displaying the IDR_MAINFRAME menu in design mode.

☐ Display the ClassWizard dialog box by selecting ClassWizard from the Project menu of Visual C++.

☐ Select the Message Maps tab at the top of ClassWizard's dialog box.

☐ Use ClassWizard to select the event (See Figure 16.18.):

```
CFileitView -> ID_FILE_TRYIT -> COMMAND
```

Figure 16.18. Adding a member function that will be executed whenever the user selects the Try It item from the File menu.

☐ Click the Add Function button and name the function `OnFileTryit()`, which is the default name that Visual C++ suggests. (See Figure 16.19.)

Figure 16.19. Adding the `OnFileTryit()` member function.

☐ Click the Edit Code button of ClassWizard.

ClassWizard responds by opening the file FileIVW.CPP, with the function `OnFileTryit()` ready to be edited by you.

☐ Write code inside the `OnFileTryit()` function so that it looks like this:

```
void CFileitView::OnFileTryit()
{
// TODO: Add your command handler code here


    //////////////////////////
    // MY CODE STARTS HERE
    //////////////////////////

    // Display the dlg dialog box.
    dlg.DoModal();

    //////////////////////////
    // MY CODE ENDS HERE
    //////////////////////////

}
```

In this code, you display the dialog box `dlg` by using the `DoModal()` function:

```
dlg.DoModal();
```

Although you have not yet finished writing the FileIt application, compile, link, and execute it so that you can verify that everything that you typed so far is working.

☐ Select Rebuild All FileIt.EXE from the Project menu.

☐ Execute the FileIt application by selecting Execute FileIt.EXE from the Project menu.

☐ Select Try It from the File menu of the FileIt program.

> *FileIt responds by displaying the Try It dialog box.*

☐ Type something inside the edit box.

☐ Click the OK button.

> *FileIt responds by closing the dialog box.*

Because you connected the edit box with the variable `m_EditBoxContents`, the program automatically updates the `m_EditBoxContents` variable with the contents of the edit box when you click the OK button. To verify that FileIt indeed maintains the contents of the edit box do the following:

☐ Select Try It from the File menu.

> *FileIt responds by displaying the Try It dialog box. The contents of the edit box are the same as they were before you closed the dialog box with the OK button.*

☐ Close the Try It dialog box and then select Exit from the File menu to terminate the FileIt application.

Providing Your User with a Save Button

Maintaining the contents of the edit box during the life of the FileIt application is nice, but once the user terminates the FileIt application, the contents of the edit box are lost forever. You'll now learn how to save the contents of the edit box to a file.

You can save to a file the text that you type inside the edit box by clicking the Save It As MyFile.TXT button. As implied by its caption, this button should cause the contents of the edit box to be saved to the MyFile.TXT file. You'll now attach code to this button.

☐ Display the ClassWizard dialog box by selecting ClassWizard from the Project menu of Visual C++.

☐ Select the Message Maps tab at the top of ClassWizard's dialog box.

☐ Use ClassWizard to select the event (See Figure 16.20.):

```
CTryitDlg -> IDC_SAVE_IT -> BN_CLICKED
```

☐ Click the Add Function button.

> *Visual C++ responds by suggesting `OnSaveIt()` as the name of the new function.*

Figure 16.20. Adding a member function that will be executed whenever the user selects the Save It As MyFile.TXT button inside the Try It dialog box.

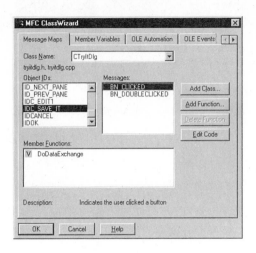

☐ Accept the function name that Visual C++ suggests.

☐ Click the Edit Code button of ClassWizard.

> *ClassWizard responds by opening the file TryItDlg.CPP, with the function* OnSaveIt() *ready to be edited by you.*

☐ Write code inside the OnSaveIt() function so that it looks like this:

```
void CTryItDlg::OnSaveIt()
{
// TODO: Add your control notification handler code here

    //////////////////////////
    // MY CODE STARTS HERE
    //////////////////////////

    // Create an object TheFile of class CFile
    CFile TheFile;

    // Prepare the file for creation OR writing
    TheFile.Open ( "C:\\MyFile.TXT",
            CFile::modeCreate¦CFile::modeWrite );


    // Update the value of m_EditBoxContents
    UpdateData (TRUE);

    // Write into the TheFile
    TheFile.Write ( m_EditBoxContents,
                m_EditBoxContents.GetLength() );

    // Close the file
    TheFile.Close();

    //////////////////////
    // MY CODE ENDS HERE
    //////////////////////

}
```

The *CFile* MFC Class

The code you typed inside the `OnSaveIt()` function creates an object called `TheFile` of class `CFile`:

```
CFile TheFile;
```

What is the `CFile` class, and why do you need to create an object of this class? This class has a lot of "goodies" (useful member functions) in it that enable you to manipulate files with great ease.

The code that you typed then uses the `Open()` member function of `CFile` to create the MyFile.TXT file in the root directory of the C: drive:

```
TheFile.Open ( "C:\\MyFile.TXT",
            CFile::modeCreate¦CFile::modeWrite );
```

The first parameter of `Open()` is the path and name of the file that you want to create or write into, and the second parameter is this:

```
CFile::modeCreate ¦ CFile::modeWrite
```

These constants tell the `Open()` function to create the file if the file does not exist already (`CFile::modeCreate`) and to open the file for writing (`CFile::modeWrite`) if it does already exist. (Note that the OR operator (¦) is used between the two constants.)

The `OnSaveIt()` function then uses the `UpdateData()` function to update the variable `m_EditBoxContents` with the contents of the edit box:

```
UpdateData (TRUE);
```

Now that `m_EditBoxContents` is updated with the contents of the edit box, you can use the `Write()` member function of the `CFile` class to write data into the MyFile.TXT file:

```
TheFile.Write ( m_EditBoxContents,
            m_EditBoxContents.GetLength() );
```

The first parameter of the `Write()` function is the data that you want to write into the MyFile.TXT file. The second parameter is the length of the data that you want to write into the file. Note that the length is specified as this:

```
m_EditBoxContents.GetLength()
```

Because the `m_EditBoxContents` variable is of type `CString`, you can use the `GetLength()` member function of `CString` to extract the length of `m_EditBoxContents`.

To summarize, the `Write()` function writes the contents of the `m_EditBoxContents` into the C:\MyFile.TXT file.

Finally, MyFile.TXT is closed by using the `Close()` member function of the `CFile` class:

```
TheFile.Close();
```

NOTE

The `TheFile` object is local to the `OnSaveIt()` function. This means that when the `OnSaveIt()` function is terminated, the `TheFile` object is destroyed (because the destructor function of the `CFile` class is executed). Therefore, the statement `TheFile.Close();` is not really needed.

Once the `TheFile` object is destroyed (or the `TheFile.Close()` function is executed), you can't perform any file manipulations on the file.

The only reason for using the `Close()` function is to illustrate its use.

Now look at the Save It As MyFile.TXT button in action:

☐ Compile, link, and execute the FileIt application.

☐ Write something inside the edit box.

☐ Click the Save It As MyFile.TXT button.

> *FileIt responds by saving the contents of the edit box into the C:\MyFile.TXT file.*

☐ Close the Try It dialog box and then select Exit from the File menu to terminate the FileIt application.

☐ Verify that indeed the data was written into the C:\MyFile.TXT file by using Notepad to open the file and examining its contents.

Reading the MyFile.TXT File

You've successfully written code that writes data into the MyFile.TXT file. Of course, knowing how to write data to a file is only half of the knowledge that you need—you also need to know how to load and read the saved files.

You'll now attach code to the Read It menu item. The code that you'll write will cause the FileIt program to read the data of MyFile.TXT and display it whenever the user selects Read It from the File menu.

☐ Select fileit.rc from the Window menu, double-click the Menu item, and then double-click the IDR_MAINFRAME item that appears under the Menu item.

> *Visual C++ responds by displaying the IDR_MAINFRAME menu.*

☐ Display the ClassWizard dialog box by selecting ClassWizard from the Project menu of Visual C++.

☐ Select the Message Maps tab at the top of ClassWizard's dialog box.

☐ Use ClassWizard to select the event (See Figure 16.21):

```
CFileitView -> ID_FILE_READIT -> COMMAND
```

Figure 16.21. Adding a member function that will be executed whenever the user selects the Read It item from the File menu.

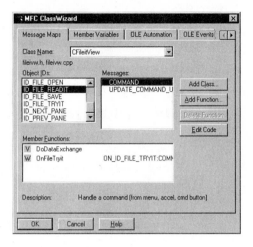

☐ Click the Add Function button.

Visual C++ responds by suggesting OnReadit() *as the name of the new function.*

☐ Accept the OnReadit() name as the name of the new function.

☐ Click the Edit Code button of ClassWizard.

ClassWizard responds by opening the file FileIVW.CPP, with the function OnReadit() *ready to be edited by you.*

☐ Write code inside the OnFileReadit() function so that the function looks like this:

```
void CFileitView::OnFileReadit()
{
// TODO: Add your command handler code here

    //////////////////////////
    // MY CODE STARTS HERE
    //////////////////////////

    UINT BytesRead;
    char FromFile[1000];


    // Create an object readMe of class CFile
     CFile readMe("C:\\MyFile.TXT",
                  CFile::modeRead );

    // Read the file into FromFile
    BytesRead = readMe.Read ( FromFile,
                              200 );
```

```
// Add a null terminator
FromFile[BytesRead] = 0;

// Display it
MessageBox ( FromFile );

//////////////////////
// MY CODE ENDS HERE
//////////////////////
```

```
}
```

The code that you typed declares two local variables:

```
UINT BytesRead;
char FromFile[1000];
```

Then an object `readMe` of class `CFile` is created:

```
CFile readMe("C:\\MyFile.TXT",
             CFile::modeRead );
```

Note that in this object creation statement, the first parameter is

```
"C:\\MyFile.TXT"
```

which is the name of the file from which data will be read, and the second parameter specifies that the file is to be read.

The `Read()` member function of `CFile` is then executed:

```
BytesRead = readMe.Read ( FromFile,
                          200 );
```

The first parameter of the `Read()` function specified the name of the buffer that will hold the read data, and the second parameter is the maximum number of bytes that will be read.

The actual number of bytes read is returned from the `Read()` function and is assigned to the `BytesRead` variable.

The `OnFileReadit()` function then attaches a null terminator character to the `FromFile` buffer:

```
FromFile[BytesRead] = 0;
```

Finally, the read data is displayed with the `MessageBox()` function:

```
MessageBox ( FromFile );
```

Note that the null terminator was attached to the `FromFile` buffer because the `MessageBox()` function expects a null terminated string as its parameter.

☐ Compile, link, and execute the FileIt application.

☐ Select Read It from the File menu.

FileIt responds by displaying a message box with the contents of the C:\MyFile.TXT file inside the message box.

☐ Experiment with the FileIt program by first selecting Try It from the File menu, typing something inside the edit box of the Try It dialog box, and then saving the contents of the edit box to the C:\\MyFile.TXT file by clicking the Save File As MyText.TXT button. Then select Read It from the File menu to display the contents of the MyFile.TXT file that you saved.

The SeekIt Application

One of the most important member functions of the CFile class is the Seek() function. This function lets you position the file pointer at any desired location. Therefore, your program will be able to read any number of bytes from any desired location in the file. The SeekIt application demonstrates how you can use the Seek() function to determine the sampling rate of a WAV file.

The Sampling Rate of a WAV File

A WAV file is a standard sound file used by Windows to play sound. A WAV file can be recorded at various sampling rates. For example, you can record a WAV file at a sampling rate of 8,000 Hertz. To play back the WAV file, the program that plays the WAV file must determine the sampling rate at which the WAV file was recorded. Every WAV file has a header section at its beginning. This header section contains information about the WAV file. One piece of this information is the sampling rate.

You can display a WAV file by using Visual C++:

☐ Select Open from the File menu of Visual C++.

Visual C++ responds by displaying the Open dialog box.

On the lower-left corner of the Open dialog box you'll see the Open As drop-down list box.

☐ Click the arrow icon of the Open As drop-down list box and select the Binary item (because you want to view the TADA.WAV file as a binary file).

☐ Use the Open dialog box to load the \Windows\Media\TADA.WAV file.

Your Open dialog box should now look like the one shown in Figure 16.22.

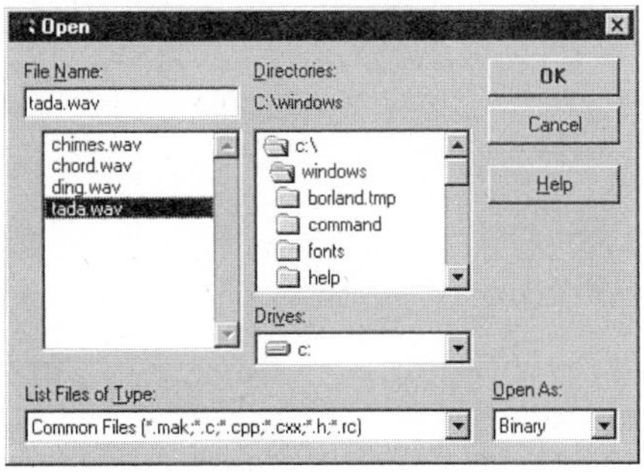

Figure 16.22. Using the Open as binary capability of Visual C++ to load the TADA.WAV file as a binary file.

☐ Click the OK button of the Open dialog box.

Visual C++ responds by displaying the TADA.WAV file in a binary format. (See Figure 16.23.)

Figure 16.23. Viewing the TADA.WAV file.

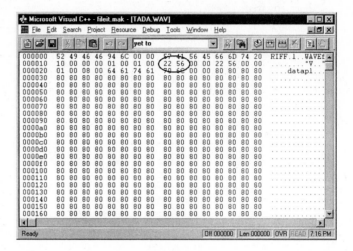

As shown in Figure 16.23, the first byte of the Tada.WAV byte is 52, the second byte is 49, and so on. As stated, these bytes represent various information about the WAV file. The 2 bytes of interest are the 25th and 26th bytes.

As shown in Figure 16.23, the 25th byte is 22, and the 26th byte is 56. (In Figure 16.23, these 2 bytes are circled.)

What is the meaning of these 2 bytes? To understand their meaning, you have to reverse their order. Therefore, these 2 bytes become

```
56 22
```

5622 (hex) is equal to

```
5*16*16*16 + 6*16+16 + 2*16 + 2 =
  20480    +   1536  +  32  + 2 = 22050
```

So to summarize, 5622 (hex) is the same as 22050 (decimal).

Therefore, the TADA.WAV was recorded at 22,050 Hertz.

Figure 16.24 shows the result of displaying the bytes of the X:\WAV\8Kenned3.WAV file of the book's CD (where *X* represents the letter drive of your CD-ROM drive). As shown, the 25th and 26th bytes of this file are 11 and 2B. Reversing these 2 bytes produces

```
2B 11
```

which represents this value:

```
2*16*16*16 + 11 *16*16 + 1*16 + 1 =

   8192    +   2816   + 16  + 1 = 11025
```

To summarize, the 8Keened3.WAV file was recorded at 11,025 Hertz.

Figure 16.24.
Displaying the bytes of
8Kenned3.WAV.

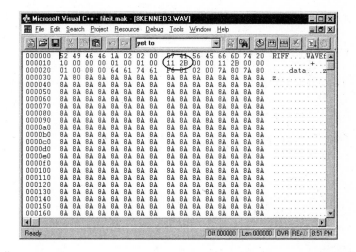

SeekIt reads and displays the sampling rate of the file \MVCPROG\WAV\8Kenned3.WAV.

Executing the SeekIt Application

Before writing the SeekIt program yourself, execute it. To execute the SeekIt application do the following:

☐ Select Run from the Start menu of Windows and execute the X:\MVCPROG\SeekIt.EXE program (where *X* represents the drive letter of your CD-ROM drive).

The main window of SeekIt.EXE appears, as shown in Figure 16.25.

Figure 16.25. The main window of the SeekIt application.

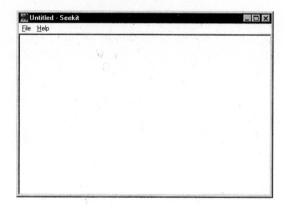

The SeekIt application has two pop-up menus: File and Help.

These pop-up menus are shown in Figures 16.26 and 16.27.

Figure 16.26. The File menu of the SeekIt application

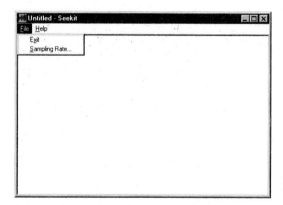

Figure 16.27. The Help menu of the SeekIt application.

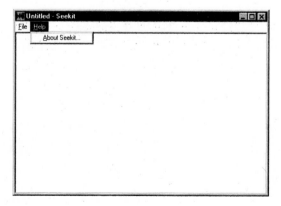

☐ Select Sampling Rate from the File menu.

SeekIt responds by displaying the sampling rate of the \MVCPROG\WAV\8Kenned3.WAV file.

☐ Close the message box and then select Exit from the File menu.

Now that you know what the SeekIt application does, you can write it.

Creating the Project of the SeekIt Application

To create the project of the SeekIt application do the following:

☐ Start Visual C++ and close all the open windows that appear inside the desktop of Visual C++ (if there are any).

☐ Select New from the File menu.

Visual C++ responds by displaying the New dialog box.

☐ Select Project inside the New dialog box and then click the OK button of the New dialog box.

Visual C++ responds by displaying the New Project dialog box.

☐ Set the project name to SeekIt.

☐ Set the project path to \MVCPROG\CH16\SeekIt\SeekIt.MAK.

Your New Project dialog box should now look like the one shown in Figure 16.28.

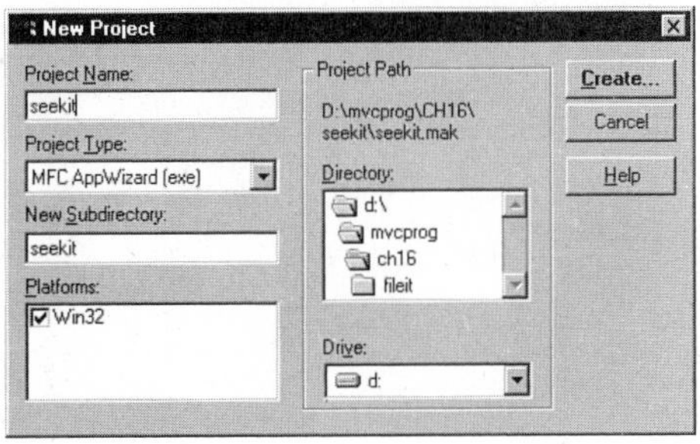

Figure 16.28. The New Project dialog box of the SeekIt.MAK project.

☐ Click the Create button of the New Project dialog box.

Visual C++ responds by displaying the AppWizard—Step 1 window.

☐ Set the Step 1 window as shown in Figure 16.29. As shown in Figure 16.29, the SeekIt.MAK project is set as a single-document interface application, and U.S. English (APPWIZUS.DLL) is used as the language for the application's resources.

*Figure 16.29. The
AppWizard—Step 1
window for the SeekIt
application.*

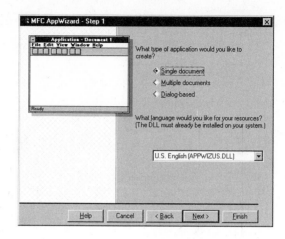

☐ Click the Next button of the Step 1 window.

Visual C++ responds by displaying the AppWizard—Step 2 of 6 window.

☐ Set the Step 2 of 6 window as shown in Figure 16.30. That is, in the SeekIt application you don't want any database support.

*Figure 16.30. The
AppWizard—Step 2 of 6
window for the SeekIt
application.*

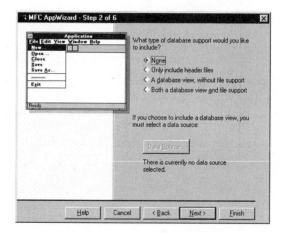

☐ Click the Next button of the Step 2 of 6 window.

Visual C++ responds by displaying the AppWizard—Step 3 of 6 window.

☐ Set the Step 3 of 6 window as shown in Figure 16.31. That is, in the SeekIt application you don't want any OLE support.

Figure 16.31. The
AppWizard—Step 3
of 6 window for the
SeekIt application.

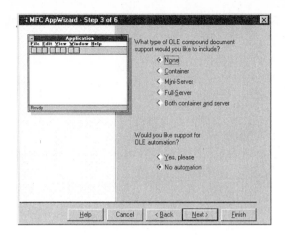

☐ Click the Next button of the Step 3 of 6 window.

Visual C++ responds by displaying the AppWizard—Step 4 of 6 window.

☐ Set the Step 4 of 6 window as shown in Figure 16.32.

Figure 16.32. The
AppWizard—Step 4
of 6 window for the
SeekIt application.

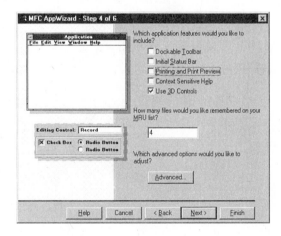

As shown in Figure 13.32, the features Dockable Toolbar, Initial Status Bar, Printing and Print Preview, and Context Sensitive Help will not be included in the SeekIt application.

☐ Click the Next button of the Step 4 of 6 window.

Visual C++ responds by displaying the AppWizard—Step 5 of 6 window.

☐ Set the Step 5 of 6 window as shown in Figure 16.33.

As shown in Figure 16.33, the project will be generated with comments, a Visual C++ makefile will be generated, and the application will use the MFC library from a DLL.

Figure 16.33. The AppWizard—Step 5 of 6 window for the SeekIt application.

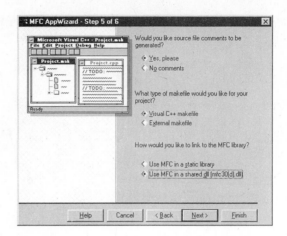

☐ Click the Next button of the Step 5 of 6 window.

Visual C++ responds by displaying the AppWizard—Step 6 of 6 window.

You'll now use the AppWizard—Step 6 of 6 window to tell AppWizard to derive the view class of the application from the MFC class `CFormView`:

☐ Select the `CFileitView` class inside the AppWizard—Step 6 of 6 window.

☐ Set the Base Class drop-down list box to `CFormView`.

Your AppWizard—Step 6 of 6 window should now look like the one shown in Figure 16.34.

Figure 16.34. The AppWizard—Step 6 of 6 window after you set the base class of the application view class to `CFormView`.

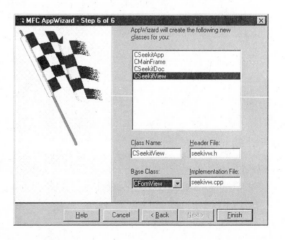

☐ Click the Finish button of the Step 6 of 6 window.

Visual C++ responds by displaying the New Project Information window, as shown in Figure 16.35.

Figure 16.35. The New Project Information window of the SeekIt.MAK project.

☐ Click the OK button of the New Project Information window.

Visual C++ responds by creating the project file and all the skeleton files of the application.

The Visual Implementation of the SeekIt Application Main Window

You'll now customize the IDD_SEEKIT_FORM dialog box (the dialog box that serves as the main window of the SeekIt application).

☐ Select seekit.rc from the Window menu, double-click the Dialog item to drop down a list of all the dialog boxes on the SeekIt.MAK project, and then double-click the IDD_SEEKIT_FORM item.

Visual C++ responds by displaying the IDD_SEEKIT_FORM dialog box in design mode.

☐ Delete the TODO: Place form controls on this dialog static text.

☐ Select Save from the File menu to save your work.

The Visual Implementation of the Menu of the SeekIt Application

The SeekIt application should have a menu, as shown in Figures 16.26 and 16.27.

☐ Implement the menu of the SeekIt program as specified in Table 16.3.

Table 16.3. The menu of the SeekIt application.

Menu Item	ID
&File	
E&xit	ID_APP_EXIT
&Sampling Rate	ID_FILE_SAMPLINGRATE
&Help	
&About Seekit	ID_APP_ABOUT

To save your work do the following:

☐ Select Save from the File menu.

The visual implementation of the menu of the SeekIt application is complete.

Modifying the About Dialog Box

Now take a look at the About dialog box that Visual C++ prepared for you.

☐ Compile and execute the SeekIt program.

☐ Select the About item from the Help menu.

> *SeekIt responds by displaying the About dialog box. (See Figure 16.36.)*

As shown in Figure 16.36, the default icon of the About dialog box is the Microsoft AFX icon.

Figure 16.36. The About dialog box with its default AFX icon.

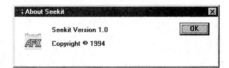

You'll now modify the icon of the About SeekIt dialog box.

Replace the icon of the About SeekIt dialog box with the X:\MVCProg\Icons\Sampling.ico icon. (See Fig-ure 16.37.)

Figure 16.37. The Sampling.ICO icon.

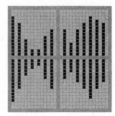

NOTE

To view *.ICO files, you can use a drawing program that lets you view *.ICO files.

Alternatively (and more conveniently), you can use Visual C++ to view *.ICO file by selecting Open from the File menu of Visual C++, setting the Open As edit box of the Open dialog box to Auto, and loading the *.ICO file that you want to view. Visual C++ loads the icon file and displays it as shown in Figure 16.38.

Figure 16.38. Viewing an icon file with Visual C++.

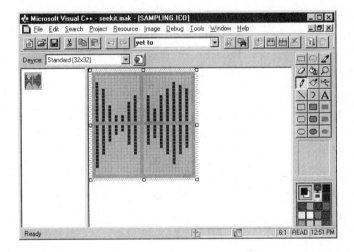

NOTE

The icon that appears inside the About SeekIt dialog box is presented for cosmetic reasons only. You should assign an icon that is related to the topic of the application. For example, the topic of the SeekIt application is sampling rate. Therefore, the icon in the About dialog box is Sampling.ICO, which represents audio samples.

Note that this icon also appears as the SeekIt application's icon when the window of the application is minimized. As you can see, now the user can easily identify the SeekIt application when its window is minimized.

Here is how you create the icon of the SeekIt application:

☐ Select seekit.rc from the Window menu.

☐ Double-click the Icon item that appears in the seekit.rc window.

  Visual C++ responds by dropping down a list of all the icons that the SeekIt.RC file contains. (See Figure 16.39.)

As shown in Figure 16.39, the SeekIt.RC file contains one icon, the IDR_MAINFRAME icon.

*Figure 16.39. Listing the
icons of the SeekIt.RC file.*

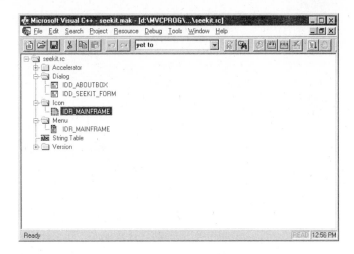

☐ Double-click the IDR_MAINFRAME icon item to display the icon.

Visual C++ responds by displaying the icon, as shown in Figure 16.40.

*Figure 16.40. The default
icon of the SeekIt
application (in design
mode).*

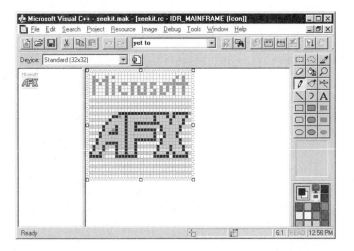

☐ Display the X:\MVCPROG\ICONS\Sampling.ICO file. (Take a look at the Window menu—it should contain the Sampling.ICO file because you loaded this file in the preceding steps.) If you already closed the Sampling.ICO file, then load it by selecting Open from the File menu and selecting X:\MVCPROG\ICONS\Sampling.ICO.

☐ Make sure that the icon picture is selected (that is, that the icon picture is enclosed by a rectangle), and then select Copy from the Edit menu.

Visual C++ responds by copying the icon to the Clipboard.

☐ Select seekit.rc—IDR_MAINFRAME (Icon) from the Window menu.

Visual C++ responds by displaying the IDR_MAINFRAME icon.

☐ Select Paste from the Edit menu to copy the contents of the Clipboard to the IDR_MAINFRAME icon.

Your IDR_MAINFRAME icon now contains the Sampling icon shown in Figure 16.37.

☐ Select Save from the File menu to save your work.

To see your design in action do the following:

☐ Compile, link, and execute the SeekIt application.

☐ Select About from the Help menu.

SeekIt responds by displaying the About dialog box, as shown in Figure 16.41. As shown, the About dialog box now contains the Sampling icon.

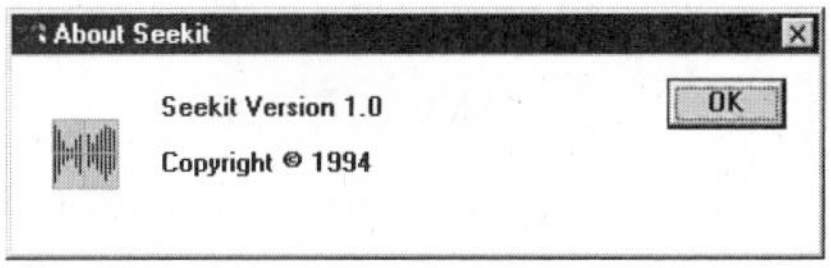

Figure 16.41. The modified About dialog box with the Sampling icon as the icon that appears inside the About dialog box.

☐ Click the OK button of the About dialog box to close the About dialog box, and then minimize the application.

As you can see, the icon of the minimized SeekIt application is the Sampling icon.

☐ Terminate the SeekIt application.

NOTE

When releasing commercial applications (as well as applications for in-house use), don't forget to replace the icon of the application as you did in the preceding steps.

There is nothing technically wrong with distributing your application with the default AFX icon as the icon of the application, but it gives the impression that you forgot to complete your application!

If you don't have a nice icon for your application, draw one yourself. For example, you can use the visual tools of Visual C++ to load the AFX icon, erase its contents, and to draw something else as the icon of your application. (For example, a simple icon such as the one shown in Figure 16.42.)

Note that you use the visual tools of Visual C++ in the same way that you use the visual tools of Paintbrush. One of the very useful visual tools of Visual C++ is the text tool (the icon that has the A character in it). This tool lets you type characters inside the icon that you are designing, so that you can design icons such as the one shown in Figure 16.42 without needing to have any artistic talent.

Figure 16.42. Using the visual tools of Visual C++ to draw a simple icon with the text tool.

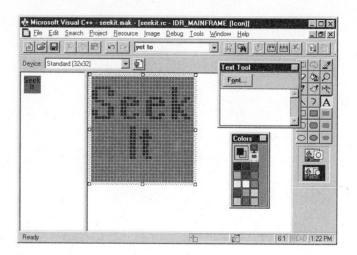

Attaching Code to the Sampling Rate Menu Item of the SeekIt Application

You'll now attach code to the Sampling Rate item of the File menu. Recall that when you select the Sampling Rate menu item, the SeekIt application should display the sampling rate of the 8Kenned3.WAV file.

☐ Select seekit.rc from the Window menu, double-click the Menu item, and then double-click the IDR_MAINFRAME item that appears under the Menu item.

   Visual C++ responds by displaying the menu of the SeekIt program in design mode.

NOTE

Sometimes, after performing various manipulations on the various components of the RC file (such as the manipulation that you performed on the icon of the application), you'll manage to confuse Visual C++, and Visual C++ will not be able to display the components of the RC file. In such cases, don't panic. Instead, close all the files, close the MAK file, and then load the MAK file again.

☐ Select ClassWizard from the Project menu, and add a new function to the following event (see Figure 16.43):

```
CSeekitView -> ID_FILE_SAMPLINGRATE -> COMMAND
```

Figure 16.43. Adding the
`OnFileSamplingRate()`
new member function.

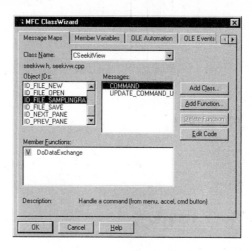

☐ Accept `OnFileSamplingRate()` as the name that Visual C++ suggests for the new function, click the Edit Code button to display the new function, and add code to the new function. After you add the code, your `OnFileSamplingRate()` function should look like this:

```
void CSeekitView::OnFileSamplingrate()
{
// TODO: Add your command handler code here


    ////////////////////////
    // MY CODE STARTS HERE
    ////////////////////////

    WORD  MyWord;
    char sSamplingRate[10];
CString Message;

    // Create an object (for reading the .WAV file)
    CFile theWAVfile ("\\MVCPROG\\WAV\\8Kenned3.WAV",
                    CFile::modeRead ) ;

    // Seek to byte number 24 (base 0)
    theWAVfile.Seek ( 24, CFile::begin );

    // Read 2 bytes from the WAV file into MyWord
    theWAVfile.Read ( &MyWord, 2 );


    // Display the sampling rate
    itoa ( (unsigned int)MyWord, sSamplingRate, 10 );
    Message =
    (CString)"The sampling rate of 8Kenned3.WAV is: " +
                        sSamplingRate ;
    MessageBox (Message);
```

```
///////////////////
// MY CODE ENDS HERE
///////////////////
```

```
}
```

The code you typed starts by declaring various local variables:

```
WORD  MyWord;
char sSamplingRate[10];
CString Message;
```

An object theWAVfile of class CFile is created:

```
CFile theWAVfile ("\\MVCPROG\\WAV\\8Kenned3.WAV",
                CFile::modeRead ) ;
```

Note that the first parameter in this object creation statement is \\MVCPROG\\WAV\\8Kenned3.WAV and the second parameter is CFile::modeRead. This means that the 8Kenned3.WAV file (on the current drive) is opened for reading.

The next statement utilizes the Seek() member function of CFile to seek the file to byte 24:

```
theWAVfile.Seek ( 24, CFile::begin );
```

You're interested in reading the 25th and 26th bytes of the 8Kenned3.WAV file. When seeking the file, byte 0 is considered the first byte of the file, byte 1 the second byte, and so on. This is the reason for supplying 24 as the first parameter of the Seek() function. The second parameter of the Seek() function is CFile::begin.

These parameters tell the Seek() function to count 24 bytes from the beginning of the file.

The next statement uses the Read() member function to read 2 bytes into the MyWord buffer:

```
theWAVfile.Read ( &MyWord, 2 );
```

Which 2 bytes will be read? The 2 bytes starting with the current file position. Because you set the current file position to 24 (with the Seek() function), the 2 bytes that will be read are byte 24 and byte 25. (Because byte 24 is actually the 25th byte, and byte 25 is actually the 26th byte, the 2 bytes to be read are the 2 bytes that contain the sampling rate).

The rest of the statements that you typed display the read data.

The itoa() function is used:

```
itoa ( (unsigned int)MyWord, sSamplingRate, 10 );
```

The CString message is constructed:

```
Message =
(CString)"The sampling rate of 8Kenned3.WAV is: " +
           sSamplingRate ;
```

Finally, the MessageBox() function is executed:

```
MessageBox (Message);
```

When you use the Seek() function with CFile:begin as its second parameter, the Seek() function positions the file to a certain number of bytes from the beginning of the file. For example, the function

```
theWAVfile.Seek (100, CFile::begin);
```

seeks the file 100 bytes from the beginning of the file.

In a similar manner, you can supply as the second parameter of the Seek() function the value

```
CFile::current
```

or the value

```
CFile::end
```

When supplying CFile::current as the second parameter of Seek(), the Seek() function will position the file a certain number of bytes from the current position. For example, the statements

```
theWAVfile.Seek(100, Cfile::begin);
theWAVfile.Seek(-25, Cfile::current);
theWAVfile.Seek(200, CFile::current);
```

set the position of the file 100 bytes from its beginning, then 25 bytes backward from the current position (that is, back to byte 75), and then 200 bytes forward from the current position.

The statement

```
theWAVfile (-100, CFile::end);
```

sets the file 100 bytes back from the end of the file.

☐ Compile, link, and execute the SeekIt application, and verify its operation. When you select Sampling Rate from the File menu, the program should display the sampling rate of 8Kenned3.WAV, as shown in Figure 16.44.

Figure 16.44. Displaying
the sampling rate of the
8Kenned3.WAV file.

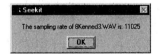

17

The Mouse

In this chapter you'll learn how to detect and respond to mouse events from within your programs, and how to draw with the mouse. As you know, the mouse is the recommended input device for Windows.

You've already learned how to attach code to mouse-clicking events on controls. For example, in previous chapters you attached code to the BN_CLICKED event that occurs whenever the user clicks the left button of the mouse.

In this chapter you'll attach code to other mouse events.

The MyMouse Application

Before you start writing the MyMouse application yourself, execute the copy of it that resides in the \MVCPROG\EXE directory of the book's CD.

To execute the MyMouse application do the following:

☐ Select Run from the Start menu of Windows and execute the X:\MVCPROG\EXE\MyMouse.EXE program (where *X* represents the drive letter of your CD-ROM drive).

  The main window of MyMouse.EXE appears, as shown in Figure 17.1.

Figure 17.1. The main window of the MyMouse application.

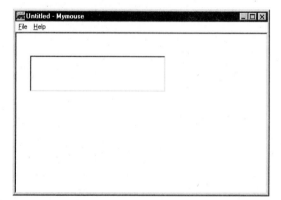

The MyMouse application has two pop-up menus: File and Help. These pop-up menus are shown in Figures 17.2 and 17.3.

☐ While the mouse cursor is inside the application's window but not inside the edit box, press the Ctrl key, and then while holding the Ctrl key down, push the left button of the mouse.

  MyMouse responds by displaying the following inside the edit box (See Figure 17.4.):

  [v] Left Mouse Down
  [v] Ctrl
  [ ] Right Button down

  [ ] SHIFT

Figure 17.2. The File menu of the MyMouse application.

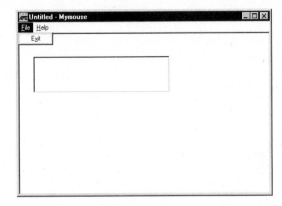

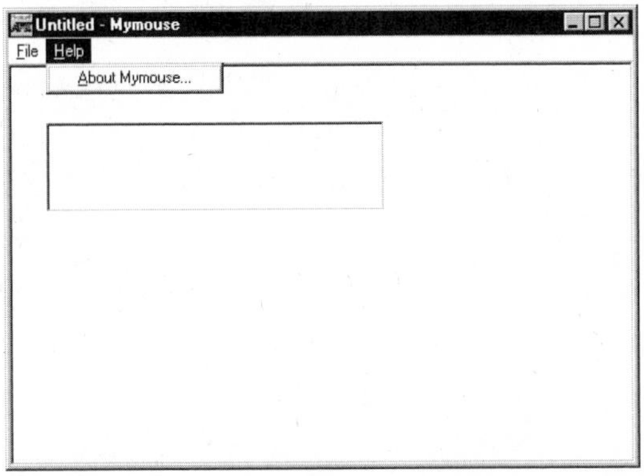

Figure 17.3. The Help menu of the MyMouse application.

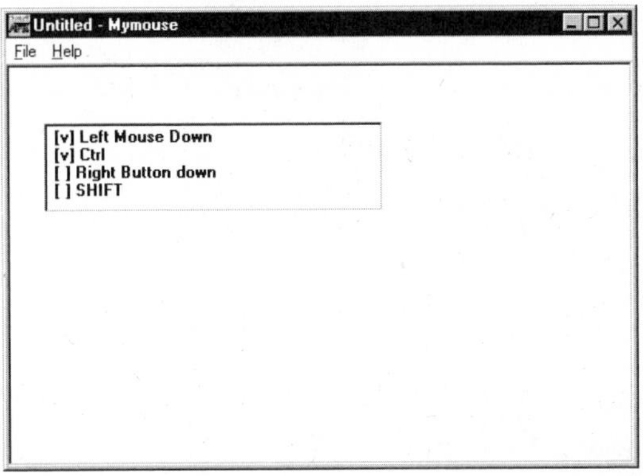

Figure 17.4. Displaying the status of the Ctrl key, the Shift key, and the right button of the mouse.

This means that the program detected that the Ctrl key was pressed down when you pushed the left button of the mouse.

☐ Experiment with the MyMouse program by first pressing the Ctrl key and/or the Shift key, and/or the right button of the mouse, and then push the left button of the mouse.

   MyMouse should display inside the edit box the status of these keys. Note that you can't write inside the edit box. That is, the edit box is a read-only control in the MyMouse application.

NOTE

The MyMouse application does not detect clicking of the right mouse button by itself. MyMouse will detect the clicking of the right button provided that while holding down the right mouse button, you push down the left button.

Similarly, MyMouse will not detect the pressing of the Shift or Ctrl keys unless they are pressed when the left button of the mouse is pushed.

Now that you know what MyMouse should do, you can write it.

Creating the Project of the MyMouse Application

To create the project of the MyMouse application do the following:

☐ Start Visual C++ and close all the open windows that appear inside the desktop of Visual C++ (if there are any).

☐ Select New from the File menu.

   Visual C++ responds by displaying the New dialog box.

☐ Select Project inside the New dialog box and then click the OK button of the New dialog box.

   Visual C++ responds by displaying the New Project dialog box.

☐ Set the Project Name to MyMouse.

☐ Set the Project Path to \MVCPROG\CH17\MyMouse\MyMouse.MAK.

Your New Project dialog box should now look like the one shown in Figure 17.5.

☐ Click the Create button of the New Project dialog box.

   Visual C++ responds by displaying the AppWizard—Step 1 window.

☐ Set the Step 1 window as shown in Figure 17.6. As shown in Figure 17.6, the MyMouse.MAK project is set as a single-document interface application, and U.S. English (APPWIZUS.DLL) is used as the language for the application's resources.

☐ Click the Next button of the Step 1 window.

   Visual C++ responds by displaying the AppWizard—Step 2 of 6 window.

Figure 17.5. The New
Project dialog box of the
MyMouse.MAK project.

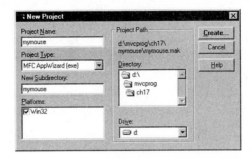

Figure 17.6. The
AppWizard—Step 1
window for the MyMouse
application.

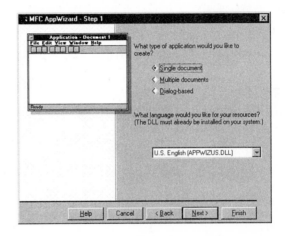

☐ Set the Step 2 of 6 window as shown in Figure 17.7. That is, in the MyMouse application
you don't want any database support.

Figure 17.7. The
AppWizard—Step 2 of 6
window for the MyMouse
application.

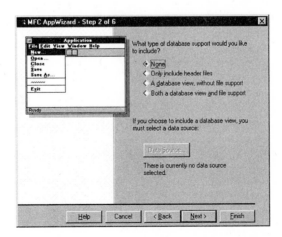

☐ Click the Next button of the Step 2 of 6 window.

  Visual C++ responds by displaying the AppWizard—Step 3 of 6 window.

☐ Set the Step 3 of 6 window as shown in Figure 17.8. That is, in the MyMouse application you don't want any OLE support.

Figure 17.8. The AppWizard—Step 3 of 6 window for the MyMouse application.

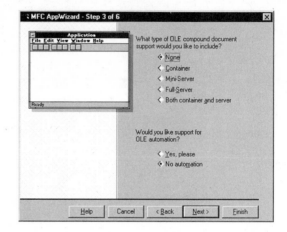

☐ Click the Next button of the Step 3 of 6 window.

  Visual C++ responds by displaying the AppWizard—Step 4 of 6 window.

☐ Set the Step 4 of 6 window as shown in Figure 17.9.

Figure 17.9. The AppWizard—Step 4 of 6 window for the MyMouse application.

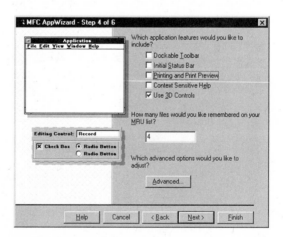

As shown in Figure 17.9, the features Dockable Toolbar, Initial Status Bar, Printing and Print Preview, and Context Sensitive Help will not be included in the MyMouse application.

☐ Click the Next button of the Step 4 of 6 window.

Visual C++ responds by displaying the AppWizard—Step 5 of 6 window.

☐ Set the Step 5 of 6 window as shown in Figure 17.10.

As shown in Figure 17.10, the project will be generated with comments, a Visual C++ makefile will be generated, and the application will use the MFC library from a DLL.

Figure 17.10. The AppWizard—Step 5 of 6 window for the MyMouse application.

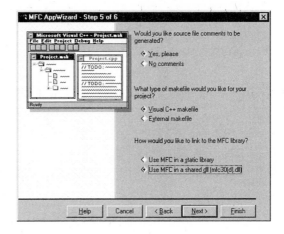

☐ Click the Next button of the Step 5 of 6 window.

Visual C++ responds by displaying the AppWizard—Step 6 of 6 window.

You'll now use the AppWizard—Step 6 of 6 window to tell AppWizard to derive the view class of the application from the MFC class CFormView:

☐ Select the CMymouseView class inside the AppWizard—Step 6 of 6 window.

☐ Set the Base Class drop-down list box to CFormView.

Your AppWizard—Step 6 of 6 window should now look as shown in Figure 17.11.

☐ Click the Finish button of the Step 6 of 6 window.

Visual C++ responds by displaying the New Project Information window, as shown in Figure 17.12.

☐ Click the OK button of the New Project Information window.

Visual C++ responds by creating the project file and all the skeleton files of the application.

Figure 17.11. The AppWizard—Step 6 of 6 window after you set the base class of the application view class to CFormView.

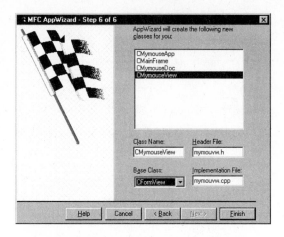

Figure 17.12. The New Project Information window of the MyMouse.MAK project.

The Visual Implementation of the Application's Form

Because in AppWizard you specified that the base class of the application's view class is CFormView, AppWizard created for you a form (a dialog box) that is attached to the view class of the application. This dialog box serves as the main window of the application. AppWizard named this dialog box IDD_MYMOUSE_FORM. You'll now customize the IDD_MYMOUSE_FORM dialog box.

☐ Double-click mymouse.rc inside the mymouse.mak window.

   Visual C++ responds by displaying the mymouse.rc window.

☐ Double-click Dialog inside the mymouse.rc window and then double-click IDD_MYMOUSE_FORM.

   Visual C++ responds by displaying the IDD_MYMOUSE_FORM dialog box in design mode.

☐ Delete the text TODO: Place form controls on this dialog. that Visual C++ placed inside the dialog box.

☐ Implement the dialog box according to the specifications in Table 17.1. When you finish implementing the dialog box, it should look like the one shown in Figure 17.13.

Table 17.1. The Properties table of the IDD_MYMOUSE_FORM dialog box.

Object	Property	Setting
Dialog box	ID	IDD_MYMOUSE_FORM
Edit box	ID	IDC_MOUSESTATUS_EDIT

Figure 17.13. The dialog box that serves as the main window of the MyMouse application (in design mode).

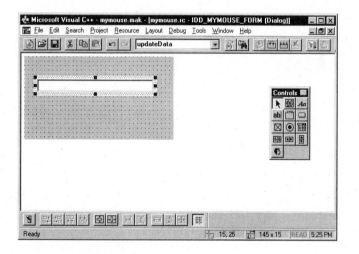

☐ Save your work by selecting Save from the File menu.

Attaching Variables to the Controls Inside the IDD_MYMOUSE_FORM Dialog Box

You'll now attach variables to the controls inside the IDD_MYMOUSE_FORM dialog box.

☐ Display the ClassWizard dialog box by selecting ClassWizard from the Project menu of Visual C++.

☐ Select the Member Variables tab at the top of ClassWizard's dialog box.

☐ Make sure the Class Name drop-down list is set to CMymouseView.

☐ Attach variables to the controls of the IDD_MYMOUSE_FORM dialog box as specified in Table 17.2.

Table 17.2. The Variables table of the IDD_MYMOUSE_FORM dialog box.

Control ID	Variable Name	Category	Variable Type
IDC_MOUSESTATUS_EDIT	m_MouseStatus	Value	Cstring

☐ To save your work, select Save from the File menu.

To see your visual design in action do the following:

☐ Select Build MyMouse.EXE from the Project menu.

Visual C++ responds by compiling and linking the MyMouse application.

☐ Select Execute MyMouse.EXE from the Project menu.

Visual C++ responds by executing the MyMouse.EXE application.

As expected, the IDD_MYMOUSE_FORM dialog box that you designed appears as the main window of the application. (See Figure 17.14.)

Figure 17.14. The main window of the MyMouse application.

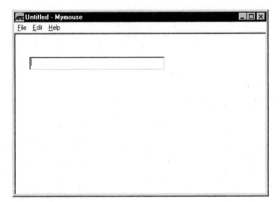

As you can see from Figure 17.14, the menu bar of the MyMouse application (the menu bar that AppWizard created for you) has an Edit pop-up menu. However, the menu bar of the MyMouse application should not have an Edit pop-up menu. (Refer back to Figure 17.1.) Later you'll customize the menu bar of the MyMouse application so that it will not have an Edit pop-up menu.

☐ Terminate the MyMouse application by selecting Exit from the File menu.

Changing the Properties of the Edit Box

You'll now make the IDC_MOUSESTATUS_EDIT edit box read-only.

☐ Display the IDD_MYMOUSE_FORM dialog box in design mode by selecting mymouse.rc-IDD_MYMOUSE_FORM [Dialog] from the Window menu of Visual C++.

☐ Double-click the IDC_MOUSESTATUS_EDIT edit box.

> *Visual C++ responds by displaying the Edit Properties dialog box for the*
> *IDC_MOUSESTATUS_EDIT edit box.*

☐ Select the Styles tab of the Edit Properties dialog box.

☐ Set the Styles properties of the IDC_MOUSESTATUS_EDIT edit box by placing a
checkmark inside the Read Only check box.

The Style properties window of your IDC_MOUSESTATUS_EDIT edit box should now look
like the one shown in Figure 17.15.

Figure 17.15. Setting the
Style properties of the
IDC_MOUSESTATUS_EDIT
edit box.

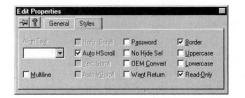

☐ Save your work by selecting Save from the File menu of Visual C++.

The Visual Implementation of the Menu Bar

The MyMouse application should have a menu, as shown in Figures 17.2 and 17.3.

Implementing this menu is very easy, because the menu bar that AppWizard created for you
(IDR_MAINFRAME) is almost what you need. All you have to do is delete the Edit pop-up menu
and modify the File menu.

Follow these steps to customize the IDR_MAINFRAME menu:

☐ Select mymouse.rc from the Window menu of Visual C++.

> *Visual C++ responds by displaying the mymouse.rc window.*

☐ Double-click Menu inside the mymouse.rc window and then double-click
IDR_MAINFRAME.

> *Visual C++ responds by displaying the IDR_MAINFRAME menu bar in design mode.*

As you can see, the IDR_MAINFRAME menu currently has three pop-up menus: File, Edit, and
Help.

Because the MyMouse application should not have an Edit menu, you have to remove the Edit
pop-up menu:

☐ Click the Edit item on the menu bar.

> *Visual C++ responds by opening the Edit pop-up menu.*

☐ Now press the Delete key on your keyboard.

   Visual C++ responds by displaying a dialog box warning you that you're about to delete an entire pop-up menu.

☐ Click the OK button of the warning dialog box.

   Visual C++ responds by deleting the Edit pop-up menu.

Take a look at the Help menu. (See Figure 17.16.) As you can see, the Help menu is exactly as you want it to be, so there is no need to modify this menu. However, the File menu is not exactly as you want it to be. (See Figure 17.17.)

Figure 17.16. The default Help menu of the MyMouse program.

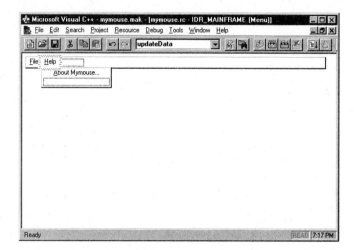

Figure 17.17. The default File menu of the MyMouse program.

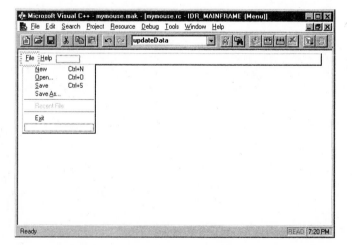

You'll now modify the File menu.

☐ Delete all the items in the File menu except the Exit item. After you delete the items, the File menu should look like the one shown in Figure 17.18.

Figure 17.18. The modified File menu of the MyMouse program.

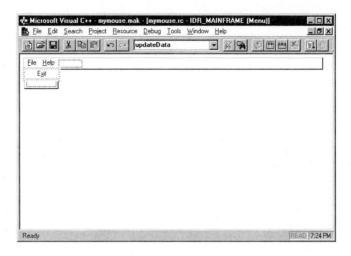

☐ Save your work by selecting Save from the File menu of Visual C++.

The visual implementation of the menu of the MyMouse application is complete. To see your visual design in action do the following:

☐ Select Build MyMouse.EXE from the Project menu.

Visual C++ responds by compiling and linking the MyMouse application.

☐ Select Execute MyMouse.EXE from the Project menu.

Visual C++ responds by executing the MyMouse.EXE application.

As expected, the menu bar of the application appears as you customized it—it now has only two pop-up menus: File and Help.

☐ Verify that the edit box is read-only (that is, you can't type inside the edit box).

☐ Verify that the File and Help menus look as shown in Figures 17.2 and 17.3.

☐ Terminate the MyMouse application by selecting Exit from the File menu.

Attaching Code to the *OnLButtonDown()* Function

You'll now attach code that will be executed whenever the user pushes the left button of the mouse.

☐ Display the ClassWizard dialog box by selecting ClassWizard from the Project menu of Visual C++.

☐ Select the Message Maps tab at the top of ClassWizard's dialog box.

☐ Use ClassWizard to select the event:

```
CMymouseView -> CMymouseView -> WM_LBUTTONDOWN
```

☐ Click the Add Function button.

> *Visual C++ responds by adding the* OnLButtonDown() *member function to the* CMymouseView *class.*

☐ Click the Edit Code button of ClassWizard.

> *ClassWizard responds by opening the file MyMouVW.CPP, with the function* OnLButtonDown() *ready to be edited by you.*

☐ Write code inside the OnLButtonDown() function so that it looks like this:

```
void CMymouseView::OnLButtonDown(UINT nFlags, CPoint point)
{
// TODO: Add your message handler code
// here and/or call default


    /////////////////////////
    // MY CODE STARTS HERE
    /////////////////////////

    MessageBeep((WORD)-1);

    /////////////////////////
    // MY CODE ENDS HERE
    /////////////////////////


CFormView::OnLButtonDown(nFlags, point);
}
```

☐ Save your work by selecting Save from the File menu.

The code that you typed uses the MessageBeep() function to cause the PC to beep.

As you can see, you are just demonstrating the operation of the OnLButtonDown() function by executing the MessageBeep() function. In other words, whenever you click the left button of the mouse, the MyMouse application should beep.

Note that the WORD cast is used when executing the MessageBeep() function:

```
MessageBeep((WORD)-1);
```

The cast is required because MessageBeep() expects WORD as its parameter. When you supply -1 as the parameter of the MessageBeep(), the MessageBeep() function causes the PC to beep.

> **NOTE**
>
> The trick of beeping for the purpose of testing whether the code is attached to the proper function is very useful.
>
> However, as you gain more experience with Visual C++ and write more complex applications, you'll soon discover that this trick does not always work! This is because sometimes Windows generates a beep when a certain error occurs (such as clicking the left mouse button inside an invalid area).
>
> Suppose that you compile the MyMouse application, execute it, and discover that whenever you click the left button of the mouse, the PC beeps. Does the beeping occur because of the `MessageBeep()` statement that you inserted inside the `OnLButtonDown()` function, or because every time you click the mouse Windows generates a beeping error?
>
> In the case of the MyMouse application you can trust us that the beeping will occur because of the clicking of the mouse. However, in more complex applications, you might want to resort to another testing mechanism. An alternate way of testing whether a certain code that you typed is being executed is to insert the `MessageBox()` statement with a string as its parameter. For example, you may consider replacing the `MessageBeep(-1)` statement with the statement
>
> ```
> MessageBox (
> "I'm inside the OnLButtonDown() function"
> );.
> ```

☐ To save your work, select Save All from the File menu.

To see your code in action do the following:

☐ Select Build MyMouse.EXE from the Project menu.

 Visual C++ responds by compiling and linking the MyMouse application.

☐ Select Execute MyMouse.EXE from the Project menu.

 Visual C++ responds by executing the MyMouse.EXE application.

☐ Push the left button of the mouse inside a free area of the window (but not inside the edit box).

 MyMouse responds by beeping. This proves that indeed the `OnLButtonDown()` function is executed whenever you push the left button of the mouse.

☐ Experiment with the MyMouse application and then terminate the application by selecting Exit from the File menu.

☐ Edit the OnLButtonDown() function by changing the MessageBeep((WORD)-1) statement to this:

```
MessageBox ("I'm Here!");
```

☐ Compile, link, and execute the MyMouse application, and verify that every time you push the left button of the mouse over a free area of the window, the application displays the message I'm Here! inside the message box.

☐ Experiment with the MyMouse application and then select Exit from the File menu.

Attaching Code to the Left Button Up Event

The term *click* means that two separate events occur: the mouse button is pushed down and the mouse button is released.

In the previous section you attached code to the pushing of the left button event. Here is how you attach code to the event of releasing the left button:

☐ Display the ClassWizard dialog box by selecting ClassWizard from the Project menu of Visual C++.

☐ Select the Message Maps tab at the top of ClassWizard's dialog box.

☐ Use ClassWizard to select the event:

```
CMymouseView -> CMymouseView -> WM_LBUTTONUP
```

☐ Click the Add Function button.

Visual C++ responds by adding the function OnLButtonUp() *member function to the* CMymouseView *class.*

☐ Click the Edit Code button of ClassWizard.

ClassWizard responds by opening the file MYMOUVW.CPP, with the function OnLButtonUp() *ready to be edited by you.*

☐ Write code inside the OnLButtonUp() function so that it looks like this:

```
void CMymouseView::OnLButtonUp(UINT nFlags, CPoint point)
{
// TODO: Add your message handler code
// here and/or call default


/////////////////////////
// MY CODE STARTS HERE
/////////////////////////

m_MouseStatus = "Left button of mouse is up";
UpdateData(FALSE);
```

```
/////////////////////
// MY CODE ENDS HERE
/////////////////////
```

```
CFormView::OnLButtonUp(nFlags, point);
}
```

☐ Save your work by selecting Save from the File menu.

The code that you typed is executed whenever the user releases the left button of the mouse. This code places inside the edit box text that tells the user the status of the mouse's left button:

```
m_MouseStatus = "Left button of mouse is up";
UpdateData(FALSE);
```

☐ Display the ClassWizard dialog box by selecting ClassWizard from the Project menu of Visual C++.

☐ Select the Message Maps tab at the top of ClassWizard's dialog box.

☐ Use ClassWizard to select the event:

```
CMymouseView -> CMymouseView -> WM_LBUTTONDOWN
```

☐ Click the Edit Code button of ClassWizard.

ClassWizard responds by opening the file MYMOUVW.CPP, with the function OnLButtonDown() *ready to be edited by you.*

☐ Edit the code inside the OnLButtonDown() function so that it looks like this:

```
void CMymouseView::OnLButtonDown(UINT nFlags, CPoint point)
{
// TODO: Add your message handler code
// here and/or call default


    ///////////////////////
    // MY CODE STARTS HERE
    ///////////////////////

    //MessageBeep((WORD)-1);

        //MessageBox ("I'm Here!");

    m_MouseStatus = "Left button of mouse is down";
    UpdateData(FALSE);


    /////////////////////
    // MY CODE ENDS HERE
    /////////////////////


CFormView::OnLButtonDown(nFlags, point);
}
```

The code you typed is executed whenever the user presses the left button of the mouse. This code places inside the edit box text that tells the user the status of the mouse's left button:

```
m_MouseStatus = "Left button of mouse is down";
UpdateData(FALSE);
```

☐ To save your work, select Save All from the File menu.

To see your code in action do the following:

☐ Select Build MyMouse.EXE from the Project menu.

Visual C++ responds by compiling and linking the MyMouse application.

☐ Select Execute MyMouse.EXE from the Project menu.

Visual C++ responds by executing the MyMouse.EXE application.

☐ Push the left button of the mouse while the mouse cursor is inside a free area of the window of the MyMouse application, and hold down the button.

MyMouse responds by displaying the text `Left button of mouse is down` *in the edit box.*

☐ Release the left button of the mouse.

MyMouse responds by displaying the text `Left button of mouse is up` *in the edit box. (See Figures 17.19 and 17.20.)*

Figure 17.19. The string inside the edit box when the left button of the mouse is down.

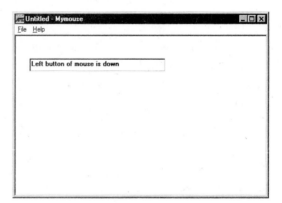

☐ Experiment with the MyMouse application and then terminate the application by selecting Exit from the File menu.

Who Receives the Messages?

When the left mouse button is released, Windows sends the message WM_LBUTTONUP. The question is Who receives and acts on the message? It depends on where the mouse pointer was located when the left button was released. If the mouse pointer was inside a free area of the window of the MyMouse application, Windows sends the message WM_LBUTTONUP to the MyMouse application. If the left mouse button was released outside the MyMouse window, however, MyMouse doesn't receive the message. You can easily verify that by completing the following steps:

☐ Execute the MyMouse program, push the left button of the mouse while the mouse cursor is inside the window of MyMouse, and keep holding the left button of the mouse down. While the left button of the mouse is down, move the mouse until the cursor of the mouse is outside the window of MyMouse, and then release the left button of the mouse.

Figure 17.20. The string inside the edit box when the left button of the mouse is up.

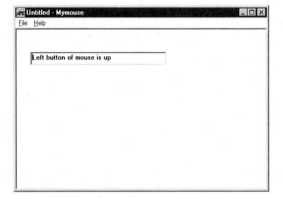

As you can see, the edit box does not reflect the fact that the left button of the mouse was released. This, of course, means that the OnLButtonUp() function was not executed. It was not executed because the left button was released outside the window of MyMouse, and hence Windows did not send the WM_LBUTTONUP message to MyMouse.

NOTE

Experiment with the MyMouse application, and note that if you release the left button of the mouse inside the rectangle that encloses the menu bar, Windows does not send the WM_LBUTTONUP message to MyMouse. In other words, Windows sends the WM_LBUTTONUP message to MyMouse only if the left button of the mouse is released inside the area that is enclosed by the bottom edge of the menu bar, and the left, right, and bottom edges of the window's frame. This area is called the client area.

In a similar manner, Windows sends the WM_LBUTTONDOWN message to MyMouse only if the left button of the mouse is pushed while the mouse cursor is inside the client area.

The Parameters of the *OnLButtonDown()* Function

Take a look at the parameters of the `OnLButtonDown()` function:

```
void CMymouseView::OnLButtonDown(UINT nFlags, CPoint point)
{
....
....
....
}
```

The parameters are `nFlags` and `point`. These parameters provide you with additional information about the event. In particular, the `point` parameter contains the location of the mouse cursor when the left button of the mouse was pushed. The `nFlags` parameter contains information regarding the status of the right button of the mouse, the Shift key, and the Ctrl key, at the time the left button was pushed.

The value of `nFlags` can be tested as follows:

If `nFlags & MK_CONTROL` is equal to `MK_CONTROL`, you know that the user pushed the left button of the mouse while the Ctrl key was pressed.

If `nFlags & MK_SHIFT` is equal to `MK_SHIFT`, you know that the user pushed the left button of the mouse while the Shift key was pressed.

If `nFlags & MK_RBUTTON` is equal to `MK_RBUTTON`, you know that the user pushed the left button of the mouse while the right button of the mouse was pushed down.

☐ Modify the `OnLButtonDown()` function. After the modification, your `OnLButtonDown()` function inside the MYMOUVW.CPP file should look like this:

```
void CMymouseView::OnLButtonDown(UINT nFlags, CPoint point)
{
// TODO: Add your message handler code
// here and/or call default

        ////////////////////////
        // MY CODE STARTS HERE
        ////////////////////////

        char LFCR[3]; // Variable to hold LF+CR

        LFCR[0] = 13;   // CR
        LFCR[1] = 10;   // LF
        LFCR[2] = 0;

        // Update the variable of the edit box.
        m_MouseStatus =
           (CString)" [v] Left Mouse Down " + LFCR;

        // Was the Ctrl key pressed?
        if ( (nFlags & MK_CONTROL) == MK_CONTROL )
           m_MouseStatus =
                  m_MouseStatus + " [v] Ctrl " + LFCR;
        else
           m_MouseStatus =
                  m_MouseStatus + " [ ] Ctrl " + LFCR;
```

```
    // Was the mouse right button pressed?
    if ( (nFlags & MK_RBUTTON) == MK_RBUTTON )
        m_MouseStatus =
                m_MouseStatus + " [v] Right Button down "
             + LFCR;
    else
        m_MouseStatus =
                m_MouseStatus + " [ ] Right Button down "
             + LFCR;

    // Was the SHIFT key pressed?
    if ( (nFlags & MK_SHIFT) == MK_SHIFT )
        m_MouseStatus =
           m_MouseStatus + " [v] SHIFT ";
    else
        m_MouseStatus =
           m_MouseStatus + " [ ] SHIFT ";

    // Update the screen with the new
    // value of m_MouseStatus
    UpdateData(FALSE);

    /////////////////////
    // MY CODE ENDS HERE
    /////////////////////
```

```
CFormView::OnLButtonDown(nFlags, point);
}
```

This code declares a local variable called LFCR:

```
char LFCR[3]; // Variable to hold LF+CR
```

This variable is updated with the values of the carriage return character (13), the line feed character (10), and the string null terminator (0):

```
LFCR[0] = 13;  // CR
LFCR[1] = 10;  // LF
LFCR[2] = 0;
```

The variable m_MouseStatus is then updated:

```
m_MouseStatus =
   (CString)" [v] Left Mouse Down " + LFCR;
```

Note that the CString casting is used in this statement. This is necessary because the statement adds strings to m_MouseStatus, which is an object of class CString. When you add strings, as in the preceding statement, at least one of the strings must be of class CString. If none of the added strings is of class CString, then you have to cast one of the strings as CString. (If you don't use the casting, you'll get a compiling error: Can't add two pointers.)

The next statements use if to determine whether the Ctrl, Shift, and right button of the mouse were pressed while the left button of the mouse was pushed. Here is the if statement that determines whether the Ctrl key was pressed:

```
if ( (nFlags & MK_CONTROL) == MK_CONTROL )
   m_MouseStatus =
```

```
        m_MouseStatus + " [v] Ctrl " + LFCR;
else
   m_MouseStatus =
        m_MouseStatus + " [ ] Ctrl " + LFCR;
```

If the if condition is satisfied, then m_MouseStatus is equal to this:

```
[v] Left Mouse Down
[v] Ctrl
```

If the if condition is not satisfied, then m_MouseStatus is equal to this:

```
[v] Left Mouse Down
[ ] Ctrl
```

Note that the contents of m_MouseStatus will spread over two lines because of the carriage return/line feed.

In a similar manner, the next if statement checks whether the Shift key was pressed at the time that the left button of the mouse was clicked, and the last if statement checks whether the right button of the mouse was pushed at the time the left button was clicked.

The MyMouse application did not check whether the middle button of the mouse was pushed. If you write an application that makes use of the middle button on a mouse with three buttons, then use the following if statement:

```
if ( (nFlags & MK_MBUTTON) == MK_MBUTTON )
    {
    Here you write the code that should
    be executed whenever the left button
    of the mouse is pushed while the middle
    button is down.
    }
```

The last statement uses the UpdateData(FALSE) function to transfer the contents of m_MouseStatus to the edit box:

```
UpdateData(FALSE);
```

Because of the insertion of the carriage return/line feed in between the strings, the edit box should display the string on multiple lines.

If you compile, link, and execute the MyMouse application, you'll discover that the strings the edit box is supposed to display are not displayed on multiple lines! Why? You did not set the Multiple Lines property of the edit box. Here is how you set the Multiple Lines property of the edit box:

☐ Display the IDD_MYMOUSE_FORM dialog box in design mode by selecting mymouse.rc-IDD_MYMOUSE_FORM [Dialog] from the Window menu of Visual C++.

☐ Double-click the IDC_MOUSESTATUS_EDIT edit box.

   Visual C++ responds by displaying the Edit Properties dialog box for the IDC_MOUSESTATUS_EDIT edit box.

☐ Select the Styles tab of the Edit Properties dialog box.

☐ Set the Styles properties of the IDC_MOUSESTATUS_EDIT edit box by placing a checkmark inside the Multiline check box.

The Style properties window of your IDC_MOUSESTATUS_EDIT edit box should now look like the one shown in Figure 17.21. (The Multiline check box is located on the lower-left corner of the dialog box.)

Figure 17.21. Setting the Style properties of the IDC_MOUSESTATUS_EDIT edit box.

☐ Save your work by selecting Save All from the File menu of Visual C++.

☐ While in design mode, increase the size of the edit box. When you finish increasing the size of the edit box, it should look like the edit box shown in Figure 17.22.

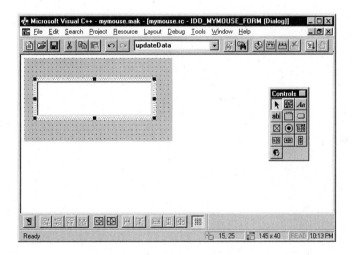

Figure 17.22. Increasing the size of the IDC_MOUSESTATUS_EDIT edit box.

Currently, you have code inside the OnLButtonUp() function (inside the MYMOUVW.CPP file). Recall that you used ClassWizard to add this function, and then you typed code inside this function. At this point, you don't need this function anymore, so delete it. Here is how you delete this function:

☐ Start ClassWizard from the Project menu, select the Messages Map tab, select the OnLButtonUp() function in the list box at the bottom of the ClassWizard dialog box, and then click the Delete Function button.

Visual C++ responds by displaying the dialog box shown in Figure 17.23.

Figure 17.23. The dialog box that Visual C++ displays when you click the Delete Function button.

☐ Click the Yes button of the dialog box shown in Figure 17.23.

Note that the dialog box shown in Figure 17.23 tells you that you have to manually delete the `OnLButtonUp()` function. In other words, Visual C++ removed the declaration of this member function from the `CMymouseView` class declaration, but it is your responsibility to actually remove the function.

☐ Delete the `OnLButtonUp()` function from the MyMouVW.CPP file so that the `OnLButtonUp()` function looks like this:

```
//void CMymouseView::OnLButtonUp(UINT nFlags, CPoint point)
//{
// TODO: Add your message handler code
// here and/or call default


/////////////////////////
// MY CODE STARTS HERE
/////////////////////////

//m_MouseStatus = "Left button of mouse is up";
//UpdateData(FALSE);


/////////////////////////
// MY CODE ENDS HERE
/////////////////////////


//      CFormView::OnLButtonUp(nFlags, point);
//}
```

In other words, you commented all the lines of the `OnLButtonUp()` function. (You could have deleted these lines instead of commenting them out.)

Earlier you learned the meaning of the `nFlags` parameter of the `OnLButtonDown()` function. As you can imagine, there are hundreds of other event-related functions in Visual C++. Are you supposed to remember the meanings of the parameters of all the functions? Not at all! You should remember that the `OnLButtonDown()` function is executed whenever the left button of the mouse is down. (This is not hard to remember, because the name of the function implies its purpose.) To figure out the meanings of the parameters of the function do the following:

☐ Double-click on any of the characters of the `OnLButtonDown()` function inside MYMOUVW.CPP.

Visual C++ responds by highlighting the `OnLButtonDown()` *characters.*

☐ Press F1.

Visual C++ responds by displaying the Help window for this function. (See Figure 17.24.)

This Help window tells you everything you need to know about the parameters of the function.

*Figure 17.24. The Help
window for the
OnLButtonDown()
function.*

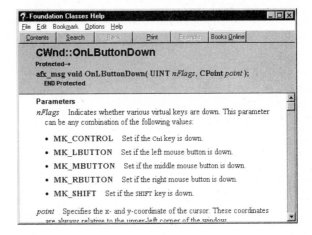

The MyMouse application is now ready to be compiled, linked, and tested.

☐ To save your work, select Save All from the File menu.

To see your code in action do the following:

☐ Select Build MyMouse.EXE from the Project menu.

Visual C++ responds by compiling and linking the MyMouse application.

☐ Select Execute MyMouse.EXE from the Project menu.

Visual C++ responds by executing the MyMouse.EXE application.

☐ Experiment with the MyMouse program and verify its proper operation. For example, press the Shift key and the right button of the mouse, and then push the left button of the mouse. MyMouse should respond by displaying the corresponding strings inside the edit box. Note that there is a v for the Shift key and for the right button of the mouse. But there is no v for the Ctrl key, because you did not press the Ctrl key. (See Figure 17.25.)

☐ Terminate the application by selecting Exit from the File menu.

NOTE

The OnLButtonDown() function will detect the fact that the Shift key, the Ctrl key, or the right button of the mouse are pressed together with the left button of the mouse, provided that you pressed the Shift key, the Ctrl key, or the right button of the mouse prior to pressing the left button.

For example, if you press the Shift key and only then press the left button of the mouse, OnLButtonDown() will report that the Shift key and the left button of the mouse are pressed. However, if you push the left button of the mouse, and then press the Shift key, then the OnLButtonDown() function will not report that the Shift key is pressed. This makes sense because once you push the left button of the mouse, the OnLButtonDown() function is executed. The fact that you later pressed the Shift key will not be known because it is too late! The OnLButtonDown() function was executed already.

This is an important fact that should be noted in the documentation of your program. For example, suppose that you write a program that lets your user perform a certain operation whenever the user presses the Shift key and then pushes the left button of the mouse. Your code might look like this:

```
void CMymouseView::OnLButtonDown(UINT nFlags, CPoint point)
{
// TODO: Add your message handler code here and/or call
// default

    /////////////////////////
    // MY CODE STARTS HERE
    /////////////////////////


    if ( (nFlags & MK_SHIFT) == MK_SHIFT )
       {
       Here is the code that is executed
       whenever the user presses the SHIFT
       key, and while holding the SHIFT key,
       then presses the left button of the
       mouse.
       }


    ////////////////////
    // MY CODE ENDS HERE
    ////////////////////


    CFormView::OnLButtonDown(nFlags, point);
}
```

Note that the OnLButtonUp() function has identical parameters to the OnLButtonDown() function.

Figure 17.25. The edit box
showing that the right
button of the mouse and the
Shift key are pressed
together with the left button
of the mouse.

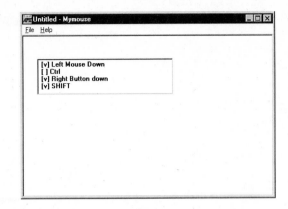

The *point* Parameter of the *OnLButtonUp()* and *OnLButtonDown()* Functions

As you have seen, the OnLButtonDown() and OnLButtonUp() functions have point as their second parameter. This parameter contains the coordinates of the mouse cursor when the event took place. This is a very useful piece of information!

The next application that you write in this chapter is called the WhereAmI application. This application demonstrates how you can use the point parameter.

The WhereAmI Application

Before you start writing the WhereAmI application yourself, execute the copy of it that resides in the \MVCPROG\EXE directory of the book's CD.

To execute the WhereAmI application do the following:

☐ Select Run from the Start menu of Windows and execute the X:\MVCPROG\EXE\WhereAmI.EXE program (where *X* represents the drive letter of your CD-ROM drive).

   The main window of WhereAmI.EXE appears, as shown in Figure 17.26.

The MyMouse application has two pop-up menus: File and Help. These pop-up menus are shown in Figures 17.27 and 17.28.

☐ Move the mouse inside the window of the WhereAmI application.

WhereAmI responds by displaying the coordinates of the mouse cursor. (See Figure 17.29.) In Figure 17.29, the center of the black dot represents the mouse cursor position. As shown, the coordinates of this point are 324 pixels from the left edge of the window and 161 pixels from the top edge of the window.

☐ Experiment with the WhereAmI application, and then select Exit from the File menu to terminate the application.

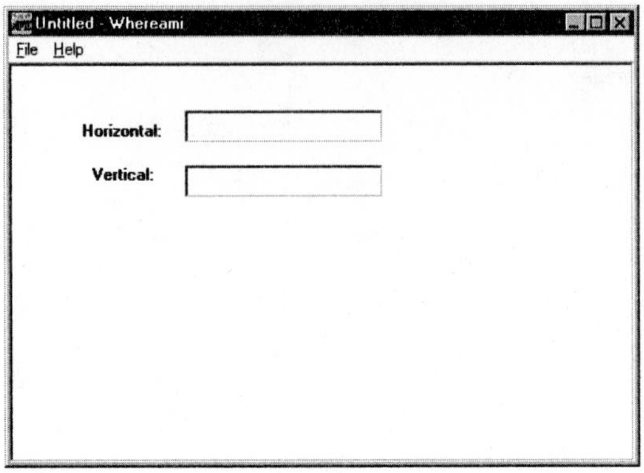

Figure 17.26. The main window of the WhereAmI application.

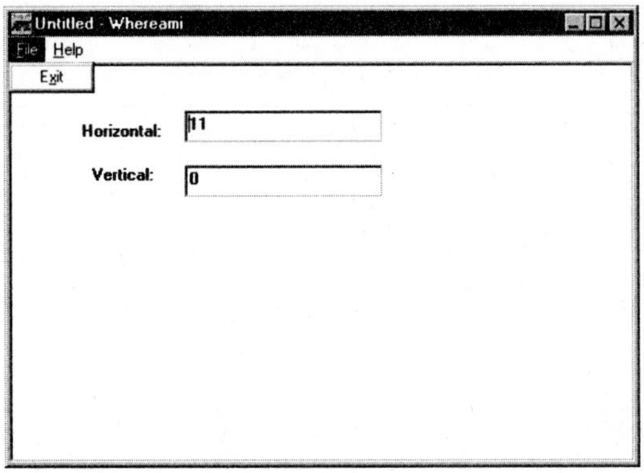

Figure 17.27. The File menu of the WhereAmI application.

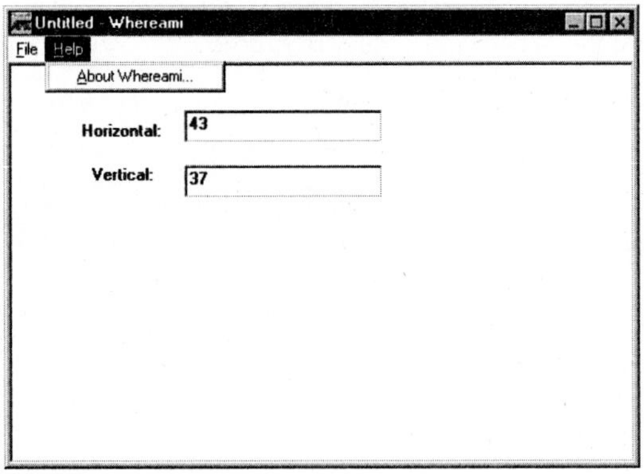

Figure 17.28. The Help menu of the WhereAmI application.

Figure 17.29. Placing the mouse cursor at coordinates (324,161).

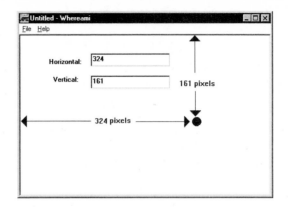

Creating the Project of the WhereAmI Application

To create the project of the WhereAmI application do the following:

☐ Start Visual C++ and close all the open windows that appear inside the desktop of Visual C++ (if there are any).

☐ Select New from the File menu.

Visual C++ responds by displaying the New dialog box.

☐ Select Project inside the New dialog box and then click the OK button of the New dialog box.

Visual C++ responds by displaying the New Project dialog box.

☐ Set the project name to WhereAmI.

☐ Set the project path to \MVCPROG\CH17\WhereAmI\WhereAmI.MAK.

Your New Project dialog box should now look like the one shown in Figure 17.30.

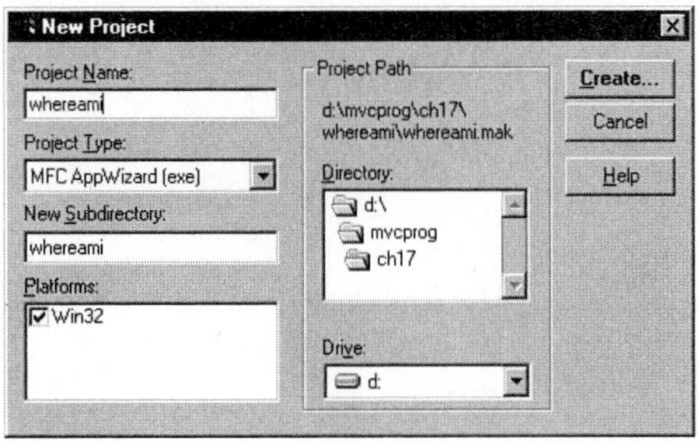

Figure 17.30. The New Project dialog box of the WhereAmI.MAK project.

☐ Click the Create button of the New Project dialog box.

   Visual C++ responds by displaying the AppWizard—Step 1 window.

☐ Set the Step 1 window as shown in Figure 17.31. As shown in Figure 17.31, the WhereAmI.MAK project is set as a single-document interface application, and U.S. English (APPWIZUS.DLL) is used as the language for the application's resources.

Figure 17.31. The AppWizard—Step 1 window for the WhereAmI application.

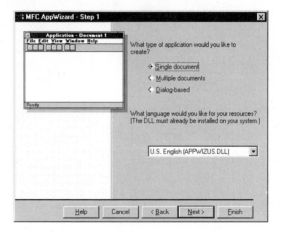

☐ Click the Next button of the Step 1 window.

   Visual C++ responds by displaying the AppWizard—Step 2 of 6 window.

☐ Set the Step 2 of 6 window as shown in Figure 17.32. That is, in the WhereAmI application you don't want any database support.

Figure 17.32. The AppWizard—Step 2 of 6 window for the WhereAmI application.

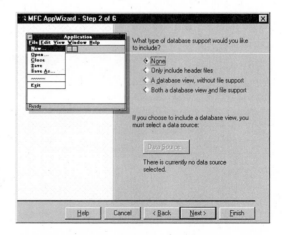

☐ Click the Next button of the Step 2 of 6 window.

   Visual C++ responds by displaying the AppWizard—Step 3 of 6 window.

☐ Set the Step 3 of 6 window as shown in Figure 17.33. That is, in the WhereAmI application you don't want any OLE support.

Figure 17.33. The AppWizard—Step 3 of 6 window for the WhereAmI application.

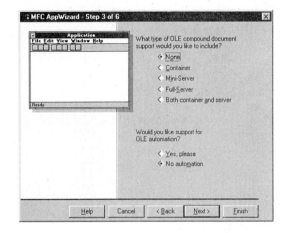

☐ Click the Next button of the Step 3 of 6 window.

Visual C++ responds by displaying the AppWizard—Step 4 of 6 window.

☐ Set the Step 4 of 6 window as shown in Figure 17.34.

Figure 17.34. The AppWizard—Step 4 of 6 window for the WhereAmI application.

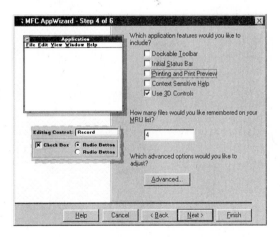

As shown in Figure 17.34, the features Dockable Toolbar, Initial Status Bar, Printing and Print Preview, and Context Sensitive Help will not be included in the WhereAmI application.

☐ Click the Next button of the Step 4 of 6 window.

Visual C++ responds by displaying the AppWizard—Step 5 of 6 window.

☐ Set the Step 5 of 6 window as shown in Figure 17.35.

*Figure 17.35. The
AppWizard—Step 5 of 6
window for the WhereAmI
application.*

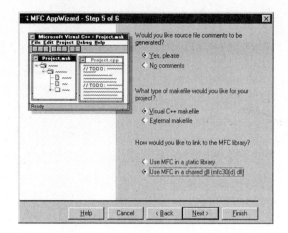

As shown in Figure 17.35, the project will be generated with comments, a Visual C++ makefile will be generated, and the application will use the MFC library from a DLL.

☐ Click the Next button of the Step 5 of 6 window.

Visual C++ responds by displaying the AppWizard—Step 6 of 6 window.

You'll now use the AppWizard—Step 6 of 6 window to tell AppWizard to derive the view class of the application from the MFC class `CFormView`:

☐ Select the `CWhereamiView` class inside the AppWizard—Step 6 of 6 window.

☐ Set the Base Class drop-down list box to `CFormView`.

Your AppWizard—Step 6 of 6 window should now look like the one shown in Figure 17.36.

*Figure 17.36. The
AppWizard—Step 6 of 6
window after you set the
base class of the application
view class to `CFormView`.*

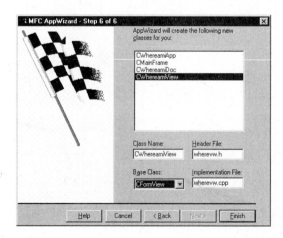

☐ Click the Finish button of the Step 6 of 6 window.

Visual C++ responds by displaying the New Project Information window, as shown in Figure 17.37.

☐ Click the OK button of the New Project Information window.

Visual C++ responds by creating the project file and all the skeleton files of the application.

The Visual Implementation of the Application's Form

Because in AppWizard you specified that the base class of the application's view class is CFormView, AppWizard created for you a form (a dialog box) that is attached to the view class of the application. This dialog box serves as the main window of the application. AppWizard named this dialog box IDD_WHEREAMI_FORM. You'll now customize the IDD_WHEREAMI_FORM dialog box.

☐ Double-click whereami.rc inside the whereami.mak window.

Visual C++ responds by displaying the whereami.rc window.

☐ Double-click Dialog inside the whereami.rc window and then double-click IDD_WHEREAMI_FORM.

Visual C++ responds by displaying the IDD_WHEREAMI_FORM dialog box in design mode.

☐ Delete the text TODO: Place form controls on this dialog. that Visual C++ placed inside the dialog box.

☐ Implement the dialog box according to the specifications in Table 17.3. When you finish implementing the dialog box, it should look like the one shown in Figure 17.38.

Table 17.3. The Properties table of the *IDD_WHEREAMI_FORM* dialog box.

Object	Property	Setting
Dialog box	ID	IDD_WHEREAMI_FORM
Static label	ID	IDC_STATIC
	Caption	Horizontal:
Static label	ID	IDC_STATIC
	Caption	Vertical:
Edit box	ID	IDC_HORIZ
Edit box	ID	IDC_VERT

Figure 17.38. The dialog box that serves as the main window of the WhereAmI application (in design mode).

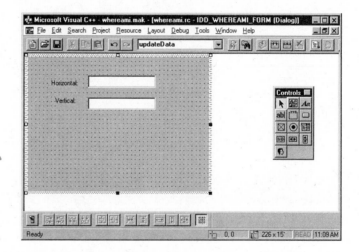

☐ Save your work by selecting Save from the File menu.

Attaching Variables to the Controls Inside the IDD_WHEREAMI_FORM Dialog Box

You'll now attach variables to the controls inside the IDD_WHEREAMI_FORM dialog box.

☐ Display the ClassWizard dialog box by selecting ClassWizard from the Project menu of Visual C++.

☐ Select the Member Variables tab at the top of ClassWizard's dialog box.

☐ Make sure the Class Name drop-down list is set to CWhereamiView.

☐ Attach variables to the controls of the IDD_WHEREAMI_FORM dialog box as specified in Table 17.4.

Table 17.4. The Variables table of the IDD_WHEREAMI_FORM dialog box.

Control ID	Variable Name	Category	Variable Type
IDC_HORIZ	m_Horiz	Value	CString
IDC_VERT	m_Vert	Value	CString

☐ To save your work, select Save from the File menu.

Changing the Properties of the Edit Box

☐ Display the IDD_WHEREAMI_FORM dialog box in design mode by selecting whereami.rc-IDD_WHEREAMI_FORM [Dialog] from the Window menu of Visual C++.

☐ Double-click the IDC_HORIZ edit box.

Visual C++ responds by displaying the Edit Properties dialog box for the IDC_HORIZ edit box.

☐ Select the Styles tab of the Edit Properties dialog box.

☐ Set the Styles properties of the IDC_HORIZ edit box by placing a checkmark inside the Read Only check box.

☐ Repeat these steps to set the Styles properties of the IDC_VERT edit box. Place a checkmark inside the Read Only check box.

☐ Save your work by selecting Save from the File menu of Visual C++.

To see your visual design in action do the following:

☐ Select Build WhereAmI.EXE from the Project menu.

Visual C++ responds by compiling and linking the WhereAmI application.

☐ Select Execute WhereAmI.EXE from the Project menu.

Visual C++ responds by executing the WhereAmI.EXE application.

As expected, the IDD_WHEREAMI_FORM dialog box that you designed appears as the main window of the application.

Of course, the edit boxes do not display the mouse coordinates yet, because you have not yet written code that accomplishes that.

As you can see from the window of the WhereAmI program, the menu bar of the WhereAmI application (the menu bar that AppWizard created for you) has an Edit pop-up menu. However, the menu bar of the WhereAmI application should not have an Edit pop-up menu. (Refer back to Figure 17.26.) In the next section you'll customize the menu bar of the WhereAmI application so that it will not have an Edit pop-up menu.

☐ Terminate the WhereAmI application by selecting Exit from the File menu.

The Visual Implementation of the Menu Bar

The WhereAmI application should have a menu, as shown in Figures 17.27 and 17.28.

Follow these steps to customize the IDR_MAINFRAME menu:

☐ Select whereami.rc from the Window menu of Visual C++.

> *Visual C++ responds by displaying the whereami.rc window.*

☐ Double-click Menu inside the whereami.rc window and then double-click IDR_MAINFRAME.

> *Visual C++ responds by displaying the IDR_MAINFRAME menu bar in design mode.*

As you can see, the IDR_MAINFRAME menu currently has three pop-up menus: File, Edit, and Help.

Take a look at the Help menu. (See Figure 17.39.) As you can see, the Help menu is exactly as you want it to be, so there is no need to modify this menu. However, the File menu is not exactly as you want it to be. (See Figure 17.40.)

Figure 17.39. The default Help menu of the WhereAmI program.

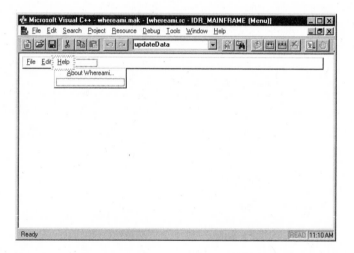

You'll now modify the File menu.

☐ Delete all the items in the file menu except the Exit item.

Because the WhereAmI application should not have an Edit menu, you have to remove the Edit pop-up menu:

☐ Click the Edit item on the menu bar.

> *Visual C++ responds by opening the Edit pop-up menu.*

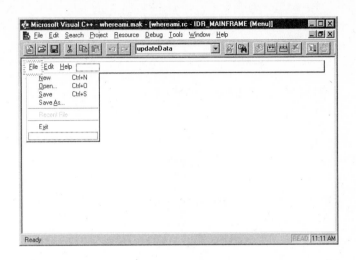

Figure 17.40. The default File menu of the WhereAmI program.

☐ Now press the Delete key on your keyboard.

Visual C++ responds by displaying a dialog box warning you that you're about to delete an entire pop-up menu.

☐ Click the OK button of the warning dialog box.

Visual C++ responds by deleting the Edit pop-up menu.

☐ Save your work by selecting Save from the File menu of Visual C++.

The visual implementation of the menu of the WhereAmI application is complete. To see your visual design in action do the following:

☐ Select Build WhereAmI.EXE from the Project menu.

Visual C++ responds by compiling and linking the WhereAmI application.

☐ Select Execute WhereAmI.EXE from the Project menu.

Visual C++ responds by executing the WhereAmI.EXE application.

As expected, the menu bar of the application appears as you customized it—it now has only two pop-up menus: File and Help.

☐ Terminate the WhereAmI application by selecting Exit from the File menu.

Responding to Mouse Events

Now that you have finished performing the visual design and all the overhead tasks, you can actually start attaching code to the WM_MOUSEMOVE event. WM_MOUSEMOVE is the message that Windows sends to WhereAmI whenever the mouse is moved inside the client area of WhereAmI.

☐ Display the ClassWizard dialog box by selecting ClassWizard from the Project menu of Visual C++.

☐ Select the Message Maps tab at the top of ClassWizard's dialog box.

☐ Use ClassWizard to select the event:

CWhereamiView -> CWhereamiView -> WM_MOUSEMOVE

☐ Click the Add Function button.

> *Visual C++ responds by adding the* OnMouseMove() *member function to the* CWhereamiView *class.*

☐ Click the Edit Code button of ClassWizard.

> *ClassWizard responds by opening the file WhereVW.CPP, with the function* OnMouseMove() *ready to be edited by you.*

☐ Write code inside the OnMouseMove() function so that it looks like this:

```
void CWhereamiView::OnMouseMove(UINT nFlags, CPoint point)
{
// TODO: Add your message handler code
// here and/or call default


/////////////////////////
// MY CODE STARTS HERE
/////////////////////////

    char XPosition[10];
    char YPosition[10];

    itoa ( point.x, XPosition, 10 );
    itoa ( point.y, YPosition, 10 );

    m_Horiz = XPosition;
    m_Vert = YPosition;

    UpdateData(FALSE);

/////////////////////////
// MY CODE ENDS HERE
/////////////////////////

CFormView::OnMouseMove(nFlags, point);
}
```

☐ Save your work by selecting Save from the File menu.

The first two statements declare two local variables:

```
char XPosition[10];
char YPosition[10];
```

Then the `itoa()` function is executed to convert the x coordinate `point.x` to the string `XPosition`, and to convert the y coordinate `point.y` to the string `YPosition`:

```
itoa ( point.x, XPosition, 10 );
itoa ( point.y, YPosition, 10 );
```

The variables of the edit boxes are then updated with the values of `XPosition` and `YPosition`:

```
m_Horiz = XPosition;
m_Vert = YPosition;
```

Finally, the `UpdateData()` function is executed to update the edit boxes with the values of their variables:

```
UpdateData(FALSE);
```

To see your visual design in action do the following:

☐ Select Build WhereAmI.EXE from the Project menu.

> *Visual C++ responds by compiling and linking the WhereAmI application.*

☐ Select Execute WhereAmI.EXE from the Project menu.

> *Visual C++ responds by executing the WhereAmI.EXE application.*

☐ Move the mouse inside the client area of the WhereAmI application's main window, and verify that the edit boxes display the mouse's coordinates.

☐ Terminate the WhereAmI application by selecting Exit from the File menu.

The DragIt Application

When the user moves the mouse, Windows generates the WM_MOUSEMOVE message from time to time. Windows does not generate the WM_MOUSEMOVE message for every move of the mouse. This makes sense, because if Windows would send a message for each and every movement of the mouse, you would not be able to execute any program while you move the mouse (that is, the CPU would be constantly busy processing the WM_MOUSEMOVE message). The DragIt application demonstrates this concept.

Determining Mouse Movement

As stated, Windows does not send the WM_MOUSEMOVE message for each movement of the mouse. Instead, Windows checks the status of the mouse periodically. In each check, the current mouse coordinates are compared with the mouse coordinates of the last check. If the coordinates are different, Windows concludes that the mouse was moved, and it generates the WM_MOUSEMOVE message. This process is shown in Figure 17.41.

The curvy line in Figure 17.41 is the actual path of the mouse. However, due to the fact that it is impractical to process each pixel movement of the mouse, Windows generates the WM_MOUSEMOVE messages only at certain time intervals.

Figure 17.41. Checking for mouse movement at various times.

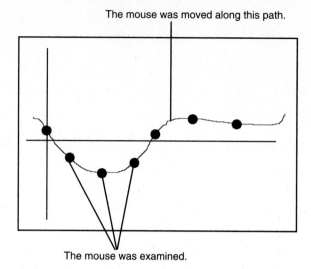

So from the point of view of the application, the mouse moved only seven times (because the application received only seven WM_MOUSEMOVE messages).

In most cases, the fact that not every pixel movement is detected does not have serious effects on the performance of the application.

As you'll soon see, when you draw a circle with the DrawIt application, the circle is drawn in accordance with the mouse movement. The quality of the drawn circle depends on how fast you move the mouse. If you move the mouse slowly, you'll be able to draw a smooth shape (such as the shape shown on the left side of Figure 17.42). On the other hand, if you draw the circle quickly, then the circle will not be smooth (as shown on the right side of Figure 17.42).

Figures 17.42. Drawing shapes with DrawIt. The left shape was drawn slowly; the right shape was drawn quickly.

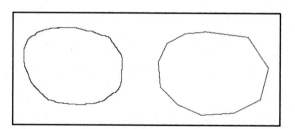

Before you start writing the DrawIt application yourself, execute the copy of it that resides in the \MVCPROG\EXE directory of the book's CD.

To execute the DrawIt application do the following:

☐ Select Run from the Start menu of Windows and execute the X:\MVCPROG\EXE\DrawIt.EXE program (where *X* represents the drive letter of your CD-ROM drive).

The main window of DrawIt.EXE appears, as shown in Figure 17.43.

Figure 17.43. The main
window of the DrawIt
application.

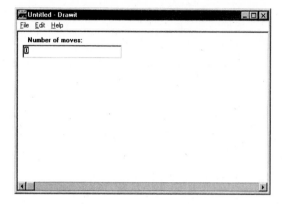

The DragIt application has two pop-up menus: File and Help.

☐ Push down the left button of the mouse, and while holding it down, move the mouse inside the window of the DrawIt application.

DrawIt responds by drawing lines in accordance with the mouse movements. (See Figure 17.44.)

Figure 17.44. Drawing
with the DrawIt
application.

☐ Experiment with the DrawIt application and then select Exit from the File menu to terminate the application.

Creating the Project of the DrawIt Application

You'll now create the DrawIt.MAK project.

To create the project of the DrawIt application do the following:

☐ Start Visual C++ and close all the open windows that appear inside the desktop of Visual C++ (if there are any).

☐ Select New from the File menu.

Visual C++ responds by displaying the New dialog box.

☐ Select Project inside the New dialog box and then click the OK button of the New dialog box.

Visual C++ responds by displaying the New Project dialog box.

☐ Set the project name to DrawIt.

☐ Set the project path to \MVCPROG\CH17\DrawIt\DrawIt.MAK.

Your New Project dialog box should now look like the one shown in Figure 17.45.

Figure 17.45. The New Project dialog box of the DrawIt.MAK project.

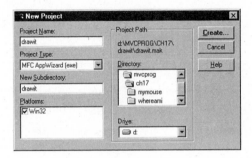

☐ Click the Create button of the New Project dialog box.

Visual C++ responds by displaying the AppWizard—Step 1 window.

☐ Set the Step 1 window as shown in Figure 17.46. As shown in Figure 17.46, the DrawIt.MAK project is set as a single-document interface application, and U.S. English (APPWIZUS.DLL) is used as the language for the application's resources.

Figure 17.46. The AppWizard—Step 1 window for the DrawIt application.

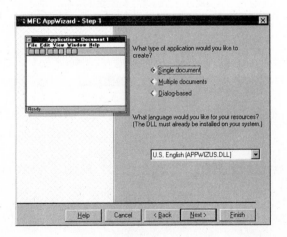

☐ Click the Next button of the Step 1 window.

  Visual C++ responds by displaying the AppWizard—Step 2 of 6 window.

☐ Set the Step 2 of 6 window as shown in Figure 17.47. That is, in the DrawIt application you don't want any database support.

Figure 17.47. The AppWizard—Step 2 of 6 window for the DrawIt application.

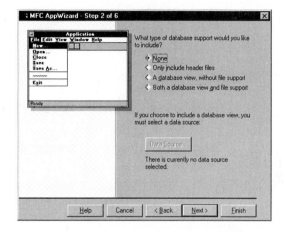

☐ Click the Next button of the Step 2 of 6 window.

  Visual C++ responds by displaying the AppWizard—Step 3 of 6 window.

☐ Set the Step 3 of 6 window as shown in Figure 17.48. That is, in the DrawIt application you don't want any OLE support.

Figure 17.48. The AppWizard—Step 3 of 6 window for the DrawIt application.

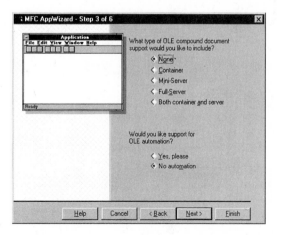

☐ Click the Next button of the Step 3 of 6 window.

  Visual C++ responds by displaying the AppWizard—Step 4 of 6 window.

☐ Set the Step 4 of 6 window as shown in Figure 17.49.

Figure 17.49. The AppWizard—Step 4 of 6 window for the DrawIt application.

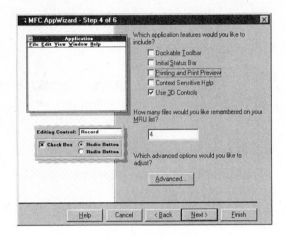

As shown in Figure 17.49, the features Dockable Toolbar, Initial Status Bar, Printing and Print Preview, and Context Sensitive Help will not be included in the DrawIt application.

☐ Click the Next button of the Step 4 of 6 window.

Visual C++ responds by displaying the AppWizard—Step 5 of 6 window.

☐ Set the Step 5 window as shown in Figure 17.50.

Figure 17.50. The AppWizard—Step 5 of 6 window for the DrawIt application.

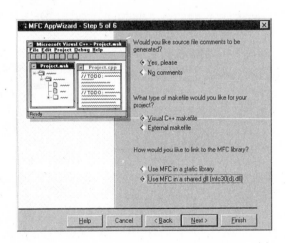

As shown in Figure 17.50, the project will be generated with comments, a Visual C++ makefile will be generated, and the application will use the MFC library from a DLL.

☐ Click the Next button of the Step 5 of 6 window.

Visual C++ responds by displaying the AppWizard—Step 6 of 6 window.

You'll now use the AppWizard—Step 6 of 6 window to tell AppWizard to derive the view class of the application from the MFC class `CFormView`:

☐ Select the `CDrawitView` class inside the AppWizard—Step 6 of 6 window.

☐ Set the Base Class drop-down list box to `CFormView`.

Your AppWizard—Step 6 of 6 window should now look like the one shown in Figure 17.51.

Figure 17.51. The AppWizard—Step 6 of 6 window after you set the base class of the application view class to `CFormView`.

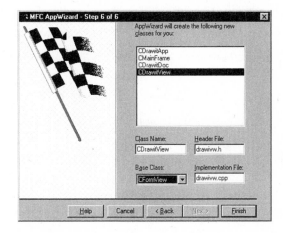

☐ Click the Finish button of the Step 6 of 6 window.

Visual C++ responds by displaying the New Project Information window, as shown in Figure 17.52.

Figure 17.52. The New Project Information window of the DrawIt.MAK project.

☐ Click the OK button of the New Project Information window.

Visual C++ responds by creating the project file and all the skeleton files of the application.

The Visual Implementation of the Application's Form

Because in AppWizard you specified that the base class of the application's view class is CFormView, AppWizard created for you a form (a dialog box) that is attached to the view class of the application. This dialog box serves as the main window of the application. AppWizard named this dialog box IDD_DRAWIT_FORM. You'll now customize the IDD_DRAWIT_FORM dialog box.

☐ Double-click drawit.rc inside the drawit.mak window.

    Visual C++ responds by displaying the drawit.rc window.

☐ Double-click Dialog inside the drawit.rc window and then double-click IDD_DRAWIT_FORM.

    Visual C++ responds by displaying the IDD_DRAWIT_FORM dialog box in design mode.

☐ Delete the text TODO: Place form controls on this dialog. that Visual C++ placed inside the dialog box.

☐ Implement the dialog box according to the specifications in Table 17.5. When you finish implementing the dialog box, it should look like the one shown in Figure 17.53.

Table 17.5. The Properties table of the IDD_DRAWIT_FORM dialog box.

Object	Property	Setting
Dialog box	ID	IDD_DRAWIT_FORM
Static label	ID	IDC_STATIC
	Caption	Number of moves:
Edit box	ID	IDC_EDIT1
	Read Only	Checked

Figure 17.53. The dialog box that serves as the main window of the DrawIt application (in design mode).

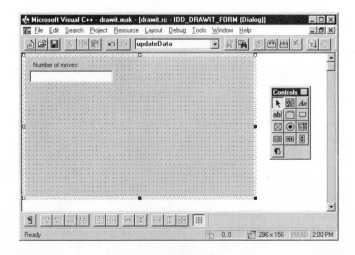

Note that in Table 17.5 you are instructed to place a checkmark inside the Read Only property of the edit box.

☐ Save your work by selecting Save from the File menu.

Attaching Variables to the Controls Inside the IDD_DRAWIT_FORM Dialog Box

You'll now attach variables to the controls inside the IDD_DRAWIT_FORM dialog box.

☐ Display the ClassWizard dialog box by selecting ClassWizard from the Project menu of Visual C++.

☐ Select the Member Variables tab at the top of ClassWizard's dialog box.

☐ Make sure the Class Name drop-down list is set to CDrawitView.

☐ Attach variables to the controls of the IDD_DRAWIT_FORM dialog box as specified in Table 17.6.

Table 17.6. The Variables table of the IDD_DRAWIT_FORM dialog box.

Control ID	Variable Name	Category	Variable type
IDC_EDIT1	m_NumberOfMoves	Value	long

NOTE

Until now, you attached a CString variable to the edit box.

The DrawIt application needs to increment the variable of the edit box. Therefore, it is most convenient to make this variable a numeric type (not a CString type). Note that in Table 17.6 you were instructed to make m_NumberOfMoves a variable of type long (not of type CString).

☐ To save your work, select Save from the File menu.

To see your visual design in action do the following:

☐ Select Build DrawIt.EXE from the Project menu.

> *Visual C++ responds by compiling and linking the DrawIt application.*

☐ Select Execute DrawIt.EXE from the Project menu.

> *Visual C++ responds by executing the DrawIt.EXE application.*

As expected, the IDD_DRAWIT_FORM dialog box that you designed appears as the main window of the application.

Of course, the edit box does not display the number of mouse movements, and you cannot yet draw with the mouse because you have not yet written code that accomplishes that.

As you can see from the window of the DrawIt program, the menu bar of the DrawIt application (the menu bar that AppWizard created for you) has an Edit pop-up menu. However, the menu bar of the DrawIt application should not have an Edit pop-up menu. You'll customize the application's menu in the next section.

☐ Terminate the DrawIt application by selecting Exit from the File menu.

The Visual Implementation of the Menu Bar

The DrawIt application should have File and Help menus, but should not have an Edit menu.

Follow these steps to customize the menu:

☐ Select drawit.rc from the Window menu of Visual C++.

Visual C++ responds by displaying the drawit.rc window.

☐ Double-click Menu inside the drawit.rc window and then double-click IDR_MAINFRAME.

Visual C++ responds by displaying the IDR_MAINFRAME menu bar in design mode.

As you can see, the IDR_MAINFRAME menu currently has three pop-up menus: File, Edit, and Help.

As you can see, the Help menu is exactly as you want it to be, so there is no need to modify this menu. However, the File menu is not exactly as you want it to be.

You'll now modify the File menu.

☐ Delete all the items in the file menu except the Exit item.

Because the DrawIt application should not have an Edit menu, you have to remove the Edit pop-up menu:

☐ Click the Edit item on the menu bar.

Visual C++ responds by opening the Edit pop-up menu.

☐ Now press the Delete key on your keyboard.

Visual C++ responds by displaying a dialog box warning you that you're about to delete an entire pop-up menu.

☐ Click the OK button of the warning dialog box.

Visual C++ responds by deleting the Edit pop-up menu.

☐ Save your work by selecting Save from the File menu of Visual C++.

The visual implementation of the menu of the DrawIt application is complete. To see your visual design in action do the following:

☐ Select Build DrawIt.EXE from the Project menu.

Visual C++ responds by compiling and linking the DrawIt application.

☐ Select Execute DrawIt.EXE from the Project menu.

Visual C++ responds by executing the DrawIt.EXE application.

As expected, the menu bar of the application appears as you customized it—it now has only two pop-up menus: File and Help.

☐ Terminate the DrawIt application by selecting Exit from the File menu.

That's it! You have completed the visual implementation of the application.

To save your work do the following:

☐ Select Save from the file menu of Visual C++.

Responding to Mouse Events

Now that you have finished performing the visual design, you can start attaching code that implements the same job that the pencil tool of Paintbrush accomplishes.

☐ Display the ClassWizard dialog box by selecting ClassWizard from the Project menu of Visual C++.

☐ Select the Message Maps tab at the top of ClassWizard's dialog box.

☐ Use ClassWizard to select the event:

```
CDrawitView -> CDrawitView -> WM_MOUSEMOVE
```

☐ Click the Add Function button.

Visual C++ responds by adding the OnMouseMove() *member function to the* CDrawitView *class.*

☐ Click the Edit Code button of ClassWizard.

ClassWizard responds by opening the file DrawiVW.CPP, with the function OnMouseMove() *ready to be edited by you.*

☐ Write code inside the OnMouseMove() function so that it looks like this:

```
void CDrawitView::OnMouseMove(UINT nFlags, CPoint point)
{
// TODO: Add your message handler
// code here and/or call default
```

```
///////////////////////
// MY CODE STARTS HERE
///////////////////////


    if ( (nFlags & MK_LBUTTON) == MK_LBUTTON )
       {
       // This code is executed provided that:
       // 1. The mouse moved inside the client area.
       // 2. The left button of the mouse was pushed down.

       // Create a dc object
       CClientDC dc(this);

       // Draw a pixel
       dc.SetPixel(point.x, point.y, RGB(0,0,0));

       // Increment the counter
       m_NumberOfMoves++;

       // Update the screen
       UpdateData(FALSE);

       }

//////////////////////
// MY CODE ENDS HERE
//////////////////////

        CFormView::OnMouseMove(nFlags, point);
   }
```

The code under the if will be executed only if the mouse is moved while the left button of the mouse is pushed down:

```
if ( (nFlags & MK_LBUTTON) == MK_LBUTTON )
    {
    // This code is executed provided that:
    // 1. The mouse moved inside the client area.
    // 2. The left button of the mouse was pushed down.
    ...
    ...
    ...
    }
```

The code under the if creates a dc object:

```
CClientDC dc(this);
```

dc stands for *device context*. What is a device context? Think of it as your software drawing tool. In other words, the device context serves as the Paintbrush program for drawing from within your programs. However, instead of drawing by clicking the mouse on one of the tools of Paintbrush and then drawing with the mouse, you perform your drawing by using the member functions of dc. As you can see, dc is an object of class CClientDC.

NOTE

The object dc lets you perform many drawing operations.

Think of it as your Paintbrush program to draw from within your programs. To use the tools of the dc object, simply apply the member functions of the CClientDC class on the dc object as in the following:

```
dc.SetPixel(point.x, point.y, RGB(0,0,0));
```

The next statement uses the SetPixel() member function:

```
dc.SetPixel(point.x, point.y, RGB(0,0,0));
```

The SetPixel() function draws a single pixel. The x coordinate of the pixel is point.x, and the y coordinate of the pixel is point.y. Recall that point is one of the parameters of the OnMouseMove() function. The third parameter of the SetPixel() function specifies the color of the pixel that will be drawn.

NOTE

RGB stands for *red green blue*. The three parameters of RGB() specify the mixing formula of the resultant color that RGB() returns. The first parameter specifies the amount of red in the final color, the second parameter specifies the amount of green in the final color, and the third parameter specifies the amount of blue in the final color.

Each parameter of RGB() can have a value between 0 and 255.

Here are some examples:

RGB(255, 0, 0) represents the color red.
RGB(0, 255, 0) represents the color green.
RGB(0, 0, 255) represents the color blue.
RGB(0, 0, 0) represents the color black.
RGB(255, 255, 255) represents the color white.

As you can see, you can figure out the basic colors by inspection. To figure out the final color that is produced by other values, you would probably need to have a Ph.D. in optical physics.

To summarize, the code that you typed draws a pixel at the current location of the mouse cursor, provided that the mouse was moved and the left button of the mouse was down.

The next statement in the OnMouseMove() function increments the value of m_NumberOfMoves:

```
m_NumberOfMoves++;
```

Finally, the UpdateData() function is executed to update the contents of the edit box with the value of its variable:

```
UpdateData(FALSE);
```

So the number that is displayed inside the edit box represents the number of times that the code inside the if block was executed. Or, the number inside the edit box represents the number of pixels that were drawn.

To see your code in action do the following:

☐ Select Build DrawIt.EXE from the Project menu.

Visual C++ responds by compiling and linking the DrawIt application.

☐ Select Execute DrawIt.EXE from the Project menu.

Visual C++ responds by executing the DrawIt.EXE application.

☐ Use the mouse to draw pictures inside the window of DrawIt. For example, Figure 17.54 shows a picture of a man and a woman drawn with the DrawIt program. Figure 17.54 shows that the picture was created by drawing 3027 pixels.

☐ Experiment with the DrawIt program, and then terminate it by selecting Exit from the File menu.

Figure 17.54. Drawing with the DrawIt program.

Figure 17.55 shows a line drawn with the DrawIt program. The left side of the line was drawn by dragging the mouse slowly, and the rest of the line was drawn by dragging the mouse quickly.

When you write a drawing program, it is unreasonable to ask the user to move the mouse slowly. Therefore, your program has to cheat. That is, instead of drawing a pixel for each WM_MOUSEMOVE message, the program draws a straight line between the current location of the mouse and the last location of the mouse.

Figure 17.55. Drawing a line with the DrawIt program.

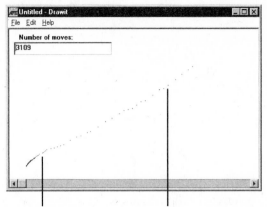

The mouse was moved slowly.   The mouse was moved quickly.

Implement the drawing by using the connecting-points-with-straight-lines technique. This technique requires the use of two variables: m_PrevX and m_PrevY. These variables hold the coordinate of the starting point of the line.

☐ Select Open from the File menu and open the DrawiVW.H file.

☐ Modify the DrawiVW.H file and add the m_PrevX and m_PrevY data members to the CDrawitView class. After you add these two variables, the CDrawitView class declaration inside the DrawiVW.H file should look like this:

```
class CDrawitView : public CFormView
{
protected: // create from serialization only
        CDrawitView();
        DECLARE_DYNCREATE(CDrawitView)

public:
        //{{AFX_DATA(CDrawitView)
        enum { IDD = IDD_DRAWIT_FORM };
        long    m_NumberOfMoves;
        //}}AFX_DATA

// Attributes
public:

/////////////////////////
// MY CODE STARTS HERE
/////////////////////////

    int m_PrevX;
    int m_PrevY;

/////////////////////////
// MY CODE ENDS HERE
/////////////////////////

        CDrawitDoc* GetDocument();
```

```
// Operations
public:

// Overrides
        // ClassWizard generated virtual function overrides
        //{{AFX_VIRTUAL(CDrawitView)
        public:
        protected:
        virtual void DoDataExchange(CDataExchange* pDX);      // DDX/DDV support
        //}}AFX_VIRTUAL

// Implementation
public:
        virtual ~CDrawitView();
#ifdef _DEBUG
        virtual void AssertValid() const;
        virtual void Dump(CDumpContext& dc) const;
#endif

protected:

// Generated message map functions
protected:
        //{{AFX_MSG(CDrawitView)
        afx_msg void OnMouseMove(UINT nFlags, CPoint point);
        //}}AFX_MSG
        DECLARE_MESSAGE_MAP()
};
```

☐ Modify the code of the OnMouseMove() function inside the DrawiVW.CPP file. After you
modify this function, the OnMouseMove() function should look like this:

```
void CDrawitView::OnMouseMove(UINT nFlags, CPoint point)
{
// TODO: Add your message handler
// code here and/or call default


    /////////////////////////
    // MY CODE STARTS HERE
    /////////////////////////


   if ( (nFlags & MK_LBUTTON) == MK_LBUTTON )
      {
      // This code is executed provided that:
      // 1. The mouse moved inside the client area.
      // 2. The left button of the mouse was pushed down.

      // Create a dc object
      CClientDC dc(this);

      // dc.SetPixel(point.x, point.y, RGB(0,0,0));

      dc.MoveTo(m_PrevX, m_PrevY);
      dc.LineTo(point.x, point.y);
      m_PrevX = point.x;
      m_PrevY = point.y;
```

```
        // Increment the counter
        m_NumberOfMoves++;

        // Update the screen
        UpdateData(FALSE);

    }

//////////////////////
// MY CODE ENDS HERE
//////////////////////


        CFormView::OnMouseMove(nFlags, point);
}
```

The code you typed creates the `dc` object of class `CClientDC`:

`CClientDC dc(this);`

The `SetPixel()` statement is commented out:

`// dc.SetPixel(point.x, point.y, RGB(0,0,0));`

The `MoveTo()` member function of the `CClientDC` class is executed on the `dc` object:

`dc.MoveTo(m_PrevX, m_PrevY);`

The `MoveTo()` function sets the current position to the coordinate (`m_PrevX`, `m_PrevY`). The current position is a coordinate that is used in several drawing functions (that is, the `CClientDC` member functions). You may think of the current position as an imaginary point that exists inside the client area. The current position is affected by several drawing functions. For example, when you use the drawing function that draws a line from one point to another, the current position is automatically updated. The new coordinates of the current position are the coordinates of the end point of the line that was drawn.

The `MoveTo()` function forces the coordinates of the current position to the coordinate specified by its parameters.

The next statement executes the `LineTo()` member function of the `CClientDC` class:

`dc.LineTo(point.x, point.y);`

As implied by its name, the `LineTo()` function draws a straight line. The question is What are the coordinates of the starting point of the line, and what are the coordinates of the end point of the line? The coordinates of the end point of the line are (`point.x`, `point.y`), as specified by the parameters of the `LineTo()` function. The coordinates of the starting point of the line are the coordinates of the current position. Because you set (`m_PrevX`, `m_PrevY`) as the current position (with the `MoveTo()` function), the line is drawn from (`m_PrevX`, `m_PrevY`) to (`point.x`, `point.y`).

As stated, once the `LineTo()` function finishes drawing the line, the coordinates of the current position are automatically updated to the coordinates of the end point of the line, which are (`point.x`, `point.y`).

The code you typed then updates the values of m_PrevX and m_PrevY with the coordinates of the end points of the line:

```
m_PrevX = point.x;
m_PrevY = point.y;
```

The rest of the code in the OnMouseMove() function increments the variable of the edit box by 1. This code is identical to the code that existed in the previous version of the DrawIt application.

To summarize, the next time the DrawIt application is executed, a line will be drawn from the end point of the previous line to the current position of the mouse. If the two points are close to each other, you won't notice that the two points are actually connected with a straight line.

The straight lines are drawn provided that the mouse moved while the left button of the mouse is pushed down. The whole process of drawing starts when the left button of the mouse is pushed down. Therefore, the OnLButtonDown() function should be used to set the starting point of the very first line of the drawing:

☐ Display the ClassWizard dialog box by selecting ClassWizard from the Project menu of Visual C++.

☐ Select the Message Maps tab at the top of ClassWizard's dialog box.

☐ Use ClassWizard to select the event:

```
CDrawitView -> CDrawitView -> WM_LBUTTONDOWN
```

☐ Click the Add Function button.

> *Visual C++ responds by adding the* OnLButtonDown() *member function to the* CDrawitView *class.*

☐ Click the Edit Code button of ClassWizard.

> *ClassWizard responds by opening the file DrawiVW.CPP, with the function* OnLButtonDown() *ready to be edited by you.*

☐ Write code inside the OnLButtonDown() function so that it looks like this:

```
void CDrawitView::OnLButtonDown(UINT nFlags, CPoint point)
{
// TODO: Add your message handler
// code here and/or call default


//////////////////////
// MY CODE STARTS HERE
//////////////////////

m_PrevX = point.x;

m_PrevY = point.y;

//////////////////////
// MY CODE ENDS HERE
//////////////////////
```

```
        CFormView::OnLButtonDown(nFlags, point);
}
```

The code you typed simply sets the values of m_PrevX and m_PrevY with the coordinates of the mouse cursor. Because immediately after the execution of this function the OnMouseMove() function will be executed, the line will be drawn from the point where the mouse cursor was when the left button of the mouse was pushed.

To see your code in action do the following:

☐ Select Build DrawIt.EXE from the Project menu.

Visual C++ responds by compiling and linking the DrawIt application.

☐ Select Execute DrawIt.EXE from the Project menu.

Visual C++ responds by executing the DrawIt.EXE application.

☐ Use the mouse to draw pictures inside the window of DrawIt. For example, the writing in Figure 17.56 was accomplished with the DrawIt program.

Figure 17.56. Writing with the DrawIt program.

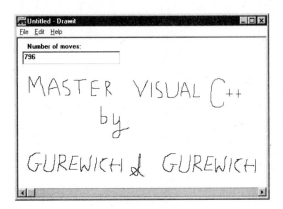

☐ Experiment with the DrawIt program, and then terminate the DrawIt application by selecting Exit from the File menu.

NOTE

When designing drawing applications such as the DrawIt application, it is best not to include the label control inside the client area. This is because the user would be able to draw on the label if it were in the client area. On the other hand, the user will not be able to draw over a control such as the edit box. Figure 17.57 illustrates that point.

Figure 17.57. Drawing over the label control (but not over the edit box control).

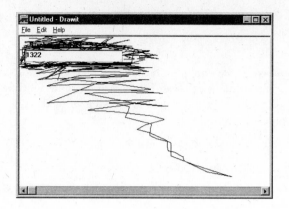

18

The Keyboard

In this chapter you'll learn how to
detect and respond to keyboard
events from within your Visual C++
programs.

The primary function of the keyboard is to type characters (the mouse can't do that). Typically, you use the edit box control to receive characters from the keyboard. As you know, the edit control already contains all the code that enables you to type characters into it. However, the keyboard is also used to perform other functions besides typing. For example, you can write code that performs certain operations when the user presses the arrow keys or other keys of the keyboard.

Generally, the user should be able to perform all the major operations of the application (except typing) by using the mouse. However, a well-designed Windows application should enable the user to operate the application by using the keyboard as well.

The MyKey Application

You'll now write the MyKey application—an example of an application that responds to keyboard events.

Before you start writing the MyKey application yourself, execute the copy of it that resides in the \MVCPROG\EXE directory of the book's CD.

To execute the MyKey application do the following:

☐ Select Run from the Start menu of Windows and execute the X:\MVCPROG\EXE\MyKey.EXE program (where *X* represents the drive letter of your CD-ROM drive).

The main window of MyKey.EXE appears, as shown in Figure 18.1.

Figure 18.1. The main window of the MyKey application.

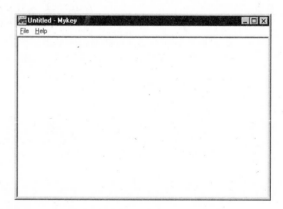

The MyKey program has File and Help menus. (See Figures 18.2 and 18.3.)

Figure 18.2. The File menu of the MyKey application.

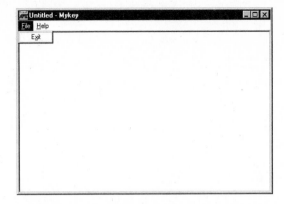

Figure 18.3. The Help menu of the MyKey application.

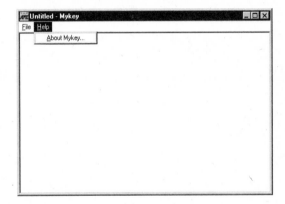

☐ Press the A key on the keyboard.

MyKey responds by printing the A character inside the window of MyKey. (See Figure 18.4.)

Figure 18.4. Displaying the pressed character.

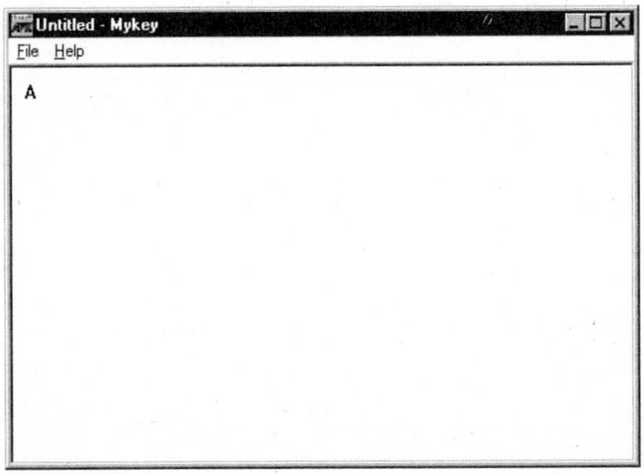

☐ Press the left-arrow key.

MyKey responds by displaying a message box that tells you that the left-arrow key was pressed, and the message box also tells you the status of the Caps Lock key.

☐ Press the Caps Lock key to toggle its state, and then press the left-arrow key.

MyKey responds by displaying a message box that tells you that the left-arrow key was pressed, and the message box also tells you the new status of the Caps Lock key.

☐ Practice with the MyKey program, and then select Exit from the File menu to terminate the program.

Creating the Project of the MyKey Application

To create the project of the MyKey application do the following:

☐ Start Visual C++ and close all the open windows that appear inside the desktop of Visual C++ (if there are any).

☐ Select New from the File menu.

Visual C++ responds by displaying the New dialog box.

☐ Select Project inside the New dialog box and then click the OK button of the New dialog box.

Visual C++ responds by displaying the New Project dialog box.

☐ Set the project name to MyKey.

☐ Set the project path to \MVCPROG\CH18\MyKey\MyKey.MAK.

Your New Project dialog box should now look like the one shown in Figure 18.5.

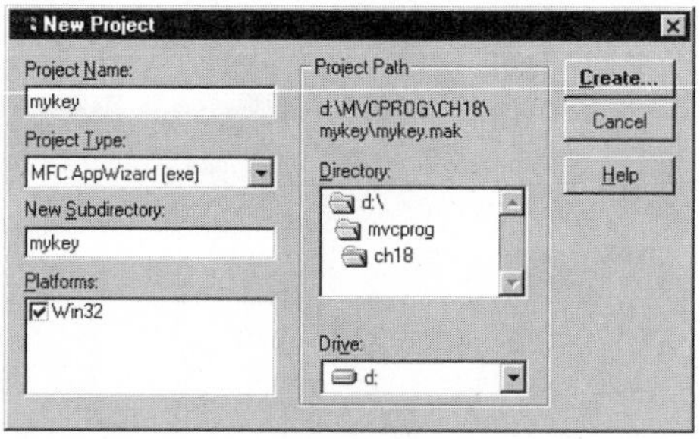

Figure 18.5. The New Project dialog box of the MyKey.MAK project.

☐ Click the Create button of the New Project dialog box.

Visual C++ responds by displaying the AppWizard—Step 1 window.

☐ Set the Step 1 window as shown in Figure 18.6. As shown in Figure 18.6, the MyKey.MAK project is set as a single-document application, and U.S. English (APPWIZUS.DLL) is used as the language for the application's resources.

Figure 18.6. The AppWizard—Step 1 window for the MyKey application.

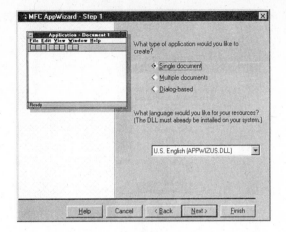

☐ Click the Next button of the Step 1 window.

Visual C++ responds by displaying the AppWizard—Step 2 of 6 window.

☐ Set the Step 2 of 6 window as shown in Figure 18.7. That is, in the MyKey application you don't want any database support.

Figure 18.7. The AppWizard—Step 2 of 6 window for the MyKey application.

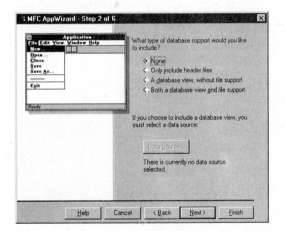

☐ Click the Next button of the Step 2 of 6 window.

Visual C++ responds by displaying the AppWizard—Step 3 of 6 window.

☐ Set the Step 3 of 6 window as shown in Figure 18.8. That is, in the MyKey application you don't want any OLE support.

*Figure 18.8. The
AppWizard—Step 3 of 6
window for the MyKey
application.*

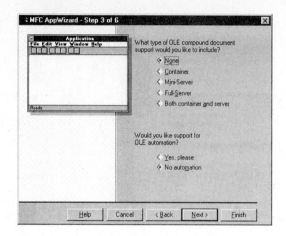

☐ Click the Next button of the Step 3 of 6 window.

> *Visual C++ responds by displaying the AppWizard—Step 4 of 6 window.*

☐ Set the Step 4 of 6 window as shown in Figure 18.9.

*Figure 18.9. The
AppWizard—Step 4 of 6
window for the MyKey
application.*

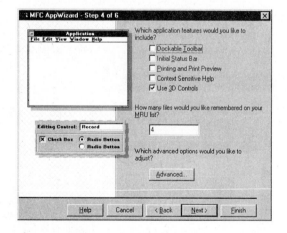

As shown in Figure 18.9, the features Dockable Toolbar, Initial Status Bar, Printing and Print Preview, and Context Sensitive Help will not be included in the MyKey application.

☐ Click the Next button of the Step 4 of 6 window.

> *Visual C++ responds by displaying the AppWizard—Step 5 of 6 window.*

☐ Set the Step 5 of 6 window as shown in Figure 18.10.

As shown in Figure 18.10, the project will be generated with comments, a Visual C++ makefile will be generated, and the application will use the MFC library from a DLL.

Figure 18.10. The AppWizard—Step 5 of 6 window for the MyKey application.

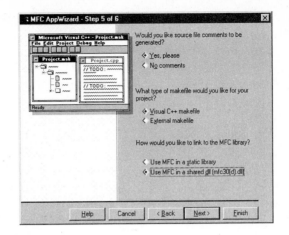

☐ Click the Next button of the Step 5 of 6 window.

Visual C++ responds by displaying the AppWizard—Step 6 of 6 window.

Note that in the AppWizard—Step 6 of 6 window, the base class of the `CMykeyView` class is set to `Cview` (the default). (See Figure 18.11.) There is no need to set the basic class to the view class to `CFormView` (as you did in the previous chapters) because the MyKey application will not have controls inside its main window.

Figure 18.11. The AppWizard—Step 6 of 6 window.

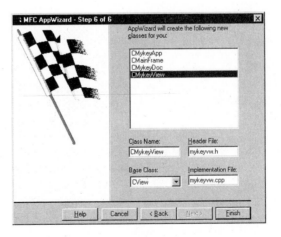

☐ Click the Finish button of the Step 6 of 6 window.

Visual C++ responds by displaying the New Project Information window, as shown in Figure 18.12.

Figure 18.12. The New
Project Information
window of the
MyKey.MAK project.

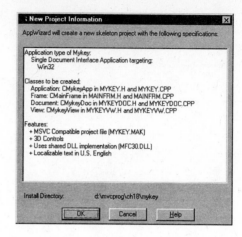

☐ Click the OK button of the New Project Information window.

Visual C++ responds by creating the project file and all the skeleton files of the application.

The Visual Implementation of the Menu Bar

The MyKey application should have a File menu and a Help menu, as shown in Figures 18.2 and 18.3.

Follow these steps to customize the IDR_MAINFRAME menu of the MyKey program:

☐ Double-click mykey.rc inside the MyKey.MAK window.

Visual C++ responds by displaying the mykey.rc window.

☐ Double-click Menu inside the mykey.rc window and then double-click IDR_MAINFRAME.

Visual C++ responds by displaying the IDR_MAINFRAME menu bar in design mode.

As you can see, the IDR_MAINFRAME menu currently has three pop-up menus: File, Edit, and Help.

Because the MyKey application should not have an Edit menu, you have to remove the Edit pop-up menu:

☐ Click the Edit item on the menu bar.

Visual C++ responds by opening the Edit pop-up menu.

☐ Now press the Delete key on your keyboard.

Visual C++ responds by displaying a dialog box warning you that you're about to delete an entire pop-up menu.

☐ Click the OK button of the warning dialog box.

Visual C++ responds by deleting the Edit pop-up menu.

You'll now modify the File menu.

☐ Delete all the items in the File menu except the Exit item.

☐ Save your work by selecting Save from the File menu of Visual C++.

The visual implementation of the menu of the MyKey application is complete.

Processing Keyboard Messages

When the user presses a key on the keyboard, Windows sends a message that corresponds to this event. The question is Who receives this message? Windows sends the message to the object that currently has the input focus.

> **NOTE**
>
> Windows sends keyboard-related messages to the object with the input focus. Therefore, whenever the user presses keys on the keyboard, Windows sends the messages that correspond to these events to the object that currently has the input focus.
>
> For example, suppose that the window contains an edit box and a push button. You can shift the input focus between the edit box and the push button by pressing the Tab key. When an edit box has the input focus, a blinking cursor appears inside the edit box, and when the push button has the input focus, a dashed rectangle appears inside the push button.

Attaching Code to the *OnKeyDown()* Function

You'll now attach code that will be executed whenever the user presses a key on the keyboard.

☐ Display the ClassWizard dialog box by selecting ClassWizard from the Project menu of Visual C++.

☐ Select the Message Maps tab at the top of ClassWizard's dialog box.

☐ Use ClassWizard to select the event:

```
CMykeyView -> CMykeyView -> WM_KEYDOWN
```

☐ Click the Add Function button.

Visual C++ responds by adding the function OnKeyDown() *member function to the* CMykeyView *class.*

☐ Click the Edit Code button of ClassWizard.

ClassWizard responds by opening the file MyKeyVW.CPP, with the function OnKeyDown() *ready to be edited by you.*

☐ Write code inside the OnKeyDown() function so that it looks like this:

```
void CMykeyView::OnKeyDown(UINT nChar, UINT nRepCnt,
                           UINT nFlags)
{
// TODO: Add your message handler code
// here and/or call default


    /////////////////////////
    // MY CODE STARTS HERE
    /////////////////////////

    MessageBox("You pressed a key on your keyboard!");

    /////////////////////////
    // MY CODE ENDS HERE
    /////////////////////////

    CView::OnKeyDown(nChar, nRepCnt, nFlags);
}
```

When the title of the MyKey window is highlighted, you know that this window has the input focus. If this window has a control in it, this control is called a child window. When the child window has the input focus, Windows sends the keyboard-related messages to the child window. MyKey has no child windows, so Windows sends the keyboard-related messages to the window of MyKey.

To see your code in action do the following:

☐ Select Build MyKey.EXE from the Project menu.

   Visual C++ responds by compiling and linking the MyKey application.

☐ Select Execute MyKey.EXE from the Project menu.

   Visual C++ responds by executing the MyKey.EXE application.

As expected, the menu bar of the application appears as you customized it—it now has only two pop-up menus: File and Help.

☐ Verify that the File and Help menus look like the ones shown in Figures 18.2 and 18.3.

☐ Press any key on the keyboard.

   MyKey responds by displaying a message box telling you that you pressed a key on the keyboard.

☐ Click the OK button of the message box to close the message box.

☐ Practice with the MyKey program. In particular, note that the program detects the pressing of any key. For example, the MyKey program detects when the user presses the Shift key, the Caps Lock key, the Num Lock key, as well as any other key on the keyboard.

☐ Terminate the MyKey application by selecting Exit from the File menu.

Determining Which Key Is Pressed

In the preceding section you performed an experiment that proved that the MyKey program detects the pressing of a key on the keyboard. In this section you'll learn how to determine which key is pressed.

☐ Display the ClassWizard dialog box by selecting ClassWizard from the Project menu of Visual C++.

☐ Select the Message Maps tab at the top of ClassWizard's dialog box.

☐ Use ClassWizard to edit the OnKeyDown() function.

ClassWizard responds by opening the file MyKeyVW.CPP, with the function OnKeyDown() *ready to be edited by you.*

☐ Edit the code inside the OnKeyDown() function so that it looks like this:

```
void CMykeyView::OnKeyDown(UINT nChar, UINT nRepCnt,
             UINT nFlags)
{
// TODO: Add your message handler
// code here and/or call default


/////////////////////////
// MY CODE STARTS HERE
/////////////////////////

// MessageBox("You pressed a key on your keyboard!");


switch (nChar)
{
case VK_LEFT:

MessageBox ("I detected that you pressed the left arrow");
break;

case VK_RIGHT:

MessageBox ("I detected that you pressed the right arrow");
break;

}

/////////////////////////
// MY CODE ENDS HERE
/////////////////////////

CView::OnKeyDown(nChar, nRepCnt, nFlags);
}
```

The code that you typed uses a switch to detect and analyze the WM_KEYDOWN message. The OnKeyDown() function has three parameters. These parameters provide information about the message that was received. One of these parameters is nChar. This parameter contains the ID of the key that was pressed. The first case under the switch is this:

```
case VK_LEFT:
MessageBox ("I detected that you pressed the left arrow");
break;
```

As implied by its name, VK_LEFT is the ID of the left-arrow key. When the WM_KEYDOWN message is received with nChar equal to VK_LEFT, you know that the user pressed the left-arrow key.

Similarly, the code you typed checks to see whether the pressed key was the right-arrow key (VK_RIGHT).

To see your code in action do the following:

☐ Select Build MyKey.EXE from the Project menu.

> *Visual C++ responds by compiling and linking the MyKey application.*

☐ Select Execute MyKey.EXE from the Project menu.

> *Visual C++ responds by executing the MyKey.EXE application.*

☐ Experiment with the MyKey application by pressing the left- and right-arrow keys.

> *MyKey responds by displaying the corresponding message box. When you press the right-arrow key, MyKey displays this message:* I detected that you pressed the right arrow. *When you press the left-arrow key, MyKey responds by displaying this message:* I detected that you pressed the left arrow.

☐ Terminate the MyKey application by selecting Exit from the File menu.

Other Virtual Keys

You detected the pressing of the left- and right-arrow keys by checking whether nChar is equal to VK_LEFT or VK_RIGHT. These keys are called virtual keys (hence the characters VK_ at the beginning of their IDs). The left- and right-arrow keys (as well as other keys such as the Page Up and Page Down) are nonprintable keys.

The OnKeyDown() function can detect both printable and nonprintable keys. When a nonprintable key is pressed, you can detect the value of the key by examining the value of nFlags (the third parameter of OnKeyDown()).

☐ Modify the OnKeyDown() function (inside the MyKeyVW.CPP file). After the modification, the OnKeyDown() function should look like this:

```
void CMykeyView::OnKeyDown(UINT nChar, UINT nRepCnt,
            UINT nFlags)
{
// TODO: Add your message handler code
// here and/or call default
```

```
/////////////////////
// MY CODE STARTS HERE
/////////////////////

switch (nChar)
{

case VK_LEFT:
 MessageBox ("I detected that you pressed the left arrow");
 break;

case VK_RIGHT:
 MessageBox ("I detected that you pressed the right arrow");
 break;

}

if ( nChar == 'A' || nChar == 'a' )
    MessageBox (" You pressed the 'A' key ");


/////////////////////
// MY CODE ENDS HERE
/////////////////////


CView::OnKeyDown(nChar, nRepCnt, nFlags);
}
```

The code you added to OnKeyDown() uses a message box to display a message whenever the A or a key is pressed.

☐ Compile and link the MyKey application, and execute it.

☐ Press the A key.

> *MyKey responds by displaying a message box telling you that you pressed the A key.*

☐ Practice with the MyKey program and then select the Exit item from the File menu to terminate the program.

NOTE

The WM_KEYDOWN message can be used to detect the pressing of printable and nonprintable keys.

The WM_CHAR message can also be used for detecting the pressing of keys. However, the WM_CHAR message does not detect the keys listed in Table 18.1. (The WM_CHAR message is discussed later in this chapter.)

Table 18.1 lists the IDs that are used for detecting nonprintable keys with the OnKeyDown() function. For example, as shown in Table 18.1, VK_RIGHT represents the right-arrow key, and VK_LEFT represents the left-arrow key.

Table 18.1. Nonprintable keys that are detected by the *OnKeyDown()* function.

ID	Key
VK_CLEAR	The 5 key on the numeric pad when Num Lock is off
VK_SHIFT	Shift
VK_CONTROL	Ctrl
VK_PAUSE	Pause
VK_CAPITAL	Caps Lock
VK_PRIOR	Page Up
VK_NEXT	Page Down
VK_END	End
VK_HOME	Home
VK_LEFT	Left-arrow
VK_UP	Up-arrow
VK_RIGHT	Right-arrow
VK_DOWN	Down-arrow
VK_INSERT	Insert
VK_DELETE	Delete
VK_F1	F1
VK_F2	F2
VK_F3	F3
VK_F4	F4
VK_F5	F5
VK_F6	F6
VK_F7	F7
VK_F8	F8
VK_F9	F9
VK_F10	F10
VK_F11	F11
VK_F12	F12
VK_NUMLOCK	Num Lock
VK_SCROLL	Scroll Lock

Checking for the Pressing of the Ctrl Key

As you can see, the OnKeyDown() function can detect the pressing of the nonprintable keys. For example, the following code fragment is used to detect whether the End key or the Ctrl key was pressed:

```
void CMykeyView::OnKeyDown(UINT nChar,
                           UINT nRepCnt,
                           UINT nFlags)
{
// TODO: Add your message handler code here and/or call
// default

/////////////////////////
// MY CODE STARTS HERE
/////////////////////////

switch (nChar)
{
...
...
...
case VK_END:
 MessageBox ("I detected that you pressed the End key");
 break;

case VK_CONTROL:
 MessageBox ("I detected that you pressed the Ctrl key");
 break;

}

/////////////////////
// MY CODE ENDS HERE
/////////////////////

CView::OnKeyDown(nChar, nRepCnt, nFlags);
}
```

But how would you detect the pressing of Ctrl+End? (Recall that many Windows applications make use of such a key combination. For example, to go immediately to the end of a document in Microsoft Word for Windows, you can press Ctrl+End.) This is accomplished by using the GetKeyState() member function.

☐ Modify the OnKeyDown() function. After the modification, your OnKeyDown() function should look like this:

```
void CMykeyView::OnKeyDown(UINT nChar,
                           UINT nRepCnt,
                           UINT nFlags)
{
// TODO: Add your message handler code
// here and/or call default

     /////////////////////////
     // MY CODE STARTS HERE
     /////////////////////////
```

```
switch (nChar)
{

case VK_HOME:

    if ( GetKeyState(VK_CONTROL) & 0x8000 )
        {
        MessageBox ("You pressed Ctrl+Home");
        }
    else
        {
        MessageBox ("You pressed Home");
        }
    break;

case VK_END:

    if ( GetKeyState(VK_CONTROL) & 0x8000 )
        {
        MessageBox ("You pressed Ctrl+End");
        }
    else
        {
        MessageBox ("You pressed End");
        }
    break;

}


/////////////////////
// MY CODE ENDS HERE
/////////////////////


CView::OnKeyDown(nChar, nRepCnt, nFlags);
}
```

The code you typed uses an `if…else` statement to detect if the key was pressed with or without the Ctrl key. The parameter of the `GetKeyState()` function contains the virtual key code that is examined. Therefore, to examine if the Ctrl key (`VK_CONTROL`) was pressed together with the Home key (`VK_HOME`), you use the following `if…else` statement:

```
case VK_HOME:

    if ( GetKeyState(VK_CONTROL) & 0x8000 )
        {
        MessageBox ("You pressed Ctrl+Home");
        }
    else
        {
        MessageBox ("You pressed Home");
        }
    break;
```

In the preceding code, the `case VK_HOME` condition is satisfied if the Home key was pressed. The `if` statement is satisfied provided that the user pressed Ctrl. So the statement under the `if` is executed whenever the user presses Ctrl+Home. Note that the `if` statement uses the AND operation (`&`). If the result of using AND is not 0, the Ctrl key was pressed.

In a similar manner, you typed code that examines whether the End key was pressed together with the Ctrl key.

☐ Compile and link the MyKey program and execute it.

☐ Press the Home key.

> *MyKey responds by displaying a message box that indicates that you pressed the Home key.*

☐ Press the Ctrl key, and while holding down the Ctrl key, press the Home key.

> *MyKey responds by displaying a message box that indicates that you pressed Ctrl+Home.*

☐ Repeat the preceding steps for testing the End and the Ctrl+End keys.

☐ Terminate the MyKey application by selecting Exit from the File menu.

Checking for Other Combinations of Keys

As stated, the GetStateKey(VK_CONTROL) function tells you whether the Ctrl key was pressed together with another key.

In a similar manner, you can use GetStateKey(VK_SHIFT) to test whether a key was pressed together with the Shift (VK_SHIFT) key.

☐ Modify the OnKeyDown() function. When you finish modifying the OnKeyDown() function, it should look like this:

```
void CMykeyView::OnKeyDown(UINT nChar,
                           UINT nRepCnt,
                           UINT nFlags)
{
// TODO: Add your message handler code
// here and/or call default

    //////////////////////////
    // MY CODE STARTS HERE
    //////////////////////////

    switch (nChar)
    {

    case VK_F1:

        if ( GetKeyState(VK_SHIFT) & 0x8000 )
            {
            MessageBox ("You pressed SHIFT+F1");
            }
        else
            {
            MessageBox ("You pressed F1");
            }
        break;

    case VK_LEFT:
```

```
            if ( GetKeyState(VK_SHIFT) & 0x8000 )
                {
                MessageBox ("You pressed SHIFT+Left arrow");
                }
            else
                {
                MessageBox ("You pressed Left arrow");
                }
            break;

        }


    //////////////////////
    // MY CODE ENDS HERE
    //////////////////////



    CView::OnKeyDown(nChar, nRepCnt, nFlags);
    }
```

The code that you typed checks whether the Shift key was pressed together with the F1 key or the left-arrow key.

☐ Compile and link the MyKey program, and execute it.

☐ Press the F1 key.

> *MyKey responds by displaying a message box that indicates that you pressed the F1 key.*

☐ Press the Shift key, and while holding down the Shift key, press the F1 key.

> *MyKey responds by displaying a message box that indicates that you pressed Shift+F1.*

☐ Repeat the preceding steps for testing the left-arrow and the Shift+left-arrow keys.

☐ Terminate the MyKey application by selecting Exit from the File menu.

☐ Check the status of the Caps Lock, Num Lock, Scroll Lock, and Insert keys.

Several keys on the keyboard are toggled. For example, pressing the Caps Lock causes the keyboard to be in a non–Caps Lock state (when you type a character, it appears as a lowercase character). Pressing the Caps Lock key again causes the keyboard to be in a Caps Lock state (when typing, the characters appear as uppercase characters). If you press the Caps Lock key again, the keyboard returns to its non-Caps Lock state.

Other toggling keys are the Num Lock, Scroll Lock, and Insert keys.

The following modification to the OnKeyDown() function demonstrates how you can detect the state of these toggling keys:

☐ Modify the OnKeyDown() function. After the modification, your OnKeyDown() function should look like this:

```
void CMykeyView::OnKeyDown(UINT nChar,
                           UINT nRepCnt,
                           UINT nFlags)
```

```
{
// TODO: Add your message handler code
// here and/or call default


/////////////////////////
// MY CODE STARTS HERE
/////////////////////////

switch (nChar)
{

case VK_F1:

 if ( GetKeyState(VK_CAPITAL) & 0x0001 )
     {
      MessageBox ("You pressed F1. Caps Lock = ON");
     }
 else
     {
     MessageBox ("You pressed F1. Caps Lock = OFF");
     }
 break;

 case VK_LEFT:

 if ( GetKeyState(VK_CAPITAL) & 0x0001 )
 {
 MessageBox ("You pressed the Left arrow. Caps Lock = ON");
 }
 else
 {
 MessageBox ("You pressed the Left arrow. Caps Lock = OFF");
 }
 break;

}

/////////////////////
// MY CODE ENDS HERE
/////////////////////


     CView::OnKeyDown(nChar, nRepCnt, nFlags);
}
```

The code you typed uses AND on VK_CAPITAL with 0x0001, and based on the result, it concludes the state of Caps Lock key:

```
if ( GetKeyState(VK_CAPITAL) & 0x0001 )
    {
     MessageBox ("You pressed F1. Caps Lock = ON");
    }
else
    {
    MessageBox ("You pressed F1. Caps Lock = OFF");
```

```
     }
```

☐ Compile and link the MyKey program, and execute it.

☐ Press the F1 key.

> *MyKey responds by displaying a message box indicating that you pressed the F1 key and showing the status of the Caps Lock key.*

☐ Press the Caps Lock and then press the F1 key.

> *MyKey responds by displaying a message box indicating that you pressed the F1 key and showing the status of the Caps Lock key.*

☐ Repeat the preceding steps for testing the left-arrow and the Caps Lock keys.

☐ Terminate the MyKey application by selecting Exit from the File menu.

In a similar manner you can check the status of the Num Lock key (by using `GetKeyStatus(VK_NUMLOCK)`), the status of the Scroll Lock key (by using `GetKeyStatus(VK_SCROLL)`), and the status of the Insert key (by using `GetKeyStatus(VK_INSERT)`).

> **NOTE**
>
> You haven't read about the Print Screen key and the Alt key in this chapter. These keys are considered to be system keys. Usually these keys are processed by Windows.

The *WM_CHAR* Message

As stated, the `WM_KEYDOWN` message can be used for processing both printable and nonprintable keys. The `WM_CHAR` message cannot be used for detecting the keys listed in Table 18.1.

☐ Display the ClassWizard dialog box by selecting ClassWizard from the Project menu of Visual C++.

☐ Select the Message Maps tab at the top of ClassWizard's dialog box.

☐ Use ClassWizard to select the event:

```
CMykeyView -> CMykeyView -> WM_CHAR
```

☐ Click the Add Function button.

> *Visual C++ responds by adding the function* `OnChar()` *member function to the* `CMykeyView` *class.*

☐ Click the Edit Code button of ClassWizard.

> *ClassWizard responds by opening the file MyKeyVW.CPP, with the function* `OnChar()` *ready to be edited by you.*

In the preceding, make sure that you are adding the function to the `CMykeyView` class. That is, make sure that the Class Name drop-down list box of ClassWizard is set to `CMykeyView`.

☐ Edit the OnChar() function that you added to the MYKEYVW.CPP file. After you edit the function, your OnChar() function should look like this:

```
void CMykeyView::OnChar(UINT nChar,
                        UINT nRepCnt,
                        UINT nFlags)
{
// TODO: Add your message handler
// code here and/or call default


        /////////////////////////
        // MY CODE STARTS HERE
        /////////////////////////

    if (nChar<32)
        {
        MessageBeep(-1);
        }
    else
        {
        CClientDC dc (this);

        dc.TextOut (10, 10, "     ");
        dc.TextOut (10, 10, nChar);
        }

        /////////////////////////
        // MY CODE ENDS HERE
        /////////////////////////


    CView::OnChar(nChar, nRepCnt, nFlags);
}
```

The code you typed uses an if statement to check whether nChar (the third parameter of OnChar()) is less than 32:

```
if (nChar<32)
    {
    MessageBeep(-1);
    }
else
    {
    .....
    .....
    .....
    }
```

If nChar is less than 32, then you know that the pressed key is a control character (for example, Enter or Tab), and the statement inside the if block causes the PC to beep.

If the if condition is not satisfied, the else is executed.

Under the else, a dc object of class CClientDC is created:

```
CClientDC dc (this);
```

The TextOut() function is executed to print several spaces on the monitor (to erase previous printing), and then the TextOut() function is executed again to print (at coordinate (10, 10)) the character that was pressed:

```
dc.TextOut (10, 10, "      ");
dc.TextOut (10, 10, nChar);
```

☐ Compile and link the MyKey application and execute it.

☐ Experiment with the MyKey application by pressing a printable key on the keyboard, and verify that the character that corresponds to the key you pressed is displayed on your monitor.

19

Writing a Multiple-Document Interface Application

In this chapter you will learn what
multiple-document interface (MDI)
applications are and how to write
such applications. Other important
topics covered in this chapter include
multiple views and splitter windows.

What Is a Multiple-Document Interface Application?

A multiple-document interface application is an application that enables the user to view and maintain several documents at one time.

All the applications that you have written so far in this book are single-document interface (SDI) applications; at any given time, the user can work with only one document. For example, the MEMO application that you wrote in Chapter 13, "Writing and Reading Data (with Serialization) to and from Files," enables the user to work with one document at a time. When the user opens a new memo (by either selecting New or Open from the File menu), the memo that is currently open is closed, and only then is the new memo opened.

In this chapter you will write an MDI application. When the user selects Open or New from the File menu, the documents that are currently open will remain open and the new document will also be opened. Each document will have its own window, and the user will be able to move from one window to another. All these windows will be inside the main window of the application.

The MDI application that you will write in this chapter will also support multiple views for the same document. That is, the user is allowed to open the same document several times and view the same document in different windows.

The PAD Application

You'll now write the PAD application. The PAD application is an example of an MDI application. As you will soon see, most of the steps necessary for writing an MDI application are identical to the steps that you took in building an SDI application. Therefore, for the most part the steps that you'll take in building the PAD application will be the same as the steps you took when you built the MEMO application in Chapter 13.

Before you start writing the PAD application, first execute the copy of it that resides in the \MVCPROG\EXE directory of the book's CD.

☐ Use Windows to execute the PAD.EXE application from the X:\MVCPROG\EXE directory (where *X* represents the letter drive of your CD-ROM drive).

> *Windows responds by executing the PAD.EXE application. The main window of PAD.EXE appears, as shown in Figure 19.1.*

As you can see from Figure 19.1, the main window of the application has another window inside it. This inner window is called a *child window* (that is, it is the "child" of the application's main window).

The title of the main window is Untitled1—Pad for Windows and the title of the child window is Untitled1.

The Untitled1 window contains a data entry form with two fields: Subject and Notes.

☐ Fill in the fields inside the Untitled1 window as shown in Figure 19.2.

Figure 19.1. The main window of the PAD application.

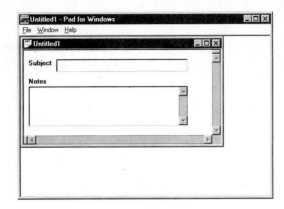

Figure 19.2. Filling in the fields of the child form.

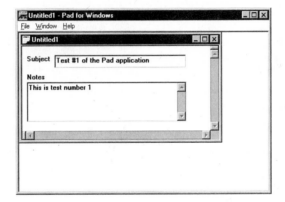

Now save the Untitled1 document:

☐ Select Save from the File menu, and save the Untitled1 document as TRY1.PAD.

> *The PAD application responds by saving your entries into the file TRY1.PAD. Note that now the titles of the main window and the child window have changed. (See Figure 19.3.)*

The title of the main window is now try1.PAD—Pad for Windows, and the title of the child window is now try1.PAD.

Because the PAD application is an MDI application, you can open more documents:

☐ Select New from the File menu.

> *The PAD application responds by opening a new document. The title of the new document's window is Untitled2. (See Figure 19.4.)*

Figure 19.3. The PAD application after you save a document as TRY1.PAD.

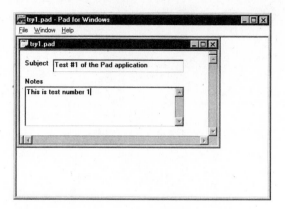

Figure 19.4. The PAD application with two open documents.

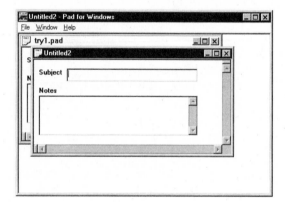

☐ Fill in the fields of the new document. Type Test #2 inside the Subject field. Type `This is test number 2 of the PAD` application inside the Notes field.

☐ Select Save from the File menu, and save the new document as TRY2.PAD.

Your PAD application should now look like the one shown in Figure 19.5.

Figure 19.5. The PAD application with two documents.

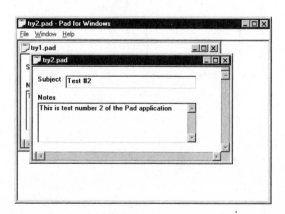

The Window menu of the PAD application has some interesting options. (See Figure 19.6.)

Figure 19.6. The Window menu of the PAD application.

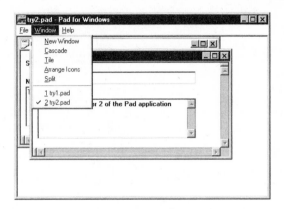

Experiment with the PAD application's Window menu options:

☐ Select Tile from the Window menu.

> *The PAD application responds by arranging the windows of TRY1.PAD and TRY2.PAD in tiled format. (See Figure 19.7.)*

Figure 19.7. Displaying the child windows in tiled format.

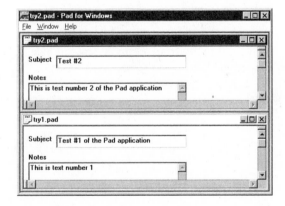

To rearrange the child windows back in cascaded format do the following:

☐ Select Cascade from the Window menu.

> *The PAD application responds by rearranging the child windows in cascaded format. (See Figure 19.5.)*

Another nice feature that the PAD application supports is displaying multiple views of the same document. To see how you can open multiple views into a single document, follow these steps:

☐ Select the window of the TRY1.PAD document (that is, click anywhere on the window of TRY1.PAD, or select TRY1.PAD from the Window menu).

☐ Select New Window from the Window menu.

> *The PAD application responds by opening another view (another window) of TRY1.DOC. (See Figure 19.8.)*

Figure 19.8. Two views of the same document.

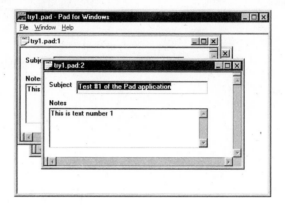

As you can see, now the document TRY1.PAD has two views (two child windows). One window has the title try1.pad:1 and the other window has the title try1.pad:2.

If you change the contents of either of these windows, the contents of the other window are updated automatically. To see this automatic updating in action do the following:

☐ Rearrange the TRY1.PAD:1 and TRY1.PAD:2 windows as shown in Figure 19.9. That is, move and size these two windows so that you are able to see the Notes fields of both windows.

Figure 19.9. Rearranging the two windows of TRY1.PAD.

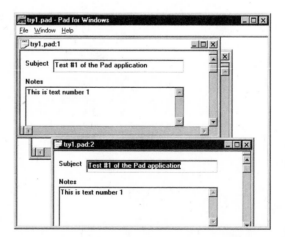

☐ Now type something inside one of the TRY1 windows.

As soon as you type something in one window of TRY1.PAD, the other window of TRY1.PAD is updated automatically. (See Figure 19.10.)

Figure 19.10. The two windows of TRY1.PAD after you type something inside one of them.

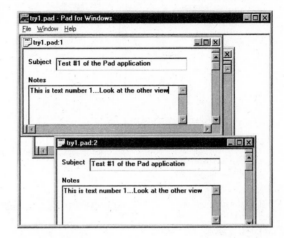

Why is the feature of displaying several views of the same document useful? Sometimes, when you have an extremely long document, you need to work on several sections of the same document at the same time. In such cases you can open several views (windows) of the same document and display in each window a different section of the document.

Another useful feature the PAD application supports is a *splitter* window. A splitter window enables the user to display several views of a document inside one window. To see a splitter window in action follow these steps:

☐ Select the window of the TRY2.PAD document (that is, click anywhere on the window of TRY2.PAD, or select TRY2.PAD from the Window menu).

☐ Maximize the window of TRY2.DOC.

Now the window of TRY2.PAD looks like the one shown in Figure 19.11.

As shown in Figure 19.11, the window of TRY2.PAD has two small split boxes. One split box is located at the top of the window's vertical scroll bar, and the other split box is located at the extreme left of the window's horizontal scroll bar.

☐ To split the window of TRY2.PAD vertically, drag the split box located at the top of the vertical scroll bar to the middle of the scroll bar and then release the mouse button.

  As soon as you release the mouse button, the window of TRY2.PAD splits into two parts. (See Figure 19.12.)

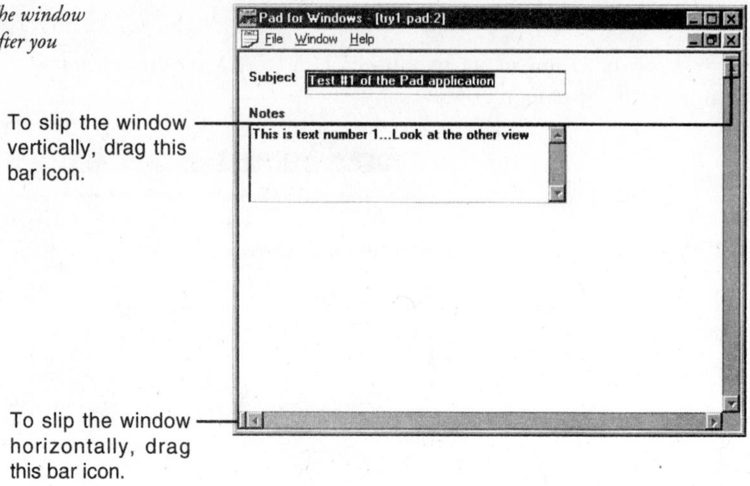

*Figure 19.11. The window
of TRY2.PAD after you
maximize it.*

To slip the window —
vertically, drag this
bar icon.

To slip the window —
horizontally, drag
this bar icon.

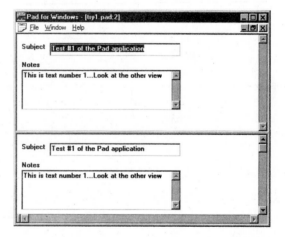

*Figure 19.12. Vertically
splitting the window of
TRY2.PAD into two parts.*

If you try to type something in one section of the split window, the other section of the window will be updated automatically.

You can now further split the window of TRY2.PAD by using the split box that is located at the left side of the horizontal scroll bar:

☐ Drag the split box located at the extreme left of the horizontal scroll bar to the middle of the scroll bar, and then release the mouse button.

As soon as you release the mouse button, the window of TRY2.PAD splits into two more parts. (See Figure 19.13.)

Figure 19.13. Splitting the window of TRY2.PAD into four parts.

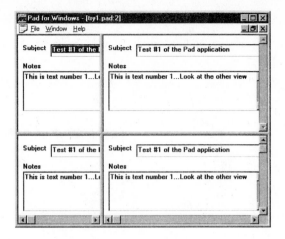

Again, if you try to type something in any of the split window's sections, the other three sections will be updated automatically.

In addition to using the split boxes to split a window, you can use the Split option in the Window menu. To see the Windows menu's Split option in action do the following:

☐ Select New from the File menu.

> *The PAD application responds by opening a new document.*

☐ Fill the Subject and Notes fields of the new document with any data.

☐ Now select Split from the Window menu.

> *The PAD application responds by displaying a horizontal axis and a vertical axis. (See Figure 19.14.)*

Figure 19.14. Splitting a window with the Split option of the Window menu.

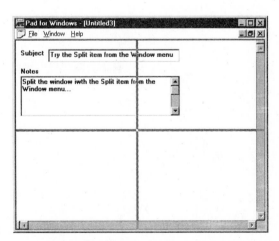

Note that as you move the mouse the intersection point of the two axes moves accordingly.

☐ Move the mouse until the two axes divide the window as you desire, and then click the mouse.

> *The PAD application responds by splitting the window in accordance with the point at which you clicked the mouse. (See Figure 19.15.)*

Figure 19.15. Using the Split item of the Window menu to split the window into four views.

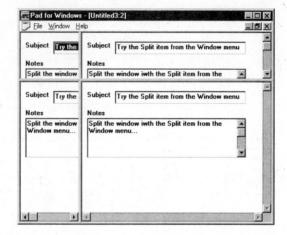

You have finished experimenting with the New Window, Cascade, Tile, and Split options of the Window menu. There is still one more menu option in the Window menu that you have not tried: Arrange Icons.

To see the Arrange Icons menu option in action do the following:

☐ Minimize all the child windows of the PAD application.

Figure 19.16 shows the main window of the PAD application, with its five minimized child windows.

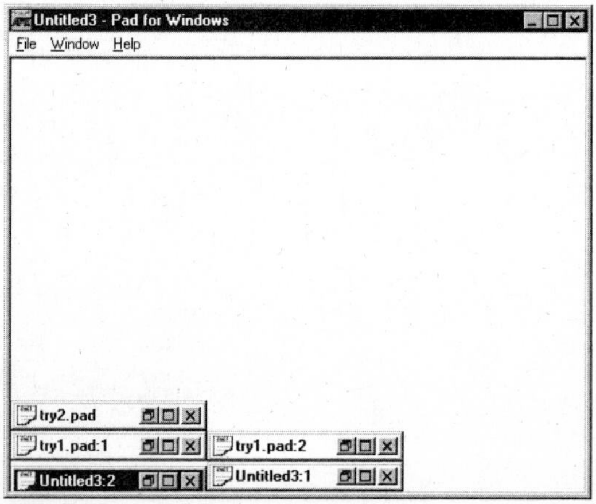

Figure 19.16. The main window of the PAD application, with five minimized child windows.

☐ Drag the minimized child windows to various random locations in the main window of the application.

Figure 19.17 shows the minimized child windows placed at various random locations.

Figure 19.17. Minimized child windows scattered at random locations in the application's main window.

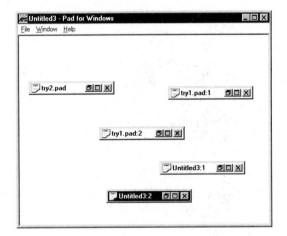

☐ Now select Arrange Icons from the Window menu.

> *The PAD application responds by arranging the minimized child windows at the bottom of the window. (See Figure 19.16.)*

Now that you are familiar with the options of the Window menu, you can experiment with the options of the File menu.

☐ Experiment with the various options of the File menu.

As you can see, the File menu of the application works as you would expect any standard Windows application to work.

Note that at any given time you can select only one child window and the operations that you perform apply to this child window. For example, if the window of TRY1.PAD is currently selected and you select Save from the File menu, TRY1.PAD will be saved.

Note that the PAD application actually has two sets of menu bars. One menu bar is displayed whenever there is at least one child window inside the application's main window. This menu bar is shown in Figure 19.18, with the File pop-up menu open.

The other menu bar is displayed when the application's main window contains no child windows (that is, the user closed all the child windows). This menu bar is shown in Figure 19.19, with the File pop-up menu open.

*Figure 19.18. The
application's menu bar
when at least one child
window is open.*

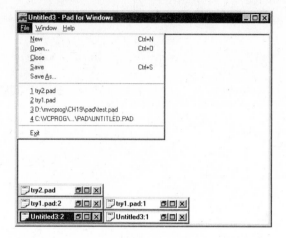

*Figure 19.19. The
application's menu bar
when no child windows
are open.*

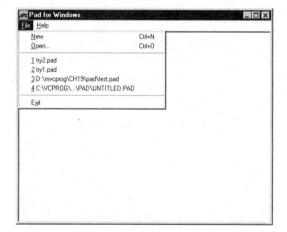

As you can see from Figure 19.19, when no child windows are in the main window of the application, the menu bar doesn't have a Window pop-up menu, and the File pop-up menu doesn't have the Close, Save, and Save As menu items.

To exit the PAD application do the following:

☐ Select Exit from the File menu.

You may think that because the PAD application supports such powerful features, the code you will have to write is more involved than the code you had to write in previous chapters (for example, the MEMO application of Chapter 13). However, this isn't the case! For the most part, the steps that you'll take to build the PAD application will be the same as the steps you took to build the MEMO application.

Now that you know what the PAD application should do, you can start writing it.

Creating the Project of the PAD Application

To create the project of the PAD application do the following:

☐ Start Visual C++ and close all the open windows that appear inside the desktop of Visual C++ (if there are any).

☐ Select New from the File menu.

> *Visual C++ responds by displaying the New dialog box.*

☐ Select Project inside the New dialog box and then click the OK button of the New dialog box.

> *Visual C++ responds by displaying the New Project dialog box.*

☐ Set the project name to pad.

☐ Set the project path to \MVCPROG\CH19\PAD\PAD.MAK.

Your New Project dialog box should now look like the one shown in Figure 19.20.

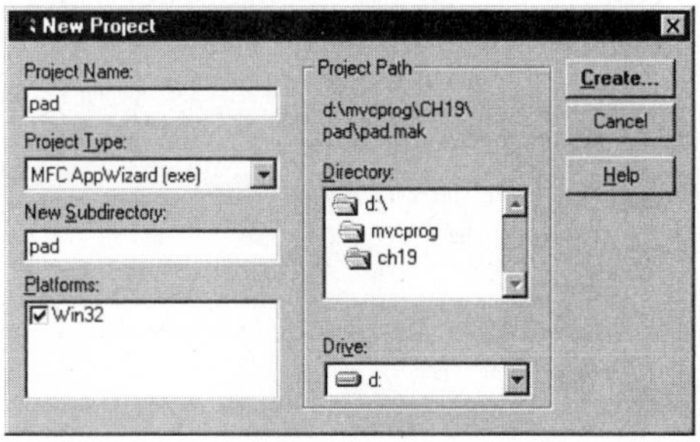

Figure 19.20. The New Project dialog box of the Pad.MAK project.

☐ Click the Create button of the New Project dialog box.

> *Visual C++ responds by displaying the AppWizard—Step 1 window.*

☐ Set the Step 1 window as shown in Figure 19.21. As shown in Figure 19.21, the Pad.MAK project is set as an MDI application, and U.S. English (APPWIZUS.DLL) is used as the language for the application's resources.

☐ Click the Next button of the Step 1 window.

> *Visual C++ responds by displaying the AppWizard—Step 2 of 6 window.*

☐ Set the Step 2 of 6 window as shown in Figure 19.22. That is, in the PAD application you don't want any database support.

Figure 19.21. The AppWizard—Step 1 window for the PAD application. Note that the Multiple documents option button is checked.

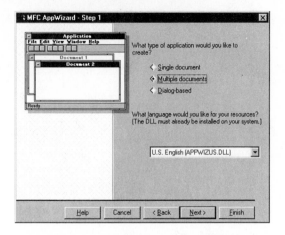

Figure 19.22. The AppWizard—Step 2 of 6 window for the PAD application.

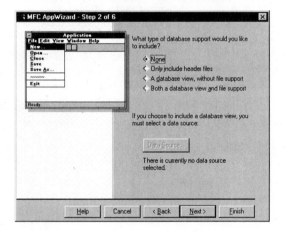

☐ Click the Next button of the Step 2 of 6 window.

Visual C++ responds by displaying the AppWizard—Step 3 of 6 window.

☐ Set the Step 3 of 6 window as shown in Figure 19.23. That is, in the PAD application you don't want any OLE support.

☐ Click the Next button of the Step 3 of 6 window.

Visual C++ responds by displaying the AppWizard—Step 4 of 6 window.

☐ Set the Step 4 of 6 window as shown in Figure 19.24.

Figure 19.23. The AppWizard—Step 3 of 6 window for the PAD application.

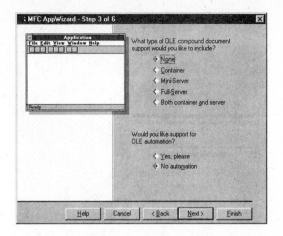

Figure 19.24. The AppWizard—Step 4 of 6 window for the PAD application.

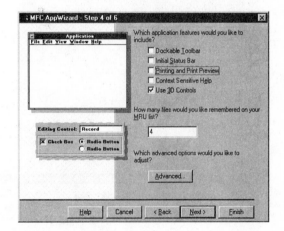

As shown in Figure 19.24, the features Dockable Toolbar, Initial Status Bar, Printing and Print Preview, and Context Sensitive Help will not be included in the PAD application.

☐ Click the Next button of the Step 4 of 6 window.

  Visual C++ responds by displaying the AppWizard—Step 5 of 6 window.

☐ Set the Step 5 of 6 window as shown in Figure 19.25.

As shown in Figure 19.25, the project will be generated with comments, a Visual C++ makefile will be generated, and the application will use the MFC library from a DLL.

Figure 19.25. The AppWizard—Step 5 of 6 window for the PAD application.

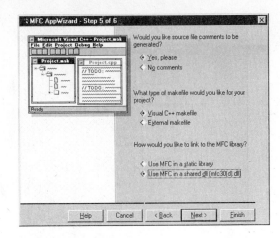

☐ Click the Next button of the Step 5 of 6 window.

Visual C++ responds by displaying the AppWizard—Step 6 of 6 window.

You'll now use the AppWizard—Step 6 of 6 window to tell AppWizard to derive the view class of the application from the MFC class CFormView:

☐ Select the CPadView class inside the AppWizard—Step 6 of 6 window.

☐ Set the base class drop-down list box to CFormView.

Your AppWizard—Step 6 of 6 window should now look like the one shown in Figure 19.26.

Figure 19.26. The AppWizard—Step 6 of 6 window after you set the base class of the application view class to CFormView.

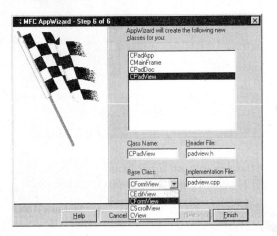

☐ Click the Finish button of the Step 6 of 6 window.

Visual C++ responds by displaying the New Project Information window, as shown in Figure 19.27.

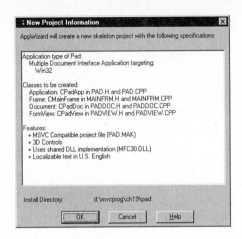

Figure 19.27. The New Project Information window of the Pad.MAK project.

☐ Click the OK button of the New Project Information window.

Visual C++ responds by creating the project file and all the skeleton files of the application.

Creating the Form of the Application

Because in AppWizard you specified that the base class of the application's view class is CFormView, AppWizard created for you a form (a dialog box) that is attached to the view class of the application. This dialog box serves as the child window of the application. AppWizard named this dialog box IDD_PAD_FORM. You'll now customize the IDD_PAD_FORM dialog box until it looks like the one shown back in Figure 19.1.

As shown in Figure 19.1, a child window of the PAD application should have inside it a data entry form with two fields: Subject and Notes.

You'll now visually design the IDD_PAD_FORM dialog box. As stated, this dialog box serves as the child window.

☐ Select pad.mak from the Window menu to display the pad.mak window, double-click pad.rc inside the pad.mak window to display the pad.rc window, double-click the Dialog item that appears inside the pad.rc window to display the list of dialog boxes, and finally, double-click the IDD_PAD_FORM item that appears under the Menu item.

Visual C++ responds by displaying the IDD_PAD_FORM dialog box in design mode. The IDD_PAD_FORM dialog box serves as the child window of the PAD application.

☐ Highlight the TODO static text, and press the Delete button on your keyboard.

Visual C++ responds by deleting the TODO static text.

☐ Design the IDD_PAD_FORM dialog box according to the specifications in Table 19.1. When you finish implementing the dialog box, it should look like the one shown in Figure 19.28.

Table 19.1. The dialog box (child window) of the PAD application.

Object	Property	Setting
Dialog box	ID	IDD_PAD_FORM
Label	ID	IDC_STATIC
	Caption	Subject
Edit box	ID	IDC_SUBJECT
Label	ID	IDC_STATIC
	Caption	Notes
Edit box	ID	IDC_NOTES
	Multiline	Yes
	Want Return	Yes
	Vert. Scroll	Yes

NOTE

Table 19.1 specifies that the Multiline, Want Return, and Vert. Scroll style properties of the IDC_NOTES edit box should be set. Recall that the Multiline and Want Return settings will enable the user to press the Enter key while editing the edit box, and the Vert. Scroll setting will provide the edit box with a vertical scroll bar. If you have forgotten how to set these properties, follow these steps:

☐ Double-click inside the IDC_NOTES edit box.

☐ Select Styles from the drop-down list box at the upper-right corner of the Properties window.

Set the Styles properties of the IDC_NOTES edit box as follows:

☐ Place a checkmark inside the Multiline check box.

☐ Place a checkmark inside the Want Return check box.

☐ Place a checkmark inside the Vert. Scroll check box (this will provide the edit box with a vertical scroll bar).

Your dialog box should now look like the one shown in Figure 19.28.

Figure 19.28. The dialog box of the PAD application (in design mode).

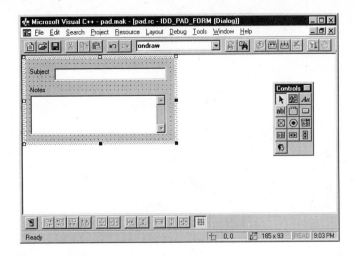

Attaching Variables to the Controls of the IDD_PAD_FORM Dialog Box

You'll now attach variables to the edit boxes of the IDD_PAD_FORM dialog box.

☐ Use ClassWizard to attach variables to the controls of the IDD_PAD_FORM dialog box as specified in Table 19.2. When you implement the variables of Table 19.2, make sure that Class Name in the ClassWizard dialog box is set to CPadView.

Table 19.2. The Variables table of the IDD_PAD_FORM dialog box.

Control ID	Variable Name	Category	Variable Type
IDC_SUBJECT	m_Subject	Value	CString
IDC_NOTES	m_Notes	Value	CString

Save your work:

☐ Select Save from the File menu.

You've finished designing the dialog box. This dialog box will serve as the child windows of the application.

The Visual Implementation of the Menus

As stated earlier, the PAD application has two menus. One menu is displayed when at least one child window is inside the main window of the application, and the other menu is displayed when no child windows are in application's main window. (See Figures 19.18 and 19.19.)

Now design these menus:

☐ Select pad.mak from the Window menu to display the pad.mak window, double-click the pad.rc item, and finally double-click the Menu item.

Visual C++ responds by listing the names of the menus of the PAD application under the Menu item. (See Figure 19.29.)

Figure 19.29. The two menus of the PAD application.

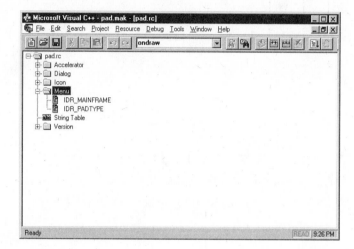

As you can see from Figure 19.29, the names of the PAD application's menus are IDR_MAINFRAME and IDR_PADTYPE.

IDR_MAINFRAME is the menu that is displayed when there are no child windows inside the application's main window. IDR_PADTYPE is the menu that is displayed when there is at least one child window inside the application's main window. Both of these menus were designed by Visual C++. Your job is to customize them (if necessary) for the particular application that you are designing.

Now take a look at the IDR_MAINFRAME menu:

☐ Double-click IDR_MAINFRAME under the Menu item inside the pad.rc window.

Visual C++ responds by displaying the IDR_MAINFRAME menu in design mode. (See Figure 19.30.)

You don't have to customize the IDR_MAINFRAME menu for the PAD application; the way Visual C++ created the IDR_MAINFRAME menu is exactly what you need for the PAD application.

Now take a look at the IDR_PADTYPE menu:

☐ Select pad.rc from the Window menu to display the pad.rc window, and double-click the IDR_PADTYPE item that appears under the Menu item.

Visual C++ responds by displaying the IDR_PADTYPE menu in design mode. (See Figure 19.31.)

Figure 19.30. The IDR_MAINFRAME menu of the PAD application.

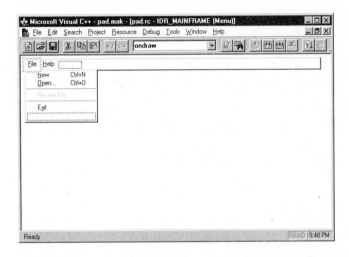

Figure 19.31. The IDR_PADTYPE menu of the PAD application.

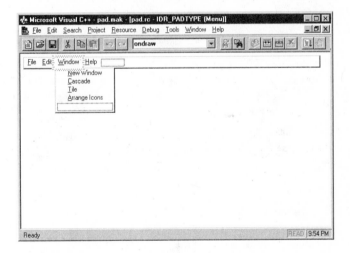

Customizing this menu for the PAD application is very easy—all you have to do is delete the Edit pop-up menu. The File pop-up menu and Help pop-up menu that Visual C++ generated for you are exactly what you need for the PAD application.

☐ Delete the Edit pop-up menu of the IDR_PADTYPE menu.

To save your work do the following:

☐ Select Save from the File menu.

The visual implementation of the two menus of the PAD application is complete.

Executing the PAD Application

Although you have not yet written a single line of code for the PAD application, execute the PAD application to see your visual design in action:

☐ Select Rebuild All PAD.EXE from the Project menu of Visual C++.

> *Visual C++ responds by compiling and linking the PAD application.*

To execute the PAD.EXE application do the following:

☐ Select Execute PAD.EXE from the Project menu.

> *Visual C++ responds by executing the PAD application. The main window of the application appears, with one child window inside it. This child window has the two fields (Subject and Notes) that you designed.*

☐ You can now experiment with various menu options of the application. However, do not experiment with the Save and Save As options of the File menu. Although you have not yet written any code that writes data, these menu options have some functionality, and if you are not careful, you can accidentally overwrite important files.

NOTE

Although you haven't written any code for opening and saving files, the menu items of the File menu have some functionality.

For example, if you select Open from the File menu, a File Open dialog box appears. Of course, once you select a file nothing will be loaded because you haven't written code to accomplish that.

Be careful with the Save and Save As menu items! Although you haven't written any code that writes data into files, the Save and Save As menu items write data. If, for example, you have a file TRY.TXT that contains some data, and you select Save As from the File menu and select the file TRY.TXT, the original TRY.TXT will be overwritten by a new, blank TRY.TXT.

Experiment with the menu of the PAD application:

☐ Select New from the File menu to add a new child window inside the application's main window.

☐ Repeat the previous step to add a few more child windows.

Experiment with the various options of the Window menu:

☐ Select Tile from the Window menu.

> *The PAD application responds by arranging the child windows in tiled format.*

☐ Select Cascade from the Window menu.

> *The PAD application responds by rearranging the child windows in cascaded format.*

Now try the Arrange Icons option:

☐ Minimize all the child windows that are currently open on the desktop.

☐ Drag the minimized child windows to various random locations in the main window of the application.

☐ Now select Arrange Icons from the Window menu.

> *The PAD application responds by arranging the minimized child windows at the bottom of the window.*

As you can see, although you haven't written a single line of code, the PAD application already has a lot of functionality. That's because Visual C++ already wrote a lot of code for you.

In the following sections you will write code that will add more life to the PAD application. You will write the code that enables the user to save documents into files and load documents from files.

Later in the chapter you will also write the code that enables the user to view the same document in several windows and the code that enables the user to split a window into several views.

To exit the PAD application do the following:

☐ Select Exit from the File menu.

The Document Class of the PAD Application

Just as you used the document class for storing the data of the application in SDI applications (for example, the MEMO application of Chapter 13), you will also use the document class for storing the application's data in the PAD application.

Recall that during the visual implementation of the dialog box you created two variables: m_Subject (the variable of the IDC_SUBJECT edit box) and m_Notes (the variable of the IDC_NOTES edit box).

Because the dialog box is connected to the view class of the application, these variables are data members of the view class.

Now add two data members to the document class. These variables will have the same names as the two data members of the view class. (Note that you don't have to name the data members of the document class with the same names as the data members of the view class, but using the same names makes the program easy to read and understand.)

The document class of the PAD application is CPadDoc, and the declaration of this class is inside the header file PADDOC.H.

☐ Open the file PADDOC.H and add code to it that defines the two variables m_Subject and m_Notes as public data members of the CPadDoc class. Declare each of these variables as type CString. After you write this code, the CPadDoc class declaration should look like this:

```
// paddoc.h : interface of the CPadDoc class
//
/////////////////////////////////////////////////////

class CPadDoc : public CDocument
{
protected: // create from serialization only
CPadDoc();
DECLARE_DYNCREATE(CPadDoc)

// Attributes
public:

    //////////////////////////
    // MY CODE STARTS HERE
    //////////////////////////

    CString m_Subject;
    CString m_Notes;

    //////////////////////////
    // MY CODE ENDS HERE
    //////////////////////////


// Operations
public:

// Overrides
// ClassWizard generated virtual function overrides
//{{AFX_VIRTUAL(CPadDoc)
public:
virtual BOOL OnNewDocument();
//}}AFX_VIRTUAL

// Implementation
public:
virtual ~CPadDoc();
virtual void Serialize(CArchive& ar);
// overridden for document i/o
#ifdef _DEBUG
virtual void AssertValid() const;
virtual void Dump(CDumpContext& dc) const;
#endif

protected:

// Generated message map functions
protected:
//{{AFX_MSG(CPadDoc)
// NOTE—the ClassWizard will add and remove member functions here.
//     DO NOT EDIT what you see in these
//     blocks of generated code !
```

```
//}}AFX_MSG
DECLARE_MESSAGE_MAP()
};
```

Save your work:

☐ Select Save from the File menu of Visual C++.

You have finished declaring the data members of the document class. Next you will initialize these variables.

Initializing the Data Members of the Document Class

Upon start-up of the application, and whenever the user selects New from the File menu, the data members of the document class should be initialized to NULL. Why? Because whenever a new document is created you want it to be blank. (See Figure 19.1.)

Recall from Chapter 13 that the code that initializes the data members of the document class should be written inside the OnNewDocument() member function of the document class. That's because OnNewDocument() is executed automatically whenever a new document is created (for example, when the user selects New from the File menu).

☐ Open the file PADDOC.CPP and edit the OnNewDocument() function. After you edit this function, your OnNewDocument() function should look like this:

```
BOOL CPadDoc::OnNewDocument()
{
if (!CDocument::OnNewDocument())
   return FALSE;

// TODO: add reinitialization code here
// (SDI documents will reuse this document)

   /////////////////////////
   // MY CODE STARTS HERE
   /////////////////////////

   // Make the new document blank.
   m_Subject = "";
   m_Notes   = "";

   /////////////////////////
   // MY CODE ENDS HERE
   /////////////////////////


return TRUE;
}
```

The code you just added to the OnNewDocument() function simply assigns null strings to the two data members of the document class. Therefore, whenever a new document is created (for example, when the user selects New from the File menu), the two data members of the document class are initialized to NULL.

Of course, you can initialize the variables to any other value. For example, you can initialize the m_Subject variable to Miscellaneous, as in the following:

```
m_Subject = "Miscellaneous";
```

As a result, whenever a new document is created, the default text inside the Subject field will be Miscellaneous.

To save your work do the following:

☐ Select Save from the File menu of Visual C++.

Initializing the Data Members of the View Class

Recall from Chapter 13 that you write the code that initializes the data members of the view class inside the OnInitialUpdate() member function of the view class. The OnInitialUpdate() function is executed automatically in the following situations:

> When the user starts the application
> When the user selects New from the File menu
> When the user selects Open from the File menu

The code you write inside the OnInitialUpdate() function should update the m_Subject and m_Notes data members of the view class with the corresponding data members of the document class.

☐ Select ClassWizard from the Project menu, set the Class Name to CPadView, select CPadView in the Object IDs list, select OnInitialUpdate() in the Messages list, and then click the Add Function button. (See Figure 19.32.)

☐ Click the Edit Code button.

> *Visual C++ responds by displaying the* OnInitialUpdate() *function of the PADVIEW.CPP file, ready to be edited by you.*

Figure 19.32. Selecting the OnInitialUpdate() *function of the* CPadView *class.*

☐ Now write the code of the OnInitialUpdate() function. After you write this function, the OnInitialUpdate() function should look like this:

```
void CPadView::OnInitialUpdate()
{
// TODO: Add your specialized code here
// and/or call the base class


/////////////////////////
// MY CODE STARTS HERE
/////////////////////////

    // Get a pointer to the document.
    CPadDoc* pDoc = (CPadDoc*) GetDocument();

    // Update the data members of the view class with the
    // current values of the document class data members.
    m_Subject = pDoc->m_Subject;
    m_Notes   = pDoc->m_Notes;

    // Update the screen with the new values.
    UpdateData(FALSE);



/////////////////////////
// MY CODE ENDS HERE
/////////////////////////

CFormView::OnInitialUpdate();
}
```

NOTE

Note that in the previous version of Visual C++ (version 1.5) you could not access the OnInitialUpdate() function from ClassWizard. In fact, in version 1.5 of Visual C++, you had to write the prototype of the OnInitialUpdate() function, and then write the function (including its first line) yourself.

As you have just seen, in the current version of Visual C++ (version 2.0) you can use ClassWizard to add the OnInitialUpdate() function. However, sometimes when you click the Add Function button and then click the Edit Code button, ClassWizard prompts you with an error message telling you that there is a problem with the PADVIEW.H file. If this happens to you, close the ClassWizard dialog box, then select ClassWizard from the Project menu, select the OnInitialUpdate() function, and click the Edit Code button.

Now go over the code of the OnInitialUpdate() function.

The first statement

```
CPadDoc* pDoc = (CPadDoc*) GetDocument();
```

extracts pDoc (the pointer for the document class).

Then the data members of the view class are updated with the current values of the document:

```
m_Subject = pDoc->m_Subject;
m_Notes   = pDoc->m_Notes;
```

Finally, the UpdateData() function is used to transfer the new values of m_Subject and m_Notes to the screen:

```
UpdateData(FALSE);
```

So what have you accomplished so far? You wrote the code that initializes the data members of the document class, and you wrote the code that initializes the data members of the view class.

NOTE

Okay, you have written enough code! To make sure that you typed the code correctly, compile and link the application:

☐ Select Build PAD.EXE from the Project menu, and make sure that there are no compiling and linking errors.

Do not execute the application. The only reason that you are instructed to compile and link the program is to verify that you entered the code correctly.

Updating the Data Members of the Document Class

Whenever the user edits the IDC_SUBJECT and IDC_NOTES edit boxes, the corresponding data members of the document class should be updated with the new values that the user types.

For example, if the user changes the contents of the IDC_SUBJECT edit box, the data member m_Subject of the document class should be updated with the m_Subject data member of the view class (because the m_Subject data member of the view class is the variable of the IDC_SUBJECT edit box).

So you need to write code that detects when the user types something inside the IDC_SUBJECT and IDC_NOTES edit boxes and then changes corresponding data members of the document class accordingly. Here is how you do that:

☐ Use ClassWizard to add a function for the event:

```
CPadView -> IDC_SUBJECT -> EN_CHANGE
```

☐ Accept the name OnChangeSubject() that Visual C++ suggests for the new function.

☐ Click the Edit Code button, and edit the OnChangeSubject() function that you added to the PADVIEW.CPP file. After you edit the function, your OnChangeSubject() function should look like this:

```
void CPadView::OnChangeSubject()
{
// TODO: Add your control notification
// handler code here


        /////////////////////////
        // MY CODE STARTS HERE
        /////////////////////////

        // Update the variables of the controls with the
        // current values inside the controls.
        UpdateData(TRUE);

        // Get a pointer to the document.
        CPadDoc* pDoc = (CPadDoc*) GetDocument();

        // Update the m_Subject data member of
        // the document class.
        pDoc->m_Subject = m_Subject;

        // Set the Modified flag of the document class to TRUE.
        pDoc->SetModifiedFlag();

        /////////////////////////
        // MY CODE ENDS HERE
        /////////////////////////


}
```

☐ Select Save from the File menu to save your work.

Now go over the code that you just typed.

The first statement in the function

```
UpdateData(TRUE);
```

updates the variables of the controls with the current values inside the controls.

The next statement

```
CPadDoc* pDoc = (CPadDoc*) GetDocument();
```

extracts pDoc (the pointer for the document class).

The next statement

```
pDoc->m_Subject = m_Subject;
```

updates the m_Subject data member of the document class with the new contents of the IDC_SUBJECT edit box.

The last statement in the function is this:

```
pDoc->SetModifiedFlag();
```

This statement executes the `SetModifiedFlag()` member function of the document class to set the Modified flag to TRUE, signaling that the document's data was modified. Recall from Chapter 13 that when the Modified flag is set to TRUE and the user tries to quit the application, the application will display a warning message, informing the user that the file has not been saved.

In a similar manner, you now need to attach code to the IDC_NOTES edit box:

☐ Use ClassWizard to add a function for the event:

```
CPadView -> IDC_NOTES -> EN_CHANGE
```

☐ Accept the name `OnChangeNotes()` that Visual C++ suggests for the new function.

☐ Click the Edit Code button and edit the `OnChangeNotes()` function that you added to the PADVIEW.CPP file. After you edit the function, your `OnChangeNotes()` function should look like this:

```
void CPadView::OnChangeNotes()
{
// TODO: Add your control notification
// handler code here

    ////////////////////////
    // MY CODE STARTS HERE
    ////////////////////////

    // Update the variables of the controls with the
    // current values inside the controls.
    UpdateData(TRUE);

    // Get a pointer to the document.
    CPadDoc* pDoc = (CPadDoc*) GetDocument();

    // Update the m_Notes data member of the document class.
    pDoc->m_Notes = m_Notes;

    // Set the Modified flag of the document class to TRUE.
    pDoc->SetModifiedFlag();

    ////////////////////////
    // MY CODE ENDS HERE
    ////////////////////////

}
```

As you can see, the `OnChangeNotes()` function is similar to the `OnChangeSubject()` function. The only difference is that now `m_Notes` (not `m_Subject`) is updated.

You have finished attaching code to the IDC_SUBJECT and IDC_NOTES edit boxes. Now whenever the user changes these edit boxes, the corresponding data members of the document class will be updated.

Don't forget to save your work:

☐ Select Save from the File menu.

Here's a review of what you have accomplished so far:

- You wrote the code that initializes the data members of the document class.
- You wrote the code that initializes the data members of the view class.
- You wrote the code that updates the data members of the document class whenever the user changes the data members of the view class (that is, when the user changes the contents of the edit boxes).

Next you will write the code that enables the user to save documents into files and load documents from files.

Writing and Reading Data to and from Files

Just as you did in previous chapters, in order to bring to life the Open, Save, and Save As menu options of the File menu, all you have to do is write code inside the Serialize() function of the document class. Follow these steps to write the code inside the document class Serialize() function:

☐ Open the file PADDOC.CPP and modify the Serialize() function of the document class until it looks like this:

```
void CPadDoc::Serialize(CArchive& ar)
{
    if (ar.IsStoring())
        {
        // TODO: add storing code here

        ////////////////////////
        // MY CODE STARTS HERE
        ////////////////////////

        // Write to the file.
        ar << m_Subject << m_Notes;

        ////////////////////////
        // MY CODE ENDS HERE
        ////////////////////////

        }
    else
        {
        // TODO: add loading code here

        ////////////////////////
        // MY CODE STARTS HERE
        ////////////////////////

        // Read from the file.
        ar >> m_Subject >> m_Notes;

        ////////////////////////
        // MY CODE ENDS HERE
        ////////////////////////

        }
}
```

The code you typed inside the Serialize() function serializes the m_Subject and m_Notes data members of the document class to and from the file that the user selects from the File menu.

> **NOTE**
>
> You have finished writing most of the PAD application's code. As you can see, even though the PAD application is an MDI application, all the steps you have taken so far are the same as the steps you took when you built an SDI application. The only difference is that when you started the PAD application, you checked the Multiple documents option in AppWizard. (See Figure 19.21.)

You have finished writing most of the code of the PAD application. To see your code in action do the following:

☐ Select Build PAD.EXE from the Project menu of Visual C++.

Visual C++ responds by compiling and linking the PAD application.

☐ Select Execute PAD.EXE from the Project menu.

Visual C++ responds by executing the PAD application. The application's main window appears with a child window in it. The title of the main window is Pad Windows Application—Pad1. The title of the child window is Pad1.

☐ Experiment with all the PAD application's menu options.

Notice that all the menu options of the PAD application are working. However, there are still a few enhancements that you need to apply to the PAD application.

In the following sections you will enhance the PAD application in three ways:

- You will use the string editor of Visual C++ to change the application windows' titles and the default document type that appears in the Save As and Open dialog boxes.
- You will add code that enables the user to display multiple views of the same document.
- You will add code that enables the user to split a window into several views.
- To exit the PAD application do the following:

☐ Select Exit from the File menu.

Using the String Editor to Enhance the PAD Application

You will now use Visual C++ string editor to change the following characteristics of the PAD application:

- You will change the title of the application's window from
Pad Windows Application—[file name] to Pad for Windows—[file name] (where *[file name]* is the name of the document whose window is currently selected).

- You will change the default filename that is displayed in the application window title when a new document is created from Pad to Untitled.

- You will change the default file type that is displayed inside the Save As and Open dialog boxes from *.* to *.PAD. This means that when the user selects Open or Save As from the File menu, the default files displayed in the File list box will have a .PAD file extension.

Complete the following steps to implement these enhancements:

☐ Select pad.mak from the Window menu to display the pad.mak window, double-click pad.rc, and finally, double-click the String Table item inside the pad.rc window.

> *Visual C++ responds by displaying the string editor.*

Recall that in previous chapters when you used the string editor you had to customize only one string—the IDR_MAINFRAME string. However, because the PAD application is an MDI application, now you need to customize two strings: IDR_MAINFRAME and IDR_PADTYPE. As you can see from the string table, IDR_MAINFRAME is the first string in the list, and IDR_PADTYPE is the second string in the list.

Why do you need to customize two strings? The first string, IDR_MAINFRAME, applies when the application's main window is empty (that is, when there are no open child windows). The second string, IDR_PADTYPE, applies when the application's main window contains at least one child window.

As you can see from the string table, the current value of the IDR_MAINFRAME string is Pad.

This string represents the left portion of the main window title. Because you want the left portion of the main window title to be Pad for Windows you need to change the IDR_MAINFRAME string as follows:

☐ Double-click the IDR_MAINFRAME string.

> *Visual C++ responds by displaying the Properties window of the IDR_MAINFRAME string.*

☐ Change the Caption property of the IDR_MAINFRAME string to Pad for Windows.

Next you need to customize the IDR_PADTYPE string. The current value of the IDR_PADTYPE string is this:

```
\nPad\nPad\n\n\nPad.Document.1\n Pad Document
```

Recall that the \n within the string serves as a separator between substrings. Therefore, the preceding string is made of the following substrings:

```
NULL
Pad
Pad
NULL
```

```
NULL
Pad.Document.1
Pad Document
```

The first \n means that the first substring is NULL.

From these seven substrings, those of interest right now are the first five.

The first substring represents the left portion of the main window title. This substring is set to NULL because the title of the main window is already specified in the IDR_MAINFRAME string (as Pad for Windows).

The second substring represents the default document name that appears in the main window title (the right portion of the title) when the user starts the application or when the user selects New from the File menu. Currently the value of this substring is Pad, and you want to change it to Untitled.

The third substring represents the document type name of the application.

The fourth and fifth substrings represent the default document type that is displayed in the Save As dialog box and Open File dialog box of the application. For example, if you set the fourth substring to this:

```
PAD Files (*.pad)
```

and you set the fifth substring to this:

```
pad
```

when the user selects Save As or Open from the File menu, the files that will be listed inside the Open and Save As dialog boxes will be files with this extension:

```
.pad
```

and the text that will appear inside the File Type box will be this:

```
PAD Files (*.pad)
```

Figure 19.33 shows the Save As dialog box listing files with the extension .pad. The text PAD Files (*.pad) appears inside the Save As dialog box.

Figure 19.33. The Save As dialog box listing files with the .pad extension.

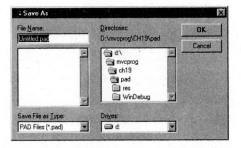

You can now customize the IDR_PADTYPE string:

☐ Double-click the IDR_PADTYPE string.

Visual C++ responds by displaying the String Properties window of the IDR_PADTYPE string.

Change the Caption property of the IDR_PADTYPE string to this:

```
\nUntitled\nPad\nPAD Files (*.pad)\n.pad\nPad.Document.1\nPad Document
```

> **NOTE**
>
> Be sure to type the string on one line. Because the string is long, Visual C++ will automatically wrap the string on two lines.

Your String Properties window for the IDR_PADTYPE string should now look like the one shown in Figure 19.34.

Figure 19.34. Changing the IDR_PADTYPE string.

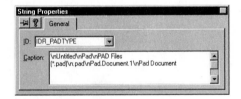

To save your work do the following:

☐ Select Save from the File menu of Visual C++.

To see the effects of the modification you made to the IDR_MAINFRAME and IDR_PADTYPE strings do the following:

☐ Select Build PAD.EXE from the Project menu of Visual C++.

☐ Execute the PAD application.

As you can see, now the main window of the application appears with the title Pad for Windows—Untitled1 and the title of the child window is Untitled1.

☐ Fill the blank form of the Untitled1 window with data.

☐ Select Save from the File menu.

The PAD application responds by displaying a Save As dialog box. As you can see, the Save As dialog box lists files with the .pad extension.

☐ Save your document as TRY.PAD.

The PAD application responds by saving the document into the file TRY.PAD, and by changing the title of the application window to Pad for Windows—TRY.PAD.

The PAD application also changes the title of the child window to TRY.PAD.

So as you can see, you have enhanced the PAD application significantly simply by customizing the IDR_MAINFRAME and IDR_PADTYPE strings using the string editor.

To terminate the PAD application do the following:

☐ Select Exit from the File menu.

Multiple Views of the Same Document

Currently the PAD application does not support multiple viewing of the same document. As discussed at the beginning of this chapter, multiple viewing of the same document means that the user is able to open several windows for the same document, and when the user changes the data inside one of the windows, the data in the rest of the windows (of the same document) is updated automatically.

To verify that currently the PAD application does not support multiple viewing, try the following experiment:

☐ Execute the PAD application.

☐ Fill the fields of the Untitled1 window; Type Test inside the Subject field and type
   Testing multiple views of the same document inside the Notes field.

☐ Select Save from the File menu, and save the new document as TEST.PAD.

☐ Select New Window from the Window menu.

   The PAD application responds by opening another view (another window) for TEST.PAD.

☐ Select Tile from the Window menu.

   Your PAD application should now look like the one shown in Figure 19.35.

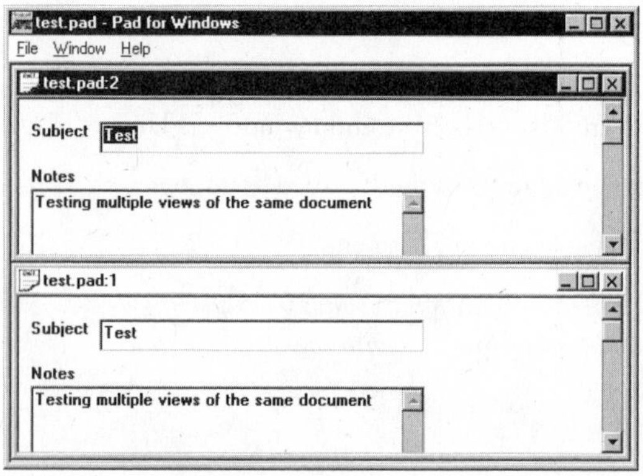

Figure 19.35. Two views of TEST.PAD.

As you can see, the document TEST.PAD has two views. One window has the title TEST.PAD:1 and the other window has the title TEST.PAD:2.

☐ Try to type something in one of the windows of TEST.PAD.

When you type something inside one view of TEST.PAD, the other view is not updated! So currently the PAD application does not support multiple viewing of the same document.

In the following sections you'll add code to the PAD application so that when the user changes one view of a document all the other views of the same document will be updated automatically.

☐ Terminate the PAD application.

The *UpdateAllViews()* and *OnUpdate()* Functions

Whenever the user changes the contents of the IDC_SUBJECT and IDC_NOTES edit boxes (that is, the user types something inside one of these edit boxes), you want to update all the views of the particular document that the user is currently changing. You do that by calling the UpdateAllViews() member function of the document class.

What does the UpdateAllViews() function do? It notifies all the views of the modified document that they need to be updated by calling the OnUpdate() member function of the view class for each view that should be updated.

So your job is this:

- Write the code that calls UpdateAllViews() whenever the user changes any view (that is, when the user types something inside an edit box).
- Write the OnUpdate() member function of the view class.

Calling the *UpdateAllViews()* Function

As stated, whenever the user changes a view of a particular document (that is, the user types something inside the IDC_SUBJECT edit box or IDC_NOTES edit box) you need to call the UpdateAllViews() member function of the document class.

You call the UpdateAllViews() function from the OnChangeSubject() and OnChangeNotes() member functions of the view class. Recall that you wrote these two functions earlier. OnChangeSubject() is executed whenever the user changes the IDC_SUBJECT edit box, and OnChangeNotes() is executed whenever the user changes the IDC_NOTES edit box.

Follow these steps to modify the OnChangeSubject() and OnChangeNotes() functions:

☐ Open the file PADVIEW.CPP and add the statement

```
// Update all the other views of the same document.
pDoc->UpdateAllViews(this);
```

to the end of the OnChangeSubject() function. After you add this statement, your OnChangeSubject() function should look like this:

```
void CPadView::OnChangeSubject()
{
// TODO: Add your control notification
// handler code here


    /////////////////////////
    // MY CODE STARTS HERE
    /////////////////////////

    // Update the variables of the controls with the
    // current values inside the controls.
    UpdateData(TRUE);

    // Get a pointer to the document.
    CPadDoc* pDoc = (CPadDoc*) GetDocument();

    // Update the m_Subject data member
    // of the document class.
    pDoc->m_Subject = m_Subject;

    // Set the Modified flag of the document class to TRUE.
    pDoc->SetModifiedFlag();


    // Update all the other views of the same document.
    pDoc->UpdateAllViews(this);


    /////////////////////////
    // MY CODE ENDS HERE
    /////////////////////////

}
```

The statement you just added

```
pDoc->UpdateAllViews(this);
```

calls the UpdateAllViews() member function of the document class. The parameter this is passed to tell UpdateAllViews() which is the current view (the this keyword is a pointer to the current view object). This way, UpdateAllWindows() will update all the views of the current document except the current view.

For example, if the user changed the IDC_SUBJECT edit box in a certain view of the document TRY.DOC, UpdateAllViews() will update all the *other* views of TRY.DOC. There is no need for UpdateAllWindows() to update the current view, because the current view has already updated itself.

You also need to modify the OnChangeNotes() function:

☐ Add the statement

```
// Update all the other views of the same document.
pDoc->UpdateAllViews(this);
```

to the end of the OnChangeNotes() function. After you add this statement, your OnChangeNotes() function should look like this:

```
void CPadView::OnChangeNotes()
{
// TODO: Add your control notification
// handler code here

    //////////////////////
    // MY CODE STARTS HERE
    //////////////////////

    // Update the variables of the controls with the
    // current values inside the controls.
    UpdateData(TRUE);

    // Get a pointer to the document.
    CPadDoc* pDoc = (CPadDoc*) GetDocument();

    // Update the m_Notes data member of the document class.
    pDoc->m_Notes = m_Notes;

    // Set the Modified flag of the document class to TRUE.
    pDoc->SetModifiedFlag();


     // Update all the other views of the same document.
     pDoc->UpdateAllViews(this);

    //////////////////////
    // MY CODE ENDS HERE
    //////////////////////

}
```

The *OnUpdate()* Member Function of the View Class

At this point, whenever the user changes one of the edit boxes in any view of a particular document, the `OnUpdateAllViews()` member function of the document class will be executed. The `OnUpdateAllViews()` function will update the contents of the other views (of the same document) by calling the `OnUpdate()` member function of the view class. Therefore, you need to write the `OnUpdate()` function.

Now write the code of the `OnUpdate()` function:

☐ Use Class Wizard to select the event:

CPadView -> CPadView -> OnUpdate

Then click the Add Function button.

☐ Click the Edit Code button and add code to the `OnUpdate()` function. After you add the code, the `OnUpdate()` function should look like this:

```
void CPadView::OnUpdate(CView* pSender, LPARAM lHint,
              CObject* pHint)
{
```

```
// TODO: Add your specialized code here
// and/or call the base class

   /////////////////////////
   // MY CODE STARTS HERE
   /////////////////////////
   // Get a pointer to the document.
   CPadDoc* pDoc = (CPadDoc*) GetDocument();

   // Update the view with the current document values.
   m_Subject = pDoc->m_Subject;
   m_Notes   = pDoc->m_Notes;

   // Update the screen with the new variables values.
   UpdateData(FALSE);

   /////////////////////////
   // MY CODE ENDS HERE
   /////////////////////////

CFormView::OnUpdate(pSender, lHint, pHint);
}
```

Now go over the code of the `OnUpdate()` function.

The first statement

```
CPadDoc* pDoc = (CPadDoc*) GetDocument();
```

extracts pDoc (the pointer for the document class).

Then the data members of the view class are updated with the current values of the document:

```
m_Subject = pDoc->m_Subject;
m_Notes   = pDoc->m_Notes;
```

Finally, the `UpdateData()` function is used to transfer the new values of `m_Subject` and `m_Notes` to the screen:

```
UpdateData(FALSE);
```

That's it! You have finished writing all the necessary code for multiple viewing of the same document.

To see in action the code that you just entered do the following:

☐ Select Build PAD.EXE from the Project menu.

☐ Execute the PAD.EXE application.

Now verify that the PAD application supports multiple viewing of the same document:

☐ Select Open from the File menu to open the document TEST.PAD (you created TEST.PAD earlier).

☐ Select New Window from the Window menu.

> *The PAD application responds by opening another view (another window) of TEST.PAD.*

☐ Arrange the two windows of TEST.PAD so that you'll be able to see the fields in both windows. (See Figure 19.35.)

☐ Try to type something in one of the windows of TEST.PAD.

As you can see, when you type something inside one view of TEST.PAD, the other view is updated automatically!

You can now add as many views as you wish for the TEST.PAD document. You'll see that when you change one view, all the other views are updated automatically.

☐ Terminate the PAD application.

Splitter Windows

Recall from the beginning of the chapter that the PAD application should support the splitter window feature. That is, each of the child windows in the application's main window should have two small split boxes located on the horizontal and vertical scroll bars of the window. (See Figure 19.11.) When the user drags these split boxes, the window splits into several views. (See Figures 19.12 and 19.13.)

To provide the user with this powerful feature, you need to use ClassWizard to create a splitter class and then modify the main application source file of the application (PAD.CPP) to use this class. After you do that, the child windows of the application will have the two small split boxes.

To create the splitter class with ClassWizard, follow these steps:

☐ Start ClassWizard from the Project menu of Visual C++.

☐ Click the Add Class button in ClassWizard's dialog box.

   ClassWizard responds by displaying the Add Class dialog box.

☐ Type CMySplit inside the Class Name box.

☐ Set the Class Type to splitter (by dropping down the list of the Class Type and selecting splitter from the list).

Your Add Class dialog box should now look like the one shown in Figure 19.36.

Figure 19.36. Adding a splitter class.

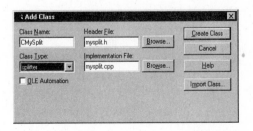

☐ Click the Create Class button of the Add Class dialog box and then click the OK button of ClassWizard's dialog box.

> *ClassWizard responds by creating the splitter class* CMySplit. *Note that the header file of this class is MYSPLIT.H and the implementation file of this class is MYSPLIT.CPP. (See Figure 19.36.)*

Now you need to modify the main application source file of the application (PAD.CPP) so that it will use the splitter class you created.

☐ Select Open from the File menu of Visual C++, open the file PAD.CPP, and look for the InitInstance() function.

One of the statements inside the InitInstance() function is this:

```
pDocTemplate = new CMultiDocTemplate(
 IDR_PADTYPE,
 RUNTIME_CLASS(CPadDoc),
 RUNTIME_CLASS(CMDIChildWnd), // standard MDI child frame
 RUNTIME_CLASS(CPadView));
```

This statement uses the CMultiDocTemplate() function with four parameters.

Currently the third parameter in the preceding statement is this:

```
RUNTIME_CLASS(CMDIChildWnd)  // standard MDI child frame.
```

Change it to this:

```
RUNTIME_CLASS(CMySplit),     // the splitter class.
```

After making this modification, the statement should look like this:

```
pDocTemplate = new CMultiDocTemplate(
    IDR_PADTYPE,
    RUNTIME_CLASS(CPadDoc),
    RUNTIME_CLASS(CMySplit), // the splitter class.
    RUNTIME_CLASS(CPadView));
```

Because the statement you just modified refers to the CMySplit class, you need to use #include on the header file of the CMySplit class (mysplit.h) at the beginning of PAD.CPP:

☐ Add the #include "mysplit.h" statement at the beginning of the PAD.CPP file (immediately before the #include statement of the mainfrm.h file). After you add this #include statement, the beginning of the PAD.CPP file should look like this:

```
// pad.cpp : Defines the class behaviors
// for the application.
//

#include "stdafx.h"
#include "pad.h"

//////////////////////////
// MY CODE STARTS HERE
//////////////////////////
```

```
#include "mysplit.h"

//////////////////////
// MY CODE ENDS HERE
//////////////////////


#include "mainfrm.h"
#include "paddoc.h"
#include "padview.h"
```

That's all you need to do! Now the PAD application supports the splitter window feature.

To see your code in action do the following:

☐ Select Build PAD.EXE from the Project menu.

☐ Execute the PAD.EXE application.

As you can see, now the child window that is displayed inside the main window (Untitled1) has small split boxes on the horizontal and vertical scroll bars of the window. (See Figure 19.11.)

☐ Drag the split boxes of the vertical and horizontal scroll bars of the window and notice how the window splits. (See Figures 19.12 and 19.13.)

☐ Terminate the PAD application.

Adding the Split Option to the Window Menu

Recall from the beginning of the chapter that besides using the split boxes, the user also should be able to split a child window by using the Split option of the Window menu. (See Figure 19.6.) Currently the Window menu of the PAD application does not include this menu item.

To add the Split option to the Window menu, you need to use the visual tools of Visual C++. You don't have to write any code!

Follow these steps to add the Split option to the Window menu:

☐ Select pad.mak from the Window menu, double-click pad.rc inside the pad.mak window, double-click the Menu item, and finally, double-click the IDR_PADTYPE item.

Visual C++ responds by displaying the IDR_PADTYPE menu in design mode.

☐ Add a new item to the Window pop-up menu: Set the Caption property of the new item to &Split and set the ID of the new item to ID_WINDOW_SPLIT.

The Properties window of your Split menu item should now look like the one shown in Figure 19.37.

Note that you must name the ID of the Split menu item ID_WINDOW_SPLIT because the application code (code that Visual C++ wrote for you) associates this constant with the action of splitting the window.

Don't forget to save your work:

☐ Select Save from the File menu of Visual C++.

Figure 19.37. The
Properties window of the
Split menu item.

Executing the Final Version of the PAD Application

To see the effects of adding the Split menu item do the following:

☐ Select Build PAD.EXE from the Project menu.

☐ Execute the PAD.EXE application and experiment with the Split option of the Window menu.

> *As you can see, the Split menu item works!*

20

Menus

So far in the book you have learned how to implement very simple menus. In this chapter you'll learn advanced menu topics: You'll learn how to implement accelerator keys, how to implement submenus, how to place and remove checkmarks in menu items, how to dim (gray) and un-dim menu items, how to take advantage of the `UPDATE_COMMAND_UI` message, and how to add menu items during the execution of the application (that is, during runtime).

The MyMenu Application

Before you start writing the MyMenu application yourself, first execute the copy of it that resides in the \MVCPROG\EXE directory of the book's CD.

To execute the MyMenu application do the following:

☐ Execute the X:\MVCPROG\EXE\MyMenu.EXE program (where *X* represents the letter drive of your CD-ROM drive).

> *The main window of MyMenu.EXE appears, as shown in Figure 20.1.*

Figure 20.1. The main window of the MyMenu application.

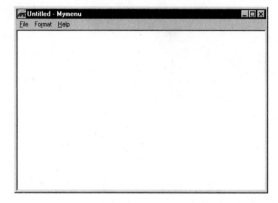

The MyMenu application has three pop-up menus: File, Format, and Help. These pop-up menus are shown in Figures 20.2, 20.3, and 20.4.

Figure 20.2. The File menu of the MyMenu application.

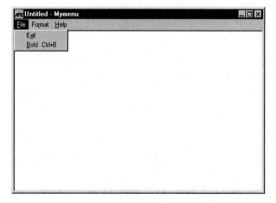

Figure 20.3. The Format menu of the MyMenu application.

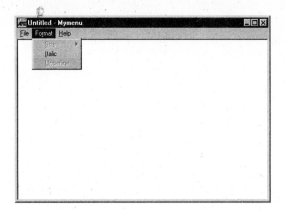

Figure 20.4. The Help menu of the MyMenu application.

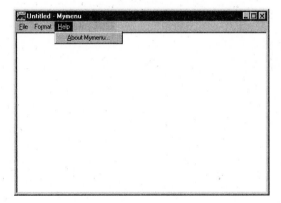

☐ Select the Format menu.

MyMenu responds by displaying the Format menu. As you can see, the Size menu item is unavailable (dimmed), and the Italic menu item is available.

To make the Size menu item available do the following:

☐ Select the Bold item from the File menu.

MyMenu responds by displaying a message box telling you that you selected Bold from the File menu.

☐ Click the OK button of the message box and then select the Format menu again.

MyMenu responds by displaying the Format menu. However, now the Size menu item is available. From now on, the Size menu item will be available in the MyMenu application.

☐ Select Size from the Format menu.

MyMenu responds by displaying the menu shown in Figure 20.5.

The checkmark that is displayed to the left of the Size point 2 menu item is an indication that currently Size point 2 is selected in the program.

*Figure 20.5. The menu
that MyMenu displays
when you select Size from
the Format menu.*

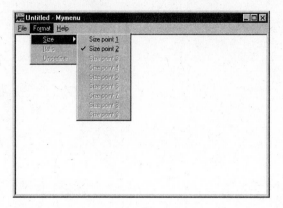

☐ Select Size point 1 from the Size menu of the Format menu.

> *MyMenu responds by displaying a message box that tells you the sequence of menus that have
> been selected. (See Figure 20.6.)*

*Figure 20.6. The message
box that MyMenu displays
after you select Format then
Size then Size point 1.*

☐ Click the OK button of the message box, and then select the Size menu item from the
Format menu.

> *MyMenu responds by again displaying the Size menu. However, now Size point 1 has a
> checkmark, and Size point 2 does not have a checkmark.*

☐ Experiment with the Size menu by selecting Size point 1 and Size point 2, and notice that
when you select the Size menu again, the checkmark appears to the left of the item that
was last selected.

As you saw, initially the Size menu was unavailable. You had to select Bold from the File menu to
make it available.

Note the text Ctrl+B that appears to the right of the Bold menu item. (See Figure 20.2.) *Ctrl+B* is
called an *accelerator key*. It serves to accelerate the process of selecting Bold. That is, instead of selecting the File menu and then selecting Bold from the File menu that pops up, you can simply
press Ctrl+B on your keyboard.

☐ Press Ctrl+B.

> *MyMenu responds in the same manner that it would respond if you had selected Bold from the File menu. To prove that indeed this is the case, take a look at the Format menu. It contains the Italic menu item.*

☐ Select Bold from the File menu and then select the Format menu.

> *MyMenu responds by displaying the Format menu. The status of the Italic item is opposite the status that existed before you selected the Bold item. (If before you selected Bold the Italic item was available, now the Italic item is dimmed, or unavailable.)*

☐ Select Bold from the File menu and verify that indeed the status of the Italic menu item toggles.

☐ Now select Bold by simply pressing Ctrl+B, and note that the status of the Italic item toggles.

☐ Experiment with the MyMenu application, and then select Exit from the File menu to terminate the MyMenu application.

Now that you know what the MyMenu application should do, you can begin to write it.

Creating the Project of the MyMenu Application

You'll now create the MyMenu.MAK project.

☐ Close all the open windows inside the desktop of Visual C++ (if there are any).

☐ Select New from the File menu.

> *Visual C++ responds by displaying the New dialog box.*

☐ Select Project inside the New dialog box and then click the OK button of the New dialog box.

> *Visual C++ responds by displaying the New Project dialog box.*

☐ Set the project name to MyMenu.

☐ Set the project path to \MVCPROG\CH20\MyMenu\MyMenu.MAK.

Your New Project dialog box should now look like the one shown in Figure 20.7.

☐ Click the Create button of the New Project dialog box.

> *Visual C++ responds by displaying the AppWizard—Step 1 window.*

☐ Set the Step 1 window as shown in Figure 20.8. As shown in Figure 20.8, the MyMenu.MAK project is set as a single-document interface application, and U.S. English (APPWIZUS.DLL) is used as the language for the application's resources.

Figure 20.7. The New Project dialog box of the MyMenu.MAK project.

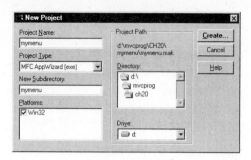

Figure 20.8. The AppWizard—Step 1 window for the MyMenu application.

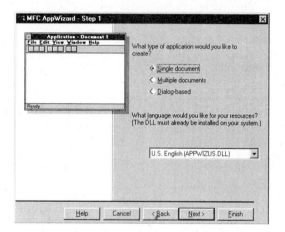

☐ Click the Next button of the Step 1 window.

Visual C++ responds by displaying the AppWizard—Step 2 of 6 window.

☐ Set the Step 2 of 6 window as shown in Figure 20.9. That is, in the MyMenu application you don't want any database support.

Figure 20.9. The AppWizard—Step 2 of 6 window for the MyMenu application.

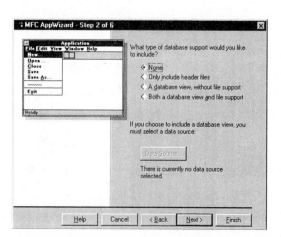

☐ Click the Next button of the Step 2 of 6 window.

> *Visual C++ responds by displaying the AppWizard—Step 3 of 6 window.*

☐ Set the Step 3 of 6 window as shown in Figure 20.10. That is, in the MyMenu application you don't want any OLE support.

Figure 20.10. The AppWizard—Step 3 of 6 window for the MyMenu application.

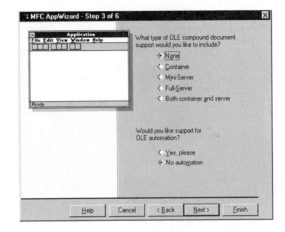

☐ Click the Next button of the Step 3 of 6 window.

> *Visual C++ responds by displaying the AppWizard—Step 4 of 6 window.*

☐ Set the Step 4 of 6 window as shown in Figure 20.11.

Figure 20.11. The AppWizard—Step 4 of 6 window for the MyMenu application.

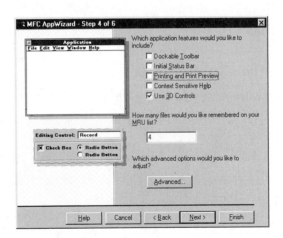

As shown in Figure 20.11, only the Use 3D Controls check box is checked.

☐ Click the Next button of the Step 4 of 6 window.

> *Visual C++ responds by displaying the AppWizard—Step 5 of 6 window.*

☐ Set the Step 5 of 6 window as shown in Figure 20.12.

As shown in Figure 20.12, the project will be generated with comments, a Visual C++ makefile will be generated, and the application will use the MFC library from a DLL.

Figure 20.12. The AppWizard—Step 5 of 6 window for the MyMenu application.

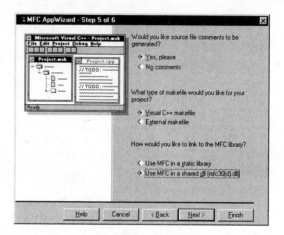

☐ Click the Next button of the Step 5 of 6 window.

> *Visual C++ responds by displaying the AppWizard—Step 6 of 6 window.*

You'll now use the AppWizard—Step 6 of 6 window to tell AppWizard to derive the view class of the application from the MFC class CFormView:

☐ Select the CMymenuView class inside the AppWizard—Step 6 of 6 window.

☐ Set the Base Class drop-down list box to CFormView.

Your AppWizard—Step 6 of 6 window should now look like the one shown in Figure 20.13.

☐ Click the Finish button of the Step 6 of 6 window.

> *Visual C++ responds by displaying the New Project Information window, as shown in Figure 20.14.*

Figure 20.13. The
AppWizard—Step 6
of 6 window after you set
the base class of the
application view class to
CFormView.

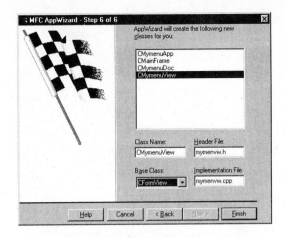

Figure 20.14. The New
Project Information
window of the
MyMenu.MAK project.

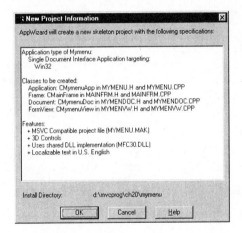

☐ Click the OK button of the New Project Information window.

Visual C++ responds by creating the project file and all the skeleton files of the application.

The Visual Design of the Menu

You'll now visually design the menu of the MyMenu application.

☐ Select MyMenu.MAK from the Window menu to display the MyMenu.MAK window,
double-click mymenu.rc inside the MyMenu.MAK window, double-click Menu, and
finally, double-click the IDR_MAINFRAME item that appears under the Menu item.

Visual C++ responds by displaying the IDR_MAINFRAME menu in design menu.

☐ Implement the menu of the MyMenu application so that it has the following items:

&File
    E&xit
    &Bold
&Help
    &About Mymenu...

As you can see, this menu is not the final menu of the MyMenu application. (You'll be instructed later in this chapter to add the Format menu.)

To save your work do the following:

☐ Select Save from the File menu.

The visual implementation of the menu of the MyMenu application is complete.

The Visual Implementation of the Main Window of MyMenu

Because in AppWizard you specified that the base class of the application's view class is CFormView, AppWizard created for you a form (a dialog box) that is attached to the view class of the application. This dialog box serves as the main window of the application. AppWizard named this dialog box IDD_MYMENU_FORM. You'll now customize the IDD_MYMENU_FORM dialog box.

☐ Select MyMenu.MAK from the Window menu to display the MyMenu.MAK window, double-click mymenu.rc inside the MyMenu.MAK window, double-click Dialog, and finally, double-click IDD_MYMENU_FORM under Dialog.

Visual C++ responds by displaying the IDD_MYMENU_FORM in design mode.

☐ Delete the TODO static text from the IDD_MYMENU_FORM dialog box.

☐ Select Save from the File menu.

Attaching Code to a Menu Item

Attaching code to a menu item is easy (you've done it many times so far in this book). Attach code to the Bold menu item. The code that you'll attach will be executed whenever the user selects Bold from the File menu.

☐ Display the IDR_MAINFRAME menu in design mode. (That is, select mymenu.rc from the Window menu, double-click Menu inside the mymenu.rc window, and finally, double-click IDR_MAINFRAME under Menu.)

☐ Use ClassWizard (from the Project menu) to select the event:

CMymenuView -> ID_FILE_BOLD -> COMMAND

Then click the Add Function button.

☐ Accept the name `OnFileBold()` that Visual C++ suggests for the new function. (Be sure that you add the function to the `CMymenuView` class.)

Visual C++ lets you attach a function either to the `COMMAND` message or to the `UPDATE_COMMAND_UI` message. The `UPDATE_COMMAND_UI` message is covered later in this chapter.

☐ Click the Edit Code button.

☐ Edit the `OnFileBold()` function that you added to the MYMENVW.CPP file. After you edit the function, your `OnFileBold()` function should look like this:

```
void CMymenuView::OnFileBold()
{
// TODO: Add your command handler code here

    /////////////////////////
    // MY CODE STARTS HERE
    /////////////////////////

    CString sMessage;

    sMessage = "I'm inside OnFileBold() ";

    MessageBox ( sMessage );

    /////////////////////
    // MY CODE ENDS HERE
    /////////////////////

}
```

The code you typed displays the message `I'm inside OnFileBold()` whenever the user clicks the Bold menu item. Of course, a real application wouldn't display this message box, but would instead carry out the operation corresponding to the selected menu item. For example, in a word processing program, the user would highlight text and then select Bold from the menu to apply bold to the highlighted text.

☐ Compile and link the MyMenu application.

☐ Execute the MyMenu application.

☐ Select Bold from the File menu.

MyMenu responds by displaying a message box. This proves that `OnFileBold()` was executed.

☐ Select Exit from the File menu to terminate the MyMenu application.

Adding Accelerator Keys to the Menu

Many Windows applications attach accelerator keys to menu items. As implied by its name, an *accelerator key* enables the user to execute a menu item's code by pressing a combination of keys instead of going through the procedure of opening the menu and then selecting the item from the menu.

Here is how you attach an accelerator key to the Bold menu item:

☐ Display the IDR_MAINFRAME menu in design mode.

☐ Double-click the Bold menu item of the File menu.

   Visual C++ responds by displaying the Properties window of the Bold menu item.

☐ Change the Caption property to &Bold\tCtrl+B. (The \t serves as a Tab character.)

The Properties window of the Bold menu item should now look like the one shown in Figure 20.15.

Figure 20.15. Changing the caption of the Bold menu item.

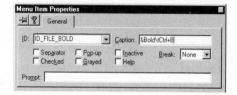

If you compile, link, and execute the MyMenu application now, in the File menu you'll see the text Ctrl+B to the right of the Bold menu item. However, pressing Ctrl+B won't pop up the Bold menu, because all you did was change this menu item's caption.

To actually add the Ctrl+B accelerator key to the Bold menu item do the following:

☐ Display the mymenu.rc window.

☐ Double-click Accelerator inside the mymenu.rc widow.

   Visual C++ responds by dropping down a list of accelerators. As shown in Figure 20.16, the MyMenu project has one accelerator table, IDR_MAINFRAME.

Figure 20.16. The IDR_MAINFRAME accelerator table.

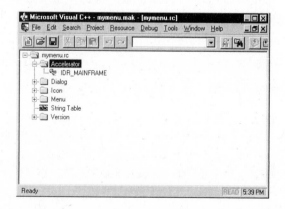

☐ Double-click IDR_MAINFRAME under the Accelerator item.

Visual C++ responds by displaying the Accelerator window. (See Figure 20.17.) As you can see from Figure 20.17, Visual C++ already assigned a variety of accelerator keys to the MyMenu application. For example, the Ctrl+Z combination of keys is assigned to the Undo item of the Edit menu. (You removed the Edit menu when you implemented the menu of MyMenu, but the accelerator key assignment remains.)

Figure 20.17. The
IDR_MAINFRAME
(Accelerator) window.

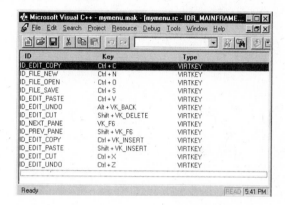

☐ Use the down-arrow key to highlight the very last item in the list of accelerators. That is, place the highlight one item after the Ctrl+Z line.

The highlight should now be on the empty line of the table.

☐ Double-click the last empty line of the Accelerator table.

Visual C++ responds by displaying the Accel Properties window of the new accelerator key that you are now adding. (See Figure 20.18.)

Figure 20.18. The empty
Accel Properties window of
the new accelerator key.

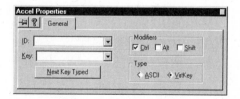

You'll now fill the Accel Properties window of Figure 20.18 so that the new accelerator key will be associated with the Bold menu item.

☐ Click the down-arrow icon of the ID list box, and select ID_FILE_BOLD. (Recall that the ID of the Bold menu item is ID_FILE_BOLD, as shown in Figure 20.15.)

NOTE

As shown in Figure 20.19, Visual C++ will automatically add the numeric value of the ID. You just have to select ID_FILE_BOLD from the list.

Figure 20.19. Selecting ID_FILE_BOLD in the Accel Properties window.

☐ Type B inside the Key box (because you want the accelerator key to be Ctrl+B).

☐ Make sure that the Ctrl check box inside the Modifiers frame is checked, and that the Alt and Shift check boxes are not checked, because the accelerator key that you are now attaching is a Ctrl key (Ctrl+B).

☐ Make sure that the VirtKey radio button is selected inside the Type frame.

The completed Accel Properties window should now look like the one shown in Figure 20.20.

Figure 20.20. The completed Accel Properties window of the new accelerator key.

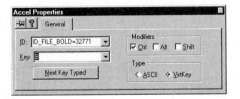

Save your work:

☐ Select Save from the File menu of Visual C++.

As you can see from Figure 20.21, the Accelerator window now contains the Ctrl+B accelerator key.

Figure 20.21. The Accelerator window with the Ctrl+B accelerator key in it.

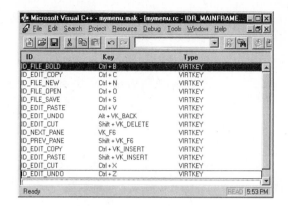

☐ Compile, link, and execute the MyMenu application.

As you can see, the text Ctrl+B appears to the right of the Bold menu item. (See Figure 20.22.)

☐ Select Bold from the File menu.

MyMenu responds by displaying a message box telling you that you did indeed select the Bold item.

☐ Click the OK button in the message box and then press Ctrl+B.

MyMenu responds in the same manner as it did when you selected Bold from the File menu.

Figure 20.22. The Bold menu item with its accelerator key.

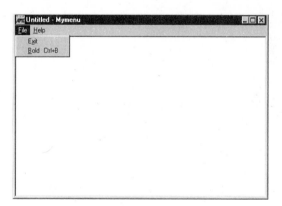

☐ Select Exit from the File menu to terminate the MyMenu application.

NOTE

As you can see in Figure 20.17, Visual C++ implemented for you several accelerator keys.

For example, Ctrl+O is the accelerator key of the Open item of the File menu (ID_FILE_OPEN). (See Figure 20.17.)

Even though you removed the Open item from the File menu, the accelerator key is functional:

☐ Execute the MyMenu application, and press Ctrl+O.

MyMenu responds by displaying the Open dialog box!

This, of course, is not desirable because MyMenu does not have an Open menu item. So you have to go over the accelerator keys and remove the ones that are not used by your program.

To delete the accelerator key of the ID_FILE_OPEN menu item do the following:

☐ Display the accelerator table.

☐ Select ID_FILE_OPEN and then press the Delete key on your keyboard.

☐ You can now repeat these steps to delete the other accelerator keys that are not used by your programs. In particular, make sure to delete the accelerator keys for the ID_FILE_NEW and ID_FILE_SAVE menu items.

Implementing Submenus

Typically, you'll implement the Bold menu in another menu heading such as Format, not in the File menu. Therefore, the menu bar of the MyMenu application should look like this: File|Format|Help.

The Format menu should contain items that are related to the process of formatting highlighted text. A typical Format menu might include the following items:

> Format
> > Size
> > Italic
> > Underline

Suppose your Format menu is used in an application that enables the user to select different widths for a line in a drawing program. One (bad) way of implementing this Format menu is this:

> Format
> > Size 1 point
> > Size 2 points
> > Size 3 points

Size 4 points
Size 5 points
Size 6 points
Size 7 points
Size 8 points
Size 9 points
Size 10 points
Italic
Underline

This implementation isn't recommended because there are simply too many items in the Format menu. In fact, there are so many Size options in the menu that the user might not notice the Italic and Underline items.

The recommended implementation of the Format menu is the following:

Format
Size
Italic
Underline

Then when the user selects the Size item, another menu should pop up:

Size 1 point
Size 2 points
Size 3 points
Size 4 points
Size 5 points
Size 6 points
Size 7 points
Size 8 points
Size 9 points
Size 10 points

Also, the Bold item should be removed from the File menu and it should be placed in the Format menu. However, in this tutorial you are just learning the topic, so leave the Bold item in the File menu.

Here is how you implement a submenu:

☐ Display the IDR_MAINFRAME menu in design mode.

☐ Implement the Format menu so that it contains the following items:

&File
E&xit
&Bold

Fo&rmat
   &Size
   &Italic
   &Underline
&Help
   &About MyMenu...

After you implement the Format menu, it should look like the one shown in Figure 20.23.

Figure 20.23. Implementing the Format menu.

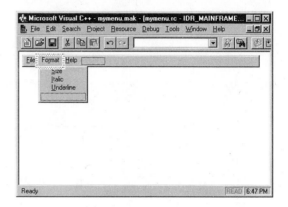

☐   Double-click the Size menu item.

    Visual C++ responds by displaying the Properties window of the Size menu item.

☐   Place an X inside the Pop-up check box. (See Figure 20.24.)

Note that once you place an X inside the Pop-up check box, Visual C++ displays a submenu to the right of the Size menu item. (See Figure 20.25.) It then removes the ID of the Size item. (See Figure 20.24.)

Figure 20.24. Making the Size menu item a pop-up menu.

☐   Double-click inside the submenu item of the Size item, and type `Size point &1` inside the Caption box of its Properties window.

    Visual C++ responds by adding Size point 1 to the submenu of the Size menu item. (See Figure 20.26.)

Figure 20.25. The submenu of the Size item (in design mode).

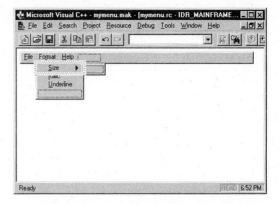

Figure 20.26. Adding items to the submenu of the Size menu item.

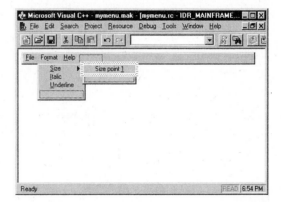

☐ Keep adding items to the submenu until the submenu looks like the one shown in Figure 20.27.

Figure 20.27. The complete submenu of Size.

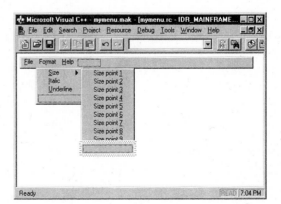

Save your work:

☐ Select Save from the File menu.

You'll now add code to the first two items of the Size submenu. (In practice, you'll add code to all nine items of the submenu, but for the sake of illustrating the concept, it is sufficient to add code to only two items.)

☐ Display the IDR_MAINFRAME menu in design mode.

☐ Use ClassWizard (from the Project menu) to select the event:

```
CMymenuView -> ID_FORMAT_SIZE_SIZEPOINT1 -> COMMAND
```

Then click the Add Function button.

☐ Accept the name OnFormatSizeSizepoint1() that Visual C++ suggests.

☐ Click the Edit Code button.

☐ Edit the OnFormatSizeSizepoint1() function that you added to the MYMENVW.CPP file.
   After you edit the function, your OnFormatSizeSizepoint1() function should look like this:

```
void CMymenuView::OnFormatSizeSizepoint1()
{
    // TODO: Add your command handler code here


    ////////////////////////
    // MY CODE STARTS HERE
    ////////////////////////

    CString sMessage;

    sMessage = "I'm inside Format->Size-> Point 1";

    MessageBox ( sMessage );

    ////////////////////////
    // MY CODE ENDS HERE
    ////////////////////////


}
```

The code you typed will be executed whenever the user selects Format|Size|Size Point 1. This code will display a message box that indicates that indeed this function is executed.

☐ Use ClassWizard (from the Project menu) to select the event:

```
CMymenuView -> ID_FORMAT_SIZE_SIZEPOINT2 -> COMMAND
```

Then click the Add Function button.

☐ Accept the name OnFormatSizeSizepoint2() that Visual C++ suggests.

☐ Click the Edit Code button.

☐ Edit the `OnFormatSizeSizepoint2()` function that you added to the MYMENVW.CPP file. After you edit the function, your `OnFormatSizeSizepoint2()` function should look like this:

```
void CMymenuView::OnFormatSizeSizepoint2()
{
// TODO: Add your command handler code here

    /////////////////////////
    // MY CODE STARTS HERE
    /////////////////////////

    CString sMessage;

    sMessage = "I'm inside Format->Size->Point 2";

    MessageBox ( sMessage );

    /////////////////////////
    // MY CODE ENDS HERE
    /////////////////////////
}
```

☐ Compile, link, and execute the MyMenu application.

☐ Select the Format menu.

> *MyMenu responds by displaying the Format menu, as shown in Figure 20.28. Note the arrow icon that is located to the right of the Size menu item. This arrow icon (placed automatically by Visual C++) is an indication to the user that upon selection of this menu item, another menu will pop up.*

Figure 20.28. The Size menu.

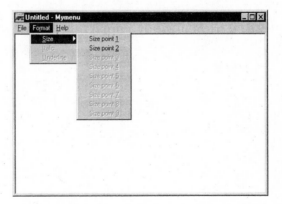

☐ Select the Size menu item.

> *MyMenu responds by displaying the submenu of Size.*

☐ Select Size point 1 from the submenu.

> *MyMenu responds by displaying a message box that indicates your selection.*

☐ Experiment with the MyMenu application and then select Exit from the File menu to terminate the application.

Placing a Checkmark in a Menu Item

Suppose the user selects Size from the Format menu, which displays the menu shown in Figure 20.28. At this point the user may select a different point size from the submenu.

To make the application easier to use, you can place a checkmark to the left of the selected submenu item. The next time the user opens the menu, the submenu item that was selected last time will have a checkmark.

You can place a checkmark in a menu item (or remove it) at design time and at runtime. Here's how you place a checkmark at design time:

☐ Display the IDR_MAINFRAME menu at design mode.

☐ Double-click the Size point 2 item and place an X in the Checked box that appears in the Properties window.

Visual C++ responds by placing a checkmark to the left of the Size point 2 menu item.

☐ Compile, link, and execute the MyMenu application.

Note that when you select Format and then Size, Size's submenu contains the menu item Size point 2 with a checkmark by it. (See Figure 20.29.) The checkmark indicates that the size is currently set to 2.

Figure 20.29. The checkmark of the Size point 2 menu item.

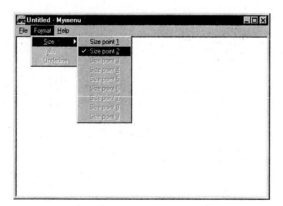

☐ Terminate the application by selecting Exit from the File menu.

Now you'll modify the MyMenu application so that when the user selects Size point 1 from the submenu the checkmark is moved from Size point 2 to Size point 1.

NOTE

If you have a large number of IDs in your application, you might sometimes want to see a list of them. You can do so as follows:

☐ Display the IDR_MAINFRAME menu in design mode.

☐ Select Symbols from the Resource menu.

Visual C++ responds by displaying the Symbol Browser dialog box. (See Figure 20.30.)

After you review the list of IDs, you can close the Symbol Browser dialog box by clicking the Close button.

Figure 20.30. The Symbol Browser dialog box.

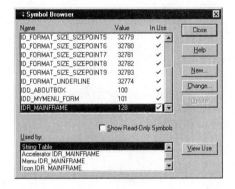

☐ Modify the `OnFormatSizeSizepoint1()` function inside the MYMENVW.CPP file. After the modification, the function should look like this:

```
void CMymenuView::OnFormatSizeSizepoint1()
{
// TODO: Add your command handler code here

    ////////////////////////
    // MY CODE STARTS HERE
    ////////////////////////

    // Extract the pointer of the parent window.
    CWnd* pParent = GetParent();

    // Extract the pointer of the menu
    CMenu* pMenu = pParent->GetMenu();

    // Remove the checkmark from the Size point 2 item
    pMenu->CheckMenuItem( ID_FORMAT_SIZE_SIZEPOINT2,
                          MF_UNCHECKED );
```

```
    // Place a checkmark to the left of
    // the Size point 1 item
    pMenu->CheckMenuItem( ID_FORMAT_SIZE_SIZEPOINT1,
                          MF_CHECKED );


    // Display a message box
    CString sMessage;
    sMessage = "I'm inside Format->Size->Point 1";
    MessageBox ( sMessage );

    ////////////////////////
    // MY CODE ENDS HERE
    ////////////////////////

}
```

The code you typed removes the checkmark from the Size point 2 menu item and places it by the Size point 1 menu item. This is accomplished with the CheckMenuItem() member function. For example, if the pointer to the menu is pMenu, you'd use the following statement to remove the checkmark from the Size point 2 menu item:

```
pMenu->CheckMenuItem( ID_FORMAT_SIZE_SIZEPOINT2,
                      MF_UNCHECKED );
```

In the preceding statement, the first parameter is ID_FORMAT_SIZE_SIZEPOINT2, which is the ID of the menu item on which you are operating. The second parameter of the CheckMenuItem() function is MF_UNCHECKED, which tells CheckMenuItem() to remove the checkmark.

In a similar manner, to place a checkmark by the Size point 1 menu item, you use this statement:

```
pMenu->CheckMenuItem( ID_FORMAT_SIZE_SIZEPOINT1,
                      MF_CHECKED );
```

The preceding statement supplies ID_FORMAT_SIZE_SIZEPOINT1 as the first parameter (the ID of the menu item), and the second parameter tells the CheckMenuItem() function to place a checkmark.

As you can see, there is a need to extract the pointer of the menu. In the preceding statements, you indicated that pMenu is the pointer of the menu.

Here is how you extract the pointer of the menu:

First you extract pParent, the pointer of the parent window of the window (the window where the menu is located):

```
CWnd* pParent = GetParent();
```

Once you've extracted pParent, you can extract pMenu, the pointer of the menu:

```
CMenu* pMenu = pParent->GetMenu();
```

You'll now add code that will be executed whenever the user selects Size point 2 from the Size menu:

☐ Modify the OnFormatSizeSizepoint2() function inside the MYMENVW.CPP file. After the modification, the function should look like this:

```
void CMymenuView::OnFormatSizeSizepoint2()
{
// TODO: Add your command handler code here

    /////////////////////////
    // MY CODE STARTS HERE
    /////////////////////////


    // Extract the pointer of the parent window.
    CWnd* pParent = GetParent();

    // Extract the pointer of the menu
    CMenu* pMenu = pParent->GetMenu();

    // Remove the checkmark from the Size point 1 item
    pMenu->CheckMenuItem( ID_FORMAT_SIZE_SIZEPOINT1,
                          MF_UNCHECKED );


    // Place a checkmark to the left of the
    //Size point 2 item
    pMenu->CheckMenuItem( ID_FORMAT_SIZE_SIZEPOINT2,
                          MF_CHECKED );

    // Display a message box
    CString sMessage;
    sMessage = "I'm inside Format->Size->Point 2";
    MessageBox ( sMessage );

    /////////////////////////
    // MY CODE ENDS HERE
    /////////////////////////

}
```

The code you typed is very similar to the code you typed inside the `OnFormatSizeSizepoint1()` function. However, now you uncheck Size point 1, and check Size point 2.

☐ Compile, link, and execute the MyMenu application.

☐ Select Size from the Format menu.

> *MyMenu responds by displaying the menu with the Size point 2 item checked (because you checked the Checked box in the Properties window of this menu item during design time).*

☐ Select Size point 1 from the menu and then click the OK button of the message box that appears.

☐ Select Size from the Format menu.

Now Size point 1 has a checkmark to its left, and there is no checkmark to the left of the Size point 2 menu item.

☐ Experiment with the MyMenu application and verify that the checkmark appears next to the menu item that was last selected.

Disabling a Menu Item

It is possible to disable a menu item at design time as well as at execution time (that is, runtime). At design time, you can disable a menu item by double-clicking the menu item of the IDR_MAINFRAME menu and placing an X inside the Grayed box in the Properties window of the item. (The term *Grayed* is used, because a disabled menu appears gray.)

☐ Display the IDR_MAINFRAME menu in design mode.

☐ Double-click the Size menu item.

   Visual C++ responds by displaying the Properties window of the Size menu item.

☐ Place an X inside the Grayed check box.

   Visual C++ responds by showing the menu item grayed (disabled).

☐ Select Save from the File menu.

☐ Compile and link the MyMenu application, and then execute it.

☐ Select the Format menu.

   The Format menu of MyMenu appears with the Size menu grayed.

> **NOTE**
>
> The Italic and Underline items are also gray, even though their Grayed boxes aren't checked. This is because you didn't attach any code to them. Visual C++ displays a menu item as gray if there is no code attached to that menu item.

☐ Select Exit from the File menu to terminate the MyMenu application.

To enable a menu item during execution, you have to use the EnableMenuItem() function. Here is how you enable the Size menu item at runtime:

☐ Modify the OnFileBold() function inside MYMENVW.CPP file.

After the modification, your OnFileBold() function should look like this:

```
void CMymenuView::OnFileBold()
{
// TODO: Add your command handler code here


    ////////////////////////
    // MY CODE STARTS HERE
    ////////////////////////

    // Extract the pointer of the parent window.
    CWnd* pParent = GetParent();
```

```
// Extract the pointer of the menu
CMenu* pMenu = pParent->GetMenu();


// Extract the pointer of the Format menu
CMenu* pMenuFormatItem = pMenu->GetSubMenu(1);


// Enable the Size menu
pMenuFormatItem->EnableMenuItem (0,
            MF_BYPOSITION ¦ MF_ENABLED );

// Display a message box
CString sMessage;
 sMessage = "I'm inside OnFileBold() ";
MessageBox ( sMessage );

//////////////////////
// MY CODE ENDS HERE
//////////////////////

}
```

The code that you typed enables the Size menu whenever you click the Bold item from the File menu. Of course, in a real application, the Bold menu item has nothing to do with the Size menu item, but the Bold menu item is used here to illustrate the concept.

The `OnFileBold()` function starts by extracting `pParent`, the pointer of the parent window:

```
CWnd* pParent = GetParent();
```

Once you have extracted `pParent`, you can extract `pMenu`, the pointer of the menu:

```
CMenu* pMenu = pParent->GetMenu();
```

The next statement uses the `GetSubMenu()` function to extract the pointer of the Format menu:

```
CMenu* pMenuFormatItem = pMenu->GetSubMenu(1);
```

In the preceding statement, the `GetSubMenu()` function operates on `pMenu`, which you extracted already. `pMenu` is the pointer of the menu bar. This means that `GetSubMenu(0)` extracts the pointer of the File menu, because File is the extreme-left item on the menu bar. Similarly, `GetSubMenu(1)` extracts the pointer of the Format menu, and `GetSubMenu(2)` extracts the pointer of the Help menu. You typed the code with `GetSubMenu(1)` because you are interested in the pointer of the Format menu.

Once you've extracted `pMenuFormatItem` (the pointer of the Format menu), you can access any of its items. The Size item is considered to be item 0 of the Format menu, Italic is considered to be item 1, and Underline is considered to be item 2.

To enable the Size item, you use this statement:

```
pMenuFormatItem->EnableMenuItem (0,
                MF_BYPOSITION ¦ MF_ENABLED );
```

The first parameter in the preceding statement is 0 because you are enabling the first item in the Format menu. How would the EnableMenuItem() function know that the first parameter is the position of the menu item (and not the ID of the menu item)? You supply MF_BYPOSITION as its second parameter.

As you can see, the second parameter of EnableMenuItem() is

MF_BYPOSITION ¦ MF_ENABLED;

which means that you are telling the EnableMenuItem() function the following:

- The first parameter of EnableMenuItem() is supplied as a position (MF_BYPOSITION).
- The menu item mentioned as the first parameter should be enabled (MF_ENABLED).

MF_BYPOSITION and MF_ENABLED are put together using the OR bitwise operator (¦).

> **NOTE**
>
> If you supply MF_BYCOMMAND as the second parameter of the EnableMenuItem(), then the EnableMenuItem() function considers the first parameter to be the ID of the menu item.
>
> If you don't mention MF_BYPOSITION or MF_BYCOMMAND as the second parameter of EnableMenuItem(), EnabledMenuItem() considers the first parameter to be the ID of the menu item.

> **NOTE**
>
> In the OnFileBold() function, you supplied MF_ENABLED as the second parameter of the EnableMenuItem() function. You can also supply MF_GRAYED as the second parameter of the EnableMenuItem() function to make a menu item gray. In addition, Visual C++ lets you supply MF_DISABLED as the second parameter of EnableMenuItem(). MF_DISABLED causes the menu item to be disabled, but it will still appear not grayed.

☐ Compile, link, and execute the MyMenu application.

☐ Select Format from the menu.

> *MyMenu responds by displaying the Format menu. The Size menu item is gray because you grayed it during design time, and the Italic and Underline items are gray because you did not attach any code to them.*

☐ Select Bold from the File menu and then select the Format menu again.

> *MyMenu responds by displaying the Format menu with the Size item enabled. This is because the code that you typed inside the OnFileBold() function was executed.*

☐ Select Exit from the File menu to terminate the application.

Using the *UPDATE_COMMAND_UI* Message

So far in this book, you have been instructed to attach code to menu items with the COMMAND event. As you've probably noticed, Visual C++ lets you attach menu code with either the COMMAND message or with the UPDATE_COMMAND_UI message.

The function that you attach to the UPDATE_COMMAND_UI message of a menu item is executed whenever the menu item is just about to be displayed. For example, if the user clicks the File menu bar, Windows will display the items of the File menu. However, before actually displaying the items of the File menu, the code that you attach to the UPDATE_COMMAND_UI of each of the menu items of the File menu will be executed.

> **NOTE**
>
> Note the difference between the COMMAND message and the UPDATE_COMMAND_UI message. If you attach code to the Bold menu item via the COMMAND message, the code is executed *after* the user clicks the Bold item. That is, when the OnFileBold() function is called, the Bold menu item is *already* drawn.
>
> On the other hand, if you attach code to the Bold item via the UPDATE_COMMAND_UI message, the code you attach will be executed when Windows is about to draw the Bold menu item. This means that the code you attach will be executed whenever the user clicks the File menu (but *before* the menu is displayed) because Windows is about to draw the Bold item after the File menu was clicked.
>
> The important thing to note is that the function that you attach via the UPDATE_COMMAND_UI message is executed *before* the Bold item is drawn.

To see the UPDATE_COMMAND_UI message in action, attach code that is executed whenever Windows is about to draw the Italic item. This means that Windows will execute the code whenever the user clicks the Format menu bar.

The code you'll attach will determine whether the Italic menu item will be drawn as a grayed or nongrayed menu item. This code will make the determination of whether to draw the Italic menu item as a gray or nongray item, based on the value of a variable called m_Italic. If m_Italic is equal to 0, the Italic item will be gray. However, if m_Italic is equal to 1, the Italic menu item will be drawn as nongray.

☐ Display the IDR_MAINFRAME menu in design mode.

☐ Use ClassWizard (from the Project menu) to select the event:

```
CMymenuView -> ID_FORMAT_ITALIC -> COMMAND
```

Then click the Add Function button.

☐ Accept the name OnFormatItalic() that Visual C++ suggests as the name of the new function.

☐ Click the Edit Code button.

> *Visual C++ responds by displaying the* OnFormatItalic() *function, ready to be edited by you.*

☐ Add code to the OnFormatItalic() function inside the MYMENVW.CPP file. After you add the code, the function should look like this:

```
void CMymenuView::OnFormatItalic()
{
// TODO: Add your command handler code here


    /////////////////////////
    // MY CODE STARTS HERE
    /////////////////////////

    MessageBox ("Format->Italic was selected");

    /////////////////////////
    // MY CODE ENDS HERE
    /////////////////////////

}
```

The code you added will display a message box whenever the user selects Italic from the Format menu.

☐ Open the file MYMENVW.H, and add the data member m_Italic to the declaration of the CMymenuView class. After you add this variable, the CMymenuView class declaration should look like this:

```
class CMymenuView : public CFormView
{
protected: // create from serialization only
CMymenuView();
DECLARE_DYNCREATE(CMymenuView)

public:
//{{AFX_DATA(CMymenuView)
enum{ IDD = IDD_MYMENU_FORM };
// NOTE: the ClassWizard will add data members here
//}}AFX_DATA

// Attributes
public:
CMymenuDoc* GetDocument();

    /////////////////////////
    // MY CODE STARTS HERE
    /////////////////////////

    // This data member is used to determine whether
    // the Italic menu will be gray.
    int m_Italic;
```

```
///////////////////
// MY CODE ENDS HERE
///////////////////


// Operations
public:

// Overrides
// ClassWizard generated virtual function overrides
//{{AFX_VIRTUAL(CMymenuView)
public:
protected:
virtual void DoDataExchange(CDataExchange* pDX);
// DDX/DDV support
//}}AFX_VIRTUAL

// Implementation
public:
virtual ~CMymenuView();
#ifdef _DEBUG
virtual void AssertValid() const;
virtual void Dump(CDumpContext& dc) const;
#endif

protected:

// Generated message map functions
protected:
//{{AFX_MSG(CMymenuView)
afx_msg void OnFileBold();
afx_msg void OnFormatSizeSizepoint1();
afx_msg void OnFormatSizeSizepoint2();
afx_msg void OnFormatItalic();
//}}AFX_MSG
DECLARE_MESSAGE_MAP()
};
```

Next, initialize the data member m_Italic to 1 (you don't want the Italic item to initially be gray).

☐ Open the file MYMENVW.CPP and initialize the data member m_Italic to 1 inside the constructor function of the CMymenuView class. After you add the initialization code, the constructor function should look like this:

```
CMymenuView::CMymenuView()
: CFormView(CMymenuView::IDD)
{
//{{AFX_DATA_INIT(CMymenuView)
// NOTE: the ClassWizard will add member
// initialization here
//}}AFX_DATA_INIT
// TODO: add construction code here

///////////////////
// MY CODE STARTS HERE
///////////////////
```

```
// Initialize the data member to 1.
m_Italic = 1;

/////////////////////
// MY CODE ENDS HERE
/////////////////////
```

}

The time and place to determine whether to display the Italic menu item as gray or nongray is when Windows is just about to draw this menu item. As discussed, the UPDATE_COMMAND_UI message was invented for this purpose.

☐ Display the IDR_MAINFRAME menu in design mode.

☐ Use ClassWizard (from the Project menu) to select the event:

CMymenuView -> ID_FORMAT_ITALIC -> UPDATE_COMMAND_UI

Then click the Add Function button.

☐ Accept the name OnUpdateFormatItalic() that Visual C++ suggests.

☐ Click the Edit Code button.

>   *Visual C++ responds by displaying the OnUpdateFormatItalic() function, ready to be edited by you.*

NOTE

Sometimes Visual C++ gets confused after you add a function. For example, once the Edit Code button is clicked, Visual C++ may prompt you with an error message, saying that the OnUpdateFormatItalic() function cannot be found.

If this happens to you, complete the following steps to correct the problem:

☐ Exit ClassWizard.

☐ Start ClassWizard from the Project menu.

☐ Delete the OnUpdateFormatItalic() function.

☐ Exit ClassWizard.

☐ Compile and link MyMenu by selecting Rebuild All from the Project menu.

☐ Start ClassWizard and add the OnUpdateFormatItalic() function all over again.

☐ Add code to the OnUpdateFormatItalic() function inside the MYMENVW.CPP file. After you add the code, the function should look like this:

```
void CMymenuView::OnUpdateFormatItalic(CCmdUI* pCmdUI)
{
// TODO: Add your command update UI handler code here
```

```
///////////////////////
// MY CODE STARTS HERE
///////////////////////

if ( m_Italic == 0 )
   pCmdUI->Enable(FALSE);
else
   pCmdUI->Enable(TRUE);

///////////////////////
// MY CODE ENDS HERE
///////////////////////

}
```

The code you typed uses if…else statements to determine whether the Italic menu item should be drawn as a gray or nongray menu item. If m_Italic is equal to 0, the menu is made gray with this statement:

```
pCmdUI->Enable(FALSE);
```

If the value of m_Italic is not equal to 0, the Italic menu item is made nongray.

Note that the OnUpdateFormatItalic() function has the parameter pCmdUI. This is the pointer to the Italic menu item (given to you as a gift from Visual C++), so that you don't have to use the GetParent() and then GetMenu() functions as you did earlier in this chapter.

To prove that indeed m_Italic determines the status of the Italic menu item, use the Bold item of the File menu to toggle the value of m_Italic.

☐ Open the file MYMENVW.CPP and modify the OnFileBold() function. After the modification, the function should look like this:

```
void CMymenuView::OnFileBold()
{
// TODO: Add your command handler code here


   ///////////////////////
   // MY CODE STARTS HERE
   ///////////////////////

   // Extract the pointer of the parent window.
   CWnd* pParent = GetParent();

   // Extract the pointer of the menu
   CMenu* pMenu = pParent->GetMenu();


   // Extract the pointer of the Format menu
   CMenu* pMenuFormatItem = pMenu->GetSubMenu(1);


   // Enable the Size menu
   pMenuFormatItem->EnableMenuItem (0,
                     MF_BYPOSITION | MF_ENABLED );
```

```
// Display a message box
CString sMessage;
 sMessage = "I'm inside OnFileBold() ";
MessageBox ( sMessage );

// Invert the value of m_Italic
if ( m_Italic == 0 )
    m_Italic = 1;
else
    m_Italic = 0;


/////////////////////
// MY CODE ENDS HERE
/////////////////////
```

}

The code you added to the OnFileBold() function checks the value of m_Italic and inverts its value:

```
if ( m_Italic == 0 )
    m_Italic = 1;
else
    m_Italic = 0;
```

So whenever the user selects Bold from the File menu, the value of m_Italic changes.

☐ Compile and link the MyMenu application, and then execute it.

☐ Select the Format menu.

> *MyMenu responds by displaying the Format menu.*

Because you initialized m_Italic to 1, the Italic item is drawn as nongray. (That is, even if you checked the Grayed check box during design time, the Italic item would appear nongray.)

☐ Select Bold from the File menu.

The OnFileBold() function is executed, and the value of m_Italic is changed to 0.

☐ Select the Format menu.

> *MyMenu responds by displaying the Format menu. Because m_Italic is now equal to 0, the Italic item is drawn as a gray menu item.*

☐ Experiment with the MyMenu application and then select Exit from the File menu.

The GROW Application

Sometimes you need to add items to the menu during the execution of an application. The GROW application demonstrates how this can be accomplished.

Before you start writing the GROW application yourself, execute the copy of it that resides in the \MVCPROG\EXE directory of the book's CD.

☐ Execute the X:\MVCPROG\EXE\GROW.EXE program (where *X* represents the drive letter of your CD-ROM drive).

The main window of Grow.EXE appears, as shown in Figure 20.31.

Figure 20.31. The main window of the GROW application.

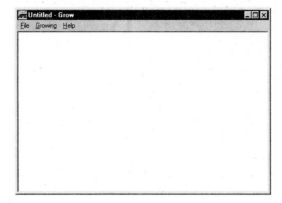

The GROW application has three pop-up menus: File, Growing, and Help. These pop-up menus are shown in Figures 20.32, 20.33, and 20.34.

Figure 20.32. The File menu of the GROW application.

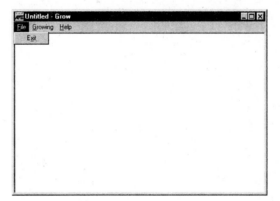

The GROW application lets you add items to the Growing menu at runtime. To see this in action do the following:

☐ Select Add Item from the Growing menu.

> *The GROW application responds by adding an item to the Growing menu.*

You can verify this:

☐ Select the Growing menu.

The GROW application responds by displaying the Growing menu with an added item, as shown in Figure 20.35.

Figure 20.33. The Growing menu of the GROW application.

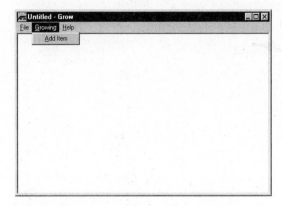

Figure 20.34. The Help menu of the GROW application.

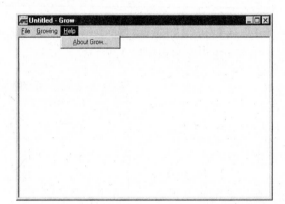

Figure 20.35. Adding an item to the Growing menu.

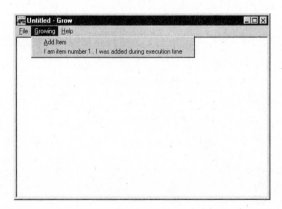

☐ Repeat the preceding steps to add additional menu items to the Growing menu. GROW lets you add a maximum of five items to the Growing menu. Figure 20.36 shows the Growing menu with five added items in it.

Figure 20.36. Adding five items to the Growing menu.

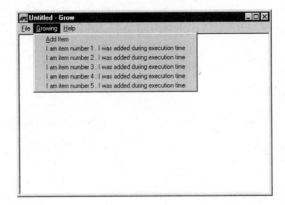

☐ Experiment with the GROW application, and then select Exit from the File menu to terminate the GROW application.

Now that you know what the GROW application does, you can begin to write it.

Creating the Project of the GROW Application

You'll now create the GROW.MAK project.

☐ Close all the open windows on the desktop of Visual C++ (if there are any).

☐ Select New from the File menu.

Visual C++ responds by displaying the New dialog box.

☐ Select Project inside the New dialog box and then click the OK button of the New dialog box.

Visual C++ responds by displaying the New Project dialog box.

☐ Set the project name to Grow.

☐ Set the project path to \MVCPROG\CH20\GROW\Grow.MAK.

Your New Project dialog box should now look like the one shown in Figure 20.37.

☐ Click the Create button of the New Project dialog box.

Visual C++ responds by displaying the AppWizard—Step 1 window.

☐ Set the Step 1 window as shown in Figure 20.38. As shown in Figure 20.38, the Grow.MAK project is set as a single-document interface application, and U.S. English (APPWIZUS.DLL) is used as the language for the application's resources.

Figure 20.37. The New Project dialog box of the Grow.MAK project.

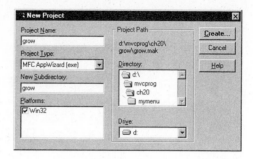

Figure 20.38. The AppWizard—Step 1 window of the GROW application.

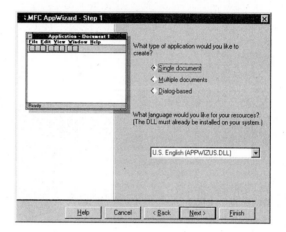

☐ Click the Next button of the Step 1 window.

Visual C++ responds by displaying the AppWizard—Step 2 of 6 window.

☐ Set the Step 2 of 6 window as shown in Figure 20.39. That is, in the GROW application you don't want any database support.

Figure 20.39. The AppWizard—Step 2 of 6 window for the GROW application.

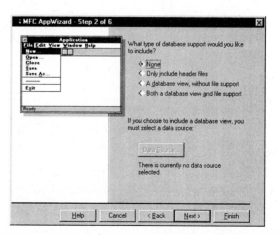

☐ Click the Next button of the Step 2 of 6 window.

Visual C++ responds by displaying the AppWizard—Step 3 of 6 window.

☐ Set the Step 3 of 6 window as shown in Figure 20.40. That is, in the GROW application you don't want any OLE support.

Figure 20.40. The AppWizard—Step 3 of 6 window for the GROW application.

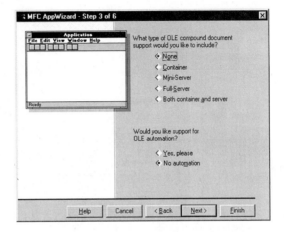

☐ Click the Next button of the Step 3 of 6 window.

Visual C++ responds by displaying the AppWizard—Step 4 of 6 window.

☐ Set the Step 4 of 6 window as shown in Figure 20.41.

Figure 20.41. The AppWizard—Step 4 of 6 window for the GROW application.

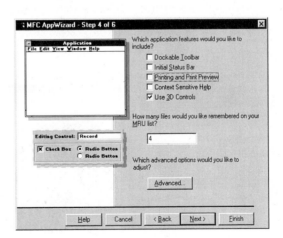

As shown in Figure 20.41, only the Use 3D Controls option is checked.

☐ Click the Next button of the Step 4 of 6 window.

Visual C++ responds by displaying the AppWizard—Step 5 of 6 window.

☐ Set the Step 5 of 6 window as shown in Figure 20.42.

As shown in Figure 20.42, the project will be generated with comments, a Visual C++ makefile will be generated, and the application will use the MFC library from a DLL.

Figure 20.42. The AppWizard—Step 5 of 6 window for the GROW application.

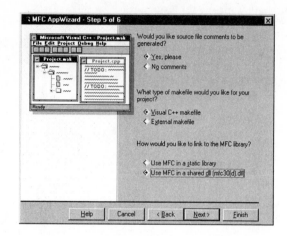

☐ Click the Next button of the Step 5 of 6 window.

> *Visual C++ responds by displaying the AppWizard—Step 6 of 6 window.*

You'll now use the AppWizard—Step 6 of 6 window to tell AppWizard to derive the view class of the application from the MFC class `CFormView`:

☐ Select the `CGrowView` class inside the AppWizard—Step 6 of 6 window.

☐ Set the Base Class drop-down list box to `CFormView`.

Your AppWizard—Step 6 of 6 window should now look like the one shown in Figure 20.43.

Figure 20.43. The AppWizard—Step 6 of 6 window after you set the base class of the application view class to `CFormView`.

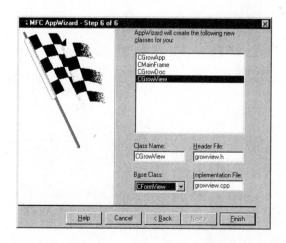

☐ Click the Finish button of the Step 6 of 6 window.

Visual C++ responds by displaying the New Project Information window, as shown in Figure 20.44.

Figure 20.44. The New Project Information window of the Grow.MAK project.

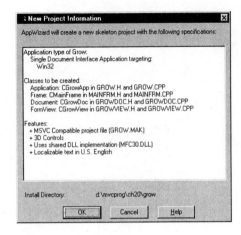

☐ Click the OK button of the New Project Information window.

Visual C++ responds by creating the project file and all the skeleton files of the application.

The Visual Design of the Menu

You'll now visually design the menu of the GROW application.

☐ Select Grow.MAK from the Window menu to display the Grow.MAK window, double-click grow.rc inside the Grow.MAK window to display the Grow.RC window, double-click Menu, and finally, double-click IDR_MAINFRAME under Menu.

Visual C++ responds by displaying the IDR_MAINFRAME menu in design mode.

☐ Implement the IDR_MAINFRAME menu so that it contains the following items:

&File
    E&xit
&Growing
    &Add Item
    Item 1
    Item 2
    Item 3
    Item 4
    Item 5
&Help
    &About Grow...

Save your work:

☐ Select Save from the File menu.

The visual implementation of the menu of the GROW application is complete.

The Visual Implementation of the Application's Main Window

You'll now visually design the main window of the GROW application.

Because in AppWizard you specified that the base class of the application's view class is `CFormView` (See Figure 20.43.), AppWizard created for you a form (a dialog box) that is attached to the view class of the application. This dialog box serves as the main window of the application. AppWizard named this dialog box IDD_GROW_FORM. You'll now customize the IDD_GROW_FORM dialog box.

☐ Double-click Dialog inside the Grow.RC window, and then double-click IDD_GROW_FORM.

    Visual C++ responds by displaying the IDD_GROW_FORM dialog box in design mode.

☐ Delete the TODO static text.

Save your work:

☐ Select Save from the File menu.

Attaching Code to the Menu Items

You'll now add functions to the Item 1, Item 2, Item 3, Item 4, and Item 5 items of the Growing menu.

☐ Display the IDR_MAINFRAME menu in design mode.

☐ Use ClassWizard (from the Project menu) to select the event:

`CGrowView -> ID_GROWING_ITEM1 -> COMMAND`

Then click the Add Function button.

☐ Accept the name `OnGrowingItem1()` that ClassWizard suggests.

☐ Click the Edit Code button to edit the `OnGrowingItem1()` function. After you add this function, your `OnGrowingItem1()` function inside the GROWVIEW.CPP file should look like this:

```
void CGrowView::OnGrowingItem1()
{
// TODO: Add your command handler code here

}
```

Note that for now you don't have to add your own code to this function.

☐ Display the IDR_MAINFRAME menu in design mode.

☐ Use ClassWizard (from the Project menu) to select the event:

```
CGrowView -> ID_GROWING_ITEM2 -> COMMAND
```

Then click the Add Function button.

☐ Accept the name OnGrowingItem2() that ClassWizard suggests.

☐ Click the Edit Code button to edit the OnGrowingItem2() function. After you add this function, your OnGrowingItem2() function inside the GROWVIEW.CPP file should look like this:

```
void CGrowView::OnGrowingItem2()
{
    // TODO: Add your command handler code here

}
```

Note that for now you don't have to add your own code to this function.

☐ Display the IDR_MAINFRAME menu in design mode.

☐ Use ClassWizard (from the Project menu) to select the event:

```
CGrowView -> ID_GROWING_ITEM3 -> COMMAND
```

Then click the Add Function button.

☐ Accept the name OnGrowingItem3() that ClassWizard suggests.

☐ Click the Edit Code button to edit the OnGrowingItem3() function. After you add this function, your OnGrowingItem3() function inside the GROWVIEW.CPP file should look like this:

```
void CGrowView::OnGrowingItem3()
{
    // TODO: Add your command handler code here

}
```

Note that for now you don't have to add your own code to this function.

☐ Display the IDR_MAINFRAME menu in design mode.

☐ Use ClassWizard (from the Project menu) to select the event:

```
CGrowView -> ID_GROWING_ITEM4 -> COMMAND
```

Then click the Add Function button.

☐ Accept the name OnGrowingItem4() that ClassWizard suggests.

☐ Click the Edit Code button to edit the `OnGrowingItem4()` function. After you add this function, your `OnGrowingItem4()` function inside the GROWVIEW.CPP file should look like this:

```
void CGrowView::OnGrowingItem4()
{
    // TODO: Add your command handler code here

}
```

Note that for now you don't have to add your own code to this function.

☐ Display the IDR_MAINFRAME menu in design mode.

☐ Use ClassWizard (from the Project menu) to select the event:

```
CGrowView -> ID_GROWING_ITEM5 -> COMMAND
```

Then click the Add Function button.

☐ Accept the name `OnGrowingItem5()` that ClassWizard suggests.

☐ Click the Edit Code button to edit the `OnGrowingItem5()` function. After you add this function, your `OnGrowingItem5()` function inside the GROWVIEW.CPP file should look like this:

```
void CGrowView::OnGrowingItem5()
{
    // TODO: Add your command handler code here

}
```

Note that for now you don't have to add your own code to this function.

Even though you haven't finished the GROW application, compile, link, and execute it to verify that you carried out the operations correctly.

☐ Compile, link, and execute the GROW application.

☐ Select the Growing menu.

Note that Item 1, Item 2, Item 3, Item 4, and Item 5 in the Growing menu are not gray. This is because you attached functions to these menu items. (It doesn't matter that you didn't type any of your own code in the functions.)

☐ Select Exit from the File menu to terminate the GROW program.

Removing the Items from the Growing Menu

Now you'll write code that is executed automatically when the application begins. This code removes Item 1, Item 2, Item 3, Item 4, and Item 5 from the Growing menu. Why? Add Item is all you want in the Growing menu when the application begins. The other menu items will be added when the user selects Add Item.

Now you'll attach code to the `WM_CREATE` event of the `CMainFrame` class.

☐ Use ClassWizard to select the event:

```
CMainFrame -> CMainFrame -> WM_CREATE
```

Then click the Add Function button.

Visual C++ responds by adding the OnCreate() function.

NOTE

Make sure that you add the function to the CMainFrame class.

WARNING

So far in this book most of the functions you added were added to the view class and document class. Note that the preceding note instructs you to add a function to the CMainFrame class! The ClassWizard dialog box should look like the one shown in Figure 20.45.

Figure 20.45. Adding a function to the WM_CREATE message of the CMainFrame class.

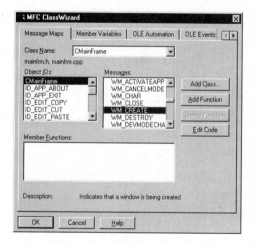

☐ Click the Edit Code button to edit the OnCreate() function.

Visual C++ responds by displaying the OnCreate() function of the MAINFRM.CPP file, ready to be edited by you.

☐ Edit the OnCreate() function inside the MAINFRM.CPP file so that it looks like this:

```
int CMainFrame::OnCreate(LPCREATESTRUCT lpCreateStruct)
{
if (CFrameWnd::OnCreate(lpCreateStruct) == -1)
return -1;
```

```
// TODO: Add your specialized creation code here


//////////////////////////
// MY CODE STARTS HERE
//////////////////////////

// Extract the pointer of the menu
CMenu* pMenu = GetMenu();

// Extract the pointer of the Growing menu
CMenu* pGrowingMenu = pMenu->GetSubMenu(1);

// Delete the current items in the Growing menu
pGrowingMenu->DeleteMenu(5, MF_BYPOSITION);
pGrowingMenu->DeleteMenu(4, MF_BYPOSITION);
pGrowingMenu->DeleteMenu(3, MF_BYPOSITION);
pGrowingMenu->DeleteMenu(2, MF_BYPOSITION);
pGrowingMenu->DeleteMenu(1, MF_BYPOSITION);

//////////////////////////
// MY CODE ENDS HERE
//////////////////////////
```

```
return 0;
}
```

Now go over the code you typed. To begin with, the OnCreate() function is automatically executed whenever the window of the application is created. You need to use this event because there is a need to delete the five menu items from the Growing menu upon start-up of the application.

The code that you typed inside the OnCreate() function starts by extracting pMenu, the pointer of the menu:

```
CMenu* pMenu = GetMenu();
```

Then pGrowingMenu, which is the pointer of the Growing menu, is extracted with the GetSubMenu(1) function:

```
CMenu* pGrowingMenu = pMenu->GetSubMenu(1);
```

Note that because the Growing menu is the second menu from the left, the parameter of GetSubMenu() is 1. (The File menu is menu #0, the Growing menu is menu #1, and the Help menu is menu #3.)

Next, the items of the Growing menu (except the Add Item) are deleted with the DeleteMenu() function:

```
pGrowingMenu->DeleteMenu(5, MF_BYPOSITION);
pGrowingMenu->DeleteMenu(4, MF_BYPOSITION);
pGrowingMenu->DeleteMenu(3, MF_BYPOSITION);
pGrowingMenu->DeleteMenu(2, MF_BYPOSITION);
pGrowingMenu->DeleteMenu(1, MF_BYPOSITION);
```

The first parameter of the DeleteMenu() function is the position of the menu item that you want to delete, and the second parameter of the DeleteMenu() function is MF_BYPOSITION. MF_BYPOSITION is an indication that the first parameter of `DeleteMenu()` is supplied by its position (not by its ID). Add Item is at position 0, Item 1 is at position 1, Item 2 is at position 2, and so on.

> **NOTE**
>
> The order of deleting the menu items is important. Suppose that you start by deleting the first item in the menu.
>
> After you delete this menu item there will be only four menu items in the menu. This means that the menu item that used to be in position 1 is now in position 0, and so on. In other words, there is no such thing as an item at position 5, because the last item is now at position 4.

Although you have not yet finished writing the GROW application, compile, link, and execute it to verify that you carried out the operations correctly:

☐ Compile and link the GROW application, and then execute it.

☐ Select the Growing menu.

> *GROW responds by displaying the Growing menu, as shown in Figure 20.46. As shown, there is only one item in the menu, the Add Item menu item. As you know, during the visual implementation of the menu, you assigned five items to the Growing menu. Four of these menu items were deleted upon start-up of the application by the* `OnCreate()` *function.*

Figure 20.46. The Growing menu (upon start-up of the GROW application).

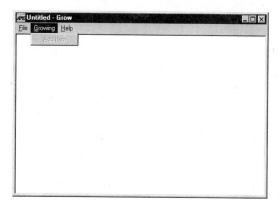

☐ Select Exit from the File menu to terminate the GROW application.

Attaching Code to the Add Item Menu Item

You'll now attach code to the Add Item of the Growing menu.

The code that you'll attach will add an item to the Growing menu whenever the user clicks the Add Item menu item.

☐ Display the IDR_MAINFRAME menu in design mode.

☐ Use ClassWizard (from the Project menu) to select the event:

```
CGrowView -> ID_GROWING_ADDITEM -> COMMAND
```

Then click the Add Function button.

> **NOTE**
>
> Make sure that you are adding the function to the `CGrowView` class.

☐ Accept the name `OnGrowingAddItem()` that Visual C++ suggests.

☐ Click the Edit Code button.

> *Visual C++ responds by displaying the* `OnGrowingAddItem()` *function, ready to be edited by you.*

☐ Edit the `OnGrowingAddItem()` function. After you edit this function, your `OnGrowingAddItem()` function inside the GROWVIEW.CPP file should look like this:

```
void CGrowView::OnGrowingAdditem()
{
// TODO: Add your command handler code here


    /////////////////////////
    // MY CODE STARTS HERE
    /////////////////////////

    // Extract the pointer of the parent pointer
    CWnd* pParent = GetParent();

    // Extract the pointer of the menu bar
    CMenu* pMenuBar = pParent->GetMenu();

    // Extract the pointer of the Growing menu
    CMenu* pMenuGrowing = pMenuBar->GetSubMenu(1);

    // Append an item to the Growing menu
    pMenuGrowing->AppendMenu ( MF_STRING | MF_ENABLED,
                               ID_GROWING_ITEM1,
"I am item number 1. I was added during execution time" );

    /////////////////////////
    // MY CODE ENDS HERE
    /////////////////////////

}
```

The code you typed uses `GetParent()` to extract the pointer of the parent window:

```
CWnd* pParent = GetParent();
```

Then the `GetMenu()` function is used to extract the pointer of the menu bar:

```
CMenu* pMenuBar = pParent->GetMenu();
```

Now that you have the pointer of the menu bar, you can use the `GetSubMenu()` function to extract the pointer of the Growing menu:

```
CMenu* pMenuGrowing = pMenuBar->GetSubMenu(1);
```

The parameter of `GetSubMenu()` is 1 because Growing is the second menu from the left on the menu bar.

The last statement you typed uses the `AppendMenu()` function on `pMenuGrowing`, the pointer of the Growing menu:

```
pMenuGrowing->AppendMenu ( MF_STRING ¦ MF_ENABLED,
                           ID_GROWING_ITEM1,
"I am item number 1. I was added during execution time" );
```

The `AppendMenu()` function uses `ID_GROWING_ITEM1` as its second parameter.

The third parameter of `AppendMenu()` contains the text that will appear in the appended menu item. This means that the `AppendMenu()` function appends a menu item to the Growing menu.

Although you have not yet finished writing the GROW application, compile, link, and execute the GROW application so that you'll see what the code you typed accomplishes.

☐ Compile and link the GROW application, and execute it.

☐ Select Add Item from the Growing menu and then select the Growing menu again.

> *GROW responds by displaying the Growing menu with the item you added.*

☐ Terminate the GROW application by selecting Exit from the File menu.

Adding Five Items at Runtime

Now that you understand how to add items to a menu at runtime, modify the code inside the `OnGrowingAddItem()` function so that it will add five items to the Growing menu.

The variable that will keep track of how many items were added to the menu is `m_CurrentAddedItem`.

☐ Add the `m_CurrentAddedItem` variable as a data member of the `CGrowView` class. After you add this data member, the `CGrowView` class declaration inside the GROWVIEW.H file should look like this:

```
class CGrowView : public CFormView
{
protected: // create from serialization only
CGrowView();
DECLARE_DYNCREATE(CGrowView)

public:
//{{AFX_DATA(CGrowView)
enum{ IDD = IDD_GROW_FORM };
```

```
// NOTE: the ClassWizard will add data members here
//}}AFX_DATA

// Attributes
public:
CGrowDoc* GetDocument();

        /////////////////////////
        // MY CODE STARTS HERE
        /////////////////////////

        int m_CurrentAddedItem;

        /////////////////////////
        // MY CODE ENDS HERE
        /////////////////////////

...
...
...

};
```

Initially there are no added items in the Growing menu. This means that you have to initialize the m_CurrentAddedItem variable to 0:

☐ Modify the constructor function of the CGrowView class. After the modification, the constructor function inside the GROWVIEW.CPP file should look like this:

```
CGrowView::CGrowView()
: CFormView(CGrowView::IDD)
{
//{{AFX_DATA_INIT(CGrowView)
// NOTE: the ClassWizard will add member
// initialization here
//}}AFX_DATA_INIT
// TODO: add construction code here

        /////////////////////////
        // MY CODE STARTS HERE
        /////////////////////////

        m_CurrentAddedItem = 0;

        /////////////////////////
        // MY CODE ENDS HERE
        /////////////////////////

}
```

☐ Modify the OnGrowingAddItem() function inside the GROWVIEW.CPP file. After the modification, the function should look like this:

```
void CGrowView::OnGrowingAdditem()
{
// TODO: Add your command handler code here
```

```
//////////////////////
// MY CODE STARTS HERE
//////////////////////

// Extract the pointer of the parent pointer
CWnd* pParent = GetParent();

// Extract the pointer of the menu bar
CMenu* pMenuBar = pParent->GetMenu();

// Extract the pointer of the Growing menu
CMenu* pMenuGrowing = pMenuBar->GetSubMenu(1);

CString Message;
char sCurrentAddedItem[10];


if (m_CurrentAddedItem == 5 )
    {
    // Display a message to the user
    MessageBox ("Sorry, no more items can be added");
    return;
    }
else
    {
    // Construct the Message variable
    itoa(m_CurrentAddedItem+1, sCurrentAddedItem, 10);
    Message = "I am item number " +
              (CString)sCurrentAddedItem +
              ". I was added during execution time";

    // Append an item to the menu
    pMenuGrowing->AppendMenu ( MF_STRING ¦ MF_ENABLED,
                               (UINT)ID_GROWING_ITEM1 +
                               (UINT)m_CurrentAddedItem,
                               (LPCSTR)Message );
    // Update m_CurrentAddedItem for the next time
    m_CurrentAddedItem++;
    }

//////////////////////
// MY CODE ENDS HERE
//////////////////////

}
```

The code you added defines two local variables:

```
CString Message;
char sCurrentAddedItem[10];
```

Then an `if` statement is used to determine whether there are five added items in the Growing menu.

If there are already five items in the menu, a message is displayed, telling the user that no more items can be added:

```
if (m_CurrentAddedItem == 5 )
    {
    // Display a message to the user
```

```
        MessageBox ("Sorry, no more items can be added");
        return;
        }
```

If there are fewer than five added items in the Growing menu, the statements inside the else block are executed:

```
else
    {
    // Construct the Message variable
    itoa(m_CurrentAddedItem+1, sCurrentAddedItem, 10);
    Message = "I am item number " +
              (CString)sCurrentAddedItem +
              ". I was added during execution time";

    // Append an item to the menu
pMenuGrowing->AppendMenu ( MF_STRING ¦ MF_ENABLED,
                           (UINT)ID_GROWING_ITEM1 +
                           (UINT)m_CurrentAddedItem,
                           (LPCSTR)Message );

    // Update m_CurrentAddedItem for the next time
    m_CurrentAddedItem++;
    return;
    }
```

The statements inside the else block construct the caption of the added menu item (Message), and then the AppendMenu() function is executed to add the item to the menu:

```
pMenuGrowing->AppendMenu ( MF_STRING ¦ MF_ENABLED,
                           (UINT)ID_GROWING_ITEM1 +
                           (UINT)m_CurrentAddedItem,
                           (LPCSTR)Message );
```

The first parameter of AppendMenu() tells the AppendMenu() function that the added item (whose caption is mentioned as the third parameter) is a string, and that the menu item should be enabled.

The second parameter of AppendMenu() is

```
(UINT)ID_GROWING_ITEM1 +
(UINT)m_CurrentAddedItem
```

For example, if currently m_CurrentAddedItem is equal to 0, the second parameter is equal to

```
(UINT)ID_GROWING_ITEM1 +
     0
```

So in this case, the second parameter is equal to the ID of Item 1 (as assigned by Visual C++).

Similarly, depending on the current value of m_CurrentAddedItem, the second parameter of AppendMenu() can be the ID of any of the added items in the Growing menu.

Note that the preceding code assumes that you created the menu items in Visual C++ sequentially (one after the other), so that Visual C++ assigned sequential ID numbers to these menu items.

☐ Compile, link, and execute the GROW application.

Add items to the Growing menu by selecting Add Item from the Growing menu. As you can see, the maximum number of items you can add to the Growing menu is five.

Deleting and Inserting Items

You can use the `RemoveMenu()` member function to remove an item from a menu, and you can use the `InsertMenu()` member function to insert an item at any particular position in the menu.

Attaching Code to the Added Menu Items

Now you'll add code that is executed whenever the user selects an added item.

☐ Use ClassWizard to modify the `OnGrowingItem1()` function inside the GROWVIEW.CPP file. After the modification, your `OnGrowingItem1()` should look like this:

```
void CGrowView::OnGrowingItem1()
{
// TODO: Add your command handler code here

        /////////////////////////
        // MY CODE STARTS HERE
        /////////////////////////

        MessageBox ("I'm now inside OnGrowingItem1()");

        /////////////////////////
        // MY CODE ENDS HERE
        /////////////////////////

}
```

Now modify the rest of the functions (inside the GROWVIEW.CPP file) of the added items of the Growing menu.

After the modifications, these functions should look like this:

```
void CGrowView::OnGrowingItem2()
{
// TODO: Add your command handler code here

        /////////////////////////
        // MY CODE STARTS HERE
        /////////////////////////

        MessageBox ("I'm now inside OnGrowingItem2()");

        /////////////////////////
        // MY CODE ENDS HERE
        /////////////////////////

}

void CGrowView::OnGrowingItem3()
{
```

```
// TODO: Add your command handler code here

    ////////////////////////
    // MY CODE STARTS HERE
    ////////////////////////

    MessageBox ("I'm now inside OnGrowingItem3()");

    ////////////////////////
    // MY CODE ENDS HERE
    ////////////////////////


}

void CGrowView::OnGrowingItem4()
{
// TODO: Add your command handler code here

    ////////////////////////
    // MY CODE STARTS HERE
    ////////////////////////

    MessageBox ("I'm now inside OnGrowingItem4()");

    ////////////////////////
    // MY CODE ENDS HERE
    ////////////////////////


}

void CGrowView::OnGrowingItem5()
{
// TODO: Add your command handler code here

    ////////////////////////
    // MY CODE STARTS HERE
    ////////////////////////

    MessageBox ("I'm now inside OnGrowingItem5()");

    ////////////////////////
    // MY CODE ENDS HERE
    ////////////////////////


}
```

☐ Compile, link, and execute the GROW application.

☐ Add items to the Growing menu, then select the added items and verify that the appropriate function is executed.

21

The Toolbar and
Status Bar

In this chapter you'll learn how to

implement a toolbar and a status bar.

Take a look at Figure 21.1. It shows the window of the Microsoft Word for Windows program. As shown, the window contains a toolbar (below the menu bar). The toolbar serves as a pictorial menu. For example, instead of selecting Save from the File menu, the user can click the diskette icon that appears on the toolbar.

Figure 21.1 also shows the status bar (below the horizontal scroll bar). The status bar serves as a placeholder for various types of messages to the user during the execution of the program. For example, the status bar can inform the user about the status of the Num Lock key. The status bar also serves as a place to display messages that correspond to the currently selected menu item. This helps the user decide which menu items should be selected for performing tasks.

Figure 21.1. The toolbar and status bar of Word for Windows.

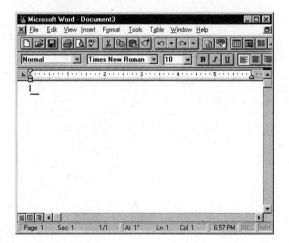

The MyTool Application

The MyTool application demonstrates how to incorporate and design a toolbar and status bar.

Before you start writing the MyTool application yourself, execute the copy of the it that resides in the \MVCPROG\EXE directory of the book's CD.

To execute the MyTool application do the following:

☐ Execute the MyTool.EXE program that resides inside the X:\MVCPROG\EXE directory of the book's CD (where *X* represents the letter drive of your CD-ROM drive).

 Windows responds by executing the MyTool.EXE application.

The main window of MyTool.EXE appears, as shown in Figure 21.2.

Figure 21.2. The main window of the MyTool application.

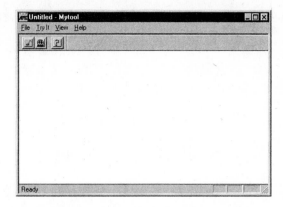

The MyTool application has four pop-up menus: File, Try It, View, and Help. These pop-up menus are shown in Figures 21.3, 21.4, 21.5, and 21.6.

Figure 21.3. The File menu of the MyTool application.

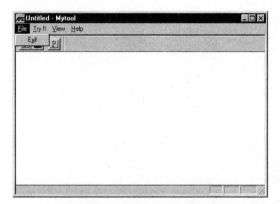

Figure 21.4. The Try It menu of the MyTool application.

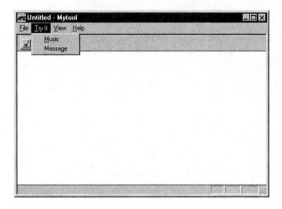

Figure 21.5. The View menu of the MyTool application.

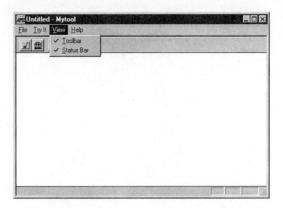

Figure 21.6. The Help menu of the MyTool application.

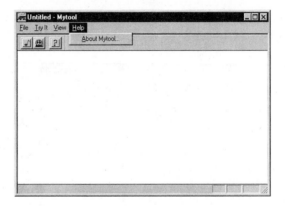

☐ Select Message from the Try It menu.

> *MyTool responds by displaying a message telling you which menu item you selected.*

☐ Click the OK button of the message box to close it.

☐ Select Music from the Try It menu.

> *MyTool responds by playing music through the PC speaker.*

The MyTool application contains a toolbar. The left icon on the toolbar is a picture of a music note.

☐ Click the extreme-left icon on the toolbar.

> *MyTool responds in the same way as when you select the Music item from the Try It menu.*

☐ Click the middle icon on the toolbar.

> *MyTool responds in the same way as when you select the Message item from the Try It menu.*

☐ Click the extreme-right icon on the toolbar.

> *MyTool responds in the same way as when you select the About item from the Help menu.*

☐ Terminate the MyTool application by selecting Exit from the File menu.

Now that you know what the MyTool application should do, you can begin to write it.

Creating the Project of the MyTool Application

You'll now create the MyTool.MAK project.

☐ Close all the open windows on the desktop of Visual C++ (if there are any).

☐ Select New from the File menu.

> *Visual C++ responds by displaying the New dialog box.*

☐ Select Project inside the New dialog box and then click the OK button of the New dialog box.

> *Visual C++ responds by displaying the New Project dialog box.*

☐ Set the project name to MyTool.

☐ Set the project path to \MVCPROG\CH21\MyTool\MyTool.MAK.

Your New Project dialog box should now look like the one shown in Figure 21.7.

Figure 21.7. The New Project dialog box of the MyTool.MAK project.

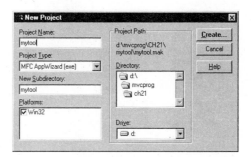

☐ Click the Create button of the New Project dialog box.

> *Visual C++ responds by displaying the AppWizard—Step 1 window.*

☐ Set the Step 1 window as shown in Figure 21.8. As shown in Figure 21.8, the MyTool.MAK project is set as a single-document interface application, and U.S. English (APPWIZUS.DLL) is used as the language for the application's resources.

Figure 21.8. The
AppWizard—Step 1
window for the MyTool
application.

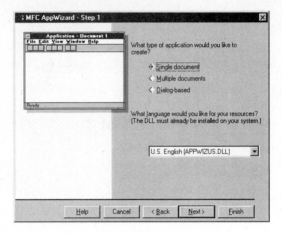

☐ Click the Next button of the Step 1 window.

   Visual C++ responds by displaying the AppWizard—Step 2 of 6 window.

☐ Set the Step 2 of 6 window as shown in Figure 21.9. That is, in the MyTool application you don't want any database support.

Figure 21.9. The
AppWizard—Step 2 of 6
window for the MyTool
application.

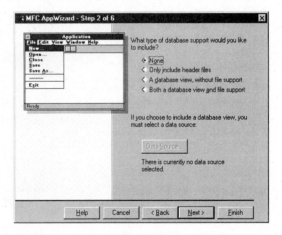

☐ Click the Next button of the Step 2 of 6 window.

   Visual C++ responds by displaying the AppWizard—Step 3 of 6 window.

☐ Set the Step 3 of 6 window as shown in Figure 21.10. That is, in the MyTool application you don't want any OLE support.

Figure 21.10. The AppWizard—Step 3 of 6 window for the MyTool application.

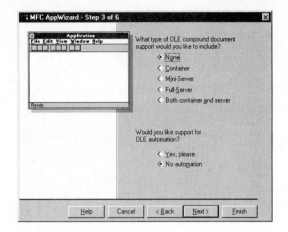

☐ Click the Next button of the Step 3 of 6 window.

Visual C++ responds by displaying the AppWizard—Step 4 of 6 window.

☐ Set the Step 4 of 6 window as shown in Figure 21.11.

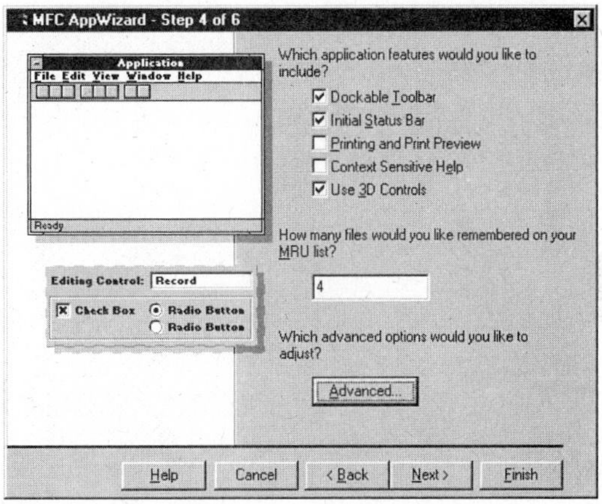

Figure 21.11. The AppWizard—Step 4 of 6 window for the MyTool application.

As shown in Figure 21.11, the features Dockable Toolbar and Initial Status Bar are checked (because you want to include a toolbar and a status bar in the application). Also, the Use 3D Controls check box is checked, but the Printing and Print Preview and Context Sensitive Help features will not be included in the MyTool application.

☐ Click the Next button of the Step 4 of 6 window.

Visual C++ responds by displaying the AppWizard—Step 5 of 6 window.

☐ Set the Step 5 of 6 window as shown in Figure 21.12.

As shown in Figure 21.12, the project will be generated with comments, a Visual C++ makefile will be generated, and the application will use the MFC library from a DLL.

Figure 21.12. The AppWizard—Step 5 of 6 window for the MyTool application.

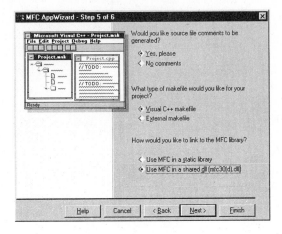

☐ Click the Next button of the Step 5 of 6 window.

> *Visual C++ responds by displaying the AppWizard—Step 6 of 6 window.*

You'll now use the AppWizard—Step 6 of 6 window to tell AppWizard to derive the view class of the application from the MFC class CFormView:

☐ Select the CMytoolView class inside the AppWizard—Step 6 of 6 window.

☐ Set the Base Class drop-down list box to CFormView.

Your AppWizard—Step 6 of 6 window should now look like the one shown in Figure 21.13.

Figure 21.13. The AppWizard—Step 6 of 6 window after you set the base class of the application view class to CFormView.

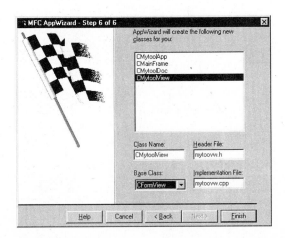

☐ Click the Finish button of the Step 6 of 6 window.

   Visual C++ responds by displaying the New Project Information window, as shown in Figure 21.14.

Figure 21.14. The New Project Information window of the MyTool.MAK project.

☐ Click the OK button of the New Project Information window.

   Visual C++ responds by creating the project file and all the skeleton files of the application.

The Visual Design of the Menu

You'll now visually design the menu of the MyTool application.

☐ Select MyTool.MAK from the Window menu to display the MyTool.MAK window, double-click mytool.rc inside the MyTool.MAK window, double-click Menu, and finally, double-click the IDR_MAINFRAME item that appears under the Menu item.

   Visual C++ responds by displaying the IDR_MAINFRAME menu in design mode.

☐ Implement the menu of the MyTool application so that it has the following items:

   &File
      E&xit
   &Try It
      &Music
      Messa&ge
   &View
      &Toolbar
      &Status Bar
   &Help
      &About Mytool…

The various menus in design mode are shown in Figures 21.15 through 21.18.

Figure 21.15. The File menu in design mode.

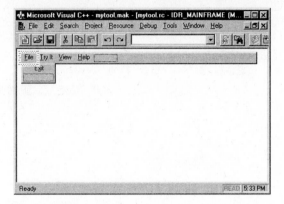

Figure 21.16. The Try It menu in design mode.

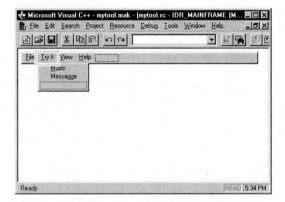

Figure 21.17. The View menu in design mode.

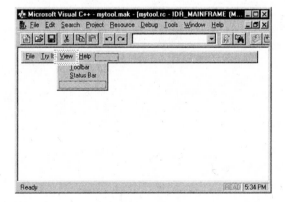

*Figure 21.18. The Help
menu in design mode.*

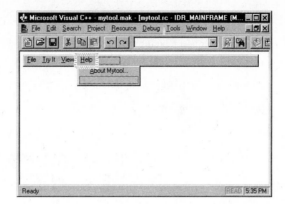

*Figure 21.18. The Help
menu in design mode.*

NOTE

Note that you did not have to design the View pop-up menu! AppWizard designed it for
you because you checked the Dockable Toolbar and Initial Status Bar check boxes when
you created the project. (See Figure 21.11.)

Save your work:

☐ Select Save from the File menu of Visual C++.

The visual implementation of the menu of the MyTool application is complete.

The Visual Implementation of the MyTool Application's Main Window

Because in AppWizard you specified that the base class of the application's view class is CFormView
(See Figure 21.13.), AppWizard created for you a form (a dialog box) that is attached to the view
class of the application. This dialog box serves as the main window of the application. AppWizard
named this dialog box IDD_MYTOOL_FORM. You'll now customize the IDD_MYTOOL_FORM
dialog box until it looks like the one shown back in Figure 21.2.

☐ Select MyTool.MAK from the Window menu to display the MyTool.MAK window,
double-click mytool.rc inside the MyTool.MAK window, double-click Dialog inside the
mytool.rc window, and finally, double-click IDD_MYTOOL_FORM under the Dialog
item.

*Visual C++ responds by displaying the IDD_MYTOOL_FORM dialog box in design mode.
This dialog box serves as the main window of the MyTool application.*

☐ Delete the TODO static text from the dialog box.

☐ Select Save from the File menu to save your work.

Note that at this point you haven't written a single line of code! Nevertheless, the MyTool application already has in it some powerful features. Do the following to see these features in action:

☐ Compile and link the MyTool application, and then execute it.

> *The main window of MyTool appears, as shown in Figure 21.19. As shown, the main window has a toolbar and a status bar.*

Figure 21.19. The main window of the MyTool application, with toolbar and status bar.

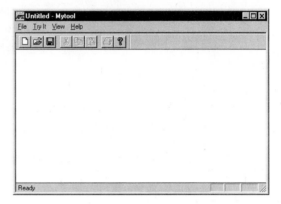

The Music and Message menu items of the Try It menu are dimmed because you have not yet attached any code to them. However, the items of the View menu are available and operational. Currently, the toolbar and the status bar are visible. To hide the status bar do the following:

☐ Click the View menu.

> *MyTool responds by dropping down the View menu. (See Figure 21.20.)*

Figure 21.20. The View menu.

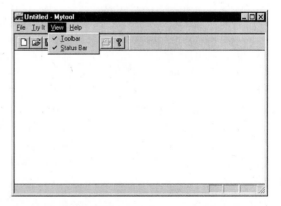

As shown in Figure 21.20, the Toolbar item has a checkmark and the Status Bar item has a checkmark. This means that currently MyTool displays its toolbar and status bar. (See Figures 21.19 and 21.20.)

☐ Select Toolbar from the View menu. (The View menu currently displays the Toolbar menu item with a checkmark to its left. To remove the checkmark, select the Toolbar menu item.)

MyTool responds by removing the checkmark from the Toolbar menu item and hiding the toolbar.

Figure 21.21. *The window of the MyTool program without a toolbar.*

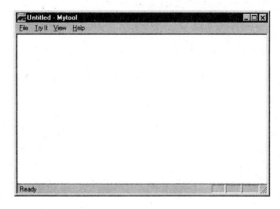

In a similar manner, you can show or hide the status bar. That is, select the Status Bar menu item from the View menu to show or hide the status bar.

☐ Select Status Bar from the View menu again.

MyTool responds by removing the checkmark from the Status Bar menu item and hiding the status bar.

☐ Display the status bar and then press the Caps Lock key several times.

MyTool responds by displaying on the status bar the status of the Caps Lock key.

☐ Press the Scroll Lock key several times.

MyTool responds by displaying the status of the Scroll Lock on the status bar.

☐ Make sure that the status bar is displayed, then press the Alt key and then use the up- and down-arrow keys and the left- and right-arrow keys to move from menu to menu.

MyTool responds by displaying a message on the status bar. This message tells you the purpose of the highlighted menu item. (Later in this chapter, you'll design the status bar messages of the Try It menu.)

☐ Select Exit from the File menu to terminate the MyTool application.

As you can see, MyTool includes a sophisticated toolbar and status bar (a gift from Visual C++). All you have to do is customize the toolbar and the status bar according to your application.

Attaching Code to the Menu Items

You'll now attach code to the Music and Message menu items of the Try It menu.

☐ Display the IDR_MAINFRAME menu in design mode.

☐ Use ClassWizard (from the Project menu) to select the event:

CMytoolView -> ID_TRYIT_MESSAGE -> COMMAND

Then click the Add Function button.

☐ Accept `OnTryitMessage()` as the name ClassWizard suggests for the new function.

☐ Click the Edit Code button.

> *Visual C++ responds by opening the MyTooVW.CPP file, with the* `OnTryitMessage()` *function ready to be edited by you.*

☐ Add code to the `OnTryitMessage()` function so that it looks like this:

```
void CMytoolView::OnTryitMessage()
{
// TODO: Add your command handler code here


    /////////////////////////
    // MY CODE STARTS HERE
    /////////////////////////

    MessageBox ("Try It -> Message was selected");


    /////////////////////////
    // MY CODE ENDS HERE
    /////////////////////////


}
```

The code you typed displays a message whenever the user selects Message from the Try It menu.

You'll now attach code to the Music menu items of the Try It menu.

☐ Display the IDR_MAINFRAME menu in design mode.

☐ Use ClassWizard (from the Project menu) to select the event:

CMytoolView -> ID_TRYIT_MUSIC -> COMMAND

Then click the Add Function button.

☐ Accept `OnTryitMusic()`, which ClassWizard suggests as the name of the new function.

☐ Click the Edit Code button.

> *Visual C++ responds by opening the MyTooVW.CPP file, with the* `OnTryitMusic()` *function ready to be edited by you.*

☐ Add code to the OnTryitMusic() function so that it looks like this:

```
void CMytoolView::OnTryitMusic()
{
// TODO: Add your command handler code here


     //////////////////////////
     // MY CODE STARTS HERE
     //////////////////////////

     // Play the music
     m_wav.SetStrProperty ("Command", "Prev" );
     m_wav.SetStrProperty ("Command", "Play" );


     ////////////////////////
     // MY CODE ENDS HERE
     ////////////////////////

}
```

The code you typed rewinds the WAV file and then plays music through the PC speaker.

Of course, the code you typed assumes that the m_wav object was created already and that the WAV file was opened already. So do that:

☐ Add an #include statement (that includes the class declaration of the CTegMM class) inside MyTooVW.H. After you add the #include statement, the beginning of the MyTooVW.H file should look like this:

```
// mytoovw.h : interface of the CMytoolView class
//
/////////////////////////////////////////////////


//////////////////////////
// MY CODE STARTS HERE
//////////////////////////

// Include the CTegMM.H file (because this program
// plays music).
#include "\MVCPROG\LIB\CTegMM.H"

//////////////////////////
// MY CODE ENDS HERE
//////////////////////////
...
...
...
```

You'll now create the m_wav object, an object of class CTegMM.

☐ Open the MyTooVW.H file, and declare the m_wav object as a public data member of the CMytoolView class. After you declare the m_wav object, the CMytoolView class declaration should look like this:

```
class CMytoolView : public CFormView
{
protected: // create from serialization only
CMytoolView();
DECLARE_DYNCREATE(CMytoolView)

public:
//{{AFX_DATA(CMytoolView)
enum{ IDD = IDD_MYTOOL_FORM };
// NOTE: the ClassWizard will add data members here
//}}AFX_DATA

// Attributes
public:
CMytoolDoc* GetDocument();


/////////////////////////
// MY CODE STARTS HERE
/////////////////////////

// Create an object m_wav (of class CTegMM)
// as a data member of the CMytoolView class.
CTegMM m_wav;

/////////////////////////
// MY CODE ENDS HERE
/////////////////////////


// Operations
public:

// Overrides
// ClassWizard generated virtual function overrides
//{{AFX_VIRTUAL(CMytoolView)
public:
protected:
virtual void DoDataExchange(CDataExchange* pDX);
// DDX/DDV support
//}}AFX_VIRTUAL

// Implementation
public:
virtual ~CMytoolView();
#ifdef _DEBUG
virtual void AssertValid() const;
virtual void Dump(CDumpContext& dc) const;
#endif

protected:

// Generated message map functions
protected:
//{{AFX_MSG(CMytoolView)
afx_msg void OnTryitMessagge();
afx_msg void OnTryitMusic();
//}}AFX_MSG
DECLARE_MESSAGE_MAP()
};
```

You'll now write the code that opens the WAV file:

☐ Use ClassWizard (from the Project menu) to select the event (See Figure 21.22.):

```
CMytoolView -> CMytoolView -> OnInitialUpdate
```

Then click the Add Function button.

Figure 21.22. Adding the `OnInitialUpdate()` *member function of the view class.*

☐ Click the Edit Code button.

> *Visual C++ responds by displaying the* `OnInitialUpdate()` *member function of the* `CMytoolView` *class (inside the MyTooVW.CPP file), ready to be edited by you.*

☐ Edit the `OnInitialUpdate()` function so that it looks like this:

```
void CMytoolView::OnInitialUpdate()
{
// TODO: Add your specialized code here
// and/or call the base class

///////////////////////////
// MY CODE STARTS HERE
///////////////////////////

m_wav.SetStrProperty ("DeviceType", "PCSpeaker");
// m_wav.SetStrProperty ("DeviceType", "WaveAudio");

char sFileName[256];
strncpy ( sFileName,
          __argv[0],
          2 );

sFileName[2] = 0;

strcat ( sFileName,
         "\\MVCPROG\\WAV\\Regga1M1.WAV" );
```

```
m_wav.SetStrProperty ("FileName", sFileName );

m_wav.SetStrProperty ("Command", "Open" );

////////////////////
// MY CODE ENDS HERE
////////////////////

CFormView::OnInitialUpdate();
}
```

The code you typed sets DeviceType to PCSpeaker:

```
m_wav.SetStrProperty ("DeviceType", "PCSpeaker");
```

Note that if you want to play the WAV file through a sound card, you have to set DeviceType to WaveAudio as follows (instead of setting DeviceType to PCSpeaker):

```
m_wav.SetStrProperty ("DeviceType", "WaveAudio");
```

Next, FileName is set to play the \MVCPROG\WAV\Regga1M1.WAV file:

```
char sFileName[256];
strncpy ( sFileName,
          __argv[0],
           2 );

sFileName[2] = 0;

strcat ( sFileName,
         "\\MVCPROG\\WAV\\Regga1M1.WAV" );

m_wav.SetStrProperty ("FileName", sFileName );
```

Note that the drive letter of the drive from which the program is executed is extracted by using the __argv[0] variable, and then the strcat() function is used to add the pathname and filename.

Finally, the Open command is issued:

```
m_wav.SetStrProperty ("Command", "Open" );
```

Of course, if you now compile and link the MyTool.MAK application you'll get linking errors. (Why? You have not yet added the CTegMM.LIB library to the project.)

☐ Select Files from the Project menu.

Visual C++ responds by displaying the Project Files dialog box.

☐ Select the \MVCPROG\LIB\CTegMM.LIB file, and click the Add button.

Visual C++ responds by adding the CTegMM.LIB file to the MyTool.MAK project.

☐ Click the Close button to close the Project Files dialog box.

Now look at your code in action:

☐ Compile, link, and execute the MyTool application.

☐ Select Message from the Try It menu.

> *MyTool responds by displaying a message box.*

☐ Close the message box.

☐ Select Music from the Try It menu.

> *MyTool responds by playing the WAV file.*

☐ Experiment with the MyTool program, and then terminate the program.

What About the Toolbar?

At this point, the MyTool application displays the default toolbar that was automatically created for you.

You'll now learn how to modify the default toolbar so that it is appropriate for your application. The important thing to remember is that clicking the icon on the toolbar produces the same result as selecting the corresponding item from the menu. In other words, the toolbar is just another way of executing a menu item. (You can design an icon on the toolbar that does not have a corresponding menu item, but usually Windows applications have a menu item for each icon in the toolbar.)

Take a look at Figure 21.23, which shows the icons on the default toolbar. (For your convenience, the figure is enlarged so that you can take a better look at these icons.)

Figure 21.23. The icons on the default toolbar.

The file MAINFRM.CPP includes code (that Visual C++ wrote for you) that declares an array called `buttons[]`. This array corresponds to the buttons (icons) of the toolbar. Take a look at this code:

☐ Open the MAINFRM.CPP file (by selecting Open from the File menu) and search for the declaration of the `buttons[]` array inside the MAINFRM.CPP file.

Currently the declaration of the `buttons[]` array looks like this:

```
// toolbar buttons-IDs are command buttons
static UINT BASED_CODE buttons[] =
{
// same order as in the bitmap 'toolbar.bmp'
ID_FILE_NEW,
ID_FILE_OPEN,
ID_FILE_SAVE,
    ID_SEPARATOR,
ID_EDIT_CUT,
ID_EDIT_COPY,
ID_EDIT_PASTE,
```

```
    ID_SEPARATOR,
ID_FILE_PRINT,
ID_APP_ABOUT,
};
```

In the MyTool application you need only three icons on the toolbar: the Music icon, the Message icon, and the Help icon.

For cosmetic reasons, it would be nice if there were a separator between the Message icon and the Help icon.

☐ Modify the declaration of the buttons[] array (inside the MAINFRM.CPP file). After the modification, the declaration of the buttons[] array should look like this:

```
// toolbar buttons—IDs are command buttons
static UINT BASED_CODE buttons[] =
{
// same order as in the bitmap 'toolbar.bmp'

    ////////////////////////
    // MY CODE STARTS HERE
    ////////////////////////

    ID_TRYIT_MUSIC,
    ID_TRYIT_MESSAGE,
        ID_SEPARATOR,
    ID_APP_ABOUT,

    ////////////////////////
    // MY CODE ENDS HERE
    ////////////////////////

};
```

The code you typed defines the first icon on the tool bar to correspond to the menu item ID_TRYIT_MUSIC, the second icon to correspond to the ID_TRYIT_MESSAGE menu item, and the third icon to correspond to the ID_APP_ABOUT menu item. Between ID_TRYIT_MESSAGE and ID_APP_ABOUT an ID_SEPARATOR is inserted. ID_SEPARATOR represents a separator (space) between the icons.

Save the MAINFRM.CPP file:

☐ Select Save from the File menu of Visual C++.

Although you have not yet finished writing the MyTool application, compile, link, and execute it so that you can see the effect of changing the buttons[] array in action:

☐ Compile, link, and execute the MyTool application.

The main window of MyTool appears, as shown in Figure 21.24.

Figure 21.24. The main window of the MyTool application (with three incorrect icons).

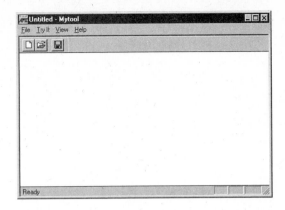

As shown in Figure 21.24, the toolbar of MyTool contains only three icons. However, these are the wrong icons! That is, the icons are operational, but the pictures of the icons have nothing to do with the particular task that is executed when the icon is clicked.

☐ Click the extreme left icon.

MyTool responds in the same manner as it does when you select Music from the Try It menu.

☐ Click the middle icon.

MyTool responds in the same manner as it does when you select Message from the Try It menu.

☐ Click the extreme right icon.

MyTool responds in the same manner as it does when you select About from the Help menu.

☐ Select Exit from the File menu to terminate the MyTool application.

Replacing the Icons on the Toolbar

You'll now replace the icons on the toolbar with more appropriate icons.

☐ Select MyTool.MAK from the Window menu to display the MyTool.MAK window, double-click the mytool.rc item to display the mytool.rc window, and double-click the Bitmap item to display a list of bitmaps that the MyTool.MAK project includes.

Visual C++ responds by listing the BMP files that the MyTool.MAK file contains. (See Figure 21.25.) As shown, the MyTool project has a single item under the Bitmap item.

*Figure 21.25. The
mytool.rc window after you
double-click the Bitmap
item.*

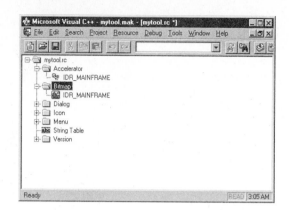

☐ Double-click the IDR_MAINFRAME item that appears under the Bitmap item.

Visual C++ responds by displaying the IDR_MAINFRAME bitmap. (See Figure 21.26.)

*Figure 21.26. The
IDR_MAINFRAME
bitmap.*

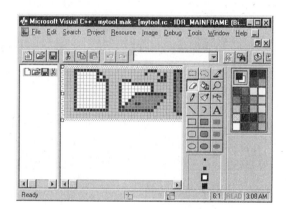

☐ Select Cut from the Edit menu to clear the picture.

Visual C++ responds by clearing the contents of the picture. (See Figure 21.27.)

You'll now use the visual tools shown in Figure 21.27 to edit the picture.

The bitmap that you'll now draw will include three toolbar icons. The size of each icon on the toolbar is 15 pixels vertically, and 16 pixels horizontally. Because there are three icons on the toolbar, the size of the bitmap you are now drawing should have 16×3=48 pixels horizontally, and 15 pixels vertically. Don't worry about the separator between the icons because Visual C++ will insert the separator automatically. (Recall that you specified a separator when you declared the buttons[] array.)

Figure 21.27. The
IDR_MAINFRAME
bitmap after you clear the
picture.

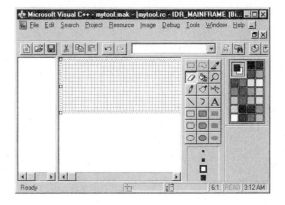

Now you'll use the drawing tools to draw icons that are more appropriate to the particular tasks
that are being performed when the icons are clicked. Recall that the extreme-left button serves as
the Music item of the Try It menu, the middle icon serves as the Message item of the Try It menu,
and the extreme-right icon serves as the About item of the Help menu.

☐ Use your artistic talent to draw the icons of the toolbar.

If you put a little efforts into the drawings, you may draw the extreme-left icon as shown in Figure
21.28. The extreme-left icon shows a picture of a music note.

Figure 21.28. Drawing a
music note as the extreme-
left icon.

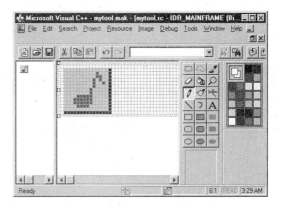

When drawing the icons, remember to draw the extreme-left icon so that it will fit within the first
16 pixels, the middle icon so that it fits within the next 16 pixels, and the extreme-right icon so that
it fits within the next 16 pixels.

Figure 21.29 shows the picture after you draw the second icon, and Figure 21.30 shows the middle
and extreme-right icons. Note that to display the area where you'll draw the extreme-right icon,
you may need to scroll the bitmap to the left.

Figure 21.29. The left and middle icons.

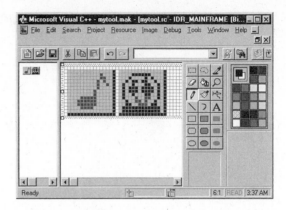

Figure 21.30. The middle and right icons.

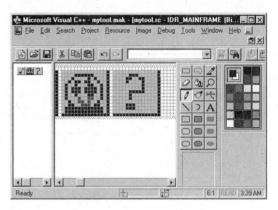

☐ Select Save from the File menu to save your work.

☐ Compile, link, and execute the MyTool application.

The window of MyTool appears. As you can see, the toolbar contains the icons that you designed.

Note that there is a space between the middle icon and the extreme-right icon on the toolbar. (Recall that you inserted ID_SEPARATOR between these icons in the definition of the buttons[ ] array array).

Customizing the Status Bar for Menu Prompts

Take a look at Figure 21.31. It shows that when the Toolbar menu item is highlighted the prompt on the status bar is this:

```
Show or hide the toolbar
```

Similarly, Figure 21.32 shows the status bar when the Status Bar menu item is highlighted. In this case, the status bar displays this message:

```
Show or hide the status bar
```

Figure 21.31. The status bar when the Toolbar menu item is highlighted.

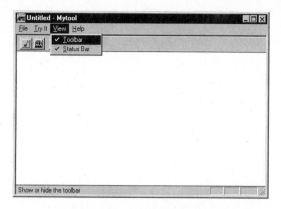

Figure 21.32. The status bar when the Status Bar menu item is highlighted.

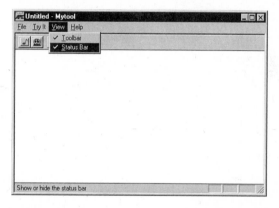

However, when you highlight the Music or Message menu items of the Try It menu, the status bar does not display any message. Why? You have not set the prompts of the status bar for these menu items. Here is how you set the prompts of the status bar:

☐ Display the IDR_MAINFRAME menu in design mode. (That is, double-click Menu inside the mytool.rc window, and then double-click the IDR_MAINFRAME item that appears below the Menu item.)

☐ Double-click the Music menu item.

Visual C++ responds by displaying the properties of the Music menu item. (See Figure 21.33).

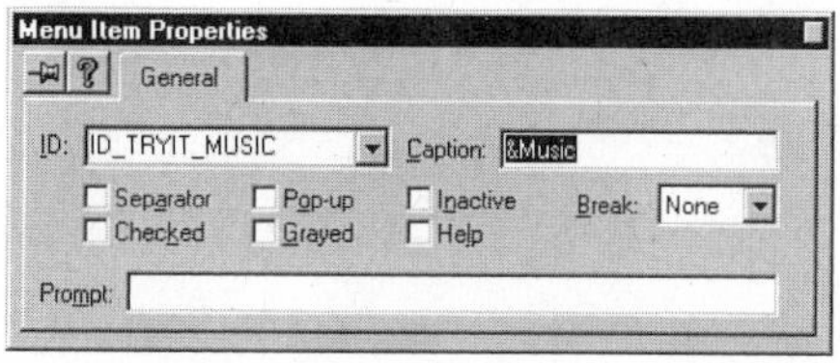

Figure 21.33. The Properties window of the Music menu item (without a status bar prompt).

As shown in Figure 21.33, the Prompt box is empty. This means that when the user highlights the Music menu item, the status bar will not display any message.

☐ Type the following inside the Prompt box (See Figure 21.34.):

```
Play music through the PC Speaker
```

Figure 21.34. Assigning a message prompt to the Music menu item.

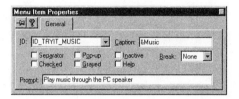

☐ Double-click the Message menu item, and type the following inside the Prompt box of its Properties window:

```
Display a message
```

☐ Select Save from the File menu.

☐ Compile and link the MyTool application, and then execute it.

☐ Press the Alt key and then use the arrow keys to highlight the Music menu item.

As shown in Figure 21.35, MyTool displays the following inside the status bar this message:

```
Play music through the PC speaker
```

Figure 21.35. The prompt on the status bar when the Music menu item is highlighted.

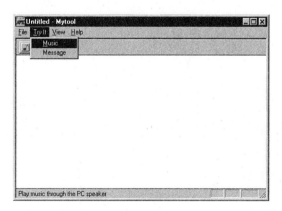

Similarly, when you highlight the Message menu item, the status bar displays the following message (See Figure 21.36.):

```
Display a message
```

Figure 21.36. The prompt on the status bar when the Message menu item is highlighted.

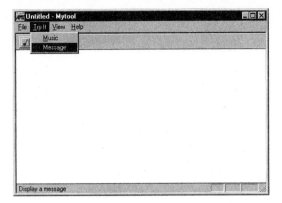

Figure 21.36. The prompt on the status bar when the Message menu item is highlighted.

NOTE

As discussed in this chapter, the toolbar is a pictorial representation of the menu. The status bar also displays the menu prompts when you place the mouse cursor on the icon of the toolbar. For example, place the mouse cursor on the extreme-left icon of the tool bar (which has the same result as selecting Music from the Try It menu). While the mouse cursor is on the extreme-left icon, the status bar displays the message that corresponds to the prompt of the Music menu item.

Further Helping the User...

In the previous section you learned that when you place the mouse cursor over an icon of the toolbar, the status bar indicates the purpose of the icon.

Perform the following experiment:

☐ Place the mouse cursor (without pushing any of its buttons) on the extreme-left icon of the toolbar.

> *MyTool responds by displaying a message that corresponds to the extreme-left icon on the status bar.*

☐ Repeat the preceding step for the middle icon.

> *MyTool responds by displaying a message that corresponds to the middle icon on the status bar.*

And now here's the interesting part:

☐ Place the mouse cursor on the About icon of the toolbar.

> *MyTool responds by displaying a message that corresponds to the About icon on the status bar. MyTool also displays a small rectangle with the word About in it. (See Figure 21.37.)*

Figure 21.37. The extra
help that MyTool displays
when you place the mouse
cursor on the About icon.

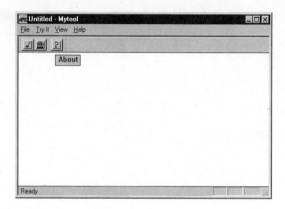

It will be nice if you can implement this extra help for the extreme-left and middle icons of the toolbar.

Can you guess how to implement this feature? It is probably implemented in the string table. Verify that the string table is indeed responsible for this extra help:

☐ Select MyTool.MAK from the Window menu to display the MyTool.MAK window, double-click mytool.rc inside the MyTool.MAK window to display the MyTool.RC window, and finally, double-click String Table inside the MyTool.RC window.

Visual C++ responds by displaying the string table. (See Figure 21.38.)

Figure 21.38. The
IDR_MAINFRAME
string table.

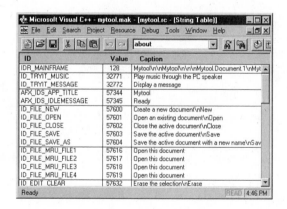

☐ Use the vertical scroll bar of the string table to scroll down the table, and then double-click the ID_APP_ABOUT item.

Visual C++ responds by displaying the String Properties dialog box of the
ID_APP_ABOUT item. (See Figure 21.39.)

Figure 21.39. The String Properties dialog box of the ID_APP_ABOUT item.

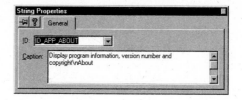

As shown in the Caption edit box of Figure 21.39, there are two strings associated with ID_APP_ABOUT, separated with the \n characters.

The first string is this:

```
Display program information, version and copyright
```

The second string is this:

```
About
```

The two strings are separated by the \n character.

The first string is the string that appears on the status bar when the user places the mouse cursor on the About icon, and the second icon is the text that appears below the About icon when the user places the mouse cursor on the About icon.

☐ For the sake of exercise, change the second string from About to About MyTool.

☐ Select Save from the File menu.

☐ Compile, link, and then execute the MyTool program.

☐ Place the mouse cursor over the About icon.

> *MyTool responds by displaying the text* About MyTool *below the About icon.*

☐ Experiment with the MyTool program and then terminate the program.

You'll now edit the string table so that when the user places the mouse cursor over the Music and Message icons of the toolbar the appropriate text will be displayed.

☐ Display the string table, and set the string of the ID_TRYIT_MUSIC item to this:

```
Play music through the PC speaker\nPlay Music
```

☐ Set the string of the ID_TRYIT_MESSAGE item inside the string table to the following:

```
Display a message\n Display a Message
```

☐ Select Save from the File menu.

☐ Compile, link, and execute the MyTool program.

☐ Place the mouse cursor over the icons.

> *MyTool responds by displaying a text that is associated with the icon on which you placed the mouse cursor.*

☐ Experiment with the MyTool program and then terminate the program.

22

Multimedia: Playing and Recording WAV Files

In this chapter you'll write an
application that lets the user play and
record a WAV file through a
Windows-compatible sound card by
using the CTegMM.LIB advanced
multimedia library.

You'll learn what the CTegMM.LIB library is and how to use it to play and record WAV files.

In this chapter you'll also learn how to use the CTegMM.LIB library for playing sound through the PC speaker.

The application you'll write in this chapter requires a Windows-compatible sound card. However, even if you don't have a sound card, you'll still be able to play the WAV file through your PC speaker.

What Is the CTegMM.LIB Advanced Multimedia Library?

The CTegMM.LIB library is a file that enables you to write multimedia programs easily. You can use it to play multimedia files such as WAV files and MIDI files through a Windows-compatible sound card. You can also use the CTegMM.LIB library for controlling multimedia devices such as audio CD drives. The CTegMM.LIB library can also be used for playing WAV files through the PC speaker. That is, if your end user does not have a sound card, you can use the CTegMM.LIB library to play WAV files through the internal PC speaker.

In this chapter you'll learn how to use the CTegMM.LIB library from within your Visual C++ programs to play and record WAV files with a sound card.

The most common uses of the CTegMM.LIB library are the following:

- To play and record WAV sound files with a sound card
- To play MIDI files
- To play CD audio
- To play video files (real movie files)
- To play WAV files through the PC speaker (without a sound card)

NOTE

The CTegMM.LIB file that is included with the book's CD is the limited version of the CTegMM.LIB library. This limited version lets you write programs that play only the multimedia files that are included with the book's CD.

The full version of the CTegMM.LIB library enables you to play your own multimedia files. The price of the full version CTegMM.LIB library is $29.95 (plus $5.00 for shipping and handling).

To order the full version of the CTegMM.LIB library, contact TegoSoft:

TegoSoft, Inc.
Box 389
Bellmore, NY 11710
Attn: CTegMM.LIB for Visual C++
Phone: (516)783-4824

The WAVE.EXE Application

You'll now write the WAVE.EXE application. The WAVE.EXE application is an example of a multimedia application that enables the user to play and record a wave file. Wave files are standard Windows sound files that have the extension .WAV (for example, MySong.WAV and MySpeech.WAV).

Before you start writing the WAVE.EXE application, execute the copy of it that resides in the \MVCPROG\EXE directory of the book's CD.

☐ Execute the \MVCPROG\EXE\WAVE.EXE program from the book's CD.

> *Windows responds by executing the WAVE.EXE application. The WAVE application first displays a limited-version message box from the CTegMM.LIB multimedia library. (See Figure 22.1.)*

Figure 22.1. The limited-version message box from the CTegMM.LIB library.

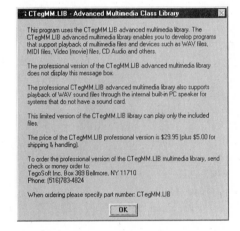

☐ Click the OK button of the message box.

> *The main window of WAVE.EXE appears, as shown in Figure 22.2.*

Figure 22.2. The main window of the WAVE application.

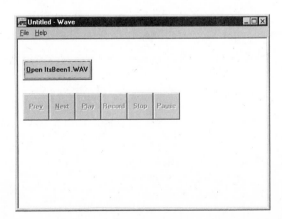

As you can see, the main window of the application has inside it an Open button (Open ITSBEEN1.WAV) and six tape-recorder buttons: Previous, Next, Play, Record, Stop, and Pause. Notice that currently the six tape-recorder buttons are disabled (dimmed). That's because currently there is no open WAV file.

To open a WAV file do the following:

☐ Click the Open ITSBEEN1.WAV button.

The WAVE.EXE application responds by opening the ITSBEEN1.WAV file and making the tape-recorder buttons available. Notice that the Stop and Pause buttons are still dimmed because currently there is no playback in progress.

To start the playback of a WAV file do the following:

☐ Click the Play button.

The WAVE application responds by playing the WAV file ItsBeen1.WAV, which resides in the book's CD \MVCPROG\WAV directory. Notice that during the playback the Stop and Pause buttons are enabled, and the Play and Record buttons are disabled.

NOTE

If you don't have a sound card, you can play the WAV file through the PC speaker. However, you'll need to change a single statement in the source code of the WAVE.EXE application. You'll have an opportunity to do so later in this chapter when you write the code of the WAVE.EXE application yourself. So if the buttons of the WAVE.EXE application are currently dimmed (because you don't have a sound card), don't worry, you'll take care of that later.

To record something do the following:

☐ Click the Prev button.

The WAVE.EXE application responds by changing the playback position to the beginning of the WAV file.

☐ Prepare yourself for recording, then click the Record button.

☐ Speak into the microphone of your sound card. When you are done, click the Stop button.

To hear your recording do the following:

☐ Click the Prev button (to rewind the playback position), then click the Play button.

The WAVE.EXE application responds by playing your recording followed by the playback of the original ItsBeen1.WAV file.

☐ Experiment with the other buttons of the WAVE.EXE application.

Note that during the playback of the WAV file the Stop and Pause buttons are available, and you can use them to stop/pause the playback. Note also that the Pause button serves as a Pause/Resume button. That is, when you click the Pause button while there is playback in progress, the playback is paused, and when you click the Pause button while the playback is paused, the playback resumes.

The WAVE.EXE application has two pop-up menus: File and Help. These pop-up menus are shown in Figures 22.3 and 22.4.

Figure 22.3. The File pop-up menu of the WAVE.EXE application.

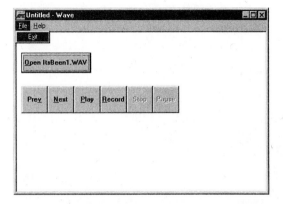

Figure 22.4. The Help pop-up menu of the WAVE.EXE application.

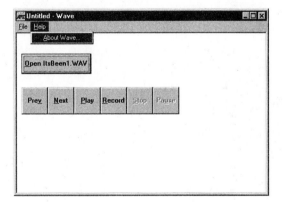

To exit the WAVE.EXE application do the following:

☐ Select Exit from the File menu.

You might think that because the WAVE.EXE application supports such powerful multimedia features, you will have to write a lot of code. However, this is not the case! All the multimedia features you've seen and heard are built into the CTegMM.LIB library. All you have to do is write code that uses the CTegMM.LIB library. As you will soon see, using the functions of the CTegMM.LIB library from within your Visual C++ application is easy and requires a small amount of code writing.

Now that you know what the WAVE.EXE application should do, you can start writing it.

Creating the Project of the WAVE.EXE Application

To create the project of the WAVE.EXE application do the following:

☐ Start Visual C++ and close all the open windows that appear inside the desktop of Visual C++ (if there are any).

☐ Select New from the File menu.

Visual C++ responds by displaying the New dialog box.

☐ Select Project inside the New dialog box and then click the OK button of the New dialog box.

Visual C++ responds by displaying the New Project dialog box.

☐ Set the project name to wave.

☐ Set the project path to \MVCPROG\CH22\WAVE\WAVE.MAK.

Your New Project dialog box should now look like the one shown in Figure 22.5.

Figure 22.5. The New Project dialog box of the WAVE.MAK project.

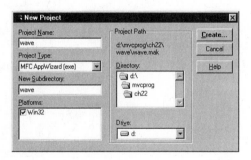

☐ Click the Create button of the New Project dialog box.

Visual C++ responds by displaying the AppWizard—Step 1 window.

☐ Set the Step 1 window as shown in Figure 22.6. As shown in Figure 22.6, the WAVE.MAK project is set as a single-document interface application, and U.S. English (APPWIZUS.DLL) is used as the language for the application's resources.

Figure 22.6. The AppWizard—Step 1 window for the WAVE application.

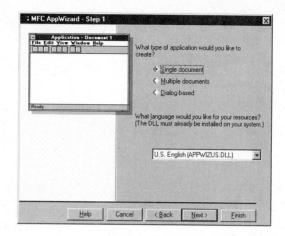

☐ Click the Next button of the Step 1 window.

  Visual C++ responds by displaying the AppWizard—Step 2 of 6 window.

☐ Set the Step 2 of 6 window as shown in Figure 22.7. That is, in the WAVE application you don't want any database support.

Figure 22.7. The AppWizard—Step 2 of 6 window for the WAVE application.

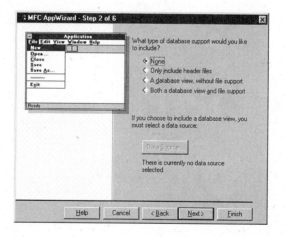

☐ Click the Next button of the Step 2 of 6 window.

  Visual C++ responds by displaying the AppWizard—Step 3 of 6 window.

☐ Set the Step 3 of 6 window as shown in Figure 22.8 That is, in the WAVE application you don't want any OLE support.

Figure 22.8. The AppWizard—Step 3 of 6 window for the WAVE application.

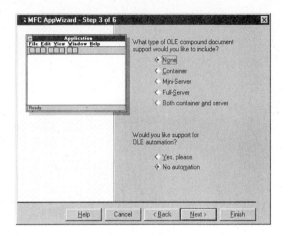

☐ Click the Next button of the Step 3 of 6 window.

Visual C++ responds by displaying the AppWizard—Step 4 of 6 window.

☐ Set the Step 4 of 6 window as shown in Figure 22.9.

Figure 22.9. The AppWizard—Step 4 of 6 window for the WAVE application.

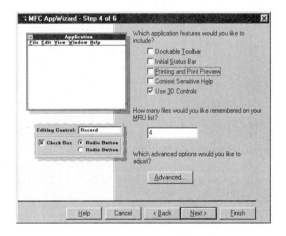

As shown in Figure 22.9, the features Dockable Toolbar, Initial Status Bar, Printing and Print Preview, and Context Sensitive Help will not be included in the WAVE application.

☐ Click the Next button of the Step 4 of 6 window.

Visual C++ responds by displaying the AppWizard—Step 5 of 6 window.

☐ Set the Step 5 of 6 window as shown in Figure 22.10.

As shown in Figure 22.10, the project will be generated with comments, a Visual C++ makefile will be generated, and the application will use the MFC library from a DLL.

Figure 22.10. The AppWizard—Step 5 of 6 window for the WAVE application.

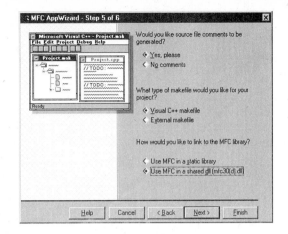

☐ Click the Next button of the Step 5 of 6 window.

> *Visual C++ responds by displaying the AppWizard—Step 6 of 6 window.*

You'll now use the AppWizard—Step 6 of 6 window to tell AppWizard to derive the view class of the application from the MFC class CFormView:

☐ Select the CWaveView class inside the AppWizard—Step 6 of 6 window.

☐ Set the Base Class drop-down list box to CFormView.

Your AppWizard—Step 6 of 6 window should now look like the one shown in Figure 22.11.

Figure 22.11. The AppWizard—Step 6 of 6 window after you set the base class of the application view class to CFormView.

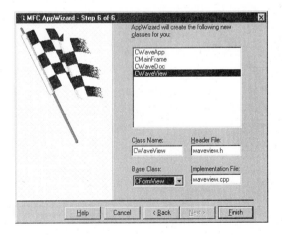

☐ Click the Finish button of the Step 6 of 6 window.

> *Visual C++ responds by displaying the New Project Information window, as shown in Figure 22.12.*

Figure 22.12. The New Project Information window of the WAVE.MAK project.

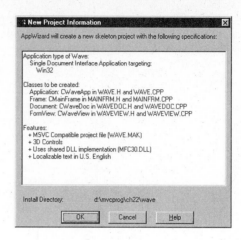

☐ Click the OK button of the New Project Information window.

Visual C++ responds by creating the project file and all the skeleton files of the application.

Creating the Form of the Application

Because in AppWizard you specified that the base class of the application's view class is CFormView, AppWizard created for you a form (a dialog box) that is attached to the view class of the application. This dialog box serves as the main window of the application. AppWizard named this dialog box IDD_WAVE_FORM. You'll now customize the IDD_WAVE_FORM dialog box until it looks like the one shown back in Figure 22.2.

☐ Select wave.mak from the Window menu to display the wave.mak window, double-click wave.rc inside the wave.mak window to display the wave.rc window, double-click the Dialog item that appears inside the wave.rc window to display a list of dialog boxes, and finally, double-click the IDD_WAVE_FORM item that appears under the Dialog item.

Visual C++ responds by displaying the IDD_WAVE_FORM dialog box in design mode.

☐ Delete the TODO static text by clicking on it and pressing the Delete key on your keyboard.

☐ Design the IDD_WAVE_FORM dialog box according to the specifications in Table 22.1. When you finish implementing the dialog box, it should look like the one shown in Figure 22.13.

Table 22.1. The Properties table for the IDD_WAVE_FORM dialog box.

Object	Property	Setting
Dialog box	ID	IDD_WAVE_FORM

Object	Property	Setting
Push button	ID	IDC_OPEN_BUTTON
	Caption	&Open ItsBeen1.WAV
Push button	ID	IDC_PREV_BUTTON
	Caption	Pre&v
	Disabled	TRUE (Checked)
Push button	ID	IDC_NEXT_BUTTON
	Caption	&Next
	Disabled	TRUE (Checked)
Push button	ID	IDC_PLAY_BUTTON
	Caption	&Play
	Disabled	TRUE (Checked)
Push button	ID	IDC_RECORD_BUTTON
	Caption	&Record
	Disabled	TRUE (Checked)
Push button	ID	IDC_STOP_BUTTON
	Caption	&Stop
	Disabled	TRUE (Checked)
Push button	ID	IDC_PAUSE_BUTTON
	Caption	Pa&use
	Disabled	TRUE (Checked)

NOTE

As specified in Table 22.1, the Disabled property of all the push buttons (except the Open push button) should be set to TRUE. Therefore, upon start-up of the WAVE.EXE application, all the push buttons (except the Open push button) will be disabled.

To set the Disabled property of a button to TRUE simply double-click the push button and place a checkmark inside the Disabled check box.

As shown in Figure 22.13, all the push buttons except the Open push button are disabled.

*Figure 22.13. The
IDD_WAVE_FORM
dialog box (in design
mode).*

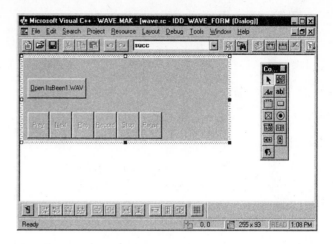

Attaching Variables to the Controls of the IDD_WAVE_FORM Dialog Box

You'll now attach variables to the push buttons of the IDD_WAVE_FORM dialog box.

> **NOTE**
>
> You need to attach variables to the push buttons of the IDD_WAVE_FORM dialog box because later when you write the code of the WAVE.EXE application, you'll use these variables to enable and disable the push buttons, depending on the current playback mode. For example, when there is playback in progress, the Play button should be disabled.

☐ Use ClassWizard to attach variables to the controls of the IDD_WAVE_FORM dialog box according to the specifications in Table 22.2. When implementing the variables of Table 22.2, make sure that the class name in the ClassWizard dialog box is set to CWaveView.

Table 22.2. The Variables table of the IDD_WAVE_FORM dialog box.

Control ID	Variable Name	Category	Variable Type
IDC_PREV_BUTTON	m_PrevButton	Control	CButton
IDC_NEXT_BUTTON	m_NextButton	Control	CButton
IDC_PLAY_BUTTON	m_PlayButton	Control	CButton
IDC_RECORD_BUTTON	m_RecordButton	Control	CButton
IDC_STOP_BUTTON	m_StopButton	Control	CButton
IDC_PAUSE_BUTTON	m_PauseButton	Control	CButton

Save your work:

☐ Select Save from the File menu.

You've finished designing the IDD_WAVE_FORM dialog box. This dialog box will serve as the main window of the application.

The Visual Implementation of the Menu

You'll now visually implement the menu of the WAVE.EXE application.

☐ Select wave.rc from the Window menu to display the wave.rc window, double-click Menu, and finally double-click IDR_MAINFRAME.

Visual C++ responds by displaying the IDR_MAINFRAME menu in design mode.

☐ Implement the IDR_MAINFRAME menu so that it contains the following items:

&File
   E&xit
&Help
   &About Wave…

Save your work:

☐ Select Save from the File menu.

The visual implementation of the menu of the WAVE.EXE application is complete.

To see your visual design in action do the following:

☐ Select Build WAVE.EXE from the Project menu of Visual C++.

☐ Select Execute WAVE.EXE from the Project menu.

Visual C++ responds by executing the WAVE.EXE application. The main window of the application appears with the form that you designed inside it—seven push buttons. As you can see, all the push buttons (except the Open push button) are disabled.

In the following sections you'll write the code that brings these push buttons to life.

To exit the WAVE.EXE application do the following:

☐ Select Exit from the File menu.

Adding the CTegMM.LIB Library to the Wave.MAK Project

Later you will write code that uses a multimedia class from the CTegMM.LIB multimedia library. Therefore, you need to add the CTegMM.LIB library to the WAVE.MAK project file. Here is how you do that:

☐ Select Files from the Project menu of Visual C++.

   Visual C++ responds by displaying the Project Files dialog box for the WAVE.MAK project.

☐ Type `C:\MVCPROG\LIB\CTEGMM.LIB` inside the File Name edit box of the Project Files dialog box. (Note that if you installed the book's CD to your D: drive you need to type `D:\MVCPROG\LIB\CTEGMM.LIB`.)

☐ Click the Add button.

   Visual C++ responds by adding the CTEGMM.LIB file to the WAVE.MAK project.

☐ Click the Close button of the Project Files dialog box.

The CTEGMM.LIB library is now part of the WAVE.MAK project. In the following sections you'll use a multimedia class from the CTEGMM.LIB library.

Declaring an Object of Class *CTegMM*

The CTEGMM.LIB library includes a powerful multimedia class called CTegMM. Using this class you can declare multimedia objects that play and control various multimedia files and devices such as WAV files, CD Audio, MIDI files, and movie files (AVI files). You can also use the CTegMM class to play WAV files through the internal PC speaker for system that do not have a sound card.

You'll now declare an object of class CTegMM. You'll name this object m_wav and you will make this object a data member of the view class. This way, m_wav will be visible in all the member functions of the view class. As implied by its name, you will use the m_wav multimedia object for playing a WAV file.

Follow these steps to declare the m_wav object:

☐ Select Open from the File menu of Visual C++ and open the WAVEVIEW.H header file.

☐ Declare the m_wav object as a public data member of the CWaveView class. After you declare m_wav, the CWaveView class declaration should look like this:

```
class CWaveView : public CFormView
{
protected: // create from serialization only
    CWaveView();
    DECLARE_DYNCREATE(CWaveView)

public:
    //{{AFX_DATA(CWaveView)
    enum { IDD = IDD_WAVE_FORM };
    Cbutton m_OpenButton;
    Cbutton m_PrevButton;
    Cbutton m_NextButton;
    Cbutton m_RecordButton;
    Cbutton m_StopButton;
    Cbutton m_PlayButton;
    Cbutton m_PauseButton;
    //}}AFX_DATA
```

```
// Attributes
public:
    CWaveDoc* GetDocument();

    /////////////////////////
    // MY CODE STARTS HERE
    /////////////////////////

    CTegMM m_wav;

    ///////////////////////
    // MY CODE ENDS HERE
    ///////////////////////

// Operations
public:

// Overrides
// ClassWizard generated virtual function overrides
//{{AFX_VIRTUAL(CWaveView)
public:
protected:
virtual void DoDataExchange(CDataExchange* pDX);
//}}AFX_VIRTUAL

// Implementation
public:
    virtual ~CWaveView();
#ifdef _DEBUG
    virtual void AssertValid() const;
    virtual void Dump(CDumpContext& dc) const;
#endif

protected:

// Generated message map functions
protected:
    //{{AFX_MSG(CWaveView)
// NOTE—the ClassWizard will add and remove member
//        functions here.
// DO NOT EDIT what you see in these blocks of generated
// code !
    //}}AFX_MSG
    DECLARE_MESSAGE_MAP()
};
```

If you try to compile and link the WAVE application now, you'll get a compiling error. Why? In the preceding code you declared an object of class CTegMM, but the CTegMM class is not known in the WAVEVIEW.H file. Therefore, you need to use #include on the header file of the CTegMM class at the beginning of the WAVEVIEW.H file:

☐ Add the statement #include "\MVCPROG\LIB\CTEGMM.H" at the beginning of the WAVEVIEW.H file. After you add this statement, the beginning of the WAVEVIEW.H file should look like this:

```
// waveview.h : interface of the CWaveView class
//
//////////////////////////////////////////////////

/////////////////////
// MY CODE STARTS HERE
/////////////////////

#include "\MVCPROG\LIB\CTEGMM.H"

/////////////////////
// MY CODE ENDS HERE
/////////////////////
```

☐ Save your work by selecting Save from the File menu.

Opening the WAV File

At this point you have an object of class CTegMM (a multimedia object) called m_wav. You'll now write the code that initializes the m_wav object. This code will open a WAV file. You'll attach this code to the Open button. This way, when the user will click the Open button, a WAV file will be opened.

☐ Display the ClassWizard dialog box by selecting ClassWizard from the Project menu of Visual C++.

☐ Select the Message Maps tab at the top of ClassWizard's dialog box.

☐ Use ClassWizard to select the event:

```
CWaveView -> IDC_OPEN_BUTTON -> BN_CLICKED
```

Then click the Add Function button.

☐ Name the new function OnOpenButton().

To write the code of the OnOpenButton() function do the following:

☐ Click the Edit Code button of ClassWizard.

> *ClassWizard responds by opening the file WaveView.CPP, with the function* OnOpenButton() *ready to be edited by you.*

☐ Write code inside the OnOpenButton() function so that it looks like this:

```
void CWaveView::OnOpenButton()
{
// TODO: Add your control notification handler code here

/////////////////////
// MY CODE STARTS HERE
/////////////////////

// Specify the window handler for Windows messages.
m_wav.SetNumProperty("hWnd", (long)m_hWnd);

// Set the device type for playback of WAV files.
m_wav.SetStrProperty("DeviceType","WaveAudio");
```

```
//// Note:
//// To play through the PC speaker, set the DeviceType
//// to "PCSpeaker" as follows:
////m_wav.SetStrProperty("DeviceType","PCSpeaker");

// Fill the string file_name with the full pathname
// of the ITSBEEN1.WAV file.
char file_name[300];
strncpy(file_name,__argv[0],2);
file_name[2]=0;
strcat(file_name,"\\MVCPROG\\WAV\\ITSBEEN1.WAV");

// Set the FileName property.
m_wav.SetStrProperty("FileName", file_name);

// Open the WAV file.
m_wav.SetStrProperty("Command", "Open");

// Was file opened successfully?
long err;
m_wav.GetNumProperty("Error", &err);
if ( err == 0 )
    {
    // File was opened successfully, so enable
    // the Prev, Next, Play, and Record buttons.
    m_PrevButton.EnableWindow(TRUE);
    m_NextButton.EnableWindow(TRUE);
    m_PlayButton.EnableWindow(TRUE);
    m_RecordButton.EnableWindow(TRUE);
    }
else
    {
    // Open command failed, so disable
    // the Prev, Next, Play, and Record buttons.
m_PrevButton.EnableWindow(FALSE);
    m_NextButton.EnableWindow(FALSE);
    m_PlayButton.EnableWindow(FALSE);
    m_RecordButton.EnableWindow(FALSE);
    }

// Currently no playback is in progress, so
// disable the Stop and Pause buttons.
m_StopButton.EnableWindow(FALSE);
m_PauseButton.EnableWindow(FALSE);

/////////////////////
// MY CODE ENDS HERE
/////////////////////

}
```

Now go over the code of the OnOpenButton() function.

The first statement

```
m_wav.SetNumProperty("hWnd", (long)m_hWnd);
```

sets the hWnd property of the m_wav multimedia object to the handler of the application's main window (m_hWnd). The hWnd property specifies which window should receive messages that pertain to the multimedia object. For example, when playback or recording is done, Windows sends a

MM_MCINOTIFY message. By setting the hWnd property of the multimedia object to m_hWnd you are specifying that the MM_MCINOTIFY message should be sent to the application's main window. Note that m_hWnd is a data member of the application's view class (inherited from the MFC class CWnd). The m_hWnd data member of the view class specifies the handler of the window that is associated with the view class (that is, the handler of the application's main window).

> **NOTE**
>
> The SetNumProperty() function is a member function of the CTegMM multimedia class. Recall that earlier you declared m_wav as an object of class CTegMM.
>
> The Num in the name of the SetNumProperty() function signifies that SetNumProperty() is used for setting a numeric property. The first parameter of the SetNumProperty() function is the name of the property to be changed. The second parameter is the numeric value that you want to assign to the property. For example, in the preceding statement you used the SetNumProperty() function:
>
> ```
> m_wav.SetNumProperty("hWnd", (long)m_hWnd);
> ```
>
> This statement sets the hWnd property of the m_wav multimedia object to m_hWnd.
>
> Note that the second parameter of the SetNumProperty() function is casted to long, because the SetNumProperty() function expects a long type for its second parameter.
>
> As you will soon see, the CTegMM class has many other properties. You manipulate and control an object of class CTegMM (a multimedia object) by setting its properties.

The next statement is

```
m_wav.SetStrProperty("DeviceType","WaveAudio");
```

This statement uses the SetStrProperty() member function of the CTegMM class to set the DeviceType property of the m_wav multimedia object to WaveAudio. The DeviceType property specifies the type of device to be opened. WaveAudio is the device type that you have to specify when you want to use the multimedia object for playing WAV files through a sound card.

> **NOTE**
>
> As implied by its name, the SetStrProperty() member function of the CTegMM class is used for setting a string property. The first parameter of the SetStrProperty() function is the name of the property to be changed. The second parameter is the string value that you want to assign to the property. For example, in the preceding statement you used the SetStrProperty() function as follows:
>
> ```
> m_wav.SetStrProperty("DeviceType", "WaveAudio");
> ```
>
> This statement, sets the DeviceType property of the m_wav multimedia object to WaveAudio.

If you don't have a sound card, instead of specifying WaveAudio as the DeviceType, specify PCSpeaker. In that case, the statement that sets the DeviceType property should look like this:

```
m_wav.SetStrProperty("DeviceType","PCSpeaker");
```

The next four statements

```
char file_name[300];
strncpy(file_name,__argv[0],2);
file_name[2]=0;
strcat(file_name,"\\MVCPROG\\WAV\\ITSBEEN1.WAV");
```

fill the local string variable file_name with the full pathname of the WAV file to be played (ITSBEEN1.WAV).

> **NOTE**
>
> In the preceding code, argv[0] is preceded with two underscores (__). __argv[0] is a string that holds the full pathname of the application's EXE file. For example, if the WAVE.EXE application is executed from the C:\TRY directory, __argv[0] will hold the string C:\TRY\WAVE.EXE.
>
> Therefore, the statement
>
> ```
> strncpy(file_name,__argv[0],2);
> ```
>
> fills the first two characters of the file_name variable with the letter drive (for example, C:) of the drive in which the application's EXE file resides.

At this point, the string variable file_name holds the full pathname of the ITSBEEN1.WAV file. For example, if you are executing the WAVE.EXE application from the D: drive, the file_name variable is filled with the string D:\MVCPROG\WAV\ITSBEEN1.WAV.

The next statement in the OnOpenButton() function is

```
m_wav.SetStrProperty("FileName", file_name);
```

This statement uses the SetStrProperty() function to set the FileName property of the m_wav multimedia object to file_name. So now the FileName property of the m_wav multimedia object holds the full pathname of the ITSBEEN1.WAV file.

The next statement in the OnOpenButton() function is this:

```
m_wav.SetStrProperty("Command", "Open");
```

This statement issues an Open command to the m_wav multimedia object. Note that this statement also uses the SetStrProperty() function—it sets the Command property of the m_wav multimedia object to Open. Issuing an Open command opens the WAV file that is specified by the FileName property. So now the ITSBEEN1.WAV file is open (that is, it is ready for playback).

The next group of statements determines whether the Open command was successful by extracting the Error property of the m_wav object:

```
// Was file opened successfully?
long err;
m_wav.GetNumProperty("Error", &err);
if ( err == 0 )
    {
    // File was opened successfully, so enable
    // the Prev, Next, Play, and Record buttons.
    m_PrevButton.EnableWindow(TRUE);
    m_NextButton.EnableWindow(TRUE);
    m_PlayButton.EnableWindow(TRUE);
    m_RecordButton.EnableWindow(TRUE);
    }
else
    {
    // Open command failed, so disable
    // the Prev, Next, Play, and Record buttons.
    m_PrevButton.EnableWindow(FALSE);
    m_NextButton.EnableWindow(FALSE);
    m_PlayButton.EnableWindow(FALSE);
    m_RecordButton.EnableWindow(FALSE);
    }
```

As you can see, the Error property is extracted by using the GetNumProperty() function:

```
long err;
m_wav.GetNumProperty("Error", &err);
```

The first parameter of the GetNumProperty() function is the name of the numeric property whose value you want to extract, and the second parameter is the address of the variable that will be filled with the value of the property.

So after executing the statements

```
long err;
m_wav.GetNumProperty("Error", &err);
```

the err local variable is filled with the value of the Error property.

The if...else statement

```
if ( err == 0 )
    {
    // File was opened successfully, so enable
    // the Prev, Next, Play, and Record buttons.
    m_PrevButton.EnableWindow(TRUE);
    m_NextButton.EnableWindow(TRUE);
    m_PlayButton.EnableWindow(TRUE);
    m_RecordButton.EnableWindow(TRUE);
    }
else
    {
    // Open command failed, so disable
    // the Prev, Next, Play, and Record buttons.
    m_PrevButton.EnableWindow(FALSE);
    m_NextButton.EnableWindow(FALSE);
```

```
    m_PlayButton.EnableWindow(FALSE);
    m_RecordButton.EnableWindow(FALSE);
    }
```

evaluates the value of the Error property. If the value of the Error property is 0, you know that the last issued command (the Open command) was successful. If this is the case, the statements under the if enable the Prev, Next, Play, and Record buttons.

If, however, the value of the Error property is not 0, you know that the last issued command (the Open command) has failed. If this is the case, the statements under the else disable the Prev, Next, Play, and Record buttons.

The last two statements in the OnOpenButton() function are

```
m_StopButton.EnableWindow(FALSE);
m_PauseButton.EnableWindow(FALSE);
```

These statements disable the Stop and Pause buttons. This is necessary because currently there is no playback in progress and the user should be able to click the Stop and Pause buttons only while there is playback in progress.

Here's a summary of what the code you wrote inside the OnOpenButton() function does:

- It sets the hWnd property of the m_wav multimedia object to m_hWnd (because you want Windows to send messages that pertain to the m_wav multimedia object to the application's main window).

- It sets the DeviceType property of m_wav to WaveAudio (because you want to use the m_wav multimedia object for playing a WAV file through the sound card).

- It sets the FileName property of the m_wav multimedia object to \\VCPROG\\WAV\\ITSBEEN1.WAV (because this is the WAV file that you want to play).

- It issues the Open command to the m_wav multimedia object by setting the Command property of the multimedia object to Open.

- It evaluates the Error property of the m_wav multimedia object to see whether the Open command has been issued successfully.

Don't forget to save your work:

☐ Select Save from the File menu.

Attaching Code to the Play Button

When the user clicks the Play button, the WAVE.EXE application should start playing the WAV file.

Follow these steps to attach code to the Play button:

☐ Display the ClassWizard dialog box by selecting ClassWizard from the Project menu of Visual C++.

☐ Select the Message Maps tab at the top of ClassWizard's dialog box.

☐ Use ClassWizard to select the event:

```
CWaveView -> IDC_PLAY_BUTTON -> BN_CLICKED
```

Then click the Add Function button.

☐ Name the new function `OnPlayButton()`.

To write the code of the `OnPlayButton()` function do the following:

☐ Click the Edit Code button of ClassWizard.

> *ClassWizard responds by opening the file WaveView.CPP, with the function*
> `OnPlayButton()` *ready to be edited by you.*

☐ Write code inside the `OnPlayButton()` function so that it looks like this:

```
void CWaveView::OnPlayButton()
{
// TODO: Add your control notification handler code here

/////////////////////////
// MY CODE STARTS HERE
/////////////////////////

// Issue a Play command.
m_wav.SetStrProperty("Command", "Play");

// Disable the Play and Record buttons.
m_PlayButton.EnableWindow(FALSE);
m_RecordButton.EnableWindow(FALSE);

// Enable the Stop and Pause buttons.
m_StopButton.EnableWindow(TRUE);
m_PauseButton.EnableWindow(TRUE);

/////////////////////////
// MY CODE ENDS HERE
/////////////////////////

}
```

☐ Save your work by selecting Save from the File menu.

The first statement inside the `OnPlayButton()` function

```
m_wav.SetStrProperty("Command", "Play");
```

issues a `Play` command to the `m_wav` multimedia object. As you can see, the `Play` command is issued by setting the Command property of the `m_wav` multimedia object to `Play`. Setting the Command property to `Play` starts the playback of the currently open WAV file. Note that because inside the `OnOpenButton()` function you opened the ITSBEEN1.WAV file, the `Play` command will play the ITSBEEN1.WAV file.

NOTE

In the WAVE.EXE application, after you issue the Play command the WAV file is played from the current playback position until the end of the WAV file.

In some applications you might find it useful to play a particular section of the WAV file. For example, you might have an application that uses one WAV file that contains several recordings of audio prompts. Depending on the user actions, you'll play a particular section from the WAV file.

To play a particular section of a WAV file you have to specify the desired section with the From and To properties of the multimedia object. For example, if the WAV file is 15 seconds long (15,000 milliseconds long), the following code will play the last 5 seconds (5000 milliseconds) of the WAV file:

```
m_wav.SetNumProperty("From", 10000);
m_wav.SetNumProperty("To",   15000);
m_wav.SetStrProperty("Command", "Play");
```

In order for the From and To properties to be effective you have to set their values immediately prior to issuing the Play command. If the From property is not specified (as in the WAVE.EXE application), the playback starts at the current playback position. If the To property is not specified (as in the WAVE.EXE application), the playback continues until the end of the WAV file.

The next two statements

```
m_PlayButton.EnableWindow(FALSE);
m_RecordButton.EnableWindow(FALSE);
```

disable the Play and Record buttons. This is necessary because during playback the user should not be able to click these buttons.

The last two statements

```
m_StopButton.EnableWindow(TRUE);
m_PauseButton.EnableWindow(TRUE);
```

enable the Stop and Pause buttons (because during playback the user should be able to click these buttons).

To hear your code in action do the following:

☐ Select Build WAVE.EXE from the Project menu.

☐ Select Execute WAVE.EXE from the Project menu.

☐ Click the Open ItsBeen1.WAV button.

☐ Click the Play button.

> *The WAVE.EXE application responds by playing the WAV file ITSBEEN1.WAV. During the playback, the Play and Record buttons are disabled, and the Stop and Pause buttons are enabled.*

As you can see, the program has a problem. Once the playback of the WAV file is done, the Play button remains disabled so you cannot play the WAV file again. You'll take care of this problem in the next section.

☐ Terminate the WAVE.EXE application by selecting Exit from the File menu.

Attaching Code to the *MM_MCINOTIFY* Event

As you have just seen, once the playback is done, the Play button remains disabled, and the user cannot play the WAV file again. You'll now attach code to the MM_MCINOTIFY event. The MM_MCINOTIFY event occurs when the WAV files is done playing (for example, when the playback position reaches the end of the WAV file).

The code that you will attach to the MM_MCINOTIFY event will enable the Play and Record buttons and disable the Stop and Pause buttons. Therefore, whenever playback is done, the Play and Record buttons will become available and the Stop and Pause buttons will become dimmed.

The MM_MCINOTIFY event is not listed inside the ClassWizard dialog box. Therefore, to process the MM_MCINOTIFY message you have to attach code to the WindowProc() member function of the view class. You can use the WindowProc() function to process any message that is not listed in the ClassWizard dialog box.

Attach code to the WindowProc() member function of the view class as follows:

☐ Display the ClassWizard dialog box by selecting ClassWizard from the Project menu of Visual C++.

☐ Select the Message Maps tab at the top of ClassWizard's dialog box.

☐ Use ClassWizard to select the event:

CWaveView -> CWaveView -> WindowProc

☐ Click the Add Function button.

> *Visual C++ responds by adding the WindowProc() member function to the CWaveView class.*

☐ Click the Edit Code button of ClassWizard.

> *ClassWizard responds by opening the file WaveView.CPP, with the function WindowProc() ready to be edited by you.*

☐ Write code inside the WindowProc() function so that it looks like this:

```
LRESULT CWaveView::WindowProc(UINT message, WPARAM wParam,
                              LPARAM lParam)
{
// TODO: Add your specialized code here and/or call the base
//       class

//////////////////////////
// MY CODE STARTS HERE
//////////////////////////

switch ( message )
        {
        case MM_MCINOTIFY:
                {
                MessageBox("DONE!!!");
                break;
                }
        }

//////////////////////////
// MY CODE ENDS HERE
//////////////////////////

return CFormView::WindowProc(message, wParam, lParam);
}
```

☐ Save your work by selecting Save from the File menu.

The code you typed inside the WindowProc() function is made of a switch statement:

```
switch ( message )
        {
        case MM_MCINOTIFY:
                {
                MessageBox("DONE!!!");
                break;
                }
        }
```

This switch statement evaluates the message parameter of the WindowProc() function to determine which event (message) has just occurred. If, for example, an MM_MCINOTIFY event has just occurred (that is, an MM_MCINOTIFY message has just arrived), the code under the MM_MCINOTIFY case will be executed:

```
case MM_MCINOTIFY:
        {
        MessageBox("DONE!!!");
        break;
        }
```

As you can see, the code under the MM_MCINOTIFY case simply displays a DONE!!! message box. This is done so that you'll be able to verify that the MM_MCINOTIFY event occurs whenever playback is done. Soon you will replace the MessageBox() statement with the code that enables the Play and Record buttons and disables the Stop and Pause buttons.

To verify that the MM_MCINOTIFY event occurs whenever playback is done, execute the WAVE.EXE application:

☐ Select Build WAVE.EXE from the Project menu.

☐ Select Execute WAVE.EXE from the Project menu.

☐ Click the Open ItsBeen1.WAV button.

☐ Click the Play button.

     The WAVE.EXE application responds by playing the WAV file ITSBEEN1.WAV.

As expected, once playback is done, a message box with the text DONE!!! is displayed.

Note that the MM_MCINOTIFY occurs whenever playback is done (not just when the playback reaches the end of the WAV file). To verify this, try the following experiment:

☐ Click the Open ItsBeen1.WAV button.

☐ Click the Play button and then immediately click the Open button.

The playback stops and the message box DONE!!! is displayed again.

So as you can see, the MM_MCINOTIFY event occurs whenever playback is done.

☐ Terminate the WAVE.EXE application by selecting Exit from the File menu.

You'll now write code under the MM_MCINOTIFY case that enables the Play and Record buttons and disables the Stop and Pause buttons. This way, whenever playback stops the Play, Record, Stop, and Pause buttons will be enabled or disabled as they should be.

☐ Open the file WAVEVIEW.CPP and modify the WindowProc() function until it looks like this:

```
LRESULT CWaveView::WindowProc(UINT message, WPARAM wParam,
                              LPARAM lParam)
{
// TODO: Add your specialized code here and/or call the base
//       class

/////////////////////////
// MY CODE STARTS HERE
/////////////////////////

switch ( message )
      {
      case MM_MCINOTIFY:
           {
           /////MessageBox("DONE!!!");

           // Enable the Play and Record buttons.
           m_PlayButton.EnableWindow(TRUE);
           m_RecordButton.EnableWindow(TRUE);

           // Disable the Stop and Pause buttons.
           m_StopButton.EnableWindow(FALSE);
           m_PauseButton.EnableWindow(FALSE);
```

```
            break;
            }
        }
```

```
/////////////////////
// MY CODE ENDS HERE
/////////////////////
```

```
return CFormView::WindowProc(message, wParam, lParam);
}
```

☐ Save your work by selecting Save from the File menu.

To see the code that you attached to the MM_MCINOTIFY event in action:

☐ Select Build WAVE.EXE from the Project menu.

☐ Select Execute WAVE.EXE from the Project menu.

☐ Click the Open ItsBeen1.WAV button.

☐ Click the Play button.

> *The WAVE.EXE application responds by playing the WAV file ITSBEEN1.WAV. During the playback, the Play and Record buttons are disabled, and the Stop and Pause buttons are enabled.*

As expected, once the playback is done, the code that you attached to the MM_MCINOTIFY event enables the Play and Record buttons and disables the Stop and Pause buttons.

☐ Click the Play button again.

This time nothing happens! Why? The current playback position is at the end of the WAV file.

In the next section you'll attach code to the Prev button. This code will enable the user to rewind the playback position to the beginning of the WAV file.

☐ Terminate the WAVE.EXE application by selecting Exit from the File menu.

Attaching Code to the Prev Button

When the user clicks the Prev button, the playback position should be rewound to the beginning of the WAV file.

Follow these steps to attach code to the Prev button:

☐ Display the ClassWizard dialog box by selecting ClassWizard from the Project menu of Visual C++.

☐ Select the Message Maps tab at the top of ClassWizard's dialog box.

☐ Use ClassWizard to select the event:

```
CWaveView -> IDC_PREV_BUTTON -> BN_CLICKED
```

Then click the Add Function button.

☐ Name the new function OnPrevButton().

To write the code of the OnPrevButton() function do the following:

☐ Click the Edit Code button of ClassWizard.

> *ClassWizard responds by opening the file WaveView.CPP, with the function OnPrevButton() ready to be edited by you.*

☐ Write code inside the OnPrevButton() function so that it looks like this:

```
void CWaveView::OnPrevButton()
{
// TODO: Add your control notification handler code here

/////////////////////////
// MY CODE STARTS HERE
/////////////////////////

// Issue a Prev command.
m_wav.SetStrProperty("Command", "Prev");

/////////////////////////
// MY CODE ENDS HERE
/////////////////////////

}
```

☐ Save your work by selecting Save from the File menu.

The code that you just typed inside the OnPrevButton() function is made of one statement:

```
m_wav.SetStrProperty("Command", "Prev");
```

This statement issues a Prev command to the m_wav multimedia object. Issuing a Prev command sets the playback position to the beginning of the WAV file.

To see the code that you attached to the Prev button in action do the following:

☐ Select Build WAVE.EXE from the Project menu.

☐ Select Execute WAVE.EXE from the Project menu.

☐ Click the Open ItsBeen1.WAV button.

☐ Click the Play button.

> *The WAVE.EXE application responds by playing the ITSBEEN1.WAV file.*

☐ Click the Play button again.

This time nothing happens because the current playback position is the end of the WAV file.

☐ Click the Prev button.

> *The WAVE.EXE application responds by rewinding the playback position to the beginning of the WAV file.*

☐ Click the Play button.

As expected, the ITSBEEN1.WAV file is played.

☐ Terminate the WAVE.EXE application by selecting Exit from the File menu.

Attaching Code to the Next Button

When the user clicks the Next button, the playback position should be set to the end of the WAV file.

Follow these steps to attach code to the Next button:

☐ Display the ClassWizard dialog box by selecting ClassWizard from the Project menu of Visual C++.

☐ Select the Message Maps tab at the top of ClassWizard's dialog box.

☐ Use ClassWizard to select the event:

```
CWaveView -> IDC_NEXT_BUTTON -> BN_CLICKED
```

Then click the Add Function button.

☐ Name the new function `OnNextButton()`.

To write the code of the `OnNextButton()` function do the following:

☐ Click the Edit Code button of ClassWizard.

> *ClassWizard responds by opening the file WaveView.CPP, with the function* `OnNextButton()` *ready to be edited by you.*

☐ Write code inside the `OnNextButton()` function so that it looks like this:

```
void CWaveView::OnNextButton()
{
// TODO: Add your control notification handler code here

/////////////////////////
// MY CODE STARTS HERE
/////////////////////////

// Issue a Next command.
m_wav.SetStrProperty("Command", "Next");

/////////////////////////
// MY CODE ENDS HERE
/////////////////////////

}
```

☐ Save your work by selecting Save from the File menu.

The code that you just typed inside the `OnNextButton()` function is made of one statement:

```
m_wav.SetStrProperty("Command", "Next");
```

This statement issues a `Next` command to the `m_wav` multimedia object. Issuing a `Next` command sets the playback position to the end of the WAV file.

To see the code that you attached to the Next button in action do the following:

☐ Select Build WAVE.EXE from the Project menu.

☐ Select Execute WAVE.EXE from the Project menu.

☐ Click the Open ItsBeen1.WAV button.

☐ Click the Next button.

> *The WAVE.EXE application responds by setting the playback position to the end of the WAV file.*

☐ Click the Play button again.

As expected, nothing is being played because the playback position is at the end of the WAV file.

☐ Click the Prev button.

> *The WAVE.EXE application responds by rewinding the playback position to the beginning of the WAV file.*

☐ Click the Play button.

As expected, the ITSBEEN1.WAV file is played.

☐ Terminate the WAVE.EXE application by selecting Exit from the File menu.

Rewinding the Playback Position Automatically

As you have just seen, once the playback reaches the end of the WAV file, in order for the user to hear the WAV file again, the user needs to click the Prev button before clicking the Play button.

You will now add code to the WAVE.EXE application so that when the playback position reaches the end of the WAV file, the playback position is automatically rewound to the beginning of the WAV file, thus relieving the user from the task of clicking the Prev button.

You will attach this Auto Rewinding code to the `MM_MCINOTIFY` event. Recall that you already attached some code to this event.

☐ Open the file WAVEVIEW.CPP and modify the `WindowProc()` function until it looks like this:

```
LRESULT CWaveView::WindowProc(UINT message, WPARAM wParam,
                              LPARAM lParam)
{
// TODO: Add your specialized code here and/or call the base
//       class
```

```
/////////////////////
// MY CODE STARTS HERE
/////////////////////

switch ( message )
        {
        case MM_MCINOTIFY:
                {
                /////MessageBox("DONE!!!");

                // Enable the Play and Record buttons.
                m_PlayButton.EnableWindow(TRUE);
                m_RecordButton.EnableWindow(TRUE);

                // Disable the Stop and Pause buttons.
                m_StopButton.EnableWindow(FALSE);
                m_PauseButton.EnableWindow(FALSE);

                // Get the total length of the WAV file.
                long length;
                m_wav.GetNumProperty("Length", &length);

                // Get the current playback position.
                long position;
                m_wav.GetNumProperty("Position", &position);

                // Has playback reached the end of the WAV file?
                if ( position == length )
                    m_wav.SetStrProperty("Command", "Prev");

                break;
                }
        }

/////////////////////
// MY CODE ENDS HERE
/////////////////////

return CFormView::WindowProc(message, wParam, lParam);
}
```

☐ Save your work by selecting Save from the File menu.

The statements that you just added under the MM_MCINOTIFY case check whether the current playback position is the end of the WAV file. If this is the case, the playback position is rewound to the beginning of the WAV file by issuing a Prev command.

The first two statements that you added

```
long length;
m_wav.GetNumProperty("Length", &length);
```

extract the value of the Length property of the m_wav multimedia object and store this value in the local variable length. The Length property reports the total length of the currently open file. So at this point, the variable length holds the total length of the WAV file.

> **NOTE**
>
> As implied by its name, the `GetNumproperty()` member function of the `CTegMM` class returns the current value of a numeric property of a multimedia object. For example, the statement
>
> ```
> m_wav.GetNumProperty("Length", &length);
> ```
>
> assigns the current value of the Length property of the `m_wav` multimedia object to the `length` variable.

The next two statements

```
long position;
m_wav.GetNumProperty("Position", &position);
```

extract the value of the Position property of the `m_wav` multimedia object and store this value in the local variable `position`. The Position property reports the current playback position. So at this point, the variable `position` holds the current playback position.

Finally, an `if` statement is used to compare the value of the Position property with the value of the Length property:

```
if ( position == length )
   m_wav.SetStrProperty("Command", "Prev");
```

If the value of the Position property is equal to the value of the Length property (that is, the playback position has reached the end of the WAV file), the `if` condition is satisfied, and the statement under the `if` issues a `Prev` command to rewind the playback position to the beginning of the WAV file.

Here's a summary of how the code that you added under the `MM_MCINOTIFY` case automatically rewinds the WAV file:

- Whenever the playback stops (for example, when the user clicks the Stop button or when the playback reaches the end of the WAV file), the code you wrote under the `MM_MCINOTIFY` case is automatically executed.
- The code you wrote under the `MM_MCINOTIFY` case checks whether the Position and Length properties of the multimedia object are equal. If they are equal (that is, the playback stopped because it reached the end of the WAV file), the code you wrote under the `MM_MCINOTIFY` case rewinds the multimedia object by setting the Command property of the multimedia object to `Prev`.

To see your Auto Rewind code in action do the following:

☐ Select Build WAVE.EXE from the Project menu.

☐ Select Execute WAVE.EXE from the Project menu.

☐ Click the Open ItsBeen1.WAV button.

☐ Click the Play button.

> *The WAVE application responds by playing the ITSBEEN1.WAV sound file.*

☐ Once the playback is done, click the Play button again.

> *As you can hear, the WAVE.EXE application responds by playing the WAV file again. You did not have to click the Prev button before clicking the Play button. The code that you wrote under the* MM_MCINOTIFY *case automatically rewinds the playback position whenever the playback reaches the end of the WAV file.*

☐ Terminate the WAVE.EXE application by selecting Exit from the File menu.

Attaching Code to the Stop Button

When the user clicks the Stop button, the playback should stop.

Follow these steps to attach code to the Stop button:

☐ Display the ClassWizard dialog box by selecting ClassWizard from the Project menu of Visual C++.

☐ Select the Message Maps tab at the top of ClassWizard's dialog box.

☐ Use ClassWizard to select the event:

CWaveView -> IDC_STOP_BUTTON -> BN_CLICKED

Then click the Add Function button.

☐ Name the new function OnStopButton().

To write the code of the OnStopButton() function do the following:

☐ Click the Edit Code button of ClassWizard.

> *ClassWizard responds by opening the file WaveView.CPP, with the function* OnStopButton() *ready to be edited by you.*

☐ Write code inside the OnStopButton() function so that it looks like this:

```
void CWaveView::OnStopButton()
{
// TODO: Add your control notification handler code here

/////////////////////////
// MY CODE STARTS HERE
/////////////////////////

// Issue a Stop command.
m_wav.SetStrProperty("Command", "Stop");

/////////////////////////
// MY CODE ENDS HERE
/////////////////////////

}
```

☐ Save your work by selecting Save from the File menu.

The code you just typed inside the `OnStopButton()` function is made of one statement:

```
m_wav.SetStrProperty("Command", "Stop");
```

This statement issues a `Stop` command to the m_wav multimedia object. Issuing a `Stop` command stops the playback.

To see the code that you attached to the Stop button in action do the following:

☐ Select Build WAVE.EXE from the Project menu.

☐ Select Execute WAVE.EXE from the Project menu.

☐ Click the Open ItsBeen1.WAV button.

☐ Click the Play button.

> *The WAVE.EXE application responds by playing the ITSBEEN1.WAV file.*

☐ While the WAV file is playing click the Stop button.

> *As expected, the playback stops.*

☐ Terminate the WAVE.EXE application by selecting Exit from the File menu.

Attaching Code to the Pause Button

When the user clicks the Pause button while there is playback in progress, the playback should be paused. When the user clicks the Pause button while the playback is paused, the playback should resume.

Follow these steps to attach code to the Pause button:

☐ Display the ClassWizard dialog box by selecting ClassWizard from the Project menu of Visual C++.

☐ Select the Message Maps tab at the top of ClassWizard's dialog box.

☐ Use ClassWizard to select the event:

```
CWaveView -> IDC_PAUSE_BUTTON -> BN_CLICKED
```

Then click the Add Function button.

☐ Name the new function `OnPauseButton()`.

To write the code of the `OnPauseButton()` function do the following:

☐ Click the Edit Code button of ClassWizard.

> *ClassWizard responds by opening the file WaveView.CPP, with the function* `OnPauseButton()` *ready to be edited by you.*

☐ Write code inside the `OnPauseButton()` function so that it looks like this:

```
void CWaveView::OnPauseButton()
{
// TODO: Add your control notification handler code here

/////////////////////////
// MY CODE STARTS HERE
/////////////////////////

// Issue a Pause command.
m_wav.SetStrProperty("Command", "Pause");

/////////////////////////
// MY CODE ENDS HERE
/////////////////////////

}
```

☐ Save your work by selecting Save from the File menu.

The code you just typed inside the `OnPauseButton()` function is made of one statement:

```
m_wav.SetStrProperty("Command", "Pause");
```

This statement issues a `Pause` command to the `m_wav` multimedia object. Issuing a `Pause` command pauses or resumes the playback, depending on the current playback mode. If the multimedia object is currently playing, the `Pause` command will pause the playback. If, however, the multimedia object is currently paused, the `Pause` command will resume the playback.

To see the code that you attached to the Pause button in action do the following:

☐ Select Build WAVE.EXE from the Project menu.

☐ Select Execute WAVE.EXE from the Project menu.

☐ Click the Open ItsBeen1.WAV button.

☐ Click the Play button.

> *The WAVE.EXE application responds by playing the ITSBEEN1.WAV file.*

☐ While the WAV file is playing click the Pause button.

> *The playback pauses.*

☐ Click the Pause button again.

> *As expected, the playback resumes.*

☐ Terminate the WAVE.EXE application by selecting Exit from the File menu.

Attaching Code to the Record Button

When the user clicks the Record button a recording session should begin. That is, immediately after you click the Record button, any sound that is picked up by the sound card's microphone should be inserted into the WAV file.

Follow these steps to attach code to the Record button:

☐ Display the ClassWizard dialog box by selecting ClassWizard from the Project menu of Visual C++.

☐ Select the Message Maps tab at the top of ClassWizard's dialog box.

☐ Use ClassWizard to select the event:

```
CWaveView -> IDC_RECORD_BUTTON -> BN_CLICKED
```

Then click the Add Function button.

☐ Name the new function OnRecordButton().

To write the code of the OnRecordButton() function do the following:

☐ Click the Edit Code button of ClassWizard.

> *ClassWizard responds by opening the file WaveView.CPP, with the function* OnRecordButton() *ready to be edited by you.*

☐ Write code inside the OnRecordButton() function so that it looks like this:

```
void CWaveView::OnRecordButton()
{
// TODO: Add your control notification handler code here

/////////////////////////
// MY CODE STARTS HERE
/////////////////////////

// Issue a Record command.
m_wav.SetStrProperty("Command", "Record");

// Disable the Play and Record buttons.
m_PlayButton.EnableWindow(FALSE);
m_RecordButton.EnableWindow(FALSE);

// Enable the Stop and Pause buttons.
m_StopButton.EnableWindow(TRUE);
m_PauseButton.EnableWindow(TRUE);

/////////////////////
// MY CODE ENDS HERE
/////////////////////

}
```

☐ Save your work by selecting Save from the File menu.

The first statement inside the OnRecordButton() function

```
m_wav.SetStrProperty("Command", "Record");
```

starts a recording session by issuing a Record command. The recording will be inserted to the current playback position, and the recording will continue until the user clicks the Stop button.

NOTE

In the WAVE.EXE application, after the user issues the `Record` command the user's recording is inserted at the current playback position, and the recording continues without any limitation (until the user clicks the Stop button).

You can set the maximum recording length by setting the From and To properties of the multimedia object prior to issuing the `Record` command. For example, the following code starts a recording session where the user's recording is inserted at the beginning of the WAV file, and the maximum recording length will be one minute (60000 milliseconds):

```
m_wav.SetNumProperty("From", 0);
m_wav.SetNumProperty("To", 60000);
m_wav.SetStrProperty("Command", "Record");
```

In order for the From and To properties to be effective, you have to set their values immediately prior to issuing the `Record` command. If the From property is not specified (as in the WAVE.EXE application), the playback starts at the current playback position. If the To property is not specified (as in the WAVE.EXE application), the recording continues until the user clicks the Stop button.

The next two statements

```
m_PlayButton.EnableWindow(FALSE);
m_RecordButton.EnableWindow(FALSE);
```

disable the Play and Record buttons. This is necessary because during the recording session the user should not be able to click these buttons.

The last two statements

```
m_StopButton.EnableWindow(TRUE);
m_PauseButton.EnableWindow(TRUE);
```

enable the Stop and Pause buttons (because during the recording session the user should be able to click these buttons).

To test your recording code do the following:

☐ Select Build WAVE.EXE from the Project menu.

☐ Select Execute WAVE.EXE from the Project menu.

☐ Click the Open ItsBeen1.WAV button.

☐ Click the Record button and speak into your sound card's microphone.

> *The WAVE.EXE application responds by inserting your recording to the current playback position (that is, at the beginning of the WAV file).*

☐ Click the Stop button to stop the recording.

☐ Click the Prev button to rewind the playback position to the beginning of the WAV file.

☐ Click the Play button.

> *The WAVE.EXE application responds by playing your recording followed by the original sound of the ITSBEEN1.WAV file.*

☐ Terminate the WAVE.EXE application by selecting Exit from the File menu.

Saving the User's Recording in the WAV File

As you have seen and heard, the WAVE.EXE application uses the m_wav multimedia object to open the WAV file ITSBEEN1.WAV. The user can then play the WAV file by clicking the Play button, and record sound into the sound file by clicking the Record button. However, the recording that the user records is not saved into the disk. In other words, once the user exits the application, the recording that the user performed is gone.

To save the WAV file to the disk, you need to issue a Save command to the multimedia object. You can do that by adding a Save button to the dialog box of the application and then attaching code to the Save button. The code that you need to attach to the Save button involves only one statement:

```
m_wav.SetStrProperty("Command", "Save");
```

This statement sets the Command property of the m_wav multimedia object to Save. In other words, it issues a Save command to the multimedia object. As stated earlier, when you issue a Save command to the multimedia object, the WAV file is saved to the disk.

Using the CTegMM.LIB Multimedia Library for Playing Through the PC Speaker

It is very easy to use the CTegMM.LIB library for other devices. For example, to play the WAV file through the internal PC speaker, all you have to do is set the DeviceType property to PCSpeaker (instead of WaveAudio).

Typically, your application will check whether your user owns a sound card and accordingly set the DeviceType property to either WaveAudio or PCSpeaker.

You can determine whether the user has a sound card as follows:

- Set the DeviceType property to WaveAudio.

- Issue an Open command.

- Check the value of the Error property. If the value of the Error property is 0 (that is, the last command was executed successfully), you know that the user has a sound card. Otherwise the user has no sound card and you should set the DeviceType property to PCSpeaker.

The following sample code opens the WAV file MySong.WAV for playback through a sound card or through the PC speaker, depending on whether the user's PC has a sound card:

```
// Set the FileName property.
m_wav.SetStrProperty("FileName", "MySong.WAV");

// Try to open the WAV file for playback
// through the sound card.
m_wav.SetStrProperty("DeviceType", "WaveAudio");
m_wav.SetStrProperty("Command", "Open");

// If the WAV file did not open successfully for a
// sound card, open it for playback through the
// PC speaker.
long error;
m_wav.GetNumProperty("Error", &error);
if (error != 0)
    {
    m_wav.SetStrProperty("DeviceType", "PCSpeaker");
    m_wav.SetStrProperty("Command", "Open");
    }
```

23

Multimedia: Playing MIDI Files

In Chapter 22, "Multimedia: Playing and
Recording WAV Files," you wrote an
application that utilizes the CTegMM.LIB
library to play a WAV file. In this chapter
you will write an application that uses the
CTegMM.LIB library to play a MIDI file.
The application that you'll write will also
illustrate how you can play a MIDI file and a
WAV file simultaneously.

The MIX Application

You'll now write the MIX application. The MIX application is an example of a multimedia application that enables the user to play a MIDI file. MIDI files are standard music files that store a series of instructions that tells the sound card how to play a piece of music. Unlike WAV files, which can play any sound (for example, music or a human voice), MIDI files are used only for playing music. MIDI files have the .MID extension (for example, MyMusic.MID).

The MIX application illustrates two programming techniques:

- How to use the CTegMM.LIB library to play a MIDI file.
- How to incorporate two multimedia objects into one application. One multimedia object is used for playing a WAV file, and the other multimedia object is used for playing a MIDI file. The user can play the WAV file and the MIDI file simultaneously.

As you will soon see, the code you need to write for playing a MIDI file is almost identical to the code you wrote in the previous chapter for playing a WAV file.

Before you start writing the MIX application, first execute the copy of it that resides in the \MVCPROG\EXE directory of the book's CD.

☐ Execute the \MVCPROG\EXE\MIX.EXE program from the book's CD.

> *Windows responds by executing the MIX.EXE application. The MIX application first displays a limited version message box from the CTegMM.LIB multimedia library. (See Figure 23.1.)*

Figure 23.1. The limited version message box of the CTegMM.LIB library.

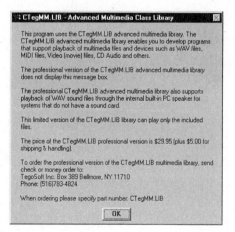

☐ Click the OK button of the message box.

The main window of MIX.EXE appears, as shown in Figure 23.2.

Figure 23.2. The main window of the MIX application.

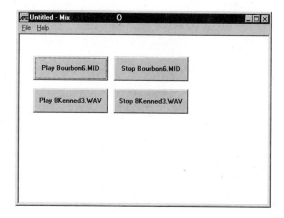

As you can see, the main window of the application has inside it four buttons: Play Bourbon6.MID, Stop Bourbon6.MID, Play 8Kenned3.WAV, and Stop 8Kenned3.WAV. As implied by the captions of these buttons, these buttons let you start the playback and stop the playback of the MIDI file Bourbon6.MID and the WAV file 8Kenned3.WAV.

To start the playback of the 8Kenned3.WAV WAV file do the following:

☐ Click the Play 8Kenned3.WAV button.

The MIX application responds by playing the WAV file 8Kenned3.WAV. As you can hear, this WAV file contains a portion of a famous speech given by former President John F. Kennedy.

☐ Now click the Play Bourbon6.MID button.

The MIX application responds by playing the MIDI file BOURBON6.MID.

You can play the WAV file and the MIDI file simultaneously:

☐ Click the Play Bourbon6.MID button, and while the music is playing, click the Play 8Kenned3.WAV button.

As you can hear, the MIX application plays the MIDI file and the WAV file simultaneously. That is, the speech of Kennedy is played with background MIDI music.

The MIX application has two pop-up menus: File and Help. These pop-up menus are shown in Figures 23.3 and 23.4.

Figure 23.3. The File pop-up menu of the MIX application.

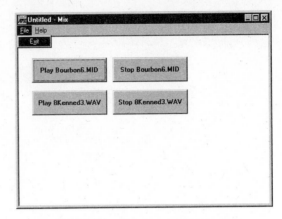

Figure 23.4. The Help pop-up menu of the MIX application.

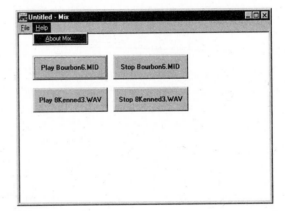

To exit the MIX application do the following:

☐ Select Exit from the File menu.

Now that you know what the MIX application should do, you can start writing it.

Creating the Project of the MIX.EXE Application

To create the project of the MIX.EXE application do the following:

☐ Start Visual C++ and close all the open windows that appear inside the desktop of Visual C++ (if there are any).

☐ Select New from the File menu.

> *Visual C++ responds by displaying the New dialog box.*

☐ Select Project inside the New dialog box and then click the OK button of the New dialog box.

> *Visual C++ responds by displaying the New Project dialog box.*

☐ Set the project name to mix.

☐ Set the project path to \MVCPROG\CH23\MIX\MIX.MAK.

Your New Project dialog box should now look like the one shown in Figure 23.5.

Figure 23.5. The New Project dialog box of the MIX.MAK project.

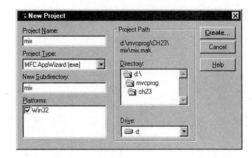

☐ Click the Create button of the New Project dialog box.

Visual C++ responds by displaying the AppWizard—Step 1 window.

☐ Set the Step 1 window as shown in Figure 23.6. As shown in Figure 23.6, the MIX.MAK project is set as a single-document interface application, and U.S. English (APPWIZUS.DLL) is the language used for the application's resources.

Figure 23.6. The AppWizard—Step 1 window for the MIX application.

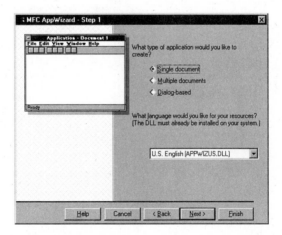

☐ Click the Next button of the Step 1 window.

Visual C++ responds by displaying the AppWizard—Step 2 of 6 window.

☐ Set the Step 2 of 6 window as shown in Figure 23.7. That is, in the MIX application you don't want any database support.

Figure 23.7. The
AppWizard—Step 2 of 6
window for the MIX
application.

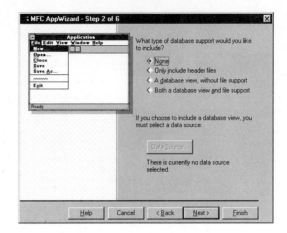

☐ Click the Next button of the Step 2 of 6 window.

  Visual C++ responds by displaying the AppWizard—Step 3 of 6 window.

☐ Set the Step 3 of 6 window as shown in Figure 23.8. That is, in the MIX application you don't want any OLE support.

Figure 23.8. The
AppWizard—Step 3 of 6
window for the MIX
application.

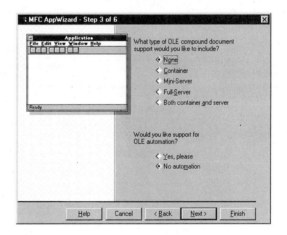

☐ Click the Next button of the Step 3 of 6 window.

  Visual C++ responds by displaying the AppWizard—Step 4 of 6 window.

☐ Set the Step 4 of 6 window as shown in Figure 23.9.

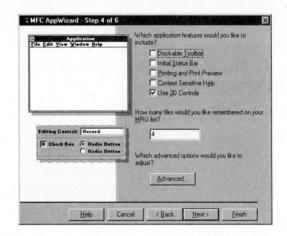

Figure 23.9. The AppWizard—Step 4 of 6 window for the MIX application.

As shown in Figure 23.9, the features Dockable Toolbar, Initial Status Bar, Printing and Print Preview, and Context Sensitive Help will not be included in the MIX application.

☐ Click the Next button of the Step 4 of 6 window.

Visual C++ responds by displaying the AppWizard—Step 5 of 6 window.

☐ Set the Step 5 of 6 window as shown in Figure 23.10.

As shown in Figure 23.10, the project will be generated with comments, a Visual C++ makefile will be generated, and the application will use the MFC library from a DLL.

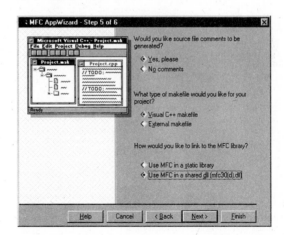

Figure 23.10. The AppWizard—Step 5 of 6 window for the MIX application.

☐ Click the Next button of the Step 5 of 6 window.

Visual C++ responds by displaying the AppWizard—Step 6 of 6 window.

You'll now use the AppWizard—Step 6 of 6 window to tell AppWizard to derive the view class of the application from the MFC class `CFormView`:

☐ Select the `CMixView` class inside the AppWizard—Step 6 of 6 window.

☐ Set the Base Class drop-down list box to `CFormView`.

Your AppWizard—Step 6 of 6 window should now look like the one shown in Figure 23.11.

Figure 23.11. The AppWizard—Step 6 of 6 window after you set the base class of the application view class to `CFormView`.

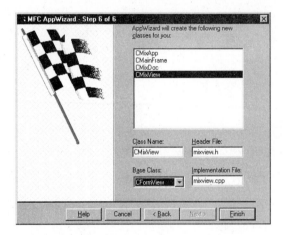

☐ Click the Finish button of the Step 6 of 6 window.

Visual C++ responds by displaying the New Project Information window, as shown in Figure 23.12.

Figure 23.12. The New Project Information window of the MIX.MAK project.

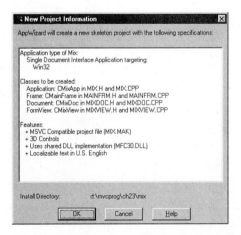

☐ Click the OK button of the New Project Information window.

Visual C++ responds by creating the project file and all the skeleton files of the application.

Creating the Form of the Application

Because in AppWizard you specified that the base class of the application's view class is CFormView, AppWizard created for you a form (a dialog box) that is attached to the view class of the application. This dialog box serves as the main window of the application. AppWizard named this dialog box IDD_MIX_FORM. You'll now customize the IDD_MIX_FORM dialog box until it looks like the one shown back in Figure 23.2.

☐ Select mix.mak from the Window menu to display the mix.mak window, double-click mix.rc inside the mix.mak window to display the mix.rc window, double-click the Dialog item that appears inside the mix.rc window to display a list of dialog boxes, and finally, double-click the IDD_MIX_FORM item that appears under the Dialog item.

Visual C++ responds by displaying the IDD_MIX_FORM dialog box in design mode.

☐ Delete the TODO static text by clicking on it and pressing the Delete key on your keyboard.

☐ Design the IDD_MIX_FORM dialog box according to the specifications in Table 23.1. When you finish implementing the dialog box, it should look like the one shown in Figure 23.13.

Table 23.1. The Properties table for the IDD_MIX_FORM dialog box.

Object	Property	Setting
Dialog box	ID	IDD_MIX_FORM
Push button	ID	IDC_PLAY_MIDI_BUTTON
	Caption	Play Bourbon6.MID
Push button	ID	IDC_STOP_MIDI_BUTTON
	Caption	Stop Bourbon6.MID
Push button	ID	IDC_PLAY_WAV_BUTTON
	Caption	Play 8Kenned3.WAV
Push button	ID	IDC_STOP_WAV_BUTTON
	Caption	Stop 8Kenned3.WAV

Figure 23.13. The IDD_MIX_FORM dialog box (in design mode).

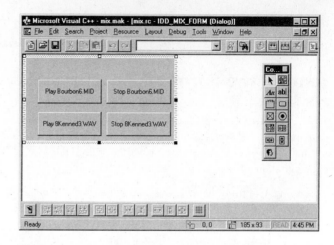

The Visual Implementation of the Menu

You'll now visually implement the menu of the MIX application.

☐ Select mix.rc from the Window menu to display the mix.rc window, double-click Menu, and finally, double-click IDR_MAINFRAME.

Visual C++ responds by displaying the IDR_MAINFRAME menu in design mode.

☐ Implement the IDR_MAINFRAME menu so that it includes the following items:

&File
    E&xit
&Help
    &About Wave...

Save your work:

☐ Select Save from the File menu.

The visual implementation of the menu of the MIX.EXE application is complete.

To see your visual design in action do the following:

☐ Select Build MIX.EXE from the Project menu of Visual C++.

☐ Select Execute MIX.EXE from the Project menu.

Visual C++ responds by executing the MIX.EXE application. The main window of the application appears with the form that you designed inside it. The form includes four push buttons.

In the following sections you'll write the code that brings these push buttons to life.

To exit the MIX.EXE application do the following:

☐ Select Exit from the File menu.

Adding the CTegMM.LIB Library to the MIX.MAK Project

Later you will write code that uses the CTegMM multimedia class from the CTegMM.LIB library. Therefore, you need to add the CTegMM.LIB library to the MIX.MAK project file. Here is how you do that:

☐ Select Files from the Project menu of Visual C++.

Visual C++ responds by displaying the Project Files dialog box for the MIX.MAK project.

☐ Type C:\MVCPROG\LIB\CTEGMM.LIB inside the File Name edit box of the Project Files dialog box. (Note that if you installed the book's CD to your D: drive you need to type D:\MVCPROG\LIB\CTEGMM.LIB.)

☐ Click the Add button.

Visual C++ responds by adding the CTEGMM.LIB file to the MIX.MAK project.

☐ Click the Close button of the Project Files dialog box.

The CTEGMM.LIB library is now part of the MIX.MAK project. In the following sections you'll use the CTegMM multimedia class from the CTEGMM.LIB library.

Declaring Two Objects of Class *CTegMM*

In the WAVE.EXE application of Chapter 22 you declared a multimedia object (m_wav) of class CTegMM and you used this object to open and play a WAV file. In the MIX.EXE application you will declare two multimedia objects: m_wav and m_mid. You'll use the m_wav object to play a WAV file and you'll use the m_mid object to play a MIDI file.

You'll declare the m_wav and m_mid objects as public data members of the view class. This way m_wav and m_mid will be visible in all the member functions of the view class.

Follow these steps to declare the m_wav and m_mid objects:

☐ Select Open from the File menu of Visual C++ and open the MIXVIEW.H header file.

☐ Declare the m_wav and m_mid objects as public data members of the CMixView class. After you declare m_wav and m_mid, the CMixView class declaration should look like this:

```
class CMixView : public CFormView
{
protected: // create from serialization only
   CMixView();
   DECLARE_DYNCREATE(CMixView)
```

```
public:
    //{{AFX_DATA(CMixView)
    enum{ IDD = IDD_MIX_FORM };
    // NOTE: the ClassWizard will add data members here
    //}}AFX_DATA

// Attributes
public:
    CMixDoc* GetDocument();

    /////////////////////////
    // MY CODE STARTS HERE
    /////////////////////////

    CTegMM m_mid;
    CTegMM m_wav;

    /////////////////////////
    // MY CODE ENDS HERE
    /////////////////////////

// Operations
public:

// Overrides
// ClassWizard generated virtual function overrides
//{{AFX_VIRTUAL(CMixView)
public:
protected:
virtual void DoDataExchange(CDataExchange* pDX);
//}}AFX_VIRTUAL

// Implementation
public:
    virtual ~CMixView();
#ifdef _DEBUG
    virtual void AssertValid() const;
    virtual void Dump(CDumpContext& dc) const;
#endif

protected:

// Generated message map functions
protected:
    //{{AFX_MSG(CMixView)
    afx_msg void OnPlayMidiButton();
    afx_msg void OnStopMidiButton();
    afx_msg void OnPlayWavButton();
    afx_msg void OnStopWavButton();
    //}}AFX_MSG
DECLARE_MESSAGE_MAP()
};
```

If you try to compile and link the MIX application now, you'll get a compiling error. Why? In the preceding code you declared two objects of class CTegMM, but the CTegMM class is not known in the MIXVIEW.H file. Therefore, you need to use #include on the header file of the CTegMM class at the beginning of the MIXVIEW.H file:

☐ Add the statement `#include "\MVCPROG\LIB\CTEGMM.H"` at the beginning of the MIXVIEW.H file. After you add this statement, the beginning of the MIXVIEW.H file should look like this:

```
// mixview.h : interface of the CMixView class
//
/////////////////////////////////////////////////

////////////////////////
// MY CODE STARTS HERE
////////////////////////

#include "\mvcprog\lib\ctegmm.h"

////////////////////////
// MY CODE ENDS HERE
////////////////////////
```

☐ Save your work by selecting Save from the File menu.

Attaching Code to the Play Bourbon6.MID Button

When the user clicks the Play Bourbon6.MID button, the MIX.EXE application should start playing the Bourbon6.MID file.

The code that you'll now attach to the Play Bourbon6.MID button will perform two tasks:

- Open the Bourbon6.MID file if the file has not been opened already. That is, when the user clicks the Play Bourbon6.MID button for the first time, the code will open the Bourbon6.MID file.
- Play the Bourbon6.MID file.

Follow these steps to attach code to the Play Bourbon6.MID button:

☐ Display the ClassWizard dialog box by selecting ClassWizard from the Project menu of Visual C++.

☐ Select the Message Maps tab at the top of ClassWizard's dialog box.

☐ Use ClassWizard to select the event:

`CWaveView -> IDC_PLAY_MIDI_BUTTON -> BN_CLICKED`

Then click the Add Function button.

☐ Name the new function `OnPlayMidiButton()`.

To write the code of the `OnPlayMidiButton()` function do the following:

☐ Click the Edit Code button of ClassWizard.

> *ClassWizard responds by opening the file MixView.CPP, with the function* `OnPlayMidiButton()` *ready to be edited by you.*

☐ Write code inside the `OnPlayMidiButton()` function so that it looks like this:

```
void CMixView::OnPlayMidiButton()
{
// TODO: Add your control notification handler code here

/////////////////////////
// MY CODE STARTS HERE
/////////////////////////

// Declare and initialize the FileIsOpen flag.
static int FileIsOpen = 0;

// If file has not been opened yet, open it.
if ( FileIsOpen == 0 )
    {

    // Fill the string file_name with the full pathname
    // of the BOURBON6.MID file.
    char file_name[300];
    strncpy(file_name,__argv[0],2);
    file_name[2]=0;
    strcat(file_name,"\\MVCPROG\\MIDI\\BOURBON6.MID");

    // Open the BOURBON6.MID file.
    m_mid.SetStrProperty("DeviceType", "Sequencer");
    m_mid.SetStrProperty("FileName", file_name);
    m_mid.SetStrProperty("Command", "Open");

    // If Open command failed, display an error message box.
    long error;
    m_mid.GetNumProperty("Error", &error);
    if (error != 0 )
        {
        // Display an error message box.
        char err_msg[300];
        m_mid.GetStrProperty("ErrorMessage", err_msg);
        ::MessageBox(NULL, err_msg, "Error", 0);
        }
    else
        {
        // File has been opened successfully.
        FileIsOpen = 1;
        }

    }

// Rewind the playback position to the beginning
// of the file.
m_mid.SetStrProperty("Command", "Prev");

// Start playing.
m_mid.SetStrProperty("Command", "Play");

/////////////////////////
// MY CODE ENDS HERE
/////////////////////////

}
```

☐ Save your work by selecting Save from the File menu.

The first statement in the `OnPlayMidiButton()` function

```
static int FileIsOpen = 0;
```

declares and initializes the static variable `FileIsOpen`. This variable is used as a flag to indicate whether the Bourbon6.MID file has already been opened. When the user clicks the Play Bourbon6.MID button for the first time, the preceding statement initializes the `FileOpen` flag to 0 to indicate that the Bourbon6.MID file has not been opened yet.

The next statement is an `if` statement that evaluates the `FileIsOpen` flag:

```
// If file has not been opened yet, open it.
if ( FileIsOpen == 0 )
    {
    ...
    ...
    ...
    ...
    }
```

This `if` statement checks whether the `FileIsOpen` flag is equal to 0. If it is equal to 0, you know that the Bourbon6.MID file has not been opened yet (that is, this is the first time the user is clicking the Play Bourbon6.MID button) and the statements under the `if` are executed:

```
// Fill the string file_name with the full pathname
// of the BOURBON6.MID file.
char file_name[300];
strncpy(file_name,__argv[0],2);
file_name[2]=0;
strcat(file_name,"\\MVCPROG\\MIDI\\BOURBON6.MID");

// Open the BOURBON6.MID file.
m_mid.SetStrProperty("DeviceType", "Sequencer");
m_mid.SetStrProperty("FileName", file_name);
m_mid.SetStrProperty("Command", "Open");

// If Open command failed, display an error message box.
long error;
m_mid.GetNumProperty("Error", &error);
if (error != 0 )
    {
    // Display an error message box.
    char err_msg[300];
    m_mid.GetStrProperty("ErrorMessage", err_msg);
    ::MessageBox(NULL, err_msg, "Error", 0);
    }
else
    {
    // File has been opened successfully.
    FileIsOpen = 1;
    }
```

These statements perform the following tasks:

- The Bourbon6.MID file is opened.

- If the file is not opened successfully (that is, the Error property of the multimedia object is not 0), an error message box is displayed. The message box displays the ErrorMessage property of the multimedia object. As implied by its name, the ErrorMessage property holds a message (string) that corresponds to the last error that occurred.

- If the file is opened successfully, the `FileIsOpen` flag is set to 1 to indicate that the Bourbon6.MID file is open. This is done so that the next time the user clicks the Play Bourbon6.MID button, the program will not open the Bourbon6.MID file again.

The Bourbon6.MID file is opened as follows:

First the local string variable `file_name` is filled with the full pathname of the BOURBON6.MID file:

```
char file_name[300];
strncpy(file_name,__argv[0],2);
file_name[2]=0;
strcat(file_name,"\\MVCPROG\\MIDI\\BOURBON6.MID");
```

NOTE

In the preceding code, `argv[0]` is preceded with two underscores (`__`). `__argv[0]` is a string that holds the full pathname of the application's EXE file. For example, if the MIX.EXE application is executed from the C:\TRY directory, `__argv[0]` will hold the string `"C:\TRY\MIX.EXE"`.

Therefore, the statement

```
strncpy(file_name,__argv[0],2);
```

fills the first two characters of the `file_name` variable with the letter drive (for example, C:) of the drive in which the application's EXE file resides.

At this point, the string variable `file_name` holds the full pathname of the BOURBON6.MID file. For example, if you are executing the MIX.EXE application from the D: drive, the `file_name` variable is filled with the string `"D:\MVCPROG\MIDI\BOURBON6.MID"`.

The next three statements open the BOURBON6.MID file by setting the DeviceType and FileName properties of the `m_mid` multimedia object and by issuing an `Open` command:

```
m_mid.SetStrProperty("DeviceType", "Sequencer");
m_mid.SetStrProperty("FileName", file_name);
m_mid.SetStrProperty("Command", "Open");
```

NOTE

When you want to use a multimedia object for playing a MIDI file, you need to set the DeviceType property of the multimedia object to Sequencer. For example, the following statements open the file MyMusic.MID:

```
m_mid.SetStrProperty("DeviceType","Sequencer");
m_mid.SetStrProperty("FileName","MyMusic.MID");
m_mid.SetStrProperty("Command","Open");
```

The last two statements inside the OnPlayMidiButton() function are

```
// Rewind the playback position to the beginning
// of the file.
m_mid.SetStrProperty("Command", "Prev");

// Start playing.
m_mid.SetStrProperty("Command", "Play");
```

The first statement rewinds the playback position of the MIDI file to the beginning of the file by issuing a Prev command, and the second statement starts the playback by issuing a Play command.

To hear the code that you attached to the Play Bourbon6.MID file in action do the following:

☐ Select Build MIX.EXE from the Project menu.

☐ Select Execute MIX.EXE from the Project menu.

☐ Click the Play Bourbon6.MID button.

> *The MIX.EXE application responds by opening and playing the MIDI file BOURBON6.MID.*

Because the BOURBON6.MID file is now open, if you click the Play Bourbon6.MID button again, the code that you wrote will not open the BOURBON6.MID file again; it will just play the file.

Attaching Code to the Stop Bourbon6.MID Button

When the user clicks the Stop Bourbon6.MID button, the playback of the Bourbon6.MID file should stop.

Follow these steps to attach code to the Stop Bourbon6.MID button:

☐ Display the ClassWizard dialog box by selecting ClassWizard from the Project menu of Visual C++.

☐ Select the Message Maps tab at the top of ClassWizard's dialog box.

☐ Use ClassWizard to select the event:

```
CMixView -> IDC_STOP_MIDI_BUTTON -> BN_CLICKED
```

Then click the Add Function button.

☐ Name the new function `OnStopMidiButton()`.

To write the code of the `OnStopMidiButton()` function do the following:

☐ Click the Edit Code button of ClassWizard.

> *ClassWizard responds by opening the file MixView.CPP, with the function* `OnStopMidiButton()` *ready to be edited by you.*

☐ Write code inside the `OnStopMidiButton()` function so that it looks like this:

```
void CMixView::OnStopMidiButton()
{
// TODO: Add your control notification handler code here

/////////////////////////
// MY CODE STARTS HERE
/////////////////////////

// Issue a Stop command.
m_mid.SetStrProperty("Command", "Stop");

/////////////////////////
// MY CODE ENDS HERE
/////////////////////////

}
```

☐ Save your work by selecting Save from the File menu.

The code you just typed inside the `OnStopMidiButton()` function is made of one statement:

```
m_mid.SetStrProperty("Command", "Stop");
```

This statement stops the playback of the MIDI file by issuing a `Stop` command to the `m_mid` multimedia object.

To see the code that you attached to the Stop Bourbon6.MID button in action do the following:

☐ Select Build MIX.EXE from the Project menu.

☐ Select Execute MIX.EXE from the Project menu.

☐ Click the Play Bourbon6.MID button.

> *The MIX.EXE application responds by playing the Bourbon6.MID file.*

☐ While the MIDI file is playing click the Stop Bourbon6.MID button.

> *As expected, the playback stops.*

☐ Terminate the MIX.EXE application by selecting Exit from the File menu.

Attaching Code to the Play 8Kenned3.WAV Button

When the user clicks the Play 8Kenned3.WAV button, the MIX.EXE application should start playing the 8Kenned3.WAV file.

Follow these steps to attach code to the Play 8Kenned3.WAV button:

☐ Display the ClassWizard dialog box by selecting ClassWizard from the Project menu of Visual C++.

☐ Select the Message Maps tab at the top of ClassWizard's dialog box.

☐ Use ClassWizard to select the event:

```
CWaveView -> IDC_PLAY_WAV_BUTTON -> BN_CLICKED
```

Then click the Add Function button.

☐ Name the new function `OnPlayWavButton()`.

To write the code of the `OnPlayWavButton()` function do the following:

☐ Click the Edit Code button of ClassWizard.

> *ClassWizard responds by opening the file MixView.CPP, with the function* `OnPlayWavButton()` *ready to be edited by you.*

☐ Write code inside the `OnPlayWavButton()` function so that it looks like this:

```
void CMixView::OnPlayWavButton()
{
// TODO: Add your control notification handler code here

/////////////////////////
// MY CODE STARTS HERE
/////////////////////////

// Declare and initialize the FileIsOpen flag.
static int FileIsOpen = 0;

// If file has not been opened yet, open it.
if ( FileIsOpen == 0 )
   {
   // Fill the string file_name with the full pathname
   // of the 8KENNED3.WAV file.
   char file_name[300];
   strncpy(file_name,__argv[0],2);
   file_name[2]=0;
   strcat(file_name,"\\MVCPROG\\WAV\\8KENNED3.WAV");

   // Open the 8KENNED3.WAV file.
   m_wav.SetStrProperty("DeviceType", "WaveAudio");
   m_wav.SetStrProperty("FileName", file_name);
   m_wav.SetStrProperty("Command", "Open");

   // If Open command failed, display an error message box.
```

```
    long error;
    m_wav.GetNumProperty("Error", &error);
    if (error != 0 )
        {
        // Display an error message box.
        char err_msg[300];
        m_mid.GetStrProperty("ErrorMessage", err_msg);
        ::MessageBox(NULL, err_msg, "Error", 0);
        }
    else
        {
        // File has been opened successfully.
        FileIsOpen = 1;
        }

    }

// Rewind the playback position to the beginning
// of the file.
m_wav.SetStrProperty("Command", "Prev");

// Start playing.
m_wav.SetStrProperty("Command", "Play");

/////////////////////
// MY CODE ENDS HERE
/////////////////////

}
```

☐ Save your work by selecting Save from the File menu.

As you can see, the code you just typed inside the OnPlayWavButton() function is almost identical to the code you wrote earlier inside the OnPlayMidiButton() function. The only difference is that now all the statements are working on the m_wav multimedia object (not on the m_mid multimedia object) and the DeviceType property is set to WaveAudio (not to Sequencer).

Attaching Code to the Stop 8Kenned3.WAV Button

When the user clicks the Stop 8Kenned3.WAV button, the playback of the 8Kenned3.WAV file should stop.

Follow these steps to attach code to the Stop 8Kenned3.WAV button:

☐ Display the ClassWizard dialog box by selecting ClassWizard from the Project menu of Visual C++.

☐ Select the Message Maps tab at the top of ClassWizard's dialog box.

☐ Use ClassWizard to select the event:

```
CMixView -> IDC_STOP_WAV_BUTTON -> BN_CLICKED
```

Then click the Add Function button.

☐ Name the new function OnStopWavButton().

To write the code of the `OnStopWavButton()` function do the following:

☐ Click the Edit Code button of ClassWizard.

> *ClassWizard responds by opening the file MixView.CPP, with the function*
> `OnStopWavButton()` *ready to be edited by you.*

☐ Write code inside the `OnStopWavButton()` function so that it looks like this:

```
void CMixView::OnStopWavButton()
{
// TODO: Add your control notification handler code here

/////////////////////////
// MY CODE STARTS HERE
/////////////////////////

// Issue a Stop command.
m_wav.SetStrProperty("Command", "Stop");

/////////////////////////
// MY CODE ENDS HERE
/////////////////////////

}
```

☐ Save your work by selecting Save from the File menu.

The code that you just typed inside the `OnStopWavButton()` function is made of one statement:

```
m_wav.SetStrProperty("Command", "Stop");
```

This statement stops the playback of the 8Kenned3.WAV file by issuing a `Stop` command to the `m_wav` multimedia object.

To see the code that you attached to the Play 8Kenned3.WAV button and to the Stop 8Kenned3.WAV button in action do the following:

☐ Select Build MIX.EXE from the Project menu.

☐ Select Execute MIX.EXE from the Project menu.

☐ Click the Play 8Kenned3.WAV button.

> *The MIX.EXE application responds by playing the 8Kenned3.WAV file.*

☐ While the 8Kenned3.WAV file is playing, click the Stop 8Kenned3.WAV button.

> *As expected, the playback of the 8Kenned3.WAV file stops.*

☐ Experiment with the MIX.EXE application. In particular, verify that you can play the 8Kenned3.WAV file and Bourbon6.MID file simultaneously.

24

Multimedia: Video for Windows

In Chapter 22, "Multimedia: Playing and Recording WAV Files," and Chapter 23, "Multimedia: Playing MIDI Files," you wrote applications that use the CTegMM.LIB library for playing a WAV file and a MIDI file. In this chapter you will write an application that uses the CTegMM.LIB library to play a Windows-compatible video file (AVI file).

Playing Video Files

Video files contain real movies. A video file includes the video (that is, the pictures) as well as the sound track of a movie. When you play a video file on your PC, the pictures of the movie are displayed on your PC's monitor and the sound is played through your sound card.

If you don't have a sound card, you can still see the video portion of the movie. As you will soon see, playing a video file on your PC is quite impressive even if you don't have a sound card.

Before You Can Play Video Files on Your PC...

Before you can play video files on your PC, you have to install special software drivers that enable your Windows system to play video files.

To see if your Windows system currently has the software drivers necessary for playing video files do the following:

☐ Start the Media Player program of Windows. The Media Player program is usually in the Accessories group of programs.

Windows responds by running the Media Player program. (See Figure 24.1.)

NOTE

Windows includes a program called Media Player that enables you to play various multimedia files.

The Media Player program is usually in the Accessories group.

Figure 24.1. The Media Player program.

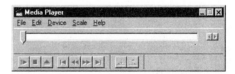

If your Windows system has the software drivers needed for playing video files, your Media Player program can play video files.

To see if your Media Player program can play video files do the following:

☐ Open the Device menu of Media Player. (See Figure 24.2.)

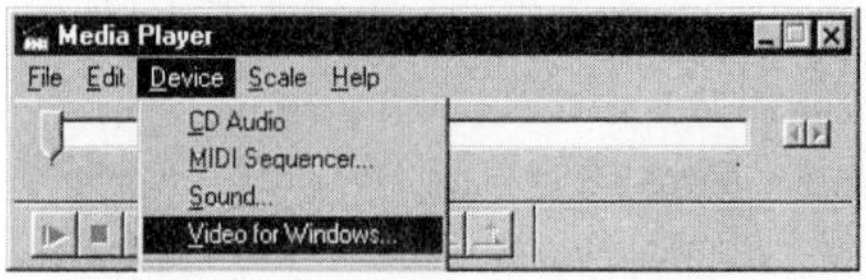

Figure 24.2. The Device menu of Media Player.

As you can see from Figure 24.2, one of the items in the Device menu is Video for Windows. If the Device menu of your Media Player program does not include this item, you know that your Windows system does not have the necessary software drivers to play video files.

☐ Terminate the Media Player program by selecting Exit from the File menu.

The following section describes how to install the software drivers necessary for playing video files.

Installing the Video for Windows Software Drivers

As discussed earlier, if the Device menu of your Media player program does not include the Video for Windows option, your Windows system does not have the software drivers necessary for playing video files.

To install the Video for Windows software drivers you need to run a special Setup program that includes in it all the necessary video drivers. After running this Setup program, you will be able to play video files in Windows. This Setup program is included with the book's CD.

To install the Video for Windows software drivers using the Setup program that is included with the book's CD, complete the following steps:

☐ Prepare a blank high-density disk and insert it into your A: drive (or B: drive).

☐ Insert the book's CD into your CD-ROM drive.

☐ Copy all the files from the \MVCPROG\VIDEO directory of the book's CD into the root directory of the blank disk.

☐ Execute the A:\Setup.EXE (or B:\Setup.EXE) program from the disk that you prepared.

> *The Setup program initializes itself, and after a while it displays a Welcome dialog box. (See Figures 24.3 and 24.4.)*

Figure 24.3. The Setup program initializing itself.

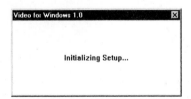

☐ Click the Continue button of the Welcome dialog box.

> *The Setup program responds by installing all the necessary video software drivers in your Windows system. When the installation is complete, the Setup program displays a Setup Successful dialog box. (See Figure 24.5.)*

Figure 24.4. The Welcome window of the Setup program.

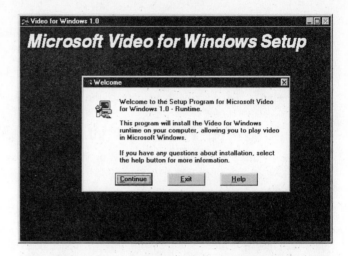

Figure 24.5. The Setup Successful dialog box of the Setup program.

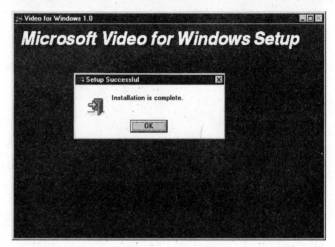

☐ Click the OK button of the Setup Successful dialog box.

Now that you've finished installing the Video for Windows software drivers, you can start playing video files.

The following section describes how to play a video file with the Media Player program of Windows. Later in the chapter you'll write your own program (a Visual C++ application) that plays a Video file.

Playing a Video File with Media Player

Windows-compatible video files have an AVI file extension (for example, MyMovie.AVI). Just as WAV files are used in Windows to play sound, AVI files are used to play movies.

In the following steps, you will use Media Player to play an AVI file (MOVIE.AVI) from the \MVCPROG\AVI directory of the book's CD.

To play the MOVIE.AVI video file with Media Player do the following:

☐ Start the Media Player program.

> *The window of Media Player appears, as shown back in Figure 24.1.*

☐ Insert the book's CD into your CD-ROM drive.

☐ Select Video for Windows from the Device menu of Media Player. (See Figure 24.2.)

> *Media Player responds by displaying an Open dialog box. (See Figure 24.6.)*

Figure 24.6. The Open dialog box of Media Player.

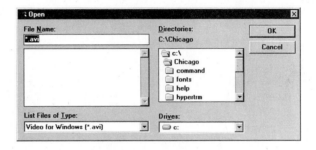

☐ Select the file X:\MVCPROG\AVI\MOVIE.AVI (where *X* is the letter drive of your CD-ROM drive).

> *Media Player responds by opening the MOVIE.AVI video file and by displaying the first frame (picture) of the movie.*

To start playing the movie do the following:

☐ Click the Play button (the extreme left button) of Media Player.

> *Media Player responds by playing the MOVIE.AVI video file.*

To stop the playback of the file do the following:

☐ Click the Stop button (the second button from the left).

You can use the horizontal scroll bar of Media Player to navigate to a particular frame in the movie. For example, to start the playback from the middle of the movie, drag the thumb tab of the horizontal scroll bar to the middle of the scroll bar and then click the Play button.

To terminate the Media Player program do the following:

☐ Select Exit from the File menu of Media player.

Creating Your Own Video Files

To create a video file yourself, you need the following hardware and software:

- A video device such as a VCR or a camcorder
- A video capture card
- A video capture program

You create the video file by connecting the video device (the VCR or camcorder) to the video card with cables. The video capture program processes the video that is received from the video device and it creates the video file. (See Figure 24.7.)

Figure 24.7. Creating your own video file.

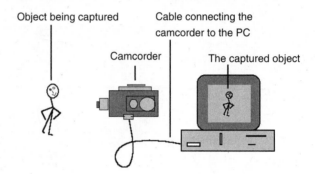

Object being captured   Cable connecting the camcorder to the PC

Camcorder   The captured object

The AVI Application

You'll now write the AVI application. The AVI application is an example of a multimedia application that enables the user to play an AVI file.

As you will soon see, the code you need to write to play an AVI file is similar to the code you wrote in Chapters 22 and 23 to play a WAV file and a MIDI file.

Before you start writing the AVI application, first execute the copy of it that resides in the \MVCPROG\EXE directory of the book's CD.

☐ Execute the \MVCPROG\EXE\AVI.EXE program from the book's CD.

   Windows responds by executing the AVI.EXE application. The AVI application first displays a limited version message box from the CTegMM.LIB multimedia library. (See Figure 24.8.)

☐ Click the OK button of the message box.

   The main window of AVI.EXE appears, as shown in Figure 24.9.

As you can see, the main window of the application has inside it five buttons (Open Movie.AVI, Play, Stop, Step, and Back) and two check boxes (Auto Repeat and Silent).

As you can see, the Play, Stop, Step, and Back buttons are currently disabled. That's because you have not opened the AVI file yet.

Figure 24.8. The limited version message box of the CTegMM.LIB library.

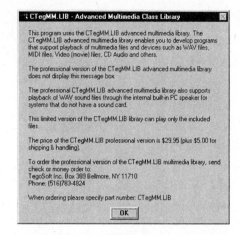

Figure 24.9. The main window of the AVI application.

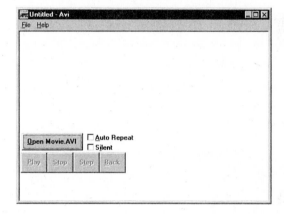

To open the MOVIE.AVI video file do the following:

☐ Click the Open Movie.AVI button.

> *The AVI application responds by opening the MOVIE.AVI file and by displaying the first frame (picture) of the MOVIE.AVI video. (See Figure 24.10.)*

Note that now the Play, Step, and Back buttons are enabled. The Stop button is disabled because there is currently no playback in progress.

To start the playback of the Movie.AVI video do the following:

☐ Click the Play button.

> *The AVI application responds by playing the Movie.AVI video. As you can see and hear, the Movie.AVI video has both pictures and sound.*

Note that during the playback, the Stop button is enabled, and the Play button is disabled.

Figure 24.10. The AVI application after you click the Open Movie.AVI button.

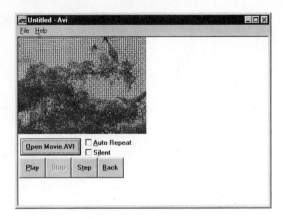

You can use the Step and Back buttons to view the video frame by frame:

☐ Click the Step button several times.

As you can see, each time you click the Step button, the next frame of the video is displayed.

☐ Click the Back button several times.

As you can see, each time you click the Back button, the previous frame is displayed.

The AVI application includes an Auto Repeat feature. To see Auto Repeat in action do the following:

☐ Place a checkmark inside the Auto Repeat check box and then click the Play button.

The AVI application responds by playing the video file. Once the playback reaches the end of the file, the playback automatically repeats itself. The playback will keep repeating in an endless loop until you either click the Stop button or uncheck the Auto Repeat check box.

The AVI application enables you to play the video without sound. To see this feature in action do the following:

☐ Place a checkmark inside the Silent check box and then click the Play button.

As you can hear (or rather, not hear), the movie is played without sound.

Note that you can check and uncheck the Silent check box while playback is in progress. As soon as you check or uncheck the Silent check box, the movie immediately becomes silent or not silent.

The AVI application has two pop-up menus: File and Help. These pop-up menus are shown in Figures 24.11 and 24.12.

To exit the AVI application do the following:

☐ Select Exit from the File menu.

Now that you know what the AVI application should do, you can start writing it.

Figure 24.11. The File pop-up menu of the AVI application.

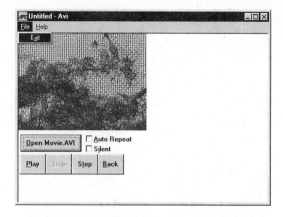

Figure 24.12. The Help pop-up menu of the AVI application.

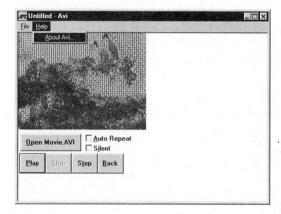

Creating the Project of the AVI Application

To create the project of the AVI application do the following:

☐ Start Visual C++ and close all the open windows that appear inside the desktop of Visual C++ (if there are any).

☐ Select New from the File menu.

Visual C++ responds by displaying the New dialog box.

☐ Select Project inside the New dialog box and then click the OK button of the New dialog box.

Visual C++ responds by displaying the New Project dialog box.

☐ Set the project name to avi.

☐ Set the project path to \MVCPROG\CH24\AVI\AVI.MAK.

Your New Project dialog box should now look like the one shown in Figure 24.13.

Figure 24.13. The New Project dialog box of the AVI.MAK project.

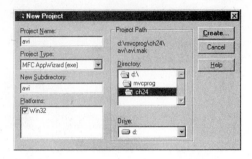

☐ Click the Create button of the New Project dialog box.

   Visual C++ responds by displaying the AppWizard—Step 1 window.

☐ Set the Step 1 window as shown in Figure 24.14. As shown in Figure 24.14, the AVI.MAK project is set as a single-document application, and U.S. English (APPWIZUS.DLL) is used as the language for the application's resources.

Figure 24.14.   The AppWizard—Step 1 window for the AVI application.

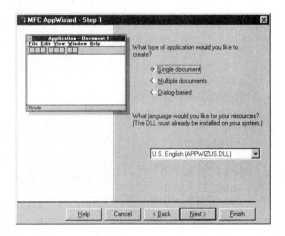

☐ Click the Next button of the Step 1 window.

   Visual C++ responds by displaying the AppWizard—Step 2 of 6 window.

☐ Set the Step 2 of 6 window as shown in Figure 24.15. That is, in the AVI application you don't want any database support.

☐ Click the Next button of the Step 2 of 6 window.

   Visual C++ responds by displaying the AppWizard—Step 3 of 6 window.

☐ Set the Step 3 of 6 window as shown in Figure 24.16. That is, in the AVI application you don't want any OLE support.

☐ Click the Next button of the Step 3 of 6 window.

   Visual C++ responds by displaying the AppWizard—Step 4 of 6 window.

Figure 24.15. The AppWizard—Step 2 of 6 window for the AVI application.

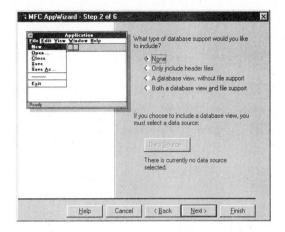

Figure 24.16. The AppWizard—Step 3 of 6 window for the AVI application.

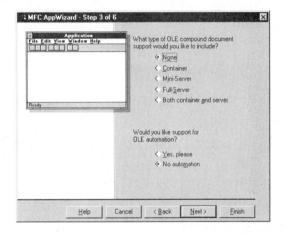

☐ Set the Step 4 of 6 window as shown in Figure 24.17.

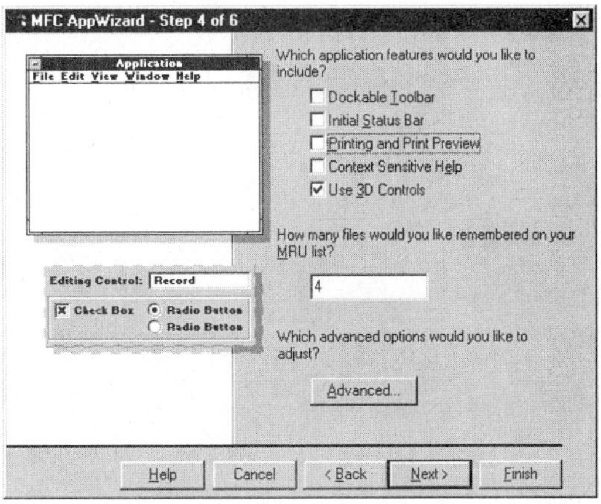

Figure 24.17. The AppWizard—Step 4 of 6 window for the AVI application.

As shown in Figure 24.17, the features Dockable Toolbar, Initial Status Bar, Printing and Print Preview, and Context Sensitive Help will not be included in the AVI application.

☐ Click the Next button of the Step 4 of 6 window.

> *Visual C++ responds by displaying the AppWizard—Step 5 of 6 window.*

☐ Set the Step 5 of 6 window as shown in Figure 24.18.

As shown in Figure 24.18, the project will be generated with comments, a Visual C++ makefile will be generated, and the application will use the MFC library from a DLL.

Figure 24.18. The AppWizard—Step 5 of 6 window for the AVI application.

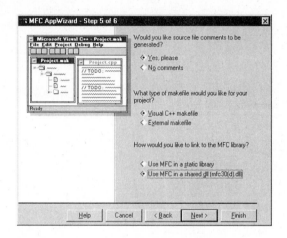

☐ Click the Next button of the Step 5 of 6 window.

> *Visual C++ responds by displaying the AppWizard—Step 6 of 6 window.*

You'll now use the AppWizard—Step 6 of 6 window to tell AppWizard to derive the view class of the application from the MFC class CFormView:

☐ Select the CAviView class inside the AppWizard—Step 6 of 6 window.

☐ Set the Base Class drop-down list box to CFormView.

Your AppWizard—Step 6 of 6 window should now look like the one shown in Figure 24.19.

☐ Click the Finish button of the Step 6 of 6 window.

> *Visual C++ responds by displaying the New Project Information window, as shown in Figure 24.20.*

☐ Click the OK button of the New Project Information window.

> *Visual C++ responds by creating the project file and all the skeleton files of the application.*

Figure 24.19. The
AppWizard—Step 6 of 6
window after you set the
base class of the application
view class to CFormView.

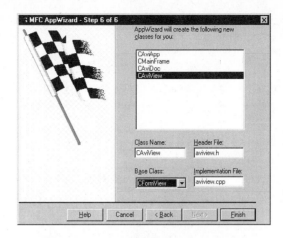

Figure 24.20. The New
Project Information
window of the AVI.MAK
project.

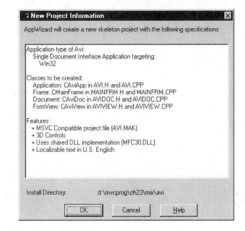

Creating the Form of the Application

Because in AppWizard you specified that the base class of the application's view class is CFormView, AppWizard created for you a form (a dialog box) that is attached to the view class of the application. This dialog box serves as the main window of the application. AppWizard named this dialog box IDD_AVI_FORM. You'll now customize the IDD_AVI_FORM dialog box until it looks like the one shown back in Figure 24.9.

☐ Select avi.mak from the Window menu to display the avi.mak window, double-click avi.rc inside the avi.mak window to display the avi.rc window, double-click Dialog inside the avi.rc window to display a list of dialog boxes, and finally, double-click the IDD_AVI_FORM item under Dialog.

   Visual C++ responds by displaying the IDD_AVI_FORM dialog box in design mode.

☐ Delete the TODO static text by clicking on it and pressing the Delete key on your keyboard.

☐ Design the IDD_AVI_FORM dialog box according to the specifications in Table 24.1. When you finish implementing the dialog box, it should look like the one shown in Figure 24.21.

Table 24.1. The Properties table of the IDD_AVI_FORM dialog box.

Object	Property	Setting
Dialog box	ID	IDD_AVI_FORM
Push button	ID	IDC_OPEN_BUTTON
	Caption	&Open Movie.AVI
Push button	ID	IDC_PLAY_BUTTON
	Caption	&Play
	Disabled	TRUE (Checked)
Push button	ID	IDC_STOP_BUTTON
	Caption	&Stop
	Disabled	TRUE (Checked)
Push button	ID	IDC_STEP_BUTTON
	Caption	S&tep
	Disabled	TRUE (Checked)
Push button	ID	IDC_BACK_BUTTON
	Caption	&Back
	Disabled	TRUE (Checked)
Check box	ID	IDC_AUTO_REPEAT_CHECK
	Caption	&Auto Repeat
Check box	ID	IDC_SILENT_CHECK
	Caption	S&ilent

NOTE

As specified in Table 24.1, the Disabled property of all the push buttons (except the Open push button) should be set to TRUE. Therefore, upon start-up of the AVI.EXE application, all the push buttons (except the Open push button) will be disabled.

To set the Disabled property of a button to TRUE simply double-click the push button and place a checkmark inside the Disabled check box.

Figure 24.21. The IDD_AVI_FORM dialog box (in design mode).

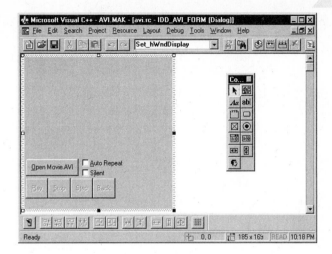

NOTE

As shown in Figure 24.21, the buttons and check boxes of the AVI.EXE application should be placed at the bottom of the dialog box. That's because the top section of the dialog box is where the pictures of the movie will be displayed.

Your dialog box should now look like the one shown in Figure 24.21. As shown in Figure 24.21, all the push buttons (except the Open push button) are disabled.

Attaching Variables to the Controls of the IDD_AVI_FORM Dialog Box

You'll now attach variables to the push buttons and check boxes of the IDD_AVI_FORM dialog box.

NOTE

You need to attach variables to the push buttons of the IDD_AVI_FORM dialog box because later when you write the code of the AVI.EXE application, you'll use these variables to enable and disable the push buttons, depending on the current playback mode. For example, when there is playback in progress, the Play button should be disabled.

☐ Use ClassWizard to attach variables to the controls of the IDD_AVI_FORM dialog box as specified in Table 24.2. When implementing the variables of Table 24.2, make sure that the class name in the ClassWizard dialog box is set to `CAviView`.

Table 24.2. The Variables table of the IDD_AVI_FORM dialog box.

Control ID	Variable Name	Category	Variable Type
IDC_PLAY_BUTTON	m_PlayButton	Control	CButton
IDC_STOP_BUTTON	m_StopButton	Control	CButton
IDC_STEP_BUTTON	m_StepButton	Control	CButton
IDC_BACK_BUTTON	m_BackButton	Control	CButton
IDC_AUTO_REPEAT_CHECK	m_AutoRepeat	Value	BOOL
IDC_SILENT_CHECK	m_Silent	Value	BOOL

☐ Save your work by selecting Save from the File menu.

You've finished designing the IDD_AVI_FORM dialog box. This dialog box will serve as the main window of the application.

The Visual Implementation of the Menu

You'll now visually implement the menu of the AVI.EXE application.

☐ Select avi.rc from the Window menu to display the avi.rc window, double-click Menu, and finally double-click IDR_MAINFRAME.

> *Visual C++ responds by displaying the IDR_MAINFRAME menu in design mode.*

☐ Implement the IDR_MAINFRAME menu so that it includes the following items:

&File
    E&xit
&Help
    &About Avi…

Save your work:

☐ Select Save from the File menu.

The visual implementation of the menu of the AVI.EXE application is complete.

To see your visual design in action do the following:

☐ Select Build AVI.EXE from the Project menu of Visual C++.

☐ Select Execute AVI.EXE from the Project menu.

> *Visual C++ responds by executing the AVI.EXE application. The main window of the application appears with the form that you designed inside it. As you can see, all the push buttons (except the Open push button) are disabled.*

In the following sections you'll write the code that brings these push buttons to life.

To exit the AVI.EXE application do the following:

☐ Select Exit from the File menu.

Adding the CTegMM.LIB Library to the AVI.MAK Project

Later you will write code that uses the CTegMM multimedia class from the CTegMM.LIB library. Therefore, you need to add the CTegMM.LIB library to the AVI.MAK project file. Here is how you do that:

☐ Select Files from the Project menu of Visual C++.

Visual C++ responds by displaying the Project Files dialog box for the AVI.MAK project.

☐ Type `C:\MVCPROG\LIB\CTEGMM.LIB` inside the File Name edit box of the Project Files dialog box. (Note that if you installed the book's CD to your D: drive you should type `D:\MVCPROG\LIB\CTEGMM.LIB`.)

☐ Click the Add button.

Visual C++ responds by adding the CTEGMM.LIB file to the AVI.MAK project.

☐ Click the Close button of the Project Files dialog box.

The CTEGMM.LIB library is now part of the AVI.MAK project. In the following sections you'll use the CTegMM multimedia class from the CTEGMM.LIB library.

Declaring an Object of Class *CTegMM*

You'll now declare a multimedia object of class CTegMM. You'll name this object m_avi and you will make this object a data member of the view class. This way, m_avi will be visible in all the member functions of the view class. As implied by its name, you will use the m_avi multimedia object for playing an AVI file.

Follow these steps to declare the m_avi object:

☐ Select Open from the File menu of Visual C++ and open the AVIVIEW.H header file.

☐ Declare the m_avi object as a public data member of the CAviView class. After you declare m_avi, the CAviView class declaration should look like this:

```
class CAviView : public CFormView
{
protected: // create from serialization only
    CAviView();
    DECLARE_DYNCREATE(CAviView)

public:
    //{{AFX_DATA(CAviView)
    enum { IDD = IDD_AVI_FORM };
    Cbutton m_BackButton;
    Cbutton m_StepButton;
```

```
        Cbutton m_StopButton;
        CButton.m_PlayButton;
        BOOL   m_AutoRepeat;
        BOOL   m_Silent;
        //}}AFX_DATA

// Attributes
public:
    CAviDoc* GetDocument();


    ///////////////////////
    // MY CODE STARTS HERE
    ///////////////////////

    CTegMM m_avi;

    ///////////////////////
    // MY CODE ENDS HERE
    ///////////////////////


// Operations
public:

// Overrides
// ClassWizard generated virtual function overrides
//{{AFX_VIRTUAL(CAviView)
protected:
virtual void DoDataExchange(CDataExchange* pDX);
virtual LRESULT WindowProc(UINT message, WPARAM wParam,
                          LPARAM lParam);
//}}AFX_VIRTUAL

// Implementation
public:
    virtual ~CAviView();
#ifdef _DEBUG
    virtual void AssertValid() const;
    virtual void Dump(CDumpContext& dc) const;
#endif

protected:

// Generated message map functions
protected:
    //{{AFX_MSG(CAviView)
    afx_msg void OnOpenButton();
    afx_msg void OnPlayButton();
    afx_msg void OnStopButton();
    afx_msg void OnStepButton();
    afx_msg void OnBackButton();
    afx_msg void OnSilentCheck();
    afx_msg void OnPaint();
    //}}AFX_MSG
    DECLARE_MESSAGE_MAP()
};
```

Because in the preceding code you declared an object of class CTegMM, you need to use #include on the header file of the CTegMM class at the beginning of the AVIVIEW.H file:

☐ Add the statement #include "\MVCPROG\LIB\CTEGMM.H" at the beginning of the AVIVIEW.H file. After you add this statement, the beginning of the AVIVIEW.H file should look like this:

```
// aviview.h : interface of the CAviView class
//
/////////////////////////////////////////////

/////////////////////////
// MY CODE STARTS HERE
/////////////////////////

#include "\MVCPROG\LIB\CTEGMM.H"

/////////////////////////
// MY CODE ENDS HERE
/////////////////////////
```

☐ Save your work by selecting Save from the File menu.

Opening the AVI File

At this point you have an object of class CTegMM (a multimedia object) called m_avi. You'll now write the code that initializes the m_avi object. This code will open an AVI file. You'll attach this code to the Open button. This way, when the user clicks the Open button, an AVI file will be opened.

☐ Display the ClassWizard dialog box by selecting ClassWizard from the Project menu of Visual C++.

☐ Select the Message Maps tab at the top of ClassWizard's dialog box.

☐ Use ClassWizard to select the event:

CAviView -> IDC_OPEN_BUTTON -> BN_CLICKED

Then click the Add Function button.

☐ Name the new function OnOpenButton().

To write the code of the OnOpenButton() function do the following:

☐ Click the Edit Code button of ClassWizard.

> *ClassWizard responds by opening the file AviView.CPP, with the function* OnOpenButton() *ready to be edited by you.*

☐ Write code inside the OnOpenButton() function so that it looks like this:

```
void CAviView::OnOpenButton()
{
// TODO: Add your control notification handler code here
```

```
/////////////////////
// MY CODE STARTS HERE
/////////////////////

// Specify the window handler for Windows messages.
m_avi.SetNumProperty("hWnd", (long)m_hWnd);

// Specify the handler of the window where the movie
// will be displayed.
m_avi.SetNumProperty("hWndDisplay", (long)m_hWnd);

// Set the device type for playback of AVI video files.
m_avi.SetStrProperty("DeviceType","AVIVideo");

// Fill the string file_name with the full pathname
// of the MOVIE.AVI file.
char file_name[300];
strncpy(file_name,__argv[0],2);
file_name[2]=0;
strcat(file_name,"\\MVCPROG\\AVI\\MOVIE.AVI");

// Set the FileName property.
m_avi.SetStrProperty("FileName", file_name);

// Open the AVI file.
m_avi.SetStrProperty("Command", "Open");

// Was file opened successfully?
long err;
m_avi.GetNumProperty("Error", &err);
if ( err == 0 )
    {
    // File was opened successfully, so enable
    // the Play, Step, and Back buttons.
    m_PlayButton.EnableWindow(TRUE);
    m_StepButton.EnableWindow(TRUE);
    m_BackButton.EnableWindow(TRUE);
    }
else
    {
    // Open command failed, so disable
    // the Play, Step, and Back buttons.
    m_PlayButton.EnableWindow(FALSE);
    m_StepButton.EnableWindow(FALSE);
    m_BackButton.EnableWindow(FALSE);

    // Display an error message box.
    char msg[300];
    m_avi.GetStrProperty("ErrorMessage", msg);
    MessageBox(msg);

    }

// Currently no playback is in progress, so
// disable the Stop button.
m_StopButton.EnableWindow(FALSE);

// Display the first frame of the movie.
m_avi.SetNumProperty("From", 1);
```

```
m_avi.SetNumProperty("To", 1);
m_avi.SetStrProperty("Command", "Play");

/////////////////////
// MY CODE ENDS HERE
/////////////////////

}
```

Now go over the code of the OnOpenButton() function.

The first statement

```
m_avi.SetNumProperty("hWnd", (long)m_hWnd);
```

sets the hWnd property of the m_avi multimedia object to the handler of the application's main window (m_hWnd). The hWnd property specifies which window should receive messages that pertain to the multimedia object. For example, when playback or recording is done, Windows sends an MM_MCINOTIFY message. By setting the hWnd property of the multimedia object to m_hWnd you are specifying that the MM_MCINOTIFY message should be sent to the application's main window. Note that m_hWnd is a data member of the application's view class (inherited from the MFC class CWnd). The m_hWnd data member of the view class specifies the handler of the window that is associated with the view class (that is, the handler of the application's main window).

The next statement

```
m_avi.SetNumProperty("hWndDisplay", (long)m_hWnd);
```

sets the hWndDisplay property of the m_avi multimedia object to the handler of the application's main window (m_hWnd). The hWndDisplay property specifies in which window the movie should be displayed. Therefore, the preceding statement specifies that the movie should be displayed inside the application's main window.

> **NOTE**
>
> The hWndDisplay property of a multimedia object specifies in which window the movie will be displayed.
>
> In the AVI.EXE application, the hWndDisplay property is set to m_hWnd (the handler of the application's main window). Therefore, in the AVI.EXE application, the movie is displayed inside the application's main window.
>
> If you set the hWndDisplay property of a multimedia object to 0, the movie will be displayed inside a separate window called a stage window.

The next statement is

```
m_avi.SetStrProperty("DeviceType","AVIVideo");
```

This statement uses the SetStrProperty() member function of the CTegMM class to set the DeviceType property of the m_avi multimedia object to AVIVideo. AVIVideo is the device type that you have to specify when you want to use the multimedia object for playing AVI video files.

The next four statements

```
char file_name[300];
strncpy(file_name,__argv[0],2);
file_name[2]=0;
strcat(file_name,"\\MVCPROG\\AVI\\MOVIE.AVI");
```

fill the local string variable file_name with the full pathname of the AVI file to be played (MOVIE.AVI).

> **NOTE**
>
> In the preceding code, argv[0] is preceded with two underscores (__). __argv[0] is a string that holds the full pathname of the application's EXE file. For example, if the AVI.EXE application is executed from the C:\TRY directory, __argv[0] will hold the string "C:\TRY\AVI.EXE".
>
> Therefore, the statement
>
> ```
> strncpy(file_name,__argv[0],2);
> ```
>
> fills the first two characters of the file_name variable with the letter (for example, C:) of the drive in which the application's EXE file resides.

At this point, the string variable file_name holds the full pathname of the MOVIE.AVI file. For example, if you are executing the AVI.EXE application from the D: drive, the file_name variable is filled with the string D:\MVCPROG\AVI\MOVIE.AVI.

The next statement

```
m_avi.SetStrProperty("FileName", file_name );
```

sets the FileName property of the m_avi object with the file_name string (that is, with the full pathname of the MOVIE.AVI file).

The next statement in the OnOpenButton() function is

```
m_avi.SetStrProperty("Command", "Open");
```

This statement opens the MOVIE.AVI file by issuing an Open command to the m_avi multimedia object.

The next group of statements determine whether the Open command was successful by extracting the Error property of the m_avi object:

```
// Was file opened successfully?
long err;
m_avi.GetNumProperty("Error", &err);
if ( err == 0 )
   {
   // File was opened successfully, so enable
   // the Play, Step, and Back buttons.
```

```
   m_PlayButton.EnableWindow(TRUE);
   m_StepButton.EnableWindow(TRUE);
   m_BackButton.EnableWindow(TRUE);
   }
else
   {
   // Open command failed, so disable
   // the Play, Step, and Back buttons.
   m_PlayButton.EnableWindow(FALSE);
   m_StepButton.EnableWindow(FALSE);
   m_BackButton.EnableWindow(FALSE);

   // Display an error message box.
   char msg[300];
   m_avi.GetStrProperty("ErrorMessage", msg);
   MessageBox(msg);

   }
```

As you can see, the Error property is extracted by using the `GetNumProperty()` function:

```
long err;
m_avi.GetNumProperty("Error", &err);
```

So at this point, the `err` local variable is filled with the value of the Error property.

The `if...else` statement evaluates the value of the Error property:

```
if ( err == 0 )
   {
   // File was opened successfully, so enable
   // the Play, Step, and Back buttons.
   m_PlayButton.EnableWindow(TRUE);
   m_StepButton.EnableWindow(TRUE);
   m_BackButton.EnableWindow(TRUE);
   }
else
   {
   // Open command failed, so disable
   // the Play, Step, and Back buttons.
   m_PlayButton.EnableWindow(FALSE);
   m_StepButton.EnableWindow(FALSE);
   m_BackButton.EnableWindow(FALSE);

   // Display an error message box.
   char msg[300];
   m_avi.GetStrProperty("ErrorMessage", msg);
   MessageBox(msg);
   }
```

If the value of the Error property is 0, the last issued command (the Open command) was success-ful. If this is the case, the statements under the `if` enable the Play, Step, and Back buttons.

If, however, the value of the Error property is not 0, the last issued command (the Open command) has failed. If this is the case, the statements under the `else` disable the Play, Step, and Back buttons, and display an error message box. The error message box simply displays the ErrorMessage prop-erty. As implied by its name, the ErrorMessage property holds an error message (string) that corre-sponds to the last error that occurred.

The next statement in the `OnOpenButton()` function

```
m_StopButton.EnableWindow(FALSE);
```

disables the Stop button. This is necessary because currently there is no playback in progress and the user should be able to click the Stop button only while there is playback in progress.

The last three statements in the `OnOpenButton()` function are

```
m_avi.SetNumProperty("From", 1);
m_avi.SetNumProperty("To", 1);
m_avi.SetStrProperty("Command", "Play");
```

These statements play the first frame of the movie. That is, the From and To properties of the `m_avi` multimedia objet are both set to 1, and then a `Play` command is issued. Doing this results in the displaying of frame number 1.

Here's a summary of what the code you wrote inside the `OnOpenButton()` function does:

- It sets the hWnd property of the `m_avi` multimedia object to m_hWnd (because you want Windows to send messages that pertain to the `m_avi` multimedia object to the application's main window).
- It sets the DeviceType property of `m_avi` to `"AVIVideo"` (because you want to use the `m_avi` multimedia object for playing an AVI video file).
- It sets the FileName property of the `m_avi` multimedia object to the full pathname of the MOVIE.AVI file (because this is the AVI file that you want to play).
- It issues the `Open` command to the `m_avi` multimedia object, by setting the Command property of the multimedia object to `Open`.
- It evaluates the Error property of the `m_avi` multimedia object to see whether or not the `Open` command has been issued successfully.
- It plays the first frame of the movie so that whenever the user clicks the Open button, the first frame of the movie is displayed.

Don't forget to save your work:

☐ Select Save from the File menu.

Attaching Code to the Play Button

When the user clicks the Play button, the AVI.EXE application should start playing the AVI file.

Follow these steps to attach code to the Play button:

☐ Display the ClassWizard dialog box by selecting ClassWizard from the Project menu of Visual C++.

☐ Select the Message Maps tab at the top of ClassWizard's dialog box.

☐ Use ClassWizard to select the event:

```
CAviView -> IDC_PLAY_BUTTON -> BN_CLICKED
```

Then click the Add Function button.

☐ Name the new function `OnPlayButton()`.

To write the code of the `OnPlayButton()` function do the following:

☐ Click the Edit Code button of ClassWizard.

> *ClassWizard responds by opening the file AviView.CPP, with the function `OnPlayButton()` ready to be edited by you.*

☐ Write code inside the `OnPlayButton()` function so that it looks like this:

```
void CAviView::OnPlayButton()
{
// TODO: Add your control notification handler code here

/////////////////////////
// MY CODE STARTS HERE
/////////////////////////

// Issue a Play command.
m_avi.SetStrProperty("Command", "Play");

// Disable the Play, Step, and Back buttons.
m_PlayButton.EnableWindow(FALSE);
m_StepButton.EnableWindow(FALSE);
m_BackButton.EnableWindow(FALSE);

// Enable the Stop button.
m_StopButton.EnableWindow(TRUE);

/////////////////////////
// MY CODE ENDS HERE
/////////////////////////

}
```

☐ Save your work by selecting Save from the File menu.

The first statement inside the `OnPlayButton()` function

```
m_avi.SetStrProperty("Command", "Play");
```

starts the playback of the movie by issuing a `Play` command to the `m_avi` multimedia object.

The next three statements

```
m_PlayButton.EnableWindow(FALSE);
m_StepButton.EnableWindow(FALSE);
m_BackButton.EnableWindow(FALSE);
```

disable the Play, Step, and Back buttons. This is necessary because during playback the user should not be able to click these buttons.

The last statement

```
m_StopButton.EnableWindow(TRUE);
```

enables the Stop button (because during playback the user should be able to click this buttons).

To see and hear your code in action do the following:

☐ Select Build AVI.EXE from the Project menu.

☐ Select Execute AVI.EXE from the Project menu.

☐ Click the Open Movie.AVI button.

> *The AVI.EXE application responds by displaying the first frame of the movie inside the application's main window.*

☐ Click the Play button.

> *The AVI.EXE application responds by playing the video file Movie.AVI. The pictures of the movie are displayed inside the application's main window, and the sound of the movie is played through the sound card. During the playback, the Play button is disabled, and the Stop button is enabled.*

As you can see, the program has a problem. Once the playback of the movie is done, the Play button remains disabled so that you cannot play the AVI file again. You'll take care of this problem in the next section.

☐ Terminate the AVI.EXE application by selecting Exit from the File menu.

Attaching Code to the *MM_MCINOTIFY* Event

As you have just seen, once the playback is done, the Play button remains disabled, and the user cannot play the AVI file again. You'll now attach code to the MM_MCINOTIFY event. The MM_MCINOTIFY event occurs when the multimedia object is done playing (for example, when the playback position reaches the end of the AVI file).

The code that you will attach to the MM_MCINOTIFY event will enable the Play button and will evaluate the status of the Auto Repeat check box. If the playback has reached the end of the AVI file and the Auto Repeat check box is checked, the code will play the AVI file again.

The MM_MCINOTIFY event is not listed inside the ClassWizard dialog box. Therefore, to process the MM_MCINOTIFY message, you have to attach code to the WindowProc() member function of the view class. You can use the WindowProc() function to process any message that is not listed in the ClassWizard dialog box.

Attach code to the WindowProc() member function of the view class as follows:

☐ Display the ClassWizard dialog box by selecting ClassWizard from the Project menu of Visual C++.

☐ Select the Message Maps tab at the top of ClassWizard's dialog box.

☐ Use ClassWizard to select the event:

```
CAviView -> CAviView -> WindowProc
```

☐ Click the Add Function button.

> *Visual C++ responds by adding the* WindowProc() *member function to the* CAviView *class.*

☐ Click the Edit Code button of ClassWizard.

> *ClassWizard responds by opening the file AviView.CPP, with the function* WindowProc() *ready to be edited by you.*

☐ Write code inside the WindowProc() function so that it looks like this:

```
LRESULT CAviView::WindowProc(UINT message, WPARAM wParam,
                             LPARAM lParam)
{
// TODO: Add your specialized code here and/or call the base
//       class

//////////////////////////
// MY CODE STARTS HERE
//////////////////////////

switch ( message )
      {
      case MM_MCINOTIFY:
            {

            // Enable the Play, Step, and Back buttons.
            m_PlayButton.EnableWindow(TRUE);
            m_StepButton.EnableWindow(TRUE);
            m_BackButton.EnableWindow(TRUE);

            // Disable the Stop button.
            m_StopButton.EnableWindow(FALSE);

            // Get the total length of the AVI file.
            long length;
            m_avi.GetNumProperty("Length", &length);

            // Get the current playback position.
            long position;
            m_avi.GetNumProperty("Position", &position);

            // Has playback reached the end of the AVI file?
            if ( position == length )
                  {
                  // Rewind the playback position to the
                  // beginning of the file.
                  m_avi.SetStrProperty("Command", "Prev");

                  // If the Auto Repeat check box is checked,
                  // start playback again.
                  UpdateData(TRUE);
                  if (m_AutoRepeat == TRUE)
                     OnPlayButton();
                  }

            break;
            }
```

```
      }

//////////////////////
// MY CODE ENDS HERE
//////////////////////

return CFormView::WindowProc(message, wParam, lParam);
}
```

☐ Save your work by selecting Save from the File menu.

The code you typed inside the `WindowProc()` function is made of a `switch` statement:

```
switch ( message )
      {
      case MM_MCINOTIFY:
            {
            ....
            ....
            ....
            }
      }
```

This `switch` statement evaluates the `message` parameter of the `WindowProc()` function to determine which event (message) has just occurred. If, for example, an `MM_MCINOTIFY` event has just occurred (that is, an `MM_MCINOTIFY` message has just arrived), then the code under the `MM_MCINOTIFY` case will be executed:

```
case MM_MCINOTIFY:
    {

    // Enable the Play, Step, and Back buttons.
    m_PlayButton.EnableWindow(TRUE);
    m_StepButton.EnableWindow(TRUE);
    m_BackButton.EnableWindow(TRUE);

    // Disable the Stop button.
    m_StopButton.EnableWindow(FALSE);

    // Get the total length of the AVI file.
    long length;
    m_avi.GetNumProperty("Length", &length);

    // Get the current playback position.
    long position;
    m_avi.GetNumProperty("Position", &position);

    // Has playback reached the end of the AVI file?
    if ( position == length )
        {
        // Rewind the playback position to the
        // beginning of the file.
        m_avi.SetStrProperty("Command", "Prev");

        // If the Auto Repeat check box is checked,
        // start playback again.
        UpdateData(TRUE);
        if (m_AutoRepeat == TRUE)
           OnPlayButton();
```

```
      }

   break;
   }
```

The first three statements under the `MM_MCINOTIFY` case

```
m_PlayButton.EnableWindow(TRUE);
m_StepButton.EnableWindow(TRUE);
m_BackButton.EnableWindow(TRUE);
```

enable the Play, Step, and Back buttons. This is necessary because playback has just stopped, and when there is no playback in progress, the user should be able to click these buttons.

The next statement

```
m_StopButton.EnableWindow(FALSE);
```

disables the Stop button (because the user should not be able to click this button when there is no playback in progress).

The next two statements

```
long length;
m_avi.GetNumProperty("Length", &length);
```

extract the value of the Length property of the `m_avi` multimedia object and store this value in the local variable `length`. The Length property reports the total length of the currently open file. So at this point, the variable `length` holds the total length of the AVI file.

The next two statements

```
long position;
m_avi.GetNumProperty("Position", &position);
```

extract the value of the Position property of the `m_avi` multimedia object and store this value in the local variable `position`. The Position property reports the current playback position. So at this point, the variable `position` holds the current playback position.

Finally, an `if` statement is used to compare the value of the Position property with the value of the Length property:

```
if ( position == length )
   {
   // Rewind the playback position to the
   // beginning of the file.
   m_avi.SetStrProperty("Command", "Prev");

   // If the Auto Repeat check box is checked,
   // start playback again.
   UpdateData(TRUE);
   if (m_AutoRepeat == TRUE)
      OnPlayButton();
   }
```

If the value of the Position property is equal to the value of the Length property (that is, the playback position has reached the end of the AVI file), the `if` condition is satisfied, and the statements under the `if` do the following:

- Issue a `Prev` command to rewind the playback position to the beginning of the AVI file.
- Call the `OnPlayButton()` function that you wrote earlier, provided that the Auto Repeat check box is checked.

Note that before the value of the `m_AutoRepeat` variable (the variable of the Auto Repeat check box) is checked, the `UpdateData()` function with its parameter set to `TRUE` is called so that the `m_AutoRepeat` variable will be updated with the current status of the Auto Repeat check box.

Here's a summary of how the code you added under the `MM_MCINOTIFY` case automatically repeats the playback when the Auto Repeat check box is checked:

- Whenever the playback stops (for example, when the user clicks the Stop button or when the playback reaches the end of the AVI file), the code you wrote under the `MM_MCINOTIFY` case is automatically executed.
- The code you wrote under the `MM_MCINOTIFY` case checks whether the Position and Length properties of the multimedia object are equal. If they are equal (that is, the playback stopped because it reached the end of the AVI file), the code you wrote under the `MM_MCINOTIFY` case rewinds the `m_avi` multimedia object by setting the Command property of the multimedia object to `Prev` and plays the AVI file again (by calling the `OnPlayButton()` function), provided that the Auto Repeat check box is checked.

To see the code that you typed under the `MM_MCINOTIFY` case in action do the following:

☐ Select Build AVI.EXE from the Project menu.

☐ Select Execute AVI.EXE from the Project menu.

☐ Click the Open Movie.AVI button.

☐ Place a checkmark inside the Auto Repeat check box.

☐ Click the Play button.

> *The AVI application responds by playing the Movie.AVI video file.*

As you can see and hear, once the playback is done, the playback repeats itself.

☐ Terminate the AVI.EXE application by selecting Exit from the File menu.

Attaching Code to the Stop Button

When the user clicks the Stop button, the playback should stop.

Follow these steps to attach code to the Stop button:

☐ Display the ClassWizard dialog box by selecting ClassWizard from the Project menu of Visual C++.

☐ Select the Message Maps tab at the top of ClassWizard's dialog box.

☐ Use ClassWizard to select the event:

```
CAviView -> IDC_STOP_BUTTON -> BN_CLICKED
```

Then click the Add Function button.

☐ Name the new function `OnStopButton()`.

To write the code of the `OnStopButton()` function do the following:

☐ Click the Edit Code button of ClassWizard.

> *ClassWizard responds by opening the file AviView.CPP, with the function `OnStopButton()` ready to be edited by you.*

☐ Write code inside the `OnStopButton()` function so that it looks like this:

```
void CAviView::OnStopButton()
{
// TODO: Add your control notification handler code here

////////////////////////
// MY CODE STARTS HERE
////////////////////////

// Issue a Stop command.
m_avi.SetStrProperty("Command", "Stop");

////////////////////////
// MY CODE ENDS HERE
////////////////////////

}
```

☐ Save your work by selecting Save from the File menu.

The code you just typed inside the `OnStopButton()` function is made of one statement:

```
m_avi.SetStrProperty("Command", "Stop");
```

This statement issues a `Stop` command to the `m_avi` multimedia object. Issuing a `Stop` command stops the playback.

To see the code that you attached to the Stop button in action do the following:

☐ Select Build AVI.EXE from the Project menu.

☐ Select Execute AVI.EXE from the Project menu.

☐ Click the Open Movie.AVI button.

☐ Click the Play button.

> *The AVI.EXE application responds by playing the Movie.AVI video file.*

☐ While the AVI file is playing click the Stop button.

As expected, the playback stops.

☐ Terminate the AVI.EXE application by selecting Exit from the File menu.

Attaching Code to the Step Button

When the user clicks the Step button, the AVI.EXE application should display the next frame.

Follow these steps to attach code to the Step button:

☐ Display the ClassWizard dialog box by selecting ClassWizard from the Project menu of Visual C++.

☐ Select the Message Maps tab at the top of ClassWizard's dialog box.

☐ Use ClassWizard to select the event:

```
CAviView -> IDC_STEP_BUTTON -> BN_CLICKED
```

Then click the Add Function button.

☐ Name the new function `OnStepButton()`.

To write the code of the `OnStepButton()` function do the following:

☐ Click the Edit Code button of ClassWizard.

> *ClassWizard responds by opening the file AviView.CPP, with the function* `OnStepButton()` *ready to be edited by you.*

☐ Write code inside the `OnStepButton()` function so that it looks like this:

```
void CAviView::OnStepButton()
{
// TODO: Add your control notification handler code here

/////////////////////////
// MY CODE STARTS HERE
/////////////////////////

// Issue a Step command.
m_avi.SetStrProperty("Command", "Step");

/////////////////////////
// MY CODE ENDS HERE
/////////////////////////

}
```

☐ Save your work by selecting Save from the File menu.

The code you just typed inside the `OnStepButton()` function is made of one statement:

```
m_avi.SetStrProperty("Command", "Step");
```

This statement issues a `Step` command to the `m_avi` multimedia object. Issuing a `Step` command displays the next frame of the movie.

Attaching Code to the Back Button

When the user clicks the Back button, the AVI.EXE application should display the previous frame.

Follow these steps to attach code to the Back button:

☐ Display the ClassWizard dialog box by selecting ClassWizard from the Project menu of Visual C++.

☐ Select the Message Maps tab at the top of ClassWizard's dialog box.

☐ Use ClassWizard to select the event:

```
CAviView -> IDC_BACK_BUTTON -> BN_CLICKED
```

Then click the Add Function button.

☐ Name the new function `OnBackButton()`.

To write the code of the `OnBackButton()` function do the following:

☐ Click the Edit Code button of ClassWizard.

ClassWizard responds by opening the file AviView.CPP, with the function `OnBackButton()` *ready to be edited by you.*

☐ Write code inside the `OnBackButton()` function so that it looks like this:

```
void CAviView::OnBackButton()
{
// TODO: Add your control notification handler code here

/////////////////////////
// MY CODE STARTS HERE
/////////////////////////

// Issue a Back command.
m_avi.SetStrProperty("Command", "Back");

/////////////////////////
// MY CODE ENDS HERE
/////////////////////////

}
```

☐ Save your work by selecting Save from the File menu.

The code you just typed inside the `OnBackButton()` function is made of one statement:

```
m_avi.SetStrProperty("Command", "Back");
```

This statement issues a `Back` command to the `m_avi` multimedia object. Issuing a `Back` command displays the previous frame of the movie.

To see the code that you attached to the Step and Back buttons in action do the following:

☐ Select Build AVI.EXE from the Project menu.

☐ Select Execute AVI.EXE from the Project menu.

☐ Click the Open Movie.AVI button.

☐ Click the Step button several times.

> *As you can see, every time you click the Step button, the next frame of the movie is displayed.*

☐ Click the Back button several times.

> *As you can see, every time you click the Back button, the previous frame of the movie is displayed.*

☐ Terminate the AVI.EXE application by selecting Exit from the File menu.

Attaching Code to the Silent Check Box

When the user places a checkmark inside the Silent check box, the movie should be played without sound. When the user removes the checkmark from the Silent check box, the movie should be played with sound.

Follow these steps to attach code to the Silent check box:

☐ Display the ClassWizard dialog box by selecting ClassWizard from the Project menu of Visual C++.

☐ Select the Message Maps tab at the top of ClassWizard's dialog box.

☐ Use ClassWizard to select the event:

```
CAviView -> IDC_SILENT_CHECK -> BN_CLICKED
```

Then click the Add Function button.

☐ Name the new function `OnSilentCheck()`.

To write the code of the `OnSilentCheck()` function do the following:

☐ Click the Edit Code button of ClassWizard.

> *ClassWizard responds by opening the file AviView.CPP, with the function* `OnSilentCheck()` *ready to be edited by you.*

☐ Write code inside the `OnSilentCheck()` function so that it looks like this:

```
void CAviView::OnSilentCheck()
{
// TODO: Add your control notification handler code here

/////////////////////////
// MY CODE STARTS HERE
/////////////////////////

// Update the m_Silent variable.
```

```
UpdateData(TRUE);

// Set the Silent property.
m_avi.SetNumProperty("Silent", m_Silent);

/////////////////////
// MY CODE ENDS HERE
/////////////////////

}
```

☐ Save your work by selecting Save from the File menu.

The first statement you typed inside the `OnSilentCheck()` function

```
UpdateData(TRUE);
```

updates the variables of the controls with the current status of the controls. Therefore, after this statement is executed, the variable of the Silent check box (`m_Silent`) is updated with the current status of the Silent check box. If the Silent check box is checked, `m_Silent` is equal to `TRUE`. If the Silent check box is not checked, `m_Silent` is equal to `FALSE`.

The second statement in the `OnSilent()` function is

```
m_avi.SetNumProperty("Silent", m_Silent);
```

This statement sets the Silent property of the `m_avi` multimedia object with the current value of the Silent check box (`m_Silent`). When the Silent property of the `m_avi` object is set to `TRUE`, the multimedia object will play the movie without sound. Therefore, whenever the user checks the Silent check box, the movie will be played without sound.

To see the code you attached to the Silent check box in action do the following:

☐ Select Build AVI.EXE from the Project menu.

☐ Select Execute AVI.EXE from the Project menu.

☐ Click the Open Movie.AVI button.

☐ Place a checkmark inside the Silent check box and then click the Play button.

> *As expected, the movie is played without sound.*

☐ Terminate the AVI.EXE application by selecting Exit from the File menu.

Attaching Code to the *WM_PAINT* Event

The AVI.EXE application is not complete yet. There is still one problem that needs to be resolved—whenever the application's window needs to be repainted (for example, after you resize the window), the current frame is not repainted.

Before you fix this problem you should "see" this problem:

☐ Select Execute AVI.EXE from the Project menu.

☐ Click the Open Movie.AVI button.

> *The AVI.EXE application responds by displaying the first frame of the Movie.AVI video inside the application's main window.*

☐ Minimize the application's window and then restore its original size.

> *As you can see, the frame disappears. That is, after you resize the window, the AVI.EXE application does not repaint the movie area of the window.*

In a similar manner, if you cover the window of the AVI.EXE application by placing it beneath other windows, when you uncover the window, the section of the frame that was covered will not be repainted.

So when there is a need to repaint the AVI.EXE application's window, the AVI.EXE application does not repaint the frame.

☐ Terminate the AVI.EXE application by selecting Exit from the File menu.

To solve this "repaint" problem, you have to attach code to the WM_PAINT event of the CAviView class. The WM_PAINT event occurs whenever there is a need to repaint the window (for example, when the user minimizes the window and then restores the window's original size).

Attach code to the WM_PAINT event of the CAviView class as follows:

☐ Display the ClassWizard dialog box by selecting ClassWizard from the Project menu of Visual C++.

☐ Select the Message Maps tab at the top of ClassWizard's dialog box.

☐ Use ClassWizard to select the event:

```
CAviView -> CAviView -> WM_PAINT
```

☐ Click the Add Function button.

> *Visual C++ responds by adding the OnPaint() member function to the CAviView class.*

☐ Click the Edit Code button of ClassWizard.

> *ClassWizard responds by opening the file AviView.CPP, with the function OnPaint() ready to be edited by you.*

☐ Write code inside the OnPaint() function so that it looks like this:

```
void CAviView::OnPaint()
{
CPaintDC dc(this); // device context for painting

// TODO: Add your message handler code here

/////////////////////////
// MY CODE STARTS HERE
/////////////////////////
```

```
// Issue a RePaint command.
m_avi.SetStrProperty("Command", "Repaint");

///////////////////////
// MY CODE ENDS HERE
///////////////////////

// Do not call CFormView::OnPaint() for painting messages

}
```

☐ Save your work by selecting Save from the File menu.

The code you just typed inside the OnPaint() function is made of one statement:

```
m_avi.SetStrProperty("Command", "Repaint");
```

This statement issues a Repaint command to the m_avi multimedia object. Issuing a Repaint command repaints the current frame.

The AVI.EXE application is now complete! To see the code you attached to the OnPaint() function in action do the following:

☐ Select Build AVI.EXE from the Project menu.

☐ Select Execute AVI.EXE from the Project menu.

☐ Click the Open Movie.AVI button.

> *The AVI.EXE application responds by displaying the first frame of the Movie.AVI video inside the application's main window.*

☐ Minimize the application's window and then restore its original size.

> *As you can see, once you restore the original size of the window, the current frame is repainted.*

Experimenting with Other Video Files

The code of the AVI application plays the video file MOVIE.AVI. The book's CD includes other video files (AVI files) with which you can experiment. These AVI files reside in the \MVCPROG\AVI directory of the book's CD.

You can experiment with these AVI files as follows:

☐ Copy an AVI file from the \MVCPROG\AVI directory of the book's CD to your \MVCPROG\AVI hard drive directory.

☐ Change the statement that sets the FileName property of the m_avi multimedia object so that it will specify the appropriate AVI filename. (The statement that sets the FileName property is in the function OnOpenButton() inside the file AVIVIEW.CPP.)

25

Multimedia: CD Audio

In the previous three chapters you
wrote applications that use the
CTegMM.LIB multimedia library for
playing a WAV file, a MIDI file, and
a video (AVI) file. In this chapter you
will write an application that uses the
CTegMM.LIB multimedia library to
play an audio CD.

NOTE

In this chapter you'll write an application that plays an audio CD. Therefore, you'll need a Windows-compatible CD-ROM drive that supports playback of audio CDs. If your system doesn't have such a CD-ROM drive, you may skip this chapter or just browse through it.

This chapter also covers the topic of Windows timers. It shows you how to write code that installs and uses a Windows timer.

If you don't have a CD-ROM drive capable of playing an audio CD, you can still learn about Windows timers in Chapter 26, "The Timer," which covers the topic of using Windows without multimedia hardware.

Playing an Audio CD with Media Player

Before you start writing an application that plays an audio CD, first verify that your system is capable of playing audio CDs.

☐ Start the Media Player program of Windows. (Media Player usually resides in the Accessories group of programs.)

> *Windows responds by running the Media Player program. (See Figure 25.1.)*

NOTE

Windows includes a program called Media Player, which enables you to play various multimedia files as well as control various multimedia devices (for example, a CD-ROM drive that supports audio CDs).

The Media Player program usually resides in the Accessories group.

Figure 25.1. The Media Player program.

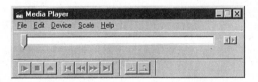

If your system has the hardware and software needed for playing an audio CD, your Media Player program can play audio CDs.

To see if your Media Player program can play audio CDs do the following:

☐ Open the Device menu of Media Player. (See Figure 25.2.)

Figure 25.2. The Device menu of Media Player.

As you can see in Figure 25.2, one of the items in the Device menu is CD Audio. If your Device menu doesn't include this item, your system doesn't have the necessary hardware or software to play audio CDs. In order to make your system support playback of audio CDs, you need to install the software that comes with your CD-ROM drive.

In the following steps, you will use Media Player to play an audio CD. If you are already familiar with Media Player's ability to play audio CDs, you may skip these steps and start reading the next section, which shows you how to write a Visual C++ application that plays audio CDs.

☐ Insert an audio CD into your CD-ROM drive.

NOTE

There are two types of CDs: data CDs and audio CDs.

Data CDs are used to store regular data files. For example, the CD that comes with this book is a data CD. Data CDs may contain any type of file (for example, EXE, CPP, WAV, MIDI, BMP).

Audio CDs do not store files. They contain audio only. Typically, an audio CD is purchased in a music store.

☐ Select CD Audio from the Device menu of Media Player. (See Figure 25.2.)

> *Media Player responds by making its buttons available and changing its title to Media Player—CD Audio [stopped]. (See Figure 25.3.)*

To start the playback of the audio CD do the following:

☐ Click the Play button (the extreme-left button) in Media Player.

> *Media Player responds by playing the first track (song) of the audio CD.*

Figure 25.3. Media Player, after you select CD Audio from the Device menu.

NOTE

Some CD-ROM drives require that you connect the CD-ROM drive to earphones (or to external speakers) before you can hear the audio CD playing. Other types of CD-ROM drives are internally connected to the speakers of your sound card.

If your CD-ROM drive is the type that needs to be connected to earphones or to external speakers, you need to connect the plug of the earphones (or the plug of the speakers) into your CD-ROM drive. The plug is usually connected to the front panel of the CD-ROM drive.

To stop the playback do the following:

☐ Click the Stop button (the second button from the left).

☐ Experiment with the other buttons of Media Player.

To terminate the Media Player program do the following:

☐ Select Exit from the File menu of Media player.

The CD Application

You'll now write the CD application. The CD application is an example of a multimedia application that enables the user to play an audio CD.

As you will soon see, the code that you need to write for playing an audio CD is very similar to the code you wrote in the previous chapters for playing a WAV file, a MIDI file, and a video file.

Before you start writing the CD application, first execute the copy of it that resides in the \MVCPROG\EXE directory of the book's CD. However, because you need to use your CD-ROM drive for the playback of the audio CD, you need to copy the CD.EXE file from the book's CD to your hard drive and then run the CD.EXE program from your hard drive. This way your CD-ROM drive will be free for the audio CD.

☐ Copy the file \MVCPROG\EXE\CD.EXE from the book's CD to any directory on your hard drive.

☐ Insert an audio CD into your CD-ROM drive.

☐ Execute the CD.EXE program from your hard drive.

Windows responds by executing the CD.EXE application. The CD application first displays a limited version message box from the CTegMM.LIB multimedia library. (See Figure 25.4.)

Figure 25.4. The limited
version message box of the
CTegMM.LIB library.

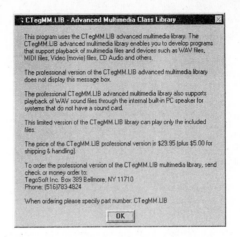

☐ Click the OK button of the message box.

The main window of CD.EXE appears, as shown in Figure 25.5.

Figure 25.5. The main
window of the CD
application.

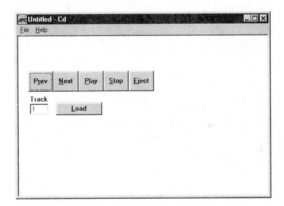

As you can see, the main window of the application has inside it several buttons (Prev, Next, Play, Stop, Eject, and Load) and an edit box that displays the current track number (song number) of the audio CD.

NOTE

Because prior to running the CD.EXE application you placed an audio CD inside your CD-ROM drive, the CD.EXE application automatically loaded the audio CD.

If prior to executing the CD.EXE application you do not place an audio CD inside your CD-ROM drive, the CD.EXE application will not be able to load the audio CD, and the Track edit box will display the number 0.

If you do not place an audio CD prior to executing the CD.EXE application, you can still load an audio CD while the CD.EXE application is running: Place an audio CD inside your CD-ROM drive and then click the Load button.

To start the playback of track 1 do the following:

☐ Click the Play button.

> *The CD application responds by playing track number 1 of the audio CD.*

To stop the playback do the following:

☐ Click the Stop button.

> *The CD application responds by stopping the playback.*

You can use the Next and Prev buttons to navigate to any particular track on the CD.

☐ Experiment with the Next and Prev buttons and notice how the Track edit box changes.

When you click the Next button, the playback position changes to the beginning of the next track. When you click the Prev button, the playback position changes to the beginning of the previous track.

The CD.EXE application also has an Eject button. You can use the Eject button only if your CD-ROM drive supports the Eject feature.

☐ Click the Eject button.

> *The CD.EXE application responds by opening the door of your CD-ROM drive (only if your CD-ROM drive supports this feature).*

Note that while the door of the CD-ROM drive is open, the Track edit box displays the number 0.

☐ Click the Eject button again.

> *The CD.EXE application responds by closing the door of your CD-ROM drive (only if your CD-ROM drive supports the Close Door feature).*

To exit the CD application do the following:

☐ Select Exit from the File menu.

Now that you know what the CD application should do, you can start writing it.

Creating the Project of the CD Application

To create the project of the CD application do the following:

☐ Start Visual C++ and close all the open windows that appear inside the desktop of Visual C++ (if there are any).

☐ Select New from the File menu.

Visual C++ responds by displaying the New dialog box.

☐ Select Project inside the New dialog box and then click the OK button of the New dialog box.

Visual C++ responds by displaying the New Project dialog box.

☐ Set the project name to cd.

☐ Set the project path to \MVCPROG\CH25\CD\CD.MAK.

Your New Project dialog box should now look like the one shown in Figure 25.6.

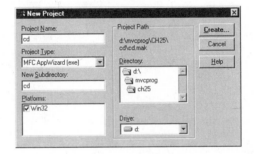

Figure 25.6. The New Project dialog box of the CD.MAK project.

☐ Click the Create button of the New Project dialog box.

Visual C++ responds by displaying the AppWizard—Step 1 window.

☐ Set the Step 1 window as shown in Figure 25.7. As shown in Figure 25.7, the CD.MAK project is set as a single-document application, and U.S. English (APPWIZUS.DLL) is used as the language for the application's resources.

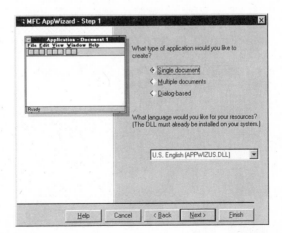

Figure 25.7. The AppWizard—Step 1 window for the CD application.

☐ Click the Next button of the Step 1 window.

Visual C++ responds by displaying the AppWizard—Step 2 of 6 window.

☐ Set the Step 2 of 6 window as shown in Figure 25.8. That is, in the CD application you don't want any database support.

Figure 25.8. The AppWizard—Step 2 of 6 window for the CD application.

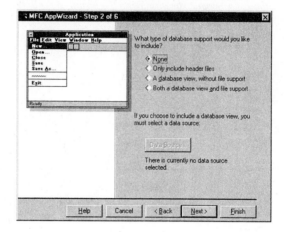

☐ Click the Next button of the Step 2 of 6 window.

Visual C++ responds by displaying the AppWizard—Step 3 of 6 window.

☐ Set the Step 3 of 6 window as shown in Figure 25.9. That is, in the CD application you don't want any OLE support.

Figure 25.9. The AppWizard—Step 3 of 6 window for the CD application.

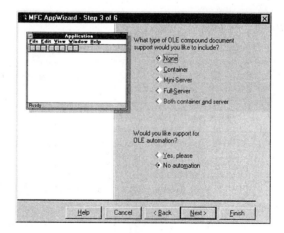

☐ Click the Next button of the Step 3 of 6 window.

Visual C++ responds by displaying the AppWizard—Step 4 of 6 window.

☐ Set the Step 4 of 6 window as shown in Figure 25.10.

Figure 25.10. The AppWizard—Step 4 of 6 window for the CD application.

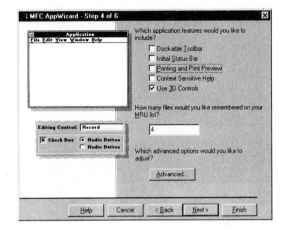

As shown in Figure 25.10, the features Dockable Toolbar, Initial Status Bar, Printing and Print Preview, and Context Sensitive Help will not be included in the CD application.

☐ Click the Next button of the Step 4 of 6 window.

Visual C++ responds by displaying the AppWizard—Step 5 of 6 window.

☐ Set the Step 5 of 6 window as shown in Figure 25.11.

As shown in Figure 25.11, the project will be generated with comments, a Visual C++ makefile will be generated, and the application will use the MFC library from a DLL.

Figure 25.11. The AppWizard—Step 5 of 6 window for the CD application.

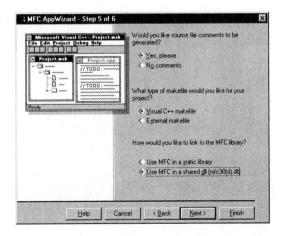

☐ Click the Next button of the Step 5 of 6 window.

> *Visual C++ responds by displaying the AppWizard—Step 6 of 6 window.*

You'll now use the AppWizard—Step 6 of 6 window to tell AppWizard to derive the view class of the application from the MFC class CFormView:

☐ Select the CCdView class inside the AppWizard—Step 6 of 6 window.

☐ Set the Base Class drop-down list box to CFormView.

Your AppWizard—Step 6 of 6 window should now look like the one shown in Figure 25.12.

Figure 25.12. The AppWizard—Step 6 of 6 window after you set the base class of the application view class to CFormView.

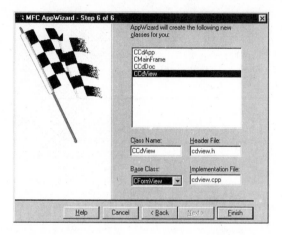

☐ Click the Finish button of the Step 6 of 6 window.

> *Visual C++ responds by displaying the New Project Information window, as shown in Figure 25.13.*

Figure 25.13. The New Project Information window of the CD.MAK project.

☐ Click the OK button of the New Project Information window.

Visual C++ responds by creating the project file and all the skeleton files of the application.

Creating the Form of the Application

Because in AppWizard you specified that the base class of the application's view class is CFormView, AppWizard created for you a form (a dialog box) that is attached to the view class of the application. This dialog box serves as the main window of the application. AppWizard named this dialog box IDD_CD_FORM. You'll now customize the IDD_CD_FORM dialog box so that it looks like the one shown back in Figure 25.5.

☐ Select cd.mak from the Window menu to display the cd.mak window, double-click cd.rc inside the cd.mak window to display the cd.rc window, double-click Dialog inside the cd.rc window to display a list of dialog boxes, and finally, double-click the IDD_CD_FORM item under the Dialog item.

Visual C++ responds by displaying the IDD_CD_FORM dialog box in design mode.

☐ Delete the TODO static text by clicking on it and pressing the Delete key on your keyboard.

☐ Design the IDD_CD_FORM dialog box according to the specifications in Table 25.1. When you finish implementing the dialog box, it should look like the one shown in Figure 25.14.

Table 25.1. The Properties table for the IDD_CD_FORM dialog box.

Object	Property	Setting
Dialog box	ID	IDD_CD_FORM
Push button	ID	IDC_PREV_BUTTON
	Caption	P&rev
Push button	ID	IDC_NEXT_BUTTON
	Caption	&Next
Push button	ID	IDC_PLAY_BUTTON
	Caption	&Play
Push button	ID	IDC_STOP_BUTTON
	Caption	&Stop
Push button	ID	IDC_EJECT_BUTTON
	Caption	&Eject
Push button	ID	IDC_LOAD_BUTTON
	Caption	&Load

continues

Table 25.1. continued.

Object	Property	Setting
Static text	ID	IDC_STATIC
	Caption	Track
Edit box	ID	IDC_CURRENT_TRACK
	Disabled	TRUE

NOTE

As specified in Table 25.1, the Disabled property of the IDC_CURRENT_TRACK edit box should be set to TRUE. This is necessary because the IDC_CURRENT_TRACK edit box is going to be a read-only edit box. That is, the application will use this edit box to display the current track number, and the user will not be able to type anything inside this edit box.

To set the Disabled property of the IDC_CURRENT_TRACK edit box to TRUE, simply double-click the edit box and then place a checkmark inside the Disabled check box.

Figure 25.14. The IDD_CD_FORM dialog box (in design mode).

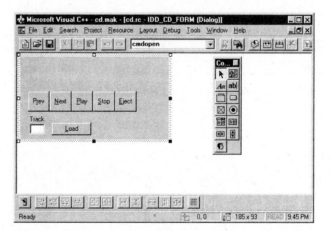

Attaching Variables to the Controls of the IDD_CD_FORM Dialog Box

You'll now attach a variable to the IDC_CURRENT_TRACK edit box of the IDD_CD_FORM dialog box.

☐ Use ClassWizard to attach a variable to the IDC_CURRENT_TRACK edit box according to the specifications in Table 25.2. When you attach the variable, make sure that the class name in the ClassWizard dialog box is set to CCdView.

Table 25.2. The Variables table of the IDD_CD_FORM dialog box.

Control ID	Variable Name	Category	Variable Type
IDC_CURRENT_TRACK	m_CurrentTrack	Value	long

> **NOTE**
>
> Note that Table 25.1 instructs you to set the variable m_CurrentTrack as a long type. This is necessary because as you will see later, the current track number of the CD is stored as a long type.

☐ Save your work by selecting Save from the File menu.

You've finished designing the IDD_CD_FORM dialog box. This dialog box will serve as the main window of the application.

The Visual Implementation of the Menu

You'll now visually implement the menu of the CD application.

☐ Select cd.rc from the Window menu to display the cd.rc window, double-click Menu, and finally, double-click IDR_MAINFRAME.

   Visual C++ responds by displaying the IDR_MAINFRAME menu in design mode.

☐ Implement the IDR_MAINFRAME menu so that it contains the following items:

   &File
      E&xit
   &Help
      &About Cd...

Save your work:

☐ Select Save from the File menu.

The visual implementation of the menu of the CD application is complete.

To see your visual design in action do the following:

☐ Select Build CD.EXE from the Project menu of Visual C++.

☐ Select Execute CD.EXE from the Project menu.

   Visual C++ responds by executing the CD.EXE application. The main window of the application appears with the form that you designed inside it.

To exit the CD application do the following:

☐ Select Exit from the File menu.

Adding the CTegMM.LIB Library to the CD.MAK Project

Later you will write code that uses the CTegMM multimedia class from the CTegMM.LIB library. Therefore, you need to add the CTegMM.LIB library to the CD.MAK project file. Here is how you do that:

☐ Select Files from the Project menu of Visual C++.

Visual C++ responds by displaying the Files dialog box for the CD.MAK project.

☐ Type `C:\MVCPROG\LIB\CTEGMM.LIB` inside the File Name edit box of the Files dialog box. (Note that if you installed the book's CD to your D: drive, you should type `D:\MVCPROG\LIB\CTEGMM.LIB`.)

☐ Click the Add button.

Visual C++ responds by adding the CTEGMM.LIB file to the CD.MAK project.

☐ Click the Close button of the Project Files dialog box.

The CTEGMM.LIB library is now part of the CD.MAK project. In the following sections you'll use the CTegMM multimedia class from the CTEGMM.LIB library.

Declaring an Object of Class *CTegMM*

You'll now declare a multimedia object of class CTegMM. You'll name this object m_cd and you will make this object a data member of the view class. This way, m_cd will be visible in all the member functions of the view class. As implied by its name, you will use the m_cd multimedia object for playing an audio CD.

Follow these steps to declare the m_cd object:

☐ Select Open from the File menu of Visual C++ and open the CDVIEW.H header file.

☐ Declare the m_cd object as a public data member of the CCdView class. After declaring m_cd, the CCdView class declaration should look like this:

```
class CCdView : public CFormView
{
protected: // create from serialization only
    CCdView();
    DECLARE_DYNCREATE(CCdView)

public:
    //{{AFX_DATA(CCdView)
    enum { IDD = IDD_CD_FORM };
    long m_CurrentTrack;
    //}}AFX_DATA
```

```
// Attributes
public:
     CCdDoc* GetDocument();

     /////////////////////////
     // MY CODE STARTS HERE
     /////////////////////////

     CTegMM m_cd;

     /////////////////////////
     // MY CODE STARTS HERE
     /////////////////////////

// Operations
public:

// Overrides
     // ClassWizard generated virtual function overrides
     //{{AFX_VIRTUAL(CCdView)
     public:
     protected:
     virtual void DoDataExchange(CDataExchange* pDX);
     //}}AFX_VIRTUAL

// Implementation
public:
     virtual ~CCdView();
#ifdef _DEBUG
     virtual void AssertValid() const;
     virtual void Dump(CDumpContext& dc) const;
#endif

protected:

// Generated message map functions
protected:
     //{{AFX_MSG(CCdView)
     //}}AFX_MSG
     DECLARE_MESSAGE_MAP()
};
```

Because in the above code you declared an object of class CTegMM, you need to use #include on the header file of the CTegMM class at the beginning of the CDVIEW.H file:

☐ Add the statement #include "\MVCPROG\LIB\CTEGMM.H" at the beginning of the CDVIEW.H file. After you add this statement, the beginning of the CDVIEW.H file should look like this:

```
// cdview.h : interface of the CCdView class
//
/////////////////////////////////////////////////

/////////////////////////
// MY CODE STARTS HERE
/////////////////////////
```

```
#include "\MVCPROG\LIB\CTEGMM.H"

/////////////////////
// MY CODE ENDS HERE
/////////////////////
```

☐ Save your work by selecting Save from the File menu.

Loading an Audio CD

At this point you have an object of class `CTegMM` (a multimedia object) called `m_cd`. You'll now write the code that initializes the `m_cd` object. This code will set the DeviceType property of the `m_cd` multimedia object for playback of CD audio and will issue an `Open` command. You'll attach this code to the `OnInitialUpdate()` member function of the view class. This way the audio CD that is inside the CD-ROM drive will be loaded upon start-up of the application.

☐ Display the ClassWizard dialog box by selecting ClassWizard from the Project menu of Visual C++.

☐ Select the Message Maps tab at the top of ClassWizard's dialog box.

☐ Use ClassWizard to select the event:

```
CCdView -> CCdView -> OnInitialUpdate
```

Then click the Add Function button.

> *Visual C++ responds by adding the* `OnInitialUpdate()` *member function to the* `CCdView` *class.*

☐ Click the Edit Code button of ClassWizard.

> *ClassWizard responds by opening the file CdView.CPP, with the function* `OnInitialUpdate()` *ready to be edited by you.*

☐ Write code inside the `OnInitialUpdate()` function so that it looks like this:

```
void CCdView::OnInitialUpdate()
{
// TODO: Add your specialized code here and/or call the base
//       class

/////////////////////////
// MY CODE STARTS HERE
/////////////////////////

// Call the OnLoadButton() function
// (to open the CD Audio device).
OnLoadButton();

// Install a system timer with 500 milliseconds interval.
if ( SetTimer (1, 500, NULL) == 0 )
   MessageBox (" Error: Cannot install timer!!!");
```

```
////////////////////
// MY CODE ENDS HERE
////////////////////
```

```
CFormView::OnInitialUpdate();
```

```
}
```

☐ Save your work by selecting Save from the File menu.

The first statement you typed in the `OnInitialUpdate()` function

```
OnLoadButton();
```

calls the `OnLoadButton()` function. You will write the code of the `OnLoadButton()` function soon. This code sets the DeviceType property of the `m_cd` multimedia object for playback of an audio CD and it issues an `Open` command.

The second (and last) statement you typed in the `OnInitialUpdate()` function is an `if` statement:

```
if ( SetTimer (1, 500, NULL) == 0 )
    MessageBox (" Error: Cannot install timer!!!");
```

This `if` statement uses the `SetTimer()` function to install a Windows timer with a 500-millisecond interval.

What does it mean to install a Windows timer? After you install a Windows timer, a `WM_TIMER` event will occur at regular intervals (for example, every 500 milliseconds). You can then attach code to the `WM_TIMER` event, and this code will be executed automatically at regular intervals (for example, every 500 milliseconds). You will attach code to the `WM_TIMER` event later in this chapter.

The `if` statement

```
if ( SetTimer (1, 500, NULL) == 0 )
    MessageBox (" Error: Cannot install timer!!!");
```

uses the `SetTimer()` function to install a timer with a 500-millisecond interval. If the `SetTimer()` function fails, it returns 0, in which case this `if` condition is satisfied and the user is prompted with an error message:

```
MessageBox ("Error: Cannot install timer!!!");
```

> **NOTE**
>
> The returned value of the `SetTimer()` function indicates whether `SetTimer()` was successful in installing a timer. If the returned value of `SetTimer()` is 0, `SetTimer()` was not able to install a timer.

The `SetTimer()` function takes three parameters. The first parameter is the ID you are assigning to the timer. In the preceding code, the first parameter is 1. Therefore, the ID of the timer will be 1.

The second parameter of the `SetTimer()` function is the interval time of the timer (in milliseconds). The interval time specifies how often a `WM_TIMER` event should occur for this timer. For example, in the preceding code, the second parameter is 500 milliseconds ($\frac{1}{2}$ second). Therefore, a WM_TIMER event will be generated every 500 milliseconds.

The third parameter of the SetTimer() function is the address of the function that should be executed whenever a WM_TIMER event occurs for the timer. If this parameter is NULL (as it is in the preceding code), the function that will be executed whenever a WM_TIMER event occurs is the function that is attached to the WM_TIMER event of the application. You will write this function later in the chapter.

To summarize, the code that you typed inside the OnInitialUpdate() function performs the following two tasks:

- It calls the OnLoadButton() function to open the CD audio device (you'll write the code of the OnLoadButton() function in the following section).
- It installs a Windows timer with a 500-millisecond delay. Therefore, a WM_TIMER event will occur every 500 milliseconds. You'll attach code to the WM_TIMER event later in this chapter.

Attaching Code to the Load Button

When the user clicks the Load button, the CD application should load the audio CD that is currently inside the CD-ROM drive.

Follow these steps to attach code to the Load button:

☐ Display the ClassWizard dialog box by selecting ClassWizard from the Project menu of Visual C++.

☐ Select the Message Maps tab at the top of ClassWizard's dialog box.

☐ Use ClassWizard to select the event:

CCdView -> IDC_LOAD_BUTTON -> BN_CLICKED

Then click the Add Function button.

☐ Name the new function OnLoadButton().

To write the code of the OnLoadButton() function do the following:

☐ Click the Edit Code button of ClassWizard.

> *ClassWizard responds by opening the file CdView.CPP, with the function OnLoadButton() ready to be edited by you.*

☐ Write code inside the OnLoadButton() function so that it looks like this:

```
void CCdView::OnLoadButton()
{
// TODO: Add your control notification handler code here

/////////////////////////
// MY CODE STARTS HERE
/////////////////////////
```

```
// Set the device type for playback of CD Audio.
m_cd.SetStrProperty("DeviceType","CDAudio");

// Issue an Open command.
m_cd.SetStrProperty("Command", "Open");

//////////////////////
// MY CODE ENDS HERE
//////////////////////

}
```

☐ Save your work by selecting Save from the File menu.

The first statement inside the OnLoadButton() function

```
m_cd.SetStrProperty("DeviceType","CDAudio");
```

sets the DeviceType property of the m_cd multimedia object to CDAudio. This is necessary because you want to use the m_cd multimedia object to play an audio CD.

> **NOTE**
>
> When you want to use a multimedia object for playing an audio CD, you need to set the DeviceType property of the multimedia object to CDAudio. For example, to set the m_cd multimedia object so that it can be used for playing audio CDs, use the statement
>
> ```
> m_cd.SetStrProperty("DeviceType","CDAudio");
> ```

The second (and last) statement inside the OnLoadButton() function

```
m_cd.SetStrProperty("Command", "Open");
```

issues an Open command to the m_cd multimedia object. After issuing the Open command, the CD audio inside the CD-ROM drive is ready for playback. You will write the code that starts the playback of the audio CD in the following section.

> **NOTE**
>
> The code you just typed inside the OnLoadButton() function is executed on two occasions:
>
> - Whenever the user clicks the Load button (because you attached the OnLoadButton() function to the BN_CLICKED event of the Load push button).
> - When the application first starts (because the OnInitialUpdate() function that you wrote earlier calls the OnLoadButton() function).

Attaching Code to the Play Button

When the user clicks the Play button, the CD-ROM drive should start playing the audio CD.

Follow these steps to attach code to the Play button:

☐ Display the ClassWizard dialog box by selecting ClassWizard from the Project menu of Visual C++.

☐ Select the Message Maps tab at the top of ClassWizard's dialog box.

☐ Use ClassWizard to select the event:

```
CCdView -> IDC_PLAY_BUTTON -> BN_CLICKED
```

Then click the Add Function button.

☐ Name the new function OnPlayButton().

To write the code of the OnPlayButton() function do the following:

☐ Click the Edit Code button of ClassWizard.

> *ClassWizard responds by opening the file CdView.CPP, with the function* OnPlayButton() *ready to be edited by you.*

☐ Write code inside the OnPlayButton() function so that it looks like this:

```
void CCdView::OnPlayButton()
{
// TODO: Add your control notification handler code here

/////////////////////////
// MY CODE STARTS HERE
/////////////////////////

// Issue a Play command.
m_cd.SetStrProperty("Command", "Play");

/////////////////////////
// MY CODE ENDS HERE
/////////////////////////

}
```

☐ Save your work by selecting Save from the File menu.

The code of the OnPlayButton() function is made up of one statement:

```
m_cd.SetStrProperty("Command", "Play");
```

This statement starts the playback of the audio CD by issuing a Play command to the m_cd multimedia object.

Attaching Code to the Stop Button

When the user clicks the Stop button, the CD-ROM drive should stop the playback of the CD audio.

Follow these steps to attach code to the Stop button:

☐ Display the ClassWizard dialog box by selecting ClassWizard from the Project menu of Visual C++.

☐ Select the Message Maps tab at the top of ClassWizard's dialog box.

☐ Use ClassWizard to select the event:

```
CCdView -> IDC_STOP_BUTTON -> BN_CLICKED
```

Then click the Add Function button.

☐ Name the new function `OnStopButton()`.

To write the code of the `OnStopButton()` function do the following:

☐ Click the Edit Code button of ClassWizard.

> *ClassWizard responds by opening the file CdView.CPP, with the function* `OnStopButton()` *ready to be edited by you.*

☐ Write code inside the `OnStopButton()` function so that it looks like this:

```
void CCdView::OnStopButton()
{
// TODO: Add your control notification handler code here

/////////////////////////
// MY CODE STARTS HERE
/////////////////////////

// Issue a Stop command.
m_cd.SetStrProperty("Command", "Stop");

/////////////////////////
// MY CODE ENDS HERE
/////////////////////////

}
```

☐ Save your work by selecting Save from the File menu.

The code of the `OnStopButton()` function is made up of one statement:

```
m_cd.SetStrProperty("Command", "Stop");
```

This statement stops the playback of the audio CD by issuing a `Stop` command to the `m_cd` multimedia object.

To hear the code that you wrote so far in action do the following:

☐ Select Build CD.EXE from the Project menu.

☐ Select Execute CD.EXE from the Project menu.

☐ If your CD-ROM drive does not have an audio CD inside it, insert an audio CD into your CD-ROM drive and then click the Load button.

☐ Click the Play button.

> *The CD.EXE application responds by playing the first track of your audio CD.*

To stop the playback do the following:

☐ Click the Stop button.

> *The CD application responds by stopping the playback.*

Note that at this point the Track edit box does not display the correct current track number. You'll write the code that is responsible for displaying the current track number inside the Track edit box later in the chapter.

☐ Terminate the CD application by selecting Exit from the File menu.

Attaching Code to the Prev Button

When the user clicks the Prev button, the CD application should change the playback position to the previous track.

Follow these steps to attach code to the Prev button:

☐ Display the ClassWizard dialog box by selecting ClassWizard from the Project menu of Visual C++.

☐ Select the Message Maps tab at the top of ClassWizard's dialog box.

☐ Use ClassWizard to select the event:

```
CCdView -> IDC_PREV_BUTTON -> BN_CLICKED
```

Then click the Add Function button.

☐ Name the new function `OnPrevButton()`.

To write the code of the `OnPrevButton()` function do the following:

☐ Click the Edit Code button of ClassWizard.

> *ClassWizard responds by opening the file CdView.CPP, with the function `OnPrevButton()` ready to be edited by you.*

☐ Write code inside the `OnPrevButton()` function so that it looks like this:

```
void CCdView::OnPrevButton()
{
// TODO: Add your control notification handler code here

////////////////////////
// MY CODE STARTS HERE
////////////////////////

// Issue a Prev command
m_cd.SetStrProperty("Command", "Prev");
```

```
////////////////////
// MY CODE ENDS HERE
////////////////////
```

}

☐ Save your work by selecting Save from the File menu.

The code you just typed inside the `OnPrevButton()` function is made of one statement:

```
m_cd.SetStrProperty("Command", "Prev");
```

This statement issues a `Prev` command to the `m_cd` multimedia object. Issuing a `Prev` command changes the playback position to the previous track.

Attaching Code to the Next Button

When the user clicks the Next button, the CD application should change the playback position to the next track.

Follow these steps to attach code to the Next button:

☐ Display the ClassWizard dialog box by selecting ClassWizard from the Project menu of Visual C++.

☐ Select the Message Maps tab at the top of ClassWizard's dialog box.

☐ Use ClassWizard to select the event:

```
CCdView -> IDC_NEXT_BUTTON -> BN_CLICKED
```

Then click the Add Function button.

☐ Name the new function `OnNextButton()`.

To write the code of the `OnNextButton()` function do the following:

☐ Click the Edit Code button of ClassWizard.

>   *ClassWizard responds by opening the file CdView.CPP, with the function* `OnNextButton()` *ready to be edited by you.*

☐ Write code inside the `OnNextButton()` function so that it looks like this:

```
void CCdView::OnNextButton()
{
// TODO: Add your control notification handler code here

////////////////////
// MY CODE STARTS HERE
////////////////////

// Issue a Next command
m_cd.SetStrProperty("Command", "Next");
```

```
/////////////////////
// MY CODE ENDS HERE
/////////////////////
```

}

☐ Save your work by selecting Save from the File menu.

The code you just typed inside the `OnNextButton()` function is made of one statement:

`m_cd.SetStrProperty("Command", "Next");`

This statement issues a `Next` command to the `m_cd` multimedia object. Issuing a `Next` command changes the playback position to the next track.

To see the code that you attached to the Prev and Next buttons in action do the following:

☐ Select Build CD.EXE from the Project menu.

☐ Select Execute CD.EXE from the Project menu.

☐ If your CD-ROM drive does not have an audio CD inside it, insert an audio CD into your CD-ROM drive and then click the Load button.

☐ Click the Play button.

 The CD application responds by playing the first track of the CD.

☐ Click the Next button.

 The CD.EXE application responds by changing the playback position to the next track (that is, to the second track).

☐ Click the Play button.

 The CD.EXE application responds by playing the second track of the CD.

☐ In a similar manner, experiment with the Prev button and verify that after you click the Prev button the playback position changes to the previous track.

Note that at this point the Track edit box is not being updated when you move from one track to another. You'll write the code that is responsible for displaying the current track number inside the Track edit box later.

☐ Terminate the CD application by selecting Exit from the File menu.

Attaching Code to the Eject Button

When the user clicks the Eject button, the CD application should either open or close the door of the CD-ROM drive. If the door of the CD-ROM drive is currently closed, clicking the Eject button should open the door. If the door of the CD-ROM drive is currently open, clicking the Eject button should close the door.

Follow these steps to attach code to the Eject button:

☐ Display the ClassWizard dialog box by selecting ClassWizard from the Project menu of Visual C++.

☐ Select the Message Maps tab at the top of ClassWizard's dialog box.

☐ Use ClassWizard to select the event:

```
CCdView -> IDC_EJECT_BUTTON -> BN_CLICKED
```

Then click the Add Function button.

☐ Name the new function OnEjectButton().

To write the code of the OnEjectButton() function do the following:

☐ Click the Edit Code button of ClassWizard.

> *ClassWizard responds by opening the file CdView.CPP, with the function OnEjectButton() ready to be edited by you.*

☐ Write code inside the OnEjectButton() function so that it looks like this:

```
void CCdView::OnEjectButton()
{
// TODO: Add your control notification handler code here

/////////////////////////
// MY CODE STARTS HERE
/////////////////////////

// Get the current playback mode.
long CurrentMode;
m_cd.GetNumProperty("Mode", &CurrentMode);

// If the CD-ROM drive door is open, close it.
// otherwise, open the CD-ROM drive door.
if ( CurrentMode == 530 )
   m_cd.SetStrProperty("Command", "CloseDoor");
else
   m_cd.SetStrProperty("Command", "Eject");

/////////////////////////
// MY CODE ENDS HERE
/////////////////////////

}
```

☐ Save your work by selecting Save from the File menu.

The first two statements in the OnEjectButton() function

```
long CurrentMode;
m_cd.GetNumProperty("Mode", &CurrentMode);
```

fill the local variable CurrentMode with the value of the Mode property of the m_cd multimedia object. The Mode property reports the current playback mode.

The next statement is an if...else statement that evaluates the value that was extracted from the Mode property:

```
if ( CurrentMode == 530 )
   m_cd.SetStrProperty("Command", "CloseDoor");
else
   m_cd.SetStrProperty("Command", "Eject");
```

If the value of the Mode property is 530, the door of the CD-ROM drive is currently open. If this is the case, the statement under the if closes the door of the CD-ROM drive by issuing a CloseDoor command:

```
m_cd.SetStrProperty("Command", "CloseDoor");
```

If, however, the value of the Mode property is not 530, the statement under the else is executed:

```
m_cd.SetStrProperty("Command", "Eject");
```

This statement opens the door of the CD-ROM drive by issuing an Eject command.

To see the code that you attached to the Eject button in action do the following:

☐ Select Build CD.EXE from the Project menu.

☐ Select Execute CD.EXE from the Project menu.

☐ If your CD-ROM drive does not have an audio CD inside it, insert an audio CD into your CD-ROM drive and then click the Load button.

☐ Click the Eject button.

> *The CD application responds by opening the door of your CD-ROM drive (only if your CD-ROM drive supports the Eject feature).*

☐ Click the Eject button again.

> *The CD application responds by closing the door of your CD-ROM drive (only if your CD-ROM drive supports the Close Door feature).*

☐ Terminate the CD application by selecting Exit from the File menu.

Updating the Track Edit Box Continuously

You'll now write the code that updates the Track edit box with the current track number. You'll attach this code to the WM_TIMER event of the view class.

Recall that inside the OnInitialUpdate() function you wrote code that installs a Windows timer with a 500-millisecond interval. Therefore, the code that you'll now attach to the WM_TIMER event will be executed every 500 milliseconds.

Attach code to the WM_TIMER event of the view class as follows:

☐ Display the ClassWizard dialog box by selecting ClassWizard from the Project menu of Visual C++.

☐ Select the Message Maps tab at the top of ClassWizard's dialog box.

☐ Use ClassWizard to select the event:

```
CCdView -> CCdView -> WM_TIMER
```

☐ Click the Add Function button.

> *Visual C++ responds by adding the* OnTimer() *member function to the* CCdView *class.*

☐ Click the Edit Code button of ClassWizard.

> *ClassWizard responds by opening the file CdView.CPP, with the function* OnTimer() *ready to be edited by you.*

☐ Write code inside the OnTimer() function so that it looks like this:

```
void CCdView::OnTimer(UINT nIDEvent)
{
// TODO: Add your message handler code here and/or call
//        default

////////////////////////
// MY CODE STARTS HERE
////////////////////////

// Set the TimeFormat property to "tmsf".
// (so that the Position property will report
//  the current position in units of tracks).
m_cd.SetStrProperty("TimeFormat", "tmsf");

// Fill the m_CurrentTrack variable with the value
// of the Position property.
m_cd.GetNumProperty("Position", &m_CurrentTrack);

// Update the Track edit box with the new value
// of the m_CurrentTrack variable.
UpdateData(FALSE);

////////////////////////
// MY CODE ENDS HERE
////////////////////////

CFormView::OnTimer(nIDEvent);

}
```

☐ Save your work by selecting Save from the File menu.

The first statement inside the OnTimer() function

```
m_cd.SetStrProperty("TimeFormat", "tmsf");
```

sets the TimeFormat property of the m_cd multimedia object to tmsf. The TimeFormat property determines in which units the Position property will report the current playback position. After you set the TimeFormat property to tmsf, the Position property will report the current playback position in units of tracks.

The next statement inside the `OnTimer()` function

```
m_cd.GetNumProperty("Position", &m_CurrentTrack);
```

fills the variable `m_CurrentTrack` with the value of the Position property. Recall that `m_CurrentTrack` is the variable that you attached to the IDC_CURRENT_TRACK edit box during the visual design of the IDD_CD_FORM dialog box.

So at this point, the variable of the IDC_CURRENT_TRACK edit box (`m_CurrentTrack`) is filled with the number of the current track.

The last statement inside the `OnTimer()` function

```
UpdateData(FALSE);
```

updates the value that is displayed inside the IDC_CURRENT_TRACK edit box with the new value of the `m_CurrentTrack` variable.

Here's a summary of how the code you attached to the WM_TIMER event updates the IDC_CURRENT_TRACK edit box continuously:

- Every 500 milliseconds a WM_TIMER event occurs (because inside the `OnInitialUpdate()` function you wrote code that installs a timer with a 500-millisecond interval).
- The code that you attached to the WM_TIMER event extracts the value of the Position property (in units of tracks) and sets the IDC_CURRENT_TRACK edit box with this value. Therefore, the IDC_CURRENT_TRACK edit box is being updated every 500 milliseconds.

To see the code that you attached to the WM_TIMER event in action do the following:

☐ Select Build CD.EXE from the Project menu.

☐ Select Execute CD.EXE from the Project menu.

☐ If your CD-ROM drive does not have an audio CD inside it, insert an audio CD into your CD-ROM drive and then click the Load button.

As you can see, the Track edit box displays the current track number (track 1).

☐ Experiment with the Next and Prev buttons and verify that the Track edit box displays the correct track number.

☐ Open the door of your CD-ROM drive.

  The CD application responds by displaying the number 0 inside the Track edit box (because the current playback position is not valid).

☐ Close the door of your CD-ROM drive.

The CD-ROM drive initializes itself for a while, and then the CD application displays the number 1 inside the Track edit box.

So as you have just seen, the code you attached to the WM_TIMER event continuously updates the Track edit box.

26

The Timer

In this chapter you will learn how to utilize a Windows timer. You will learn what a Windows timer is and how to install and utilize a Windows timer from within your Visual C++ applications. In this chapter you'll also learn how to change the default characteristics of the application's main window.

The MyTimer Application

The MyTimer application is an example of a Visual C++ application that installs and uses a Windows timer.

Before you start writing the MyTimer application, first execute the copy of it that resides in the \MVCPROG\EXE directory of the book's CD.

☐ Execute X:\MVCPROG\EXE\MyTimer.EXE (where *X* represents the drive letter of your CD-ROM drive).

Windows responds by executing the MyTimer.EXE application. The main window of MyTimer.EXE appears, as shown in Figure 26.1.

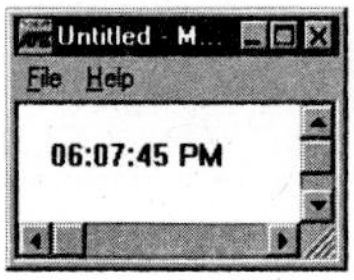

Figure 26.1. The main window of the MyTimer application.

As you can see, the main window of the application displays the current time, and the application keeps updating the displayed time.

Note that the MyTimer application has two special characteristics:

* Whenever the application is started, the application's window appears with the size shown in Figure 26.1.
* The application's window always appears on top of the desktop.

To prove that the application's main window is always on top of the desktop do the following:

☐ While the MyTimer application is running, switch to any other Windows application.

As you can see, the window of the MyTimer application always remains on the top of the desktop, even when another application's window is active. Figure 26.2 shows the window of the MyTimer application when the Paintbrush application's window is active.

The MyTimer application has two pop-up menus: File and Help. These pop-up menus are shown in Figures 26.3 and 26.4.

To exit the MyTimer application do the following:

☐ Select Exit from the File menu.

Now that you know what the MyTimer application should do, you can start writing it.

Figure 26.2. The window
of MyTimer while
Paintbrush is active.

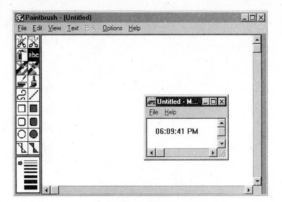

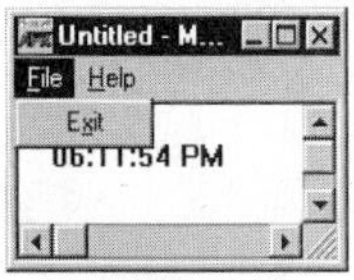

Figure 26.3. The File
pop-up menu of the
MyTimer application.

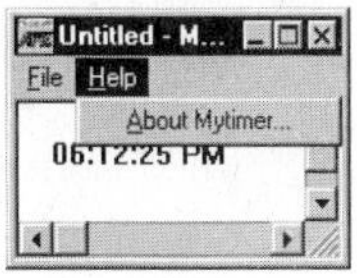

Figure 26.4. The Help
pop-up of the MyTimer
application.

Creating the Project of the MyTimer Application

You'll now create the MyTimer.MAK project.

☐ Close all the open windows on the desktop of Visual C++ (if there are any).

☐ Select New from the File menu.

Visual C++ responds by displaying the New dialog box.

☐ Select Project inside the New dialog box and then click the OK button of the New dialog box.

Visual C++ responds by displaying the New Project dialog box.

☐ Set the project name to MyTimer.

☐ Set the project path to \MVCPROG\CH26\MyTimer\MyTimer.MAK.

Your New Project dialog box should now look like the one shown in Figure 26.5.

Figure 26.5. The New Project dialog box of the MyTimer.MAK project.

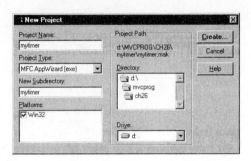

☐ Click the Create button of the New Project dialog box.

Visual C++ responds by displaying the AppWizard—Step 1 window.

☐ Set the Step 1 window as shown in Figure 26.6. As shown in Figure 26.6, the MyTimer.MAK project is set as a single-document application, and U.S. English (APPWIZUS.DLL) is used as the language for the application's resources.

Figure 26.6. The AppWizard—Step 1 window for the MyTimer application.

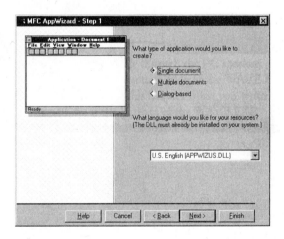

☐ Click the Next button of the Step 1 window.

Visual C++ responds by displaying the AppWizard—Step 2 of 6 window.

☐ Set the Step 2 of 6 window as shown in Figure 26.7. That is, in the MyTimer application you don't want any database support.

☐ Click the Next button of the Step 2 of 6 window.

Visual C++ responds by displaying the AppWizard—Step 3 of 6 window.

☐ Set the Step 3 of 6 window as shown in Figure 26.8. That is, in the MyTimer application you don't want any OLE support.

*Figure 26.7. The
AppWizard—Step 2 of 6
window for the MyTimer
application.*

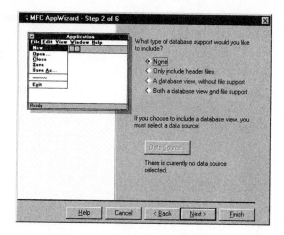

*Figure 26.8. The
AppWizard—Step 3 of 6
window for the MyTimer
application.*

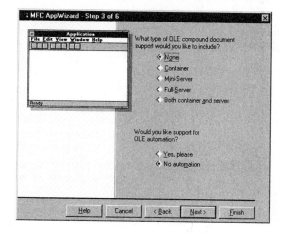

☐ Click the Next button of the Step 3 of 6 window.

    Visual C++ responds by displaying the AppWizard—Step 4 of 6 window.

☐ Set the Step 4 of 6 window as shown in Figure 26.9.

As shown in Figure 26.9, only the Use 3D Controls check box is checked.

☐ Click the Next button of the Step 4 of 6 window.

    Visual C++ responds by displaying the AppWizard—Step 5 of 6 window.

☐ Set the Step 5 of 6 window as shown in Figure 26.10.

As shown in Figure 26.10, the project will be generated with comments, a Visual C++ makefile will
be generated, and the application will use the MFC library from a DLL.

Figure 26.9. The AppWizard—Step 4 of 6 window for the MyTimer application.

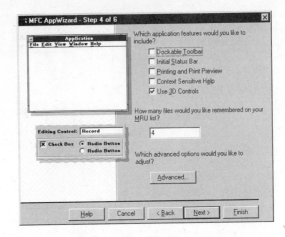

Figure 26.10. The AppWizard—Step 5 of 6 window for the MyTimer application.

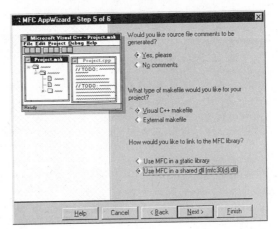

☐ Click the Next button of the Step 5 of 6 window.

Visual C++ responds by displaying the AppWizard—Step 6 of 6 window.

You'll now use the AppWizard—Step 6 of 6 window to tell AppWizard to derive the view class of the application from the MFC class CFormView:

☐ Select the CMytimerView class inside the AppWizard—Step 6 of 6 window.

☐ Set the Base Class drop-down list box to CFormView.

Your AppWizard—Step 6 of 6 window should now look like the one shown in Figure 26.11.

Figure 26.11. The
AppWizard—Step 6 of 6
window after you set the
base class of the application
view class to CFormView.

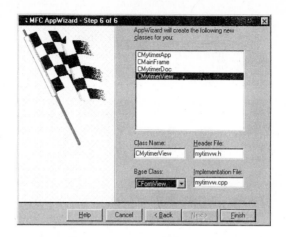

☐ Click the Finish button of the Step 6 of 6 window.

Visual C++ responds by displaying the New Project Information window, as shown in
Figure 26.12.

Figure 26.12. The New
Project Information
window of the
MyTimer.MAK project.

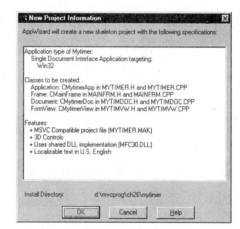

☐ Click the OK button of the New Project Information window.

Visual C++ responds by creating the project file and all the skeleton files of the application.

The Visual Implementation of the MyTimer Application's Menu

The MyTimer application should have a menu with two pop-up menus, as shown in Figures 26.3
and 26.4. Now implement this menu:

☐ Select MyTimer.MAK from the Window menu to display the MyTimer.MAK window, double-click mytimer.rc inside the MyTimer.MAK window, double-click Menu inside the mytimer.rc window, and finally, double-click IDR_MAINFRAME under Menu.

Visual C++ responds by displaying the IDR_MAINFRAME menu in design mode.

☐ Implement the menu of the MyTimer application so that it contains the following items:

&File
    E&xit
&Help
    &About Mytimer...

Don't forget to delete the accelerator keys of the menu items that you removed:

☐ Select mytimer.rc from the Window menu, double-click Accelerator inside the mytimer.rc window, double-click IDR_MAINFRAME under Accelerator.

Visual C++ responds by displaying the accelerator table of the MyTimer.MAK project.

☐ Delete the accelerator keys that are not used by the application. In particular, delete the accelerator keys of the ID_FILE_NEW, ID_FILE_OPEN, and ID_FILE_SAVE menu items.

If you do not delete these accelerator keys, they will be active during runtime. If, for example, the user presses Ctrl+N, it will be as if the user selected New from the File menu (even though you removed the New item from the File menu).

Save your work:

☐ Select Save from the File menu.

The visual implementation of the menu of the MyTimer application is complete.

The Visual Implementation of the MyTimer Application's Main Window

Because in AppWizard you specified that the base class of the application's view class is CFormView, AppWizard created for you a form (a dialog box) that is attached to the view class of the application. This dialog box serves as the main window of the application. AppWizard named this dialog box IDD_MYTIMER_FORM. You'll now customize the IDD_MYTIMER_FORM dialog box.

☐ Select MyTimer.MAK from the Window menu to display the MyTimer.MAK window, double-click mytimer.rc inside the MyTimer.MAK window, double-click Dialog inside the mytimer.rc window, and finally, double-click IDD_MYTIMER_FORM under the Dialog item.

Visual C++ responds by displaying the IDD_MYTIMER_FORM dialog box in design mode. This dialog box serves as the main window of the MyTimer application.

☐ Delete the TODO static text from the dialog box.

☐ Select Save from the File menu to save your work.

Installing a Timer in the MyTimer Application

The MyTimer application installs and utilizes a Windows timer. What does it mean to install a Windows timer? After you install a Windows timer, a WM_TIMER event will occur at regular intervals (for example, every 500 milliseconds). You can then attach code to the WM_TIMER event, and this code will be executed automatically at regular intervals (for example, every 500 milliseconds).

You will now write the code that installs a Windows timer in the MyTimer application. You will write this code inside the OnCreate() member function of the view class, because you want the timer to be installed upon start-up of the application.

☐ Use ClassWizard (from the Project menu) to select the event:

```
CMytimerView -> CMytimerView -> WM_CREATE
```

Then click the Add Function button.

> *Visual C++ responds by adding the OnCreate() function.*

☐ Click the Edit Code button.

> *Visual C++ responds by displaying the OnCreate() function ready to be edited by you.*

☐ Edit the OnCreate() function that you added to the MYTIMVW.CPP file. After you edit this function, it should look like this:

```
int CMytimerView::OnCreate(LPCREATESTRUCT lpCreateStruct)
{
if (CFormView::OnCreate(lpCreateStruct) == -1)
return -1;

// TODO: Add your specialized creation code here

/////////////////////////
// MY CODE STARTS HERE
/////////////////////////

// Install a system timer with 500 milliseconds interval.
if ( SetTimer (1, 500, NULL) == 0 )
    MessageBox ("Cannot install timer!!!");

/////////////////////////
// MY CODE ENDS HERE
/////////////////////////


return 0;
}
```

The code you typed is made of a single if statement:

```
if ( SetTimer (1, 500, NULL) == 0 )
    MessageBox ("Cannot install timer!!!");
```

This *if* statement uses the SetTimer() function to install a timer. If the SetTimer() function fails, it returns 0, the *if* condition is satisfied, and the user is prompted with an error message:

```
MessageBox ("Cannot install timer!!!");
```

> **NOTE**
>
> The returned value of the SetTimer() function indicates whether SetTimer() was successful in installing a timer. If the returned value of SetTimer() is 0, you know that SetTimer() was not able to install a timer.
>
> For example, Windows version 3.1 allows a total of 32 timers to be active at one time. Therefore, if all 32 timers are in use by other applications, you will not be able to install a timer, and SetTimer() will return 0.

The SetTimer() function takes three parameters. The first parameter is the ID you are assigning to the timer. In the preceding code, the first parameter is 1. Therefore, the ID of the timer is 1.

The second parameter of the SetTimer() function is the interval time of the timer (in milliseconds). The interval time specifies how often a WM_TIMER event should occur for this timer. For example, in the preceding code, the second parameter is 500 milliseconds $^1/_2$ second). Therefore, a WM_TIMER event is generated every 500 milliseconds.

The third parameter of the SetTimer() function is the address of the function that should be executed whenever a WM_TIMER event occurs for the timer. If this parameter is NULL (as it is in the preceding code), the function that will be executed whenever a WM_TIMER event occurs is the function that is attached to the WM_TIMER event of the application. You will write this function in the following section.

Attaching Code to the *WM_TIMER* Event

The code you wrote inside the OnCreate() function of the view class installed a timer with a 500-millisecond interval. This means that a WM_TIMER event will occur every 500 milliseconds. You will now attach code to the WM_TIMER event. Therefore, this code will be executed every 500 milliseconds.

☐ Use ClassWizard (from the Project menu) to select the event:

```
CMytimerView -> CMytimerView -> WM_TIMER
```

Then click the Add Function button.

Visual C++ responds by adding the OnTimer() *function.*

☐ Click the Edit Code button.

Visual C++ responds by displaying the OnTimer() *function, ready to be edited by you.*

☐ Edit the OnTimer() function that you added to the MYTIMVW.CPP file. After you edit this function, it should look like this:

```
void CMytimerView::OnTimer(UINT nIDEvent)
{
// TODO: Add your message handler code
// here and/or call default


    /////////////////////////
    // MY CODE STARTS HERE
    /////////////////////////

    MessageBeep((WORD)-1);

    /////////////////////////
    // MY CODE ENDS HERE
    /////////////////////////


CFormView::OnTimer(nIDEvent);
}
```

The code you just typed inside the OnTimer() function simply calls the MessageBeep() function to beep:

```
MessageBeep((WORD)-1);
```

Later you will change this code so that instead of beeping, the code of OnTimer() will display the current time inside the application window. For now, you are using the MessageBeep() function to illustrate the timer concept.

Here's a summary of what you've done so far:

- You wrote code inside the OnCreate() function of the view class that installs a timer with a 500-millisecond interval. Therefore, a WM_TIMER event will occur every 500 milliseconds.

- You attached code to the WM_TIMER event. This code uses the MessageBeep() function to beep. Therefore, when you run the MyTimer application, you should hear the PC speaker beep every 500 milliseconds.

NOTE

Note that the OnTimer() function has one parameter: nIDEvent.

This parameter specifies the ID of the timer for which the WM_TIMER event occurred. In the MyTimer application you did not have to use this parameter because you installed only one timer. However, in applications in which you install more than one timer, you need to use this parameter to check for which timer the WM_TIMER event has occurred. You can use a series of if statements or a switch statement to check the value of nIDEvent and then execute the appropriate code.

Don't forget to save your work:

☐ Select Save from the File menu.

Executing the MyTimer Application

Now execute the MyTimer application and hear the code that you attached to the WM_TIMER event in action:

☐ Select Rebuild MYTIMER.EXE from the Project menu of Visual C++.

☐ Select Execute MYTIMER.EXE from the Project menu.

> *Visual C++ responds by executing the MyTimer application. As you can hear, the MyTimer application beeps every 500 milliseconds.*

☐ Switch to another Windows application.

The MyTimer application keeps on beeping every 500 milliseconds, even when the window of another Windows application is active!

☐ Switch back to the MyTimer application and terminate it.

In the following sections, you'll enhance the MyTimer application as follows:

- You'll change the code inside OnTimer() so that instead of beeping every 500 milliseconds, it will display the current time in the application's main window.

- You'll change the default characteristics of the application's main window so that upon start-up of the application the size of the window will be as shown in Figure 26.1 and so that the main window will always be on top of the desktop (even when another application is active).

Displaying the Current Time in the MyTimer Application's Window

You'll now modify the OnTimer() function so that instead of beeping every 500 milliseconds, it will display the current time inside the application window.

☐ Modify the OnTimer() function inside the MYTIMVW.CPP file until it looks like this:

```
void CMytimerView::OnTimer(UINT nIDEvent)
{
// TODO: Add your message handler code here and/or call default


    /////////////////////////
    // MY CODE STARTS HERE
    /////////////////////////

    //MessageBeep((WORD)-1);

    // Create an object of class CTime.
```

```
CTime tNow;

// Update tNow with the current time.
tNow = CTime::GetCurrentTime();

// Format the current time.
CString sNow = tNow.Format("%I:%M:%S %p");

// Display the current time.
CClientDC dc(this);
dc.TextOut(15,15,sNow);

/////////////////////
// MY CODE ENDS HERE
/////////////////////
```

```
CFormView::OnTimer(nIDEvent);
}
```

In the modification you just made to the OnTimer() function, you commented out (//) the MessageBeep() statement, and you added the statements that display the current time inside the application window.

The first statement

```
CTime tNow;
```

creates an object tNow of class CTime.

The next statement

```
tNow = CTime::GetCurrentTime();
```

uses the GetCurrentTime() member function of the CTime class to update the tNow object with the current time.

The next statement is

```
CString sNow = tNow.Format("%I:%M:%S %p");
```

This statement creates a CString object (sNow) and fills this object with a string that corresponds to the time stored in tNow. In the preceding statement, you converted tNow to a string (sNow) by using the Format() member function of the CTime class. The parameter passed to the Format() function is

```
"%I:%M:%S %p"
```

The %I represents the hour portion of the time in 12-hour format (01 through 12), the %M represents the minutes portion of the time (00 through 59), the %S represents the seconds portion of the time (00 through 59), and the %p represents the AM/PM portion of the time. For example, if currently the value of tNow is 23:30:45 (11:30:45 PM), the statement

```
CString sNow = tNow.Format("%I:%M:%S %p");
```

updates sNow with the string "11:30:45 PM".

The last two statements in `OnTimer()` display the sNow string:

```
CClientDC dc(this);
dc.TextOut(15,15,sNow);
```

Now execute the MyTimer application and see the code that you just entered in action:

☐ Select Build MYTIMER.EXE from the Project menu of Visual C++.

☐ Select Execute MYTIMER.EXE from the Project menu.

> *Visual C++ responds by executing the MyTimer application. As you can see, the MyTimer application displays the current time inside the application window. The code you wrote inside* `OnTimer()` *keeps updating the displayed time every 500 milliseconds.*

In the following sections you'll add code that changes the default characteristics of the application's main window:

- Upon start-up of the application the size of the window will be as shown in Figure 26.1
- The application's main window will always be on top of the desktop (even when another application is active).

Changing the Default Characteristics of the MyTimer Application's Main Window

Recall that upon start-up of the application, the default size of the application window should be as shown in Figure 26.1. You want the window to appear like that for cosmetic reasons. That is, because the area that is needed for displaying the current time is small, the application window should be sized accordingly. In addition, the main window of the application should always be on top of the desktop. That is, even when the window of another application is active, you want the window of the MyTimer application to remain on top.

You need to write the code that sets the default characteristics of the application window inside the `PreCreateWindow()` member function of the `CMainFrame` class.

The header file of the `CMainFrame` class is MAINFRM.H and the implementation file of the `CMainFrame` class is MAINFRM.CPP.

☐ Use ClassWizard (from the Project menu) to select the event:

```
CMainFrame -> CMainFrame -> PreCreateWindow
```

Then click the Add Function button.

> *Visual C++ responds by adding the* `PreCreateWindow()` *function.*

☐ Click the Edit Code button.

> *Visual C++ responds by displaying the* `PreCreateWindow()` *function ready to be edited by you.*

☐ Now write the code of the `PreCreateWindow()` function. After you write this function, the end of the MAINFRM.CPP file should look like this:

```
BOOL CMainFrame::PreCreateWindow(CREATESTRUCT& cs)
{
// TODO: Add your specialized code here
// and/or call the base class


/////////////////////////
// MY CODE STARTS HERE
/////////////////////////

    // Set the width of the window.
    cs.cx = 160;

    // Set the height of the window.
    cs.cy = 120;

    // Make the window a topmost window.
    cs.dwExStyle = WS_EX_TOPMOST;

/////////////////////////
// MY CODE ENDS HERE
/////////////////////////

return CFrameWnd::PreCreateWindow(cs);
}
```

As its name implies, the `PreCreateWindow()` function is automatically executed prior to the creation of the window.

You can use this function to override the default characteristics of the window. The parameter of `PreCreateWindow()`, `cs`, is a structure of type `CREATESTRUCT`.

You set the characteristics of the window by setting the members of the `cs` structure.

Now go over the code you typed inside the `PreCreateWindow()` function.

The first statement is

```
cs.cx = 160;
```

This statement sets the value of the `cx` member of the `cs` structure to 160. The `cx` member specifies the width of the window. Therefore, the width of the window will be 160.

The next statement is

```
cs.cy = 120;
```

This statement sets the value of the `cy` member of the `cs` structure to 120. The `cy` member specifies the height of the window. Therefore, the height of the window will be 90.

The next statement is

```
// Make the window a topmost window.
cs.dwExStyle = WS_EX_TOPMOST;
```

This statement sets the value of the dwExStyle member of the cs structure to the constant WS_EX_TOPMOST. The dwExStyle member specifies the extended style of the window. When dwExStyle is set to WS_EX_TOPMOST the window is created as a topmost window. That is, the window will always remain on top of the desktop (even when another window is active).

Don't forget to save your work:

☐ Select Save from the File menu.

Executing the Final Version of the MyTimer Application

To see the code that you attached to the PreCreateWindow() function in action do the following:

☐ Select Build MYTIMER.EXE from the Project menu of Visual C++.

☐ Select Execute MYTIMER.EXE from the Project menu.

Visual C++ responds by executing the MyTimer application. As you can see, the window of the MyTimer application appears, as you specified inside the PreCreateWindow() function. (See Figure 26.1.)

You can now verify that the window of the MyTimer application is the topmost window (as you specified in the PreCreateWindow() function):

☐ Switch to another application.

As you can see, the window of the MyTimer application remains on the top of the desktop, even when you switch to another application.

Killing the Timer

In the MyTimer application you did not have to kill (that is, remove) the timer because MyTimer needed the timer throughout the lifetime of the application. Once the application is terminated, the timer is killed automatically.

However, in some applications, you will need to kill the timer during runtime (from within your code). To do this, you need to use the KillTimer() function. The KillTimer() function takes one parameter: the ID of the timer to be killed.

Recall from earlier in the chapter that when you install a timer with the SetTimer() function you specify the ID of the timer. For example, in the MyTimer application you called the SetTimer() function as follows:

```
SetTimer (1, 500, NULL)
```

This statement defines the ID of the timer as 1 (the first parameter). Therefore, if later in the program you want to kill this timer, you need to call `KillTimer()` as follows:

```
KillTimer(1);
```

Note that both `SetTimer()` and `KillTimer()` are member functions of the `CWnd` class. You can call these functions from the view class of the application because the view class (`CView` or `CFormView`) is derived from `CWnd`.

27

Animation

In this chapter you will learn
about animation. You'll learn
what animation is and how to
write Visual C++ applications
that perform animation.

The BALL Application

Animation is the process of displaying pictures one after the other, thereby creating the illusion that the objects shown inside the pictures are moving.

You will now write the BALL application, which is an example of a Visual C++ application that displays an animation show. The animation show of the BALL application is silent. That is, it does not include any sound. In Chapter 29, "Animation and Sound with and Without Synchronization," you will write other Visual C++ animation applications that include sound.

Before you start writing the BALL application, first execute the copy of it that resides in the \MVCPROG\EXE directory of the book's CD.

☐ Execute the X:\MVCPROG\EXE\Ball.EXE program (where *X* represents the letter drive of your CD-ROM drive).

> *Windows responds by executing the Ball.EXE application. The main window of Ball.EXE appears, as shown in Figure 27.1.*

Figure 27.1. The main window of the BALL application.

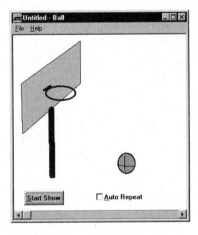

As you can see, the main window of the application contains a picture of a basketball and a basket, a push button (Start Show), and a check box (Auto Repeat).

To start the animation show do the following:

☐ Click the Start Show button.

> *The BALL application responds by displaying an animation show. The animation show creates the illusion that the basketball is thrown up into the basket and then falls down.*

To make the animation show automatically repeat itself do the following:

☐ Check the Auto Repeat check box and then click the Start Show button.

The BALL application now keeps displaying the animation show continuously—that is, once the animation show is over, the show starts automatically all over again.

The animation show takes place even when another Windows application is active. To verify this fact do the following:

☐ While the animation show is running (with the Auto Repeat check box checked), switch to another Windows application (for example, Paintbrush).

☐ Place the window of the other application so that you can see both the window of the BALL application and the window of the other application.

As you can see, the animation show inside the window of the BALL application is running even when the window of the other application is active. Figure 27.2 shows a snapshot of the BALL application animation while the window of Paintbrush is active.

Figure 27.2. The show must go on (even when the window of Paintbrush is active).

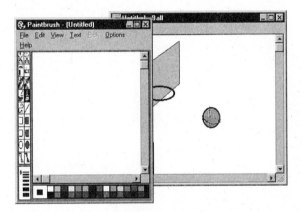

You can also run several instances of the BALL application and view several animation shows simultaneously! To see this do the following:

☐ Terminate the BALL application by selecting Exit from its File menu.

☐ Execute the X:\MVCPROG\EXE\BALL.EXE program.

☐ Repeat the preceding step to run another copy of the BALL.EXE application.

You now have two instances of the BALL.EXE application running.

☐ Arrange the two windows of the BALL.EXE applications so that you are able to see both of them, and then start the animation in both windows with the Auto Repeat check box checked. That is, in each of the two windows, check the Auto Repeat check box, and then click the Start Show button.

You now have two animation shows! Figure 27.3 shows a snapshot of the two animation shows.

Figure 27.3. Running two
animation shows
simultaneously.

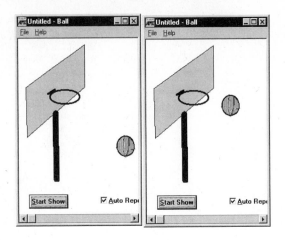

The BALL application has two pop-up menus: File and Help. These pop-up menus are shown in Figures 27.4 and 27.5.

Terminate the two instances of the BALL application that you just started:

☐ Select Exit from the File menu of each of the two instances of the BALL.EXE application.

Now that you know what the BALL application should do, you can start writing it.

Figure 27.4. The File
pop-up menu of the
BALL application.

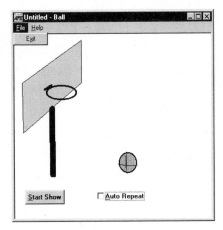

*Figure 27.5. The Help
pop-up menu of the BALL
application.*

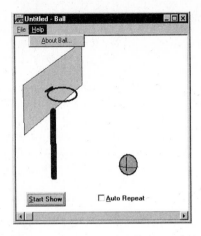

Creating the Project of the BALL Application

You'll now create the BALL.MAK project.

☐ Close all the open windows on the desktop of Visual C++ (if there are any).

☐ Select New from the File menu.

Visual C++ responds by displaying the New dialog box.

☐ Select Project inside the New dialog box and then click the OK button of the New dialog box.

Visual C++ responds by displaying the New Project dialog box.

☐ Set the project name to Ball.

☐ Set the project path to \MVCPROG\CH27\Ball\Ball.MAK.

Your New Project dialog box should now look like the one shown in Figure 27.6.

*Figure 27.6. The New
Project dialog box of the
Ball.MAK project.*

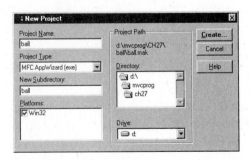

☐ Click the Create button of the New Project dialog box.

Visual C++ responds by displaying the AppWizard—Step 1 window.

☐ Set the Step 1 window as shown in Figure 27.7. As shown in Figure 27.7, the Ball.MAK project is set as a single-document application, and U.S. English (APPWIZUS.DLL) is used as the language for the application's resources.

Figure 27.7. The AppWizard—Step 1 window for the BALL application.

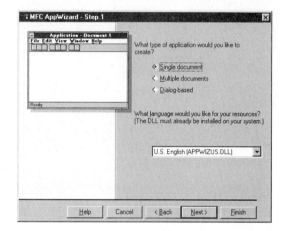

☐ Click the Next button of the Step 1 window.

Visual C++ responds by displaying the AppWizard—Step 2 of 6 window.

☐ Set the Step 2 of 6 window as shown in Figure 27.8. That is, in the BALL application you don't want any database support.

Figure 27.8. The AppWizard—Step 2 of 6 window for the BALL application.

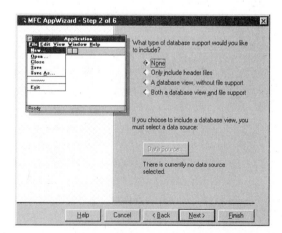

☐ Click the Next button of the Step 2 of 6 window.

   Visual C++ responds by displaying the AppWizard—Step 3 of 6 window.

☐ Set the Step 3 of 6 window as shown in Figure 27.9. That is, in the BALL application you
   don't want any OLE support.

*Figure 27.9. The
AppWizard—Step 3 of 6
window for the BALL
application.*

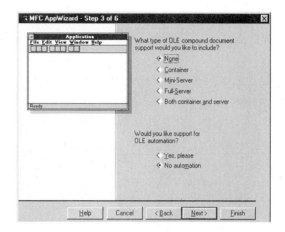

☐ Click the Next button of the Step 3 of 6 window.

   Visual C++ responds by displaying the AppWizard—Step 4 of 6 window.

☐ Set the Step 4 of 6 window as shown in Figure 27.10.

*Figure 27.10. The
AppWizard—Step 4 of 6
window for the BALL
application.*

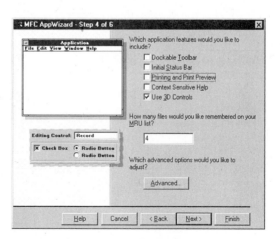

As shown in Figure 27.10, only the Use 3D Controls check box is checked.

☐ Click the Next button of the Step 4 of 6 window.

   Visual C++ responds by displaying the AppWizard—Step 5 of 6 window.

☐ Set the Step 5 of 6 window as shown in Figure 27.11.

As shown in Figure 27.11, the project will be generated with comments, a Visual C++ makefile will be generated, and the application will use the MFC library from a DLL.

Figure 27.11. The AppWizard—Step 5 of 6 window for the BALL application.

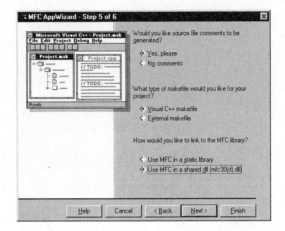

☐ Click the Next button of the Step 5 of 6 window.

Visual C++ responds by displaying the AppWizard—Step 6 of 6 window.

You'll now use the AppWizard—Step 6 of 6 window to tell AppWizard to derive the view class of the application from the MFC class CFormView:

☐ Select the CBallView class inside the AppWizard—Step 6 of 6 window.

☐ Set the Base Class drop-down list box to CFormView.

Your AppWizard—Step 6 of 6 window should now look like the one shown in Figure 27.12.

Figure 27.12. The AppWizard—Step 6 of 6 window after you set the base class of the application view class to CFormView.

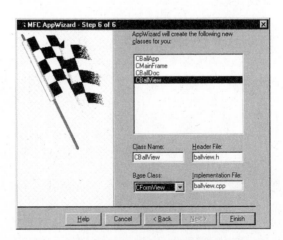

☐ Click the Finish button of the Step 6 of 6 window.

Visual C++ responds by displaying the New Project Information window, as shown in Figure 27.13.

Figure 27.13. *The New Project Information window of the Ball.MAK project.*

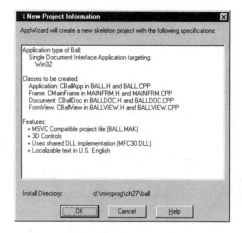

☐ Click the OK button of the New Project Information window.

Visual C++ responds by creating the project file and all the skeleton files of the application.

The Visual Implementation of the BALL Application's Main Window

Because in AppWizard you specified that the base class of the application's view class is CFormView (See Figure 27.12.), AppWizard created for you a form (a dialog box) that is attached to the view class of the application. This dialog box serves as the main window of the application. AppWizard named this dialog box IDD_BALL_FORM. You'll now customize the IDD_BALL_FORM dialog box.

☐ Select Ball.MAK from the Window menu to display the Ball.MAK window, double-click ball.rc inside the Ball.MAK window, double-click Dialog inside the ball.rc window, and finally, double-click IDD_BALL_FORM under the Dialog item.

Visual C++ responds by displaying the IDD_BALL_FORM dialog box in design mode. This dialog box serves as the main window of the BALL application.

☐ Delete the TODO static text from the dialog box.

☐ Implement the IDD_BALL_FORM dialog box according to the specifications in Table 27.1.

Table 27.1. The dialog box of the BALL application.

Object	Property	Setting
Dialog box	ID	IDD_BALL_FORM
Push button	ID	IDC_START_BUTTON
	Caption	&Start Show
Check box	ID	IDC_AUTO_REPEAT
	Caption	&Auto Repeat

Your dialog box should now look like the one shown in Figure 27.14.

Figure 27.14. The dialog box of the BALL application.

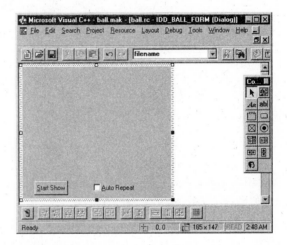

Save your work:

☐ Select Save from the File menu.

Attaching Variables to the Controls of the IDD_BALL_FORM Dialog Box

You'll now attach variables to the controls of the IDD_BALL_FORM dialog box.

☐ Use ClassWizard (from the Project menu) to attach the variable shown in Table 27.2. (See Figure 27.15.)

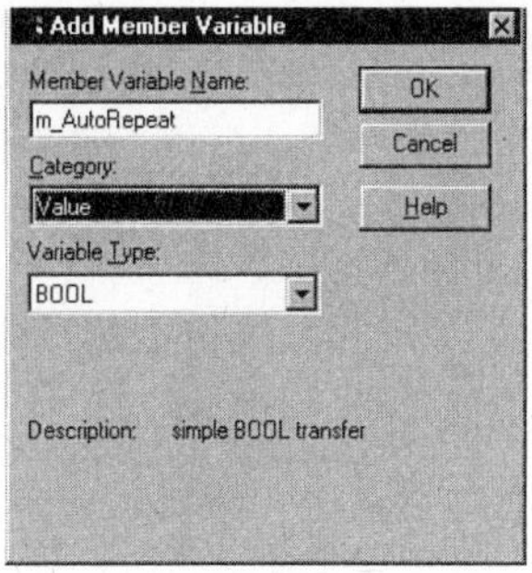

Figure 27.15. Attaching a variable to the check box.

Table 27.2. The Variables table of the IDD_BALL_FORM dialog box.

ID	Variable Name	Category	Variable Type
IDC_AUTO_REPEAT	m_AutoRepeat	Value	BOOL

Save your work:

☐ Select Save from the File menu.

The Visual Implementation of the Menu

You'll now visually design the menu of the BALL application.

☐ Select Ball.MAK from the Window menu to display the Ball.RC window, double-click Menu inside the Ball.RC window, and finally, double-click the IDR_MAINFRAME item that appears under the Menu item.

Visual C++ responds by displaying the IDR_MAINFRAME menu in design menu.

☐ Implement the menu of the BALL application so that it contains the following items:

&File
  E&xit
&Help
  &About Ball...

The visual implementation of the menu of the BALL application is complete.

Adding Bitmap Files to the BALL Application

The BALL application uses 11 bitmap (BMP) files for the animation. As you'll see later, the code of the BALL application displays these bitmaps one after the other to create the illusion that the object shown in these bitmaps (a basketball) is moving. (See Figures 27.16 through 27.26.)

Figure 27.16. The BALL1.BMP bitmap file.

Figure 27.17. The BALL2.BMP bitmap file.

Figure 27.18. The BALL3.BMP bitmap file.

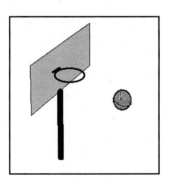

Figure 27.19. The BALL4.BMP bitmap file.

Figure 27.20. The BALL5.BMP bitmap file.

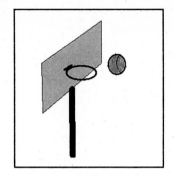

Figure 27.21. The BALL6.BMP bitmap file.

Figure 27.22. The BALL7.BMP bitmap file.

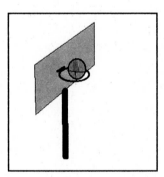

Figure 27.23. The BALL8.BMP bitmap file.

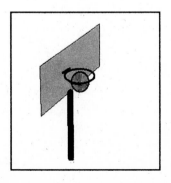

Figure 27.24. The
BALL9.BMP bitmap file.

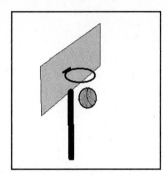

Figure 27.25. The
BALL10.BMP bitmap file.

Figure 27.26. The
BALL11.BMP bitmap file.

NOTE

In the following steps you'll be instructed to import BMP files. These BMP files were copied from the \MVCPROG\BMP directory of the book's CD to the \MVCPROG\BMP directory of your hard drive. The file attribute of these files is r (read-only).

Before proceeding with the following steps, make sure to remove the read-only attribute from these files.

To add the 11 bitmaps to the BALL application, follow these steps:

☐ Select Import from the Resource menu.

Visual C++ responds by displaying the Import dialog box.

☐ Select the \MVCPROG\BMP\BALL1.BMP file and then click the OK button.

Visual C++ responds by importing the \MVCPROG\BMP\BALL1.BMP file into the BALL application and displaying the bitmap. Note that the ID that Visual C++ assigned to the BALL1.BMP bitmap is IDB_BITMAP1.(See Figure 27.27.)

Figure 27.27. The IDB_BITMAP1 window after you import the BALL1.BMP file.

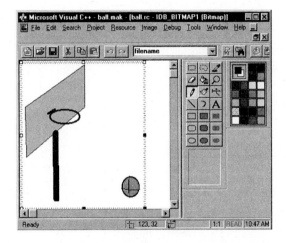

You'll now have to repeat the preceding steps to create more bitmap resources and then import the BMP files. That is, you have to select Import from the Resource menu and then select the BMP file that you want to import.

Repeat the preceding steps to import the rest of the BMP files:

☐ Import C:\MVCPROG\BMP\BALL2.BMP.

☐ Import C:\MVCPROG\BMP\BALL3.BMP.

☐ Import C:\MVCPROG\BMP\BALL4.BMP.

☐ Import C:\MVCPROG\BMP\BALL5.BMP.

☐ Import C:\MVCPROG\BMP\BALL6.BMP.

☐ Import C:\MVCPROG\BMP\BALL7.BMP.

☐ Import C:\MVCPROG\BMP\BALL8.BMP.

☐ Import C:\MVCPROG\BMP\BALL9.BMP.

☐ Import C:\MVCPROG\BMP\BALL10.BMP.

☐ Import C:\MVCPROG\BMP\BALL11.BMP.

When you finish importing the BMP files, your project should have the following bitmaps:

Name of New Resource	*Name of Imported BMP File*
IDB_BITMAP1	Ball1.BMP
IDB_BITMAP2	Ball2.BMP
IDB_BITMAP3	Ball3.BMP
IDB_BITMAP4	Ball4.BMP
IDB_BITMAP5	Ball5.BMP
IDB_BITMAP6	Ball6.BMP
IDB_BITMAP7	Ball7.BMP
IDB_BITMAP8	Ball8.BMP
IDB_BITMAP9	Ball9.BMP
IDB_BITMAP10	Ball10.BMP
IDB_BITMAP11	Ball11.BMP

NOTE

In the preceding steps you were instructed to import 11 BMP files into the BALL application. The order in which you imported the BMP files is important (that is, first BALL1.BMP, then BALL2.BMP, then BALL3.BMP, and so on). The order is important because as you import the BMP files, Visual C++ assigns to the BMP files the constant names IDB_BITMAP1, IDB_BITMAP2, IDB_BITMAP3, and so on. Later, when you write the code of the BALL application, it will be assumed that IDB_BITMAP1 corresponds to BALL1.BMP, IDB_BITMAP2 corresponds to BALL2.BMP, IDB_BITMAP3 corresponds to BALL3.BMP, and so on.

You've finished importing 11 bitmaps into the BALL application. To verify that you imported the bitmaps properly do the following:

☐ Select ball.rc from the Window menu, and then double-click Bitmap.

   Visual C++ responds by displaying a list of all the bitmaps of the Ball.MAK project. (See Figure 27.28.)

You can examine each of the bitmaps as follows:

☐ Double-click IDB_BITMAP1.

   Visual C++ responds by displaying the IDB_BITMAP1 window.

In a similar manner, you can display the windows of the other bitmaps you added to the project.

To save your work do the following:

☐ Select Save from the File menu.

Figure 27.28. The Ball.RC
window with a list of all
the bitmaps that the project
includes.

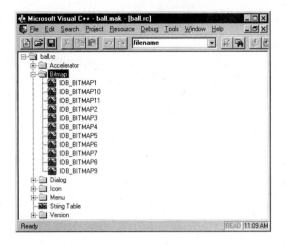

NOTE

When you import bitmaps to your application (as you just did), the bitmaps become an integral part of the application's EXE file. That is, after you compile and link your application, these bitmap files will be part of the EXE file. Therefore, the more bitmaps you import into your application, the larger your EXE file will be!

Executing the BALL Application

Although you have not yet written any code, execute the BALL application to see your visual design in action:

☐ Select Build All BALL.EXE from the Project menu of Visual C++.

☐ Select Execute BALL.EXE from the Project menu.

Visual C++ responds by executing the BALL application.

The main window of the application appears with the form that you designed inside it (including a push button and a check box). Of course, none of the bitmaps that you imported into the BALL application are displayed yet because you have not written any code to accomplish that. In the following sections, you'll write code that brings the BMP files to life.

To exit the BALL application do the following:

☐ Select Exit from the File menu.

Declaring Variables for the Animation Show

You'll now write the code that declares variables that are used by the animation show. You will declare these variables as data members of the view class because these variables need to be visible in several member functions of the view class.

☐ Open the file BALLVIEW.H and write code that declares two data members inside the CBallView class. When you finish writing this code, the CBallView class declaration should look like this:

```
class CBallView : public CFormView
{
protected: // create from serialization only
CBallView();
DECLARE_DYNCREATE(CBallView)

public:
//{{AFX_DATA(CBallView)
enum { IDD = IDD_BALL_FORM };
BOOL    m_AutoRepeat;
//}}AFX_DATA

// Attributes
public:
CBallDoc* GetDocument();


    ///////////////////////////
    // MY CODE STARTS HERE
    ///////////////////////////

    // The current frame number.
    int m_CurrentFrame;

    // An array for the 11 bitmaps.
    CBitmap* m_pB[11];

    ///////////////////////////
    // MY CODE ENDS HERE
    ///////////////////////////


// Operations
public:

// Overrides
// ClassWizard generated virtual function overrides
//{{AFX_VIRTUAL(CBallView)
public:
protected:
virtual void DoDataExchange(CDataExchange* pDX);
// DDX/DDV support
//}}AFX_VIRTUAL

// Implementation
public:
virtual ~CBallView();
#ifdef _DEBUG
```

```
virtual void AssertValid() const;
virtual void Dump(CDumpContext& dc) const;
#endif

protected:

// Generated message map functions
protected:
//{{AFX_MSG(CBallView)
// NOTE—the ClassWizard will add and remove member functions here.
//    DO NOT EDIT what you see in these blocks of generated code !
//}}AFX_MSG
DECLARE_MESSAGE_MAP()
};
```

In the preceding code, you declared two data members for the view class. You declared the first data member as this:

```
int m_CurrentFrame;
```

`m_CurrentFrame` is an integer that is used for maintaining the current frame number (bitmap) that is being displayed.

During the animation show, the code of the application will display the bitmaps one after the other. `m_CurrentFrame` indicates which bitmap is currently displayed. For example, when `m_CurrentFrame` is 0, the program should display the first bitmap (IDB_BITMAP1), when `m_CurrentFrame` is 1, the program should display the second frame (IDB_BITMAP2), and so on. As the animation show progresses, the code that you will write will increment the `m_CurrentFrame` variable.

You declared the second data member as this:

```
CBitmap* m_pB[11];
```

`m_pB[]` is an array with 11 elements that is used for storing pointers to objects of class `CBitmap`. `CBitmap` is an MFC that was designed to work specifically with bitmaps.

As you'll see in the next section, the `m_pB[]` array is used to load the 11 bitmaps of the animation show. `m_pB[0]` is used for the first bitmap (IDB_BITMAP1), `m_pB[1]` is used for the second bitmap (IDB_BITMAP2), `m_pB[2]` is used for the third bitmap (IDB_BITMAP3), and so on.

Don't forget to save your work:

☐ Select Save from the File menu of Visual C++.

Loading the Bitmaps

Before you can display the bitmaps, you need to first load them. In the BALL application you will write the code that loads the bitmaps inside the `OnInitialUpdate()` function because you want to load the bitmaps upon start-up of the application. This way, the code that performs the animation show will not need to load the bitmaps, and the animation will be performed smoothly. That is, loading the bitmaps takes time, and if you do it during the animation show, it will affect the performance of the animation.

☐ Use ClassWizard (from the Project menu) to select the event (See Figure 27.29.):

```
CBallView -> CBallView -> OnInitialUpdate
```

Then click the Add Function button.

Visual C++ responds by adding the `OnInitialUpdate()` *function.*

Figure 27.29. Adding the `OnInitialUpdate()` *function.*

☐ Click the Edit Code button.

Visual C++ responds by displaying the `OnInitialUpdate()` *function, ready to be edited by you.*

☐ Now add code to the `OnInitialUpdate()` function. After you add this code, the `OnInitialUpdate()` function should look like this:

```
void CBallView::OnInitialUpdate()
{
// TODO: Add your specialized code here
// and/or call the base class

/////////////////////////
// MY CODE STARTS HERE
/////////////////////////

    // Load IDB_BITMAP1
    m_pB[0] = new CBitmap;
    m_pB[0]->LoadBitmap(IDB_BITMAP1);

    // Load IDB_BITMAP2
    m_pB[1] = new CBitmap;
    m_pB[1]->LoadBitmap(IDB_BITMAP2);

    // Load IDB_BITMAP3
    m_pB[2] = new CBitmap;
    m_pB[2]->LoadBitmap(IDB_BITMAP3);
```

```
// Load IDB_BITMAP4
m_pB[3] = new CBitmap;
m_pB[3]->LoadBitmap(IDB_BITMAP4);

// Load IDB_BITMAP5
m_pB[4] = new CBitmap;
m_pB[4]->LoadBitmap(IDB_BITMAP5);

// Load IDB_BITMAP6
m_pB[5] = new CBitmap;
m_pB[5]->LoadBitmap(IDB_BITMAP6);

// Load IDB_BITMAP7
m_pB[6] = new CBitmap;
m_pB[6]->LoadBitmap(IDB_BITMAP7);

// Load IDB_BITMAP8
m_pB[7] = new CBitmap;
m_pB[7]->LoadBitmap(IDB_BITMAP8);

// Load IDB_BITMAP9
m_pB[8] = new CBitmap;
m_pB[8]->LoadBitmap(IDB_BITMAP9);

// Load IDB_BITMAP10
m_pB[9] = new CBitmap;
m_pB[9]->LoadBitmap(IDB_BITMAP10);

// Load IDB_BITMAP11
m_pB[10] = new CBitmap;
m_pB[10]->LoadBitmap(IDB_BITMAP11);


//////////////////////
// MY CODE ENDS HERE
//////////////////////


CFormView::OnInitialUpdate();
}
```

Now go over the code of the OnInitialUpdate() function.

The first statement is

```
m_pB[0] = new CBitmap;
```

This statement creates an object of class CBitmap and fills the first element of the m_pB[] array (m_pB[0]) with the address of this object. So now m_pB[0] points to an object of class CBitmap.

The next statement

```
m_pB[0]->LoadBitmap(IDB_BITMAP1);
```

uses the LoadBitmap() member function of the CBitmap class to load the first bitmap of the animation show (IDB_BITMAP1). So now, for all intents and purposes, m_pB[0] points to the first bitmap of the animation show.

In a similar manner, the rest of the statements of the OnInitialUpdate() function load the other bitmaps of the animation show. That is, after the code of OnInitialUpdate() is executed, m_pB[0] points to the first bitmap (IDB_BITMAP1), m_pB[1] points to the second bitmap (IDB_BITMAP2), m_pB[2] points to the third bitmap (IDB_BITMAP3), and so on.

NOTE

As stated earlier, the BMP files that you imported with Visual C++ into the application become an integral part of the EXE file. When you use the LoadBitmap() function, the bitmap is loaded from the application's EXE file.

Don't forget to save your work:

☐ Select Save from the File menu of Visual C++.

Displaying the First Frame of the Show

You have written the code that loads the 11 bitmaps of the show. Now write the code that displays the first bitmap of the show. Upon start-up of the application, the first bitmap of the show should be displayed. You'll now attach code to the OnDraw() member function of the view class.

The OnDraw() function is automatically executed whenever there is a need to repaint the view window. For example, if the user minimizes the window and then maximizes the window again, the OnDraw() function will be executed automatically.

The OnDraw() function is also executed upon start-up of the application.

☐ Use ClassWizard (from the Project menu) to select the event (See Figure 27.30.):

CBallView -> CBallView -> OnDraw

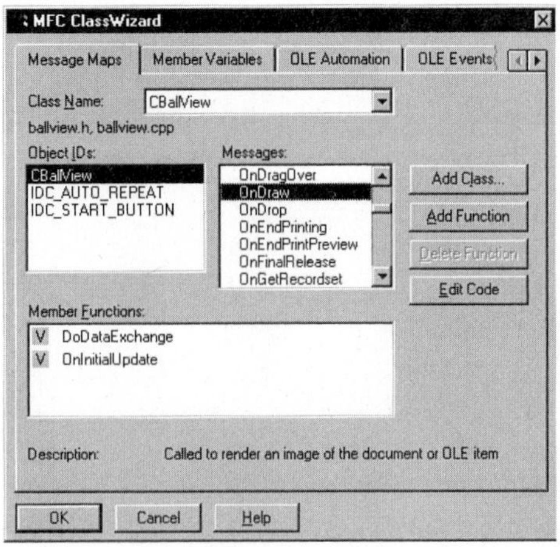

Figure 27.30. Adding the OnDraw() function.

Then click the Add Function button.

> *Visual C++ responds by adding the* OnDraw() *function.*

☐ Click the Edit Code button.

> *Visual C++ responds by displaying the* OnDraw() *function, ready to be edited by you.*

☐ Now add code to the OnDraw() function. After you add this code, the OnDraw() function should look like this:

```
void CBallView::OnDraw(CDC* pDC)
{
// TODO: Add your specialized code here and/or call the base class

/////////////////////////
// MY CODE STARTS HERE
/////////////////////////

 // Create a memory DC.
 CDC* pMemDC = new CDC;
 pMemDC->CreateCompatibleDC(pDC);

 // Select the bitmap into the memory DC.
 pMemDC->SelectObject( m_pB[0] );

 // Copy the bitmap from the memory DC into the screen DC.
 pDC->BitBlt(10,10,500,500,pMemDC,0,0,SRCCOPY);

 // Delete the memory DC.
 delete pMemDC;


/////////////////////////
// MY CODE ENDS HERE
/////////////////////////


CFormView::OnDraw(pDC);
}
```

As stated previously, the OnDraw() function is automatically executed whenever there is a need to paint the window (for example, upon start-up of the application). The parameter of the OnDraw() function (pDC) is the *device context* (or DC, for short) that corresponds to the window. You draw on the screen (inside the window) by calling data members of the CDC class. (pDC is a pointer to an object of class CDC.)

The code you just typed inside the OnDraw() function places the first bitmap of the show inside the screen (inside the application's window). Now go over this code.

The first two statements you typed

```
CDC* pMemDC = new CDC;
pMemDC->CreateCompatibleDC(pDC);
```

create a memory DC called pMemDC. You need a memory DC because you cannot select a bitmap directly into the screen DC. You must first select the bitmap into a memory DC and then copy the bitmap from the memory DC into the screen DC.

The next statement is

```
pMemDC->SelectObject( m_pB[0] );
```

This statement selects the m_pB[0] bitmap into the memory DC. Recall that m_pB[0] points to the first bitmap of the animation show (IDB_BITMAP1). So at this point, the memory DC pMemDC contains the first bitmap of the show.

The next statement

```
pDC->BitBlt(10,10,500,500,pMemDC,0,0,SRCCOPY);
```

uses the BitBlt() function to copy the bitmap from the memory DC (pMemDC) into the screen DC (pDC). So after this statement is executed, the screen DC (the window of the application) contains the first bitmap of the animation show.

Now take a close look at the BitBlt() statement:

```
pDC->BitBlt(10,10,500,500,pMemDC,0,0,SRCCOPY);
```

As stated earlier, this statement copies the bitmap from the pMemDC DC (the fifth parameter) into the pDC DC (that is, into the screen DC).

The first parameter (10), specifies the x coordinate of the upper-left corner of the destination bitmap. The second parameter (10), specifies the y coordinate of the upper-left corner of the destination bitmap. Therefore, the upper-left corner of the bitmap will be at coordinate 10,10 of the window.

The third parameter (500) specifies the width of the bitmap, and the fourth parameter (500), specifies the height of the bitmap.

The fifth parameter (pMemDC) specifies the DC from which the bitmap will be copied. That is, you are copying the bitmap from the memory DC pMemDC.

The sixth parameter (0), specifies the x coordinate of the upper-left corner of the source bitmap. The seventh parameter (0), specifies the y coordinate of the upper-left corner of the source bitmap. Therefore, the upper-left corner of the source bitmap is 0,0.

The seventh parameter (SRCCOPY) is a constant that specifies the operation to be performed. When the constant SRCCOPY is supplied as the seventh parameter, the operation that will be performed is this: Copy source bitmap into destination bitmap.

The last statement you typed inside the OnDraw() function

```
delete pMemDC;
```

deletes the memory DC.

Here's a summary of what the code you typed inside the OnDraw() function does:

- It creates a memory DC.
- It selects the first bitmap of the animation show into the memory DC.
- It copies the bitmap from the memory DC into the screen DC by using the BitBlt() function.
- It deletes the memory DC.

The code you typed inside the OnDraw() function places the first bitmap of the animation show inside the screen DC. Therefore, upon start-up of the application, and whenever there is a need to repaint the window of the application, the first bitmap of the animation show will be displayed inside the application window. (See Figure 27.1.)

Don't forget to save your work:

☐ Select Save from the File menu of Visual C++.

Deleting the Bitmaps

Inside the OnInitialUpdate() function you wrote code that creates 11 CBitmap objects:

```
void CBallView::OnInitialUpdate()
{

   // Load IDB_BITMAP1
   m_pB[0] = new CBitmap;
   m_pB[0]->LoadBitmap(IDB_BITMAP1);

   // Load IDB_BITMAP2
   m_pB[1] = new CBitmap;
   m_pB[1]->LoadBitmap(IDB_BITMAP2);

   ...
   ...
   ...

   // Load IDB_BITMAP10
   m_pB[10] = new CBitmap;
   m_pB[10]->LoadBitmap(IDB_BITMAP10);

}
```

You need to write code that deletes these objects when the application terminates. If you do not do this, the memory that is occupied by these objects will not be released, and the available memory of the user's system will be decreased every time the user executes your application.

You'll now write the code that deletes the 11 bitmaps inside the destructor function of the view class. Here is how you do that:

☐ Open the file BALLVIEW.CPP and add code to the destructor function ~CBallView() so that it looks like this:

```
CBallView::~CBallView()
{

    /////////////////////////
    // MY CODE STARTS HERE
    /////////////////////////

    // Delete the 11 bitmaps.
    for (int i=0; i<11; i++)
        delete m_pB[i];

    /////////////////////////
    // MY CODE ENDS HERE
    /////////////////////////

}
```

The code you just typed uses a for loop to delete the 11 bitmaps:

```
for (int i=0; i<11; i++)
    delete m_pB[i];
```

Therefore, upon termination of the application, the memory occupied by these bitmaps will be freed.

Execute the BALL application to see in action the code you typed inside the OnDraw() function:

☐ Select Build BALL.EXE from the Project menu of Visual C++.

☐ Select Execute BALL.EXE from the Project menu.

> *As you can see, now the main window of the application appears, with the first bitmap of the animation show.*

☐ Try to minimize the window and then maximize it.

> *Again, the application window appears, with the first bitmap of the animation show inside it.*

Whenever there is a need to redraw the window (for example, upon start-up of the application), the code you wrote inside the OnDraw() function is automatically executed, and this code displays the IDB_BITMAP1 bitmap (pB[0]) inside the window.

To terminate the BALL application do the following:

☐ Select Exit from the File menu.

NOTE

If you did not design the IDD_BALL_FORM dialog box so that it's large enough, the main window of the BALL application will appear as shown in Figure 27.31. If you did not make the dialog box large enough, simply display the IDD_BALL_FORM dialog box, enlarge the dialog box, and move the check box and push button down. Then compile, link, and execute the BALL application again.

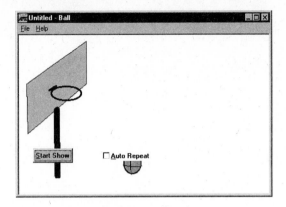

Figure 27.31. The main window of the BALL application if you did not make the dialog box large enough.

Starting the Animation Show

You'll now write the code that starts the animation show.

The animation show should start running when the user clicks the Start Show button. Therefore, you'll attach the code that starts the animation show to the Start Show button.

Here is how you attach code to the Start Show button:

☐ Use ClassWizard (from the Project menu) to select the event:

```
CBallView -> IDC_START_BUTTON -> BN_CLICKED
```

Then click the Add Function button.

☐ Accept the name OnStartButton() that Visual C++ suggests.

☐ Click the Edit Code button.

> *Visual C++ responds by displaying the* OnStartButton() *function, ready to be edited by you.*

☐ Add code to the OnStartButton() function. After you add the code, your OnStartButton() function should look like this:

```
void CBallView::OnStartButton()
{
// TODO: Add your control notification
// handler code here

//////////////////////////
// MY CODE STARTS HERE
//////////////////////////

// Initialize the current frame number to 0.
m_CurrentFrame = 0;

// Install a system timer.
```

```
    if ( SetTimer (1, 200, NULL) == 0 )
        MessageBox ("Cannot install timer!!!");

    /////////////////////
    // MY CODE ENDS HERE
    /////////////////////

}
```

The code you just typed is made of two statements.

The first statement

```
m_CurrentFrame = 0;
```

initializes the m_CurrentFrame variable to 0.

As stated earlier, the m_CurrentFrame variable is used to store the index number of the current bitmap. Initially (upon start-up of the animation) the first bitmap is displayed, so in the preceding statement m_CurrentFrame is set to 0.

The next statement

```
if ( SetTimer (1, 200, NULL) == 0 )
    MessageBox ("Cannot install timer!!!");
```

starts the animation. Recall (from Chapter 26, "The Timer") that the SetTimer() function installs a timer. In the preceding statement, the second parameter of SetTimer() is 200. Therefore, from now on, every 200 milliseconds a WM_TIMER event will occur. In the following section you'll attach code to the WM_TIMER event.

The Animation Show

The code you attached to the Start Show button installed a timer with an interval of 200 milliseconds. You'll now attach code to the WM_TIMER event. This code will be automatically executed every 200 milliseconds.

Here is how you attach code to the WM_TIMER event:

☐ Use ClassWizard (from the Project menu) to select the event:

```
CBallView -> CBallView -> WM_TIMER
```

Then click the Add Function button.

☐ Click the Edit Code button.

> *Visual C++ responds by displaying the OnTimer() function, ready to be edited by you.*

☐ Add code to the OnTimer() function. After you add the code, your OnTimer() function should look like this:

```
void CBallView::OnTimer(UINT nIDEvent)
{
// TODO: Add your message handler code
```

```
// here and/or call default

//////////////////////
// MY CODE STARTS HERE
//////////////////////

// Increment the current frame number.
m_CurrentFrame++;

// Is it the end of the show?
if (m_CurrentFrame==11)
   {

   // Reset the frame number.
   m_CurrentFrame=0;

   // If Auto Repeat not requested, kill the timer.
   UpdateData(TRUE);
   if (m_AutoRepeat == FALSE)
      KillTimer(1);

   }

// Get a dc for the screen.
CClientDC dc(this);

// Create a memory DC.
CDC* pMemDC = new CDC;
pMemDC->CreateCompatibleDC(&dc);

// Select the bitmap into the memory DC.
pMemDC->SelectObject( m_pB[m_CurrentFrame] );

// Copy the bitmap from the memory DC into the screen DC.
dc.BitBlt(10,10,550,500,pMemDC,0,0,SRCCOPY);

// Delete the memory DC.
delete pMemDC;

//////////////////////
// MY CODE ENDS HERE
//////////////////////

CFormView::OnTimer(nIDEvent);
}
```

The purpose of the code you just typed inside the OnTimer() function is to display the next bitmap of the animation show. That is, every 200 milliseconds the code of the OnTimer() function will be executed automatically, and the next bitmap of the show will be displayed. This creates the illusion that the object inside the bitmaps (the basketball) is moving.

The first statement you typed inside the OnTimer() function is this:

```
m_CurrentFrame++;
```

This statement increments the m_CurrentFrame variable because you want to display the next bitmap. For example, if m_CurrentBitmap is 0, you know that currently the m_pB[0] bitmap is displayed.

Therefore, you increment m_CurrentFrame by 1 because the next bitmap you want to display is the m_pB[1] bitmap.

The next statement is an if statement that checks whether the last bitmap of the show was displayed:

```
if (m_CurrentFrame==11)
   {

   // Reset the frame number.
   m_CurrentFrame=0;

   // If Auto Repeat not requested, kill the timer.
   UpdateData(TRUE);
   if (m_AutoRepeat == FALSE)
      KillTimer(1);

   }
```

If m_CurrentFrame is 11, the last bitmap of the show has been displayed (that is, if m_CurrentFrame is 11, the animation show is over). If this is the case, the code under the if statement is executed. The first statement inside the if statement

```
m_CurrentFrame=0;
```

resets the m_CurrentFrame to 0. That is, because the last bitmap of the show has been displayed, you now want to display the first bitmap of the show.

The next two statements inside the if statement

```
UpdateData(TRUE);
if (m_AutoRepeat == FALSE)
   KillTimer(1);
```

check the current status of the Auto Repeat check box. If the Auto Repeat check box is not checked, the condition m_AutoRepeat == FALSE is satisfied and the preceding code kills the timer by using the KillTimer() function. After the timer is killed, the animation show stops (because the code of the OnTimer() function will not execute every 200 milliseconds). Note that the parameter that is passed to the KillTimer() function is 1. That's because when you wrote the code that installs the timer (inside OnStartButton()), you made the ID of the timer 1.

The next statement in the OnTimer() function

```
CClientDC dc(this);
```

creates a DC called dc for the screen (that is, for the view window).

The remaining code of the OnTimer() function is like the code you wrote inside the OnDraw() function. It displays the bitmap (as specified by m_CurrentFrame) inside the application window.

The first two statements create a memory DC (pMemDC):

```
CDC* pMemDC = new CDC;
pMemDC->CreateCompatibleDC(&dc);
```

Then the bitmap (as specified by m_CurrentFrame) is selected into the memory DC:

```
pMemDC->SelectObject( m_pB[m_CurrentFrame] );
```

For example, if currently m_CurrentFrame is 3, this statement selects the bitmap m_pB[3] into the memory DC.

Then the bitmap from the memory DC (pMemDC) is copied into screen DC:

```
dc.BitBlt(10,10,550,500,pMemDC,0,0,SRCCOPY);
```

Finally, the memory DC is deleted:

```
delete pMemDC;
```

You have finished writing the code that performs the animation. To see your animation code in action do the following:

☐ Build the BALL application, and then execute it.

☐ Experiment with the Start Show button and Auto Repeat check box.

As expected, the animation code that you wrote is performing the animation.

In the following section you will add code to the BALL application that makes the default size of the application's window appear as shown in Figure 27.1.

☐ Terminate the BALL application by selecting Exit from the File menu.

Setting the Default Size of the Application's Window

Upon start-up of the application, the default size of the application window should be as shown in Figure 27.1. You want the window to appear like that for cosmetic reasons. That is, because the bitmaps of the animation show are displayed on a small area of the screen, the application window should be sized accordingly.

You need to write the code that sets the default size of the application window inside the PreCreateWindow() member function of the CMainFrame class. The header file of the CMainFrame class is MAINFRM.H and the implementation file of the CMainFrame class is MAINFRM.CPP.

☐ Use ClassWizard (from the Project menu) to select the event (See Figure 27.32.):

```
CMainFrame -> CMainFrame -> PreCreateWindow
```

Then click the Add Function button.

☐ Click the Edit Code button.

> *Visual C++ responds by displaying the* PreCreateWindow() *function, ready to be edited by you.*

Figure 27.32. Adding the `PreCreateWindow()` *function.*

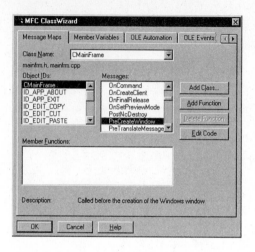

☐ Add code to the `PreCreateWindow()` function. After you add the code, your
`PreCreateWindow()` function should look like this:

```
BOOL CMainFrame::PreCreateWindow(CREATESTRUCT& cs)
{
// TODO: Add your specialized code here
// and/or call the base class

/////////////////////////
// MY CODE STARTS HERE
/////////////////////////

    // Set the width of the window to 335.
    cs.cx = 335;

    // Set the height of the window to 385.
    cs.cy = 385;


/////////////////////
// MY CODE ENDS HERE
/////////////////////


return CFrameWnd::PreCreateWindow(cs);
}
```

Recall from previous chapters that the `PreCreateWindow()` function is automatically executed prior
to the creation of the window. You can use this function to override the default characteristics of
the window. The parameter of `PreCreateWindow()`—cs—is a structure of type CREATESTRUCT. You
set the characteristics of the window by setting the members of the cs structure.

Now go over the code you typed inside the `PreCreateWindow()` function.

The first statement

```
cs.cx = 335;
```

sets the value of the `cx` member of the `cs` structure to `335`. The `cx` member specifies the width of the window. Therefore, the width of the window will be `335`.

The next statement

```
cs.cy = 385;
```

sets the value of the `cy` member of the `cs` structure to `385`. The `cy` member specifies the height of the window. Therefore, the height of the window will be `385`.

Don't forget to save your work:

☐ Select Save from the File menu.

To see the code that you attached to the `PreCreateWindow()` function in action do the following:

☐ Compile, link, and execute the BALL application.

As you can see, now the size of the main window of the application is as shown in Figure 27.1.

28

The **OnIdle()** *Function*

In this chapter you will learn about the `OnIdle()` member function of the `CWinApp` class. You will learn when this function is executed and how you can utilize this function in your Visual C++ applications.

What Is the *OnIdle()* Function?

Whenever an event occurs, Windows sends a message to the application that is associated with that event, informing the application about the event. For example, if your application has a dialog box with a button whose ID is IDC_MY_BUTTON inside it, and the user clicks this button, Windows sends a BN_CLICKED message to your application, telling it that the IDC_MY_BUTTON button was clicked. Your application then executes the code that you attached to the BN_CLICKED event of the IDC_MY_BUTTON button.

When no events are occurring in your application (that is, when your application is *idle*), the OnIdle() member function of the CWinApp class is automatically executed. You can write code inside the OnIdle() function, and this code will be executed whenever your application is idle.

Note that the OnIdle() function is *not* executed in the following situations:

- When other applications are not idle. That is, if another application is currently processing messages that Windows sent it, the OnIdle() function of your application will not be executed. Once all other applications are idle, the OnIdle() function of your application will automatically be executed.

- When the menu of your application (or the system menu of your application) is active. That is, if the user clicks the icon on the upper-left corner of your application window, or if the user opens any of the pop-up menus of your application, the OnIdle() function of your application will not be executed.

- When the user opens a modal dialog box in your application. That is, if the user opens any modal dialog box in your application, the OnIdle() function of your application will not be executed.

To summarize, the OnIdle() function of your application is automatically executed whenever all applications (including your applications) are idle.

The ANNOUNCE application is an example of a Visual C++ application that utilizes the OnIdle() function.

The ANNOUNCE Application

Before you start writing the ANNOUNCE application, execute the copy of it that resides in the \MVCPROG\EXE directory of the book's CD.

To execute the Announce.EXE application do the following:

☐ Use Windows to execute the X:\MVCPROG\EXE\Announce.EXE program (where *X* represents the drive letter of your CD-ROM drive).

   Windows responds by executing the Announce.EXE application.

An hourglass icon is displayed for a while and then the main window of ANNOUNCE.EXE appears, as shown in Figure 28.1.

Figure 28.1. The
main window of the
ANNOUNCE application.

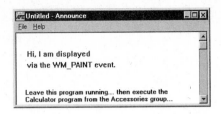

As you can see, the main window of the application instructs the user to leave the ANNOUNCE application running and then to execute the Calculator program (which resides inside the Accessories group).

☐ Execute the Calculator program.

The ANNOUNCE application detects the presence of the Calculator window, and it responds by playing a WAV file through the PC speaker.

As you have just heard, the ANNOUNCE application continuously monitors the Windows session, and when it discovers that the Calculator window is on the desktop, it plays a WAV file through the PC speaker.

The ANNOUNCE application has two pop-up menus: File and Help. These pop-up menus are shown in Figures 28.2 and 28.3.

Figure 28.2. The File
pop-up menu of the
ANNOUNCE application.

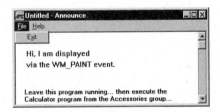

Figure 28.3. The Help
pop-up menu of the
ANNOUNCE application.

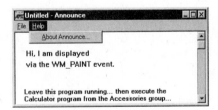

To exit the ANNOUNCE application do the following:

☐ Terminate the Calculator program.

The ANNOUNCE program responds by stopping the playing of the WAV file.

☐ Select Exit from the File menu of the ANNOUNCE program.

Now that you know what the ANNOUNCE application should do, you can start writing it.

Creating the Project of the ANNOUNCE Application

You'll now create the Announce.MAK project.

☐ Close all the open windows of Visual C++ (if there are any).

☐ Select New from the File menu.

    Visual C++ responds by displaying the New dialog box.

☐ Select Project inside the New dialog box and then click the OK button of the New dialog box.

    Visual C++ responds by displaying the New Project dialog box.

☐ Set the project name to Announce.

☐ Set the project path to \MVCPROG\CH28\Announce\Announce.MAK.

Your New Project dialog box should now look like the one shown in Figure 28.4.

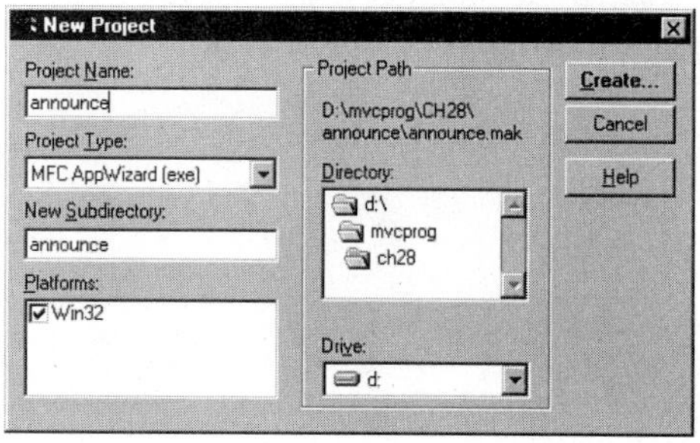

Figure 28.4. The New Project dialog box of the Announce.MAK project.

☐ Click the Create button of the New Project dialog box.

    Visual C++ responds by displaying the AppWizard—Step 1 window.

☐ Set the Step 1 window as shown in Figure 28.5. As shown in Figure 28.5, the Announce.MAK project is set as a single-document interface application, and U.S. English (APPWIZUS.DLL) is used as the language for the application's resources.

☐ Click the Next button of the Step 1 window.

    Visual C++ responds by displaying the AppWizard—Step 2 of 6 window.

☐ Set the Step 2 of 6 window as shown in Figure 28.6. That is, in the ANNOUNCE application you don't want any database support.

Figure 28.5. The AppWizard—Step 1 window for the ANNOUNCE application.

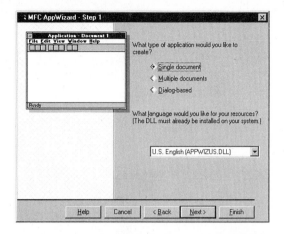

Figure 28.6. The AppWizard—Step 2 of 6 window for the ANNOUNCE application.

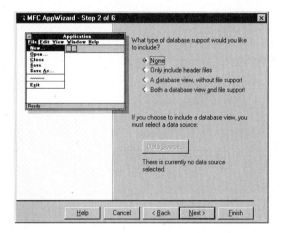

☐ Click the Next button of the Step 2 of 6 window.

   Visual C++ responds by displaying the AppWizard—Step 3 of 6 window.

☐ Set the Step 3 of 6 window as shown in Figure 28.7. That is, in the ANNOUNCE application you don't want any OLE support.

☐ Click the Next button of the Step 3 of 6 window.

   Visual C++ responds by displaying the AppWizard—Step 4 of 6 window.

☐ Set the Step 4 of 6 window as shown in Figure 28.8.

*Figure 28.7. The
AppWizard—Step 3 of 6
window for the
ANNOUNCE application.*

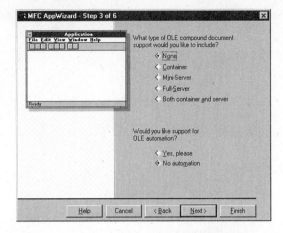

*Figure 28.8. The
AppWizard—Step 4 of 6
window for the
ANNOUNCE application.*

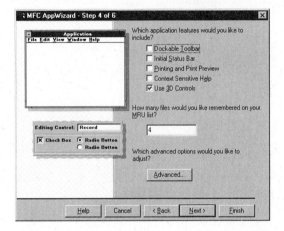

As shown in Figure 28.8, the features Dockable Toolbar, Initial Status Bar, Printing and Print Preview, and Context Sensitive Help will not be included in the ANNOUNCE application.

☐ Click the Next button of the Step 4 of 6 window.

Visual C++ responds by displaying the AppWizard—Step 5 of 6 window.

☐ Set the Step 5 of 6 window as shown in Figure 28.9.

As shown in Figure 28.9, the project will be generated with comments, a Visual C++ makefile will be generated, and the application will use the MFC library from a DLL.

Figure 28.9. The AppWizard—Step 5 of 6 window for the ANNOUNCE application.

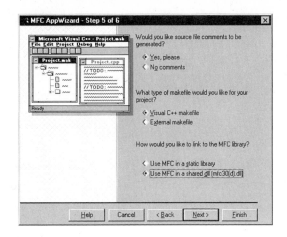

☐ Click the Next button of the Step 5 of 6 window.

> *Visual C++ responds by displaying the AppWizard—Step 6 of 6 window.*

You'll now use the AppWizard—Step 6 of 6 window to tell AppWizard to derive the view class of the application from the MFC class `CFormView`:

☐ Select the `CAnnounceView` class inside the AppWizard—Step 6 of 6 window.

☐ Set the Base Class drop-down list box to `CFormView`.

Your AppWizard—Step 6 of 6 window should now look like the one shown in Figure 28.10.

Figure 28.10. The AppWizard—Step 6 of 6 window after you set the base class of the application view class to `CFormView`.

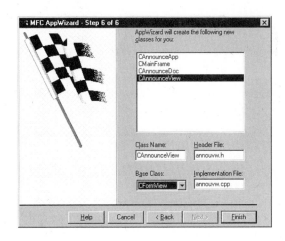

☐ Click the Finish button of the Step 6 of 6 window.

Visual C++ responds by displaying the New Project Information window, as shown in Figure 28.11.

Figure 28.11. The New Project Information window of the Announce.MAK project.

☐ Click the OK button of the New Project Information window.

Visual C++ responds by creating the project file and all the skeleton files of the application.

The Visual Implementation of the ANNOUNCE Application's Main Window

The ANNOUNCE application should have a menu with two pop-up menus, as shown in Figures 28.2 and 28.3.

☐ Select Announce from the Window menu to display the Announce.MAK window, double-click announce.rc inside the Announce.MAK window, double-click Dialog, and finally, double-click the IDD_ANNOUNCE_FORM item.

Visual C++ responds by displaying the IDD_ANNOUNCE_FORM dialog box in design mode. Visual C++ created the IDD_ANNOUNCE_FORM dialog box (a dialog box that serves as the main window of the application) because you set the base class to CFormView in step 6. (See Figure 28.10.)

☐ Delete the TODO static text from the IDD_ANNOUNCE_FORM dialog box.

☐ Implement the IDD_ANNOUNCE_FORM dialog box according to the specifications in Table 28.1. When you finish implementing the dialog box, it should look like the one shown in Figure 28.12.

☐ Select Save from the File menu to save your work.

Table 28.1. The Properties table of the IDD_ANNOUNCE_FORM dialog box.

Object	ID	Property
Static text	IDC_STATIC	Leave this program running, then execute the Calculator program from the Accessories group.

Figure 28.12. The IDD_ANNOUNCE_FORM dialog box (in design mode).

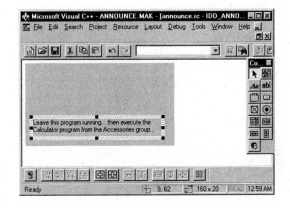

The Visual Implementation of the Menu

You'll now visually implement the menu of the ANNOUNCE application.

☐ Select announce.rc from the Window menu to display the announce.rc window, double-click Menu, and finally, double-click IDR_MAINFRAME.

   Visual C++ responds by displaying the IDR_MAINFRAME menu in design mode.

☐ Implement the IDR_MAINFRAME menu so that it contains the following elements:

   &File
       E&xit
   &Help
       &About Announce…

The File menu should look like the one shown in Figure 28.13.

Save your work:

☐ Select Save from the File menu.

The visual implementation of the menu of the ANNOUNCE application is complete.

Figure 28.13. The IDR_MAINFRAME menu of the ANNOUNCE program (in design mode).

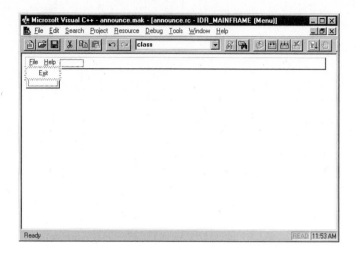

Writing Code in the ANNOUNCE Application's *OnIdle()* Function

As stated earlier, whenever the ANNOUNCE application is idle the `OnIdle()` member function of the `CWinApp` class is automatically executed. The code of the ANNOUNCE application (code that Visual C++ wrote for you) declares a class called `CAnnounceApp` that is derived from `CWinApp`. The header file of the `CAnnounceApp` class is ANNOUNCE.H, and the implementation file is ANNOUNCE.CPP.

You will now add the `OnIdle()` function.

☐ Use ClassWizard (from the Project menu) to select the event (See Figure 28.14.):

```
CAnnounceApp -> CAnnounceApp -> OnIdle
```

Then click the Add Function button.

Figure 28.14. Adding the OnIdle() function.

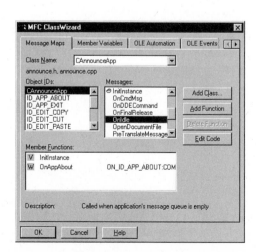

☐ Click the Edit Code button.

> *Visual C++ responds by displaying the* OnIdle() *function, ready to be edited by you.*

☐ Add code to the OnIdle() function. After you add the code, the OnIdle() function should look like this:

```
BOOL CAnnounceApp::OnIdle(LONG lCount)
{
// TODO: Add your specialized code here
// and/or call the base class


//////////////////////
// MY CODE STARTS HERE
//////////////////////

   // Beep.
   MessageBeep((WORD)-1);

   // Delay of 500 ms
   Sleep(500);

   return TRUE;

//////////////////////
// MY CODE ENDS HERE
//////////////////////


return CWinApp::OnIdle(lCount);
}
```

The statements you typed simply calls the MessageBeep() function to beep:

```
MessageBeep((WORD)-1);
```

Later in the chapter you will change this code so that instead of just beeping, the code of OnIdle() will monitor the Windows session and check whether the Calculator window is on the desktop. If the Calculator window is on the desktop, your code will play a WAV file through the PC speaker. For now, you are just using the MessageBeep() function to illustrate the OnIdle() concept.

The next statement you typed uses the Sleep() function to create a 500-millisecond delay:

```
// Delay of 500 ms
   Sleep(500);
```

The next statement you typed returns TRUE:

```
return TRUE;
```

When OnIdle() returns TRUE, Windows knows that OnIdle() should be called again. That is, when OnIdle() returns TRUE, OnIdle() will be called continuously for as long as the application is idle. If OnIdle() returns FALSE, OnIdle() will be executed only the first time the application is idle.

Don't forget to save your work:

☐ Select Save from the File menu.

Executing the ANNOUNCE Application

Execute the ANNOUNCE application and hear the code you wrote inside the `OnIdle()` function in action:

☐ Compile and link the ANNOUNCE program.

☐ Select Execute ANNOUNCE.EXE from the Project menu.

   Visual C++ responds by executing the ANNOUNCE application.

As you can hear, the ANNOUNCE application plays a series of beeps with a half-second (that is 500-millisecond) delay between the beeps. That is, whenever the ANNOUNCE application is idle, the `OnIdle()` function you wrote is executed. Because the `OnIdle()` function you typed returns TRUE, the `OnIdle()` function is executed many times, and each time a beep is played. This generates a series of beeps.

The `OnIdle()` function is executed even when the window of another application is active. To verify this do the following:

☐ Leave the ANNOUNCE application running and start any other Windows application.

As you can hear, the ANNOUNCE application keeps on beeping.

That is, even though the window of another application is active, the `OnIdle()` function of the ANNOUNCE application keeps on executing in the background.

As stated earlier, the `OnIdle()` function is not executed in the following situations:

- When other applications are not idle.
- When the menu of your application (or the system menu of your application) is active.
- When the user opens a modal dialog box in your application.

Verify this:

☐ While the ANNOUNCE application is still running, start the Paintbrush program.

☐ Use the pencil tool of Paintbrush to draw something.

Note that as you are drawing (that is, when Paintbrush is not idle), the PC speaker stops beeping. That is, for as long as Paintbrush is not idle, the `OnIdle()` function of the ANNOUNCE application is not executed.

☐ Terminate the Paintbrush application and switch back to the ANNOUNCE application.

☐ Now try to open any of the menus of the ANNOUNCE application.

As you can hear (or rather *not* hear), when you open a menu (a regular menu or the system menu), the PC does not beep. That is, when a menu is open, the OnIdle() function is not executed.

☐ Now select About from the Help menu of the ANNOUNCE application.

Again, as long as the About dialog box is active, the ANNOUNCE application stops beeping. That is, because the About dialog box of the ANNOUNCE application is a modal dialog box, while this dialog box is active, the OnIdle() function of the ANNOUNCE application is not executed.

However, if you open a menu of another application (or a modal dialog box of another application), the OnIdle() function of the ANNOUNCE application will be executed.

In the following sections, you'll enhance the ANNOUNCE application in the following ways:

- You'll change the code inside OnIdle() so that instead of just beeping it monitors the Windows session and plays an audio recording through the PC speaker whenever the Calculator window is on the desktop.
- You'll write code that displays text inside the main window of the application, as shown in Figure 28.1.
- You'll write code so that upon start-up of the application the default size of the application window will be as shown in Figure 28.1.

Declaring the *CTegMM* Advanced Multimedia Class

Later in this chapter you'll modify the OnIdle() function so that instead of beeping it will monitor the Windows session and play a WAV file whenever the Calculator window is on the desktop.

Because the code that plays sound resides inside the Announce.CPP file, you need to declare the CTegMM class declaration inside the Announce.H file.

☐ Open the file ANNOUNCE.H and add the #include "\MVCPROG\LIB\CTegMM.H" statement at the beginning of the file. After you add this statement, the beginning of ANNOUNCE.H should look like this:

```
// announce.h : main header file
//for the ANNOUNCE application
//

#ifndef __AFXWIN_H__
#error include 'stdafx.h' before including this file for PCH
#endif

#include "resource.h"       // main symbols


/////////////////////////
// MY CODE STARTS HERE
/////////////////////////

// Include the TegoSoft CTegMM class declaration
#include "\MVCPROG\LIB\CTegMM.H"
```

```
///////////////////////
// MY CODE ENDS HERE
///////////////////////
```

```
....
....
....
```

Creating a Multimedia Object of Class *CTegMM*

The ANNOUNCE application uses the WAV file \\MVCProg\\WAV\\Rolli2M0.WAV.

You'll now create the m_wav object of class CTegMM.

☐ Open the file ANNOUNCE.H, and add code to the CAnnounceApp class declaration that defines the m_wav object of class CTegMM class. After you write this code, the CAnnounceApp class declaration should look like this:

```
class CAnnounceApp : public CWinApp
{
public:
CAnnounceApp();

///////////////////////////
// MY CODE STARTS HERE
///////////////////////////

// Create the m_wav object of class CTegMM class
// as a data member of the CAnnounceApp class.
CTegMM m_wav;


///////////////////////
// MY CODE ENDS HERE
///////////////////////

// Overrides
// ClassWizard generated virtual function overrides
//{{AFX_VIRTUAL(CAnnounceApp)
public:
virtual BOOL InitInstance();
virtual BOOL OnIdle(LONG lCount);
//}}AFX_VIRTUAL

// Implementation

//{{AFX_MSG(CAnnounceApp)
afx_msg void OnAppAbout();
// NOTE—the ClassWizard will add and remove member functions here.
//     DO NOT EDIT what you see in these blocks of generated code !
//}}AFX_MSG
DECLARE_MESSAGE_MAP()
};
```

The code you typed creates an object m_wav of class CTegMM:

```
CTegMM m_wav;
```

Now that you have created the m_wav object as a data member, you can write the code that opens the WAV sound file:

☐ Open the file ANNOUNCE.CPP, and add code to the constructor function of the CAnnounceApp class. After you add this code, the constructor of the CAnnounceApp class should look like this:

```
CAnnounceApp::CAnnounceApp()
{
// TODO: add construction code here,
// Place all significant initialization in InitInstance


////////////////////////
// MY CODE STARTS HERE
////////////////////////

// Set the DeviceType property to PC speaker
m_wav.SetStrProperty ("DeviceType", "PCSpeaker");
//m_wav.SetStrProperty ("DeviceType", "WaveAudio");

// Set the FileName property.
m_wav.SetStrProperty ("FileName",
            "\\MVCProg\\WAV\\Rolli2M0.WAV");

// Issue an Open command.
m_wav.SetStrProperty ("Command", "Open");

// If Open command fails, display an error message.
long lError;
char msg[250];
m_wav.GetNumProperty ("Error", &lError );
if (lError != 0 )
   {
   // Error
   m_wav.GetStrProperty ("ErrorMessage", msg );
   MessageBox (NULL,
            msg,
            "Error",
            0);
   }


////////////////////////
// MY CODE ENDS HERE
////////////////////////

}
```

The code you typed sets DeviceType to PCSpeaker:

```
m_wav.SetStrProperty ("DeviceType", "PCSpeaker");
```

This means that the WAV file will be played through the PC speaker.

> **NOTE**
>
> If you prefer you can set DeviceType to `WaveAudio`:
>
> `m_wav.SetStrProperty ("DeviceType", "WaveAudio");`
>
> This means that the WAV file will be played through the sound card.

Next, FileName is set to the filename and path of the Rolli2M0.WAV file:

```
m_wav.SetStrProperty ("FileName",
           "\\MVCProg\\WAV\\Rolli2M0.WAV");
```

Finally, the `Open` command is issued:

```
m_wav.SetStrProperty ("Command", "Open");
```

The rest of the statements that you typed check whether the WAV file was opened successfully. Two local variables are declared:

```
long lError;
char msg[250];
```

The `lError` variable is updated with the number that represents the error (if any) that occurred during the execution of the last command (the `Open` command):

```
m_wav.GetNumProperty ("Error", &lError );
```

An `if` statement is executed to check the value of `lError`:

```
if (lError != 0 )
   {
   // Error
   m_wav.GetStrProperty ("ErrorMessage", msg );
   MessageBox (NULL,
             msg,
             "Error",
             0);
   }
```

The code under the `if` statement is executed if an error occurred.

Adding the CTegMM.LIB Library to the Announce.MAK Project

You'll now add the CTegMM.LIB library to the Announce.MAK project.

☐ Select Files from the Project menu.

   Visual C++ responds by displaying the Project Files window. (See Figure 28.15.)

Figure 28.15. The Project Files window.

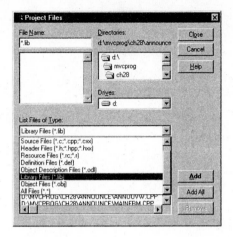

As you can see from Figure 28.15, the Project Files window lists all the files used by the Announce.MAK project.

☐ Select the CTegMM.LIB file from the \MVCPROG\LIB directory, and then click the Add button. (See Figure 28.16.)

Visual C++ responds by adding the CTegMM.LIB file to the Announce project.

Figure 28.16. Adding the CTegMM.LIB library to the Announce.MAK project.

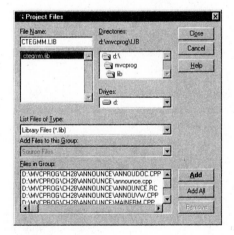

Monitoring the Windows Session

You'll now modify the OnIdle() function so that instead of beeping, it will monitor the Windows session and play the WAV file whenever the Calculator program (of the Accessories group) is on the desktop.

☐ Open the ANNOUNCE.CPP file and modify the `OnIdle()` function until it looks like this:

```cpp
BOOL CAnnounceApp::OnIdle(LONG lCount)
{
// TODO: Add your specialized code here
// and/or call the base class


/////////////////////////
// MY CODE STARTS HERE
/////////////////////////

    // Beep.
    //MessageBeep((WORD)-1);

    // Delay of 500 ms
    //Sleep(500);


    // Is the Calculator window on the desktop?
    HWND hWindow = FindWindow (NULL, "Calculator" );
    if (hWindow > 0  )
       {

       m_wav.SetStrProperty ("Command", "Prev" );
       m_wav.SetStrProperty ("Command", "Play" );


       Sleep (3000);

       }



    return TRUE;

/////////////////////////
// MY CODE ENDS HERE
/////////////////////////


return CWinApp::OnIdle(lCount);
}
```

In the modification you just made to the `OnIdle()` function, you commented out (`//`) the `MessageBeep((WORD)-1)` and `Sleep()` statements, and you added the statements that monitor the Windows session.

The code checks whether the Calculator window is on the desktop by using the `FindWindow()` function:

```cpp
// Is the Calculator window on the desktop?
HWND hWindow = FindWindow (NULL, "Calculator" );

if (hWindow > 0  )
   {
```

```
     . . . . .
     . . . . .
     . . . . .
     }
```

If the return value of FindWindow() is greater than 0, you know that the Calculator window is on the desktop, and therefore the code under the if statement is executed.

NOTE

The FindWindow() function is a Windows API function. The second parameter of the FindWindow() function contains the text that appears inside the caption of the window to be found by the FindWindow() function.

Figure 28.17 shows the Calculator window of the Calculator program that resides inside the Accessories group of programs. As shown, the caption of the window is Calculator.

The second parameter of the FindWindow() function must be identical (including the case) to the text that appears inside the caption of the window you are trying to find. That is, you must supply Calculator as the second parameter of the FindWindow() function. For example, if you supply CALCULATOR as the second parameter of the FindWindow() function, then the returned value will report that no window with caption CALCULATOR resides on the desktop.

Figure 28.17. The Calculator program.

If the Calculator is on the desktop, the WAV file is rewound:

```
m_wav.SetStrProperty ("Command", "Prev" );
```

The Play command is issued:

```
m_wav.SetStrProperty ("Command", "Play" );
```

Finally, the Sleep() function is executed:

```
Sleep (3000);
```

This means that as long as the Calculator window is on the desktop, the WAV file will be played repeatedly, with a 3-second interval between the playbacks.

Don't forget to save your work:

☐ Select Save from the File menu.

To see the code that you wrote inside the `OnIdle()` function in action do the following:

☐ Compile, link, and execute the ANNOUNCE application.

☐ Execute the Calculator program from the Accessories group of programs.

> *As you can hear, the ANNOUNCE application responds by playing the WAV file as long as the Calculator window is on the desktop.*

Displaying Text in the Main Window of the ANNOUNCE Application

The main window of the application should contain text, as shown in Figure 28.1. To display the last lines of the text, you attached static text during the visual implementation of the ANNOUNCE window.

For the sake of learning about the `WM_PAINT` event, you'll now attach another two lines to the window of the ANNOUNCE application.

Here is how you do that:

☐ Use ClassWizard to select the event:

```
CAnnounceView -> CAnnounceView -> WM_PAINT
```

Then click the Add Function button.

☐ Click the Edit Code button.

> *Visual C++ responds by displaying the* `OnPaint()` *function, ready to be edited by you.*

☐ Edit the `OnPaint()` function that you added to the ANNOUVW.CPP file. After you edit the function, your `OnPaint()` function should look like this:

```
void CAnnounceView::OnPaint()
{
CPaintDC dc(this); // device context for painting

// TODO: Add your message handler code here

        ////////////////////////
        // MY CODE STARTS HERE
        ////////////////////////

        // Display text inside the application window.
        dc.TextOut(20,30,"Hi, I am displayed");
        dc.TextOut(20,50,"via the WM_PAINT event.");
```

```
//////////////////////
// MY CODE ENDS HERE
//////////////////////

// Do not call CFormView::OnPaint() for
// painting messages
}
```

Save your work:

☐ Select Save from the File menu.

The code you typed displays two lines of text:

```
dc.TextOut(20,30,"Hi, I am displayed");
dc.TextOut(20,50,"via the WM_PAINT event.");
```

Note that the first line of the OnPaint() function (which was written by ClassWizard) declares the dc object for you:

```
CPaintDC dc(this); // device context for painting
```

dc stands for *device contents*. Think of dc as the object on which you perform an operation (that is, it is the screen).

The first parameter of the TextOut() function indicates that the text should be displayed 20 pixels from the left edge of the window.

The second parameter of the TextOut() function indicates the vertical coordinate of the text. Therefore, the first TextOut() function displays the text 30 pixels from the top, and the second TextOut() function displays the text 50 pixels from the top.

☐ Compile, link, and execute the ANNOUNCE program, and verify that the window of the ANNOUNCE program looks like the one shown in Figure 28.18.

Figure 28.18. The window of the ANNOUNCE program.

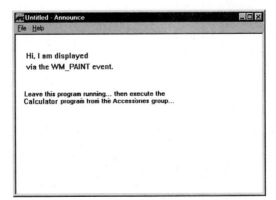

Changing the Default Size of the ANNOUNCE Application's Main Window

Recall that upon start-up of the application, the default size of the application window should be as shown in Figure 28.1 (which is different from the size of the window shown in Figure 28.18).

You need to write the code that sets the default characteristics of the application's window inside the `PreCreateWindow()` member function of the `CMainFrame` class.

The header file of the `CMainFrame` class is MAINFRM.H and the implementation file of the `CMainFrame` class is MAINFRM.CPP.

You'll now write the code of the `PreCreateWindow()` function.

☐ Select ClassWizard from the Project menu and select the event (see Figure 28.19):

```
CMainFrame -> CMainFrame -> PreCreateWindow
```

Then click the Add Function button.

Figure 28.19. Adding the
PreCreateWindow()
function.

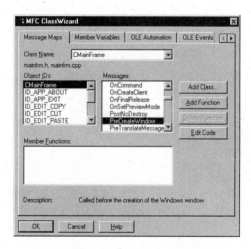

☐ Click the Edit Code button.

> *Visual C++ responds by displaying the PreCreateWindow() function, ready to be edited by you.*

☐ Edit the `PreCreateWindow()` function. After you edit this function, it should look like this:

```
BOOL CMainFrame::PreCreateWindow(CREATESTRUCT& cs)
{
// TODO: Add your specialized code
// here and/or call the base class
```

```
/////////////////////
// MY CODE STARTS HERE
/////////////////////


// Set the width of the window to 270.
cs.cx = 270;

// Set the height of the window to 180.
cs.cy = 180;

/////////////////////
// MY CODE ENDS HERE
/////////////////////


return CFrameWnd::PreCreateWindow(cs);
}
```

The PreCreateWindow() function is automatically executed prior to the creation of the window. You can use this function to override the default characteristics of the window. The parameter of PreCreateWindow(), cs, is a structure of type CREATESTRUCT. You set the characteristics of the window by setting the members of the cs structure.

Now go over the code you typed inside the PreCreateWindow() function.

The first statement

```
cs.cx = 270;
```

sets the value of the cx member of the cs structure to 270. The cx member specifies the width of the window. Therefore, the width of the window is 270.

The next statement

```
cs.cy = 180;
```

sets the value of the cy member of the cs structure to 180. The cy member specifies the height of the window. Therefore, the height of the window is 180.

Don't forget to save your work:

☐ Select Save from the File menu.

To see the code that you attached to the OnPaint() and PreCreateWindow() functions in action do the following:

☐ Compile, link, and execute the ANNOUNCE application.

As you can see, now the main window of the ANNOUNCE application looks like the one shown in Figure 28.1.

NOTE

In this chapter you learned about the OnIdle() function.

You also learned about the TextOut() function (to display text), and about the PreCreateWindow() function.

There is no relationships between the OnIdle() function and the TextOut() function, and there is no relationship between the OnIdle() function and the PreCreateWindow() function. The only reason for introducing these functions together with the OnIdle() function is to illustrate that the inclusion of the OnIdle() function in your project has no effect on the other sections of your project.

29

Animation and Sound with and Without Synchronization

Chapter 27, "Animation," explains the
basics of animation. In this chapter
you'll learn how to write Visual C++
Windows applications that combine
animation and sound. As you'll soon
see, there are two types of animation/
sound programs—animation with
asynchronous sound and animation with
synchronized sound.

Animation with Asynchronous Sound—The DANCE Application

The code you wrote for the BALL application in Chapter 27 performs animation without sound. Now you'll write another Visual C++ application—the DANCE application—which performs animation and plays sound (music) in the background.

> **NOTE**
>
> The DANCE application requires a Windows-compatible sound card. If you do not have a sound card you may skip this section or just browse through it.

Before you start writing the DANCE application, first execute the copy of it that resides in the \MVCPROG\EXE directory of the book's CD.

☐ Execute the X:\MVCPROG\EXE\Dance.EXE program (where *X* represents the drive letter of your CD-ROM drive).

> *Windows responds by executing the Dance.EXE application. The main window of Dance.EXE appears, as shown in Figure 29.1.*

Figure 29.1. The main window of the DANCE application.

As you can see, the main window of the application has inside it a picture of a couple standing up, a Start Show button, and a Stop button.

To start the animation show do the following:

☐ Click the Start Show button.

> *The DANCE application responds by displaying an animation show and by playing background music. The animation show creates the illusion that the couple is dancing to the music.*

To stop the animation show do the following:

☐ Click the Stop button.

The DANCE application stops the playback of the music and displays the couple standing up.

The DANCE application has two pop-up menus: File and Help. These pop-up menus are shown in Figures 29.2 and 29.3.

Figure 29.2. The File pop-up menu of the DANCE application.

Figure 29.3. The Help pop-up menu of the DANCE application.

☐ Terminate the DANCE application by selecting Exit from the File menu.

Now that you know what the DANCE application should do, you can start writing it.

Creating the Project of the DANCE Application

You'll now create the Dance.MAK project.

☐ Close all the open windows on the desktop of Visual C++ (if there are any).

☐ Select New from the File menu.

Visual C++ responds by displaying the New dialog box.

☐ Select Project inside the New dialog box and then click the OK button of the New dialog box.

Visual C++ responds by displaying the New Project dialog box.

☐ Set the project name to Dance.

☐ Set the project path to \MVCPROG\CH29\Dance\Dance.MAK.

Your New Project dialog box should now look like the one shown in Figure 29.4.

Figure 29.4. The New Project dialog box of the Dance.MAK project.

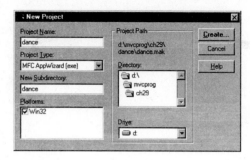

☐ Click the Create button of the New Project dialog box.

    Visual C++ responds by displaying the AppWizard—Step 1 window.

☐ Set the Step 1 window as shown in Figure 29.5. As shown in Figure 29.5, the Dance.MAK project is set as a single-document application, and U.S. English (APPWIZUS.DLL) is used as the language for the application's resources.

Figure 29.5. The AppWizard—Step 1 window for the DANCE application.

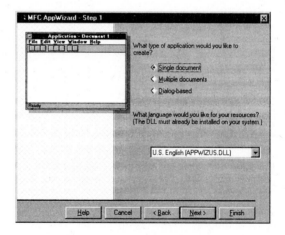

☐ Click the Next button of the Step 1 window.

    Visual C++ responds by displaying the AppWizard—Step 2 of 6 window.

☐ Set the Step 2 of 6 window as shown in Figure 29.6. That is, in the DANCE application you don't want any database support.

*Figure 29.6. The
AppWizard—Step 2 of 6
window for the DANCE
application.*

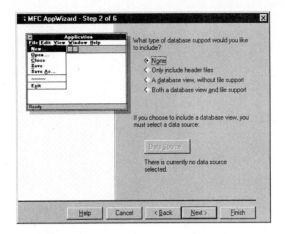

☐ Click the Next button of the Step 2 of 6 window.

　　Visual C++ responds by displaying the AppWizard—Step 3 of 6 window.

☐ Set the Step 3 of 6 window as shown in Figure 29.7. That is, in the DANCE application
you don't want any OLE support.

*Figure 29.7. The
AppWizard—Step 3 of 6
window for the DANCE
application.*

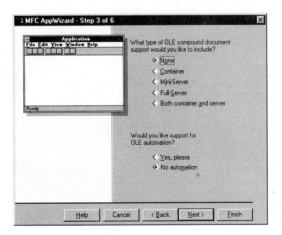

☐ Click the Next button of the Step 3 of 6 window.

　　Visual C++ responds by displaying the AppWizard—Step 4 of 6 window.

☐ Set the Step 4 of 6 window as shown in Figure 29.8.

As shown in Figure 29.8, only the Use 3D Controls check box is checked.

*Figure 29.8. The
AppWizard—Step 4 of 6
window for the DANCE
application.*

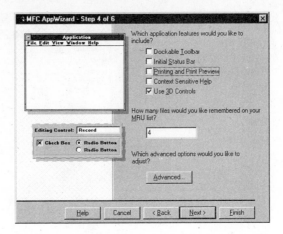

☐ Click the Next button of the Step 4 of 6 window.

   Visual C++ responds by displaying the AppWizard—Step 5 of 6 window.

☐ Set the Step 5 of 6 window as shown in Figure 29.9.

As shown in Figure 29.9, the project will be generated with comments, a Visual C++ makefile will
be generated, and the application will use the MFC library from a DLL.

*Figure 29.9. The
AppWizard—Step 5 of 6
window for the DANCE
application.*

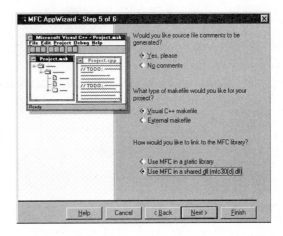

☐ Click the Next button of the Step 5 of 6 window.

   Visual C++ responds by displaying the AppWizard—Step 6 of 6 window.

You'll now use the AppWizard—Step 6 of 6 window to tell AppWizard to derive the view class of
the application from the MFC class CFormView:

☐ Select the CDanceView class inside the AppWizard—Step 6 of 6 window.

☐ Set the Base Class drop-down list box to CFormView.

Your AppWizard—Step 6 of 6 window should now look like the one shown in Figure 20.10.

Figure 29.10. The AppWizard—Step 6 of 6 window after you set the base class of the application view class to CFormView.

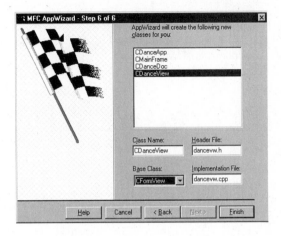

☐ Click the Finish button of the Step 6 of 6 window.

> *Visual C++ responds by displaying the New Project Information window, as shown in Figure 29.11.*

Figure 29.11. The New Project Information window of the Dance.MAK project.

☐ Click the OK button of the New Project Information window.

> *Visual C++ responds by creating the project file and all the skeleton files of the application.*

Creating the Form of the DANCE Application

As shown in Figure 29.1, the main window of the DANCE application should have inside it two push buttons: Start Show and Stop.

Because in AppWizard you specified that the base class of the application's view class is `CFormView` (See Figure 29.10.), AppWizard created for you a form (a dialog box) that is attached to the view class of the application. This dialog box serves as the main window of the application. AppWizard named this dialog box IDD_DANCE_FORM. You'll now customize the IDD_DANCE_FORM dialog box.

☐ Select Dance.MAK from the Window menu to display the Dance.MAK window, double-click dance.rc inside the Dance.MAK window, double-click Dialog inside the dance.rc window, and finally, double-click IDD_DANCE_FORM under the Dialog item.

> *Visual C++ responds by displaying the IDD_DANCE_FORM dialog box in design mode. This dialog box serves as the main window of the DANCE application.*

☐ Delete the TODO static text from the IDD_DANCE_FORM dialog box.

☐ Implement the IDD_DANCE_FORM dialog box according to the specifications in Table 29.1. When you finish implementing the IDD_DANCE_FORM dialog box, it should look like the one shown in Figure 29.12.

Table 29.1. The dialog box of the DANCE application.

Object	Property	Setting
Dialog box	ID	IDD_DANCE_FORM
Push button	ID	IDC_START_BUTTON
	Caption	&Start Show
Push button	ID	IDC_STOP_BUTTON
	Caption	&Stop

Figure 29.12. The IDD_DANCE_FORM dialog box (in design mode).

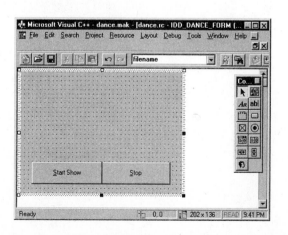

NOTE

When you place controls inside a dialog box during design time, it is best to check the Snap to Grid check box. Here is how you display and check this check box:

☐ Select Grid Settings from the Layout menu.

Visual C++ responds by displaying the Grid Settings dialog box. (See Figure 29.13.)

☐ Place an X inside the Snap to Grid check box.

☐ Click the OK button.

From now on, when you place a control inside a dialog box, you don't have to "struggle" with the mouse as you try to place the control at a certain point. That is, when you drag the control inside the dialog box, and then release the mouse, Visual C++ will place the control so that the upper-left corner of the control will be placed at the grid-point that is closest to the upper-left corner of the control you are placing. (See Figure 29.14.)

*Figure 29.13. The Grid
Settings dialog box.*

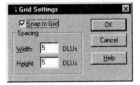

*Figure 29.14. The snap-
to-grid operation.*

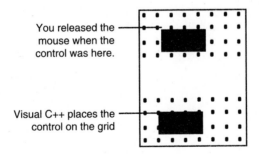

Don't forget to save your work:

☐ Select Save from the File menu.

The Visual Implementation of the Menu

The DANCE application should have a menu with two pop-up menus, as shown in Figures 29.2 and 29.3. Now implement this menu:

☐ Select dance.rc from the Window menu to display the Dance.RC window, double-click Menu, and finally double-click the IDR_MAINFRAME item that appears under the Menu item.

Visual C++ responds by displaying the IDR_MAINFRAME menu in design menu.

☐ Implement the menu of the DANCE application so that it contains the following items:

&File
    E&xit
&Help
    &About Dance…

Don't forget to delete the accelerator keys that correspond to the menu items you removed:

☐ Select dance.rc from the Window menu, double-click Accelerator, and then double-click IDR_MAINFRAME under Accelerator.

Visual C++ responds by displaying the Accelerator table.

☐ Delete the accelerator keys that are not used by the DANCE application. In particular, delete the accelerator keys of the ID_FILE_NEW, ID_FILE_OPEN, and ID_FILE_SAVE menu items.

Save your work:

☐ Select Save from the File menu.

The visual implementation of the menu of the DANCE application is complete.

Adding Bitmap Files to the DANCE Application

The DANCE application uses four bitmap (BMP) files for the animation. The code of the DANCE application will display these bitmaps one after the other to create the illusion that the objects inside these bitmaps (two people) are moving (dancing).

The four bitmaps of the DANCE application are shown in Figures 29.15 through 29.18.

Figure 29.15. The DANCE1.BMP bitmap file.

Figure 29.16. The DANCE2.BMP bitmap file.

Figure 29.17. The DANCE3.BMP bitmap file.

Figure 29.18. The DANCE4.BMP bitmap file.

NOTE

The BMP files inside the \MVCPROG\BMP directory were copied from the book's CD. The file attribute of these files is r (read-only).

Before you use the BMP files from within Visual C++, make sure that these files are not set as read-only files. (For example, you can use the File Manager program of Windows to remove the r attribute.)

To add the four bitmaps to the DANCE application, follow these steps:

☐ Select dance.rc from the Window menu of Visual C++.

> *Visual C++ responds by displaying the dance.rc window.*

☐ Select Import from the Resource menu.

> *Visual C++ responds by displaying the Import Resource dialog box.*

☐ Use the Import Resource dialog box to select the file \MVCPROG\BMP\DANCE1.BMP.

> *Visual C++ responds by importing the bitmap DANCE1.BMP into the DANCE application and by displaying the DANCE1.BMP bitmap. (See Figure 29.19.)*

Note that the ID that Visual C++ assigned to the DANCE1.BMP bitmap is IDB_BITMAP1. (See Figure 29.19.)

☐ Repeat the preceding steps to import the three other BMP files:

☐ Import \MVCPROG\BMP\DANCE2.BMP.

☐ Import \MVCPROG\BMP\DANCE3.BMP.

☐ Import \MVCPROG\BMP\DANCE4.BMP.

You have finished importing four bitmaps into the DANCE application.

Figure 29.19. Importing the DANCE1.BMP bitmap into the DANCE application.

To verify that you imported the bitmaps properly do the following:

☐ Select dance.rc from the Window menu.

☐ Double-click Bitmap inside the dance.rc window.

> *Visual C++ responds by listing all the bitmaps of the DANCE application inside the Resources list. (See Figure 29.20.)*

Figure 29.20. The bitmaps of the DANCE application.

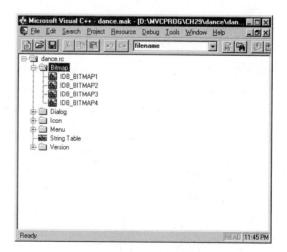

As you can see from Figure 29.20, the IDs that Visual C++ assigned to the four bitmaps that you imported are IDB_BITMAP1, IDB_BITMAP2, IDB_BITMAP3, and IDB_BITMAP4.

To inspect the properties of the IDB_BITMAP1 bitmap do the following:

☐ Click the right mouse button on the IDB_BITMAP1 item.

Visual C++ responds by displaying a menu.

☐ Select the Properties item from the menu.

Visual C++ responds by displaying the Bitmap Properties window of the IDB_BITMAP1 bitmap. (See Figure 29.21.)

Figure 29.21. The Properties window of the IDB_BITMAP1 bitmap.

As you can see from Figure 29.21, the Properties window displays the picture of the IDB_BITMAP1 bitmap as well as the filename of the bitmap. Note that the filename is res\dance1.BMP. When you imported the file \MVCPROG\BMP\DANCE1.BMP into the DANCE application, Visual C++ copied this file into the RES directory of the application. (The RES directory of the DANCE application is \MVCPROG\CH29\DANCE\RES.)

In a similar manner you can now inspect the other bitmaps that you imported to the DANCE application.

Don't forget to save your work:

☐ Select Save from the File menu.

Executing the DANCE Application

Although you have not written any code yet, execute the DANCE application to see your visual design in action:

☐ Select Build All DANCE.EXE from the Project menu of Visual C++.

☐ Select Execute DANCE.EXE from the Project menu.

Visual C++ responds by executing the DANCE application.

The main window of the application appears with the form that you designed inside it. Of course, none of the bitmaps that you imported into the DANCE application are displayed yet, because you did not write any code to accomplish that.

In the following sections you'll write code that displays the BMP files.

☐ Terminate the DANCE application by selecting Exit from the File menu.

Declaring Variables for the Animation Show

You'll now write the code that declares variables that are used by the animation show. You will declare these variables as data members of the view class (because these variables need to be visible in several member functions of the view class).

☐ Open the file DANCEVW.H and write code that declares two data members inside the CDanceView class declaration. When you finish writing this code, the CDanceView class declaration should look like this:

```
class CDanceView : public CFormView
{
protected: // create from serialization only
CDanceView();
DECLARE_DYNCREATE(CDanceView)

public:
//{{AFX_DATA(CDanceView)
enum{ IDD = IDD_DANCE_FORM };
// NOTE: the ClassWizard will add data members here
//}}AFX_DATA

// Attributes
public:
CDanceDoc* GetDocument();


        /////////////////////////
        // MY CODE STARTS HERE
        /////////////////////////

        // The current frame number.
        int m_CurrentFrame;

        // An array for the 4 bitmaps.
        CBitmap* m_pB[4];

        /////////////////////////
        // MY CODE ENDS HERE
        /////////////////////////


// Operations
public:

// Overrides
// ClassWizard generated virtual function overrides
//{{AFX_VIRTUAL(CDanceView)
public:
protected:
virtual void DoDataExchange(CDataExchange* pDX);
// DDX/DDV support
//}}AFX_VIRTUAL

// Implementation
public:
virtual ~CDanceView();
```

```
#ifdef _DEBUG
virtual void AssertValid() const;
virtual void Dump(CDumpContext& dc) const;
#endif

protected:

// Generated message map functions
protected:
//{{AFX_MSG(CDanceView)
// NOTE—the ClassWizard will add and remove member functions here.
//DO NOT EDIT what you see in these blocks of
// generated code !
//}}AFX_MSG
DECLARE_MESSAGE_MAP()
};
```

As you can see, these data members are the same as the data members you declared in the BALL application of Chapter 27. The first data member, m_CurrentFrame, is an integer that is used for maintaining the current frame (bitmap) number that is displayed. During the animation show, the code of the application will display the bitmaps one after the other. m_CurrentFrame indicates which bitmap is currently displayed. For example, when m_CurrentFrame is 0, the program should display the first bitmap (IDB_BITMAP1), when m_CurrentFrame is 1, the program should display the second frame (IDB_BITMAP2), and so on. As the animation show progresses, the code that you will write will increment the m_CurrentFrame variable.

You declared the second data member as

```
CBitmap* m_pB[4];
```

☐ m_pB[] is an array with four elements that is used for storing pointers to objects of class CBitmap. m_pB[0] is used for the first bitmap (IDB_BITMAP1), m_pB[1] is used for the second bitmap (IDB_BITMAP2), m_pB[2] is used for the third bitmap (IDB_BITMAP3), and m_pB[3] is used for the fourth bitmap (IDB_BITMAP4).

Don't forget to save your work:

☐ Select Save from the File menu of Visual C++.

Loading the Bitmaps and Creating a Multimedia Object

You'll now create the m_midi multimedia object, an object of class CTegMM.

☐ Open the DanceVW.H file, and create the m_midi object as a data member of the CDanceView class. After you create the m_midi object, the CDanceView class declaration should look like this:

```
class CDanceView : public CFormView
{
protected: // create from serialization only
CDanceView();
DECLARE_DYNCREATE(CDanceView)
```

```
public:
//{{AFX_DATA(CDanceView)
enum{ IDD = IDD_DANCE_FORM };
// NOTE: the ClassWizard will add data
// members here
//}}AFX_DATA

// Attributes
public:
CDanceDoc* GetDocument();


    /////////////////////////
    // MY CODE STARTS HERE
    /////////////////////////

    // The current frame number.
    int m_CurrentFrame;

    // An array for the 4 bitmaps.
    CBitmap* m_pB[4];


    // Create an object of class CTegMM
    CTegMM m_midi;

    /////////////////////////
    // MY CODE ENDS HERE
    /////////////////////////
....
....
....
};
```

Of course, when the compiler encounters the statement

```
CTegMM m_midi;
```

it will generate an error, because the compiler knows nothing about the CTegMM class. This means that you need to use #include on the CTegMM.H file inside the DanceVW.H file.

☐ Add an #include statement to the DanceVW.H file. After you add the #include statement, the beginning of the DanceVW.H file should look like this:

```
// dancevw.h : interface of the CDanceView class
//
///////////////////////////////////////////////////

/////////////////////////
// MY CODE STARTS HERE
/////////////////////////

#include "\MVCPROG\LIB\CTegMM.H"

/////////////////////////
// MY CODE ENDS HERE
/////////////////////////
...
...
...
```

If you now link the Dance.MAK project, you'll get errors because you have not yet added the CTegMM.LIB file to the Dance.MAK project.

☐ Select Files from the Project menu.

> *Visual C++ responds by displaying the Project Files dialog box.*

☐ Set the List Files of Type list box to Library File (*.lib) and then select the file \MVCPROG\Lib\CTegMM.LIB.

☐ Click the Add button.

> *Visual C++ responds by adding the CTegMM.LIB file to your project.*

☐ Click the Close button to close the Project Files dialog box.

Just to make sure that you added the CTegMM.LIB file correctly, compile and link the Dance.MAK project:

☐ Compile, link, and execute the Dance program, and verify that you are getting no errors.

☐ Terminate the Dance program.

You'll now write code inside the `OnInitialUpdate()` function that performs initializations.

☐ Use ClassWizard (from the Project menu) to select the event (see Figure 29.22):

```
CDanceView -> CDanceView -> OnInitialUpdate
```

Then click the Add Function button.

> *Visual C++ responds by adding the `OnInitialUpdate()` function.*

Figure 29.22. Adding the `OnInitialUpdate()` function.

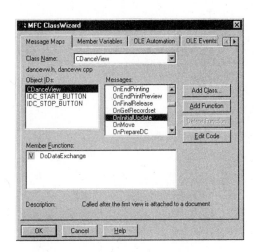

☐ Click the Edit Code button.

> *Visual C++ responds by displaying the `OnInitialUpdate()` function, ready to be edited by you.*

☐ Add code to the `OnInitialUpdate()` function. After you add the code, the `OnInitialUpdate()` function should look like this:

```
void CDanceView::OnInitialUpdate()
{
// TODO: Add your specialized code here
// and/or call the base class


/////////////////////////
// MY CODE STARTS HERE
/////////////////////////


    // Specify the window handler
    //for multimedia messages.
    m_midi.SetNumProperty("hWnd", (long)m_hWnd);

    // Fill the string file_name with the full pathname
    // of the BOURBON6.MID file.
    char file_name[300];
    strncpy(file_name,__argv[0],2);
    file_name[2]=0;
    strcat(file_name,"\\MVCPROG\\MIDI\\BOURBON6.MID");

    // Open the BOURBON6.MID file.
    m_midi.SetStrProperty("DeviceType", "Sequencer");
    m_midi.SetStrProperty("FileName", file_name);
    m_midi.SetStrProperty("Command", "Open");

    // If Open command failed, display an error message box.
    long error;
    m_midi.GetNumProperty("Error", &error);
    if (error != 0 )
        {
        // Display an error message box.
        char err_msg[300];
        m_midi.GetStrProperty("ErrorMessage", err_msg);
        ::MessageBox(NULL, err_msg, "Error", 0);
        }


// Load IDB_BITMAP1
m_pB[0] = new CBitmap;
m_pB[0]->LoadBitmap(IDB_BITMAP1);

// Load IDB_BITMAP2
m_pB[1] = new CBitmap;
m_pB[1]->LoadBitmap(IDB_BITMAP2);

// Load IDB_BITMAP3
m_pB[2] = new CBitmap;
m_pB[2]->LoadBitmap(IDB_BITMAP3);

// Load IDB_BITMAP4
m_pB[3] = new CBitmap;
m_pB[3]->LoadBitmap(IDB_BITMAP4);
```

```
///////////////////
// MY CODE ENDS HERE
///////////////////
```

```
CFormView::OnInitialUpdate();
}
```

Now go over the code of the `OnInitialUpdate()` function.

The first statement specifies the window that will receive multimedia messages:

```
m_midi.SetNumProperty("hWnd", (long)m_hWnd);
```

That is, the preceding statement specifies that the view window (`m_hWnd`) is the window that should receive multimedia messages. Multimedia messages? During the course of performing multimedia operations, various messages are generated. For example, when the playback is complete, the multimedia object generates a message that indicates that the playback is completed. By specifying `m_hWnd` as the hWnd property of the `m_midi` object, you are instructing the multimedia object to send the messages to the view window. Later in this chapter you'll see the effects of the preceding statement.

The next group of statements fills the variable `file_name` with the path and filename of the MIDI file that will be played during the show:

```
char file_name[300];
strncpy(file_name,__argv[0],2);
file_name[2]=0;
strcat(file_name,"\\MVCPROG\\MIDI\\BOURBON6.MID");
```

Next, DeviceType is set to Sequencer, and the MIDI file is opened:

```
m_midi.SetStrProperty("DeviceType", "Sequencer");
m_midi.SetStrProperty("FileName", file_name);
m_midi.SetStrProperty("Command", "Open");
```

An `if` statement is then used to check whether the MIDI file was opened successfully:

```
long error;
m_midi.GetNumProperty("Error", &error);
if (error != 0 )
   {
   // Display an error message box.
   char err_msg[300];
   m_midi.GetStrProperty("ErrorMessage", err_msg);
   ::MessageBox(NULL, err_msg, "Error", 0);
   }
```

Note that by preceding the `MessageBox()` function with `::`, you are instructing the compiler to use the Windows API `MessageBox()` function (not the `MessageBox()` member function of the `CDanceview` class).

The remaining statements in the `OnInitialUpdate()` function load the four bitmaps for the animation show. For example, the first bitmap (IDB_BITMAP1) is loaded with two statements. The first statement

```
m_pB[0] = new CBitmap;
```

creates an object of class CBitmap and fills the first element of the m_pB[ ] array (m_pB[0]) with the address of this object. So now m_pB[0] points to an object of class CBitmap.

The second statement

```
m_pB[0]->LoadBitmap(IDB_BITMAP1);
```

uses the LoadBitmap() member function of the CBitmap class to load the first bitmap of the animation show (IDB_BITMAP1). So now m_pB[0] points to the first bitmap of the animation show.

In a similar manner, the rest of the statements of the OnInitialUpdate() function load the other bitmaps of the animation show. That is, after the code of OnInitialUpdate() is executed, m_pB[0] points to the first bitmap (IDB_BITMAP1), m_pB[1] points to the second bitmap (IDB_BITMAP2), m_pB[2] points to the third bitmap (IDB_BITMAP3), and m_pB[3] points to the fourth bitmap (IDB_BITMAP4).

Don't forget to save your work:

☐ Select Save from the File menu of Visual C++.

Displaying the First Frame of the Show

So far you have written the code that initializes the m_midi multimedia object and loads the four bitmaps of the animation show. Now write the code that displays the first bitmap of the show.

Upon start-up of the application, the first bitmap of the show should be displayed. You'll now attach code to the OnDraw() member function of the view class that displays the first bitmap (IDB_BITMAP1) inside the application's window. Here is how you do that:

☐ Use ClassWizard (from the Project menu) to select the event:

```
CDanceView -> CDanceView -> OnDraw
```

Then click the Add Function button.

☐ Click the Edit Code button.

> *Visual C++ responds by displaying the* OnDraw() *function, ready to be edited by you.*

☐ Add code to the OnDraw() function. After you add the code, the OnDraw() function should look like this:

```
void CDanceView::OnDraw(CDC* pDC)
{
// TODO: Add your specialized code
// here and/or call the base class


/////////////////////
// MY CODE STARTS HERE
/////////////////////

  // Create a memory DC.
  CDC* pMemDC = new CDC;
  pMemDC->CreateCompatibleDC(pDC);
```

```
// Select the bitmap into the memory DC.
pMemDC->SelectObject( m_pB[0] );

// Copy the bitmap from the memory DC into the screen DC.
pDC->BitBlt(100,10,500,500,pMemDC,0,0,SRCCOPY);

// Delete the memory DC.
delete pMemDC;


//////////////////////
// MY CODE ENDS HERE
//////////////////////

CFormView::OnDraw(pDC);
}
```

As you can see, the OnDraw() function of the DANCE application does the same things as the OnDraw() function of the BALL application:

- It creates a memory DC.

- It selects the first bitmap of the animation show into the memory DC.

- It copies the bitmap from the memory DC into the screen DC by using the BitBlt() function.

- It deletes the memory DC.

Overall, the code you typed inside the OnDraw() function places the first bitmap of the animation show inside the screen DC. Therefore, upon start-up of the application, and whenever there is a need to repaint the window of the application (that is, whenever OnDraw() is executed), the first bitmap of the animation show will be displayed inside the application window.

Don't forget to save your work:

☐ Select Save from the File menu of Visual C++.

Deleting the Bitmaps

You wrote code inside the OnInitialUpdate() function that creates four CBitmap objects:

```
void CDanceView::OnInitialUpdate()
{

...
...
...

// Load IDB_BITMAP1
m_pB[0] = new CBitmap;
m_pB[0]->LoadBitmap(IDB_BITMAP1);

// Load IDB_BITMAP2
m_pB[1] = new CBitmap;
m_pB[1]->LoadBitmap(IDB_BITMAP2);
```

```
// Load IDB_BITMAP3
m_pB[2] = new CBitmap;
m_pB[2]->LoadBitmap(IDB_BITMAP3);

// Load IDB_BITMAP4
m_pB[3] = new CBitmap;
m_pB[3]->LoadBitmap(IDB_BITMAP4);

}
```

When the application terminates, your code should delete these objects. If you do not write this code, the memory that is occupied by these objects will not be released, and the available memory of the user's system will be decreased every time the user executes your application. (This is commonly known as having a *memory leakage* in your program.) If you write programs with memory leakage, sooner or later your users will notice that whenever they use your programs they encounter memory problems.

Just as in the BALL application, you'll write the code that deletes the four bitmaps inside the destructor function of the view class. Here is how you do that:

☐ Open the file DANCEVW.CPP and add code to the destructor function ~CDanceView() so that it looks like this:

```
CDanceView::~CDanceView()
{

    ////////////////////////
    // MY CODE STARTS HERE
    ////////////////////////

    // Delete the 4 bitmaps.
    for (int i=0; i<4; i++)
        delete m_pB[i];

    ////////////////////////
    // MY CODE ENDS HERE
    ////////////////////////

}
```

The code you just typed uses a `for` loop to delete the four bitmaps:

```
for (int i=0; i<4; i++)
    delete m_pB[i];
```

Therefore, upon termination of the application, the memory occupied by the four bitmaps will be freed.

Now execute the DANCE application to see the code you typed inside the `OnDraw()` function in action:

☐ Compile, link, and execute the DANCE.EXE application.

As you can see, now the main window of the application appears with the first bitmap of the animation show.

☐ Try to minimize the window and then maximize it.

Again, the application window appears with the first bitmap of the animation show inside it. That is, whenever there is a need to repaint the window (for example, upon start-up of the application), the code you wrote inside the OnDraw() function is automatically executed, and this code displays the IDB_BITMAP1 bitmap (pB[0]) inside the window.

☐ Terminate the DANCE application by selecting Exit from the File menu.

Starting the Animation Show

You'll now write the code that starts the animation show.

The animation show should start running when the user clicks the Start Show button. Therefore, you'll attach the code that starts the animation show to the Start Show push button.

Here is how you attach code to the Start Show push button:

☐ Use ClassWizard (from the Project menu) to select the event:

```
CDanceView -> IDC_START_BUTTON -> BN_CLICKED
```

Then click the Add Function button.

> *Visual C++ responds by suggesting the name* OnStartButton() *as the name of the new function.*

☐ Accept the name OnStartButton() as the name of the new function.

☐ Click the Edit Code button.

> *Visual C++ responds by displaying the* OnStartButton() *function, ready to be edited by you.*

☐ Edit the OnStartButton() function that you added to the DANCEVW.CPP file. After you edit the function, your OnStartButton() function should look like this:

```
void CDanceView::OnStartButton()
{
// TODO: Add your control notification
// handler code here

/////////////////////////
// MY CODE STARTS HERE
/////////////////////////

    // Disable the Start push button.
    GetDlgItem(IDC_START_BUTTON)->EnableWindow(FALSE);

    // Initialize the current frame number to 0.
    m_CurrentFrame = 0;

    // Rewind the multimedia object.
    m_midi.SetStrProperty("Command","Prev");

    // Start playing the MIDI file.
    m_midi.SetStrProperty("Command","Play");
```

```
// Install a timer with a 350 msec interval.
if ( SetTimer (1, 350, NULL) == 0 )
    MessageBox ("Cannot install timer!!!");
```

```
///////////////////////
// MY CODE ENDS HERE
///////////////////////
```

```
}
```

Now go over the code of the OnStartButton() function.

The first statement disables the Start push button:

```
GetDlgItem(IDC_START_BUTTON)->EnableWindow(FALSE);
```

You disable the Start Show push button because you don't want the user to click it while the animation show is in progress.

The next statement is

```
m_CurrentFrame = 0;
```

This statement initializes the m_CurrentFrame variable to 0.

As stated earlier, the m_CurrentFrame variable is used to store the index number of the displayed bitmap.

Initially (upon start-up of the animation) the first bitmap is displayed, so in the preceding statement m_CurrentFrame is set to 0.

The next two statements start the playback of the MIDI file. The first statement

```
m_midi->SetStrProperty("Command","Prev");
```

rewinds the m_midi multimedia object so that the playback will start from the beginning of the MIDI file. The second statement

```
m_midi->SetStrProperty("Command","Play");
```

issues a Play command to the multimedia object.

The last statement in the OnStartButton() function is

```
if ( SetTimer (1, 350, NULL) == 0 )
    MessageBox ("Cannot install timer!!!");
```

The SetTimer() function installs a timer. The second parameter of the SetTimer() function sets the interval to 350 milliseconds.

This means that from now on the OnTimer() function is automatically executed every 350 milliseconds. In the next section you'll write the code of the OnTimer() function.

As you'll see, once the timer is installed, the animation starts.

The Animation Show

The code you attached to the Start Show push button installs a timer and sets its interval to 350 milliseconds.

You'll now attach code to the WM_TIMER event. Because you set the interval of the timer to 350 milliseconds, the code you will now write will be automatically executed every 350 milliseconds.

☐ Use ClassWizard (from the Project menu) to select the event:

```
CDanceView -> CDanceView -> WM_TIMER
```

Then click the Add Function button.

☐ Click the Edit Code button.

> *Visual C++ responds by displaying the* OnTimer() *function, ready to be edited by you.*

☐ Edit the OnTimer() function that you added to the DanceVW.CPP file. After you edit it, your OnTimer() function should look like this:

```
void CDanceView::OnTimer(UINT nIDEvent)
{
// TODO: Add your message handler
// code here and/or call default

///////////////////////
// MY CODE STARTS HERE
///////////////////////

    // Increment the current frame number.
    m_CurrentFrame++;

    // Was the last frame of the dance displayed?
    if (m_CurrentFrame==4)
       m_CurrentFrame=0;

    // Get a DC for the screen.
    CClientDC dc(this);

    // Create a memory DC.
    CDC* pMemDC = new CDC;
    pMemDC->CreateCompatibleDC(&dc);

    // Select the bitmap into the memory DC.
    pMemDC->SelectObject( m_pB[m_CurrentFrame] );

    // Copy the bitmap from the memory DC into the screen DC.
    dc.BitBlt(100,10,500,500,pMemDC,0,0,SRCCOPY);

    // Delete the memory DC.
    delete pMemDC;

///////////////////////
// MY CODE ENDS HERE
///////////////////////
```

```
CFormView::OnTimer(nIDEvent);
}
```

The purpose of the code you just typed is to display the next bitmap of the animation show. That is, every 350 milliseconds the code will be executed automatically, and the next bitmap of the show will be displayed. This creates the illusion that the objects inside the bitmaps (the couple) are moving (dancing).

The first statement you typed inside the function is

```
m_CurrentFrame++;
```

This statement increments the `m_CurrentFrame` variable because you want to display the next bitmap. For example, if currently `m_CurrentBitmap` is 0, currently the `m_pB[0]` bitmap is displayed. Therefore, you increment `m_CurrentFrame` by 1 because the next bitmap you want to display is the `m_pB[1]` bitmap.

The next statement is an `if` statement that checks whether the last bitmap of the dance has been displayed:

```
if (m_CurrentFrame==4)
    m_CurrentFrame=0;
```

If `m_CurrentFrame` is 4, the last bitmap of the dance has been displayed. If this is the case, the `if` condition is satisfied and the `m_CurrentFrame` variable is reset to 0. This means that every 350 milliseconds `m_CurrentFrame` is incremented, and once its value is 4 it is reset to 0. Therefore, the cycle of values that `m_CurrentFrame` goes through is this:

```
0->1->2->3->0->1->2->3->0->1->2->3...
```

The next statement in the function is

```
CClientDC dc(this);
```

This statement creates a DC called `dc` for the screen (that is, for the application window).

The remaining code of the function is like the code you wrote inside the `OnDraw()` function. It displays the bitmap (as specified by `m_CurrentFrame`) inside the application window.

The first two statements create a memory DC (`pMemDC`):

```
CDC* pMemDC = new CDC;
pMemDC->CreateCompatibleDC(&dc);
```

Then the bitmap (as specified by `m_CurrentFrame`) is selected into the memory DC:

```
pMemDC->SelectObject( m_pB[m_CurrentFrame] );
```

For example, if currently `m_CurrentFrame` is 2, this statement selects the bitmap `m_pB[2]` into the memory DC.

Then the bitmap from the memory DC (`pMemDC`) is copied into screen DC:

```
dc.BitBlt(100,
          10,
          500,
```

```
        500,
    pMemDC,
        0,
        0,
    SRCCOPY);
```

Finally the memory DC is deleted:

```
delete pMemDC;
```

So every 350 milliseconds the preceding code will be executed, and in each iteration a different bitmap of the dance show is displayed. This creates the illusion that the cartoon characters of the bitmaps are dancing.

Stopping the Animation Show

The code you attached to the Start Show button starts the playback of the MIDI file and starts the animation show.

You'll now attach code to the MM_MCINOTIFY event. The MM_MCINOTIFY event occurs when the multimedia object is done playing (for example, when the playback position reaches the end of the MIDI file).

The MM_MCINOTIFY event is not listed inside the ClassWizard dialog box. Therefore, to process the MM_MCINOTIFY message, you have to attach code to the WindowProc() member function of the view class.

> **NOTE**
>
> You can use the WindowProc() function to process any message that is not listed in the ClassWizard dialog box.

Attach code to the WindowProc() member function of the view class as follows:

☐ Use ClassWizard (from the Project menu) to select the event:

```
CDanceView -> CDanceView -> WindowProc
```

Then click the Add Function button.

Visual C++ responds by adding the WindowProc() *member function to the* CDanceView *class.*

☐ Click the Edit Code button of ClassWizard.

ClassWizard responds by opening the file DanceVW.CPP, with the function WindowProc() *ready to be edited by you.*

☐ Write code inside the WindowProc() function so that it looks like this:

```
LRESULT CDanceView::WindowProc(UINT message,
            WPARAM wParam, LPARAM lParam)
```

```
{
// TODO: Add your specialized code
// here and/or call the base class

/////////////////////////
// MY CODE STARTS HERE
/////////////////////////

switch ( message )
      {
      case MM_MCINOTIFY:
           {

           // Kill the timer.
           KillTimer(1);

           // Enable the Start push button.
           GetDlgItem(IDC_START_BUTTON)
                   ->EnableWindow(TRUE);

           // Trigger a call to the OnDraw() function.
           Invalidate();

           break;
           }

      }// end of switch


/////////////////////
// MY CODE ENDS HERE
/////////////////////


return CFormView::WindowProc(message, wParam, lParam);
}
```

☐ Save your work by selecting Save from the File menu.

The code you typed inside the `WindowProc()` function is made of a `switch` statement:

```
switch ( message )
      {
      case MM_MCINOTIFY:
           {
           ....
           ....
           ....
           }
      }
```

This `switch` statement evaluates the `message` parameter of the `WindowProc()` function to determine which event (message) has just occurred. If, for example, an `MM_MCINOTIFY` event has just occurred (that is, an `MM_MCINOTIFY` message has just arrived), the code under the `MM_MCINOTIFY` case will be executed:

```
case MM_MCINOTIFY:
      {
```

```
        // Kill the timer.
        KillTimer(1);

        // Enable the Start push button.
        GetDlgItem(IDC_START_BUTTON)
                    ->EnableWindow(TRUE);

        // Trigger a call to the OnDraw() function.
        Invalidate();

        break;
        }
```

The first statement terminates the timer:

```
KillTimer(1);
```

Recall that once the timer is killed, the animation is terminated. So when the playback is complete, the MM_MCINOTIFY message is generated. You wrote code that is executed when the MM_MCINOTIFY message is received. This code kills the timer (which causes the animation to stop).

Of course, you did not have to use a switch statement. However, it is best to use a switch statement (instead of an if statement) because this way it will be very easy to add more cases to the switch if you need to process more messages in the future.

The next statement

```
GetDlgItem(IDC_START_BUTTON)->EnableWindow(TRUE);
```

enables the Start Show button.

Finally, the Invalidate() function is executed to force the execution of the OnDraw() function.

It is important to note that the MM_MCINOTIFY message will be sent to the WindowProc() function of the view class, provided that the hWnd property of the multimedia object was set to the m_hWnd data member of the view class. This is the reason that you were instructed at the beginning of this exercise to set the hWnd property of the m_midi object inside the OnInitialUpdate() function of the view class as follows:

```
void CDanceView::OnInitialUpdate()
{
// TODO: Add your specialized code here
// and/or call the base class


//////////////////////////
// MY CODE STARTS HERE
//////////////////////////


   // Specify the window handler for Windows messages.
   m_midi.SetNumProperty("hWnd", (long)m_hWnd);

....
....
....
```

Attaching Code to the Stop Button

The code you attached to the WindowProc() function terminates the animation show when the multimedia object completes the playback of the MIDI file. But what if the user wants to stop the animation and playback before the playback is done? Are you going to force your user to listen to the whole song? Of course not. To allow the user to stop the playback and animation at any time, you'll now attach code to the Stop button.

Follow these steps to attach code to the Stop push button:

☐ Use ClassWizard (from the Project menu) to select the event:

```
CDanceView -> IDC_STOP_BUTTON -> BN_CLICKED
```

Then click the Add Function button.

☐ Accept the name OnStopButton() that Visual C++ suggests.

☐ Click the Edit Code button.

> *Visual C++ responds by displaying the* OnStopButton() *function, ready to be edited by you.*

☐ Edit the OnStopButton() function that you added to the DANCEVW.CPP file. After you edit the function, it should look like this:

```
void CDanceView::OnStopButton()
{
// TODO: Add your control notification handler code here

    /////////////////////////
    // MY CODE STARTS HERE
    /////////////////////////

    // Stop the playback.
    m_midi.SetStrProperty("Command","Stop");

    /////////////////////////
    // MY CODE ENDS HERE
    /////////////////////////

}
```

The code you just typed inside the OnStopButton() function is made of one statement:

```
m_midi.SetStrProperty("Command","Stop");
```

This statement issues the Stop command to the multimedia object, which stops the playback of the MIDI file. But what about stopping the animation show? Once the multimedia object stops playing the MIDI file, an MM_MCINOTIFY message occurs, and the code that you earlier attached to the MM_MCINOTIFY message (inside the WindowProc() function) stops the animation show.

You have finished writing the code that plays the MIDI file and performs the animation. To see the animation and hear the playback of the MIDI file in action do the following:

☐ Build the DANCE application, and then execute it.

☐ Experiment with the Start Show and Stop buttons.

As expected, the animation code you wrote is performing the animation while the MIDI file plays in the background.

In the following section you will add code to the DANCE application that makes the default size of the application's window small.

☐ Terminate the DANCE application by selecting Exit from the File menu.

Setting the Default Size of the Application Window

Upon start-up of the application, the default size of the application window should be as shown in Figure 29.1.

Just as you did in the BALL application of Chapter 27, you'll write the code that sets the default size of the application window inside the PreCreateWindow() member function of the CMainFrame class.

☐ Use ClassWizard (from the Project menu) to select the event (See Figure 29.23.):

```
CMainFrmae -> CMainFrame -> PreCreateWindow
```

Then click the Add Function button.

Figure 29.23. Adding the
PreCreateWindow()
function.

☐ Click the Edit Code button.

Visual C++ responds by displaying the PreCreateWindow() *function, ready to be edited by you.*

☐ Add code to the PreCreateWindow() function (inside the MAINFRM.CPP file). After you write the code inside this function, it should look like this:

```
BOOL CMainFrame::PreCreateWindow(CREATESTRUCT& cs)
{
// TODO: Add your specialized code here
// and/or call the base class

/////////////////////////
// MY CODE STARTS HERE
/////////////////////////

    // Set the width of the window to 335.
    cs.cx = 370;

    // Set the height of the window to 275.
    cs.cy = 275;


/////////////////////////
// MY CODE ENDS HERE
/////////////////////////

return CFrameWnd::PreCreateWindow(cs);
}
```

As you can see, this code sets the width of the application window to 370 and the height of the window to 275.

Don't forget to save your work:

☐ Select Save from the File menu.

To see the code that you attached to the `PreCreateWindow()` function in action do the following:

☐ Compile, link, and execute the DANCE application.

As you can see, now the default size of the main window of the application is as you set it inside the `PreCreateWindow()` function.

☐ Experiment with the DANCE application and then terminate it.

Animation with Synchronized Sound—The KENNEDY Application

The DANCE application that you just wrote is an example of an application that creates an animation show with background sound. However, the animation show is not synchronized with the sound. That is, every 350 milliseconds a different bitmap of the animation show is displayed, without regard to the current playback position of the music. Such an animation show works well in cases in which the played sound is music and the displayed bitmaps do not have to match a specific playback position. However, in cases in which the background sound is speech, you need to write code that synchronizes the background speech with the displayed bitmaps.

The KENNEDY application is an example of a Visual C++ application that synchronizes the background sound (a speech by former President John F. Kennedy) with the displayed bitmaps. Before you start writing the KENNEDY application, first execute the copy of it that resides in the \MVCPROG\EXE directory of the book's CD.

☐ Execute the X:\MVCPROG\EXE\Kennedy.EXE program (where *X* represents the drive letter of your CD-ROM drive).

> *Windows responds by executing the Kennedy.EXE application. The main window of Kennedy.EXE appears, as shown in Figure 29.24.*

Figure 29.24. The main window of the KENNEDY application.

As you can see, the main window of the application has inside it a picture of President Kennedy and a Start button.

To start the animation do the following:

☐ Click the Start button.

> *The KENNEDY application responds by playing through the sound card a portion of a famous speech of President Kennedy and by displaying bitmaps with text that corresponds to the current playback position of the speech.*

That is, the bitmaps that display the words of the speech are synchronized with the sound of the speech.

The KENNEDY application has two pop-up menus: File and Help. These pop-up menus are shown in Figures 29.25 and 29.26.

Figure 29.25. The File pop-up menu of the KENNEDY application.

Figure 29.26. The Help pop-up menu of the KENNEDY application.

☐ Terminate the KENNEDY application by selecting Exit from the File menu.

Now that you know what the KENNEDY application should do, you can start writing it.

Creating the Project of the KENNEDY Application

You'll now create the project of the KENNEDY application.

☐ Close all the open windows on the desktop of Visual C++ (if there are any).

☐ Select New from the File menu.

> *Visual C++ responds by displaying the New dialog box.*

☐ Select Project inside the New dialog box and then click the OK button of the New dialog box.

> *Visual C++ responds by displaying the New Project dialog box.*

☐ Set the project name to Kennedy.

☐ Set the project path to \MVCPROG\CH29\Kennedy\Kennedy.MAK.

Your New Project dialog box should now look like the one shown in Figure 29.27.

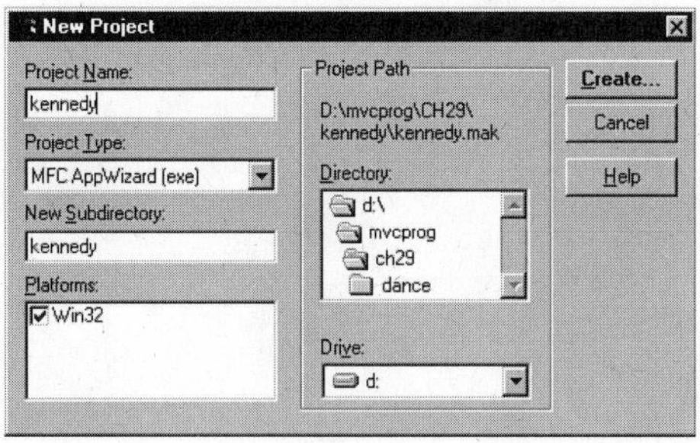

Figure 29.27. The New Project dialog box of the Kennedy.MAK project.

☐ Click the Create button of the New Project dialog box.

   Visual C++ responds by displaying the AppWizard—Step 1 window.

☐ Set the Step 1 window as shown in Figure 29.28. As shown in Figure 29.28, the Kennedy.MAK project is set as a single-document application, and U.S. English (APPWIZUS.DLL) is used as the language for the application's resources.

Figure 29.28. The AppWizard—Step 1 window for the KENNEDY application.

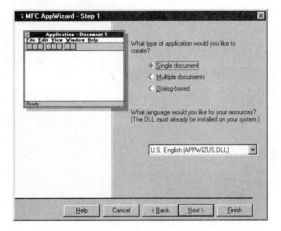

☐ Click the Next button of the Step 1 window.

   Visual C++ responds by displaying the AppWizard—Step 2 of 6 window.

☐ Set the Step 2 of 6 window as shown in Figure 29.29. That is, in the KENNEDY application you don't want any database support.

Figure 29.29. The AppWizard—Step 2 of 6 window for the KENNEDY application.

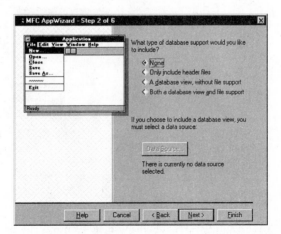

☐ Click the Next button of the Step 2 of 6 window.

Visual C++ responds by displaying the AppWizard—Step 3 of 6 window.

☐ Set the Step 3 of 6 window as shown in Figure 29.30. That is, in the KENNEDY application you don't want any OLE support.

Figure 29.30. The AppWizard—Step 3 of 6 window for the KENNEDY application.

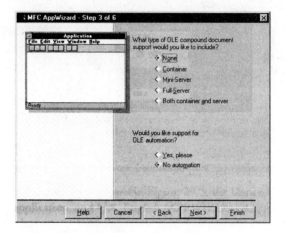

☐ Click the Next button of the Step 3 of 6 window.

Visual C++ responds by displaying the AppWizard—Step 4 of 6 window.

☐ Set the Step 4 of 6 window as shown in Figure 29.31.

Figure 29.31. The AppWizard—Step 4 of 6 window for the KENNEDY application.

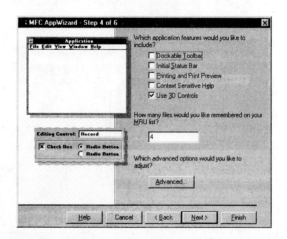

As shown in Figure 29.31, only the Use 3D Controls check box is checked.

☐ Click the Next button of the Step 4 of 6 window.

Visual C++ responds by displaying the AppWizard—Step 5 of 6 window.

☐ Set the Step 5 of 6 window as shown in Figure 29.32.

As shown in Figure 29.32, the project will be generated with comments, a Visual C++ makefile will be generated, and the application will use the MFC library from a DLL.

Figure 29.32. The AppWizard—Step 5 of 6 window for the KENNEDY application.

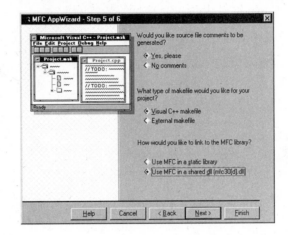

☐ Click the Next button of the Step 5 of 6 window.

Visual C++ responds by displaying the AppWizard—Step 6 of 6 window.

You'll now use the AppWizard—Step 6 of 6 window to tell AppWizard to derive the view class of the application from the MFC class `CFormView`:

☐ Select the `CKennedyView` class inside the AppWizard—Step 6 of 6 window.

☐ Set the Base Class drop-down list box to `CFormView`.

Your AppWizard—Step 6 of 6 window should now look like the one shown in Figure 29.33.

☐ Click the Finish button of the Step 6 of 6 window.

Visual C++ responds by displaying the New Project Information window, as shown in Figure 29.34.

☐ Click the OK button of the New Project Information window.

Visual C++ responds by creating the project file and all the skeleton files of the application.

Figure 29.33. The AppWizard—Step 6 of 6 window after you set the base class of the application view class to `CFormView`.

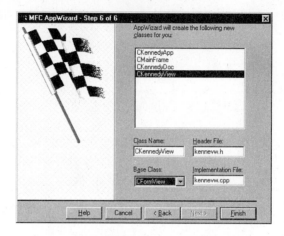

Figure 29.34. The New Project Information window of the Kennedy.MAK project.

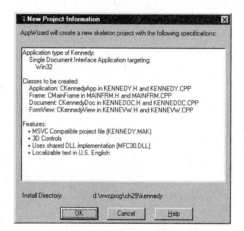

The Visual Implementation of the Dialog Box

You'll now implement the dialog box that serves as the main window of the KENNEDY application.

☐ Select Kennedy.MAK from the Window menu, double-click kennedy.rc inside the Kennedy.MAK window, double-click Dialog, and finally, double-click IDD_KENNEDY_FORM under Dialog Box.

Visual C++ responds by displaying the IDD_KENNEDY_FORM dialog box in design mode.

☐ Implement the dialog box IDD_KENNEDY_FORM according to the specifications in Table 29.2.

Table 29.2. The IDD_KENNEDY_FORM dialog box of the KENNEDY application.

Object	Property	Setting
Dialog box	ID	IDD_KENNEDY_FORM
Push button	ID	IDC_START_BUTTON
	Caption	&Start

Now your IDD_KENNEDY_FORM dialog box looks like the one shown in Figure 29.35.

Figure 29.35. The dialog box of the KENNEDY application (in design mode).

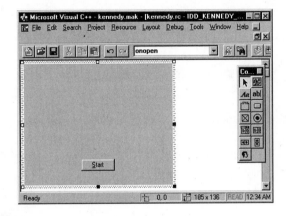

You have finished designing the dialog box of the KENNEDY application!

Don't forget to save your work:

☐ Select Save from the File menu.

The Visual Implementation of the Menu

The KENNEDY application should have a menu with two pop-up menus, as shown in Figures 29.25 and 29.26. Implement this menu:

☐ Select kennedy.rc from the Window menu to display the Kennedy.RC window, double-click Menu, and finally, double-click IDR_MAINFRAME under Menu.

Visual C++ responds by displaying the IDR_MAINFRAME menu in design mode.

☐ Implement the IDR_MAINFRAME menu so that it contains the following items:

```
&File
    E&xit
&Help
    &About Kennedy...
```

Don't forget to delete the accelerator keys of the menu items that you removed:

☐ Select kennedy.rc from the Window menu, double-click Accelerator, and then double-click IDR_MAINFRAME under Accelerator.

Visual C++ responds by displaying the Accelerator table.

☐ Delete the accelerator keys that are not used by the KENNEDY application. In particular, delete the accelerator keys of the ID_FILE_NEW, ID_FILE_OPEN, and ID_FILE_SAVE menu items.

Save your work:

☐ Select Save from the File menu.

The visual implementation of the menu of the KENNEDY application is complete.

Adding Bitmap Files to the KENNEDY Application

The KENNEDY application uses four bitmap files for the animation.

The four bitmaps of the KENNEDY application are shown in Figures 29.36 through 29.39.

*Figure 29.36. The
KENNEDY.BMP bitmap
file.*

*Figure 29.37. The
KEN1.BMP bitmap file.*

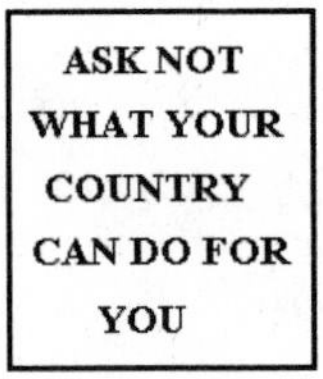

SO MY

FELLOW

AMERICANS

*Figure 29.38. The
KEN2.BMP bitmap file.*

ASK NOT
WHAT YOUR
COUNTRY
CAN DO FOR
YOU

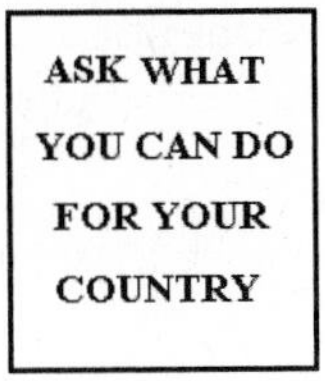

Figure 29.39. The KEN3.BMP bitmap file.

```
┌─────────────────┐
│  ASK WHAT       │
│  YOU CAN DO     │
│  FOR YOUR       │
│  COUNTRY        │
└─────────────────┘
```

To add these four bitmaps to the KENNEDY application, follow these steps:

☐ Select kennedy.rc from the Window menu to display the kennedy.rc window, and then select Import from the Resource menu.

   Visual C++ responds by displaying the Import Resource dialog box.

☐ Select the \MVCPROG\BMP\KENNEDY.BMP file and then click the OK button.

   Visual C++ responds by importing the KENNEDY.BMP file.

Now import the KEN1.BMP, KEN2.BMP, and KEN3.BMP files:

☐ Select Import from the Resource menu.

☐ Select the \MVCPROG\BMP\KEN1.BMP file and then click the OK button.

☐ Select Import from the Resource menu.

☐ Select the \MVCPROG\BMP\KEN2.BMP file and then click the OK button.

☐ Select Import from the Resource menu.

☐ Select the \MVCPROG\BMP\KEN3.BMP file and then click the OK button.

Note that the ID that Visual C++ assigned to the KENNEDY.BMP bitmap is IDB_BITMAP1. The ID that was assigned to KEN1.BMP is IDB_BITMAP2, the ID that was assigned to KEN2.BMP is IDB_BITMAP3, and the ID that was assigned to KEN3.BMP is IDB_BITMAP4.

You have finished importing four bitmaps into the KENNEDY application. Don't forget to save your work:

☐ Select Save from the File menu.

Executing the KENNEDY Application

Although you have not yet written any code, execute the application to see your visual design in action:

☐ Select Build All KENNEDY.EXE from the Project menu of Visual C++.

☐ Select Execute KENNEDY.EXE from the Project menu.

The main window of the application appears, with the form that you designed inside it.

Of course, none of the bitmaps that you imported into the application are displayed yet because you did not write code to accomplish that. In the following sections, you'll write code that brings the BMP files to life.

☐ Terminate the application by selecting Exit from the File menu.

Declaring Variables for the Animation Show

You'll now write the code that declares variables that are used by the animation show. You will declare these variables as data members of the view class because these variables need to be visible in several member functions of the view class.

☐ Open the file KENNEVW.H and write code inside the CKennedyView class declaration that declares data members. When you finish writing this code, the CKennedyView class declaration should look like this:

```
class CKennedyView : public CFormView
{
protected: // create from serialization only
CKennedyView();
DECLARE_DYNCREATE(CKennedyView)

public:
//{{AFX_DATA(CKennedyView)
enum{ IDD = IDD_KENNEDY_FORM };
// NOTE: the ClassWizard will add data members here
//}}AFX_DATA

// Attributes
public:
CKennedyDoc* GetDocument();

    /////////////////////////
    // MY CODE STARTS HERE
    /////////////////////////

    // The current frame number.
    int m_CurrentFrame;

    // An array for the 4 bitmaps.
    CBitmap* m_pB[4];

    // A multimedia object of class CTegMM
    CTegMM m_wav;

    /////////////////////////
    // MY CODE ENDS HERE
    /////////////////////////


// Operations
public:

// Overrides
// ClassWizard generated virtual function overrides
```

```
//{{AFX_VIRTUAL(CKennedyView)
public:
protected:
virtual void DoDataExchange(CDataExchange* pDX);
// DDX/DDV support
//}}AFX_VIRTUAL

// Implementation
public:
virtual ~CKennedyView();
#ifdef _DEBUG
virtual void AssertValid() const;
virtual void Dump(CDumpContext& dc) const;
#endif

protected:

// Generated message map functions
protected:
//{{AFX_MSG(CKennedyView)
// NOTE—the ClassWizard will add and remove member functions here.
// DO NOT EDIT what you see in these blocks
// of generated code !
//}}AFX_MSG
DECLARE_MESSAGE_MAP()
};
```

As you can see, these data members are the same as the data members that you declared in the DANCE application. The first data member, m_CurrentFrame, is an integer that is used for maintaining the current frame number (bitmap) that is being displayed. The array m_pB[4] is used for the four bitmaps that are used by the application.

The m_wav object is a multimedia object of class CTegMM.

Because the KenneVW.H file uses the CTegMM class, you must use #include on the CTegMM.H file:

☐ Add an #include statement to the KenneVW.H file. After you add the #include statement, the beginning of the KenneVW.H file should look like this:

```
// kennevw.h : interface of the CKennedyView class
//
/////////////////////////////////////////////////////

/////////////////////////
// MY CODE STARTS HERE
/////////////////////////

#include "\MVCPROG\LIB\CTegMM.H"

/////////////////////////
// MY CODE ENDS HERE
/////////////////////////
....
....
....
```

Also, you need to add the CTegMM.LIB file to the Kennedy.MAK project:

☐ Select Files from the Project menu.

> *Visual C++ responds by displaying the Project Files dialog box.*

☐ Select the \MVCPROG\LIB\CTegMM.LIB file, click the Add button, and then click the Close button.

Don't forget to save your work:

☐ Select Save from the File menu of Visual C++.

Loading the Bitmaps and Initializing the Multimedia Object

Just as you did in the DANCE application, you'll now write code inside the OnInitialUpdate() function that initializes the multimedia object and loads the bitmaps.

☐ Use ClassWizard (from the Project menu) to select the event:

CKennedyView -> CKennedyView -> OnInitialUpdate

Then click the Add Function button.

☐ Click the Edit Code button.

> *Visual C++ responds by displaying the* OnInitialUpdate() *function, ready to be edited by you.*

☐ Add code inside the OnInitialUpdate() function. After you add the code, the OnInitialUpdate() function should look like this:

```
void CKennedyView::OnInitialUpdate()
{
// TODO: Add your specialized code here
// and/or call the base class

/////////////////////////
// MY CODE STARTS HERE
/////////////////////////

    // Specify the window handler for Windows messages.
     m_wav.SetNumProperty("hWnd", (long)m_hWnd);

    // Fill the string file_name with the full pathname
    // of the 8Kenned3.WAV file.
    char file_name[300];
    strncpy(file_name,__argv[0],2);
    file_name[2]=0;
    strcat(file_name,"\\MVCPROG\\WAV\\8Kenned3.WAV");

    // Open the 8Kenned3.WAV file.
    m_wav.SetStrProperty("DeviceType", "WaveAudio");
    m_wav.SetStrProperty("FileName", file_name);
    m_wav.SetStrProperty("Command", "Open");
```

```
// If Open command failed, display an error message box.
long error;
m_wav.GetNumProperty("Error", &error);
if (error != 0 )
    {
    // Display an error message box.
    char err_msg[300];
    m_wav.GetStrProperty("ErrorMessage", err_msg);
    ::MessageBox(NULL, err_msg, "Error", 0);
    }


// Load IDB_BITMAP1
m_pB[0] = new CBitmap;
m_pB[0]->LoadBitmap(IDB_BITMAP1);

// Load IDB_BITMAP2
m_pB[1] = new CBitmap;
m_pB[1]->LoadBitmap(IDB_BITMAP2);

// Load IDB_BITMAP3
m_pB[2] = new CBitmap;
m_pB[2]->LoadBitmap(IDB_BITMAP3);

// Load IDB_BITMAP4
m_pB[3] = new CBitmap;
m_pB[3]->LoadBitmap(IDB_BITMAP4);


/////////////////////
// MY CODE ENDS HERE
/////////////////////


CFormView::OnInitialUpdate();
}
```

The code you typed sets the window that will receive multimedia messages to the window of the view class (m_hWnd):

```
m_wav.SetNumProperty("hWnd", (long)m_hWnd);
```

Then the multimedia object is initialized for playback of the 8Kenned3.WAV file:

```
// Fill the string file_name with the full pathname
// of the 8Kenned3.WAV file.
char file_name[300];
strncpy(file_name,__argv[0],2);
file_name[2]=0;
strcat(file_name,"\\MVCPROG\\WAV\\8Kenned3.WAV");

// Open the 8Kenned3.WAV file.
m_wav.SetStrProperty("DeviceType", "WaveAudio");
m_wav.SetStrProperty("FileName", file_name);
m_wav.SetStrProperty("Command", "Open");

// If Open command failed, display an error message box.
long error;
m_wav.GetNumProperty("Error", &error);
```

```
if (error != 0 )
    {
    // Display an error message box.
    char err_msg[300];
    m_wav.GetStrProperty("ErrorMessage", err_msg);
    ::MessageBox(NULL, err_msg, "Error", 0);
    }
```

Finally, the four bitmaps are loaded:

```
// Load IDB_BITMAP1
m_pB[0] = new CBitmap;
m_pB[0]->LoadBitmap(IDB_BITMAP1);

// Load IDB_BITMAP2
m_pB[1] = new CBitmap;
m_pB[1]->LoadBitmap(IDB_BITMAP2);

// Load IDB_BITMAP3
m_pB[2] = new CBitmap;
m_pB[2]->LoadBitmap(IDB_BITMAP3);

// Load IDB_BITMAP4
m_pB[3] = new CBitmap;
m_pB[3]->LoadBitmap(IDB_BITMAP4);
```

Note that the code you just typed is almost identical to the code you typed inside the OnInitialUpdate() function of the DANCE application. The only difference is that now instead of initializing the multimedia object for playing a MIDI file, the multimedia object is initialized for playing a WAV file (8KENNED3.WAV).

Don't forget to save your work:

☐ Select Save from the File menu of Visual C++.

Displaying the First Frame of the Show

So far, you have written the code that initializes the multimedia object and loads the four bitmaps of the animation show.

Now write the code that displays the first bitmap of the show. Upon start-up of the application, the first bitmap of the show should be displayed. You'll now attach code to the OnDraw() member function of the view class that displays the first bitmap (IDB_BITMAP1) inside the application's window. Here is how you do that:

☐ Use ClassWizard (from the Project menu) to select the event:

```
CKennedyView -> CkennedyView -> OnDraw
```

Then click the Add Function button.

☐ Click the Edit Code button.

Visual C++ responds by displaying the OnDraw() *function, ready to be edited by you.*

☐ Now write the code of the OnDraw() function. After you write this code, the OnDraw() function should look like this:

```
void CKennedyView::OnDraw(CDC* pDC)
{
// TODO: Add your specialized code here
// and/or call the base class

/////////////////////////
// MY CODE STARTS HERE
/////////////////////////

  // Create a memory DC.
  CDC* pMemDC = new CDC;
  pMemDC->CreateCompatibleDC(pDC);

  // Select the bitmap into the memory DC.
  pMemDC->SelectObject( m_pB[0] );

  // Copy the bitmap from the memory DC into the screen DC.
  pDC->BitBlt(90,10,500,500,pMemDC,0,0,SRCCOPY);

  // Delete the memory DC.
  delete pMemDC;


/////////////////////
// MY CODE ENDS HERE
/////////////////////


CFormView::OnDraw(pDC);
}
```

The code you just typed is identical to the code you typed in the OnDraw() function of the DANCE application. It does four things:

- It creates a memory DC.
- It selects the first bitmap of the animation show into the memory DC.
- It copies the bitmap from the memory DC into the screen DC by using the BitBlt() function.
- It deletes the memory DC.

In other words, the code you just typed inside the OnDraw() function places the first bitmap of the animation show inside the screen DC. Therefore, upon start-up of the application, and whenever there is a need to repaint the window of the application (that is, whenever OnDraw() is executed), the first bitmap of the animation show will be displayed inside the application window.

Don't forget to save your work:

☐ Select Save from the File menu of Visual C++.

Deleting the Bitmaps

Just as you did in the DANCE application, you'll now write the code that deletes the four bitmaps inside the destructor function of the view class. Here is how you do that:

☐ Open the file KENNEVW.CPP and add code to the destructor function ~CKennedyView( ) so that it looks like this:

```
CKennedyView::~CKennedyView( )
{

    /////////////////////////
    // MY CODE STARTS HERE
    /////////////////////////

    // Delete the 4 bitmaps.
    for (int i=0; i<4; i++)
        delete m_pB[i];

    /////////////////////////
    // MY CODE ENDS HERE
    /////////////////////////

}
```

This code is identical to the code you wrote inside the destructor of the view class of the DANCE application. It uses a for loop to delete the four bitmaps. Therefore, upon termination of the application, the memory occupied by these bitmaps will be freed.

Execute the KENNEDY application to see the code you typed inside the OnDraw( ) function in action:

☐ Select Build KENNEDY.EXE from the Project menu of Visual C++.

☐ Select Execute KENNEDY.EXE from the Project menu.

The main window of the application appears, with the first bitmap of the animation show.

☐ Terminate the KENNEDY application by selecting Exit from the File menu.

Starting the Animation Show

You'll now write the code that starts the animation show. The animation show should start running when the user clicks the Start button. Therefore, you'll attach the code that starts the animation show to the Start push button.

☐ Use ClassWizard (from the Project menu) to select the event:

CKennedyView -> IDC_START_BUTTON -> BN_CLICKED

Then click the Add Function button.

☐ Accept the name OnStartButton( ) that Visual C++ suggests.

☐ Click the Edit Code button.

Visual C++ responds by displaying the OnStartButton() *function, ready to be edited by you.*

☐ Add code to the OnStartButton() function. After you add the code, the OnStartButton() function should look like this:

```
void CKennedyView::OnStartButton()
{
// TODO: Add your control notification
// handler code here


/////////////////////////
// MY CODE STARTS HERE
/////////////////////////

    // Disable the Start button.
    GetDlgItem(IDC_START_BUTTON)->EnableWindow(FALSE);

    // Initialize the current frame number to 0.
    m_CurrentFrame = 0;

    // Rewind the multimedia object.
    m_wav.SetStrProperty("Command","Prev");

    // Start playing the WAV file.
    m_wav.SetStrProperty("Command","Play");

    // Install a timer with a 350 msec interval.
    if ( SetTimer (1, 350, NULL) == 0 )
       MessageBox ("Cannot install timer!!!");


/////////////////////////
// MY CODE ENDS HERE
/////////////////////////

}
```

This code is the same as the code you typed in the OnStartButton() function of the DANCE application. It does the following:

- It disables the Start button so that the user will not be able to click it while the animation show is in progress.

- It initializes the m_CurrentFrame variable to 0, because initially the first bitmap (m_pB[0]) is displayed.

- It rewinds the multimedia object.

- It starts the playback of the WAV file.

- It installs a timer with a 350-millisecond interval. This means that from now on the WM_TIMER event will be automatically executed every 350 milliseconds. The code that you'll attach to the WM_TIMER event is the code that performs the animation. You'll write this code in the following section.

The Synchronized Animation Show

The code you attached to the Start push button sets the interval of the timer to 350 milliseconds. You'll now attach code to the WM_TIMER event. Because you set the interval of the timer to 350 milliseconds, the code that you will now write will be automatically executed every 350 milliseconds. This code will display the bitmaps of the animation show in accordance with the current position of the playback (synchronized animation).

Here is how you attach code to the WM_TIMER event:

☐ Use ClassWizard (from the Project menu) to select the event:

CKennedyView -> CKennedyView -> WM_TIMER

Then click the Add Function button.

☐ Click the Edit code button.

   Visual C++ responds by displaying the OnTimer() *function, ready to be edited by you.*

☐ Add code to the OnTimer() function. After you add the code, the OnTimer() function should look like this:

```
void CKennedyView::OnTimer(UINT nIDEvent)
{
// TODO: Add your message handler code
// here and/or call default


///////////////////////
// MY CODE STARTS HERE
///////////////////////

    // Get the current position.
    long position;
    m_wav.GetNumProperty("Position", &position);

    // Set the frame number in accordance
    // with the current playback position.
    if (position<3000)
       m_CurrentFrame = 1;
    if (position>3000 && position<7000)
       m_CurrentFrame = 2;
    if (position>7000)
       m_CurrentFrame = 3;

    // Get a DC for the screen.
    CClientDC dc(this);

    // Create a memory DC.
    CDC* pMemDC = new CDC;
    pMemDC->CreateCompatibleDC(&dc);

    // Select the bitmap into the memory DC.
    pMemDC->SelectObject( m_pB[m_CurrentFrame] );
```

```
// Copy the bitmap from the memory DC.
// into the screen DC.
dc.BitBlt(90,
          10,
         500,
         500,
      pMemDC,
          0,
          0,
      SRCCOPY);

// Delete the memory DC.
delete pMemDC;


//////////////////////
// MY CODE ENDS HERE
//////////////////////


CFormView::OnTimer(nIDEvent);
}
```

The purpose of the code you just attached to the WM_TIMER event is to display the appropriate bitmap of the animation show, in accordance with the current playback position.

The WAV file that the multimedia object is playing (8KENNED3.WAV) contains this audio phrase:

```
So my fellow Americans,
ask not what your country can do for you,
ask what you can do for your country.
```

The animation show of the KENNEDY application uses three BMP files to display this audio phrase. Each of these BMP files displays a different section of the phrase:

Bitmap	Phrase
KEN1.BMP	So my fellow Americans. (See Figure 29.37.)
KEN2.BMP	Ask not what your country can do for you. (See Figure 29.38.)
KEN3.BMP	Ask what you can do for your country. (See Figure 29.39.)

The corresponding audio sections within the WAV file are the following:

Bitmap	Audio section (in milliseconds)
KEN1.BMP	0 through 3000
KEN2.BMP	3000 through 7000
KEN3.BMP	7000 through end of file

To determine which bitmap should be displayed, the code that you typed first retrieves the current playback position:

```
// Get the current position.
long position;
m_wav.GetNumProperty("Position", &position);
```

Then a series of three `if` statements is used to determine which bitmap should be displayed:

```
if (position<3000)
    m_CurrentFrame = 1;
if (position>3000 && position<7000)
    m_CurrentFrame = 2;
if (position>7000)
    m_CurrentFrame = 3;
```

For example, if the playback position is currently 4000 milliseconds, the second `if` statement is satisfied and `m_CurrentFrame` is set to 2.

The next statement in the function is

```
CClientDC dc(this);
```

This statement creates a DC called `dc` for the screen (that is, for the application window).

The remaining code of the function displays the bitmap (as specified by `m_CurrentFrame`) inside the application window.

The first two statements create a memory DC (`pMemDC`):

```
CDC* pMemDC = new CDC;
pMemDC->CreateCompatibleDC(&dc);
```

Then the bitmap (as specified by `m_CurrentFrame`) is selected into the memory DC:

```
pMemDC->SelectObject( m_pB[m_CurrentFrame] );
```

For example, if currently `m_CurrentFrame` is 2, this statement selects the bitmap `m_pB[2]` into the memory DC.

Then the bitmap from the memory DC (`pMemDC`) is copied into screen DC:

```
dc.BitBlt(90,10,500,500,pMemDC,0,0,SRCCOPY);
```

Finally, the memory DC is deleted:

```
delete pMemDC;
```

So every 350 milliseconds the preceding code will be executed, and in each iteration, depending on the current playback position, a different bitmap is displayed. Therefore, the speech and the bitmaps are synchronized.

Stopping the Animation Show

The code you attached to the Start button starts the playback of the WAV file and starts the animation show.

You'll now attach code to the `MM_MCINOTIFY` event. The `MM_MCINOTIFY` event occurs when the multimedia object is done playing (for example, when the playback position reaches the end of the WAV file).

The MM_MCINOTIFY event is not listed inside the ClassWizard dialog box. Therefore, to process the MM_MCINOTIFY message, you have to attach code to the WindowProc() member function of the view class. You can use the WindowProc() function to process any message that is not listed in the ClassWizard dialog box.

Attach code to the WindowProc() member function of the view class as follows:

☐ Use ClassWizard (from the Project menu) to select the event:

```
CKennedyView -> CKennedyView -> WindowProc
```

Then click the Add Function button.

> *Visual C++ responds by adding the* WindowProc() *member function to the* CKennedyView *class.*

☐ Click the Edit Code button of ClassWizard.

> *ClassWizard responds by opening the file KenneVW.CPP, with the function* WindowProc() *ready to be edited by you.*

☐ Write code inside the WindowProc() function so that it looks like this:

```
LRESULT CKennedyView::WindowProc(UINT message,
            WPARAM wParam, LPARAM lParam)
{
// TODO: Add your specialized code here
// and/or call the base class

//////////////////////////
// MY CODE STARTS HERE
//////////////////////////

switch ( message )
      {
      case MM_MCINOTIFY:
            {

            // Kill the timer.
            KillTimer(1);

            // Enable the Start push button.
            GetDlgItem(IDC_START_BUTTON)
                        ->EnableWindow(TRUE);

            // Trigger a call to the OnDraw() function.
            Invalidate();

            break;
            }

      }// end of switch
```

```
//////////////////////
// MY CODE ENDS HERE
//////////////////////
```

```
return CFormView::WindowProc(message, wParam, lParam);
}
```

☐ Save your work by selecting Save from the File menu.

The code you typed inside the `WindowProc()` function is made of a `switch` statement:

```
switch ( message )
      {
      case MM_MCINOTIFY:
            {
            ....
            ....
            ....
            }
      }
```

This `switch` statement evaluates the `message` parameter of the `WindowProc()` function to determine which event (message) has just occurred. If, for example, an `MM_MCINOTIFY` event has just occurred (that is, an `MM_MCINOTIFY` message has just arrived), the code under the `MM_MCINOTIFY` case will be executed.

The first statement terminates the timer:

```
KillTimer(1);
```

Recall that once the timer is killed, the animation is terminated.

The next statement

```
GetDlgItem(IDC_START_BUTTON)->EnableWindow(TRUE);
```

enables the Start button.

Finally, the `Invalidate()` function is executed to force the execution of the `OnDraw()` function.

It is important to note that the `MM_MCINOTIFY` message will be sent to the `WindowProc()` function of the view class, provided that the hWnd property of the multimedia object was set to `m_hWnd` of the view class. This is the reason you were instructed at the beginning of writing the Kennedy program to set the hWnd property of the `m_wav` object inside the `OnInitialUpdate()` function of the view class to `m_hWnd`:

```
m_wav.SetNumProperty("hWnd", (long)m_hWnd);
```

You have finished writing the code that plays the WAV file and displays the bitmaps in synchronization with the sound.

To see the bitmaps and hear the playback of the WAV file in action do the following:

☐ Build the KENNEDY application, and then execute it.

☐ Click the Start button.

As expected, the code you wrote plays the WAV file and displays the corresponding bitmaps in accordance with the playback position.

In the following section you will add code to the KENNEDY application that makes the default size of the application's window smaller.

☐ Terminate the KENNEDY application by selecting Exit from the File menu.

Setting the Default Size of the Application's Window

Just as you did in the BALL and DANCE applications, you'll now write the code that sets the default size of the application window inside the `PreCreateWindow()` member function of the `CMainFrame` class.

☐ Use ClassWizard (from the Project menu) to select the event:

```
CMainFrame -> CMainFrame -> PreCreateWindow
```

Then click the Add Function button.

☐ Click the Edit Code button.

> *Visual C++ responds by displaying the* `PreCreateWindow()` *function, ready to be edited by you.*

☐ Click the Edit Code button.

> *Visual C++ responds by displaying the* `PreCreateWindow()` *function, ready to be edited by you.*

☐ Add code to the `PreCreateWindow()` function. After you add the code, the `PreCreateWindow()` function should look like this:

```
BOOL CMainFrame::PreCreateWindow(CREATESTRUCT& cs)
{
// TODO: Add your specialized code here
// and/or call the base class


//////////////////////////
// MY CODE STARTS HERE
//////////////////////////

    // Set the width of the window to 335.
    cs.cx = 275;

    // Set the height of the window to 275.
    cs.cy = 300;
```

```
///////////////////////
// MY CODE ENDS HERE
///////////////////////

return CFrameWnd::PreCreateWindow(cs);
}
```

As you can see, this code sets the width of the application window to 275 and the height of the window to 300.

Don't forget to save your work:

☐ Select Save from the File menu.

To see the code that you attached to the `PreCreateWindow()` function in action do the following:

☐ Compile, link, and execute the KENNEDY application.

As you can see, now the default size of the main window of the application is as you set it inside the `PreCreateWindow()` function of the MainFRM.CPP file.

☐ Experiment with the Kennedy program and then select Exit from the File menu to terminate the program.

30

Creating C++ Classes for Distribution and Profit

As you have probably noticed in this book, Visual C++ is a highly modular programming language. This means that you create applications by "plugging in" software modules created by others. A classic example of such a software module is the MFC, which you have used extensively throughout this book.

In this chapter you'll learn how to write your own software modules. Typically, you design your own software modules for the purpose of distributing and selling them, or for distributing them inside your organization.

Why Create Professional Software Modules?

Typically, you design a software module that performs a task that is otherwise not available in the MFC library, and it is not easy to implement. For example, you can design a software module that enables programmers to display 3D graphs.

Sure, the programmer could probably design such a 3D program by himself or herself, but most programmers prefer to purchase an off-the-shelf software module that performs the task. Therefore, the programmer will be able to concentrate on his or her own program. When the application requires the displaying of 3D graphs, the programmer can plug in your software module rather than spend time designing the software module.

> **NOTE**
>
> In this book the term *programmer* means you, the reader. The term *end user* means the person who uses your application.
>
> In this chapter, however, you'll learn how to write software modules, and how to distribute them to other programmers. Therefore, in this chapter, the term *programmer* means another programmer who utilizes your software modules. In other words, in this chapter the term *end user* means a person (a Visual C++ programmer) who purchases and uses your software modules.

The question is Why not create a function or set of functions that perform the particular task, and then distribute the C++ source code to your end users?

There are several reasons for not distributing your software as a set of C++ functions:

- The person who receives your code might accidentally (or not accidentally) mess up the code.
- The names of functions and variables used by your functions may conflict with names of functions and variables already used by the program written by your customer.
- You don't want your user to know how you implemented the task. You only want your user to know how to use your software.
- Your user expects a "finished product" that can be plugged into applications without the need to compile and link the product.

Different Formats for Software Modules

As stated earlier, the trend is to supply (that is, sell and distribute) software in a form of software modules.

Naturally, the format of the software module depends on the particular software package and programming language that your user uses. For example, earlier versions of Visual C++ (prior to Visual C++ version 2.0) utilize VBX files.

Probably the best way to distribute software modules to Visual C++ 2.0 programmers is in a format of C++ libraries. For example, you can distribute a file called Circle.LIB. As implied by its name, the Circle.LIB library lets your users perform operations that are related to a circle (for example, calculate areas of a circle). Instead of writing functions that calculate the circle's area, your user simply plugs the Circle.LIB library into his or her application. Your responsibility is only to supply information to your users, telling them how they can apply your library to calculate circle areas.

> **NOTE**
>
> In the following sections you'll implement the Circle.LIB library. The code of the Circle.LIB library is very simple (so simple that nobody would really be interested in purchasing this library). The point of the project is to teach you how a library is prepared with Visual C++, and how to prepare the library for distribution.

Creating the Circle.CPP and Circle.H Files

The Circle.LIB file that you'll create will be generated from the Circle.CPP and Circle.H files. You'll now create the Circle.CPP and Circle.H files:

☐ Start Visual C++ and close all open windows (if there are any).

☐ Select New from the File menu, select Code/Text from the New dialog box, and then click the OK button.

Visual C++ responds by displaying a new window.

☐ Type the following inside the new window:

```
/////////////////
// Circle.CPP
/////////////////

// Copyright (C) 1994

// This file is used for generating the Circle.LIB file

#include "Circle.h"
```

☐ Save the text file as Circle.CPP inside the \MVCPROG\MyLib directory.

☐ Select New from the File menu, select Code/Text from the New dialog box, and then click the OK button.

Visual C++ responds by displaying a new window.

☐ Type the following inside the new window:

```
/////////////////
// Circle.H
/////////////////

// Copyright (C) 1994
```

☐ Save the text file as Circle.H inside the \MVCPROG\MyLib directory.

☐ Close all windows (that is, select Close All from the Window menu).

You now have the Circle.CPP and Circle.H files that are used for generating the Circle.LIB library. (Of course, later you'll write more code in these files.)

Creating the Circle.MAK Project

Your first step in creating the Circle.LIB library is to create a project.

☐ Start Visual C++ and close all the open windows (if there are any).

☐ Select New from the File menu.

Visual C++ responds by displaying the New dialog box.

☐ Select the Project item, and then click the OK button of the New dialog box. (See Figure 30.1.)

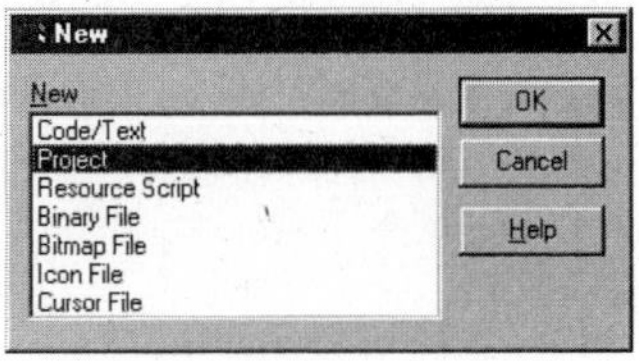

Figure 30.1. Selecting a new project for creating a new library.

Visual C++ responds by displaying the New Project dialog box.

☐ Set the project type to Static Library. (That is, click the down-arrow icon of the Project Type list box to drop down a list of options, and select the Static Library item, as shown in Figure 30.2.)

Figure 30.2. Selecting Static Library as the project type.

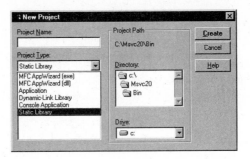

NOTE

In the preceding step you told Visual C++ that the project type is Static Library.

Static libraries have an advantage over dynamic linked libraries (DLLs): Once your customer finishes designing his or her application and plugging in your software, the application can be distributed without your software.

On the other hand, if you design the Circle library as a dynamic library (Circle.DLL), your user must distribute his or her application together with the Circle.DLL file.

This process is shown schematically in Figure 30.3.

Figure 30.3. Distributing static libraries versus distributing dynamic libraries.

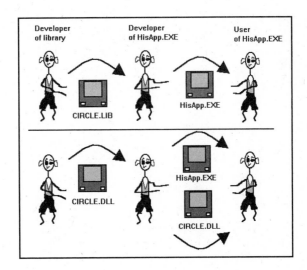

☐ Set the project path to \MVCPROG\MyLib.

☐ Set the project name to Circle.MAK

Your New Project dialog box should now look like the one shown in Figure 30.4.

Figure 30.4. The completed New Project dialog box.

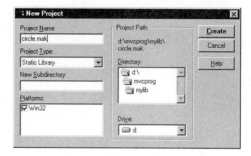

☐ Click the Create button of the New Project dialog box.

Visual C++ responds by displaying the Project Files dialog box. (See Figure 30.5.)

Figure 30.5. The Project Files dialog box.

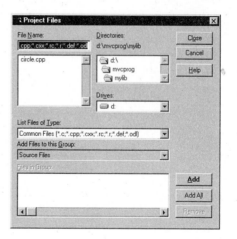

You'll now add the necessary files to the Circle.MAK project.

☐ Select the Circle.CPP file, and then click the Add button.

Visual C++ responds by adding the Circle.CPP file to the project. Your Project Files dialog box should now look like the one shown in Figure 30.6.

Figure 30.6. Adding the Circle.CPP file to the Circle.MAK project.

NOTE

Do *not* add the Circle.H file to the project.

☐ Click the Close button of the Project Files dialog box.

> *Visual Basic responds by creating the Circle.MAK project and displaying the Project.MAK window, as shown in Figure 30.7.*

Figure 30.7. The Circle.MAK window (in Win32 Debug mode).

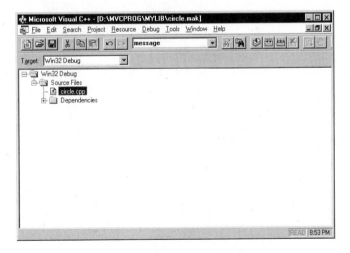

As shown in Figure 30.7, currently the target is set to Win32 Debug.

☐ Click the down-arrow icon of the Target list box, and select the Win 32 Release item. (See Figure 30.8.)

Figure 30.8. Setting the Target to Win32 Release.

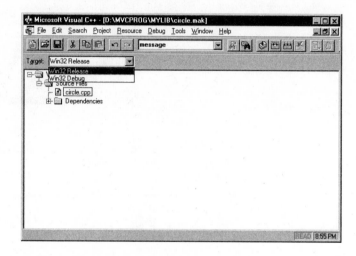

Your Circle.MAK window should now look like the one shown in Figure 30.9.

Figure 30.9. The Circle.MAK window (in Win32 Release mode).

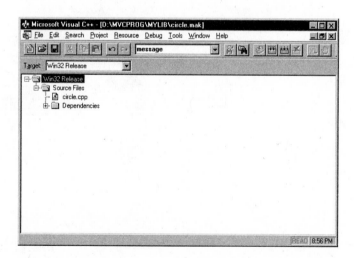

Just to make sure that you performed all the previous steps correctly do the following:

☐ Open the Project menu (but do not select any items from the Project menu).

As you can see in Figure 30.10, the Project menu includes the Build Circle.LIB item. (Recall that in previous chapters you generated EXE files, and hence the Project menu included the Build ???.EXE item.)

Figure 30.10. The Project menu with the Build Circle.LIB item.

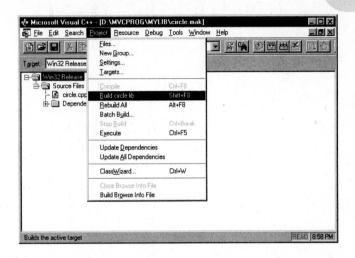

You have performed all the overhead tasks that are needed for telling Visual C++ to generate the Circle.LIB library. It is now time to start writing the code of the project.

Declaring the *CCircle* Class

You'll now declare the CCircle class.

☐ Select Open from the File menu, and select the Circle.H file.

   Visual C++ responds by opening the Circle.H file.

☐ Add code to the Circle.H file. After you add the code, your Circle.H file should look like this:

```
//////////////
// Circle.H
//////////////

// Copyright (C) 1994


// Class declaration

class CCircle
{
public:

 CCircle();  // Constructor

 void  SetRadius   ( int r );
 int   GetRadius   ( void );
 void  DisplayArea ( void );

 ~CCircle();  // Destructor

private:
```

```
int m_radius;
float CalcArea    ( void );

};
```

The code that you typed inside Circle.H declares the CCircle class:

```
class CCircle
{
...
...
...
};
```

The public section of the class contains the constructor, destructor, and three member functions:

```
public:

CCircle();  // Constructor

void  SetRadius    ( int r );
int   GetRadius    ( void );
void  DisplayArea ( void );

~CCircle();  // Destructor
```

The private section of the class contains one data member and one member function:

```
private:
int m_radius;
float CalcArea    ( void );
```

☐ Select Save from the File menu to save the Circle.H file.

Writing Code Inside the Circle.CPP File

You'll now write code inside the Circle.CPP file.

☐ Select Open from the File menu and open the Circle.CPP file.

☐ Add code to the Circle.CPP file. After you add the code, your Circle.CPP file should look like this:

```
/////////////////
// Circle.CPP
/////////////////

// Copyright (C) 1994

// This file is used for generating the Circle.LIB file


#include "Circle.h"

#include <windows.h>

#include <stdio.h>
```

```cpp
#include <stdlib.h>
#include <string.h>

/////////////////////////////
// The constructor function
/////////////////////////////
CCircle::CCircle()
{


}

/////////////////////////////
// The destructor function
/////////////////////////////
CCircle::~CCircle()
{


}

/////////////////////////////
// The SetRadius() function
/////////////////////////////
void  CCircle::SetRadius   ( int r )
{

m_radius = r;

}

/////////////////////////////
// The GetRadius() function
/////////////////////////////
int   CCircle::GetRadius   ( void  )
{

return m_radius;

}


/////////////////////////////
// The CalcArea() function
/////////////////////////////
float CCircle::CalcArea ( void )
{

return float(3.14 * m_radius * m_radius);

}


/////////////////////////////
// The DisplayArea() function
/////////////////////////////
void  CCircle::DisplayArea ( void  )
{
```

```
float   fArea;
char    sArea[100];

fArea = CalcArea ();


sprintf ( sArea, "Area is:%f", fArea );


MessageBox ( NULL,
             sArea,
             "Circle Area",
             0 );

}
```

The code you typed starts with several #include statements:

```
#include "Circle.h"

#include <windows.h>

#include <stdio.h>
#include <stdlib.h>
#include <string.h>
```

The constructor function of CCircle has no code inside it:

```
/////////////////////////////
// The constructor function
/////////////////////////////
CCircle::CCircle()
{


}
```

The destructor function of CCircle has no code inside it:

```
/////////////////////////////
// The destructor function
/////////////////////////////
CCircle::~CCircle()
{


}
```

The SetRadius() member function sets the m_radius data member:

```
/////////////////////////////
// The SetRadius() function
/////////////////////////////
void  CCircle::SetRadius   ( int r )
{

m_radius = r;

}
```

The `GetRadius()` member function returns the `m_radius` data member:

```
/////////////////////////////
// The GetRadius() function
/////////////////////////////
int   CCircle::GetRadius   ( void   )
{

return m_radius;

}
```

The `CalcArea()` member function calculates the circle's area:

```
/////////////////////////////
// The CalcArea() function
/////////////////////////////
float CCircle::CalcArea ( void )
{

return float(3.14 * m_radius * m_radius);

}
```

Finally, the `DisplayArea()` function displays the calculated area:

```
/////////////////////////////
// The DisplayArea() function
/////////////////////////////
void  CCircle::DisplayArea ( void   )
{

float  fArea;
char   sArea[100];

fArea = CalcArea ();


sprintf ( sArea, "Area is:%f", fArea );


MessageBox ( NULL,
             sArea,
             "Circle Area",
             0 );

}
```

☐ Select Save from the File menu to save the Circle.CPP file.

Making the Circle.LIB Library

You are now ready to generate the Circle.LIB file:

☐ Select Build Circle.LIB from the Project menu.

> *Visual C++ responds by creating the Circle.LIB file.*

Take a look inside your \MVCPROG\MyLib\WinRel directory. This directory now contains the Circle.LIB file!

Testing the Library—The TestLib.EXE Program

You'll now write a program called TestLib.EXE that uses the Circle.LIB library.

☐ Close all the open windows of Visual C++ (if there are any).

☐ Select New from the Project menu.

> *Visual C++ responds by displaying the New dialog box.*

☐ Select Project inside the New dialog box and then click the OK button of the New dialog box.

> *Visual C++ responds by displaying the New Project dialog box.*

☐ Set the project name to testlib.

☐ Set the project path to \MVCPROG\CH30\TestLib\TestLib.MAK.

Your New Project dialog box should now look like the one shown in Figure 30.11.

Figure 30.11. The New Project dialog box of the TestLib.MAK project.

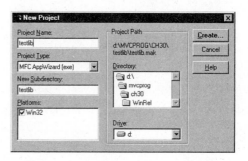

☐ Click the Create button of the New Project dialog box.

> *Visual C++ responds by displaying the AppWizard—Step 1 window.*

☐ Set the Step 1 window as shown in Figure 30.12. As shown in Figure 30.12, the TestLib.MAK project is set as a single-document interface application, and U.S. English (APPWIZUS.DLL) is used as the language for the application's resources.

☐ Click the Next button of the Step 1 window.

> *Visual C++ responds by displaying the AppWizard—Step 2 of 6 window.*

☐ Set the Step 2 of 6 window as shown in Figure 30.13. That is, in the TestLib application you don't want any database support.

Figure 30.12. The AppWizard—Step 1 window for the TestLib application.

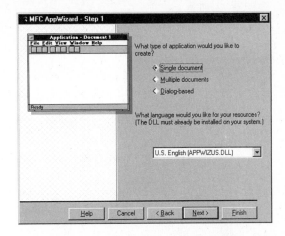

Figure 30.13. The AppWizard—Step 2 of 6 window for the TestLib application.

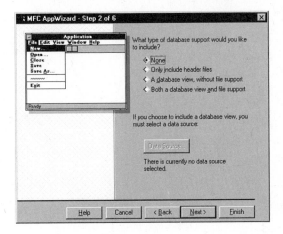

☐ Click the Next button of the Step 2 of 6 window.

Visual C++ responds by displaying the AppWizard—Step 3 of 6 window.

☐ Set the Step 3 of 6 window as shown in Figure 30.14. That is, in the TestLib application you don't want any OLE support.

☐ Click the Next button of the Step 3 of 6 window.

Visual C++ responds by displaying the AppWizard—Step 4 of 6 window.

☐ Set the Step 4 of 6 window as shown in Figure 30.15.

Figure 30.14. The AppWizard—Step 3 of 6 window for the TestLib application.

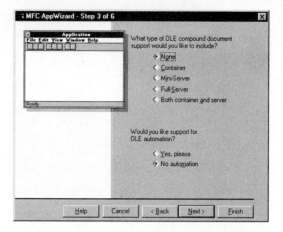

Figure 30.15. The AppWizard—Step 4 of 6 window for the TestLib application.

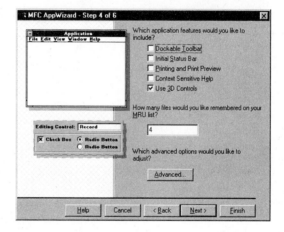

As shown in Figure 30.15, the features Dockable Toolbar, Initial Status Bar, Printing and Print Preview, and Context Sensitive Help will not be included in the TestLib application.

☐ Click the Next button of the Step 4 of 6 window.

Visual C++ responds by displaying the AppWizard—Step 5 of 6 window.

☐ Set the Step 5 of 6 window as shown in Figure 30.16.

As shown in Figure 30.16, the project will be generated with comments, a Visual C++ makefile will be generated, and the application will use the MFC library from a DLL.

☐ Click the Next button of the Step 5 of 6 window.

Visual C++ responds by displaying the AppWizard—Step 6 of 6 window.

Figure 30.16. The
AppWizard—Step 5 of 6
window for the TestLib
application.

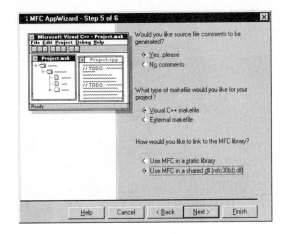

You'll now use the AppWizard—Step 6 of 6 window to tell AppWizard to derive the view class of the application from the MFC class `CFormView`:

☐ Select the `CTestlibView` class inside the AppWizard—Step 6 of 6 window.

☐ Set the Base Class drop-down list box to `CFormView`.

Your AppWizard—Step 6 of 6 window should now look like the one shown in Figure 30.17.

Figure 30.17. The
AppWizard—Step 6 of 6
window after you set the
base class of the application
view class to `CFormView`.

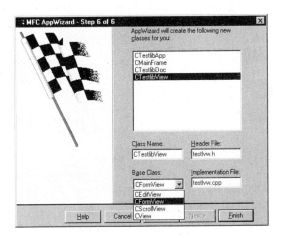

☐ Click the Finish button of the Step 6 of 6 window.

Visual C++ responds by displaying the New Project Information window, as shown in Figure 30.18.

*Figure 30.18. The New
Project Information
window of the
TestLib.MAK project.*

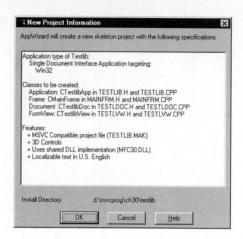

☐ Click the OK button of the New Project Information window.

> *Visual C++ responds by creating the project file and all the skeleton files of the application.*

The Visual Implementation of the TestLib Main Window

You'll now visually design the main window of the TestLib program. (Because you set the view class to CFormView, Visual C++ created the IDD_TESTLIB_FORM dialog box for you. This dialog box serves as the main window of the application.)

☐ Select TestLib.MAK from the Window menu, double-click TestLib.rc inside the TestLib.MAK window, double-click the Dialog item to drop down the list of dialog boxes that TestLib contains, and then double-click the IDD_TESTLIB_FORM item.

> *Visual C++ responds by displaying the IDD_TESTLIB_FORM dialog box in design mode. The IDD_TESTLIB_FORM dialog box serves as the main window of the TestLib application.*

☐ Click inside the TODO static text to highlight it, and then press the Delete button to delete the TODO static text.

☐ Design the IDD_TESTLIB_FORM dialog box according to the specifications in Table 30.1. When you finish designing the dialog box, it should look like the one shown in Figure 30.19.

☐ Select Save from the File menu to save your work.

Table 30.1. The Properties table of the IDD_TESTLIB_FORM dialog box.

Object	Property	Setting
Dialog box	ID	IDD_TESTLIB_FORM
Static text	ID	IDC_STATIC
	Caption	Testing the Circle.LIB library
Push button	ID	IDC_MYCIRCLE_BUTTON
	Caption	&My Circle
Push button	ID	IDC_HISCIRCLE_BUTTON
	Caption	&His Circle
Push button	ID	IDC_HERCIRCLE_BUTTON
	Caption	He&r Circle
Push button	ID	IDC_OURCIRCLE_BUTTON
	Caption	&Our Circle

Figure 30.19. The IDD_TESTLIB_FORM dialog box (in design mode).

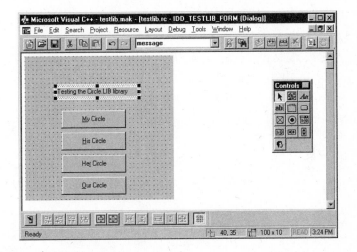

Attaching Code to the My Circle Button of the IDD_TESTLIB_FORM Dialog Box

You'll now attach code to the My Circle button of the IDD_TESTLIB_FORM dialog box.

☐ Use ClassWizard (from the Project menu) to select the event (See Figure 30.20.):

```
CTestlibView -> IDC_MYCIRCLE_BUTTON -> BN_CLICKED
```

Then click the Add Function button.

Figure 30.20. Adding the OnMycircleButton() function.

☐ Accept the name *OnMycircleButton()* that Visual C++ suggests.

☐ Click the Edit Code button.

   Visual C++ responds by displaying the OnMycircleButton() *function, ready to be edited by you.*

☐ Add code to the OnMycircleButton() function. After you add the code, the OnMycircleButton() function should look like this:

```
void CTestlibView::OnMycircleButton()
{
// TODO: Add your control notification
// handler code here


/////////////////////////
// MY CODE STARTS HERE
/////////////////////////


// Create the object
CCircle MyCircle;

// Set the radius of the circle
MyCircle.SetRadius(1);

// Display the area
MyCircle.DisplayArea();

/////////////////////////
// MY CODE ENDS HERE
/////////////////////////


}
```

The code that you typed creates the `MyCircle` object of class `CCircle`:

```
CCircle MyCircle;
```

The radius of `MyCircle` is set to 1:

```
MyCircle.SetRadius(1);
```

Finally, the area of `MyCircle` is displayed:

```
MyCircle.DisplayArea();
```

Attaching Code to the His Circle Button of the IDD_TESTLIB_FORM Dialog Box

You'll now attach code to the His Circle button of the IDD_TESTLIB_FORM dialog box.

☐ Use ClassWizard (from the Project menu) to select the event:

```
CTestlibView -> IDC_HISCIRCLE_BUTTON -> BN_CLICKED
```

Then click the Add Function button.

☐ Accept the name `OnHiscircleButton()` that Visual C++ suggests.

☐ Click the Edit Code button.

> *Visual C++ responds by displaying the* `OnHiscircleButton()` *function, ready to be edited by you.*

☐ Add code to the `OnHiscircleButton()` function. After you add the code, the `OnHiscircleButton()` function should look like this:

```
void CTestlibView::OnHiscircleButton()
{
// TODO: Add your control notification
// handler code here

/////////////////////////
// MY CODE STARTS HERE
/////////////////////////


// Create the object
CCircle HisCircle;

// Set the radius of the circle
HisCircle.SetRadius(2);

// Display the area
HisCircle.DisplayArea();

/////////////////////////
// MY CODE ENDS HERE
/////////////////////////

}
```

The code you typed is similar to the code you typed inside the OnMycircleButton() function, except that now you have created the HisCircle object and set the radius to 2.

Attaching Code to the Her Circle Button of the IDD_TESTLIB_FORM Dialog Box

You'll now attach code to the Her Circle button of the IDD_TESTLIB_FORM dialog box.

☐ Use ClassWizard (from the Project menu) to select the event:

```
CTestlibView -> IDC_HERCIRCLE_BUTTON -> BN_CLICKED
```

Then click the Add Function button.

☐ Accept the name OnHercircleButton() that Visual C++ suggests.

☐ Click the Edit Code button.

> *Visual C++ responds by displaying the* OnHercircleButton() *function, ready to be edited by you.*

☐ Add code to the OnHercircleButton() function. After you add the code, the OnHercircleButton() function should look like this:

```
void CTestlibView::OnHercircleButton()
{
// TODO: Add your control notification
// handler code here


/////////////////////////
// MY CODE STARTS HERE
/////////////////////////


// Create the object
CCircle HerCircle;

// Set the radius of the circle
HerCircle.SetRadius(3);

// Display the area
HerCircle.DisplayArea();

/////////////////////////
// MY CODE ENDS HERE
/////////////////////////

}
```

The code you typed is similar to the code you typed inside the OnMycircleButton() and the OnHiscircleButton() functions, except that now you have created the HerCircle object and set the radius to 3.

Attaching Code to the Our Circle Button of the IDD_TESTLIB_FORM Dialog Box

You'll now attach code to the Our Circle button of the IDD_TESTLIB_FORM dialog box.

☐ Use ClassWizard (from the Project menu) to select the event:

```
CTestlibView -> IDC_OURCIRCLE_BUTTON -> BN_CLICKED
```

Then click the Add Function button.

☐ Accept the name OnOurcircleButton() that Visual C++ suggests.

☐ Click the Edit Code button.

> *Visual C++ responds by displaying the* OnOurcircleButton() *function, ready to be edited by you.*

☐ Add code to the OnOurcircleButton() function. After you add the code, the OnOurcircleButton() function should look like this:

```
void CTestlibView::OnOurcircleButton()
{
// TODO: Add your control notification
// handler code here

/////////////////////////
// MY CODE STARTS HERE
/////////////////////////


// Create the object
CCircle OurCircle;

// Set the radius of the circle
OurCircle.SetRadius(4);

// Display the area
OurCircle.DisplayArea();

/////////////////////////
// MY CODE ENDS HERE
/////////////////////////

}
```

The code you typed is similar to the code you attached to the other buttons of the IDD_TESTLIB_FORM dialog box, except that now you have created the OurCircle object and set the radius to 4.

☐ Select Save from the File menu to save your work.

Plugging In the TestLib.LIB Library

If you try to compile and link the TestLib.MAK project now, you'll get plenty of errors! Why? TestLib.MAK knows nothing about the CCircle class. Therefore, you must use #include on the Circle.H file at the beginning of the TestLVW.CPP file.

☐ Open the TestLVW.CPP file and use #include on the C:\MVCPROG\MyLib\Circle.H file. (If your \MVCPROG directory is on your D: drive, you have to use #include on the D:\MVCPROG\MyLib\Circle.H file.) After you use #include on the file, the beginning of the TestLVW.CPP file should look like this:

```
// testlvw.cpp : implementation of the CTestlibView
// class
//

#include "stdafx.h"
#include "testlib.h"

#include "testldoc.h"
#include "testlvw.h"


/////////////////////////
// MY CODE STARTS HERE
/////////////////////////

#include "D:\MVCPROG\MyLib\Circle.H"

/////////////////////////
// MY CODE ENDS HERE
/////////////////////////


#ifdef _DEBUG
#undef THIS_FILE
static char BASED_CODE THIS_FILE[] = __FILE__;
#endif
....
....
....
```

You have used #include on the Circle.H file, but inside the TestLVW.CPP file you used member functions of the CCircle class. Yes, the prototypes of these member functions will be known to the compiler (because you used #include on the Circle.H file), but the linker needs to use the actual code of these member functions! The actual code resides inside the Circle.LIB file. In the following steps you'll plug the Circle.LIB file into the TestLib.MAK project.

☐ Select Files from the Project menu.

Visual C++ responds by displaying the Project Files dialog box. (See Figure 30.21.)

Figure 30.21. The Project
Files dialog box.

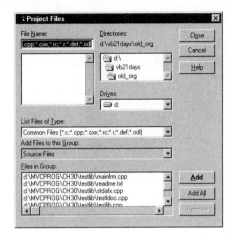

You'll now add the \MVCPROG\MyLib\WinRel\Circle.LIB file to the project:

☐ Set List Files of Type to Library Files (*.lib), select the
\MVCPROG\MyLib\WinRel\Circle.LIB file, and then click the Add button. (See Figure 30.22.)

Figure 30.22. Adding the
Circle.LIB library to the
project.

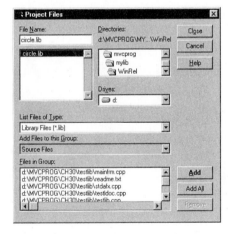

Visual C++ responds by adding the \MVCPROG\MyLib\WinRe l\Circle.LIB file to the
TestLib.MAK project.

☐ Click the Close button of the Project Files dialog box.

☐ Select Save from the File menu to save your work.

Compiling, Linking, and Executing the TestLib Program

You'll now compile, link, and execute the TestLib program.

☐ Select Build TestLib from the Project menu.

> *Visual C++ responds by compiling and linking the TestLib program.*

☐ Select Execute TestLib.EXE from the Project menu.

> *Visual C++ responds by executing the TestLib.EXE program and displaying the window shown in Figure 30.23.*

Figure 30.23. The window
of the TestLib.EXE
program.

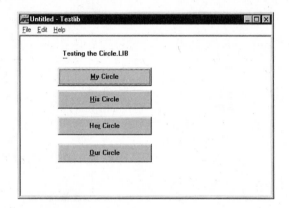

☐ Click the My Circle button.

> *TestLib responds by displaying a message box that shows the circle's area. (See Figure 30.24.)*

Figure 30.24. The message
box that TestLib displays
after you click the My
Circle button.

☐ Click the OK button of the message box to close it.

☐ Experiment with the other buttons of the TestLib program, and then terminate the TestLib program.

Distributing Your Software Modules

In the preceding section you proved that the Circle.LIB library works as expected.

So what will you distribute to your users? You have to distribute to your users the following:

- The Circle.LIB file.
- The Circle.H file.
- Documentation showing how to use Circle.LIB. (It is a good idea to distribute the TestLib program as part of your documentation because your user will be able to see how the Circle.LIB library is used.)

> **NOTE**
>
> Note that your CCircle class calculates the area of the circle by using the formula Area=3.14×radius×radius, but because you did not supply your user with the source code, the "secret" of calculating the circle's area remains with you. Your user does not know how you implemented the area calculations!
>
> Of course, the preceding discussion has more meaning when you accomplish a more complicated task.

31

Creating Your Own DLLs

In this chapter you'll learn what a

DLL is, how to create a DLL with

Visual C++, and how to use a DLL in

Visual C++.

What Is a DLL?

A *DLL (or dynamic linked library)* is a library file that contains functions. A programmer can integrate a DLL file into his or her program and use the functions of the DLL.

For example, you can create a DLL called CIRCLE.DLL that contains various functions that pertain to circles (for example, `DrawCircle()`, `CalculateCircleArea()`, and so on). You can then distribute the CIRCLE.DLL file to other programmers, and these programmers will be able to use the functions of the CIRCLE.DLL file in their programs.

As implied by its name, a DLL is a library that is linked dynamically to the application. This means that when you create the EXE file of your application, you don't link the DLL file to your application. The DLL file will be dynamically linked to your application during runtime. So when you write an application that uses a DLL, you must distribute the DLL file together with the EXE file of your application.

> **NOTE**
>
> When you create an application that uses a DLL file, you have to distribute the DLL file together with the EXE file of your application.
>
> In order for an application that uses a DLL file to work, the DLL file must reside inside any of the following directories:
>
> - The \WINDOWS\SYSTEM directory
> - Any directory that is within the DOS path
> - The directory where the application resides
>
> Typically, the INSTALL program of your application copies the DLL file into the user's \WINDOWS\SYSTEM directory, because this way other applications can also use the DLL file, and your program does not depend on the current setting of the user's DOS path.

A DLL file can be used by any programming language that supports DLLs (for example, Visual C++ and Visual Basic for Windows).

In the following sections you'll create a simple DLL file. You'll then write a Visual C++ program that uses this DLL file.

Creating a DLL

You'll now create a DLL file called MyDLL.DLL. Later in the chapter you'll write an application that uses the functions of MyDLL.DLL.

Writing the code of a DLL involves some overhead code. That is, whenever you start writing code for a DLL you need to write overhead code that is the same for all DLLs. Therefore, to save time, you can use template files that include the necessary overhead code. You can then copy these template files to your development directory whenever you start a new DLL project.

The book's CD includes such template files. In the following section, you'll use these template files to start the MyDLL.DLL project.

Using Generic Files to Start Your DLL Project

The book's CD includes generic files for developing a DLL. In the following steps you will copy these generic files to your development directory, and you'll customize these files to fit the DLL that you're currently developing (that is, MyDLL.DLL).

Begin by creating a development directory for MyDLL.DLL:

☐ Use the File Manager of Windows (or DOS) to create the subdirectory C:\MVCPROG\CH31\MYDLL. (You already have the directory \MVCPROG\CH31, so create the subdirectory MYDLL inside this directory.)

☐ Now, copy all the files from the \MVCPROG\GENDLL directory of the book's CD to your C:\MVCPROG\CH31\MYDLL directory.

Your C:\MVCPROG\CH31\MYDLL directory should now contain the two files GENDLL.CPP and GENDLL.DEF.

Rename the files that you copied to the C:\MVCPROG\CH31\MYDLL directory as follows:

☐ Rename the GENDLL.CPP file MyDLL.CPP.

☐ Rename the GENDLL.DEF file MyDLL.DEF.

Your C:\MVCPROG\CH31\MYDLL directory should now contain the two files MyDLL.CPP and MyDLL.DEF.

In the following sections you'll customize these files.

Creating the Project of MyDLL.DLL

To create the project of MyDLL.DLL do the following:

☐ Start Visual C++ and close all the open windows that appear inside the desktop of Visual C++ (if there are any).

☐ Select New from the File menu.

Visual C++ responds by displaying the New dialog box.

☐ Select Project inside the New dialog box and then click the OK button of the New dialog box.

Visual C++ responds by displaying the New Project dialog box.

☐ Set the Project Type list box to Dynamic-Link Library.

☐ Set the project name to mydll.

☐ Set the project path to \MVCPROG\CH31\MYDLL\MYDLL.MAK.

Your New Project dialog box should now look like the one shown in Figure 31.1.

Figure 31.1. The New Project dialog box of the MYDLL.MAK project.

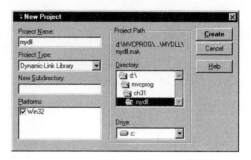

☐ Click the Create button of the New Project dialog box.

Visual C++ responds by displaying the Project Files dialog box.

You'll now use the Project Files dialog box to add the two files MYDLL.CPP and MYDLL.DEF to the MYDLL.MAK project:

☐ Select the C:\MVCPROG\CH31\MYDLL\MYDLL.CPP file and then click the Add button.

☐ Select the C:\MVCPROG\CH31\MYDLL\MYDLL.DEF file and then click the Add button.

Your Project Files dialog box should now look like the one shown in Figure 31.2.

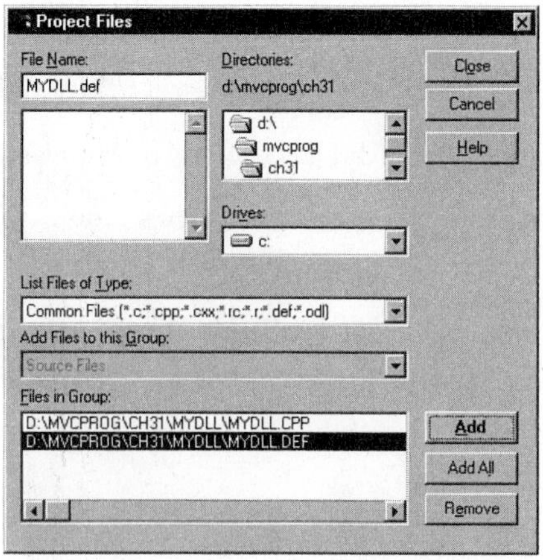

Figure 31.2. The Project Files dialog box after you add the two files MYDLL.CPP and MYDLL.DEF.

☐ Click the Close button of the Project Files dialog box.

Visual C++ responds by displaying the MYDLL.MAK window. (See Figure 31.3.)

Figure 31.3. The
MYDLL.MAK window.

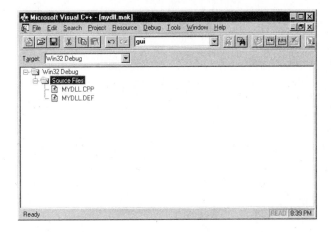

As shown in Figure 31.3, the two source files of the MYDLL.MAK project are the two files that you added to the project: MYDLL.CPP and MYDLL.DEF. In the following sections you'll customize these files.

As you can see, currently the Target drop-down list box (at the top of the MYDLL.MAK window) is set for debugging (Win32 Debug). Change the Target drop-down list box to Win32 Release:

☐ Set the Target drop-down list box at the top of the MYDLL.MAK window to `Win32 Release`. (See Figure 31.4.)

Figure 31.4. The
MYDLL.MAK window
after you change the Target
drop-down list box from
Win32 Debug to Win32
Release.

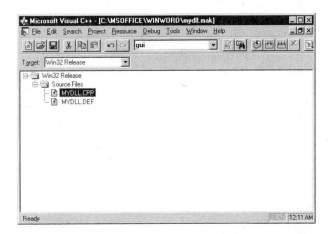

Customizing the MyDLL.CPP File

The MyDLL.CPP file was originally the GenDLL.CPP file that you copied to the C:\MVCPROG\CH31\MYDLL directory and renamed MyDLL.CPP. You'll now customize this file.

☐ Open the MyDLL.CPP file.

☐ Change the description comment lines at the beginning of the file from this:

```
/////////////////////////////////////////
// gendll.cpp
//
// Contains template code for a generic DLL
//
/////////////////////////////////////////
```

to this:

```
/////////////////////////////////////////
// mydll.cpp
//
// A simple DLL.
//
/////////////////////////////////////////
```

After you make this modification, the MyDLL.CPP file should look like this:

```
/////////////////////////////////////////
// mydll.cpp
//
// A simple DLL.
//
/////////////////////////////////////////

#include <windows.h>

/////////////////////////////////////////
// DllEntryPoint(): The entry point of the DLL
//
/////////////////////////////////////////
BOOL WINAPI DllEntryPoint (HINSTANCE hDLL, DWORD dwReason,
                           LPVOID Reserved)
{

switch (dwReason)
   {

   case DLL_PROCESS_ATTACH:
       {

       break;
       }
```

```
    case DLL_PROCESS_DETACH:
        {


        break;
        }
    }

return TRUE;

}
```

As you can see, the code inside the MyDll.CPP file (code that you borrowed from the GenDll.CPP file) is very short—it has one function inside it: `DllEntryPoint()`. (Soon you'll add more functions to the DLL.)

As implied by its name, the `DllEntryPoint()` function is the entry point of the DLL. That is, when an EXE program that uses the DLL loads the DLL, the `DllEntryPoint()` function is automatically executed. (You'll write an EXE program that loads MyDLL.DLL and uses the functions of MyDLL.DLL later in this chapter.)

As you can see, the `DllEntryPoint()` function is made up of a `switch` statement:

```
BOOL WINAPI DllEntryPoint (HINSTANCE hDLL, DWORD dwReason,
                           LPVOID Reserved)
{

switch (dwReason)
    {

    case DLL_PROCESS_ATTACH:
        {


        break;
        }


    case DLL_PROCESS_DETACH:
        {


        break;
        }
    }

return TRUE;

}
```

The switch statement evaluates `dwReason` (the second parameter of the `DllEntryPoint()` function).

The code under the `DLL_PROCESS_ATTACH` case is executed when the DLL is attached to the EXE file (that is, when the EXE file loads the DLL). Therefore, you can write initialization code under the `DLL_PROCESS_ATTACH` case.

The code under the DLL_PROCESS_DETACH case is executed when the DLL is detached from the EXE file. For example, when the EXE that uses the DLL terminates, the code under the DLL_PROCESS_DETACH case is executed. Therefore, you can write clean-up code under the DLL_PROCESS_DETACH case.

Now add two simple functions to the MyDll.CPP file. Later in the chapter you will create an EXE file that will use these functions:

☐ Add a function (called MyBeep()) to the end of the MyDLL.CPP file. The MyBeep() function looks like this:

```
int MyBeep(void)
{

// Beep
MessageBeep( (WORD) -1 );

return 1;

}
```

☐ Add another function (called MyDelay()) to the end of the MyDLL.CPP file. The MyDelay() function looks like this:

```
int MyDelay( long wait )
{

// Delay.
Sleep(wait);

return 1;

}
```

> **NOTE**
>
> As you can see, the two functions that you added to the MyDLL.DLL DLL are very simple. The only purpose of these functions is to illustrate how to add functions to a DLL.
>
> Later in the chapter you'll write an EXE program that loads MyDLL.DLL and uses its two functions (MyBeep() and MyDelay()).

You now have to declare the prototypes of the MyBeep() and MyDelay() functions:

☐ Add the prototype declarations of the MyBeep() and MyDelay() functions to the beginning of the MyDLL.CPP file (immediately after the #include <windows.h> statement). After you add these prototypes, the beginning of the MyDLL.CPP file looks like this:

```
/////////////////////////////////////////////
// mydll.cpp
//
// Contains template code for a generic DLL
//
/////////////////////////////////////////////
```

```
#include <windows.h>

// Declare the DLL functions prototypes.
int MyBeep  ( void );
int MyDelay ( long wait );
```

☐ Save your work by selecting Save from the File menu of Visual C++.

The code inside your MyDLL.CPP file should now look like this:

```
/////////////////////////////////////////
// mydll.cpp
//
// A simple DLL.
//
/////////////////////////////////////////

#include <windows.h>

// Declare the DLL functions prototypes.
int MyBeep  ( void );
int MyDelay ( long wait );

/////////////////////////////////////////////////
// DllEntryPoint(): The entry point of the DLL
//
/////////////////////////////////////////////////
BOOL WINAPI DllEntryPoint (HINSTANCE hDLL, DWORD dwReason,
                           LPVOID Reserved)
{

switch (dwReason)
   {

   case DLL_PROCESS_ATTACH:
        {


        break;
        }


   case DLL_PROCESS_DETACH:
        {


        break;
        }
   }

return TRUE;

}


int MyBeep(void)
{
```

```
// Beep
MessageBeep( (WORD) -1 );

return 1;

}


int MyDelay( long wait )
{

// Delay.
Sleep(wait);

return 1;

}
```

Customizing the MyDLL.DEF File

The last thing you have to do is customize the MyDLL.DEF file. Recall that the MyDLL.DEF file was originally the GenDLL.DEF file that you copied to the C:\MVCPROG\CH31\MYDLL directory and renamed MyDLL.DEF. You'll now customize this file.

☐ Open the MyDLL.DEF file and modify it so that it looks like this:

```
;;;;;;;;;;;;;;;;;;;;;;;;;;;;;;;;;;;;
; MyDLL.DEF
;
; The DEF file for the MyDLL.DLL DLL.
;

LIBRARY    mydll

CODE       PRELOAD MOVEABLE DISCARDABLE
DATA       PRELOAD SINGLE

EXPORTS
   ; The names of the DLL functions
   MyBeep
   MyDelay
```

☐ Save your work by selecting Save from the File menu.

The DEF file of the DLL defines various characteristics of the DLL. Notice that in a DEF file, comment lines are preceded with the ; character (not the // characters).

In the preceding code, you set the library name with the LIBRARY statement, as follows:

```
LIBRARY    mydll
```

That's because you are now creating the MyDLL.DLL DLL.

In the preceding code you also added the two function names MyBeep and MyDelay under the EXPORTS statement:

```
EXPORTS
   ; The names of the DLL functions
   MyBeep
   MyDelay
```

Therefore, an EXE program that loads MyDLL.DLL will be able to use the two functions `MyBeep()` and `MyDelay()`.

That's it! You have finished writing all the necessary code for creating MyDLL.DLL.

To create the MyDLL.DLL file do the following:

☐ Select Build MYDLL.DLL from the Project menu of Visual C++.

Visual C++ responds by creating the MYDLL.DLL file.

You can verify that Visual C++ created the MYDLL.DLL file by examining your C:\MVCPROG\CH31\MYDLL\WINREL directory.

> **NOTE**
>
> Visual C++ created the MyDLL.DLL file in the directory C:\MVCPROG\CH31\MYDLL\WINREL because earlier you set the Target drop-down list box of the MyDLL.MAK window to Win32 Release. (See Figure 31.4.)
>
> Had you left the Target drop-down list box of the MyDLL.MAK window at the default Win32 Debug (as in Figure 31.3), Visual C++ would have created the MyDLL.DLL file in the C:\MVCPROG\CH31\MYDLL\WINDEBUG directory.

You now have a DLL file called MyDLL.DLL that has two functions in it: `MyBeep()` and `MyDelay()`. You can now distribute this DLL file to any programmer of a programming language that supports DLLs (for example, Visual C++ or Visual Basic) and this programmer will be able to use the functions of your DLL.

When you distribute the DLL you should supply it with documentation that specifies the prototypes of the `MyBeep()` and `MyDelay()` functions.

In the following section you'll write a Visual C++ program that loads MyDLL.DLL and uses its two functions: `MyBeep()` and `MyDelay()`.

Writing a Visual C++ Program That Uses MyDLL.DLL

In the following sections you'll write a Visual C++ application, called TestDLL.EXE, that uses the MyDLL.DLL DLL that you created. The TestDLL.EXE application will load MyDLL.DLL and use its two functions `MyBeep()` and `MyDelay()`.

Creating the Project of the TestDLL Application

To create the project of the TestDLL application do the following:

☐ Close all the open windows that appear inside the desktop of Visual C++ (if there are any).

☐ Select New from the File menu.

> *Visual C++ responds by displaying the New dialog box.*

☐ Select Project inside the New dialog box and then click the OK button of the New dialog box.

> *Visual C++ responds by displaying the New Project dialog box.*

☐ Set the project name to testdll.

☐ Set the project path to \MVCPROG\CH31\TESTDLL\TESTDLL.MAK.

Your New Project dialog box should now look like the one shown in Figure 31.5.

Figure 31.5. The New Project dialog box of the TESTDLL.MAK project.

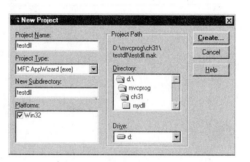

☐ Click the Create button of the New Project dialog box.

> *Visual C++ responds by displaying the AppWizard—Step 1 window.*

☐ Set the Step 1 window as shown in Figure 31.6. As shown in Figure 31.6, the TESTDLL.MAK project is set as a single-document application, and U.S. English (APPWIZUS.DLL) is used as the language for the application's resources.

☐ Click the Next button of the Step 1 window.

> *Visual C++ responds by displaying the AppWizard—Step 2 of 6 window.*

☐ Set the Step 2 of 6 window as shown in Figure 31.7. That is, in the TestDLL application you don't want any database support.

☐ Click the Next button of the Step 2 of 6 window.

> *Visual C++ responds by displaying the AppWizard—Step 3 of 6 window.*

☐ Set the Step 3 of 6 window as shown in Figure 31.8. That is, in the TestDLL application you don't want any OLE support.

Figure 31.6. The AppWizard—Step 1 window for the TestDLL application.

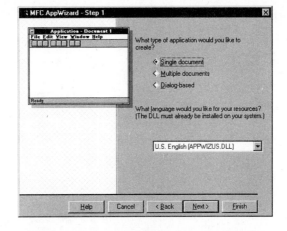

Figure 31.7. The AppWizard—Step 2 of 6 window for the TestDLL application.

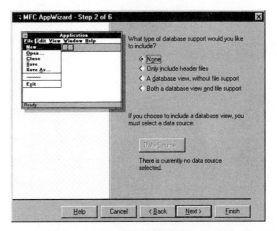

Figure 31.8. The AppWizard—Step 3 of 6 window for the TestDLL application.

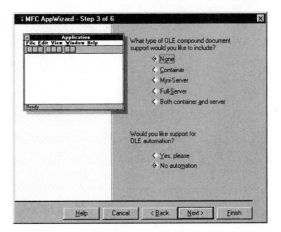

☐ Click the Next button of the Step 3 of 6 window.

Visual C++ responds by displaying the AppWizard—Step 4 of 6 window.

☐ Set the Step 4 of 6 window as shown in Figure 31.9.

Figure 31.9. The AppWizard—Step 4 of 6 window for the TestDLL application.

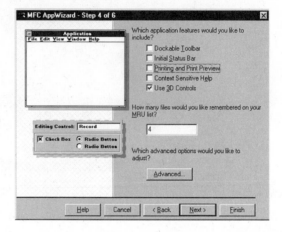

As shown in Figure 31.9, the features Dockable Toolbar, Initial Status Bar, Printing and Print Preview, and Context Sensitive Help will not be included in the TestDLL application.

☐ Click the Next button of the Step 4 of 6 window.

Visual C++ responds by displaying the AppWizard—Step 5 of 6 window.

☐ Set the Step 5 of 6 window as shown in Figure 31.10.

As shown in Figure 31.10, the project will be generated with comments, a Visual C++ makefile will be generated, and the application will use the MFC library from a DLL.

Figure 31.10. The AppWizard—Step 5 of 6 window for the TestDLL application.

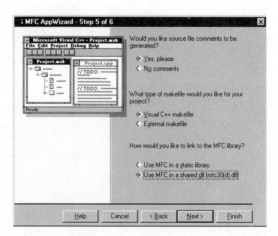

☐ Click the Next button of the Step 5 of 6 window.

Visual C++ responds by displaying the AppWizard—Step 6 of 6 window.

You'll now use the AppWizard—Step 6 of 6 window to tell AppWizard to derive the view class of the application from the MFC class CFormView:

☐ Select the CTestdllView class inside the AppWizard—Step 6 of 6 window.

☐ Set the Base Class drop-down list box to CFormView.

Your AppWizard—Step 6 of 6 window should now look like the one shown in Figure 31.11.

Figure 31.11. The AppWizard—Step 6 of 6 window after you set the base class of the application view class to CFormView.

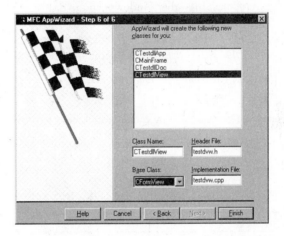

☐ Click the Finish button of the Step 6 of 6 window.

Visual C++ responds by displaying the New Project Information window, as shown in Figure 31.12.

Figure 31.12. The New Project Information window of the TestDLL.MAK project.

☐ Click the OK button of the New Project Information window.

Visual C++ responds by creating the project file and all the skeleton files of the application.

Creating the Form of the Application

Because in AppWizard you specified that the base class of the application's view class is CFormView, AppWizard created for you a form (a dialog box) that is attached to the view class of the application. This dialog box serves as the main window of the application. AppWizard named this dialog box IDD_TESTDLL_FORM. You'll now customize the IDD_TESTDLL_FORM dialog box.

☐ Select testdll.mak from the Window menu to display the testdll.mak window, double-click testdll.rc inside the testdll.mak window to display the testdll.rc window, double-click Dialog inside the testdll.rc window to display a list of dialog boxes, and finally, double-click the IDD_TESTDLL_FORM item under the Dialog item.

Visual C++ responds by displaying the IDD_TESTDLL_FORM dialog box in design mode.

☐ Delete the TODO static text by clicking on it and pressing the Delete key on your keyboard.

☐ Design the IDD_TESTDLL_FORM dialog box as specified in Table 31.1. When you finish implementing the dialog box, it should look like the one shown in Figure 31.13.

Table 31.1. The Properties table for the IDD_TESTDLL_FORM dialog box.

Object	Property	Setting
Dialog box	ID	IDD_TESTDLL_FORM
Push button	ID	IDC_LOAD_BUTTON
	Caption	&Load MyDLL.DLL
Push button	ID	IDC_TEST_BUTTON
	Caption	&Test MyDLL.DLL

*Figure 31.13. The
IDD_TESTDLL_FORM
dialog box (in design
mode).*

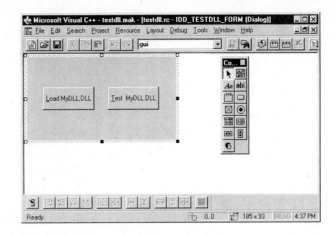

The Visual Implementation of the Menu

You'll now visually implement the menu of the TestDLL application.

☐ Select testdll.rc from the Window menu to display the testdll.rc window, double-click Menu, and finally, double-click IDR_MAINFRAME.

   Visual C++ responds by displaying the IDR_MAINFRAME menu in design mode.

☐ Implement the IDR_MAINFRAME menu so that it contains the following items:

   &File
       E&xit
   &Help
       &About Testdll...

Save your work:

☐ Select Save from the File menu.

The visual implementation of the menu of the TestDLL application is complete.

To see your visual design in action do the following:

☐ Select Build TESTDLL.EXE from the Project menu of Visual C++.

☐ Select Execute TESTDLL.EXE from the Project menu.

   Visual C++ responds by executing the TESTDLL.EXE application. The main window of the application appears, with the form that you designed inside it.

☐ Terminate the TestDLL application by selecting Exit from the File menu.

Declaring Global Variables

As you'll soon see, the code that loads and uses MyDLL.DLL uses global variables. You'll now declare these global variables.

☐ Open the file TESTDVW.CPP (the file of the application's view class) and add code to its beginning. After you add this code, the beginning of the TESTDVW.CPP file looks like this:

```
// testdvw.cpp : implementation of the CTestdllView class
//

#include "stdafx.h"
#include "testdll.h"

#include "testddoc.h"
#include "testdvw.h"

#ifdef _DEBUG
#undef THIS_FILE
static char BASED_CODE THIS_FILE[]= __FILE__;
#endif

/////////////////////////
// MY CODE STARTS HERE
/////////////////////////

// The instance of the MyDLL.DLL library.
HINSTANCE gLibMyDLL = NULL;

// Declare the MyBeep() function from the MyDLL.DLL library.
typedef int (*MYBEEP)(void);
MYBEEP MyBeep;

// Declare the MyDelay() function from
// the MyDLL.DLL library.
typedef int (*MYDELAY)(long);
MYDELAY MyDelay;


/////////////////////////
// MY CODE ENDS HERE
/////////////////////////
```

☐ Save your work by selecting Save from the File menu.

The statements that you've just added to the beginning of the TESTDVW.CPP file declare several global variables.

The first statement

```
HINSTANCE gLibMyDLL = NULL;
```

declares the gLibMyDLL variable and initializes it to NULL. As you'll see later, the code that loads MyDLL.DLL uses gLibMyDLL for storing the handle of the DLL.

The next two statements

```
typedef int (*MYBEEP)(void);
MYBEEP MyBeep;
```

declare the MyBeep() function from the MyDLL.DLL library. Notice how the MyBeep() function is declared. The first statement

```
typedef int (*MYBEEP)(void);
```

declares a variable type called MYBEEP that holds a pointer (address) of a function that returns int and takes no parameters.

Then the statement

```
MYBEEP MyBeep;
```

declares a variable MyBeep of type MYBEEP. So from now on the variable MyBeep can be considered a regular function that returns an int and takes no parameters.

Similarly, the last two statements you typed

```
typedef int (*MYDELAY)(long);
MYDELAY MyDelay;
```

declare the MyDelay() function of MyDLL.DLL. Notice that these statements declare MyDelay() as a function that returns an int type and takes one parameter of type long.

Loading MyDLL.DLL

Before you can use the functions of MyDLL.DLL you must first load MyDLL.DLL. You'll attach the code that accomplishes this to the Load push button.

NOTE

In the TestDLL.EXE application the code that loads the MyDLL.DLL is attached to the Load button. Therefore, the DLL will be loaded when the user clicks the Load button.

However, normally you want the DLL to be loaded automatically without the user having to click anything. Therefore, typically you will write the code that loads a DLL at the entry point of the program.

For example, in the TestDLL.EXE application, you can attach the code that loads a DLL to the InitApplication() member function of the CTestdllApp class.

Follow these steps to attach code to the Load button:

☐ Display the ClassWizard dialog box by selecting ClassWizard from the Project menu of Visual C++.

☐ Select the Message Maps tab at the top of ClassWizard's dialog box.

☐ Use ClassWizard to select the event:

```
CTestdllView -> IDC_LOAD_BUTTON -> BN_CLICKED
```

Then click the Add Function button.

☐ Name the new function OnLoadButton().

To write the code of the OnLoadButton() function do the following:

☐ Click the Edit Code button of ClassWizard.

> *ClassWizard responds by opening the file TESTDVW.CPP, with the function* OnLoadButton() *ready to be edited by you.*

☐ Write code inside the OnLoadButton() function so that it looks like this:

```
void CTestdllView::OnLoadButton()
{
// TODO: Add your control notification handler code here

/////////////////////////
// MY CODE STARTS HERE
/////////////////////////

// If the MyDLL.DLL has already been loaded,
// tell the user and terminate this function.
if ( gLibMyDLL != NULL )
   {
   MessageBox("The MyDLL.DLL DLL has already been loaded.");
   return;
   }

// Load the MyDLL.DLL DLL.
gLibMyDLL = LoadLibrary("MYDLL.DLL");

// If the DLL was not loaded successfully, display
// an error message box.
if ( gLibMyDLL == NULL )
   {
   char msg[300];
   strcpy (msg, "Cannot load the MYDLL.DLL DLL. ");
   strcat (msg, "Make sure that the file MYDLL.DLL ");
   strcat (msg, "is in your \\WINDOWS\\SYSTEM directory.");
   MessageBox( msg );
   }

// Get the address of the MyBeep() function
// of the MyDLL.DLL library.
MyBeep = (MYBEEP)GetProcAddress(gLibMyDLL, "MyBeep");

// Get the address of the MyDelay() function
// of the MyDLL.DLL library.
MyDelay = (MYDELAY)GetProcAddress(gLibMyDLL, "MyDelay");
```

```
///////////////////
// MY CODE ENDS HERE
///////////////////
```

```
}
```

☐ Save your work by selecting Save from the File menu.

The first statement you typed inside the `OnLoadButton()` function is an `if` statement:

```
if ( gLibMyDLL != NULL )
    {
    MessageBox("The MyDLL.DLL DLL has already been loaded.");
    return;
    }
```

This `if` statement determines whether MyDLL.DLL has already been loaded by evaluating the `gLibMyDLL` global variable. If `gLibMyDLL` is not equal to `NULL`, MyDLL.DLL has already been loaded (that is, the user clicked the Load button previously). If this is the case, the `if` condition is satisfied and the code under the `if` displays a message box telling the user that MyDLL.DLL has already been loaded, and the function is terminated with the `return` statement.

If, however, `gLibMyDLL` is equal to `NULL`, MyDLL.DLL has not been loaded yet, and the rest of the statements in the function are executed. (Recall that when you declared the global variable `gLibMyDLL` you initialized it to `NULL`. Therefore, when the user clicks the Load button for the first time, `gLibMyDLL` is `NULL`.)

The next statement

```
gLibMyDLL = LoadLibrary("MYDLL.DLL");
```

uses the `LoadLibrary()` function to load MyDLL.DLL and to assign the handle of the DLL to the `gLibMyDLL` variable. Note that the name of the DLL file—MYDLL.DLL—is specified without the full pathname of the DLL. The `LoadLibrary()` function will search for the DLL file in the current directory, in all the directories that are within the DOS path, and in the \WINDOWS\SYSTEM directory. If the `LoadLibrary()` function fails in loading the DLL, `LoadLibrary()` will return `NULL`.

The next statement is an `if` statement:

```
if ( gLibMyDLL == NULL )
    {
    char msg[300];
    strcpy (msg, "Cannot load the MYDLL.DLL DLL. ");
    strcat (msg, "Make sure that the file MYDLL.DLL ");
    strcat (msg, "is in your \\WINDOWS\\SYSTEM directory.");
    MessageBox( msg );
    }
```

This `if` statement evaluates the returned value of the `LoadLibrary()` function. If the returned value of `LoadLibrary()` was `NULL`, the DLL was not loaded successfully. If this is the case, the statements under the `if` display a message box telling the user that MYDLL.DLL cannot be loaded. The message box also tells the user to make sure that MYDLL.DLL is in the \WINDOWS\SYSTEM directory.

The next statement

```
MyBeep = (MYBEEP)GetProcAddress(gLibMyDLL, "MyBeep");
```

uses the `GetProcAddress()` function to fill the variable `MyBeep` with the address of the `MyBeep()` function of MyDLL.DLL. As you can see, the first parameter of the `GetProcAddress()` function is the handle of the DLL, and the second parameter is the name of the function whose address you want to retrieve.

So at this point the global variable `MyBeep` is filled with the address of the `MyBeep()` function of MyDLL.DLL. This means that from now on you can use the `MyBeep` variable as if it were the `MyBeep()` function. In other words, from now on you can call the `MyBeep()` function just the way you call any other function.

Similarly, the last statement in the `OnLoadButton()` function

```
MyDelay = (MYDELAY)GetProcAddress(gLibMyDLL, "MyDelay");
```

fills the `MyDelay` global variable with the address of the `MyDelay()` function of MyDLL.DLL. So from now on you can call the `MyDelay()` function of the MyDLL.DLL just as you call any other function.

Attaching Code to the Test MyDLL.DLL Button

You'll now attach code to the Test MyDLL.DLL button. This code will test MyDLL.DLL by calling its two functions `MyBeep()` and `MyDelay()`.

Follow these steps to attach code to the Test MyDLL.DLL button:

☐ Display the ClassWizard dialog box by selecting ClassWizard from the Project menu of Visual C++.

☐ Select the Message Maps tab at the top of ClassWizard's dialog box.

☐ Use ClassWizard to select the event:

```
CTestdllView -> IDC_TEST_BUTTON -> BN_CLICKED
```

Then click the Add Function button.

☐ Name the new function `OnTestButton()`.

To write the code of the `OnTestButton()` function do the following:

☐ Click the Edit Code button of ClassWizard.

> *ClassWizard responds by opening the file TESTDVW.CPP, with the function OnTestButton() ready to be edited by you.*

☐ Write code inside the `OnTestButton()` function so that it looks like this:

```
void CTestdllView::OnTestButton()
{
// TODO: Add your control notification handler code here
```

```
///////////////////////
// MY CODE STARTS HERE
///////////////////////

// If the MyDLL.DLL has not been loaded yet, tell
// the user and terminate this function.
if ( gLibMyDLL == NULL )
   {
   MessageBox ("You must first load the MyDLL.DLL DLL.");
   return;
   }

// Call the MyBeep() function of the MyDLL.DLL DLL.
MyBeep();

// Call the MyDelay() function of the MyDLL.DLL DLL.
MyDelay(500);

// Call the MyBeep() function of the MyDLL.DLL DLL.
MyBeep();

///////////////////////
// MY CODE ENDS HERE
///////////////////////

}
```

☐ Save your work by selecting Save from the File menu.

The first statement you typed inside the `OnTestButton()` function is an `if` statement:

```
if ( gLibMyDLL == NULL )
   {
   MessageBox ("You must first load the MyDLL.DLL DLL.");
   return;
   }
```

This `if` statement checks whether the `gLibMyDLL` variable is NULL. If it is, MyDLL.DLL has not been loaded yet. If this is the case, the code under the `if` displays a message box telling the user that MyDLL.DLL must be loaded, and the function is terminated with the `return` statement.

If, however, the `gLibMyDLL` variable is not NULL (that is, MyDLL.DLL has been loaded), the rest of the statements in the function are executed:

```
// Call the MyBeep() function of the MyDLL.DLL DLL.
MyBeep();

// Call the MyDelay() function of the MyDLL.DLL DLL.
MyDelay(500);

// Call the MyBeep() function of the MyDLL.DLL DLL.
MyBeep();
```

These statements simply call the `MyBeep()` and `MyDelay()` functions of MyDLL.DLL. Therefore, whenever the user clicks the Test MyDLL.DLL button, the program will beep once, then delay for 500 milliseconds (half a second), and then beep again.

To see the code that you wrote in action do the following:

☐ Select Build TESTDLL.EXE from the Project menu.

☐ Select Execute TESTDLL.EXE from the Project menu.

☐ Click the Load MyDLL.DLL button.

> *The TestDLL.EXE application responds by displaying a message box telling you that MyDLL.DLL could not be loaded.*

TestDLL.EXE could not load the MyDLL.DLL library because you did not copy the MyDLL.DLL file to any directory within the DOS path or to the directory where the TestDLL.EXE file resides or to the \WINDOWS\SYSTEM directory.

☐ Start the File Manager program of Windows and copy the MyDLL.DLL file that you created earlier from the \MVCPROG\CH31\MYDLL\WINREL directory to your \WINDOWS\SYSTEM directory.

☐ Switch back to the TestDLL.EXE program and click the Load MyDLL.DLL button again.

This time, the TestDLL.DLL application loads MyDLL.DLL successfully (that is, this time no error message is displayed).

☐ Click the Test MyDLL.DLL button.

> *As expected, the TestDLL.EXE application responds by beeping twice, with a 500-millisecond delay between the beeps.*

NOTE

If for some reason your PC speaker (or sound card) does not beep, you can modify the code of MyDLL.DLL so that the `MyBeep()` function of MyDLL.DLL displays a message box instead of beeping. After you modify and build the project of MyDLL.DLL, don't forget to copy the new version of the MyDLL.DLL file to your \WINDOWS\SYSTEM directory.

☐ Terminate the TestDLL.EXE application by selecting Exit from the File menu.

As you have just seen, the TestDLL.EXE application successfully loads the MyDLL.DLL file and successfully uses the functions of MyDLL.DLL.

32

Drawing Geometric Shapes and Text with Different Fonts

So far in this book there have been several applications in which you wrote code that displays drawing or text on the screen. For example, you learned how to draw lines with the mouse (the DrawIt program in Chapter 17, "The Mouse"), and in several applications you learned how to display text by using the TextOut() function. In this chapter you'll learn about additional drawing topics in Visual C++. You'll learn how to draw geometric shapes (such as lines and circles), and you'll learn how to draw text with different fonts and font sizes.

Drawing from Within Visual C++ Versus Drawing from Within Paintbrush

Drawing from within your Visual C++ programs is very similar to drawing with the Paintbrush program that is shipped with Windows. Recall that in Paintbrush you first click the mouse on a drawing tool (for example, pencil, circle, line), then you move the mouse to the drawing area, and finally you draw the shape.

As you'll soon see, the same technique is used when drawing from within your Visual C++ programs. The only difference is that instead of selecting the drawing tool with the mouse, you select the tool by executing a function that selects the tool, and instead of drawing the shape with the mouse, you execute a function that draws the shape.

The DRAW Application

Before you start writing the DRAW application yourself, execute the copy of it that resides in the \MVCPROG\EXE directory of the book's CD.

To execute the DRAW application do the following:

☐ Select Run from the Start menu of Windows and execute the
X:\MVCPROG\EXE\Draw.EXE program (where *X* represents the drive letter of your
CD-ROM drive).

The main window of Draw.EXE appears, as shown in Figure 32.1.

Figure 32.1. The main window of the DRAW application.

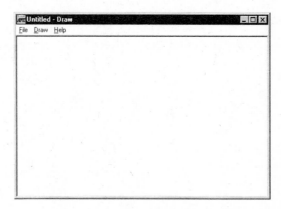

The DRAW application has three pop-up menus: File, Draw, and Help. These pop-up menus are shown in Figures 32.2, 32.3, and 32.4.

Figure 32.2. The File menu of the DRAW application.

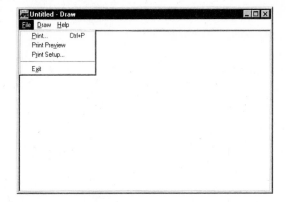

Figure 32.3. The Draw menu of the DRAW application.

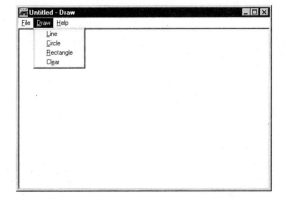

Figure 32.4. The Help menu of the DRAW application.

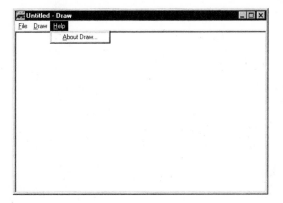

The DRAW application demonstrates how to draw various shapes.

☐ Select Line from the Draw menu.

> *The DRAW application responds by drawing a line composed of two parts. The left part of the line is a thick green line, and the right part of the line is a thin black line.*

☐ Select Clear from the Draw menu to clear the window.

☐ Select Circle from the Draw menu.

> *The DRAW application responds by drawing a red circle with thick boundaries.*

☐ Select Rectangle from the Draw menu.

> *The DRAW application responds by drawing a rectangle filled with diagonal lines.*

The DRAW application has the standard Print menu items. (See Figure 32.2.)

☐ Select Print Preview from the File menu.

> *The DRAW application responds by displaying a window that shows how the printout will look. (See Figure 32.5.) Note that the cursor of the mouse looks like a magnifying glass tool.*

☐ Click the area you want to magnify.

> *The DRAW application responds by magnifying that section of the Print Preview window. (See Figure 32.6.)*

Figure 32.5. The Print Preview window.

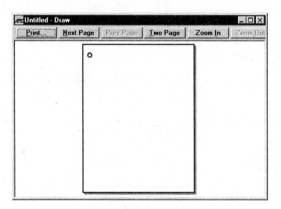

☐ Click the Close button of the Preview window.

NOTE

The Close button is the extreme-right button on the toolbar. If you don't see this button, maximize the window.

> *The DRAW application responds by returning to its main window.*

Figure 32.6. The magnified section of the Print Preview window.

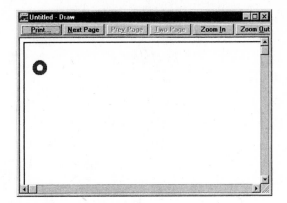

The DRAW application lets you print the contents of the window:

☐ Select Print from the File menu.

> *The DRAW application responds by displaying the Print dialog box. (See Figure 32.7.)*

☐ Press the OK button of the Print dialog box to send the contents of the window to the printer.

Figure 32.7. The Print dialog box.

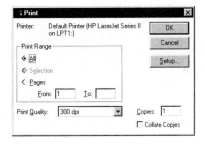

☐ Experiment with the DRAW application, and then select Exit from the File menu to terminate the DRAW application.

Now that you know what DRAW should do, you can begin to write it.

Creating the Project of the DRAW Application

To create the project of the DRAW application do the following:

☐ Start Visual C++ and close all the open windows that appear inside the desktop of Visual C++ (if there are any).

☐ Select New from the File menu.

> *Visual C++ responds by displaying the New dialog box.*

☐ Select Project inside the New dialog box and then click the OK button of the New dialog box.

   Visual C++ responds by displaying the New Project dialog box.

☐ Set the project name to draw.

☐ Set the project path to \MVCPROG\CH32\Draw\Draw.MAK.

Your New Project dialog box should now look like the one shown in Figure 32.8.

Figure 32.8. The New Project dialog box of the Draw.MAK project.

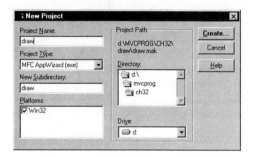

☐ Click the Create button of the New Project dialog box.

   Visual C++ responds by displaying the AppWizard—Step 1 window.

☐ Set the Step 1 window as shown in Figure 32.9. As shown in Figure 32.9, the Draw.MAK project is set as a single-document interface application, and U.S. English (APPWIZUS.DLL) is used as the language for the application's resources.

Figure 32.9. The AppWizard—Step 1 window for the DRAW application.

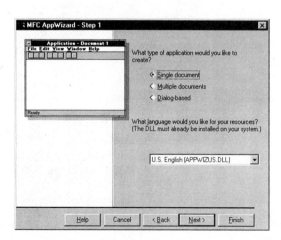

☐ Click the Next button of the Step 1 window.

   Visual C++ responds by displaying the AppWizard—Step 2 of 6 window.

☐ Set the Step 2 of 6 window as shown in Figure 32.10. That is, in the DRAW application you don't want any database support.

Figure 32.10. The AppWizard—Step 2 of 6 window for the DRAW application.

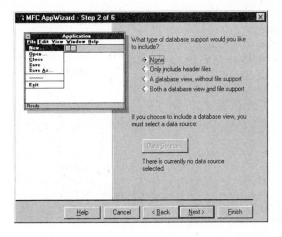

☐ Click the Next button of the Step 2 of 6 window.

Visual C++ responds by displaying the AppWizard—Step 3 of 6 window.

☐ Set the Step 3 of 6 window as shown in Figure 32.11. That is, in the DRAW application you don't want any OLE support.

Figure 32.11. The AppWizard—Step 3 of 6 window for the DRAW application.

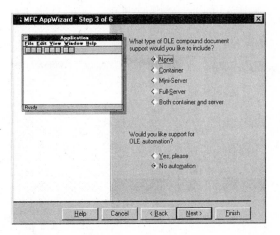

☐ Click the Next button of the Step 3 of 6 window.

Visual C++ responds by displaying the AppWizard—Step 4 of 6 window.

☐ Set the Step 4 of 6 window as shown in Figure 32.12.

Figure 32.12. The AppWizard—Step 4 of 6 window for the DRAW application.

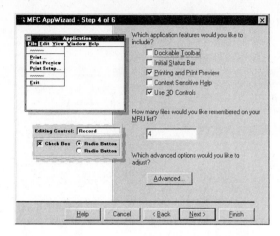

As shown in Figure 32.12, the features Dockable Toolbar, Initial Status Bar, and Context Sensitive Help will not be included in the DRAW application. However, the program will include the Printing and Print Preview and the 3D Controls features.

☐ Click the Next button of the Step 4 of 6 window.

Visual C++ responds by displaying the AppWizard—Step 5 of 6 window.

☐ Set the Step 5 of 6 window as shown in Figure 32.13.

As shown in Figure 32.13, the project will be generated with comments, a Visual C++ makefile will be generated, and the application will use the MFC library from a DLL.

Figure 32.13. The AppWizard—Step 5 of 6 window for the DRAW application.

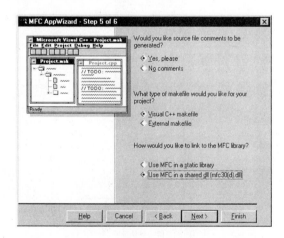

☐ Click the Next button of the Step 5 of 6 window.

Visual C++ responds by displaying the AppWizard—Step 6 of 6 window.

You'll now use the AppWizard—Step 6 of 6 window to tell AppWizard to derive the view class of the application from the MFC class `CView`:

☐ Select the `CDrawView` class inside the AppWizard—Step 6 of 6 window.

☐ Make sure that Base Class is set to `CView` (which is the default class that Visual C++ suggests for the base class).

Your AppWizard—Step 6 of 6 window should now look like the one shown in Figure 32.14.

Figure 32.14. The AppWizard—Step 6 of 6 window with the base class of the application view class set to `CView`.

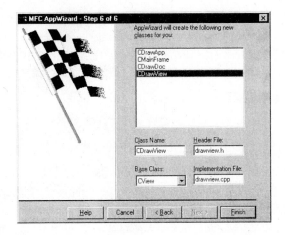

NOTE

As you can see from Figure 32.1, the main window of the DRAW program does not have any controls inside it. Therefore, you were instructed to set the base class of the `CDrawView` class to `CView` as indicated in Figure 32.14.

☐ Click the Finish button of the Step 6 of 6 window.

Visual C++ responds by displaying the New Project Information window, as shown in Figure 32.15.

☐ Click the OK button of the New Project Information window.

Visual C++ responds by creating the project file and all the skeleton files of the application.

Figure 32.15. The New
Project Information
window of the
DRAW.MAK project.

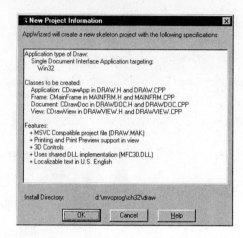

The Visual Design of the Menu

You'll now visually design the menu of the DRAW application.

☐ Select draw.mak from the Window menu, double-click draw.rc inside the draw.mak window, double-click Menu inside the draw.rc window, and then double-click IDR_MAINFRAME under the Menu item.

> *Visual C++ responds by displaying the IDR_MAINFRAME menu in design mode.*

☐ Implement the menu so that it contains the following items:

&File
    &Print...
    Print Pre&view
    P&rint Setup...
    Separator
    E&xit
&Draw
    &Line
    &Circle
    &Rectangle
    Cl&ear
&Help
    &About Draw...

Note that the Print, Print Preview, and the Print Setup items in the File menu were prepared by Visual C++ (because you placed a checkmark inside the Printing and Print Preview check box in the window shown in Figure 32.12).

Figures 32.16, 32.17, and 32.18 show the File, Draw, and Help menus in design mode.

Figure 32.16. The File menu (in design mode).

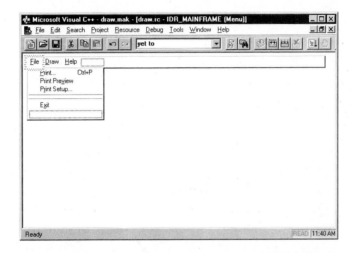

Figure 32.17. The Draw menu (in design mode).

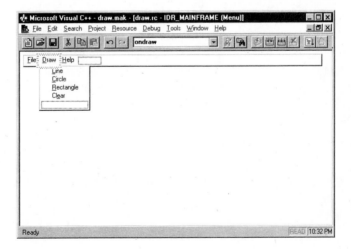

Figure 32.18. The Help
menu (in design mode).

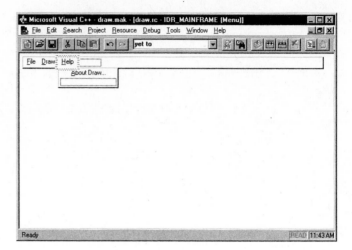

To save your work do the following:

☐ Select Save from the File menu of Visual C++.

The visual implementation of the menu of the DRAW application is complete.

The *OnDraw( )* Function

One of the most important concepts of drawing in Windows with Visual C++ is the OnDraw() function. As you'll soon see, the OnDraw() function is automatically executed whenever there is a need to draw the window of the application. Who will decide that there is a need to draw the window of the application? Windows may decide that, and so may your own code.

As stated, Windows may decide that it is time to draw the window of the application, and the OnDraw() function will be automatically executed. This happens, for example, when the application is started. (This makes sense because upon start-up of an application, the window of the application should be drawn.)

Another example of a situation in which Windows decides to cause the execution of the OnDraw() function is when you minimize the window of the application and then restore its size or maximize it. Under these conditions, there is a need to redraw the window of the application.

Another example of a situation in which Windows decides to cause the execution of the OnDraw() function is when you cover the window of the application with a window of another application, and then move the window of the other application to expose the window of your application.

As you can see, Windows is working very hard for you. It constantly monitors the user's operations, and whenever there is a need to draw the window of the application, it causes the execution of the OnDraw() function.

As stated, you can cause the execution of the OnDraw() function. However, in Visual C++ you don't call the OnDraw() function directly. Instead, you call another function, called the Invalidate() function, that causes the execution of the OnDraw() function. You'll have a chance to experiment with the Invalidate() function later in this chapter.

NOTE

Note that the names of the OnDraw() function make sense. The OnDraw() function is executed whenever Windows decides that there is a need to draw the window of the application. That is, if you have a push button called Try It, then the appropriate function's name for the function that is executed whenever the user clicks the Try It button is OnTryIt(). Similarly, whenever the user does an operation that requires the redrawing of the window, Windows executes the OnDraw() function. Windows constantly monitors the user's operations, and when it decides that the user performed an operation that justifies the execution of the OnDraw() function, Windows sets an internal "invalid window" flag. When the user completes the operation, Windows checks the status of the invalid window flag, and if this flag is set, the OnDraw() function is executed.

As stated, if you want to force Windows to draw the window, you use the Invalidate() function (as will be demonstrated later in this chapter).

Attaching Code to the *OnDraw( )* Function

In the previous section you read about the capability of Windows to cause the execution of the OnDraw() function. You'll now prove to yourself that indeed the OnDraw() function is automatically executed under these conditions.

☐ Select ClassWizard from the Project window, set Class Name to CDrawView, set Object ID to CDrawView, set Message to OnDraw(), and then click the Edit Code button. (See Figure 32.19.)

Figure 32.19. Accessing the OnDraw( ) function inside the DRAWVIEW.CPP file.

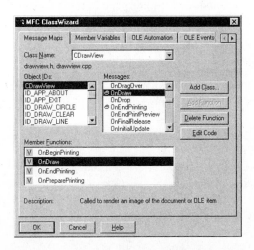

☐ Modify the OnDraw() function. (Visual C++ wrote the skeleton of the OnDraw() function for you.) After you modify the OnDraw() function, it should look like this:

```
void CDrawView::OnDraw(CDC* pDC)
{
CDrawDoc* pDoc = GetDocument();
ASSERT_VALID(pDoc);

// TODO: add draw code for native data here

/////////////////////////
// MY CODE STARTS HERE
/////////////////////////

// Beep (to demonstrate that the OnDraw() function
// was executed)
MessageBeep((WORD)-1);

/////////////////////////
// MY CODE ENDS HERE
/////////////////////////


}
```

The code you typed executes the MessageBeep() function. This means that whenever the OnDraw() function is executed, you'll hear a beep.

☐ Compile, link, and execute the DRAW application.

> *When the application displays its window, you hear a beep. This means that the OnDraw() function was executed.*

☐ Minimize the window of the application, and then maximize it.

> *When you maximize the window, you'll hear a beep because the window of the application is redrawn (which means that the OnDraw() function is executed).*

☐ Cover the window of the application with a window of another application, and then remove the window of the other application to expose the window of the DRAW application.

> *The DRAW application responds by beeping (because as soon as you expose its window, the window has to be redrawn, which means that the OnDraw() function is executed).*

☐ Experiment with the DRAW application, and then select Exit from the File menu to terminate the application.

NOTE

If you move the window of the application just a little by dragging its title, you won't hear the beep (which means that the OnDraw() function is not executed). OnDraw() is not executed in this case because in this case Windows is responsible for the redrawing (without causing the execution of OnDraw()).

Drawing Inside the Window

You'll now declare a data member called m_Shape. This variable serves as an indication of which shape to draw.

☐ Open the file DRAWVIEW.H, and add the data member m_Shape to the class declaration of CDrawView. After you add this data member, the CDrawView class declaration should look like this:

```
class CDrawView : public CView
{
protected: // create from serialization only
CDrawView();
DECLARE_DYNCREATE(CDrawView)

// Attributes
public:
CDrawDoc* GetDocument();

        /////////////////////////
        // MY CODE STARTS HERE
        /////////////////////////

        int m_Shape;

        /////////////////////////
        // MY CODE ENDS HERE
        /////////////////////////


// Operations
public:

// Overrides
// ClassWizard generated virtual function overrides
//{{AFX_VIRTUAL(CDrawView)
public:
virtual void OnDraw(CDC* pDC);
// overridden to draw this view
protected:
virtual BOOL OnPreparePrinting(CPrintInfo* pInfo);
virtual void OnBeginPrinting(CDC* pDC, CPrintInfo* pInfo);
virtual void OnEndPrinting(CDC* pDC, CPrintInfo* pInfo);
//}}AFX_VIRTUAL

// Implementation
public:
virtual ~CDrawView();
#ifdef _DEBUG
virtual void AssertValid() const;
virtual void Dump(CDumpContext& dc) const;
#endif

protected:

// Generated message map functions
protected:
//{{AFX_MSG(CDrawView)
```

```
// NOTE—the ClassWizard will add and remove member functions here.
//    DO NOT EDIT what you see in these blocks of generated code !
//}}AFX_MSG
DECLARE_MESSAGE_MAP()
};
```

The value of the data member m_Shape is set like this:

When the value of m_Shape is equal to 0, OnDraw() clears the window.

When the value of m_Shape is equal to 1, OnDraw() draws a line.

When the value of m_Shape is equal to 2, OnDraw() draws a circle.

When the value of m_Shape is equal to 3, OnDraw() draws a rectangle.

Initially, set the value of m_Shape to 0:

☐ Open the DRAWVIEW.CPP file, and initialize the value of m_Shape to 0 inside the constructor function of the CDrawView class. After the modification, the constructor function should look like this:

```
CDrawView::CDrawView()
{
// TODO: add construction code here

    /////////////////////////
    // MY CODE STARTS HERE
    /////////////////////////

    m_Shape = 0;

    /////////////////////////
    // MY CODE ENDS HERE
    /////////////////////////

}
```

In the preceding step you were instructed to set the value of m_Shape to 0. As you know, when C++ creates the m_Shape integer, it sets the value of m_Shape to 0. So why do you need to set the m_Shape integer to 0 inside the constructor function? You want to demonstrate where you should initialize the m_Shape variable (in case you want to initialize it to a value other than 0).

Attaching Code to the Menu Items

You'll now add code to the Line menu item of the Draw menu.

☐ Use ClassWizard to select the event:

```
CDrawView -> ID_DRAW_LINE -> COMMAND
```

Then click the Add Function button.

☐ Accept the name OnDrawLine() that ClassWizard suggests.

☐ Click the Edit Code button.

☐ Edit the `OnDrawLine()` function that you added to the DRAWVIEW.CPP file. After you edit the function, your `OnDrawLine()` function should look like this:

```
void CDrawView::OnDrawLine()
{
// TODO: Add your command handler code here

    ///////////////////////
    // MY CODE STARTS HERE
    ///////////////////////


    // Set the flag to 1 (Line)
    m_Shape = 1;

    // Trigger a call to OnDraw()
    Invalidate();


    ///////////////////////
    // MY CODE ENDS HERE
    ///////////////////////

}
```

The code you typed sets the value of `m_Shape` to 1:

```
m_Shape = 1;
```

The `Invalidate()` function causes the execution of the `OnDraw()` function:

```
Invalidate();
```

So when you select Line from the Draw menu, your code sets the value of `m_Shape` to 1, and then the `OnDraw()` function is executed.

You'll now add code to the Circle item of the Draw menu.

☐ Use ClassWizard to select the event:

```
CDrawView -> ID_DRAW_CIRCLE -> COMMAND
```

Then click the Add Function button.

☐ Accept the name `OnDrawCircle()` that ClassWizard suggests.

☐ Click the Edit Code button.

☐ Edit the `OnDrawCircle()` function that you added to the DRAWVIEW.CPP file. After you edit the function, your `OnDrawCircle()` function should look like this:

```
void CDrawView::OnDrawCircle()
{
// TODO: Add your command handler code here
```

```
////////////////////////
// MY CODE STARTS HERE
////////////////////////

// Set the flag to 2 (Circle)
m_Shape = 2;

// Trigger a call to OnDraw()
Invalidate();


////////////////////////
// MY CODE ENDS HERE
////////////////////////

}
```

The code you typed sets the value of m_Shape to 2:

```
m_Shape = 2;
```

The Invalidate() function causes the execution of the OnDraw() function:

```
Invalidate();
```

So when you select Circle from the Draw menu, your code sets the value of m_Shape to 2, and then the OnDraw() function is executed.

You'll now add code to the Rectangle item of the Draw menu.

☐ Use ClassWizard to select the event:

```
CDrawView -> ID_DRAW_RECTANGLE -> COMMAND
```

Then click the Add Function button.

☐ Accept the name OnDrawRectangle() that ClassWizard suggests.

☐ Click the Edit Code button.

☐ Edit the OnDrawRectangle() function that you added to the DRAWVIEW.CPP file. After you edit the function, your OnDrawRectangle() function should look like this:

```
void CDrawView::OnDrawRectangle()
{
// TODO: Add your command handler code here


////////////////////////
// MY CODE STARTS HERE
////////////////////////

// Set the flag to 3 (Rectangle)
m_Shape = 3;

// Trigger a call to OnDraw()
Invalidate();
```

```
///////////////////
// MY CODE ENDS HERE
///////////////////
```

```
}
```

The code you typed sets the value of `m_Shape` to 3:

```
m_Shape = 3;
```

The `Invalidate()` function causes the execution of the `OnDraw()` function:

```
Invalidate();
```

So when you select Line from the Draw menu, your code sets the value of `m_Shape` to 3, and then the `OnDraw()` function is executed.

You'll now add code to the Clear menu item of the Draw menu.

☐ Use ClassWizard to select the event:

```
CDrawView -> ID_DRAW_CLEAR -> COMMAND
```

Then click the Add Function button.

☐ Accept the name `OnDrawClear()` that ClassWizard suggests.

☐ Click the Edit Code button.

☐ Edit the `OnDrawClear()` function that you added to the DRAWVIEW.CPP file. After you edit the function, your `OnDrawClear()` function should look like this:

```
void CDrawView::OnDrawClear()
{
// TODO: Add your command handler code here

    ///////////////////
    // MY CODE STARTS HERE
    ///////////////////

    // Set the flag to 0 (clear)
    m_Shape = 0;

    // Trigger a call to OnDraw()
    Invalidate();


    ///////////////////
    // MY CODE ENDS HERE
    ///////////////////

}
```

So when you select Clear from the Draw menu, your code sets the value of `m_Shape` to 0, and then the `OnDraw()` function is executed.

Drawing a Line from within the *OnDraw()* Function

So far you have attached code to the Line, Circle, Rectangle, and Clear menu items of the Draw menu. The code that you attached sets the value of m_Shape to 0, 1, 2, or 3, and then the OnDraw() function is executed (by calling the Invalidate() function).

Of course if you compile, link, and execute the DRAW application, nothing will be drawn because the fact that you change the value of m_Shape does not cause any drawing.

To actually draw the shapes, you have to add code to the OnDraw() function. The code that you'll add to the OnDraw() function will draw a shape in accordance with the value of m_Shape.

☐ Open the DRAWVIEW.CPP file, and add the following code to the OnDraw() function. After you add the code, your OnDraw() function should look like this:

```
void CDrawView::OnDraw(CDC* pDC)
{
CDrawDoc* pDoc = GetDocument();
ASSERT_VALID(pDoc);

// TODO: add draw code for native data here

     ////////////////////////
     // MY CODE STARTS HERE
     ////////////////////////

     // Beep (to demonstrate that the OnDraw() function
     // was executed)
     // MessageBeep((WORD)-1);

     if ( m_Shape == 1 )
        {
        pDC->MoveTo ( 10, 30 );
        pDC->LineTo ( 50, 30 );
        }

     ////////////////////////
     // MY CODE ENDS HERE
     ////////////////////////

}
```

The code that you typed comments out (//) the MessageBeep() function:

```
// MessageBeep((WORD)-1);
```

Then an if statement is used to determine whether m_Shape is currently equal to 1:

```
if ( m_Shape == 1 )
   {
   pDC->MoveTo ( 10, 30 );
   pDC->LineTo ( 50, 30 );
   }
```

If m_Shape is equal to 1, the MoveTo() function is executed:

```
pDC->MoveTo ( 10, 30 );
```

Note that pDC is the parameter of the OnDraw() function. pDC is a pointer to the device context (DC stands for *device context*). The device context represents the screen. The MoveTo() function moves the current position to position (10, 30).

The next statement under the if statement draws a line from the current position to the position (50, 30):

```
pDC->LineTo ( 50, 30 );
```

So a line is drawn from position (10, 30) to position (50,3 0).

To see in action the code that you typed do the following:

☐ Compile, link, and execute the DRAW application.

The main window of the DRAW application appears without a drawing in it.

☐ Select Line from the Draw menu.

The DRAW application responds by drawing a line, as shown in Figure 32.20.

Figure 32.20. Drawing a line.

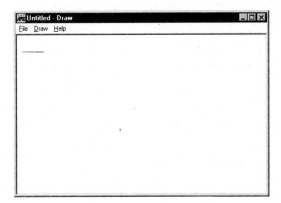

Note that the Print, Print Review, and Print Setup items of the File menu are operational.

☐ Select Print from the File menu.

The DRAW application responds by sending the contents of the DRAW window to the printer.

☐ Experiment with the items of the File menu, and then select Exit from the File menu to terminate the application.

Changing the Characteristics of the Line

The width of the line that you drew is 1 pixel. (See Figure 32.20.) This is the default width of the pen that Windows uses to draw lines. However, just like in Paintbrush, you can change the width of the pen.

☐ Modify the OnDraw() function (inside DRAWVIEW.CPP) so that it looks like this:

```
void CDrawView::OnDraw(CDC* pDC)
{
CDrawDoc* pDoc = GetDocument();
ASSERT_VALID(pDoc);

// TODO: add draw code for native data here

    ////////////////////////
    // MY CODE STARTS HERE
    ////////////////////////

    // Beep (to demonstrate that the OnDraw() function
    // was executed)
    // MessageBeep((WORD)-1);


    if ( m_Shape == 1 )
        {

        // Create a new pen
        CPen NewPen (PS_SOLID,          // The Style
                     10,                // The width
                     RGB(0,255,0) );    // The color

        // Set the new pen (and save the original pen)
        CPen* pOriginalPen = pDC->SelectObject ( &NewPen );

        pDC->MoveTo ( 10, 30 );
        pDC->LineTo ( 50, 30 );

        // Restore the original pen
         pDC->SelectObject ( pOriginalPen );


        pDC->MoveTo ( 50, 30 );
        pDC->LineTo ( 80, 30 );


        }

    ///////////////////////
    // MY CODE ENDS HERE
    ///////////////////////

}
```

The code you typed creates an object called NewPen of class CPen:

```
CPen NewPen (PS_SOLID,          // The Style
             10,                // The width
             RGB(0,255,0) );    // The color
```

The constructor function of CPen takes three parameters. The first parameter is PS_SOLID. This means that the pen will draw a solid line.

The second parameter is the width of the pen. You typed 10 as the second parameter, because you want the width to be 10 pixels.

The third parameter is the color of the pen. You supplied the value RGB(0,255,0) because you want the pen to be a green pen.

The next statement executes the SelectObject() function:

```
CPen* pOriginalPen = pDC->SelectObject ( &NewPen );
```

Note that the SelectObject() function "works" on pDC (which was received as the parameter of the OnDraw() function). As implied by its name, the SelectObject() function selects the object that will be used to draw. Think of it as selecting a drawing tool in Paintbrush. The parameter of SelectObject() is the address of the drawing tool. You typed &NewPen as the parameter of SelectObject() because you want the drawing tool to be the NewPen tool that you declared in the previous statement (that is, a solid green pen with width equal to 10).

Note that the return value of SelectObject() is saved as pOriginalPen. pOriginalPen is the pointer to the current pen. SelectObject() returns this value because in many cases you want to change the drawing tool, draw something with it, and then return to the original drawing tool.

Now that the pen of your choice has been selected, you can draw the line:

```
pDC->MoveTo ( 10, 30 );
pDC->LineTo ( 50, 30 );
```

To prove that indeed pOriginalPen (which was previously was returned from the SelectObject() function) is the original pen, you execute the SelectObject() function again with pOriginalPen as its parameter:

```
pDC->SelectObject ( pOriginalPen );
```

Then you continue to draw the line:

```
pDC->MoveTo ( 50, 30 );
pDC->LineTo ( 80, 30 );
```

So you first draw a thick, green line, and then you continue to draw the line with the original thin, black pen.

To see your code in action do the following:

☐ Compile, link, and execute the DRAW application.

☐ Select Line from the Draw menu.

The DRAW application responds by drawing the line as shown in Figure 32.21.

☐ Experiment with the DRAW application and then select Exit from the File menu to terminate the application.

Figure 32.21. A line drawn with two pens.

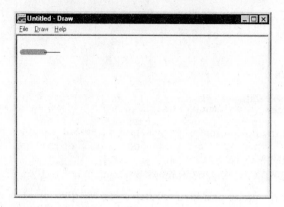

NOTE

The Clear menu item is operational because the `Invalidate()` function causes the execution of `OnDraw()`, and when `m_Shape` is equal to 0, the `OnDraw()` function does not draw any shape inside the window. In other words, the `Invalidate()` function erases the current contents of the window because `OnDraw()` draws nothing (because the `if` condition is not satisfied). So a clear-window operation is performed.

You should know, however, that the `Invalidate()` function has a parameter. The parameter can be `TRUE` or `FALSE`. When the parameter of `Invalidate()` is `TRUE`, the `Invalidate()` function erases the background of the window, and when the parameter of `Invalidate()` is `FALSE`, the background of the window is not erased.

So why did you type `Invalidate()` instead of `Invalidate(TRUE)`? The default value of the parameter is `TRUE`. So executing `Invalidate()` produces the same results as executing `Invalidate(TRUE)`.

Drawing a Circle

You'll now attach code to the `OnDraw()` function that draws a circle.

☐ Open the DRAWVIEW.CPP file, and add code to the `OnDraw()` function. After you add the code, your `OnDraw()` function should look like this:

```
void CDrawView::OnDraw(CDC* pDC)
{
CDrawDoc* pDoc = GetDocument();
ASSERT_VALID(pDoc);

// TODO: add draw code for native data here

    ///////////////////////////
    // MY CODE STARTS HERE
    ///////////////////////////
```

```
// Beep (to demonstrate that the OnDraw() function
// was executed)
// MessageBeep((WORD)-1);


// Draw the line.
if ( m_Shape == 1 )
   {

   // Create a new pen
    CPen NewPen (PS_SOLID,          // The Style
               10,                  // The width
               RGB(0,255,0) );      // The color

   // Set the new pen (and save the original pen)
   CPen* pOriginalPen = pDC->SelectObject ( &NewPen );

   pDC->MoveTo ( 10, 30 );
   pDC->LineTo ( 50, 30 );

   // Restore the original pen
    pDC->SelectObject ( pOriginalPen );


   // Draw a line with the original pen
   pDC->MoveTo ( 50, 30 );
   pDC->LineTo ( 80, 30 );

   }


// Draw the circle
if ( m_Shape == 2 )
   {

   // Create a new pen
   CPen NewPen (PS_SOLID,           // The Style
               40,                  // The width
               RGB(255, 0, 0) );    // The color

   // Set the new pen (and save the original pen)
   CPen* pOriginalPen = pDC->SelectObject ( &NewPen );


   // Create a rectangle object
   CRect theRect ( 20, 100, 120, 200 );

   // Draw the Circle
   pDC->Ellipse ( &theRect );

   // Restore the original pen
    pDC->SelectObject ( pOriginalPen );


   }
```

```
///////////////////
// MY CODE ENDS HERE
///////////////////
```

}

The code you added to the OnDraw() function is executed whenever m_Shape is equal to 2:

```
if ( m_Shape == 2 )
    {
    ....
    // A circle is drawn here
    ....
    }
```

The code starts by creating a new pen:

```
CPen NewPen (PS_SOLID,          // The Style
             40,                // The width
             RGB(255, 0, 0) );  // The color
```

The new pen is called NewPen. The pen has the following characteristics:

It is a solid pen (first parameter).

The width is 40 (second parameter).

The color of the pen is red (third parameter).

Next, you put this pen to use by selecting it with the SelectObject() function:

```
CPen* pOriginalPen = pDC->SelectObject ( &NewPen );
```

Again, the original pen is returned from the SelectObject() function.

The next statement creates an object of type CRect:

```
CRect theRect ( 20, 100, 120, 200 );
```

As implied by its name, the CRect class defines a rectangular area. The upper-left corner of the rectangle is at point (20, 100), and the lower-right corner of the rectangle is at point (100, 200).

You can now draw the circle:

```
pDC->Ellipse ( &theRect );
```

Note that the parameter of the Ellipse() function is &theRect. This means that the ellipse will be drawn bounded by theRect. Because you defined theRect as a square, the ellipse will be drawn as a circle. (Recall that an ellipse bounded by a square is called a circle.)

The last statement restores the original pen:

```
pDC->SelectObject ( pOriginalPen );
```

This means that if you now draw something the drawing will be done with the original pen.

To see your code in action do the following:

☐ Compile, link, and execute the DRAW application.

☐ Select the Circle item from the Draw menu.

   The DRAW application responds by drawing the circle, as shown in Figure 32.22.

Figure 32.22. Drawing a circle.

Drawing a Rectangle

You'll now attach code to the OnDraw() function that draws a rectangle.

☐ Open the DRAWVIEW.CPP file, and add code to the OnDraw() function. After you add the code, your OnDraw() function should look like this:

```
void CDrawView::OnDraw(CDC* pDC)
{
    CDrawDoc* pDoc = GetDocument();
    ASSERT_VALID(pDoc);

// TODO: add draw code for native data here

    /////////////////////////
    // MY CODE STARTS HERE
    /////////////////////////

    // Beep (to demonstrate that the OnDraw() function
    // was executed)
    // MessageBeep(-1);

    // Draw the line.
    if ( m_Shape == 1 )
        {
```

```
    // Create a new pen
     CPen NewPen (PS_SOLID,          // The Style
                  10,                // The width
                  RGB(0,255,0) );    // The color

    // Set the new pen (and save the original pen)
    CPen* pOriginalPen = pDC->SelectObject ( &NewPen );

    pDC->MoveTo ( 10, 30 );
    pDC->LineTo ( 50, 30 );

    // Restore the original pen
    pDC->SelectObject ( pOriginalPen );


    // Draw a line with the original pen
    pDC->MoveTo ( 50, 30 );
    pDC->LineTo ( 80, 30 );


    }


// Draw the circle
if ( m_Shape == 2 )
   {

    // Create a new pen
    CPen NewPen (PS_SOLID,           // The Style
                 40,                 // The width
                 RGB(255, 0, 0) );   // The color

    // Set the new pen (and save the original pen)
    CPen* pOriginalPen = pDC->SelectObject ( &NewPen );


    // Create a rectangle object
    CRect theRect ( 20, 100, 120, 200 );

    // Draw the Circle
    pDC->Ellipse ( &theRect );

    // Restore the original pen
    pDC->SelectObject ( pOriginalPen );


    }


// Draw the rectangle
if ( m_Shape == 3 )
    {
    // Create a rectangle object
    CRgn theRgn;
    theRgn.CreateRectRgn ( 50, 100, 150, 200 );

    // Create a new brush
    CBrush MyBrush( HS_BDIAGONAL, RGB(0, 0, 255) );

    // Draw the rectangle
```

```
      pDC->FillRgn ( &theRgn, &MyBrush );

      }

//////////////////////
// MY CODE ENDS HERE
//////////////////////

}
```

The code you typed will be executed whenever the user selects Rectangle from the Draw menu:

```
if ( m_Shape == 3 )
   {
   ...
   ...
   ...
   // Draw the rectangle
   ...
   ...
   ...
   }
```

The first statement under the `if` block creates an object `theRgn` of class `CRgn`:

```
CRgn theRgn;
```

Then the region is defined with the `CreateRectRgn()` member function of `CRgn`:

```
theRgn.CreateRectRgn ( 50, 100, 150, 200 );
```

The upper-left corner of the rectangular region is `(50, 100)`, and the lower-right corner of the region is `(150, 200)`.

The next statement creates a brush (an object `MyBrush` of class `CBrush`):

```
CBrush MyBrush( HS_BDIAGONAL, RGB(0, 0, 255) );
```

The first parameter of the constructor function `MyBrush()` is `HS_BDIAGONAL`. This means that the brush will cause the drawing of diagonal lines.

The second parameter of the constructor function is `RGB(0,0,255)`. This means that the color of the brush is blue.

Now that you have defined the brush and the region, you can execute the `FillRgn()` function:

```
pDC->FillRgn ( &theRgn, &MyBrush );
```

The first parameter of `FillRgn()` is the address of the region that you defined, and the second parameter is the address of the brush that will be used to fill the region.

To see your code in action do the following:

☐ Compile, link, and execute the DRAW application.

☐ Select Rectangle from the Draw menu.

The DRAW application responds by drawing the rectangle shown in Figure 32.23.

Figure 32.23. Drawing a rectangle.

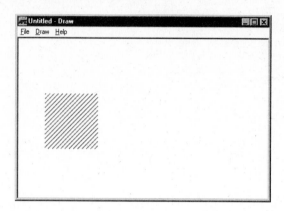

☐ Experiment with the DRAW program and then select Exit from the File menu to terminate the program.

The CircleIt Application

So far in this chapter you have drawn shapes by taking advantage of the OnDraw() function. The OnDraw() function is a good focal place to draw, because it is automatically executed whenever there is a need to redraw the window.

If, for example, you minimize the window and then restore its size, the OnDraw() function will be executed, and all the drawings that OnDraw() draws will be redrawn.

As you can see, this is a great advantage, because you don't have to write code that detects when the window of the application has to be redrawn. Nevertheless, there are occasions on which you'll need to draw outside the OnDraw() function. The CircleIt application demonstrates how this is accomplished.

Before you start writing the CircleIt application yourself, first execute the copy of it that resides in the \MVCPROG\EXE directory of the book's CD.

To execute the CircleIt.EXE application do the following:

☐ Execute the X:\MVCPROG\EXE\CircleIt.EXE program (where *X* represents the drive letter of your CD-ROM drive).

Windows responds by executing the CircleIt.EXE application. The main window of CircleIt.EXE appears, as shown in Figure 32.24.

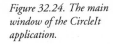

Figure 32.24. The main window of the CircleIt application.

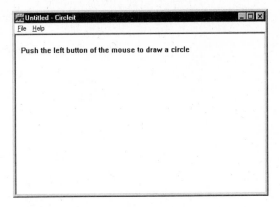

The CircleIt application has two pop-up menus: File and Help. The File menu contains the standard Print menu items. (See Figure 32.25.)

Figure 32.25. The File menu of the CircleIt application.

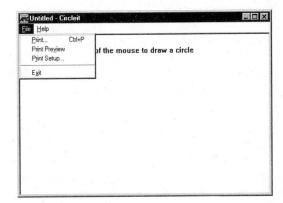

☐ Click the left mouse button inside the window of the CircleIt application.

The CircleIt application responds by drawing a circle with a thick boundary. (See Figure 32.26.)

☐ Keep clicking the mouse at various points inside the window of the CircleIt application.

The CircleIt application responds by drawing a circle for each click. (See Figures 32.27 and 32.28.)

Figure 32.26. Drawing a circle with the CircleIt application.

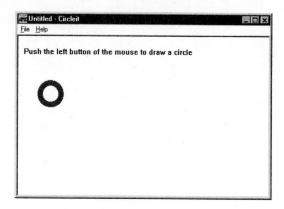

Figure 32.27. Drawing the text C++ with circles.

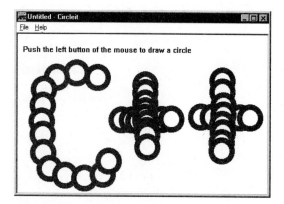

Figure 32.28. Drawing a face with the CircleIt application.

☐ Drag the title of the CircleIt window down until half of it is outside the screen.

☐ Drag the title of the CircleIt window upward.

As shown in Figure 32.29, the part of the window that went off the screen isn't redrawn. This is because the drawing wasn't performed from within the OnDraw() function.

Figure 32.29. The area that went off the screen is not redrawn.

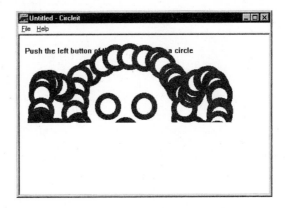

☐ Minimize the window of CircleIt and then restore it to its original size.

> *The CircleIt application responds by displaying its window without any circles in it, because the original circles weren't drawn from within* OnDraw()*. However, the original text,* Push the left button of the mouse to draw a circle, *does appear, because the text is drawn from within* OnDraw()*.*

☐ Experiment with the CircleIt application, and then select Exit from the File menu to terminate the CircleIt application.

Now that you know what the CircleIt application should do, you can write it.

Creating the Project of the CircleIt Application

To create the project of the CircleIt application do the following:

☐ Start Visual C++ and close all the open windows that appear inside the desktop of Visual C++ (if there are any).

☐ Select New from the File menu.

> *Visual C++ responds by displaying the New dialog box.*

☐ Select Project inside the New dialog box and then click the OK button of the New dialog box.

> *Visual C++ responds by displaying the New Project dialog box.*

☐ Set the project name to CircleIt.

☐ Set the project path to \MVCPROG\CH32\CircleIt\CircleIt.MAK.

Your New Project dialog box should now look like the one shown in Figure 32.30.

*Figure 32.30. The New
Project dialog box of the
CircleIt.MAK project.*

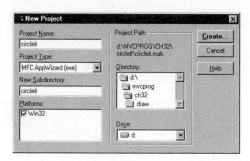

☐ Click the Create button of the New Project dialog box.

 Visual C++ responds by displaying the AppWizard—Step 1 window.

☐ Set the Step 1 window as shown in Figure 32.31. As shown in Figure 32.31, the CircleIt.MAK project is set as a single-document interface application, and U.S. English (APPWIZUS.DLL) is used as the language for the application's resources.

*Figure 32.31. The
AppWizard—Step 1
window for the DRAW
application.*

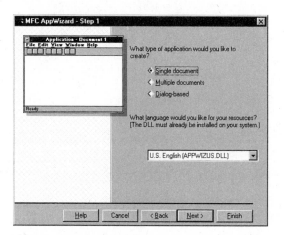

☐ Click the Next button of the Step 1 window.

 Visual C++ responds by displaying the AppWizard—Step 2 of 6 window.

☐ Set the Step 2 of 6 window as shown in Figure 32.32. That is, in the CircleIt application you don't want any database support.

☐ Click the Next button of the Step 2 of 6 window.

 Visual C++ responds by displaying the AppWizard—Step 3 of 6 window.

☐ Set the Step 3 of 6 window as shown in Figure 32.33. That is, in the CircleIt application you don't want any OLE support.

Figure 32.32. The AppWizard—Step 2 of 6 window for the CircleIt application.

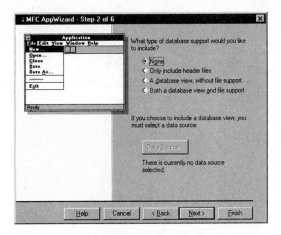

Figure 32.33. The AppWizard—Step 3 of 6 window for the CircleIt application.

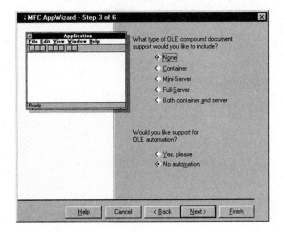

☐ Click the Next button of the Step 3 of 6 window.

Visual C++ responds by displaying the AppWizard—Step 4 of 6 window.

☐ Set the Step 4 of 6 window as shown in Figure 32.34.

As shown in Figure 32.34, the features Dockable Toolbar, Initial Status Bar, and Context Sensitive Help will not be included in the CircleIt application. However, the Printing and Print Preview and 3D Controls features will be included.

☐ Click the Next button of the Step 4 of 6 window.

Visual C++ responds by displaying the AppWizard—Step 5 of 6 window.

☐ Set the Step 5 of 6 window as shown in Figure 32.35.

As shown in Figure 32.35, the project will be generated with comments, a Visual C++ makefile will be generated, and the application will use the MFC library from a DLL.

Figure 32.34. The AppWizard—Step 4 of 6 window for the CircleIt application.

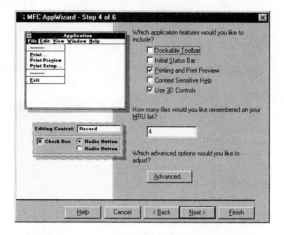

Figure 32.35. The AppWizard—Step 5 of 6 window for the CircleIt application.

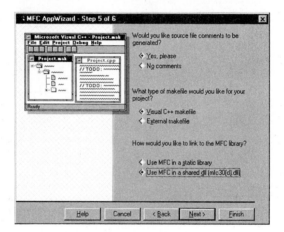

☐ Click the Next button of the Step 5 of 6 window.

Visual C++ responds by displaying the AppWizard—Step 6 of 6 window.

You'll now use the AppWizard—Step 6 of 6 window to tell AppWizard to derive the view class of the application from the MFC class CView:

☐ Select the CCircleItView class inside the AppWizard—Step 6 of 6 window.

☐ Make sure that the base class is set to CView (which is the default class that Visual C++ suggests for the base class).

Your AppWizard—Step 6 of 6 window should now look like the one shown in Figure 32.36.

Figure 32.36. The AppWizard—Step 6 of 6 window.

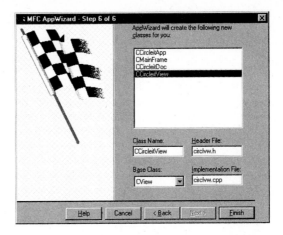

> **NOTE**
>
> As you can see from Figure 32.26, the main window of the CircleIt program does not have any controls inside it. Therefore, you were instructed to set the base class of the `CCircleItView` class to `CView` (as indicated in Figure 32.36).

☐ Click the Finish button of the Step 6 of 6 window.

> *Visual C++ responds by displaying the New Project Information window, as shown in Figure 32.37.*

Figure 32.37. The New Project Information window of the CircleIt.MAK project.

☐ Click the OK button of the New Project Information window.

> *Visual C++ responds by creating the project file and all the skeleton files of the application.*

The Visual Design of the Menu of the CircleIt Application

You'll now implement the menu of the CircleIt program.

☐ Select circleit.mak from the Window menu to display the CircleIt.MAK file, double-click circleit.rc inside the CircleIt.MAK window to display the circleit.rc window, double-click Menu inside the circleit.rc window, and finally double-click IDR_MAINFRAME under the Menu item.

> *Visual C++ responds by displaying the menu of the CircleIt program in design mode.*

☐ Delete the Edit menu.

☐ Modify the menu of the CircleIt so that it contains the following items:

&File
    &Print...
    Print Pre&view
    P&rint Setup...
    Separator
    E&xit
&Help
    &About Circleit...

To save your work do the following:

☐ Select Save from the File menu.

The visual implementation of the menu of the CircleIt application is complete.

Adding Code to the *OnDraw()* Function

Before adding "drawing code" outside the OnDraw() function, add code inside the OnDraw() function. This way you'll be able to see the differences between drawing that is generated inside and outside the OnDraw() function.

☐ Open the CIRCLVW.CPP file, and add the following code to the OnDraw() function.
After you add the code, your OnDraw() function should look like this:

```
void CCircleitView::OnDraw(CDC* pDC)
{
CCircleitDoc* pDoc = GetDocument();
ASSERT_VALID(pDoc);

// TODO: add draw code for native data here
```

```
/////////////////////
// MY CODE STARTS HERE
/////////////////////

CString MyString =
   "Push the left button of the mouse to draw a circle";

pDC->TextOut( 10,
              20,
              MyString );



/////////////////////
// MY CODE ENDS HERE
/////////////////////

}
```

The code you typed creates an object MyString of type CString:

```
CString MyString =
   "Push the left button of the mouse to draw a circle";
```

Then the TextOut() function is executed:

```
pDC->TextOut( 10,            // X-coordinate
              20,            // Y-coordinate
              MyString );
```

Note that in the preceding statement, TextOut() "works" on the pDC. pDC was received as the parameter of the OnDraw() function.

NOTE

Here is how you can learn more about the TextOut() function:

☐ Display the help window of TextOut() by highlighting the TextOut text. Then press F1 for help.

Visual C++ responds by displaying the help window of the TextOut() *function, as shown in Figure 32.38.*

As shown in Figure 32.38, there are two TextOut() functions: one has four parameters, and one has three parameters. In the code that you typed inside OnDraw(), you used the TextOut() function with three parameters. In C++ you may have more than one function with the same name (and a different number of parameters); such a function is called an *overload function*.

Figure 32.38. The help window of the TextOut() function.

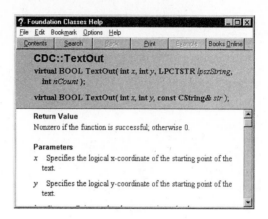

Drawing Outside the *OnDraw()* Function

You'll now attach code to the CIRCLVW.CPP file that is executed whenever the left button of the mouse is pressed. The code will draw a circle whenever the left button of the mouse is pressed.

☐ Select ClassWizard from the Project menu to select the event (see Figure 32.39):

CCircleitView -> CCircleitView -> WM_LBUTTONDOWN

Then click the Add Function button.

> *Visual C++ responds by creating the* OnLButtonDown() *member function. The* OnLButtonDown() *function is executed when the user presses the left button of the mouse.*

Figure 32.39. Adding the OnLButtonDown() function.

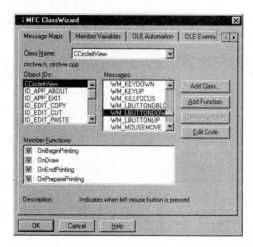

☐ Click the Edit Code button and edit the `OnLButtonDown()` function that you added to the CIRCLVW.CPP file. After you edit the function, your `OnLButtonDown()` function should look like this:

```
void CCircleitView::OnLButtonDown(UINT nFlags, CPoint point)
{
// TODO: Add your message handler code
// here and/or call default

    ////////////////////////
    // MY CODE STARTS HERE
    ////////////////////////

    CDC* pDC = GetDC();

    // Create a new pen
    CPen NewPen (PS_SOLID,              // The Style
                10,                     // The width
                RGB(255, 0, 0) );       // The color

    // Set the new pen (and save the original pen)
    CPen* pOriginalPen = pDC->SelectObject ( &NewPen );


    // Create a rectangle object
    CRect theRect ( point.x-20,
                    point.y-20,
                    point.x+20,
                    point.y+20 );

    // Draw the Circle
    pDC->Ellipse ( &theRect );

    // Restore the original pen
    pDC->SelectObject ( pOriginalPen );


    ReleaseDC (pDC);


    ////////////////////////
    // MY CODE ENDS HERE
    ////////////////////////

CView::OnLButtonDown(nFlags, point);
}
```

The code you typed uses the `GetDC()` member function to get a device context called `pDC`:

```
CDC* pDC = GetDC();
```

This was not necessary when you used the `OnDraw()` function, because `pDC` was supplied as the parameter of the `OnDraw()` function.

Because you extracted pDC with GetDC(), it is your responsibility to release it with the ReleaseDC() function. This means that your code must look like this:

```
CDC* pDC = GetDC();
    ......
    ......
    ......
    // Draw whatever you want to draw
    ......
    ......
    ......
ReleaseDC (pDC);
```

Between the GetDC() and the ReleaseDC() you can write "drawing code" in the same way you write it inside the OnDraw() function.

> **NOTE**
>
> As stated, when using the GetDC() function, it is your responsibility to release the DC with the ReleaseDC() function.
>
> However, when drawing from within OnDraw(), do not use the ReleaseDC() function to release the pDC (because this is done automatically for you).
>
> Sometimes, when developing programs, you'll change your mind and you'll move code from the OnDraw() function to another function, or vice versa. When doing so, don't forget the business of the GetDC() and ReleaseDC() functions.

Now take a look at the code you typed between GetDC() and ReleaseDC():

First, you created a new pen object:

```
CPen NewPen (PS_SOLID,          // The Style
             10,                // The width
             RGB(255, 0, 0) );  // The color
```

Then you used the SelectObject() function to put this new pen in use:

```
CPen* pOriginalPen = pDC->SelectObject ( &NewPen );
```

Note that in the preceding statement the pen that existed before the new pen was created is saved as pOriginalPen.

The next statement creates the object theRect of class CRect:

```
CRect theRect ( point.x-20,
                point.y-20,
                point.x+20,
                point.y+20 );
```

The rectangle is defined in reference to the point where the left button of the mouse was pushed. Note that point was received as the parameter of the OnLButtonDown() function.

So the theRect rectangle is defined as shown in Figure 32.40.

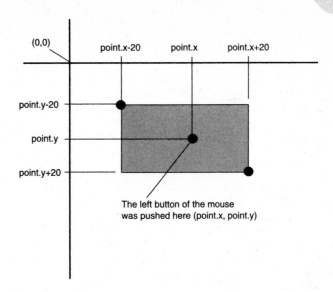

Figure 32.40. Defining theRect *in reference to the* point *parameter.*

Now that the pen and the rectangle are defined, you can use the `Ellipse()` function to draw the circle:

```
pDC->Ellipse ( &theRect );
```

Finally, the `SelectObject()` function is used to restore the original pen:

```
pDC->SelectObject ( pOriginalPen );
```

NOTE

It is a good programming habit to restore the original pen.

Consider, for example, the case of an application that uses `Function1()` to draw something with a particular pen. Imagine that `Function1()` draws something and then calls `Function2()`. `Function2()` draws something with a different pen, and then `Function1()` continues the drawing.

The process looks like this:

```
void Function1(void)
{
// Create a pen,(pen1)
...
...
...

// Draw with pen1
```

```
...
...
...

// Execute Function2()
Function2();

// Continue the drawing (with pen1)
...
...
...
}
```

If `Function2()` uses a different pen but returns the original pen, then when `Function1()` continues the drawing with the current pen (`Pen1`), there is no need for `Function1()` to create `pen1` all over again.

So the rule of thumb is this: A function that changes the current pen should be responsible for restoring the original pen.

This, of course, is not a C++ requirement, but it makes a program easy to read and maintain.

To see your code in action do the following:

☐ Compile, link, and execute the CircleIt application.

☐ Click inside the window of the application.

> *The CircleIt application responds by drawing a circle. The center of the circle is at the point where you clicked the mouse.*

☐ Keep clicking the mouse to draw circles at various places.

☐ Drag the window of the application (or minimize it and then restore its size).

The CircleIt application displays the text that was drawn inside the `OnDraw()` function, but the circles that you drew disappear! This is because the circles were not drawn inside `OnDraw()`.

☐ Select Exit from the File menu to terminate the CircleIt application.

The MyText Application

The MyText application demonstrates how your Visual C++ application can draw text with various fonts.

Before you start writing the MyText application yourself, execute the copy of it that resides in the \MVCPROG\EXE directory of the book's CD.

☐ Execute the X:\MVCPROG\EXE\MyText.EXE program (where *X* represents the letter drive of your CD-ROM drive).

> *Windows responds by executing the MyText.EXE application. The main window of MyText.EXE appears, as shown in Figure 32.41. As shown the program displays test in its main window.*

Figure 32.41. The main window of the MyText application.

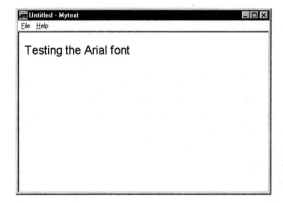

The MyText application has two pop-up menus: File and Help. The File menu of the MyText application contains the standard Print menu items. (See Figure 32.42.)

Figure 32.42. The File menu of the MyText application.

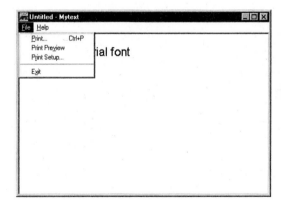

Now that you know what the MyText should do, you can write it.

Creating the Project of the MyText Application

To create the project of the MyText application do the following:

☐ Start Visual C++ and close all the open windows that appear inside the desktop of Visual C++ (if there are any).

☐ Select New from the File menu.

   Visual C++ responds by displaying the New dialog box.

☐ Select Project inside the New dialog box and then click the OK button of the New dialog box.

   Visual C++ responds by displaying the New Project dialog box.

☐ Set the project name to MyText.

☐ Set the project path to \MVCPROG\CH32\MyText\MyText.MAK.

Your New Project dialog box should now look like the one shown in Figure 32.43.

Figure 32.43. The New Project dialog box of the MyText.MAK project.

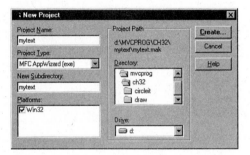

☐ Click the Create button of the New Project dialog box.

   Visual C++ responds by displaying the AppWizard—Step 1 window.

☐ Set the Step 1 window as shown in Figure 32.44. As shown in Figure 32.44, the MyText.MAK project is set as a single-document interface application, and U.S. English (APPWIZUS.DLL) is used as the language for the application's resources.

Figure 32.44. The AppWizard—Step 1 window for the MyText application.

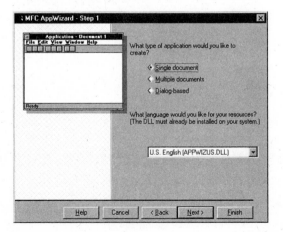

☐ Click the Next button of the Step 1 window.

Visual C++ responds by displaying the AppWizard—Step 2 of 6 window.

☐ Set the Step 2 of 6 window as shown in Figure 32.45. That is, in the MyText application you don't want any database support.

Figure 32.45. The AppWizard—Step 2 of 6 window for the MyText application.

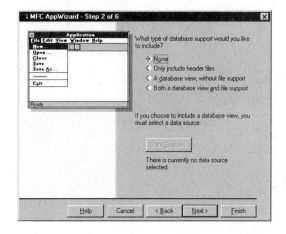

☐ Click the Next button of the Step 2 of 6 window.

Visual C++ responds by displaying the AppWizard—Step 3 of 6 window.

☐ Set the Step 3 of 6 window as shown in Figure 32.46. That is, in the MyText application you don't want any OLE support.

Figure 32.46. The AppWizard—Step 3 of 6 window for the MyText application.

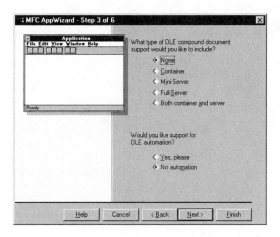

☐ Click the Next button of the Step 3 of 6 window.

Visual C++ responds by displaying the AppWizard—Step 4 of 6 window.

☐ Set the Step 4 of 6 window as shown in Figure 32.47.

Figure 32.47. The AppWizard—Step 4 of 6 window for the MyText application.

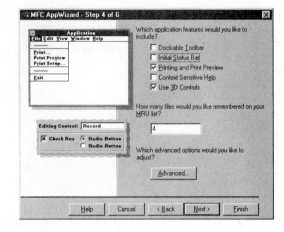

As shown in Figure 32.47, the features Dockable Toolbar, Initial Status Bar, and Context Sensitive Help will not be included in the MyText application. However, the Printing and Print Preview and 3D Controls features will be included.

☐ Click the Next button of the Step 4 of 6 window.

Visual C++ responds by displaying the AppWizard—Step 5 of 6 window.

☐ Set the Step 5 of 6 window as shown in Figure 32.48.

As shown in Figure 32.48, the project will be generated with comments, a Visual C++ makefile will be generated, and the application will use the MFC library from a DLL.

Figure 32.48. The AppWizard—Step 5 of 6 window for the MyText application.

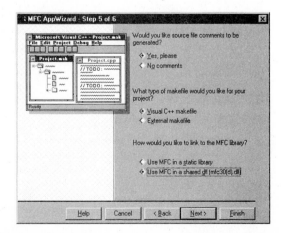

☐ Click the Next button of the Step 5 of 6 window.

> *Visual C++ responds by displaying the AppWizard—Step 6 of 6 window.*

You'll now use the AppWizard—Step 6 of 6 window to tell AppWizard to derive the view class of the application from the MFC class `CView`:

☐ Select the `CMytextView` class inside the AppWizard—Step 6 of 6 window.

☐ Make sure that the base class is set to `CView` (which is the default class that Visual C++ suggests for the base class).

Your AppWizard—Step 6 of 6 window should now look like the one shown in Figure 32.49.

Figure 32.49. The AppWizard—Step 6 of 6 window.

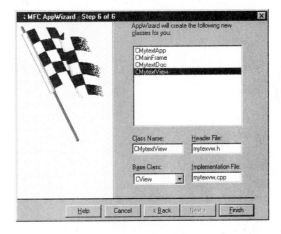

NOTE

As you can see from Figure 32.41, the main window of the MyText program does not have any controls inside it. Therefore, you were instructed to set the base class of the `CMytextView` class to `CView` (not to `CFormView`) as instructed by Figure 32.49.

☐ Click the Finish button of the Step 6 of 6 window.

> *Visual C++ responds by displaying the New Project Information window, as shown in Figure 32.50.*

☐ Click the OK button of the New Project Information window.

> *Visual C++ responds by creating the project file and all the skeleton files of the application.*

*Figure 32.50. The New
Project Information
window of the
MyText.MAK project.*

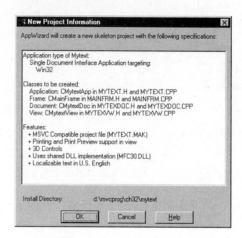

The Visual Design of the Menu of the MyText Application

You'll now visually design the menu of the MyText application.

☐ Select mytext.mak from the Window menu to display the mytext.mak window, double-click mytext.rc inside the mytext.mak window to display the mytext.rc window, double-click the Menu item inside the mytext.rc window, and finally, double-click IDR_MAINFRAME under the Menu item.

> *Visual C++ responds by displaying the menu of the MyText program in design mode.*

☐ Delete the Edit menu.

☐ Design the menu so that it contains the following items:

&File
    &Print...
    Print Pre&view
    P&rint Setup...
    Separator
    E&xit
&Help
    &About Mytext...

The visual implementation of the menu of the MyText application is complete.

Displaying Text with Different Fonts

You've already had several opportunities in this book to display text with the TextOut() function. The MyText application demonstrates how to use the TextOut() function for displaying text with various fonts.

☐ Open the MYTEXVW.CPP file and add code to the `OnDraw()` function. After you add the code, your `OnDraw()` function should look like this:

```
void CMytextView::OnDraw(CDC* pDC)
{
CMytextDoc* pDoc = GetDocument();
ASSERT_VALID(pDoc);

// TODO: add draw code for native data here


        //////////////////////
        // MY CODE STARTS HERE
        //////////////////////

        CFont MyFont;

        MyFont.CreateFont     ( 25,
                                0,
                                0,
                                0,
                                400,
                                FALSE,
                                FALSE,
                                0,
                                ANSI_CHARSET,
                                OUT_DEFAULT_PRECIS,
                                CLIP_DEFAULT_PRECIS,
                                DEFAULT_QUALITY,
                                DEFAULT_PITCH¦FF_SWISS,
                                "Arial");

        CFont* pOldFont = (CFont*)pDC->SelectObject(&MyFont);

        pDC->TextOut(10,
                     20,
                     "Testing the Arial font");

        //////////////////////
        // MY CODE ENDS HERE
        //////////////////////


}
```

The code you typed creates an object `MyFont` of class `CFont`:

```
CFont MyFont;
```

The next statement uses the `CreateFont()` function to create the font:

```
MyFont.CreateFont     ( 25,
                        0,
                        0,
                        0,
                        400,
                        FALSE,
                        FALSE,
                        0,
```

```
ANSI_CHARSET,
OUT_DEFAULT_PRECIS,
CLIP_DEFAULT_PRECIS,
DEFAULT_QUALITY,
DEFAULT_PITCH|FF_SWISS,
"Arial");
```

As you can see, the `CreateFont()` function has many parameters. To see the purpose of each of the parameters do the following:

☐ Highlight the CreateFont text, and then press F1 for help.

Visual C++ responds by displaying the help window for the `CreateFont()` function. (See Figure 32.51.)

Figure 32.51. The help window for the `CreateFont()` function.

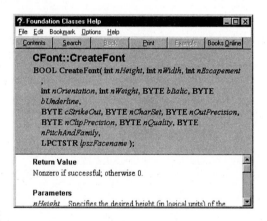

For now, pay attention to the first and last parameters. The first parameter is the height of the text, and the last parameter is the name of the font.

The next statement you typed actually puts the font to use by using the `SelectObject()` function:

```
CFont* pOldFont = (CFont*)pDC->SelectObject(&MyFont);
```

Note that as usual, the returned value of `SelectObject()` is the pointer of the object that was re-placed. So after you execute the `SelectObject()` function, `pOldFont` is updated with the pointer of the font that existed before the Arial font was selected with the `SelectObject()` function.

Finally, the `TextOut()` function is executed to display text with the font specified in the `CreateFont()` function:

```
pDC->TextOut(10,
             20,
             "Testing the Arial font");
```

☐ Compile, link, and execute the MyText application.

The MyText application responds by displaying its main window, as shown in Figure 32.52.

Figure 32.52. The main window of the MyText application, which contains text in the Arial font, with height of 25.

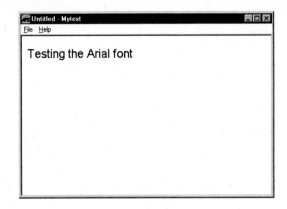

You can now experiment by changing the value of the first parameter of the CreateFont() function.

☐ Open the MYTEXVW.CPP file, and change the first parameter of the CreateFont() function inside the OnDraw() function.

After you change the value of the first parameter, the statement that calls the CreateFont() function should look like this:

```
MyFont.CreateFont    ( 100,
                       0,
                       0,
                       0,
                       400,
                       FALSE,
                       FALSE,
                       0,
                       ANSI_CHARSET,
                       OUT_DEFAULT_PRECIS,
                       CLIP_DEFAULT_PRECIS,
                       DEFAULT_QUALITY,
                       DEFAULT_PITCH¦FF_SWISS,
                       "Arial");
```

☐ Compile, link, and execute the MyText application.

The main window of the MyText application appears with text in it. The text is in the Arial font, with height equal to 100.

☐ Experiment with the MyText application by changing its first parameter as well as its last parameter.

For example, modify the OnDraw() function so that it looks like this:

```
void CMytextView::OnDraw(CDC* pDC)
{
    CMytextDoc* pDoc = GetDocument();
    ASSERT_VALID(pDoc);

    // TODO: add draw code for native data here
```

```
/////////////////////
// MY CODE STARTS HERE
/////////////////////

CFont MyFont;

MyFont.CreateFont    ( 25,
                        0,
                        0,
                        0,
                        400,
                        FALSE,
                        FALSE,
                        0,
                        ANSI_CHARSET,
                        OUT_DEFAULT_PRECIS,
                        CLIP_DEFAULT_PRECIS,
                        DEFAULT_QUALITY,
                        DEFAULT_PITCH¦FF_SWISS,
                        "Courier New");


CFont* pOldFont = (CFont*)pDC->SelectObject(&MyFont);

pDC->TextOut(10,
             20,
             "Testing the Courier New font");

/////////////////////
// MY CODE ENDS HERE
/////////////////////

}
```

This code will display the text as Courier New with height of 25.

> **NOTE**
>
> At first glance, it looks as if drawing text with Visual C++ is a long and complex business. After all, look how many lines of code you had to type for displaying simple text!
>
> Don't forget that the program will display the text no matter what monitor or VGA card your user uses. That is, you are writing code without knowing the system on which this code will be executed. In fact, if you specify a font that the system of your user does not have, Windows will automatically substitute the font that most closely matches that font.
>
> So don't complain about the code that you have to type for displaying text. After all, it is Windows that does all the hard work.

33

Creating OCX Controls

In this chapter and in the following
two chapters you'll learn about OCX
controls (OLE controls). You'll learn
what an OCX control is, how to
create OCX controls, and how to test
OCX controls.

What Is an OCX Control?

Before we answer the question What is an OCX control?, first review what a standard Visual C++ control is. In this book, you've used many standard controls. The standard controls are the controls that appear inside the Tools window of Visual C++: the push button control, the horizontal scroll bar control, the combo box control, and so on. (See Figure 33.1.)

Figure 33.1. The Tools window of Visual C++.

As you know, a control has properties and events. For example, the push button control has properties such as Caption and it has events such as Click and Double-click. The programmer who uses a control in a program places the control inside a dialog box, sets the properties of the control, and attaches code to the events of the control. The code that the programmer attaches to a certain event of the control is automatically executed when the event occurs. For example, if the user attaches code to the Click event of a push button control, this code will be automatically executed whenever the user clicks the push button.

Now, wouldn't it be nice if you could build your own custom control and then add this control to the Tools window so that you (and other programmers, as well) could use your control as if it were a regular control? Well, that's what OCX controls are all about. After you build your own OCX control, you can distribute it to other programmers (that is, programmers of languages that support OCX controls) and these programmers will be able to install your OCX control inside the Tools window and use your custom control just as they use other standard controls. That is, the programmer who uses your OCX control will be able to set the properties of your OCX control as well as attach code to the events of your OCX control.

Unfortunately, the current version of Visual C++ (version 2.0 for 32-bit or version 1.51 for 16-bit) does not allow programmers to add an OCX control to the Tools window of Visual C++. However, future versions of Visual C++ will enable programmers to add an OCX control to the Tools window. The programmer could then place the OCX control inside a dialog box and use ClassWizard to attach code to the events of the OCX control.

In the near future, most popular visual programming languages will enable programmers to add OCX controls to their Tools window. Therefore, learning how to create OCX controls is essential.

The question is Once you create your OCX control how will you be able to test it? As you'll soon see, the OLE Custom Development Kit (CDK) that comes with Visual C++ includes a program that lets you test your OCX controls.

The MYCLOCK OCX Control

In the remainder of this chapter and in the following two chapters, you'll develop and test your own OCX control, called MyClock.OCX. As implied by its name, the MyClock.OCX control will be used for displaying the current time. That is, when a programmer places a MyClock.OCX control inside a form (or a dialog box), the MyClock.OCX control will keep displaying the current time.

To develop the MyClock.OCX control you can use either Visual C++ 2.0 or Visual C++ 1.51. If you develop the OCX control using Visual C++ 1.51, the resultant OCX control will be compatible with the 16-bit platform. If you develop the OCX control using Visual C++ 2.0, the resultant OCX control will be compatible with the 32-bit platform.

As you'll soon see, the steps you need to take in order to develop a 16-bit OCX control (using Visual C++ 1.51) and the steps that you need to take in order to develop a 32-bit OCX control (using Visual C++ 2.0) are almost identical.

NOTE

As discussed, you can use Visual C++ 1.51 to develop 16-bit OCX controls and you can use Visual C++ 2.0 to develop 32-bit OCX controls.

Another type of custom control that you can develop with Visual C++ 1.51 is a VBX control. However, you cannot develop VBX controls with Visual C++ 2.0.

To learn about VBX controls (what they are and how to develop them with Visual C++ 1.51) you can refer to the Sams Publishing book *Master Visual C++ 1.5* by Gurewich & Gurewich. *Master Visual C++ 1.5* includes a VBX tutorial (similar to the tutorial presented here) that shows you how to implement a sample VBX control called MyClock.VBX.

Creating the Project of the MyClock.OCX Control

Follow these steps to create the project of the MyClock.OCX control:

☐ Start Visual C++ 2.0 (or Visual C++ 1.51).

☐ Close all open files (if there are any).

☐ Select ControlWizard from the Tools window of Visual C++.

Visual C++ responds by displaying the MFC ControlWizard dialog box. (See Figure 33.2.)

NOTE

If you do not see the option ControlWizard inside your Visual C++ Tools menu you have not installed the OLE Custom Development Kit that comes with Visual C++.

To install the OLE Custom Development Kit, you need to run the SETUP program of Visual C++ (from the original CD of Visual C++) and then click the OLE Custom Development Kit (CDK) button.

After you finish installing the OLE Custom Development Kit, the Tools menu of Visual C++ will include the ControlWizard item.

Figure 33.2. The ControlWizard dialog box.

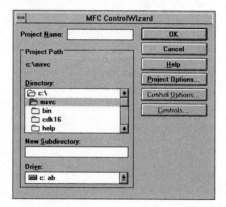

What is ControlWizard? ControlWizard is a very useful "wizard" that writes for you the skeleton of your OCX control. Instead of writing overhead code every time you start creating a new OCX control, ControlWizard writes this overhead code for you.

NOTE

Whenever you begin creating a new OCX control, start by running ControlWizard. ControlWizard writes the skeleton code for your control; it creates all the necessary files and subdirectories for your new control.

To tell ControlWizard the directory in which you want to create the new OCX control do the following:

☐ Use the directory list box to select the directory C:\MVCPROG\CH33. (See Figure 33.2.)

Your ControlWizard dialog box should now look like the one shown in Figure 33.3.

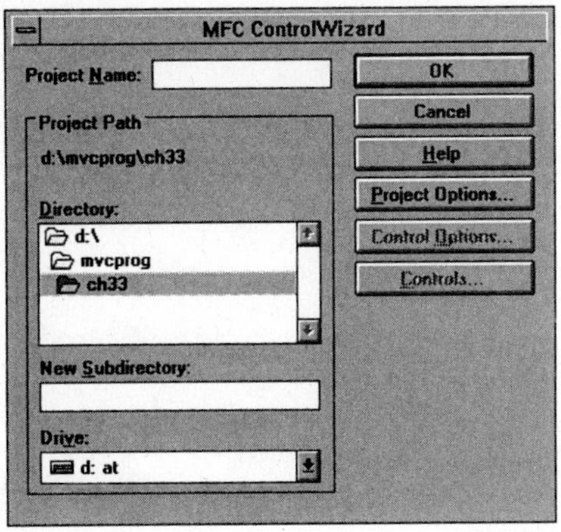

Figure 33.3. The ControlWizard dialog box after you select the directory C:\MVCPROG\CH33.

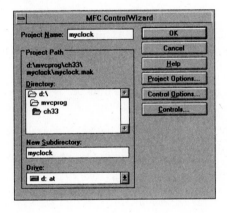

Now tell ControlWizard the name of the project:

☐ Type `myclock` inside the Project Name edit box.

Now the full pathname of the project is c:\mvcprog\ch33\myclock\myclock.mak. (See Figure 33.4.)

Figure 33.4. The ControlWizard dialog box after you specify the directory and name of the project.

Next you have to set various options for the project:

☐ Click the Project Options button.

   Visual C++ responds by displaying the Project Options dialog box. (See Figure 33.5.)

☐ Make sure that your Project Options dialog box is set as shown in Figure 33.5. That is, the only check box that should have a checkmark inside it is the Source Comments check box. By placing a checkmark inside the Source Comments option, you are telling ControlWizard to place comments inside the code that ControlWizard will write for you.

☐ Click the OK button of the Project Options dialog box.

   Visual C++ responds by closing the Project Options dialog box.

*Figure 33.5. The Project
Options dialog box.*

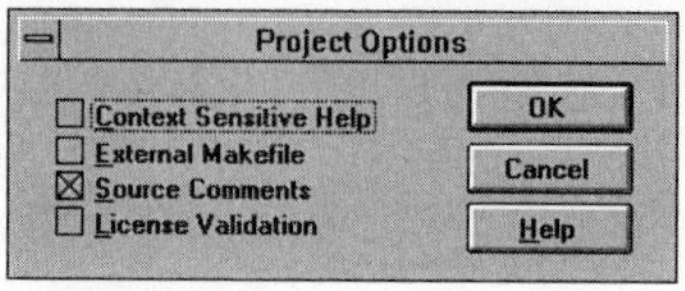

*Figure 33.6. The Control
Options dialog box.*

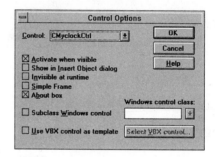

☐ Now click the Control Options button.

> *Visual C++ responds by displaying the Control Options dialog box. (See Figure 33.6.)*

☐ Make sure that your Control Options dialog box is set as shown in Figure 33.6. That is, the only two check boxes that should have checkmarks inside them are Activate when visible and About box.

Notice in Figure 33.6 that the Control box is set to CMyclockCtrl. CMyclockCtrl is the name of the class that ControlWizard will declare for the MYCLOCK control.

☐ Click the OK button of the Control Options dialog box.

> *Visual C++ responds by closing the Control Options dialog box.*

☐ Now click the Controls button.

> *Visual C++ responds by displaying the Controls dialog box. (See Figure 33.7.)*

The Controls dialog box lists the names of the control's classes and files that ControlWizard will create for you.

☐ Leave the names in the Controls dialog box at their default settings (as shown in Figure 33.7).

☐ Click the OK button of the Controls dialog box.

> *Visual C++ responds by closing the Controls dialog box.*

You can now tell ControlWizard to create the skeleton files of the MYCLOCK control:

☐ Click the OK button of the ControlWizard dialog box.

> *ControlWizard responds by displaying the New Control Information dialog box. (See Figure 33.8.)*

Figure 33.7. The Controls dialog box.

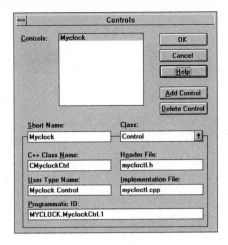

Figure 33.8. The New Control Information dialog box.

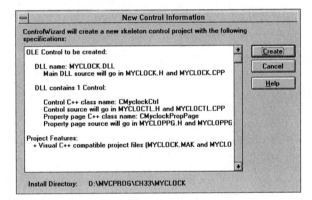

☐ Click the Create button.

> *ControlWizard responds by creating the project file (MAK file) and the skeleton files of the MYCLOCK OCX control.*

Note that now the title of the main window of Visual C++ has the name of the project file of the MYCLOCK OCX control.

NOTE

If you are using Visual C++ 1.51, the name of the project file is MYCLOCK.MAK.

If you are using Visual C++ 2.0, the name of the project file is MYCLOC32.MAK.

What exactly did ControlWizard do for you? If you examine your hard drive, you'll see that ControlWizard created several files in your C:\MVCPROG\CH33\MYCLOCK directory. These files are the "bones" (that is, skeleton) of your MYCLOCK control. Your job, with the aid of Visual C++, is to customize these files so that the MYCLOCK control will look and behave as you want it to.

Testing the MYCLOCK Control Before Customizing It

Before you start customizing the files of the MYCLOCK control, first compile, link, and test the MYCLOCK control in its current state. As you'll see, the skeleton files that ControlWizard created have code in them that actually produces a working OCX control.

To compile and link the MYCLOCK control do the following:

☐ If you are using Visual C++ 1.51, select Make TypeLib from the Tools menu.

> *Visual C++ 1.5 responds by creating a type library (.tlb file) for the MYCLOCK control and by displaying an OK message box with the text* Successfully generated type library tlb16\MYCLOCK.tlb.

☐ Click the OK button of the message box.

NOTE

The preceding two steps are applicable only if you are creating the control with Visual C++ 1.51. If you are creating the control with Visual C++ 2.0, the preceding two steps are not applicable.

☐ Select Build MYCLOCK.DLL (or Build MYCLOCK.OCX) from the Project menu of Visual C++.

> *Visual C++ responds by compiling and linking the files of the MYCLOCK control and by creating the file MYCLOCK.DLL (or MYCLOCK.OCX).*

NOTE

The preceding step asks you to select Build MYCLOCK.DLL (or Build MYCLOCK.OCX) from the Project menu of Visual C++.

If you are using Visual C++ 2.0, your Project menu has the menu item Build MYCLOCK.OCX.

If you are using Visual C++ 1.51, your Project menu has the menu item Build MYCLOCK.DLL.

But wait a minute. How come Visual C++ 1.51 creates for you the file MYCLOCK.DLL? Shouldn't Visual C++ 1.51 create the file MYCLOCK.OCX? After all, you are trying to create an OCX file, not a DLL file.

Well, an OCX control is actually a DLL (dynamic linked library). Once you complete the development of the MYCLOCK control (using Visual C++ 1.51) and you are ready to distribute the MYCLOCK control, you can rename the MYCLOCK.DLL file MYCLOCK.OCX and distribute it to your users as an OCX file. This way your users will know that your MYCLOCK.OCX file is an OCX control. However, while you develop, test, and debug the MYCLOCK control you can leave the extension of the file DLL.

> **NOTE**
>
> As discussed, an OCX control is actually a DLL.
>
> As discussed in Chapter 31, "Creating Your Own DLLs," a DLL is a library that is linked dynamically to the program that uses the DLL.
>
> So when you (or other programmers) write a program that uses your OCX control, you have to distribute to your users the OCX control together with the EXE file of the program.

> **NOTE**
>
> As discussed earlier, to create an OCX control for the 16-bit platform, use Visual C++ 1.51. To create an OCX control for the 32-bit platform, use Visual C++ 2.0.
>
> Once you finish developing an OCX control using Visual C++ 1.51, you should rename the OCX control so that it has a name that identifies it as a 16-bit OCX control (for example, CLOCK16.OCX).
>
> Similarly, once you finish developing an OCX control using Visual C++ 2.0, you should rename the OCX control so that it has a name that identifies it as a 32-bit OCX control (for example, CLOCK32.OCX).
>
> Renaming an OCX control in a way that identifies it as a 16-bit or a 32-bit OCX control is not a requirement, but it will help you (as well as other programmers) identify the platform of the control immediately.

Although you have not yet written a single line of code, thanks to the code that ControlWizard wrote for you, you have in your hands a working OCX control (MYCLOCK). In the following section you'll test the MYCLOCK control. In the next two chapters, you'll customize the files of the MYCLOCK control so that it will look and behave as you want it to.

Registering the MYCLOCK Control

Before you can use the MYCLOCK control, you must first register the control with Windows. That is, you have to provide Windows with some information about the MYCLOCK control. Here is how you do that:

☐ Select Register Control from the Tools menu.

> *Visual C++ responds by registering the MYCLOCK control. Visual C++ knows that you want to register the MYCLOCK control (and not another control) because the project of the MYCLOCK control is currently open. Note that the code that actually registers the MYCLOCK control is inside the MYCLOCK control. This code was written for you by ControlWizard.*

Once Visual C++ finishes registering the MYCLOCK control, an OK message box appears, telling you that the control has been registered successfully.

☐ Click the OK button of the message box.

The registration process of the MYCLOCK control saved information about the MYCLOCK control (such as the name and path of the control) inside a Windows database. This Windows database is called the Registration Database.

Testing the MYCLOCK Control

The ultimate way to test an OCX control is to use a visual programming language that lets the programmer add the OCX control to the Tools window. Once you add the OCX control to the Tools window, you can test the OCX control by placing it inside forms (dialog boxes), by changing the properties of the control, and by attaching code to the events of the control. As discussed at the beginning of this chapter, in the near future, most visual programming languages will allow programmers to add OCX controls to the Tools window.

Another way to test an OCX control is to use the Test Container program that comes with Visual C++. As implied by its name, the Test Container program lets you test an OCX control by placing it inside the window of the Test Container program.

Now use the Test Container program to test the MYCLOCK control:

☐ Select Test Container from the Tools menu of Visual C++.

> *Visual C++ responds by executing the Test Container program. (See Figure 33.9.)*

To place the MYCLOCK control inside the window of the Test Container program do the following:

☐ Select Insert OLE Control from the Edit menu of the Test Container program.

Test Container responds by displaying the Insert OLE Control dialog box. The Insert OLE Control dialog box lists all the names of the controls that are currently registered in Windows.

Figure 33.9. The Test Container program.

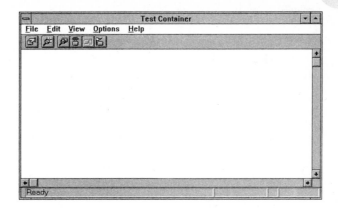

☐ Select the MYCLOCK control and then click the OK button.

> *Test Container responds by inserting the MYCLOCK control. As shown in Figure 33.10, the MYCLOCK control now appears inside the window of Test Container, and the tool icon of the MYCLOCK control appears inside the toolbar of Test Container. (See Figure 33.10.)*

Figure 33.10. The Test Container program after you insert the MYCLOCK control.

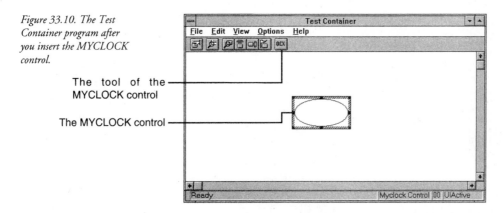

The tool of the MYCLOCK control

The MYCLOCK control

Notice that the tool icon of the MYCLOCK control displays the letters *OCX*. Later, you'll customize the MYCLOCK control so that the tool icon will display a more appropriate picture (namely, a picture of a clock).

Notice also that the MYCLOCK control displays an ellipse inside it. The code that ControlWizard wrote for you is displaying an ellipse inside the control. Later, you'll customize the code of the MYCLOCK control so that it will do what it is supposed to do (that is, display the current time).

As shown in Figure 3.10, the MYCLOCK control is surrounded by a frame with eight small black dots on it. These small dots are the handles of the control. You can use them to size the MYCLOCK control to any desired size. For example, to increase the height of the control do the following:

☐ Drag any of the handles at the bottom of the control's frame downward and then release the mouse.

Once you release the mouse, the control changes its size, and the size of the ellipse inside the control changes accordingly. (See Figure 33.11.)

Figure 33.11. The Test Container program after you increase the size of the MYCLOCK control.

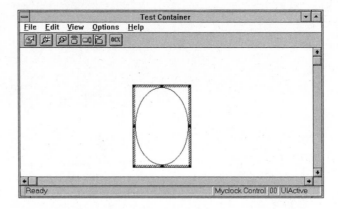

Besides sizing the control, Test Container also allows you to move the control. Here is how you move the control:

☐ Drag the frame of the control to the point where you want to move the control. Do not drag the handles of the control. That is, drag any point of the control's frame except the points where the handles of the control are.

Once you release the mouse, the control moves to the point where you released the mouse. Figure 33.12 shows the window of Test Container after you move the MYCLOCK control to the top-left corner of the window.

Figure 33.12. The Test Container program after you move the MYCLOCK control to the top-left corner of the window.

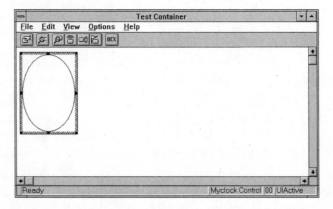

You can place several MYCLOCK controls inside the window of Test Container. Here is how you do that:

☐ Click the tool of the MYCLOCK control on the toolbar of Test Container. (See Figure 33.10.)

> *Test Container responds by placing another MYCLOCK control inside its window. (See Figure 33.13.)*

Figure 33.13. Placing another MYCLOCK control inside the window of Test Container.

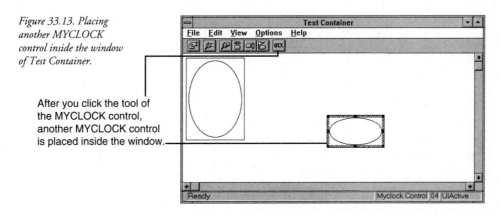

After you click the tool of the MYCLOCK control, another MYCLOCK control is placed inside the window.

☐ Place several more MYCLOCK controls by clicking the tool of the MYCLOCK control.

In the preceding steps, you used Test Container to test the visual aspect of the MYCLOCK control: You placed the control inside the window of Test Container, you sized the control, you moved the control, and you placed several controls inside the window.

Test Container also lets you test the events and properties of the control. However, at this point the MYCLOCK control does not have any events or properties (because ControlWizard could not guess which events and properties you want the control to have). Later when you add properties and events to the MYCLOCK control, you'll use Test Container to test these properties and events.

So as you have just verified with the aid of Test Container, the code that ControlWizard wrote for you produces a functional OCX control. Of course, the code ControlWizard wrote for you does not make the MYCLOCK control behave and look the way that you want it to behave and look. Therefore, in the following section and in the next two chapters, you'll customize the files of the MYCLOCK control until it looks and behaves as you want it to.

☐ Terminate Test Container by selecting Exit from the File menu.

> *Test Container responds by terminating itself.*

Customizing the Picture of the MYCLOCK Control Tool

As shown in Figure 33.10, the icon of the MYCLOCK control tool (inside the toolbar of Test Container) displays a picture of the letters *OCX*. You'll now customize the MYCLOCK control so that the tool of the MYCLOCK control will display a more appropriate picture: a picture of a clock.

To customize the picture of the MYCLOCK control tool, you need to work on the bitmap IDB_MYCLOCK. This bitmap was created by ControlWizard.

To display the IDB_MYCLOCK bitmap with Visual C++ 1.51 do the following:

☐ Select AppStudio from the Tools menu of Visual C++ 1.51, then select Bitmap inside the Type list, and finally, double-click IDB_MYCLOCK inside the Resources list.

To display the IDB_MYCLOCK bitmap with Visual C++ 2.0 do the following:

☐ Double-click myclock.rc inside the MYCLOC32.MAK window, then double-click Bitmaps inside the MYCLOCK.RC window, and finally, double-click IDB_MYCLOCK under the Bitmaps item.

☐ After you display the IDB_MYCLOCK bitmap, use the visual tools of Visual C++ to change the picture of the IDB_MYCLOCK bitmap from the letters *OCX* to a picture of a simple clock—a circle with two hands (lines) inside it.

Figure 33.14 shows the IDB_MYCLOCK bitmap before customization, and Figure 33.15 shows the IDB_MYCLOCK bitmap after customization.

Figure 33.14. The IDB_MYCLOCK bitmap before customization.

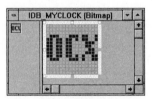

Figure 33.15. The IDB_MYCLOCK bitmap after customization (a simple picture of a clock).

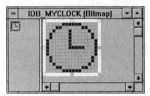

☐ Save your work by selecting Save from the File menu.

To see your work in action do the following:

☐ Select Build MYCLOCK.DLL (or Build MYCLOCK.OCX) from the Project menu of Visual C++.

   Visual C++ responds by compiling and linking the MYCLOCK control.

☐ Select Test Container from the Tools menu of Visual C++.

 Visual C++ responds by running the Test Container program.

☐ Select Insert OLE Control from the Edit menu of the Test Container program.

 Test Container responds by displaying the Insert OLE Control dialog box.

☐ Select the MYCLOCK control and then click the OK button.

 Test Container responds by inserting the MYCLOCK control. As shown in Figure 33.16, the tool icon of the MYCLOCK tool now displays your picture—a picture of a clock!

Figure 33.16. The tool icon of the MYCLOCK control (with a picture of a clock).

The tool of the MYCLOCK control

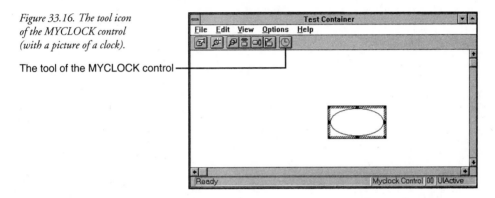

☐ Terminate Test Container by selecting Exit from the File menu.

What You Have Accomplished So Far

In this chapter you used ControlWizard to create the skeleton files for the MYCLOCK OCX control.

As you have seen, even though you have not yet written a single line of code, the skeleton code that ControlWizard wrote for you produces a working control. This control displays an ellipse inside it.

In this chapter you customized the icon of the MYCLOCK control tool so that it displays a picture of a clock.

In the next two chapters you will further customize the MYCLOCK control: You will write the code that is responsible for displaying the current time inside the MYCLOCK control, you'll add properties to the MYCLOCK control, and you'll add events to the MYCLOCK control.

34

Customizing OCX Controls

In this chapter you'll continue

developing the MYCLOCK control

that you created in the previous

chapter—you'll write the code that

makes the control continuously

display the current time, you'll add

properties to the control, and you'll

write the code that sets the initial size

of the control.

Drawing Inside the MYCLOCK Control

Currently, the MYCLOCK control displays an ellipse inside it. That's because the code that ControlWizard wrote for you draws an ellipse. However, you want the MYCLOCK control to display the current time. Therefore, you have to write code that displays the current time inside the control.

You'll now write code that draws text inside the MYCLOCK control.

☐ Start Visual C++.

☐ Open the project file (MAK file) of the MYCLOCK control that you created in the previous chapter (if it's not already open).

☐ Open the file MYCLOCTL.CPP (which is inside the directory \MVCPROG\CH33\MYCLOCK).

The MYCLOCTL.CPP is the implementation file of the MYCLOCK control. It was created for you by ControlWizard and it's where you'll write your own code for customizing the MYCLOCK control.

☐ Locate the function OnDraw() inside the MYCLOCTRL.CPP file.

The OnDraw() function currently looks like this:

```
/////////////////////////////////////////////
// CMyclockCtrl::OnDraw—Drawing function

void CMyclockCtrl::OnDraw(
  CDC* pdc, const CRect& rcBounds, const CRect& rcInvalid)
{
```

```
// TODO: Replace the following code with your own drawing
//       code.
pdc->FillRect(rcBounds,
              CBrush::FromHandle
               ((HBRUSH)GetStockObject(WHITE_BRUSH)));
pdc->Ellipse(rcBounds);

}
```

The OnDraw() function is automatically executed whenever there is a need to draw the control (for example, when someone places the control inside a dialog box for the first time).

The code that is currently inside the OnDraw() function (code that ControlWizard wrote) draws an ellipse inside the control.

Change the code inside the OnDraw() function so that the control will display your own text:

☐ Delete the code that is currently inside the OnDraw() function and replace it with your own custom code so that the OnDraw() function looks like this:

```
void CMyclockCtrl::OnDraw(
  CDC* pdc, const CRect& rcBounds, const CRect& rcInvalid)
{

// TODO: Replace the following code with your own drawing
//       code.

/////////////////////////
// MY CODE STARTS HERE
/////////////////////////

// Draw text inside the control.
pdc->ExtTextOut(rcBounds.left,
                rcBounds.top,
                ETO_CLIPPED,
                rcBounds,
                "This is my first OCX control",
                28,
                NULL);


/////////////////////////
// MY CODE ENDS HERE
/////////////////////////
}
```

☐ Save your work by selecting Save from the File menu.

The code you typed inside the OnDraw() function is made up of one statement:

```
pdc->ExtTextOut(rcBounds.left,
                rcBounds.top,
                ETO_CLIPPED,
                rcBounds,
                "This is my first OCX control",
                28,
                NULL);
```

This statement executes the `ExtTextOut()` function on the `pdc` object to display text inside the control. `pdc` (the first parameter of the `OnDraw()` function) is a pointer to an object of class `CDC`. `pdc` holds the DC (device context) of the control. Therefore, after the preceding statement is executed, the text `This is my first OCX control` will be displayed inside the MYCLOCK control.

Notice that the preceding statement uses the variable `rcBounds`. `rcBounds` (an object of class `CRect`) is the second parameter of the `OnDraw()` function. It specifies the rectangular dimensions (boundaries) of the control. For example, `rcBounds.left` is the x-coordinate of the top-left corner of the control.

> **NOTE**
>
> Use the `ExtTextOut()` member function of the MFC `CDC` to display text inside the control. The first two parameters of the `ExtTextOut()` function are the x,y coordinates of the text to be displayed. The third parameter specifies how the text will be displayed. When the third parameter is set to `ETO_CLIPPED`, the text will be clipped to a rectangle. The fourth parameter specifies the rectangle area in which the text will be displayed. The fifth parameter is a string that holds the text to be displayed, and the sixth parameter is the length of the string to be displayed. The seventh parameter specifies the spacing between the displayed characters. When the seventh parameter is set to `NULL`, the characters will be displayed with the default spacing.

To see your drawing code in action do the following:

☐ Select Build MYCLOCK.DLL (or Build MYCLOCK.OCX) from the Project menu of Visual C++.

   Visual C++ responds by compiling and linking the files of the MYCLOCK control.

☐ Select Test Container from the Tools menu of Visual C++.

   Visual C++ responds by running the Test Container program.

☐ Select Insert OLE Control from the Edit menu of the Test Container program.

   Test Container responds by displaying the Insert OLE Control dialog box.

☐ Select the MYCLOCK control and then click the OK button.

   Test Container responds by inserting the MYCLOCK control. (See Figure 34.1.) As shown in Figure 34.1, the text `This is my first` is displayed inside the control.

☐ Increase the width of the MYCLOCK control so that it will look as shown in Figure 34.2. (To increase the width of the control, drag the handle on the right edge of the control's frame to the right.)

Figure 34.1. The
MYCLOCK control with
the text This is my
first inside it.

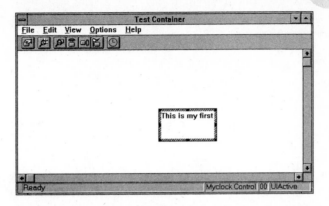

Figure 34.2. The
MYCLOCK control after
you increase its width.

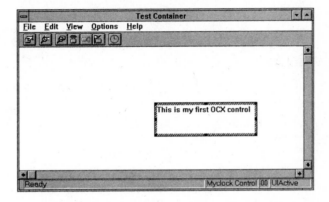

So as you can see, the code that you wrote inside the OnDraw() function is working! Whenever there is a need to redraw the MYCLOCK control (for example, when you place the MYCLOCK control inside the window or after you resize the control), the OnDraw() function is automatically executed, and the code that you wrote inside OnDraw() displays the text This is my first OCX control inside the control.

☐ Place several more controls inside the window of Test Container (by clicking the tool of the MYCLOCK control inside the toolbar of Test Container) and observe how each control has the text This is my first OCX control inside it. Figure 34.3 shows the window of Test Container with several MYCLOCK controls inside it.

Recall that after you place a control inside the window, you can move it to any desired location in the window by dragging any point on the frame of the control except the points where the control's handles are located.

☐ Terminate Test Container by selecting Exit from the File menu.

Figure 34.3. The Test Container window with four MYCLOCK controls inside it.

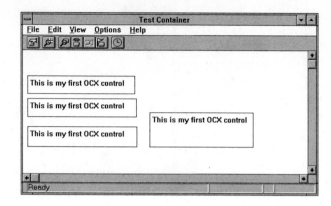

Displaying the Current Time Inside the MYCLOCK Control

Currently the code of the MYCLOCK control displays the text This is my first OCX control. You'll now change the code of the MYCLOCK control so that it will display the current time.

☐ Open the file MYCLOCTL.CPP (if it's not open already).

☐ Modify the OnDraw() function until it looks like this:

```
void CMyclockCtrl::OnDraw(
   CDC* pdc, const CRect& rcBounds, const CRect& rcInvalid)
{

// TODO: Replace the following code with your own drawing
//       code.

/////////////////////////
// MY CODE STARTS HERE
/////////////////////////

char CurrentTime[30];
struct tm *newtime;
long lTime;

// Get the current time
time(&lTime);
newtime=localtime(&lTime);

// Convert the time into a string.
strcpy(CurrentTime, asctime(newtime));

// Pad the string with 1 blank.
CurrentTime[24]=' ';

// Terminate the string.
CurrentTime[25] = 0;
```

```
// Display the current time
pdc->ExtTextOut(rcBounds.left,
                rcBounds.top,
                ETO_CLIPPED,
                rcBounds,
                CurrentTime,
                strlen(CurrentTime),
                NULL);

//////////////////////////
// MY CODE ENDS HERE
//////////////////////////
}
```

☐ Save your work by selecting Save from the File menu.

The first three statements that you typed inside the OnDraw() function declare three local variables:

```
char CurrentTime[30];
struct tm *newtime;
long lTime;
```

The rest of the code you typed uses these three variables to get the current time and to display it:

```
// Get the current time
time(&lTime);
newtime=localtime(&lTime);

// Convert the time into a string.
strcpy(CurrentTime, asctime(newtime));

// Pad the string with 1 blank.
CurrentTime[24]=' ';

// Terminate the string.
CurrentTime[25] = 0;

// Display the current time
pdc->ExtTextOut(rcBounds.left,
                rcBounds.top,
                ETO_CLIPPED,
                rcBounds,
                CurrentTime,
                strlen(CurrentTime),
                NULL);
```

The first statement

```
time(&lTime);
```

uses the time() function to store inside the variable lTime the number of seconds that have elapsed since midnight January 1, 1970. Of course, this number is not friendly enough, so you use the next statement

```
newtime=localtime(&lTime);
```

to convert the number that is stored in lTime into a friendlier representation of time. This statement uses the localtime() function to convert lTime into a structure of type tm and assigns the result to the structure newtime. So at this point, the fields of the structure newtime store the current time.

The next statement is

```
strcpy(CurrentTime, asctime(newtime));
```

This statement uses the asctime() function to convert the current time that is stored in newtime into a string. The resultant string is assigned to the CurrentTime string. So at this point CurrentTime contains a string with 24 characters that represents the current time. This string includes the day of week, month, time, and year.

The next statement

```
CurrentTime[24]=' ';
```

fills the 24th character of the CurrentTime string with a blank. This is done because you want to pad the end of the CurrentTime string with one blank (for cosmetic reasons).

The next statement

```
CurrentTime[25]=0;
```

terminates the CurrentTime string.

Finally, the last statement you typed inside the OnDraw() function uses the ExtTextOut() function to display the CurrentTime string inside the control:

```
pdc->ExtTextOut(rcBounds.left,
                rcBounds.top,
                ETO_CLIPPED,
                rcBounds,
                CurrentTime,
                strlen(CurrentTime),
                NULL);
```

Now see the code you typed inside the OnDraw() function in action:

☐ Select Build MYCLOCK.DLL (or Build MYCLOCK.OCX) from the Project menu of Visual C++.

   Visual C++ responds by compiling and linking the files of the MYCLOCK control.

☐ Select Test Container from the Tools menu of Visual C++.

   Visual C++ responds by running the Test Container program.

☐ Select Insert OLE Control from the Edit menu of the Test Container program.

   Test Container responds by displaying the Insert OLE Control dialog box.

☐ Select the MYCLOCK control and then click the OK button.

   Test Container responds by inserting the MYCLOCK control.

☐ Increase the width of the MYCLOCK control so that it looks as shown in Figure 34.4.

*Figure 34.4. The
MYCLOCK control
displaying the current time.*

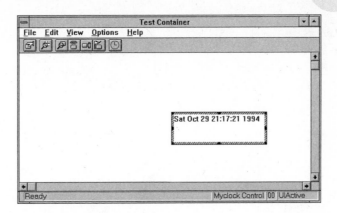

As you can see, the code you wrote inside the OnDraw() function displays the current time inside the control. However, the time is not updated continuously. In the following section you will enhance the code of the MYCLOCK project so that the control will display the current time continuously.

☐ Terminate Test Container by selecting Exit from the File menu.

Displaying the Current Time Continuously

In order to display the time continuously, you will now do the following:

- Write code that installs a timer for the MYCLOCK control with a 1,000-millisecond interval.
- Attach code to the WM_TIMER event of the MYCLOCK control.

After you install such a timer, Windows sends a WM_TIMER message every 1000 milliseconds (that is, every second) to the MYCLOCK control, and the code that you attach to the WM_TIMER event of the MYCLOCK control is executed. The code you will attach to the WM_TIMER event will simply display the current time. Therefore, the current time will be displayed continuously.

Because you want to install the timer when the control is first created, you need to attach the code that installs the timer to the WM_CREATE event of the control:

☐ Display the ClassWizard dialog box (by selecting ClassWizard from the Browse menu of Visual C++ 1.51 or by selecting ClassWizard from the Project menu of Visual C++ 2.0).

☐ Select the Message Maps tab of ClassWizard.

☐ Use ClassWizard to select the following event:

> Class Name: CMyclockCtrl
> Object ID: CMyclockCtrl
> Message: WM_CREATE

Your ClassWizard dialog box should now look like the one shown in Figure 34.5.

Figure 34.5. Selecting the
WM_CREATE event in
ClassWizard.

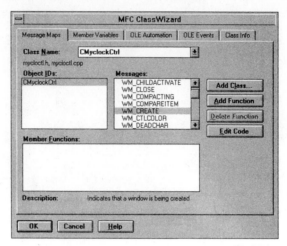

☐ Click the Add Function button.

> *Visual C++ responds by adding the* OnCreate() *member function to the* CMyclockCtrl *class.*

☐ Click the Edit Code button of ClassWizard.

> *ClassWizard responds by opening the file MYCLOCTL.CPP, with the function* OnCreate()
> *ready to be edited by you.*

☐ Write code inside the OnCreate() function so that it looks like this:

```
int CMyclockCtrl::OnCreate(LPCREATESTRUCT lpCreateStruct)
{

if (COleControl::OnCreate(lpCreateStruct) == -1)
   return -1;

// TODO: Add your specialized creation code here

///////////////////////////
// MY CODE STARTS HERE
///////////////////////////

// Install a timer.
SetTimer(1, 1000, NULL);

///////////////////////////
// MY CODE ENDS HERE
///////////////////////////

return 0;

}
```

☐ Save your work by selecting Save from the File menu.

The code you typed inside the OnCreate() function is made of one statement:

```
SetTimer(1, 1000, NULL);
```

This statement uses the SetTimer() function to install a timer with a 1000-millisecond interval. From now on, Windows will send a WM_TIMER message to the control every 1000 milliseconds.

Now you need to attach code to the WM_TIMER event of the control:

☐ Display the ClassWizard dialog box (by selecting ClassWizard from the Browse menu of Visual C++ 1.51 or by selecting ClassWizard from the Project menu of Visual C++ 2.0).

☐ Select the Message Maps tab of ClassWizard.

☐ Use ClassWizard to select the following event:

Class Name:	CMyclockCtrl
Object ID:	CMyclockCtrl
Message:	WM_TIMER

☐ Click the Add Function button.

Visual C++ responds by adding the OnTimer() *member function to the* CMyclockCtrl *class.*

☐ Click the Edit Code button of ClassWizard.

ClassWizard responds by opening the file MYCLOCTL.CPP, with the function OnTimer() *ready to be edited by you.*

☐ Write code inside the OnTimer() function so that it looks like this:

```
void CMyclockCtrl::OnTimer(UINT nIDEvent)
{

// TODO: Add your message handler code here and/or call
//       default

/////////////////////////
// MY CODE STARTS HERE
/////////////////////////

// Trigger a call to the OnDraw() function.
InvalidateControl();

/////////////////////////
// MY CODE ENDS HERE
/////////////////////////

COleControl::OnTimer(nIDEvent);

}
```

☐ Save your work by selecting Save from the File menu.

The code you typed inside the OnTimer() function is made of one statement:

```
InvalidateControl();
```

This statement uses the InvalidateControl() function to trigger a call to the OnDraw() function that you wrote earlier. That is, calling the InvalidateControl() function causes the control to redraw itself.

So the code you wrote inside the OnCreate() function installs a timer with a 1000-millisecond interval. As a result, the code you wrote inside the OnTimer() function is automatically executed every 1000 milliseconds. This code causes the execution of the OnDraw() function by calling the InvalidateControl() function. The code you wrote inside the OnDraw() function displays the current time. Therefore, every 1000 milliseconds (1 second) the displayed time is updated.

To see your code in action do the following:

☐ Select Build MYCLOCK.DLL (or Build MYCLOCK.OCX) from the Project menu of Visual C++.

   Visual C++ responds by compiling and linking the files of the MYCLOCK control.

☐ Select Test Container from the Tools menu of Visual C++.

   Visual C++ responds by running the Test Container program.

☐ Select Insert OLE Control from the Edit menu of the Test Container program.

   Test Container responds by displaying the Insert OLE Control dialog box.

☐ Select the MYCLOCK control and then click the OK button.

   Test Container responds by inserting the MYCLOCK control.

☐ Increase the width of the MYCLOCK control so that it will look as shown back in Figure 34.4 (that is, increase the width of the control so that you are able to see the seconds portion of the time).

   As you can see, now the MYCLOCK control displays the current time continuously. That is, the seconds portion of the time keeps changing.

☐ Terminate Test Container by selecting Exit from the File menu.

Adding Stock (Standard) Properties to the MYCLOCK Control

Stock properties (or standard properties) are predefined. As you'll soon see, adding a stock property to a control is very easy. Table 34.1 lists all the stock properties you can add to an OCX control.

Table 34.1. Stock properties.

Property	Stored Value
BackColor	The control's background color
BorderStyle	The control's border style

Property	Stored Value
Caption	The control's caption
Enabled	The control's enabled/disabled status
Font	The control's font for drawing text
ForeColor	The control's foreground color
hWnd	The control's window handle
Text	The control's text

For practice, add two stock properties to the MYCLOCK control: BackColor and ForeColor. The BackColor property determines the background color of the control, and the ForeColor property determines the foreground color of the control.

Follow these steps to add the BackColor property to the MYCLOCK control:

☐ Display the ClassWizard dialog box (by selecting ClassWizard from the Browse menu of Visual C++ 1.51 or by selecting ClassWizard from the Project menu of Visual C++ 2.0).

☐ Select the OLE Automation tab of ClassWizard. (See Figure 34.6.)

Figure 34.6. Selecting the OLE Automation tab of ClassWizard.

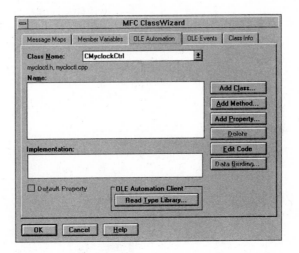

☐ Make sure that the Class Name box is set to CMyclockCtrl, as shown in Figure 34.6.

☐ Click the Add Property button.

Visual C++ responds by displaying the Add Property dialog box. (See Figure 34.7.)

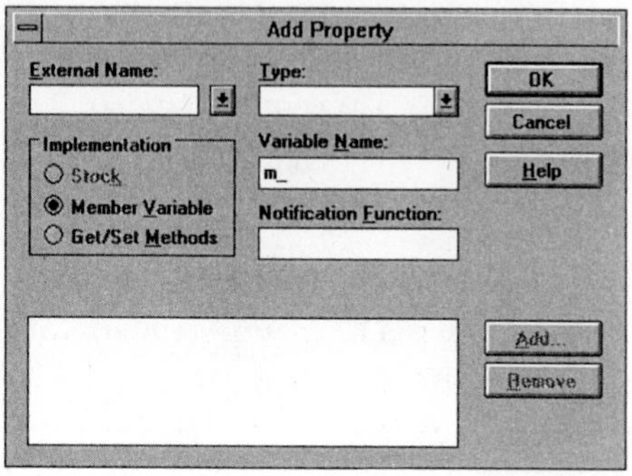

Figure 34.7. The Add Property dialog box.

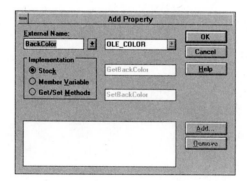

☐ Click the down arrow of the External Name combo box, and select BackColor from the list that pops up.

Your Add Property dialog box should now look like the one shown in Figure 34.8.

Figure 34.8. The Add Property dialog box after you set the External Name combo box to BackColor.

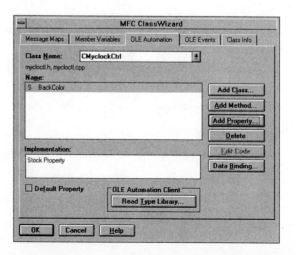

☐ Click the OK button of the Add Property dialog box.

The ClassWizard dialog box reappears, as shown in Figure 34.9.

Figure 34.9. The ClassWizard dialog box after you add the BackColor stock property.

As shown in Figure 34.9, the Name list now contains the property BackColor. Notice that the letter *S* appears to the left of BackColor. This *S* serves as an indication that the BackColor property is a stock property.

Now add the ForeColor property:

☐ Click the Add Property button.

Visual C++ responds by displaying the Add Property dialog box.

☐ Click the down arrow of the External Name combo box, and select ForeColor from the list that pops up.

☐ Click the OK button of the Add Property dialog box.

The ClassWizard dialog box reappears, as shown in Figure 34.10.

Figure 34.10. The ClassWizard dialog box after you add the ForeColor stock property.

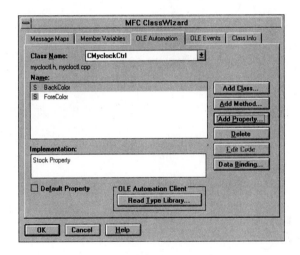

As shown in Figure 34.10, now the Name list contains both the BackColor property and ForeColor property. The letter *S* appears to the left of both properties, because both the BackColor property and the ForeColor property are stock properties.

☐ Click the OK button of ClassWizard.

That's it! You have finished adding the BackColor and ForeColor properties to the MYCLOCK control.

To verify that the MYCLOCK control now has the BackColor and ForeColor properties, do the following:

☐ If you are using Visual C++ 1.51, select Make TypeLib from the Tools menu.

Visual C++ 1.5 responds by creating the type library (.tlb file) for the MYCLOCK control and by displaying an OK message box with the text `Successfully generated type library tlb16\MYCLOCK.tlb`.

☐ Click the OK button of the message box.

> **NOTE**
>
> The preceding two steps are applicable only if you are creating the control with Visual C++ 1.51. If you are creating the control with Visual C++ 2.0, the preceding two steps are not applicable.
>
> In Visual C++ 1.51, after you add a property (or an event or a method) to the control, you have to rebuild the type library prior to building the project. You don't have to do that in Visual C++ 2.0.

☐ Select Build MYCLOCK.DLL (or Build MYCLOCK.OCX) from the Project menu of Visual C++.

> *Visual C++ responds by compiling and linking the files of the MYCLOCK control.*

☐ Select Test Container from the Tools menu of Visual C++.

> *Visual C++ responds by running the Test Container program.*

☐ Select Insert OLE Control from the Edit menu of the Test Container program.

> *Test Container responds by displaying the Insert OLE Control dialog box.*

☐ Select the MYCLOCK control and then click the OK button.

> *Test Container responds by inserting the MYCLOCK control.*

☐ Increase the width of the MYCLOCK control so that it looks as shown back in Figure 34.4 (that is, increase the width of the control so that you are able to see the entire text of the current time).

☐ Select Properties from the View menu of Test Container.

> *Test Container responds by displaying the Properties dialog box. (See Figure 34.11.)*

Figure 34.11. The Properties dialog box of Test Container.

☐ Click the down arrow of the Property combo box.

> *Test Container responds by popping up a list with the properties of the MYCLOCK control. (See Figure 34.12.) As you can see, the only properties listed are the BackColor and ForeColor properties (because so far these are the only properties you've added to the MYCLOCK control).*

Figure 34.12. Selecting a
property from a list
(currently the MYCLOCK
control has only the
BackColor and ForeColor
properties).

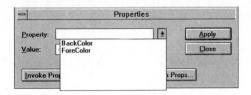

☐ Select the BackColor property.

Your Properties dialog box should now look like the one shown in Figure 34.13.

Figure 34.13. The
Properties dialog box after
you select the BackColor
property.

As you can see from Figure 34.13, the Properties dialog box displays the current value of the
BackColor property, and it enables you to change this value. You can specify a color by typing the
corresponding value of the color, or you can select the color visually by clicking the three dots button (…) to the right of the Value edit box.

☐ Click the three dots button to the right of the Value edit box.

A Color dialog box appears. (See Figure 34.14.)

Figure 34.14. The Colors
dialog box.

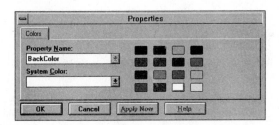

If you try to set the BackColor property of the MYCLOCK control to any color, you'll see that
nothing happens to the control. That is, the background color of the control will not change to the
color you selected. Why not? You have not yet written the code that accomplishes that. All you did
is add the BackColor property to the MYCLOCK control—you did not write the code that makes
the BackColor property functional.

In other words, at this point the MYCLOCK control has the BackColor property. Therefore, the
user can see this property in the Properties dialog box and the user can even select a color from a
Colors dialog box. However, when the user selects a color, nothing happens.

In the following section, you'll write the code that adds functionality to the BackColor and ForeColor properties. When the user sets the BackColor property to a certain value, your code will change the background color of the control to the color that the user selected. When the user sets the ForeColor property to a certain value, your code will change the foreground color of the control to the color the user selected.

☐ Terminate Test Container by selecting Exit from the File menu.

Making the BackColor and ForeColor Properties Functional

As you have seen, at this point the MYCLOCK control has the BackColor and ForeColor properties, but the MYCLOCK control does not make use of the values that are stored in these properties. That is, when the user changes these properties, the control does not change its background and foreground colors.

You'll now write the code that makes use of the values that are stored in the BackColor and ForeColor properties. You'll write this code inside the OnDraw() function.

☐ Open the file MYCLOCTL.CPP (if it's not open already).

☐ Insert the following statements at the beginning of the OnDraw() function:

```
// Set the foreground color (i.e. the text color)
// according to the ForeColor property.
pdc->SetTextColor(TranslateColor(GetForeColor()));

// Set the background mode to transparent mode.
pdc->SetBkMode(TRANSPARENT);

// Create a brush based on the BackColor property.
CBrush bkBrush(TranslateColor(GetBackColor()));

// Paint the background using the BackColor property
pdc->FillRect(rcBounds, &bkBrush);
```

The remaining code in the OnDraw() function (code that you wrote earlier) should remain as is. After inserting the preceding statements at the beginning of the OnDraw() function, your OnDraw() function should look like this:

```
void CMyclockCtrl::OnDraw(
  CDC* pdc, const CRect& rcBounds, const CRect& rcInvalid)
{

// TODO: Replace the following code with your own drawing
//       code.

///////////////////////////
// MY CODE STARTS HERE
///////////////////////////

// Set the foreground color (i.e. the text color)
// according to the ForeColor property.
pdc->SetTextColor(TranslateColor(GetForeColor()));
```

```
// Set the background mode to transparent mode.
pdc->SetBkMode(TRANSPARENT);

// Create a brush based on the BackColor property.
CBrush bkBrush(TranslateColor(GetBackColor()));

// Paint the background using the BackColor property
pdc->FillRect(rcBounds, &bkBrush);

char CurrentTime[30];
struct tm *newtime;
long lTime;

// Get the current time
time(&lTime);
newtime=localtime(&lTime);

// Convert the time into a string.
strcpy(CurrentTime, asctime(newtime));

// Pad the string with 1 blank.
CurrentTime[24]=' ';

// Terminate the string.
CurrentTime[25] = 0;

// Display the current time
pdc->ExtTextOut(rcBounds.left,
                rcBounds.top,
                ETO_CLIPPED,
                rcBounds,
                CurrentTime,
                strlen(CurrentTime),
                NULL);

////////////////////////
// MY CODE ENDS HERE
////////////////////////

}
```

☐ Save your work by selecting Save from the File menu.

The statements you added to the beginning of the OnDraw() function change the background color and foreground color of the MYCLOCK control according to the current values of the BackColor and ForeColor properties. Therefore, whenever there is a need to redraw the control (that is, whenever the OnDraw() function is executed), the control will be painted with the background and foreground colors that are currently stored in the BackColor and ForeColor properties.

The first statement you added to the beginning of the OnDraw() function

```
pdc->SetTextColor(TranslateColor(GetForeColor()));
```

sets the text color (that is, the foreground color) of the control according to the current value of the ForeColor property. Notice that the value of the ForeColor property is retrieved with the GetForeColor() function.

The next statement

```
pdc->SetBkMode(TRANSPARENT);
```

sets the background mode to transparent mode.

The last two statements you added to the beginning of the OnDraw() function are

```
// Create a brush based on the BackColor property.
CBrush bkBrush(TranslateColor(GetBackColor()));

// Paint the background using the BackColor property
pdc->FillRect(rcBounds, &bkBrush);
```

The first statement

```
CBrush bkBrush(TranslateColor(GetBackColor()));
```

creates a brush (bkBrush) based on the current value of the BackColor property. Notice that you retrieve the BackColor property by using the GetBackColor() function.

The second statement

```
pdc->FillRect(rcBounds, &bkBrush);
```

fills the control with the color of the bkBrush brush (that is, with the color of the BackColor property). Notice that the first parameter of the FillRect() function is rcBounds. rcBounds (an object of class CRect) is the second parameter of the OnDraw() function. It specifies the rectangular dimensions (boundaries) of the control.

To see the code that you added to the OnDraw() function in action do the following:

☐ Select Build MYCLOCK.DLL (or Build MYCLOCK.OCX) from the Project menu of Visual C++.

   Visual C++ responds by compiling and linking the files of the MYCLOCK control.

☐ Select Test Container from the Tools menu of Visual C++.

   Visual C++ responds by running the Test Container program.

☐ Select Insert OLE Control from the Edit menu of the Test Container program.

   Test Container responds by displaying the Insert OLE Control dialog box.

☐ Select the MYCLOCK control and then click the OK button.

   Test Container responds by inserting the MYCLOCK control.

☐ Increase the width of the MYCLOCK control so that you are able to see the entire text of the current time.

☐ Select Properties from the View menu of Test Container.

   Test Container responds by displaying the Properties dialog box.

☐ Click the down arrow of the Property combo box.

> *Test Container responds by popping up a list with the properties of the MYCLOCK control.*

☐ Select the BackColor property.

☐ Click the three dots button to the right of the Value edit box.

> *A Colors dialog box appears. (See Figure 34.14.)*

☐ Select the red color (by clicking the rectangle that is painted red) and then click the Apply Now button.

☐ Click the OK button of the Colors dialog box and then click the Close button of the Properties dialog box.

> *As you can see, the control changed its background color to red! The code that you added to the* OnDraw() *function is working!*

Similarly, you can experiment with the ForeColor property—you will see that after you set the ForeColor property to a certain color, the foreground color of the control (that is, the color of the text) changes accordingly. When you select a color in the Colors dialog box, don't forget to first click the Apply Now button of the Colors dialog box, then the OK button of the Colors dialog box, and finally the Close button of the Properties dialog box.

☐ Terminate Test Container by selecting Exit from the File menu.

Setting the Initial Size of the MYCLOCK Control

As you have seen in the preceding steps, when you place the MYCLOCK control inside the window of Test Container, the initial size of the MYCLOCK control is not wide enough. That is, in order to see the seconds portion of the displayed time, you have to increase the width of the control.

Now add code that sets the initial size of the MYCLOCK control so that when the user places the MYCLOCK control inside a window, the control will be wide enough.

☐ Open the file MYCLOCTRL.CPP (if it's not open already).

☐ Locate the constructor function of the CMyclockCtrl class inside the MYCLOCTRL.CPP file.

The constructor function currently looks like this:

```
/////////////////////////////////////////////////
// CMyclockCtrl::CMyclockCtrl—Constructor
CMyclockCtrl::CMyclockCtrl()
{
InitializeIIDs(&IID_DMyclock, &IID_DMyclockEvents);

// TODO: Initialize your control's instance data here.

}
```

☐ Add code to the constructor function so that it looks like this:

```
CMyclockCtrl::CMyclockCtrl()
{
InitializeIIDs(&IID_DMyclock, &IID_DMyclockEvents);

// TODO: Initialize your control's instance data here.

///////////////////////////
// MY CODE STARTS HERE
///////////////////////////

// Set initial size of control to width=200, height=15.
SetInitialSize(200, 15);

///////////////////////////
// MY CODE ENDS HERE
///////////////////////////


}
```

☐ Save your work by selecting Save from the File menu.

The code you typed inside the constructor function is made of one statement:

```
SetInitialSize(200, 15);
```

This statement uses the `SetInitialSize()` function to set the initial width of the control to 200 and the initial height of the control to 15.

To see your code in action do the following:

☐ Select Build MYCLOCK.DLL (or Build MYCLOCK.OCX) from the Project menu of Visual C++.

   Visual C++ responds by compiling and linking the files of the MYCLOCK control.

☐ Select Test Container from the Tools menu of Visual C++.

   Visual C++ responds by running the Test Container program.

☐ Select Insert OLE Control from the Edit menu of the Test Container program.

   Test Container responds by displaying the Insert OLE Control dialog box.

☐ Select the MYCLOCK control and then click the OK button.

   Test Container responds by inserting the MYCLOCK control.

As you can see, the MYCLOCK control is now wide enough! That is, you don't have to increase the size of the control in order to see the seconds portion of the time.

☐ Terminate Test Container by selecting Exit from the File menu.

Adding a Custom Property to the MYCLOCK Control

In many cases, you will have to add a property to your OCX control that is not a standard property. Such a property is called a custom property (a property that is custom-made by you).

In the following steps you'll add an additional property to the MYCLOCK control. The name of this property will be UpdateInterval and it will be used for storing numbers. For now, don't concern yourself with the purpose of the UpdateInterval property. Later you will make use of this property, but now all you want to do is add this property to the MYCLOCK control.

Follow these steps to add the UpdateInterval custom property to the MYCLOCK control:

☐ Display the ClassWizard dialog box (by selecting ClassWizard from the Browse menu of Visual C++ 1.51 or by selecting ClassWizard from the Project menu of Visual C++ 2.0).

☐ Select the OLE Automation tab of ClassWizard. (See Figure 34.15.)

Figure 34.15. The OLE Automation tab.

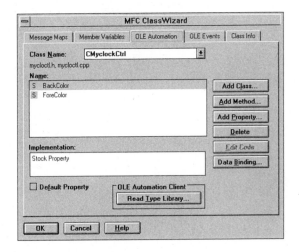

☐ Make sure that the Class Name box is set to CMyclockCtrl, as shown in Figure 34.15.

☐ Click the Add Property button.

> *Visual C++ responds by displaying the Add Property dialog box.*

☐ Type inside the External Name combo box UpdateInterval.

☐ Set the Type list box to long.

☐ Make sure that the Member Variable option is selected inside the Implementation frame.

Your Add Property dialog box should now look like the one shown in Figure 34.16.

Figure 34.16. The Add Property dialog box after you set the External Name combo box to UpdateInterval and set the Type list box to long.

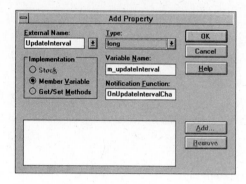

By setting the Add Property dialog box as shown in Figure 34.16, you are specifying that the name of the new property should be UpdateInterval and that this property will be used to hold numbers of type long.

As shown in Figure 34.16, the Variable Name box is set to m_updateInterval. This means that the variable that will be associated with the UpdateInterval property will be m_updateInterval. m_updateInterval will be a data member of the CMyclockCtrl class.

As shown in Figure 34.16, the Notification Function box is set to OnUpdateIntervalChange. This means that whenever someone changes the value of the UpdateInterval property, the function OnUpdateIntervalChange() will be executed automatically. You'll write the code of the OnUpdateIntervalChange() function later.

☐ Click the OK button of the Add Property dialog box.

The ClassWizard dialog box reappears, as shown in Figure 34.17.

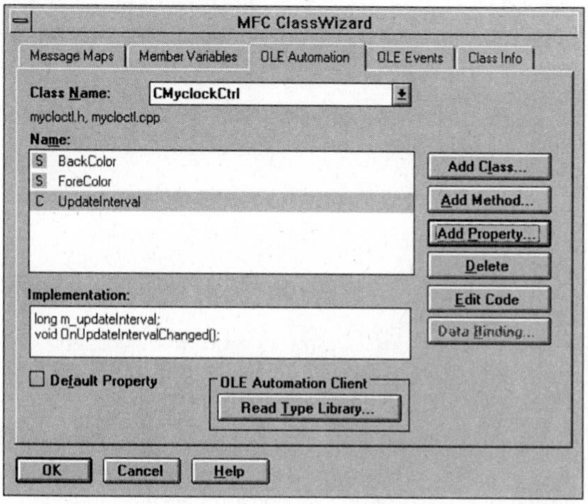

Figure 34.17. The ClassWizard dialog box after you add the UpdateInterval custom property.

As shown in Figure 34.17, the Name list now contains the property UpdateInterval. Notice that the letter *C* appears to the left of UpdateInterval. This *C* serves as an indication that the UpdateInterval property is a custom property.

That's it! You've finished adding the UpdateInterval custom property to the MYCLOCK control.

To verify that the MYCLOCK control now has the UpdateInterval property do the following:

☐ If you are using Visual C++ 1.51, select Make TypeLib from the Tools menu.

> *Visual C++ 1.51 responds by creating the type library (.tlb file) for the MYCLOCK control and by displaying an OK message box with the text* `Successfully generated type library tlb16\MYCLOCK.tlb`.

☐ Click the OK button of the message box.

> **NOTE**
>
> The preceding two steps are applicable only if you are creating the control with Visual C++ 1.51. If you are creating the control with Visual C++ 2.0, the preceding two steps are not applicable.
>
> As stated earlier, in Visual C++ 1.51, after adding a property (or an event or a method) to the control, you have to rebuild the type library prior to building the project. You don't have to do that in Visual C++ 2.0.

☐ Select Build MYCLOCK.DLL (or Build MYCLOCK.OCX) from the Project menu of Visual C++.

> *Visual C++ responds by compiling and linking the files of the MYCLOCK control.*

☐ Select Test Container from the Tools menu of Visual C++.

> *Visual C++ responds by running the Test Container program.*

☐ Select Insert OLE Control from the Edit menu of the Test Container program.

> *Test Container responds by displaying the Insert OLE Control dialog box.*

☐ Select the MYCLOCK control and then click the OK button.

> *Test Container responds by inserting the MYCLOCK control.*

☐ Select Properties from the View menu of Test Container.

☐ Click the down arrow of the Property combo box.

> *Test Container responds by popping up a list with the properties of the MYCLOCK control. (See Figure 34.18.) As you can see, the UpdateInterval property that you added to the control is in the list.*

Figure 34.18. Selecting a property from a list. (The MYCLOCK control now has three properties: BackColor, ForeColor, and UpdateInterval.)

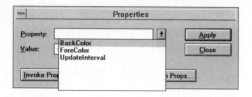

☐ Select the UpdateInterval property.

> *Your Properties dialog box should now look like the one shown in Figure 34.19.*

Figure 34.19. The Properties dialog box after you select the UpdateInterval property.

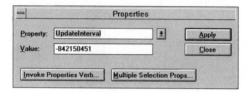

As you can see from Figure 34.19, the Properties dialog box displays the current value of the UpdateInterval property, and it enables you to change this value. You can specify a new value for the UpdateInterval property by typing the desired value inside the Value edit box and then clicking the Apply button.

If you try to set the UpdateInterval property of the MYCLOCK control to any value, the UpdateInterval property will be changed to the new value, but nothing will happen to the control. Why not? You have not yet written the code that makes the UpdateInterval property functional. In other words, at this point the MYCLOCK control has the UpdateInterval property. Therefore, the user can see this property in the Properties dialog box and the user can even change the value of this property. However, when the user changes the value of the property, nothing happens to the control.

You'll write the code that makes the UpdateInterval property functional later in this chapter.

☐ Terminate Test Container by selecting Exit from the File menu.

Initializing the UpdateInterval Property

At this point, when the user places the MYCLOCK control inside a dialog box (or inside a form), the UpdateInterval property is not initialized to any specific value. As shown in Figure 34.19, the initial value of the UpdateInterval property is some large negative value.

You'll now write code that initializes the UpdateInterval property to 1000. Why to 1000 and not to some other value? As you'll see later, the UpdateInterval property will be used for setting the timer interval of the MYCLOCK control. Recall that in the OnCreate() function you set the interval of the timer to 1000 milliseconds. Therefore, the initial value of the UpdateInterval property should be 1000.

To write the code that initializes the UpdateInterval property to 1000 do the following:

☐ Open the file MYCLOCTRL.CPP (if it's not open already).

☐ Locate the function `DoPropExchange()` inside the MYCLOCTRL.CPP file.

The `DoPropExchange()` function currently looks like this:

```
void CMyclockCtrl::DoPropExchange(CPropExchange* pPX)
{
ExchangeVersion(pPX, MAKELONG(_wVerMinor, _wVerMajor));
COleControl::DoPropExchange(pPX);

// TODO: Call PX functions for each persistent custom
//       property.

}
```

☐ Add code to the `DoPropExchange()` function so that it looks like this:

```
void CMyclockCtrl::DoPropExchange(CPropExchange* pPX)
{
ExchangeVersion(pPX, MAKELONG(_wVerMinor, _wVerMajor));
COleControl::DoPropExchange(pPX);

// TODO: Call PX_ functions for each persistent custom
//       property.

//////////////////////////
// MY CODE STARTS HERE
//////////////////////////

// Initialize the UpdateInterval property to 1000.
PX_Long(pPX, _T("UpdateIntrval"), m_updateInterval, 1000);

//////////////////////////
// MY CODE ENDS HERE
//////////////////////////

}
```

☐ Save your work by selecting Save from the File menu.

The code you typed inside the `DoPropExchange()` is made up of one statement:

```
PX_Long(pPX, _T("UpdateIntrval"), m_updateInterval, 1000);
```

This statement uses the `PX_Long()` function to initialize the value of the UpdateInterval property to 1000. The `PX_Long()` function is used because the UpdateInterval property is of type `long`. To initialize other types of properties you can use other `PX_` functions such as `PX_Bool()`, `PX_Short`, and `PX_String()`.

NOTE

Be careful when you type the statement

```
PX_Long(pPX, _T("UpdateIntrval"), m_updateInterval, 1000);
```

> The second parameter is _T("UpdateInterval") because UpdateInterval is the property you are initializing.
>
> The third parameter is m_updateInterval (not m_UpdateInterval) because m_updateInterval is the variable that is associated with the UpdateInterval property. (Refer back to Figure 34.16.) That is, as you can see from Figure 34.16, when you added the UpdateInterval property, you specified the name of the variable as m_updateInterval (not m_UpdateInterval).

To see your initialization code in action do the following:

☐ Select Build MYCLOCK.DLL (or Build MYCLOCK.OCX) from the Project menu of Visual C++.

   Visual C++ responds by compiling and linking the files of the MYCLOCK control.

☐ Select Test Container from the Tools menu of Visual C++.

   Visual C++ responds by running the Test Container program.

☐ Select Insert OLE Control from the Edit menu of the Test Container program.

   Test Container responds by displaying the Insert OLE Control dialog box.

☐ Select the MYCLOCK control and then click the OK button.

   Test Container responds by inserting the MYCLOCK control.

☐ Select Properties from the View menu of Test Container.

☐ Click the down arrow of the Property combo box and then select the UpdateInterval property from the list that pops up.

Your Properties dialog box should now look like the one shown in Figure 34.20. As expected, the initial value of the UpdateInterval property is 1000. The code you wrote inside the DoPropExchange() function is working!

Figure 34.20. The Properties dialog box after you select the UpdateInterval property. (The value of the UpdateInterval property is initially 1000.)

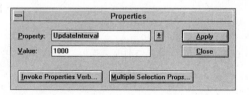

☐ Terminate Test Container by selecting Exit from the File menu.

Making the UpdateInterval Property Functional

At this point the MYCLOCK control has the UpdateInterval property (Figure 34.20), but this property does not do anything. That is, you managed to add the UpdateInterval property to the

MYCLOCK control, and you managed to initialize the value of this property to 1000, but if someone sets the UpdateInterval property to any value, it has no effect on the control. You'll now add code to the MYCLOCK control that makes the UpdateInterval property functional.

What should the UpdateInterval property do? As its name implies, this property should determine the interval at which the MYCLOCK control updates itself. Currently, the MYCLOCK control updates the displayed time every 1000 milliseconds (because you installed the timer of the control in the `OnCreate()` function with a 1000-millisecond interval). You'll now enhance the code of the MYCLOCK control, so that the MYCLOCK control will update the displayed time every X milliseconds, where X is the current value of the UpdateInterval property. Here is how you do that:

☐ Open the file MYCLOCTRL.CPP (if it's not open already).

☐ Locate the function `OnUpdateIntervalChanged()` inside the MYCLOCTRL.CPP file.

The `OnUpdateIntervalChanged()` function currently looks like this:

```
void CMyclockCtrl::OnUpdateIntervalChanged()
{

// TODO: Add notification handler code

SetModifiedFlag();

}
```

ClassWizard wrote for you the `OnUpdateIntervalChanged()` function when you added the UpdateInterval property. As implied by its name, the `OnUpdateIntervalChanged()` function is automatically executed whenever someone changes the value of the UpdateInterval property.

☐ Add code to the `OnUpdateIntervalChanged()` function so that it looks like this:

```
void CMyclockCtrl::OnUpdateIntervalChanged()
{

// TODO: Add notification handler code

/////////////////////////
// MY CODE STARTS HERE
/////////////////////////

// Re-install the timer with interval set
// to the current value of the UpdateInterval
// property.
SetTimer(1, (UINT)m_updateInterval, NULL);

/////////////////////////
// MY CODE ENDS HERE
/////////////////////////

SetModifiedFlag();

}
```

☐ Save your work by selecting Save from the File menu.

The code you added to the `OnUpdateIntervalChanged()` function is made up of a single statement:

```
SetTimer(1, (UINT)m_updateInterval, NULL);
```

This statement re-installs the timer and sets the interval of the timer to the value of the variable `m_updateInterval`. Recall that `m_updateInterval` is the variable of the UpdateInterval property. Therefore, whenever someone changes the value of the UpdateInterval property, the interval of the timer changes accordingly. Note that in the preceding statement the cast (`UINT`) is used, because the `SetTimer()` function expects its second parameter to be of type `UINT`, and the UpdateInterval property is defined as type `long`.

> **NOTE**
>
> Be careful when you type the statement
>
> ```
> SetTimer(1, (UINT)m_updateInterval, NULL);
> ```
>
> The second parameter is `m_updateInterval` (not `m_UpdateInterval`).

Recall that in the `OnCreate()` function you set the interval of the timer to 1000 milliseconds with the statement

```
SetTimer(1, 1000, NULL);
```

Now change the `OnCreate()` function so that it will use the current value of the UpdateInterval property and not the hard-coded value of 1000. This way, whenever a MYCLOCK control is created, the initial value of the timer interval will be the same as the current value of the UpdateInterval property.

☐ Locate the `OnCreate()` function inside the MYCLOCTRL.CPP file and change it so that it looks like this:

```
int CMyclockCtrl::OnCreate(LPCREATESTRUCT lpCreateStruct)
{

if (COleControl::OnCreate(lpCreateStruct) == -1)
    return -1;

// TODO: Add your specialized creation code here

////////////////////////
// MY CODE STARTS HERE
////////////////////////

// Install a timer.
SetTimer(1, (UINT)m_updateInterval, NULL);

////////////////////////
// MY CODE ENDS HERE
////////////////////////

return 0;

}
```

Again, when you type the preceding code, make sure that you type `m_updateInterval` (not `m_UpdateInterval`).

☐ Save your work by selecting Save from the File menu.

To see in action the code that you attached to the `OnUpdateIntervalChanged()` function do the following:

☐ Select Build MYCLOCK.DLL (or Build MYCLOCK.OCX) from the Project menu of Visual C++.

Visual C++ responds by compiling and linking the files of the MYCLOCK control.

☐ Select Test Container from the Tools menu of Visual C++.

Visual C++ responds by running the Test Container program.

☐ Select Insert OLE Control from the Edit menu of the Test Container program.

Test Container responds by displaying the Insert OLE Control dialog box.

☐ Select the MYCLOCK control and then click the OK button.

Test Container responds by inserting the MYCLOCK control.

☐ Select Properties from the View menu of Test Container.

☐ Click the down arrow of the Property combo box and then select the UpdateInterval property from the list that pops up.

As you can see, the initial value of the UpdateInterval property is 1000. That's because earlier you wrote code inside the `DoPropExchange()` function that initializes the UpdateInterval property to 1000.

☐ Observe the seconds portion of the displayed time inside the MYCLOCK control and verify that the time is updated every 1000 milliseconds (that is, every second).

☐ Change the value of the UpdateInterval property to 5000 and then click the Apply button.

☐ Observe the MYCLOCK control again, and notice that now the time is updated every 5000 milliseconds (that is, every five seconds).

As soon as you changed the UpdateInterval property to 5000, the code that you wrote inside the `OnUpdateIntervalChanged()` function was automatically executed, and this code set the interval period of the timer to the new value of the UpdateInterval property.

☐ Terminate Test Container by selecting Exit from the File menu.

Validating the Value of the UpdateInterval Property

You can write code that validates the value that the user enters for the UpdateInterval property. Suppose, for example, that you don't want the user to enter negative values for the UpdateInterval property. When the user enters a negative value for the UpdateInterval property, your validation code will prompt the user with a message box and will set the UpdateInterval property to a valid value.

To write such validation code, follow these steps:

☐ Open the file MYCLOCTRL.CPP (if it's not open already).

☐ Locate the function `OnUpdateIntervalChanged()` inside the MYCLOCTRL.CPP file.

☐ Add code to the `OnUpdateIntervalChanged()` function so that it looks like this:

```
void CMyclockCtrl::OnUpdateIntervalChanged()
{

// TODO: Add notification handler code

////////////////////////
// MY CODE STARTS HERE
////////////////////////

// Make sure the user did not set the property to a
// negative value.
if (m_updateInterval < 0)
   {
   MessageBox("This property cannot be negative!");
   m_updateInterval = 1000;
   }

// Re-install the timer with interval set
// to the current value of the UpdateInterval
// property.
SetTimer(1, (UINT)m_updateInterval, NULL);

////////////////////////
// MY CODE ENDS HERE
////////////////////////

SetModifiedFlag();

}
```

☐ Save your work by selecting Save from the File menu.

The validation code you added to the `OnUpdateIntervalChanged()` function is made up of a single if statement:

```
if (m_updateInterval < 0)
   {
   MessageBox("This property cannot be negative!");
   m_updateInterval = 1000;
   }
```

This `if` statement evaluates the value of the UpdateInterval property (`m_updateInterval`) to see if it is less than 0. If `m_updateInterval` is less than 0, the code under the `if` displays an error message box and sets the value of `m_updateInterval` to a valid value (`1000`).

To see your validation code in action, follow these steps:

☐ Select Build MYCLOCK.DLL (or Build MYCLOCK.OCX) from the Project menu of Visual C++.

   Visual C++ responds by compiling and linking the files of the MYCLOCK control.

☐ Select Test Container from the Tools menu of Visual C++.

   Visual C++ responds by running the Test Container program.

☐ Select Insert OLE Control from the Edit menu of the Test Container program.

   Test Container responds by displaying the Insert OLE Control dialog box.

☐ Select the MYCLOCK control and then click the OK button.

   Test Container responds by inserting the MYCLOCK control.

☐ Select Properties from the View menu of Test Container.

☐ Set the Property combo box to UpdateInterval.

☐ Change the value of the UpdateInterval property to a negative value (for example, `-1000`) and then click the Apply button.

   As expected, the message box shown in Figure 34.21 appears.

Figure 34.21. The message
box that appears after you
set the UpdateInterval
property to a negative
value.

☐ Click the OK button of the message box.

☐ Observe the value of the UpdateInterval. It should be 1000.

So as you have just verified, the validation code that you wrote inside the `OnUpdateIntervalChanged()` function is working. When someone tries to set the UpdateInterval property to a negative value, your validation code displays a message box and sets the UpdateInterval property to 1000.

☐ Terminate Test Container by selecting Exit from the File menu.

Adding a Properties Page to the MYCLOCK Control

So far, you accessed the properties of the MYCLOCK control by selecting Properties from the View menu of the Test Container program and then using the Properties dialog box to view and to set values of properties.

Another way to enable the user to view or set properties during design time is by providing the user with *properties pages*. Properties pages let the user view or change properties in a friendly visual manner. Each properties page lets the user view/set properties that are related. For example, the Colors properties page lets the user view/set color properties; the Fonts properties page lets the user view/set font properties, and so on.

To illustrate what a properties page is and how to add it to a control, in this section you'll add a Colors properties page to the MYCLOCK control. The user will be able to use the Colors properties page to view or set the values of the color properties of the MYCLOCK control (that is, the BackColor and ForeColor properties).

Before you write the code that adds the Colors properties page to the MYCLOCK control, first run the Test Container program and verify that currently the MYCLOCK control does not have the Colors properties page.

☐ Select Test Container from the Tools menu of Visual C++.

> *Visual C++ responds by running the Test Container program.*

☐ Select Insert OLE Control from the Edit menu of the Test Container program.

> *Test Container responds by displaying the Insert OLE Control dialog box.*

☐ Select the MYCLOCK control and then click the OK button.

> *Test Container responds by inserting the MYCLOCK control.*

☐ Double-click any point on the frame of the MYCLOCK control.

> *The Myclock Control Properties dialog box appears, as shown in Figure 34.22.*

Figure 34.22. The Myclock Control Properties dialog box.

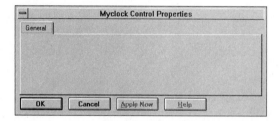

As shown in Figure 34.22, the Myclock Control Properties dialog box includes one tab—the General tab. The dialog box contains only the General tab, because at this point the MYCLOCK control has only one properties page (the General properties page). When you add more properties pages to the MYCLOCK control, the Myclock Control Properties dialog box will include more tabs. For example, soon you'll write the code that adds the Colors properties page to the MYCLOCK control. After you write this code, the Myclock Properties dialog box will have another tab called Colors. The user will be able to use the Colors tab to set the Color properties of the control.

As shown in Figure 34.22, the General tab (that is, the General properties page) is blank. As implied by its name, the General properties page should contain general properties—properties that do not belong to any other properties page. Later in this chapter, you'll customize the General properties page so that it will not be blank.

☐ Close the Myclock Control Properties dialog box by clicking its OK button.

☐ Terminate the Test Container program by selecting Exit from the File menu.

In the following steps, you'll add the Colors properties page. To write the code that adds the Colors properties page to the MYCLOCK control, follow these steps:

☐ Open the file MYCLOCTRL.CPP (if it's not open already).

☐ Locate the Properties pages table inside the MYCLOCTRL.CPP file.

The Properties pages table currently looks like this:

```
/////////////////////////////////////////////////
// Properties pages

// TODO: Add more properties pages as needed.
//       Remember to increase the count!
BEGIN_PROPPAGEIDS(CMyclockCtrl, 1)
    PROPPAGEID(CMyclockPropPage::guid)
END_PROPPAGEIDS(CMyclockCtrl)
```

☐ Modify the Properties pages table so that it looks like this:

```
/////////////////////////////////////////////////
// Properties pages

// TODO: Add more properties pages as needed.
//       Remember to increase the count!
BEGIN_PROPPAGEIDS(CMyclockCtrl, 2)
    PROPPAGEID(CMyclockPropPage::guid)
    PROPPAGEID(CLSID_CColorPropPage)
END_PROPPAGEIDS(CMyclockCtrl)
```

That is, you have to modify the second parameter in the statement

```
BEGIN_PROPPAGEIDS(CMyclockCtrl, 1)
```

from 1 to 2:

```
BEGIN_PROPPAGEIDS(CMyclockCtrl, 2)
```

You also have to add the statement

```
PROPPAGEID(CLSID_CColorPropPage)
```

☐ Save your work by selecting Save from the File menu.

Now take a close look at how the Properties pages table is constructed:

```
BEGIN_PROPPAGEIDS(CMyclockCtrl, 2)
    PROPPAGEID(CMyclockPropPage::guid)
    PROPPAGEID(CLSID_CColorPropPage)
END_PROPPAGEIDS(CMyclockCtrl)
```

The first statement

```
BEGIN_PROPPAGEIDS(CMyclockCtrl, 2)
```

begins the table. The first parameter, `CMyclockCtrl`, is the class name of the MYCLOCK control. The second parameter, 2, specifies the total number of properties pages. As you add more properties pages to the control, you have to change this parameter accordingly. For example, currently the table lists two properties pages. Therefore, the second parameter is set to 2.

The next two statements

```
PROPPAGEID(CMyclockPropPage::guid)
PROPPAGEID(CLSID_CColorPropPage)
```

list the IDs of the properties pages. The first statement

```
PROPPAGEID(CMyclockPropPage::guid)
```

lists the ID of the General properties page. This statement was written for you by ControlWizard when you created the project of the MYCLOCK project. That's why the MYCLOCK control already has a General properties page. (See Figure 34.22.) As discussed earlier, the General properties page is currently blank. Later you'll customize the General properties page so that it will not be blank.

The second statement

```
PROPPAGEID(CLSID_CColorPropPage)
```

lists the ID of the Colors properties page.

The last statement of the Properties Pages table is

```
END_PROPPAGEIDS(CMyclockCtrl)
```

This statement ends the table.

So by adding the ID of the Colors properties page to the Properties Pages table, you added the Colors properties page to the MYCLOCK control. You don't have to write any additional code!

To verify that the MYCLOCK control now has the Colors properties page follow these steps:

☐ Select Build MYCLOCK.DLL (or Build MYCLOCK.OCX) from the Project menu of Visual C++.

   Visual C++ responds by compiling and linking the files of the MYCLOCK control.

☐ Select Test Container from the Tools menu of Visual C++.

   Visual C++ responds by running the Test Container program.

☐ Select Insert OLE Control from the Edit menu of the Test Container program.

   Test Container responds by displaying the Insert OLE Control dialog box.

☐ Select the MYCLOCK control and then click the OK button.

   Test Container responds by inserting the MYCLOCK control.

☐ Double-click any point on the frame of the MYCLOCK control.

   The Myclock Control Properties dialog box appears, as shown in Figure 34.23.

Figure 34.23. The Myclock Control Properties dialog box. (Now there are two properties pages: General and Colors.)

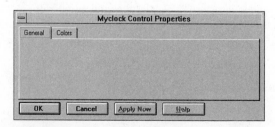

As shown in Figure 34.23, the Myclock Control Properties dialog box now includes two properties pages (that is, two tabs): General and Colors.

☐ Select the Colors Properties page. (See Figure 34.24.)

Figure 34.24. The Colors properties page of the MYCLOCK control.

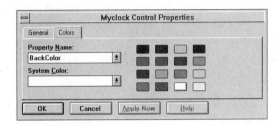

As you can see, the Colors Properties page provides you with a very easy and user-friendly interface to view and set the color properties of the MYCLOCK control.

You can select the desired Color property from the Property Name combo box, and you can then set the value of the property by clicking the desired color.

Note that after you click the down arrow of the Property Name combo box, the combo box lists only the color properties of the MYCLOCK control. (See Figure 34.25.) This way, the user can concentrate on the color aspect of the control.

Figure 34.25. The Property Name combo box of the Colors properties page lists only the Colors properties.

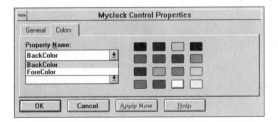

☐ Experiment with the Colors properties page and observe how easy it is use. Verify that after you click the OK button of the dialog box, the MYCLOCK control changes its foreground and background colors per your selections.

☐ Close the Myclock Control Properties dialog box by clicking its OK button.

☐ Terminate the Test Container program by selecting Exit from the File menu.

Customizing the General Properties Page

As you have seen in the previous steps, the MYCLOCK control now has two properties pages: General and Colors. The Colors properties page is fully functional. However, the General properties page is currently blank. (See Figure 34.23.)

You'll now customize the General properties page so that it will not be blank. You'll customize it in such a way that the user will use it for viewing/setting the value of the UpdateInterval property.

To customize the General properties page, you need to work on the IDD_PROPPAGE_MYCLOCK dialog box. This dialog box was created for you by ControlWizard.

To display the IDD_PROPPAGE_MYCLOCK dialog box with Visual C++ 1.51 do this:

☐ Select App Studio from the Tools menu of Visual C++ 1.51, then select Dialog inside the Type list, and finally double-click IDD_PROPPAGE_MYCLOCK inside the Resources list.

To display the IDD_PROPPAGE_MYCLOCK dialog box with Visual C++ 2.0 do this:

☐ Double-click myclock.rc inside the MYCLOC32.MAK window, then double-click Dialog inside the MYCLOCK.RC window, and finally double-click IDD_PROPPAGE_MYCLOCK under the Dialog item.

The IDD_PROPPAGE_MYCLOCK dialog box is shown in Figure 34.26. As you can see, it is currently blank.

Figure 34.26. The IDD_PROPPAGE_MYCLOCK dialog box (before customization).

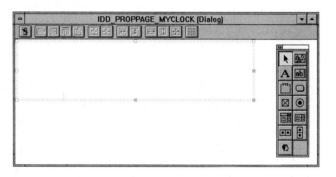

☐ Place a static label control inside the dialog box, double-click it, set its ID property to IDC_STATIC and its Caption property to UpdateInterval:.

☐ Place an edit box control inside the dialog box, double-click it, and set its ID property to IDC_UPDATE_INTERVAL.

☐ Save your work by selecting Save from the File menu.

Your IDD_PROPPAGE_MYCLOCK dialog box should now look like the one shown in Figure 34.27.

☐ Save your work by selecting Save from the File menu.

☐ If you are using Visual C++ 1.51, terminate App Studio by selecting Exit from the File menu of App Studio.

Figure 34.27. The IDD_PROPPAGE_MYCLOCK dialog box (after customization).

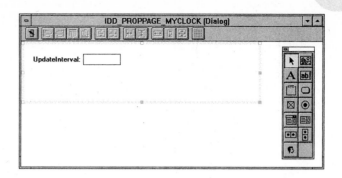

Now you have to attach a variable to the IDC_UPDATE_INTERVAL edit box and you have to associate this variable with the UpdateInterval property. Here is how you do that:

☐ Display the ClassWizard dialog box (by selecting ClassWizard from the Browse menu of Visual C++ 1.51 or by selecting ClassWizard from the Project menu of Visual C++ 2.0).

☐ Select the Member Variables tab.

☐ Set the Class Name combo box to CMyclockPropPage.

Your ClassWizard dialog box should now look like the one shown in Figure 34.28.

Figure 34.28. The Member Variables tab of ClassWizard after you select the CMyclockPropPage class.

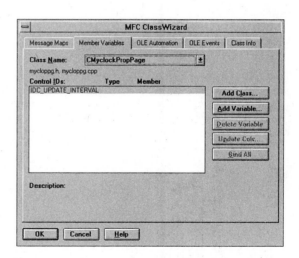

☐ Make sure that IDC_UPDATE_INTERVAL is selected in the Control IDs list and then click the Add Variable button.

   Visual C++ responds by displaying the Add Member Variable dialog box.

☐ In the Member Variable Name edit box type m_updateInterval.

☐ Set the Category field to Value.

☐ Set the Variable Type field to long.

☐ In the Optional OLE Property Name combo box type UpdateInterval.

Your Add Member Variable dialog box should now look like the one shown in Figure 34.29.

*Figure 34.29. Attaching a
variable to the
IDC_UPDATE_INTERVAL
edit box.*

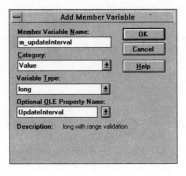

☐ Click the OK button of the Add Member Variable dialog box and then click the OK
button of ClassWizard.

☐ Save your work by selecting Save from the File menu.

That's it! You have completed the implementation of the General properties page.

To verify that the General properties page is no longer blank and that it enables the user to view and
set the UpdateInterval property, follow these steps:

☐ Select Build MYCLOCK.DLL (or Build MYCLOCK.OCX) from the Project menu of
Visual C++.

Visual C++ responds by compiling and linking the files of the MYCLOCK control.

☐ Select Test Container from the Tools menu of Visual C++.

Visual C++ responds by running the Test Container program.

☐ Select Insert OLE Control from the Edit menu of the Test Container program.

Test Container responds by displaying the Insert OLE Control dialog box.

☐ Select the Myclock control and then click the OK button.

Test Container responds by inserting the MYCLOCK control.

☐ Double-click any point on the frame of the MYCLOCK control.

The Myclock Control Properties dialog box appears, as shown in Figure 34.30.

As shown in Figure 34.30, the General properties page is not blank anymore! It appears just as you
designed it—with a label UpdateInterval: and with an edit box. The edit box contains the value
1000 because this is the current value of the UpdateInterval property. The edit box contains the
value of the UpdateInterval property because when you created the variable of this edit box with

ClassWizard (Figure 34.29), you set the Optional OLE Property Name combo box to UpdateInterval.

Figure 34.30. The Myclock Control Properties dialog box (the General properties page is not blank anymore).

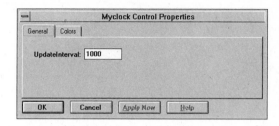

☐ Try to set the UpdateInterval property to various values, then click the OK button and verify that the MYCLOCK control updates itself in accordance with the new value that you set. For example, if you set the UpdateInterval to 5000, then the seconds portion of the clock should change once every 5 seconds.

☐ Terminate the Test Container program by selecting Exit from the File menu.

What You Have Accomplished So Far

In this chapter you enhanced the MYCLOCK OCX control. You wrote the code that makes the MYCLOCK control display the current time, you added to the control two stock properties (BackColor and ForeColor) and one custom property (UpdateInterval). You also wrote validation code for the UpdateInterval property, so that when the user enters a negative value for the UpdateInterval property, a message box is displayed and the value of the UpdateInterval property is reset to 1000.

At the end of the chapter, you added a Colors properties page to the MYCLOCK control and you customized the General properties page of the MYCLOCK control. As you have seen, providing the user with properties pages makes the control very user-friendly.

In the next chapter you'll further customize the MYCLOCK control: You will add to the MYCLOCK control a stock event, a custom event, and a method.

35

Adding Events and Methods to OCX Controls

In this chapter you'll continue

developing the MYCLOCK

control that you created in the

previous two chapters—you'll add

both events and methods to

the control.

> **NOTE**
>
> This chapter assumes that you have read and implemented all the steps of the previous two chapters.
>
> In this chapter you'll continue working on the project of the previous two chapters.

Adding Stock Events to the MYCLOCK Control

In the previous chapter you added two stock properties and one custom property to the MYCLOCK control. Now you'll learn how to add a stock event to the control. As you'll soon see, the steps necessary to add a stock event are as easy as the steps you took when you added a stock property.

Stock events are events such as Click (mouse click) and DblClick (mouse double-click). These events are predefined, and adding them to an OCX control is easy. You can add any of the following stock events to an OCX control:

```
Click

DblClick

Error

KeyDown

KeyPress

KeyUp

MouseDown

MouseMove

MouseUp
```

The names of these events are self-explanatory: the Click event occurs when the user clicks the control; the DblClick event occurs when the user double-clicks the control; the Error event occurs when an error has occurred within the control; the KeyDown event occurs when the user presses down a key while the control has the keyboard focus; and so on.

Note that the mouse events apply to any of the mouse buttons. For example, the Click event occurs when the user clicks any of the mouse buttons (left, middle, or right).

For practice, add two stock events to the MYCLOCK control: Click and DblClick.

Follow these steps to add the Click event to the MYCLOCK control:

☐ Start Visual C++.

☐ Open the project file (MAK file) of the MYCLOCK control that you created in the previous two chapters (if it's not already open).

NOTE

When you created the project and skeleton files of the MYCLOCK control, Visual C++ created for you two project (MAK) files: MYCLOCK.MAK and MYCLOC32.MAK.

If you are using Visual C++ 1.51, you should open the \MVCPROG\CH33\MYCLOCK\MYCLOCK.MAK project.

If you are using Visual C++ 2.0, you should open the \MVCPROG\CH33\MYCLOCK\MYCLOC32.MAK project.

☐ Display the ClassWizard dialog box (by selecting ClassWizard from the Browse menu of Visual C++ 1.51 or by selecting ClassWizard from the Project menu of Visual C++ 2.0).

☐ Select the OLE Events tab of ClassWizard.

☐ Make sure that the Class Name box is set to `CMyclockCtrl`.

Your ClassWizard dialog box should now look like the one shown in Figure 35.1.

Figure 35.1. Selecting the OLE Events tab of ClassWizard and setting the Class Name to `CMyclockCtrl`.

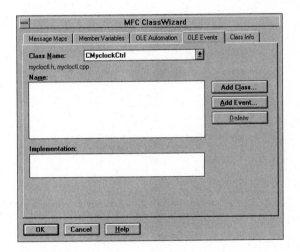

☐ Click the Add Event button.

Visual C++ responds by displaying the Add Event dialog box. (See Figure 35.2.)

Figure 35.2. The Add Event dialog box.

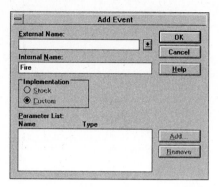

☐ Click the down arrow of the External Name combo box and select Click from the list that pops up.

Your Add Event dialog box should now look like the one shown in Figure 35.3.

Figure 35.3. The Add Event dialog box after you set the External Name combo box to Click.

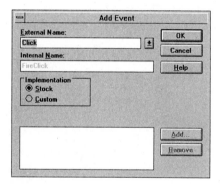

☐ Click the OK button of the Add Event dialog box.

The ClassWizard dialog box reappears, as shown in Figure 35.4.

*Figure 35.4. The
ClassWizard dialog box
after you add the* Click
stock event.

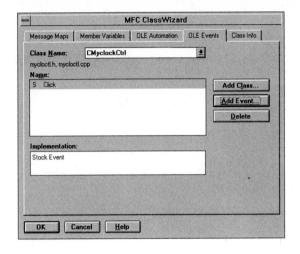

As shown in Figure 35.4, the Name list now contains the event Click. Notice that the letter *S* appears to the left of Click. This *S* serves as an indication that the Click event is a stock event.

Now add the DblClick event:

☐ Click the Add Event button.

    Visual C++ responds by displaying the Add Event dialog box.

☐ Click the down arrow of the External Name combo box and select DblClick from the list
that pops up.

☐ Click the OK button of the Add Event dialog box.

    The ClassWizard dialog box reappears, as shown in Figure 35.5.

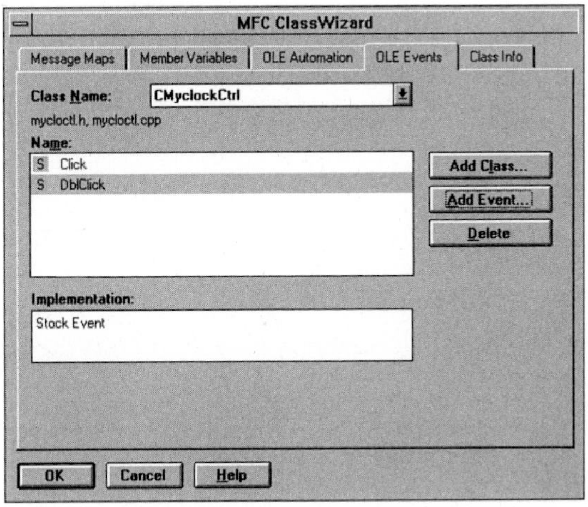

*Figure 35.5. The
ClassWizard dialog box
after you add the
DblClick stock event.*

As shown in Figure 35.5, now the Name list contains both the Click event and DblClick event. The letter *S* appears to the left of both events, because both the Click event and the DblClick event are stock events.

☐ Click the OK button of ClassWizard.

That's it! You've finished adding the Click and DblClick events to the MYCLOCK control.

The fact that the MYCLOCK control now has the Click and DblClick events means that programmers who will use your MYCLOCK control in their programs will be able to attach code to these events. The code a programmer attaches to the Click event will be automatically executed whenever someone clicks the MYCLOCK control. The code a programmer attaches to the DblClick event will be automatically executed whenever someone double-clicks the MYCLOCK control.

To verify that the MYCLOCK control now has the Click and DblClick events do the following:

☐ If you are using Visual C++ 1.51, select Make TypeLib from the Tools menu.

Visual C++ 1.51 responds by creating the type library (.tlb file) for the MYCLOCK control and by displaying an OK message box with the text Successfully generated type library tlb16\MYCLOCK.tlb.

☐ Click the OK button of the message box.

NOTE

The preceding two steps are applicable only if you are creating the control with Visual C++ 1.51. If you are creating the control with Visual C++ 2.0, the preceding two steps are *not* applicable.

In Visual C++ 1.51, after you add an event (or a property or a method) to the control, you have to rebuild the type library prior to building the project. You don't have to do that in Visual C++ 2.0.

☐ Select Build MYCLOCK.DLL (or Build MYCLOCK.OCX) from the Project menu of Visual C++.

Visual C++ responds by compiling and linking the files of the MYCLOCK control.

☐ Select Test Container from the Tools menu of Visual C++.

Visual C++ responds by running the Test Container program.

☐ Select Insert OLE Control from the Edit menu of the Test Container program.

Test Container responds by displaying the Insert OLE Control dialog box.

☐ Select the MYCLOCK control and then click the OK button.

Test Container responds by inserting the MYCLOCK control.

☐ Select Event Log from the View menu of Test Container.

Test Container responds by displaying the Event Log dialog box. (See Figure 35.6.)

Figure 35.6. The Event Log dialog box of Test Container.

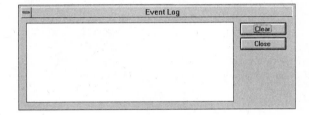

As implied by its name, the Event Log dialog box displays a log of events as they occur.

To verify that the MYCLOCK control has a Click event do the following:

☐ Leave the Event Log dialog box open (that is, do not close it).

☐ Click inside the MYCLOCK control. (Don't click on the frame of the control, but click inside it.)

The Event Log dialog box logs a Click event. (See Figure 35.7.)

Figure 35.7. The Event Log dialog box after you click the MYCLOCK control.

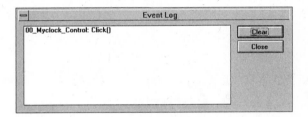

So as you have just verified, the MYCLOCK control has a Click event.

☐ Click the MYCLOCK control several more times and notice how the Event Log dialog box logs a Click event for each time you click the MYCLOCK control. (See Figure 35.8.)

Note that it does not matter which of the mouse buttons you use to click the MYCLOCK control. The Click event occurs when you click the mouse using the left, middle, or right buttons.

To verify that the MYCLOCK control has a DblClick event do the following:

☐ Double-click inside the MYCLOCK control.

The Event Log dialog box logs a DblClick event. (See Figure 35.9.)

Figure 35.8. The Event Log dialog box after you click the MYCLOCK control four times.

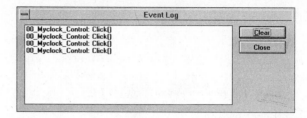

Figure 35.9. The Event Log dialog box after you double-click the MYCLOCK control.

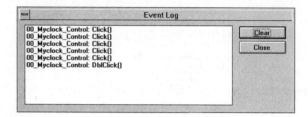

☐ Double-click the MYCLOCK control several more times, and notice how the Event Log dialog box logs a DblClick event for each time you click the MYCLOCK control. Notice also that for each time you double-click the control, the Event Log dialog box also logs a Click event. That's because every time you double-click the control, two events occur: a regular click and a double-click. That is, the first click of a double-click is a regular click.

Note that it does not matter which of the mouse buttons you use to double-click the MYCLOCK control. The DblClick event occurs when you double-click the mouse using the left, middle, or right buttons.

☐ Terminate Test Container by selecting Exit from the File menu.

Adding a Custom Event to the MYCLOCK Control

In many cases, you'll have to add an event to your OCX control that isn't a standard event. Such an event is called a custom event (an event that is custom-made by you).

Now add an additional event to the MYCLOCK control. The name of this event will be NewMinute. For now, don't concern yourself with the purpose of the NewMinute event. Later you will make this event functional, but now all you want to do is add it to the MYCLOCK control.

Follow these steps to add the NewMinute custom event to the MYCLOCK control:

☐ Display the ClassWizard dialog box (by selecting ClassWizard from the Browse menu of Visual C++ 1.51 or by selecting ClassWizard from the Project menu of Visual C++ 2.0).

☐ Select the OLE Events tab of ClassWizard.

☐ Make sure that the Class Name box is set to `CMyclockCtrl`.

Your ClassWizard dialog box should now look like the one shown in Figure 35.10.

Figure 35.10. The OLE Events tab.

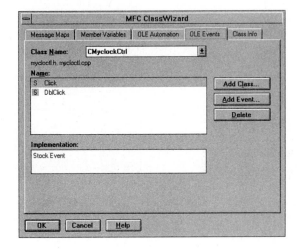

☐ Click the Add Event button.

> *Visual C++ responds by displaying the Add Event dialog box.*

☐ Type inside the External Name combo box `NewMinute`.

Notice that as you type `NewMinute` inside the External Name combo box, Visual C++ automatically fills the Internal Name edit box with the text `FireNewMinute`.

Your Add Event dialog box should now look like the one shown in Figure 35.11.

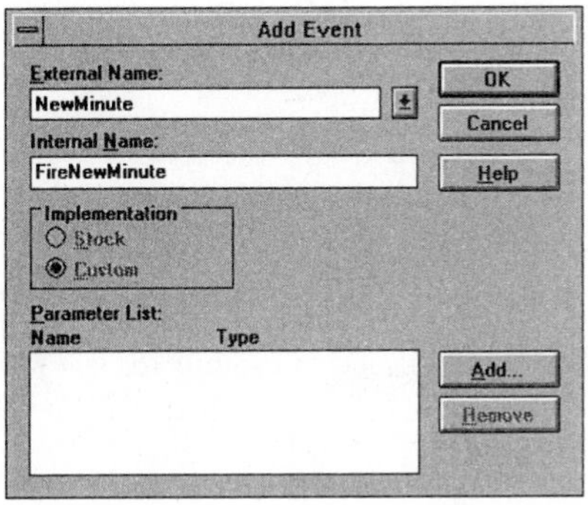

Figure 35.11. The Add Event dialog box after you type inside the External Name combo box NewMinute.

☐ Click the OK button of the Add Event dialog box.

The ClassWizard dialog box reappears, as shown in Figure 35.12.

*Figure 35.12. The
ClassWizard dialog
box after you add the
NewMinute custom event.*

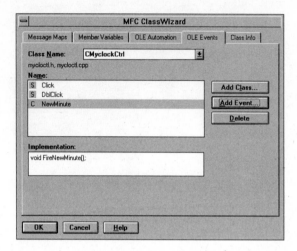

As shown in Figure 35.4, the Name list now contains the event NewMinute. Notice that the letter *C* appears to the left of NewMinute. This *C* serves as an indication that the NewMinute event is a custom event.

NOTE

When you add a custom event to a control, you can add parameters to the event. You do that by clicking the Add button inside the Add Event dialog box. (See Figure 35.11.)

In the preceding steps you were not instructed to click the Add button inside the Add Event dialog box, because you don't want the NewMinute event to have any parameters.

In your future OCX projects you may have a need to add parameters to a certain event. When an event has parameters, whoever receives the event (that is, an event procedure) can make use of these parameters to get more information about the event.

That's it! You have finished adding the NewMinute custom event to the MYCLOCK control.

To verify that the MYCLOCK control now has the NewMinute event do the following:

☐ If you are using Visual C++ 1.51, select Make TypeLib from the Tools menu.

Visual C++ 1.51 responds by creating the type library (.tlb file) for the MYCLOCK control and by displaying an OK message box with the text Successfully generated type library tlb16\MYCLOCK.tlb.

☐ Click the OK button of the message box.

> **NOTE**
>
> The preceding two steps are applicable only if you are creating the control with Visual C++ 1.51. If you are creating the control with Visual C++ 2.0, the preceding two steps are *not* applicable.
>
> As stated earlier, in Visual C++ 1.51, after you add an event (or a property or a method) to the control, you have to rebuild the type library prior to building the project. You don't have to do that in Visual C++ 2.0.

☐ Select Build MYCLOCK.DLL (or Build MYCLOCK.OCX) from the Project menu of Visual C++.

Visual C++ responds by compiling and linking the files of the MYCLOCK control.

☐ Select Test Container from the Tools menu of Visual C++.

Visual C++ responds by running the Test Container program.

☐ Select Insert OLE Control from the Edit menu of the Test Container program.

Test Container responds by displaying the Insert OLE Control dialog box.

☐ Select the MYCLOCK control and then click the OK button.

Test Container responds by inserting the MYCLOCK control.

To see a list of all the events of the MYCLOCK control do the following:

☐ Select View Event List from the Edit menu of Test Container.

Test container responds by displaying the Events for Myclock Control dialog box. (See Figure 35.13.)

Figure 35.13. The
Events for Myclock
Control dialog box.

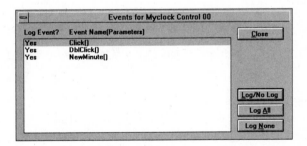

As you can see, the NewMinute event is listed! The MYCLOCK control has three events: Click, DblClick, and NewMinute.

☐ Close the Events for Myclock Control dialog box by clicking its Close button.

☐ Terminate Test Container by selecting Exit from the File menu.

Firing the *NewMinute* Event

As you have just verified, the MYCLOCK control has the `NewMinute` event that you added to it. However, this event never happens. To make the `NewMinute` event occur, you need to write some code.

When you add to a control a stock event, such as the `DblClick` event that you added earlier, you do not need to write any code to make the event happen. That is, a standard event already includes built-in code that makes the event happen. For example, in the case of the `DblClick` event, the event occurs automatically whenever the user double-clicks the MYCLOCK control.

However, when you add a custom event to a control, you need to write code that makes the event happen. Your code needs to recognize that the event has occurred and then use the `Fire` function of the event to fire the event (that is, to make the event happen).

The `Fire` function of the `NewMinute` event is `FireNewMinute()`. To make the `NewMinute` event happen, your code needs to detect when the `NewMinute` event occurs, and then call the `FireNewMinute()` function.

The question is When should the `NewMinute` event occur? As its name implies, the `NewMinute` event should occur whenever a new minute begins.

Follow these steps to write the code that fires the `NewMinute` event:

☐ Open the file MYCLOCTRL.CPP (if it's not open already).

☐ Locate the function `OnDraw()` inside the MYCLOCTRL.CPP file.

☐ Add the following `if` statement to the end of the `OnDraw()` function:

```
// If new minute has just begun, fire a NewMinute event.
if (newtime->tm_sec==0)
   FireNewMinute();
```

After you add this `if` statement to the end of the `OnDraw()` function, the `OnDraw()` function should look like this:

```
void CMyclockCtrl::OnDraw(
  CDC* pdc,const CRect& rcBounds,const CRect& rcInvalid)
{
// TODO: Replace the following code with your own drawing
//       code.

/////////////////////////////
// MY CODE STARTS HERE //
/////////////////////////////

// Set the foreground color (i.e. the text color)
// according to the ForeColor property.
pdc->SetTextColor(TranslateColor(GetForeColor()));

// Set the background mode to transparent mode.
pdc->SetBkMode(TRANSPARENT);

// Create a brush based on the BackColor property.
CBrush bkBrush(TranslateColor(GetBackColor()));
```

```
// Paint the background using the BackColor property
pdc->FillRect(rcBounds, &bkBrush);

char CurrentTime[30];
struct tm *newtime;
long lTime;

// Get the current time
time(&lTime);
newtime=localtime(&lTime);

// Convert the time into a string.
strcpy(CurrentTime, asctime(newtime));

// Pad the string with 1 blank.
CurrentTime[24]=' ';

// Terminate the string.
CurrentTime[25] = 0;

// Display the current time
pdc->ExtTextOut(rcBounds.left,
                rcBounds.top,
                ETO_CLIPPED,
                rcBounds,
                CurrentTime,
                strlen(CurrentTime),
                NULL);

// If new minute has just begun, fire a NewMinute event.
if (newtime->tm_sec==0)
   FireNewMinute();

//////////////////////////
// MY CODE ENDS HERE //
//////////////////////////

}
```

The code you just added to the OnDraw() function is one if statement:

```
if (newtime->tm_sec==0)
   FireNewMinute();
```

This if statement checks whether the tm_sec field of the newtime structure is currently 0. If it is, a new minute has just begun, and the FireNewMinute() function is executed to fire the NewMinute event:

```
FireNewMinute();
```

Note that the FireNewMinute() event is called without any parameters. That's because earlier when you added the NewMinute event to the control (See Figure 35.11.) you did not specify any parameters for it. That is, you did not use the Add button of the Add Event dialog box to add parameters to the NewMinute event.

You have finished writing the code that fires the NewMinute event! Now whenever a new minute begins, the code you wrote will fire a NewMinute event, and the code that the user of your MYCLOCK control will attach to the NewMinute event will be executed automatically.

Note that the code you wrote for detecting the NewMinute event is not perfect. This code is executed whenever the OnDraw() function is executed, which is determined by the value of the UpdateInterval property. So if the UpdateInterval property will be set to a value greater than 1000 milliseconds, there is a chance that a new minute will begin without your code detecting it.

Verify that the code you wrote actually fires the NewMinute event:

☐ Select Build MYCLOCK.DLL (or Build MYCLOCK.OCX) from the Project menu of Visual C++.

Visual C++ responds by compiling and linking the files of the MYCLOCK control.

☐ Select Test Container from the Tools menu of Visual C++.

Visual C++ responds by running the Test Container program.

☐ Select Insert OLE Control from the Edit menu of the Test Container program.

Test Container responds by displaying the Insert OLE Control dialog box.

☐ Select the MYCLOCK control and then click the OK button.

Test Container responds by inserting the MYCLOCK control.

☐ Select Event Log from the View menu of Test Container.

Test Container responds by displaying the Event Log dialog box.

☐ Leave the Event Log dialog box open.

☐ Observe the time that the MYCLOCK control displays, and wait for a new minute to begin.

As expected, as soon as a new minute begins, the Event Log dialog box logs the NewMinute event! (See Figure 35.14.)

Figure 35.14. The Event Log dialog box after a new minute has begun.

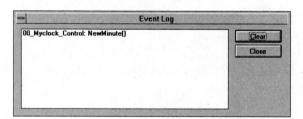

So as you have just verified, the NewMinute event is working. Whenever a new minute begins, the code you wrote inside the OnDraw() function detects that a new minute has begun, and your code fires the NewMinute event by calling the FireNewMinute() function.

☐ Terminate Test Container by selecting Exit from the File menu.

Adding Methods to the MYCLOCK Control

Besides adding properties and events to a control, you can also add methods to a control. What are methods? Methods are like C++ member functions. After you add a method to your control, the programmers who use your control can use your method in their programs. For example, suppose you add a method called MyMethod() to the MYCLOCK control. The programmers who use your MYCLOCK control will be able to call the MyMethod() method in their programs. If, for example, a programmer adds a MYCLOCK object in his or her program and names this MYCLOCK control Clock1, the programmer will be able to use a statement such as the following:

```
Clock1.MyMethod()
```

This statement would execute the MyMethod() method on the Clock1 control.

The *AboutBox()* Method—A Gift from ControlWizard

Although you haven't yet written any code to add a method to the MYCLOCK control, the MYCLOCK control already has a method called AboutBox(). The code that implements the AboutBox() method was written for you by ControlWizard.

As implied by its name, the AboutBox() method displays an About dialog box for the MYCLOCK control. When programmers who use your MYCLOCK control call the AboutBox() method from their programs, an About dialog box appears.

Before you add your own methods to the MYCLOCK control, test the AboutBox() method that ControlWizard implemented for you:

☐ Select Test Container from the Tools menu of Visual C++.

   Visual C++ responds by running the Test Container program.

☐ Select Insert OLE Control from the Edit menu of the Test Container program.

   Test Container responds by displaying the Insert OLE Control dialog box.

☐ Select the MYCLOCK control and then click the OK button.

   Test Container responds by inserting the MYCLOCK control.

☐ Select Invoke Methods from the Edit menu of Test Container.

   Test Container responds by displaying the Invoke Control Method dialog box. (See Figure 35.15.)

Figure 35.15. The Invoke
Control Method dialog box.

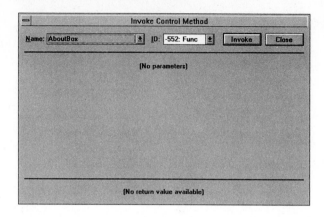

As shown in Figure 35.15, the Name list box of the Invoke Control Method dialog box is set to AboutBox. This means that if you now click the Invoke button, Test Container will execute the AboutBox() method of the MYCLOCK control.

☐ Click the Invoke button.

> *Test Container responds by executing the AboutBox() method of the MYCLOCK control.*
> *The AboutBox() method displays an About dialog box, as shown in Figure 35.16.*

Figure 35.16. The About
dialog box that the
AboutBox() method of the
MYCLOCK control
displays.

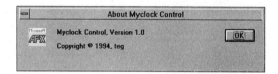

☐ Close the About dialog box by clicking its OK button.

☐ Close the Invoke Control Method dialog box by clicking its Close button.

☐ Terminate Test Container by selecting Exit from the File menu.

Currently, the MYCLOCK control has only one method—the AboutBox() method (a gift from ControlWizard). In the following sections you'll add more methods to the MYCLOCK control.

NOTE

Currently the About dialog box that the AboutBox() method displays looks like the one shown in Figure 35.16.

If you wish, you can customize this About dialog box. To customize it, you need to work on the IDD_ABOUTBOX_MYCLOCK dialog box. This dialog box was created for you by ControlWizard.

To display the IDD_ABOUTBOX_MYCLOCK dialog box with Visual C++ 1.51 do the following:

☐ Select App Studio from the Tools menu of Visual C++ 1.51, then select Dialog inside the Type list, and finally, double-click IDD_ABOUTBOX_MYCLOCK inside the Resources list.

To display the IDD_ABOUTBOX_MYCLOCK dialog box with Visual C++ 2.0 do the following:

☐ Double-click `myclock.rc` inside the MYCLOC32.MAK window, then double-click `Dialog` inside the MYCLOCK.RC window, and finally, double-click IDD_ABOUTBOX_MYCLOCK under the `Dialog` item.

Adding a Stock Method to the MYCLOCK Control

Stock methods are predefined. As you'll soon see, adding a stock method to a control is very easy. The current version of Visual C++ (Visual C++ 2.0 for the 32-bit platform or Visual C++ 1.51 for the 16-bit platform) supports two stock methods: `DoClick()` and `Refresh()`.

The `DoClick()` method simulates a clicking of the control. In other words, executing the `DoClick()` method has the same effect as the user clicking the control.

The `Refresh()` method causes the control to redraw itself. That is, executing the `Refresh()` method triggers a call to the `OnDraw()` function of the control.

For practice, add the `Refresh()` stock method to the MYCLOCK control.

Follow these steps to add the `Refresh()` stock method to the MYCLOCK control:

☐ Display the ClassWizard dialog box (by selecting ClassWizard from the Browse menu of Visual C++ 1.51 or by selecting ClassWizard from the Project menu of Visual C++ 2.0).

☐ Select the OLE Automation tab of ClassWizard. (See Figure 35.17.)

☐ Make sure that the Class Name box is set to `CMyclockCtrl`, as shown in Figure 35.17.

☐ Click the Add Method button.

Visual C++ responds by displaying the Add Method dialog box. (See Figure 35.18.)

☐ Click the down arrow of the External Name combo box, and select `Refresh` from the list that pops up.

Your Add Method dialog box should now look like the one shown in Figure 35.19.

☐ Click the OK button of the Add Method dialog box.

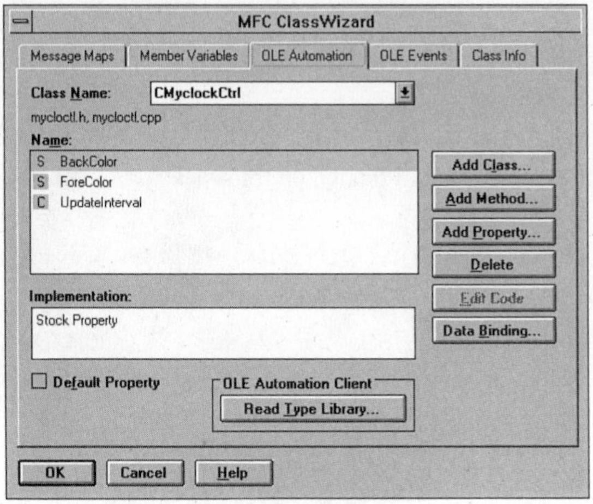

Figure 35.17. Selecting the OLE Automation tab of ClassWizard.

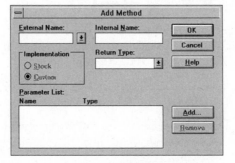

Figure 35.18. The Add Method dialog box.

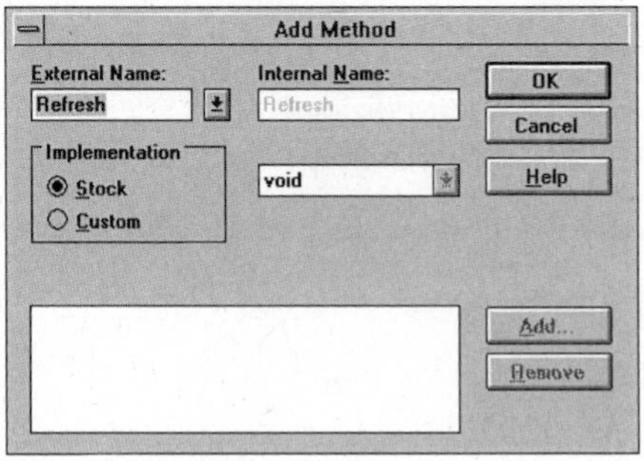

Figure 35.19. The Add Method dialog box, after you set the External Name combo box to Refresh.

The ClassWizard dialog box reappears, as shown in Figure 35.20.

As shown in Figure 35.20, the Name list now contains the method Refresh. Notice that the letter

Figure 35.20. The ClassWizard dialog box after you add the Refresh stock method.

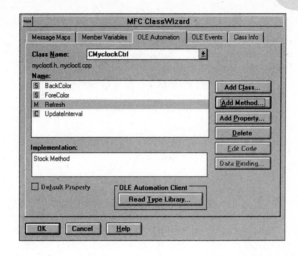

M appears to the left of Refresh. This *M* serves as an indication that Refresh is a method.

☐ Close the ClassWizard dialog box by clicking its OK button.

That's it! You have finished adding the Refresh stock method to the MYCLOCK control.

To verify that the MYCLOCK control now has the Refresh method and to see the Refresh method in action do the following:

☐ If you are using Visual C++ 1.51, select Make TypeLib from the Tools menu.

Visual C++ 1.5 responds by creating the type library (.tlb file) for the MYCLOCK control and by displaying an OK message box with the text Successfully generated type library tlb16\MYCLOCK.tlb.

☐ Click the OK button of the message box.

NOTE

The preceding two steps are applicable only if you are creating the control with Visual C++ 1.51. If you are creating the control with Visual C++ 2.0, the preceding two steps are *not* applicable.

As stated earlier, in Visual C++ 1.51, after you add a method (or an event or a property) to the control, you have to rebuild the type library prior to building the project. You don't have to do that in Visual C++ 2.0.

☐ Select Build MYCLOCK.DLL (or Build MYCLOCK.OCX) from the Project menu of Visual C++.

Visual C++ responds by compiling and linking the files of the MYCLOCK control.

☐ Select Test Container from the Tools menu of Visual C++.

Visual C++ responds by running the Test Container program.

☐ Select Insert OLE Control from the Edit menu of the Test Container program.

Test Container responds by displaying the Insert OLE Control dialog box.

☐ Select the MYCLOCK control and then click the OK button.

Test Container responds by inserting the MYCLOCK control.

To see the Refresh() method in action, you first have to increase the value of the UpdateInterval property. Why? Currently the UpdateInterval property is set to 1000 milliseconds (1 second). Therefore, the MYCLOCK control keeps updating itself every second, and when you invoke the Refresh() method you will not be able to see the effects of the Refresh() method.

Increase the value of the UpdateInterval property as follows:

☐ Select Properties from the View menu of Test Container.

Test Container responds by displaying the Properties dialog box.

☐ Click the down arrow of the Property combo box and select the UpdateInterval property.

☐ Change the value of the UpdateInterval property to 15000, then click the Apply button, and finally, click the OK button.

☐ Observe the MYCLOCK control and verify that the displayed time is being refreshed every 15000 milliseconds (15 seconds).

> **NOTE**
>
> In the preceding steps you changed the UpdateInterval property of the MYCLOCK control by selecting Properties from the View menu of Test Container. Alternatively, you could have double-clicked the frame of the MYCLOCK control and then set the UpdateInterval property in the General properties page. (Recall that you customized the General properties page of the MYCLOCK control in the previous chapter.)

Now test the Refresh() method as follows:

☐ Select Invoke Methods from the Edit menu of Test Container.

Test Container responds by displaying the Invoke Control Method dialog box.

☐ Make sure that the Name list box of the Invoke Control Method dialog box is set to Refresh, as shown in Figure 35.21 (because you want to test the Refresh() method).

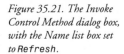

Figure 35.21. The Invoke Control Method dialog box, with the Name list box set to Refresh.

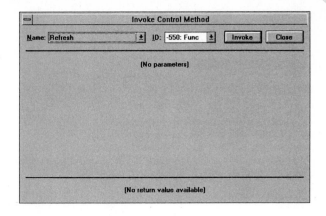

☐ Move the Invoke Control Method dialog box (by dragging its title) so that you are able to see the MYCLOCK control. That is, move the Invoke Control Method dialog box downward so that it does not overlap the MYCLOCK control.

☐ Click the Invoke button.

> *Test Container responds by executing the* Refresh() *method of the MYCLOCK control. As you can see, as soon as you click the Invoke button, the MYCLOCK control redraws itself. The* Refresh() *method that you added to the MYCLOCK control is working!*

☐ Click the Invoke button several more times, and notice that after each click the MYCLOCK control redraws itself.

☐ Close the Invoke Control Method dialog box by clicking its Close button.

☐ Terminate Test Container by selecting Exit from the File menu.

Adding a Custom Method to the MYCLOCK Control

In many cases you'll want to add a method to your OCX control that isn't a standard method. Such a method is called a custom method.

Add a simple custom method to the MYCLOCK control. The name of this method will be Beep(), and as implied by its name, calling this method will generate a beep.

Follow these steps to add the Beep() custom method to the MYCLOCK control:

☐ Display the ClassWizard dialog box (by selecting ClassWizard from the Browse menu of Visual C++ 1.51 or by selecting ClassWizard from the Project menu of Visual C++ 2.0).

☐ Select the OLE Automation tab of ClassWizard.

☐ Make sure that the Class Name box is set to CMyclockCtrl.

☐ Click the Add Method button.

Visual C++ responds by displaying the Add Method dialog box.

☐ Inside the External Name combo box type Beep.

Notice that as you type Beep inside the External Name combo box, Visual C++ automatically fills the Internal Name edit box with the text Beep. The Internal Name edit box specifies the function name of the MYCLOCK control that will be executed when anyone executes the Beep() method. You'll write the code of the Beep() function soon.

☐ Set the Return Type list box to void. (You don't want the Beep() method to return any value.)

Your Add Method dialog box should now look like the one shown in Figure 35.22.

Figure 35.22. Adding the Beep() method to the MYCLOCK control.

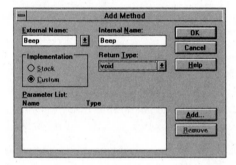

☐ Click the OK button of the Add Method dialog box.

The ClassWizard dialog box reappears, as shown in Figure 35.23.

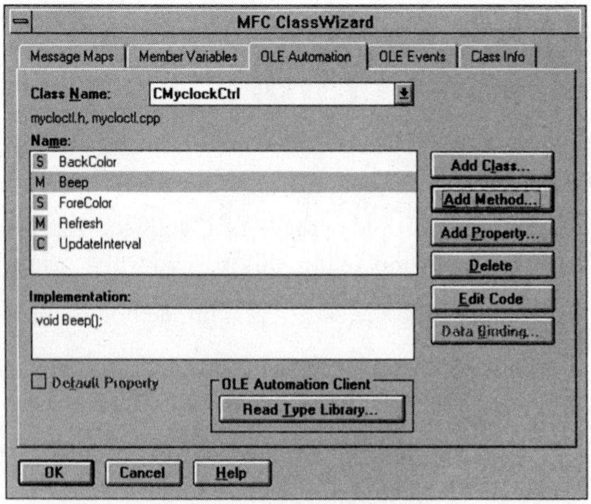

Figure 35.23. The ClassWizard dialog box after you add the Beep custom method.

As shown in Figure 35.23, the Name list now contains the method Beep. Notice that the letter *M* appears to the left of Beep. This *M* serves as an indication that Beep is a method.

> **NOTE**
>
> When you add a custom method to a control, you can add parameters to the method. You do that by clicking the Add button inside the Add Method dialog box. (See Figure 35.22.)
>
> In the preceding steps you were not instructed to click the Add button inside the Add Method dialog box because you don't want the Beep() method to have any parameters.
>
> In your future OCX projects you may need to implement a method that has parameters. When a method has parameters, whoever calls the method needs to pass these parameters to the method.

☐ Close the ClassWizard dialog box by clicking its OK button.

To write the code of the Beep() method do the following:

☐ Open the file MYCLOCTRL.CPP (if it's not open already).

☐ Locate the function Beep() inside the MYCLOCTRL.CPP file (Visual C++ wrote for you the skeleton of this function when you added the Beep() method.)

☐ Write code inside the Beep() function so that it looks like this:

```
void CMyclockCtrl::Beep()
{
// TODO: Add your dispatch handler code here

/////////////////////////
// MY CODE STARTS HERE
/////////////////////////

MessageBeep((WORD)-1);

/////////////////////////
// MY CODE ENDS HERE
/////////////////////////

}
```

☐ Save your work by selecting Save from the File menu.

The code you just typed inside the Beep() function is made of one statement:

```
MessageBeep((WORD)-1);
```

This statement uses the MessageBeep() function to beep.

That's it! You have finished adding the Beep custom method to the MYCLOCK control.

To verify that the MYCLOCK control now has the `Beep()` method and to see (or rather, hear) the `Beep()` method in action do the following:

☐ If you are using Visual C++ 1.51, select Make TypeLib from the Tools menu.

Visual C++ 1.5 responds by creating the type library (.tlb file) for the MYCLOCK control and by displaying an OK message box with the text `Successfully generated type library tlb16\MYCLOCK.tlb`.

☐ Click the OK button of the message box.

NOTE

The preceding two steps are applicable only if you are creating the control with Visual C++ 1.51. If you are creating the control with Visual C++ 2.0, the preceding two steps are *not* applicable.

As stated earlier, in Visual C++ 1.51, after you add a method (or an event or a property) to the control, you have to rebuild the type library prior to building the project. You don't have to do that in Visual C++ 2.0.

☐ Select Build MYCLOCK.DLL (or Build MYCLOCK.OCX) from the Project menu of Visual C++.

Visual C++ responds by compiling and linking the files of the MYCLOCK control.

☐ Select Test Container from the Tools menu of Visual C++.

Visual C++ responds by running the Test Container program.

☐ Select Insert OLE Control from the Edit menu of the Test Container program.

Test Container responds by displaying the Insert OLE Control dialog box.

☐ Select the MYCLOCK control and then click the OK button.

Test Container responds by inserting the MYCLOCK control.

Now test the `Beep()` method as follows:

☐ Select Invoke Methods from the Edit menu of Test Container.

Test Container responds by displaying the Invoke Control Method dialog box.

☐ Set the Name list box of the Invoke Control Method dialog box to `Beep` as shown in Figure 35.24 (because you want to test the `Beep()` method).

Figure 35.24. The Invoke Control Method dialog box with the Name list box set to Beep.

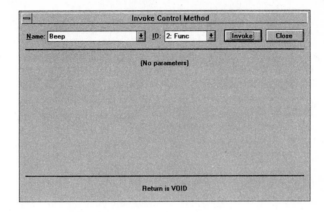

☐ Click the Invoke button several times.

As you can hear, each time you click the Invoke button your PC beeps. The Beep() custom method that you added to the MYCLOCK control is working!

☐ Close the Invoke Control Method dialog box by clicking its Close button.

☐ Terminate Test Container by selecting Exit from the File menu.

Final Words...

In this chapter you further enhanced the MYCLOCK OCX control. You added to the MYCLOCK control a stock event, a custom event, a stock method, and a custom method.

As you have seen in this chapter and in the previous two chapters, developing an OCX control with Visual C++ is easy.

As stated in Chapter 33, in the near future most Visual programming languages will support OCX controls. Therefore, once you finish developing an OCX control, many programmers will be able to use your control.

Index

SYMBOLS

& (ampersand) in dialog-
box-item names, 105
// characters, in comments,
27-28
; (semicolon), declaring
classes, 34
<< characters
insertion operator,
375-376
stream direction, 28
>> (extractor) operator, 376
\ character, 440
{} (curly brackets), declaring
classes, 34
~ (tilde), destructors, 35
8Kenned3.WAV file
playing, 753-754
stopping, 754-755

A

About dialog box, modify-
ing, 478-481
AboutBox( ) method
(MYCLOCK control),
1133-1135
Accel Properties dialog box,
623-624
accelerator keys, attaching to
commands, 621-626
Accelerator table, MyMenu
application, 622-626
access functions, 50-54
Add button, attaching code
to BN_CLICKED event of,
420-422
Add Class dialog box, 132
Add Event dialog box, 1121

Add Member Function dialog box, 111

Add Member Variable dialog box, 152

Add Method dialog box, 1141

AddHead( ) function, 403

AddString( ) function, 238, 260

AddTail( ) function, 422

allocating memory, 83-85

Alt key, 564

ampersand (&) in dialog-box-item names, 105

animation, 842

    declaring variables for
        BALL application, 858-859
        DANCE application, 912-913
        KENNEDY application, 940-942
    frames, displaying first
        BALL application, 862-865
        DANCE application, 918-919
        KENNEDY application, 944-945
    starting
        BALL application, 867-868
        DANCE application, 921-922
        KENNEDY application, 946-947
    stopping
        DANCE application, 925-929, 952-953
        KENNEDY application, 950-953
    timer, 868-871
        DANCE application, 923-925

    KENNEDY application, 948-950
    see also BALL application; DANCE application; KENNEDY application

ANNOUNCE application

    declaring
        CTegMM class, 887-888
        CTegMM class objects, 888-890
    default dialog box size, changing, 896-898
    executing, 876-877, 886-887
    OnIdle( ) function
        beeping, 884-886
        playing WAV files, 891-894
    project
        adding CTegMM.LIB library, 890-891
        creating, 878-882
    static text, displaying, 894-895
    visual implementation
        dialog box form, 882-883
        menu bar, 883

AppendMenu( ) function, 659, 662

application classes, 333

applications

    ANNOUNCE, *see* ANNOUNCE application
    ARCH, *see* ARCH application
    AVI, *see* AVI application
    BALL, *see* BALL application
    Beep, *see* Beep application
    CD, *see* CD application
    ChkBox, *see* ChkBox application

    CircleIt, *see* CircleIt application
    console, *see* console applications
    DANCE, *see* DANCE application
    dialog-based, 92
    distributing DLLs, 984
    DRAW, *see* DRAW application
    DrawIt, *see* DrawIt application
    FileIt, *see* FileIt application
    GROW, *see* GROW application
    idling, 876
        beeping, 884-886
    KENNEDY, *see* KENNEDY application
    MDI (multiple-document interface), 568
        versus SDI (single-document interface) applications, 324-325
    MEMO, *see* MEMO application
    MIX, *see* MIX application
    MyCombo, *see* MyCombo application
    MyDialog, *see* MyDialog application
    MyEdit, *see* MyEdit application
    MyKey, *see* MyKey application
    MyList, *see* MyList application
    MyMenu, *see* MyMenu application
    MyMouse, *see* MyMouse application
    MyRadio, *see* MyRadio application
    MyText, *see* MyText application

MyTimer, *see* MyTimer application

MyTool, *see* MyTool application

PAD, *see* PAD application

PHN, *see* PHN application

SAY, *see* SAY application

ScrollMe, *see* ScrollMe application

SeekIt, *see* SeekIt application

Test, *see* Test application

TestDLL, *see* TestDLL application

testing during visual design process, 274-276

TestLib, *see* TestLib application

WAVE.EXE, *see* WAVE.EXE application

WhereAmI, *see* WhereAmI application

see also programs

AppWizard, 91-97
SDI applications, 331-335

ARCH application
attaching variables to controls, 440

executing, 432-434, 446

project, creating, 434-439

visual implementation
dialog box form, 439-440

menu bar, 441

archives
serializing contents to edit boxes, 444-446

serializing edit-box contents to, 441-444

areas, calculating
circles, 967

rectangles, 68-72

asctime( ) function, 366, 1084

asynchronous sound, *see* **DANCE application**

audio CDs
ejecting, 818-820

loading, 810-813

next track, 817-818

playing, 814

previous track, 816-817

stopping, 814-816

updating Track edit box continuously, 820-822

automatic rewind, WAV files, 724-727

AVI application
attaching variables to dialog box controls, 771-772

declaring CTegMM class objects, 773-775

executing, 762-764

project
adding CTegMM.LIB library, 773

creating, 765-768

reactivating Play button, 782-786

video (AVI) files
opening, 775-780

playing, 780-782

playing without sound, 790-791

previous frame, 789-790

repainting frames, 791-793

stepping through, 788

stopping, 786-787

visual implementation
dialog box form, 769-771

menu bar, 772-773

AVI files, *see* **video files**

B

Back button, attaching code to BN_CLICKED event of, 789-790

BackColor property (MyClock.OCX control), 1089-1091, 1094-1097

background sound, *see* **DANCE application**

BALL application
attaching variables to dialog box controls, 850-851

bitmaps
deleting, 865-866

importing, 851-857

loading, 859-862

changing default dialog box, 871-873

declaring variables, 858-859

displaying first frame, 862-865

executing, 842-844, 857

project, creating, 845-849

starting animation, 867-868

timer, 868-871

visual implementation
dialog box form, 849-850

menu bar, 851

base classes, 72

Beep application
associating menus with classes, 131-132

attaching
code to buttons, 140-143

code to menu items, 135-140

menus to dialog boxes, 133-135

executing, 118-119
project, creating, 119-122
visual implementation
   dialog boxes, 122-124
   menu bar, 124-131
**Beep( ) custom method,
1139-1143**
**beeping while idling,
884-886**
BitBlt( ) function, 864
bitmaps (BMP)
   deleting
      BALL application,
      865-866
      DANCE application,
      919-921
      KENNEDY applica-
      tion, 946
   importing
      BALL application,
      851-857
      DANCE application,
      908-911
      KENNEDY applica-
      tion, 938-939
   loading
      BALL application,
      859-862
      DANCE application,
      913-918
      KENNEDY applica-
      tion, 942-944
**BN_CLICKED events,
attaching code to, 109**
   Add button, 420-422
   Back button, 789-790
   check boxes, 179-181,
   790-791
   Clear 1 button, 153-155
   Clear 2 button, 161-163
   Clear button, 345-347
   Copy button, 163-165
   Delete button, 422-424
   Disable button, 186-188,
   216-218

Display Data button,
   304-305
Display Speed button,
   313-314
Eject button, 818-820
Enable button, 186-188,
   216-218
Enter Speed button,
   312-313
Exit button, 114-116,
   178-179, 200-201,
   238-239, 260-261,
   283-284, 296-297
Her Circle button, 976
Hide button, 181-186,
   213-216
His Circle button,
   975-976
Load button, 444-446,
   812-813, 1001-1004
Max. button, 219-220
Min. button, 218-219
My Circle button, 973-975
Next button, 419-420,
   723-724, 817-818
Open button, 710-715,
   775-780
Our Circle button, 977
Paste button, 165-167
Pause button, 728-729
Play 8Kenned3.WAV
   button, 753-754
Play Bourbon6.MID
   button, 747-751
Play button, 715-718,
   780-782, 814
Prev button, 721-723,
   816-817
Previous button, 416-419
Record button, 729-732
Report Status button,
   284-287
Reset button, 220-222
Save button, 441-444,
   463-464

Say Hello button, 108-116
Show button, 181-186,
   213-216
Start button, 946-947
Start Show button,
   867-868, 921-922
Step button, 788
Stop 8Kenned3.WAV
   button, 754-755
Stop Bourbon6.MID
   button, 751-752
Stop button, 727-728,
   786-787, 814-816,
   928-929
Test 1 button, 153-155
Test 2 button, 159-161
Test button, 345-347
Test MyDLL.DLL button,
   1004-1005
**BN_DOUBLECLICKED
events, 109**
**BN_HSCROLL events of
IDD_DIALOG2 dialog
box, attaching code to,
317-322**
Bourbon6.MID file
   playing, 747-751
   stopping, 751-752
**brackets ({ }), declaring
classes, 34**
**Build xxx command (Project
menu), 26**
buttons
   adding to dialog boxes,
   156
   attaching code to
      COMMAND event of
      Beep 1 Time, Beep 2
      Times, and Beep 3 Times
      buttons,140-143
   attaching code to
      BN_CLICKED event of,
      see BN_CLICKED
      events, attaching code to

attaching variables to
  AVI application,
  771-772
  WAVE.EXE applica-
  tion, 706-707
creating, 103-107
deleting from dialog boxes,
  102-103
left mouse
  pushing down,
    499-504, 1046-1050
  releasing, 502-503
moving, 106
properties, changing, 107
radio
  grouping, 276-278
  initializing, 280-282
  status, determining,
    284-287
  see also MyRadio
    application
reactivating
  Play button, 718-721,
    782-786
  Record button,
    718-721
renaming, 106
resizing, 105-106

C

C++ versus C, 32
  classes versus structures,
    32-33
  declaring variables, 62
CalcArea( ) function, 967
**CalculateArea( ) function,
  40, 42-43**
**Calculator program, playing
  WAV files, 891-894**
CArchive class, 432
CBallView class
  declaring, 858-859
  destructor function,
    865-866

**CCdView class, declaring,
  808-810**
**CCircle class, declaring,
  39-40, 46, 57, 963-964**
CD application
  attaching variables to
    dialog box controls,
    806-807
  audio CDs
    ejecting, 818-820
    loading, 810-813
    next track, 817-818
    playing, 814
    previous track, 816-817
    stopping, 814-816
  declaring CTeggMM class
    objects, 808-810
  executing, 798-800
  project
    adding CTegMM.LIB
      library, 808
    creating, 800-805
  updating Track edit box
    continuously, 820-822
  visual implementation
    dialog box form,
      805-806
    menu bar, 807-808
CD drives, controlling, 696
**CDanceView class, destruc-
  tor function, 920**
CDialog class, 116, 184
**CDrawView class, declaring,
  1021-1022**
CDs
  audio, 796-798
  contents on accompanying
    disc, 2
CFile class, 465-466
**check box tool (Tools
  window), 175**
check boxes
  attaching
    code to BN_CLICKED
      event of, 179-181,
      790-791

variables to (AVI
  application), 771-772
enabling/disabling,
  186-188
hiding/displaying, 181-186
status, displaying, 179-181
see also ChkBox application
**checkmarks, placing in
  commands, 632-635**
**CheckMenuItem( ) function,
  634**
**CheckRadioButton( )
  function, 282**
ChkBox application
  attaching code to
    BN_CLICKED event of
      check boxes, 179-181
    Enable/Disable buttons,
      186-188
    Exit button, 178-179
    Hide/Show buttons,
      181-186
  attaching variables to
    dialog box controls,
    175-176
  executing, 170
  initializing controls,
    176-178
  project, creating, 171-174
  visual implementation,
    dialog box form, 174-175
Circle class, declaring, 33-35
**Circle.CPP program (Listing
  2.2), 36-44**
Circle.LIB library, 957
  Circle.CPP file, 957,
    964-967
  Circle.H file, 958,
    963-964
  declaring CCircle class,
    963-964
  distributing, 981
  generating, 967-968
  including files in TestLib
    application, 978-979
  project, creating, 958-963
  testing, 980

**Circle2.CPP program
(Listing 2.3), 44-48**
**Circle3.CPP program
(Listing 2.4), 50-54**
**Circle4.CPP program
(Listing 2.5), 54-61**
CircleIt application
  drawing circles, 1046-1050
  executing, 1036-1039
  OnDraw( ) function,
    1044-1045
  project, creating,
    1039-1043
  visual implementation,
    menu bar, 1044
circles
  area, calculating, 967
  drawing, 1023-1024,
    1030-1033
      by pressing left mouse
        button, 1046-1050
class keyword, 34
classes
  application, 333
  associating menus with,
    131-132
  attaching to dialog boxes,
    458-459
  base, 72
  CArchive, 432
  CBallView, 858-859
      destructor function,
        865-866
  CCdView, 808-810
  CCircle, 39-40, 46, 57
      declaring, 963-964
  CDanceView, destructor
    function, 920
  CDialog, 116, 184
  CDrawView, declaring,
    1021-1022
  CFile, 465-466
  Circle, 33-35
  CListBox, member
    functions, 246-250

CMainFrame, 333
CMyclockCtrl, constructor
  function, 1097-1098
CMyDlg
  creating, 299-300
  objects, creating,
    301-303
CNewRectangle, 75-76, 80
  class-hierarchy
    relationship with
    CRectangle class,
    78-79
CObList, creating objects
  of, 400-401
CPhone, creating, 396-398
creating for new dialog
  boxes, 299-300, 309
CRectangle, 70-71, 75
CSayDlg, 109
CSpeedDlg
  creating, 309
  objects, creating,
    309-312
CTegMM
  declaring, 887-888
  declaring objects,
    708-710, 745-747,
    773-775, 808-810,
    888-890, 913-918,
    942-944
CTestApp, 333
CTestDoc, 333
CTestView, 333
declaring, 33-35
derived, 72
  creating, 72-78
document, 333
  MEMO application,
    363-366, 369-376
  PAD application,
    589-592, 594-598
  PHN application,
    400-404, 413-416
hierarchies (inheritance),
  72-79

main frame window, 333
names, 39
serializeable, constructor
  functions, 397
versus C structures, 32-33
view, 333
  deriving from
    CFormView class,
    335
  FileIt application,
    460-461
  MEMO application,
    366-369
  PAD application,
    592-594
  PHN application,
    408-412
**ClassWizard command
(Project menu), 108-116,
132, 1121**
**ClassWizard dialog box,
132, 1121**
  Member Variables tab, 152
  Message Maps tab,
    108-116
**Clear 1 button, attaching
code to BN_CLICKED
event, 153-155**
**Clear 2 button, attaching
code to BN_CLICKED
event, 161-163**
**Clear button, attaching code
to BN_CLICKED event,
345-347**
clearing drawing area, 1025
**Click event, attaching to
OCX controls, 1120-1126**
clicking mouse, 502
**CListBox class, member
functions, 246-250**
Close command
  File menu, 37
  System menu, 108
**Close( ) function, 443-444,
465**

closing
 programs, 108
 windows, 37
CMainFrame class, 333
CMultiDocTemplate( )
function, 608
CMyclockCtrl class,
constructor function,
1097-1098
CMyDlg class
 creating, 299-300
 objects, creating, 301-303
CNewRectangle class
 class-hierarchy relationship
  with CRectangle class,
  78-79
 declaring, 75-76, 80
CObList class, creating
objects of, 400-401
colors for OCX controls
 background, 1089-1091,
  1094-1097
 foreground, 1091,
  1094-1097
Colors properties page,
adding to MyClock.OCX
control, 1109-1113
combo box tool (Tools
window), 255
combo boxes, 250
 placing items in combo
  boxes, 258-260
 reading list box items,
  261-264
 transferring contents to
  edit boxes, 265
 see also MyCombo
  application
COMMAND event
 attaching code to Beep 1
  Time, Beep 2 Times,
  and Beep 3 Times
  buttons,140-143
 comparing with UPDATE
  _COMMAND_UI
  message, 639

commands
 adding at runtime,
  657-662
 adding to menus (PAD
  application), 609-610
 attaching accelerator keys
  to, 621-626
 attaching code to,
  620-621, 657-662
  DRAW application,
   1022-1025
  GROW application,
   652-654
  runtime-added
   commands, 663-664
  MyTool application,
   678-683
  with UPDATE_
   COMMAND_UI
   message, 639-644
 deleting from menus,
  654-657, 663
 disabling, 636-638
 File menu
  Close, 37
  Exit, attaching code to,
   135-136
  in FileIt application,
   455
  in MEMO application,
   before customizing,
   360
  in Test application
   before customizing,
   338-339
  in Test application,
   customizing, 343-344
  New, 23
  Open, 28, 373-376,
   597-598
  Save, 373-376, 597-598
  Save As, 25
 Help menu, Foundation
  Classes, 183-184
 inserting into menus, 663

 placing checkmarks in,
  632-635
 Project menu
  Build xxx, 26
  ClassWizard, 108-116,
   132, 1121
  Execute xxx, 98
  Files, 398-399
  Resource menu, Symbols,
   277
  Start menu (Windows),
   Run, 118
  System menu, Close, 108
  Tools menu
   Register Control, 1070
   Test Container, 1070
   Toolbars, 104
  Window menu, filename,
   27
   Output, 26
 see also menu bars
comments, 27-28
companion CD, 2
compiling programs, 25-27
console applications, 22
constructor functions
 CBrush class, 1035
 CCircle class, 966
 CDrawView class, 1022
 CMyclockCtrl class,
  1097-1098
 CNewRectangle class,
  76-77
 CRectangle class, 70, 76
 declaring prototypes,
  34-35
 of serializeable classes, 397
Control Options dialog box,
1066
controls
 OCX, 1062-1063
  attaching custom
   events, 1126-1132
  custom methods,
   1139-1143

custom properties, 1099

moving, 1072

MyClock, *see* MyClock OCX control

naming, 1069

picture display, customizing, 1074-1075

properties pages, 1109-1113

stock (standard) properties, 1088-1094

Test Container program, 1070

VBX, 1063

Controls dialog box, 1066

ControlWizard, 1064

Copy button, attaching code to BN_CLICKED event, 163-165

cout statement, 28

CPhone class, creating, 396-398

CreateFont( ) function, 1057-1060

CreateRectRgn( ) function, 1035

CRectangle class

class-hierarchy relationship with CNewRectangle class, 78-79

declaring, 70-71, 75

CSayDlg class, 109

CSpeedDlg class

creating, 309

objects, creating, 309-312

CTegMM class

declaring, 887-888

declaring objects, 708-710, 745-747, 808-810

ANNOUNCE application, 888-890

AVI application, 773-775

DANCE application, 913-918

KENNEDY application, 942-944

GetNumproperty( ), 726

CTegMM.LIB library, 696

adding to projects

ANNOUNCE application, 890-891

AVI application, 773

CD application, 808

MIX application, 745

WAVE.EXE application, 707-708

playing through PC speakers, 732-733

CTestApp class, 333

CTestDoc class, 333

CTestView class, 333

Ctrl key combinations, detecting, 559-561

curly brackets ({ }), declaring classes, 34

cursor, coordinates, 513

D

DANCE application

animation

starting, 921-922

stopping, 925-929, 952-953

bitmaps

deleting, 919-921

importing, 908-911

loading, 913-918

changing default dialog box, 929-930

declaring

CTegMM class objects, 913-918

variables, 912-913

displaying first frame, 918-919

executing, 900-901, 911

project, creating, 901-905

timer, 923-925

visual implementation

dialog box form, 906-907

menu bar, 907-908

data members, 33

declaring, 34

FileIt application view class, 460-461

MEMO application document class, 363-364

PHN application document class, 400-401

PHN application view class, 408-409

initializing

MEMO application document class, 364-366

MEMO application view class, 366-369

PAD application document class, 591-592

PAD application view class, 592-594

PHN application document class, 401-404

PHN application view class, 409-412

names, 39

reading/writing, 49-54

serializing

MEMO application document class, 373-376

PAD application document class, 597-598

updating
MEMO application
document class,
369-373
PAD application
document class,
594-597
PHN application
document class,
413-416
DblClick event, attaching to OCX controls, 1123-1129
debug targets, 30-31
debugging
creating EXE files for, 97
ScrollMe application,
222-227
DECLARE_SERIAL macro, 427
declaring
classes, 33-35
CBallView, 858-859
CCdView, 808-810
CCircle, 963-964
CDrawView,
1021-1022
CNewRectangle, 75, 80
CRectangle, 70-71, 75
CTegMM, 887-888
CTegMM class objects,
708-710, 745-747,
808-810
ANNOUNCE
application, 888-890
AVI application,
773-775
DANCE application,
913-918
KENNEDY applica-
tion, 942-944
data members, 34
FileIt application view
class, 460-461
MEMO application
document class,
363-364

PHN application
document class,
400-401
PHN application view
class, 408-409
member function proto-
types, 34
variables
BALL application,
858-859
DANCE application,
912-913
global, TestDLL
application,
1000-1001
in C++ versus C, 62
KENNEDY applica-
tion, 940-942
defaults
ANNOUNCE application
dialog box size, changing,
896-898
BALL application dialog
box, changing, 871-873
DANCE application dialog
box, changing, 929-930
KENNEDY application
dialog box, changing,
953-954
MEMO application file
extension displays,
changing, 378-381
MyTimer application
dialog box, changing,
836-838
parameters, 62-65
definition files,
MyDLL.DEF, 992-993
Delete button, attaching code to BN_CLICKED event of, 422-424
delete operator, 83-85
DeleteContents( ) member function, 404-407

DeleteMenu( ) function, 656-657
deleting
bitmaps
BALL application,
865-866
DANCE application,
919-921
KENNEDY applica-
tion, 946
buttons from dialog boxes,
102-103
commands from menus,
654-657, 663
phone list objects, 422-424
from memory, 404-408
derived classes, 72
creating, 72-78
destructor functions
CBallView class, 865-866
CCircle class, 966
CDanceView class, 920
CNewRectangle class, 77
CRectangle class, 76
declaring prototypes,
35-36
development directories (DLLs), 985
device context, 536-537
DeviceType property, multimedia objects, 712
dialog boxes
About, 478-481
Accel Properties, 623-624
Add Class, 132
Add Event, 1121
Add Member Function,
111
Add Member Variable,
152
Add Method, 1141
adding controls, 156
attaching classes, 458-459
attaching menus to,
133-135

attaching variables to controls
ARCH application, 440
AVI application, 771-772
BALL application, 850-851
CD application, 806-807
ChkBox application, 175-176
DrawIt application, 533-534
edit boxes, 152-153, 157-158
FileIt application, 459
IDD_DIALOG1 dialog box (MyDialog application), 300-301
IDD_DIALOG2 dialog box (MyDialog application), 309
MEMO application, 359-361
MyCombo application, 256-258
MyList application, 236
MyMouse application, 495-496
MyRadio application, 278-280
PAD application, 585
PHN application, 395
ScrollMe application, 196-197
Test application, 341
WAVE application, 706-707
WhereAmI application, 520-521
ClassWizard, 132, 1121
Member Variables tab, 152
Message Maps tab, 108-116

Control Options, 1066
Controls, 1066
ControlWizard, 1064
creating
creating classes for, 309
creating for accepting user input, 297-298
creating multiple, 306-307
creating with scroll bars, 307-308
declaring classes for, 299-300
dialog box object, creating, 301-303, 309-312
displaying, 303-304
implementing, 305-306
initializing scroll bars, 314-317
customizing, 101-107
IDD_ABOUTBOX_MYCLOCK, 1134-1135
IDD_ANNOUNCE_FORM, 882-883
IDD_ARCH_FORM, 439-440
IDD_AVI_FORM, 769-771
IDD_BALL_FORM, 849-850
IDD_BEEP_DIALOG, 122-124
IDD_CD_FORM, 805-806
IDD_CHKBOX_DIALOG, 174-175
IDD_DANCE_FORM, 906-907
IDD_DIALOG1, 457-458
IDD_DIALOG2, 307-308
IDD_DRAWIT_FORM, 532-533

IDD_FILEIT_FORM, 456-457
IDD_KENNEDY_FORM, 936-937
IDD_MEMO_FORM, 357-359
IDD_MIX_FORM, 743
IDD_MYCOMBO_DIALOG, 255-256
IDD_MYDIALOG_DIALOG, 295-296
IDD_MYEDIT_DIALOG, 150-151
IDD_MYLIST_DIALOG, 234-235
IDD_MYMENU_FORM, 620
IDD_MYMOUSE_FORM, 494-495
IDD_MYRADIO_DIALOG, 272-276
IDD_MYTIMER_FORM, 830-831
IDD_MYTOOL_FORM, 675-677
IDD_PAD_FORM, 583-585
IDD_PHN_FORM, 393-395
IDD_PROPPAGE_MYCLOCK, 1114-1117
IDD_SAY_DIALOG, 101-107
IDD_SCROLLME_DIALOG, 194-195
IDD_SEEKIT_FORM, 477
IDD_TEST_FORM, 339-340
IDD_TESTDLL_FORM, 998
IDD_TESTLIB_FORM, 972-973

IDD_WAVE_FORM, 704-705

IDD_WHEREAMI_FORM, 519-520

declaring as class data members, 460-461

defaults, changing
  ANNOUNCE application sizes, 896-898
  BALL application, 871-873
  DANCE application, 929-930
  KENNEDY application, 953-954
  MyTimer application, 836-838

Dialog Properties, 134

drawing, 1018-1020

Edit Properties, Style tab, 158

Event Log, 1125

Events for Myclock Control, 1129

hiding all controls, 224-227

initializing controls, 176-178
  MyCombo application, 258-260
  MyList application, 237-238
  MyRadio application, 280-282
  ScrollMe application, 197-200

Insert OLE Control, 1070

item names, underlining letters, 105

Menu Item Properties, 126-131

MFC AppWizard—Step 1, 92-93

MFC AppWizard—Step 2, 93-94

MFC AppWizard—Step 3 of 4, 94-96

MFC AppWizard—Step 4 of 4, 96

MFC AppWizard—Step 5 of 6, 331-332

MFC AppWizard—Step 6 of 6, 332-335

modal, 304

New, 90
  Code/Text item, 23

New Control Information, 1066-1067

New Project, 90-91

New Project Information, 96-97

Project Files, 398-399

Project Options, 1065

Properties
  Group check box, 276
  Style tab, 227

Push Button Properties, 104-106

read-only edit boxes, 227-228

Run Application, 118

Save As, 25

Search, 183-184

Select Class, 132

String Properties, 692

String Table, 378-381

Toolbars, 104

see also MyDialog application

Dialog Properties dialog box, 134

dialog-based applications, 92

Disable button, attaching code to, 186-188, 216-218

disabling commands, 636-638

Display Data button, attaching code to BN_CLICKED event of, 304-305

Display Speed button, attaching code to BN_CLICKED event of, 313-314

DisplayArea( ) function, 41-42, 47-48, 70, 76, 81, 967

distributing DLLs, 984

DllEntryPoint( ) function, 989-990

DLLs (dynamic linked libraries), 959, 984
  creating, 984-985
    customizing CPP files, 988-992
    customizing DEF files, 992-993
    development directories, 985
    projects, creating, 985-987
  OCX controls, *see* MyClock.OCX control
  TestDLL application
    declaring global variables, 1000-1001
    executing, 1006
    loading MyDLL.DLL, 1001-1004
    project creation, 994-998
    testing MyDLL.DLL, 1004-1005
    visual implementation, dialog box form, 998
    visual implementation, menu bar, 999
  versus static libraries, 95

DoClick( ) method, 1135

document classes, 333
  MEMO application
    declaring data members, 363-364
    initializing data members, 364-366

serializing data
members, 373-376
updating data members,
369-373
PAD application, 589-591
initializing data
members, 591-592
serializing data
members, 597-598
updating data members,
594-597
PHN application, 400
initializing data
members, 401-404
updating data members,
413-416
documents, multiple views
of single documents
displaying, 602-603
splitter windows, 607-610
updating, 603-607
DoPropExchange( ) func-
tion, 1103-1104
DOS console applications,
22
DRAW application
attaching code to com-
mands, 1022-1025
drawing
application windows,
1019-1020
circles, 1030-1033
lines, 1026-1027
rectangles, 1033-1036
shapes, 1021-1022
executing, 1008-1011
line attributes, changing,
1027-1030
project, creating,
1011-1015
visual implementation,
menu bar, 1016-1018
drawing
application windows,
1018-1020

circles, 1023-1024,
1030-1033
by pressing left mouse
button, 1046-1050
clearing area, 1025
from within Visual C++
versus from within
Paintbrush, 1008
lines, 1022-1023,
1026-1027
changing attributes,
1027-1030
rectangles, 1024-1025,
1033-1036
shapes, 1021-1022
text
inside MyClock.OCX
control, 1078-1081
with various fonts,
1056-1060
DrawIt application
attaching
codes to mouse
movements, 535-543
variables to dialog box
controls, 533-534
executing, 526-527
project, creating, 527-531
visual implementation
dialog box form,
532-533
menu bar, 534-535
drivers, video
determining if available,
758-759
installing, 759-760
dynamic linked libraries,
***see* DLLs**

E

edit box tool (Tools
window), 151, 358

edit boxes
adding to dialog boxes,
156
attaching variables to,
152-153, 157-158
CD application,
806-807
IDD_DIALOG1 dialog
box (MyDialog
application), 300-301
IDD_DIALOG2 dialog
box (MyDialog
application), 309
PAD application, 585
Test application, 341
properties
changing, 158-159
properties, changing
MEMO application,
361-362
MyMouse application,
496-497
WhereAmI application,
521
read-only, 227-228
saving contents to file,
463-464
see also combo boxes
see also MyEdit application
serializing archive contents
to, 444-446
serializing contents to
archives, 441-444
transferring list box/combo
box contents to, 265
user input
updating data members
after, 369-373
Edit Properties dialog box
Style tab, 158
Eject button
attaching code to
BN_CLICKED event of,
818-820
ejecting audio CDs, 818-820

Ellipse( ) function, 1032, 1049

EN_CHANGE event
attaching code to, 369-373

Enable button
attaching code to, 186-188, 216-218

EnableMenuItem( ) function, 636-638

Enter Speed button
attaching code to BN_CLICKED event of, 312-313

error messages
going directly to lines causing errors, 30
out-of-heap-space, 98
out-of-memory, 98
This program cannot be run in DOS mode, 27
xxx( ) function cannot be found, 642

Error property
multimedia objects, 714-715

Event Log dialog box, 1125

events
BN_CLICKED, attaching code to
Add button, 420-422
Back button, 789-790
check boxes, 179-181, 790-791
Clear 1 button, 153-155
Clear 2 button, 161-163
Copy button, 163-165
Delete button, 422-424
Display Data button, 304-305
Display Speed button, 313-314
Eject button, 818-820
Enter Speed button, 312-313

Exit button, 178-179, 200-201, 238-239, 260-261, 283-284, 296-297
Her Circle button, 976
His Circle button, 975-976
Load button, 444-446, 812-813, 1001-1004
My Circle button, 973-975
Next button, 419-420, 723-724, 817-818
Open button, 710-715, 775-780
Our Circle button, 977
Paste button, 165-167
Pause button, 728-729
Play 8Kenned3.WAV button, 753-754
Play Bourbon6.MID button, 747-751
Play button, 715-718, 780-782, 814
Prev button, 721-723, 816-817
Previous button, 416-419
Record button, 729-732
Report Status button, 284-287
Save button, 441-444, 463-464
Start button, 946-947
Start Show button, 867-868, 921-922
Step button, 788
Stop 8Kenned3.WAV button, 754-755
Stop Bourbon6.MID button, 751-752
Stop button, 727-728, 786-787, 814-816, 928-929

Test 1 button, 153-155
Test 2 button, 159-161
Test MyDLL.DLL button, 1004-1005
BN_HSCROLL, of IDD_DIALOG2 dialog box, attaching code to, 317-322
COMMAND
attaching code to Beep 1 Time/Beep 2 Times/Beep 3 Times buttons, 140-143
comparing with UPDATE_COMMAND_UI message, 639
custom, attaching to OCX controls, 1126-1132
EN_CHANGE, attaching code to, 369-373
MM_MCINOTIFY, attaching code to, 718-721, 782-786, 925-927, 950-953
stock (standard), attaching to OCX controls, 1120-1126
WM_CREATE, attaching code to, 1085-1087
WM_HSCROLL, attaching code to, 201-204
WM_INITDIALOG, attaching code to, 197-200, 258-260, 280-282
IDD_CHKBOX_DIALOG dialog box, 176-178
list boxes, 237-238
WM_LBUTTONDOWN, attaching code to, 1046-1050
WM_MOUSEMOVE, attaching code to, 523-525, 535-543

WM_PAINT, attaching
code to, 791-793
WM_TIMER, attaching
code to, 820-822,
832-834, 1087-1088
BALL application,
868-871
DANCE application,
923-925
KENNEDY applica-
tion, 948-950
see also messages
**Events for Myclock Control
dialog box, 1129**
**EXE files, creating for
debugging, 97**
**Execute xxx command
(Project menu), 98**
**Exit button, attaching code
to BN_CLICKED event of,
114-116, 178-179,
200-201, 238-239,
260-261, 283-284,
296-297**
**Exit command (File menu),
attaching code to, 135-136**
exiting programs, 30
WAVE.EXE application,
699
extractor (>>) operator, 376
**ExtTextOut( ) function,
1080, 1084**

F

File menu commands
Close, 37
Exit, attaching code to,
135-136
in FileIt application, 455
in MEMO application,
before customizing, 360

in Test application
before customizing,
338-339
customizing, 343-344
New, 23
Open, 28, 373-376,
597-598
Save, 373-376, 597-598
Save As, 25, 373-376,
597-598
FileIt application
attaching
classes to dialog boxes,
458-459
code to menu items,
461-463, 466-469
variables to dialog-box
controls, 459
executing, 448-450
project, creating, 450-454
view class, declaring data
members, 460-461
visual implementation
dialog box form,
456-457
menu bar, 454-456
Try It dialog box, 457
**filename commands
(Window menu), 27**
files
AVI (video), 758
experimenting with,
793
hardware/software
requirements, 762
opening, 775-780
playing, 760-761,
780-782
playing without sound,
790-791
previous frame,
789-790
repainting frames,
791-793

stepping through, 788
stopping, 786-787
BMP (bitmap)
deleting, 865-866,
919-921, 946
importing, 851-857,
908-911, 938-939
loading, 859-862,
913-918, 942-944
Circle.CPP, 957, 964-967
displaying, 27
EXE, creating for debug-
ging, 97
extensions
MEMO application
default display,
changing, 378-381
PAD application,
changing display,
598-602
header
Circle.H, 958, 963-964
PHONE.H, 397,
425-426
ICO, 479
MIDI, 736
MRU (most recently used)
lists, 377
MyDLL.CPP, 988-992
MyDLL.DEF definition,
992-993
opening, 28
RC (resource), 100
reading data from,
466-469
MEMO application,
373-376
PAD application,
597-598
PHN application,
428-429
text, creating, 23
WAV, 469-471
format, 697
pausing playback,
728-729

playing, 715-718
playing through PC
speakers, 732-733
recording, 729-732
rewinding, 721-727
saving, 732
setting plackback
position to end of
files, 723-724
stopping, 727-728
testing recording code,
731-732
writing
edit-box contents to,
463-464
to MEMO application,
373-376
to PAD application,
597-598
to PHN application,
428-429
**Files command (Project
menu), 398-399**
FillRect( ) function, 1096
FillRgn( ) function, 1035
**FindWindow( ) function,
892-893**
**FireNewMinute( ) dialog
box, 1130**
**FireNewMinute( ) function,
1131**
**fonts, drawing text with
various, 1056-1060**
**ForeColor property,
MyClock.OCX control,
1091, 1094-1097**
Format( ) function, 835
forms (dialog boxes)
ANNOUNCE application,
882-883
ARCH application,
439-440
AVI application, 769-771
BALL application,
849-850

CD application, 805-806
ChkBox application,
174-175
DANCE application,
906-907
DrawIt application,
532-533
FileIt application, 456-457
KENNEDY application,
936-937
MEMO application,
357-359
MIX application, 743
MyCombo application,
255-256
MyDialog application,
295-296
MyEdit application,
150-151
MyList application,
234-235
MyMenu application, 620
MyMouse application,
494-495
MyRadio application,
272-276
MyTimer application,
830-831
MyTool application,
675-677
PAD application, 583-585
PHN application, 393-395
SAY application, 100-107
ScrollMe application,
194-195
SeekIt application, 477
Test application, 339-340
TestDLL application, 998
TestLib application,
972-973
WAVE application,
704-705
WhereAmI application,
519-520

**Foundation Classes com-
mand (Help menu),
183-184**
frames, displaying first
BALL application,
862-865
DANCE application,
918-919
KENNEDY application,
944-945
freeing memory, 83-85
**xxx( ) function cannot be
found error message, 642**
functions
access, 50-54
AddHead( ), 403
AddString( ), 238, 260
AddTail( ), 422
AppendMenu( ), 659, 662
asctime( ), 366, 1084
BitBlt( ), 864
CalcArea( ), 967
CalculateArea( ), 40, 42-43
CheckMenuItem( ), 634
CheckRadioButton( ), 282
CListBox class, 246-250
Close( ), 443-444, 465
CMultiDocTemplate( ),
608
constructor
CBrush class, 1035
CCircle class, 966
CDrawView class, 1022
CMyclockCtrl class,
1097-1098
CNewRectangle class,
76-77
CRectangle class,
70, 76
declaring prototypes,
34-35
of serializeable classes,
397
CreateFont( ), 1057-1060
CreateRectRgn( ), 1035

DeleteContents( ), 404-407

DeleteMenu( ), 656-657

destructor
    CBallView class, 865-866
    CCircle class, 966
    CDanceView class, 920
    CNewRectangle class, 77
    CRectangle class, 76
    declaring prototypes, 35-36

DisplayArea( ), 41-42, 47-48, 70, 76, 81, 967

DllEntryPoint( ), 989-990

DLLs, *see* DLLs

DoPropExchange( ), 1103-1104

Ellipse( ), 1032, 1049

EnableMenuItem( ), 636-638

ExtTextOut( ), 1080, 1084

FillRect( ), 1096

FillRgn( ), 1035

FindWindow( ), 892-893

FireNewMinute( ), 1130-1131

Format( ), 835

GetAt( ), 411

GetBackColor( ), 1096

GetCheckedRadioButton( ), 286

GetCount( ), 246, 249

GetCurrentTime( ), 835

GetCurSel( ), 241

GetDC( ), 1047, 1048

GetDlgItem( ), 181-185, 224, 315-316

GetDocument( ), 368

GetForeColor( ), 1095

GetKeyState( ), 559-562

GetMenu( ), 659

GetNumProperty( ), 714, 726

GetParent( ), 658

GetPrev( ), 418

GetProcAddress( ), 1004

GetRadius( ), 53-54, 58, 967

GetSubMenu( ), 637, 659

GetText( ), 241-242

GetWindowText( ), 263

InitApplication( ), 1001

InitInstance( ), 608

InsertMenu( ), 663

Invalidate( ), 927, 1023-1025, 1030

IsEmpty( ), 407, 424

itoa( ), 249, 484, 525

KillTimer( ), 838-839, 927

LineTo( ), 541-542

LoadBitmap( ), 861, 918

LoadLibrary( ), 1003

localtime( ), 1083

main( )
    Circle.CPP program, 40-42
    Circle2.CPP program, 46-48
    Circle4.CPP program, 58-60
    CNewRectangle class, 77-78, 82, 84-85
    CRectangle class, 70-72
    Hello.CPP program, 28

member
    adding to classes through inheritance, 72-78
    declaring prototypes, 34
    overriding, 79-81

MessageBeep( ), 500-501, 833, 885

MessageBox( ), 314, 468, 484, 917

MoveTo( ), 541

MyBeep( ), 990-992, 1001

MyDelay( ), 990-992, 1001, 1004

OnAddButton( ), 421-422

OnBackButton( ), 789

OnBeep1Button( ), 141

OnBeep2Button( ), 142

OnBeep3Button( ), 142-143

OnBeepBeep1time( ), 137-138

OnBeepBeep2times( ), 138-139

OnBeepBeep3times( ), 139-140

OnChangeDate( ), 369-371

OnChangeMemo( ), 371-372

OnChangeName( ), 413-414

OnChangeNotes( ), 596, 603-605

OnChangePhone( ), 415-416

OnChangeRef( ), 372-373

OnChangeSubject( ), 594-596, 603-604

OnChar( ), 564-566

OnClear1Button( ), 154-155

OnClear2Button( ), 161-162

OnClearButton( ), 346-347

OnCopyButton( ), 164-165

OnCreate( ), 655-657, 831-832, 1086-1087, 1106

OnDblclkMyList( ), 241-242

OnDeleteButton( ), 423-424

OnDisableButton( ), 187, 216-217, 222-223

OnDisplaydataButton( ), 304-305

OnDisplayspeedButton( ), 313-314

OnDraw(), 862-865,
918-919, 944-945,
1018-1020, 1026-1036,
1044-1045, 1057-1060,
1078-1085, 1094-1097,
1130-1132
OnDrawCircle(),
1023-1024
OnDrawClear(), 1025
OnDrawLine(),
1022-1023
OnDrawRectangle(),
1024-1025
OnEjectButton(), 819-820
OnEnableButton(),
187-188, 217, 223-224
OnEnterdataButton(), 304
OnEnterspeedButton(),
312-313
OnExitButton(), 114-116,
178-179, 200-201,}
238-239, 260, 283,
296-297
OnFileBold(), 621,
636-637, 643-644
OnFileExit(), 135-136
OnFileSamplingRate(),
483-485
OnFileTryit(), 462-463
OnFormatItalic(),
639-640
OnFormatSizeSizepoint1(),
630, 633-634
OnFormatSizeSizepoint2(),
630-631, 634-635
OnGetcountButton(),
248-249
OnGrowingAddItem(),
658-662
OnGrowingItemx(),
652-654, 663-664
OnHercircleButton(), 976
OnHideButton(),
181-182, 213-214,
225-226

OnHiscircleButton(),
975-976
OnHScroll(), 202-208,
212
OnHScrollUpdate(),
318-321
OnIdle(), 876, 891-894
OnInitDialog(), 177-178,
198-199, 237-238,
259-260, 281-282,
314-317
OnInitialUpdate(),
366-368, 410-412,
592-594, 681-682,
810-812, 860-862,
865-866, 915-921,
942-944, 946
OnKeyDown(), 553-564
OnLButtonDown(), 500,
503-513, 1046-1050
OnLButtonUp(),
502-503, 513
OnLoadButton(),
444-446, 811-813,
1002-1004
OnMaxButton(), 220
OnMinButton(), 219
OnMouseMove(),
524-525, 535-543
OnMyCheckbox(),
179-180
OnMycircleButton(),
974-975
OnNewDocument(),
365-366, 401-403,
591-592
OnNextButton(),
419-420, 723-724,
817-818
OnOK(), 115-116
OnOpenButton(),
710-715, 775-780
OnOurcircleButton(), 977
OnPaint(), 792-793,
894-895
OnPasteButton(), 166

OnPauseButton(),
728-729
OnPlayButton(), 716-717,
781-782, 814
OnPlayMidiButton(),
747-751
OnPlayWavButton(),
753-754
OnPrevButton(), 722,
816-817
OnPreviousButton(),
416-419
OnReadit(), 467-469
OnRecordButton(),
730-731
OnReportButton(),
284-287
OnResetButton(), 221
OnSaveButton() function,
442-444
OnSaveIt(), 463-464
OnSayhelloButton(),
111-113
OnShowButton(), 182,
214-215, 226
OnSilentCheck(),
790-791
OnStartButton(),
867-868, 921-922,
946-947
OnStepButton(), 788
OnStopButton(),
727-728, 787, 815,
928-929
OnStopMidiButton(), 752
OnStopWavButton(),
754-755
OnTest1Button(),
153-154
OnTest2Button(),
160-161
OnTestButton(), 345-346,
1004-1006
OnTimer(), 821-822,
832-836, 868-871,
923-925, 948-950,
1087-1088

OnToEditBox(), 262
OnToListboxButton(),
 244-245
OnTryitMessage(), 678
OnTryitMusic(), 678-679
OnUpdate(), 603-606
OnUpdateAllViews(), 605
OnUpdateFormatItalic(),
 642-643
OnUpdateIntervalChanged(),
 1105-1109
Open(), 465
overloading, 54-61, 1045
parameters, default, 62-65
PreCreateWindow(),
 836-838, 871-873,
 896-898, 953-954
PX_Long(), 1103-1104
Read(), 468, 484
ReleaseDC(), 1048
RemoveAt(), 424
RemoveHead(), 407
RemoveMenu(), 663
ReplaceSel(), 199
RGB(), 537
Seek(), 469, 484-485
SelectObject(), 1029,
 1048-1049, 1058
Serialize(), 373-375,
 427-429, 432, 597-598
SetHeight(), 71, 77
SetInitialSize(), 1098
SetModifiedFlag(),
 370-371
SetNumProperty(), 712
SetPixel(), 537, 541
SetRadius(), 53, 58, 966
SetScrollPos(), 199
SetScrollRange(), 199
SetSel(), 199
SetStrProperty(), 712-713
SetTimer(), 811-812, 832,
 839, 922, 1087
SetWidth(), 71, 77
ShowScrollBar(), 214

ShowWindow(), 182,
 186, 214
Sleep(), 885
strcat(), 249
TextOut(), 895,
 1045, 1058
time(), 1083
UpdateAllViews(),
 603-605
UpdateData(), 154, 285,
 368, 411, 465, 525
WindowProc(), 718-721,
 724-726, 782-786,
 925-927, 951-953
Write(), 465

G

General properties page,
 customizing, 1113-1117
GetAt() function, 411
GetBackColor() function,
 1096
GetCheckedRadioButton()
 function, 286
GetCount() function,
 246, 249
GetCurrentTime() function,
 835
GetCurSel() function, 241
GetDC() function,
 1047-1048
GetDlgItem() function, 181,
 183-185, 224, 315-316
GetDocument() function,
 368
GetForeColor() function,
 1095
GetKeyState() function,
 559-562
GetMenu() function, 659
GetNumProperty()
 function, 714, 726
GetParent() function, 658

GetPrev() function, 418
GetProcAddress() function,
 1004
GetRadius() function,
 53-54, 58, 967
GetSubMenu() function,
 637, 659
GetText() function, 241-242
GetWindowText() function,
 263
global variables, declaring
 (TestDLL application),
 1000-1001
going to lines causing errors
 from error messages, 30
grayed commands, 636-638
 code for determining,
  639-644
grouping radio buttons,
 276-278
GROW application
 executing, 644-647
 menu items
  adding at runtime,
   657-662
  attaching code to,
   652-654
  attaching code to
   runtime-added
   commands, 663-664
  deleting, 654-657
 project, creating, 647-651
 visual implementation,
  menu bar, 651-652

H

hardware requirements, AVI
 (video) files, 762
header files
 Circle.H, 958
 PHONE.H, 397, 425-426
Hello.CPP program
 (Listings 2.1/2.2), 25-30

help, adding to toolbar
(MyTool application),
691-694

Help menu, Foundation
Classes command,
183-184

Her Circle button, attaching
code to BN_CLICKED
event of, 976

Hide button, attaching code
to, 181-186, 213-216

hiding
all controls, 224-227
check boxes, 181-186
scroll bars, 213-216
status bar, 677
toolbar, 676-677

hierarchies (classes), 72-79

His Circle button, attaching
code to BN_CLICKED
event of, 975-976

horizontal scroll bar tool
(Tools window), 195

horizontal scroll bars,
201-204

I–J

ICO files, 479

icons
About SeekIt dialog box,
479-481
replacing in toolbar,
685-688

ID numbers
checking, 277
listing, 633

IDC_EDIT1 edit box,
152-153

IDC_EDIT2 edit box,
157-159

IDD_ABOUTBOX_
MYCLOCK dialog box,
1134-1135

IDD_ANNOUNCE_FORM
dialog box, 882-883

IDD_ARCH_FORM dialog
box, 439-440

IDD_AVI_FORM dialog
box, 769-771

IDD_BALL_FORM dialog
box, 849-850

IDD_BEEP_DIALOG
dialog box, 122-124
attaching IDR_MENU1
menu to, 133-135

IDD_CD_FORM dialog
box, 805-806

IDD_CHKBOX_DIALOG
dialog box, 174-175

IDD_DANCE_FORM
dialog box, 906-907

IDD_DIALOG1 dialog box
attaching variables to edit
boxes, 300-301
creating, 297-298
declaring class for,
299-300
displaying, 303-304
FileIt application, 457-458

IDD_DIALOG2 dialog box,
307-308
attaching code to
BN_HSCROLL event
of, 317-322
attaching variables to edit
boxes, 309
declaring class for, 309
initializing scroll bars,
314-317

IDD_DRAWIT_FORM
dialog box, 532-533

IDD_FILEIT_FORM dialog
box, 456-457

IDD_KENNEDY_FORM
dialog box, 936-937

IDD_MEMO_FORM dialog
box, 357-359

IDD_MIX_FORM dialog
box, 743

IDD_MYCOMBO_DIALOG
dialog box, 255-256

IDD_MYDIALOG_DIALOG
dialog box, 295-296

IDD_MYEDIT_DIALOG
dialog box, 150-151

IDD_MYLIST_DIALOG
dialog box, 234-235

IDD_MYMENU_FORM
dialog box, 620

IDD_MYMOUSE_FORM
dialog box, 494-495

IDD_MYRADIO_DIALOG
dialog box, 272-276

IDD_MYTIMER_FORM
dialog box, 830-831

IDD_MYTOOL_FORM
dialog box, 675-677

IDD_PAD_FORM dialog
box, 583-585

IDD_PHN_FORM dialog
box, 393-395

IDD_PROPPAGE_MYCLOCK
dialog box, 1114-1117

IDD_SAY_DIALOG dialog
box, 101-107

IDD_SCROLLME_DIALOG
dialog box, 194-195

IDD_SEEKIT_FORM
dialog box, 477

IDD_TEST_FORM dialog
box, 339-340

IDD_TESTDLL_FORM
dialog box, 998

IDD_TESTLIB_FORM
dialog box, 972-973

IDD_WAVE_FORM dialog
box, 704-705

IDD_WHEREAMI_FORM
dialog box, 519-520

idling applications, 876
beeping, 884-886
see also ANNOUNCE
application

IDR_MENU1 menu
associating with classes,
131-132
attaching to
IDD_BEEP_DIALOG
dialog box, 133-135
customizing, 124-131
IMPLEMENT_SERIAL
macro, 427
importing bitmap files
to BALL application,
851-857
to DANCE application,
908-911
to KENNEDY application,
938-939
#include statement, 28
inheritance (class hierar-
chies), 72-79
InitApplication( ) function,
1001
initializing
data members
MEMO application
document class,
364-366
MEMO application
view class, 366-369
PAD application
document class,
591-592
PAD application view
class, 592-594
PHN application docu-
ment class, 401-404
PHN application view
class, 409-412
dialog box controls
ChkBox application,
176-178
MyCombo application,
258-260
MyList application,
237-238
MyRadio application,
280-282

ScrollMe application,
197-200
scroll bars in dialog boxes,
314-317
UpdateInterval custom
property (MyClock.OCX
control), 1102-1104
InitInstance( ) function, 608
input focus, sending
keyboard messages to
objects with, 553
Insert OLE Control dialog
box, 1070
inserting commands into
menus, 663
insertion (<<) operator,
375-376
InsertMenu( ) function, 663
installing
timer (Windows)
MyClock.OCX control,
1085-1088
MyTimer application,
831-832
video drivers, 759-760
int variables, serializing
(MEMO application), 382
Invalidate( ) function, 927,
1023-1025, 1030
IsEmpty( ) function, 407,
424
Italic menu item, code for
determining if grayed/
active, 639-644
itoa( ) function, 249, 484,
525

K

KENNEDY application
animation
starting, 946-947
stopping, 950-953

bitmaps
deleting, 946
importing, 938-939
loading, 942-944
changing default dialog
box, 953-954
declaring
CTegMM class objects,
942-944
variables, 940-942
displaying first frame,
944-945
executing, 930-932,
939-940
project, creating, 932-935
timer, 948-950
visual implementation
dialog box form,
936-937
menu bar, 937-938
keyboard
messages, processing, 553
pressing keys, 553-554
Ctrl key combinations,
559-561
determining which
keys, 555-556
printable keys, 556,
564-566
Shift key combinations,
561-562
toggle keys, 562-564
virtual (nonprintable)
keys, 556-558
see also MyKey application
keys
accelerator, attaching to
commands (MyMenu
application), 621-626
Close (Alt+F4), 108
keywords
class, 34
private, 36
public, 36
KillTimer( ) function,
838-839, 927

L

left mouse button, attaching code to
  pushing down, 499-504, 1046-1050
  releasing, 502-503
libraries
  Circle.LIB, 957
    Circle.CPP file, 957, 964-967
    Circle.H file, 958, 963-964
    distributing, 981
    generating, 967-968
    including files in TestLib application, 978-979
    project, creating, 958-963
    testing, 980
  CTegMM.LIB, 696
    adding to ANNOUNCE application project, 890-891
    adding to AVI application project, 773
    adding to CD application project, 808
    adding to MIX application project, 745
    adding to WAVE.EXE application project, 707-708
    playing through PC speakers, 732-733
  DLLs, *see* DLLs
  static, 959
    versus DLLs (dynamic linked libraries), 95
lines
  changing attributes, 1027-1030
  drawing, 1022-1023, 1026-1027

LineTo( ) function, 541
linking programs, 25-27
list box tool (Tools window), 235
list boxes
  adding list items, 243-246
  placing items in list boxes, 237-238
  reading items from, 239-242
  transferring contents to edit boxes, 265
  see also combo boxes; MyList application
listings
  2.1. Hello.CPP program, 25
  2.2. Circle.CPP program, 37-39
  2.3. Circle2.CPP program, 44-46
  2.4. Circle3.CPP program, 50-52
  2.5. Circle4.CPP program, 54-57
  3.1. Rect.CPP program, 68-69
  3.2. RECT2.CPP program, 72-75
lists
  MRU (most recently used) files, 377
  phone
    adding blank objects, 420-422
    creating, 400-401
    deleting objects, 422-424
    deleting objects from memory, 404-408
    moving to next object, 419-420
    moving to previous object, 416-419
    serializing, 425-430
    see also PHN application

Load button, attaching code to BN_CLICKED event of, 444-446, 812-813, 1001-1004
LoadBitmap( ) function, 861, 918
loading
  audio CDs, 810-813
  bitmaps
    BALL application, 859-862
    DANCE application, 913-918
    KENNEDY application, 942-944
    MyDLL.DLL, 1001-1004
LoadLibrary( ) function, 1003
localtime( ) function, 1083

M

m_Edit1 variable, 152-153
m_Edit2 variable, 157-158
macros
  DECLARE_SERIAL, 427
  IMPLEMENT_SERIAL, 427
main frame window classes, 333
main windows, *see* **dialog boxes**
main( ) function
  Circle.CPP program, 40-42
  Circle2.CPP program, 46-48
  Circle4.CPP program, 58-60
  CNewRectangle class, 77-78, 82, 84-85
  CRectangle class, 70-72
  Hello.CPP program, 28
.mak windows, Target drop-down list box, 97

Max. button, attaching code to, 219-220

MDI (multiple-document interface) applications, 568

Media Player (Windows), 758-761, 796-798

member functions, 33
adding to classes through inheritance, 72-78
CListBox class, 246-250
declaring prototypes, 34
overriding, 79-81
see also functions

MEMO application
document class
declaring data members, 363-364
initializing data members, 364-366
serializing data members, 373-376
updating data members, 369-373
edit boxes, changing properties, 361-362
executing, 350-353, 377, 381
file extension default displays, changing, 378-381
project, creating, 353-356
reading data from files, 373-376
title, changing, 378-381
variables
attaching to controls, 359-361
serializing, 382
view class, initializing data members, 366-369
visual implementation
dialog box form, 357-359
menu bar, 362-363
writing data to files, 373-376

memory
allocating/freeing, 83-85
deleting phone list objects from, 404-408

menu bars
customizing
IDR_MENU1 menu, 124-131
Test application, 341-345
visual implementation
ANNOUNCE application, 883
ARCH application, 441
AVI application, 772-773
BALL application, 851
CD application, 807-808
CircleIt application, 1044
DANCE application, 907-908
DRAW application, 1016-1018
DrawIt application, 534-535
FileIt application, 454-456
GROW application, 651-652
KENNEDY application, 937-938
MEMO application, 362-363
MIX application, 744-745
MyKey application, 552-553
MyMenu application, 619-620
MyMouse application, 497-499
MyText application, 1056
MyTimer application, 829-830

MyTool application, 673-675
PAD application, 585-587
PHN application, 395-396
SeekIt application, 477-478
TestDLL application, 999
WAVE application, 707
WhereAmI application, 522-523

Menu Item Properties dialog box, 126-131

menus
adding commands
at runtime, 657-662
PAD application, 609-610
associating with classes, 131-132
attaching accelerator keys to commands, 621-626
attaching code to commands, 135-140, 620-621, 652-654, 657-662
DRAW application, 1022-1025
FileIt application, 461-463, 466-469
MyTool application, 678-683
runtime-added commands, 663-664
SeekIt application, 482-485
with UPDATE_ COMMAND_UI message, 639-644
attaching to dialog boxes, 133-135
deleting commands, 654-657, 663

disabling commands,
636-638
inserting commands, 663
placing checkmarks in
commands, 632-635
submenus, 626-632
see also GROW
application; MyMenu
application
**MessageBeep( ) function,
500-501, 833, 885**
**MessageBox( ) function,
314, 468, 484, 917**
messages
keyboard, processing, 553
SB_LINEDOWN,
208-209
SB_LINEUP, 209
SB_PAGEDOWN, 210
SB_PAGEUP, 210-211
SB_THUMBPOSITION,
203
SB_THUMBTRACK, 212
scroll bar, attaching code
to, 206-211
UPDATE_COMMAND_UI,
639-644
WM_CHAR, 557,
564-566
WM_KEYDOWN,
555-558
WM_LBUTTONDOWN,
recipients, 505
WM_LBUTTONUP,
recipients, 504-505
WM_MOUSEMOVE,
processing, 525-526
see also events
methods
DoClick( ), 1135
MyClock.OCX control,
1133
AboutBox( ),
1133-1135
custom, 1139-1143

parameters for custom,
1141
Refresh( ), 1135-1139
stock (standard),
1135-1139
**MFC AppWizard—Step 1
dialog box, 92-93**
**MFC AppWizard—Step 2
dialog box, 93-94**
**MFC AppWizard—Step 3
of 4 dialog box, 94-96**
**MFC AppWizard—Step 4
of 4 dialog box, 96**
**MFC AppWizard—Step 5
of 6 dialog box, 331-332**
**MFC AppWizard—Step 6
of 6 dialog box, 332-335**
MIDI files, 696, 736
playing
8Kenned3.WAV,
753-754
Bourbon6.MID,
747-751
stopping
8Kenned3.WAV,
754-755
Bourbon6.MID,
751-752
see also MIX application
**Min. button, attaching code
to, 218-219**
MIX application
declaring CTegMM class
objects, 745-747
executing, 736-738
playing MIDI files
8Kenned3.WAV,
753-754
Bourbon6.MID,
747-751
project
adding CTegMM.LIB
to, 745
creating, 738-743

stopping MIDI files
8Kenned3.WAV,
754-755
Bourbon6.MID,
751-752
visual implementation
dialog box form, 743
menu bar, 744-745
**MM_MCINOTIFY event,
attaching code to,
718-721, 925-927,
950-953**
AVI application, 782-786
modal dialog boxes, 304
**most-recently used (MRU)
file lists, 377**
mouse
left button
pushing down,
499-504, 1046-1050
releasing, 502-503
messages, processing,
504-505
movements
attaching codes to
(DrawIt application),
535-543
attaching codes to
(WhereAmI applica-
tion), 523-525
processing, 525-526
see also DrawIt application;
MyMouse application;
WhereAmI application
**mouse cursor, coordinates,
513**
MoveTo( ) function, 541
moving
buttons, 106
OCX controls, 1072
**MRU (most-recently used)
file lists, 377**
multimedia
audio CDs
ejecting, 818-820
loading, 810-813

next track, 817-818
playing, 814
previous track, 816-817
stopping, 814-816
updating Track Edit
box continuously,
820-822
AVI (video) files, 758
hardware/software
requirements, 762
playing, 760-761
CTegMM.LIB library,
696, 732-733
MIDI files
playing, 747-754
stopping, 751-752,
754-755
video (AVI) files
opening, 775-780
playing, 780-782
playing without sound,
790-791
previous frame,
789-790
reactivating Play
button, 782-786
stepping through, 788
stopping, 786-787
video drivers
determining if available,
758-759
installing, 759-760
WAV files, 697
CTegMM.LIB library,
696, 732-733
opening, 698, 710-715
pausing playback,
728-729
playing, 698, 715-718
playing through PC
speakers, 732-733
recording, 698,
729-732

rewinding, 721-723,
724-727
sampling rate, 469-471
saving, 732
setting plackback
position to end of
files, 723-724
stopping, 727-728
testing recording code,
731-732
see also AVI application;
MIX application; WAV
application
**multiple-document interface
(MDI) applications, 568**
**My Circle button, attaching
code to BN_CLICKED
event of, 973-975**
**MyBeep( ) function,
990-992, 1001**
MyClock.OCX control
development versions,
1063
displaying current time,
1082-1085
continuously,
1085-1088
drawing text, 1078-1081
events
custom, 1126-1132
stock (standard),
1120-1126
initial size, setting,
1097-1098
methods, 1133
AboutBox( ),
1133-1135
custom, 1139-1143
stock (standard),
1135-1139
picture display, customizing, 1074-1075
project, creating,
1063-1068

properties
BackColor and
ForeColor,
1094-1097
stock (standard),
1088-1094
UpdateInterval custom,
1099-1109, 1138
properties pages
Colors, adding,
1109-1113
General, customizing,
1113-1117
registering, 1070
testing, 1068-1073
update intervals, setting,
1104-1107
MyCombo application
attaching code to
BN_CLICKED event of
Exit button, 260-261,
283-284
Report Status button,
284-287
attaching variables to
dialog box controls,
256-258
executing, 250-251
initializing dialog box
controls, 258-260
project, creating, 251-254
reading list box items,
261-264
transferring contents of list
boxes/combo boxes to
edit boxes, 265
visual implementation,
dialog box form, 255-256
**MyDelay( ) function,
990-992, 1001, 1004**
MyDialog application
attaching code to
BN_CLICKED event of
Display Data button,
304-305

Display Speed button,
313-314
Enter Speed button,
312-313
Exit button, 296-297
attaching code to
BN_HSCROLL event of
IDD_DIALOG2 dialog
box, 317-322
attaching variables to
controls
IDD_DIALOG1 dialog
box, 300-301
IDD_DIALOG2 dialog
box, 309
class objects, creating,
301-303, 309-312
creating dialog boxes
for accepting user
input, 297-298
multiple, 306-307
declaring classes for
new dialog boxes,
299-300, 309
displaying
IDD_DIALOG1 dialog
box, 303-304
executing, 290-291
implementing dialog
boxes, 305-306
initializing scroll bars,
314-317
project, creating, 291-294
visual implementation
dialog box form,
295-296
dialog boxes with scroll
bars, 307-308
MyDLL.DLL
development directory,
985
loading, 1001-1004
MyDLL.CPP file,
customizing, 988-992
MyDLL.DEF file,
customizing, 992-993

project, creating, 985-987
testing, 1004-1005
MyEdit application
adding buttons and edit
boxes, 156
attaching code to
BN_CLICKED events
of, 153-155
Clear 2 button,
161-163
Copy button, 163-165
Paste button, 165-167
Test 2 button, 159-161
attaching variables to edit
boxes, 152-153, 157-158
edit box properties,
changing, 158-159
executing, 146-147
project, creating, 147-150
visual implementation,
dialog box form, 150-151
MyKey application
executing, 546-548
keyboard messages,
processing, 553
pressing keys, 553-554
Ctrl key combinations,
559-561
determining which
keys, 555-556
printable keys, 556,
564-566
Shift key combinations,
561-562
toggle keys, 562-564
virtual (nonprintable)
keys, 556-558
project, creating, 548-552
visual implementation,
menu bar, 552-553
MyList application
adding list box items,
243-246
attaching code to
BN_CLICKED event of
Exit button, 238-239

CListBox class member
functions, 246-250
dialog box controls
attaching variables to,
236
initializing, 237-238
executing, 230-231
project, creating, 231-234
reading list box items,
239-242
visual implementation,
dialog box form, 234-235
MyMenu application
executing, 612-615
menu items
attaching accelerator
keys to, 621-626
attaching code to,
620-621
attaching code to
with UPDATE_
COMMAND_UI
message, 639-644
disabling, 636-638
placing checkmarks in,
632-635
project, creating, 615-619
submenus, 626-632
visual implementation
dialog box form, 620
menu bar, 619-620
MyMouse application
attaching code to left
mouse button
pushing down, 499-504
releasing, 502-503
attaching variables to
controls, 495-496
edit box properties,
changing, 496-497
executing, 488-490
mouse cursor, coordinates,
513
mouse messages, process-
ing, 504-505
project, creating, 490-493

visual implementation
  dialog box form,
    494-495
  menu bar, 497-499
MyRadio application
  dialog box controls
    attaching variables to,
      278-280
    initializing, 280-282
  executing, 268
  grouping radio buttons,
    276-278
  project, creating, 269-272
  visual implementation,
    dialog box form, 272-276
MyText application
  drawing text with various
    fonts, 1056-1060
  executing, 1050-1051
  project, creating,
    1051-1055
  visual implementation,
    menu bar, 1056
MyTimer application
  attaching code to
    WM_TIMER event,
    832-834
  changing default dialog
    box, 836-838
  current time, displaying,
    834-836
  executing, 824, 834
    final version, 838
  project, creating, 825-829
  timer
    installing, 831-832
    killing, 838-839
  visual implementation
    dialog box form,
      830-831
    menu bar, 829-830
MyTool application
  attaching code to com-
    mands, 678-683

customizing status bar,
  688-691
executing, 666-669
project, creating, 669-673
toolbar
  customizing, 683-685
  help, adding, 691-694
  replacing icons,
    685-688
visual implementation
  dialog box form,
    675-677
  menu bar, 673-675

N

names
  classes, 39
  data members, 39
  dialog-box items, underlin-
    ing letters, 105
  OCX controls, 1069
  renaming buttons, 106
**New command (File menu),
  23**
**New Control Information
  dialog box, 1066-1067**
New dialog box, 90
  Code/Text item, 23
new operator, 83-85
**New Project dialog box,
  90-91**
**New Project Information
  dialog box, 96-97**
**NewMinute custom event
  (MyClock.OCX control),
  1126-1132**
**Next button, attaching code
  to BN_CLICKED event of,
  419-420, 723-724,
  817-818**
**nonprintable (virtual) keys,
  556-558**

O

objects
  creating, 40
  CTegMM class, declaring,
    708-710, 745-747,
    773-775, 808-810,
    888-890, 913-918,
    942-944
  pointers to, 82-83
OCX controls, 1062-1063
  custom events, 1126-1132
  custom methods,
    1139-1143
  moving, 1072
  naming, 1069
  picture display, customiz-
    ing, 1074-1075
  properties
    custom, 1099
    stock (standard),
      1088-1094
  properties pages,
    1109-1113
  Test Container program,
    1070
  MyClock, *see*
    MyClock.OCX control
**OnAddButton( ) function,
  421-422**
**OnBackButton( ) function,
  789**
**OnBeep1Button( ) function,
  141**
**OnBeep2Button( ) function,
  142**
**OnBeep3Button( ) function,
  142-143**
**OnBeepBeep1time( )
  function, 137-138**
**OnBeepBeep2times( )
  function, 138-139**
**OnBeepBeep3times( )
  function, 139-140**

OnChangeDate() function,
369-371
OnChangeMemo() function, 371-372
OnChangeName() function,
413-414
OnChangeNotes() function,
596, 603-605
OnChangePhone() function, 415-416
OnChangeRef() function,
372-373
OnChangeSubject()
function, 594-596,
603-604
OnChar() function,
564-566
OnClear1Button() function,
154-155
OnClear2Button() function,
161-162
OnClearButton() function,
346-347
OnCopyButton() function,
164-165
OnCreate() function,
655-657, 831-832,
1086-1087, 1106
OnDblclkMyList() function, 241-242
OnDeleteButton() function,
423-424
OnDisableButton()
function, 187, 216-217,
222-223
OnDisplaydataButton()
function, 304-305
OnDisplayspeedButton()
function, 313-314
OnDraw() function,
862-865, 918-919,
944-945, 1018-1020,
1026-1036, 1044-1045,
1057-1060, 1078-1085,
1094-1097, 1130-1132

OnDrawCircle() function,
1023-1024
OnDrawClear() function,
1025
OnDrawLine() function,
1022-1023
OnDrawRectangle()
function, 1024-1025
OnEjectButton() functions,
819-820
OnEnableButton() function,
187-188, 217, 223-224
OnEnterdataButton()
function, 304
OnEnterspeedButton()
function, 312-313
OnExitButton() function,
114-116, 178-179,
200-201, 238-239, 260,
283, 296-297
OnFileBold() function, 621,
636-637, 643-644
OnFileExit() function,
135-136
OnFileSamplingRate()
function, 483-485
OnFileTryit() function,
462-463
OnFormatItalic() function,
639-640
OnFormatSizeSizepoint1()
function, 630, 633-634
OnFormatSizeSizepoint2()
function, 630-631,
634-635
OnGetcountButton()
function, 248-249
OnGrowingAddItem()
function, 658-662
OnGrowingItemx() functions, 652-654, 663-664
OnHercircleButton()
function, 976
OnHideButton() function,
181-182, 213-214,
225-226

OnHiscircleButton()
function, 975-976
OnHScroll() function,
202-208, 212
OnHScrollUpdate()
function, 318-321
OnIdle() function, 876
   attaching code to, 884-886
   playing WAV files,
   891-894
OnInitDialog() function,
177-178, 198-199,
237-238, 259-260,
281-282, 314-317
OnInitialUpdate() function,
366-368, 410-412,
592-594, 681-682,
810-812, 860-862,
865-866, 915-921,
942- 946
OnKeyDown() function,
553-564
OnLButtonDown()
function, 500, 503-513,
1046-1050
OnLButtonUp() function,
502-503, 513
OnLoadButton() function,
444-446, 811-813,
1002-1004
OnMaxButton() function,
220
OnMinButton() function,
219
OnMouseMove() function,
524-525, 535-543
OnMyCheckbox() function,
179-180
OnMycircleButton()
function, 974-975
OnNewDocument()
function, 365-366,
401-403, 591-592
OnNextButton() function,
419-420, 723-724,
817-818

OnOK() function, 115-116

OnOpenButton() function, 710-715, 775-780

OnOurcircleButton() function, 977

OnPaint() function, 792-793, 894-895

OnPasteButton() function, 166

OnPauseButton() function, 728-729

OnPlayButton() function, 716-717, 781-782, 814

OnPlayMidiButton() function, 747-751

OnPlayWavButton() function, 753-754

OnPrevButton() function, 722, 816-817

OnPreviousButton() function, 416-419

OnReadit() function, 467-469

OnRecordButton() function, 730-731

OnReportButton() function, 284-287

OnResetButton() function, 221

OnSaveButton() function, 442-444

OnSaveIt() function, 463-464

OnSayhelloButton() function, 111-113

OnShowButton() function, 182, 214-215, 226

OnSilentCheck() function, 790-791

OnStartButton() function, 867-868, 921-922, 946-947

OnStepButton() function, 788

OnStopButton() function, 727-728, 787, 815, 928-929

OnStopMidiButton() function, 752

OnStopWavButton() function, 754-755

OnTest1Button() function, 153-154

OnTest2Button() function, 160-161

OnTestButton() function, 345-346, 1004-1006

OnTimer() function, 821-822, 832-836, 868-871, 923-925, 948-950, 1087-1088

OnToEditBox() function, 262

OnToListboxButton() function, 244-245

OnTryitMessage() function, 678

OnTryitMusic() function, 678-679

OnUpdate() function, 603-606

OnUpdateAllViews() function, 605

OnUpdateFormatItalic() function, 642-643

OnUpdateIntervalChanged() function, 1105-1109

Open button, attaching code to BN_CLICKED event of, 710-715, 775-780

Open command (File menu), 28, 373-376, 597-598

Open() function, 465

opening files, 28
    video (AVI) files, 775-780
    WAV files, 698, 710-715

operators
    << (insertion), 375-376
    >> (extractor), 376
    delete, 83-85
    new, 83-85

option buttons, *see* radio buttons

Our Circle button, attaching code to BN_CLICKED event of, 977

out-of-heap-space error message, 98

out-of-memory error message, 98

Output command (Window menu), 26

output window, 26

overloaded functions, 54-61, 1045

overriding member functions, 79-81

P–Q

PAD application
    adding commands to menus, 609-610
    attaching variables to dialog-box controls, 585
    document class, 589-591
        initializing data members, 591-592
        serializing data members, 597-598
        updating data members, 594-597
    executing, 568-578, 588-589, 610
    multiple views of single documents
        displaying, 602-603
        splitter windows, 607-610
        updating, 603-607
    project, creating, 579-583
    reading data from files, 597-598
    titles, changing, 598-602
    view class, initializing data members, 592-594

visual implementation
dialog box form,
583-585
menu bar, 585-587
writing data to files,
597-598

**Paintbrush, drawing from
within, versus from within
Visual C++, 1008**

parameters
custom events, 1128
custom methods, 1141
default, 62-65

**Paste button, attaching code
to BN_CLICKED event of,
165-167**

**Pause button, attaching code
to BN_CLICKED event of,
728-729**

**pausing playback (WAV
files), 728-729**

pens
changing attributes,
1027-1030
restoring original,
1049-1050

PHN application
attaching code to
BN_CLICKED event of
Add button, 420-422
Delete button, 422-424
Next button, 419-420
Previous button,
416-419
attaching variables to
controls, 395
CObList class, creating
objects of, 400-401
CPhone class, creating,
396-398
document class, 400
initializing data
members, 401-404
updating data members,
413-416

executing, 386-388, 396,
424-425
phone lists
deleting objects from
memory, 404-408
serializing, 425-430
project
adding PHONE.CPP
program, 398-399
creating, 389-393
title, changing, 430
view class
declaring data mem-
bers, 408-409
initializing data
members, 409-412
visual implementation
dialog box form,
393-395
menu bar, 395-396

phone lists
adding blank objects,
420-422
creating, 400-401
deleting objects, 422-424
from memory, 404-408
moving to
next object, 419-420
previous object,
416-419
serializing, 425-430

**PHONE.CPP program,
397-398, 426-427**
adding to PHN application
project, 398-399

**PHONE.H header file, 397,
425-426**

**picture display (OCX
controls), customizing,
1074-1075**

**Play 8Kenned3.WAV
button, attaching code to
BN_CLICKED event of,
753-754**

**Play Bourbon6.MID button,
attaching code to
BN_CLICKED event of,
747-751**

Play button
attaching code to
BN_CLICKED event of,
715-718, 780-782, 814
reactivating
AVI application,
782-786
WAVE application,
718-721

playback (WAV files)
pausing, 728-729
position
rewinding, 724-727
setting to end of WAV
files, 723-724
stopping, 727-728

playing
audio CDs, 814
AVI (video) files, 760-761,
780-782
without sound,
790-791
MIDI files
8Kenned3.WAV,
753-754
Bourbon6.MID,
747-751
WAV files, 698
OnIdle( ) function,
891-894
through PC speakers,
732-733

pointers to objects, 82-83

**pop-up menus (WAVE.EXE
application), 699**

**PreCreateWindow( )
function, 836-838,
871-873, 896-898,
953-954**

**Prev button, attaching code
to BN_CLICKED event of,
721-723, 816-817**

Previous button, attaching code to BN_CLICKED event of, 416-419
Print Screen key, 564
private keyword, 36
programs
Circle.CPP (Listing 2.2), 36-44
Circle2.CPP (Listing 2.3), 44-48
Circle3.CPP (Listing 2.4), 50-54
Circle4.CPP (Listing 2.5), 54-61
closing, 108
compiling, 25-27
executing, 27
exiting, 30
Hello.CPP (Listings 2.1, 2.2), 25-30
linking, 25-27
Media Player (Windows), 758-759
PHONE.CPP, 397-398, 426-427
adding to PHN application project, 398-399
Rect.CPP (Listing 3.1), 68-72
RECT2.CPP (Listing 3.2), 72-78
RECT3.CPP, 79-81
RECT4.CPP, 82-83
RECT5.CPP, 83-85
saving, 25
Test Container, 1070
see also applications
Project Files dialog box, 398-399
Project menu commands
Build xxx, 26
ClassWizard, 108-116, 132, 1121
Execute xxx, 98
Files, 398-399

Project Options dialog box, 1065
projects
adding CTegMM.LIB library to
ANNOUNCE application, 890-891
AVI application, 773
CD application, 808
MIX application, 745
WAVE application, 707-708
creating
ANNOUNCE application, 878-882
ARCH application, 434-439
BALL application, 845-849
Beep application, 119-122
CD application, 800-805
ChkBox application, 171-174
Circle.LIB library, 958-963
CircleIt application, 1039-1043
DANCE application, 901-905
DLLs, 985-987
DRAW application, 1011-1015
DrawIt application, 527-531
FileIt application, 450-454
GROW application, 647-651
KENNEDY application, 932-935
MEMO application, 353-356
MIX application, 738-743

MyClock.OCX control, 1063-1068
MyCombo application, 251-254
MyDialog application, 291-294
MyEdit application, 147-150
MyKey application, 548-552
MyList application, 231-234
MyMenu application, 615-619
MyMouse application, 490-493
MyRadio application, 269-272
MyText application, 1051-1055
MyTimer application, 825-829
MyTool application, 669-673
PAD application, 579-583
PHN application, 389-393
SAY application, 90-97
ScrollMe application, 191-193
SeekIt application, 473-477
Test application, 328-335
TestDLL application, 994-998
TestLib application, 968-972
WAVE application, 700-704
WhereAmI application, 515-519
PHN application, adding PHONE.CPP program, 398-399

properties
   BackColor
      (MyClock.OCX control),
      1089-1091, 1094-1097
   buttons, changing, 107
   custom, adding to controls,
      1099
   DeviceType (multimedia
      objects), 712
   edit boxes, changing,
      158-159
      MEMO application,
         361-362
      MyMouse application,
         496-497
      WhereAmI application,
         521
   Error (multimedia objects),
      714-715
   ForeColor (MyClock.OCX
      control), 1091,
      1094-1097
   stock (standard),
      1088-1094
   UpdateInterval custom
      (MyClock.OCX control),
      1099-1109
      increasing values, 1138
Properties dialog box
   Group check box, 276
   Style tab, 227
properties pages
   adding to controls, 1109
   Colors, adding to
      MyClock.OCX control,
      1109-1113
   General, customizing,
      1113-1117
**Properties Pages tables
   (MYCLOCTRL.CPP file),
   1111-1113**
Properties tables, 123
   IDD_ANNOUNCE_FORM
      dialog box, 883
   IDD_ARCH_FORM
      dialog box, 439

IDD_AVI_FORM dialog
   box, 770
IDD_BALL_FORM
   dialog box, 850
IDD_BEEP_DIALOG
   dialog box, 123
IDD_CD_FORM dialog
   box, 805-806
IDD_CHKBOX_DIALOG
   dialog box, 174
IDD_DANCE_FORM
   dialog box, 906
IDD_DIALOG1 dialog
   box, 458
IDD_DIALOG2 dialog
   box, 308
IDD_DRAWIT_FORM
   dialog box, 532
IDD_KENNEDY_FORM
   dialog box, 937
IDD_MEMO_FORM
   dialog box, 358
IDD_MIX_FORM dialog
   box, 743
IDD_MYCOMBO_DIALOG
   dialog box, 255
IDD_MYDIALOG_DIALOG
   dialog box, 295
IDD_MYEDIT_DIALOG
   dialog box, 150-151
IDD_MYLIST_DIALOG
   dialog box, 235
IDD_MYMOUSE_FORM
   dialog box, 495
IDD_MYRADIO_DIALOG
   dialog box, 273
IDD_PAD_FORM dialog
   box, 584
IDD_PHN_FORM dialog
   box, 394
IDD_SCROLLME_DIALOG
   dialog box, 195
IDD_TEST_FORM
   dialog box, 340
IDD_TESTDLL_FORM
   dialog box, 998

IDD_TESTLIB_FORM
   dialog box, 973
IDD_WAVE_FORM
   dialog box, 704-705
IDD_WHEREAMI_FORM
   dialog box, 520
public keyword, 36
push button controls,
   see **buttons**
**Push Button Properties
   dialog box, 104-106**
**push button tool (Tools
   window), 103, 123**
**PX_Long( ) function,
   1103-1104**

R

**radio button tool (Tools
   window), 274**
radio buttons
   grouping, 276-278
   initializing, 280-282
   status, determining,
      284-287
   see also MyRadio
      application
RC (resource) files, 100
Read( ) function, 468, 484
**read-only edit boxes,
   227-228**
   MyMouse application,
      496-497
   WhereAmI application,
      521
reading
   data from files, 466-469
      MEMO application,
         373-376
      PAD application,
         597-598
      PHN application,
         428-429
   data members, 49-54

list box items, 239-242
  in combo boxes,
    261-264
Record button
  attaching code to
    BN_CLICKED event of,
    729-732
  reactivating (WAVE
    application), 718-721
**recording WAV files, 698,
  729-732**
**Rect.CPP program (Listing
  3.1), 68-72**
**RECT2.CPP program
  (Listing 3.2), 72-78**
**RECT3.CPP program,
  79-81**
**RECT4.CPP program,
  82-83**
**RECT5.CPP program,
  83-85**
rectangles
  areas, calculating, 68-72
  drawing, 1024-1025,
    1033-1036
**Refresh( ) method,
  1135-1139**
**Register Control command
  (Tools menu), 1070**
**registering MyClock.OCX
  control, 1070**
release targets, 30-31
ReleaseDC( ) function, 1048
RemoveAt( ) function, 424
**RemoveHead( ) function,
  407**
**RemoveMenu( ) function,
  663**
**repainting video frames,
  791-793**
ReplaceSel( ) function, 199
**Report Status button,
  attaching code to
  BN_CLICKED event of,
  284-287**

**Reset button, attaching
  code to, 220-222**
resource (RC) files, 100
**Resource menu, Symbols
  command, 277**
**resources, adding to resource
  files, 125-126**
**restoring original pens,
  1049-1050**
**rewinding WAV files,
  721-727**
RGB( ) function, 537
**Run Application dialog box,
  118**
**Run command (Windows
  Start menu), 118**

S

**sampling rate (WAV files),
  469-471**
**Save As command (File
  menu), 25, 373-376,
  597-598**
Save As dialog box, 25
**Save button, attaching code
  to, 441-444, 463-464**
**Save command (File menu),
  373-376, 597-598**
saving
  edit box contents to file,
    463-464
  programs, 25
  WAV files, 732
SAY application
  attaching code to
    Exit button, 114-116
    Say Hello button,
    108-114
  executing, 88-89
    before customizing,
    98-100
  project, creating, 90-97
  visual implementation,
    dialog box form, 100-107

**Say Hello button, attaching
  code to, 108-116**
**SB_LINEDOWN message,
  208-209**
SB_LINEUP message, 209
**SB_PAGEDOWN message,
  210**
**SB_PAGEUP message,
  210-211**
**SB_THUMBPOSITION
  message, 203**
**SB_THUMBTRACK
  message, 212**
scroll bars
  attaching variables to
    IDD_DIALOG2 dialog
    box (MyDialog applica-
    tion), 309
  creating dialog boxes with,
    307-308
  determining which is
    associated with events,
    204-205
  enabling/disabling,
    216-218, 222-224
  hiding/displaying, 213-216
  horizontal, 201-204
  initializing in dialog boxes,
    314-317
  positions
    maximum, 219-220
    minimum, 218-219
    resetting, 220-222
  minimum/maximum
    values, setting, 197-200
  responding to messages,
    206-211
  split boxes, 607
  thumb tabs
    displaying position
      while being dragged,
      211-213
    setting, 197-200
  see also ScrollMe
    application

ScrollMe application

attaching code to

Disable/Enable buttons, 216-218

Exit button, 200-201

Hide/Show buttons, 213-216

Max. button, 219-220

Min. button, 218-219

Reset button, 220-222

scroll bar messages, 206-211

WM_HSCROLL event, 201-204

debugging, 222-227

dialog box controls

attaching variables to, 196-197

initializing, 197-200

executing, 190-191

project, creating, 191-193

read-only edit boxes, 227-228

scroll bars, determining which is associated with events, 204-205

thumb tab, displaying position while being dragged, 211-213

visual implementation, dialog box form, 194-195

SDI (single-document interface) applications versus MDI (multiple-document interface) applications, 324-325

Search dialog box, 183-184

Seek( ) function, 469, 484-485

SeekIt application, 469

About dialog box, modifying, 478-481

attaching code to Sampling Rate menu item, 482-485

executing, 471-473

project, creating, 473-477

visual implementation

dialog box form, 477

menu bar, 477-478

Select Class dialog box, 132

SelectObject( ) function, 1029, 1048-1049, 1058

semicolon (;), declaring classes, 34

Serialize( ) function, 373-375, 427-429, 432, 597-598

serializeable classes, constructor functions, 397

serializing

archive contents to edit boxes, 444-446

data members

MEMO application document class, 373-376

PAD application document class, 597-598

edit-box contents to archives, 441-444

phone lists, 425-430

variables (MEMO application), 382

SetHeight( ) function, 71, 77

SetInitialSize( ) function, 1098

SetModifiedFlag( ) function, 370-371

SetNumProperty( ) function, 712

SetPixel( ) function, 537, 541

SetRadius( ) function, 53, 58, 966

SetScrollPos( ) function, 199

SetScrollRange( ) function, 199

SetSel( ) function, 199

SetStrProperty( ) function, 712-713

SetTimer( ) function, 811-812, 832, 839, 922, 1087

SetWidth( ) function, 71, 77

Shift key combinations, detecting, 561-562

Show button, attaching code to, 181-186, 213-216

ShowScrollBar( ) function, 214

ShowWindow( ) function, 182, 186, 214

single-document interface (SDI) applications versus multiple-document interface (MDI) applications, 324-325

sizes, setting initial (MyClock.OCX control), 1097-1098

sizing

output window, 26

resizing buttons, 105-106

Sleep( ) function, 885

software modules

distributing, 981

formats, 957

reasons for creating, 956

software requirements, AVI (video) files, 762

sound

background, *see* DANCE application

playing video (AVI) files without, 790-791

synchronous, *see* KENNEDY application

sound files, *see* WAV files

splitter windows, 607-610

standard, *see* stock

Start button, attaching code to BN_CLICKED event of, 946-947

Start menu, Run command (Windows), 118

Start Show button, attaching code to BN_CLICKED event of, 867-868, 921-922
starting
animation
BALL application, 867-868
DANCE application, 921-922
KENNEDY application, 946-947
Visual C++, 23
statements
cout, 28
#include, 28
static libraries, 959
versus DLLs (dynamic linked libraries), 95
static text, displaying (ANNOUNCE application), 894-895
static text tool (Tools window), 358
status bar
creating, 665-666
customizing, 688-691
hiding, 677
see also MyTool application
Step button, attaching code to BN_CLICKED event of, 788
stepping through video (AVI) files, 788
stock (standard)
events, attaching to OCX controls, 1120-1126
methods, 1135-1139
properties, 1088-1094
Stop 8Kenned3.WAV button, attaching code to BN_CLICKED event of, 754-755
Stop Bourbon6.MID button, attaching code to BN_CLICKED event of, 751-752

Stop button, attaching code to BN_CLICKED event of, 727-728, 786-787, 814-816, 928-929
stopping
animation
DANCE application, 925-929
KENNEDY application, 950-953
audio CDs, 814-816
MIDI files
8Kenned3.WAV, 754-755
Bourbon6.MID, 751-752
playback (WAV files), 727-728
video (AVI) files, 786-787
strcat( ) function, 249
String Properties dialog box, 692
String Table dialog box, 378-381
string tables (status bar help), 692
structures versus C++ classes, 32-33
submenus, 626-632
Symbols command (Resource menu), 277
synchronous sound, *see* KENNEDY application
System menu, Close command, 108

T

tables
Accelerator (MyMenu application), 622-626
Properties, 123
IDD_ANNOUNCE_ FORM dialog box, 883

IDD_ARCH_FORM dialog box, 439
IDD_AVI_FORM dialog box, 770
IDD_BALL_FORM dialog box, 850
IDD_BEEP_DIALOG dialog box, 123
IDD_CD_FORM dialog box, 805-806
IDD_CHKBOX_DIALOG dialog box, 174
IDD_DANCE_FORM dialog box, 906
IDD_DIALOG1 dialog box, 458
IDD_DIALOG2 dialog box, 308
IDD_DRAWIT_FORM dialog box, 532
IDD_KENNEDY_FORM dialog box, 937
IDD_MEMO_FORM dialog box, 358
IDD_MIX_FORM dialog box, 743
IDD_MYCOMBO_ DIALOG dialog box, 255
IDD_MYDIALOG_ DIALOG dialog box, 295
IDD_MYEDIT_DIALOG dialog box, 150-151
IDD_MYLIST_DIALOG dialog box, 235
IDD_MYMOUSE_ FORM dialog box, 495
IDD_MYRADIO_ DIALOG dialog box, 273
IDD_PAD_FORM dialog box, 584
IDD_PHN_FORM dialog box, 394

IDD_SCROLLME_
DIALOG dialog box,
195
IDD_TEST_FORM
dialog box, 340
IDD_TESTDLL_FORM
dialog box, 998
IDD_TESTLIB_FORM
dialog box, 973
IDD_WAVE_FORM
dialog box, 704-705
IDD_WHEREAMI_
FORM dialog box,
520
Properties Pages
(MYCLOCTRL.CPP
file), 1111-1113
string (status bar help),
692
Variables
ChkBox application,
175
IDD_ARCH_FORM
dialog box, 440-446
IDD_AVI_FORM
dialog box, 772
IDD_BALL_FORM
dialog box, 851
IDD_CD_FORM
dialog box, 807
IDD_DIALOG1 dialog
box, 459
IDD_DIALOG2 dialog
box, 309
IDD_DRAWIT_FORM
dialog box, 533
IDD_MEMO_FORM
dialog box, 359
IDD_MYCOMBO_
DIALOG dialog box,
257
IDD_MYLIST_DIALOG
dialog box, 236
IDD_MYMOUSE_
FORM dialog box,
496

IDD_MYRADIO_
DIALOG dialog box,
279
IDD_PAD_FORM
dialog box, 585
IDD_PHN_FORM
dialog box, 395
IDD_TEST_FORM
dialog box, 341
IDD_WAVE_FORM
dialog box, 706
IDD_WHEREAMI_
FORM dialog box,
521
ScrollMe dialog box,
196
**Target drop-down list box
(.mak windows), 97**
targets
debug, 30-31
release, 30-31
**Test 1 button, attaching
code to BN_CLICKED
event of, 153-155**
**Test 2 button, attaching
code to BN_CLICKED
event of, 159-161**
Test application, 326
attaching
code to BN_CLICKED
events of Test/Clear
buttons, 345-347
variables to controls,
341
variables to edit boxes,
341
executing, 326-328
before customizing,
336-339
project, creating, 328-335
visual implementation
dialog box form,
339-340
menu bar, 341-345

**Test button, attaching code
to BN_CLICKED event of,
345-347**
**Test Container command
(Tools menu), 1070**
**Test Container program,
1070**
**Test MyDLL.DLL button,
attaching code to
BN_CLICKED event of,
1004-1005**
TestDLL application
declaring global variables,
1000-1001
executing, 1006
loading MyDLL.DLL,
1001-1004
project, creating, 994-998
testing MyDLL.DLL,
1004-1005
visual implementation
dialog box form, 998
menu bar, 999
testing
Circle.LIB library, 980
during visual design
process, 274-276
for code attachment to
functions, 500-501
MyClock.OCX control,
1068-1073
MyDLL.DLL, 1004-1005
stock events (OCX
controls), 1124
WAV file recordings,
731-732
TestLib application
buttons
Her Circle, 976
His Circle, 975-976
My Circle, 973-975
Our Circle, 977
executing, 980
including Circle.LIB files,
978-979
project, creating, 968-972

visual implementation,
    dialog box form, 972-973
text
    drawing
        inside MyClock.OCX
            control, 1078-1081
        with various fonts,
            1056-1060
    static, displaying
        (ANNOUNCE
        application), 894-895
text files, creating, 23
**TextOut( ) function, 895,
    1045, 1058**
**This program cannot be run
    in DOS mode error
    message, 27**
thumb tab (scroll bars)
    displaying position while
        being dragged, 211-213
    initializing position,
        197-200
tilde (~), destructors, 35
time, displaying current
    MyClock.OCX control,
        1082-1085
        continuously,
            1085-1088
    MyTimer application,
        834-836
time( ) function, 1083
timer (Windows), 811-812
    BALL application,
        868-871
    DANCE application,
        923-925
    KENNEDY application,
        948-950
    MyClock.OCX control,
        installing, 1085-1088
    MyTimer application
        installing, 831-832
        killing, 838-839
titles, changing
    MEMO application,
        378-381

PAD application, 598-602
PHN application, 430
**toggle keys, detecting,
    562-564**
toolbars
    adding help, 691-694
    creating, 665-666
    customizing, 683-685
    hiding, 676-677
    replacing icons, 685-688
    see also MyTool application
**Toolbars command (Tools
    menu), 104**
Toolbars dialog box, 104
Tools menu commands
    Register Control, 1070
    Test Container, 1070
    Toolbars, 104
Tools window
    check box tool, 175
    combo box tool, 255
    displaying, 104
    edit box tool, 151, 358
    horizontal scroll bar tool,
        195
    list box tool, 235
    push button tool, 103, 123
    radio button tool, 274
    static text tool, 358

U

**underlining letters in dialog-
    box item names, 105**
**UPDATE_COMMAND_UI
    message, 639-644**
**UpdateAllViews( ) member
    function, 603-605**
**UpdateData( ) function,
    154, 285, 368, 411,
    465, 525**
**UpdateInterval custom
    property (MyClock.OCX
    control)**
    adding, 1099-1102

attaching code to,
    1104-1107
increasing values, 1138
initializing, 1102-1104
validating values,
    1107-1109
updating
    data members
        MEMO application
            document class,
            369-373
        PAD application docu-
            ment class, 594-597
        PHN application
            document class,
            413-416
    edit boxes continuously
        (CD application),
        820-822
    multiple views of single
        documents (PAD
        application), 603-607
    MyClock.OCX control,
        setting intervals,
        1104-1107
    video (AVI) files, repaint-
        ing frames, 791-793
user input
    creating dialog boxes for
        accepting, 297-298
    in edit boxes, updating
        data members after,
        369-373

V

**validating values
    (MyClock.OCX control),
    1107-1109**
variables
    attaching to dialog box
        controls, 806-807
        ARCH application, 440
        AVI application,
            771-772

BALL application,
850-851
ChkBox application,
175-176
DrawIt application,
533-534
edit boxes, 152-153,
157-158
FileIt application, 459
IDD_DIALOG1 dialog
box (MyDialog
application), 300-301
IDD_DIALOG2 dialog
box (MyDialog
application), 309
MEMO application,
359-361
MyCombo application,
256-258
MyList application, 236
MyMouse application,
495-496
MyRadio application,
278-280
PAD application, 585
PHN application, 395
ScrollMe application,
196-197
Test application, 341
WAVE application,
706-707
WhereAmI application,
520-521
declaring
BALL application,
858-859
DANCE application,
912-913
global (TestDLL
application),
1000-1001
in C++ versus C, 62
KENNEDY applica-
tion, 940-942
serializing (MEMO
application), 382

Variables tables
ChkBox application, 175
IDD_ARCH_FORM
dialog box, 440-446
IDD_AVI_FORM dialog
box, 772
IDD_BALL_FORM
dialog box, 851
IDD_CD_FORM dialog
box, 807
IDD_DIALOG1 dialog
box, 459
IDD_DIALOG2 dialog
box, 309
IDD_DRAWIT_FORM
dialog box, 533
IDD_MEMO_FORM
dialog box, 359
IDD_MYCOMBO_DIALOG
dialog box, 257
IDD_MYLIST_DIALOG
dialog box, 236
IDD_MYMOUSE_FORM
dialog box, 496
IDD_MYRADIO_DIALOG
dialog box, 279
IDD_PAD_FORM dialog
box, 585
IDD_PHN_FORM dialog
box, 395
IDD_TEST_FORM
dialog box, 341
IDD_WAVE_FORM
dialog box, 706
IDD_WHEREAMI_FORM
dialog box, 521
ScrollMe dialog box, 196
VBX controls, 1063
video (AVI) files, 758
experimenting with, 793
frames
previous, 789-790
repainting, 791-793
hardware/software
requirements, 762

opening, 775-780
playing, 760-761, 780-782
without sound,
790-791
stepping through, 788
stopping, 786-787
see also AVI application
video drivers
determining if available,
758-759
installing, 759-760
view classes, 333
deriving from CFormView
class, 335
FileIt application,
declaring data members,
460-461
MEMO application,
initializing data mem-
bers, 366-369
PAD application, initializing data members,
592-594
PHN application
declaring data mem-
bers, 408-409
initializing data
members, 409-412
**virtual (nonprintable) keys,
556-558**
Visual C++, starting, 23
visual implementation
dialog box forms
ANNOUNCE
application, 882-883
ARCH application,
439-440
AVI application,
769-771
BALL application,
849-850
Beep application,
122-124
CD application,
805-806

ChkBox application, 174-175

DANCE application, 906-907

DrawIt application, 532-533

FileIt application, 456-457

FileIt application Try It dialog box, 457

KENNEDY application, 936-937

MEMO application, 357-359

MIX application, 743

MyCombo application, 255-256

MyDialog application, 295-296

MyDialog application dialog boxes with scroll bars, 307-308

MyDLL application, 998

MyEdit application, 150-151

MyList application, 234-235

MyMenu application, 620

MyMouse application, 494-495

MyRadio application, 272-276

MyTimer application, 830-831

MyTool application, 675-677

PAD application, 583-585

PHN application, 393-395

SAY application, 100-107

ScrollMe application, 194-195

SeekIt application, 477

Test application, 339-340

TestLib application, 972-973

WAVE application, 704-705

WhereAmI application, 519-520

menu bars

ANNOUNCE application, 883

ARCH application, 441

AVI application, 772-773

BALL application, 851

Beep application, 124-131

CD application, 807-808

CircleIt application, 1044

DANCE application, 907-908

DRAW application, 1016-1018

DrawIt application, 534-535

FileIt application, 454-456

GROW application, 651-652

KENNEDY application, 937-938

MEMO application, 362-363

MIX application, 744-745

MyKey application, 552-553

MyMenu application, 619-620

MyMouse application, 497-499

MyText application, 1056

MyTimer application, 829-830

MyTool application, 673-675

PAD application, 585-587

PHN application, 395-396

SeekIt application, 477-478

Test application, 341-345

TestDLL application, 999

WAVE application, 707

WhereAmI application, 522-523

W–Z

WAV files, 697

CTegMM.LIB library, 696, 732-733

opening, 698, 710-715

pausing playback, 728-729

playing, 698, 715-718

through PC speakers, 732-733

recording, 698, 729-732

rewinding, 721-727

sampling rate, 469-471

saving, 732

setting plackback position to end of files, 723-724

stopping, 727-728

testing recording code, 731-732

WAVE application

attaching code to BN_CLICKED event of Play button, 715-718

attaching variables to dialog box controls, 706-707

CTegMM class, declaring objects of, 708-710
executing, 697-699
exiting, 699
opening WAV files, 710-715
playback
  pausing, 728-729
  setting position to end of WAV files, 723-724
  stopping, 727-728
playing WAV files, 715-718
  through PC speakers, 732-733
pop-up menus, 699
project
  adding CTegMM.LIB to, 707-708
  creating, 700-704
reactivating Play/Record buttons, 718-721
recording WAV files, 729-732
rewinding WAV files, 721-727
saving recordings, 732
visual implementation
  dialog box form, 704-705
  menu bar, 707
WhereAmI application
attaching codes to mouse movements, 523-525
attaching variables to controls, 520-521
edit box properties, changing, 521
executing, 513
project, creating, 515-519
visual implementation
  dialog box form, 519-520
  menu bar, 522-523

Window menu commands
filename, 27
Output, 26
WindowProc( ) function, 718-721, 724-726, 782-786, 925-927, 951-953
Windows
Media Player program, 758-759
timer, 811-812
  installing (MyClock.OCX control), 1085-1088
  killing, 838-839
  MyTimer application, 831-832
windows
closing, 37
.mak, Target drop-down list box, 97
multiple views of single documents
  displaying, 602-603
  splitter windows, 607-610
  updating, 603-607
output, 26
Tools, *see* Tools window
see also dialog boxes
wizards
AppWizard, 91-97
  SDI applications, 331-335
ClassWizard, 108-116
ControlWizard, 1064
WM_CHAR message, 557, 564-566
WM_CREATE event, attaching code to, 1085-1087
WM_HSCROLL event, attaching code to, 201-204
WM_INITDIALOG event
attaching code to, 197-200, 258-260, 280-282

attaching to IDD_CHKBOX_DIALOG dialog box, 176-178
of list boxes, attaching code to, 237-238
WM_KEYDOWN message, 555-558
WM_LBUTTONDOWN event
attaching code to, 1046-1050
recipients, 505
WM_LBUTTONUP message, recipients, 504-505
WM_MOUSEMOVE event
attaching code to, 523-525, 535-543
processing, 525-526
WM_PAINT event, attaching code to, 791-793
WM_TIMER event, 820-822, 1087-1088
BALL application, 868-871
DANCE application, 923-925
KENNEDY application, 948-950
MyTimer application, 832-834
Write( ) function, 465
writing
console applications, reasons for, 22
data members, 49-54
data to files
  MEMO application, 373-376
  PAD application, 597-598
  PHN application, 428-429
edit-box contents to files, 463-464

Add to Your Sams Library Today with the Best Books for Programming, Operating Systems, and New Technologies

The easiest way to order is to pick up the phone and call

1-800-428-5331

between 9:00 a.m. and 5:00 p.m. EST.

For faster service please have your credit card available.

ISBN	Quantity	Description of Item	Unit Cost	Total Cost
0-672-30468-6		Master Visual C++ 1.5 (book/CD-ROM)	$49.95	
0-672-30364-7		Win32 API Desktop Reference (book/CD-ROM)	$49.95	
0-672-30284-5		Secrets of the Visual C++ Masters (book/disk)	$34.95	
0-672-30440-6		Database Developer's Guide with Visual Basic 3 (book/disk)	$44.95	
0-672-30286-1		C Programmer's Guide to Serial Communications, Second Edition	$39.95	
0-672-30514-3		Master Visual Basic 3 (book/CD-ROM)	$45.00	
0-672-30568-2		Teach Yourself OLE 2 in 21 Days (book/disk)	$39.99	
0-672-30594-1		Programming WinSock (book/disk)	$35.00	
0-672-30507-0		Tricks of the Game-Programming Gurus (book/CD-ROM)	$45.00	
0-672-30160-1		Multimedia Developer's Guide (book/CD-ROM)	$49.95	
0-672-30546-1		Mastering Borland C++ 4.5, 2E (book/disk)	$49.99	

❑ 3 ½" Disk

❑ 5 ¼" Disk

Shipping and Handling: See information below.		
TOTAL		

Shipping and Handling: $4.00 for the first book, and $1.75 for each additional book. Floppy disk: add $1.75 for shipping and handling. If you need to have it NOW, we can ship product to you in 24 hours for an additional charge of approximately $18.00, and you will receive your item overnight or in two days. Overseas shipping and handling adds $2.00 per book and $8.00 for up to three disks. Prices subject to change. Call for availability and pricing information on latest editions.

201 W. 103rd Street, Indianapolis, Indiana 46290

1-800-428-5331 — Orders   1-800-835-3202 — FAX   1-800-858-7674 — Customer Service

Book ISBN 0-672-30532-1

Special
Disk Offer

The CTegMM multimedia class that is included on the book's CD is the limited version.

To purchase the full professional version of the CTegMM advanced multimedia class, send check or money order to:

TegoSoft Inc.
Box 389
Bellmore, NY 11710
Attn: CTegMM
Phone (516)783-4824

The price of the full professional version is $29.95 plus $5.00 for shipping and handling. New York State residents please add appropriate sales tax.

The CTegMM advanced multimedia class enables you to develop Visual C++ 2.0 applications that support sound cards, record and play WAV files, MIDI files, AVI movie files, CD audio, and PC speaker (playing WAV files through the PC speaker without any hardware and without any drivers).

The CD

The following page gives instructions on installing the CD.

This page also indicates what is available to you on the CD that comes with the book.

How to Install the CD

Here is how you install the CD on your hard drive:

- ☐ Start Windows.
- ☐ Insert the CD into your CD-ROM drive.
- ☐ Execute the INSTALL.EXE program that resides in the root directory of the CD.
- ☐ Follow the directions of the INSTALL.EXE program.
- ☐ Make sure to read the README.TXT file that resides in the root directory of the CD.

What's on the CD

The CD contains many "goodies." It includes all the files that you'll encounter and use throughout this book. It contains the following:

- ☐ All the project (MAK) files and source code files of the applications that the book covers.
- ☐ All the EXE files of the applications that the book covers (so that you can immediately execute the applications).
- ☐ All the BMP files (picture files) and ICO (icon files) that are used by the applications of the book.
- ☐ All the movie files (AVI files) that are used by the applications of the book.
- ☐ All the sound files (WAV, MIDI) that are used by the applications of the book.
- ☐ A limited version of the CTegMM class, an advanced multimedia class that lets you play and record WAV files, MIDI files, CD Audio, movie AVI files, and perform synchronized and non-synchronized animation. This class also lets you determine whether the PC has a sound card installed in it, and accordingly, WAV files can be played through the sound card or through the PC speaker without any hardware or drivers.
- ☐ The source files of the tutorial that teaches you how to create your own OCX control files.